Business & Society

Ethics, Sustainability, and Stakeholder Management

NINTH EDITION

ARCHIE B. CARROLL
University of Georgia

ANN K. BUCHHOLTZ
Rutgers University

Australia • Brazil • Japan • Korea • Mexico • Singapore • Spain • United Kingdom • United States

Business & Society: Ethics, Sustainability, and Stakeholder Management, Ninth Edition

Archie B. Carroll
Ann K. Buchholtz

Senior Vice President, Global Product Management—Higher Ed: Jack W. Calhoun

Vice President, General Manager, Social Science & Softside Business: Erin Joyner

Product Director: Michael Schenk

Senior Product Manager: Mike Roche

Associate Content Developer: Josh Wells

Product Assistant: Tamara Grega

Marketing Brand Manager: Robin LeFevre

Marketing Coordinator: Michael Saver

Art and Cover Direction, Production Management, and Composition: Integra Software Services Pvt.Ltd.

Senior Media Developer: Sally Nieman

Rights Acquisition Director: Audrey Pettengill

Senior Rights Acquisition Specialist, Text and Image: John Hill

Manufacturing Planner: Ron Montgomery

Cover Image(s): Paul Anderson/© Images. com/Corbis

For product information and technology assistance, contact us at
Cengage Learning Customer & Sales Support, 1-800-354-9706

For permission to use material from this text or product,
submit all requests online at **www.cengage.com/permissions**
Further permissions questions can be emailed to
permissionrequest@cengage.com

ExamView ® is a registered trademark of eInstruction Corp. Windows is a registered trademark of the Microsoft Corporation used herein under license. Macintosh and Power Macintosh are registered trademarks of Apple Computer, Inc. used herein under license. © 2008 Cengage Learning. All Rights Reserved.

Cengage Learning WebTutor™ is a trademark of Cengage Learning.

Library of Congress Control Number: 2013949386

ISBN-13: 978-1-285-73429-3

ISBN-10: 1-285-73429-7

Cengage Learning
200 First Stamford Place, 4th Floor
Stamford, CT 06902
USA

Cengage Learning is a leading provider of customized learning solutions with office locations around the globe, including Singapore, the United Kingdom, Australia, Mexico, Brazil, and Japan. Locate your local office at: **www.cengage.com/global**

Cengage Learning products are represented in Canada by Nelson Education, Ltd.

To learn more about Cengage Learning Solutions, visit **www.cengage.com**

Purchase any of our products at your local college store or at our preferred online store **www.cengagebrain.com**

Printed in the United States of America
2 3 4 5 6 7 17 16 15 14

Brief Contents

Contents

ETHICS IN PRACTICE CASES

CASES

Preface

Business & Society: Ethics, Sustainability, and Stakeholder Management, Ninth Edition, provides a conceptual framework, analysis, and discussion of the issues surrounding the business and society relationship. The book's structure, chapters, and cases identify and engage the major topics involved in developing a strong understanding of business *and* society, or business *in* society. The latest research, examples, and cases provide you with a broad, yet detailed analysis of the subject matter; they also offer a solid basis for thoughtful reflection and analysis of the domestic and global issues facing businesses today.

The book employs a managerial perspective that identifies and integrates current and relevant thought and practice. The managerial perspective is embedded within the book's major themes of business ethics, sustainability, and stakeholder management. Each of these themes is crucial today. Each theme takes its own perspective but is consistent with and overlaps with the others. Taken together, they capture the challenges of the past and provide frameworks for thinking about the current and future role of business in society.

The *business ethics* dimension is central because it has become clear that value considerations are woven into the fabric of the public issues that organizations face today. An emphasis is placed on business ethics fundamentals and how ethics integrates into personal and organizational decision making. Special spheres of business ethics discussed include the realms of technology and global capitalism, where ethical questions increasingly have arisen for the past 20 years. The subject of each chapter, moreover, is imbued with ethics considerations that are vital to their full treatment.

Sustainability has become one of business's most recent and pressing mandates. This dimension has been developed further since the eighth edition of this book because it has become more evident in the business world today that a concern for the natural, social, and financial environments are interrelated and that all three must be maintained in balance for both current and future generations.

The *stakeholder management* perspective is crucial and enduring because it requires managers to (1) identify the various groups or individuals who have stakes in the firm or its actions, decisions, policies, and practices and (2) incorporate the stakeholders' concerns into the firm's daily operations and strategic plans. Stakeholder management is an approach that increases the likelihood decision makers will integrate ethical wisdom with management wisdom with respect to all salient parties to the business and society relationship.

As this edition goes to press, the country and world economies have been striving to recover from one of the most perilous financial periods since the Great Depression. The world stock market collapse beginning in the fall of 2008 had devastating repercussions for economies, governments, businesses, and individuals, and still we have not resolved the uncertainty associated with what began as financial turmoil and bankruptcies on Wall Street. This major event and its consequences will be with us for many years, and we urge readers to keep in mind the extent to which our world has now changed as they read through the book and consider its content and application. Major events have the power to change the business and society relationship in significant ways—and instantaneously—so it is essential that the book's topics be read with an ever present eye on the events breaking in the news each day.

Applicable Courses for Text

This text is appropriate for college and university courses that carry such titles as Business and Society; Business *in* Society; Business and Its Environment; Business Ethics; Business and Public Policy; Social Issues in Management; Business, Government, and Society; Social Responsibility of Business; and Stakeholder Management. The book is appropriate for either a required or an elective course seeking to meet the most recent accrediting standards of the Association to Advance Collegiate Schools of Business (AACSB International). The book has been used successfully in both undergraduate and graduate courses.

Though the AACSB does not require any specific courses in this subject matter, its recently adopted (April 8, 2013) standards specify that a business school's curriculum should include the topics covered throughout this textbook in both undergraduate and graduate degree programs. For undergraduate and graduate degree programs, learning experiences should be addressed and are addressed in General Skill Areas such as *ethical understanding and reasoning* and *diverse and multicultural work environments*. In terms of General Business and Management Knowledge Areas, the following topics should be addressed and are addressed in this textbook: *Economic, political, regulatory, legal, technological, and social contexts of organizations in a globalized society;* and *Social responsibility, including sustainability, and ethical behavior and approaches to management.*

This book is ideal for coverage of perspectives that form the context for business: ethical and global issues; the influence of political, social, legal, environmental, technological and regulatory issues; and the impact of diversity on organizations. The book provides perspectives on business, society, and ethics in the United States, along with examples from Europe, Asia, and other parts of the world. As the world has grown closer due to technology, communications, and transportation, there has been more convergence than divergence in applicability of the ideas presented herein. The book has proved suitable in a number of different countries outside of the United States. In previous editions, versions were published in Canada and China. Publication in Japan is under consideration. Though written from the perspective of American society, a special effort has been made to include some examples from different parts of the world to illustrate major points. Most of the book applies in developed economies around the world.

Objectives in Relevant Courses

Depending on the placement of a course in the curriculum or the individual instructor's philosophy or strategy, this book could be used for a variety of objectives. The courses for which it is intended typically include several essential goals, including the following:

1. Students should be made aware of the expectations and demands that emanate from stakeholders and are placed on business firms.
2. As prospective managers, students need to understand appropriate business responses and management approaches for dealing with social, political, environmental, technological, and global issues and stakeholders.
3. An appreciation of ethical and sustainability issues and the influence these have on society, management decision-making, behavior, policies, and practices is important.
4. The broad question of business's legitimacy as an institution in a global society is at stake and must be addressed from both business and societal perspectives. These topics are essential to business building trust with society and all stakeholders.
5. The increasing extent to which social, ethical, public, environmental, and global issues must be considered from a strategic perspective is critical in such courses.

New to the Ninth Edition

This ninth edition has been updated and revised to reflect recent research, laws, cases, and examples. Material in this new edition includes

- New research, surveys, and examples throughout all the chapters
- Coverage throughout the text on the most recent ethics scandals and their influence on business, society, organizations, and people
- New concepts and examples on the developing theme of "behavioral ethics"
- Discussion of recent developments with the Sarbanes–Oxley Act and Alien Tort Claims Act, and other laws with significant importance to managers today
- Expanded coverage of insider trading
- Coverage of competing corporate governance perspectives
- Incorporation of the issue of risk management and its relation to business in society
- New coverage of social entrepreneurship and Bottom of the Pyramid
- Expanded coverage of sustainability reporting and integrated reports
- Extended coverage of Citizens United, Super PACs and Dark Money, and the importance of Corporate Political Accountability and Transparency
- Consideration of recent legislation such as the Credit Card Act, which was implemented in 2010, and the Dodd Frank Wall Street Reform and Consumer Financial Protection Act of 2010
- "Spotlight on Sustainability" features in each chapter, which demonstrate how sustainability is relevant and applicable to each chapter's topics
- Forty-four "Ethics in Practice Cases" embedded in chapters throughout the book, 37 of which are brand new to this edition.
- Forty-one end-of-text cases that may be assigned with any of the book's chapter topics, 16 of which are brand new to this edition.
- A revised and updated Instructor's Manual.
- A brand new set of writing prompts incorporated into the powerful Write Experience platform, providing both students and instructors with instant feedback and robust tools to assess and improve writing skills.

"Ethics in Practice Cases"

Continuing in this ninth edition are in-chapter features titled "Ethics in Practice Cases." Interspersed throughout the chapters, these short cases present (1) actual ethical situations faced by companies, managers, or employees (2) topics currently being discussed in the news, or (3) dilemmas faced personally in the work experiences of our former students in university or executive education classes. These latter types of cases are real-life situations actually encountered in their full- and part-time work experiences. Students and managers wrote some of these cases and we are pleased they gave us permission to use them. They provide ready examples of the types of ethical issues people face today. We would like to acknowledge them for their contributions to the book. Instructors may wish to use these as mini-cases for class discussion when a lengthier case is not assigned. They can be read quickly, but they contain considerable substance for class discussion and analysis.

"Spotlight on Sustainability" Features

The "Spotlight on Sustainability" features in each chapter highlight an important and relevant linkage of sustainability concepts that augment each chapter's text material. The feature sometimes highlights a pertinent organization covered in the chapter and further discusses its activities or issues. Other features highlight a sustainability challenge that a range of organizations face or a sustainability success that organizations or individuals can emulate. These features permit students to quickly and easily discover how the sustainability theme applies to each topic covered in the text. The concept of sustainability extends to virtually all business, society, and ethics topics, and embraces people and profits, as well as the planet.

Structure of the Book

Part 1. Business, Society, and Stakeholders

Part 1 of the book provides introductory coverage of pertinent business, society, and stakeholder topics and issues. Because most courses that will use this book relate to the issue of corporate social responsibility, this concept is discussed at the outset. Part 1 documents and discusses how corporate social responsiveness evolved from social responsibility and how these two matured into a concern for corporate social performance, sustainability and corporate citizenship. Also given early coverage is the stakeholder management concept, because it provides a way of thinking and analyzing all topics in the book, as well as a helpful perspective for thinking about organizations.

Part 2. Corporate Governance and Strategic Management Issues

The second part of the text addresses corporate governance and strategic management for stakeholder responsiveness. The purpose of this part is to discuss management considerations and implications for dealing with the issues discussed throughout the text. Corporate governance is covered early because in the past decade this topic has been identified as critical to effective strategic management. The strategic management perspective is useful because these issues have impacts on the total organization and have become intense ones for many upper-level managers. Special treatment is given to corporate public policy; issue, risk, and crisis management; and public affairs management.

Some instructors may elect to cover Part 2 later in their courses. It could easily be covered after Part 4 or 5. This option would be most appropriate for those who use the book for a business ethics course or who desire to spend less time on the governance, strategy, and management perspectives.

Part 3. Business Ethics and Management

Four chapters dedicated to business ethics topics are presented in Part 3. In actuality, business ethics cannot be separated from the full range of external and internal stakeholder concerns, but the topic's importance merits the more detailed treatment presented here. Part 3 focuses on business ethics fundamentals, personal and organizational ethics, business ethics and technology, and ethical issues in the global arena. Taken together, they cover business and society issues that require ethical thinking.

Part 4. External Stakeholder Issues

Vital topics here include business's relations with government, consumers, the natural environment, and the community. In each of these topic areas we encounter social and ethical issues that dominate business today. The business-government relationship is divided into the regulatory initiatives to monitor business practices and business's attempts to influence government. Consumers, environment, and community stakeholders are then treated in separate chapters.

Part 5. Internal Stakeholder Issues

The primary internal stakeholders addressed in this part are employees. Here, we consider workplace issues and the key themes of employee rights, employment discrimination, and affirmative action. Two chapters address the changing social contract between business and employees and the urgent subjects of employee rights. A final chapter treats the vital topic of employment discrimination and affirmative action. Owner stakeholders may be seen as internal stakeholders, but we cover them in Part 2, where the subject of corporate governance has been placed.

Case Studies

Throughout each of the chapters, there are "Ethics in Practice Cases," 44 in total, that pertain to the chapter in which they are located, but also can be used with other chapters as needed. The 41 cases at the end of the book address a broad range of topics and decision situations. The cases are of varying length. They include classic cases (involving such corporate giants as Walmart, The Body Shop, Nike, McDonald's) with ongoing deliberations, as well as new cases touching upon issues that have arisen in the past several years, such as political accountability in a post-Citizens United world and the environmental and worker-safety issues related to fast fashion. All the cases are intended to provide instructors and students with real-life situations within which to further analyze course issues, concepts, and topics covered throughout the book. These cases have intentionally been placed at the end of the text material so that instructors will feel freer to use them with any text material they desire. Many of the cases in the book carry ramifications that spill over into several subject areas or issues. Almost all of them may be used for different chapters. Immediately preceding the cases is a set of guidelines for case analysis that the instructor may wish to use in place of or in addition to the questions that appear at the end of each case. A case matrix, located inside the front cover of the instructor edition of the textbook and in the instructor's manual, provides guidance as to which of the cases in the book, both Ethics in Practice and End of Text, work best with each chapter.

Support for the Student

CourseMate Student Resources

The CourseMate site, accessible at www.cengagebrain.com, includes many student support resources to enhance and assess learning, including chapter quizzes, PowerPoint slides, key terms, learning objectives, and BBC video clips.

Write Experience

New to this edition is a robust set of engaging writing prompts, correlated to each part of the text and covering such topics as the environment, personal integrity, and employment law. These prompts allow students to write and submit their open-ended responses for immediate autoscoring and feedback on their writing skills, while providing instructors with powerful, time-saving tools for evaluating those results.

Support for the Instructor

Instructor's Manual

The Instructor's Manual includes learning objectives, teaching suggestions, complete chapter outlines, highlighted key terms, answers to discussion questions, case notes, and group exercises. The Instructor's Manual is available on the Web site.

Test Bank

Cengage Learning Testing Powered by Cognero is a flexible, online system that allows you to author, edit, and manage test-bank content from multiple Cengage Learning solutions; create multiple test versions in an instant; and deliver tests from your LMS, your classroom, or wherever you want. The test bank for each chapter includes true/false, multiple-choice, short-answer, and essay questions, all correlated to AACSB guidelines and learning standards, and questions are identified by the level of difficulty.

PowerPoint Slides

The PowerPoint presentations are colorful and varied, designed to hold students' interest and reinforce each chapter's main points. The PowerPoint presentations are available on the Web site.

Videos with Instructor Guide

Available within CourseMate, a new set of BBC videos chosen for this edition emphasize textual concepts within real-world scenarios. Through the Instructor Companion site, instructors can also access a guide that includes chapter correlation suggestions, topic overviews, and discussion questions.

Online Instructor Resources

To access the online course materials, please visit www.cengage.com, and log in with your credentials.

Acknowledgments

First, we would like to express gratitude to our professional colleagues in the Social Issues in Management (SIM) Division of the Academy of Management, the International Association for Business and Society (IABS), and the Society for Business Ethics (SBE). Over the years members of these organizations have meant a great deal to us and have helped provide a stimulating environment in which we could intellectually pursue these topics in which we have a common interest. Many of these individuals are cited in this book and their work is sincerely appreciated.

Second, we would like to thank the many reviewers of the eight previous editions who took the time to provide us with helpful critiques. Many of their ideas and suggestions have been used for this ninth edition and led to improvements in the text:

Steven C. Alber, Hawaii Pacific University
Paula Becker Alexander, Seton Hall University
Laquita C. Blockson, St. Leo University
Mark A. Buchanan, Boise State University
Peter Burkhardt, Western State College of Colorado
Preston D. Cameron, Mesa Community College
William B. Carper, University of West Florida
George S. Cole, Shippensburg University
Brenda Eichelberger, Portland State University
Jeanne Enders, Portland State University
Joshua S. Friedlander, Baruch College
John William Geranios, George Washington University
Kathleen Getz, American University
Peggy A. Golden, University of Northern Iowa
Russell Gough, Pepperdine University
Michele A. Govekar, Ohio Northern University
Wade Graves, Grayson College
Frank J. Hitt, Mountain State University
Robert H. Hogner, Florida International University
Sylvester R. Houston, University of Denver
Ralph W. Jackson, University of Tulsa
David C. Jacobs, American University

Leigh Redd Johnson, Murray State University

Ed Leonard, Indiana University–Purdue University Fort Wayne

Timothy A. Matherly, Florida State University

Kenneth R. Mayer, Cleveland State University

Douglas M. McCabe, Georgetown University

Douglas McCloskey, Washington University School of Law

Bill McShain, Cumberland University

Geralyn Miller, Indiana University–Purdue University Fort Wayne

Nana Lee Moore, Warner University

Harvey Nussbaum, Wayne State University

Nathan Oliver, University of Alabama Birmingham

E. Leroy Plumlee, Western Washington University

Richard Raspen, Wilkes University

Dawna Rhoades, Embry-Riddle Aeronautical University

William T. Rupp, Austin Peay State University

Robert J. Rustic, The University of Findlay

John K. Sands, Western Washington University

Valarie Spiser-Albert, University of Texas at San Antonio

David S. Steingard, St. Joseph's University

John M. Stevens, The Pennsylvania State University

Diane L. Swanson, Kansas State University

Dave Thiessen, Lewis-Clark State College

Jeff R. Turner, Howard Payne University

Ivan R. Vernon, Cleveland State University

Marion Webb, Cleveland State University

George E. Weber, Whitworth College

Ira E. Wessler, Robert Morris University

We would also like to express gratitude to our students, who have not only provided comments on a regular basis but also made this ninth edition even more interesting with the ethical dilemmas they have personally contributed, as highlighted in the Ethics in Practice Cases features found in many of the chapters or at the end of the text. In addition to those who are named in the Ethics in Practice Cases features and End of Text Cases and have given permission for their materials to be used, we would like to thank the following individuals for their contributions: Michelle Alen, Kristine Calo, Chad Cleveland, Ken Crowe, Lee Askew Elkins, William Megathlin, Jr., Madeline Meibauer, Laura Rosario, Paul Rouland, Sr., and Clayton Wilcox. We express grateful appreciation to the authors of the other cases that appear at the end of the text, and their names are mentioned there. We also would like to thank Bruce F. Freed and Karl Sandstrom of the Center for Political Accountability for their support as we incorporated the issues stemming from Citizens United into our discussion of corporate political activity.

Finally, we wish to express heartfelt appreciation to our family members and friends for their patience, understanding, and support when work on the book altered our priorities and plans.

Archie B. Carroll
Ann K. Buchholtz

About the Authors

Archie B. Carroll

Archie B. Carroll is Robert W. Scherer Chair of Management & Corporate Public Affairs *Emeritus* and professor of management *emeritus* in the Terry College of Business, University of Georgia. For twelve years (2000–2012) he served as Director of the Non-profit Management & Community Service Program in the Terry College of Business. Dr. Carroll received his three academic degrees from The Florida State University in Tallahassee. Recently, he co-authored *Corporate Responsibility: The American Experience* (Cambridge University Press, 2012) and was recognized with the first Lifetime Achievement Award in Corporate Social Responsibility (2012) given by the Institute of Management, Humboldt University, Berlin, Germany.

Professor Carroll has published numerous books, chapters, articles, and encyclopedia entries. His research has appeared in the *Academy of Management Journal, Academy of Management Review, Business and Society, Journal of Management, Business Ethics Quarterly, Journal of Business Ethics,* and many others. Professionally, he has served on the editorial review boards of *Business and Society, Business Ethics Quarterly, Academy of Management Review, Journal of Management,* and the *Journal of Public Affairs.*

He is former Division Chair of the Social Issues in Management (SIM) Division of the Academy of Management, a founding board member of the International Association for Business and Society (IABS), and past president of the Society for Business Ethics (SBE). He has been elected a Fellow of the Southern Management Association (1995), Fellow of the Academy of Management (2005), and Fellow of the International Association for Business and Society (2012).

Other important professional recognitions include the Sumner Marcus Award (1992) for Distinguished Service by the SIM Division of the Academy of Management; Distinguished Research Award (1993) by Terry College of Business, University of Georgia; and Distinguished Service Award (2003) by the Terry College of Business. He was named professor *emeritus* (2005) at the University of Georgia and in 2008 he was recognized with the Outstanding Ph.D. Award from the College of Business, Florida State University.

Ann K. Buchholtz

Ann K. Buchholtz is Professor of Leadership and Ethics at Rutgers University and serves as Research Director of the Institute for Ethical Leadership at the Rutgers Business School. She received her Ph.D. from the Stern School of Business at New York University.

Professor Buchholtz's research focuses on the social and ethical implications of corporate governance, in particular, and the relationship of business and society in general. Journals in which her work has appeared include *Business and Society, Business Ethics Quarterly,* the *Academy of Management Journal,* the *Academy of Management Review,* the *Journal of Management, Organization Science,* the *Journal of Management Studies,* and *Corporate Governance an International Review,* among others. She serves on the editorial board of *Business & Society.* Her research on board processes received an ANBAR citation of excellence award.

Her teaching and consulting activities are in the areas of business ethics, social issues, strategic leadership, and corporate governance. Her service learning activities in the classroom received a Trailblazer Advocate of the Year award from the Domestic Violence Council of Northeast Georgia. She is the recipient of numerous teaching awards, including Profound Effect on a Student Leader, and was named a Senior Teaching Fellow at the University of Georgia.

Professor Buchholtz is past Division Chair of the Social Issues in Management Division of the Academy of Management. She served on the ethics task force that designed a Code of Ethics for the Academy of Management and then became the inaugural chairperson of the Academy's Ethics Adjudication Committee when the Academy's ethics code was put into effect. She now serves on the Academy of Management's Board of Governors. Prior to entering academe, Dr. Buchholtz's work focused on the education, vocational, and residential needs of individuals with disabilities. She has worked in a variety of organizations, in both managerial and consultative capacities, and has consulted with numerous public and private firms.

Business, Society, and Stakeholders

Chapter 1
The Business and Society Relationship

Chapter 2
Corporate Citizenship: Social Responsibility, Performance, Sustainability

Chapter 3
The Stakeholder Approach to Business, Society, and Ethics

1

The Business and Society Relationship

The business and society relationship has generated a number of economic, social, ethical, and environmental challenges over the decades. Though the business system has served society well, criticism of business and its practices has become commonplace in recent decades. This may be a reflection of the natural tendency to take for granted the beneficial aspects of the relationship and to focus on the negative or stressful ones.

Since the early 2000s, beginning with the Enron scandal, a number of major companies have been in the news because of their ethical violations. In the first decade of the 2000s, companies accused of committing violations of the public trust or for raising questions regarding corporate ethics included Martha Stewart, Rite Aid, WorldCom, HealthSouth, and Boeing. As *BusinessWeek* observed, "Watching executives climb the courthouse steps became a spectator sport...."[1] More recently, companies such as Fannie Mae, Freddie Mac, Bear Stearns, and Lehman Brothers have occupied the spotlight.

The business system and society suffered a major blow when the BP oil spill occurred in the spring of 2010. Called the worst environmental disaster in history, the ongoing challenges of the cleanup, dealing with ecological and business consequences, and assigning responsibility would take years to settle. It heightened the public's awareness of the impact business can have on the natural environment and heightened support of the sustainability movement which was already well underway. In November 2012, BP agreed to a $4.5 billion settlement of the criminal charges against it for gross negligence in the Deepwater Horizon oil spill. But, it was clear this would not settle all of the future liabilities facing the company.[2]

In the fall of 2008, a collapsing U.S. stock market and worldwide recession had a deeper and more far-reaching impact on the economy and began to raise questions about the future of the business system as we have known it. In what is now believed to be the most serious financial collapse since the 1920s, this financial crisis centered on Wall Street and many of the major firms that historically had been the backbone of the U.S. financial system. The epicenter of the financial calamity that brought about untold financial damage around the world was the Wall Street district and a handful of financial institutions located in what has been called "the neighborhood that wrecked the world."[3]

The causes of the financial collapse and the ensuing economic chaos are still being debated. The housing bubble burst and years of lax lending standards put big investment banks and Wall Street at the center of the collapse.[4] Faced with an unprecedented financial crisis, the federal government entered the bailout business as Congress approved a $700 billion rescue plan[5] for Wall Street financial firms, including Merrill Lynch, Bear Stearns, Citigroup, Lehman Brothers, and AIG. It also approved a plan to bail out the auto industry.

There was plenty of blame to go around for the financial crisis, and the finger-pointing continues to this day. Some of those named as guilty parties included home buyers who took on more debt than they could handle; mortgage lenders who ceased using conventional lending standards; credit rating agencies not doing their job; commission-hungry brokers; builders who conspired with crooked appraisers; and the Federal Reserve, which was accused of flooding the market with easy money.[6] In 2013, the U.S. Department of Justice decided to sue Standard & Poor's Ratings Services for fraud because investors relied on its deceptively high ratings of bonds that signified low default risk.[7] Significant criticism also was directed towards Wall Street and the businesses themselves as being central to the financial collapse. Others have claimed that the Wall Street firms were just doing what the capitalist system encourages, and that it is actually capitalism itself that is behind the mess.

Also in the fall of 2011, Big Business and the capitalistic system were targeted by a new protest movement which called itself "Occupy Wall Street." The movement reflected some of the built up discontent with the business system which had resulted in high unemployment and financial stress for millions. Hundreds and then thousands of protestors assembled in lower Manhattan, claimed Zuccotti Park as their operating base camp, and began the most energetic anti-capitalism movement that has been seen in years. It didn't take long before the protests spread to other countries and the sit-in that started in New York soon sprouted up in major cities all over the globe.[8] In spite of protests that continued beyond 2012, the Occupy Wall Street (OWS) movement never had a distinct list of criticisms or demands, but it was understood that the enemy was the big business system and modern capitalism.

Though the OWS movement never seemed to forge a clear goal, its list of complaints included crony capitalism, inequality of wealth, the lack of affordable housing, obscenely high executive compensation, business greed, frustration at the lack of good jobs, a culture that puts profits before people, and a general discontent with capitalism and the economic system.[9]

Some observers criticized the protestors because they failed to see the complicity of big government in developing and supporting housing policies that led to the financial crisis in the first place. Throughout the 1990s and 2000s, politicians were pushing mortgage lenders Fannie Mae and Freddie Mac to direct a substantial portion of their mortgage financing to borrowers who had blemished credit or whose income was so low they would never be able to afford their loans. Then private lenders and banks joined in and the cumulative effect was a housing crisis whose bubble burst and threw the entire economic system into disarray and near bankruptcy.[10] In short, though OWS was preoccupied with Wall Street and the capitalistic system, Big Government also had a hand in the crisis as well.

Business is a more inviting target than government, however, because it is seen as being motivated only by profit, while government is not seeking profits but is charged with acting in the public interest. As a consequence, business and the capitalistic system have become the primary targets of the critics. The Wall Street protestors framed the battle as being between the 99 percent of citizens they represented and the wealthy 1 percent of citizens, primarily businesspeople, they were angry about. The OWS movement had some success as a few public opinion polls showed more of the public supported its cause than opposed it. Further, businesses which claimed to represent enlightened social change, such as Ben & Jerry's ice cream, began donating to the movement beginning in 2012.[11] This group of OWS supporters named themselves the Movement Resource Group. Only time will tell where this movement will go, but in the meantime it has raised public awareness of weaknesses in the capitalistic system. And, more and more commentaries questioning the capitalistic system have been coming out, so it appears to be an issue the business community must address to repair its bruised image.[12]

In addition to the financial crisis, the OWS movement and growing anti-capitalism sentiments, along with the BP oil spill, other serious questions continue to be raised about other ongoing day-to-day business issues: corporate governance, ethical conduct, executive compensation, hiring of illegal immigrants, fluctuating energy prices, government involvement in the economy, healthiness of fast food, international corruption, and so on. The listing of such issues could go on and on, but these examples illustrate the enduring tensions between business and society, which in part can be traced to recent high-profile incidents, trends, or events.

Many other familiar issues carrying social or ethical implications continue to be debated within the business and society interface. Some of these issues have included businesses moving offshore, downsizing of pension programs, high unemployment, reduced health insurance benefits, sexual harassment in the workplace, abuses of corporate power, toxic waste disposal, insider trading, whistle-blowing, product liability, deceptive marketing, and questionable lobbying by business to influence the outcome of legislation. These examples of both specific incidents and general issues are typical of the kinds of stories about business and society in newspapers and magazines and on television and the Internet.

At the broadest level, the role of business in society is the subject of this book. Many key concerns will be addressed—the role of business relative to the role of government in the socioeconomic system; what a firm must do to be considered socially responsible; what managers must do to be considered ethical; and what responsibilities companies have to consumers, employees, shareholders, and communities in an age of economic uncertainty and globalization. And, throughout all this, a growing mandate for sustainability has captured the attention of business leaders, critics, and public policy makers.

Spotlight on Sustainability

Perspectives on Sustainability

- Sustainability is…providing for the needs of the present generation while not compromising the ability of future generations to meet theirs (*original definition in the U.N. Brundtland Commission Report on "Our Common Future," 1987*).
- Sustainability is…creating shareholder and social value while decreasing the environmental footprint along the value chains in which we operate (*DuPont*).
- Sustainability is generally considered to have three interdependent, coevolutionary dimensions: the economy, the society, and the natural environment (Jean Garner Stead and W. Edward Stead, *Management for a Small Planet*, 3d Ed., 2009).
- Corporate sustainability is a business approach that creates long-term shareholder value by embracing opportunities and managing risks deriving from economic, environmental, and social developments (3BL Media, 2009).
- Corporate sustainability can be broadly defined as the pursuit of a business growth strategy by allocating financial or in-kind resources of the corporation to a social or environmental initiative (The Conference Board, *Sustainability Matters*, 2011).
- Sustainability is continuous reduction of our environmental footprint throughout our own facilities and our value or supply chain. We also define it from a social perspective as making sure that the community in general, and certainly communities where we sell products, are viable and healthy and that their needs are met (A consumer products company).

In the middle of the second decade of the new millennium, many economic, legal, ethical, and technological issues concerning business and society continue on. This period is turbulent and has been characterized by significant changes in the world, the economy, society, technology, and global relationships. Against this setting of ongoing instability in the business and society relationship, some basic concepts and ideas are worth considering first.

Business and Society

There are some basic concepts that are central to understanding the continuing business and society relationship. These concepts include pluralism, our special-interest society, business criticism, corporate power, and corporate social response to stakeholders. First, it is essential to define and describe two key terms that are central to the discussion: *business* and *society*.

Business Defined

Business may be defined as the collection of private, commercially oriented (profit-oriented) organizations, ranging in size from one-person proprietorships (e.g., DePalma's Restaurant, Gibson's Men's Wear, and Taqueria la Parrilla) to corporate giants (e.g., Coca-Cola, Microsoft, Apple, Google, Delta Airlines, and UPS). Between these two extremes are many medium-sized proprietorships, partnerships, and corporations.

When businesses are referred to in this collective sense, businesses of all sizes and in all types of industries are included. However, in embarking on a study of business and society, there is a tendency to focus more on big businesses in selected industries. Big Business is highly visible and assumes a huge profile. Its products, services and advertising are widely known. Consequently, it is more frequently in the critical public eye. Size is often associated with power, and the powerful are given closer scrutiny. Although small businesses far outnumber large ones, the prevalence, power, visibility, and impact of large firms keep them on the front page most of the time.

In addition, some industries are simply more conducive than others with respect to the creation of visible, social problems. For example, many manufacturing firms by their nature cause observable air, water, and solid waste pollution. They contribute to climate changes. Such firms, therefore, are more likely to be subject to criticism than a life insurance company, which emits no obvious pollutants. The auto industry with the manufacture of sport utility vehicles (SUVs) and trucks is a specific case in point. Much of the criticism of General Motors (GM) and other automakers is raised because of their high profile as manufacturers, the products they make (which are the largest single source of air pollution), and the popularity of their products (many families own multiple cars and road congestion is experienced daily).

Some industries are highly visible because of the intensive advertising of their products (e.g., Procter & Gamble, FedEx, Anheuser-Busch, and Home Depot). Other industries (e.g., the cigarette, toy, and fast-food industries) are scrutinized because of the possible effects of their products on health or because of their roles in providing health-related products (e.g., pharmaceutical firms, vitamin firms).

For these reasons, when discussing business in its relationship with society, the focus of attention tends to be on large businesses in particular industries. However, we should not lose sight of the fact that our discussions also apply to small- and medium-sized companies. In recent years, the social responsibilities of smaller enterprises and the developing movement towards social entrepreneurship has captivated considerable attention.

Society Defined

Society may be defined as a community, a nation, or a broad grouping of people with common traditions, values, institutions, and collective activities and interests. As such, business and society relationships may be between business and the local community (business and Atlanta, for example), business and the United States as a whole, global business, or business and a specific group of stakeholders (consumers, employees, investors, environmentalists).

When discussing business and the entire society, society is thought of as being composed of numerous interest groups, more or less formalized organizations, and a variety of institutions. Each of these groups, organizations, and institutions is a purposeful aggregation of people who have united because they represent a common cause or share common beliefs about a particular issue. Examples of interest groups or purposeful organizations are numerous: Friends of the Earth, Common Cause, chambers of commerce, National Association of Manufacturers, People for the Ethical Treatment of Animals (PETA), and the Forest Stewardship Council.

Society as the Macroenvironment

The environment of society is a key element in analyzing business and society relationships. At its broadest level, the societal environment might be thought of as a **macroenvironment** which includes the total environment outside the firm. The macroenvironment is the comprehensive societal context in which organizations reside. The idea of the macroenvironment is just another way of thinking about society. In fact, early courses on business and society were sometimes (and some still are) titled "Business and Its Environment." The concept of the macroenvironment evokes different images or ways of thinking about business and society relationships and is therefore useful in terms of framing and understanding the total business context.

A useful conceptualization of the macroenvironment is to think of it as being composed of four identifiable but interrelated segments: social, economic, political, and technological.[13]

The **social environment** focuses on demographics, lifestyles, culture, and social values of the society. Of particular interest here is the manner in which shifts in these factors affect the organization and its functioning. For example, the influx of undocumented workers over the past decade has brought changes to the demographic profile of countries. The **economic environment** focuses on the nature and direction of the economy in which business operates. Variables of interest include such indices as gross national product, inflation, interest rates, unemployment rates, foreign exchange fluctuations, national debt, global trade, balance of payments, and various other indices of economic activity. In the past decade, hypercompetition in the world economy has dominated the economic segment of this environment and global competitiveness is now a huge issue for businesses.[14] Slow business growth during the past decade has been a serious problem. Businesses moving jobs offshore has been a controversial trend. Enduring levels of high unemployment, underemployment and use of part-time workers have been problematic.

The **political environment** focuses on the processes by which laws get passed and officials get elected and all other aspects of the interaction between firms, political processes, and government. Of particular interest to business in this segment are the regulatory process and the changes that occur over time in business regulation of various industries, products, and various issues. The passage of the Sarbanes–Oxley Act in 2002 continues to be a contentious issue for many businesses. Beginning in 2009, Congress ramped up its regulatory ambitions as it sought to improve the global economic system. Passage of the Affordable Care Act (ACA) in 2010 introduced considerable uncertainty in business decision making because of its dramatic impact on business costs. Finally, the **technological environment** represents the total set of technology-based advancements taking place in society and the world. This segment includes new products, processes, materials, and means of communication (social networking, for example), as well as the status of knowledge and scientific advancement. The process of technological change is of significant importance here.[15] In recent years, computer-based information technologies and biotechnology have been driving this segment of environmental turbulence.

Understanding that business and society relationships are embedded in a macroenvironment provides us with a constructive way of understanding the kinds of issues that constitute the broad milieu in which business functions. Throughout this book, evidence of these turbulent environmental segments will become apparent and it will become easier to appreciate what challenges managers face as they strive to develop effective organizations while interfacing with society. Each of the thousands of specific groups and organizations that make up our pluralistic society can typically be traced to one of these four environmental segments.

A Pluralistic Society

Societies as macro environments are typically pluralistic. Pluralistic societies make for business and society relationships that are complex and dynamic. **Pluralism** refers to a diffusion of power among society's many groups and organizations. A long-standing definition of a pluralistic society is helpful: "A pluralistic society is one in which there is wide decentralization and diversity of power concentration."[16]

The key descriptive terms in this definition are *decentralization* and *diversity*. In other words, power is dispersed among many groups and people. It is not in the hands of any single institution (e.g., business, government, labor, or the military) or a small number of groups. Many years ago, in *The Federalist Papers*, James Madison speculated that

FIGURE 1-1

The Virtues of a Pluralistic Society

A pluralistic society ...
- Prevents power from being concentrated in the hands of a few
- Maximizes freedom of expression and action and strikes a balance between monism (social organization into one institution), on the one hand, and anarchy (social organization into an infinite number of persons), on the other[a]
- Is one in which the allegiance of individuals to groups is dispersed

- Creates a widely diversified set of loyalties to many organizations and minimizes the danger that a leader of any one organization will be left uncontrolled[b]
- Provides a built-in set of checks and balances, in that groups can exert power over one another with no single organization (business or government) dominating and becoming overly influential

Sources: [a]Keith Davis and Robert L. Blomstrom, *Business and Society: Environment and Responsibility*, 3d ed. (New York: McGraw- Hill, 1975), 63. [b]Joseph W. McGuire, *Business and Society* (New York: McGraw-Hill, 1963), 132. Also see "Pluralistic Society," http://www.education.com/definition/pluralistic-society/, Accessed March 18, 2013.

pluralism was a virtuous scheme. He correctly anticipated the rise of numerous organizations in society as a consequence of it. Pluralistic societies are found all over the world now, and some of the virtues of a pluralistic society are summarized in Figure 1-1.

Pluralism and Its Strengths and Weaknesses

All social systems have strengths and weaknesses. A pluralistic society prevents power from being concentrated in the hands of a few. It also maximizes freedom of expression and action. Pluralism provides for a built-in set of checks and balances so that no single group dominates. However, a weakness of a pluralistic system is that it creates an environment in which diverse institutions pursue their own self-interests with the result that there is no unified direction to bring together individual pursuits. Another weakness is that groups and institutions proliferate to the extent that their goals start to overlap, thus causing confusion as to which organizations best serve which functions. Pluralism forces conflict onto center stage because of its emphasis on autonomous groups, each pursuing its own objectives. In light of these concerns, a pluralistic system does not appear to be very efficient though it does provide a greater balance of power among groups in society.

Multiple Publics, Systems, and Stakeholders

Knowing that society is composed of so many different semiautonomous and autonomous groups might cause one to question whether we can realistically speak of society in a definitive sense that has any generally agreed-upon meaning. Nevertheless, we do speak in such terms, knowing that, unless we specify a particular societal subgroup or subsystem, we are referring to the collectivity of all those persons, groups, and institutions that constitute society. Thus, references to business and society relationships usually refer either to particular segments or subgroups of society (consumers, women, minorities, environmentalists, senior citizens) or to business and some *system* in our society (politics, law, custom, religion, economics). These groups of people or systems may also be referred to in an institutional form (business and the courts, business and labor unions, business and the church, business and the Federal Trade Commission, and so on).

Figure 1-2 depicts in graphic form the points of interface between business and some of the multiple publics, systems, or stakeholders with which business interacts. Stakeholders are those groups or individuals with whom an organization interacts or has interdependencies. The stakeholder concept will be developed further in Chapter 3. It also should be noted that each stakeholder group may be further subdivided into more specific subgroups.

FIGURE 1-2 Business and Selected Stakeholder Relationships

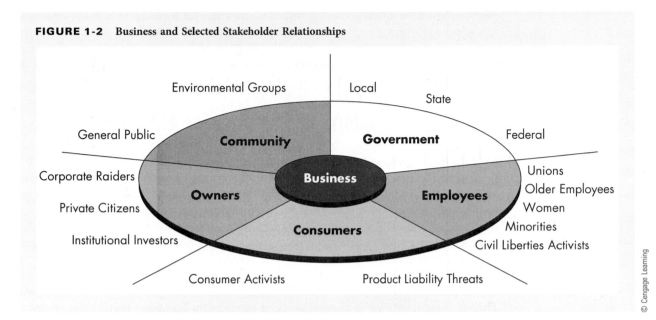

If sheer numbers of relationships and interactions are an indicator of complexity, business's current relationships with different segments of society constitute a truly complex macro environment. Today, managers must deal with these interfaces on a daily basis, and the study of business and society is designed to improve that understanding.

A Special-Interest Society

A pluralistic society often becomes a **special-interest society**. As the concept of pluralism is pursued to an extreme, a society is created that is characterized by tens of thousands of special-interest groups, each pursuing its own focused agenda. General-purpose interest organizations, often called *advocacy groups*, such as Common Cause and the U.S. Chamber of Commerce, still exist. However, the past three decades have been characterized by increasing specialization on the part of interest groups representing all sectors of society—consumers, employees, investors, communities, the natural environment, government, and business itself. One newspaper headline noted that "there is a group for every cause." Special-interest groups not only have grown in number at an accelerated pace, but they also have become increasingly activist, intense, and focused on single issues. Such groups are strongly committed to their causes and strive to put pressure on businesses to meet their needs and on governments to accommodate their agendas.

The health-care debate that began raging in the United States in the fall of 2009 illustrates how a pluralistic, special-interest society works. Consider that the following special-interest groups were all active and continued to be so in the fine-tuning of the health-care legislation. The major interest groups included doctors, hospitals, drug companies, insurance companies, employers, insured people, seniors, and uninsured people.[17] Each of these groups has much at stake in resolving this society-level issue that has significant implications for many sectors, including business. Though the Affordable Care Act was passed in 2010, its implementation has been gradual and contentious details are still in the process of being worked out. The full implications for business are not yet clear.

The consequence of interest-group specialization is that each of these groups has been able to attract a significant following that is dedicated to the group's goals. Increased memberships have meant increased revenues and a sharper focus as each of these groups has aggressively sought its specific, narrow purposes. The likelihood of these groups working at cross-purposes and with no unified set of goals has made life immensely more complex for the major institutions, such as business and government. But this is how a pluralistic society works.

Business Criticism and Corporate Response

It is inevitable in a pluralistic, special-interest society that the major institutions that make up that society, such as business and government, will become the subjects of considerable analysis and criticism. The purpose here is not so much to focus on the negative as it is to illustrate how the process of business criticism has shaped the evolution of the business and society relationship today. Were it not for the fact that individuals and groups have been critical of business and have such high expectations and demands, there would be no books or courses on this subject, and few improvements would occur in the business and society relationship over time.

Figure 1-3 illustrates how certain factors that have arisen in the social environment have created an atmosphere in which business criticism has taken place and flourished. Though some resistance to change has been apparent on business's part, the more positive responses on the part of business have been (1) an increased awareness and concern for the social environment and (2) a changed social contract (relationship) between business and society. Each of these factors merits closer attention.

Factors in the Social Environment

Over the decades, many factors in the social environment have created a climate in which criticism of business has taken place and flourished. Some of these factors occur relatively independently of one another, but some are interrelated; that is, they occur and grow hand in hand.

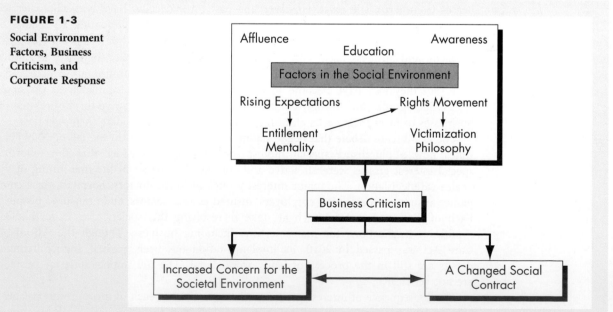

FIGURE 1-3

Social Environment Factors, Business Criticism, and Corporate Response

© Cengage Learning

Affluence and Education. Two factors that have advanced side by side in developed economies are affluence and education. As a society becomes more prosperous and better educated, higher expectations of its major institutions, such as business, naturally follow.

Affluence refers to the level of wealth, disposable income, and standard of living of the society. Measures of the U.S. standard of living indicate that it has been rising for decades, but leveling off during the past five years or so. In the past several years, questions have been raised as to whether successive generations will be better off or not. In spite of recent events, overall affluence remains elevated, but this could change. This movement toward affluence is found in many of the world's developed countries and is also occurring in emerging economies as global capitalism spreads. The recent, worldwide economic recession raises valid questions about continuing affluence, however.[18]

Alongside a relatively high standard of living has been a growth in the average formal **education** of the populace. The U.S. Census Bureau reported that between 1970 and 2010, when the last census data were published, the number of American adults who graduated from high school grew from 55 percent to 85 percent, and the numbers who graduated from college increased from 11 percent to 28 percent.[19] As citizens continue to gain more education, their expectations of life generally increase. The combination of relative affluence and growing education has formed the underpinning for a society in which criticism of major institutions, such as business, naturally arises. Moderating factors such as high unemployment, underemployment, and rising educational costs resulting in huge student loans are also at work. And when income and educational levels decline, business is often singled out as a major culprit. There is significant uncertainty today as to whether past trends will continue.

Awareness Through Television, Movies, and the Internet. Closely related to formal education is the broad and growing level of public awareness in society today. Although newspapers and magazines are read by a declining fraction of the population, more powerful media—television, movies, and the Internet—are accessed by virtually the entire society. Through television, people receive a profusion of information that contributes to a climate of business criticism. In recent decades especially, movies have bashed both business and the capitalist system. In addition, the Internet and smart phone explosion have brought elevated levels of awareness around the world. Through e-mails, texts, blogs, tweets, and other social media, the average citizen is extraordinarily aware of what is going on in the world on a real-time basis.

The prevalence and power of TV touches all socioeconomic classes. According to data compiled by the A. C. Nielsen Co., the average daily time spent viewing television per household is more than four hours per day.[20] In the United States today, more than 98 percent of homes have color TVs, and a great majority of homes have two or more televisions. In developed countries around the world, statistics such as this are becoming more common. Television remains a pervasive and powerful medium in society.

24/7 News and Investigative Programs   There are at least three ways in which information that leads to criticism of business appears on television. First, there are straight news shows, such as the 24-hour cable news channels, the evening news on the major networks, and investigative news programs. It is debatable whether or not the major news programs are treating business fairly, but in one major study conducted by Corporate Reputation Watch, senior executives identified media criticism, along with unethical behavior, as the biggest threats to a company's reputation. Reflecting on the lessons learned from high-profile cases of corporate wrongdoing, half the executives surveyed thought unethical behavior and media criticism were the biggest threats to their corporate reputations.[21] Coverage of Wall Street's complicity in the recent worldwide recession has been particularly damaging because it has called into question society's basic trust of corporate executives and the business system. And, business has demonstrated a low level of preparedness for dealing with the social media criticism receives.[22]

Business has to deal not only with the scrutiny of 24/7 news coverage but also with investigative news programs such as *60 Minutes, 20/20, Dateline NBC, Rock Center*, and PBS's *Frontline*, that sometimes present exposés of corporate wrongdoings or questionable practices. Whereas the straight news programs make an effort to be objective, the investigative shows are tougher on business, tending to favor stories that expose the dark side of the enterprises or their executives. These shows are enormously popular and influential, and many companies squirm when reporters show up on their premises complete with camera crews.

Prime-Time Television Programs   The second way in which criticisms of business appear on TV is through prime-time programs. Television's depiction of businesspeople in negative ways always brings to mind the scheming oilman J. R. Ewing of *Dallas*, whose backstabbing shenanigans dominated prime-time TV for years (1978–1991) before it went off the air. In 2012, *Dallas* came roaring back on TV and J. R. and his son were typically up to no good. Just as the second season of *Dallas* was being filmed, Larry Hagman, who played J. R., died of cancer, and TV's most charming scoundrel would no longer be around. Doubtless his son will try to fill J. R.'s boots to become the new, Texas-sized villain viewers love to hate.[23] The popular TV reality shows *The Apprentice* and *Celebrity Apprentice* featuring billionaire businessman Donald Trump, have depicted aspiring and well-known business executives in often questionable roles.

More often than not, the businessperson has been portrayed across the nation's television screens as smirking, scheming, cheating, and conniving "bad guys." A study released by the Business & Media Institute reported an investigation of 12 prime-time dramas in which 77 percent of the plots involving business were negative toward businesspeople. In this study, business characters committed almost as many serious felonies as drug dealers, child molesters, and serial killers combined. On one show, *Law & Order*, half of the felons were businesspeople.[24] A few other TV shows where this unfavorable portrayal has been evident include *CSI, Mad Men, Horrible Bosses, Damages, Banshee*, and *Criminal Minds*. Any redeeming social values that business and businesspeople may have rarely show up on television. Rather, businesspeople are often cast as evil and greedy social parasites whose efforts to get more for themselves are justly condemned and usually thwarted.[25]

Commercials   A third way in which television contributes to business criticism is through commercials. This may be business's own fault. To the extent that business does not accurately and fairly portray its products and services on TV, it undermines its own credibility. Commercials are a two-edged sword. On the one hand, they may sell more products and services in the short run. On the other hand, they could damage business's long-term credibility if they promote products and services deceptively and dishonestly. It is also believed by many that TV today promotes excessive commercialism as well as sedentary lifestyles.

In three specific TV settings—news coverage, prime-time programming, and commercials—a strained environment is fostered by this "awareness" factor made available through the power and pervasiveness of television.

Movies   Movies are also a significant birthplace of business criticism. Hollywood seems to perceive corporations as powerful, profit-seeking enterprises that have no redeeming values. The Oscar-winning movie *Avatar*, along with *Up in the Air*, portrayed corporations as greedy, cruel, and destructive. Michael Moore's documentary, *Capitalism: A Love Story* slammed the free enterprise system as corrupt and doomed. Other popular movies to stigmatize the business system include *The Informant, The International, Syriana*, and *Duplicity*. In these movies, corporate life is depicted as amoral, at best, and possibly deadly. In 2010, the sequel to *Wall Street* was released—*Wall Street: Money Never Sleeps*—with Michael Douglas again playing the malevolent Gordon Gekko. Gekko is released from 14 years in prison just in time to witness the financial system's collapse and to visit his old ways. Hollywood writers seem to love advancing the "greed is good" portrayal of business, and they go out of their way to perpetuate this image of the corporate community.[26] The release of *The Social Network* did not focus on the positive aspects of Facebook, but portrayed its co-founder Mark Zuckerberg as a conniving, antisocial individual who had to make a few enemies to succeed. The movie *Margin Call* cast its characters as flawed and cynical as they sought to save their financial institution from imminent collapse.[27] *Side Effects* (2013) portrayed a hotshot trader on Wall Street who had just done time for insider trading. The movie appears to be a modest film about the victims of a greedy pharmaceutical industry, but it turns into a murder mystery set in the world of white-collar crime.[28]

To be fair, business cannot blame the media for all its problems. If some businesses did not engage in questionable behavior, the media might not be as inclined to create such an environment. The media makes the public more aware of questionable practices and should be seen as only one factor that influences the environment in which business continues to find itself criticized.

Revolution of Rising Expectations. In addition to affluence, formal education, and awareness through the media, other societal trends have fostered the climate in which business criticism has flourished. Growing out of these factors has been a **revolution of rising expectations**. This is a belief or an attitude that each succeeding generation ought to have a standard of living higher than that of its predecessor. A Pew Charitable Trust study has revealed that, according to census data, today this is more a dream than reality. A continuing unemployment crisis has been hitting many people very hard, and some writers have been asking if we have now reached the "end of prosperity." It is more frequently being questioned whether the next generation will be better off than the current one. A recent Boston Consulting Group poll has revealed that the West is a glum place to be right now. Only 12 percent of the French, 21 percent of Americans, and 28 percent of the British think the next generation will be better off than the current one.[29] This decline in confidence characterized the first decade of the new millennium[30] and is continuing today.[31]

If rising expectations continue as they have for decades, people's hopes for major institutions, such as business, should be greater too. Building on this line of thinking, it could be argued that business criticism is evident today because society's rising expectations of business's social performance have outpaced business's ability to meet these growing expectations. To the extent that this has occurred over the past and continues, business will find itself with a larger social problem.[32] To be fair, some have observed that we may have entered an era of diminishing economic expectations,[33] but whether this turns out to apply to business' social performance remains to be seen.

A **social problem** has been described as a gap between society's expectations of social conditions and the current social realities.[34] From the viewpoint of a business firm, the social problem is experienced as the gap grows between society's *expectations* of the firm's social performance and its *actual* social performance. Rising expectations typically outpace the responsiveness of institutions such as business, thus creating a constant predicament in that it is subject to criticism. Figure 1-4 illustrates the larger "social

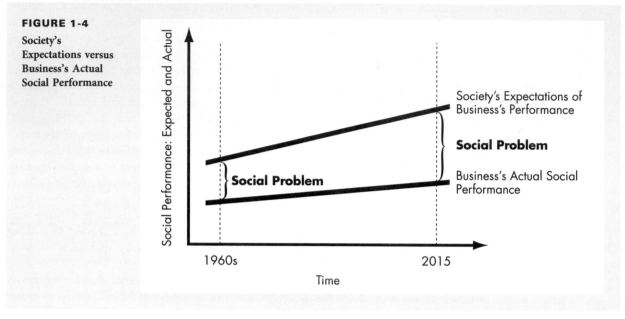

FIGURE 1-4

Society's Expectations versus Business's Actual Social Performance

problem" that business faces today. It is depicted by the "gap" between society's expectations of business and business's actual social performance.

Although the general trend of rising expectations may continue, the revolution moderates at times when the economy is not as robust. Historically, job situations, health, family lives, and overall quality of life have continued to improve, though the effect of the recent recession makes their future hard to predict. The persistence of problems in society such as crime, poverty, homelessness, unemployment, environmental pollution, alcohol and drug abuse, along with terrorism and potential pandemics are always present to moderate rising expectations.[35]

Entitlement Mentality. One notable outgrowth of the revolution of rising expectations has been the emergence of an **entitlement mentality** on the part of some. The entitlement mentality is the general belief that someone is owed something (e.g., a job, an education, a living wage, or health care) just because she or he is a member of society. Several years ago, the Public Relations Society conducted a study of public expectations, with particular focus on public attitudes toward the philosophy of entitlement. In the national survey, a significant gap was found between what people thought they were entitled to have and what they actually had—a steadily improving standard of living, a guaranteed job for all those willing and able to work, and products certified as safe and not hazardous to one's health.[36]

In the middle of the second decade of the 2000s, jobs, fair wages, insurance, retirement programs, and health care continue to be issues on which entitlement thinking has centered though these have been moderated by the weak and unpredictable economy. Each of these issues has significant implications for business when they are perceived to be "entitlements" but are not received.

Rights Movement. The revolution of rising expectations, the entitlement mentality, and all of the factors discussed so far have contributed to what has been termed the **rights movement** that has been evident in society for several decades now. In the past several decades, and continuing, the U.S. Supreme Court has heard increasing numbers of cases aimed at establishing for some groups various legal rights that perhaps never occurred to the founders of the nation.[37]

Some of these rights, such as the right to privacy and the right to due process, have been perceived as generic for all citizens. However, in addition to these generalized rights, there has been activism for rights for particular groups in society. This modern movement began with the civil rights cases of the 1950s. Many groups have been inspired by the success of African Americans and have sought progress by similar means. Thus, we have seen the protected status of minorities grow to include many other groups. At various levels—federal, state, and local—there have been claims for the rights of many different groups each claiming they are due special protection.

Business, as one of society's major institutions, has been affected with an ever-expanding array of expectations as to how people want to be treated, not only as employees but also as shareholders, consumers, environmentally conscious citizens, and members of the community. The "rights" movement is related to the special-interest society discussed earlier and sometimes follows an "entitlement" mentality among some people and within some sectors of society.

Victimization Philosophy. It has become apparent during the past several decades that there are growing numbers of individuals and groups who see themselves as having been victimized by society. The *New York* magazine featured a cover story on "The New Culture of Victimization," with the title "Don't Blame Me!"[38] *Esquire* probed what it called "A Confederacy of Complainers."[39] Charles Sykes published *A Nation of Victims: The Decay of the American Character.*[40] Sykes's thesis, with which these other observers might agree, is that modern cultures have become a "society of victims."

What is particularly interesting about the novel **victimization philosophy** is the wide-spread extent to which it is dispersing in the population. According to these writers, the victim mentality is just as likely to be seen among all groups in society—regardless of race, gender, age, or any other classification. Sykes observed that previous movements may have been seen as a "revolution of rising expectations," but the victimization movement might be called a "revolution of rising sensitivities" in which grievance begets grievance. In such a society of victims, feelings rather than reason or facts prevail, and people start perceiving that they are being unfairly "hurt" by society's institutions—business, government, and education. The victimization philosophy is intimately related to and sometimes inseparable from the rights movement and the entitlement mentality. Taken together, these unusual ways of viewing one's plight—as someone else's unfairness—pose special challenges for future business managers.

In summary, affluence and education, awareness through television, movies and the Internet, the revolution of rising expectations, an entitlement mentality, the rights movement, and the victimization philosophy have formed a backdrop against which criticism of business has grown and flourished. This helps explain why we have a societal environment that is conducive to criticism of business. Though the U.S. and world economies have been through their worst fiscal slump since World War II, some of these trends are bound to continue but may be moderated if economies improve.

In the next two subsections, some of the general criticisms of business, and some of the general responses to such criticisms, are identified and discussed.

General Criticism of Business: Use and Abuse of Power

A number of different criticisms have been directed toward business over the years: Business is too big, it is too powerful, it pollutes the environment and exploits people for its own gain, it takes advantage of workers and consumers, it does not tell the truth, its executives are too highly paid, and so on. If one were to identify a common thread that

---

ETHICS IN PRACTICE CASE

Working for My Cup or the House?

Service industry employees are paid minimally by the company they work for and so their pay is largely determined by the tips they receive from customers. Bartenders have to deal with peoples' needs as well as employee competition and standard operating procedures set forth by management. Every time they pour a drink, they must decide whether to follow company standards or give away extra alcohol in order to receive a larger tip.

When first being promoted to bartender at an established golf resort, I witnessed firsthand the different factors that can affect a "pour." A pour can be defined as how much liquor is added to a customer's drink. The three factors that affect a pour are comparisons to other employees' pours, the requests of customers for extra pours with promise of a larger tip, or what the company designates as a pour.

When working as a team or having repeat customers, bartenders are compared based on their pour. If one bartender uses two pours and another uses one pour (the latter is the standard for the company), the rule-following bartender is not viewed as favorably as the one using the larger pour. This is clearly reflected in tips from customers. Similarly, the customer might say, "Put a little extra in there and I'll take care of you." The employee is put on the spot to choose between the company and him or herself.

The bartender with the heavier pour or who gives away drinks for free may receive more money in their tip cup, but the company suffers from lost revenues. If a bartender makes an average of 100 drinks a night and uses two pours instead of one for each drink, that bartender is giving away 100 drinks worth of alcohol each night which reduces nightly revenues, and has a huge effect on yearly liquor revenues.

In this highly competitive and profitable industry, over pouring is a practice that can cripple a business. New bartenders want to fit in with the others and earn as much money as possible. Which is more important, filling their own tip cup, or maximizing the house's profits, which does not directly benefit the bartender?

1. Is it ethical to over pour customers' drinks in order to develop better customer relations to earn more tips at the expense of company revenues? Are the bartenders using the "entitlement mentality" here to justify their self-serving actions? Do bartenders have a "right" to take care of their own cups?

2. If the customer wants or expects over pouring, should the companies allow over pouring in order to satisfy the customers' wants and desires?

3. Is it ethical to witness and not report over pouring on the part of fellow bartenders who have been there longer? Should the over pouring bartenders be reported to management?

Contributed by Matthew DePasquale

---

seems to run through all the grievances, it seems to be business's use and perceived abuse of power. This is an issue that will not go away. In a cover story, *BusinessWeek* posed the question: "Too Much Corporate Power?" In this featured article, the magazine presented its surveys of the public regarding business power.

Most Americans are willing to acknowledge that Corporate America gets much credit for the good fortunes of the country. In spite of this, 72 percent said business has too much power over too many aspects of their lives.[41] In the relatively new book, *Power, Inc.*, the case is made that companies, not kings, now rule the world. The author suggests that global corporations wield greater power today than most nation-states.[42] In Michael Moore's provocative movie, *Capitalism: A Love Story*, the filmmaker continued his assault on business power by laying the blame for the worldwide recession on both big business and government. Whether at the general level or the level of the firm, questions about business's use or abuse of power continue to be raised.

Some of the points of friction between business and the public, in which corporate power is identified as partially the culprit, include such issues as corporate governance,

CEO pay, investor losses, wholesale job losses, outsourcing jobs, health care availability and costs, drug and gas prices, poor airline service, HMOs that override doctors' decisions, in-your-face marketing, e-mail spam, globalization, corporate bankrolling of politicians, sweatshops, urban sprawl, and low wages.

So, what is **business power**? Business power refers to the capacity or ability to produce an effect or to bring influence to bear on a situation or people. Power, in and of itself, may be either positive or negative. In the context of business criticism, however, power typically is perceived as being abused. Business certainly does have enormous power, but whether it abuses power is an issue that needs to be carefully examined. The allegation that business abuses power remains the central theme behind the details.

Levels of Power. Business power exists and may be manifested at several different levels. Four such levels include the macrolevel, the intermediate level, the microlevel, and the individual level.[43] The *macrolevel* refers to the entire corporate system—Corporate America, Big Business—the totality of business organizations. Power here emanates from the sheer size, resources, and dominance of the corporate system over our lives. As the corporate system has become more global, its impact has become more far reaching as well. At the 2012 World Economic Forum, it was noted that the worlds' major companies are now larger than many governments and are operating in a universe that is increasingly supranational, often disconnected from local issues and home markets.[44]

The *intermediate level* of business power refers to groups of corporations acting in concert in an effort to produce a desired effect—to set prices, control markets, dominate purchasers, promote an issue, or pass or defeat legislation. Prime examples include OPEC (gas prices), airlines, cable TV companies, banks, pharmaceutical companies, and defense contractors pursuing interests they have in common. The combined effect of companies acting in concert is substantial. The *microlevel* of business power is the level of the individual firm. This might refer to the exertion of power or influence by any major corporation—Google, Walmart, Apple, Microsoft, Nike, or Exxon—for example. The final level is the *individual level.* This refers to the individual corporate leader exerting power—for example, Indra Nooyi (Pepsi), Daniel Amos (Aflac), Virginia Rometty (IBM), Tim Cook (Apple), Muhtar Kent (Coca-Cola), or Warren Buffett (Berkshire Hathaway).

The key point here is that as one analyzes corporate power, one should think in terms of the different levels at which that power is manifested. When this is done, it is not easy to generalize whether corporate power is excessive or has been abused. Specific levels of power need to be delineated and examined before conclusions can be reached.

Spheres of Power. In addition to levels of power, there are also many different spheres or arenas in which business power may be manifested. Figure 1-5 depicts one way of looking at the four levels identified and some of the spheres of power that also exist. *Economic power* and *political power* are two dominant spheres, but business has other, more subtle forms of power as well. These other spheres include *social and cultural power, power over the individual, technological power*, and *environmental power.*[45]

Is the power of business excessive? Does business abuse its power? Apparently, many people think so. To provide sensible and fair answers to these questions, however, one must carefully specify which level of power is being referred to and in which sphere the power is being exercised. When this is done, it is not simple to arrive at answers that are generalizable. Furthermore, the nature of power is such that it is sometimes wielded unintentionally. Sometimes the use of power is consequential; that is, it is not wielded intentionally, but nevertheless exerts its influence even though no attempt is made to exercise it.[46]

FIGURE 1-5   Levels and Spheres of Corporate Power

Levels / Spheres	Macrolevel (the business system)	Intermediate Level (several firms)	Microlevel (single firm)	Individual Level (single executive)
Economic				
Social/Cultural				
Individual				
Technological				
Environmental				
Political				

ETHICS IN PRACTICE CASE

Does Business Have Too Much Power?

The "business system," that totality of all businesses in a nation or the world, is said to be one of the most powerful institutions known to humankind. The other major candidates for this honor are typically government and the military. One of the most often repeated accusations about large businesses is that they have too much power. It is also claimed that they abuse this power.

What is business power? It is the ability to produce an effect—to get things done, to bring about its desired state of affairs. It's about business getting its way. Business can exercise its power at the macro level, the industry level, the firm level, and the level of the individual corporate leader.

One way to think about business power is to frame it in terms that analysts have claimed are relevant. John French and Bertram Raven have argued that business has five types of power: coercive power, legitimate power, reward power, referent power, and expert power. Each of these may be thought of from the perspective of a large business.

Coercive power occurs when someone in authority forces someone to do something—usually with some threat of punishment. *Legitimate* power exists when a person in the chain of command has a title or position that implies he or she has the right to take some action. *Reward* power is manifested when a boss uses rewards to get things done. The rewards may be monetary (pay increases, promotions) but also may be psychological such as praise. *Referent* power is gained by leaders due to others admiring him or her as a role model. *Expert* power arises when someone becomes highly regarded due to their superior training and/or experience.

1. Which type of power do businesses display the most? Give an example.
2. As an employee, with which type of power would you be most concerned?
3. As a consumer, with which type of power would you be most troubled?
4. Have you been the "victim" of business power? Explain.
5. Does business have too much power? Does business abuse its power?

Sources: John French and Bertram Raven, "Bases of Social Power." *Studies in Social Power.* Dorwin Cartwright (ed.) University of Michigan, Ann Arbor, 1959. Jeffrey Pfeffer, *Power—Why Some People Have It—and Others Don't,* Harper Business, 2010; Justin Johnson, "Five Types of Power," *Chron,* http://smallbusiness.chron.com/ 5-types-power-businesses-18221.html, Accessed March 18, 2013.

Balance of Power and Responsibility

Whether or not business abuses its power or allows its use of power to become excessive is a central issue that cuts through all the topics examined in this book. But power should not be viewed in isolation from responsibility, and this power–responsibility relationship is the foundation of pleas for corporate social responsibility which are at the heart of business and society discussions. The **Iron Law of Responsibility** is a concept that addresses this: "In the long run, those who do not use power in a manner which society considers responsible will tend to lose it."[47] Stated another way, whenever power and responsibility become substantially out of balance, forces will be generated to bring them into closer balance.

When power gets out of balance, a variety of forces come to bear on business to be more responsible and more responsive to the criticisms being made against it. Some of these more obvious forces include governmental actions such as increased regulations, or consumer actions such as boycotts. The investigative news media become interested in what is going on, and a whole host of special-interest groups bring pressure to bear. In the *BusinessWeek* story cited earlier, the point was made that "it's this power imbalance that's helping to breed the current resentment against corporations."[48]

The tobacco industry is an excellent example of an industry that has felt the brunt of efforts to address allegations of abuse of power. Eventually, the Food and Drug Administration (FDA) was given additional authority to address the power imbalance between the industry and customers.

In 2002, the U.S. Congress quickly passed the Sarbanes–Oxley Act, which was designed to rein in the power and abuse that were manifested in such corporate scandals as Enron, WorldCom, Arthur Andersen, and Tyco. Beginning in 2011, a new federal regulatory body began its work. The Consumer Financial Protection Bureau was created to make markets fairer for consumers wanting to apply for a mortgage, choose among competing credit cards, or engage in a number of other consumer financial transactions in which business has traditionally held the upper hand.[49] A major argument presented in this book is that such governmental regulations may have been avoided by business if it had done a better job of balancing its power with responsibly in these sectors.

Business Response: Concern and Changing Social Contract

Growing out of criticisms of business and unease regarding the power–responsibility imbalance has been an increased concern on the part of business for the stakeholder environment and a changed social contract. Previously it was indicated that the social environment was composed of such factors as demographics, lifestyles, and social values of the society. It may also be seen as a collection of conditions, events, and trends that reflect how people think and behave and what they value. As firms have sensed that the social environment and the expectations of business have been changing, they have realized that they must adapt as well.

One way of thinking about the business–society relationship is through the concept of **social contract**. The social contract is a set of reciprocal understandings that characterize the relationship between major institutions—in our case, business and society. The social contract has been changing, and these changes have been a direct outgrowth of the increased importance of the social environment to stakeholders. The social contract has been changing to reflect society's expanded expectations of business, especially in the social, ethical, and environmental realms.

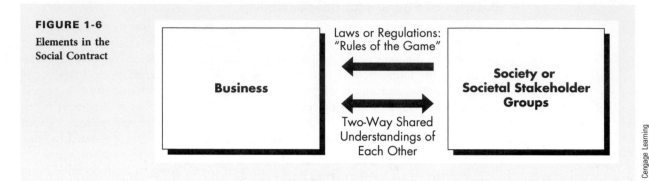

FIGURE 1-6

Elements in the Social Contract

Business

Laws or Regulations: "Rules of the Game"

Two-Way Shared Understandings of Each Other

Society or Societal Stakeholder Groups

© Cengage Learning

The social contract between business and society, as illustrated in Figure 1-6, is articulated in two main ways. The social contract is expressed through:

1. *Laws and regulations* that society has established as the framework within which business must operate, and
2. *Shared understandings* that evolve over time as to each group's expectations of the other.

Laws and regulations spell out the "rules of the game" for business for which they are held accountable. Shared understandings, on the other hand, are more subtle and create room for misunderstandings. These shared understandings reflect mutual expectations regarding each other's roles, responsibilities, and ethics. These unspoken elements of the social contract represent what might be called the normative perspective on the relationship (i.e., what "ought" to be done by each party to the social contract).[50] The growing importance of social responsibility and business ethics are reflected here.

If these shared understandings were spelled out, a company might adopt the following principles as part of its social contract with consumers:

- We believe our company has a right to innovation, entrepreneurship, and profit-making while our consumers have a right to a healthy society and planet.
- We believe that the interests of our company and our customers are best served through a sustainable practice of capitalism—economically, morally, environmentally, and socially.
- We believe that our company and our customers are duty-bound to serve as custodians of global well-being for this and all future generations.[51]

Unfortunately, the shared understandings dimension of the social contract is seldom expressed in written form such as this.

A *BusinessWeek* editorial on the subject of the social contract argued that the social contract between business and society has been changing significantly and that businesses are expected to take on more responsibilities than they once had. Business is expected to accommodate a broader range of human values than in the past, and because business's existence is based on its willingness and ability to serve society, it must meet these expanded expectations if it expects to prosper in the future.

Another *BusinessWeek* editorial commented on the new social contract by saying, "Listen up, Corporate America. The American people are having a most serious discussion about your role in their lives." The editorial was referring to the criticisms coming out about the abuse of corporate power.[52] Such a statement suggests that changes in the social contract between business and society will be ongoing.

Focus of the Book

This book takes a **managerial approach** to the business and society relationship. This managerial approach emphasizes three main themes that are of vital importance to managers and organizations today: business ethics, sustainability, and stakeholder management.

Managerial Approach

Managers are practical, and they have begun to deal with social and ethical concerns in ways similar to those they have used to manage traditional business functions—marketing, finance, operations, risk management, and so forth—in a rational, systematic, and administratively sound fashion. By viewing issues of social and ethical concern and sustainability from a managerial frame of reference, managers have been able to convert seemingly unmanageable concerns into ones that can be dealt with in a balanced and impartial fashion. At the same time, managers have had to integrate traditional economic and financial considerations with ethical and social considerations.

Urgent Versus Enduring Issues. From the standpoint of urgency in organizational response, management is concerned with two broad types or classes of social issues. First, there are those issues or crises that arise instantaneously and for which management must formulate relatively quick responses. A typical example might be a protest group that shows up on management's doorstep one day, arguing vehemently that the company should withdraw its sponsorship of a violent television show scheduled to air the next week. Or a crisis could occur with respect to a company's products, services, or operations.

Second, there are issues that management has time to deal with on a long-term basis. These enduring issues include product safety, environmental pollution, sustainability, employment discrimination, and occupational safety and health. These are continuing long-term issues that will be of concern to society on an ongoing basis and for which management must develop planned, thoughtful organizational responses. Management must be concerned with both short-term and long-term capabilities for dealing with social problems and the organization's social performance.

The measure of success of the managerial approach will be the extent to which leaders can improve an organization's social, ethical, and sustainability performance by taking a managerial approach rather than dealing with issues and crises on an ad hoc basis. This managerial approach will require balancing the needs of urgency with the requirements of enduring issues.

Business Ethics Theme

The managerial focus attempts to take a practical look at the social issues and expectations business faces, but ethical questions inevitably and continually come into play. In the workplace, **ethics** basically refers to issues of fairness and justice, and **business ethics** focuses on ethical issues that arise in the commercial realm. Ethical factors appear throughout our discussion because questions of fairness and justice, no matter how slippery they are to deal with, permeate business's activities as it attempts to interact successfully with major stakeholder groups: employees, customers, shareholders, government, and the global and local communities. In light of the ethical scandals in recent years, the ethics theme resonates as one of the most urgent dimensions of business and society relationships.

Sustainability Theme

The concept of **sustainability** has become one of business's most pressing mandates. Discussions of sustainability began with respect to the natural environment. As time has passed, however, it has become evident that it is a broader concept that applies not only to the natural environment but to the entirety of business's operations and processes as well, especially business's global role and development. At a basic level, sustainability is about business's ability to survive and thrive over the long term.[53] The concept of sustainability is derived from the notion of **sustainable development**, which is a pattern of resource use that aims to meet current human needs while preserving the environment so that these needs can be met not only in the present but also for future generations. The term *sustainability* was initiated by the Brundtland Commission, which coined what has become the most often-quoted definition of sustainable development:

> *Development that meets the needs of the present without compromising the ability of future generations to meet their own needs.*[54]

Today, sustainability is understood to embrace environmental, economic, and social criteria, and this is the general sense in which it will be used in this book. Thus, discussions of sustainability and its implications will be explicit or implicit in most chapters, not just in the chapter on the natural environment.

Stakeholder Management Theme

As suggested throughout this chapter, **stakeholders** are individuals or groups with which business interacts who have a "stake," or vested interest, in the firm. Stakeholders are integral constituents in the business and society relationship.

Two broad groups of stakeholders are considered in this book—external and internal. Though all chapters touch on the **stakeholder management** theme, Chapter 3 develops the concept in detail and Chapter 4 provides early treatment of shareholding stakeholders within the topic of corporate governance.

Later, *external stakeholders*, which include government, consumers, the natural environment, and community members, are considered. Both domestic and global stakeholders are major concerns. Government is treated first because ostensibly it represents the public. It is helpful to understand the role and workings of government to best appreciate business's relationships with other groups. Consumers may be business's most important external stakeholders. Members of the community are crucial, too, and they are concerned about a variety of issues. One of the most important is the natural environment and the topic of sustainability.

The second broad grouping of stakeholders is *internal stakeholders*. Shareholders are treated in our discussion of corporate governance (Chapter 4), but then later in the book (Chapters 17–19) employees are addressed as the principal group of internal stakeholders. We live in an organizational society, and many people think that their roles as employees are just as important as their roles as shareholders. Both of these groups have legitimate legal and ethical claims on the organization, and the management's task is to address their needs and balance these needs against those of the firm and of other stakeholder groups.

Structure of the Book

The structure and flow of the parts and chapters of this book are outlined in Figure 1-7.

In Part 1, "Business, Society, and Stakeholders," there are three chapters. Chapter 1 provides an overview of the business and society relationship. Chapter 2 introduces corporate citizenship: social responsibility, social performance and sustainability. Chapter 3 defines and elaborates on stakeholder management. These chapters provide a crucial foundation or context for understanding the business and society relationship.

FIGURE 1-7

Organization and Flow of the Book

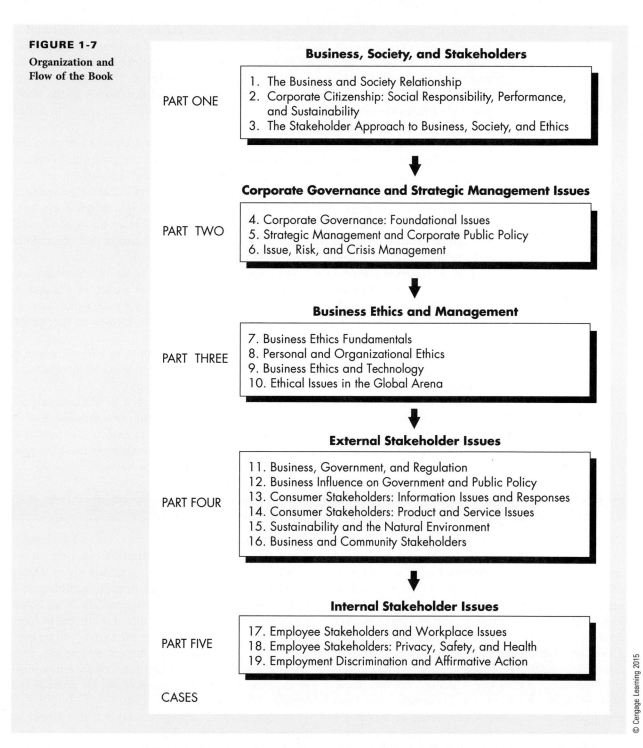

Business, Society, and Stakeholders

PART ONE
1. The Business and Society Relationship
2. Corporate Citizenship: Social Responsibility, Performance, and Sustainability
3. The Stakeholder Approach to Business, Society, and Ethics

Corporate Governance and Strategic Management Issues

PART TWO
4. Corporate Governance: Foundational Issues
5. Strategic Management and Corporate Public Policy
6. Issue, Risk, and Crisis Management

Business Ethics and Management

PART THREE
7. Business Ethics Fundamentals
8. Personal and Organizational Ethics
9. Business Ethics and Technology
10. Ethical Issues in the Global Arena

External Stakeholder Issues

PART FOUR
11. Business, Government, and Regulation
12. Business Influence on Government and Public Policy
13. Consumer Stakeholders: Information Issues and Responses
14. Consumer Stakeholders: Product and Service Issues
15. Sustainability and the Natural Environment
16. Business and Community Stakeholders

Internal Stakeholder Issues

PART FIVE
17. Employee Stakeholders and Workplace Issues
18. Employee Stakeholders: Privacy, Safety, and Health
19. Employment Discrimination and Affirmative Action

CASES

Part 2 is titled "Corporate Governance and Strategic Management Issues." Chapter 4 covers the highly relevant and timely topic of corporate governance, which has become more prominent during the past decade. The next two chapters address management-related topics. Chapter 5 covers strategic management and corporate public policy. Chapter 6 addresses issues, risk and crisis management.

Part 3, "Business Ethics and Management," focuses exclusively on business ethics. Business ethics fundamentals are established in Chapter 7, and personal and organizational ethics are further developed in Chapter 8. Chapter 9 addresses business ethics and technology. Chapter 10 treats business ethics in the global or international sphere. Although ethical issues cut through and permeate virtually all discussions in the book, this dedicated treatment of business ethics is warranted by a need to explore in added detail the ethical dimension in management.

Part 4, "External Stakeholder Issues," deals with the foremost external stakeholders of business. Because government is such an active participant in all the groups to follow, in Chapter 11 business–government relationships and government regulations are discussed. Chapter 12 discusses how business endeavors to shape and influence government and public policy. Chapters 13 and 14 address consumer stakeholders, arguably the most important because without them businesses fail. Chapter 15 addresses sustainability and the natural environment as stakeholder. Chapter 16 addresses business and community stakeholder issues, including corporate philanthropy.

Part 5, "Internal Stakeholder Issues," addresses employees as the sole stakeholders because the treatment of shareholding stakeholders is discussed earlier in Chapter 4. Chapter 17 examines employees and major workplace issues. Chapter 18 looks carefully at the issues of employee privacy, safety, and health. Chapter 19 focuses on the special case of employment discrimination and diversity.

Depending on the emphasis desired in the course, Part 2 could be covered where it appears, or it could be postponed until after Part 5. Alternatively, it could be omitted if a strategic management orientation is not desired.

Taken as a whole, this book strives to take the reader through a building-block progression of foundational and then more developed concepts and ideas that are vital to the business and society relationship. It also allows the reader to explore the nature of social and ethical issues and stakeholder groups with which management must interact. It considers the external and internal stakeholder groups in some depth.

Summary

The business and society relationship has faced severe testing over the past decades. The Occupy Wall Street movement has been a recent manifestation of the tensions. In spite of this, the pluralistic system is still at work, presenting business firms with a variety of challenges. The pluralistic business system throughout the developed world has several advantages and some disadvantages. Within this context, business firms must deal with a multitude of stakeholders and an increasingly special-interest society. A major force that shapes the public's view of business is the criticism that business receives from a variety of sources. Factors in the social environment that have contributed to an atmosphere in which business criticism thrives include affluence, education, public awareness developed through the media (especially TV, movies, and the Internet), the revolution of rising expectations, a growing entitlement mentality, the rights movement, and a philosophy of victimization. The global economic situation may result in changes in business criticism and its antecedents. In addition, actual questionable practices on the part of business have made it a natural target. Ethics scandals perpetrated by individuals, including the Enron and post-Enron scandals, and the Wall Street financial scandals, have perpetuated criticisms of business. Not all firms are guilty, but the guilty attract negative attention to the entire business community. One result is that the trust and legitimacy of the entire business system is called into question and the reputational capital of businesses decline.

A common criticism of business is that it abuses its power. Power operates on four different levels: the level of the entire business system, groups of companies acting in concert, the individual firm, and the individual corporate executive. Business power may be manifested in several different spheres—economic, political, technological, environmental, social, and individual. It is difficult to conclude whether business is actually abusing its power, but it is clear that business has enormous power and that it must exercise it carefully. Power evokes responsibility, and this is the central reason that calls for corporate responsibility have continued. The Iron Law of Responsibility calls for greater

balance in business power and its responsible use. These concerns have led to a changing social environment for business and a changed social contract. The changing terms of the social contract will become evident throughout the book's chapters.

Key Terms

affluence, p. 11
business, p. 5
business ethics, p. 21
business power, p. 17
economic environment, p. 7
education, p. 11
entitlement mentality, p. 14
ethics, p. 21
Iron Law of Responsibility, p. 19

macroenvironment, p. 6
managerial approach, p. 21
pluralism, p. 7
political environment, p. 7
revolution of rising expectations, p. 13
rights movement, p. 14
social contract, p. 19
social environment, p. 7
social problem, p. 13

society, p. 6
special-interest society, p. 9
stakeholder management, p. 22
stakeholders, p. 22
sustainability, p. 21
sustainable development, p. 22
technological environment, p. 7
victimization philosophy, p. 15

Discussion Questions

1. In discussions of business and society, why is there a tendency to focus on large firms rather than small- or medium-sized firms? Have the corporate ethics scandals of the past decade affected small- and medium-sized firms? If so, in what ways have these firms been affected?
2. What is the greatest strength of a pluralistic society? What is the greatest weakness? Do these characteristics work for or against business?
3. Identify and explain the major factors in the social environment that create an atmosphere in which business criticism takes place and prospers. Provide examples. How are the factors

related to one another? Has the revolution of rising expectations run its course, or is it still a reality among young people today?
4. Give an example of each of the four levels of power discussed in this chapter. Also give an example of each of the spheres of business power.
5. Explain in your own words the Iron Law of Responsibility and the social contract. Give an example of a shared understanding between you as a consumer or an employee and a firm with which you do business or for which you work. Is Congress justified in creating new regulations to govern the financial services industry?

Endnotes

1. "The Perp Walk," *BusinessWeek* (January 13, 2003), 86.
2. Steve Hargreaves, "BP Settlement not the final word in spill story," CNNMoney, November 15, 2012, http://money.cnn.com/2012/11/15/news/companies/bp-settlement/index.html. Accessed December 10, 2012.
3. Matthew Philips, "The Neighborhood That Wrecked the World," *Newsweek* (December 29, 2008/January 5, 2009), 16–17.
4. Niall Ferguson, "The End of Prosperity?" *Time* (October 13, 2008), 36–44.
5. Ellen Simon, "Business Year in Review: At Least You've Got Your Health," *The Atlanta Journal-Constitution* (December 26, 2008), E4.
6. Mara Der Hovanesian, "Pointing a Finger at Wall Street," *BusinessWeek* (August 11, 2008), 80.
7. Kevin McCoy, "U. S. to sue S&P for fraud in mortgage case," *USA Today*, February 5, 2013, 1A.
8. "Story of an Occupation," *Time*, October 31, 2012.
9. L. Gordon Crovitz, "Occupy Wall Street's Crony Capitalism," *The Wall Street Journal*, October 17, 2011, A15.
10. Peter J. Wallison, "Wall Street's Gullible Occupiers," *The Wall Street Journal*, October 12, 2011, A21.
11. Jessica Firger, "Occupy Groups Get Funding," *The Wall Street Journal*, February 28, 2012, A6.

12. Lynn Forester de Rothschild and Adam S. Posen, "How Capitalism Can Repair its Bruised Image," *The Wall Street Journal*, January 2, 2013, A17.

13. Liam Fahey and V. K. Narayanan, *Macroenvironmental Analysis for Strategic Management* (St. Paul: West, 1986), 28–30.

14. Michael Porter and Jan Rivkin, "What Business Should Do to Restore U.S. Competiveness," *Fortune*, October 29, 2012, 168–171.

15. Ibid.

16. Joseph W. McGuire, *Business and Society* (New York: McGraw-Hill 1963), 130.

17. "Interest Groups Have a Lot at Stake in Health Care Debate," *USA Today* (November 23, 2009), 15A.

18. Conor Dougherty and Anna Wilde Mathews, "Household Income Sinks to '95 Level," *The Wall Street Journal*, September 13, 2012, A1.

19. United States Census Bureau, USA Quickfacts, http://quickfacts.census.gov/qfd/states/00000.html, Accessed March 18, 2013.

20. "Television and Health," *The Sourcebook for Teaching Science*, http://www.csun.edu/science/health/docs/tv&health.html#tv_stats, Accessed November 6, 2012.

21. "Executives See Unethical Behavior, Media Criticisms as Threats," *Nashville Business Journal* (June 11, 2002).

22. Social Marketing Forum, "Shocking low levels of preparedness to deal with social media criticism," http://www.socialmarketingforum.net/2012/08/major-fail-businesses-are-unprepared-for-social-media-criticism/, Accessed March 18, 2013.

23. Karen Valby, "Remembering Larry Hagman," *EW.COM*, December 7, 2012, 12–13; James Poniewozik, "Milestones: Larry Hagman Texas-size Villain," *Time*, December 10, 2012, 23.

24. Timothy Lamer, "Crooks in Suits," *World* (July 29, 2006), 29.

25. Linda S. Lichter, S. Robert Lichter, and Stanley Rothman, "How Show Business Shows Business," *Public Opinion* (November 1982), 10–12.

26. Michael Medved, "Hollywood's Business-Bashing: Biting the Hand That Is You," *USA Today* (February 3, 2010), 9A.

27. Rachel Dodes, "Hollywood's Favorite Villain," *The Wall Street Journal*, October 14, 2011, D1.

28. Logan Hill, "Movie Math," *Bloomberg Businessweek*, February 11–17, 2013, 70.

29. Bagehot, "Britain's cheering gloom," *The Economist*, June 30, 2012, 62.

30. Gerald F. Seib, "U.S. Hurting in Wallet—and Spirit," *The Wall Street Journal* (December 18, 2009), A2.

31. Jon Meacham, "Keeping the Dream Alive," *Time*, July 2, 2012, 24–39.

32. Robert J. Samuelson, *The Good Life and Its Discontents: The American Dream in the Age of Entitlement, 1945–1995* (New York: Times Books, 1996).

33. "The age of diminished expectations," *The Economist*, February 20, 2013, Accessed March 18, 2013.

34. Neil H. Jacoby, *Corporate Power and Social Responsibility* (New York: Macmillan, 1973), 186–188.

35. Linda DeStefano, "Looking Ahead to the Year 2000: No Utopia, but Most Expect a Better Life," *The Gallup Poll Monthly* (January 1990), 21.

36. Joseph Nolan, "Business Beware: Early Warning Signs for the Eighties," *Public Opinion* (April/May 1981), 16.

37. Charlotte Low, "Someone's Rights, Another's Wrongs," *Insight* (January 26, 1987), 8.

38. John Taylor, "Don't Blame Me!" *New York* (June 3, 1991).

39. Pete Hamill, "A Confederacy of Complainers," *Esquire* (July 1991).

40. Charles J. Sykes, *A Nation of Victims: The Decay of the American Character* (New York: St. Martin's Press, 1991).

41. Aaron Bernstein, "Too Much Corporate Power?" *BusinessWeek* (September 11, 2000), 144–155.

42. David Rothkopf, *Power, Inc.: The Epic Rivalry Between Big Business and Government—and the Reckoning that Lies Ahead*, (New York: Farrar, Straus & Giroux, 2012).

43. Edwin M. Epstein, "Dimensions of Corporate Power: Part I," *California Management Review* (Winter 1973), 11.

44. Rana Foroohar, "Companies are the New Countries," *Time*, February 13, 2012, 21.

45. Epstein, ibid.

46. Ibid.

47. Keith Davis and Robert L. Blomstrom, *Business and Its Environment* (New York: McGraw-Hill, 1966), 174–175.

48. Bernstein, 146.

49. Consumer Financial Protection Bureau, http://www.consumerfinance.gov/the-bureau/, Accessed March 11, 2013.

50. Thomas Donaldson and Thomas W. Dunfee, "Toward a Unified Conception of Business Ethics: Integrative Social Contracts Theory," *Academy of Management Review* (April 1994), 252–253.

51. Simon Mainwaring, "The Corporate Social Contract," *CR Magazine*, May/June 2011, 13–14.

52. "New Economy, New Social Contract," *BusinessWeek* (September 11, 2000), 182.

53. Wayne Visser, "Sustainability," in Wayne Visser, Dirk Matten, Manfred Pohl, and Nick Tolhurst, *The A to Z of Corporate Social Responsibility*, 2007 (West Sussex, England: John Wiley & Sons), 445–446.

54. United Nations, "Sustainable Development," 1987. *Report of the World Commission on Environment and Development*. General Assembly Resolution 42/187, December 11, 1987.

2

Corporate Citizenship: Social Responsibility, Performance, Sustainability

CHAPTER LEARNING OUTCOMES

After studying this chapter, you should be able to:

1. Explain how corporate social responsibility (CSR) evolved and encompasses economic, legal, ethical, and philanthropic components.

2. Provide business examples of CSR and corporate citizenship.

3. Differentiate between and among corporate citizenship, social responsibility, social responsiveness, social performance, and sustainability.

4. Elaborate on the concept of corporate social performance (CSP).

5. Explain how corporate citizenship develops in stages in companies.

6. Describe the triple bottom line and its relevance to sustainability.

7. Describe the socially responsible investing movement's characteristics.

For several decades business has been undergoing the most intense scrutiny it has ever received from the public. Allegations levied against it are that it has little concern for the consumer, cares nothing about the deteriorating social order, has no concept of acceptable ethical behavior, and is indifferent to the problems of minorities and the environment. Issues about what responsibilities business has to society continue to be raised. These claims have generated an unprecedented number of pleas for companies to be more socially responsible. For some, the concept of corporate social responsibility (CSR) has been embraced in the broader term *corporate citizenship*. Other terms that have been derived from CSR include *corporate social responsiveness, corporate social responsibility, corporate responsibility,* and *corporate sustainability.* These terms are often expressed as synonyms for CSR. For others they represent similar but somewhat distinct terms. In the final analysis, the meaning of these expressions often overlap. The terms are frequently used interchangeably, but a careful inspection of each is needed to understand the user's intent. Without question, sustainability thinking is tracking towards popular usage, and this is a vital theme in this book.

CSR has been a "front-burner" issue within the business community and continues to grow in importance each year. An example of this growth was the formation of an organization called **Business for Social Responsibility (BSR)**. BSR claims to have been formed to fill an urgent need for a national business alliance that fosters socially responsible corporate policies. In 2012, BSR celebrated its twentieth anniversary and reported among its membership such recognizable firms as Apple, Inc., Bristol-Myers Squibb Co., Coca-Cola Co., Google, Inc., Target Corp., Hitachi, Novo Nordisk A/S, Xerox Corp., and hundreds of others. The mission statement of BSR is succinct: "We work with business to create a just and sustainable world."[1] Today many of the world's leading corporations have a high echelon officer who is responsible for the firm's corporate social responsibility or sustainability.[2]

This chapter explores several different aspects of the CSR topic and offers some insights into what CSR means and how businesses carry it out. This entire chapter is dedicated to CSR-related issues, concepts, and practices that have emerged because it is a core idea that serves as the basis for most of the discussions in this book.

Corporate Social Responsibility (CSR) as a Concept

Chapter 1 illustrated how criticisms of business led to increased concern for the social environment and a changed social contract. Out of these developments has grown the notion of CSR. Before providing some historical perspective, it is useful to impart an initial view of what CSR means.

An early view of CSR stated: "Corporate social responsibility is seriously considering the impact of the company's actions on society."[3] Another early definition was that "social responsibility ... requires the individual to consider his [or her] acts in terms of a whole social system, and holds him [or her] responsible for the effects of his [or her] acts anywhere in that system."[4] Both of these early definitions provide useful insights into the idea of social responsibility. Figure 2-1 illustrates the business criticism–social response cycle, depicting how the concept of CSR developed out of the ideas introduced in Chapter 1—business criticism, the increased concern for the social environment, and the changed social contract. Figure 2-1 also clarifies that businesses' commitment to social responsibility has led

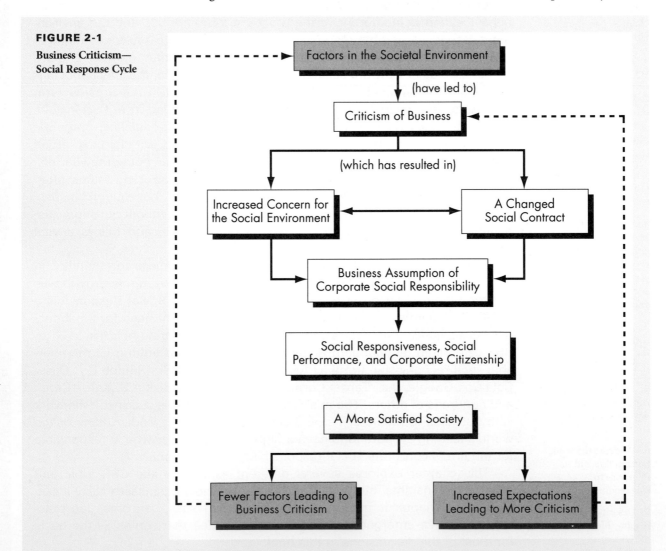

FIGURE 2-1

Business Criticism—Social Response Cycle

FIGURE 2-2

Corporate
Citizenship
Concepts

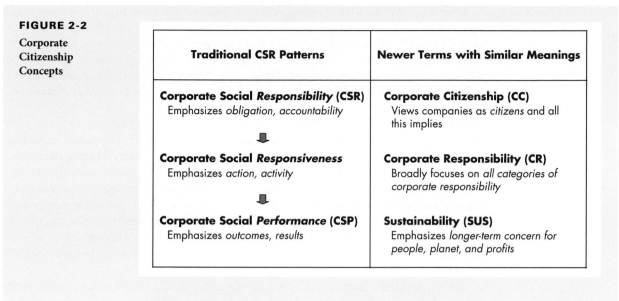

Traditional CSR Patterns	Newer Terms with Similar Meanings
Corporate Social *Responsibility* (CSR) Emphasizes *obligation, accountability*	**Corporate Citizenship (CC)** Views companies as *citizens* and all this implies
Corporate Social *Responsiveness* Emphasizes *action, activity*	**Corporate Responsibility (CR)** Broadly focuses on *all categories of corporate responsibility*
Corporate Social *Performance* (CSP) Emphasizes *outcomes, results*	**Sustainability (SUS)** Emphasizes *longer-term concern for people, planet, and profits*

to increased corporate *responsiveness* toward stakeholders and improved social (stakeholder) *performance*—ideas that are developed more fully in this chapter.

Some academics and practitioners today prefer to use the term **corporate citizenship** to collectively embrace the host of concepts related to CSR. For now, a useful summary of the themes or emphases of each of these concepts helps to clarify how the flow of ideas has extended as these concepts have developed. In Figure 2-2, a summary of the various terminologies in use today are presented along with a brief definition. These terms will be developed further in later discussions.

The growth of social responsibility ideas has brought about a society more satisfied with business. However, this satisfaction, despite reducing the number of factors leading to business criticism, has at the same time led to increased expectations that have resulted in more criticism. Figure 2-1 illustrates this double effect. The net result is that overall levels of business social performance and societal satisfaction should increase with time in spite of this interplay of positive and negative factors. If business is not responsive to societal expectations, it could conceivably enter a downward spiral, resulting in significant deterioration in the business and society relationship. The tidal wave of corporate fraud scandals beginning in 2001–2002, followed by the Wall Street financial collapse beginning in 2008, has seriously called businesses' concern for society into question, and this concern continues today.

Historical Perspective on CSR

The concept of business responsibility that prevailed in the United States and among free market societies since the Industrial Revolution of the 1800s was fashioned after the traditional, or classical, *economic model*.[5] Adam Smith's concept of the "invisible hand" was its major starting point. The classical view holds that a society can best determine its needs and wants through the marketplace. If business is rewarded on the basis of its ability to respond to the demands of the market, the self-interested pursuit of that reward will result in society getting what it wants. In this view, the "invisible hand" of the market transforms self-interest into societal interest. Although the marketplace has done a fairly good job in deciding what goods and services should be produced, it has not fared quite as well in ensuring that business always acts fairly and ethically.

Over the decades, when laws constraining business behavior began to proliferate, a *legal model* emerged. Society's expectations of business changed from being strictly economic in nature to encompassing issues that had been previously at business's discretion. Over time, a *social model*, eventually transforming to a *stakeholder model,* has evolved. Throughout there has been a tension between the interests of shareholders and other stakeholders. In the stakeholder model, sustainability has become a prominent dimension.

Modifications of the Economic Model

Early on, adaptations of the classical economic model were seen in practice in at least three areas: philanthropy, community obligations, and paternalism.[6] History documents that businesspeople engaged in **philanthropy**—contributions to charity and other worthy causes—even during periods dominated by the traditional economic view. Voluntary **community obligations** to improve, beautify, and uplift were also evident. An early example of this was the post–Civil War cooperative effort between the railroads and the YMCA to provide community services in railroad-served areas. Although these services economically benefited the railroads, they were at the same time philanthropic in nature.[7]

During the latter part of the 19th century and into the 20th century, **paternalism** appeared in many forms. One of the most visible examples was the company town. Although business's motives for creating company towns (e.g., the Pullman, Illinois, experiment) were mixed, business had to do a considerable amount of the work in governing them. Thus, some companies took on a kind of protective, paternalistic social responsibility.[8]

The emergence of large corporations during the late 1800s played a major role in hastening movement away from the classical economic view. As society developed from the economic structure of small, powerless firms governed primarily by the marketplace to large corporations in which power was more concentrated, questions of the responsibility of business to society surfaced more frequently.[9]

Although the idea of CSR had not yet fully developed in the 1920s, managers even then had a more positive view of their role. Community service was in the forefront. The most visible example was the Community Chest movement. This was the first large-scale endeavor in which business leaders became involved with other nongovernmental community groups for a common, non-business purpose that required their contribution of time and money to community welfare projects.[10] The social responsibility of business, then, had received a further broadening of its meaning.

The 1930s signaled a transition from a predominantly laissez-faire economy to a mixed economy in which business found itself one of the constituencies monitored by a more activist government. From this time well into the 1950s, business's social responsibilities grew to include employee welfare (pension and insurance plans), safety, medical care, retirement programs, and so on. These new developments were spurred both by governmental compulsion and by a broadened concept of business responsibility.[11]

In his book *The Generous Corporation*, Neil J. Mitchell presents an interesting thesis regarding how CSR evolved.[12] He argued that American business leaders developed the ideology of CSR, particularly philanthropy, as a strategic response to the antibusiness fervor that was beginning in the late 1800s and early 1900s. The antibusiness reaction was the result of questionable practices, such as railroad price gouging, and public resentment of the emerging gigantic fortunes being made by late 19th-century moguls such as John D. Rockefeller and Andrew Carnegie.[13]

As business leaders came to realize that the government had the power to intervene in the economy and, in fact, was being encouraged to do so by public opinion, there was a need for a philosophy that promoted large corporations as a force for social good. Thus,

Mitchell argued, business leaders attempted to persuade those affected by business power that such power was being used properly. An example of this early progressive business ideology was reflected in Carnegie's 1889 essay, "The Gospel of Wealth," in which he asserted that business must pursue profits but that business wealth should be used for the benefit of the community. Philanthropy, or corporate giving, became the most popular means of using corporate wealth for public benefit. A prime example of this was Carnegie's funding and building of more than 2,500 libraries.[14]

In a discussion of little-known history, Mitchell documents by specific examples how business developed this idea of the generous corporation and how it had distinct advantages: It helped business gain support from national and local governments, and it helped achieve in America a social stability that was unknown in Europe during that period. Berenbeim in his review of Mitchell's book argues that the main motive for corporate generosity in the early 1900s was essentially the same as it is now—to keep the government at arm's length.[15]

Over the last half century the concept of CSR has gained considerable acceptance and its meaning has broadened. During this time, the emphasis has moved from little more than a general awareness of social and moral concerns to a period in which specific issues, such as corporate governance, product safety, honesty in advertising, employee rights, affirmative action, environmental sustainability, ethical behavior, and global CSR have taken center stage. The *issue* orientation eventually gave way to the more recent focus on corporate citizenship, social performance, and sustainability. It is helpful to expand upon the modern view of CSR by examining a few definitions or understandings of this term that have developed in recent years.

Evolving Meanings of CSR

It is helpful to return to the basic question: What does CSR really mean? Up to this point, a rather simple definition of corporate social responsibility has been used:

> *Corporate social responsibility is seriously considering the impact of the company's actions on society.*

Although this definition has inherent ambiguities, most of the definitions presented by others also have limitations. A second definition is worth considering:

> *Social responsibility is the obligation of decision makers to take actions which protect and improve the welfare of society as a whole along with their own interests.*[16]

This description suggests two active aspects of social responsibility—*protecting* and *improving*. To protect the welfare of society implies the avoidance of negative impacts on society. To improve the welfare of society implies the creation of positive benefits for society. Like the first definition, this second characterization contains several words that are perhaps unavoidably vague.

A third definition that has been useful is also rather general. But, unlike the previous two, it places social responsibilities in context vis-à-vis economic and legal objectives of business:

> *The idea of social responsibility supposes that the corporation has not only economic and legal obligations, but also certain responsibilities to society which extend beyond these obligations.*[17]

This description is attractive in that it acknowledges the importance of economic objectives (e.g., profits) side by side with legal obligations while also encompassing a broader conception of the firm's responsibilities. It is limited, however, in that it does not clarify what the *certain* responsibilities that extend beyond these are. Over the years, a number of different definitions or views on CSR have evolved.[18] One recent study found 37 different definitions of CSR, and that is why it is important that we focus on one popular definition that will be helpful to us in moving through the book.[19]

A Four-Part Definition of CSR

Each of the definitions of CSR presented earlier is valuable. At this point, it is useful to present Carroll's four-part definition of CSR that focuses on the *types* of social responsibilities business has. This definition helps us identify and understand the component parts that make up CSR, and it is the definition that will be used most frequently in this book:

> *Corporate social responsibility encompasses the economic, legal, ethical, and discretionary (philanthropic) expectations that society has of organizations at a given point in time.*[20]

This four-part definition places economic and legal expectations of business in context by linking them to more socially oriented concerns. These social concerns include ethical responsibilities and philanthropic (voluntary/discretionary) responsibilities. This set of four responsibilities creates a foundation or infrastructure that helps to delineate and frame businesses' responsibilities to the society of which it is part.

Economic Responsibilities Business has **economic responsibilities**. It may seem odd to call an economic responsibility a social responsibility, but, in effect, this is what it is. First and foremost, free enterprise social systems call for business to be an economic institution; as an institution it should have the objective to produce goods and services that society wants and to sell them at fair prices—prices that societal members think represent the value of the goods and services delivered and that provide business with profits sufficient to ensure its survival and growth and to reward its investors. While thinking about its economic responsibilities, business employs many management concepts that are directed toward financial effectiveness—attention to revenues, costs, investments, strategic decision making, and the host of business concepts focused on augmenting the long-term financial performance of the organization. Today, global competition in business has underscored the importance of business's economic responsibilities. Economic sustainability has become an urgent topic. Though economic responsibilities are needed, they are not enough; without them, everything else is moot because firms go out of business. With them, this is just part of what they must do.

Legal Responsibilities Business also has **legal responsibilities**. Just as society has sanctioned economic systems by permitting businesses to assume the productive role, as a partial fulfillment of the social contract, it has also established the ground rules—the laws—under which businesses are expected to operate. Legal responsibilities reflect society's view of "codified ethics" in the sense that they articulate basic notions of fair practices as established by lawmakers. It is business's responsibility toward society to comply with these laws. It is not an accident that compliance officers now have an important role on company organization charts. If business does not agree with laws that have been passed or are about to be passed, however, society has provided a mechanism by which dissenters can be heard through the political process. In the past decades, society has witnessed a proliferation of laws and regulations striving to monitor and control business behavior. A notable *Newsweek* cover story titled "Lawsuit Hell: How Fear of Litigation Is Paralyzing Our Professions" emphasizes the burgeoning role that the legal responsibility of organizations has assumed.[21] The legal aspect of the business and society relationship will be examined further in other chapters as pertinent issues arise.

As important as legal responsibilities are, legal responsibilities do not capture the full range of standards and practices expected of business by society. On its own, law is inadequate for at least three reasons. First, the law cannot possibly address all the topics or issues that business may face. New issues continuously emerge in such realms as e-commerce, genetically modified foods, dealing with undocumented immigrants, and the use of cell phones while driving—just to mention a few examples. Second, the law often lags behind more recent interpretations of what is considered appropriate behavior. For example, as technology permits more precise measurements of environmental contamination, laws based on measures made by obsolete equipment become outdated but not frequently updated. Third, laws are made by elected lawmakers and may reflect the personal interests and political motivations of legislators rather than appropriate ethical justifications. A wise sage once said: "Never go to see how sausages or laws are made." It may not be a pretty picture. Although we would like to believe that lawmakers are focusing on "what is right and best for society," the history of political maneuvering, compromising, and self-interested decision-making often suggests otherwise.

Ethical Responsibilities Because laws are essential but not sufficient, **ethical responsibilities** are needed to embrace those activities, standards, and practices that are expected or prohibited by society even though they are not codified into law. Ethical responsibilities embody the full scope of norms, standards, values, and expectations that reflect what consumers, employees, shareholders, and the community regard as fair, just, and consistent with respect for or protection of stakeholders' moral rights.[22]

Initially, changes in ethics or values precede the establishment of new laws and they become the driving forces behind the initial creation of laws and regulations. For example, the civil rights, environmental, and consumer movements activated in the 1960s reflected basic alterations in societal values and thus were ethical bellwethers foreshadowing and leading to later legislation. Secondly, ethical responsibilities may be seen as embracing and reflecting newly emerging values and norms that society expects business to meet, and they may reflect a higher standard of performance than currently required by law. Ethical responsibilities in this sense are continually evolving. As a result, debate about their acceptability continues. Regardless, business is expected to be responsive to newly emerging concepts of what constitutes ethical practices. One example might be Whole Foods Market selling only those foods it considers organic. In recent years, ethics issues in the global arena have multiplied and extended the study of acceptable business norms and practices.

Superimposed on these ethical expectations originating from societal and stakeholder groups are the implicit levels of ethical performance suggested by a consideration of the great universal ethical principles of moral philosophy, such as justice, rights, and utilitarianism.[23] Because ethical responsibilities are so important, Part 3 of the text, composed of four chapters, is dedicated to the subject. For the moment, it is useful to think of ethical responsibilities as encompassing those decision and behavior arenas in which society expects certain levels of moral or principled performance but for which it has not yet articulated or codified them into law.

Philanthropic Responsibilities Finally, there are business's voluntary, discretionary, or **philanthropic responsibilities**. Though not responsibilities in the literal sense of the word, these are perceived as responsibilities because they reflect current expectations of business by the public. The amount and nature of these activities are voluntary or discretionary, guided only by business's desire to engage in social activities that are not mandated, not required by law, and not generally expected of business in an ethical sense. Nevertheless, the public has an expectation that business will "give back," thus this category has become a part of the social contract between business and society. Such activities might include corporate giving, product and service donations, employee volunteerism, community development, and any other kind of voluntary involvement of the organization's resources and its employees with the community or other stakeholders.

Examples of companies expressing their philanthropic responsibilities, and "doing well by doing good," are many:

- Chick-fil-A, the fast-food restaurant, through the WinShape Centre® Foundation, operates foster homes, sponsors a summer camp that hosts more than 1,900 campers every year, and has provided college scholarships for thousands of students.[24]
- Aflac, Inc., the insurance provider, recently was honored for its overall commitment to pediatric cancer. For two decades, Aflac has raised and contributed more than $62 million for the treatment and research of childhood cancer, and has made the Aflac Cancer Center and Blood Disorders Service at Children's Healthcare of Atlanta its primary philanthropic cause.[25] It is little wonder the Aflac Duck has become an international icon.
- General Mills, the food company, goes the extra mile to support community causes. *Box Tops for Education* is one of its most important causes. General Mills supports schools across the United States by funding essential items such as books, computers, musical instruments, and other supplies. Since 1996 General Mills has raised more than $340 million for K–8 schools.[26]
- Timberland, the products company, underwrites skills training for women working for its suppliers in China. In Bangladesh, it helps provide micro-loans and health services for laborers.[27]

Although there is sometimes an ethical motivation for companies getting involved in philanthropy,[28] it typically is considered a practical way for the company to demonstrate that it is a good corporate citizen. A major distinction between ethical and philanthropic responsibilities is that the latter typically are not *expected* in a moral or an ethical sense. Communities desire and expect business to contribute its money, facilities, and employee time to humanitarian programs or purposes, but they do not regard firms as unethical if they do not provide these services at the desired levels. Therefore, these responsibilities are more discretionary, or voluntary, on business's part, although the societal expectation that these be provided has been around for some time. This category of responsibilities is often referred to as good "corporate citizenship."

To summarize, the four-part CSR definition forms a conceptualization that includes the economic, legal, ethical, and discretionary/philanthropic expectations society places on organizations at a given point in time. Figure 2-3 summarizes the four components, society's expectation regarding each component, and explanations.

This four-part definition provides us with a structure within which to identify and situate the different expectations that society has of business. With each of these categories considered to be indispensable to the total social responsibility of business, they comprise a conceptual model that more completely and specifically describes the kinds of expectations that society has of business. A major advantage of this definitional model is its ability to accommodate those who have argued against CSR by characterizing an economic emphasis as separate from a social emphasis.

The Pyramid of Corporate Social Responsibility

A useful way of graphically depicting the four-part definition of CSR is to envision it as a pyramid with four layers. This **Pyramid of Corporate Social Responsibility** is shown in Figure 2-4[29]

FIGURE 2-3   Understanding the Four Components of CSR

Type of Responsibility	Societal Expectation	Explanations
Economic	REQUIRED of business by society	Be profitable. Maximize sales, minimize costs. Make sound strategic decisions. Be attentive to dividend policy. Provide investors with adequate and attractive returns on their investments.
Legal	REQUIRED of business by society	Obey all laws, adhere to all regulations. Environmental and consumer laws. Laws protecting employees. Fulfill all contractual obligations. Honor warranties and guarantees.
Ethical	EXPECTED of business by society	Avoid questionable practices. Respond to spirit as well as to letter of law. Assume law is a floor on behavior, operate above the minimum required. Do what is right, fair, and just. Assert ethical leadership.
Philanthropic	DESIRED/EXPECTED of business by society	Be a good corporate citizen. Give back. Make corporate contributions. Provide programs supporting community—education, health or human services, culture and arts, and civic. Provide for community betterment. Engage in volunteerism.

© Cengage Learning 2015

The pyramid portrays the four components of CSR, beginning with the basic building block of economic performance at the base. The infrastructure of CSR begins at the point of a successful, profit-making enterprise that has demonstrated its economic sustainability. At the same time, business is expected to obey the law, because the law is society's codification of acceptable and unacceptable practices. In addition, business has the responsibility to be ethical. At its most basic level, this is the obligation to do what is right, just, and fair and to avoid or minimize harm to stakeholders (employees, consumers, the environment, and others). Finally, business is expected to be a good corporate citizen—to fulfill its philanthropic responsibility to contribute financial and human resources to the community and to improve the quality of life.

No metaphor is perfect, and the Pyramid of CSR is no exception. It intends to illustrate that the *total* social responsibility of business is composed of four distinct components which, when taken together, make up the whole. Although the components have been treated as separate concepts for discussion purposes, they are not mutually exclusive and are not intended to juxtapose a firm's economic responsibilities with its other responsibilities. At the same time, a consideration of the separate components helps the manager see that the different types or kinds of obligations are in constant and dynamic tension with one another. The most critical tensions, of course, are those between economic and legal, economic and ethical, and economic and philanthropic. Some might see this as a conflict between a firm's "concern for profits" and its "concern for society," but it is suggested here that this is an oversimplification because the two are so intertwined. Their reconciliation is what CSR is all about.

FIGURE 2-4   The Pyramid of Corporate Social Responsibility

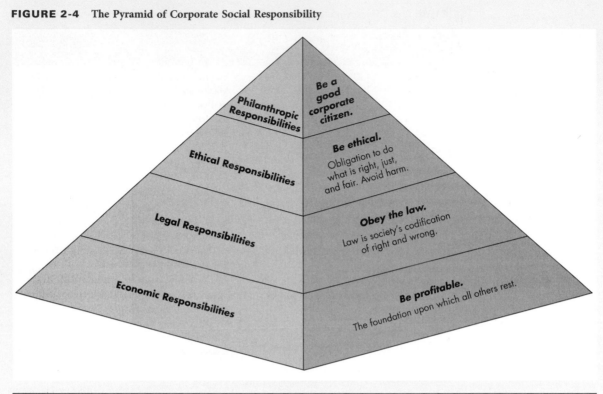

Source: Adapted from: Archie B. Carroll, "The Pyramid of Corporate Social Responsibility: Toward the Moral Management of Organizational Stakeholders," *Business Horizons* (July–August 1991), 42. Copyright © 1991 by the Foundation for the School of Business at Indiana University. Used with permission. Also see Archie B. Carroll, "Managing Ethically with Global Stakeholders: A Present and Future Challenge," *Academy of Management Executive*, Vol. 18, No. 2, May 2004, 114–120.

Pyramid as a Unified Whole   A CSR or stakeholder perspective would focus on the total pyramid as a unified whole and on how the firm might engage in decisions, actions, policies, and practices that *simultaneously* fulfill its four component parts. This pyramid should *not* be interpreted to mean that business is expected to fulfill its social responsibilities in some sequential fashion, starting at the base. Rather, business is expected to fulfill *all* its responsibilities simultaneously. The positioning of economic, legal, ethical, and philanthropic strives to portray the fundamental or basic nature of these four categories to business's existence in society. Economic and legal are *required*; ethical and philanthropic are *expected and desired*.

In summary, the total social responsibility of business entails the concurrent fulfillment of the firm's economic, legal, ethical, and philanthropic responsibilities. This might be illustrated in the form of an equation, as follows:

Economic Responsibilities + Legal Responsibilities + Ethical Responsibilities

+ Philanthropic Responsibilities = Total Corporate Social Responsibility

Stated in more practical and managerial terms, the socially responsible firm should strive to

- Make a profit.
- Obey the law.
- Be ethical.
- Be a good corporate citizen.

CSR Definition and Pyramid Are Sustainable Stakeholder Models Note especially that the four-part CSR definition and the Pyramid of CSR represent sustainable stakeholder models. Each of the four components of responsibility addresses different stakeholders in terms of the varying priorities in which the stakeholders are affected. Economic responsibilities most dramatically impact shareholders and employees (because if the business is not financially successful, shareholders and employees will be directly affected). When the latest economic recession hit, employees were displaced and significantly affected. Legal responsibilities are certainly crucial with respect to owners, but in today's society, the threat of litigation against businesses emanates frequently from employees and consumer stakeholders. Ethical responsibilities affect all stakeholder groups, but an examination of the ethical issues business faces today suggests that they involve consumers, employees, and the environment most frequently. Finally, philanthropic responsibilities most affect the community, but it could be reasoned that employees are next affected because some research has suggested that a company's philanthropic performance significantly affects its employees' morale. The definition and pyramid are sustainable in that they represent long-term responsibilities that overarch into future generations of stakeholders as well.

The role of stakeholders in discussions of CSR is inseparable. In fact, there have been recent calls for CSR to be redefined as corporate "stakeholder" responsibility, rather than corporate "social" responsibilities.[30] Others have suggested that CSR stands for corporate "sustainability" responsibilities. These views would be entirely consistent with the models presented in this chapter because a concern for stakeholders and sustainability is implicit in their understanding.

The four major areas of social concern for business—economic, legal, ethical, and philanthropic—provide a useful framework for conceptualizing the issue of CSR. The social contract between business and society is, to a large extent, formulated from mutual understandings that exist in each of these areas. But the ethical and philanthropic categories, taken together, more frequently capture the essence of what many people generally mean today when they speak of the social responsibility of business. Situating these two categories relative to the legal and economic obligations, however, keeps them in proper perspective and provides a more comprehensive understanding of CSR.

CSR in Practice in Business

CSR in practice is seen both in those firms that are generally perceived to be socially responsible and also in firms that are beginning to be known as CSR Exemplar firms.

Activities of Socially Responsible Firms What do companies have to do to be seen as socially responsible? A study by Walker Information, a research organization, sought to discover what the general public perceived to be the activities or characteristics of socially responsible companies. Figure 2-5 summarizes what the sample said were the top 20 activities or characteristics of socially responsible companies.[31] The items in this listing are quite compatible with our discussion of CSR. Most of these characteristics would be representative of the legal, ethical, and philanthropic or discretionary components of our four-part CSR definition.

Walker Information concluded that the public thinks CSR factors impact a company's reputation just as do traditional business factors such as quality, service, and price. A related question on its survey pertained to the impact of social *irresponsibility* on firm reputation. The study found that ethical and law-abiding companies can reap rewards from CSR activities and enjoy enhanced reputations. However, those companies perceived to be unethical or non–law abiding can do little in the way of other CSR activities to correct their images. Thus, the penalties for disobeying the law are greater than the rewards for helping society.

FIGURE 2-5

Top 20 Activities or Characteristics of Socially Responsible Companies

Following are activities or characteristics of socially responsible companies as seen by citizens.

- Makes products that are safe.
- Does not pollute air or water.
- Obeys the law in all aspects of business.
- Promotes honest or ethical employee behavior.
- Commits to safe workplace ethics.
- Does not use misleading or deceptive advertising.
- Upholds stated policy banning discrimination.
- Utilizes "environmentally friendly" packaging.
- Protects employees against sexual harassment.

- Recycles within company.
- Shows no past record of questionable activity.
- Responds quickly to customer problems.
- Maintains waste reduction program.
- Provides or pays portion of medical costs.
- Promotes energy conservation program.
- Helps displaced workers with placement.
- Gives money toward charitable or educational causes.
- Utilizes only biodegradable or recyclable materials.
- Employs friendly or courteous or responsive personnel.
- Tries continually to improve quality.

Sources: Walker Information. Used with permission.

Rise of CSR Exemplar Firms In the past several decades, a number of socially responsible firms have become models for other firms. We call these CSR exemplar firms because they have tended to go well beyond the typical and established patterns for business firms in terms of their social responsibility excellence. These firms have taken the lead in advocating a social, environmental, or sustainability dimension to their missions. There are at least three main categories of socially responsible firms worth considering: social entrepreneurship firms, social intrapreneurship firms, and mainstream adopters.

Social entrepreneurship firms began their CSR initiatives at the very beginning of their founding and strategically carried them forward. A large part of their initial mission was to bring about social change or to reflect certain social values as a part of their organization's character. Porter and Kramer have argued that social entrepreneurship has been moving capitalism toward the creation of "shared value" in which economic value is created in a way that also creates value for society by "addressing its needs and challenges."[32] Three examples of social entrepreneurship would be The Body Shop International, founded by social activist Anita Roddick; Ben & Jerry's Ice Cream also founded by two social activists, Ben Cohen and Jerry Greenfield; and more recently, Tom's Shoes, founded by Blake Mycoskie. Since its beginning, Tom's Shoes has sought to produce and sell quality products and to bring about social change by giving away to poor children a pair of shoes for every pair it sells: "one for one."[33]

Social intrapreneurship firms are companies that did not have a specific social agenda as part of their initial formation but later developed a highly visible social agenda or program. Social intrapreneurs are people who work inside major companies to develop and promote practical solutions to social, environmental, or sustainability challenges as a part of their financial missions. Sustainability, a leading nonprofit advocacy organization, says, "These corporate changemakers work inside big business, often against the prevailing status quo, to innovate and deliver market solutions to some of the world's most pressing social and environmental challenges."[34] Companies today that illustrate this model might include Timberland, Starbucks, Panera Bread, Microsoft, and Patagonia. As a result of innovation and risk taking, these firms have become high-profile exemplars of social responsibility and sustainability.

Mainstream adopters, a third group, would include all other conventional businesses that have adopted, practiced, and achieved some degree of excellence or recognition for socially responsible policies and practices. Their motives might include one of the following: gaining competitive advantage; reducing costs; enhancing their reputations; emulating what other firms are doing; or fulfilling their own concept of corporate citizenship. Firms that would fall into this third category include, but are not limited to, General Electric, Xerox, Aflac, Coca-Cola, IBM, DuPont, AT&T, UPS, General Mills, and Walmart. While it is not always easy to clearly identify which category each firm is in, the three types do offer a good way to understand the range of strategies by which different business firms have taken on a socially conscious mission and have become highly visible role models for other firms seeking to integrate social responsibility and sustainability into their everyday operations.[35]

Traditional Arguments Against and For CSR

In an effort to provide a balanced, historical view of CSR, it is useful to consider the arguments that traditionally have been raised against and for it.[36] It should be stated clearly at the outset, however, that those who argue *against* CSR are not using in their considerations the comprehensive four-part CSR definition and model presented in this chapter. Rather, it appears that the critics are viewing CSR more narrowly—as only the organizations' efforts to pursue social goals (primarily the philanthropic category). Some critics equate CSR with only the philanthropic category.

Very few businesspeople and academics argue against the fundamental notion of CSR today. The debate among businesspeople more often centers on the kinds and degrees of CSR and on subtle ethical questions, rather than on the basic question of whether or not business should be socially responsible, sustainable, or a good corporate citizen. Today, very few resist CSR on the grounds of economic theory or arguments. The following arguments have historically been cited regarding CSR, and it is helpful to appreciate them to see CSR's progress over the years.

Arguments Against CSR

Classical Economics This traditional view holds that management has one responsibility—to maximize shareholder wealth. This classical economic school, often attributed to the late Milton Friedman, argued that social issues are not the concern of businesspeople and that these problems should be resolved by the unfettered workings of the free market system.[37] Further, this view holds that if the free market cannot solve the social problem, then it falls upon government and legislation to do the job. This view is consistent with the prevailing Anglo-American view of corporate governance, which is based on shareholder primacy. We discuss this in more detail in Chapter 4.

Friedman softened his argument somewhat by his assertion that management is "to make as much money as possible *while conforming to the basic rules of society, both those embodied in the law and those embodied in ethical customs.*"[38] When Friedman's entire statement is considered, it appears that he accepts three of the four categories of the four-part model—economic, legal, and ethical. The only category not specifically embraced in his quote is the voluntary or philanthropic category. It is clear that the economic argument views CSR more narrowly than depicted in the four-part model.

Business Not Equipped This objection holds that managers are oriented toward finance and operations and do not have the necessary expertise (social skills) to make social decisions.[39] Although this may have been true at one point in time, it is less true today as CSR has become integral to business school education and integrated into corporate strategic decisions.

Dilutes Business Purpose Closely related to business not being equipped is a third issue: If managers were to pursue CSR vigorously, it would tend to dilute business's primary purpose.[40] The objection here is that CSR would put business into fields not related to its "proper aim."[41] There is virtually no practical evidence, however, that this dilution has been realized.

Too Much Power Already A fourth argument against CSR is that business already has enough power—economic, environmental, and technological—and so why place in its hands the opportunity to wield additional power?[42] In reality, today business has this social power regardless of CSR. Further, this view tends to ignore the potential use of business's social power for the public good.

Global Competitiveness Another argument that merits consideration is that by encouraging business to assume social responsibilities, businesses might be placed in a vulnerable position in terms of global competition. One consequence of being socially responsible is that business must internalize costs that it formerly passed on to society in the form of dirty air, unsafe products, consequences of discrimination, and so on. The increase in the costs of products caused by inclusion of social or environmental considerations in the price structure might necessitate raising the prices of products, thereby making them less competitive in international markets. This argument weakens considerably when we consider the reality that social responsibility has become widespread globally, not one restricted to domestic firms and operations.

The arguments presented here constitute the principal claims that have historically been made by those who oppose the CSR concept as it once was narrowly conceived. Many of the reasons given appear engaging. Value choices as to the type of society the citizenry would like to have, at some point, become part of the total social responsibility decision. Whereas some of these objections might have had validity at one point in time, most of them do not carry much weight today.

Arguments for CSR

Enlightened Self-Interest The long-range self-interest view, sometimes referred to as "enlightened self-interest," holds that if business is to have a healthy climate in which to operate in the future, it must take actions now to ensure its long-term viability. The reasoning behind this view is that society's expectations are such that if business does not respond on its own, its role in society may be altered by the public—for example, through government regulation or, more dramatically, through alternative economic systems for the production and distribution of goods and services.

For managers who often have a short-term orientation, it is sometimes difficult to appreciate that their rights and roles in the economic system are determined by society. Business must be responsive to society's expectations over the long term if it is to survive in its current form or in a less restrained form. This concern for the long-term viability of society is the primary driver in the current emphasis on sustainability, which has become a synonym for CSR in the minds of many.

Warding Off Government Regulations One of the most practical reasons for business to be socially responsible is to ward off government intervention and regulations. Today there are numerous areas in which government intervenes with an expensive, elaborate regulatory apparatus to fill a void left by business's self-regulatory inaction. To the extent that business polices itself with self-disciplined standards and guidelines, future government intervention can be somewhat forestalled.

Resources Available Two additional arguments supporting CSR deserve mention together—"Business has the resources" and "Let business try."[43] These two views maintain that because business has a reservoir of management talent, functional expertise, and capital, and because so many others have tried and failed to solve societal problems, business should be given a chance. These arguments have some merit, because there are some social problems that best can be handled, in the final analysis, only by business. Examples include creating a fair workplace, providing safe products, and engaging in fair advertising. Admittedly, government can and does assume a role in these areas, but business also has responsibility for the decisions.

Proaction Better than Reaction Another argument supporting CSR is that "proaction is better than reaction." This position holds that *proacting* (anticipating and initiating) is more practical and less costly than simply *reacting* to problems that have already occurred. Environmental pollution is a good example, particularly business's experience with attempting to clean up rivers, lakes, and other waterways that have been neglected for decades. A wiser approach would have been to prevent environmental deterioration in the first place. *Proaction* is a basic idea that undergirds the notion of sustainable development.

Public Support A final argument in favor of CSR is that the public strongly supports it.[44] A *BusinessWeek*/Harris poll revealed that a stunning 95 percent of the public believes that companies should not only focus on profits for shareholders but should also be responsible toward their workers and communities, even if making things better for workers and communities requires companies to sacrifice some profits.[45] This public support for CSR has grown over the years.[46]

The Business Case for CSR

After considering the pros and cons of CSR, most businesses and managers today embrace the idea. In recent years, the "business case" for CSR has been unfolding.[47] At the same time, the business case for sustainability has been advancing as well.[48] The "business case" reveals why businesspeople believe that CSR brings distinct benefits or advantages to their organizations and the business community. In this argument, CSR directly benefits the "bottom line." The astute business guru, Michael Porter, perhaps the most respected consultant today in upper-level management circles and boardrooms, has pointed out how corporate and social initiatives are intertwined. According to Porter, "Today's companies ought to invest in corporate social responsibility as part of their business strategy to become more competitive." In a competitive context, "the company's social initiatives—or its philanthropy—can have great impact. Not only for the company but also for the local society."[49]

In Simon Zadek's perceptive book, *The Civil Corporation*, Zadek has identified four ways in which firms respond to CSR pressures, and he holds that these form a composite business case for CSR. His four approaches are as follows:[50]

1. *Defensive approach.* This is an approach designed to alleviate pain. Companies will do what they have to do to avoid pressure that makes them incur costs.
2. *Cost–benefit approach.* This traditional approach holds that firms will undertake those activities if they can identify direct benefits that exceed costs.
3. *Strategic approach.* In this approach, firms will recognize the changing environment and engage with CSR as part of a deliberate emergent strategy.
4. *Innovation and learning approach.* In this approach, an active engagement with CSR provides new opportunities to understand the marketplace and enhances organizational learning, which leads to competitive advantage.

FIGURE 2-6

The Business Case for CSR

Six Business Reasons for Embracing CSR
Companies that understand CSR are using it to push the following business processes in the organization:
1. Innovation
2. Cost savings
3. Brand differentiation
4. Long-term thinking
5. Customer engagement
6. Employee engagement

Business Benefits of Corporate Social Responsibility
Carefully implemented CSR policies can help the organization:
1. Win new business
2. Increase customer retention
3. Develop and enhance relationships with customers, suppliers, and networks
4. Attract, retain, and maintain a happy workforce and be an Employer of Choice
5. Save money on energy and operating costs and manage risk
6. Differentiate itself from competitors
7. Improve its business reputation and standing
8. Provide access to investment and funding opportunities
9. Generate positive publicity and media opportunities due to media interest in ethical business activities

Sources: James Epstein-Reeves, "Six Reasons Companies Should Embrace CSR," http://www.forbes.com/sites/csr/2012/02/21/six-reasons-companies-should-embrace-csr/, Accessed January 5, 2013. Simply CSR, "Business Benefits of CSR," http://www.simplycsr.co.uk/the-benefits-of-csr.html, Accessed January 5, 2013.

Companies may vary as to why they pursue a CSR strategy, but these approaches, taken together, build a strong business rationale for the pursuit of socially responsible business. Figure 2-6 summarizes some of the business case (reasons and benefits) for CSR taken from two different studies.

Corporate Social Responsiveness

To this point, the progress of CSR has been documented, a definitional model for understanding CSR has been presented, and the arguments for and against it have been outlined. It is now worthwhile to consider a related idea that arose over the distinction between the terms *responsibility* and *responsiveness*. **Corporate social responsiveness** represents an *action-oriented* variant of CSR.

A general argument that has generated much discussion holds that the term "responsibility" is too suggestive of efforts to pinpoint accountability or obligation. Therefore, it is not dynamic enough to fully describe business's willingness and activity—apart from obligation—to respond to social demands. For example, Ackerman and Bauer criticized CSR by stating, "The connotation of 'responsibility' is that of the process of assuming an obligation. It places an emphasis on motivation rather than on performance." They go on to say, "Responding to social demands is much more than deciding what to do. There remains the management task of *doing* what one has decided to do, and this task is far from trivial."[51] They argue that "social responsiveness" is a more appropriate description of what is essential in the social arena.

This point has some merit. *Responsibility*, taken quite literally, does imply more of a state or condition of having assumed an obligation, whereas *responsiveness* connotes a dynamic, action-oriented condition. It should not be overlooked, however, that much of what business has done and is doing has resulted from a particular motivation—an assumption of obligation—whether assigned by government, forced by special-interest groups, or voluntarily assumed. Perhaps business, in some instances, has failed to accept and internalize the obligation, and thus it may seem odd to refer to it as a responsibility. Nevertheless, some motivation that led to social responsiveness had to be present, even

ETHICS IN PRACTICE CASE

The Socially Responsible Shoe Company

When Blake Mycoskie visited Argentina in 2006, a bright idea struck him. He was wearing *alpargatas*— resilient, lightweight, canvas slip-ons—shoes typically worn by Argentinian farmworkers, during his visit to poor villages where many of the residents had no shoes at all. He formulated the plan to start a shoe company and give away a pair of shoes to some needy child or person for every shoe the company sold. This became the basic mission of his company.

Initially, Mycoskie had to self-finance his company. He decided to name his company "Toms: Shoes for Tomorrow." Mycoskie is from Texas, and he liked to read books about such business success stories as those of Ted Turner, Richard Branson, and Sam Walton. He appends the following message to his e-mails: *"Disclaimer: you will not win the rat race wearing Toms."*

In the summer of 2006, he unveiled his first collection of Toms shoes. Stores such as American Rag and Fred Segal in Los Angeles, and Scoop in New York, started stocking his shoes. By fall, the company had sold 10,000 pairs and he was off to the Argentinian countryside, along with several volunteers, to give away 10,000 pairs of shoes. In an article in *Time*, Mycoskie was quoted as saying, "I always thought I'd spend the first half of my life making money and the second half giving it away. I never thought I could do both at the same time."

By February 2007, Mycoskie's company had orders from 300 stores for 41,000 of his spring and summer collection of shoes, and he had big plans to go international by entering markets in Japan, Australia, Canada, France, and Spain in the summer of 2008. In 2011, Mycoskie published his book *Start Something that Matters* in which he presents a lot of gushy do-goodism but also presents an energetic and convincing story. In 2012, the company also launched its Toms Eyewear line and adopted a program called "One for One," in which "with every pair you purchase, Toms will give sight to a person in need. One for One."

1. How would you assess Toms' CSR using the four-part CSR definition? Is the company based on the typical business case for CSR or more of an ethical or philanthropic model?

2. Is Blake Mycoskie a social entrepreneur, intrapreneur, or mainstream adopter? Explain.

3. Do you believe Mycoskie's twin goal of economic and social success is sustainable? Review the company's Web site to see additional information: http://www.toms.com

4. What challenges do you foresee for the company's future?

Sources: Nadia Mustafa, "A Shoe That Fits So Many Souls," *Time* (February 5, 2007), C2; Blake Mycoskie, *Start Something that Matters*, 2011; Philip Broughton, "Doing Good by Shoeing Well," *The Wall Street Journal*, September 9, 2011, A17; "Good Guy of the Month," *The Oprah Magazine*, February 1, 2007; Toms Shoes, http://www.toms.com/our-movement, Accessed January 5, 2013.

though in some cases it was not articulated as a responsibility or an obligation. Figure 2-7 summarizes other experts' views regarding corporate social *responsiveness*. Accordingly, the corporate social responsiveness dimension that has been discussed by some as an alternative focus to that of social responsibility is, practically speaking, an *action phase* of management's response in the social sphere.

Corporate Social Performance

For many years there has been a trend toward making the concern for social, environmental, and ethical issues more and more *practical and tangible*. The responsiveness thrust was a step in this direction. It is possible to integrate these concerns into a **corporate social performance (CSP) model**. The performance focus suggests that what really matters is what companies are able to achieve—the results or outcomes of their

FIGURE 2-7

Corporate Social Responsiveness: Other Views

Sethi's Three-Stage Schema

Sethi proposes a three-stage schema for classifying corporate behavior: social obligation, social responsibility, and social *responsiveness*. Social responsiveness suggests that what is important is that corporations be "anticipatory" and "preventive." This third stage is concerned with business's long-term role in a dynamic social system.

Frederick's CSR₁, CSR₂, and CSR₃

CSR_1 refers to the traditional *accountability* concept of CSR. CSR_2 is *responsiveness* focused. It refers to the capacity of a corporation to *respond* to social pressures. It involves the literal act of responding to, or achieving, a responsive posture to society. It addresses the mechanisms, procedures, arrangements, and patterns by which business responds to social pressures. CSR_3 refers to corporate social rectitude, which is concerned with the moral correctness of the actions or policies taken. CSR_3 integrates business ethics into responsiveness.

Epstein's Process View

Responsiveness is a part of the corporate social policy process. The emphasis is on the *process* aspect of social responsiveness. It focuses on both individual and organizational processes "for determining, implementing, and evaluating the firm's capacity to anticipate, respond to, and manage the issues and problems arising from the diverse claims and expectations of internal and external stakeholders."

Sources: S. Prakash Sethi, "Dimensions of Corporate Social Performance: An Analytical Framework," *California Management Review* (Spring 1975), 58–64; William C. Frederick, "From CSR1 to CSR2: The Maturing of Business-and-Society Thought," Working Paper No. 279 (Graduate School of Business, University of Pittsburgh, 1978). See also William Frederick, *Business and Society* (Vol. 33, No. 2, August 1994), 150–164; and Edwin M. Epstein, "The Corporate Social Policy Process: Beyond Business Ethics, Corporate Social Responsibility and Corporate Social Responsiveness," *California Management Review* (Vol. 29, No. 3, 1987), 104.

acceptance of social responsibility and the adoption of a responsiveness viewpoint. Performance is a bottom-line concept.

In developing a conceptual framework for CSP, it is important to specify the nature (economic, legal, ethical, or philanthropic) of the responsibility, and also to identify a particular philosophy, pattern, mode, or strategy of responsiveness. Finally, it is important to identify the stakeholder issues to which these responsibilities are manifested and applied. The issues, and especially the degree of organizational interest in the issues, are always in a state of flux. As times change, so does the emphasis on the range of social or ethical issues that business feels compelled to address.

Also of interest is that businesses' concerns toward particular issues vary depending on the industry in which they exist as well as other factors. A bank, for example, is not as pressed about environmental issues as a manufacturer. Likewise, a manufacturer is considerably more concerned with the issue of environmental protection than is an insurance company.

Carroll'S CSP Model

Figure 2-8 presents Carroll's corporate social performance (CSP) model, which brings together the three major dimensions in a graphical depiction:

1. *Social responsibility categories*—economic, legal, ethical, and discretionary (philanthropic).
2. *Philosophy (or mode) of social responsiveness*—strategies ranging from reaction, defense, accommodation, and proaction.
3. *Social (or stakeholder) issues involved*—consumers, environment, employees, and others.[52]

FIGURE 2-8 Carroll's Corporate Social Performance Model

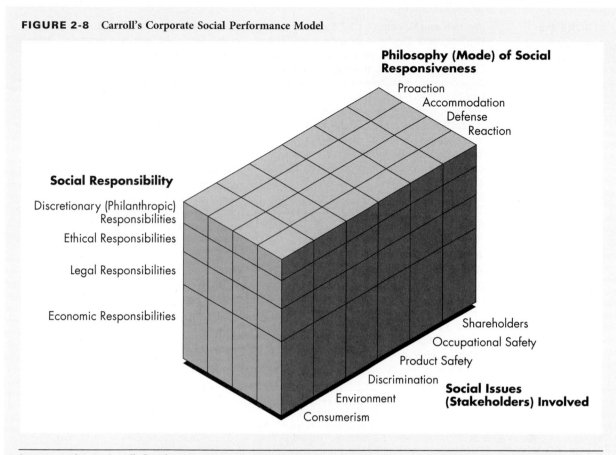

Sources: Archie B. Carroll, "A Three-Dimensional Conceptual Model of Corporate Social Performance," *Academy of Management Review* (Vol. 4, No. 4, 1979), 503. Reproduced with permission.

The first dimension of this model pertains to all that is included in the *definition of social responsibility* presented earlier—the economic, legal, ethical, and discretionary (philanthropic) components. The second is a *social responsiveness continuum* or dimension. The model in Figure 2-8 suggests that responsiveness is just one additional aspect to be addressed if CSP is to be achieved. The third dimension concerns the *scope or range of social or stakeholder issues* (e.g., consumerism, environment, product safety, and discrimination) that management must address in the first two dimensions.

The CSP model is intended to be useful to both academics and managers. For academics, the model is primarily a conceptual aid to understanding the distinctions among the concepts of CSR that have appeared in the literature. What were previously regarded as separate definitions of CSR are treated here as three separate aspects of CSP. The model's major academic use, therefore, is in helping to organize the important concepts that must be understood in an effort to clarify the CSP concept.

The conceptual model can assist managers in understanding that social responsibility is not separate and distinct from economic performance. The model integrates economic concerns into a social performance framework. Also, it places ethical and philanthropic expectations into a rational economic and legal framework. The model provides a template for the manager to systematically think through major stakeholder issues. Although it does not provide the answer to how far the organization should go, it does provide a

FIGURE 2-9

Corporate Social
Performance:
Extensions,
Reformulations,
Reorientations

Wartick and Cochran's CSP Extensions

Wartick and Cochran proposed several changes/extensions to the CSP model. They proposed that the "social issues" dimension had matured into a new management field known as "social issues management." They extended the CSP model further by proposing that the three dimensions be viewed as depicting *principles* (corporate social responsibilities, reflecting a philosophical orientation), *processes* (corporate social responsiveness, reflecting an institutional orientation), and *policies* (social issues management, reflecting an organizational orientation).

Wood's Reformulated CSP Model

Wood elaborated and reformulated Carroll's model and Wartick and Cochran's extensions and set forth a reformulated model. Her definition of corporate social performance was "A business organization's configuration of principles of social responsibility, processes of social responsiveness, and policies, programs, and

other observable outcomes as they relate to the firm's societal relationships." Wood took this definition further by proposing that each of the three components—principles, processes, and outcomes—is composed of specific elements.

Swanson's Reorientation of CSP

Swanson elaborated on the dynamic nature of the principles, processes, and outcomes reformulated by Wood. Relying on research from corporate culture, Swanson's reoriented model links CSP to the personally held values and ethics of executive managers and other employees. She proposed that the executive's sense of morality highly influences the policies and programs of environmental assessment, stakeholder management, and issues management, carried out by employees. These internal processes are means by which organizations can impact society through *economizing* (efficiently converting inputs into outputs) and *ecologizing* (forging community-minded collaborations).

Sources: Steven L. Wartick and Philip L. Cochran, "The Evolution of the Corporate Social Performance Model," *Academy of Management Review* (Vol. 10, 1985), 765–766; Donna J. Wood, "Corporate Social Performance Revisited," *Academy of Management Review* (October 1991), 691–718; D. L. Swanson, "Addressing a Theoretical Problem by Reorienting the Corporate Social Performance Model," *Academy of Management Review* (Vol. 20, No. 1, 1995), 43–64; D. L. Swanson, "Toward an Integrative Theory of Business and Society: A Research Strategy for Corporate Social Performance," *Academy of Management Review* (Vol. 24, No. 3, 1999), 596–521.

framework that may lead to more effective social performance. In addition, the model could be used as a planning and diagnostic problem-solving tool. It can assist the manager by identifying categories within which the organization and its decisions can be situated. There have been several extensions, reformulations, or reorientations of the CSP model. Figure 2-9 summarizes some of these.

Corporate Citizenship

Business practitioners and academics alike have grown fond of the term "corporate citizenship" in reference to businesses' CSR and CSP. Earlier in the chapter, corporate citizenship was presented as a collective term embracing the concepts of *corporate social responsibility, responsiveness*, and *performance*, which have also been described earlier in the text. *Sustainability* might fall under this umbrella as well. However, it is appropriate to ask whether it has a meaning distinct from these concepts. A careful look at the concept and its literature shows that although *corporate citizenship* is a useful and attractive term, it is not distinct from the other terminologies, except in the eyes of some writers who have attempted to give it a specific, narrow meaning. Nevertheless, it is a popular term and one worth exploring.

If one thinks about companies as "citizens" of the countries in which they reside, corporate citizenship means that these companies have certain responsibilities they must fulfill in order to be perceived as good corporate citizens. One view is that "corporate citizenship is not a new concept, but one whose time has come."[53] In today's global business environment, some have argued that multinational enterprises are citizens of the world. Windsor has argued that corporate citizenship has become an important practitioner-based movement and that it conveys a sense of responsibility for social impacts or a sense of neighborliness in local communities.[54]

Broad Views

Corporate citizenship has been described by some as a broad, inclusive term that essentially embraces all that is implied in the concepts of social responsibility, responsiveness, and performance. Corporate citizenship has been defined as "serving a variety of stakeholders well."[55] Fombrun proposed a broad conception. He holds that corporate citizenship is composed of a three-part view that encompasses (1) a reflection of shared moral and ethical principles, (2) a vehicle for integrating individuals into the communities in which they work, and (3) a form of enlightened self-interest that balances all stakeholders' claims and enhances a company's long-term value.[56]

Davenport's research also resulted in a broad definition of corporate citizenship that requires a commitment to ethical business behavior and balancing the needs of stakeholders, while working to protect the environment.[57] Carroll framed his four categories of CSR as embracing the "four faces of corporate citizenship"—economic, legal, ethical, and philanthropic. Each face, aspect, or responsibility category reveals an important facet that contributes to the whole. He suggests that "just as private citizens are expected to fulfill these responsibilities, companies are as well."[58]

Narrow Views

At the narrow end of the spectrum, Altman speaks of corporate citizenship in terms of "corporate community relations." In this view, it embraces the functions through which business intentionally interacts with nonprofit organizations, citizen groups, and other stakeholders at the community level.[59] The focus in the narrow view is on one stakeholder group—the community. Other definitions of corporate citizenship fall between these broad and narrow perspectives, and some refer to global corporate citizenship as well, because increasingly companies are expected to conduct themselves appropriately wherever they do business around the world.[60]

Drivers of Corporate Citizenship

A pertinent question is, "What drives companies to embrace corporate citizenship?" According to one major survey, both internal (to the companies) motivators and external pressures drive companies toward corporate citizenship.[61]

Internal motivators **include:**

> Traditions and values
>
> Reputation and image
>
> Business strategy
>
> Recruiting or retaining employees

External pressures **include:**

> Customers and consumers
>
> Expectations in the community
>
> Laws and political pressures

Benefits of Corporate Citizenship to Business Itself

The benefits of good corporate citizenship to stakeholders are readily apparent. But what are the benefits of good corporate citizenship to business itself? Following are the benefits of corporate citizenship to companies, defined broadly:[62]

- Improved employee relations (e.g., improves employee recruitment, retention, morale, loyalty, motivation, and productivity)
- Improved customer relationships (e.g., increases customer loyalty, acts as a tiebreaker for consumer purchasing, and enhances brand image)
- Improved business performance (e.g., positively impacts bottom-line returns, increases competitive advantage, and encourages cross-functional integration)
- Enhanced company's marketing efforts (e.g., helps create a positive company image, helps a company manage its reputation, supports higher prestige pricing, and enhances government affairs activities)

Stages of Corporate Citizenship

Like individual development, companies develop and grow in their maturity for dealing with corporate citizenship issues. A major contribution to how this growth occurs has been presented by Philip Mirvis and Bradley Googins at the Center for Corporate Citizenship at Boston College. The center holds that the essence of corporate citizenship is how companies deliver on their core values in a way that minimizes harm, maximizes benefits, is accountable and responsive to key stakeholders, and supports strong financial results.[63] This definition is quite compatible with the four-part definition of CSR presented earlier. The **stages of corporate citizenship model** helps to explain their points.

The development of the corporate citizenship model reflects a stage-by-stage process in which seven dimensions (citizenship concept, strategic intent, leadership, structure, issues management, stakeholder relationships, and transparency) evolve as companies move through five stages and become more sophisticated in their approaches to corporate citizenship. This is a five-stage model beginning with Stage 1, which is Elementary, and growing toward Stage 5, which is Transforming.

As seen in Figure 2-10, the citizenship concept starts with an emphasis on "jobs, profits, and taxes" in Stage 1 and progresses through several emphases such as "philanthropy, environmental protection," "stakeholder management," "sustainability or triple bottom-line," and, finally, "change the game." Similarly, the other vital dimensions change orientations as they evolve through the five stages.

Another aspect of the five stages is that companies face different *developmental challenges* at each stage. Thus, in Stage 1 the challenge is to "gain credibility." As the companies grow toward Stage 5, the challenges are to build capacity, create coherence, and deepen commitment. Figure 2-11 graphically depicts the developmental challenges that trigger the movement of corporate citizenship through the five stages of growth.

Company examples that illustrate the various stages have been identified by Mirvis and Googins. GE is pictured as a company coming to the realization in Stage 1 that it must extend its emphases beyond financial success. Chiquita, Nestlé, and Shell Oil are depicted as companies becoming engaged in Stage 2. In Stage 3, Baxter International and ABB are identified as innovative companies striving to create coherence. BP's commitment to sustainability is provided as an example of Stage 4, where the theme is integration. Finally, the experiences of Unilever, widely noted for its socioeconomic investments in emerging markets, is presented as a company at Stage 5, with an emphasis on transformation in its corporate citizenship.

FIGURE 2-10   Stages of Corporate Citizenship

Stages of Corporate Citizenship

CENTER FOR
CORPORATE CITIZENSHIP

BOSTON COLLEGE
CARROLL SCHOOL
OF MANAGEMENT

Dimensions		Stage 1: Elementary	Stage 2: Engaged	Stage 3: Innovative	Stage 4: Integrated	Stage 5: Transforming
	Citizenship Concept	Jobs, Profits & Taxes	Philanthropy, Environmental Protection	Stakeholder Management	Sustainability or Triple Bottom Line	Change the Game
	Strategic Intent	Legal Compliance	License to Operate	Business Case	Value Proposition	Market Creation or Social Change
	Leadership	Lip Service, Out of Touch	Supporter, In the Loop	Steward, On Top of It	Champion, In Front of It	Visionary, Ahead of the Pack
	Structural	Marginal: Staff Driven	Functional Ownership	Cross-Functional Coordination	Organizational Alignment	Mainstream: Business Driven
	Issues Management	Defensive	Reactive, Policies	Responsive, Programs	Pro-Active, Systems	Defining
	Stakeholder Relationships	Unilateral	Interactive	Mutual Influence	Partnership Alliance	Multi-Organization
	Transparency	Flank Protection	Public Relations	Public Reporting	Assurance	Full Disclosure

Sources: Philip Mirvis and Bradley K. Googins, *Stages of Corporate Citizenship:* A Boston: Carroll School of Management's Center for Corporate Citizenship at Boston College Monograph, 2006, p. 3. Used with permission.

FIGURE 2-11

Developmental
Challenges
Triggering
Movement of
Corporate
Citizenship

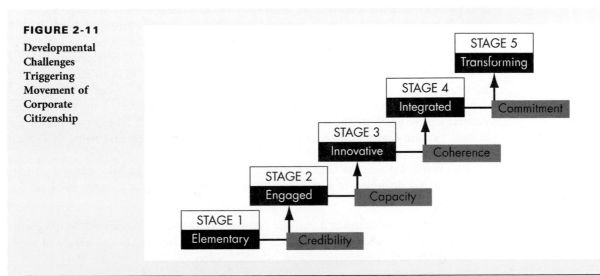

Sources: Philip Mirvis and Bradley K. Googins, *Stages of Corporate Citizenship: A Developmental Framework* (Center for Corporate Citizenship at Boston College, Boston, 2006), 5. Used with permission.

The stages of corporate citizenship framework effectively presents the challenges of credibility, capacity, coherence, and commitment that firms move through as they come to grips with developing more comprehensive and integrated citizenship agendas. From the researchers' work, it is apparent that corporate citizenship is not a static position but is one that progresses through different themes and challenges as firms get better and better over time.[64]

The terminology and concepts of corporate citizenship are especially attractive because they resonate so well with the business community's attempts to describe its own socially responsive activities and practices. Therefore, it is expected that this concept will be around for some years to come. When reference is made to CSR, social responsiveness, social performance, and sustainability, these also embrace activities, programs, and practices that would typically fall under the purview of a firm's corporate citizenship.[65]

As indicated earlier, in addition to CSR and corporate citizenship, related concepts that have competed to become central terms in the field include *business ethics, stakeholder management*, and *sustainability*. These five concepts are overlapping and complementary and they each have attributes that help reveal vital dimensions of interest in the pursuit of a common core in the business and society field.[66] All of these topics are dealt with fully throughout the book.

Global Corporate Citizenship

Global CSR and **global corporate citizenship** are topics that are becoming more relevant with each passing year. As global capitalism has become the marketplace stage for large- and medium-sized companies, the expectations that they address citizenship issues at a world level also multiply. Chapter 10 examines global business ethics in detail. Here, it is noted that there are also challenges for global CSR and citizenship. To some extent, these are international extensions of the concepts treated throughout this book. Because cultures have features that are both divergent and common, however, adaptations of traditional CSR and corporate citizenship concepts often are necessary. Over time, countries are adapting CSR to best fit their cultures and economies.

There are two aspects of the global dimension worthy of mention. First, U.S.-based and other multinational enterprises from countries around the world are expected to be good corporate citizens in the countries in which they conduct business. Further, they are expected to tailor as carefully as possible their citizenship initiatives to conform to the cultural environment in which they find themselves. Second, it is important to note that academics and businesspeople around the world are now doing research on and advocating CSR and corporate citizenship concepts. In fact, there has been a virtual explosion of interest in these topics, especially in the United Kingdom, Europe, and Australia/New Zealand, and also in Asia and South America.[67] These two points are related because academic interest is sparked by business interest and helps to explain the growing appeal of the topic.

Two items illustrate the kind of thinking behind the idea of global corporate citizenship. First is a definition of a global business citizen presented in a recent book on the topic:

> *A global business citizen is a business enterprise (including its managers) that responsibly exercises its rights and implements its duties to individuals, stakeholders, and societies within and across national and cultural borders.*[68]

This view of a global business citizen is consistent with the discussions of this topic from a domestic perspective, but it also applies across national and cultural borders. With this working definition, it can be understood how the citizenship concepts presented in this chapter can be naturally expanded and adapted to embrace multinational enterprises.

A second illustration of the global reach is provided by a distinction between frameworks for understanding CSR in America versus Europe, especially in the United Kingdom. This distinction illustrates how CSR around the world has much in common, but specific, national contexts must be considered to fully grasp the topic. Dirk Matten and Jeremy Moon maintain that CSR is more "explicit" in America whereas it is more "implicit" in Europe. In their distinctions, they argue that *explicit CSR* would normally consist of voluntary, self-interest driven policies, programs, and strategies as is typical in U.S.-based understandings of CSR. By contrast, *implicit CSR* would embrace the entirety of a country's formal and informal institutions that assign corporations an agreed-upon share of responsibility for society's concerns. Implicit CSR, such as that seen in the United Kingdom and Europe, would embrace the values, norms, and rules evident in the local culture.[69] The authors contend that CSR is more implicit, or understood, in Europe because it is more a part of the culture than in the United States. In Europe, some aspects of CSR are more or less decreed or imposed by institutions, such as government, whereas in the United States CSR is more voluntary, often pressured, and driven by companies' specific, explicit, actions. And, when thinking about CSR and corporate citizenship in the global context, a special case has to be made for their applications in developing countries.[70]

In short, although CSR and corporate citizenship have much in common in terms of their applicability around the world and in diverse countries, national differences may also exist, which might suggest divergent or dissimilar strategies depending on where business is being conducted. A 2012 study of firms from 42 countries found that the *political* system followed by the *labor* and *education* systems and the *cultural* system were the most important variables that affected corporate social performance and citizenship in different countries.[71] As the world economic stage becomes more common as the environment within which businesses function, convergence in CSR approaches seems predictable.

Corporate Citizenship Awards by Business Press

Although there has been considerable academic research on the subjects of CSR, CSP corporate citizenship, and sustainability over the past decades, we should stress that the business community is also quite interested in this topic. Prominent business organizations and periodicals that report on corporate citizenship and social performance and provide awards for company social performance include *Fortune* magazine, the Conference Board, *CR: Corporate Responsibility* magazine, and the U.S. Chamber of Commerce. In addition, there are many other business groups with a keen interest in the topic. For many years now, *Fortune* magazine has conducted rankings of the "World's Most Admired Companies" and has included the classification of "Social Responsibility" among its categories of performance. The rankings are the result of a poll of more than 12,600 senior executives, outside directors, and financial analysts. In its 2012 rankings of most socially responsible were: GDF Suez, Marquard & Bahls, RWE, Altria Group, Starbucks, and Walt Disney.[72] In a related vein, *Fortune* also publishes "The 100 Best Companies to Work For," on an annual basis. Recent winners have included Google, Boston Consulting Group, SAS Institute, Wegman's Food Markets, and Edwards Jones.[73] It is not clear what specific impact the *Fortune* rankings have on these businesses, but surely they have some positive impact on the firms' reputational capital. The important point to note here is that the social responsibility category is one major indicator of corporate citizenship and that it continues to be included as a criterion of admired companies by one of the country's leading business magazines.

Annual Business Corporate Citizenship Awards are also given each year by *CR: Corporate Responsibility* magazine. The magazine calls its program "The 100 Best Corporate Citizens List." For 2012, the top five firms were Bristol Myers Squibb, IBM, Microsoft, Intel, and Johnson Controls.[74] Many firms today have corporate responsibility officers, and these individuals are charged with exerting CSR leadership in their respective companies. Each year, through its Business Civic Leadership Center, the U.S. Chamber of Commerce awards its Corporate Citizenship Awards. These awards are designed to recognize leading business firms and their performance in the following four categories: U.S. Community Service Award, International Community Service Award, Partnership Award, and Corporate Stewardship Award. Recent award recipients include Kraft Foods, UnitedHealth Group, and Grainger and American Red Cross.[75]

Social Performance and Financial Performance Relationship

An issue that surfaces frequently in considerations of CSR or corporate citizenship is whether or not there is a demonstrable relationship between a firm's social responsibility/performance and its financial performance. Unfortunately, attempts to measure this relationship have typically been hampered by measurement problems. The appropriate performance criteria for measuring financial performance and social responsibility are subject to debate. Furthermore, the accurate measurement of social responsibility is difficult at best.

Over the years, many studies on the social responsibility–financial performance relationship have produced mixed results.[76] In a comprehensive meta-analysis, one review of research on the relationship supports the conclusion that social and financial performance are positively related. The researchers conclude by saying, "...portraying managers' choices with respect to CSP and CFP as an either/or trade-off is not justified in light of 30 years of empirical data."[77] In another study, the conclusion was reached that "there is a small, but positive relationship between corporate social performance and company financial performance."[78] Finally, another major study concluded that research supports a positive association between corporate social and financial performance.[79]

Three Perspectives on the Social-Financial-Reputation Relationship

In understanding the relationship between social and financial performance and reputation, it is important to note that there have been at least three different perspectives that have dominated these discussions and research.

Perspective 1 Perhaps the most popular view is the belief that *socially responsible firms are more financially profitable*. To those who advocate the concept of social performance, it is apparent why they would like to think that social performance is a driver of financial performance and, in addition, a corporation's reputation. If it could be demonstrated that socially responsible firms, in general, are more financially successful and have better reputations, this would significantly bolster the CSP view, even in the eyes of its critics.

Perspective 1 has been studied extensively. The findings of many of the studies that have sought to demonstrate this relationship have been inconclusive. In spite of this, some studies have claimed to have successfully established this linkage. The most positive conclusion linking CSP with CFP were the two studies reported earlier in the text.[80] Despite the lack of conclusive evidence, a 2012 Deloitte study found that chief financial officers (CFOs) of major firms are not only engaging with sustainability practices, but

---

ETHICS IN PRACTICE CASE
Burgers with a Soul: Fresh, Local, Sustainable

Burgerville sells not only burgers but also good work. But if you don't live in Oregon or the State of Washington, you may have never heard about Burgerville, a company founded in 1961 in Vancouver, Washington. Today, there are 39 Burgerville restaurants spanning those two states with more scheduled to come.

In the 1990s, when Burgerville began losing sales of its burgers to the national chains, Chief Executive Tom Mears decided to differentiate his product and sell "burgers with a soul." Mears, the son-in-law of the founder, decided to combine good food with good works. The company began to build its strategy around three key words: "fresh, local, and sustainable." It pursued this strategy through partnerships with local businesses, farms, and producers. In 2003, *Gourmet* magazine recognized Burgerville the home of the nation's freshest fast food.

According to the company Web site, "At Burgerville, doing business responsibly means doing business sustainably. One example of this is our commitment to purchasing 100 percent local wind power equal to the energy use of all our restaurants and corporate office." The company purchases its electricity from local windmills. Burgerville uses "sustainable agriculture," which means that its meat and produce are free from genetically modified seeds or livestock. In its cooking, the company avoids trans-fats, and once the cooking oils are used up, they are converted

into biodiesel. The company buys its antibiotic- and hormone-free beef locally.

In addition to burgers, Burgerville offers a wild Coho salmon and Oregon Hazelnut Salad. Meals for children often come with seeds and gardening tools rather than the usual cheap toy offered at the national chains.

Burgerville extends its good works to its employees. The company pays 95 percent of the health insurance for its hundreds of workers. This adds $1.5 million to its annual compensation expense. To get its affordable health care, employees have to work a minimum of 20 hours a week for at least six months, a more generous arrangement than most provided by stores.

Being a good corporate citizen is expensive. Though the company won't reveal its financial bottom line, one industry consultant estimated that its margin is closer to 10 percent compared with McDonald's 15 percent.

1. Is the world ready for a socially responsible, sustainable hamburger? How much extra would you be willing to pay, assuming the burgers taste really good?
2. What tensions among its economic, legal, ethical, and philanthropic responsibilities do you think are most pressing to Burgerville?
3. Does Burgerville sound like a business that might work in Oregon and Washington, but maybe not elsewhere? What is the future of Burgerville?

Sources: "Fast Food: Want a Cause with That?" *Forbes* (January 8, 2007), 83. Also see the company Web site: http://www.burgerville.com/. Accessed March 14, 2013; Vancouver SW Washington Business Journal, "Burgerville Fundraiser," February 6, 2013, http://www.vbjusa.com/news/news-briefs/8879-burgerville-fundraiser-to-benefit-crestline-elementary, Accessed March 22, 2013.

---

that 49 percent of all CFOs see a strong link between sustainability performance and financial performance. These CFOs perceive sustainability to be a key driver of financial performance.[81]

Perspective 2 This view, which has not been studied as extensively, argues that *a firm's financial performance is a driver of its social performance.* This perspective is built somewhat on the notion that social responsibility is a "fair weather" concept. That is, when times are good and companies are enjoying financial success, higher levels of social performance are witnessed. In one major study, it was found that financial performance either precedes or is contemporaneous with social performance. This evidence supports the view that social–financial performance correlations are best explained by positive synergies or by "available funding."[82]

Spotlight on Sustainability

Sustainability's Stock Is Rising

A comprehensive study conducted by Deloitte Touche Tohmastsu Ltd., a private financial services provider, interviewed 250 CFOs representing 14 countries and 15 different industries with annual revenues averaging US$12 billion and found the following:

- Sustainability is seen as a key driver of financial performance.
- Organizations are transforming to meet the sustainability imperative.
- Sustainability is becoming operationalized.
- CFO involvement with sustainability is deepening.
- Sustainability aspects of tax and financial reporting have gained significant mindshare among CFOs.
- Energy management still tops the list of issues.
- CFOs strongly believed employees are becoming increasingly concerned with sustainability.

Sources: Summarized from "Sustainability: CFOs are Coming to the Table," Deloitte Touche Tohmatsu, Ltd., 2012, unpublished report. Also see "Nearly 50% of CFOs Say Sustainability Is Key Driver of Financial Performance," September 9, 2012, *Environmental Leader*, http://www.environmentalleader.com/2012/09/19/nearly-50-of-cfos-say-sustainability-is-key-driver-of-financial-performance/, Accessed March 22, 2013; "How to align Profit and Sustainability," *Environmental Leader*, March 8, 2013, http://www.environmentalleader.com/2013/03/08/how-to-align-profit-and-sustainability/, Accessed March 22, 2013.

Perspective 3 A third perspective argues that there is *an interactive relationship between and among social performance, financial performance, and corporate reputation.* In this symbiotic view, the three major factors influence each other, and, because they are so interrelated, it is not easy to identify which factor is driving the process. Regardless of the perspective taken, each view advocates a significant role for CSP, and it is expected that researchers will continue to explore these perspectives for years to come. Figure 2-12 depicts the essentials of each of these views.

Finally, it should be mentioned that a "contingency" view suggests that CSP should be seen as a function of the "fit" between specific strategies and structures and the nature of the social issue. According to this research, the social issue is determined by the expectational gaps between the firm and its stakeholders that occur within or between views of what is and/or ought to be, and high CSP is achieved by closing these expectational gaps with the appropriate strategy and structure.[83]

A basic premise of all these perspectives is that there is only one "bottom line"—a corporate *financial* bottom line—that addresses primarily the shareholders' investments in the firm. An alternative view is that the firm has "multiple bottom lines" that benefit from CSP. This stakeholder–bottom line perspective argues that the impacts or benefits of social performance cannot be fully measured or appreciated by considering only the impact on the firm's financial bottom line.

To truly employ a stakeholder perspective, companies need to accept the multiple-bottom line view as reflective of reality. Thus, CSP cannot be fully comprehended unless its impacts on stakeholders, such as consumers, employees, the community, and other stakeholder groups, are recognized and measured. Research may never conclusively demonstrate a simple relationship between CSP and financial performance. If a stakeholder perspective is taken, however, it may be more straightforward to assess the impact of CSP on multiple stakeholders.

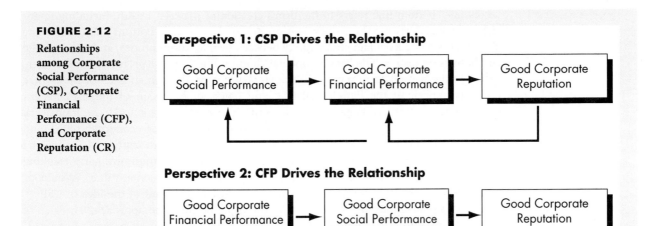

FIGURE 2-12

Relationships
among Corporate
Social Performance
(CSP), Corporate
Financial
Performance (CFP),
and Corporate
Reputation (CR)

Sustainability—Profits, People, Planet

As introduced in Chapter 1, sustainability is one of the major themes of this book. It is also one of the key concepts or terms that often has been used interchangeably in recent years with CSR, CSP, and Corporate Citizenship. Because of this rising status, it is important to highlight it in this chapter as well. As first used by the Bruntland Commission, the term *sustainability* was derived from the idea of **sustainable development** which is a pattern of resource use that aims to meet human needs while preserving the environment so that these needs can be met not only in the present but also for future generations. Taking a future-oriented, longer-term perspective is a key to sustainability thinking. Earlier versions of sustainability focused primarily on the natural environment, and that use continues as will be apparent throughout the book. More recently, it has become evident that sustainability is a broader concept that applies not only to the natural environment but to other environments of business as well. In recent years, the idea of sustainability has been expressed in the well-known concept of the triple bottom line. A brief examination of this concept conveys why it has become so popular.

The Triple Bottom Line

A variant of the multiple-bottom-line perspective discussed earlier is popularly known as the **triple bottom line** concept. The phrase *triple bottom line* has been attributed to John Elkington. The concept seeks to encapsulate for business the three key spheres of **sustainability** that it must attend to—*economic, social,* and *environmental.* The "economic" bottom line refers to the firm's creation of material wealth, including financial income and assets. The emphasis is on *profits*. The "social" bottom line is about the quality of people's lives and about equity between people, communities, and nations. The emphasis is on *people*. The "environmental" bottom line is about protection and conservation of the natural environment.[84] The emphasis is on the *planet*. Each of these three topics is implicit in the Pyramid of CSR and represent a version of the stakeholder–bottom line concept. At its narrowest, the term *triple bottom line* is used as a framework for measuring and reporting corporate performance in terms of economic, social, and environmental indicators. At its broadest, the concept is used to capture the whole set of values, issues, and processes that companies must address to minimize harm resulting from their activities and to create economic, social, and environmental value.[85] As a popular concept, it is often thought of as a more detailed spelling out of the idea of CSP.

Corporate sustainability is the goal of the triple bottom line approach. The goal of sustainability is to create long-term shareholder value by taking advantage of opportunities and managing risks related to economic, environmental, and social developments. Leaders in this area try to take advantage of the market's demand for sustainable products and services while successfully reducing and avoiding sustainability costs and risks. To help achieve these goals, the Dow Jones Sustainability Indexes were created to monitor and assess the sustainability of corporations.[86] As it will become apparent throughout the book, the concept of sustainability overlaps considerably with other social responsibility concepts and terminology, and it has become so important in business and academic usage that it needs to be emphasized in various contexts.

Spotlight on Sustainability

Myths About Sustainability

There are many misconceptions about sustainability. Often these misconceptions, or myths, serve as barriers to companies pursuing sustainable development. Myths about sustainability are eliminated when the experiences of leading companies are considered. Here are some of the myths about sustainability followed by insights that dispel them.

1. *Sustainability is a cost we can't afford right now.* Xerox CEO Anne Mulcahy said that being "a good corporate citizen" saved the company from bankruptcy.
2. *There's no money to be made from sustainability.* Johnson & Johnson has undertaken 80 sustainability projects since 2005 and achieved $187 million in savings with an ROI of nearly 19 percent, and rising.
3. *It's just for big companies.* Actually, smaller companies have an advantage because their competitiveness often depends on being lean, resourceful, and nimble, which sustainability makes possible.
4. *We'll be accused of greenwashing if we pursue sustainability.* Companies that set and achieve meaningful goals have the right to publicize their successes.
5. *We don't make things, so we don't have to worry about the supply chain.* Walmart doesn't make things, but it is developing a supplier index for its thousands of suppliers to gauge the carbon impact from supplies they sell to the business.

Sources: Vijay Kanal, "The Eight Biggest Myths about Sustainability in Business," November 23, 2009, http://www.greenbiz.com/blog/2009/11/23/8-myths-about-sustainability-business. Accessed January 7, 2013; Michael D. Lemonick, "Top 10 Myths about Sustainability," http://web.chem.ucsb.edu/~feldwinn/greenworks/Top%2010%20Myths%20about%20Sustainability.pdf, Accessed March 14, 2013: "Twelve Myths about Sustainability," *Everblue*, 12/12/12, http://www.everblue.edu/blog/12-myths-about-sustainability-12122012, Accessed March 22, 2013.

Socially Responsible, Sustainable, Ethical Investing

Special-interest groups, business, the media, and academics are not alone in their interest in business's social performance. Investors are also interested. The **socially responsible, sustainable or ethical investing movement** arrived on the scene in the 1970s and has continued to grow and prosper. By 2013, socially responsible and sustainable investing (SRI) had matured into a comprehensive investing approach complete with social and environmental screens, shareholder activism, and community investment, accounting for more than $3.74 trillion of investments in the United States, according to the Forum for Sustainable and Responsible Investing.[87] Today, the socially responsible investing movement embraces social screening, shareholder advocacy, and community investing.

Socially responsible investing can be traced back to the early 1900s, when church endowments refused to buy so-called "sin" stocks—then defined as shares in tobacco, alcohol, and gambling companies. During the Vietnam War era of the 1960s and early 1970s, antiwar investors refused to invest in defense contracting firms. In the early 1980s, universities, municipalities, and foundations sold off their shares of companies that had operations in South Africa to protest apartheid. By the 1990s, self-styled socially responsible investing came into its own.[88] In the 2000s, social investing began celebrating the fact that it is now part of the mainstream.

Socially conscious investments have been continuing to grow.[89] However, managers of socially conscious mutual funds do not use only ethical or social responsibility criteria to decide which companies to invest in. They consider a company's financial health before all else. Moreover, a growing corps of brokers, financial planners, and portfolio managers are available to help people evaluate investments for their social impacts.[90]

The concept of *social screening* is the backbone of the socially conscious investing movement. Investors seeking to put their money into socially responsible firms want to *screen out* those firms they consider to be socially irresponsible or to actively *screen in* those firms they think of as socially responsible or sustainable. Thus, there are negative social screens and positive social screens. Some of the *negative social screens* that have been used in recent years include the avoidance of investing in tobacco manufacturers, gambling casino operators, defense or weapons contractors, and firms doing business in South Africa.[91] In 1994, however, with the elimination of the official system of apartheid in South Africa, this was eliminated as a negative screen by many.

It is more difficult, and thus more challenging, to implement *positive social screens*, because these require the potential investor to make judgment calls as to what constitutes an acceptable or a strong level of social performance on social investment criteria. Criteria that may be used as either positive or negative screens, depending on the firm's performance, might include the firm's demonstrated record on issues such as equal employment opportunity and affirmative action, environmental sustainability, treatment of employees, corporate citizenship (broadly defined), and treatment of animals.

One experience of Pax World Funds, a socially responsible investor, illustrates how tricky social screening can be. When Starbucks introduced a coffee liqueur containing Jim Beam bourbon, Pax World Fund thought it had no choice but to sell its $23 million stake in Starbucks, even though it had long believed Starbucks to have a strong record of social responsibility. Pax World did divest of its Starbucks stock. By 2006, however, Pax World shareholders concluded that the company needed to eliminate its zero-tolerance policy on alcohol and gambling and they approved more flexible guidelines for the future. Under the new guidelines, the company would focus more on positive social screens, like a company's record on corporate governance, climate change, and other social issues.[92]

The financial performance of socially conscious mutual funds shows that investors do not have to sacrifice profitability for principles. An increasing number of studies have demonstrated that socially responsible funds perform competitively with non-CSR funds over time. A study from Morningstar showed that in a comparison of five year returns, non-socially responsible returns for large-cap stock funds was 2.9% whereas the returns from socially responsible firms during the same period was 3.0%.[93] The fast growth of socially conscious investing is the most convincing evidence that competitive returns are being achieved.[94]

Over the past 20 years, the total dollars invested in SRI has grown exponentially, as has the number of institutional, professional, and individual investors involved in the field. The Council on Economic Priorities has suggested that there are at least three reasons why there has been an upsurge in social or ethical investing: more reliable research on CSP than in the past; firms using social criteria have established a solid track record demonstrating that investors do not have to sacrifice gains for principles; and the socially conscious 1960s generation is now making investment decisions through their own IRAs and 401(k) plans.[95] Further, more citizens are seeing social investments as a way in which they can exert their priorities concerning the balance of financial and social concerns.

Whether it be called social investing, ethical investing, socially responsible investing, or sustainable investing, it is clear that social investing has "arrived" on the scene and has become a major part of the mainstream. Socially responsible investing is growing globally as well.[96] Socially conscious mutual funds will continue to be debated in the investment community. The fact that they exist, have grown, and have prospered, however, provides evidence that the practice is serious and that there truly are investors in the real world who take the social responsibility and sustainability issue quite seriously.

Summary

Corporate citizenship, corporate social responsibility, responsiveness, and performance, and sustainability are important and related concepts. The CSR concept has a rich history. It has grown out of many diverse views. A four-part conceptualization broadly conceives CSR as encompassing economic, legal, ethical, and philanthropic obligations. The four responsibilities were also depicted as part of the Pyramid of CSR-building upon the basic economic foundations of business.

The concern for CSR has been expanded to include a concern for social responsiveness and social performance. The responsiveness theme suggests more of an action-oriented focus by which firms not only must address their basic obligations, but also must decide on basic strategies of responding to these obligations. A CSP model was presented that brought the responsibility and responsiveness dimensions together into a framework that also identified categories of social or stakeholder issues that must be considered.

The term *corporate citizenship* arrived on the scene to embrace a whole host of socially conscious activities and practices on the part of businesses. This term has become quite popular in the business community. It is not clear that the concept is different from the emphases on corporate social responsibility, responsiveness, and performance, but it is a term being used more frequently. A "stages of corporate citizenship" model depicts how companies progress and grow in their increasing sophistication and maturity in dealing with corporate citizenship issues.

Today, a concern for sustainability has taken its place at the table. Sustainability is frequently expressed through the triple bottom line and may be viewed as a narrow concept focusing on the natural environment or more broadly as including economic (profits), social (people), and environmental (planet) arenas.

The interest in CSR extends beyond the academic community. The business media is interested as well. Such publications from *Fortune, Forbes, CR: Corporate Responsibility* as well as the U.S. Chamber of Commerce recognize outstanding "corporate citizens" in a variety of ways each year. Achieving such status has become a symbol of pride for the companies receiving these recognitions.

Finally, the socially responsible, sustainable, or ethical investing movement is flourishing. This documents that there is a growing body of investors who are sensitive to business's social and ethical (as well as financial) performance. Studies of social investing have demonstrated that investors do not have to give up financial performance to achieve social performance. The industry has been growing consistently and is now considered to be a part of the mainstream of investing.

Key Terms

Business for Social Responsibility (BSR), p. 27
community obligations, p. 30
corporate citizenship, p. 29
corporate social performance (CSP) model, p. 43
corporate social responsibility (CSR), p. 32
corporate social responsiveness, p. 42
corporate sustainability, p. 56

economic responsibilities, p. 32
ethical responsibilities, p. 33
global corporate citizenship, p. 50
legal responsibilities, p. 32
mainstream adopters (of CSR), p. 39
paternalism, p. 30
philanthropic responsibilities, p. 33
philanthropy, p. 30
Pyramid of Corporate Social Responsibility, p. 34

social entrepreneurship, p. 38
social intrapreneurship, p. 38
socially responsible, sustainable, or ethical investing, p. 57
stages of corporate citizenship model, p. 48
sustainability (SUS), p. 55
sustainable development, p. 55
triple bottom line, p. 55

Discussion Questions

1. Explain the Pyramid of Corporate Social Responsibility. Provide several examples of each "layer" of the pyramid. Identify and discuss some of the tensions among the layers or components. How do the different layers of the pyramid "overlap" with each other?

2. In your view, what is the single strongest argument *against* the idea of corporate social responsibility? What is the single strongest argument *for* corporate social responsibility? Briefly explain.

3. Differentiate between corporate social responsibility and corporate social responsiveness. Give an example of each. How does corporate social performance relate to these terms?

Where do corporate citizenship and sustainability fit in?

4. Analyze how the triple bottom line and the Pyramid of CSR are similar and different. Draw a schematic that shows how the two concepts relate to one another.

5. Research two different companies and try to identify at which stage of corporate citizenship these companies reside. What are the best examples you can find of companies in Stage 5 of corporate citizenship?

6. Does socially responsible, sustainable, or ethical investing seem to you to be a legitimate way in which the average citizen might demonstrate her or his concern for CSR? Discuss.

Endnotes

1. Business for Social Responsibility, "Our Mission and How We Work," https://www.bsr.org/en/about/how-we-work. Accessed March 21, 2013.

2. Robert Strand, "The Chief Officer of Corporate Social Responsibility: A Study of Its Presence in Top Management Teams," *Journal of Business Ethics* (2013), 112: 721–734.

3. Quoted in John L. Paluszek, *Business and Society: 1976–2000* (New York: AMACOM, 1976), 1.

4. Keith Davis, "Understanding the Social Responsibility Puzzle," *Business Horizon* (Winter 1967), 45–50.

5. For a more complete history of corporate responsibility in the U. S. see Archie B. Carroll, Kenneth J. Lipartito, James E. Post, Patricia H. Werhane, and Kenneth E. Goodpaster, executive editor, 2012, *Corporate Responsibility: The American Experience.* Cambridge: Cambridge University Press.

6. Davis, 45–50.

7. See Morrell Heald, *The Social Responsibilities of Business: Company and Community, 1900–1960* (Cleveland: Case Western Reserve University Press, 1970), 12–14.

8. James W. McKie, "Changing Views," in *Social Responsibility and the Business Predicament* (Washington, DC: The Brookings Institute, 1974), 22–23.

9. Ibid., 25. Also see Carroll et al 2012.

10. Heald, 119.

11. McKie, 27–28.

12. Neil J. Mitchell, *The Generous Corporation: A Political Analysis of Economic Power* (New Haven, CT: Yale University Press, 1989).

13. Ronald E. Berenbeim, "When the Corporate Conscience Was Born" (A review of Mitchell's book), *Across the Board* (October 1989), 60–62.

14. For more on Andrew Carnegie, see his biography, *Andrew Carnegie*, by David Nasaw, The Penguin Press, 2006. For a book review, see Bob Dowling, "The Robin Hood Robber Baron," *BusinessWeek* (November 27, 2006), 116.

15. Berenbeim, 62.

16. Keith Davis and Robert L., Blomstrom, *Business and Society: Environment and Responsibility*, 3rd ed. (New York: McGraw-Hill, 1975), 39.

17. Joseph W. McGuire, *Business and Society* (New York: McGraw-Hill, 1963), 144.

18. For a more complete history of the CSR concept, see Archie B. Carroll, "Corporate Social Responsibility: Evolution of a Definitional Construct," *Business and Society* (Vol. 38, No. 3, September 1999), 268–295.

19. Alexander Dahlsrud, "How Corporate Social Responsibility is Defined: an Analysis of 37 Definitions," *Corporate Social Responsibility and Environmental Management*, 15, 2008, 1–13.

20. Archie B. Carroll, "A Three-Dimensional Conceptual Model of Corporate Social Performance," *Academy of Management Review* (Vol. 4, No. 4, 1979), 497–505. Also see Archie B. Carroll, "The Pyramid of Corporate Social Responsibility: Toward the Moral Management of Organizational Stakeholders," *Business Horizons* (July–August 1991), 39–48.

21. Stuart Taylor, Jr., and Evan Thomas, "Civil Wars," *Newsweek* (December 15, 2003), 43–53.

22. Archie B. Carroll, "The Pyramid of Corporate Social Responsibility: Toward the Moral Management of Organizational Stakeholders," *Business Horizons* (July–August 1991), 39–48. Also see Archie B. Carroll, "The Four Faces of Corporate Citizenship," *Business and Society Review* (Vol. 100–101, 1998), 1–7.

23. Ibid. Also see Mark S. Schwartz, *Corporate Social Responsibility: An Ethical Approach* (Peterborough, Ontario: Broadview Press, 2011).

24. Winshape Foundation, http://www.chick-fil-a.com/Company/Winshape. Accessed March 21, 2013.

25. "Aflac receives two awards for its social responsibility," March 4, 2011, http://www.aflac.com/aboutaflac/pressroom/pressreleasestory.aspx?rid=1535927 Accessed March 21, 2013.

26. General Mills Charitable Contributions and Brand Philanthropy," 2011, http://generalmills.com/~/media/Files/CSR/2011_csr_final.ashx. Accessed March 21, 2013.

27. Unmesh Kher, "Getting Smart at Being Good…Are Companies Better Off for It?" *Time, Inside Business* (January 2006), A8. Also see http://responsibility.timberland.com/factories/?story=1#sustainable-living. Accessed January 5, 2013.

28. Mark Schwartz and Archie Carroll, "Corporate Social Responsibility: A Three Domain Approach," *Business Ethics Quarterly*, 13:4, 2003, 503–530.

29. Carroll, Ibid., 1–7.

30. R. Edward Freeman, S. Ramakrishna Velamuri, and Brian Moriarty, "Company Stakeholder Responsibility: A New Approach to CSR," *Business Roundtable Institute for Corporate Ethics Bridge Paper* (2006), 10.

31. Walker Group, "Corporate Character: It's Driving Competitive Companies: Where's It Driving Yours?" Unpublished document, 1994.

32. M. E. Porter and M. R. Kramer, "Creating shared value," *Harvard Business Review*, January–February 2011, 64.

33. http://www.toms.com/. Accessed December 6, 2012.

34. "The Social Intraprenuer," Sustainability, http://www.sustainability.com/library/the-social-intrapreneur?path=library/the-social-intrapreneurs#.ULfAZaxZUn0. Accessed November 30, 2012.

35. Carroll, et al. 2012, 373–374.

36. For further discussion, see Duane Windsor, "Corporate Social Responsibility: Cases For and Against It," in Marc J. Epstein and Kirk O. Hanson, eds., *The Accountable Corporation: Corporate Social Responsibility*, Volume 3 (Westport, CN and London: Praeger, 2006), 31–50.

37. Milton Friedman, "The Social Responsibility of Business Is to Increase Its Profits," *The New York Times* (September 1962), 126. Also see "Special Report: Milton Friedman," *The Economist* (November 25, 2006), 79.

38. Ibid., 33 (emphasis added).

39. Christopher D. Stone, *Where the Law Ends* (New York: Harper Colophon Books, 1975), 77.

40. Keith Davis, "The Case For and Against Business Assumption of Social Responsibilities," *Academy of Management Journal* (June 1973), 312–322.

41. F. A. Hayek, "The Corporation in a Democratic Society: In Whose Interest Ought It and Will It Be Run?" in H. Ansoff (ed.), *Business Strategy* (Middlesex: Penguin, 1969), 225.

42. Davis, 320.

43. Davis, 316.

44. For further discussion, see Duane Windsor, "Corporate Social Responsibility: Cases For and Against," in Marc J. Epstein and Kirk O. Hanson (eds.), *The Accountable*

Corporation, Volume 3, Corporate Social Responsibility (Westport, Connecticut: Praeger, 2006), 31–50.

45. Cited in Aaron Bernstein, "Too Much Corporate Power," *BusinessWeek* (September 11, 2000), 149.

46. James Epstein-Reeves, "Consumers Overwhelmingly want CSR," *Forbes*, December 15, 2010, http://www.forbes.com/sites/csr/2010/12/15/new-study-consumers-demand-companies-implement-csr-programs/. Accessed March 21, 2013.

47. Archie B. Carroll and Kareem M. Shabana, "The Business Case for Corporate Social Responsibility: A Review of Concepts, Research and Practice," *International Journal of Management Reviews*, Vol. 12, Issue 1, March 2010, 85–105.

48. Archie B. Carroll and Shabana, K. M. "The Business Case for Sustainability," in *Sustainability Matters: Why and How Corporate Boards Should Become Involved*," Matteo Tonello (ed.), Research Report R-1481-11-RR, New York: The Conference Board, 2011, pp. 21–26

49. "CSR—A Religion with Too Many Priests," *European Business Forum* (Issue 15, Autumn 2003). Also see "Getting Smart at Being Good…" *Time Inside Business* (January 2006), A1–A38.

50. Simon Zadek, *The Civil Corporation: New New Economy of Corporate Citizenship* (London: Earthscan, 2001). See also Lance Moir, "Social Responsibility: The Changing Role of Business," Cranfield School of Management, U.K.

51. Robert Ackerman and Raymond Bauer, *Corporate Social Responsiveness: The Modern Dilemma* (Reston, VA: Reston Publishing Company, 1976), 6.

52. Carroll, 1979, 502–504.

53. See special issue on "Corporate Citizenship," *Business and Society Review* (Vol. 105, No. 1, Spring 2000), edited by Barbara W. Altman and Deborah Vidaver-Cohen.

54. Duane Windsor, "Corporate Citizenship: Evolution and Interpretation," in Jörg Andriof and Malcom McIntosh (eds.), *Perspectives on Corporate Citizenship* (Sheffield, UK: Greenleaf Publishing, 2001), 39–52.

55. Samuel P. Graves, Sandra Waddock, and Marjorie Kelly, "How Do You Measure Corporate Citizenship?" *Business Ethics* (March/April 2001), 17.

56. Charles J. Fombrun, "Three Pillars of Corporate Citizenship," in Noel Tichy, Andrew McGill, and Lynda St. Clair (eds.), *Corporate Global Citizenship* (San Francisco: The New Lexington Press), 27–61.

57. Kimberly S. Davenport, *Corporate Citizenship: A Stakeholder Approach for Defining Corporate Social Performance and Identifying Measures for Assessing It*, doctoral dissertation, The Fielding Institute, Santa Barbara, CA.

58. Archie B. Carroll, "The Four Faces of Corporate Citizenship," *Business and Society Review* (100/101, 1998), 1–7.

59. Barbara W. Altman, *Corporate Community Relations in the 1990s: A Study in Transformation*, unpublished doctoral dissertation, Boston University.

60. Andreas G. Scherer and Guido Palazzo (eds.), *Handbook of Research on Global Corporate Citizenship* (Cheltenham, UK: Edward Elgar Publishing, 2008).

61. *The State of Corporate Citizenship in the U.S.: Business Perspective 2005*, Center for Corporate Citizenship at Boston College, U.S. Chamber of Commerce Center for Corporate Citizenship, and the Hitachi Foundation.

62. Archie B. Carroll, Kim Davenport, and Doug Grisaffe, "Appraising the Business Value of Corporate Citizenship: What Does the Literature Say?" Proceedings of the International Association for Business and Society, Essex Junction, VT, 2000.

63. Philip Mirvis and Bradley K. Googins, *Stages of Corporate Citizenship: A Developmental Framework* (monograph) (Boston: The Center for Corporate Citizenship at Boston College, 2006), i.

64. Ibid., 1–18.

65. For more on corporate citizenship, see the special issue "Corporate Citizenship," *Business and Society Review* (Vol. 105, No. 1, Spring 2000), edited by Barbara W. Altman and Deborah Vidaver-Cohen. Also see Jorg Andriof and Malcolm McIntosh (eds.), *Perspectives on Corporate Citizenship* (London: Greenleaf Publishing, 2001). Also see Isabelle Maignan, O. C. Ferrell, and G. Tomas M. Hult, "Corporate Citizenship: Cultural Antecedents and Business Benefits," *Journal of the Academy of Marketing Science* (Vol. 27, No. 4, Fall 1999), 455–469. Also see Malcolm McIntosh, Deborah Leipziger, Keith Jones, and Gill Coleman, *Corporate Citizenship: Successful Strategies for Responsible Companies* (London: Financial Times/Pitman Publishing), 1998.

66. Mark S. Schwartz and Archie B. Carroll, "Integrating and Unifying Competing and Complementary Frameworks: The Search for a Common Core in the Business and Society Field," *Business and Society* (Vol. 47, No. 2, June 2008), 148–186. Also see, Schwartz, 2011.

67. One of the most important meetings held on the subject of Global CSR are the International Conferences on CSR held at Humboldt University in Berlin every other year. The most recent meeting was held in October 2012. http://www.csr-hu-berlin.org/5th-csr-conference/. Accessed January 7, 2013.

68. Donna J. Wood, Jeanne M. Logsdon, Patsy G. Lewellyn, and Kim Davenport, *Global Business Citizenship: A Transformative Framework for Ethics and Sustainable Capitalism* (Armonk, NY: M. E. Sharpe, 2006), 40.

69. Dirk Matten and Jeremy Moon, "Implicit and Explicit CSR: A Conceptual Framework for Understanding CSR in Europe," *Research Paper Series, International Centre for Corporate Social Responsibility*, Nottingham University Business School, United Kingdom, 2004, 9.

70. Wayne Visser, "Corporate Social Responsibility in Developing Countries," in Andrew Crane, Abagail McWilliams, Dirk Matten, and Jeremy Moon (eds.), *The Oxford Handbook of Corporate Social Responsibility* (Oxford: Oxford University Press, 2008), 473–502.

71. Ioannis Ioannou and George Serafeim, "What drives corporate social performance? The role of nation-level institutions," *Journal of International Business Studies,* 43, December 2012, 834–864.

72. "Best and Worst in Social Responsibility," http://money. cnn.com/magazines/fortune/most-admired/2012/best_worst/best4.html. Accessed March 22, 2013.

73. "100 Best Companies to Work For," http://money.cnn. com/magazines/fortune/best-companies/2012/full_list/. Accessed November 27, 2012.

74. CRO Magazine's 100 Best Corporate Citizens for 2012," http://www.thecro.com/files/100Best2012_List_3.8.pdf. Accessed November 27, 2012.

75. Business Civic Leadership Center, U.S. Chamber of Commerce, 2011 Corporate Citizenship Award Winners, http://bclc.uschamber.com/article/2011-corporate-citizenship-awards. Accessed November 27, 2012.

76. See, for example, Mark Starik and Archie B. Carroll, "In Search of Beneficence: Reflections on the Connections Between Firm Social and Financial Performance," in Karen Paul (ed.), *Contemporary Issues in Business and Society in the United States and Abroad* (Lewiston, NY: The Edwin Mellen Press, 1991), 79–108; and I. M. Herremans, P. Akathaporn, and M. McInnes, "An Investigation of Corporate Social Responsibility, Reputation, and Economic Performance," *Accounting, Organizations, and Society* (Vol. 18, No. 7/8, 1993), 587–604.

77. Marc Orlitzky, Frank Schmidt, and Sara Rynes, "Corporate Social and Financial Performance: A Meta-Analysis," *Organization Studies* (Vol. 24, No. 3, 2003), 369–396. Also see Marc Orlitzky, "Payoffs to Social and Environmental Performance," *Journal of Investing* (Fall 2005), 48–51. Also see Lee E. Preston and Douglas P. O'Bannon, "The Corporate Social–Financial Performance Relationship: A Typology and Analysis," *Business and Society* (Vol. 36, No. 4, December 1997), 419–429; Sandra Waddock and Samuel Graves, "The Corporate Social Performance–Financial Performance Link," *Strategic Management Journal* (Vol. 18, No. 4, 1997), 303–319; Jennifer Griffin and John Mahon, "The Corporate Social Performance and Corporate Financial Performance Debate," *Business and Society* (Vol. 36, No. 1, March 1997), 5–31; Ronald Roman, Sefa Hayibor, and Bradley Agle, "The Relationship between Social and Financial Performance," *Business and Society* (Vol. 38, No. 1, March 1999), 121. For a reply to this study, see John Mahon and Jennifer Griffin, "Painting a Portrait: A Reply," *Business and Society* (Vol. 38, No. 1, March 1999), 126–133.

78. John Peloza, "The Challenge of Measuring Financial Impacts from Investments in Corporate Social Performance," *Journal of Management* (December 2009), 1518–1541.

79. Heli Wang and Jaepil Choi, "A New Look at the Corporate Social-Financial Performance Relationship: The Moderating Roles of Temporal and Interdomain Consistency in Corporate Social Performance," *Journal of Management,* February 2013, 416–441.

80. Orlitzky, Schmidt and Rynes, 2005 and Peloza, 2009. For an excellent overview of this research see Marc Orlitzky, "Corporate Social Performance and Financial Performance," Chapter 5, in Crane, et al (eds.), 2008, 113–136.

81. "Sustainability: CFOs are Coming to the Table," 2012 Deloitte Global Services Limited, 3–4.

82. Preston and O'Bannon, 428.

83. Bryan Husted, "A Contingency Theory of Corporate Social Performance," *Business and Society* (Vol. 39, No. 1, March 2000), 24–48, 41.

84. Zadek, 105–114.

85. Sustainability, "Environmental, Social and Governance Goals," http://www.sustainability.com/. Accessed July 5, 2010.

86. Dow Jones Sustainability Indexes, http://www.sustainability-index.com/. Accessed November 30, 2012.

87. The Forum for Sustainable and Responsive Investment, http://ussif.org/, Accessed March 22, 2013.

88. See, for example, Lawrence A. Armour, "Who Says Virtue Is Its Own Reward?" *Fortune* (February 16, 1998), 186–189; Thomas D. Saler, "Money & Morals," *Mutual Funds* (August 1997), 55–60; and Keith H. Hammonds, "A Portfolio with a Heart Still Needs a Brain," *BusinessWeek* (January 26, 1998), 100.

89. "Investing for Good," Domini Social Investments, http://www.domini.com/, Accessed March 25, 2013.

90. See Jack A. Brill and Alan Reder, *Investing from the Heart* (New York: Crown Publishers, 1992); Performance and SRI Investments, http://www.ussif.org/content.asp?contentid=35, Accessed March 22, 2013.

91. William A. Sodeman, *Social Investing: The Role of Corporate Social Performance in Investment Decisions,* unpublished Ph.D. dissertation, University of Georgia, 1993. See also William A. Sodeman and Archie B. Carroll, "Social Investment Firms: Their Purposes, Principles, and Investment Criteria," in International Association for Business and Society 1994 Proceedings, edited by Steven Wartick and Denis Collins, 339–344.

92. Daniel Akst, "The Give and Take of 'Socially Responsible,'" *The New York Times* (October 8, 2006), 28 BU; Jia Lynn Yang, "New Rules for Do-Good Funds," *Fortune* (February 5, 2007), 109–112.

93. "Invest with your conscience," *Money*, July 2011, 62.

94. "Performance and SRI Investments," http://www.ussif.org/content.asp?contentid=35. Accessed March 22, 2013.

95. Samuel B. Graves and Sandra A. Waddock, "Institutional Owners and Corporate Social Performance," *Academy of Management Journal* (Vol. 37, No. 4, August 1994), 1034–1046.

96. The Forum for Sustainable and Responsible Investment, http://ussif.org/projects/iwg/. Accessed March 22, 2013.

3

The Stakeholder Approach to Business, Society, and Ethics

After studying this chapter, you should be able to:

1. Define stake and stakeholder, and describe the origins of these concepts.

2. Differentiate among the production, managerial, and stakeholder views of the firm.

3. Differentiate among the three values of the stakeholder model.

4. Expound upon the concept of stakeholder management.

5. Identify and describe the five major questions that capture the essence of stakeholder management.

6. Identify the three levels of stakeholder management capability (SMC).

7. Describe the key principles of stakeholder management.

The business organization today, especially the modern corporation, is the institutional centerpiece of a complex society. Society today consists of many people with a multitude of interests, expectations, and demands regarding what major organizations ought to provide to accommodate people's lives and lifestyles. Business responds to many of the expectations placed on it. There has been an ever-changing social contract. There have been many assorted legal, ethical, and philanthropic expectations and demands being met by organizations willing to change as long as the economic incentives were present and honored. What was once viewed as a specialized means of providing profit through the manufacture and distribution of goods and services has become a multipurpose social institution that many people and groups depend on for their livelihoods, prosperity, and fulfillment.

Even in recessionary times, members of our society expect a quality, sustainable lifestyle, with more individuals and groups every day laying claim to their share of the good life. Business organizations today need to be responsive to individuals and groups they once viewed as powerless and unable to make such claims on them. We call these individuals and groups *stakeholders*. The stakeholder approach to management is an accepted framework that is constantly undergoing development, especially in the business-and-society arena. In the academic and business community, advances in stakeholder theory have illustrated the crucial development of the stakeholder concept.[1]

In terms of corporate application, a model for the "stakeholder corporation" has even been proposed. It has been argued that "stakeholder inclusion" is the key to company success in the 21st century.[2] A book titled *Stakeholder Power* presents a "winning plan for building stakeholder commitment and driving corporate growth."[3] Another book titled *Redefining the Corporation: Stakeholder Management and Organizational Wealth* argues that the corporate model needs redefinition because of business size and socioeconomic power and the inadequacy of the "ownership" model and its implications.[4] Yet another, titled simply *Stakeholders,* traces the theory and practice of the concept and brings us up to date on both strategic and ethical perspectives on stakeholders.[5] The topic of stakeholders is of crucial interest in this book.

An outgrowth of these developments is that it has become apparent that business organizations must address the legitimate needs and expectations of stakeholders if they want to be successful in the long run.[6] Business must also address stakeholders because it is the ethical course of action. They must recognize and factor in the stakeholders' needs, expectations, claims, and rights. For sustainable development to become a reality, the stakeholder approach offers the best opportunity. It is for these reasons that the stakeholder concept and orientation have become central to the vocabulary and thinking in the study of business, society, and ethics.

Origins of the Stakeholder Concept

The stakeholder concept has become a key to understanding business and society relationships. The term stakeholder is a variant of the more familiar and traditional concepts of *stockholders* or *shareholders*—the investors in or owners of businesses. Just as an individual might own his or her own private house, automobile, or iPhone, a stockholder owns a portion or a share of one or more businesses. Thus, a shareholder is also a type of stakeholder. However, shareholders are just one of many legitimate stakeholders that business and organizations deal with today to be effective.

What Is the *Stake* in Stakeholder?

To appreciate the concept of stakeholders, it helps to understand the idea of a stake. A **stake** is an interest in or a share in an undertaking. If a group plans to go out to dinner and a movie for the evening, each person in the group has a stake, or interest, in the group's decision. No money has been spent yet, but each member sees his or her interests (preference, taste, priority) in the decision. A stake may also be a claim. A claim is a demand for something due or believed to be due. We can see clearly that an owner or a shareholder has an interest in and an ownership of a share of a business.

The idea of a stake can range from simply an interest in an undertaking at one extreme to a legal claim of ownership at the other. Between these extremes might be a "need" for something or a "right." It might be a legal right to certain treatment rather than a legal claim of ownership, such as that of a shareholder. Legal rights might include the right to fair treatment (e.g., not to be discriminated against) or the right to privacy (not to have one's privacy invaded or abridged). A right also might be thought of as a moral right, such as that expressed by an employee: "I've got a right not to be fired because I've worked here 30 years, and I've given this firm the best years of my life." Or a consumer might say, "I've got a right to a safe product after all I've paid for this."

In short, stakeholders have a stake in the "value" they expect to receive from firms with which they interact. Harrington and Wicks have recently contended that stakeholders, in general, desire utility associated with (1) the actual goods and services companies provide, (2) organizational justice (fair treatment), (3) affiliating with companies that exhibit practices consistent with the things they value, and (4) getting a good deal from the company based on the opportunity costs they spend compared with value received from other companies.[7] Stakeholders, thus, have a significant stake in the value provided them by firms.

As we have seen, stakes take on a variety of different forms. Figure 3-1 summarizes various categories or types of stakes and provides examples.

FIGURE 3-1   Types of Stakes

	An Interest	A Right	Ownership
Definitions	When a person or group will be affected by a decision, it has an interest in that decision.	(1) Legal Right: When a person or group has a legal claim to be treated in a certain way or to have a particular right protected.	When a person or group has a legal title to an asset or a property.
Examples	This plant closing will affect the community. This TV commercial demeans women. I'm concerned about the environment for future generations.	Employees expect due process, privacy; customers or creditors have certain legal rights.	"This company is mine. I founded it, and I own it," or "I own 1,000 shares of this corporation."
Definitions		(2) Moral Right: When a person or group thinks it has a moral or ethical right to be treated in a certain way or to have a particular right protected.	
Examples		Fairness, justice, equity.	

© Cengage Learning

What Is a Stakeholder?

It follows, then, that a **stakeholder** is an individual or a group that has one or more of the various kinds of stakes in the organization. Just as stakeholders may be *affected by* the actions, decisions, policies, or practices of the business firm, these stakeholders may also *affect* the organization's actions, decisions, policies, or practices. With stakeholders, therefore, there is a real two-way interaction or exchange of influence. In short, a stakeholder may be thought of as "any individual or group who can affect or is affected by the actions, decisions, policies, practices, or goals of the organization."[8]

Who Are Business's Stakeholders?

In today's hypercompetitive, global business environment, any individuals and groups may be business's stakeholders. From the business point of view, certain individuals and groups have more *legitimacy* in the eyes of management; that is, they have a legitimate (authentic, justified), direct interest in, or claim on, the operations of the firm. The most obvious of these groups are shareholders, employees, and customers. However, from the point of view of a highly pluralistic society, stakeholders include not only these groups, but other groups as well. These other groups include the community, competitors, suppliers, special-interest groups, the media, and society (the public at large). Regulators, activists, and geographic communities also have been identified as stakeholders.[9] Charles Holliday, former chairperson and CEO of DuPont, stated, "We have traditionally defined four stakeholder groups important to DuPont—shareholders, customers, employees, and society."[10] But, the list of relevant stakeholders obviously extends beyond these major groups.

Because sustainability is one of the key themes in this textbook, special attention is called to the natural environment as stakeholder. The natural environment, along with the economic and social environments, was identified in Chapter 2 as central to the triple bottom line concept. When the concept of sustainability first became popular, however, the natural environment was given priority, but the natural environment has often been neglected. In keeping with sustainability, the natural environment, nonhuman species, and future generations should be considered among business's important stakeholders.[11] One reason these groups have been neglected is that they have never had a direct spokesperson. Who is to speak for the mountain ranges, the biosphere, the oceans, and the flora and fauna? The answer is interest groups such as Greenpeace, Friends of the Earth, and other environmental groups.[12] But, these nonprofit organizations and non-governmental organizations (NGOs) are indirect stakeholders, and consequently there has been a failure to fully incorporate their concerns by some organizations. This is why explicit consideration for the natural environment needs to be emphasized in this stakeholder chapter.

Three Views of the Firm: Production, Managerial, and Stakeholder

From an historical perspective, the advancement of the stakeholder concept parallels the growth and expansion of the business enterprise. In what has been termed the traditional **production view of the firm**, owners thought of stakeholders as only those individuals or groups that supplied resources or bought products or services.[13] Later, as we witnessed the growth of corporations and the resulting separation of ownership from control, business firms began to see their responsibilities toward other major constituent groups to be essential if they were to be successful. Thus, the **managerial view of the firm** emerged. Finally, as major internal and external changes occurred in business and its environment, managers were required to undergo a radical conceptual shift in how they perceived the firm and its multilateral relationships with constituent or stakeholder groups. The result was the **stakeholder view of the firm**.[14] Figure 3-2 depicts the evolution from the production view to the managerial view of the firm, and Figure 3-3 illustrates the stakeholder view of the firm. The stakeholder view encompasses numerous different individuals and groups that are embedded in the firm's internal and external environments. The diagram in Figure 3-3 is called a **stakeholder map** because it charts out a firm's stakeholders.

In the stakeholder view of the firm, management must perceive as stakeholders not only those groups that *management* thinks have some stake in the firm but also those who themselves think or perceive they have a stake in the firm. This is an essential perspective that management must take, at least until it has had a chance to weigh carefully the legitimacy of the claims and the power of various stakeholders. Of particular note is that each stakeholder group is composed of subgroups; for example, the government stakeholder group includes federal, state, and local government subgroups as stakeholders.

Primary and Secondary Stakeholders

A useful way to categorize stakeholders is to think of them as *primary* and *secondary* as well as *social* and *nonsocial*; thus, stakeholders may be thought of as follows[15]:

Primary social **stakeholders include:**	*Secondary social* **stakeholders include:**
• Shareholders and investors	• Government and regulators
• Employees and managers	• Civic institutions
• Customers	• Social pressure/activist groups
• Local communities	• Media and academic commentators
• Suppliers and other business partners	• Trade bodies
	• Competitors

FIGURE 3-2

The Production and Managerial Views of the Firm

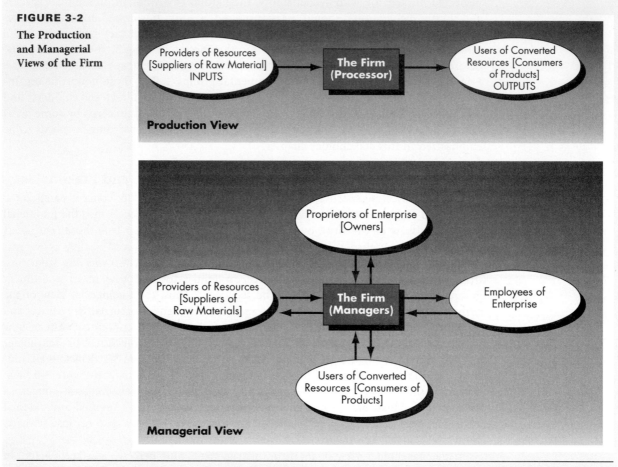

Source: Adapted from Freeman's *Strategic Management: A Stakeholder Approach*, Copyright © 1984 by R. Edward Freeman. Reprinted with permission from Pitman Publishing Company.

Primary social stakeholders have a *direct* stake in the organization and its success and, therefore, are most influential. **Secondary social stakeholders** may be extremely *influential* as well, especially in affecting reputation and public standing, but their stake in the organization is more *indirect*. Therefore, a firm's responsibility toward secondary stakeholders may be less, but it is not avoidable. These groups may wield significant power and quite often represent legitimate public concerns that make it impossible for them to be ignored.[16]

Primary nonsocial stakeholders include:	*Secondary nonsocial* stakeholders include:
• Natural environment	• Environmental interest groups (e.g., Friends of the Earth, Greenpeace, Rainforest Alliance)
• Future generations	• Animal welfare organizations (e.g., People for the Ethical Treatment of Animals—PETA, American Society for the Prevention of Cruelty to Animals—ASPCA, The Humane Society)
• Nonhuman species	

FIGURE 3-3   The Stakeholder View of the Firm

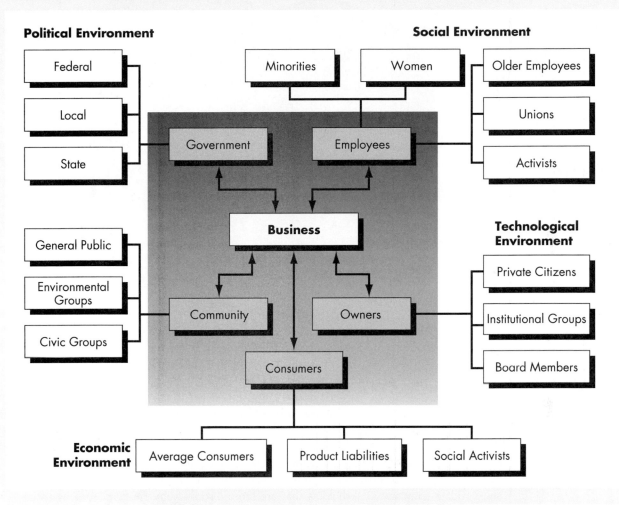

The terms primary and secondary may be defined differently depending on the situation. Secondary stakeholders can quickly become primary, for example. This often occurs through the media or special-interest groups when a claim's *urgency* (as in a boycott or demonstration) takes precedence over its legitimacy. In today's business environment, the media and social media have the power to instantaneously transform a stakeholder's status within minutes or hours. Thus, it may be useful to think of primary and secondary classes of stakeholders for discussion purposes, but we should understand how easily and quickly those categories can shift.

A Typology of Stakeholder Attributes: Legitimacy, Power, Urgency

How do managers decide which stakeholders deserve their attention? Stakeholders have attributes including legitimacy, power, and urgency. A typology of stakeholders has been developed based on these three attributes.[17] When these three attributes are superimposed, as depicted in Figure 3-4, seven stakeholder categories may be seen.

The three attributes of legitimacy, power, and urgency help us see how stakeholders may be thought of and analyzed in terms of their characteristics. The stakeholders are more or less salient depending on these factors. **Legitimacy** refers to the perceived validity or

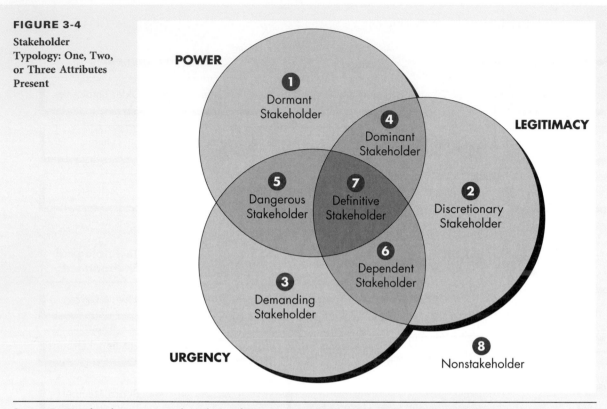

FIGURE 3-4

Stakeholder Typology: One, Two, or Three Attributes Present

Source: Reprinted with permission of Academy of Management, PO Box 3020, Briar Cliff Manor, NY 10510-8020. Stakeholder Typology: One, Two, or Three Attributes Present (Figure), R. K. Mitchell, B. R. Agle, and D. J. Wood, *Academy of Management Review*, October 1997. Reproduced by permission of the publisher via Copyright Clearance Center, Inc.

appropriateness of a stakeholder's claim to a stake. Therefore, owners, employees, and customers represent a high degree of legitimacy due to their explicit, formal, and direct relationships with a company. Stakeholders that are more distant from the firm, such as social activist groups, NGOs, competitors, or the media, might be thought to have less legitimacy.

Power refers to the ability or capacity to produce an effect—to get something done that otherwise may not be done. Therefore, whether one has legitimacy or not, power means that the stakeholder could affect the business. For example, with the help of the media, a large, vocal, activist group such as the People for the Ethical Treatment of Animals (PETA) could wield extraordinary power over a business firm. In recent years, PETA has been successful in influencing the practices and policies of virtually all the fast-food restaurants regarding their suppliers' treatment of chickens and cattle.

Urgency refers to the degree to which the stakeholder claim on the business calls for the business's *immediate* attention or response. Urgency may imply that something is critical—it really needs to get done. Or it may imply that something needs to be done immediately or on a timely basis. A management group may perceive a union strike, a consumer boycott, a contaminated product, or a social activist group picketing outside headquarters as urgent.

Research has suggested that at least one other criterion should be considered in addition to legitimacy, power, and urgency—**proximity**.[18] The spatial distance between the organization and its stakeholders is a relevant consideration in evaluating stakeholders' importance and priority. Stakeholders that share the same physical space or are adjacent to the organization may affect and be affected by the organization. In a global example, nation states may share borders, introducing spatially related stakeholders. It is evident, therefore, that the greater the proximity, the greater the likelihood of relevant and important stakeholder relationships.[19]

An appropriate example of a stakeholder action that illustrated both power and urgency occurred in several dozen Home Depot stores around the country. In each of the stores, strange announcements began blaring from the intercom systems: *"Attention shoppers, on aisle seven you'll find mahogany ripped from the heart of the Amazon."* Shocked store managers raced through the aisles trying to apprehend the environmental activists behind the stunt. The activists had apparently gotten the access codes to the intercoms. After months of similar antics, Home Depot bowed to the demands of the environmental group and announced that it would stop selling wood from endangered forests and, instead, stock wood products certified by the Forest Stewardship Council (FSC).[20] This group of environmental activists was not even on Home Depot's stakeholder radar screen and then, all of a sudden, the company was convinced it had to sell only FSC-certified wood. This was an awesome display of stakeholder power.

ETHICS IN PRACTICE CASE

Are Plants and Flowers Stakeholders? Do They Have Rights?

Scientists in Switzerland for years have created genetically modified produce, such as rice, corn, and apples. Recently, the question has been raised whether they ever stopped to think that their experiments may be "humiliating" to plants. A recently passed constitutional rule came into existence after the Swiss Parliament asked a panel of philosophers, geneticists, theologians, and lawyers to establish the "meaning" of a flora's dignity. The panel wrote a lengthy treatise on the "moral consideration of plants for their own sake." The document argued that vegetation has an inherent value and that it is immoral to harm plants arbitrarily. One example of this would be the "decapitation of wildflowers at the roadside without any apparent reason."

Defenders of the new law state that it reflects a broader, progressive effort to protect the sanctity of living things and promote sustainability. Switzerland also granted new rights to all "social animals." For example, prospective dog owners now have to take a four-hour course on pet care before they can acquire a dog. Anglers now have to learn how to catch fish humanely. Goldfish can no longer be flushed down the toilet as a means of disposal. First, they must be anesthetized with special chemicals. One Swiss scientist recently exclaimed, "Where does it stop? Should we now defend the dignity of microbes and viruses?" In a related decision, the people of Ecuador passed a new constitution that is said to be the first to recognize ecosystem rights enforceable in a court of law. Now, the nation's rivers, forests, and air are right-bearing entities with "the right to exist, persist, and regenerate."

One nonprofit organization that has formed to support this point of view is "Fair Flowers Fair Plants" an independent foundation representing international stakeholders in the flower industry striving for social and environmental standards.

1. Are plants stakeholders? Are they primary or secondary stakeholders? Do flora have rights? What about dogs and goldfish?
2. Are the Swiss and Ecuadorian decisions too extreme? What are the limits of stakeholders' rights? Is this taking sustainability too far or pushing the idea to its natural limits?
3. What are the implications for business decisions of the Swiss and Ecuadorian decisions? Are these unique to these countries and won't apply elsewhere?

Sources: James Wandersee and Renee Clary, Gautam Naik, *Human Flower Project*, "Do Plants Have Rights?" http://www.humanflo werproject.com/index.php/weblog/comments/do_plants_have_rights/, Accessed March 25, 2013. Also see "Switzerland's Green Power Revolution: Ethicists Ponder Plants' Rights," *The Wall Street Journal*, October 10, 2008, A1. Human Flower Project, "Do Plants Have Rights?" "Fair Flowers Fair Plants, http://www.fairflowersfairplants.com/home-en/ffp-standard.aspx, Accessed March 25, 2013.

The typology of stakeholder attributes suggests that managers must attend to stakeholders on the basis of their assessment of the extent to which competing stakeholder claims reflect legitimacy, power, and urgency and are salient. Using the categories shown in Figure 3-4, the stakeholder groups represented by overlapping circles (e.g., those with two or three attributes such as Categories 4, 5, 6, and 7) are highly "salient" to the management and would likely receive priority attention.

Stakeholder Approaches

Strategic, Multifiduciary, and Synthesis Approaches

A major challenge embedded in the stakeholder approach is to determine whether it should be seen primarily as a way to *manage better* or as a way to *treat more ethically* those groups known as stakeholders. Both of these concerns have sustainability implications. This issue may be addressed by considering the stakeholder approach used. Kenneth Goodpaster has suggested three approaches: the strategic approach, the multifiduciary approach, and the stakeholder synthesis approach.[21]

Strategic Approach The **strategic approach** views stakeholders primarily as factors to be taken into consideration and managed while the firm pursues profits for its shareholders. In this view, managers take stakeholders into account because offended stakeholders might resist or retaliate (e.g., through political action, protest, or boycott). This approach sees stakeholders as instruments that may facilitate or impede the firm's pursuit of its strategic, business objectives; thus, it is an instrumental view.

Multifiduciary Approach The **multifiduciary approach** views stakeholders as more than just individuals or groups who can wield economic or legal power. This view holds that the management has a fiduciary responsibility toward stakeholders just as it has this same responsibility toward shareholders. In this approach, the management's traditional fiduciary, or trust, duty is expanded to embrace stakeholders on roughly an equal footing with shareholders. Thus, shareholders are no longer of exclusive importance as they are under the strategic approach.[22] This view broadens the idea of a fiduciary responsibility to include stockholders and other important stakeholders.

Stakeholder Synthesis Approach An innovative, stakeholder **synthesis approach** is preferred because it holds that business does have moral responsibilities to stakeholders but that they should not be seen as part of a fiduciary obligation. As a consequence, the management's basic fiduciary responsibility toward shareholders is kept intact, but it is also expected to be implemented within a context of ethical responsibility. This ethical responsibility is business's duty not to harm, coerce, lie, cheat, steal, and so on.[23] The result is the same in the multifiduciary and stakeholder synthesis views. However, the reasoning or rationale is different.

As we continue our discussion of stakeholder management, it should become clear that we are pursuing it from a balanced perspective, which suggests that we are integrating the strategic approach with the stakeholder synthesis approach. We should be managing strategically and morally at the same time.[24] The stakeholder approach should not be just a better way to manage. It also should be a more ethical and sustainable way to manage.

Three Values of the Stakeholder Model

In addition to the strategic, multifiduciary, and stakeholder synthesis approaches, the stakeholder model of the firm has three aspects or values that should be appreciated. Although interrelated, these include the descriptive, instrumental, and normative values or aspects.[25]

Descriptive Value

First, the stakeholder model has value because it is *descriptive*; that is, **descriptive value** provides language and concepts to describe effectively the corporation or organization in inclusive terms. The corporation is a constellation of cooperative and competitive interests possessing both instrumental and intrinsic value. Understanding organizations in this way allows us to have a fuller description and explanation of how they function. The language and terms used in stakeholder theory are useful in helping us understand organizations. As a result, stakeholder language and concepts are being used more and more in many fields of endeavor—business, government, politics, education, nonprofit organizations, and so on.

Instrumental Value

Second, the stakeholder model has **instrumental value** because it is *instrumental* in portraying the relationship between the practice of stakeholder management and the resulting achievement of corporate performance goals. The fundamental premise here is that practicing effective stakeholder management should lead to the achievement of traditional business goals, such as profitability, stability, and growth.[26] This is similar to the *strategic approach* discussed earlier. Business school courses in strategic management often employ the instrumental model of stakeholders.

Normative Value

Third, the stakeholder model has **normative value** because stakeholders are seen as possessing value irrespective of their instrumental use to management. This is often considered the moral or ethical view because it emphasizes how stakeholders *should* be treated. The "principle of stakeholder fairness" has been suggested as the moral underpinning, or normative justification, for the stakeholder model.[27] Thus, the normative value of stakeholder thinking is of central importance in business ethics and business and society.

In summarizing, stakeholder theory is *managerial* in the broad sense of the term in that it not only describes or predicts but also recommends attitudes, structures, and practices that constitute stakeholder management. Effective management requires simultaneous attention to the legitimate interests of all appropriate stakeholders in the creation of organizational structures and policies and in decision making.[28]

Key Questions in Stakeholder Management

The managers of a business firm are responsible for establishing the firm's overall direction (its governance, mission, strategies, goals, and policies) and ensuring implementation of these plans. As a consequence, they have some long-term responsibilities and many that are of more immediate concern. Before the stakeholder environment became as turbulent and dynamic as it now is, the managerial task was relatively straightforward because the external environment was stable. As managers have transitioned to the stakeholder view of the firm, however, the managerial task has become an inevitable consequence of the changing trends and developments described in the first two chapters.

The challenge of stakeholder management is to see to it that while the firm's primary stakeholders achieve their objectives, the other stakeholders are dealt with ethically and are also relatively satisfied. At the same time, the firm's profitability must be ensured. This is the classic "win–win" situation. The management's second-best alternative is to meet the goals of its primary stakeholders, keeping in mind the important role of its owner-investors. Without economic sustainability, all other stakeholders' interests become unresolved.

With these perspectives in mind, it is possible to approach stakeholder management with the idea that managers can become successful stewards of their stakeholders' resources by gaining knowledge about stakeholders and using this knowledge to predict and improve their company's behaviors and actions. Thus, the important functions of stakeholder management are to describe, to analyze, to understand, and, finally, to manage. The quest for stakeholder management embraces social, legal, ethical, and economic considerations. Normative as well as instrumental objectives and perspectives are essential.

Five **key questions** are critical to capturing the essential information needed for stakeholder management:

1. *Who* are our organization's stakeholders?
2. What are our stakeholders' *stakes*?
3. What *opportunities and challenges* do our stakeholders present to the firm?
4. What *responsibilities* (economic, legal, ethical, and philanthropic) does the firm have to its stakeholders?
5. What *strategies or actions* should the firm take to best address stakeholder challenges and opportunities?[29]

Figure 3-5 presents a schematic of the decision process outlining the five questions and key issues with respect to each.

Who Are the Organization's Stakeholders?

To manage them effectively, each firm and its management group must ask and answer this question: *Who are our stakeholders?* This stage is often called "stakeholder identification." To answer this question fully, management must identify not only *generic* stakeholder groups but also *specific* subgroups. A generic stakeholder group is a general or broad grouping, such as employees, shareholders, environmental groups, or consumers. Within each of these generic categories, there may be a few or many specific subgroups. Figure 3-6 illustrates some of the generic and specific stakeholder subgroups of a large organization.

McDonald's Continuing Experience To illustrate the process of stakeholder identification, it is helpful to consider some events in the life of the McDonald's Corporation that resulted in their broadening significantly who the company considered its stakeholders. The case study begins when the social activist group PETA, which claims more than two million members and supporters, decided it was dissatisfied with some of McDonald's practices and launched a billboard and bumper sticker campaign against the hamburger giant.[30] PETA, convinced that McDonald's was dragging its feet on animal welfare issues, went on the offensive. The group announced that it would put up billboards saying "The animals deserve a break today" and "McDonald's: Cruelty to Go" in Norfolk, Virginia, PETA's hometown. The ad campaign was announced when talks broke down between PETA and McDonald's on the subject of ways the company might foster animal rights issues within the fast-food industry. Using terminology introduced earlier, PETA was a secondary social or nonsocial stakeholder and, therefore, had low legitimacy. However, its power and urgency were extremely high as it was threatening the company with a very visible, potentially destructive campaign that was being reported by a cooperative and empathetic media.

PETA's pressure tactics continued and escalated. In the early 2000s, McDonald's announced significant changes in the requirements it was placing on its chicken and egg suppliers. Egg suppliers were required to improve the "living conditions" of their chickens. Specifically, McDonald's insisted that its suppliers no longer cage the chickens wingtip to wingtip. Suppliers were required to increase the space allotted to each hen

FIGURE 3-5

Stakeholder Management: Five Key Questions

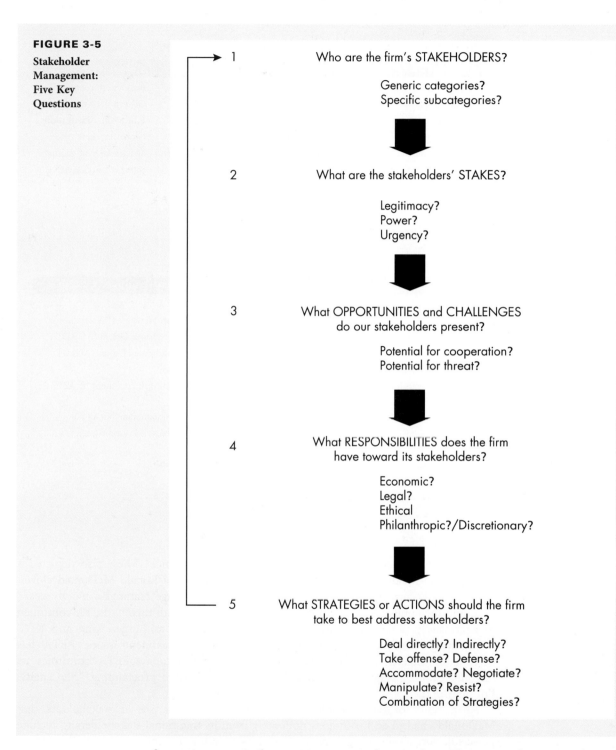

1   Who are the firm's STAKEHOLDERS?

Generic categories?
Specific subcategories?

2   What are the stakeholders' STAKES?

Legitimacy?
Power?
Urgency?

3   What OPPORTUNITIES and CHALLENGES
do our stakeholders present?

Potential for cooperation?
Potential for threat?

4   What RESPONSIBILITIES does the firm
have toward its stakeholders?

Economic?
Legal?
Ethical
Philanthropic?/Discretionary?

5   What STRATEGIES or ACTIONS should the firm
take to best address stakeholders?

Deal directly? Indirectly?
Take offense? Defense?
Accommodate? Negotiate?
Manipulate? Resist?
Combination of Strategies?

© Cengage Learning

from 48 square inches to 72 square inches per hen. They were also required to stop "forced molting," a process that increases egg production by denying hens food and water for up to two weeks.[31]

PETA then escalated its pressure tactics against the firm by distributing "*unhappy meals*" at restaurant playgrounds and outside the company's shareholder meeting venues. The kits came in boxes similar to that of Happy Meal™, McDonald's meal for children,

FIGURE 3-6   Generic and Specific Stakeholders of a Large Firm

Owners	Employees	Governments	Customers
Trusts	Young employees	Federal	Business purchasers
Foundations	Middle-aged employees	• EPA	Government purchasers
Mutual funds	Older employees	• FTC	Educational institutions
Universities	Women	• OSHA	Global markets
Board members	Minority groups	• CPSC	Special-interest groups
Employee pension funds	Disabled	State	Internet purchasers
Management owners	Special-interest groups	Local	
Individual owners	Unions		

Community	Competitors	Social Activist Groups
General fund-raising	Firm A	Rainbow/PUSH
United Way	Firm B	Rainforest Action Network (RAN)
YMCA/YWCA	Firm C	Mothers Against Drunk Driving (MADD)
Middle schools	Indirect competition	American Civil Liberties Union (ACLU)
Elementary schools	Global competition	Consumers Union
Residents who live close by	Internet-based competition	People for the Ethical Treatment of Animals (PETA)
All other residents		National Rifle Association (NRA)
Neighborhood associations		National Resources Defense Council
Local media		Citizens for Health
Chamber of Commerce		Greenbiz.com
Environments		

but were covered instead with pictures of slaughtered animals. These also depicted a bloody, knife-wielding "Son of Ron" doll that resembled the Ronald McDonald clown, as well as toy farm animals with slashed throats. One image featured a bloody cow's head and the familiar fast-food phrase "Do you want fries with that?"[32] PETA continued to aggressively pursue McDonald's and other firms, such as Burger King and KFC, for their chicken-slaughter methods and other animal treatment issues. PETA has become the stakeholder that refuses to go away. Even today, PETA continues its ongoing campaign against McDonald's with its Web page proclaiming "McCruelty: I'm Hating It."[33]

As a result of this example, it can be seen how the set of stakeholders that McDonald's had to deal with grew noticeably from its traditional stakeholders to include powerful, special-interest groups such as PETA. With the cooperation of the media, especially major newspapers, magazines and TV, PETA moved from being a secondary stakeholder to a primary stakeholder in McDonald's life.

Wool Industry Under Fire Not only does PETA attack companies, it also takes on whole *industries*. Under pressure from PETA, many companies began to ban Australian wool. PETA's complaint against Australia's $2.2 billion industry has been targeted toward its use of wool from so-called mulesed merino sheep. Mulesing is a process of removing folds of skin from a sheep's hindquarters. The technique developed over 70 years ago and named after John Mules, who devised it, is performed without anesthetics. The intention is to protect the sheep against infestation by blowflies whose eggs hatch into flesh-eating maggots while in the wool. When PETA first started lobbying against this process in 2004, most apparel makers had never heard of the process or the issue. PETA began its attacks on Benetton, the Italian company that produces sweaters. It dispatched protestors wielding signs that read "Benetton—Baaad to Sheep" to picket stores stocking the product. In New York City, PETA also put up billboards with the question "Did your sweater cause a bloody butt?" The protests worked. Benetton soon publicly came out in favor of phasing out mulesing. Other companies followed. As one European retailer observed, "who wants to be on PETA's radar screen?" More than 30 companies signed on to the ban, including well-known brands such as Abercrombie & Fitch, Timberland, Hugo Boss, and adidas. Meanwhile, Australia's 55,000 sheep farmers are unhappy because they believe mulesing is the best way to protect their flocks.[34]

These actual experiences of companies illustrate the evolving nature of the question, "Who are our stakeholders?" In actuality, stakeholder identification is an unfolding process. However, by recognizing early the potential of failure if one does not think in stakeholder terms, the value and usefulness of stakeholder thinking can be readily seen. Had McDonald's, KFC, Benetton, and other firms perceived PETA as a stakeholder with power and some moral legitimacy, earlier on, perhaps they could have dealt with these situations more effectively. These firms should have been aware of one of the basic principles of stakeholder responsibility: "Recognize that stakeholders are real and complex people with names, faces, and values."[35]

Getting to know your company's stakeholders requires managers to go beyond simple list making of their characteristics. It means getting to know your stakeholders just like you get to know your customers. A McKinsey study found a strong positive correlation between in-depth profiling of stakeholders and success at engaging them.[36] But, many businesses do not carefully identify their generic stakeholder groups, much less their specific stakeholder groups. This must be done, however, if the management is to be in a position to answer the second major question, "What are our stakeholders' stakes?"

What Are Our Stakeholders' Stakes?

Once stakeholders have been identified, the next step is to address the question: *What are our stakeholders' stakes?* Even groups in the same generic category frequently have different specific interests, concerns, perceptions of rights, and expectations. Management's challenge is to identify the nature, legitimacy, and saliency of a group's stake(s) and the group's power to affect the organization. As discussed earlier, urgency is another critical factor.

Nature or Legitimacy of a Group's Stakes Stakeholders may possess varying types of stakes. Think about a large corporation with several hundred million shares of stock outstanding. Among the shareholder population of this corporation are these more specific subgroups:

1. Institutional owners (trusts, foundations, churches, universities)
2. Large mutual fund organizations (Fidelity, Vanguard, Pax World)
3. Board of director members who own shares
4. Members of management who own shares
5. Millions of small, individual shareholders

For all these subgroups, the nature of stakeholder claims on this corporation is *ownership*. All these groups have legitimate claims—they are all owners. Because of other factors, such as power or urgency, however, these stakeholders may have to be dealt with differently.

Power of a Group's Stakes When power is considered, significant differences become apparent. Which of the groups in the previous list are the most powerful? Certainly not the small, individual investors, unless they have found a way to organize and thus wield power. The powerful stakeholders in this case are (1) the institutional owners and mutual fund organizations, because of the sheer magnitude of their investments and (2) the board and management shareholders, because of their dual roles of ownership and management (control).

Sub-groups within a Generic Group Consider a manufacturing firm in Ohio that is faced with a generic group of environmental stakeholders. Within the generic group of environmental stakeholders might be the following specific sub-groups:

1. Residents living within a 25-mile radius of the plant
2. Other residents in the city
3. Residents who live in the path of the jet stream hundreds of miles away (some in Canada) who are being impacted by acid rain
4. Environmental Protection Agency (federal government)
5. Ohio's Environmental Protection Division (state government)
6. Sierra Club (environmental activist group)
7. Earth Liberation Front (environmental activist group)
8. Ohio Environmental Council (special interest group)

It would require some degree of time and care for the firm to identify the nature, legitimacy, power, and urgency of each of these specific groups. However, the firm can and should do this if it wants to better engage and manage its environmental stakeholders. Companies have an ethical responsibility to be sensitive to legitimate stakeholder claims even if the stakeholders have no power or leverage with the management.

Return for a moment to the fast-food and wool industry examples. One may conclude that PETA, as a special-interest animal welfare group, did not have much *legitimacy* vis-à-vis these companies. It did claim animals' rights and treatment as a moral issue, and thus had some general legitimacy through the issues it represented. Unfortunately for PETA, not all of the public shares its concerns or degree of concern with these issues. However, PETA had tremendous power and urgency. It was this power, wielded in the form of adverse publicity and media attention that without a doubt played a significant role in bringing about changes in these companies' policies.

What Opportunities and Challenges Do Our Stakeholders Present?

Opportunities and challenges represent opposite sides of the coin when it comes to stakeholder analysis. The opportunities are for business to build decent, productive working relationships with the stakeholders. Challenges, on the other hand, usually present themselves in such a way that the firm must handle the stakeholders acceptably or be hurt in some way—financially (short term or long term) or in terms of its public image or reputation in the community.

Stakeholder challenges typically take the form of varying degrees of expectations, demands, or threats. In most instances, they arise because stakeholders think or believe that their needs or points of view are not being met adequately. The example of PETA illustrated this point quite well. The challenges also arise when stakeholder groups think that any crisis that occurs is the responsibility of the firm or that the firm caused the crisis in some way.

Another example of a stakeholder crisis illustrates this point[37]: Rainforest Action Network (RAN) launched a campaign to transform the entire logging industry, starting with Boise, Inc., an international distributor of office supplies and paper and an integrated manufacturer and distributor of paper, packaging, and building materials. At the time, Boise was one of the top loggers and distributors of old-growth forest products in the United States and a top distributor of wood products from the world's most endangered forests, including the tropical rainforests of the Amazon and the boreal forests of Canada. Boise was also the largest logger of U.S. public lands and the sole logging company to oppose the U.S. Forest Service Roadless Area Conservation Policy in court.

As a result of RAN's campaigning, Boise implemented a domestic old-growth policy, committing to "no longer harvesting timber from old-growth forests in the United States." To catch up with public values and meet the new marketplace standards, Boise dropped its opposition to the Roadless Policy and became the first U.S. logging and distribution company to commit to "eliminate the purchase of wood products from endangered areas."[38] RAN's aggressive protection of rainforests continues to this day. Currently, RAN has campaigns against Chevron, Cargill, Bank of America, and APP and APRIL (in Indonesia).[39]

If one looks at the recent experiences of businesses, including the crisis mentioned here, it is evident that there is a need to think in stakeholder terms to understand fully the potential threats that businesses of all kinds face on a daily basis.

Opportunities and challenges might also be viewed in terms of *potential for cooperation* and *potential for threat*. Arguments abound that such assessments of cooperation and threat are necessary to enable managers to identify strategies for dealing with stakeholders.[40] In terms of potential for threat, managers need to consider stakeholders' relative power and its relevance to a particular issue facing the organization. In terms of potential for cooperation, the firm needs to be sensitive to the possibility of joining forces with stakeholders for the advantage of all parties involved. Several examples of how cooperative alliances were formed include the following.

Several companies have entered into cooperative partnerships with the sustainability group Environmental Defense Fund (EDF). Companies such as Facebook, Google, Boeing, and Procter & Gamble have begun participating in EDF's Climate Corps which was launched in 2008. In this program, students from leading business and public policy schools are trained and sent to major companies and organizations for summer fellowships. These Climate Corps Fellows have as their main task searching for energy savings. To date, these EDF Climate Corps Fellows have identified $1 billion in energy savings.[41] In another collaboration, EDF and FedEx joined together in a cooperative relationship to launch the first "street ready" hybrid trucks ever built. Today, hundreds of these trucks are in the corporate fleets of UPS, Coca-Cola, and the U.S. Postal Service.

What Responsibilities Does a Firm Have toward Its Stakeholders?

The next logical question after identifying and understanding stakeholders' threats and opportunities is "*What responsibilities does a firm have in its relationships with its stakeholders?"* Responsibilities may be thought of in terms of the corporate social responsibility discussion presented in Chapter 2. What economic, legal, ethical, and philanthropic responsibilities does management have toward each stakeholder? Because most of the firm's economic responsibilities are principally to itself and its shareholders, the analysis naturally turns to legal, ethical, and philanthropic questions. The most pressing threats are typically presented as legal and ethical questions. Often, opportunities are reflected in areas of philanthropy or "giving back" to the community.

It should be pointed out, however, that the firm itself has an economic stake in most legal and ethical issues it faces. For example, when Johnson & Johnson (J&J) faced the Tylenol poisoning crisis, it had to decide what legal and ethical actions to take and what actions were in the firm's best economic interests. In this classic case, J&J concluded that recalling the tainted Tylenol products was not only the ethical choice but also one that would preserve its reputation of being concerned about consumers' health and well-being. Figure 3-7 illustrates the **stakeholder responsibility matrix** that management faces when assessing the firm's responsibilities to stakeholders. The matrix may be seen as a template that managers might use to systematically think through its various responsibilities to each stakeholder group.

What Strategies or Actions Should Management Take?

Once responsibilities have been assessed, an organization must contemplate strategies and actions for addressing its stakeholders. In every decision situation, a multitude of alternative courses of action are available, and management must choose one or several that seem best. Important questions or decision choices for management in dealing with stakeholders include:

- Do we deal *directly* or *indirectly* with stakeholders?
- Do we take the *offense* or the *defense* in dealing with stakeholders?
- Do we *accommodate, negotiate, manipulate,* or *resist* stakeholder overtures?
- Do we employ a *combination of these* strategies or pursue a *singular course* of action?[42]

FIGURE 3-7

Stakeholder
Responsibility
Matrix

Stakeholders	Types of Responsibilities			
	Economic	Legal	Ethical	Philanthropic
Owners				
Customers				
Employees				
Community				
Public at Large				
Social Activist Groups				
Others				

© Cengage Learning

In actual practice, managers need to prioritize stakeholder expectations and demands before deciding on the appropriate strategy.[43] In addition, strategic thinking in terms of forms of communication, degree of collaboration, development of policies or programs, and allocation of resources would need to be thought through carefully.[44] The development of specific strategies should be based on a classification of stakeholders' *potentials for cooperation and threat* discussed earlier. If these two factors are used, four stakeholder types and resultant generic strategies emerge: supportive, marginal, nonsupportive, and mixed blessing.[45]

Type 1: **The** *Supportive* **Stakeholder** The **supportive stakeholder** has a high potential for cooperation and a low potential for threat. This is the ideal stakeholder. To a well-managed organization, supportive stakeholders might include its board of directors, managers, employees, and loyal customers. Others might be suppliers and service providers. The strategy with supporters is one of involvement. An example of this might be the strategy of engaging employee stakeholders through participative management or employee volunteerism.

Type 2: **The** *Marginal* **Stakeholder** The **marginal stakeholder** is low on both potential for threat and potential for cooperation. For large organizations, these stakeholders might include professional associations of employees, inactive consumer interest groups, or shareholders—especially those that hold few shares and are not organized. The strategy here is for the organization to *monitor* the marginal stakeholder. Monitoring is especially called for to make sure circumstances do not change.

Type 3: **The** *Nonsupportive* **Stakeholder** The **nonsupportive stakeholder** has a high potential for threat but a low potential for cooperation. Examples of this group could include competing organizations, unions, federal or other levels of government, and the media. Special-interest groups often fall in this category. The recommended strategy is to defend against the nonsupportive stakeholder. An example of a special-interest group that many would regard as nonsupportive is the Earth Liberation Front (ELF), a movement that originated in the Pacific Northwest. It claimed responsibility for a string of arsons in the suburbs of Los Angeles, Detroit, and Philadelphia. ELF's attacks targeted luxury homes and sports utility vehicles (SUVs), the suburban status symbols that some environmentalists regard as despoilers of the Earth. Many such radical environmental groups have been called "eco-terrorists."[46] Such organizations do not seem interested in establishing positive, or supportive, relationships with companies and industries. In the examples discussed earlier, PETA typically comes across as a non-supportive stakeholder because of its high potential for threat and reticence toward cooperation.

Type 4: **The** *Mixed-Blessing* **Stakeholder** The **mixed-blessing stakeholder** is high on both potential for threat and potential for cooperation. Examples of this group, in a well-managed organization, might include employees who are in short supply, clients, or customers. A mixed-blessing stakeholder could become a supportive or a nonsupportive stakeholder. The recommended strategy here is to collaborate with the mixed-blessing stakeholder. By maximizing collaboration, the likelihood that this stakeholder will remain supportive is enhanced. Today, many companies regard sustainability groups as mixed blessings rather than nonsupportive. These firms are turning environmentalists into allies by building alliances with them for mutual gain.[47] Figure 3-8 summarizes an analysis of stakeholder types and recommended strategies and actions.

FIGURE 3-8   Analyzing Stakeholders and Recommended Strategies and Actions

Stakeholder Type	Examples of Stakeholder Type	Stakeholder *Potential for Threat*	Stakeholder *Potential for Cooperation*	Strategy/Action Recommended
Supportive Stakeholder	Board of directors, some employees	Low	High	Involve; take offense, accommodate, proact; keep satisfied
Marginal Stakeholder	Professional associations, interest groups	Low	Low	Monitor; watch carefully; minimal effort; offense or defense
Nonsupportive Stakeholder	Competitors, unions, governments, some activist groups	High	Low	Defend; be prepared; guard against; negotiate
Mixed Blessing Stakeholder	Employees, clients, customers	High	Medium-to-high	Collaborate; take offense, partnership, pool resources; keep informed

Sources: Compiled from multiple sources: Grant T. Savage, Timothy W. Nix, Carlton J. Whitehead, and John D. Blair, "Strategies for Assessing and Managing Organizational Stakeholders," *Academy of Management Executive* (Vol. V, No. 2, May 1991), 61–75; Ian C. MacMillan and Patricia E. Jones, *Strategy Formulation: Power and Politics* (St. Paul, MN: West, 1986), 66; "Stakeholder Management," http://pubs.opengroup.org/architecture/togaf9-doc/arch/chap24. html. Accessed February 1, 2013.

A summary guideline regarding these four stakeholder types might be stated in the following way[48]:

> *Managers should attempt to satisfy minimally the needs of marginal stakeholders and to satisfy maximally the needs of supportive and mixed blessing stakeholders, enhancing the latter's support for the organization.*

The four stakeholder types and recommended strategies illustrate what was referred to earlier in this chapter as the "strategic" or instrumental view of stakeholders. It also could be argued that by taking stakeholders' needs and concerns into consideration, businesses' ethical treatment of them may be improved. It takes more than just consideration, however. Management still has an ethical responsibility toward stakeholders that extends beyond the strategic view. A fuller appreciation of this ethical responsibility is developed in Chapters 7 through 10.

Tapping Expertise of Stakeholders Especially with "supportive" stakeholders, but potentially with the other categories as well, it has been proposed that managers can turn "gadflies into allies." Nonprofit special-interest groups, especially activist NGOs, hold great promise for cooperation if managements refrain from seeing them as "pests" and strive to get them to join in the company initiatives.[49] These NGOs have resources such as legitimacy, awareness of social forces, distinct networks, and specialized technical expertise that can be tapped by companies to gain competitive advantage.

Effective Stakeholder Management

Effective stakeholder management is at the top of the list in terms of executive priorities today. This process requires a strong commitment on the part of management and demands a careful assessment of the five key questions posed in this chapter. To

---

ETHICS IN PRACTICE CASE

Where Did the Corn Go?

When I was serving at another institution, I found myself in a bit of an ethics quandary. As I was at work one day, a part broke on our corn auger. This particular time it occurred on a weekend. So I had to find a way to feed the animals. I decided my best course of action was to go to an adjacent research unit, get the corn from their bin, and shovel it into our mixer that had scales so the animals could get fed.

As I was pulling in the driveway of the other unit in my farm truck, I met the farm foreman in his personal truck as he was leaving with a pickup load filled with corn. I told him what I was planning to do and he just agreed with my plan and continued out the drive toward his house. I did as I had planned and noticed there were other workers present at the research unit and they just seemed to not care about any coming or going at the unit.

These activities seemed strange, so I talked to other workers and asked if they had noticed any unusual things happening on the weekend. They said it was happening on a regular basis and the Center Director

was aware of it but did nothing to stop it. The Center Director and I did not see eye to eye on several issues, but I could not imagine his disregard for what seemed to be happening. At one time he had told me I didn't fit in there because I could not communicate on a working man's level and didn't understand what it took to work within an established system. This Center Director has a PhD in Weed Science but saw things from a very different vantage point.

1. Who are the stakeholders in this scenario and what are their stakes?
2. Is the Center Director a stakeholder? Should I go to the Center Director with my questions or would I just risk losing my job?
3. If I went above him to a higher manager what would be the repercussions?
4. Should I just turn my back on this situation and hope that one day someone will discover the truth?

Contributed by Bobby Smith

---

deal successfully with those who assert claims on the organization, managers must understand these core questions. Business has been and will continue to be subjected to careful scrutiny of its actions, practices, policies, and ethics. Stakeholder management helps deal with these issues.

Criticisms of business and calls for better corporate citizenship have been the consequences of the changes in the business–society relationship, and the stakeholder approach to viewing the organization has become one needed response. To do less is to deny the realities of business's plight in the modern world, which is increasingly global in scope, and to fail to see the kinds of adaptations that are essential if businesses are to prosper now and in the future.

Stakeholder Thinking

Stakeholder thinking undergirds stakeholder management and is the process of always reasoning in stakeholder terms throughout the management process, and especially when organizations' decisions and actions have important implications for others. Some managers continue to think in shareholder terms because it is simpler. To think in stakeholder terms increases the complexity of decision making, and it is quite taxing for some managers to assess which stakeholders' claims take priority in a given situation. Despite its complexity, however, the stakeholder view is most consistent with the environment that business faces today, and "stakeholder thinking" has become a vital characteristic of effective stakeholder management.

In fairness, we should also note that there are criticisms and limitations of the stakeholder approach. One major criticism relates to the complexity and time-consuming

Spotlight on Sustainability

Walmart's "Sustainability 360" Initiative

An excellent example of a company tapping the expertise of its stakeholders and building on cooperative stakeholder relationships is Walmart's innovative "Sustainability 360" initiative. Walmart not only has pushed its suppliers to be more concerned about the environment, but it has engaged its employees, communities, and customers in its sustainability efforts. Walmart has challenged its associates and suppliers to come up with new ways to remove nonrenewable energy from products that it sells. Major suppliers such as Unilever, PepsiCo, and Universal Music have provided strong support. The sustainability initiative has created new allies with groups such as Environmental Defense Fund, which plans to work cooperatively with Walmart, as well as with several other environmental groups. EDF works with Walmart on seven issues that are sustainability-focused: China, global warming, packaging, toxic materials, product innovation, plastic bag waste, and sustainable agriculture.

A consulting firm developed and implemented for a consumer products distributor a strategy that included a networkwide AMP Workforce Motivation program, client team training, facility expansion planning, and support of Walmart's Sustainability 360 initiative. Cutting through corporate silos, the consultants tapped the intelligence of different senior executives. That gave them a broad-ranging perspective, which made implementation more effective.

Sources: EDF+Business, "Why we work with Wal-Mart," Environmental Defense Fund, http://business.edf.org/projects/walmart. Accessed March 25, 2013; Jayne O'Donnell, "Wal-Mart Includes Workers, Suppliers in Environment Efforts," *USA Today* (February 2, 2007) 7B; "Meeting the Wal-Mart Challenge," Awareness into Action, http://www.awarenessintoaction.com/casestudies/Case-study-walmart-360-Sustainability-XCD-Workforce-motivation.html. Accessed March 25, 2013.

nature of identifying, assessing, and responding to stakeholder claims, which constitute an extremely demanding process. Also, the ranking of stakeholder claims is no easy task. These challenges must be kept in mind as the approach is used in practice.

Effective stakeholder management is facilitated by a number of other useful concepts. The following concepts—stakeholder culture, stakeholder management capability, the stakeholder corporation model, and principles of stakeholder management—round out a useful approach to stakeholder management effectiveness. Each of these is considered in more detail.

Developing a Stakeholder Culture

In management circles, the importance of developing a strong, values-based corporate culture has been recognized as a key to successful enterprises. Corporate culture refers to the taken-for-granted beliefs, functional guidelines, ways of doing things, priorities, and values important to managers.[50] Within that context, developing a strong **stakeholder culture** is a major factor supporting successful stakeholder management. Stakeholder culture embraces the beliefs, values, and practices that organizations have developed for addressing stakeholder issues and relationships. There are at least five categories of stakeholder cultures that reside on a continuum from little concern to great concern for stakeholders.[51]

First is *agency* culture, which basically is not concerned with others. Next are two cultures characterized by limited morality considerations—*corporate egoist* and *instrumentalist*—which focus mostly on the firm's shareholders as the important stakeholders. These cultures focus on short-term profit maximization. Finally are two cultures that are broadly moral—*moralist* and *altruist*. Both of these cultures are morally based and provide the broadest concern for stakeholders.[52] Effective stakeholder management requires the development of a corporate culture that most broadly conceives of responsibilities to others. In the above scheme, the moralist and altruist cultures would be most compatible with stakeholder management and a stakeholder corporation.

Stakeholder Management Capability

Effective stakeholder management is also greatly affected by the extent to which the organization has developed its **stakeholder management capability (SMC)**.[53] Stakeholder management capability describes an organization's integration of stakeholder thinking into its processes and it may reside at one of three levels of increasing sophistication: rational, process, transactional

Level 1: Rational Level

This introductory level of SMC simply entails the company identifying who their stakeholders are and what their stakes happen to be. This is the level that would enable management to create a basic stakeholder map, such as that depicted in Figure 3-3. The **rational level** is descriptive and somewhat analytical, because the legitimacy of stakes, the stakeholders' power, and urgency are identified. This represents a beginning, or entry level of SMC. Most organizations have at least identified who their stakeholders are, but not all have analyzed the nature of the stakes or the stakeholders' power. This first level has also been identified by Mark Starik as the element of *familiarization* and *comprehensiveness*, because the management operating at Level 1 is seeking to become familiar with their stakeholders and to develop a comprehensive assessment of their identification and stakes.[54]

Level 2: Process Level

At the **process level**, organizations go a step further than Level 1 and actually develop and implement processes—approaches, procedures, policies, and practices—by which the firm may scan the environment and gather pertinent information about stakeholders, which is then used for decision-making purposes. An applicable stakeholder principle here is "constantly monitoring and redesigning processes to better serve stakeholders."[55] Typical approaches at the process level include portfolio analysis processes, strategic review processes, and environmental scanning processes, which are used to assist managers in their strategic management.[56] Other approaches, such as issue, risk, or crisis management (Chapter 6), also might be considered examples of Level 2 SMC. This second level has been described as *planning integrativeness*, because the management does focus on planning processes for stakeholders and integrating a consideration for stakeholders into organizational decision making.[57]

Level 3: Transactional Level

The **transactional level** is the highest and most developed of the three levels. This is the highest goal for stakeholder management—the extent to which managers actually engage in transactions (relationships) with stakeholders.[58] At this highest level of SMC, in which a *transformation* of the business and society relationship occurs, management must take the initiative in meeting stakeholders face to face and attempting to be responsive to their needs. The transactional level may require actual negotiations with stakeholders.[59] Level 3 is the *communication* level, which is characterized by *communication proactiveness, interactiveness, genuineness, frequency, satisfaction*, and *resource adequacy*. Resource adequacy refers to the management actually spending resources on stakeholder transactions.[60] Regarding stakeholder communications, a relevant principle is that business must "engage in intensive communication and dialogue with (all) stakeholders, not just those who are friendly."[61]

An example of Level 3 has been the relationship established between General Motors Corporation (GM) and the Coalition for Environmentally Responsible Economies (Ceres). Over a decade ago, these two organizations actually began to talk with one another, and the result was a mutually beneficial collaboration. The arrangement became a high-profile example of a growing trend within the sustainability movement—that of using quiet discussions, engagement, and negotiations rather than noisy protests to change corporate behavior. Beginning in the early 2000s, for example, Ceres and other environmental groups began demanding tougher governmental fuel economy standards, while automakers such as GM intensified their lobbying to keep existing rules in place, probably because of the popularity of high-fuel-consumption SUVs.[62] In spring of 2009, when fuel economy standards for 2012–2016 were under development, Ceres partnered with Citi Investment Research and the University of Michigan to analyze the impact of strong standards on the auto industry. The resulting analysis made the economic case for an average fuel economy standard for passenger vehicles of 35.5 mpg, the standard that was eventually adopted by the Obama Administration.[63] In 2012, President Obama raised the bar when he set strict new standards for 2025.[64] A moving target such as this will require significant efforts by companies striving to maintain their "transactional level" status.

Stakeholder Engagement

Recently there has been growing interest in the topic of stakeholder engagement. **Stakeholder engagement** may be seen as an approach by which companies successfully implement the transactional level of strategic management capability. Companies may employ different strategies in terms of the degree of engagement with their stakeholders, but best practices suggest that interaction with stakeholders must be integrated into every level of decision making in the organization.[65]

Ladder of Stakeholder Engagement A ladder of stakeholder engagement, which depicts a number of steps from low engagement to high engagement, has been set forth as a continuum of engagement postures that companies might follow.[66] Lower levels of

---

ETHICS IN PRACTICE CASE

Overbooked

It is Friday on a football weekend; the hotel has been booked solid for nine months. All guests have made a two-night commitment that is non-refundable. It will be a packed house and the hotel management has intentionally overbooked the hotel. In all likelihood, the hotel will come up short of rooms and then someone with a confirmed, paid reservation will be going down the road, late at night, extremely angry.

1. Who are the stakeholders in this case and what are their stakes?
2. How can a stakeholder commitment be a commitment if only one party honors it?
3. Can a stakeholder relationship be one-way?
4. As an employee stakeholder of the hotel, how do you take an ethical stand on this issue and retain your position?

Contributed by Danny Bivins

stakeholder engagement might be used for informing and explaining. Middle levels might involve token gestures of participation such as placation, consultation, and negotiation. Higher levels of stakeholder engagement might be active or responsive attempts to involve stakeholders in company decision making. At the highest level, terms such as "involvement," "collaboration," or "partnership" might be appropriate descriptions of the relationship established. An example of this highest level would be when a firm enters into a strategic alliance with a stakeholder group to seek the group's opinion of a product design that would be sensitive to the group's concerns, such as environmental impact or product safety. This was illustrated when McDonald's entered into an alliance with the Environmental Defense Fund to eliminate polystyrene packaging that was not biodegradable.[67]

Transparency The concept of stakeholder engagement is relevant to developing what Tapscott and Ticoll refer to as *The Naked Corporation*. In their book, they argue that in the characteristics of the open enterprise, "environmental engagement" and "stakeholder engagement" are two critical factors. Environmental engagement calls for an open operating environment: sustainable ecosystems, peace, order, and good public governance. Stakeholder engagement calls for these open enterprises to put resources and effort into reviewing, managing, recasting, and strengthening relationships with stakeholders, old and new.[68] The "open enterprise" with an emphasis on "transparency" has become crucial because of the corporate scandals of the past decade.

Engaging on Sustainability One of the latest emphases has been engaging stakeholders on sustainability. The idea here has been to involve stakeholders such as the social media, consumers, NGOs, and communities as early as possible on sustainability developments and initiatives. "Sustainability Stakeholder Engagement" conferences are now being held to facilitate this process. One of the unique aspects of these conferences has been the increasing use of social media technologies, such as Twitter, to engage stakeholders in a more timely fashion.[69] Some of the conclusions about stakeholder engagement that have emerged include the following:

- Engage stakeholders sooner rather than later
- Sustainability is important to companies of all sizes
- Companies do best when an internal champion facilitates
- Internal education takes more time than external engagement
- Engage your most vocal critics to find a common ground

Another element in stakeholder engagement is stakeholder dialogue. **Stakeholder dialogue** is primarily focused on exchanging communications with stakeholder groups and thus it is one form of engagement. When considering stakeholder dialogue among global stakeholders, it is worth noting that different countries are characterized by different approaches. In one major study, for example, it was found that stakeholder dialogue varied among three major countries—Germany, Italy, and the United States. Both Germany and Italy employed a more *implicit* approach while the United States used a more *explicit* approach.[70] This followed the different CSR approaches found to be present in Europe versus the United States.[71] The approaches to stakeholder dialogue were more *focused* in Germany, more *engaging* in Italy, and more *strategic* in the United States. A major conclusion of this study was that stakeholder dialogue has to be tailored to the national business system and that attempts to develop universal principles or guidelines may be imprudent.

The Stakeholder Corporation

Perhaps the ultimate form the stakeholder approach or stakeholder management might take is to be called the **stakeholder corporation**. The central element of this concept is **stakeholder inclusiveness.**[72]

> *In the future, development of loyal relationships with customers, employees, share-holders, and other stakeholders will become one of the most important determinants of commercial viability and business success. Increasing shareholder value will be best served if your company cultivates the support of all who may influence its importance.*

Advocates of the stakeholder corporation would embrace the idea of **stakeholder symbiosis**, which recognizes that all stakeholders depend on each other for their success and financial well-being.[73] It is the acceptance of this mutuality of interests that makes the difference in a firm becoming a stakeholder corporation. As James Post has summarized, "The stakeholder corporation is characterized by leaders who understand the need to balance, prioritize, and adjust to the needs of all constituencies."[74]

Principles of Stakeholder Management

On the basis of years of observation and research, a set of **principles of stakeholder management** has been developed for use by managers and organizations. These principles, also known as the **Clarkson Principles**, were named after the late Max Clarkson, a dedicated researcher on the topic of stakeholder management. The principles are intended to provide managers with guiding precepts regarding how stakeholders should be treated. Figure 3-9 summarizes these principles. The key words in the principles are action words that reflect the kind of cooperative spirit that should be used in building stakeholder relationships: *acknowledge, monitor, listen, communicate, adopt, recognize, work, avoid, and acknowledge conflicts.*

Strategic Steps toward Global Stakeholder Management

The global competition that characterizes business firms in the 21st century necessitates a stakeholder approach for both effective and ethical management. The stakeholder approach requires that stakeholders be moved to the center of the management's vision. Three strategic steps may be taken that can lead today's global competitors toward the more balanced view that is needed in today's changing business environment.[75]

1. **Governing Philosophy.** *Integrating stakeholder management into the firm's governing philosophy.* Boards of directors and top management groups should move the organization from the idea of "shareholder agent" to "stakeholder trustee." Long-term shareholder value, along with sustainability, will be the objective of this transition in corporate governance.
2. **Values Statement.** *Create a stakeholder-inclusive "values statement."* Various firms have done this. J&J's is called a "credo," Microsoft's is called a "values statement." Microsoft emphasizes integrity and honesty, and accountability to customers, shareholders, partners, and employees. Regardless of what such a values statement is called, such a pledge publicly reinforces the organization's commitment to stakeholders.
3. **Measurement System.** *Implement a stakeholder performance measurement system.* Such a system should be integrated, monitored, and auditable as stakeholder

FIGURE 3-9 The "Clarkson Principles" of Stakeholder Management

Principle 1	Managers should **acknowledge** and actively **monitor** the concerns of all legitimate stakeholders, and should take their interests appropriately into account in decision making and operations.
Principle 2	Managers should **listen** to and openly **communicate** with stakeholders about their respective concerns and contributions, and about the risks that they assume because of their involvement with the corporation.
Principle 3	Managers should **adopt** processes and modes of behavior that are sensitive to the concerns and capabilities of each stakeholder constituency.
Principle 4	Managers should **recognize the interdependence** of efforts and rewards among stakeholders, and should attempt to achieve a fair distribution of the benefits and burdens of corporate activity among them, taking into account their respective risks and vulnerabilities.
Principle 5	Managers should **work cooperatively** with other entities, both public and private, to ensure that risks and harms arising from corporate activities are minimized and, where they cannot be avoided, appropriately compensated.
Principle 6	Managers should **avoid altogether** activities that might jeopardize inalienable human rights (e.g., the right to life) or give rise to risks that, if clearly understood, would be patently unacceptable to relevant stakeholders.
Principle 7	Managers should **acknowledge the potential conflicts** between (a) their own role as corporate stakeholders and (b) their legal and moral responsibilities for the interests of stakeholders, and should address such conflicts through open communication, appropriate reporting, incentive systems and, where necessary, third-party review.

Source: *Principles of Stakeholder Management* (Toronto: The Clarkson Centre for Business Ethics, Joseph L. Rotman School of Management, University of Toronto, 1999), 4.

relations are improved. Measurement is evidence of serious intent to achieve results, and such a system will motivate a sustainable commitment to the stakeholder view. One recent example of a measurement system has been Walmart's creation of a *worldwide sustainability index*. With this initiative, the company is helping to create a more transparent supply chain, driving product innovation, and ultimately providing customers with information they need to assess products' sustainability.[76]

Implementation

The key to effective stakeholder management is in its *implementation*. Implementation implies the following key activities: execution, application, operationalization, and enactment. Corporate social responsibility and sustainability are made operable when companies translate their stakeholder dialogue into practice.[77] After studying three large, successful companies in detail—Cummins Engine Company, Motorola, and the Royal Dutch/Shell Group—prominent researchers concluded that the key to effective implementation is in recognizing and using stakeholder management as a *core competence.*

When this is done, at least four indicators or manifestations of successful stakeholder management will be apparent. First, stakeholder management results in *survival*. Second, there are *avoided costs*. Third, there was *continued acceptance and use* in the companies studied, implying success. Fourth, there was evidence of *expanded recognition and adoption* of stakeholder-oriented policies by other companies and consultants.[78] These indicators suggest the value and practical benefits that may be derived from the stakeholder approach. Finally, it should be noted that organizations develop learning processes over time in implementing their changing or evolving stakeholder orientations.[79]

Summary

A stakeholder is an individual or a group that claims to have one or more stakes in an organization. Stakeholders may affect the organization and, in turn, be affected by the organization's actions, policies, practices, and decisions. The stakeholder approach extends beyond the traditional production and managerial views of the firm and warrants a much broader conception of the parties involved in the organization's functioning and success. Both primary and secondary social and nonsocial stakeholders assume important roles in the eyes of management. A typology of stakeholders suggests that three attributes are especially significant: legitimacy, power, and urgency. Proximity also may be salient.

Strategic, multifiduciary, and stakeholder synthesis approaches help us appreciate the strategies that may be adopted with regard to stakeholders. The stakeholder synthesis approach is encouraged because it highlights the ethical responsibility business has to its stakeholders. The stakeholder view of the firm has three values that make it useful: descriptive, instrumental, and normative. In a balanced perspective, managers are concerned with both goal achievement and ethical treatment of stakeholders.

Five key questions assist managers in stakeholder management: (1)Who are the firm's stakeholders? (2) What are our stakeholders' stakes? (3) What challenges or opportunities are presented to a firm by stakeholders? (4) What responsibilities does a firm have to its stakeholders? (5) What strategies or actions should a firm take with respect to its stakeholders? Effective stakeholder management requires the assessment and appropriate response to these five questions. In addition, the use of other relevant stakeholder thinking concepts is helpful. The concept of SMC illustrates how firms can grow and mature in their approach to stakeholder management. The stakeholder corporation is a model that represents stakeholder thinking in its most advanced form. Other key ideas include stakeholder culture and stakeholder engagement.

Seven principles of stakeholder management are helpful in guiding managers toward more effective stakeholder thinking. Although the stakeholder management approach is quite complex and time consuming, it is in tune with the complex, dynamic environment that business organizations face today. Successful steps in stakeholder management include making stakeholders a part of the guiding philosophy, creating corporate value statements, and developing measurement systems that monitor results. In the final analysis, implementation is the key to effective stakeholder management.

Key Terms

Clarkson Principles, p. 88
descriptive value (of stakeholder model), p. 73
instrumental value (of stakeholder model), p. 73
key questions (in stakeholder management), p. 74
legitimacy, p. 69
managerial view of the firm, p. 67
marginal stakeholder, p. 81
mixed-blessing stakeholder, p. 81

multifiduciary approach (to stakeholders), p. 72
nonsupportive stakeholder, p. 81
normative value (of stakeholder model), p. 73
power, p. 70
primary social stakeholders, p. 68
principles of stakeholder management, p. 88
process level, p. 85
production view of the firm, p. 67
proximity, p. 70

rational level, p. 85
secondary social stakeholders, p. 68
stake, p. 65
stakeholder, p. 66
stakeholder corporation, p. 88
stakeholder culture, p. 84
stakeholder dialogue, p. 87
stakeholder engagement, p. 86
stakeholder inclusiveness, p. 88
stakeholder management capability (SMC), p. 85

Discussion Questions

1. Explain the concepts of stake and stakeholder from your perspective as an individual. What kinds of stakes and stakeholders do you have? Discuss.

2. Explain in your own words the differences between the production, managerial, and stakeholder views of the firm. Which view is best and why?

3. Differentiate between primary and secondary social and nonsocial stakeholders in a business situation. Give examples of each.

4. How is effective stakeholder management related to sustainability and sustainable development on the part of companies?

5. How can a firm transition from Level 1 to Level 3 of stakeholder management capability (SMC)? Where does stakeholder engagement fit in?

6. Is the stakeholder corporation a realistic model for business firms? Will stakeholder corporations become more prevalent in the 21st century?

Endnotes

1. See, for example, Jill A. Brown and William R. Forster, "CSR and Stakeholder Theory: A Tale of Adam Smith," *Journal of Business Ethics* (2013), 112: 301–312; Robert A. Phillips, "Stakeholder Theory and a Principle of Fairness," *Business Ethics Quarterly* (Vol. 7, No. 1, January 1997), 51–66; Sandra A. Waddock and Samuel B. Graves, "Quality of Management and Quality of Stakeholder Relations," *Business and Society* (Vol. 36, No. 3, September 1997), 250–279; James P. Walsh, "Taking Stock of Stakeholder Management," *Academy of Management Review* (Vol. 30, No. 2, 2005), 426–438; Thomas Jones and Andrew Wicks, 1999, "Convergent Stakeholder Theory," *Academy of Management Review* (Vol. 20, 1999), 404–437.

2. David Wheeler and Maria Sillanpää, *The Stakeholder Corporation: A Blueprint for Maximizing Stakeholder Value* (London: Pitman Publishing, 1997).

3. Steven F. Walker and Jeffrey W. Marr, *Stakeholder Power: A Winning Plan for Building Stakeholder Commitment and Driving Corporate Growth* (Cambridge, MA: Perseus Publishing, 2001).

4. James E. Post, Lee E. Preston, and Sybille Sachs, *Redefining the Corporation: Stakeholder Management and Organizational Wealth* (Stanford: Stanford University Press, 2002).

5. Robert Phillips and R. Edward Freeman, *Stakeholders,* Edward Elgar Pub, 2010.

6. Jeanne M. Logsdon, Donna J. Wood, and Lee E. Benson, "Research in Stakeholder Theory, 1997–1998: The Sloan Foundation Minigrant Project" (Toronto: The Clarkson Centre for Business Ethics, 2000).

7. Jeffrey S. Harrison and Andrew C. Wicks, "Stakeholder Theory, Value and Firm Performance," *Business Ethics Quarterly,* January 2013, 97–124.

8. This definition is similar to that of R. Edward Freeman in *Strategic Management: A Stakeholder Approach* (Boston: Pitman, 1984), 25.

9. George Kassinis, "The Value of Managing Stakeholders," in Pratima Bansal and Andrew Hoffman (eds.), *The Oxford Handbook of Business and the Natural Environment* (Oxford: Oxford University Press, 2012).

10. "A Thought Leader Commentary with Charles O. Holliday, Chairman and Chief Executive Officer, DuPont," *Company Stakeholder Responsibility: A New Approach to CSR,* Business Roundtable Institute for Corporate Ethics, 2006, 12.

11. Mark Starik, "Is the Environment an Organizational Stakeholder? Naturally!" *International Association for Business and Society (IABS) 1993 Proceedings,* 466–471.

12. David Woodward, "Is the natural environment a stakeholder? Of course it is (no matter what the Utilitarians might say)," in *Critical Perspectives on Accounting Conference,* New York, April 25–27, 2002, New York: Baruch College, City University of New York.

13. Freeman, 5.

14. Freeman, 24–25. Also see James E. Post, Lee E. Preston, and Sybille Sachs, *Redefining the Corporation: Stakeholder Management and Organizational Wealth* (Stanford: Stanford University Press), 2002.

15. Wheeler and Sillanpää (1997), 167.

16. Ibid., 168.

17. Ronald K. Mitchell, Bradley R. Agle, and Donna J. Wood, "Toward a Theory of Stakeholder Identification and Salience: Defining the Principle of Who and What Really Counts," *Academy of Management Review* (October 1997), 853–886.

18. Mark Starik and Cathy Driscoll, "The Primordial Stakeholder: Advancing the Conceptual Consideration of Stakeholder Status for the Natural Environment," in A. J. Zakhem, D. E. Palmer, and M. L. Stoll (eds.) *Stakeholder Theory: Essential Readings in Ethical Leadership and Management* (Amherst, NY: Prometheus Books, 2007), 219–222.

19. Ibid.

20. Jim Carlton, "How Home Depot and Activists Joined to Cut Logging Abuse," *The Wall Street Journal* (September 26, 2000), A1.

21. Kenneth E. Goodpaster, "Business Ethics and Stakeholder Analysis," *Business Ethics Quarterly* (Vol. 1, No. 1, January 1991), 53–73.

22. Ibid.

23. Ibid.

24. Johanna Kujala, Anna Heikkinen, and Hanna Lehtimaki, "Understanding the Nature of Stakeholder Relationships: An Empirical Examination of a Conflict Situation," *Journal of Business Ethics* 2012, 109: 53–65.

25. Thomas Donaldson and Lee Preston, "The Stakeholder Theory of the Corporation: Concepts, Evidence, Implications," *Academy of Management Review* (Vol. 20, No. 1, 1995), 65–91.

26. Ibid.

27. Robert Phillips, *Stakeholder Theory and Organizational Ethics*, San Francisco: Berrett-Koehler Publishers, Inc., 2003, 85–118.

28. Donaldson and Preston.

29. Parallel questions are posed with respect to corporate strategy by Ian C. MacMillan and Patricia E. Jones, *Strategy Formulation: Power and Politics* (St. Paul, MN: West, 1986), 66.

30. "Animal Rights Group Aims Ad Attack at McDonald's," *The Wall Street Journal* (August 30, 1999), B7. Also see http://www.mccruelty.com/why.aspx, Accessed January 15, 2013

31. Marcia Yablon, "Happy Hen, Happy Meal: McDonald's Chick Fix," *U.S. News   World Report* (September 4, 2000), 46.

32. Ibid.

33. "McCruelty: I'm Hatin' It," http://www.mccruelty.com/. Accessed January 15, 2013.

34. Kerry Capell, "The Wool Industry Gets Bloodied," *BusinessWeek* (July 14 & 21, 2008), 40. Also see http://www.peta.org/issues/animals-used-for-clothing/wool-industry.aspx. Accessed January 15, 2013.

35. R. Edward Freeman, S.R. Velamuri, and Brian Moriarty, *"Company Stakeholder Responsibility: A New Approach to CSR,"* Business Roundtable Institute for Corporate Ethics, Bridge Paper, 2006, 11.

36. John Browne and Robin Nuttall, "Beyond Corporate Social Responsibility: Integrated External Engagement," *McKinsey Quarterly*, March 2013, https://www.mckinseyquarterly.com/Beyond_corporate_social_responsibility_Integrated_external_engagement_3069. Accessed March 22, 2013.

37. "Does It Pay to Be Ethical?," *Business Ethics* (March/April 1997), 14. "What's Your Poison?" *The Economist* (August 9, 2003), 50. Web site of Rain Forest Action Network: http://www.ran.org/. Accessed June 25, 2010. Also see Jeanne Whalen, "Drug Giant Is Targeted by Attacks," *The Wall Street Journal* (August 5, 2009), 1.

38. Rainforest Action Network, "Forests," http://ran.org/forests. Accessed January 15, 2013.

39. Rainforest Action Network, http://ran.org/challenging-corporations. Accessed January 15, 2013.

40. Grant T. Savage, Timothy W. Nix, Carlton J. Whitehead, and John D. Blair, "Strategies for Assessing and Managing Organizational Stakeholders," *Academy of Management Executive* (Vol. V, No. 2, May 1991), 61–75.

41. Environmental Defense Fund, "Corporate partnerships achieve strong results," http://www.edf.org/approach/partnerships/corporate, Accessed January 23, 2013.

42. MacMillan and Jones, 66–70.

43. John F. Preble, "Toward a Comprehensive Model of Stakeholder Management," *Business and Society Review* (Vol. 110, No. 4, 2005), 421–423.

44. Ibid., 415.

45. Savage, Nix, Whitehead, and Blair, 65.

46. Seth Hettena and Laura Wides, "Eco-Terrorists Coming Out of the Wild," *USA Today* (October 3, 2003), 22A. Also see Anti-Defamation League, "Extremism in America," http://www.adl.org/learn/ext_us/default.asp?LEARN_Cat=ExtremismLEARN_SubCat=Extremism_in_Americaxpicked=1item=0. Accessed January 15, 2013.

47. Geewax, E7.

48. Savage, Nix, Whitehead, and Blair, 72.

49. Michael Yaziji, "Turning Gadflies into Allies," *Harvard Business Review* (February 2004), 110–115.

50. C. Geertz, *The Interpretation of Cultures: Selected Essays* (New York: Basic Books, 1973). See also, M. J. Hatch, "The Dynamics of Organizational Culture," *Academy of Management Review* (Vol. 18, 1993), 657–693.

51. Thomas M. Jones, Will Felps, and Gregory A. Bigley, "Ethical Theory and Stakeholder-Related Decisions: The Role of Stakeholder Culture," *Academy of Management Review* (Vol. 32, No. 1, 2007), 137–155.

52. Ibid.

53. Freeman, 53.

54. Mark Starik, "Stakeholder Management and Firm Performance: Reputation and Financial Relationships to

U.S. Electric Utility Consumer-Related Strategies," unpublished Ph.D. dissertation, University of Georgia, 1990, 34.

55. Freeman, Velamur, and Moriarty (2006), 11.

56. Freeman, 64.

57. Starik (1990), 36.

58. Freeman, 69–70.

59. Freeman, Velamur, and Moriarty (2006), 11.

60. Starik (1990), 36–42.

61. Freeman, Velamur, and Moriarty (2006), 11.

62. Jeffrey Ball, "After Long Détente, GM, Green Group Are at Odds Again," *The Wall Street Journal* (July 30, 2002), A1.

63. Ceres: mobilizing business leadership for a sustainable world, "Transportation: Driving a Sustainable Economy," http://www.ceres.org/industry-initiatives/transportation. Accessed January 23, 2013.

64. Juliet Eilperin, "EPA Issues New Fuel Efficiency Standard," Washington Post, August 28, 2012, http://articles.washingtonpost.com/2012-08-28/national/35490347_1_fuel-efficiency-fuel-standards-vehicle-fuel-efficiency-standards. Accessed January 16, 2013.

65. Browne and Nuttall, 2013, ibid.

66. Andrew L. Friedman and Samantha Miles, *Stakeholders: Theory and Practice* (Oxford: Oxford University Press, 2006), 160–179.

67. Ibid., 175. Also see Laura Dunham, R. Edward Freeman, and Jeanne Liedtka, "Enhancing Stakeholder Practice: A Particularized Exploration of Community," *Business Ethics Quarterly* (Vol. 16, 1, 2006), 23–42.

68. Don Tapscott and David Ticoll, *The Naked Corporation: How the Age of Transparency Will Revolutionize Business* (Free Press, 2003).

69. Perry Goldschein and Beth Bengston, "How to Engage Stakeholders on Sustainability," *GreenBiz.com* (September 17, 2009), http://www.greenbiz.com/blog/2009/09/17/how-engage-stakeholders-sustainability. Accessed January 15, 2013.

70. Lorenzo Patelli, "Stakeholder Dialogue in Germany, Italy, and the United States," *Director Notes, The Conference Board*, New York: The Conference Board, July 2012.

71. Dirk Matten and Jeremy Moon, "Implicit and Explicit CSR: A Conceptual Framework for a Comparative Understanding of Corporate Social Responsibility," *Academy of Management Review* 33, no 2 2008, 404–424.

72. Wheeler and Sillanpää (1997), book cover.

73. "Stakeholder Symbiosis," *Fortune* (March 30, 1998), S2–S4, special advertising section.

74. James Post, "Governance and the Stakeholder Corporation: New challenges for Global Business," Corporate Public Affairs Oration, Melbourne, 24 June 2004. Cited on http://trevorcook.typepad.com/weblog/2005/07/the_stakeholder.html. Accessed January 15, 2013.

75. "Measurements," *Measuring and Managing Stakeholder Relationships* (Indianapolis: Walker Information Global Network, 1998).

76. "Sustainability Index," http://corporate.walmart.com/global-responsibility/environment-sustainability/sustainability-index. Accessed January 15, 2013.

77. Esben Rahbek Pedersen, "Making Corporate Social Responsibility (CSR) Operable: How Companies Translate Stakeholder Dialogue into Practice," *Business and Society Review* (Vol. 111, No. 2, 2006), 137–163.

78. James E. Post, Lee E. Preston, Sybille Sachs, "Managing the Extended Enterprise: The New Stakeholder View," *California Management Review* (Vol. 45, No. 1, Fall 2002), 22–25.

79. Marc Maurer and Sybille Sachs, "Implementing the Stakeholder View," *Journal of Corporate Citizenship* (Vol. 17, Spring 2005), 93–107.

PART 2

Corporate Governance and Strategic Management Issues

4

Corporate Governance: Foundational Issues

CHAPTER LEARNING OUTCOMES

After studying this chapter, you should be able to:

1. Link the issue of legitimacy to corporate governance.

2. Identify the best practices that boards of directors can follow.

3. Discuss the problems that have led to the recent spate of corporate scandals and the efforts that are currently underway to keep them from happening again.

4. Discuss the principal ways in which shareholder activism exerted pressure on corporate management groups to improve governance.

5. Discuss the ways in which managers relate to shareholders and the issues arising from that relationship.

6. Compare and contrast the shareholder-primacy and director-primacy models of corporate governance. What are their respective strengths and weaknesses? Which do you prefer and why?

I n this second part of the book, we more closely examine how management has responded and should respond to the social, ethical, and stakeholder issues developed throughout this book. This chapter explores the ways in which the board and top managers govern the corporation. In Chapters 5 and 6, the view expands to look at how these social, ethical, and stakeholder issues fit into not only the strategic management and corporate public affairs functions of the firm but also the management of issues and crises.

The 21st century has been fraught with corporate scandals that have shaken the public's trust in business institutions. The global financial crisis further undermined public confidence and threatened the legitimacy of business as a whole. As the Organisation for Economic Co-operation and Development (OECD) observed, "If there is one major lesson to draw from the financial crisis, it is that corporate governance matters."[1]

We begin by examining the concept of legitimacy and the part that corporate governance plays in establishing the legitimacy of business. We then explore how good corporate governance can mitigate the problems created by the separation of ownership and control and examine some of the specific challenges facing those involved in corporate governance today.

Legitimacy and Corporate Governance

Corporate governance took center stage at the dawn of the 21st century. The bankruptcy of Enron, once the seventh-largest company in the United States, as well as those of corporate giants WorldCom, Global Crossing, and Parmalat, sent shock waves through the corporate world. When a host of firms subsequently issued earnings restatements, investors throughout the world began wondering where they could place their trust. A few years later, the global financial crisis struck and investors were stunned as they watched their life savings shrivel. These worldwide events threatened more than one industry, more than one company, and more than the investors who lost great portions of their wealth. As Monks and Minnow put it, "every one of the mechanisms set up to provide checks and balances failed at the same time."[2] These events threatened the institution of business as a whole by calling the legitimacy of the institution of business into question. At a Harvard Business School summit designed to explore the legitimacy of business in the context of the global financial crisis, thought leaders concluded that the crisis could precipitate a general rethinking of the legitimacy of capitalism.[3]

To understand corporate governance, it is important to understand the idea of **legitimacy**. Legitimacy is a somewhat abstract concept, but it is vital in that it helps explain the importance of the relative roles of a corporation's charter, shareholders, board of directors, management, and employees—all of which are components of the modern corporate governance system. He argued, "Organizations are legitimate to the extent that their activities are congruent with the goals and values of the social system within which they function."[4] From this definition, we may see legitimacy as a condition that prevails when there is congruence between the organization's activities and society's expectations. Thus, whereas legitimacy is a condition, **legitimation** is a dynamic process by which business seeks to perpetuate its acceptance. We emphasize the dynamic process aspect because society's norms and values change, and business must change if its legitimacy is to continue. It is also useful to consider legitimacy at both the micro, or company, level and the macro, or business institution, level.

At the *micro level of legitimacy*, we refer to individual business firms achieving and maintaining legitimacy by conforming to societal expectations. Companies seek legitimacy in several ways. First, a company may adapt its methods of operating to conform to what it perceives to be the prevailing standard. For example, a company may discontinue door-to-door selling if that marketing approach comes to be viewed in the public mind as a shoddy sales technique,[5] or a pharmaceutical company may discontinue offering free drug samples to medical students if this practice begins to take on the aura of a bribe. Second, a company may try to change the public's values and norms to conform to its own practices by advertising and other techniques.[6] Amazon.com was successful at this when it began marketing through the Internet.

Finally, an organization may seek to enhance its legitimacy by identifying itself with other organizations, people, values, or symbols that have a powerful legitimate base in society.[7] This occurs at several levels. At the national level, companies proudly announce appointments of celebrities, former politicians, or other famous people to managerial positions or board directorships. At the community level, a company may ask the winning local football coach to provide an endorsement by sitting on its board or promoting its products.[8]

The *macro level of legitimacy* is the level with which we are most concerned in this chapter. The macro level refers to the corporate system—the totality of business enterprises. It is difficult to talk about the legitimacy of business in pragmatic terms at this level. American business is such a potpourri of institutions of different shapes, sizes, and industries that making general conclusions about it is difficult. Yet this is an important level at which business needs to be concerned about its legitimacy. What is at stake is the acceptance of the form of business as an institution in our society. William Dill has suggested that business's social (or societal) legitimacy is a fragile thing:

> Business has evolved by initiative and experiment. It never had an overwhelmingly clear endorsement as a social institution. The idea of allowing individuals to joust with one another in pursuit of personal profit was an exciting and romantic one when it was first proposed as a way of correcting other problems in society; but over time, its ugly side and potential for abuse became apparent.[9]

Business must now accept that it has a **fragile mandate**. It must realize that its legitimacy is constantly subject to ratification; and it must realize that it has no inherent right to exist. Business exists solely because society has given it that right.[10] In this sense, business is a public institution as well as a private entity.[11] When the legitimacy of business as an institution is in question, political and social factors may overshadow economic factors to change the future of the institution of business in profound ways.[12]

In comparing the micro view of legitimacy with the macro view, it is clear that, although specific business organizations try to perpetuate their own legitimacy, the corporate or business system as a whole rarely addresses the issue at all. This is unfortunate because the spectrum of powerful issues regarding business conduct clearly indicates that such institutional introspection is necessary if business is to survive and prosper. If business is to continue to justify its right to exist, we must remember the question of legitimacy and its operational ramifications.

The Purpose of Corporate Governance

The purpose of corporate governance is a direct outgrowth of the question of legitimacy. The word *governance* comes from the Greek word for steering.[13] The way in which a corporation is governed determines the direction in which it is steered. Owners of small private firms can steer the firm on their own; however, the shareholders who are the owners of public firms must count on boards of directors to make certain that their companies are steered properly in their absence. For business to be legitimate and to maintain its legitimacy in the eyes of the public, it must be steered in a way that corresponds to the will of the people.

Corporate governance refers to the method by which a firm is being governed, directed, administered, or controlled and to the goals for which it is being governed. Corporate governance is concerned with the relative roles, rights, and accountability of such stakeholder groups as owners, boards of directors, managers, employees, and others who have a stake in the firm's governance.

Components of Corporate Governance

This chapter focuses on the **Anglo-American model** toward which much of the world is converging.[14] Institutional investors largely drive this convergence because, as they invest more globally, they seek governance mechanisms with which they are familiar and comfortable.[15] The Anglo-American model is a **shareholder-primacy model** because shareholders have primary importance. Later in this chapter, we will discuss a director-primacy model of corporate governance that is receiving increasing attention.[16]

Roles of Four Major Groups   The four major groups we need to mention in setting the stage for the shareholder-primacy model of corporate governance are the shareholders (owner-stakeholders), the board of directors, the managers, and the employees. Overarching these groups is the **charter** issued by the state, giving the corporation the right to exist and stipulating the basic terms of its existence. Figure 4-1 presents these four groups, along with the state charter, in a hierarchy of corporate governance authority.

Shareholders own stock in the firm and, according to the shareholder-primacy model, that makes them the firm's owners and gives them ultimate control over the corporation. This control is manifested in the right to select the board of directors of the company and to vote on resolutions. Generally, the degree of each shareholder's right is determined by the number of shares of stock owned. The individual who owns 100 shares of Apple Computer, for example, has 100 "votes" when electing the board of directors. By contrast, the large public pension fund that owns 10 million shares has 10 million "votes."

Because large organizations may have hundreds of thousands of shareholders, they elect a smaller group, known as the **board of directors**, to govern and oversee the management of the business. Under the shareholder-primacy model, the purpose of the board is to ascertain that the manager puts the interests of the shareholders first. The third major group in the authority hierarchy is the **management**—the group of

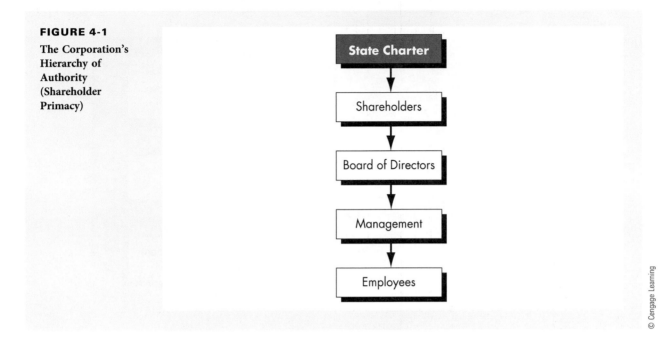

FIGURE 4-1

The Corporation's Hierarchy of Authority (Shareholder Primacy)

individuals hired by the board to run the company and manage it on a daily basis. Along with the board, the top management establishes the overall policy. Middle- and lower-level managers carry out this policy and conduct the daily supervision of the operative employees. **Employees** are those hired by the company to perform the actual operational work. Managers are employees, too, but in this discussion, we use the term employees to refer to nonmanagerial employees.

Separation of Ownership from Control   The major condition embedded in the Anglo-American model of modern corporations that has contributed to the corporate governance problem has been the **separation of ownership from control**. This problem did not exist before corporations came into being. In the precorporate period, owners were typically the managers themselves; thus, the system worked the way it was intended, with the owners also controlling the business. Even when firms grew larger and managers were hired, the owners were often on the scene to hold the management group accountable. For example, if a company got in trouble, the Carnegies, or Mellons, or Morgans, were always there to fire the president.[17]

As the public corporation grew and stock ownership became widely dispersed, shareholders (owners) became more distant from managers and a separation of ownership from control became the prevalent condition. Figure 4-2 illustrates the precorporate and corporate periods. The dispersion of ownership into hundreds of thousands or millions of shares meant that essentially no one person or group owned enough shares to exercise control. This being the case, the most effective control that owners could exercise was the election of the board of directors to serve as their representative and watch over the management.

The problem with this evolution was that true authority, power, and control began to rest with the group that had the most concentrated interest at stake—the management. The shareholders were owners in a technical sense, but most of them did not perceive themselves as owners. If you owned 100 shares of Walt Disney Co. and there were

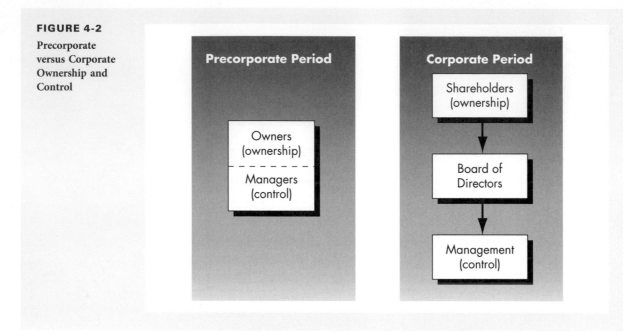

FIGURE 4-2

Precorporate versus Corporate Ownership and Control

10 million shares outstanding, you would be more likely to see yourself as an investor than you would be to see yourself as an owner. With just a telephone call issuing a sell order to your stockbroker, your "ownership" stake could be gone. Furthermore, with stock ownership so dispersed, no real supervision of corporate boards was possible.

The other factors that added to management's power were the corporate laws and traditions that gave the management group control over the proxy process—the method by which the shareholders elected boards of directors. Technically, the board hires and fires managers, but eventually managers were able to subvert that process. Over time, managers were able to influence board member selection so that boards of directors became filled with like-minded executives who would too often defer to the management on whatever it wanted. The result of this process was the opposite of what was originally intended: power, authority, and control began to flow upward from the management rather than downward from the shareholders (owners). **Agency problems** developed when the interests of the shareholders were not aligned with the interests of the manager, and the manager (who is a hired *agent* with the responsibility of representing the owners' best interests) began to pursue self-interest instead of the owners' best interests.

Problems in Corporate Governance

It is clear from the preceding discussion that a potential governance problem is built into the corporate system because of the separation of ownership from control and the agency problems that result. The duty of the board of directors is to oversee management on behalf of the shareholders and with full regard for the stakeholders. However, this is where the system can break down. For corporate governance to function effectively, the board of directors must be an effective, potent body carrying out its roles and responsibilities.

With mechanisms for corporate governance in place, how could debacles like Enron, WorldCom, and Global Crossing still occur? Why did corporate governance mechanisms not prevent the global financial crisis from occurring? Surprisingly, most of the behavior that led to these crises fell within the letter of the law. Therefore, the response to them has been geared toward changing the law. The Sarbanes–Oxley Act (SOX) was a response to the problems that stemmed from Enron and WorldCom and the like, and the Dodd–Frank Wall Street Reform and Consumer Protection Act was a response to the global financial crisis. We will discuss them later in this chapter.

To be fair, corporate governance is a complex process and even a well-designed board is no guarantee of success. Nevertheless, boards have improved and they strive to continue to improve in many ways. In the 2012 PWC survey of corporate directors, 66 percent of the responding boards indicated that they made changes in the board based on the regular self-evaluation they conducted.[18] More than a third said their changes included bringing more expertise on the board.[19] In the "What Directors Think" survey, 86 percent of respondents indicated that their boards do regular analyses of director skill sets and board composition strengths and weaknesses.[20] As we discuss the failings of corporate governance in the past decade, we must keep in mind that boards share in the blame but are not responsible for all of it. They are not superheroes, and we should not expect them to be.[21]

The Need for Board Independence

Board independence from management is a crucial aspect of good governance. It is here that the difference between **inside directors** and **outside directors** becomes most pronounced. Outside directors are independent from the firm and its top managers. They can come from a variety of backgrounds (e.g., top managers of other firms, academics, former government officials) but the one thing they have in common is that they have no other substantive relationship to the firm or its CEO. In contrast, inside directors have ties of some sort to the firm. They can be top managers in the firm, family members, or others with a professional or personal relationship to the firm or to the CEO. To varying degrees, each of these parties is "beholden" to the CEO and, therefore, might be hesitant to speak out when necessary. Since the implosion of Enron and its aftermath, changes in public policy and public opinion have led to an increase in the percentage of independent directors.

Issues Surrounding Compensation

The issue of executive pay is a lightning rod for those who feel that CEOs are placing their own interests over those of their shareholders. For example, people became outraged when they heard that Wall Street firms gave out $18.2 billion as bonuses in 2008 as the economy crumbled. Two issues are at the heart of the CEO pay controversy: (1) the extent to which CEO pay is tied to firm performance and (2) the overall size of CEO pay.

The CEO Pay–Firm Performance Relationship   The move to tie CEO pay more closely to firm performance grew in momentum when shareholders observed CEO pay rising as firm performance fell. Many executives had received staggering salaries even while profits were falling, workers were being laid off, and shareholder return was dropping. Since then shareholders have focused not only on limiting the pay initially rewarded but also on taking back pay that, in retrospect, seems undeserved. **Clawback provisions** allow shareholders to regain compensation from executives who have fallen short of the mark in some way, such as financial performance or ethical behavior.[22] In 2012, compensation research firm Equilar reported 86.5% of the Fortune 100 had adopted Clawback provisions.[23] This is up from 72 percent in 2009 and only 17.6 percent in 2006.[24]

Efforts to strengthen the CEO pay–firm performance relationship have centered on the use of **stock options**. While they have improved the pay–performance relationship, they have also created a host of new problems. Stock options are designed to motivate the recipient to improve the value of the firm's stock. Put simply, an option allows the recipient to purchase stock in the future at the price it is today, that is, "at the money." If the stock value rises after the granting of the option, the recipient will make money. The logic behind giving CEOs stock options is that those CEOs will want to increase the value of the firm's stock so that they will be able to exercise their options, buying stock in the future at a price that is lower than its worth. Of course, this logic only works if the option is granted at the true "at the money" price. The possibility of quick gains through misrepresentation of the pricing has led to numerous abuses. The following are the ones most frequently in the news.

Stock option **backdating** occurs when the recipient is given the option of buying stock at yesterday's price, resulting in an immediate and guaranteed wealth increase. This puts the stock option "in the money" rather than "at the money," which is where an option should be granted. Of course, backdating results in an immediate gain and is not in keeping with the purpose of stock options. This is not the only stock option abuse that has been observed. Even stock options granted "at the money" can be problematic when coupled with inside knowledge that the stock price is soon going to change. **Spring-loading** is the granting of a stock option at today's price but with the inside knowledge that something good is about to happen that will improve the stock's value. **Bullet-dodging** is the delaying of a stock option grant until right after bad news. Backdating is not inherently illegal, but it can be deemed so if documents were falsified to conceal the backdating. Spring-loading and bullet-dodging have been subjects of intense debate: The role of insider information in these two practices is a cause for concern. Adam Lashinsky of *Fortune* questions whether the benefits of stock options are worth the problems they create. Lashinsky suggests removing stock options from employee compensation packages and instead paying them competitively, increasing their compensation when the company is doing well through profit-sharing and bonuses. He states, "Outsized riches should be reserved for the company founders, not the hired help, which, let's face it, is what most executives are."[25]

Excessive CEO Pay Concern about the size of executive compensation has been around for a long time. In ancient Greece, Plato recommended that no one in a community receive a wage higher than five times that of the lowest paid worker. Today, CEO salaries have skyrocketed while worker salaries have waned. Executive Paywatch, the annual CEO compensation survey by the AFL-CIO, reported that, by 2011, the ratio of CEO pay to the average worker was 380 to 1.[26] This represents a significant decline from 2000, when the gap between CEO pay and average worker pay had risen to a staggering 531 to 1. Nevertheless, it is more than nine times as large as the 42-to-1 ratio found in 1980.[27] The Economic Policy Institute provides another measure of the CEO to worker pay ratio. Among the largest 350 firms and based on the value of executive option grants, the pay ratio went from 18.3 in 1965 to 209 in 2011.[28] To add insult to injury, Executive Excess 2012 notes that 25 of the 100 highest-paid U.S. corporate chief executives in 2012 were given more in CEO pay than their companies paid in income taxes.[29] Typically, the issue of excessive executive pay is a United States phenomenon. However, at this writing, European Union officials are considering letting bank shareholders set a limit for the allowable difference between the firm's highest and lowest paid employees.[30]

The **Say on Pay movement** evolved from concerns over excessive executive compensation. It began in the United Kingdom in 2002 with regulations that included the requirement to put a remuneration report to a shareholder vote at each annual meeting.[31] Soon after the United Kingdom instituted its regulations, Say on Pay requirements spread through Europe and Australia, with the Netherlands making the vote binding on the company.[32] In the United States, the Dodd–Frank Wall Street Reform Act requires companies to submit their executive pay packages to a nonbinding shareholder vote at least once every three years.[33] From 2010, when the Act was instituted, to 2012, 1,911 say on pay resolutions came to a vote: Institutional Shareholder Services (ISS) advised shareholders to vote against 265 of them.[34] Shareholders voted against 36.[35] Pay consultant Daniel Ryterbrand says that Say on Pay is more of a success than the numbers might indicate: "Say on pay has had a significant impact on the design and magnitude of pay packages." Boards are nervous about how proxy advisers such as ISS and Glass Lewis will react to packages, so they're reaching out to shareholders and reducing pay that's not tied to performance."[36] Executive pay also has begun to have an impact on a firm's larger reputation. In Corporate Knights' ranking of the Global 100 most sustainable firms, executive pay is a part of two clean capitalism key performance indicators: the ratio of CEO to average employee pay and the linking of executive pay to clean capitalism goals.[37] Corporate Knights defines *clean capitalism* as "an economic system in which prices fully incorporate social, economic, and ecological costs and benefits, and actors are clearly aware of the consequences of their marketplace actions."[38]

When the executive's high level of pay results from dubious practices, such as financial misconduct or the exercising of options in a questionable way, shareholders have a right to try to recover those funds, but in the past, they have lacked a mechanism for doing so. This is changing due to the increasing adoption of clawback provisions, which are compensation recovery mechanisms that enable a company to recoup compensation funds, typically in the event of a financial restatement or executive's misbehavior.[39] In the United States, the Dodd–Frank Reform Act mandated that securities exchanges and associations require a compensation recovery policy in listing standards.[40] The SEC is required to implement a policy, but as of this writing has yet to do so. The Council for Institutional Investors (CII) issued a policy that both current and former executive officers should be subject to clawback in cases of financial misstatements or fraud.[41] The CII does not have power over listings, but its members are large shareholders with voting power.[42]

Individual investors and other parties concerned do not have to wade through proxy statements to learn about CEO compensation. The AFL-CIO sponsors CEO PayWatch (http://www.aflcio.org/paywatch), a Web site that is an "online center for learning about the excessive salaries, bonuses, and perks of the CEOs of major corporations."[43] Visitors to the Web site can enter their pay and a firm's name and find out how many years they would have to work to make what the CEO of that firm makes in one year (or how many workers are at your salary that the CEO's pay could support). The Web site also provides instructions for assessing the pay of CEOs at public corporations and beginning a campaign of shareholder activism in any company.

Executive Retirement Plans and Exit Packages Executive retirement packages have traditionally flown under the radar, escaping the notice of shareholders, employees, and the public. However, as details of some retirement packages have become public, those packages have come under increased scrutiny. The issue took center stage when former General Electric (GE) chairman and CEO Jack Welch's retirement package was disclosed during his divorce proceedings. Country club memberships, wine and laundry services, luxurious housing, and access to corporate jets were but a few of the perks that Welch had enjoyed.[44] These packages are negotiated well in advance and so they often are unrelated to performance. The $210-million exit package Robert Nardelli received following his ouster from Home Depot inflamed shareholder activists and outraged the public.[45] After Bank of America took $45 billion in federal bailout funds and became the subject of investigation by federal and state officials, outgoing CEO Ken Lewis received nearly $64 million in retirement pay and left the firm with what some compensation analysts estimate to be $125 million.[46]

Part of the public's frustration is that these CEO retirement packages stand in stark contrast to the retirement packages that workers receive. Many of today's workers do not have retirement packages, and those who do are far more likely to have the less lucrative defined contribution plans (that specify what will be put into the retirement fund) rather than the defined benefit plans (that specify the benefit the retiree will receive).[47] These defined contribution plans are more vulnerable to stock market fluctuations than defined benefit plans, and so the majority of workers saw their retirement funds plummet as the global financial crisis hit. Now top executives want to avoid that level of uncertainty, and so some U.S. companies are designing supplemental retirement plans to get around ERISA, the federal pension law that was intended to avoid the favoring of high-ranking managers.[48]

Outside Director Compensation Paying board members is a relatively recent idea. Ninety years ago, it was illegal to pay nonexecutive board members. The logic was that because board members represented the shareholders, paying them out of the company's (i.e., shareholders') funds would be self-dealing.[49] Today, outside board members are paid for their efforts. From 2003 through 2010, median total outside director pay rose about a third from $175,800 to $233,800: At the same time, the average time directors spent on the job increased 46%.[50]

Transparency SEC rules on disclosure of executive compensation are designed to address some of the more obvious problems by making the entire pay packages of top executives transparent. In the past they have included such items as deferred pay, severance, accumulated pension benefits, and perks over $10,000.[51] There is evidence that improvements in disclosure even have an impact prior to implementation. Michael S. Melbinger, a compensation lawyer, tells the story of a CEO who had a contract provision that not only reimbursed all his medical expenses (including deductibles and co-pays) but also provided a **tax gross-up**, which reimbursed him for the taxes he would have to pay on his medical benefits. In contrast, employees in this company were required to cover their own medical expenses. So when the CEO realized how bad it would look that the company not only paid all his medical bills but also the taxes on that benefit, he quickly gave up that perk.[52]

The Dodd–Frank Wall Street Reform Act includes provisions intended to have the SEC improve the transparency of firm operations. One is an equity pay provision that requires firms to reveal the difference in salaries between executives and rank-and-file workers. At this writing, the SEC has not implemented the policy but is receiving letters from both opponents and proponents. The Chamber of Commerce opposes the new rule. "The ratio is not going to be a meaningful way to help investors but will be used as a political tool to attack companies," says David Hirschmann, president of the U.S. Chamber of Commerce's Center for Capital Markets.[53] Other opponents say that calculating the ratio would be cumbersome given a global marketplace with different payroll systems.[54] Proponents of the measure include labor unions and institutional investors who believe that the requirement could slow down the high rate of growth in CEO pay, as well as motivate boards to think more often of their front-line workers.[55]

Another Dodd–Frank requirement focuses on the transparency of the compensation setting process. In 2012, the SEC approved a new exchange listing standards rule that will require listing standards to include issues such as the independence of compensation committee members, the compensation adviser hiring process, and the nature of the relationship between the compensation adviser and the committee.[56]

The Governance Impact of the Market for Corporate Control

Mergers and acquisitions are another form of corporate governance, one that comes from outside the corporation. The expectation from the Anglo-American shareholder-primacy perspective is that the threat of a possible takeover will motivate top managers to pursue shareholder, rather than self, interest (the expectation of the director-primacy perspective will be explained later in the chapter). The merger, acquisition, and hostile takeover craze of the 1980s motivated many corporate CEOs and boards to go to great lengths to protect themselves from these takeovers. Two of the controversial practices to emerge from the hostile takeover wave were poison pills and golden parachutes. We briefly consider each of these and see how they fit into the corporate governance problem being discussed. Then we examine the issue of insider trading.

Poison Pills A **poison pill** is intended to discourage or prevent a hostile takeover. They work much like their name suggests—when an acquirer tries to swallow (i.e., acquire) a company, the poison pill makes the company very difficult to ingest. Poison pills can take a variety of forms but, typically, when a hostile suitor acquires more than a certain percentage of a company's stock, the poison pill provides that other shareholders be able to purchase shares, thus diluting the suitor's holdings and making the acquisition prohibitively expensive (i.e., difficult to swallow). Poison pills have fallen out of favor, going from 2,218 such defenses in 2001 to 1,206 at the start of 2009, largely due to institutional shareholder pressure.[57] A decline in hostile takeovers has also contributed to the decline in poison pills.[58] Nevertheless, they remain within the corporate arsenal. In 2012, Netflix adopted a poison pill to fend off a corporate takeover by corporate raider, Carl Icahn.[59]

Golden Parachutes A **golden parachute** is a contract in which a corporation agrees to make payments to key officers in the event of a change in the control of the corporation.[60] Advocates argue that golden parachutes provide top executives involved in takeover battles with an incentive for not fighting a shareholder wealth-maximizing takeover attempt in an effort to preserve their employment. However, a study of more than 400 takeover attempts found that golden parachutes had no effect on takeover resistance.[61] Critics argue that executives are already being paid sufficiently well and that these parachutes essentially reward them for failure.[62] Others argue that lavish exit packages might make CEOs too eager to accept a takeover offer.[63] In a recent Equilar Inc. study of Fortune 100 companies, 82 percent of the CEOs were promised exit packages if they lost their jobs following a corporate takeover, or "change in control."[64] The trend in the percentage of executives awarded packages is holding steady but the multiple involved (the percentage of payout relative to salary) has been declining.[65]

Insider Trading

Insider trading is the practice of buying or selling a security by someone who has access to material information that is not available to the public. **Material information** is information that a reasonable investor might want to use and that is likely to affect the price of a firm's stock once that information is released to the public. Although insider trading is typically thought of as illegal conduct, insider trading can be legal in some cases.[66] Whether or not inside trading is legal depends on when the trade occurs. If the trade is made while the information is still not public, then it is illegal because members of the

FIGURE 4-3
An Insider
Trading Quiz

Which of the following are considered to be illegal inside trading, prosecutable by the SEC?

1. A lower-level employee of the company learns the company will have higher-than-expected earnings in the next quarterly statement and buys shares of the company's stock before the statement is released to the public. Can that employee be prosecuted by the SEC?

2. The above employee who learned the information does not trade on the information but tells his or her spouse and that spouse buys company stock shares before the information goes public. Can the spouse be prosecuted by the SEC?

3. In example 2 above, can the employee who did not trade be prosecuted by the SEC?

4. While playing basketball on the weekend, the employee shares the information with a casual friend. That friend then buys shares of the company's stock before the statement is released to the public. Can the friend be prosecuted by the SEC?

The answer to all the questions in this quiz is 'yes.'

© Cengage Learning 2015

public do not have access to that information.[67] The market system is based on trust and fair play. Investor confidence relies on fairness and integrity in the securities markets and illegal insider trading erodes that confidence.[68]

The SEC has brought charges against people who received or revealed inside information in a variety of ways. One can be a **tipper** who provides that information or a **tippee** who receives the information. Both types are prosecutable and both have been prosecuted by the SEC.[69] It is clear that these include corporate directors, executives, and employees, but the SEC has also brought charges against friends, family members, and business associates of insiders. If an employee of a law, banking, or printing firm receives inside information in the process of providing services to a company and then trades on that information knowing it is non-public, that person is prosecutable. The same is true for government employees, including employees of the SEC.[70] In November 2012 cases were filed against a former portfolio manager at a leading hedge fund, a former major league baseball player accused both of trading illegally and sharing information with three friends, and six high-school buddies accused of tipping while playing basketball.[71] It even does not matter if the person gained or lost money, insider trading is prosecutable whether or not it is successful, although your defense attorney may be able to argue the information was not material if only losses occur.[72] Fast computing and the Internet have made it much easier to catch illegal inside traders: The SEC now brings more cases in one year than it did throughout the 1990s.[73] Cases are also growing in size.

One of the complications of insider trading prosecutions is determining whether a person who possesses insider information actually used it in the decision to trade. **SEC Rule 10b5-1** specifies that if a trader is aware of material nonpublic information, that trader is assumed to be trading on that information except in very specific circumstances. Proving *intent* would be difficult and so prosecution is based on *timing* and the onus is on the person being charged. The only way a person can show that inside information was not a factor in the trading decision is to prove that the trader had a pre-existing contract or plan to make the trade.[74] Another complication is the determination of who is an insider and thus liable for prosecution. **SEC Rule 10b5-2** expands that definition beyond the insider who works for the company. People in relationships that include a duty of confidentiality can also be considered insiders. For example, a spouse, parent, child, sibling, or friend would generally be considered to have a duty of confidentiality. For this reason, the answer to all the questions in the Insider Trading Quiz in Figure 4-3, page 106, is yes. Please note that the quiz asks if the person's deed is prosecutable. Someone charged with insider trading can mount a defense, which may or may not be successful. Illegal insider trading is not defined by any federal statute and so the definition of it has proven malleable as the SEC pursues cases and the courts weigh their merits.[75] The Supreme Court ruled illegal insider trading is a "breach of a fiduciary duty or other relationship of trust and confidence."[76] A Court of Appeals rejected SEC arguments that a marital relationship was sufficient for the person to be liable for insider trading; Nevertheless, at this writing, the SEC is bringing charges against a tippee and tipper who were close friends.[77] If the SEC succeeds, the boundary of fiduciary duty will expand, and we are likely to see even more inside trading cases in the future.[78]

Insider trading allegations cause the general public to lose faith in the stability and security financial industry because **information asymmetry** (one party having information that another does not) favors one group over another. Information asymmetry can also arise if companies release information to one group before another receives it. If large investors can act on information that smaller investors do not have, the playing field is not level. To prop up investor confidence, the SEC instituted disclosure rules designed to aid the small investor who historically did not have access to the information large investors hold. **Regulation FD (fair disclosure)** set limits on the common company practice of selective disclosure. When companies disclose meaningful information to shareholders and securities professionals, they must do so publicly so that small investors can enjoy a more level playing field.[79]

ETHICS IN PRACTICE CASE
Playing with Presets

According to Rule 10b5-1, inside trading can be legal if the trade simply carries out a plan that was set in place before the information arrived, i.e., a preset plan. This is helpful to executives who want to trade in their own company's stock because it enables them to trade even when they possess inside knowledge, as they almost always do. The existence of the plan can be used as evidence that the inside information was not a factor in the decision to trade. Executives are not required to file these plans with a federal agency or to disclose when they open or close one. Various studies have found that insiders do better in the stock market than one would normally expect. Some observers point to these higher returns and argue that executives are benefitting from insider trading. However, it is virtually impossible for an outside observer to determine if inside information played a factor in executive trades because the preset plans allow for intermittent buying and selling of shares, and they are not filed with a federal agency. Some observers argue that not letting executives trade when they have inside information is absurd because executives always have nonpublic material information about their firms and they should be able to trade in their firm's stock. They suggest that the problem is relatively small and need not form the basis of new regulation. Others argue that executive insider trading gives the executives an unfair advantage over the average investor.

1. With whom do you agree? Do you believe that executives have a right to trade in their own firm's shares? Please justify your answer and explain what restrictions you would place on their trades.

2. If you do not believe that executives should be able to trade in their own shares, please explain your rationale for limiting their behavior. Do you consider other aspects of being an executive (e.g., salary, bonuses, options) to compensate for not being permitted to trade?

3. Given the current situation, what policy recommendation would you give to the SEC? Could transparency play a part in resolving this issue? If so, how?

Sources: http://www.sec.gov/answers/insider.htm. Accessed March 29, 2013; Lauren Cohen, Christopher Malloy, and Lukasz Pomorski. "Decoding Inside Information," *Journal of Finance* (Vol. 67, No. 3, 2012): 1009–1043; Susan Pulliam and Rob Barry, "Executives' Good Luck in Trading Own Stock," *The Wall Street Journal* (November 27, 2012), http://online.wsj.com/article/SB10000872396390444100404577 641463717344178.html. Accessed March 29, 2013; Felix Salmon, "Is Executive Insider Trading a Problem? (November 28, 2012), http://blogs.reuters.com/felix-salmon/2012/11/28/is-executive-insider-trading-a-problem/. Accessed March 29, 2013.

Improving Corporate Governance

We first discuss legislative efforts to improve corporate governance. The Sarbanes–Oxley Act was passed in response to the public outcry for greater protection following the financial scandals of 2001. The Dodd–Frank Wall Street Reform Act was passed in response to the global financial crisis. We then proceed to discussing other efforts to improve corporate governance through changes in the composition, structure, and functioning of boards of directors.

Legislative Efforts

The **Accounting Reform and Investor Protection Act of 2002,** also known as the **Sarbanes–Oxley Act (aka SOX or Sarbox)**, amends the securities laws to provide better protection to investors in public companies by improving the financial reporting of companies. According to the Senate committee report, "the issue of auditor independence is at the center of [SOX]."[80] Some of the ways the act endeavors to ensure auditor independence are by limiting the nonauditing services an auditor can provide, requiring auditing firms to rotate the auditors who work with a specific company, and making it unlawful for accounting firms to provide auditing services where conflicts of interest (as defined by the act) exist. In addition, the act enhances financial disclosure with requirements such as the reporting of offbalance-sheet transactions, the prohibiting of personal loans to executives and directors, and the requirement that auditors assess and report upon the internal controls employed by the company. Other key provisions include the requirement that audit committees have at least one financial expert, that CEOs and chief financial officers (CFOs) certify and be held responsible for financial representations of the company, and that whistle-blowers are afforded protection. Corporations must also disclose whether they have adopted a code of ethics for senior financial officers, and, if they have not, provide an explanation for why they have not.[81] The penalties for noncompliance with SOX are severe. A CEO or CFO who misrepresents company finances may face a fine of up to $1 million and imprisonment for up to ten years. If that misrepresentation is willful, the fine may go up to $5 million with up to 20 years' imprisonment.[82] Since the passage of SOX, debate has continued regarding its costs and benefits with attitudes becoming more positive as firms have more experience with SOX's requirements. Protiviti conducted a 10-year retrospective survey of nearly 600 executives and professionals involved in SOX compliance. According to Brian Christensen, Protiviti's executive vice president, global internal audit and Jim DeLoach, a Protiviti managing director and the firm's senior SOX practice leader, "While Sarbanes-Oxley has had its share of controversy in the past, nearly 70 percent of respondents in the survey reported that the internal control over financial reporting structure in their organizations has improved since compliance with Sarbanes-Oxley.[83] They go on to say, "While initial compliance costs and efforts involved are burdensome for new Sarbanes-Oxley filers, over the long term, many organizations view the benefits of Sarbanes-Oxley compliance to outweigh the costs." **The Dodd-Frank Wall Street Reform and Consumer Protection Act** was passed in the wake of the global financial crisis and signed into law on July 21, 2010. At this writing, it is still being put into place and so some time will have to pass before we truly know its costs and benefits. This comprehensive legislation covers a range of areas including banks, credit card companies, credit rating agencies, insurance companies, hedge funds, and futures trading. We discussed its impact on executive compensation previously and will continue to discuss the Act in applicable parts of the book.[84]

Legislative efforts are important and governments have a responsibility to respond when crises such as the Enron and WorldCom bankruptcies and the global occur.

Government has a responsibility to protect the public interest but no amount of legislative oversight will fully protect the public from the next crisis. In their study of the global financial crisis, Michael Santoro and Ronald Strauss acknowledge that government has a crucial role to play but conclude, "no amount of government regulation can succeed where the moral core is corrupt... Unless Wall Street itself formulates a coherent moral response to the crisis, no amount of regulatory oversight will prevent another, potentially more destabilizing, crisis from occurring."[85]

Changes in Boards of Directors

Because of the growing belief that CEOs and executive teams need to be made more accountable to shareholders and other stakeholders, boards have been undergoing a variety of changes. Here we focus on several key areas that need to change as well as some of the recommendations that were set forth for improving board functioning. Figure 4-4 presents a ranked list of nine "red flags" that signal that a board member should increase his or her involvement, and the National Association of Corporate Directors' nine steps that provide a roadmap for board repair.

Board Diversity

Prior to the 1960s, boards were composed primarily of white, male inside directors. It was not until the 1960s that pressure from Washington, Wall Street, and various stakeholder groups began to emphasize the concept of board diversity.

The Alliance for Board Diversity conducted a 2010 census, *Missing Pieces: Women and Minorities on Fortune 500 Boards*, which showed women and minorities are severely under-represented in the Fortune 100 companies. They found a gain of 11 seats for white women, a gain of three seats each for Asian Pacific Islander women and Hispanic women, and a loss of one seat for African American women. That represents 16 gained board seats for women overall, representing a dismal 1.1 percent increase over six years. For men, Asia-Pacific Islanders gained twelve seats, Hispanic men lost three seats, and African American men lost five seats. The Fortune 500 was even less diverse. [86]

Problems with achieving board diversity issue are not confined to the United States. Only 15 percent of FTSE 100 board seats are occupied by women: 6.6 percent are executives and 22.4 percent are non-executives.[87] A 2012 European Commission report noted that, in Europe's top firms, only one in seven board members are women. The leader in

---

FIGURE 4-4 Ranking of Red Flags That Signal Board Problems and Steps to Take for Board Repair

Ranking of Red Flags	Steps to Take for Board Repair
1. Company has to restate earnings	1. Spread risk oversight among multiple committees
2. Poor employee morale	2. Seek outside help in identifying potential risks
3. Negative risk assessment from auditor	3. Deepen involvement in corporate strategy
4. Poor customer satisfaction track record	4. Align board size and skill mix with strategy
5. Management misses strategic performance goals	5. Revamp executive compensation
6. Company is target of employee lawsuits	6. Pick compensation committee members who will question the status quo
7. Stock price declines	7. Use independent compensation consultants
8. Quarterly financial results miss analysts' expectations	8. Evaluate CEO on grooming potential successors
9. Low corporate governance quotient rating	9. Know what matters to your investors

Sources: "What Directors Think Study 2008," Corporate Board Member, http://www.boardmember.com. (This list results from a 2008 Corporate *Board Member* and PricewaterhouseCoopers LLP survey of 1,040 corporate directors.) Joanne S. Lublin, "Corporate Directors Give Repair Plan to Boards," *The Wall Street Journal* (March 24, 2009), B4.

having women on corporate boards of directors is Norway. The 500 publicly traded firms in Norway were told they would face closure if they did not meet a January 2008 deadline for achieving 40 percent female representation on their boards.[88] By 2008, every major Norwegian corporation was in compliance. The number of women on Norway's corporate board had almost quadrupled in five years.[89] By 2010, the percentage of women on publicly traded Norwegian boards was greater than 40 percent, and, even on private boards, the percentage of women had risen to more than 25 percent.[90] Not surprisingly, this dramatic shift ignited a fierce debate about the use of quotas to create change and the role of women in the workplace.[91] Regulators in Spain, Belgium, the Netherlands, and France have now followed Norway's lead, with their regulators making compulsory or quasi-compulsory recommendations for female representation.[92]

Do diverse boards make a difference? Given the diversity of stakeholders, a diverse board is better able to hear their concerns and respond to their needs.[93] Diverse boards are also less likely to fall prey to groupthink because they would have the range of perspectives necessary to question the assumptions that drive group decisions.[94] There is some evidence of board diversity being associated with better financial performance.[95] However, a cause–effect relationship is very difficult to determine because so many factors influence the performance of a firm.

Outside Directors

As we discussed earlier, legislative, investor, and public pressure have led firms to seek a greater ratio of outside to inside board members. Do outside board members make a difference for both shareholders and stakeholders? As with diversity, a relationship between the proportion of outside directors and financial performance is difficult to find. For that reason, scholars have looked to more targeted measures. One study found outside directors to be associated with fewer shareholder lawsuits.[96] Regarding stakeholders, researchers found that outside directors correlated positively with dimensions of social responsibility associated with both people and product quality.[97] A recent study examined 20,000 board members from 2,080 firms and found that as board connections to the firm increased, so did earnings restatements and mergers that hurt firm performance.[98] This independence can come at a cost, however, as inside directors have greater knowledge of the firm because of their connections to it. Some observers have expressed concern that the call for more outside directors has pushed chief financial officers (CFOs) off the board. The number of CFOs on a Fortune 500 board dropped from 37 to 19 in two years.[99]

Outside directors are a heterogeneous group and so the impact of appointing more outside directors to boards can be expected to vary with the characteristics of the appointees, such as their expertise, their experience, and the time they have available to give to their post. Arguably, the most important characteristic for outside directors is the ability to ask difficult questions and speak truthfully about concerns, without letting ties to the firm get in the way. Julie Daum, co-head of SpencerStuart's North American board and CEO search practice, said in 2012, "Boards are becoming much more independent each year."[100] Sarbanes-Oxley (SOX) had a major impact as it prompted U.S. stock exchanges to require that public companies have boards in which a majority of members are independent.[101] In spite of these steps forward, the issue of board independence is one that will always merit attention.

Use of Board Committees

The **audit committee** is responsible for assessing the adequacy of internal control systems and the integrity of financial statements. Recent scandals, such as Enron,

WorldCom, and the many companies that have subsequently needed to restate earnings, underscore the importance of a strong audit committee. SOX mandates that the audit committee be composed entirely of independent board members and that there be at least one identified financial expert, as defined in SOX.[102] The principal responsibilities of an audit committee are as follows:[103]

1. To ensure that published financial statements are not misleading
2. To ensure that internal controls are adequate
3. To follow up on allegations of material, financial, ethical, and legal irregularities
4. To ratify the selection of the external auditor

While the audit committee has taken center stage in the current corporate governance environment, other committees still play key roles. The **nominating committee**, which should be composed of outside directors, has the responsibility of ensuring that competent, objective board members are selected. The function of the nominating committee is to nominate candidates for the board and for senior management positions. The suggested role and responsibility of this committee notwithstanding, in most companies, the CEO continues to exercise a powerful role in the selection of board members. The **compensation committee** has the responsibility of evaluating executive performance and recommending terms and conditions of employment. This committee should be composed of outside directors. Both the New York Stock Exchange (NYSE) and NASDAQ require that the compensation committee be composed of independent board members. One might ask, however, how objective these board members are when the CEO has played a significant role in their being elected to the board. Finally, each board has committees that respond to the needs of their industries and that address public policy and social issues. The committees have a variety of names. For example, Johnson & Johnson has a regulatory, compliance, and governmental affairs committee as well as a science, technology, and sustainability committee.[104] Unilever has a corporate responsibility and reputation committee.[105] Although it is recognized that most management structures have some sort of formal mechanism for responding to public or social issues, this area is important enough to warrant a board committee that would become sensitive to these issues, provide policy leadership, and monitor the management's performance on these issues. Most major companies today have committees that typically deal with such issues as diversity, equal employment opportunity, environmental affairs, employee health and safety, consumer affairs, political action, and other areas in which public or ethical issues are present. Debate continues over the extent to which large firms actually use such committees, but the fact that they have institutionalized such concerns by way of formal corporate committees is encouraging.

The Board's Relationship with the CEO

Boards of directors have always been responsible for monitoring CEO performance and dismissing poorly performing CEOs. Historically, however, CEOs were protected from the axe that hit other employees when times got rough. This is no longer true. Tough, competitive economic times, the rising vigilance of outside directors, and the increasing power of large institutional investors has resulted in CEOs "dropping like flies."[106] As the *Christian Science Monitor* commented, "While the perks of sitting in a corner office are great, job security isn't one of them."[107]

Part of the protection that CEOs once felt came from **CEO duality**, which occurs when the CEO serves the dual function of CEO and chairman of the board. One can only wonder how the board's responsibility to monitor the CEO can be fulfilled effectively when the CEO is heading the process, and so it is not surprising that activist shareholders have pushed to separate the CEO and board chairman functions. As is true with outside directors, CEO duality is "a double-edged sword."[108] CEOs who also serve as chairs are able act decisively in responding to a competitive marketplace; however, that comes at the cost of a reduced ability for the board to monitor effectively.[109] Activist shareholders have been successful in getting companies to split the CEO and board chair function. In 2012, 20 percent of the S&P 500 companies have independent outsiders as board chairs: That is up from 12 percent in 2007.[110]

"You have to perform or perish," according to John A. Challenger, CEO of outplacement firm Challenger, Gray & Christmas Inc. "If you don't produce immediate results, you just don't have much room to move."[111] A record number of CEOs lost their jobs in the first nine months of 2008.[112] Some analysts see increased turnover in CEOs as a positive thing. "I take it as a good sign, because it says boards of directors are tougher on CEOs than they used to be," says Donald P. Jacobs, former dean of the Kellogg School of Business at Northwestern University.[113] Still others express their concern. Rakesh Khurana of Harvard Business School opines, "We've made this a superhero job. Boards look at the CEO as a panacea and get fixated on the idea that one single individual will solve all the company's problems."[114]

Board Member Liability

Concerned about increasing legal hassles emanating from stockholder, customer, and employee lawsuits, directors have been quitting board positions or refusing to accept them in the first place. In the past, courts rarely held board members personally liable in the hundreds of shareholder suits filed every year. Instead, the **business judgment rule** prevailed. The business judgment rule holds that courts should not challenge board members who act in good faith, making informed decisions that reflect the company's best interests instead of their own self-interest. The argument for the business judgment rule is that board members need to be free to take risks without fear of liability. The issue of good faith is central here because the rule was never intended to absolve board members completely from personal liability. In cases where the good faith standard was not upheld, board members have paid a hefty price.

The TransUnion Corporation case involved an agreement among the directors to sell the company for a price the owners later decided was too low. A suit was filed, and the court ordered that the board members be held personally responsible for the difference between the price the company was sold for and a later-determined "fair value" for the deal.[115] In addition to the TransUnion case, Cincinnati Gas and Electric reached a $14-million settlement in a shareholder suit that charged directors and officers with improper disclosure concerning a nuclear power plant.[116]

The Caremark case then further heightened directors' concerns about **personal liability**. Caremark, a home health-care company, paid substantial civil and criminal fines for submitting false claims and making illegal payments to doctors and other health-care providers. The Caremark board of directors was then sued for breach of fiduciary duties because the board members had failed in their responsibility to monitor effectively the Caremark employees who violated various state and federal laws. The Delaware Chancery Court ruled that it is the duty of the board of directors to ensure that a company has an effective reporting and monitoring system in place. If the board fails to do this, individual directors can be held personally liable for losses that are caused by their failure to meet appropriate standards.[117]

The issue of board members paying personal liability costs from their personal funds (also known as **out-of-pocket liability**) came to the forefront following the Enron and WorldCom debacles. Twelve WorldCom directors were ordered to pay $24.75 million out of their personal funds instead of drawing on their D&O insurance.[118] Ten former Enron directors agreed to pay $13 million from their personal funds.[119] In a November 2006 decision, the Delaware Supreme Court affirmed the "Caremark Standard" which states that directors can only be held liable if "1. The director utterly failed to implement any reporting or information system or controls, or 2. having implemented such a system or controls, consciously failed to monitor or oversee its operations, disabling their ability to be informed of risks or problems requiring their attention."[120] The economic meltdown raised new concerns about personal liability as directors realized they could be held personally liable when employees seek redress for the impacts of layoffs and plant closings.[121]

ETHICS IN PRACTICE CASE
Monitoring the Monitors

News leaks seemed to plague Hewlett Packard. The first leaks surrounded the ouster of chairwoman and chief executive Carly Fiorina. In the midst of this internal turmoil, *The Wall Street Journal* published an article with details of closed-door board discussions about the planned management reorganization. An external legal counsel interviewed board members but did not succeed in identifying the leak. Evidence of more leaks appeared a year later as news organizations once again described the deliberations of closed-door board and senior management meetings in extensive detail. It was clear that someone from inside was leaking information. In addition to board members, reporters from such publications as the *The New York Times, The Wall Street Journal, BusinessWeek*, and CNET became targets of the ensuing investigation into ten different leaks. The methods used to try to plug these news leaks led eventually to a board shake-up, which included the departure of nonexecutive chairwoman Patricia Dunn.

Investigating board members is a difficult proposition. As the source of the potential leaks, the board could not supervise what was essentially an investigation of itself. Neither could the employees handle the investigation because that would have put them in the untenable position of investigating their own bosses. Left with few options, HP board chairwoman Dunn turned the investigation over to a network of private investigators. According to Dunn, she could not supervise the investigation because she was a potential target. Dunn asked the head of corporate security to handle the investigation, as this was the person who handled employee investigations, but he still had conflicts of interest as an employee of the board. So the company outsourced the investigation to a network of outside investigators, telling them to conduct it within the confines of the law.

The primary source of the leaks was uncovered, but questions remained about the process of the investigations. Although no recording or eavesdropping occurred, investigators had used a form of "pretexting" to elicit phone records. Pretexting is a way of obtaining information by disguising one's identify. In this case, investigators used pretexting to obtain phone records of not only HP board members but also reporters who covered the story. In addition, investigators followed board members and journalists and watched their homes. They also planted false messages with journalists in an effort to get them to reveal their sources inadvertently through the tracking software included in the fake messages.

1. Who should be responsible for taking action when a board member engages in problematic behavior? If the chairperson is responsible, when should he or she involve the whole board? What are the costs of early full board involvement? What are the costs of late full board involvement?
2. One complaint lodged was that HP provided board members' home phone numbers to investigators. Was this out of line? Do board members have a responsibility to provide certain basic information, or was their privacy breached when their home phone numbers were given? A board member whose phone records proved he was not involved in any leaks still resigned the board in protest that his privacy was invaded by the pretexting. Was he right?
3. The law regarding pretexting is unclear. While it is illegal when used to obtain financial records, the use of pretexting in other situations—such as the phone records in this example—was not necessarily against the law. Should it be?
4. How might things have evolved differently if the ethicality rather than the legality of the practice had been the issue? Are the two synonymous or is there a difference?

Sources: Damon Darlin, Julie Cresswell, and Eric Dash, "H.P. Chairwoman Aims Not to Be the Scapegoat," *The New York Times* (September 9, 2006), C1; Ellen Nakashima and Yuke Noguchi, "HP CEO Allowed 'Sting' of Reporter," *Washington Post* (September 21, 2006), A1.

The Role of Shareholders

Shareholders are a varied group with a range of interests and expectations. They, however, have one aspect in common: In the Anglo-American system of corporate governance, they are the owners of the corporation. As such, they have a right to have their voices heard. Putting that right into practice, however, has presented an ongoing challenge for shareholders and managers.

Our discussion begins with an overview of the state of shareholder democracy, which relates to strengthening shareholder voice and participation in corporate governance. We then discuss shareholder activism and close with recommendations for improved shareholder relations.

Shareholder Democracy

Throughout the world, shareholders have been fighting to have their voices heard in corporate governance. This **shareholder democracy** movement stems from the lack of power shareholders have felt, particularly in board elections. In the United States, votes against board members have generally not been counted and corporations have been free to ignore shareholder resolutions.[122] Withholding a vote for a board member has typically had no impact because only the votes that were actually cast were counted.[123] Similarly, many European firms have not had one vote for each share issued.[124] Of course, the ability of shareholders to elect board members is central to the governance process

Spotlight on Sustainability

Shareholder Impact on Sustainability

Shareholder resolutions can appear to be frustrating propositions. Boards of directors and top management usually oppose them, and, even when resolutions are put forth, they typically get only a fraction of the votes needed to pass. In spite of these discouraging statistics, shareholders often can have a greater impact than one would first believe. Erin Reid and Michael Toffel conducted a study of the results of a campaign by the Carbon Disclosure Project (CDP), a London-based NGO that represents more than 300 institutional investors. The CDP targeted firms in the S&P 500 and asked that they become transparent about greenhouse gas emissions: They then publicized the names of companies that responded as well as the companies that declined to do so. The authors found that the existence of an environmental resolution not only caused managers of the target firm to become more transparent, but it also had a spillover effect leading non-targeted firms in the same industry to become more transparent as well. Apparently being targeted by shareholder activists, or being in an industry with other firms that have been targeted, "primes the pump," making firms more receptive to implementing changes. That receptivity is likely to continue as there is an upward trend in attention to environmental, social, and governance (ESG) issues. According to the *2012 Report on Sustainable and Responsible Investing Trends in the United States*, more investors, both individual and institutional, are factoring their values into their investments. Of the 272 money managers surveyed in the *Trends* report, 72 percent said that their incorporation of formal ESG analysis was driven by requests from investors.

Sources: Erin M. Reid and Michael W. Toffel, "Responding To Public and Private Politics: Corporate Disclosure of Climate Change Strategies," *Strategic Management Journal* (Vol. 30, No. 11, 2009), 1157–1178; Michael Kramer, "How Sustainable Investors Impact Industries and Corporate Policies," *Greenbiz.com* (November 26, 2012), http://www.greenbiz.com/blog/2012/11/26/how-sustainable-investors-impact-industries-and-corporate-policies. Accessed March 17, 2013; "2012 Report on Sustainable and Responsible Investing Trends in the United States," http://www.ussif.org/resources/pubs/trends/. Accessed March 17, 2013.

because the elected board members will be governing the corporation.[125] However, pundits and scholars disagree over the value of the recommended reforms.

Proponents of shareholder democracy argue that if shareholders are not able to select their own representatives, the board is likely to become a self-perpetuating oligarchy.[126] They contend that increased shareholder power and involvement will lead to improved firm performance.[127] Opponents counter that shareholders are not "owners" in the traditional sense of the word because they can exit their ownership relatively easily by simply selling their shares.[128] They contend that increased shareholder power will lead to inefficient and short-term-oriented decision making, as well as infighting among competing interests.[129]

Shareholder democracy begins with board elections and so we focus our discussion there. Three key issues that have arisen are majority vote, classified boards, and proxy access.

Majority vote is the requirement that board members be elected by a majority of votes cast. This is in contrast to the previously prevailing norm of plurality voting. With plurality voting, the board members with the greatest number of "yes" votes are elected to the available seats on the board. The "no" and withheld votes are not counted. With "plurality plus," board members who receive less than a majority of votes cast must submit their resignation; however, boards of directors have not always accepted the resignations.[130]

Classified boards (also known as **staggered boards**) are those that elect their members in staggered terms. For example, in a board of 12 members, 4 might be elected each year, and each would serve a three-year term. It would then take three years for the entire board slate to be replaced. Many shareholder activists oppose classified boards because of the time required to replace the board. Proponents of classified boards argue that board members need a longer time frame to get to make longer-term-oriented strategic decisions.

Proxy access provides shareholders with the opportunity to propose nominees for the board of directors. This has been an issue of contention for years. In the prevailing system, shareholders must file a separate ballot if they want to nominate their own candidates for director positions. This procedure is time-consuming and costly, so shareholder groups are asking for the ability to place their candidates directly on the proxy materials.

The Role of the SEC

The role of the SEC in the United States is clear; the commission is responsible for protecting investor interests. However, many critics argue that the SEC often appears more focused on the needs of business than on that of investors. In one of the worst scandals in the SEC's 75-year history, the SEC failed to stop the Bernard Madoff Ponzi scheme that cost investors around the world tens of billions of dollars. A **Ponzi scheme** lures investors in with the fake promise of profit but actually pays earlier investors with later investors' money until the scheme collapses.

The SEC failed to stop Madoff in spite of having been warned of the scheme nearly a decade earlier. Harry Markopolos, an independent financial fraud investigator, provided the SEC with both the reasons and the roadmap for investigating Madoff, but they failed to stop the scheme. According to Markopolos, "I gift wrapped and delivered the largest Ponzi scheme in history to them and somehow they couldn't be bothered to conduct a thorough and proper investigation because they were too busy on matters of higher priority."[131] In addition to characterizing the regulatory agency as "financially illiterate," Markopolos considers it plagued by infighting and captive to big industry.[132] It appears that Madoff might agree. In a jailhouse interview, he said he was "astonished" that the regulators did not follow simple procedures such as checking his clearinghouse accounts when complaints surfaced.[133] The first substantive complaint the SEC received about

Madoff was in 1992, 16 years before the scheme imploded.[134] A 2011 movie, *Chasing Madoff*, about Markopolis's ten-year quest to catch Madoff draws heavily from his aptly named book, *No One Would Listen.*[135]

By all accounts, the failure to catch Madoff would be unlikely to happen today. The SEC may be "outmanned" and "outgunned" but, according to Bloomberg BusinessWeek, they are "on a roll."[136]

Shareholder Activism

One major reason that relations between management groups and shareholders have heated up is that shareholders have discovered the benefits of organizing and wielding power. **Shareholder activism** is not a new phenomenon. It dates back 60 years to 1932, when Lewis Gilbert, then a young owner of ten shares, was appalled by the absence of communication between the New York-based Consolidated Gas Company's management and its owners. Supported by a family inheritance, Gilbert decided to quit his job as a newspaper reporter and "fight this silent dictatorship over other people's money." He resolved to devote himself "to the cause of the public shareholder."[137] Today, technology has made it easier for even the smallest investor to obtain information and share news, ideas, and any issues they have with the companies in which they invest.[138] Today, shareholder activism is thriving. Shareholder activists have put forth a record number of proposals that have led to a shift toward greater shareholder power, but they have also created tensions between shareholders and board members.[139]

The History of Shareholder Activism

The history of shareholder activism is too detailed to report fully here, but Gilbert's efforts planted a seed that grew, albeit slowly. The major impetus for the movement came in the 1960s and early 1970s. The early shareholder activists were an unlikely conglomeration—corporate gadflies, political radicals, young lawyers, an assortment of church groups, and a group of physicians.[140] The movement grew out of a period of political and social upheaval—civil rights, the Vietnam War, pollution, and consumerism.

The watershed event for shareholder activism was Campaign GM in the early 1970s, also known as the Campaign to Make General Motors Responsible. Among those involved in this effort was, not surprisingly, Ralph Nader, who is discussed in more detail in Chapter 13. The shareholder group did not achieve all its objectives, but it won enough to demonstrate that shareholder groups could wield power if they worked at it hard enough. Two of Campaign GM's most notable early accomplishments were that (1) the company created a public policy committee of the board, composed of five outside directors, to monitor social performance and (2) GM appointed the Reverend Leon Sullivan as its first black director.[141]

One direct consequence of the success of Campaign GM was the growth of church activism. Church groups were the early mainstay of the corporate social responsibility movement and were among the first shareholder groups to adopt Campaign GM's strategy of raising social issues with corporations. Church groups began examining the relationship between their portfolios and corporate practices, such as minority hiring and companies' presence in South Africa. Church groups remain among the largest groups of institutional stockholders willing to take on the management and press for what they think is right. Many churches' activist efforts are coordinated by the Interfaith Center on Corporate Responsibility (ICCR), which coordinates the shareholder advocacy of about 275 religious orders with about $90 billion in investments. The ICCR was instrumental in convincing Kimberly-Clark to divest the cigarette paper business and pressuring PepsiCo to move out of Burma.[142]

Shareholder activists have historically been socially oriented; that is, they want to exert pressure to make the companies in which they own stock more socially responsive. While that still remains true for many, activist shareholders are now also driven by a concern for profit. Home Depot CEO Robert Nardelli was ousted following pressure from activist shareholders, most notably Ralph Whitworth, cofounder of Relational Investors.[143] The successful ouster was not Whitworth's only goal. He continued to pressure Home Depot to nominate candidates for the board election and to have input in the firm's strategic direction.[144]

The growth of shareholder activism shows no signs of abating.[145] Activist shareholders, known also as **corporate gadflies**, are no longer dismissed as nuisance and are instead viewed as credible, powerful, and a force with which to be reckoned.[146] In fact, money managers and hedge funds advertise their activist orientation in the belief that being seen as aggressive gives them an edge.[147]

Shareholder Resolutions

One of the major vehicles by which shareholder activists communicate their concerns to management groups is through the filing of **shareholder resolutions**. An example of such a resolution is, "The company should name women and minorities to the board of directors." To file a resolution, a shareholder or a shareholder group must obtain a stated number of signatures to require management to place the resolution on the proxy statement so that it can be voted on by all the shareholders. Resolutions that are defeated (fail to get majority votes) may be resubmitted provided they meet certain SEC requirements for such resubmission.

Although an individual could initiate a shareholder resolution, she or he probably would not have the resources or means to obtain the required signatures to have the resolution placed on the proxy. Thus, most resolutions are initiated by large institutional investors that own large blocks of stock or by activist groups that own few shares of stock but have significant financial backing. Foundations, religious groups, universities, and other such large shareholders are in the best position to initiate resolutions. The issues on which shareholder resolutions are filed vary widely, but they typically concern some aspect of a firm's social performance. Resolutions have addressed such issues as executive compensation, animal testing, board structure, sustainability reporting, board diversity, and climate change.[148]

Most shareholder resolutions never pass, and even those that pass are typically nonbinding. So one might ask why groups pursue them. Meredith Benton, research associate with Walden Asset Management, describes why she would come to the point of wanting to put forth a resolution. When an issue arises, the group examines the issue and whether it poses a potential long-term negative impact for the company. The group then approaches the company, and the company may ignore the group, or it may engage in conversation with the group. "If they're ignoring us or strongly disagreeing with our viewpoint," Benton states, "we have one more option, which is shareholder resolution."[149] Benton notes that resolutions are the most public aspect of what they do but that they actually have constructive conversations far more often.[150]

Shareholder Lawsuits

An earlier reference was made to the **shareholder lawsuit** in the TransUnion case. Shareholders sued the board of directors for approving a buyout offer that the shareholders argued should have had a higher price tag. Their suit charged that the directors had been negligent in failing to secure a third-party opinion from experienced investment bankers. The case went to trial and resulted in a $23.5-million judgment against the directors.[151] The TransUnion case may have been one of the largest successful shareholder suits at that time, but it was dwarfed by the Enron settlement of $7.2 billion.[152] At this writing, the largest settlement from the global financial crisis is Bank of America's $2.4 billion settlement with shareholders.

A recent study by the Stanford Law School Securities Class Action Clearinghouse found that federal securities fraud class-action filing activity increased in 2011, but only slightly. A total of 188 federal securities class actions were filed, representing a small increase over the 176 filings the previous year.[153] The study goes on to say that this is 3.1 percent below the annual average of 194 filings observed between 1997 and 2010.[154] The **Private Securities Litigation Reform Act of 1995** was intended to rein in excessive levels of private securities litigation and the trend is downward.[155] Filings also decreased in the first half of 2012, so it is possible things are settling down until another issue appears.[156]

Investor Relations

Over the years, corporate boards have neglected their shareholders. As share ownership has dispersed, there are several legitimate reasons why this separation has taken place. However, the tide seems to be turning as a majority of boards now communicate with their major investors. In the 2012 PWC Corporate Directors Survey, 62 percent of boards indicated they speak with their institutional investors, though one-third said they do not, and should not, have dialogue with investors. These opposing views suggest that boards have a range of relationships with their investors and still struggle with how that relationship should be handled.[157]

Public corporations have obligations to existing shareholders as well as potential shareholders. **Full disclosure** (also known as **transparency**) is one of these responsibilities. Disclosure should be made at regular and frequent intervals and should contain information that might affect the investment decisions of shareholders. This information might include the nature and activities of the business, financial, and policy matters; tender offers; and special problems and opportunities in the near future and in the longer term.[158] Of paramount importance are the interests of the investing public, not the interests of the incumbent management team. Board members should avoid conflicts between personal interests and the interests of shareholders. Company executives and directors have an obligation to avoid taking personal advantage of information that is not disclosed to the investing public and to avoid any personal use of corporation assets and influence.

Another responsibility of management is to communicate with shareholders. Successful shareholder programs do exist. Berkshire Hathaway Inc. is known for attending to its shareholders, and CEO Warren Buffett is praised by shareholders in return.[159] One indication of Berkshire Hathaway's relationship with shareholders is the annual meeting. Buffett calls the annual shareholders' meeting "Woodstock weekend for capitalists." It is not unusual for shareholders to attend a minor league baseball game decked out in their forest green Berkshire Hathaway T-shirts and caps. Many wait in line to have a picture taken with Buffett or get his autograph.[160] Even in a difficult year, Buffett is honest with his shareholders. In his chairman's letter that followed the global financial crisis, Buffett said bluntly, "I did some dumb things in investments."[161] Of course, communicating is easier when you have Buffett's record of serving his shareholders well. Companies that have incidents to explain like Massey Energy's coal facility explosion or BP's Deepwater Horizon rig explosion make communication with shareholders more challenging.[162]

Technology has made investor relations easier to accomplish, and companies have begun to take advantage of it. Companies such as Dell Computer have set up investor relations blogs that not only share information but also give readers an opportunity to communicate with Dell executives.[163] Intel Corporation was the first company to let shareholders use the Internet to vote and submit questions to the annual meeting, and Walmart provides live Twitter and video updates from their annual meetings.[164] Herman Miller, the furniture company, has switched to virtual shareholder meetings, not only enhancing shareholder access but also saving money in the process.[165]

With good investor relations, many serious problems can be averted and those that are unavoidable are less likely to fester. If shareholders are able to make their concerns heard outside the annual meeting, they are less likely to confront managers with hostile questions when the meeting is in session. If their recommendations receive serious consideration, they are less likely to put them in the form of a formal resolution. Constructive engagement is easier for all involved.[166]

An Alternative Model of Corporate Governance

As we mentioned in the beginning of this chapter, the material presented so far is based on the Anglo-American model of corporate governance: It is one of shareholder primacy, that is, it considers shareholders to be of primary importance. As we discussed previously, the shareholder-primacy model asserts that maximizing share value is the ultimate firm goal and that improving corporate governance entails reducing board power, maximizing shareholder power and tying incentives to share price. Activist shareholders have been pursuing these goals with some success, but sometimes that pursuit has strained relations between shareholders and the board.[167] A new perspective is emerging to challenge the traditional model of shareholder primacy. A **director-primacy model** of corporate governance is challenging the status quo and asking whether the balance of power in corporate governance should favor shareholders or board members.[168] Some observers argue that the current push to increase shareholder power represents a sorely needed improvement in corporate governance.[169] Others express skepticism about the value of an increase in shareholder power and argue for a different conception of corporate governance.[170]

A director-primacy model of corporate governance is based on the concept of a corporation that is not owned, but instead is an independent legal entity that owns itself.[171] In it, boards are "mediating hierarchs" who are responsible for balancing the often-competing interests of a variety of stakeholders. In this model, boards have a duty to shareholders, but board members are the ultimate decision makers and their primary duty is to the corporation. From this perspective, board members should be given the autonomy and discretion needed to balance demands that sometimes conflict with each other.[172] Instead of a principal-agent based model, the director-primacy view stems from a **team production model** of corporate governance. Team production notes that the work of a corporation requires the combined input of two or more individuals or groups.[173] From this perspective, corporations are cooperative teams charged with the responsibility of not only creating new wealth but also attending to the interests and needs of stakeholders—and boards should be reflective of that cooperative team.[174] Some analysts suggest that corporations will not be able to fulfill their sustainability and corporate social responsibility goals until corporate boards move away from a singular focus on shareholder wealth maximization.[175]

Many of the proponents for a director-primacy model of corporate governance come from the field of law. They argue that the laws used to support a shareholder-primacy model of corporate governance have been misinterpreted and that shareholders do not own corporations—they only own stock and thus have no legal right to control the firm.[176] Nevertheless, those in support of director primacy place value on shareholder welfare; they simply argue that a director-primacy model of corporate governance will ultimately serve shareholders best because it provides boards of directors the autonomy needed to do what is in the long-term best interests of the corporation.[177] These proponents contend that focusing on share value promotes "short-termism," which eventually can cause harm to firms and all their stakeholders, including shareholders.[178] The pursuit of share value is coming under question by practitioners as well as academics. Between 1997 and 2008, older firms went private and new firms opted not to sell shares, causing the number of U.S. public corporations to drop by more than a third.[179] Former GE CEO Jack Welch, once known as "Neutron Jack," drastically cut employees and basic research expenditures in single-minded pursuit of shareholder value.[180] After the global financial crisis, however, Welch had a different perspective on shareholder primacy[181]:

> *Your main constituents are your employees, your customers, and your products… The idea that shareholder value is a strategy is insane. It is the product of your combined efforts—from the management to the employees.*

The arguments for and against shareholder primacy and director primacy continue to evolve and are not likely to be settled soon. In the meantime, awareness and understanding of both perspectives is helpful in developing a richer understanding of the complexities of corporate governance.

Summary

Recent events in corporate America have served to underscore the importance of good corporate governance and the legitimacy it is supposed to provide for business. To remain legitimate, corporations must be governed according to the intended and legal pattern. Governance debacles, such as the global financial crisis, call not only the legitimacy of individual companies into question but also that of business as a whole.

The modern corporation is a complex entity and so it is not surprising that reasonable people would differ on the model on which corporate governance should be based. The Anglo-American shareholder-primacy model has been a dominant model for years but the director primacy-based team production model is making inroads. In the shareholder-primacy model, the key issue is a separation between ownership and control, which has resulted in problems with managers not always doing what the owners would prefer. From this perspective, boards of directors are responsible for ensuring that managers represent the best interests of owners, but boards sometimes lack the independence needed to monitor management effectively. This has led to serious problems in the corporate governance arena, such as excessive levels of CEO pay and a weak relationship between CEO pay and firm performance. Of course, at times an effort to solve one problem can create another. The use of stock options in CEO compensation has helped tie CEO pay to firm performance more closely, but it has resulted in sky-

rocketing levels of pay, as well as in the manipulation of option timing and pricing. Other issues are lavish executive retirement plans and outside director compensation. New SEC rules for transparency may have an impact on the compensation issue in the future.

In the director-primacy model, the board is a mediating hierarch, responsible for balancing the needs of all the stakeholders. At times, the two models of corporate governance converge but more often they diverge. The Market for Corporate Control is an example. From the shareholder-primacy perspective, the market for corporate control should rein in CEO excesses. The threat of a takeover should motivate a CEO to represent shareholders' best interests. Poison pills become problems because they can blunt the takeover threat by making it prohibitively expensive for an acquirer. In contrast, the director-primacy model would see poison pills as an opportunity to slow the speed of a hostile takeover attempt, providing an opportunity to assure that all stakeholders are well-represented.

SOX was a landmark piece of legislation, drafted in response to the financial scandals of 2001. As with all efforts to improve corporate governance, it has held both costs and benefits. The demands of SOX have led many firms to go private to avoid the costs involved in compliance; however, evidence indicates that firms have adjusted to the requirements and seen positive outcomes from the requirements. The global financial crisis ushered in the Dodd–Frank Wall Street Reform

Act. At this writing, the Act is relatively new and so implementation is still unfolding.

In many ways, corporate governance has improved. CEOs no longer enjoy job security when firm performance suffers. Corporations can no longer release false or misleading reports without threat of consequences. The growth in CEO pay has tapered off, although it remains at extremely high levels. These improvements are worthy of note, but they are insufficient to protect the legitimacy of business. Steps were taken to lessen the likelihood of another Enron or another global financial crisis occurring. Continual vigilance must be maintained if corporate governance is to realize its promise and its purpose, that of being responsive to the needs shareholders and the many individuals and groups who have a stake in the firm, as well as enabling business to be a positive force in society.

Key Terms

Accounting Reform and Investor Protection Act of 2002, p. 108
agency problems, p. 100
Anglo-American model, p. 98
audit committee, p. 110
backdating, p. 102
board of directors, p. 98
bullet-dodging, p. 102
business judgment rule, p. 112
CEO duality, p. 111
charter, p. 98
classified boards, p. 115
clawback provisions, p. 101
compensation committee, p. 111
corporate gadflies, p. 117
corporate governance, p. 98
director-primacy model, p. 119
Dodd–Frank Wall Street Reform and Consumer Protection Act, p. 108
employees, p. 99
fragile mandate, p. 97
full disclosure, p. 118

golden parachute, p. 105
information asymmetry, p. 107
inside directors, p. 101
insider trading, p. 105
legitimacy, p. 97
legitimation, p. 97
majority vote, p. 115
management, p. 98
material information, p. 105
nominating committee, p. 111
out-of-pocket liability, p. 112
outside directors, p. 101
personal liability, p. 112
poison pill, p. 105
Ponzi scheme, p. 115
Private Securities Litigation Reform Act of 1995, p. 118
proxy access, p. 115
Regulation FD (fair disclosure), p. 107
Sarbanes–Oxley Act (aka SOX or Sarbox), p. 108

Say on Pay movement, p. 103
SEC Rule 10b5-1, p. 106
SEC Rule 10b5-2, p. 106
separation of ownership from control, p. 99
shareholder activism, p. 116
shareholder democracy, p. 114
shareholder lawsuit, p. 117
shareholder-primacy model, p. 98
shareholder resolutions, p. 117
shareholders, p. 98
spring-loading, p. 102
staggered boards, p. 115
stock options, p. 102
tax gross-up, p. 104
team production model, p. 119
tippee, p. 106
tipper, p. 106
transparency, p. 118

Discussion Questions

1. Explain the evolution of corporate governance. What problems developed? What are the current trends?
2. What are the major criticisms of boards of directors? Which single criticism do you find to be the most important? Why?
3. Explain how governance failures such as Enron and the global financial crisis could happen. How might they be avoided?

4. Outline the major suggestions that have been set forth for improving corporate governance. In your opinion, which suggestions are the most important? Why?
5. Discuss the pros and cons of the shareholder-primacy and director-primacy models of corporate governance. Which do you prefer and why?

Endnotes

1. OECD Observer No 273 (June 2009): http://www.oec
    dobserver.org/news/fullstory.php/aid/2931/Corporate_
    governance:_Lessons_from_the_financial_crisis.html.
    Accessed November 12, 2012.

2. Robert A. G. Monks and Nell Minow, *Corporate gover-
    nance* (4th. ed.) (West Sussex, England: John Wiley &
    Sons, 2008), 3.

3. Curtis C. Verschoor, "Can Government Manage More
    Ethically Than Capitalism," *Strategic Finance* (October,
    2009), 15–16 & 73.

4. Cited in Edwin M. Epstein and Dow Votaw (eds.)
    *Rationality, Legitimacy, Responsibility: Search for New
    Directions in Business and Society* (Santa Monica, CA:
    Goodyear Publishing Co., 1978), 72.

5. Ibid., 73.

6. Ibid.

7. Ibid.

8. Ibid.

9. William R. Dill (ed.), *Running the American Corpora-
    tion* (Englewood Cliffs, NJ: Prentice Hall, 1978), 11.

10. Ibid.

11. Richard C. Warren, "The Evolution of Business Legiti-
    macy," *European Business Review* (Vol. 15, No. 3, 2003),
    153–163.

12. Ibid.

13. "Special Report: Corporate America's Woes, Continued—
    Enron: One Year On," *The Economist* (November 30,
    2002).

14. Ewald Engelen, "Corporate Governance, Property and
    Democracy: A Conceptual Critique of Shareholder Ide-
    ology," *Economy & Society* (August, 2002), 391–413;
    Henry Hansmann, H. and R. Kraakman, "The End of
    History for Corporate Law," *Georgetown Law Journal*
    (January, 2001), 439.

15. Christine Mallin, "Corporate Governance Develop-
    ments in the U.K.," in Christine Mallin (ed.) *Handbook
    on International Corporate Governance* (Northampton,
    MA: Edward Elgar, 2006).

16. Lynn Stout, *The Shareholder Value Myth* (San Fran-
    cisco, CA: Berrett-Koehler Publishers, Inc., 2012).

17. Carl Icahn, "What Ails Corporate America—And What
    Should Be Done," *BusinessWeek* (October 17, 1986),
    101.

18. *Insights from the Boardroom 2012: Board Evolution:
    Progress Made, Yet Challenges Persist*, pwc.com/us/
    CenterForBoardGovernance [Accessed December 20,
    2012].

19. Ibid.

20. "What Directors Think Study 2011," *Corporate Board
    Member*, http://www.boardmember.com. Accessed
    December 21, 2012.

21. Jack Welch and Suzy Welch, "How Much Blame Do
    Boards Deserve?" *BusinessWeek* (January 14, 2009),
    http://www.businessweek.com/stories/2009-01-13/how-
    much-blame-do-boards-deserve. Accessed January 2,
    2013.

22. Elizabeth G. Olson, "Executive Pay Clawbacks: Just a
    Shareholder Pacifier?," *CNNMoney*, http://management
    .fortune.cnn.com/2012/08/16/executive-pay-clawbacks/.
    Accessed December 28, 2012.

23. Ibid.

24. David Chun, "From '06 to '09, Fortune 100 Companies
    Disclosing Clawbacks Jump From 17 to 72 Percent,"
    Equilar CEO Blog (November 18, 2009), http://www
    .executive-compensation.com/ceo_blog/?p=240. Accessed
    December 28, 2012.

25. Adam Lashinsky, "Why Option Backdating Is a Big
    Deal," *Fortune* (July 26, 2006), http://money.cnn.com/
    2006/07/26/magazines/fortune/lashinsky.fortune/index
    .htm. Accessed January 1, 2013.

26. http://www.aflcio.org/Corporate-Watch/CEO-Pay-and-
    the-99. Accessed January 2, 2013.

27. Ibid.

28. Chris Gay, "Can Huge CEO Golden Parachutes Hurt You?"
    U.S. News Money (November 4, 2012), http://money.us
    news.com/money/personal-finance/mutual-funds/articles/
    2012/11/14/can-huge-ceo-golden-parachutes-hurt-you.
    Accessed December 10, 2012.

29. Sarah Anderson, Chuck Collins, Scott Klinger, and Sam
    Pizzigati, "Executive Excess 2012: The CEO Hands in
    Uncle Sam's Pocket," http://www.ips-dc.org/reports/
    executive_excess_2012. Accessed January 2, 2013.

30. Leslie Kwoh, "Firms Resist New Pay-Equity Rules," *The
    Wall Street Journal* (June 26, 2012), http://online.wsj
    .com/article/SB10001424052702304458604577490842258
    4787190.html?mod=WSJ_hp_LEFTWhatsNewsCollection.
    Accessed January 2, 2013.

31. Paul Hodgson, "A Brief History of Say on Pay," *Ivey Busi-
    ness Journal* (September/October 2009), http://www.ivey
    businessjournal.com/topics/leadership/a-brief-history-of-
    say-on-pay. Accessed January 1, 2013.

32. Ibid.

33. Diane Brady, "Say on Pay: Boards Listen When Share-
    holders Speak," *Bloomberg BusinessWeek* (June 7, 2012),
    http://www.businessweek.com/articles/2012-06-07/say-on-
    pay-boards-listen-when-shareholders-speak. Accessed
    December 30, 2012.

34. Ibid.

35. Ibid.

36. Ibid.

37. http://www.global100.org/methodology/selection-criteria
    .html. Accessed March 17, 2013.

38. Clean Capitalism Defined, http://www.corporateknights .com/article/clean-capitalism-defined?page=show. Accessed June 4, 2013.

39. Gretchen Morgenson, "Making Managers Pay, Literally," *The New York Times* (March 25, 2007), 1.

40. Deborah Lifshey, "Summary of Clawback Policies Under Dodd–Frank Reform Act," Boardmember.com, https:// www.boardmember.com/summary-of-clawback-policies-under-dodd-frank-reform-act.aspx. Accessed January 1, 2013.

41. Randy Diamond "CII Gets Specific on Its Clawback Recommendations," Pensions & Investments (October 5, 2012), http://www.pionline.com/article/20121005/DAI LYREG/121009896

42. Ibid.

43. ALF-CIO. ExecutivePayWatch, http://www.aflcio.org/ paywatch. Accessed January 3, 2013.

44. John J. Sweeney, "Commentary: The Foxes Are Still Guarding the Henhouse," *Los Angeles Times* (September 19, 2003), B13.

45. "Relentless Activism," *Directorship* (January/February, 2007), 1–13.

46. Alyce Gomstin, "Why Bank of America's Ken Lewis Will Take Home More Than Peers," *ABC News Business Unit* (October 8, 2009), http://abcnews.go.com/Business/bank-america-ceo-ken-lewis-retirement-pay-higher/story?id=87 75299#.UOX7POQpiDk. Accessed December 29, 2012.

47. Stephanie Costo, "Trends in Retirement Plan Coverage Over the Last Decade," *Bureau of Labor Statistics* (February, 2006), http://www.bls.gov/opub/mlr/2006/02/art5full. pdf. Accessed December 29, 2012.

48. Fran Hawthorne, "For Top Executives, Richer Retirement Plans," *The New York Times* (September 11, 2012), http://www.nytimes.com/2012/09/12/business/retirement special/companies-beef-up-retirement-plans-for-top-exec utives.html?pagewanted=all&_r=0. Accessed December 30, 2012.

49. Geoffrey Colvin, "Is the Board Too Cushy?" *Director* (February 1997), 64–65.

50. Peter Miterko and Richard King, "A New Elephant In the Room: Corporate Director Pay," https://www.board member.com/Article_Details.aspx?id=7116. Accessed January 2, 2013.

51. Nanette Byrnes and Jane Sasseen, "Board of Hard Knocks," *BusinessWeek* (January 22, 2007), 35–39.

52. Ibid.

53. Kwoh, 2012.

54. Ibid.

55. Ibid.

56. Matt Orsagh, "SEC: "More Transparency Please" on Executive Compensation," *Market Integrity Insights* (June 22, 2012), http://blogs.cfainstitute.org/marketin tegrity/2012/06/22/sec-more-transparency-please-on-exe cutive-compensation/.

57. Heidi N. Moore, "The Demise of Poison Pills?: Why Takeover Defenses Have Been on the Wane; Shareholders vs. Boards," *The Wall Street Journal* (February 24, 2009), C4.

58. David Futrelle, "Corporate Raiders Beware: A Short History of the "Poison Pill" Defense," *Time* (November 7, 2012), http://business.time.com/2012/11/07/corporate-raiders-beware-a-short-history-of-the-poison-pill-takeover-defense/. Accessed November 5, 2012.

59. Dealbook, "Netflix Adopts Poison Pill," DealBook (November 5, 2012), http://dealbook.nytimes.com/2012/ 11/05/netflix-adopts-poison-pill/. Accessed November 29, 2012.

60. Philip L. Cochran and Steven L. Wartick, "Golden Parachutes: Good for Management and Society?" in S. Prakash Sethi and Cecilia M. Falbe (eds.) *Business and Society: Dimensions of Conflict and Cooperation* (Lexington, MA: Lexington Books, 1987), 321.

61. Ann K. Buchholtz and Barbara A. Ribbens, "Role of Chief Executive Officers in Takeover Resistance: Effects of CEO Incentives and Individual Characteristics," *Academy of Management Journal* (June 1994), 554–579.

62. Cochran and Wartick, 325–326.

63. Gay, 2012.

64. Phred Dvorak, "Companies Cut Holes in CEOs' Golden Parachutes: New Disclosure Rules Prompt More Criticism of Guaranteed Payouts," *The Wall Street Journal* (September 15, 2008), B4.

65. Equilar Study: Change in Control Case Severance Analysis, http://www.equilar.com/knowledge-network/research-arti cles/2011/201108-change-in-control.php. Accessed January 2, 2013.

66. http://www.sec.gov/answers/insider.htm/. Accessed December 30, 2012.

67. Josh Clark, "How Insider Trading Works," *howstuffworks*, http://money.howstuffworks.com/insider-trading .htm. Accessed December 29, 2012.

68. http://www.sec.gov/answers/insider.htm. Accessed December 30, 2012.

69. http://www.investopedia.com/articles/03/100803.asp#ax zz2H1MnmQGw. Accessed December 30, 2012.

70. Ibid.

71. Peter Henning, "String of Inside Trading Cases Shows Prosecutors Casting a Wider Net," *The New York Times* (December 3, 2012), http://dealbook.nytimes.com/2012/ 12/03/string-of-insider-trading-cases-shows-prosecutors-casting-a-wider-net/. Accessed December 30, 2012.

72. Alex Berenson, "A Deal That Lost Millions for Galleon," *The New York Times* (October 20, 2009), http:// www.nytimes.com/2009/10/21/business/21insider.html. Accessed January 1, 2013.

73. "SEC Enforcement Cases Hit Record High in 2011," *Thomson Reuters Insight* (November 9, 2011), _November/ SEC_enforcement_cases_hit_record_high_in_2011/. Accessed December 29, 2012.; Josh Clark, "How Insider Trading

Works," *howstuffworks*, http://money.howstuffworks .com/insider-trading.htm. Accessed December 29, 2012.

74. http://www.sec.gov/answers/insider.htm. Accessed December 30, 2012.

75. Peter J. Henning, "The Evolving Contours of Inside Trading," *The New York Times* (July 30, 2012), http:// dealbook.nytimes.com/2012/07/30/the-evolving-contours-of-insider-trading/. Accessed January 1, 2013.

76. Ibid.

77. Ibid.

78. Ibid.

79. Christopher H. Schmitt, "The SEC Lifts the Curtain on Company Info," *BusinessWeek* (August 11, 2000).

80. Michael Schlesinger, "2002 Sarbanes–Oxley Act," *Business Entities* (November/December 2002), 42–49.

81. Ibid.

82. Jonathon A. Segal, "The Joy of Uncooking," *HR Magazine* (November 2002), 52–57.

83. Brian Christensen and Jim DeLoach, "How Sarbanes-Oxley Has Affected Internal Controls and Compliance: A 10th Anniversary Review," (August 16, 2012), http:// cfocompass.bpmcpa.com/sarbanes-oxley-part-i-look ing-back-and-looking-ahead-a-10-year-review-of-sox/. Accessed January 1, 2013.

84. Ibid.

85. Michael Santoro and Ronald Strauss, *Wall Street Values: Business Ethics and the Financial Crisis* (New York: Cambridge University Press, 2013), 19.

86. http://theabd.org/Reports.html, Accessed December 31, 2012.

87. Johanne Grosvold, Stephen Pavelin, and Ian Tonks, "Gender Diversity on Company Boards," *Vox* (March 27, 2012), http://www.voxeu.org/article/women-board-room. Accessed January 4, 2013.

88. Joan Warner, "Get Ready for a Red-Hot Season," *Directorship* (December 2006–January 2007), 1–27.

89. Stephanie Holmes, "Smashing the Glass Ceiling," *BBC News* (January 11, 2008), http://news.bbc.co.uk/2/hi/ business/7176879.stm. Accessed January 4, 2013.

90. Nicola Clark, "Getting Women into Boardrooms, by Law," *The New York Times* (January 28, 2010), http://www .nytimes.com/2010/01/28/world/europe/28iht-quota.html? pagewanted=all. Accessed January 5, 2013.

91. Ibid.

92. Grosvold *et al.*, 2012.

93. Thomas W. Joo, "A Trip through the Maze of 'Corporate Democracy': Shareholder Voice and Management Composition," *St. John's Law Review* (Fall, 2003), 735–767.

94. Steven A. Ramirez, "A Flaw in the Sarbanes–Oxley Reform: Can Diversity in the Boardroom Quell Corporate Corruption?" *St. John's Law Review* (Fall, 2003), 837–866.

95. Niclas L. Erhardt, James D. Werbel, and Charles B. Shrader, "Board of Director Diversity and Firm Financial Performance," *Corporate Governance: An International Review* (April 2003), 102–111.

96. Eric Helland and Michael Sykuta, "Who's Monitoring the Monitor? Do Outside Directors Protect Shareholders' Interests?" *Financial Review* (May 2005), 155–172.

97. Richard A. Johnson and Daniel W. Greening, "The Effects of Corporate Governance and Institutional Ownership Types on Corporate Social Performance," *Academy of Management Journal* (October 1999), 564–576.

98. Del Jones, "Board, CEO Ties Found among TARP Companies," *USA Today* (April 3, 2009).

99. Maxwell Murphy, "A 'Waste of a Board Seat,'" *The Wall Street Journal* (October 16, 2012), B1.

100. Ibid.

101. Michael W. Peregrine, "The Independent Director: A Key Sarbanes Legacy," Boardmember.com: https://www .boardmember.com/the-independent-director-a-key-sarb anes-legacy.aspx. Accessed December 30, 2012.

102. The Sarbanes–Oxley Act 2002, LegalArchiver.Org, http://www.legalarchiver.org/soa.htm. Accessed January 4, 2013.

103. Charles A. Anderson and Robert N. Anthony, *The New Corporate Directors: Insights for Board Members and Executives* (New York: John Wiley & Sons, 1986), 141.

104. http://www.investor.jnj.com/governance/committee .cfm. Accessed March 29, 2013.

105. http://www.unilever.com/investorrelations/corp_gover nance/boardandmanagementcommittees/. Accessed March 29, 2013.

106. Anthony Bianco and Louis Lavelle, "The CEO Trap," *BusinessWeek* (December 11, 2000), 86–92.

107. David R. Francis and Seth Stern, "Era of Shaky Job Security for the CEO," *Christian Science Monitor* (December 4, 2003), Web edition. http://www.csmon itor.com/2003/ 1204/p01s01-usec.html. Accessed January 5, 2013.

108. Sydney Finkelstein and Richard D'Aveni, "CEO Duality as a Double-Edged Sword: How Boards of Directors Balance Entrenchment Avoidance and Unity of Command," *Academy of Management Journal* (Vol. 37, No. 5, 1994), 1079–1106.

109. Ibid.

110. Joann S. Lublin, "More CEOs Sharing Control at the Top," *The Wall Street Journal* (June 7, 2012), B1–B2.

111. Nanette Byrnes and David Kiley, "Hello, You Must Be Going," *BusinessWeek* (February 12, 2007), 30–32.

112. Penny Herscher, "The Rise in CEO Turnover Is a Sign of the Times—Both Good and Bad," *The Huffington Post* (January 17, 2009), http://www.huffingtonpost .com/penny-herscher/the-rise-in-ceo-turnover_b_158736 .html. Accessed January 5, 2013.

113. Anthony Bianco and Louis Lavelle, "The CEO Trap," *BusinessWeek* (December 11, 2000), 86–92.

114. Ibid.

115. "A Landmark Ruling That Puts Board Members in Peril," *BusinessWeek* (March 18, 1985), 56–57.

116. Laurie Baum and John A. Byrne, "The Job Nobody Wants: Outside Directors Find That the Risks and Hassles Just Aren't Worth It," *BusinessWeek* (September 8, 1986), 57.

117. Paul E. Fiorella, "Why Comply? Directors Face Heightened Personal Liability After Caremark," *Business Horizons* (July/August 1998), 49–52.

118. "Liability & Litigation," *Corporate Board* (January/February 2007), 28–29.

119. J. P. Donlon. "The Flaw of Law," *Directorship* (February 2005), 3.

120. "Liability & Litigation," 28.

121. Jennifer B. Rubin, "A View from the Bar: Directors Can Be Liable for Layoffs, Plant Closings," *Corporate Board Member* (Third Quarter 2009), https://www.boardmember.com/MagazineArticle_Details.aspx?id=3879&terms=Rubin+view+from+bar. Accessed January 4, 2013.

122. "Ownership Matters," *The Economist* (March 11, 2006), 10.

123. Joo, 735–767.

124. "What Shareholder Democracy?" *The Economist* (March 26, 2005), 62.

125. "Who Selects, Governs," *Directorship* (May 2004), 6.

126. Dennis M. Ray, "Corporate Boards and Corporate Democracy," *Journal of Corporate Citizenship* (Winter, 2005), 93–105.

127. Lucien A. Bebchuk. "The Case for Increasing Shareholder Power," *Harvard Law Review* (January 2005), 835–914.

128. Iman Anabtawi and Lynn A. Stout, "Fiduciary Duties for Activist Shareholders," *Stanford Law Review* (February 2008), 1255–1329.

129. Lynn A. Stout, "Corporations Shouldn't Be Democracies," *The Wall Street Journal—Eastern Edition* (September 27, 2007), A17.

130. Joann S. Lublin, "Directors Lose Elections but Not Seats: Staying Power of Board Members Raises Questions about Investor Democracy," *The Wall Street Journal* (September 28, 2009), B4.

131. Allan Chernoff, "Madoff Whistleblower Blasts SEC," CNNMoney.com (February 4, 2009), http://money.cnn.com/2009/02/04/news/newsmakers/madoff_whistleblower/. Accessed June 25, 2010.

132. Ibid.

133. Diana B. Henriquez, "Lapses Helped Scheme, Madoff Told Investigators," *The New York Times* (October 30, 2009), A1.

134. Ibid.

135. Daniel M. Gold, "The High Human Cost of Following the Money in the Madoff Fraud Case," *The New York Times* (August 25, 2011), http://movies.nytimes.com/2011/08/26/movies/chasing-madoff-a-documentary-of-a-fraud-review.html?_r=0. Accessed January 4, 2013.

136. Devin Leonard, "Outmanned, Outgunned, and On a Roll," *Bloomberg BusinessWeek* (April 23–29, 2012), 59–66.

137. Lauren Tainer, *The Origins of Shareholder Activism* (Washington, DC: Investor Responsibility Research Center, July 1983), 2.

138. Rob Curran, "Small Investor, Bigger Voice," *The Wall Street Journal* (December 3, 2009), R8.

139. Jennifer G. Hill 2010. "The Rising Tension between Shareholder and Director Power in the Common Law World," *Corporate Governance: An International Review* (July 2010), 344–359.

140. Ibid., 1.

141. Ibid., 12–22.

142. "Religious Activists Raise Cain with Corporations," *Chicago Tribune* (June 7, 1998), *Business Section*, 8.

143. Charles Duhigg, "Gadflies Get Respect, and Not Just at Home Depot," *The New York Times* (January 5, 2007), 1.

144. Ibid.

145. Joan Warner, "Get Ready for a Red-Hot Season," *Directorship* (December 2006–January 2007), 1–27.

146. Duhigg, 2007.

147. Ibid.

148.

149. "How Shareholder Resolutions Influence Corporate Behavior," *Christian Science Monitor Daily Online Newspaper* (May 1, 2006).

150. Ibid.

151. Thomas J. Neff, "Liability Panic in the Board Room," *The Wall Street Journal* (November 10, 1986), 22.

152. Dan Fitzpatrick, Christian Berthelson, and Robin Sidel, "BofA Takes New Crisis-Era Hit," *The Wall Street Journal* (September 29–30, 2012), B1–B2.

153. Cornerstone Research, "Securities Class Action Filings 2011: *A Year in Review,*" http://www.cornerstone.com/securities_class_action_filings_2011_year_in_review/ Accessed January 5, 2013.

154. Ibid.

155. Ibid.

156. Kevin LaCroix, "Cornerstone Research Releases Mid-Year 2012 Securities Litigation Report," *Cornerstone Research* (July 25, 2012), http://www.dandodiary.com/2012/07/articles/securities-litigation/cornerstone-research-releases-midyear-2012-securities-litigation-report/. Accessed January 4, 2013.

157. *Insights from the Boardroom 2012: Board Evolution: Progress Made, Yet Challenges Persist,* pwc. com/us/CenterForBoardGovernance. Accessed December 20, 2012.

158. "The Responsibility of a Corporation to Its Shareholders," *Criteria for Decision Making* (C. W. Post Center, Long Island University, 1979), 14.

159. Mel Duvall and Kim S. Nash, "Auditing an Oracle: Shareholders Nearly Deify Warren Buffett for the Way He Manages His Diverse Holding Company, Bershire Hathaway of Omaha," *Baseline* (August 1, 2003), 30.

160. Amy Kover, "Warren Buffett: Revivalist," *Fortune* (May 29, 2000), 58–60.

161. Alex Crippen, "Warren Buffet Tells Shareholders he Did "Some Dumb Things" in 2008," *CNBC* (February 28, 2009), http://www.cnbc.com/id/29441086/Warren_ Buffett_Tells_Shareholders_He_Did_quotSome_Dumb_ Thingsquot_In_2008. Accessed January 5, 2013.

162. Michael McGinn, "Disclose No Evil," *Newsweek* (February 28, 2011), 5.

163. Rob Curran, "Small Investor, Bigger Voice," *The Wall Street Journal* (December 3, 2009), R8.

164. Ibid.

165. Ibid.

166. Warner, 2007.

167. Hill, 2010.

168. Margaret M. Blair and Lynn A. Stout, "A Team Production Theory Of Corporate Law," *Virginia Law Review* (March, 1999), 247–329; Stephen M. Bainbridge, "Director Primacy and Shareholder Disempowerment," *Harvard Law Review* (April 2006), 1735–1758; Luh Luh Lan and Loizos Heracleous, "Rethinking Agency Theory: The View From the Law," *Academy of Management Review* (April 2010) 223–239.

169. Lucien A. Bebchuk, Cohen A, Ferrell A. 2009. "What matters in corporate governance?" *Review of Financial Studies* (February 2009), 783–827.

170. Iman Anabtawi, "Some skepticism about increasing shareholder power," *UCLA Law Review* (February 2006), 561–599.

171. Lynn A. Stout, *The Shareholder Value Myth* (San Francisco, CA: Berrett-Koehler, 2012).

172. Blair and Stout, 1999.

173. Ibid.

174. Allen Kaufman and Ernie Englander, "A Team Production Model of Corporate Governance," *Academy of Management Executive* (August 1, 2005), 9–22.

175. Edward E. Lawler and Christopher G. Worley, "Why Boards Need to Change," *MIT Sloan Management Review* (Fall 2012), 10–12.

176. Stout, 2010.

177. Stout, 2012.

178. Ibid.

179. Ibid.

180. Ibid.

181. Francesco Guerrera, "Welch condemns share price focus," *Financial Times* (March 12, 2009), http://www.ft .com/cms/s/0/294ff1f2-0f27-11de-ba10-0000779fd2ac .html. Accessed December 17, 2012.

5

Strategic Management and Corporate Public Policy

CHAPTER LEARNING OUTCOMES

After studying this chapter, you should be able to:

1. Describe the concept of corporate public policy and relate it to strategic management.

2. Articulate the four major strategy levels and explain enterprise-level strategy.

3. Explain social entrepreneurship and relate it to the benefit corporation.

4. Explain sustainability reports and integrated reporting.

5. Link public affairs with the strategic management function.

6. Indicate how public affairs may be incorporated into every manager's job.

I n this chapter and the next, we more closely examine how management has responded and should respond to the kinds of social, ethical, and stakeholder issues developed in this book. In this chapter, we provide a broad overview of strategic management and discuss how social, ethical, and public issues fit into this concept. We introduce the term **corporate public policy** to describe that component of management decision making that embraces these issues. Then we discuss corporate public affairs, or public affairs management, as the formal organizational approach companies use in implementing these initiatives. The overriding goal of this chapter is to focus on planning for the turbulent social/ethical stakeholder environment, and this encompasses the strategic management process, integrated and social reporting, and public affairs management.

The Concept of Corporate Public Policy

While the impact of the environmental/social/ethical/global stakeholder environment on business organizations has always been powerful, it seems to grow stronger each year. Ford Motor Company and its disastrous Pinto gas tank problem, Johnson & Johnson and its tainted Tylenol capsules, Exxon's catastrophic *Valdez* oil spill, and Enron's financial meltdown are *classic* reminders of how social issues can directly affect a firm and its stakeholders. More recently, we have seen the LIBOR scandal that involved banks manipulating key interest rates and the Walmart bribery scandal that involved the alleged bribing of Mexican officials to obtain permission to build a store on the site of ancient ruins. These scandals, along with the terrible tragedy of the Tazreen Fashions Factory fire in Bangladesh that killed 122 people, remind us of the toll that corporate inattention to public policy matters can take.

What started as a simple awareness of social issues and social responsibility has matured into a focus on the management of sustainability, reflected in the triple bottom line. Sustainability is now a strategic issue with far-reaching implications for organizational purpose, direction, and functioning. This issue comes under *corporate public policy*, which can also be called *corporate sustainability policy, corporate public affairs,* or *corporate citizenship.*

Corporate Public Policy Defined

What is corporate public policy?

Corporate public policy is a firm's posture, stance, strategy, or position regarding the environmental, social, global, and ethical aspects of stakeholders and corporate functioning.

Later in the chapter, we discuss how businesses formalize this concern under the rubric of **corporate public affairs**, or public affairs management. Businesses encounter several situations daily that involve highly visible public and ethical issues, including those that are subject to intensive public debate for specific periods before being institutionalized. Examples of such issues have included sexual harassment, affirmative action, product safety, and employee privacy. Other issues that are more basic, more enduring, and more philosophical might include the broad role of business in society, the corporate governance question, and the relative balance of business versus government direction that is best for our society.

The idea behind corporate public policy is that a firm must give specific attention to issues in which basic questions of justice, fairness, ethics, or public policy reside. Today's dynamic stakeholder environment necessitates that managers employ a policy perspective to these issues. At one time, the social environment was thought to be a relatively constant backdrop against which the real work of business took place. Today, these issues are central, and managers at all levels must address them. Corporate public policy is the process by which management addresses these significant concerns.

Corporate Public Policy and Strategic Management

Where does corporate public policy fit into strategic management? First, let us briefly discuss strategic management. Strategic management refers to the overall management process that strives to identify corporate purpose and to position a firm to succeed in its market environment. A basic way in which the firm relates to its market environment is through the products and services it produces and the markets in which it chooses to participate. **Strategic management** incorporates environmental, ethical, and social concerns, with the realization that the long-term viability of a corporation is linked inextricably with its impact on the economy, society, and the environment—it requires that firms operate very differently from the way that many do.[1]

Corporate public policy incorporates sustainability as that part of the overall strategic management of the organization that focuses on the environmental, economic, social, and ethical stakeholder issues that are embedded in the decision processes of the firm. Therefore, just as a firm needs to develop policy on functional areas such as human resources, operations, marketing, or finance, it also must develop corporate *public* policy to address proactively the host of issues discussed throughout this book.

Citizens Bank of Canada is a company that concluded it needed a formal corporate public policy. As a company trying to build a strong reputation in the CSR area since opening its doors more than a decade ago, the bank's management concluded that it needed to do more than establish a few enlightened policies. It needed something that would set a systematic course and foundation for "doing well by doing good." Citizens' first step was to establish a document of guiding principles, called an *ethical policy*, which would steer the firm's practices toward its social and environmental commitments. To implement its policy and follow up on implementation, the bank created an "ethical policy compliance" unit.[2] The Citizens' initiatives illustrate the value of a formalized public policy. It became the first North American-based bank to become carbon neutral, and it achieved this goal two years ahead of schedule.[3] In that same year, the bank donated $50,000 to Habitat for Humanity and one day of volunteering to nonprofit causes.[4]

Relationship of Ethics to Strategic Management

A consideration of ethics is implicit in corporate public policy discussions, but it is useful to make this relationship more explicit. Over the years, a growing number of observers have stressed this point. The leadership challenge of determining future strategy in the face of rising moral and ethical standards may be the most strenuous in strategic decision making, particularly stressful within the inherently amoral corporation.[5]

The focus of linking ethics and strategy moved to center stage in the book *Corporate Strategy and the Search for Ethics,* which argued that if business ethics were to have any meaning beyond pompous moralizing, it should be linked to business strategy. The theme was that the concept of corporate strategy could be revitalized by linking ethics to strategy. This linkage permits addressing the most pressing management issues of the day in ethical terms. The book introduces the idea of *enterprise strategy* as the one that best links these two vital notions, and this concept is examined in more detail in the next section.[6]

The concept of corporate public policy and the linkage between ethics and strategy are better understood when we think about the

1. four key levels at which strategy decisions arise, and
2. steps in the strategic management process in which these decisions are embedded.

Four Key Strategy Levels

Because organizations are hierarchical, it is not surprising to find that strategic management also is hierarchical in nature; that is, the firm has several levels at which strategic decisions are made, or the strategy process occurs. These levels range from the broadest or highest levels (where missions, visions, goals, and decisions entail higher risks and are characterized by longer time horizons, more subjective values, and greater uncertainty) to the lowest levels (where planning is done for specific functional areas and are characterized by shorter time horizons, less complex information needs, and less uncertainty). Four key strategy levels are important: (1) enterprise-level strategy, (2) corporate-level strategy, (3) business-level strategy, and (4) functional-level strategy.

Four Strategy Levels Described

Enterprise-Level Strategy. The broadest level of strategic management is known as *societal-level strategy* or *enterprise-level strategy.* **Enterprise-level strategy** is the overarching strategy level that poses such basic questions as, "What is the role of the organization in society?" and "For what do we stand?" As will be evident from the detailed discussion later, this encompasses the development and articulation of corporate public policy and may be considered the first and most important level at which ethics and strategy are linked. Corporate governance is one of the most important topics at this level.

Corporate-Level Strategy. **Corporate-level strategy** addresses what is often posed as the most defining business question for a firm, "In what business(es) should we be?" Thus, mergers, acquisitions, and divestitures, as well as whether and how to participate in global markets, are examples of decisions made at this level. A host of issues related to ethics and sustainability arise at this level as well.

Business-Level Strategy. **Business-level strategy** is concerned with the question, "How should we compete in a given business or industry?" Thus, a company whose products or services take it into many different businesses, industries, or markets will need a business-level strategy to define its competitive posture in each of them. A competitive strategy might address whether a product should be low cost or differentiated, as well as whether it should compete in broad or narrow markets and how to do so in a sustainable way.

Functional-Level Strategy. **Functional-level strategy** addresses the question, "How should a firm integrate its various subfunctional activities and how should these activities be related to changes taking place in the diverse functional areas (finance, marketing, human resources, and operations)?"[7] Companies need to ascertain that their functional areas conduct themselves in ways that are consistent with the values for which the firm stands.

The purpose of identifying the four strategy levels is to clarify that corporate public policy is primarily a part of enterprise-level strategy, which, in turn, is but one level of strategic decision making that occurs in organizations. In terms of its implementation, however, the other strategy levels inevitably come into play, and all levels play a part in fulfilling a firm's commitment to its values. Figure 5-1 illustrates that enterprise-level strategy is the broadest strategy level and that the other levels are narrower concepts that cascade from it.

Emphasis on Enterprise-Level Strategy

The term *enterprise-level strategy* is not used frequently in the business community, but it is helpful to understand the concept. Although many firms address the issues with which enterprise-level strategy is concerned, use of this terminology is concentrated primarily in the academic community. This terminology describes the level of strategic thinking necessary if firms are to be fully responsive to today's complex and dynamic stakeholder environment. Most organizations convey their enterprise or societal strategy in their vision, missions, or values statements. Others embed their enterprise strategies in codes of conduct. Increasingly, these strategies reflect a global level of application.

Enterprise-level strategy needs to be thought of as a concept that more closely aligns social and ethical concerns with traditional business concerns.[8] In setting the direction for a firm, a manager needs to understand the impact of changes in business strategy on the underlying values of the firm and the new stakeholder relations that will consequently emerge and take shape. Thus, at the enterprise level, the task of setting strategic direction involves understanding the role in

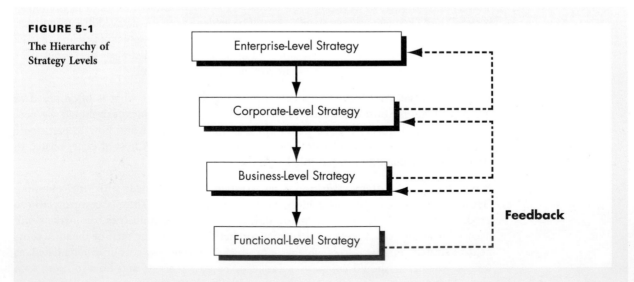

FIGURE 5-1

The Hierarchy of Strategy Levels

Enterprise-Level Strategy

Corporate-Level Strategy

Business-Level Strategy

Feedback

Functional-Level Strategy

society of a particular firm as a whole and its relationships to other social institutions. Important questions then become

- What is the role of our organization in society?
- How do our stakeholders perceive our organization?
- What principles or values does our organization represent?
- What obligations do we have to society, including to the world?
- What are the broad implications for our current mix of businesses and allocation of resources?

Many firms have addressed some of these questions—perhaps only in part or in an ad hoc way. The point of enterprise-level strategy, however, is that the firm needs to address these questions intentionally, specifically, and cohesively in such a way that a corporate public policy is articulated.

How have business firms addressed these questions? What are the manifestations of enterprise-level thinking and corporate public policy? The manifestations show up in various ways in different companies, such as a firm's response when faced with public crises. Does it respond to its stakeholders in a positive, constructive, and sensitive way or in a negative, defensive, and insensitive way? Corporate decisions and actions reveal the presence or absence of soundly developed enterprise-level strategy. Companies also demonstrate the degree of thinking that has gone into public issues by the presence or absence and use or nonuse of codes of ethics, codes of conduct, mission statements, values statements, corporate creeds, vision statements, or other such policy-oriented codes and statements.

Social Entrepreneurship Although enterprise strategy is relevant for all firms, it holds special importance in **social entrepreneurship.** Social entrepreneurship is a cultural phenomenon that has been growing exponentially.[9] In spite of its popularity, it remains "a term in search of a good definition."[10] Social entrepreneurs differ from traditional entrepreneurs in that the social entrepreneurship enterprise has a mission of societal value creation as its reason for being. Socially responsible businesses may create social value en route to creating wealth, but wealth creation remains their ultimate goal. Social entrepreneurs must create wealth to survive and thrive as well, but it is a means to an end of social value creation. The social mission is fundamental to social entrepreneurship. J. Gregory Dees, Professor of the Practice of Social Entrepreneurship at Duke University, provides the following definition of social entrepreneurship[11]:

Social entrepreneurs play the role of change agents in the social sector by:

- *Adopting a mission to create and sustain social value (not just private value)*
- *Recognizing and relentlessly pursuing new opportunities to serve that mission*
- *Engaging in a process of continuous innovation, adaptation, and learning*
- *Acting boldly without being limited by resources currently in hand*
- *Exhibiting heightened accountability to the constituencies served and for the outcomes created*

Social entrepreneurship can address a range of societal goals, including education, the environment, and the arts. However, alleviating poverty has been a central focus.

The **bottom of the pyramid (BOP)** is a term used to characterize the largest and poorest socio-economic group of people, the billions of people who live on less than $2 a day.[12] A decade ago, C. K. Prahalad and Stuart L. Hart introduced the concept that businesses could make a fortune by engaging with this typically forgotten segment of society because it contains innovative entrepreneurs as well as value-demanding customers.[13] Prahalad and Hart envisioned large, multinational corporations (MNCs) being the ones that would be able to take advantage of the BOP concept. A review of the work that has happened in the decade since their article was published shows that only a small number of MNCs have been involved.[14] Instead, smaller enterprises and social entrepreneurs have led the effort.[15]

Social entrepreneurship helps to highlight the enterprise strategy of business and to provide a mechanism by which entrepreneurial individuals can draw on their business-based skills to make a positive difference in the world. At the same time, social entrepreneurship holds a mirror up to traditional business, showing it the potential the marketplace has for creating societal as well as economic value. Michael E. Porter and Mark R. Kramer have proposed the concept of **shared value** which holds that economic and social goals are not mutually exclusive—business can pursue profit while also promoting the common good.[16] In an interview about social entrepreneurship, Porter talked about the "crisis of purpose" that he is seeing in his work with the main CEOs in the world.[17] He said, "The profit that comes from benefitting society is a higher form of profit that corporations should aspire to," and that redefining aspirations in this way will lead to "a sense of much greater purpose."[18]

The Benefit Corporation   A new corporate form has arisen that helps companies that wish to emphasize enterprise-level strategy. This new corporate form is designed to aid companies that have found it challenging to fulfill their social good-oriented missions in traditional for-profit corporations that entail a fiduciary duty for profit maximization and shareholder primacy. The **benefit corporation** permits corporations to pursue stakeholder and societal welfare maximization as well as shareholder wealth maximization because benefit corporations have a broader mission that includes having a positive impact on society. With benefit corporations, that societal mission does not take a backseat to shareholder wealth maximization. Benefit corporations give managers the opportunity to build, investors the opportunity to finance, and customers the opportunity to patronize businesses that promise to make social responsibility an important goal. The law grew out of B Lab, a nonprofit group that certifies companies as B Corporations based on their accountability, transparency, and social responsibility.[19]

In the United States, individual states have the authority to create and charter corporations and so the benefit corporation movement is growing state by state. In 2010, Maryland and Vermont were the first states to pass benefit corporation legislation: By 2012, Massachusetts became the eleventh state and Pennsylvania became the twelfth to permit companies to incorporate as benefit corporations.[20]

At this writing, California, Hawaii, Illinois, Maryland, Massachusetts, Louisiana, New Jersey, New York, Pennsylvania, South Carolina, Vermont, and Virginia have all made it possible for firms to incorporate as benefit corporations. Five other states have introduced benefit corporation legislation.[21]

Rob Thomas, founder and president of Social(k), a Springfield, Massachussets-based retirement planning company that screens for social funds, plans to apply for benefit corporation status for his company. He says, "It sends a message that we take seriously the opportunity for a business to bake into its DNA that we're here for more than just financial return."[22] Benefit corporation status does not give firms tax or other incentives. According to Andrew Kassoy, co-founder of B-Lab, "It expands the fiduciary duties of a business to include having a material, positive impact on society and the environment, not just value for shareholders."

Spotlight on Sustainability

Enterprise-Level Strategy in Action

One of the best ways to appreciate a company's public policy or enterprise-level strategy is to examine its posture on sustainability. Wegmans, a regional U.S. supermarket chain with stores in the Mid-Atlantic region, has made a formal and effective commitment to promoting sustainability through a sustainability mission statement, a sourcing philosophy, and a sustainability coordinator.

Wegmans' mission statement begins with the Native American proverb, "We do not inherit the earth from our ancestors; we borrow it from our children." It goes on to say, "There are no simple solutions to these challenges. Still, we all have a responsibility to be aware and be accountable. We promise to take steps to protect our world for future generations—it's part of our commitment to make a difference in every community we serve."

To learn more about Wegmans' commitment to sustainability, check out its Web site: http://www.wegmans.com.

The enterprise-level strategy and corporate values of Unilever are reflected in their purpose and principles statement shown in Figure 5-2. Just as the character of a person will be evident in his or her actions, the values of an organization can be seen in that organization's activities. Ranked #1 for food and beverages in the Dow Jones Sustainability Index, Unilever lives its values in a variety of ways, including buying cage-free eggs, lowering salt in its foods, and selling water purifiers to poor people.[23] Marc Gunther of

---

FIGURE 5-2

Unilever Purpose and Principles

Purpose & principles
Our corporate purpose states that to succeed requires "the highest standards of corporate behavior towards everyone we work with, the communities we touch, and the environment on which we have an impact."

Always working with integrity
Conducting our operations with integrity and with respect for the many people, organizations and environments our business touches has always been at the heart of our corporate responsibility.

Positive impact
We aim to make a positive impact in many ways: through our brands, our commercial operations and relationships, through voluntary contributions, and through the various other ways in which we engage with society.

Continuous commitment
We're also committed to continuously improving the way we manage our environmental impacts and are working towards our longer-term goal of developing a sustainable business.

Setting out our aspirations
Our corporate purpose sets out our aspirations in running our business. It's underpinned by our code of business Principles which describes the operational standards that everyone at Unilever follows, wherever they are in the world. The code also supports our approach to governance and corporate responsibility.

Working with others
We want to work with suppliers who have values similar to our own and work to the same standards we do. Our Business partner code, aligned to our own Code of business principles, comprises ten principles covering business integrity and responsibilities relating to employees, consumers and the environment.

Source: Unilever: Purpose and Principles, http://www.unileverusa.com/aboutus/purposeandprinciples/. Accessed June 6, 2013. Reproduced with kind permission of Unilever PLC and group companies.

Greenbiz.com says, "In my opinion, no big company is doing more to limit its environmental footprint while improving health and well-being and growing its business. Unilever's commitments are wide and deep."[24]

Importance of Core Values It is crucial for firms to not only have values statements that provide guidance but also for these values to "mean something." Ever since Jim Collins and Jerry Porras published *Built to Last: Successful Habits of Visionary Companies*, firms have felt they needed such statements. The authors made the case that many of the best companies adhere to a set of principles called **core values**. Core values are the deeply ingrained principles that guide all of a company's actions and decisions, and they serve as cultural cornerstones.[25] Though many companies have written publicly proclaimed values statements, many have been sullied because they are not followed. To be effective, companies need to weave core values into everything they do. If a company's core values are not upheld, they become hollow or empty and may do more harm than good.

In contrast, deeply felt and strongly held values have the power to transform. A good example of that came from when Tim Cook, the man tapped to run Apple's operations in Steve Jobs' absence, was asked by investors how the company would function without Jobs. Cook's seemingly extemporaneous response created what *Fortune's* Adam Lashinsky described as a "magical moment." Cook stated, "don't settle for anything less than excellence in every group in the company, and we have the self-honesty to admit when we're wrong and the courage to change. And I think regardless of who is in what job those values are so embedded in this company that Apple will do extremely well."[26]
According to Lashinsky, Cook had been considered uncharismatic and uninspiring, but he came across in this response as "forceful, eloquent, and passionate about Apple."[27]

In what do value-based companies believe? It has been argued that three basic organizational values undergird all others: transparency, sustainability, and responsibility.[28] Transparency emphasizes that the company is open and honest, especially with employees. Sustainability is about conducting today's business in a way that does not rob the future, and responsibility invokes the idea of commitment to integrity and social responsibility. A good example of a values-based business is Stonyfield Farms, a small New Hampshire yogurt company. The company's mission is devoted to healthy food, healthy people, a healthy planet, and healthy business.[29] "In 1983, we had a wonderful business, just no supply and no demand, no one knew what organic was, no one ate yogurt," says CEO Gary Hirshberg.[30] Today the company has succeeded through offering a high quality differentiated product, focusing on customer engagement, and undertaking a variety of initiatives to lessen the impact of its operations on the planet.[31]

Other Manifestations of Enterprise-Level Strategic Thinking Enterprise-level strategic thinking is manifested in other ways. It may include the extent to which firms have established board or senior management committees. Such committees might include the following: public policy or issues committees, sustainability committees, ethics committees, governance committees, social audit committees, corporate philanthropy committees, and ad hoc committees to address specific public issues. The firm's public affairs function can also reflect the firm's level of enterprise-level thinking. Does the firm have an established public affairs office? To whom does the director of corporate public affairs report? What role does public affairs play in corporate-level and strategic decision-making?

Another major indicator of enterprise-level strategic thinking is the extent to which the firm attempts to identify social or public issues, analyze them, and integrate them into its strategic management processes. For many firms, it will be necessary to undergo a **value shift** in order to integrate environmental, ethical, and social considerations into its strategic plans. Such a value shift, according to Lynn Sharp Paine, requires firms to get back to basics and adopt a different kind of management than that often practiced by companies.[32] More and more, superior performers are those companies that meet both the social and financial expectations of their stakeholders, a theme we seek to develop in this chapter and book. Following is a discussion of how corporate public policy is integrated into the strategic management process.

The Strategic Management Process

To understand how corporate public policy is just one part of the larger system of management decision making, it is useful to identify the major steps that make up the **strategic management process**. Boards and top management teams are responsible for activating the process. One conceptualization includes six steps: (1) goal formulation, (2) strategy formulation, (3) strategy evaluation, (4) strategy implementation, (5) strategic control, and (6) environmental analysis.[33] Figure 5-3 graphically portrays an expanded view of this process.

The environmental analysis component requires collection of information on trends, events, and issues that occur in the stakeholder environment, and this information is then fed into the other steps of the process. Although the tasks or steps are often discussed sequentially, they are in fact interactive and do not always occur in a neatly ordered pattern or sequence. Figure 5-3 also captures the relationship between the strategic management process and corporate public policy.

Strategic Corporate Social Responsibility

In recent years, the term "strategic corporate social responsibility" has captured the idea of integrating a concern for society into the strategic management processes of the firm.[34] Such a perspective insures that CSR is fully integrated into the firm's strategy, mission, and vision. Strategic CSR and the firm's level of strategic management reflect a firm's enterprise-level strategy discussed earlier.

The notion of strategic CSR got a huge boost when strategy expert Michael Porter began advocating the importance of the linkage between competitive advantage, a crucial strategy concept, and CSR.[35] Though Porter had been preceded by others in advocating this linkage, the strength of his reputation has furthered the cause. He and co-author Mark Kramer argued that the interdependence between business and society takes two forms: "inside-out linkages" wherein company operations affect society, and "outside-in linkages" wherein external societal forces affect companies.[36] In order to prioritize social issues, they proceed to categorize three broad ways corporations intersect with society. First, there are "generic social issues" wherein a company's operations do not significantly affect society and the issue is not material to the firm's long-term competitiveness. Second, there are "value chain social impacts" where a company's normal operations significantly affect society. Finally, there are "social dimensions of competitive context," wherein social issues affect the underlying drivers of a company's competitiveness.[37]

Porter and Kramer next divide these three categories into two primary modes of corporate involvement. *Responsive CSR* addresses "generic social impacts" through good corporate citizenship and "value chain social impacts" by mitigating harm from negative

© Cengage Learning 2015

FIGURE 5-3 The Strategic Management Process and Corporate Public Policy

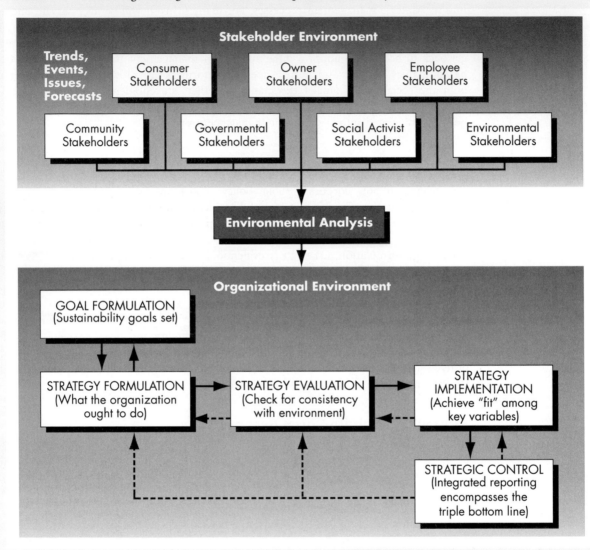

corporate impacts on society. *Strategic CSR* transforms "value chain social impacts" into activities that benefit society, while simultaneously reinforcing corporate strategy and advancing strategic philanthropy that leverages relevant areas of competitiveness.[38]

These ideas are integrated into a series of steps that intend to integrate business and society strategically. These steps include:

1. Identifying the points of intersection (inside-out and outside-in).
2. Choosing which social issues to address (generic, value chain social impacts, social dimensions of competitiveness).
3. Creating a corporate social agenda (responsive and strategic).
4. Integrating inside-out and outside-in practices (getting practices to work together).
5. Creating a social dimension to the value proposition. (The company adds a social dimension to its value proposition, thus making social impact integral to the overall strategy.)[39]

Porter and Kramer offer Whole Foods Market (WFM) as an example of this final point. The value proposition of WFM is to sell natural, organic, healthy food products to customers who passionately care about the environment. Social issues are central to WFM's mission and are implemented through sourcing approaches, commitment to the environment, and use of environment-friendly policies and practices.[40]

The Porter–Kramer framework is useful because it applies strategic thinking to both leverage positive social and environmental benefits and mitigate negative social and environmental impacts in ways that enhance competitive advantage.[41] The challenge for companies, therefore, has been to find the ways in which the environmental and social dimensions can be incorporated into the business as part of the whole rather than a separate part. Integrated reporting represents a major step in that direction.

Measuring Sustainable Corporate Performance

Achieving sustainability requires performance accountability and that necessitates a change in the way many firms operate. Organizations can only perform well financially, socially, and environmentally if performance information and performance accountability reflect those goals.[42] When firms only measure financial performance and the board holds them responsible for only maximizing shareholder value, environmental and social considerations become side issues. Social or environmental initiatives might be approved if they add to corporate image or the bottom line but they are not viewed as central to the business.[43] To achieve sustainable corporate performance, corporations need a "fundamental change in their goals and how they achieve them."[44] The triple bottom line must be reflected in every aspect of the firm's operations to achieve sustainability. Figure 5-4 lists the "Clean Capitalism Key Performance Indicators" that Corporate Knight uses in compiling its list of the Global 100 most sustainable corporations.

Sustainability Reporting A **sustainability report** represents an effort to measure a firm's overall value creation and to spur integrated thinking that recognizes the interconnections of the range of business functions, as well as the multiple business bottom lines.[45] Sustainability reports are also known as **integrated reports (IR)** because they reflect the extent to which the firm is creating value in the triple bottom line. In contrast, **social audits, social responsibility reports**, and **environmental impact reports** focus on specific areas. The movement toward sustainability reports is new but gaining momentum. The International Integrated Reporting Council (IIRC) is spearheading the development of a global framework for IR. The group is composed of regulators, investors,

---

FIGURE 5-4		
Corporate Knight's Clean Capitalism Key Performance Indicators	***Energy Productivity:*** Revenue per gigajoule of energy consumption. ***Carbon Productivity:*** Revenue per metric ton of direct/indirect GHG emissions. ***Water Productivity:*** Revenue per cubic meter of water withdrawal. ***Waste Productivity:*** Revenue per metric ton of produced waste. ***Leadership Diversity:*** Percentage of women and visible minority on board of directors. ***Clean Capitalism Pay Link:*** At least one senior executive's compensation tied to clean capitalism-themed performance targets.	***% Tax Paid:*** Percentage of reported tax obligation paid in tax. ***CEO-Average Worker Pay:*** How much more CEO gets paid (expressed as a multiple) compared to average worker. ***Safety Productivity:*** Revenue divided by (lost-time incidents * $1K + fatalities * $1M) ***Innovation Capacity:*** Revenue per R&D dollar spent (3-year average) ***Employee Turnover:*** Percentage of employees that voluntarily leave the company

Source: http://www.corporateknights.com/report/8th-annual-global-100-most-sustainable-corporations/global-100

businesses, NGOs, standard setters, and representatives from the accounting profession.[46] According to Professor Mervyn King, Chairman of the IIRC:

> *We define Integrated Reporting as the language evidencing sustainable business. It is the means by which companies communicate how value is created and will be enhanced over the short, medium and long term... The journey towards Integrated Reporting therefore also entails a mindset change about how the company makes its money.*[47]

IR does not necessarily replace other reports. Firms may still issue financial statements, environmental impact reports and social responsibility reports, etc. However, by pulling that information together into an integrated format, decision makers become more aware of the interconnectedness of decisions and the fact that sustainability considerations cut across all the individual areas. The IIRC mounted a pilot program to assess the value of integrated reporting: eighty businesses participated. They surveyed the participating businesses to assess any behavioral changes during the first year of the program and reported their findings. They found that 93 percent of the respondents agree that IR leads to a greater management focus on sustainability issues.[48] One respondent noted that boards do not meet that often and so IR helps to get their attention on sustainability issues by putting them on the agenda.[49]

Novo Nordisk was one of the first companies to commit to integrated reporting when they discontinued the use of separate financial, social, and environmental reports in 2004.[50] Ranked at the top of the 2012 Global 100 list of most sustainable corporations in the world, Novo Nordisk incorporates sustainability into every decision.[51] It is the only pharmaceutical company that reports linking the CEO's pay to indicators of sustainability, and it sells insulin to some of the world's poorest countries at no more than 20 percent of the average price in the Western world.[52] The company considers sustainability to be a driver or innovation and a means of engaging with stakeholders that illuminates opportunities and warns of potential trouble.[53]

Implicit in our discussion of control is the idea that some sustainability performance planning has already taken place. Although we refer to the sustainability report here as a control process, it is a planning and control system as well.[54] For example, Alcoa's 2012 sustainability report sets strategic sustainability goals for 2020 and 2030: When they meet or exceed them, they revise their goals upward.[55] In the context of strategic control, the sustainability report can assume a role much like that portrayed in Figure 5-5. This figure is similar to the diagram of the strategic management process and corporate public policy shown in Figure 5-3, but it is modified to highlight sustainability goals and the first three steps in the strategic control process.

The impetus for sustainability reports in recent years has come both from inside the firm and from societal and public interest groups' expectations that firms report their achievements in the triple bottom line. Such reports typically require monitoring and measuring progress, and this is valuable to management groups wanting to track their own progress as well as be able to report it to other interested parties. Some companies create and issue such reports because it helps their competitive positions. Sustainability helps companies to manage their brands and reputations more effectively, bring coherence to their communications, and benchmark their performance.[56] Globalization is another driver for sustainability reports. As more and more companies do business globally, they need to document their achievements when critics raise questions about their contributions, especially in developing countries. Companies such as Apple and Walmart have been criticized for their use of sweatshops abroad, so they have an added incentive to issue such reports. Sustainability reports can also help companies to engage with stakeholders. Novo Nordisk offers interactive Web site games that provide stakeholders with an opportunity to address ethical dilemmas, develop strategies that balance

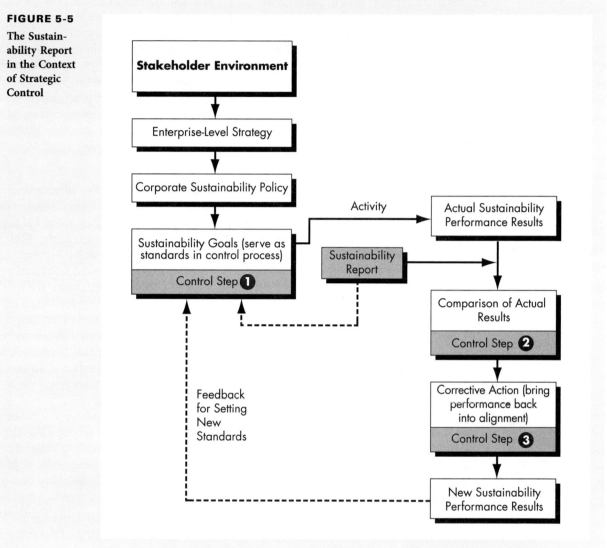

FIGURE 5-5

The Sustainability Report in the Context of Strategic Control

environmental and economic concerns, and convince the Minister of Health to invest more in diabetes research.[57]

Ceres The nonprofit organization Ceres (pronounced "series") is a national network of investors, environmental organizations, and other public interest groups working with companies and investors to address sustainability challenges and promote sustainability reporting. Ceres's mission is "mobilizing investor and business leadership to build a thriving, sustainable global economy."[58]

A specific initiative of Ceres has been its annual award for sustainability reporting. The awards are called the *Ceres-ACCA Awards for Sustainability Reporting*, recognizing the joint initiative with the Association of Chartered Certified Accountants (ACCA). Nike won the most recent Ceres-ACCA North American Awards for Best Sustainability Reporting. Ceres said that Nike's report "addresses the new context within which business must operate—one with a rising global population, decreasing natural resources, and an unstable climate—and reveals how Nike, in an effort to take a competitive advantage, is shifting to a more sustainable business model. In the report, Nike recognizes that "sustainability is a route to profitability," and to that end the report details how the company is integrating sustainability into strategic planning and decision-making, from its board of directors, to its product designers and across its supply chain. The report also demonstrates the company's commitment to scaling sustainability solutions through the open sourcing of its audit and design tools and its integral role in the creation of the Green Xchange platform."[59] As it heads into the future, Ceres plans to "work with its core constituencies to accelerate the adoption of sustainable business practices, integrate sustainability risks and opportunities into corporate and investor strategies, and establish new rules of the road."[60] The Scaling Sustainability plan is divided into four mutually reinforcing areas of impact: Sustainable Business Strategies, Sustainable Capital Markets, Climate & Clean Energy, and Water Resources.[61]

Global Reporting Initiative One of the major impediments to the advancement of effective sustainability reporting has been the absence of standardized measures. Standardization is a challenge that has been undertaken by a consortium of more than 300 global organizations called the **Global Reporting Initiative (GRI)**. Ceres launched the GRI in conjunction with the UN Environment Programme (UNEP) with the mission of developing globally applicable guidelines for reporting on the economic, environmental, and social performance of corporations, governments, and non-governmental organizations (NGOs).[62] GRI is now considered the de facto international standard for corporate reporting on environmental, social, and economic performance. It includes the participation of corporations, NGOs, accountancy organizations, business associations, and other worldwide stakeholders.[63] The GRI's Sustainability Reporting Guidelines represented the first global framework for comprehensive sustainability reporting, encompassing the triple bottom line of economic, environmental, and social issues. The mission of GRI is to maintain, enhance, and disseminate the guidelines through ongoing consultation and stakeholder engagement.[64]

As firms develop enterprise-level strategies and corporate public policies, the potential for sustainability reporting remains high. Sustainability reporting is best appreciated not as an isolated, periodic attempt to assess social performance but rather as an *integral part* of the overall strategic management process as it described here. Because the need to improve planning and control will remain as long as the management desires to evaluate its corporate social performance, the need for approaches such as sustainability reporting will likely be with us for some time, too. The net result of continued use and refinement should be improved sustainability and enhanced credibility of business in the eyes of its stakeholders and the public.

Public Affairs As a Part of Strategic Management

In a comprehensive management system, the overall flow of activity would be as follows: A firm engages in strategic management, part of which includes the development of enterprise-level strategy. Enterprise-level strategy poses the question, "For what do we stand?" The answers to this question help the organization form a corporate public policy, which is a more specific posture on the public, social, or stakeholder environment or specific issues within this environment. Some firms call this a **public affairs strategy**.

Public affairs (PA) and **public affairs management** are umbrella terms companies use to describe the management processes that focus on the formalization and institutionalization of corporate public policy. The PA function is a logical and increasingly prevalent component of the overall strategic management process. PA experts argue that it has grown significantly into one of the most important parts of strategic management over the past decade and today may be seen as the strategic core business function for companies wanting to compete successfully internationally.[65]

ETHICS IN PRACTICE CASE

Reporting Bad News—Whose Interests Matter?

The rules about disclosing bankruptcy to the public are unclear, and so companies are able to make their own decisions about when to disclose the fact that they are filing for bankruptcy protection. *The Wall Street Journal* analyzed the bankruptcy filings of 90 large public companies and found that 29 did not disclose their bankruptcy preparations in any way. A few collapsed too quickly to report, but most made the decision not to let the public know. Is that a bad thing?

On one hand, a free market relies on transparency and honesty. Bankruptcy filings are material information and, as such, investors have a right to know that a company is in distress. On the other hand, filing for bankruptcy protection is intended to help the company to get out from under debt and keep operating. Disclosure can work against that process. With the introduction of innovations such as credit default swaps, creditors are less likely to be motivated to work with the company. Furthermore, employees with mobility are likely to begin departing once they know the company's future is in doubt. Investors have a right to know, while stakeholders have a right to their livelihood. Where do you draw the line?

1. Do investors have the right to full information about a company's plans to file for bankruptcy?
2. Does a company have the right to keep bankruptcy procedures private prior to filing in order to work out an arrangement that will allow the business to continue?
3. Whose interests are more important—the investors or the stakeholders who depend on the business?
4. If you were writing the rules for corporate disclosure, where would you draw the line?

Sources: Robert Fishman, John Henry Squires, Steven Towbin, and Daniel Zazove, "The Importance of Being Earnest: Bankruptcy Disclosure Rules." *Depaul Business & Commercial Law Journal* (Vol. 7, No. 4, 2009), 627–653; Mike Spector, "Keeping Mum About the 'B' Word," *The Wall Street Journal*" (November 7, 2012); "What's Your Position? Amending the Bankruptcy Disclosure Rules to Keep Pace with Financial Innovation." *UCLA Law Review* 58, no. 3 (February 2011): 803–841.

As an overall concept, PA management embraces corporate public policy, discussed earlier, along with **issues and crisis management**, which we cover in more detail in Chapter 6. Indeed, many issues management and crisis management programs are housed in **public affairs departments** or intimately involve PA professionals. Corporate PA also embraces the broad areas of governmental relations and corporate communications.

We now consider how the PA function has evolved in business firms, what concerns PA departments currently face, and how PA thinking might be incorporated into the operating manager's job. This last issue is crucial, because PA management is most effective when considered an indispensable part of every manager's job, rather than an isolated function or department.

The Corporate Public Affairs Function Today

PA blossomed in the United States because of four primary reasons: (1) the growing magnitude and impact of government; (2) the changing nature of the political system, especially its progression from a patronage orientation to an issues orientation; (3) the growing recognition by business that it was being outflanked by interests that were counter to its own on a number of policy matters; and (4) the need to be more active in politics outside the traditional community-related aspects, such as the symphony and art museums.[66]

Thus, the PA function as we know it today was an outgrowth of the social activism begun decades ago. Just as significant federal laws were passed in the early 1970s to address such issues as discrimination, environmental protection, occupational health and safety, and consumer safety, corporations responded with a surge of PA activities and creation of PA departments.[67] The Public Affairs Council (PAC), the leading professional organization of executives who do the PA work of companies, provides the following definition of *public affairs*:

> *Public affairs represents an organization's efforts to monitor and manage its business environment. It combines government relations, communications, issues management, and corporate citizenship strategies to influence public policy, build a strong reputation, and find common ground with stakeholders.[68]*

Public Affairs Activities and Functions

Public affairs as a management function progressed out of isolated company initiatives designed to handle such diverse activities as community relations, corporate philanthropy and contributions, governmental affairs, lobbying, grassroots programs, corporate responsibility, and public relations. In some firms, the public relations staff handled issues involving communication with external publics, so it is not surprising that public affairs often evolved from public relations. Part of the confusion between public relations and public affairs is traceable to the fact that some corporate public relations executives changed their titles to public affairs, but not their functions. The key difference between public affairs and public relations relates to their goals. Public relations focuses on selling a product, while public affairs is designed to influence public policy.[69] The range of fields that PA encompasses can be seen by the areas of expertise of PAC staff, which include lobbying, global public affairs, social media, corporate responsibility, campaign finance, grassroots advocacy, crisis communication, and many other areas.[70]

An important element of the public affairs function is the influence it has on corporate strategy and planning. If the public affairs function is to be effective in representing the "noncommercial" factors and issues affecting business decision making, it is important that public affairs has influence at the top management level. Public affairs can help to identify and prioritize issues as well as provide input on emerging social and political trends. For public affairs to fulfill this function it is important that it has a seat at the table for corporate planning sessions.

Another way for public affairs to have an impact on top management is to think of the CEO as the company's chief public affairs officer. The idea here is that the public affairs function needs a transformation from reacting to proacting and that the best way to make this happen is to place the CEO in charge of the function.[71] This might not work as a practical reality, but the spirit of the idea is appropriate. It is an excellent idea in terms of elevating the importance of public affairs and its relationship to corporate strategy.

PA's Place at the Table

An important element of the PA function is the influence it has on corporate strategy and planning. If the PA function is to be effective in representing the "noncommercial" factors and issues affecting business decision making, it is important that PA has influence at the top management level. PA can help to identify and prioritize issues, as well as provide input on emerging social and political trends. As mentioned earlier, for PA to fulfill this function it is important that it has a seat at the table for corporate planning sessions. Unfortunately, that goal is not yet fully realized. A 2012 *Public Affairs Journal* retrospective of the PA function notes that, "PA activity generally remains a peripheral element in the strategic management of most companies."[72]

Part of the problem may be that, in today's highly specialized business world, it is easy for the day-to-day operating managers to let PA departments worry about government affairs, community relations, issues management, PR, or any of the numerous other PA functions. It is not surprising, therefore, that a 2012 study showed that PA remained a largely specialist function.[73] The problem may stem largely from ambiguity surrounding the definition of public affairs and the differences in the activities undertaken by different PA departments.[74] More promising, however, was the finding that relationships with senior management were strong. Senior managers might not always understand what PA does, but they recognize the value and importance of the PA function.[75]

Future of Corporate PA in the 21st Century

With growing worldwide sensitivity to corporate social performance and business ethics, it is easy to argue that corporate PA should have a bright future. Because of the tsunami of ethical crises in corporations in the early 2000s, PA specialists have an ideal opportunity to solidify their strategic roles and help to transform companies' approaches to handling business and society relationships. Three different opportunities for PA executives have been set forth for future consideration.[76]

First, PA can help develop value-based enterprises. Such enterprises actively seek out stakeholders and work cooperatively with them on social issues. An example cited was when Whirlpool reached agreements with the National Resource Defense Council, Friends of the Earth, and the Sierra Club to work together in solving energy efficiency challenges. By proactively engaging stakeholders, competitive advantages may be created.[77] Second, PA executives can assert themselves as thought leaders in their companies. As thought leaders, they should not just toe the company line, but actively engage academics, researchers, media, and public opinion formers about the great issues of the day and how companies can best respond to the latest thinking about social and public issues. As PA executives increasingly have the ear of the top management, they are uniquely positioned to have great influence. Finally, PA specialists have the opportunity to seek alternative arenas of resolution as they can broaden issues to embrace global considerations while they pay close attention to domestic matters. Today, public issues migrate across geographical boundaries and political jurisdictions, and PA executives are in a perfect position to track these issues and employ preemptive initiatives. A case in point might be their opportunities in the global debate over genetically modified organisms that are controversial in the United Kingdom while being largely ignored in the United States.[78] In short, the PA function within firms is strategically positioned to wield more and better influence in the years ahead to help business build bridges between its strategic management and its corporate social performance.

Summary

Corporate public policy is a firm's posture or stance regarding the public, social, or ethical aspects of stakeholders and corporate functioning. It is a part of strategic management, particularly enterprise-level strategy. Enterprise-level strategy is the broadest, overarching level of strategy, and its focus is on the role of the organization in society. A major aspect of enterprise-level strategy is the integration of important core values into company strategy. The other strategy levels include the corporate, business, and functional levels. The strategic management process entails six stages, and a concern for social, ethical, and public issues may be seen at each stage. In the control stage, the social audit or social performance report is crucial.

Social entrepreneurship holds the mission of the firm as its ultimate purpose. Creating wealth is necessary for social entrepreneurs if they are to survive and thrive but wealth is more of a means to an end the benefits society. The benefit corporation is a new corporate form that makes it possible for social entrepreneurs and other like-minded business people to promote the social good as well as wealth creation. Sustainability reports measure how well the firm achieves the triple bottom line of planet, people, and profit. Social audits and social responsibility reports measure the extent to which a firm achieves its social goals and is socially responsible.

Public affairs can be described as the management function that is responsible for monitoring and interpreting a corporation's noncommercial environment and managing its response to that environment. PA is inti-

mately linked to corporate public policy, environmental analysis, issues management, and crisis management. The major functions of PA departments today include government relations, political action, community involvement or responsibility, issues management, global PA, and corporate philanthropy. PA executives are positioned to increase their future status and influence as they embark on such challenges as helping to create values-based enterprises, exerting themselves as thought leaders in their companies, and helping seek alternative arenas of resolution as they broaden issues to embrace global considerations.

Key Terms

benefit corporation, p. 132
bottom of the pyramid, p. 131
business-level strategy, p. 129
core values, p. 134
corporate-level strategy, p. 129
corporate public affairs, p. 128
corporate public policy, p. 127
enterprise-level strategy, p. 129
environmental impact reports, p. 137

functional-level strategy, p. 130
Global Reporting Initiative (GRI), p. 140
issues and crisis management, p. 141
integrated reports (IR), p. 137
public affairs (PA), p. 140
public affairs departments, p. 141
public affairs management, p. 140
public affairs strategy, p. 140

shared value, p. 132
social audit, p. 137
social entrepreneurship, p. 131
social responsibility report, p. 137
strategic management, p. 128
strategic management processes, p. 135
sustainability report, p. 137
value shift, p. 135

Discussion Questions

1. Which of the four strategy levels is most concerned with social, ethical, or public issues? Discuss the characteristics of this level.
2. Identify the steps involved in the strategic management process.
3. What is the difference between integrated reporting and a social performance report?

4. What is social entrepreneurship and how is it related to the bottom of the pyramid (BOP)?
5. Why are integrated reports increasing in popularity?
6. What are the major ways in which public affairs might be incorporated into every manager's job? Rank them in terms of what you think their impact might be.

Endnotes

1. Edward E. Lawler and Christopher G. Worley, "Why Boards Need to Change," *MIT Sloan Management Review* (Fall, 2012), 10–12.
2. Victoria Miles, "Auditing Promises: One Bank's Story," *CMA Management* (Vol. 74, No. 5, June 2000), 42–46.
3. https://www.citizensbank.ca/AboutUs/CorporateSocial Responsibility/. Accessed January 24, 2013.
4. Ibid.
5. Kenneth R. Andrews, *The Concept of Corporate Strategy*, 3d ed. (Homewood, IL: Irwin, 1987), 68–69.
6. R. Edward Freeman and Daniel R. Gilbert, Jr., *Corporate Strategy and the Search for Ethics* (Englewood Cliffs, NJ: Prentice Hall, 1988), 20. Also see R. Edward Freeman,

Daniel R. Gilbert, Jr., and Edwin Hartman, "Values and the Foundations of Strategic Management," *Journal of Business Ethics* (Vol. 7, 1988), 821–834; and Daniel R. Gilbert, Jr., "Strategy and Ethics," in *The Blackwell Encyclopedic Dictionary of Business Ethics* (Malden, MA: Blackwell Publishers Ltd., 1997), 609–611.
7. Charles W. Hofer, Edwin A. Murray, Jr., Ram Charan, and Robert A. Pitts, *Strategic Management: A Casebook in Policy and Planning*, 2d ed. (St. Paul, MN: West Publishing Co., 1984), 27–29. Also see Gary Hamel and C. K. Prahalad, *Competing for the Future* (Boston: Harvard Business School Press, 1994).
8. R. Edward Freeman, *Strategic Management: A Stakeholder Approach* (Boston: Pitman, 1984), 90.

9. Nicola M. Pless, "Social Entrepreneurship in Theory and Practice: An Introduction," *Journal of Business Ethics* (Vol. 111, 2012) 317–320.

10. Samer Abu-Saifan, "Social Entrepreneurship: Definition and Boundaries," *Technology Innovation Management Review* (February 2012), 22–27.

11. http://www.caseatduke.org/documents/dees_sedef.pdf. Accessed February 1, 2013.

12. C. K. Prahalad and Stuart L. Hart. "The Fortune at the Bottom of the Pyramid," *Strategy+Business* (Vol. 20, 1998) 1–13.

13. Ibid.

14. Kolk, Ans, Rivera-Santos, Miguel and Rufin, Carlos R., "Reviewing a Decade of Research on the 'Base/Bottom of the Pyramid' (BOP) Concept," *Business & Society*, Forthcoming, doi 10.1177/0007650312474928. Available at SSRN: http://ssrn.com/abstract=2193938. Accessed February 1, 2013.

15. Ibid.

16. Michael E. Porter and Mark R. Kramer, "Creating Shared Value," *Harvard Business Review* (Jan/Feb 2011), 62–77

17. Michaela Driver, "An Interview with Michael Porter: Social Entrepreneurship and the Transformation of Capitalism," *Academy of Management Learning and Education* (Vol. 11, No. 3, 2012), 436.

18. Ibid.

19. Shira Schoenberg, "Massachusetts Companies Create Socially Responsible "Benefit Corporations," Masslive. com (December 4, 2012), http://www.masslive.com/politics/index.ssf/2012/12/massachusetts_companies_create.html. Accessed January 24, 2013.

20. Ibid.

21. http://www.benefitcorp.net/state-by-state-legislative-status. Accessed January 24, 2013.

22. Schoenberg, 2012.

23. http://www.sustainability-indexes.com/review/supersector-leaders-2012.jsp. March 16, 2013.

24. Marc Gunther, "Will Unilever's Sustainability Leadership Pay Off?," *Greenbiz.com* (April 25, 2012), http://www.greenbiz.com/blog/2012/04/25/will-unilevers-sustainability-leadership-pay. Accessed March 16, 2013.

25. James C. Collins and Jerry I. Porras, *Built to Last: Successful Habits of Visionary Companies* (HarperBusiness, 1994).

26. Adam Lashinsky, "The Cook Doctrine at Apple," *Fortune* (January 22, 2009), http://features.blogs.fortune.cnn.com/2009/01/22/the-cook-doctrine-at-apple/. Accessed January 24, 2013.

27. Ibid.

28. Mark Albion, *True to Yourself: Leading a Values-Based Business* (San Francisco, CA: Berrett-Koehler, 2006).

29. http://www.stonyfield.com/about-us/our-mission. Accessed January 21, 2013.

30. http://www.triplepundit.com/2012/04/economics-stonyfield-yogurt/. Accessed January 21, 2013.

31. http://www.triplepundit.com/2012/03/starbucks-stonyfield-recycling-extended-producer-responsibility/. Accessed January 21, 2013.

32. Lynn Sharp Paine, *Value Shift: Why Companies Must Merge Social and Financial Imperatives to Achieve Superior Performance* (New York: McGraw-Hill, 2003).

33. C. W. Hofer and D. E. Schendel, *Strategy Formulation: Analytial Concepts* (St. Paul: West, 1978), 52–55. Also see J. David Hunger and Thomas L. Wheelen, *Essentials of Strategic Management* (Reading, MA: Addison-Wesley, 2000).

34. William B. Werther, Jr. and David Chandler, *Strategic Corporate Social Responsibility: Stakeholders in a Global Environment* (Thousand Oaks, CA: Sage Publications), 2006.

35. Michael E. Porter and Mark R. Kramer, "Strategy and Society: The Link Between Competitive Advantage and Corporate Social Responsibility," *Harvard Business Review* (December 2006), 80–92.

36. Ibid., 84.

37. Ibid., 85.

38. Ibid., 85.

39. Ibid., 83–90.

40. Ibid., 90–91.

41. Ibid.

42. Lawler and Worley, 2012, 10–12.

43. Ibid.

44. Ibid., 10.

45. http://www.theiirc.org/. Accessed January 22, 2013.

46. Ibid.

47. Black Sun Plc, *Understanding Transformation: Building the Business Case for Integrated Reporting* (2012), 1. The report is available for download from www.theiirc.org. Accessed January 22, 2013.

48. Ibid., 13.

49. Ibid.

50. http://annualreport2011.novonordisk.com/stakeholders-and-reporting/reporting/about-our-reporting.aspx. Accessed March 16, 2013.

51. http://www.global100.org/annual-lists/2012-global-100-list.html. Accessed March 16, 2013.

52. http://www.marcgunther.com/ratings-rankings-and-the-worlds-most-sustainable-company/. Accessed March 16, 2013.

53. Ibid.

54. David H. Blake, William C. Frederick, and Mildred S. Myers, *Social Auditing: Evaluating the Impact of Corporate Programs* (New York: Praeger, 1976), 3.

55. http://www.alcoa.com/sustainability/en/info_page/vision_targets.asp. Accessed March 16, 2013.

56. Karen Janowski and Kathleen Gilligan, "How to Produce a Top-Notch Sustainability Report," *Greenbiz.com* (May 10, 2010), http://www.greenbiz.com/blog/2010/05/10/how produce-topnotch-sustainability-report. Accessed January 22, 2013.

57. http://www.novonordisk.com/sustainability/games/inter active-challenges.asp. Accessed March 16, 2013.

58. http://www.ceres.org/about-us. Accessed January 22, 2013.

59. http://www.ceres.org/awards/reporting-awards. Accessed January 22, 2013.

60. http://www.ceres.org/resources/reports/strategic-plan-2012-2015/view. Accessed January 22, 2013.

61. Ibid.

62. https://www.globalreporting.org/information/about-gri/Pages/default.aspx. Accessed January 22, 2013.

63. Ibid.

64. Ibid.

65. Phil Harris and Craig S. Fleisher (eds.), *The Handbook of Public Affairs* (Thousand Oaks, CA: Sage Publications, 2005), 561–562. Also see "Public Affairs at Heart of Corporate Strategy," *Corporate Public Affairs* (Vol. 16, No. 2, 2006), 1–2.

66. Craig S. Fleisher, "Evaluating Your Existing Public Affairs Management System," in Craig S. Fleisher (ed.), *Assessing, Managing and Maximizing Public Affairs Performance* (Washington, DC: Public Affairs Council, 1997), 4.

67. For more on the origins and development of public affairs, see John M. Holcomb, "Public Affairs in North America: US Origins and Development," in Phil Harris and Craig S. Fleisher (eds.), *The Handbook of Public Affairs* (Thousand Oaks, CA: Sage Publications, 2005), 31–49.

68. http://pac.org/faq. Accessed January 24, 2013.

69. Kassandra Hannay, "Public Affairs: A Career Worth Considering," *Public Relations Out Loud* (Spring 2010), http://www.platformmagazine.com/article.cfm?alias=Public-Affairs-A-Career-Worth-Considering. Accessed July 15, 2010.

70. http://pac.org/about. Accessed March 30, 2013.

71. "Corporate Public Affairs and Organizational Change: Towards a New Positive Model," *Corporate Public Affairs* (Vol. 17, No. 1, 2007), 12.

72. Craig Fleisher, "Anniversary Retrospective, Perspective, and Prospective of Corporate Public Affairs: Moving from the 2000+ PA Model toward *Public Affairs 2.0*," *Public Affairs* (Vol. 12, No. 1, 2012), 8.

73. Danny Moss, Conor McGrath, Jane Tonge, and Phil Harris, "Exploring the Management of the Corporate Public Affairs Function in a Dynamic Global Environment," *Journal of Public Affairs* (Vol. 12 No. 1, 2012), 47–57.

74. Ibid.

75. Ibid.

76. Jennifer J. Griffin, Steven N. Brenner, and Jean J. Boddewyn, "Corporate Public Affairs: Structure, Resources, and Competitive Advantage," in Marc J. Epstein and Kirk O. Hanson (eds.) *The Accountable Corporation, Volume 4: Business-Government Relations* (Westport, CT: Praeger Publishers, 2006), 134–138.

77. Ibid., 135–136.

78. Ibid., 136–137.

6

Issue, Risk, and Crisis Management

CHAPTER LEARNING OUTCOMES

After studying this chapter, you should be able to:

1. Distinguish between issue management, risk management, and crisis management.

2. Identify and briefly explain the stages in the issue management process.

3. Describe the major categories of risk and some of the factors that have characterized risk management in actual practice.

4. Define a crisis and identify the four crisis stages.

5. List and discuss the major stages or steps involved in managing business crises.

The World Health Organization declared the China dairy industry scandal to be one of the largest food-safety crises in recent history when nearly 300 people became sick and several infants died due to tainted infant formula and food products.[1] Like most major crises, there were several causes. Dairy farmers reacted to rising feed costs by using a lower grade of feed, which led to lower-quality milk. Distributors added melamine to the milk to evade dairy standards for protein content, and dairies allowed the tainted milk to be distributed. Finally, companies such as Heinz, Mars, and Unilever unknowingly manufactured and distributed items made with the contaminated ingredients.[2] How can these things happen? The proverbial fox is often guarding the hen house as governments cut back on the few food inspections they once did.[3] This forces consumers to rely on businesses to act responsibly.

The big issue for business is that of "trust." Can the public trust business? In the past few years, business has seen the trust of consumers, employees, investors, and the public erode because of issues such as these that threatened the public's safety when they become crises. Food safety is just one of many issues that raise concerns. Enron, Health South, and Goldman Sachs created financial scandals that caused people to lose faith in business as an institution. Other continuing issues, such as employee rights, sexual harassment, workplace safety, sweatshops, bribery, corruption, and deceptive advertising contribute to the negative opinion many people hold of business.

Of course, not all issues are caused by business. External events are sometimes unavoidable but firms must still prepare for their possibilities and manage their repercussions effectively. The World Trade Center terrorist attacks affected businesses at the site as well as around the globe. The 2011 earthquake and tsunami in Japan not only devastated a nation but also led to the world's worst nuclear accident in 25 years.[4] In 2012, Superstorm Sandy became the largest Atlantic hurricane on record, causing death and destruction throughout the northeastern United States. Each of these events posed serious challenges for businesses. Throughout this book, we discuss major social and ethical issues that have become controversies in the public domain. Some have been caused by external events, while the roots of others can be traced back to business. Many are now recognizable code words, such as the Tylenol™ poisonings, the BP *Deepwater Horizon* oil spill, and the Tazreen Fashions Factory fire in Bangladesh.

Managerial decision-making processes known as issue management, risk management, and crisis management are three major ways by which business responds to these situations. These three approaches symbolize the extent to which the environment has become turbulent and the public sensitized to business's responses to the issues that have emerged from this turbulence. In today's environment of instantaneous and global communication, no event is too small to be noticed by everyone. In an ideal situation, issue, risk, and crisis management might be seen as the natural and logical by-products of a firm's development of enterprise-level strategy and overall corporate public policy, but this is not always the case. Some firms do not think seriously about public and ethical issues until they face a crisis. However, even those firms that have not experienced major crises themselves have seen what major business crises can do to companies. Such firms should still be concerned with issue, risk, and crisis management in preparing for an uncertain future because no company is immune to the threat of a crisis.

The Relationships Between Issue, Risk, and Crisis Management

Differentiating between issue, risk, and crisis management is difficult, even for the professionals who work in those fields. Many product managers cannot differentiate between risks and issues, and the apparent inseparability of issue and crisis management has led issue management practitioner and expert Tony Jaques to label them "the Siamese twins of public relations."[5] As is true with all planning processes, issue, risk, and crisis management have many characteristics in common. Though they are interrelated, we have chosen to treat them separately for discussion purposes.

The Issue Management Council defines an **issue** as "a gap between [a firm's] actions and stakeholder expectations" and issue management as "the process used to close that gap."[6] Thus, an issue is something that already exists. In contrast, "a risk is a *potential* issue that may or may not occur."[7] A crisis is an issue that has escalated into a critical state. It follows, then, that **risk management** deals with potential issues, **issue management** deals with issues that occur, and **crisis management** deals with issues that escalate into extremely serious situations. A common thread is that all three processes focus on improving stakeholder management and enabling the organization to be more ethically responsive to stakeholders' expectations. Issue, risk, and crisis management, to be effective, must have closing that gap between the firm's situation and its stakeholders' expectations as the ultimate objective. Issue, risk, and crisis management are also related in that effective risk management may keep issues from arising, and effective issue management may enable managements to either avoid a crisis or engage in more effective crisis management if a crisis occurs. Many of the crises companies face today arise out of issue categories that are being monitored and prioritized through issue management systems. In addition, effective issue management is a vital component of post-crisis management. For example, after dealing with an oil-spill crisis, a company must continue to address the issue of environmental degradation.[8] Figure 6-1 provides examples of major *issue* categories and specific *crises* that have occurred within these issue categories.

FIGURE 6-1   Issue Categories and Specific Crises within Categories

ISSUE CATEGORIES		
Food, Beverage, and Products	Health-Related Issues	Corporate Fraud and Ethics
Crises	*Crises*	*Crises*
Peanut Corporation of America: More than 125 varieties of products recalled due to salmonella contamination (2008–2009).	H1N1: A possible flu pandemic led to crises for companies and questions of how to treat employees (2009).	Bernie Madoff: Ponzi scheme cost major foundations millions of dollars jeopardizing critical medical research (2008–2009).
Taco Bell: Outbreak of *E. coli* closed outlets nationwide (2006).	Avian flu: A possible bird flu pandemic has created a crisis environment for many businesses, including mask makers who are facing short supplies (2006–2007).	Hewlett-Packard: Boardroom information was leaked causing a governance crisis (2006).
Coca-Cola and Pepsi: Allegations that soft drinks in India contained pesticide residue (2004–2007)		Hyundai's CEO: Arrested and jailed for bribery and slush fund charges (2006).
Coca-Cola's Dasani bottled water: High levels of bromate led to recall in Great Britain (2004).	Banned dietary supplements androstenedione and ephedra by FDA:	Boeing: Loses CEO and top level executive to ethics scandals (2004–2005).
Mad cow disease crisis: Outbreaks in Europe and Canada have created crises in sales and safety for meat industry (2001–2004).	Crisis for dozens of pharmaceutical and vitamin firms (2004).	Enron: Scandal began with off-the-books partnerships, aggressive accounting, and allegations of fraud and bankruptcy (2001–2004).
	Tobacco companies: Dangerous products and advertising. Allegations of addictions and death by cancer (1990–2004).	
Firestone and Ford: Tire tread separation outbreak (2001–2002).	Dow Corning: Silicone breast implants alleged to lead to serious health problems (1994).	WorldCom: CEO Bernard Ebbers charged with massive accounting fraud (2003–2004).
Food Lion: Supermarket chain accused by ABC-TV's *Prime Time Live* of selling spoiled meat (1992).	Johnson & Johnson: Cyanide-tampering Tylenol poisonings (1982).	Arthur Andersen: Involvement in Enron scandal led to dissolution of firm (2002).

Issue Management

Because it is at the heart of the public policy issues we address in this chapter, we will begin with a discussion of issue management. Risk management is an effort to keep issues from arising and crisis management is the management of issues that have become major threats. Issue management is a process by which organizations identify issues in the stakeholder environment, analyze and prioritize those issues in terms of their relevance to the organization, plan responses to the issues, and then evaluate and monitor the results. It is helpful to think of issue management in connection with concepts introduced in the preceding chapter, such as the sustainable strategic management process, enterprise-level strategy, corporate public policy, and integrated reporting.

Two Approaches to Issues Management

Thinking about the concepts mentioned here requires us to make some distinctions. A central consideration seems to be that issues management has been thought of in two major ways: (1) narrowly, in which public, or social, issues are the primary focus, and (2) broadly, in which strategic issues and the strategic management process are the focus of attention. Fahey has provided a useful distinction between these two approaches. He refers to (1) the **conventional approach** and (2) the **strategic management approach**.[9]

Conventional Approach (Narrowly Focused) This approach to issues management has the following characteristics:[10]

- Issues fall within the domain of public policy or public affairs management.
- Issues typically have a public policy or public affairs orientation or flavor.
- An issue is any trend, event, controversy, or public policy development that might affect the corporation.
- Issues originate in social, political, regulatory, or judicial environments.

Strategic Management Approach (Broadly Inclusive) This approach to issues management has evolved in a small number of companies and is typified by the following:[11]

- Issues management is typically the responsibility of senior line management or strategic planning staff.
- Issues identification is more important than it is in the conventional approach.
- Issues management is seen as an approach to the anticipation and management of external and internal challenges to the company's strategies, plans, and assumptions.

Figure 6-2 portrays strategic issues management as depicted by H. Igor Ansoff. Note the "strategic" characteristics—threats or opportunities and strengths or weaknesses—to which we alluded in the preceding chapter.

At the risk of oversimplification, we consider the primary distinction between the two perspectives on issues management to be that the conventional approach focuses on public or social issues, whereas the strategic approach is broadly inclusive of all issues. In addition, the conventional approach can be used as a "stand-alone" decision-making process, whereas the strategic approach is interconnected with the strategic management process as a whole. Another difference may be whether operating managers, strategic planners, or public affairs staff members are implementing the system. Beyond these distinctions, the two approaches have much in common.

The discussion in this chapter emphasizes the conventional approach, because this book focuses on public, social, and ethical stakeholder issues. We should point out, however, that the purpose in the preceding chapter was to convey the notion that social issues ought to be seen as just one part of the broader strategic management process. The chapter discussed environmental analysis as a broad phenomenon; here the emphasis is on social or ethical issues, although it is obvious that a consideration of these issues is embedded in a larger, more strategically focused process, such as that depicted in Figure 6-2.

Therefore, we are comfortable with both perspectives on issues management. We should point out that the conventional approach could be perceived as a subset of the strategic approach. Much of what is said about issues management applies to issues arising from social or ethical domains or strictly business domains. In a sense, the two approaches are highly inseparable, and it is difficult for organizations to operate effectively unless they address both in some way. For our purposes, however, the conventional perspective is emphasized.

The Changing Issue Mix

The emergence of "company issue management groups" and "issue managers" has been a direct outgrowth of the changing mix of issues that managers have had to handle. Economic and financial issues have always been an inherent part of the business process, although their complexity seems to have increased as global markets have broadened and competitiveness has become such a critical issue. The growth of technology, especially the Internet, has presented business with other issues to address. The most

FIGURE 6-2
Strategic Issue
Management

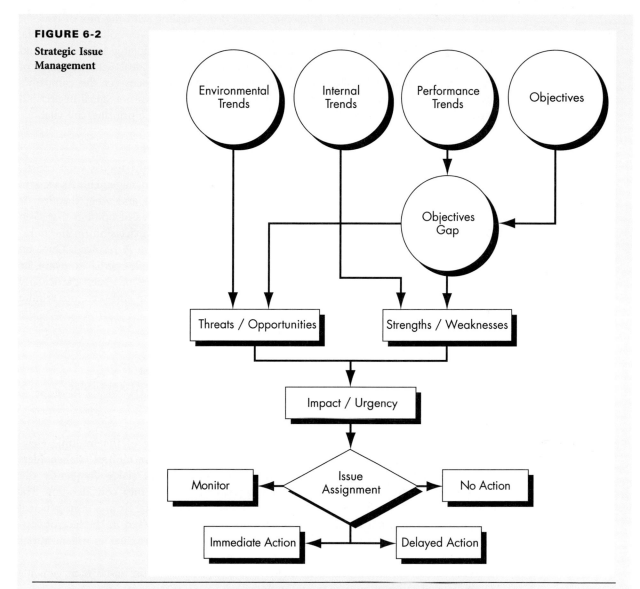

Source: H. Igor Ansoff, "Strategic Issue Management," *Strategic Management Journal* (Vol. 1, 1980), 137.

dramatic growth has been in social, ethical, and political issues—all public issues that have high visibility, media appeal, and interest among special-interest stakeholder groups. We should further observe that these issues become more interrelated over time.

For most firms, social, ethical, political, and technological issues are at the same time economic issues, because firms' success in handling them frequently has a direct bearing on their financial statuses, reputations, and well-being. Over time, management groups face an escalating challenge as a changing mix of issues creates a cumulative effect.

A Portfolio Approach Many firms get affected by so many issues that one wonders how they can deal with them all. One way is to see no connection between the issues; that is, to take things on an issue-by-issue basis. An alternative is the **portfolio approach.**[12] In this view, experience with prior issues likely influences future issues.

Such a view provides focus and coherence to the firm's dealing with the mix of issues it faces. Issues that might show up in Royal Dutch Shell's issue portfolio, for example, might be stopping climate change, protecting biodiversity, reducing wastewater, and operating in sensitive regions. A company such as Shell might deal with hundreds of issues, and the issue portfolio helps to prioritize and provide focus for the company's resources. The nonadoption of certain issues into the portfolio does not signal neglect but is part of a rational process of issue management in which strategic priorities are vital.[13]

Issue Definition and the Issue Management Process

Before describing the issue management process, we should briefly discuss what constitutes an issue and what assumptions we are making about issue management. As we said previously, an *issue* is a gap between what stakeholders expect and what the firm is doing. The gap typically evokes debate, controversy, or differences of opinion that need to be resolved. At some point, the organization needs to make a decision on the unresolved matter, but such a decision does not mean that the issue is resolved. Once an issue becomes public and subject to public debate and high-profile media exposure, its resolution becomes increasingly more difficult. One of the features of issues, particularly those arising in the social or ethical realm, is that they are ongoing and therefore require ongoing responses.

Following are some of the characteristics of an **emerging issue**:[14]

- The terms of the debate are not clearly defined.
- The issue deals with matters of conflicting values and interest.
- The issue does not lend itself to automatic resolution by expert knowledge.
- The issue is often stated in value-laden terms.
- Trade-offs are inherent.

The question of issue definition can be complicated because of the multiple viewpoints that come into play when an issue is considered. There are multiple stakeholders and motivations in any given management situation. Personal stakes frequently can be important factors but are often either ignored or not taken into consideration. For example, some of the affected parties may be interested in the issue from a deep personal perspective and will not compromise or give up their positions even in the face of concrete evidence that clearly refutes them.[15] Thus, the resolution of issues in organizations is not easy.

What about the assumptions we make when we choose to use issue management? The following assumptions are typically made:[16]

- Issues can be identified earlier, more completely, and more reliably than in the past.
- Early anticipation of issues widens the organization's range of options.
- Early anticipation permits study and understanding of the full range of issues.
- Early anticipation permits the organization to develop a positive orientation toward the issue.
- The organization will have earlier identification of stakeholders.
- The organization will be able to supply information to influential publics earlier and more positively, thus allowing them to understand the issue better.

These are not only assumptions of issue management but also benefits in that they make the organization more effective in its issue-management process.

Model of the Issue Management Process Like the strategic management process that entails a multitude of sequential and interrelated steps or stages, the issue management process has been conceptualized by many different authorities in a variety of ways.

Conceptualizations of issue management have been developed by companies, academics, consultants, and associations. The issue management process discussed here has been extracted from many of the conceptualizations previously developed. This process represents the elements or stages that seem to be common to most issue management models. This process is consistent with the stakeholder orientation we have been developing and using.

Figure 6-3 presents a model of the issue management process as is discussed here. It contains *planning aspects* (identification, analysis, ranking or prioritization of issues, and formulation of responses) and *implementation aspects* (implementation of responses and evaluation, monitoring, and control of results). Although we discuss the stages in the issue management process as though they were discrete, in reality they may be interrelated and overlap one another.

Identification of Issues   Many names have been assigned to the process of issue identification. The terms *social forecasting, futures research, environmental scanning*, and *public issues scanning* have been used at various times, and many techniques have been employed as well. All of these approaches or techniques are similar, but each has its own unique characteristics. Common to all of them, however, is the need to scan the environment and identify emerging issues or trends that might later be determined to have some relevance to or impact on the organization. In recent years, examples of identified issues that may have widespread ramifications for many organizations include natural disasters (e.g., the Great East Japan Earthquake), acts of terrorism (e.g., World Trade Center), potential pandemics (e.g., H1N1 outbreaks), and economic events (e.g., the global financial crisis).

FIGURE 6-3

The Issue Management Process

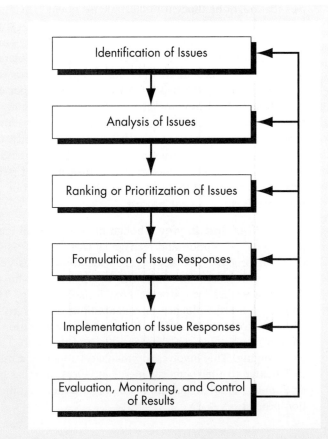

Issue identification, in its most rudimentary form, involves the assignment to some individual in the organization the tasks of continuously scanning social media and a variety of publications to build a comprehensive list of issues. Often this same person or group will also review public documents, records of congressional hearings, and other such sources of information. One result of this scanning is an internal report that is circulated throughout the organization. The next step in this evolution may be for the company to subscribe to a trend information service that is prepared by a private individual or consulting firm that specializes in environmental or issue scanning.[17]

Futurists, people who make a systematic effort to predict the future, have contributed to the body of knowledge that has helped issue identification. The field of futurism was founded over a century ago and remains strong today.[18] Futurists are common on Madison Avenue, in Washington think tanks and as corporate change experts.[19] On LinkedIn, nearly 5,000 people describe themselves as current or former futurists.[20]

Futurist Graham T. T. Molitor contends, "[e]verybody is a futurist" because forecasting is inherent in the tasks of everyday life.[21] Thus by monitoring ongoing trends, individuals can do their own forecasting of the future. Molitor proposed that there are five leading forces as predictors of social change:[22]

- Leading events
- Leading authorities or advocates
- Leading literature
- Leading organizations
- Leading political jurisdictions

If these five forces are monitored closely, impending social change can be identified and, in some cases, predicted. Figure 6-4 presents Molitor's five leading forces, as well as examples that might be thought to illustrate his points. The attacks on the World Trade Center in New York added the issue of "preparation for terrorism" to future lists of leading events portending significant social change. National security and business security are now vital issues for managers today. Similarly, the Global Financial Crisis has underscored the importance of corporate transparency and public affairs to managers.

Today social media makes it easier not only to spot emerging trends but also to spot them earlier. According to Terry Young, who is forming a new advertising agency geared toward identifying emerging trends, social media "is allowing us to do things we couldn't three, four, five years ago. We have the opportunity to identify and see pop culture trends when they're starting and incorporate our brands early in the process."[23] Social media has the same impact on the management of issues—issues can be identified as they are starting and these emerging issues can then be incorporated into issue management much earlier in the process.

Issue Selling and Buying Though the source of all issues is the external environment, the internal perception and managerial treatment of issues greatly affects the issue identification process. The key in issue identification is getting the people regularly confronted with issues in touch with top managers who can do something about them. This process has two aspects. First is **issue selling.** This relates to middle managers exerting upward influence in organizations as they try to attract the attention of top managers to issues salient to them and the organization.[24] In other words, they have to sell top management on the importance of the issue. The second part of this process is **issue buying.** This involves top managers adopting a more open mind-set for the issues that matter to their subordinates.[25] In short, internal organization members and their assessments of what matters to the organization significantly affect the issue identification process.

FIGURE 6-4   **Examples of Forces Leading Social Change**

Leading Forces	Examples	Public Issue Realm
Events	Salmonella outbreaks	Food safety
	H1N1 flu outbreaks	Public health/safety
	Enron, WorldCom, Arthur Andersen	Corporate governance, fraud
	World Trade Center attacks	Terrorism as public threat
	Three Mile Island/Chernobyl	Nuclear plant safety
	Bhopal gas leak	Plant safety
	Earth Day	Environment
	Tylenol poisonings	Product tampering
	Love Canalc	Environment—toxic waste
	Raj Rajaratnam scandal	Insider trading abuses
	Clarence Thomas hearings	Sexual harassment
	BP oil rig explosion	Environment
	Global financial crisis, subprime lending crisis	Corporate governance, regulation
Authorities/Advocates	Ralph Nader	Consumerism
	Rachel Carson	Pesticides and genetic engineering
	Rev. Martin Luther King	Civil rights
	Former Vice President Al Gore	Global warming
	General Colin Powell	Volunteerism
Literature	*Global Warming* (John Houghton)	Global warming
	Unsafe at Any Speed (Ralph Nader)	Automobile safety
	Megatrends (John Naisbitt)	Issue identification
Organizations	Friends of the Earth	Environment
	Sierra Club	Environment
	Action for Children's Television (ACT)	Children's advertising
	People for the Ethical Treatment of Animals (PETA)	Animal rights
	Mothers Against Drunk Driving (MADD)	Highway safety, alcohol abuse
Political Jurisdictions	State of Michigan—Whistle-Blower Protection Act	Employee freedom of speech
	State of Delaware	Corporate governance
	States of Connecticut, Iowa, Massachusetts, New Hampshire, Vermont	Gay Marriage

© Cengage Learning 2015

Analysis of Issues   The next two steps in the issue management process—analysis and ranking of issues—are closely related. To analyze an issue means to carefully study, dissect, break down, group, or engage in any specific process that helps management better understand the nature or characteristics of the issue. An analysis requires that managers look beyond the obvious manifestations of the issue and strive to learn more of its history, development, current nature, and potential for future relevance to the organization.

A series of key questions that focus on stakeholder groups in attempting to analyze issues has been proposed:[26]

- Who (which stakeholder) is affected by the issue?
- Who has an interest in the issue?
- Who is in a position to exert influence over the issue?
- Who has expressed opinions on the issue?
- Who ought to care about the issue?

In addition to these questions, the following key questions help with issue analysis:[27]

- Who started the ball rolling? (historical view)
- Who is now involved? (contemporary view)
- Who will get involved? (future view)

Answers to these questions place management in a better position to rank or prioritize the issues so that it will have a better sense of the urgency with which the issues need to be addressed.

Ranking or Prioritization of Issues Issues vary in the extent to which they matter to an organization, and so determining which issues matter most is essential in determining which ones should receive the most organizational resources, such as time and money. Of the many ways to analyze issues, the two most critical dimensions of issues are likelihood of occurrence and impact on the organization. Two essential questions are (1) *How likely is the issue to affect the organization?* and (2) *How much impact will the issue have?* [28]

Once these questions are answered, it is necessary to prioritize issues as to their importance or relevance to the organization. Those listed as top priority will receive the most attention and resources, while those at the bottom may even be removed from consideration because of their low likelihood or potential impact. The prioritization stage may involve a simple grouping of issues into categories ranging from the most urgent to the least important. Alternatively, a more elaborate or sophisticated scoring system may be employed.[29] Other techniques that have been used in issues identification, analysis, and prioritization include polls or surveys, expert panels, content analysis, the Delphi technique, trend extrapolation, scenario building, and the use of precursor events or bellwethers.[30] Teams of company experts are also used. For example, Baxter International, a U.S.-based health care and biotech firm, uses multidisciplinary teams because its main issues are in bioethics, and expertise in this subject cuts across a number of different knowledge-based lines of business.[31]

Earlier we described a simple issues identification process as involving an individual in the organization or a subscription to a newsletter or trend-spotting service. The analysis and ranking stages could be done by an individual, but more often, the company moves up to a next stage of formalization. This next stage involves assignment of the issue management function to a team, often as part of a public affairs department, which begins to specialize in the issue management function. This group of specialists can provide a wide range of issue management activities, depending on the commitment of the company to the process. Some companies have created issue management units or managers to alert the management on emerging trends and controversies and to help mobilize the companies' resources to deal with them.

Formulation and Implementation of Responses Formulation and implementation of responses are two steps in the issue management process combined here for discussion purposes. We should observe that the formulation and implementation stages in the issue management process are quite similar to the corresponding stages discussed in the preceding chapter, which pertained to the strategic management process as a whole.

Formulation in this case refers to the response design process. On the basis of the analysis conducted, companies can then identify options that might be pursued in dealing with the issues, in making decisions, and in implementing those decisions. Strategy formulation refers not only to the formulation of the actions that the firm intends to take but also to the creation of the overall strategy, or degree of aggressiveness, employed in carrying out those actions. Options might include aggressive pursuit, gradual pursuit, or selective pursuit of goals, plans, processes, or programs.[32] All of these more detailed plans are part of the strategy formulation process.

Once plans for dealing with issues have been formulated, *implementation* becomes the focus. Many organizational aspects need to be addressed in the implementation process, including the clarity of the plan itself, resources needed to implement the plan, top management support, organizational structure, technical competence, and timing.[33]

Evaluation, Monitoring, and Control These recognizable steps in the issue management process were also treated as steps in the strategic management process in Chapter 5. In the current discussion, they mean that companies should continually evaluate the results of their responses to the issues and ensure that these actions are kept on track. In particular, this stage requires careful monitoring of stakeholders' opinions. A form of stakeholder audit—something derivative of the social audit discussed in Chapter 5— might be used. The information gathered during this final stage in the issue management process is then fed back to the earlier stages in the process so that changes or adjustments might be made as needed. Evaluation information may be useful at each stage in the process.

The issue management process has been presented as a complete system. In practice, companies apply the stages across various degrees of formality or informality as needed or desired. For example, because issue management is more important in some situations than in others, some stages of the process may be truncated to meet the needs of different firms in different industries. In addition, some firms are more committed to issue management than others.

Issue Development Process

A vital attribute of issue management is that issues tend to develop according to an evolutionary pattern. This pattern might be thought of as a developmental or growth process or, as some have called it, a life cycle. The life cycle is often considered to have five stages—early, emerging, current, crisis, and dormant.[34] It is important for managers to have some appreciation of this **issue development process** so that they can recognize when an event or trend is becoming an issue and because it might affect the strategy the firm employs in dealing with the issue. Companies may take a variety of courses of action depending on the stage of the issue in the process.

Figure 6-5 presents a simplified view of what an issue development life cycle process might look like. In the beginning, a nascent issue emerges in the press or social media, is enunciated by public interest organizations, and is detected through public opinion polling. According to a former director of corporate responsibility at Monsanto, the issue is low-key and flexible at this stage.[35] During this time, the issue may reflect a felt need, receive media coverage, and attract interest group development and growth. A typical firm may notice the issue but take no action. More issue-oriented firms may become more active in their monitoring and in their attempts to shape or help "define the issue."[36] Active firms may have the capacity to prevent issues from going any further, through either effective responses to the issues or effective lobbying. In the next stage of the cycle, national media attention and leading political jurisdictions (e.g., cities, states, or countries) may address the issue. Quite often, federal government attention is generated in the form of studies and hearings; legislation, regulation, and litigation follow. This is simply an example of a sequence. Issues vary, and so the stages in the process, especially the early stages, might occur in a different sequence or in an iterative pattern. Further, not all issues complete the process; some are resolved before they reach the stage of legislation or regulation. It is important not to oversimplify the issue

FIGURE 6-5

Issue Development
Life Cycle Process

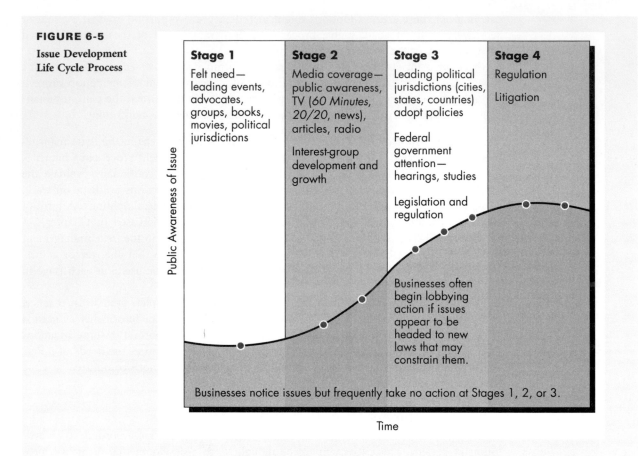

Stage 1

Felt need—
leading events,
advocates,
groups, books,
movies, political
jurisdictions

Stage 2

Media coverage—
public awareness,
TV (*60 Minutes*,
20/20, news),
articles, radio

Interest-group
development and
growth

Stage 3

Leading political
jurisdictions (cities,
states, countries)
adopt policies

Federal
government
attention—
hearings, studies

Legislation and
regulation

Stage 4

Regulation

Litigation

Businesses often
begin lobbying
action if issues
appear to be
headed to new
laws that may
constrain them.

Businesses notice issues but frequently take no action at Stages 1, 2, or 3.

Public Awareness of Issue

Time

© Cengage Learning

development process. The paths issues follow vary with the nature of the issues and the intensity and variety of stakeholder interests and values. The complex interactions of all the variables make it unlikely issues will follow a straight line.[37]

Illustrations of Issue Development This evolution may be illustrated through two examples. First, consider the issue of environmental protection. The social expectation was manifested in Rachel Carson's book *Silent Spring* (1963); it became a political issue in Eugene McCarthy's political platform (1968); it resulted in legislation in 1971–1972 with the creation of the Environmental Protection Agency (EPA); and it was reflected in social control by emissions standards, pollution fines, product recalls, and environmental permits in later years. Today, the important and pervasive issue of sustainability can be traced to these early roots. The second example involves product or consumer safety. The social expectation manifested in Ralph Nader's book *Unsafe at Any Speed* (1964). It then became a political issue through the National Traffic Auto Safety Act and Motor Vehicle Safety Hearings (1966), and that resulted in legislation in 1966 with the passage of the Motor Vehicle Safety Act and mandatory seat belt usage laws in four states (1984). It was reflected in social control through the ordering of seat belts in all cars (1967), defects litigation, product recalls, and driver fines. Today, product safety is an institutionalized issue that all companies must address.[38]

Issue Management in Practice

Issue management began as a way for companies to get in front of, and not simply respond to, public policy issues that could affect the organization. Howard Chase, the father of issue management, described it as "a methodology by which the private sector can get out of the unenviable position of being at the end of the crack-the-whip political line."[39] Today, issue management covers not only public policy activities but also a full range of public relations and management activities. There is greater use of interdepartmental issue teams, with the public affairs department often serving as coordinator and strategist but with appropriate line and staff executives charged with ultimate accountability for implementation. In practice, therefore, issue management does not function as a stand-alone activity but has been subsumed into a host of functions for which modern public affairs departments take responsibility.[40]

Issue management faces a serious challenge in business today. From the standpoint of the turbulence in the stakeholder environment, issue management is sorely needed. To become a permanent part of the organization, however, issue management will have to prove itself continuously. We can talk conceptually about the process with ease, but the field remains somewhat nebulous even though it is struggling to become more scientific and legitimate. Managers want results, and if issue management cannot deliver those results, it will be destined to failure as a management process. A practitioner of issue management warned that issue management "often attracts excessive process at the expense of real progress."[41]

Research has shown that companies that adopted issue management processes developed better overall and issue-specific reputations and had better short- and long-term financial performance than organizations not practicing issue management.[42] By combining issue management and stakeholder management, the most successful companies used stakeholder integration techniques in their implementation. This means that the firms actively sought to establish close-knit ties with a broad range of external and internal stakeholders and successfully incorporated their values and interests into management decisions.[43]

Risk Management

The difference between risk management and issue management is one of timing. Risk management concerns potential issues—it addresses an issue that has not yet occurred and endeavors to keep the issue from arising. The act of identifying and preparing for potential issues is difficult for the human psyche as our bounded rationality is not geared toward envisioning the future.[44] Robert Kaplan and Anette Mikes argue that, too often, managers adopt a compliance approach to the management of risk by basing it on rules. This can be effective in controlling preventable, internal risks but not in controlling risks that stem from a company's strategy or risks caused by major disruptions in the external environment. They provide an example of Tony Hayward's tenure as CEO of BP. When he arrived at BP in 2007, he promised to make safety his priority and, to that end, he instituted new rules. These rules included the requirement that employees not text while driving and that they use lids on their coffee cups while walking. Of course, these rules did not prevent the *Deepwater Horizon* from exploding three years later.[45]

Kaplan and Mikes provide a new framework for risk management that divides it into three categories:[46]

- *Preventable risks*—internal risks that offer no strategic benefits
- *Strategic risks*—risks taken to achieve greater returns
- *External risks*—external risks that cannot be controlled

Tony Hayward's safety program of safe driving and covered coffee cups comes under the first category of **preventable risks.** Failing to prevent these risks can cause serious damage and so risk managers should eliminate them whenever possible. Because they are internal and foreseeable, preventable risks lend themselves to a rule-based compliance approach. A corporate mission that defines the company's values, clear boundaries for employee behavior, and effective monitoring procedures are effective at preventing this category of risks. [47]

Strategic risks, unlike preventable risks, are not necessarily bad. Because risk and return are related, companies might take on additional risk in order to pursue a company strategy that promises higher returns. BP took on extra risk when it decided to drill several miles below the surface of the Gulf of Mexico, because the oil and gas there held the potential of significant returns. In this instance, a two-pronged risk management approach is needed to curtail the risk:

1. Reducing the probability of the risk event occurring, and
2. Developing the capability to manage the risk event should it occur.

A strategic risk management program does not prevent a firm from taking on strategic risks; it simply enables the firm to do so more effectively.[48]

External risks are beyond the firm's control. They come from outside the company and include such events as natural disasters and economic shocks. These usually cannot be controlled and they can be the most difficult to predict. Methods of identifying external risks should include techniques like scenario analysis and war-gaming to assist risk managers in foreseeing the unforeseeable. Some external risk events have a low probability of occurrence and so are difficult for managers to envision.[49]

Risk Management and Sustainability

Sustainability involves living in the present in a way that does not compromise the future. Risk management involves taking action today that will mitigate or prevent a problem that could arise in the future. As such, sustainability and risk management share a connection in that both are concerned with the future consequences of present-day actions. Sustainability is concerned both with not harming and with benefitting future generations. Risk management can provide a mechanism for avoiding, or at least mitigating, future harm to stakeholders and avoiding or mitigating the risk of not benefitting stakeholders in the future.[50]

Risk-shifting is an issue that merits attention in this regard. In the pursuit of sustainability for the business enterprise, some managers may use management techniques that shift risk from the firm to other parties. For example, some techniques such as credit default swaps can shift risks to the customer base, eroding the economic sustainability of the consumer.[51] This underscores the importance of a holistic approach to sustainability. Risk managers must take care not to promote the sustainability of the firm in such a way that it threatens the sustainability of stakeholders.

Crisis Management

Prudential Financial became a major player in the Japanese market over time. After entering the market in 1988, the company expanded through a 2001 acquisition of Gibraltar Life Insurance, Ltd.[52] In February 2011, the company "doubled down" on its investment in Japan with a $4.8 billion purchase of Star and Edison life insurance companies from AIG.[53] The earthquake and tsunami hit just a few weeks later, with devastating loss of life and property.[54] The first thing Prudential did was to check to make sure its 23,000 employees in Japan were safe. Then they set about responding to the crisis. The Prudential Foundation donated 500 million yen, $6.1 million, to support relief efforts. The Foundation also pledged to match individual donations that employees made.[55] Then people pitched in with volunteer efforts. In one instance, a team of volunteers, 37 people from 10 different countries and 16 different businesses, went to Japan to help with clean up in one of the worst affected areas.[56]

Prudential could not control the devastation caused by the earthquake and tsunami but the company could, and did, control its reaction to it effectively. Crises occur with regularity, making them almost routine. However, the fallout from a crisis is not routine in any way. Crises can rip the foundations of organizations to shreds if top management does not respond quickly, decisively, and effectively.[57] At the same time, a strong and effective response to a crisis can strengthen an organization in the end. Masahiro Watanabe, Head of Human Resources at Prudential Corporation Asia Life in Japan, saw value in the volunteer experience. He said, "It was a great opportunity for me to be able to support and participate in this program as a citizen of the host country. In one respect, this program is a part of the social contribution activities of a corporation. However, looking at it from a different side, it offered an occasion for training and team-building that transcended the boundaries of the local business units."

Several observers have suggested that the Tylenol poisonings in 1982 put crisis management "on the map"—it was the case that marked the beginning of the new corporate discipline known as crisis management because Johnson & Johnson's voluntary recall of some 31 million Tylenol bottles was the first important example of an organization assuming responsibility for its products without being pressured.[58] Other corporate crises include the Union Carbide Bhopal disaster, which killed more than 2,000 people in India; the attacks on the World Trade Center in New York, which resulted in the deaths of approximately 3,000 people; and Firestone and Ford being implicated in massive tire recalls due to faulty tires causing tread separations and deaths.

The Nature of Crises

There are many kinds of crises. Those mentioned here have all been associated with major stakeholder groups and have achieved high-visibility status. Injured or killed

---

Spotlight on Sustainability

Sustainable Corporations Shine in Economic Crisis

An A. T. Kearney study entitled "Green Winners: The Performance of Sustainability-Focused Companies in the Financial Crisis" analyzed 99 of the largest companies officially recognized as having a strong commitment to sustainable practice. The study defined sustainable practice as being "geared toward protecting the environment and promoting social well-being while achieving shareholder value." It found that sustainable companies outperformed their competitors by 15 percent in 16 of 18 industries, with the difference representing an average of $650 million more in market capitalization per company than their competitors.

The study found that sustainability involves characteristics that help firms weather a crisis. A long-term perspective, sound risk management practices, and green innovations such as reduced waste and emissions and the use of alternate energy sources were cited as factors that gave sustainable companies a competitive edge. Recognition for their sustainability efforts may also have enabled them to differentiate themselves from their competitors.

The report concluded that "the most sustainability-focused may well emerge from the current crisis stronger than ever … recognized by investors who appreciate the true long-term value of sustainability."

Source: Robert Kropp, "Sustainable Corporations Outperform during Economic Crisis," *Social Funds* (February 16, 2009), http://www.socialfunds.com/news/article.cgi/article2628.html.

customers, injured employees, injured stockholders, and unfair practices are the concerns of modern crisis management. Not all crises involve such public or ethical issues, but these kinds of crises almost always ensure front-page status. Major companies can be seriously damaged by such episodes, especially if the episodes are poorly handled.

What is a crisis? Dictionaries state that a **crisis** is a "turning point for better or worse," an "emotionally significant event," or a "decisive moment." We all think of crises as being emotion charged, but we do not always think of them as turning points for better or for worse. The implication here is that a crisis is a decisive moment that, if managed one way, could make things worse but, if managed another way, could make things better. Choice is present, and how the crisis is managed can make a difference.

From a managerial point of view, a line needs to be drawn between a problem and a crisis. Problems, of course, are common in business. A crisis, however, is not as common. A useful way to think about a crisis is as follows:

A crisis is an extreme event that may threaten your very existence. At the very least, it causes substantial injuries, deaths, and financial costs, as well as serious damage to your reputation.[59]

Another definition is also helpful in understanding the critical aspects of a crisis:

An organizational crisis is a low-probability, high-impact event that threatens the viability of the organization and is characterized by ambiguity of cause, effect, and means of resolution, as well as by a belief that decisions must be made swiftly.[60]

Consider, for a moment, the classic case wherein StarKist Foods, then a subsidiary of H.J. Heinz Co. but now a wholly owned subsidiary of the Dongwon Group, faced a management crisis. Gerald Clay was appointed general manager of the Canadian subsidiary and was given the mandate to develop a five-year business strategy for the firm. Just after his arrival in Canada, the crisis hit: The Canadian Broadcasting Corporation accused his company of shipping one million cans of rancid and decomposing tuna. Dubbed "Tuna-gate" by the media, the crisis dragged on for weeks. With guidance from Heinz, Clay chose to keep quiet, even as the Canadian prime minister ordered the tuna seized. The silence cost plenty. According to Clay's boss, "We were massacred in the press." The company, which had commanded half the Canadian tuna market, watched revenues plunge by 90 percent. At one point, Clay's boss observed that the company's future was in doubt.[61] StarKist survived though they had to pull out of Canada due to the loss in market share. Tunagate was such a classic crisis management scandal, however, that it has its own entry in *Wikipedia*.[62]

Figure 6-6 presents a "how not to do it" case in crisis management as experienced by golf star Tiger Woods. Woods was under fire for allegations of serial infidelity that were at odds with the family-oriented image he had cultivated.

Types of Crises Many situations may leave companies vulnerable to crises. These include industrial accidents, environmental problems, union problems or strikes, product recalls, investor relations, hostile takeovers, proxy fights, rumors or media leaks, government regulatory problems, acts of terrorism, and embezzlement.[63] Other common crises include product tampering, executive kidnapping, work-related homicides, malicious rumors, and natural disasters that destroy corporate offices or information bases.[64] Since September 11, 2001, we have had to add terrorism to this list.

Crises may be grouped into seven families[65]:

- *Economic crises* (recessions, hostile takeovers, stock market crashes)
- *Physical crises* (industrial accidents, product failures, supply breakdown)
- *Personnel crises* (strikes, exodus of key employees, workplace violence)
- *Criminal crises* (product tampering, kidnappings, acts of terrorism)

FIGURE 6-6

Crisis Management and Tiger Woods, Inc.: How Not to Do It

When Tiger Woods crashed his Cadillac Escalade into a fire hydrant and a tree in his gated Florida community, the world's media converged upon him. Allegations of serial infidelity soon arose that set the pro golfer's personal and professional life into a tailspin. As the man behind a billion dollar financial empire and the personification of the brand it sells, Woods' personal trouble quickly developed into an organizational crisis. His management of the crisis held implications not only for him but also for the business that had been built around him.

Most crisis management experts fault his management of the crisis. Woods waited days to issue a statement, and the statement that appeared spoke only vaguely of "transgressions." Robbie Vorhaus, a crisis reputation adviser in New York, believes he should have spoken more quickly. He said, "If you don't tell your story first, then you're letting someone else tell your story. Now he has to react and respond to what everyone else is saying." This advice is similar to the advice Woods gave in an ESPN interview when he was asked about Michael Vick's response after Vick was caught being involved in a dog-fighting ring:

If you made that big a mistake, you've got to come out and just be contrite, be honest and just tell the public that "I was wrong".

Waiting a long time got a lot of people polarized.... If he would have come out earlier, he would've diffused a little more of it.

It has been suggested that Woods broke three basic rules of crisis management when he failed to follow his own advice:

- **Rule No. 1: Don't Wait.** After the car crash, Woods issued a statement acknowledging the accident but nothing else. Two days later, Woods issued another statement, but it was vague and the story was shaped by others in the interim.
- **Rule No. 2: Don't Run from the Truth.** Woods' first statement pleaded for privacy and claimed that "false, unfounded, and malicious rumors" were circulating, giving the impression that the rumors were untrue. Three days later, he changed his story but admitted only to unspecified "transgressions."
- **Rule No. 3: Don't Hide.** Woods hid away long after the accident, leaving the women who alleged that they had relationships with him as the only voices telling the story.

Sources: Dana Mattoli, "Tiger Bungles Crisis Management 101," *The Wall Street Journal* (December 8, 2009), A31; Ryan Ballingee, "Tiger's Own Words May Be Cause for Concern About Anthony Galea," *Waggle Room* (December 18, 2009). http://www.waggleroom.com; Rachel Beck, AP Business Writer, "Commentary: Tiger Flubs Crisis Management 101," *Sporting News* (December 11, 2009), http://www.sportingnews.com.

- *Information crises* (theft of proprietary information, cyberattacks)
- *Reputational crises* (rumormongering or slander, logo tampering)
- *Natural disasters* (earthquakes, floods, fires)

After major crises, companies report the following outcomes: The crises escalated in intensity, were subjected to media and government scrutiny, interfered with normal business operations, and damaged the company's bottom line. For example, as a result of the horrific attacks on the World Trade Center, companies experienced major power shifts among executives as some bosses fumbled with their responsibilities and didn't handle the crisis well. Those bosses who handled the crisis well garnered more responsibility, whereas others lost responsibilities.[66]

Four Crisis Stages There are several ways of describing the stages through which a crisis may progress. One view is that a crisis may consist of as many as four distinct stages: (1) a **prodromal crisis stage**, (2) an **acute crisis stage**, (3) a **chronic crisis stage**, and (4) a **crisis resolution stage**.[67]

Prodromal Crisis Stage This is the warning stage. ("Prodromal" is a medical term that refers to a previous notice or warning.) This stage could also be thought of as a symptom stage. Although it could be called a "precrisis" stage, this presupposes that one knows that a crisis is coming. Many experts suggest that a possible outbreak of avian flu would be in this stage. It is believed that crises "send out a repeated trail of early warning signals" that managers can learn to recognize.[68] Perhaps management should adopt this perspective: Watch each situation with the thought that it could be a crisis in the making. Early symptoms may be quite obvious, such as in the case where a social activist group tells the management it will boycott the company if a certain problem is not addressed. On the other hand, symptoms may be more subtle, as in the case where defect rates for a particular product a company makes start edging up over time.

Acute Crisis Stage   This is the stage at which the crisis has actually occurred, and there is no turning back. Damage has been done, and it is now up to management to handle or contain it. If the prodromal stage is the precrisis stage, the acute stage is the *actual* crisis stage. The crucial decision point at which things may get worse or better has been reached.

Chronic Crisis Stage   This is the lingering period. It may be the period of investigations, audits, or in-depth news stories. Management may see it as a period of recovery, self-analysis, or self-doubt. A survey of major companies found that crises tended to linger as much as two-and-a-half times longer in firms without crisis management plans than in firms with such plans.

Crisis Resolution Stage   This is the final stage—the goal of all crisis management efforts. When an early warning sign of a crisis is noted, the manager should seize control swiftly and determine the most direct and expedient route to resolution. If the warning signs are missed in the first stage, the goal is to speed up all phases and reach the final stage as soon as possible.

Figure 6-7 presents one way in which these four stages might be depicted. It should be noted that the phases may overlap and that each phase varies in intensity and

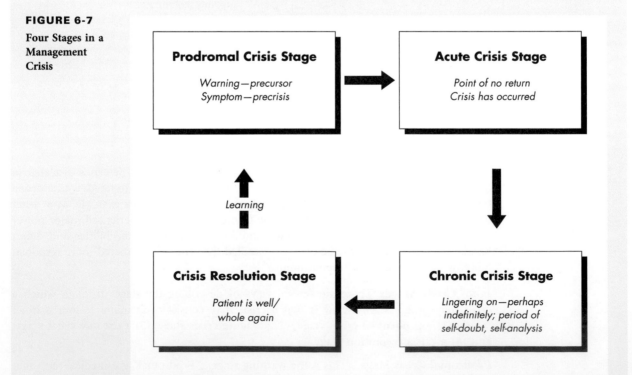

FIGURE 6-7

Four Stages in a Management Crisis

Prodromal Crisis Stage

Warning—precursor
Symptom—precrisis

Acute Crisis Stage

Point of no return
Crisis has occurred

Learning

Crisis Resolution Stage

Patient is well/
whole again

Chronic Crisis Stage

Lingering on—perhaps
indefinitely; period of
self-doubt, self-analysis

© Cengage Learning

duration. It is expected that management will learn from the crisis and thus will be better prepared for, and better able to handle, any future crisis.

Managing Business Crises

Five Practical Steps in Managing Crises The following five steps, synthesized by *BusinessWeek* magazine from the actual experiences of companies going through crises, are summarized and discussed next. They are (1) identifying areas of vulnerability, (2) developing a plan for dealing with threats, (3) forming crisis teams, (4) simulating crisis drills, and (5) learning from experience.[69]

First: Identify Areas of Vulnerability In the first step, some areas of vulnerability are obvious, such as potential chemical spills, whereas others are more subtle. The key seems to be in developing a greater consciousness of how things can go wrong and get out of hand. After the "Tunagate" incident, a vice president at Heinz set up brainstorming sessions. He said, "We're brainstorming about how we would be affected by everything from a competitor who had a serious quality problem to a scandal involving a Heinz executive."[70] A key to identifying areas of vulnerability is "recognizing the threat." The most skilled executives often fail at this stage because they are oblivious to emerging threats.[71] For example, many companies were surprised by and unprepared for the credit crisis in 2008. In contrast, AutoNation showed resilience during a crisis that devastated its industry. Years before the crisis struck, Chairman and CEO Mike Jackson considered what seemed to be unlikely scenarios. AutoNation executives asked themselves, "What if consumers bought cars every five years instead of every three?," and "What if the financing spigot turned off?"[72] Recognizing low-probability but high-consequence events is a challenge, but planning for them can help a company to survive major crises.[73]

Following are some ways that companies can identify areas of vulnerability:[74]

- *Scenario planning.* Create scenarios for crises that could occur over the next two years.
- *Risk analysis.* Estimate the probabilities and costs/benefits of estimated future events.
- *Incentives.* Reward managers for information sharing.
- *Networks.* Build formal coalitions to mobilize internal and external information suppliers.

Second: Develop a Plan for Dealing with Threats A plan for dealing with the most serious crisis threats is a logical next step. One of the most crucial issues is communications planning. After a Dow Chemical railroad car derailed near Toronto, forcing the evacuation of 250,000 people, Dow Canada prepared information kits on the hazards of its products so that executives would be knowledgeable enough to respond properly if a similar crisis were to arise in the future. Dow Canada also trained executives in interviewing techniques. This effort paid off several years later when an accident caused a chemical spill into a river that supplied drinking water for several nearby towns. The company's emergency response team arrived at the site almost immediately and established a press center that distributed information about the chemicals. In addition, the company recruited a neutral expert to speak about the hazards and how to deal with them. Officials praised Dow for its handling of this crisis.[75]

Getting an entire organization trained to deal with crises is difficult and expensive, but the CEO paraphrases what a car repairperson once said in a TV commercial: "You can pay now or pay a lot more later." Most of us would believe that now is infinitely better for everyone.[76]

Third: Form Crisis Teams   Another step that can be taken as part of an overall planning effort is the formation of **crisis teams**. Such teams have played key roles in many well-managed disasters. A good example is the team formed at Procter & Gamble when its Rely tampon products were linked with toxic shock syndrome. The team was quickly assembled, a vice president was appointed to head it, and after one week, the decision was made to remove Rely from marketplace shelves. The quick action earned the firm praise, and it paid off for P&G in the long run.

Another task in assembling crisis teams is identifying managers who can cope effectively with stress. Not every executive can handle the fast-moving, high-pressured, ambiguous decision environment that is created by a crisis, and early identification of executives who can is important. We should also note that it is not always the CEO who can best perform in such a crisis atmosphere.

Despite the careful use of crisis teams, crises can often overwhelm a carefully constructed plan. When ValuJet's Flight 592 crashed in the Florida Everglades, for example, ValuJet flawlessly executed a three-pronged, team-based crisis management plan calling for the company to (1) show compassion, (2) take responsibility, and (3) demonstrate that the airline learned from the crisis. Experts have said that the company handled the crisis well. However, a close look at the tragedy revealed that a series of complicating factors turned the crisis into something even more difficult than a well-scripted, perfectly executed crisis management plan could handle.[77]

Fourth: Simulate Crisis Drills   Some companies have gone so far as to run crisis drills in which highly stressful situations are simulated so that managers can "practice" what they might do in a real crisis. As a basis for conducting crisis drills and experiential exercises, a number of companies have adopted a crisis management software package. This software allows companies to centralize and maintain up-to-date crisis management information and allows company leaders to assign responsibilities to their crisis team, target key audiences, identify and monitor potential issues, and create crisis-response processes.[78]

Fifth: Learn From Experience   The final stage in crisis management is learn from experience. At this point, managers need to ask themselves exactly what they have learned from past crises and how that knowledge can be used to advantage in the future. Part of this stage entails an assessment of the effectiveness of the firm's crisis-handling strategies and identification of areas where improvements in capabilities need to be made. Without a crisis management system of some kind in place, the organization will find itself reacting to crises after they have occurred. If learning and preparation for the future are continuous, however, the firm may engage in more proactive behavior.[79]

It is important to note that effective crisis management requires a program tailored to a firm's specific industry, business environment, and crisis management experience. Effective crisis managers will understand that there are major crisis management factors that may vary from situation to situation, such as the type of crisis (e.g., natural disaster or human induced), the phase of the crisis, the systems affected (e.g., humans, technology, or culture), and the stakeholders affected. Managers cannot eliminate crises; however, they can become keenly aware of their vulnerabilities and make concerted efforts to understand and reduce these vulnerabilities through continuous crisis management programs.[80]

Crisis Communications

An illustration of crisis management without effective communications occurred during the Jack in the Box hamburger disaster years ago. There was an outbreak of *Escherichia coli* bacteria in the Pacific Northwest area, resulting in the deaths of four children. Following this crisis, the parent company, San Diego-based Foodmaker, entered a downward spiral after lawsuits by the families of victims enraged the public and franchisees. Foodmaker did most of the right things and did them quickly. The company immediately suspended hamburger sales, recalled suspect meat from its distribution system, increased cooking time for all foods, pledged to pay for all the medical costs related to the disaster, and hired a food safety expert to design a new food-handling system. However, it forgot to do one thing: Communicate with the public, including its own employees.[81]

The company's **crisis communications** efforts were inept. It waited a week before accepting any responsibility for the tragedy, preferring to point fingers at its meat supplier and even the Washington state health officials for not explaining the state's new guidelines for cooking hamburgers at higher temperatures. The media pounced on the company. The company was blasted for years even though within itself, the company was taking proper steps to correct the problem. The company suffered severe financial losses, and it took at least six years before the company felt it was on the road to recovery. "The crisis," as it was called around company headquarters, taught the firm an important lesson. CEO Robert Nugent was quoted later as saying, "Nobody wants to deal with their worst nightmare, but we should have recognized you've got to communicate."[82]

Virtually all crisis management plans call for effective crisis communications, but they are not always effectively executed. There are a number of different stakeholder groups with whom effective communications are critical, especially the media and those immediately affected by the crisis. Many companies have failed to manage their crises successfully because of inadequate or failed communications with key stakeholder groups. Successful communications efforts are crucial to effective crisis management. It is axiomatic that *prepared* communications will be more helpful than *reactive* communications. Ten steps of crisis communication that are worth summarizing include:[83]

1. Identify your crisis communications team.
2. Identify key spokespersons who will be authorized to speak for the organization.
3. Train your spokespersons.
4. Establish communications protocols.
5. Identify and know your audience.
6. Anticipate crises.
7. Assess the crisis situation.
8. Identify key messages you will communicate to key groups.
9. Decide on communications methods.
10. Be prepared to ride out the storm.

A brief elaboration on the importance of step 8, identifying key messages that will be communicated to key groups, is useful. It is important to communicate with internal stakeholders first because rumors are often started there, and uninformed employees can do great damage to a successful crisis management effort. Internal stakeholders are your best advocates and can be supportive during a crisis. Prepare news releases that contain as much information as possible, and get this information out to all media outlets at the same time. Communicate with others in the community who have a need to know, such as public officials, disaster coordinators, stakeholders, and others. Uniformity of response is of vital importance during a crisis and so it is important to have a key spokesperson (step 2).[84]

The Centers for Disease Control and Prevention (CDC) states as part of its crisis communications training that the first 48 hours of a crisis are the most important. The

ETHICS IN PRACTICE CASE

Crisis Management: When to Repent and When to Defend

When facing a crisis, especially one in which the organization is implicated, many crisis management experts take the approach that management or the firm needs to quickly repent of its malfeasance or wrongdoing, ask for forgiveness, and promise to do better in the future. This soft approach argues for engaging in careful communications and apologizing, if necessary. This approach, it is believed, is the best route to limiting damage and restoring the public's confidence in the company and its leaders.

In their book, *Damage Control: Why Everything You Know about Crisis Management Is Wrong* (2007), authors Eric Dezenhall and John Weber argue that this soft approach is often wrong. According to the authors, if you are facing a lawsuit, a sex scandal, a defective product, or allegations of insider trading, experts may tell you to stay positive, get your message out, and everything will be just fine. But, Dezenhall and Weber conclude, this kind of cheery talk does not help much during a real crisis, and it's easy to lose sight of your genuine priorities. If your case goes to trial, for example, you might want the public to think you're a wonderful company, but all that matters is what the jury thinks.

The authors support a political model of crisis management, which means you may have to fight back and defend yourself. When the company has done wrong, repentance is in order. When the company has been wronged, a strong defense is recommended. The authors recommend not admitting guilt and meeting each accusation with a counter claim. They say this is how Martha Stewart turned her public image around after serving a jail sentence. In another example, they say this is how Merck, the pharmaceutical company, recovered from legal defeats and bad press as it began to portray plaintiffs as selfish opportunists. They also cite how successful the mobile phone industry was in mounting a defense against the consumer complaints that the phones were causing brain tumors. The key, they say, is determining when to be conciliatory and when to defend aggressively.

1. What are the relevant issues in this debate over the best response to a crisis?
2. Is it best to apologize, repent and move on, or stand firm and aggressively defend?
3. What is the downside risk of mounting a rigorous defense?

Sources: Eric Dezenhall and John Weber, *Damage Control: Why Everything You Know about Crisis Management Is Wrong* (New York: Portfolio Hardcover, 2007); Richard Evans, "Crisis Management for a Vindictive Age," *Financial Times* (April 24, 2007), 12.

program's mantra is reported as "be *first*, be *right*, be *credible*."[85] Being first means getting your message out first, which allows you to control its accuracy and content. If a company is late in getting its message out, the media and others will fill in the blanks, and they might include rumors, their own speculations, misunderstandings, or bias. Being right means saying and doing the right thing. This is the ethical dimension of communications. This is done after the management has gathered all the facts and understands exactly what has happened in the crisis. Being credible means being open, honest, and speaking with one consistent voice. Mixed messages from mixed sources can lead to disaster. The company's spokesperson should be sincere, be empathetic, be accountable, demonstrate competence, display expertise, and put forth consistent facts.[86] For all this to happen, of course, careful crisis communications must be a priority in the crisis plan.

Successful Crisis Management

Be Prepared for Crises Being prepared for crises has become a primary activity in a growing number of companies. Today, most companies may be prepared for crises, but their degree of preparedness varies widely. In recent years, there is no better example of being well prepared than how well many business enterprises responded to the Hurricane Katrina disaster in 2005. They were applauded for their readiness and execution of disaster plans as the devastating hurricane hit the Southeast, especially the New Orleans and Gulf Coast regions of the country. Companies that stood out in their preparedness and assistance included Walmart and Home Depot.

These two companies had anticipated the impact of the hurricane, gotten their act together days beforehand, and implemented their plans to the benefit of thousands of affected residents. Some experts even observed that the Federal Emergency Management Agency (FEMA) and the Red Cross, both agencies whose mission it is to respond to crises, learned a lot from these companies and other such firms.[87] Because of the types of products and supplies they sell, these two companies and other big-box stores always seem to play key roles in natural disasters such as hurricanes, tornadoes, and other weather-related crises. Another major company that helped the government solve transportation and communication problems was FedEx. One of FedEx's radio antennae in New Orleans became the key communication link for FEMA as it sought to establish a communication system in the area.[88]

Learn from Crises Many corporate CEOs admitted that coping with Katrina taught them a great deal about preparing for crises and disasters. Major lessons learned included the following: Take care of your employees, keep communication lines open, and get ready for the next disaster.[89] General Electric (GE) chairman and CEO Jeff Immelt described himself as "humbler and hungrier" as a result of the global recession and credit crisis that sorely tested GE.[90] In addition to the expected responses of refocusing operations and cutting costs, Immelt has looked inward, changing his management style in response to the crisis and recession. He meets more regularly and individually with his 25 top executives, pushes more decision making to lower organizational levels, and, in a move that might not come naturally to a former applied math major, he has become more comfortable with ambiguity.[91]

Sometimes being prepared for one type of crisis provides valuable learning when other types of crises strike. A case in point was that of Childs Capital in New York City, a company that provides economic development in poor countries. The company's CEO, Donna Childs, put a disaster plan in place for business disruptions such as a subway fire, a scaffolding accident, a brownout, or some other smaller scale business disruption. She had made arrangements by developing a communications plan and a method for a continuous functioning off-site should the need arise. As a result of her crisis management for one type of disaster, she was back up and running one week after the collapse of the World Trade Center in New York. One result of her experience is that she is now giving weekly seminars on disaster preparedness and has even authored a book, *Prepare for the Worst, Plan for the Best: Disaster Preparedness and Recovery for Small Businesses.*[92]

A Successful Crisis Management Example We conclude this chapter with an illustration of a successful crisis management case study of one company. Earlier, we presented the handling of the J&J Tylenol crisis as a success story. This success story started with the kind of phone call every company dreads—"Your product is injuring people; we're announcing it at a press conference today." Schwan's Sales Enterprises, Inc., got such a call from the Minnesota Department of Health at about noon one fateful day. The Health Department reported that it had found a statistical link between Schwan's ice cream and confirmed cases of salmonella. Thousands of people in at least 39 states became ill with salmonella after eating tainted Schwan's ice cream, potentially setting the company up for a decade's worth of litigation. Instead, in a little more than a year after the outbreak, the vast majority of claims had been handled outside the legal system through direct settlements or as part of a class action suit in Minneapolis.[93]

Schwan's knew that its image of the smiling man in the sunshine-yellow Schwan's truck (with a Swan on the side) busily hand-delivering ice cream to grateful consumers was one of its major assets. Before the company was sure of the Health Department's findings, it halted sales and production, shut down, and invited the state health department, the department of agriculture, and the FDA into the plant to investigate. It also notified all its sales offices nationwide. Also, within the first 24 hours of the crisis, the company set up a hotline to answer consumer questions, contacted employees and managers to staff the hotline, prepared for a product recall, and began working with its insurer.[94]

By placing consumer safety as its number one priority, Schwan's was able to resolve the crisis much more quickly than would have been possible without a carefully designed crisis management plan. Whether by coincidence or preparedness, the manager of public affairs and the company's general counsel had completed a review and rewriting of the company's crisis management manual just two months before the outbreak. One vital component of the plan was a crisis management team, which went to work as soon as the news came. The crisis management team quickly set up a process for handling consumers who had been affected. The team, working with its insurance company, quickly helped customers get medical treatment and their bills paid. Settlements to customers who suffered from salmonella symptoms included financial damages, medical expenses, and other costs, such as reimbursement for workdays missed.[95]

How did the ice cream get contaminated with salmonella? After a month's investigation that kept the Marshall, Minnesota, plant closed, it was determined that the ice cream mix supplied by a few vendors was the culprit. The mix of cream, sugar, and milk had been shipped in a tanker truck that had previously held raw, unpasteurized eggs that had the bacteria. Schwan's quietly sought and received legal damages from the suppliers but stayed focused on its customers throughout the crisis.

What did Schwan's learn from this crisis? Previously, Schwan's did not repasteurize its ice cream mix once the mix arrived at the Marshall plant. Within a few weeks of the outbreak, however, the company had broken ground to build its own repasteurization plant. The company also leased a dedicated fleet of tanker trucks to deliver the ice cream mix from the suppliers to the plant, set up a system for testing each shipment, and delayed shipping the final product until the test results were known. In summary, Schwan's planning, quick response, and customer-oriented strategy combined to retain customer loyalty and minimize the company's legal exposure.[96] It was a case of good, effective crisis management.

Undoubtedly, in the years to come, stories will be told of successful crisis management in the aftermath of major traumatic events in the lives of organizations and society. Sadly, preparation for acts of terrorism is now a vital national and business issue. Clearly, the events of the past few years have made crisis management a priority topic in boardrooms and among managers.

Summary

Issue management and crisis management are two key approaches by which companies may plan for the turbulent stakeholder environment. Both these approaches are frequently found housed in a company's department of public affairs. Issue management is a process by which an organization identifies issues in the stakeholder environment, analyzes and prioritizes those issues in terms of their relevance to the organization, plans responses to the issues, and then evaluates and monitors the results. There are two approaches to issue management: the conventional approach and the strategic management approach. Issue management requires knowledge of the changing mix of issues, the issue management process, the issue development process, and how companies might implement issue management in practice. Issue management serves as a bridge to crisis management.

Crisis management, like issue management, is not a panacea for organizations. In spite of well-intended efforts by management, not all crises will be resolved in the company's favor. Nevertheless, being prepared for the inevitable makes sense, especially in today's world of instantaneous global communications and obsessive media coverage. Whether thinking about the long term, the intermediate term, or the short term, managers need to be prepared to handle crises. A crisis has a number of different stages, and managing crises requires a number of key steps before, during, and after the crisis. These steps include identifying areas of vulnerability, developing a plan for dealing with threats, forming crisis teams, using crisis drills, and learning from experience. Crisis communications is critical for successful crisis management. When used in tandem, issue and crisis management can help managers fulfill their economic, legal, ethical, and philanthropic responsibilities to stakeholders.

Key Terms

acute crisis stage, p. 163
chronic crisis stage, p. 163
conventional approach, p. 149
crisis, p. 162
crisis communications, p. 167
crisis management, p. 148
crisis resolution stage, p. 163
crisis teams, p. 166

emerging issue, p. 152
external risks, p. 160
issue, p. 148
issue buying, p. 154
issue selling, p. 154
issue development
    process, p. 157
issue management, p. 148

portfolio approach, p. 151
preventable risks, p. 159
prodromal crisis stage, p. 163
risk management, p. 148
strategic management
    approach, p. 149
strategic risks, p. 160

Discussion Questions

1. Which of the major stages in the issue management process do you think is the most important? Why?

2. Following the approach indicated in Figure 6-1, identify a new issue category not listed in Figure 6-1. Identify several examples of "crises" that have occurred in recent years under each issue category.

3. Identify one example, other than those listed in Figure 6-4, of each of the leading force categories: events, authorities/advocates, literature, organizations, and political jurisdictions.

4. Identify a crisis that has occurred in your life or in the life of someone you know, and briefly explain it in terms of the four crisis stages: prodromal, acute, chronic, and resolution.

5. Research the impacts on business organizations of the attacks on the World Trade Center in New York and the scandals that accompanied the Global Financial Recession. What have been successful and unsuccessful examples of crisis management that have come out of this research? Is terrorism a likely crisis for which business may prepare? How does preparation for terrorism (which comes from without) compare with preparation for ethical scandals (which come from within)?

Endnotes

1. Alice M. Tybout and Michelle Roehm, "Let the Response Fit the Scandal," *Harvard Business Review* (December 2009) 82–88.

2. Ibid.

3. Stephanie Armour, "Food Sickens Millions as Company-Paid Checks Find It Safe," *Bloomberg* *Markets Magazine* (October 11, 2012), http://www.bloomberg.com/news/2012-10-11/food-sickens-millions-as-industry-paid-inspectors-find-it-safe.html. Accessed January 26, 2013.

4. Danielle Demetriou, "Japan Earthquake, Tsunami and Fukushima Nuclear Disaster: 2011 Review," *The*

Telegraph (December 19, 2011), http://www.telegraph.co.uk/news/worldnews/asia/japan/8953574/Japan-earthquake-tsunami-and-Fukushima-nuclear-disaster-2011-review.html. Accessed January 26, 2013.

5. Duraideivamani Sankararajan and NK Shrivastava, "Risks vs. Issues," *PM Network* (June 2012), 28–29; Tony Jaques, "Towards a New Terminology: Optimizing the Value of Issue Management," *Journal of Communication Management* (Vol. 7, No. 2), 140–147. Cited in Tony Jaques, "Issue and Crisis Management: Quicksand in the Definitional Landscape," *Public Relations Review* (September 2009), 281.

6. http://issuemanagement.org/learnmore/clarification-of-terms/. Accessed January 26, 2013.

7. Risks vs. Issues, *The Engineer Leader* (August 16, 2012), http://www.engineerleader.com/risks-vs-issues/. Accessed January 26, 2013.

8. Tony Jaques, "Issue Management as a Post-Crisis Discipline: Identifying and Responding to Issue Impacts Beyond the Crisis," *Journal of Public Affairs* (February 2009), 35–44.

9. Liam Fahey, "Issues Management: Two Approaches," *Strategic Planning Management* (November 1986), 81, 85–96.

10. Ibid., 81.

11. Ibid., 86.

12. Pursey P. M. A. R.Heugens, John F. Mahon, Steve L. Wartick, "A Portfolio Approach to Issue Adoption," *International Association for Business and Society* (2004 Annual Meeting, Jackson Hole, WY).

13. Ibid.

14. Joseph F. Coates, Vary T. Coates, Jennifer Jarratt, and Lisa Heinz, *Issues Management* (Mt. Airy, MD: Lomond Publications, 1986), 19–20.

15. John Mahon, "Issues Management: The Issue of Definition," *Strategic Planning Management* (November 1986), 81–82. For further discussion on what constitutes an issue, see Steven L. Wartick and John F. Mahon, "Toward a Substantive Definition of the Corporate Issue Construct," *Business & Society* (Vol. 33, No. 3, December 1994), 293–311.

16. Coates et al., 18.

17. Ibid., 32.

18. Bernhard Warner, "Happy Birthday, Futurists! A Movement Turns 104." *Bloomberg Businessweek* (February 20, 2013), http://www.businessweek.com/articles/2013-02-20/happy-birthday-futurists-a-movement-turns-104. Accessed March 5, 2013.

19. Ibid.

20. Ibid.

21. Graham T. T. Molitor, "We're All Futurists," *Vital Speeches of the Day* (November 1, 2003).

22. T. Graham Molitor, "How to Anticipate Public Policy Changes," *SAM Advanced Management Journal* (Vol. 42, No. 3, Summer 1977), 4.

23. Stuart Elliott, "Spotting the Trends Before They Break Out," *The New York Times* (March 11, 2012), http://www.nytimes.com/2012/03/12/business/media/spotting-the-trends-before-they-break-out-advertising.html?_r=0. Accessed January 26, 2013.

24. J. E. Dutton, S. J. Ashford, R. M. O'Neill, E. Hayes, and E. E. Wierba, "Reading the Wind: How Middle Managers Assess the Context for Selling Issues to Top Managers," *Strategic Management Journal* (Vol. 18, 1997), 407–425; Jennifer A. Howard-Grenville, "Developing Issue-Selling Effectiveness over Time: Issue Selling as Resourcing," *Organization Science* (July/August 2007), 560–577.

25. Pursey P. M. A. R. Heugens, "Issues Management: Core Understandings and Scholarly Development," in Phil Harris and Craig S. Fleisher (eds.), *The Handbook of Public Affairs* (Thousand Oaks, CA: Sage Publications, 2005), 490–493.

26. William R. King, "Strategic Issue Management," in William R. King and David I. Cleland (eds.) *Strategic Planning and Management Handbook* (New York: Van Nostrand Reinhold, 1987), 259.

27. James K. Brown, *This Business of Issues: Coping with the Company's Environment* (New York: The Conference Board, 1979), 45.

28. Elizabeth Dougall, "Issues Management," *Essential Knowledge Project* (December 12, 2008), http://www.instituteforpr.org/essential_knowledge/detail/issues_management/. Accessed January 27, 2013.

29. Brown, 33.

30. Coates et al., 46.

31. Cited in Heugens, 2005, 488.

32. I. C. MacMillan and P. E. Jones, "Designing Organizations to Compete," *Journal of Business Strategy* (Vol. 4, No. 4, Spring 1984), 13.

33. Roy Wernham, "Implementation: The Things That Matter," in King and Cleland, 453.

34. Dougall, 2008.

35. Earl C. Gottschalk, Jr., "Firms Hiring New Type of Manager to Study Issues, Emerging Troubles," *The Wall Street Journal* (June 10, 1982), 33–36.

36. Mahon, 81–82.

37. Barbara Bigelow, Liam Fahey, and John Mahon, "A Typology of Issue Evolution," *Business & Society* (Spring 1993), 28. For another useful perspective, see John F. Mahon and Sandra A. Waddock, "Strategic Issues Management: An Integration of Issue Life Cycle Perspectives," *Business & Society* (Spring 1992), 19–32. Also see Steven L. Wartick and Robert E. Rude, "Issues Management: Fad or Function," *California Management Review* (Fall 1986), 134–140.

38. Thomas G. Marx, "Integrating Public Affairs and Strategic Planning," *California Management Review* (Fall 1986), 145.

39. W. H. Chase, "Issues and Policy," *Public Relations Quarterly* (Vol. 1, Winter 1980), 5, cited in Jaques, 2009, 282.

40. Public Affairs Council, "Public Affairs: Its Origins, Its Present, and Its Trends," http://www.pac.org (2001).

41. Tony Jaques, "Issue Management: Process Versus Progress," *Journal of Public Affairs* (February 2006), 69–74.

42. Pursey P. M. A. R. Heugens, "Strategic Issues Management: Implications for Corporate Performance," *Business & Society* (Vol. 41, No. 4, December 2002), 456–468.

43. Ibid., 459. Also see Archie B. Carroll, "Stakeholder Management: Background and Advances," in Phil Harris and Craig S. Fleisher (eds.), *The Handbook of Public Affairs* (Thousand Oaks, CA: Sage Publications, 2005), 501–516.

44. Louis Anthony Cox, Jr. "Community Resilience and Decision Theory Challenges for Catastrophic Events," *Risk Analysis: An International Journal* (November 2012), 1919–1934.

45. Robert S. Kaplan and Anette Mikes, "Managing Risks: A New Framework," *Harvard Business Review* (June 2012), 48–60.

46. Ibid.

47. Ibid.

48. Ibid.

49. Ibid.

50. Frank C. Krysiak,"Risk Management as a Tool for Sustainability," *Journal of Business Ethics* (April 2009, Supplement 3), 483–492.

51. Diane B. MacDonald, "When Risk Management Collides with Enterprise Sustainability," *Journal of Leadership, Accountability & Ethics* (January 2011), 56–66.

52. Trefis Team, "Japan Is Key To Prudential's International Success," *Forbes* (September 17, 2012), http://www.forbes.com/sites/greatspeculations/2012/09/17/japan-is-key-to-prudentials-international-success/. Accessed January 27, 2013.

53. Jack Willoughby, "For Pru, Japan Is the Land of the Rising Premium," *Barrons* (August 6, 2011), http://online.barrons.com/article/SB50001424052702304183104576488413229552474.html?mod=rss_barrons_this_week_magazine. Accessed January 27, 2013.

54. Ibid.

55. http://www.news.prudential.com/article_print.cfm?article_id=5897. Accessed January 27, 2013.

56. http://2011cr.prudential.co.uk/our-people/helping-out-in-the-earthquake-zone.aspx. Accessed January 27, 2013.

57. Ken Brumfield, "Succeeding in Crisis Leadership," *Financial Executive* (October 2012), 45–47.

58. Ian Mitroff, with Gus Anagnos, *Managing Crises Before They Happen: What Every Executive and Manager Needs to Know about Crisis Management* (New York: AMACOM, 2001), Chapter 2.

59. Ian Mitroff, "Crisis Leadership: Seven Strategies of Strength," *Leadership Excellence* (Vol. 22, No. 1, 2005), 11.

60. Christine M. Pearson and Judith Clair,"Reframing Crisis Management," *Academy of Management Review* (Vol. 23, No. 1, 1998), 60.

61. "How Companies Are Learning to Prepare for the Worst," *BusinessWeek* (December 23, 1985), 74.

62. "Tunagate," http://en.wikipedia.org/wiki/Tunagate. Accessed January 27, 2013.

63. Ibid., 68. For further discussion of types of crises, see Ian Mitroff, "Crisis Management and Environmentalism: A Natural Fit," *California Management Review* (Winter 1994), 101–113.

64. Pearson and Clair, 60.

65. Ian I. Mitroff and Mural C. Alpaslan, "Preparing for Evil," *Harvard Business Review* (April 2003), 3–9.

66. Steven Fink, *Crisis Management: Planning for the Inevitable* (New York: AMACOM, 1986), 69. Also see Sharon H. Garrison, *The Financial Impact of Corporate Events on Corporate Stakeholders* (New York: Quorem Books, 1990); and Joe Marconi, *Crisis Marketing: When Bad Things Happen to Good Companies* (Chicago: NTC Business Books, 1997). See also Carol Hymowitz, "Companies Experience Major Power Shifts as Crises Continue," *The Wall Street Journal* (October 9, 2001), B1, and Sue Shellenbarger, "Some Bosses, Fumbling in Crisis, Have Bruised Loyalty of Employees," *The Wall Street Journal* (October 17, 2001), B1.

67. Fink, 20.

68. Mitroff and Anagnos, 2001.

69. "How Companies Are Learning to Prepare for the Worst," 76.

70. Ibid.

71. Michael D. Watkins and Max H. Bazerman, "Predictable Surprises: The Disasters You Should Have Seen Coming," *Harvard Business Review* (March 2003), 3–10.

72. David Niles, "The Secret of Successful Planning," *Forbes* (August 3, 2009), http://www.forbes.com/2009/08/03/scenario-planning-advice-leadership-managing-planning.html. Accessed January 27, 2013.

73. Ibid.

74. Watkins and Bazerman (2003).

75. *BusinessWeek* (1985), 74.

76. Richard J. Mahoney, "The Anatomy of a Public Policy Crisis," *The CEO Series, Center for the Study of American Business* (May 1996), 7.

77. Greg Jaffe, "How Florida Crash Overwhelmed ValuJet's Skillful Crisis Control," *The Wall Street Journal* (June 5, 1996), S1.

78. Melissa Master, "Keyword: Crisis," *Across the Board* (September 1998), 62.

79. Ian Mitroff, Paul Shrivastava, and Firdaus Udwadia, "Effective Crisis Management," *Academy of Management Executive* (November 1987), 285.

80. Christine M. Pearson and Ian I. Mitroff, "From Crisis Prone to Crisis Prepared: A Framework for Crisis Management," *Academy of Management Executive* (Vol. 7, No. 1, February 1993), 58–59. Also see Ian Mitroff, Christine M. Pearson, and L. Katherine Harrington,

The Essential Guide to Managing Corporate Crises (New York: Oxford University Press, 1996).

81. Robert Goff, "Coming Clean," *Forbes* (May 17, 1999), 156–160.

82. Ibid.

83. Johnathan L. Bernstein, "The Ten Steps of Crisis Communications" (January 2013), http://www.crisisnaviga tor.org/The-Ten-Steps-of-Crisis-Communications.490.0. html. Accessed January 27,2013.

84. Richard Wm. Brundage, "Crisis Management – An Outline for Survival," *Crisisnavigator* (January 2013), http:// www.crisisnavigator.org/Crisis-Management-An-Outline-for-Survival.454.0.html?&no_cache=1&sword_list[]=Brund age. Accessed January 27, 2013.

85. Cited in Irene Rozansky, "Communicating in a Crisis," *Board Member* (March/April 2007), 2.

86. Ibid.

87. James C. Cooper and Kathleen Madigan, "Katrina's Impact Depends on How Business Reacts," *Business-Week* (September 19, 2005), 31; Justin Fox, "A Meditation on Risk: Hurricane Katrina Brought out the Worst in Washington and the Best in Business," *Fortune* (October 3, 2005), 50–61; Devin Leonard, "The Only Lifeline Was the Wal-Mart," *Fortune* (October 3, 2005), 74–80.

88. Ellen Florian Kratz, "For FedEx, It Was Time to Deliver," *Fortune* (October 3, 2005), 83–84.

89. "New Lessons to Learn," *Fortune* (October 3, 2005), 87–88.

90. Paul Glader, "GE's Immelt to Cite Lessons Learned," *The Wall Street Journal* (December 14, 2009), http://online. wsj.com/article/SB1000142405274870-3954904574596350 792489752.html.

91. Ibid.

92. Mike Tierney, "Disaster Planning Pushed by CEO: Business Saved Following 9/11," *Atlanta Journal Constitution* (June 2, 2007), C1.

93. Bruce Rubenstein, "Salmonella-Tainted Ice Cream: How Schwan's Recovered," Corporate Legal Times Corp., June 1998.

94. Ibid.

95. Ibid.

96. Ibid.

PART **3**

Business Ethics and Management

7

Business Ethics Fundamentals

CHAPTER LEARNING OUTCOMES

After studying this chapter, you should be able to:

1. Describe how the public regards business ethics.

2. Define business ethics and appreciate the complexities of making ethical judgments.

3. Explain the conventional approach to business ethics. Differentiate it from the principles approach and ethical tests approach.

4. Analyze economic, legal, and ethical aspects of a decision by using a Venn model.

5. Identify and explain three models of management ethics. Give examples of each.

6. Describe and discuss Kohlberg's three levels of moral development.

7. Identify and discuss the elements of moral judgment.

Public interest in business ethics is at an all-time high. Certainly, there has been an ebb and flow of interest on society's part, but lately this interest has grown to a preoccupation or, as some might say, an obsession. With the ethics scandals of the early 2000s, beginning with Enron, we witnessed the birth and accelerated maturation of the "ethics industry."[1] The impact of the Enron scandal was so great on business ethics that it has been dubbed the "Enron Effect"[2] and it is still talked about today. The effects and lessons learned from the Enron scandal have been so enormous, that business will never be the same.

We thought we would never soon see anything like the Enron era of scandals. The Enron collapse, brought to light in 2001, ushered in an avalanche of ethics scandals that brought down WorldCom, Tyco, Arthur Andersen, and other companies. The magnitude of CEO greed and contempt for the law seemed unprecedented. Congress thought it put the problems to bed with the passage in 2002 of the Sarbanes–Oxley Act (SOX). The legislation did bring about improved financial controls and it did strengthen the accountability of CEOs and CFOs for the veracity of financial statements. The public had a sense of relief that government regulations had once again solved their problems. Regrettably, SOX did not "fix" the problem of financial scandals among businesses, although it did improve conditions somewhat.

The public may have been lulled into a false sense of security over the next several years. And, it wasn't until the Wall Street financial crisis began in 2008 that the country realized that the difficulties with corporate ethics had not been fixed. The stock market collapse in 2008 began a recession that, in terms of its effects on the world economy, had not been seen since the Great Depression. It appears we have had two business ethics "eras" in a decade and a half. First, there was the Enron Era (2001–2008) and then, beginning in 2008, we found ourselves in the era of the Wall Street financial scandals that resulted in a global financial crisis.[3] This period is not yet completely behind us.

How have these two eras been similar and different? The headliners in the Enron Era included both companies and CEOs or CFOs. Among these were Enron (Kenneth Lay, Jeffrey Skilling, Andrew Fastow), WorldCom (Bernie Ebbers), Tyco (Dennis Kozlowski), Adelphia (John Rigas), and Global

Crossing (Gary Winnick). For good measure, one could toss in HealthSouth and Martha Stewart during this era. What was unique about the Enron Era is that it included chief-level executives as the poster children for poor corporate ethics.

Before Enron, many thought business ethics was a problem having to do with employees and lower- and middle-level managers; that is, the lower two-thirds of the corporate pyramid. Beginning with the Enron Era, the focus turned to the top one-third of the corporate pyramid, especially CEOs and CFOs, including negligent corporate boards. After prolonged investigations and trials, some of these chief-level executives were found guilty and were sent to prison. Ken Lay of Enron was convicted but died before he could begin his prison sentence.

The Wall Street financial crisis and scandals ushered in a new set of corporate characters, and it has been mostly companies and not their CEOs or CFOs accused of questionable dealings. The new companies we began reading about included Fannie Mae, Freddie Mac, Bear Stearns, Lehman Brothers, AIG, Countrywide Financial, and Merrill Lynch. Some will argue that these firms did not commit ethics violations, per se, but rather made bad judgments about risk and returns. This is still being debated. At a minimum, there was widespread recklessness about risk, especially with the subprime lending crisis and exotic financial instruments that few experts completely understood. These firms were led by the financial wizards who had become known as "the smartest guys in the room," and they should have known better. It is unethical to lend money to customers who, in your reasonable judgment, will not be able to pay it back. It is unethical to lend money without checking people's job status, income, and assets. It can be called bad risk–return calculations, but many think that this is just a euphemism for the questionable business practices that were taking place. Many observers have argued that the firms got greedy and were driven by profits (and bonuses) without regard for the consequences. Beginning with Bernie Madoff who concocted a multibillion dollar Ponzi scheme in which he defrauded his investors, we saw a few private individuals once again grab the limelight through deceitful schemes or insider trading.

Many of these corporate decision makers may not have broken laws and thus may not be prosecuted like those from the Enron Era; however, only time will tell. But, this latter scandal era has had drastically wider ramifications for the world economy, and it helped precipitate a worldwide recession. In the Enron Era, the immediate stakeholders suffered greatly, especially employees and shareholders. In the current era, the devastation has been all encompassing—the world is suffering from the economic calamity of these bad decisions. These businesspeople have raised serious questions about trust in the financial system.

It is difficult to say what will happen next. There are some signs that economies are improving, but it may take much longer for trust in business to be restored. What the recent scandals have revealed is that the issue of business ethics has both macro and micro effects. At the macro level, the entire business system and capitalism itself have been called into question. At the micro level, individual companies, managers, and employees still face the continuing onslaught of ethics challenges that occur daily. Using a managerial perspective, business ethics education is more focused on this latter category of ethics challenges. The broad environment, which deals with business and society relationships, however, continues to be a confounding backdrop against which these daily challenges occur.

Figure 7-1 summarizes some of the major business ethics scandals that occurred beginning in 2001. The effects of some of these continue to the present day. Many of these companies and executives have claimed their

FIGURE 7-1 Recent Ethics Scandals: From Enron to Global Financial Crisis

Companies Implicated	Major Executives Implicated	Legal/Ethical Charges and Convictions
Enron	Andrew Fastow, Jeffrey Skilling, Kenneth Lay	Securities fraud, conspiracy to inflate profits, corrupt corporate culture
WorldCom	Scott Sullivan, CFO; Bernard J. Ebbers, CEO	Accounting fraud, lying, filing false financial statements
Arthur Andersen	Entire firm; David Duncan, auditor for Enron	Accounting fraud, criminal charges, obstruction
Tyco	Mark Schwartz, CFO; Dennis Kozlowski, CEO	Sales tax evasion, stealing through corruption, fraud
Adelphia	John Rigas, sons Timothy and Michael; Michael Mulcahey; James Brown	Accounting fraud; looting the company, using it as "personal piggy bank"
HealthSouth	Richard Scrushy, CEO	Found not guilty in company scandal; later convicted of bribery, conspiracy, mail fraud
Martha Stewart	Martha Stewart	Conspiracy, securities fraud, and obstruction of justice
Parmalat (Italy)	Calisto Tanzi, chairman and CEO, and others	Flawed corporate governance
Computer Associates	Sanjay Kumar, CEO	Pleaded guilty to fraud
Fannie Mae, Freddie Mac, Bear Stearns, Lehman Brothers, AIG, Merrill Lynch, Countrywide	Most executives were not legally charged. Upper echelon executives and board implicated in list of questionable behaviors.	Recklessness, excessive risk taking, greed, bad loan decisions, governance failures, arrogance, hubris
Bernard L. Madoff Investment Securities LLC	Bernie L. Madoff	Convicted; $17.3 billion Ponzi scheme; fraud
Barclay's Bank	Robert Diamond, CEO	False reports; LIBOR scandal; heavy fines
Galleon Group Hedge Fund	Raj Rajaratnam, Founder	Insider trading; securities fraud; 11 years in prison
Peregrine Financial Group	Russell Wasendorf, Sr., Founder, Chairman	Embezzlement; fraud; doctoring bank statements; duping auditor
Stanford International Group	R. Allen Stanford, CEO; James M. Davis, CFO	Fraudulent $7 billion Ponzi scheme; Conviction: 110 years in prison
Goldman Sachs	Rajat Gupta, board member	Insider trading; securities fraud;
MF Global Holdings	Jon Corzine	Questionable risk taking; lost client funds
JPMorgan Chase	Jamie Dimon, CEO	Flawed, poorly executed and monitored derivatives trades

FIGURE 7-2

Examples of Ethical Issues Businesses Face

Stakeholder Group	Examples of Ethical Issues
Customers	Product safety/healthfulness Advertising/marketing honestly Packaging fairly/accurately Labeling accurately/completely Pricing fairly relative to quality Protecting consumer privacy
Employees	Fair compensation practices Fair day's work; fair day's pay Compliance with employment laws Avoidance of employment discrimination Safe working conditions Avoiding employee theft/embezzlement Protecting employees' privacy Dealing with distracted employees
Community/Environment	Environmental protection/sustainability Adherence to legal mandates Good corporate citizenship Philanthropy/supporting causes Adapting to foreign cultures Avoidance of bribery
Shareholders	Protecting shareholders' interests Fair compensation for executives Quality boards of directors Protection of company assets Fair returns on investments Communicating accurately Transparency

© Cengage Learning 2015

innocence, and allegations and trials are at various stages of completion. Some have been convicted and sent to prison.

To gain an appreciation of the kinds of issues that are important under the rubric of business ethics, Figure 7-2 presents a list of business ethics issues that companies typically have to face with select stakeholder groups. Against this backdrop, we begin our business ethics discussion in this chapter and continue it in the next three. This chapter introduces fundamental business ethics background and concepts. Chapter 8 extends the discussion by considering personal and organizational ethics. Chapter 9 addresses business ethics issues pertaining to newly emerging technology. Finally, Chapter 10 turns to the international sphere as it examines ethical issues in the global arena.

The Public's Opinion of Business Ethics

The public's view of business ethics has never been very high. Anecdotal evidence suggests that many citizens see business ethics as essentially a contradiction in terms, an oxymoron, and think that there is only a fine line between a business executive and a crook. Over many years now, public opinion polls have revealed the public's deep concerns about the honesty and ethical standards of business and other professions. The December 2012 Gallup Poll on the public's opinion of business executives revealed that only 21 percent of the public thought business executives had high or very high ethics. This was a slight improvement over the 12 percent who rated them highly in the same category in 2009.[4] Specific categories of businesspeople had even lower ethics rankings. These included car salespeople, advertising practitioners, stockbrokers, insurance sales-people, and HMO managers.[5]

The public's opinion of business ethics may be reported at two levels. At a broad level is the general perception of business ethics by the public and at a narrower level are specific perceptions as to what is going on inside organizations. It is apparent from the 2012 Gallup Poll that society does not consider business's ethics to be very high. There can be no doubt that the endless stream of ethical scandals over the past decade or so contributed significantly to this lack of trust.

In terms of what is going on within companies, the most recent National Business Ethics Survey (NBES) conducted by the Ethics Resource Center (ERC) had some encouraging news, but it presented mixed results. The NBES was a study of employees to determine what was going on *within* companies. Following are the major findings[6]:

- *Misconduct observed.* Forty five percent of workers reported observing misconduct. This was down slightly from two years prior.
- *Reporting bad behavior.* Sixty five percent of the workers surveyed reported that they had reported the bad behavior they had observed. This was up slightly over two years prior.
- *Retaliation against workers.* Retaliation against those reporting wrongdoing (whistle-blowers) was up sharply. Twenty-two percent of those reporting wrongdoing say they experienced some form of retaliation from their bosses.
- *Pressure to compromise.* The percentage of employees who reported they felt pressure to compromise standards in order to do their jobs was near the all-time high.
- *Weak ethical cultures.* The percentage of companies with weak ethics cultures also increased to almost record levels.

The pattern in which there existed lower unethical conduct but higher reporting and widespread retaliation was unlike findings in previous studies. What stood out were two influences: the economy and the unique experiences of those using social networking at work. Those using social networking at work tended to report wrongdoing more frequently and suffer more frequent retaliation.[7]

As we are well into the second decade of the 2000s, it appears that society is clamoring for a renewed emphasis on values, morals, and ethics and that the business ethics debate of this period is but a subset of this larger societal concern. Whether the business community will be able to close the trust gap and ratchet up its reputation to a higher plateau remains to be seen. One thing is sure: There is a continuing interest in business ethics, and the proliferation of business ethics courses in colleges and universities, along with the revitalized interest on the part of the business community, paints an encouraging picture for an ethical business environment in the future.

Are the Media Reporting Business Ethics More Vigorously?

Sometimes it is difficult to tell whether business ethics have really deteriorated or that the media is doing a more thorough job of reporting on ethics violations. There is no doubt that the media are reporting ethical problems more frequently and fervently. Spurred on by the scandals of the past few years, the media have found business ethics and, indeed, ethics questions among all institutions to be subjects of growing and sustaining interest. The media had a field day with the Bernie Madoff Ponzi scheme, in which he defrauded thousands of investors out of $50 billion. Madoff got 150 years in prison for his epic fraud, and the daily reporting of his plight was a sight to behold.[8] Of particular interest in recent years has been the in-depth investigative reporting of business ethics on such TV news shows as *60 Minutes, 20/20, Dateline NBC, Rock Center,* and *Frontline.* Such investigations keep business ethics in the public eye and make it difficult to assess whether public opinion polls are reflecting the actual business ethics of the day or simply the reactions to the latest scandals covered on a weekly basis.

Is Society Changing?

As argued in Chapter 1, many business managers subscribe to the belief that society is changing. W. Michael Blumenthal, one-time U.S. Secretary of the Treasury and CEO of the Bendix Corporation, was one of the leading advocates of this view. He argued:

> *It seems to me that the root causes of the questionable and illegal corporate activities that have come to light recently … can be traced to the sweeping changes that have taken place in our society and throughout the world and to the unwillingness of many in business to adjust to these changes.*[9]

Blumenthal went on to say, "People in business have not suddenly become immoral. What has changed are the contexts in which corporate decisions are made, the demands that are being made on business, and the nature of what is considered proper corporate conduct."[10]

Although it would be difficult to prove Blumenthal's thesis, it is an intuitively attractive one. You do not have to make a lengthy investigation of some of today's business practices to realize that a good number of what are now called unethical practices were at one time considered acceptable. Or that possibly the practices never really were acceptable to the public but that, because they were not known, they were tolerated, thus causing no moral dilemmas in the mind of the public. In spite of this analysis, one cannot help but believe that the greed by top-level business executives that has been exposed in the past two decades has elevated the ethics issue to new heights. Executive lying has contributed to the problem. Though corporate governance has become better in recent years, lack of careful oversight of top-echelon executives has been a problem as well. Corporate boards, in some cases, have fallen down in their duties to monitor top-executive behavior, and one consequence has been a continuing stream of ethics scandals.

Figure 7-3 illustrates one way of looking at this. It depicts how the magnitude of the ethics problem may be more noticeable today than it once was as a result of the public's expectations of business's ethical behavior rising more rapidly than actual business ethics. Note in the figure that actual business ethics is assumed to be slightly improving but not at the same pace as public expectations are rising. Alternatively, some perceive actual business ethics to be declining or stable. Either way, in this analysis, the magnitude of the current ethics problem is seen partially to be a function of rising societal expectations about business behavior compared with smaller increases, declines, or stability in actual business ethics.

Business Ethics: Meaning, Types, Approaches

In Chapter 2, ethical responsibilities of business were introduced and the contrast between ethics, economics, law, and philanthropy were discussed. To be sure, we all have a general idea of what business ethics means, but now it is important to probe the topic more deeply. To understand business ethics, it is useful to comment on the relationship between ethics and morality.

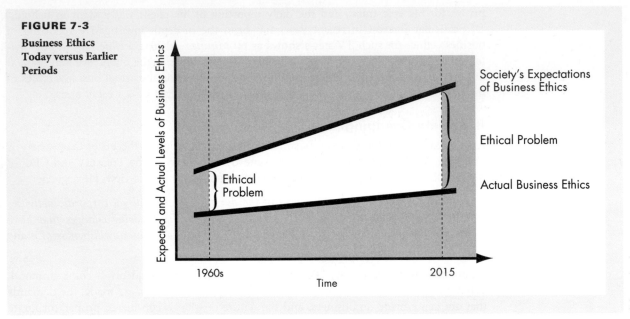

FIGURE 7-3

Business Ethics Today versus Earlier Periods

© Cengage Learning

Ethics is the discipline that deals with moral duty and obligation. Ethics can also be regarded as a set of moral principles or values. **Morality** is a doctrine or system of moral conduct. Moral conduct refers to principles of right, wrong, and fairness in behavior. For the most part, then, we can think of ethics and morality as being so similar to one another that we may use the terms interchangeably to refer to the study of fairness, justice, and moral behavior in business.

Business ethics, therefore, is concerned with morality and fairness in behavior, actions, policies, and practices that take place within a business context. Today morality is increasingly interpreted to include the often difficult and subtle questions of fairness, justice, and equity in the workplace. Business ethics is the study of practices in organizations and a quest to determine whether these practices are acceptable or not. Business ethics is also a field of study that is of interest to the public, academics, students, and managers.

Descriptive versus Normative Ethics

Two key branches of moral philosophy, or ethics, are *descriptive* ethics and *normative* ethics. Each takes a different perspective.

Descriptive ethics is concerned with describing, characterizing, and studying the morality of people, an organization, a culture, or a society. It also compares and contrasts different moral codes, systems, practices, beliefs, and values.[11] In descriptive business ethics the focus is on learning what *is* occurring in the realm of behavior, actions, decisions, policies, and practices of business firms, managers, or, perhaps, specific industries. The public opinion poll cited earlier gives us glimpses into descriptive ethics—what people believe is going on as the basis of their perceptions and understandings. Descriptive ethics focuses on "what is"—the prevailing set of ethical standards and practices in the business community, in specific organizations, or on the part of specific managers. A real danger in limiting our attention to descriptive ethics is that some people may adopt the view that "if everyone is doing it," it must be acceptable. For example, if a survey reveals that 70 percent of employees are padding their expense accounts, this describes what *is* taking place, but it does not describe what *should* be taking place. Just because many are participating in this questionable activity doesn't make it an appropriate practice. This is why normative ethics is important.

In contrast to descriptive ethics, **normative ethics** is concerned with supplying and justifying a coherent moral system of thinking and judging. Normative ethics seeks to uncover, develop, and justify basic moral principles that are intended to guide behavior, actions, and decisions.[12] Normative business ethics, therefore, seeks to propose some principle or principles for distinguishing what is ethical from what is unethical in the business context. It deals more with "what ought to be" or "what should be" in terms of business practices. Normative ethics is concerned with establishing norms or standards by which business practices might be guided or judged.

Normative business ethics might be based on moral common sense (be fair, honest, truthful), or it might require critical thinking and the pursuit of different types of ethical analysis (interest based, rights based, duty based, virtue based).[13] In our study of business ethics, we need to be ever mindful of this distinction between the descriptive and normative perspectives. It is tempting to observe the prevalence of a particular practice in business (e.g., discrimination or deceptive marketing) and conclude that because so many are *doing it* (descriptive ethics), it must be acceptable behavior. Normative ethics would insist that a practice be justified on the basis of some ethical principle, argument, philosophy, or rationale before being considered acceptable. Normative ethics demands a more meaningful moral anchor than just "everyone is doing it." Normative ethics is our primary concern in this book, though we frequently compare "what ought to be" with "what is" going on in the real world for purposes of analysis.

Three Major Approaches to Business Ethics

In this chapter and the next, three major approaches to thinking about business ethics is helpful to our discussion. These include the following:

1. **Conventional approach**—based on how common, everyday society (the average person) views business ethics today. The conventional approach is based on ordinary, common sense and prevailing practice.
2. **Principles approach**—based on the use of ethics principles or guidelines to justify and direct behavior, actions, policies, and practices.
3. **Ethical tests approach**—based on short, practical questions or "tests" to guide ethical decision making, behavior, and practices.

The conventional approach to business ethics will be used primarily in this chapter and the other two approaches will be covered in Chapter 8.

The Conventional Approach to Business Ethics

The conventional approach to business ethics is the approach whereby we compare a decision, practice, or policy with prevailing norms of acceptability in society. We call it the conventional approach because it is thought that this is the way conventional or general society thinks. The conventional approach relies on the use of common sense and a widely held sense of what is ethical. The major challenge in this approach is answering the questions, "Whose ethical norms do we use?" in making the ethical judgment, and "What ethical norms are prevailing?" This approach may be depicted by highlighting the major variables to be compared with one another:

Decision, Behavior, or Practice ⟷ *Prevailing Norms of Acceptability*

There is considerable room for variability on both of these questions. With respect to which norms are used as the basis for ethical judgments, the conventional approach would consider as legitimate those norms emanating from family, friends, religious beliefs, the local community, one's employer, law, the profession, and so on. This approach would also employ what is in one's own best self-interest as a guideline.

One's conscience or one's self-interest would be seen by many to be legitimate sources of ethical norms. Two classic "Frank & Ernest" comic strips poke fun at the use of one's conscience, however. In the first, a sign on the wall reads "Tonight's Lecture: Moral Philosophy." Then it shows Frank saying to Ernest, "I'd let my conscience be my guide, but I'm in enough trouble already!" In a second comic strip, Frank says to Ernest, while they are standing at a bar, "I always use my conscience as my guide. But, fortunately, it has a terrible sense of direction." These comic strips reveal the often limiting nature of following one's conscience.

Figure 7-4 illustrates some of the sources of ethical norms that come to bear on the individual and that might be used in various circumstances, and over time, under the conventional approach. These different sources compete in their influence on what constitutes today's "prevailing norms of acceptability."

In many circumstances, the conventional approach to ethics may be useful and applicable. What does a person do, however, if norms from one source conflict with norms from another source? Also, how can we be sure that societal norms are really appropriate or defensible? Society's culture sends us many and often conflicting messages about what is appropriate ethical behavior. These messages come from television, movies, books, music, politics, and other sources in the culture and they do not always convey high ethical standards.

TV shows such as *Survivor* and *Celebrity Apprentice* have run episodes in which questionable ethics have been depicted and sometimes celebrated. On *Survivor*, the participants are forever creating alliances (agreements of trust) with others and then breaking them (violating trust) in the interest of winning the game. On one segment of *Celebrity Apprentice*, Donald Trump, the host and CEO who gets to aim his deadly quip "You're fired!" at a person on the losing team, conveyed to the viewing public that loyalty was more important than honesty in business. When one celebrity was in the final board room, he expressed the opinion that the winning team *did* do a better job on a

FIGURE 7-4

Sources of Ethical Norms Communicated to Individuals

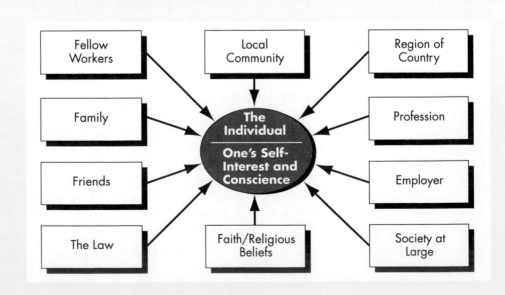

commercial than his team. Trump fired him for being "disloyal" to his team. One major Web site gave Trump the "Ethics Alarms Dunce of the Year Award" for that example of a conflicting judgment.[14]

Another example of the conflicting messages people get today from society occurs in the realm of sexual harassment in the workplace. On the one hand, today's television, movies, advertisements, and music are replete with sexual innuendo and the treatment of women and men as sex objects. This would suggest that such behavior is normal, acceptable, even desired. On the other hand, the law and the courts stringently prohibit sexual gestures or innuendo in the workplace. As we will see in Chapter 19, it does not take much sexual innuendo to constitute a "hostile work environment" and a sex discrimination charge under Title VII of the Civil Rights Act. In this example, we see a norm that is prevalent in culture and society clashing with a norm evolving from employment law and business ethics. These examples serve to illustrate how views of ethics that are acceptable to many in conventional society would not be accepted in more rigorous forms of ethical analysis.

Ethics and the Law

The issue of ethics versus the law arises often. In Chapter 2, we said that ethical behavior is typically thought to reside above behavior required by the law. This is the generally accepted view of ethics. We should make it clear, however, that in many respects the law and ethics overlap. To appreciate this, you need to recognize that the law embodies notions of ethics. That is, the law may be seen as a reflection of what society thinks are minimal standards of conduct and behavior. Both law and ethics have to do with what is deemed appropriate or acceptable, but law reflects society's *codified* ethics. Therefore, if a person breaks a law or violates a regulation, she or he is also behaving unethically. We should be open to the possibility, however, that in some rare cases the law may not be ethical, in which case standing up to the law might be the principled course of action. A case in point might be when Rosa Parks, a black woman, stood up to the authorities and refused to move to the back of the bus because she thought this was racial discrimination. In retrospect, Parks was doing the principled thing and civil rights history has borne this out.

The late legal scholar Ronald Dworkin always argued that laws should be understood to be part of a larger moral vision rather than as an ordinary set of rules. He held that law should not produce results that were not in harmony with ordinary morality.[15] In spite of this frequent intermixing of law and ethics, we continue to talk about desirable ethical behavior as behavior that extends beyond what is required by law. The *spirit* of the law often extends beyond the *letter* of the law and taps into the ethical dimension. Viewed from the standpoint of minimums, we would certainly say that obedience to the law is generally regarded to be a minimum standard of ethical behavior.

There are two good business examples in which the confusion between law and ethics led to disastrous results. In one analysis, the Enron scandal was said to have been all about the difference between the letter of the law and the spirit of the law. Interestingly, the fraud at Enron was accompanied by obsessive and careful attention to the letter of the law. One observer stated that "the people who ran Enron did back flips and somersaults as they tried to stay within the law's lines."[16] But CEO Ken Lay and CFO Jeffrey Skilling apparently missed the main point of securities law, which is that CEOs and other high-level officials should not get rich while their shareholders go broke. So, the source of all their crimes was the basic dishonesty of trying to keep Enron's stock afloat so that the officials could make money.[17] Their focus on the law to the neglect of ethics was a significant cause of their downfall.

Also note that the law does not address all realms in which ethical questions might be raised. Thus, there are clear roles for both law and ethics to play.[18] Research on illegal corporate behavior has been conducted for some time. Illegal corporate behavior, of course, comprises business practices that are in direct defiance of law or public policy. Research has focused on two dominant questions: (1) Why do firms behave illegally or what leads them to engage in illegal activities and (2) what are the consequences of behaving illegally?[19] We will not deal with these studies of law breaking in this discussion; however, we should view this body of studies and investigations as being relevant to our interest in business ethics because it represents a special case of business ethics (illegal behavior).

Making Ethical Judgments

When a decision is made about what is ethical (right, just, fair) using the conventional approach, there is room for variability on several counts (see Figure 7-5). Three key elements compose such a decision. First, we observe the *decision, action,* or *practice* that has taken place in the workplace setting. Second, we *compare the practice with prevailing norms of acceptability*—that is, society's or some other standard of what is acceptable or unacceptable. Third, we must recognize that *value judgments are being made* by someone as to what really occurred (the actual behavior) and what the prevailing norms of acceptability really are. This means that two people could look at the same behavior or practice, compare it with their beliefs of what the prevailing norms are, and reach different conclusions as to whether the behavior was ethical or not. This becomes complex as perceptions of what is ethical inevitably lead to the difficult task of ranking different values against one another.

If we can put aside for a moment the fact that perceptual differences about an incident do exist, and the fact that we might differ among ourselves because of our personal values and philosophies of acceptable behavior, we are still left with the challenging task of determining society's prevailing norms of acceptability of business practice. As a whole, members of society generally agree that certain practices are inappropriate. However, the consensus tends to disintegrate as we move from general to specific situations.

This may be illustrated with a business example. We might all agree with the general belief that "You should not steal someone else's property." As a general precept, we probably would have consensus on this. But, as we look at specific situations, our consensus may tend to disappear. Is it acceptable to take home from work such things as pencils, pens, paper clips, paper, staplers, thumb drives, and calculators? Is it acceptable to use the company telephone for personal long-distance calls? Is it acceptable to use

FIGURE 7-5

Elements Involved in Making Ethical Judgments

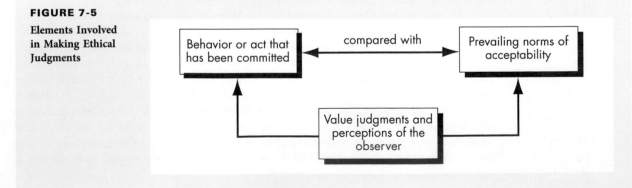

© Cengage Learning

company-bought gasoline for private use or to pad expense accounts? Is it acceptable to use company computers for personal e-mail or Web surfing? What if everyone else is doing it?

What is interesting in these examples is that we are more likely to reach consensus in principle than in practice. Some people who would say these practices are not acceptable might privately engage in them. Furthermore, a person who would not think of shoplifting even the smallest item from a local store might take pencils and paper home from work on a regular basis. A comic strip depicting the "Born Loser" illustrates this point. In the first panel, the father admonishes his son Wilberforce in the following way: "You know how I feel about stealing. Now tomorrow I want you to return every one of those pencils to school." In the second panel, the father says to Wilberforce, "I'll bring you all the pencils you need from work." This is an example of the classic double standard, and it illustrates how actions may be perceived differently by the observer or the participant.

Thus, in the conventional approach to business ethics, determinations of what is ethical and what is not require judgments to be made on at least three counts:

1. What is the *true nature* of the practice, behavior, or decision that occurred?
2. What are society's (or business's) *prevailing norms* of acceptability?
3. What *value judgments* are being made by someone about the practice or behavior, and what are that person's *perceptions* of applicable norms?

The human factor in the situation thus introduces the problem of perception and values and makes the decision process depicted in Figure 7-5 to be complicated.

The conventional approach to business ethics can be valuable, because we all need to be aware of and sensitive to the total environment in which we exist. We need to be aware of how society regards ethical issues. It has limitations, however, and we need to be cognizant of these as well. The most serious danger is that of falling into an **ethical relativism** where we pick and choose which source of norms we wish to use on the basis of what will justify our current actions or maximize our freedom. A relevant comic strip illustrates this point. In a courtroom, while swearing in, the witness stated, "I swear to tell the truth ... *as I see it.*"

In the next chapter, we maintain that a *principles approach* is needed to augment the conventional approach. The principles approach represents *normative ethics* and looks at general guidelines to ethical decision making that come from moral philosophy and practice. We also present the *ethical tests approach*, which is more of a practical approach.

Ethics, Economics, and Law—A Venn Model

In many business decisions, ethics, economics and the law all come into play. When we focus on ethics and ethical decision making, it is useful to consider these primary forces that come into tension while making ethical judgments. In Chapter 2, these were introduced as part of the four-part definition of corporate social responsibility, and they were depicted in the Pyramid of CSR. When we discuss a firm's CSR, philanthropy usually enters the discussion. This is because philanthropic initiatives are one of the primary ways many companies display their CSR in the community—through good and charitable works. In ethical decision making, however, we tend to set aside philanthropic expectations and focus on ethical expectations and, especially, those forces that primarily come into tension with ethics—economics (the quest for profits) and law (codified ethics). Thus, in most decision-making situations, ethics, economics, and law become the central variables that must be considered and balanced against each other in the quest to make wise decisions.

ETHICS IN PRACTICE CASE

To Hunt or Not to Hunt—That Is the Question

John Q. Expert from Enterprise Consulting Firm (ECF) has been working with City in South Georgia for approximately six months now on a study to reorganize the local government. The arrangement with City in South Georgia has generated nearly $50,000 in revenues for ECF so far.

A member of the City Council of City in South Georgia, Councilman Lotsoland, happens to be a prominent landowner and operates a 500-acre hunting/fishing preserve on the outskirts of City in South Georgia. Councilman Lotsoland uses the preserve to host prominent business and community leaders to City in South Georgia. Regular customers pay as much as $1,000/day for use of the property.

During the course of completing the six-month study with City in South Georgia, John Q. Expert develops a friendship with Councilman Lotsoland. Councilman Lotsoland and John Q. Expert share many mutual interests especially their love for the outdoors, and in particular their unending love for quail hunting.

Toward the end of the local government reorganization study, Councilman Lotsoland offers John Q. Expert an "all expenses paid" weekend at his hunting/fishing preserve.

1. What factors must John Q. Expert consider in his decision of whether or not to accept the complimentary weekend? Are there any conflicts of interest present that ought to be considered?

2. Is it appropriate for Councilman Lotsoland to offer the "all expenses paid" weekend? What factors make it acceptable or unacceptable?

3. Is it proper for John Q. Expert to accept the offer? Why? Why not?

Contributed by Matthew L. Bishop, PhD
J. W. Fanning Institute for Leadership Development

A firm's economic, legal, and ethical responsibilities may be depicted in a Venn diagram model illustrating how certain actions, decisions, or policies fulfill one, two, or three of these responsibility categories. Figure 7-6 presents this Venn diagram model, illustrating the overlapping potential of these three responsibility categories.

In Area 1 of the diagram, where the decision, action, or practice fulfills all three responsibilities, the management prescription is to "go for it." That is, the action is profitable, in compliance with the law, and represents ethical behavior. In Area 2a, the action under consideration is profitable and legal, but its ethical status may be uncertain. The guideline here is to "proceed cautiously." In these kinds of situations, the ethics of the action need to be carefully considered. In Area 2b, the action is profitable and ethical, but perhaps the law does not clearly address the issue or is ambiguous. If it is ethical, there is a good chance it is also legal, but the guideline again is to "proceed cautiously." In Area 3, the action is legal and ethical but not profitable. Therefore, the strategy here would be to avoid this action or find ways to make it profitable. However, there may be a compelling case to take the action if it is legal and ethical and, thus, represents the right thing to do. Schwartz and Carroll have presented a three-domain approach to CSR that employs a Venn diagram format similar to that presented in Figure 7-6. They provide corporate examples to illustrate each section of the Venn diagram.[20]

By taking philanthropy out of the picture, the ethics Venn model serves as a useful template for thinking about the more immediate expectations that society has on business in a situation in which the ethical dimension plays an important role. It illustrates clearly that many business decisions boil down to trade-offs between the influences of economics, law, and ethics.

FIGURE 7-6 A Venn Model for Ethical Decision Making

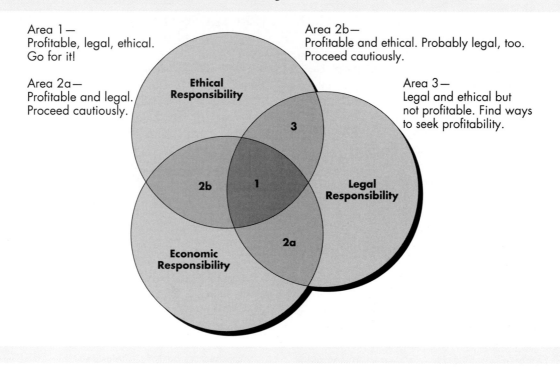

Area 1—
Profitable, legal, ethical.
Go for it!

Area 2a—
Profitable and legal.
Proceed cautiously.

Area 2b—
Profitable and ethical. Probably legal, too.
Proceed cautiously.

Area 3—
Legal and ethical but
not profitable. Find ways
to seek profitability.

Ethical
Responsibility

Legal
Responsibility

Economic
Responsibility

3

2b

1

2a

© Cengage Learning

Three Models of Management Ethics

In striving to understand the basic concepts of business ethics, it is useful to think in terms of key ethical models that might describe different types of management ethics found in the organizational world.[21] These models should provide some useful base points for discussion and comparison. The media have focused so much on immoral or unethical business behavior that it is easy to forget about the possibility of other ethical types. For example, scant attention has been given to the distinction that may be made between those activities that are *immoral* and those that are *amoral*. Similarly, little attention has been given to contrasting these two forms of behavior with ethical or *moral* management.

Believing that there is value in discussing descriptive models, or frameworks, for purposes of clearer understanding, here we describe, compare, and contrast three models or types of ethical management:

- Immoral management
- Moral management
- Amoral management

A major goal in this section is to develop a clearer understanding of the range of management postures in which ethics or morality is a defining characteristic. By seeing these approaches come to life through description and example, prospective managers will be in an improved position to assess their own ethical approaches and those of other organizational members (supervisors, subordinates, and peers). Another important objective is to identify more completely the amoral management model, which often is overlooked in the everyday rush to classify things as good or bad, moral or immoral. In

ETHICS IN PRACTICE CASE
Is Résumé Inflation and Deception Okay?

According to Steven Levitt, author of *Freakonomics*, a small bit of inflation on one's résumé is universal. Levitt estimates that at least half the people engage in this deception to some degree. Typically the small edits to one's résumé are done to disguise some unaccounted for time in between jobs. On other occasions the deceptions have been more substantial; for example, claiming an academic degree one almost acquired but didn't: "Well, I was just two courses short!" It has also been said that based on studies, the average American tells one or two lies a day, often at work. A recent survey of 2,500 hiring managers by CareerBuilder found that 30 percent of them find false or misleading information on applicants' résumés.

A résumé controversy with significant consequences occurred when Yahoo CEO Scott Thompson was questioned about a statement on his company's Web site that reported he had a degree in computer science. A dissident shareholder went public with the revelation that Thompson couldn't have a degree in computer science because the small college he graduated from didn't have a computer science *major* until *after* he graduated. The company's regulatory filing indicated that Thompson had a degree in accounting and computer science. Thompson claimed the Web site information was an inadvertent error without providing more information. According to his college, Thompson graduated with a bachelor's of science in business administration.

Days after this information came out, a person close to Yahoo's board reported that in absence of information that Thompson intentionally misled, the company probably would not force him out, indicating that his importance as CEO to the company was more important than whether he had a computer science degree or not. In spite of this, CEO Scott Thompson resigned his position soon thereafter amid the controversy over his résumé discrepancy.

1. In light of the prevalence of these practices, is résumé inflation and deception okay? Is it okay up to a point as long as the distortion doesn't get too big? Is a small amount of puffery on one's résumé just expected as part of the game of getting a job and getting ahead? What would the conventional approach to business ethics say?
2. Some small schools don't have official majors but people sometimes claim them anyway. Is this an acceptable practice?
3. If you had been on Yahoo's board, would you have supported keeping Thompson?
4. Why do you suppose Thompson resigned?

Sources: Steven Levitt, *Freakonomics*, 2005; David Wescott, "The Truth Won't Set You Free," *Bloomberg BusinessWeek*, February 4–10, 2013; "Imaginary Friends," *Bloomberg BusinessWeek*, January 21–27, 2013, 68; Amir Efrati and J. S. Lublin, "Résumé Trips Up Yahoo's Chief," *The Wall Street Journal*, May 5–6, 2012, A1, A12; Chris Smith, "Scott Thompson Quits as Yahoo CEO Following 'Fake Degree' Controversy," *Techradar*, May 12, 2012, http://www.techradar.com/us/news/internet/scott-thompson-quits-as-yahoo-ceo-following-fake-degree-controversy-1080165. Accessed April 4, 2013.

a later section, we discuss the elements of moral judgment that must be developed if the transition to moral management is to succeed. A more detailed development of each management model is valuable in coming to understand the range of ethics that leaders may intentionally or unintentionally display. The two extremes will be considered first—immoral and moral management—and then amoral management.

Immoral Management

Using *immoral* and *unethical* as synonyms, **immoral management** is defined as an approach that is devoid of ethical principles or precepts and at the same time implies a positive and active opposition to what is ethical. Immoral management decisions, behaviors, actions, and practices are discordant with ethical principles. This model holds that the management's motives are selfish and that it cares only or primarily about its own or its organization's gains. If the management's activity is actively opposed to what is regarded as ethical, this suggests that the management understands right from wrong and yet chooses to do wrong; thus, its motives are deemed greedy or selfish. In this model, the management's goals are profitability and organizational success at virtually any price. The management does not care about others' claims to be treated fairly or justly.

What about the management's orientation toward the law, considering that law is often regarded as an embodiment of minimal ethics? Immoral management regards legal standards as barriers that the management must avoid or overcome to accomplish what it wants. Immoral managers would just as soon engage in illegal activity as in immoral or unethical activity. This point is illustrated in a popular Dilbert comic strip. Dogbert, the VP of Marketing, announces at a meeting: "It's my job to spray paint the road kill." In panel 2 he says: "I'll use a process the experts call 'dishonesty.'" In panel 3, Dilbert concludes: "My motto is, 'If it isn't immoral, it probably won't work.'"[22]

Operating Strategy The operating strategy of immoral management is focused on exploiting opportunities for corporate or personal gain. An active opposition to what is moral would suggest that managers cut corners anywhere and everywhere it appears useful. Thus, the key operating question guiding immoral management is, "Can we make money with this action, decision, or behavior, *regardless of what it takes*?" Implicit in this question is that nothing else matters, at least not very much. Figure 7-7 summarizes some of the major characteristics of immoral managers.

Illustrative Cases Examples of immoral management abound. Following are several that are illustrative and enduring.

Enron No business scandal in recent times stands out as an example of immoral management as much as that of Enron Corporation. The two major players in the Enron scandal were CFO Jeffrey Skilling and CEO Ken Lay, now convicted felons. Though Enron imploded in 2001, it was not until 2006 that these two individuals were brought to justice and convicted.[23] Ken Lay, founder and CEO of Enron, died on July 5, 2006, before he had a chance to serve his prison sentence that would have taken him to the end of his life.[24] The Enron scandal became so famous that it produced a British play about the financial scandal that engulfed it, and in 2010 the play moved to Broadway in the United States but only lasted through 16 performances before it closed.[25] In addition, many books have been written about this infamous scandal.

Lay and Skilling were both convicted of securities fraud and conspiracy to inflate profits, along with a number of other charges. They used off-the-books partnerships to disguise Enron's debts, and then they lied to investors and employees about the company's disastrous financial situation while selling their own company shares.[26] In addition, Enron traders manipulated California's energy market to create phony shortages. This forced the state to borrow billions to pay off artificially inflated power bills. Voters in California were so fearful of brownouts, skyrocketing power bills, and rising state debt

FIGURE 7-7
Characteristics of Immoral Managers

- These managers intentionally do wrong.
- These managers are *self-centered* and *self-absorbed*.
- They care only about self or organization's profits or success.
- They actively oppose what is right, fair, or just.
- They *exhibit no concern* for stakeholders.
- These managers are the "bad guys."
- An ethics course probably would not help them.

© Cengage Learning

that they recalled Governor Gray Davis and replaced him with Arnold Schwarzenegger.[27] In 2013, Skilling, though in prison, was still trying to convince the courts that he was not given a fair trial and that his conviction should be overturned.[28] *The Wall Street Journal* recently observed that "the shadow of Enron still lingers."[29] Lay and Skilling were clearly immoral managers.

Bernie Madoff   Bernard Madoff perpetrated what has been called the biggest financial scandal in history, ending in his conviction at age 71. By his own account, the amount fraudulently stolen was $50 billion, but the true amount of the losses may never be known. Using what is called a Ponzi scheme, Madoff lured investors into turning their money over to him while he led them to believe their money was safely invested and yielding large returns. The scheme claimed to be making steady, double-digit returns trading options on a share index. In reality, client funds sat in an account at JPMorgan and were only withdrawn to meet redemption requirements or to be moved to other investments. Of course, Madoff spent much of the money and used it to live a lavish lifestyle all over the world. The SEC had reports on various occasions that he was swindling investors, but because of lapses in their investigations, Madoff was allowed to continue the swindle for years. When finally caught, Madoff was convicted and sentenced to 150 years in prison. The judge called the fraud "extraordinarily evil," and the sentence turned out to be the stiffest penalty ever given for a white-collar crime. Hundreds of investors lost their life savings. His victims included some of the world's largest banks and wealthiest people. Mr. Madoff, at age 71, said he would "live with this pain, with this torment, for the rest of my life."[30] He told *The New York Times* in an interview from prison in 2011 that the banks "had to know" he was committing fraud, but they chose to turn a blind eye.[31] Madoff, the immoral manager, is serving out his life-plus sentence in prison to this day.

Other insider traders didn't learn from Madoff's conviction. In 2012, Rajat Gupta, former head of McKinsey & Co. and an ex-board member of Goldman Sachs and Procter & Gamble, was convicted of insider trading. Raj Rajaratnam of Galleon hedge fund was slapped with an 11-year prison term for an insider trading scheme. And, R. Allen Stanford, the international financier well known for his extravagant lifestyle was sentenced to 110 years in prison for masterminding a $7 billion Ponzi scheme.[32] Each of these executives personifies immoral management.

Everyday Questionable Practices   In a "Deloitte & Touche USA Ethics & Workplace" survey, respondents identified a number of questionable behaviors observed in the workplace that they considered unacceptable. This list reveals everyday practices that would typically correspond with the model of immoral management[33]:

- Stealing petty cash
- Cheating on expense reports
- Taking credit for another person's accomplishments
- Lying on time sheets about hours worked
- Coming into work hung over
- Telling a demeaning joke (e.g., racist)
- Taking office supplies for personal use

In this same Deloitte & Touche survey, respondents provided what they considered to be other unethical behaviors.[34] These practices also would be characterized as immoral management:

- Showing preferential treatment toward certain employees
- Taking credit for another person's accomplishments

- Rewarding employees who display wrong behaviors
- Harassing a fellow employee (e.g., verbally, sexually, racially)

All of these are examples of immoral management wherein executives' decisions or actions were self-centered, actively opposed to what is right, focused on achieving organizational success at whatever the cost, and cutting corners where it was useful. These decisions were made without regard to the possible consequences of such concerns as honesty or fairness to others. What is apparent from the Deloitte & Touche survey findings is that immoral management can occur on an everyday basis and does not need to be in the league of the mega scandals such as Enron or Madoff to be unacceptable behavior.

Moral Management

At the opposite extreme from immoral management is **moral management**. Moral management conforms to the highest standards of ethical behavior or professional standards of conduct. Although it is not always crystal clear what level of ethical standards prevail, moral management strives to be highly ethical in terms of its focus on elevated ethical norms and professional standards of conduct, motives, goals, orientation toward the law, and general operating strategy.

In contrast to the selfish motives in immoral management, moral management aspires to succeed, but only within the confines of sound ethical precepts; that is, standards predicated on such norms as fairness, justice, respect for rights, and due process.

Spotlight on Sustainability

Ray Anderson's Epiphany

Many managers have a conversion experience before they become moral managers. In other words, they had to transition from, probably, an amoral condition to a moral style. Often this comes as a result of an epiphany, a sudden realization in understanding what they experience. A prominent example is that of Ray Anderson, former CEO of Interface Carpet, who has been ranked as one of the leading sustainable CEOs in business today. Anderson had a special moment occur when he was reading Paul Hawken's *Ecology of Commerce* in which he came to the conclusion that he, personally, was an environmental villain.

"It was an epiphanic spear in my heart, a life-changing moment; a new definition of success flooded my mind," he told the UK's *Guardian* newspaper about the revelation. He went on to report, "I realized I was a plunderer and it was not a legacy I wanted to leave behind. I wept."

Anderson then made it his new mission to change that legacy and proceeded to, as the *Guardian* puts it, "turn the company into a champion of environmental sustainability." By taking this courageous step, Anderson played a leadership role in getting many other companies into the conversation about sustainability. Without his ethical leadership, it is questionable when or if this would have occurred. Anderson was a sought-after international speaker who gave nearly 100 talks each year to audiences hungry for a message about the company that was proving the business model for sustainability works. Mr. Anderson passed away in 2011 but his memory serves as a constant reminder of the importance of sustainability.

Sources: Katherine Gustafson, "A Look at America's Most 'Sustainable' CEOs," *Tonic*, http://intentblog .com/look-americas-most-sustainable-ceos/. Accessed March 26, 2013. Also see "Founder and Chairman Ray Anderson Speaks on the Interface Journey and Sustainability," http://www.interfaceglobal.com/ company/leadership-team/ray-watch.aspx. Accessed March 26, 2013; and Ray Anderson, "The Eight Faces of Mount Sustainability," http://www.earthsayers.com/special_collection/Ray_Anderson/41/0/. Accessed April 4, 2013.

Moral management's motives would be termed fair, balanced, or unselfish. Organizational goals continue to stress profitability, but only within the confines of legal compliance and responsiveness to ethical standards.

Moral management pursues its objectives of profitability, legality, and ethics as both required and desirable. Moral management would not pursue profits at the expense of the law and sound ethics. Indeed, the focus here would be not only on the letter of the law but on the spirit of the law as well. The law would be viewed as a minimal standard of ethical behavior, because moral management strives to operate at a level above what the law mandates.

Operating Strategy The operating strategy of moral management is to live by sound ethical standards, seeking out only those economic opportunities that the organization or management can pursue within the confines of ethical boundaries. The manager or organization assumes a leadership position when ethical dilemmas arise. The central question guiding moral management's actions, decisions, and behaviors is, "Will this action, decision, behavior, or practice be fair to all stakeholders involved as well as to the organization?"

Integrity Strategy   Lynn Sharp Paine advocates an "integrity strategy" that closely resembles the moral management model.[35] The **integrity strategy** is characterized by a conception of ethics as the driving force of an organization. Ethical values shape management's search for opportunities, the design of organizational systems, and the decision-making process. Ethical values in the integrity strategy provide a common frame of reference and serve to unify different functions, lines of business, and employee groups. Organizational ethics, in this view, helps to define what an organization is and what it stands for. Some common features of an integrity strategy include the following,[36] which are all consistent with the moral management model:

- Guiding values and commitments make sense and are clearly communicated.
- Company leaders are personally committed, credible, and willing to take action on the values they espouse.
- Espoused values are integrated into the normal channels of management decision making.
- The organization's systems and structures support and reinforce its values.
- All managers have the skills, knowledge, and competencies to make ethically sound decisions on a daily basis.

Habits of Moral Leaders   Closely related to moral management is the topic of moral leadership. Carroll has set forth what he refers to as the "Seven Habits of Highly Moral Leaders."[37] Adapting the language used by Stephen Covey in his best-selling book *The Seven Habits of Highly Effective People*,[38] these qualities would need to be so common in the leader's approach that they become habitual as a leadership approach. Helping to further flesh out what constitutes a moral manager, the seven habits of highly moral leaders have been set forth as follows:

1. They (highly moral leaders) have a passion to do right.
2. They are morally proactive.
3. They consider all stakeholders.
4. They have a strong ethical character.
5. They have an obsession with fairness.
6. They undertake principled decision making.
7. They integrate ethics wisdom with management wisdom.[39]

FIGURE 7-8

Characteristics of Moral Managers

- These managers conform to a *high level of ethical or right behavior* (moral rectitude).
- They conform to a high level of personal and professional *standards*.
- *Ethical leadership* is commonplace—they search out where people may be hurt.
- Their goal is to succeed but only within the confines of *sound ethical precepts* (fairness, due process).

- *High integrity* is displayed in *thinking, speaking,* and *doing*.
- These managers embrace the letter and *spirit* of the law. Law is seen as a *minimal* ethical level. They prefer to operate *above* legal mandates.
- They possess an acute *moral sense* and *moral maturity*.
- Moral managers are the "good guys."

© Cengage Learning

Figure 7-8 summarizes the important characteristics of moral managers.

Positive Ethical Behaviors   Drawing on the "Deloitte & Touche USA Ethics & Workplace" survey cited earlier, following are examples of positive ethical behaviors identified by the survey respondents.[40] These represent everyday ways that managers can display moral management:

- Giving proper credit where it is due
- Always being straightforward and honest when dealing with other employees
- Treating all employees equally
- Being a responsible steward of company assets (e.g., no lavish entertainment)
- Resisting pressure to act unethically
- Recognizing and rewarding ethical behavior of others
- Talking about the importance of ethics and compliance on a regular basis

Illustrative Cases   A couple cases of moral management illustrate how this model of management is played out in actual practice.

Navistar   Navistar is a diesel engine manufacturer. One of its plants is located in Huntsville, Alabama. Because of the sour economy in 2009 and 2010, the company had to cut its production from 900 engines a day to 100. The company faced imminent layoffs. Plant manager Chuck Sibley wrestled with the layoff decision and finally came up with a creative solution that saved 50 jobs. Sibley's decision was not to lay off the employees but to send them out into the community, at corporate expense, to help the needy. Their initial assignments were to help Habitat for Humanity, the Salvation Army, and CASA, all nonprofit organizations deeply involved in community volunteerism. The employees were shocked but pleasantly surprised. They would still be paid by Navistar and they would keep all their benefits. The reassignments were expected to be for three months. Plant manager Sibley argued that the company will save money because they will avoid the costs of rehiring and training. The company expected an improvement in market conditions in three months and then the plan was to bring the 50 employees back to the plant.[41] The 50 employees were brought back to work as scheduled and they reported positive experiences about their time spent helping others.[42] This creative solution not only saved the employees from unemployment, but helped the community in a big way as well. Only a moral manager could come up with such a win–win solution.

Merck   Another well-known case of moral management occurred when Merck & Co., the pharmaceutical firm, invested millions of dollars to develop a drug for treating "river blindness," a Third World disease that was affecting almost 18 million people. Seeing that no government or aid organization was agreeing to buy the drug, Merck pledged to supply the drug for free forever. Merck's recognition that no effective mechanism existed to distribute the drug led to its decision to go far beyond industry practice and organize a committee to oversee the drug's distribution.[43]

We should stress at this time that not all organizations now engaging in moral management have done so all along. These companies sometimes arrived at this posture after years or decades of rising consumer expectations, increased government regulations, lawsuits, and pressure from social and consumer activists. By the same token, some moral management companies may slip from this status due to actions or practices taken. We must think of moral management, therefore, as a desirable posture that in many instances has evolved over periods of several years. If we hold management to an idealistic, 100 percent historical moral purity test, no management will fill the bill. Rather, we should consider moral those managements that now see the enlightened self-interest of responding in accordance with the moral management model rather than alternatives.

Amoral Management

Amoral management is not just a middle position on a continuum between immoral and moral management. Conceptually it has been positioned between the other two, but it is different in nature and kind from both, and it is of two kinds: **intentional amoral management** and **unintentional amoral management**.

Intentional Amoral Management   Amoral managers of this type do not factor ethical considerations into their decisions, actions, and behaviors because they believe business activity resides outside the sphere to which moral judgments apply. They simply think that different rules apply in business than in other realms of life. Intentionally amoral managers are in a distinct minority today. At one time, however, as managers first began to think about reconciling business practices with sound ethics, some managers adopted this stance. A few intentionally amoral managers are still around, but they are a vanishing breed in today's ethically conscious world.

Unintentional Amoral Management   Like intentionally amoral managers, unintentionally amoral managers do not think about business activity in ethical terms, but for different reasons. These managers are simply casual about, careless about, or inattentive to the fact that their decisions and actions may have negative or deleterious effects on others. These managers lack ethical perception and moral awareness. They have no "moral sense." That is, they blithely go through their organizational lives not thinking that what they are doing has an ethical dimension or facet. These managers are well intentioned but are either too insensitive or too self-absorbed to consider the effects of their decisions and actions on others. These managers normally think of themselves as ethical managers, but they frequently overlook these unintentional, subconscious, or unconscious aspects. As it turns out, they are more amoral than moral.

Unconscious Biases   Sometimes amoral managers may be unconscious of hidden biases that prevent them from being objective. Researchers have found that many businesspeople go through life deluded by the illusion of objectivity. Unconscious, or implicit biases, can run contrary to our consciously held, explicit beliefs.[44] Though most managers think they are ethical, sometimes even the most well-meaning person unwittingly allows unconscious thoughts and biases to influence what appear to be objective decisions. Four sources of unintentional, or unconscious, influences include implicit forms of prejudice, bias that favors one's own group, conflict of interest, and a tendency to overclaim credit.[45]

Unconscious biases were believed to be at work among accountants in some of the recent accounting scandals. Three *structural aspects* of accounting bias include ambiguity, attachment, and approval. When *ambiguity* exists, people tend to reach self-serving conclusions. For example, subjective interpretations of what constitutes a deductible expense may be made in a self-serving fashion. *Attachment* occurs when auditors, motivated to stay in their clients' good graces, approve things they might otherwise not approve. With respect to *approval*, external auditors may be reviewing the work of internal auditors, and self-serving biases may become even stronger when other people's biases are being endorsed or approved, especially if those judgments align with one's own biases.[46]

In addition, three aspects of human nature may amplify unconscious biases: familiarity, discounting, and escalation. With *familiarity*, people may be more willing to harm strangers (anonymous investors) than individuals they know (clients). *Discounting* refers to the act of overlooking or minimizing decisions that may not have immediate consequences. Finally, *escalation* occurs when an accountant or businessperson allows small judgments to accumulate and become large and then decides to cover up the unwitting mistakes through concealment. Thus, small indiscretions escalate into larger ones, and unconscious biases become conscious corruption.[47] These unconscious biases have been exposed in research within the general realm of behavioral ethics, which will be explored in further detail in Chapter 8.

Amoral management pursues profitability as its goal, but it does not consciously or cognitively attend to moral issues that may be intertwined with that pursuit. If there is an ethical guide to amoral management, it would be the marketplace as constrained by law—the letter of the law, not the spirit. The amoral manager sees the law as the parameters within which business pursuits take place.

Operating Strategy The operating strategy of amoral management is not to bridle managers with excessive ethical structure but to permit free rein within the supposedly unspoken but understood tenets of the free enterprise system. Personal ethics may periodically or unintentionally enter into managerial decisions, but it does not preoccupy management. Furthermore, the impact of decisions on others is an afterthought, if it is considered at all.

Amoral management represents a model of decision making in which the managers' ethical mental gears, to the extent that they are present, are stuck in neutral. The key management question guiding decision making is, "Can we make money with this action, decision, or behavior?" Note that the question does not imply an active or implicit intent to be either moral or immoral.

Compliance Strategy   Lynn Sharp Paine has articulated a compliance strategy that is consistent with the characteristics of amoral management. The **compliance strategy**, as contrasted with her integrity strategy discussed earlier, is more focused on submission to the law as its driving force. The compliance strategy is lawyer driven and is oriented not toward ethics or integrity but toward conformity with existing regulatory and criminal law. The compliance approach uses deterrence as its underlying assumption. This approach envisions managers as rational maximizers of self-interest, responsive to the personal costs and benefits of their choices, yet indifferent to the moral legitimacy of those choices.[48]

Figure 7-9 summarizes the major characteristics of amoral managers.

Illustrative Cases There are perhaps more examples of unintentionally amoral management than any other kind.

Early Examples   When police departments first stipulated that recruits must be at least 5′ 9″ tall and weigh at least 180 pounds, they were making an amoral decision, because

FIGURE 7-9

Characteristics of Amoral Managers

Intentionally Amoral Managers

- These managers don't think ethics and business should "mix."
- Business and ethics are seen as existing in *separate* spheres. Ethics is seen as too "Sunday schoolish" and not applicable to business.
- These managers are a vanishing breed. There are very few managers like this left in the world.

Unintentionally Amoral Managers

- These managers forget to consider the *ethical dimension* of decision making.
- They just don't "*think ethically.*"
- They may lack *ethical perception* or awareness; they have no "ethics buds" that help them sense the ethical dimension.
- They are well intentioned, but morally casual or careless; may be morally *unconscious.*
- Their ethical gears, if they exist, are in *neutral.*

© Cengage Learning

they were not considering the injurious exclusion this would impose on women and other ethnic groups who do not, on average, attain that height and weight. When companies decided to use scantily clad young women to advertise vehicles, men's cologne, and other products, these companies were not thinking of the degrading and demeaning characterization of women that would result from what they thought was an ethically neutral decision. When Domino's initially decided to deliver pizza orders within 30 minutes or the food was free, they didn't think about how such a policy might induce their drivers to speed and, sometimes, cause auto accidents. This policy was later dropped.

Nestlé   Nestlé's initial decision to market infant formula in Third World countries (see Chapter 10) could have been an amoral decision when it was first made. Nestlé may not have considered the detrimental effects such a seemingly innocent business decision would have on mothers and babies in a land of impure water, poverty, and illiteracy. In other words, Nestlé simply wasn't factoring ethical considerations into its marketing decisions.

Sears   A classic illustration of unintentionally amoral management involved the case of Sears Roebuck and Co. and its automotive service business which spanned a decade. Paine described how consumers and attorneys general in 40 states accused the company of misleading consumers and selling them unneeded parts and services.[49] In the face of declining revenues and a shrinking market share, Sears' executives instituted new goals, quotas, and incentives for auto-center service personnel. Service employees were told to meet product-specific and service-specific quotas—sell so many brake jobs, batteries, and front-end alignments—or face consequences such as reduced working hours or transfers. Some employees spoke of the "pressure" they felt to generate business. Although Sears' executives did not set out to defraud customers, they put into place a commission system that led to Sears' employees feeling pressure to sell products and services that consumers did not need. Fortunately, Sears eliminated its quota system as a partial remedy to the problem.[50]

The Sears case is an archetypal example of unintentionally amoral management—a well-intentioned company drifting into questionable practices because it just did not think ethically. The company simply did not think through the impacts that its strategic decisions would have on important stakeholders. Today, many companies do not think carefully about the effects employee rewards systems might have on customers and others.

Figure 7-10 provides a summary of the major characteristics of immoral, amoral, and moral management. It compares the three in terms of ethical norms, motives, goals, orientation toward the law, and operating strategy.

FIGURE 7-10   Three Approaches to Management Ethics

		Immoral Management	**Amoral Management**	**Moral Management**
Organizational Characteristics	Ethical Norms	Management decisions, actions, and behavior imply a positive and active opposition to what is moral (ethical). Decisions are discordant with accepted ethical principles. An active negation of what is moral is implied.	Management is neither moral nor immoral, but decisions lie outside the sphere to which moral judgments apply. Management activity is outside or beyond the moral order of a particular code. May imply a lack of ethical perception and moral awareness.	Management activity conforms to a standard of ethical, or right, behavior. Conforms to accepted professional standards of conduct. Ethical leadership is commonplace on the part of management.
	Motives	Selfish. Management cares only about its or the company's gains.	Well-intentioned but selfish in the sense that impact on others is not considered.	Good. Management wants to succeed but only within the confines of sound ethical precepts (fairness, justice, due process).
	Goals	Profitability and organizational success at any price.	Profitability. Other goals are not considered.	Profitability within the confines of legal obedience and ethical standards.
	Orientation Toward Law	Legal standards are barriers that management must overcome to accomplish what it wants.	Law is the ethical guide, preferably the letter of the law. The central question is what we can do legally.	Obedience toward letter and spirit of the law. Law is a minimal ethical behavior. Prefer to operate well above what law mandates.
	Strategy	Exploit opportunities for corporate gain. Cut corners when it appears useful.	Give managers free rein. Personal ethics may apply but only if managers choose. Respond to legal mandates if caught and required to do so.	Live by sound ethical standards. Assume leadership position when ethical dilemmas arise. Enlightened self-interest.

Source: Archie B. Carroll, "In Search of the Moral Manager," *Business Horizons* (March/April 1987), 8. Copyright © 1987 by the Foundation for the School of Business at Indiana University. Used with permission.

Two Hypotheses Regarding the Models of Management Morality

A thorough study has not been conducted to ascertain precisely what proportions of managers each model of morality represents in the total management population. However, two plausible hypotheses regarding the moral management models are worthy of consideration.

Population Hypothesis The **population hypothesis** is that the distribution of the three models might approximate a normal curve, with the amoral group occupying the large middle part of the curve and the moral and immoral categories occupying the smaller tails of the curve. It is difficult to research this question. If you asked managers what they thought they were or what others thought they were, a self-serving bias would likely enter in and you would not get an accurate, unbiased picture. Another approach would be to observe management actions. This would be nearly impossible because it is not possible to observe all management actions for any sustained period. Therefore, the supposition remains a hypothesis based on one person's judgment of what is going on in the management population.

This proposed normal curve distribution is similar to behavioral economist Dan Ariely's belief that 1 percent of people would *never* steal, 1 percent would *always* try to steal, and 98 percent would be honest as long as they were not tempted. Ariely believes that most of us are 98-percenters. One of Ariely's students told him the story about a locksmith who helped him when he locked himself out of his house. Being amazed at how easily and quickly the locksmith was able to pick the lock, the locksmith told him that the locks were there to keep the honest people from stealing. The locks remove the temptation for most people.[51] It is uncertain whether the large middle group of amoral managers would cheat or not if tempted, but the normal curve distribution pattern is strikingly similar.

Individual Hypothesis Equally disturbing as the belief that the amoral management style is common among the managerial population today is the **individual hypothesis** that, within the individual manager, these three models may operate at various times and under various circumstances. That is, the average manager himself or herself may be amoral most of the time but may slide into a moral or an immoral mode on occasion, based on a variety of factors. Like the population hypothesis, this view has not been empirically supported, but it does provide an interesting perspective for managers to ponder. This perspective would be somewhat similar to the situational ethics argument that has been around for some time. Is the individual hypothesis more likely valid than the population hypothesis? Could both exist at the same time?

Amoral Management Is a Serious Organizational Problem With the exception of the major ethics scandals witnessed in the past couple decades, it could be argued that the more insidious ethical problem in organizations today seems to be the group of managers who for one reason or another subscribe to or live out the amoral management ethic. These are managers who are driven primarily by profitability or a bottom-line ethos which regards economic success as the exclusive barometer of organizational and personal achievement. These amoral managers are not necessarily bad people, but they essentially see the competitive business world as ethically neutral. Until this group of managers moves toward the moral management ethic, we will continue to see businesses and other organizations criticized as they have been in the past.

To connect the three models of management morality with concepts introduced earlier, we show in Figure 7-11 how the components of corporate social responsibility (Chapter 2) would likely be viewed by managers using each of the three models of management morality.

Figure 7-12 displays how managers using the three models would probably embrace or reject the stakeholder concept or stakeholder thinking (Chapter 3). It is hoped that

FIGURE 7-11   Three Models of Management Morality and Emphases on CSR

Models of Management Morality	COMPONENTS OF THE CSR DEFINITION			
	Economic Responsibility	Legal Responsibility	Ethical Responsibility	Philanthropic Responsibility
Immoral management	XXX	X		
Amoral management	XXX	XX	X	X
Moral management	XXX	XXX	XXX	XXX

Weighting code:
X = token consideration (appearances only)
XX = moderate consideration
XXX = significant consideration

FIGURE 7-12 The Moral Management Models and Acceptance or Rejection of Stakeholder Thinking (SHT)

Moral Management Model	Acceptance of Stakeholder Thinking (SHT)	Stakeholder Thinking Posture Embraced
Immoral management	SHT rejected: management is self-absorbed	SHT rejected, not deemed useful. Accepts profit maximization model but does not really pursue it.
Amoral management	SHT accepted: narrow view (minimum number of stakeholders considered)	Instrumental view of SHT prevails. How will it help management?
Moral management	SHT enthusiastically embraced: wider view (maximum number of stakeholders considered)	Normative view of SHT prevails. SHT is fully embraced in all decision making.

© Cengage Learning

these suggested interrelationships among these concepts will make them easier to understand and appreciate.

Making Moral Management Actionable

The characteristics of immoral, moral, and amoral management should provide some useful benchmarks for managerial self-analysis because self-analysis and introspection significantly help managers recognize the need to move from the immoral or amoral ethic to the moral ethic. Organizational leaders must acknowledge that amoral management is a morally vacuous condition that can be quite easily disguised as just an innocent, practical, bottom-line philosophy—something to take pride in. Amoral management is, however, and will continue to be, the bane of the management profession until it is recognized for what it really is and until managers take steps to overcome it. Most managers are not "bad guys," as they sometimes are portrayed, but the idea that managerial decision making can be ethically neutral is not tenable in the society of the new millennium.[52] To make moral management actionable, both immoral and amoral management must be discarded and the process of developing moral judgment begun.

Developing Moral Judgment

As a manager, it is helpful to know something about how people, whether they are managers or employees, develop moral (or ethical) judgment. Perhaps if we knew more about this process, we could better understand our own behavior and the behavior of those around us and those we manage. Further, we might be able to better design reward systems for encouraging ethical behavior if we knew more about how employees and others think and process issues about ethics. A good starting point is to appreciate what psychologists have to say about how we as individuals develop morally. The major research on this issue are **Kohlberg's levels of moral development**.[53] After this discussion, we consider other sources of a manager's values, especially those emanating from both societal sources and from within the organization itself.

Levels of Moral Development

The psychologist Lawrence Kohlberg has done extensive research into the topic of **moral development**. He concluded, on the basis of more than 20 years of research, that there is a general sequence of three levels (each with two stages) through which individuals advance in learning to think or develop morally. There is widespread practical usage of his levels of moral development, and this suggests a general if not unanimous consensus that it is valuable. Figure 7-13 illustrates Kohlberg's three levels and six stages. There it can be seen that as one develops morally, the focus moves from the *self*, to *others*, and then to *humankind*. Understanding this progression is of great value in developing a basic foundation in business ethics and leadership.

Level 1: Preconventional Level   At the **preconventional level of moral development**, which is typically characteristic of how people behave as infants and children, the focus is mainly on the *self*. As an infant starts to grow, his or her main behavioral reactions are in response to punishments and rewards. Stage 1 is the *reaction-to-punishment stage*. If you want a child to do something (such as stay out of the street) at a very early age, scolding or spanking often is needed. The child's orientation at this stage is toward the avoidance of pain.

As the youngster gets a bit older, rewards start to work. Stage 2 is the *seeking-of-rewards stage*. The child begins to see some connection between being "good" (i.e., doing what Mom or Dad wants the child to do) and some reward that may be forthcoming. The reward may be parental praise or something tangible, such as candy, extra TV time, or getting to use Mom's iPad. At this preconventional level, children do not completely understand the moral idea of "right" and "wrong" but rather learn to behave according to the consequences—punishments or rewards—that are likely to follow.

Though we normally associate the preconventional level with the moral development of children, many adults in organizations are significantly influenced by rewards and punishments. Consequently, the preconventional level of motivation may be observed in adults as well as children and is relevant to a discussion of adult moral maturity. Like children, adults in responsible positions react to punishments (organizational sanctions) or seek rewards (approval).

FIGURE 7-13   Kohlberg's Levels of Moral Development

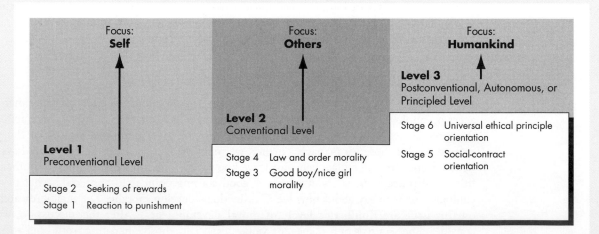

© Cengage Learning

Level 2: Conventional Level As a person matures, she or he learns that there are *others* whose ideas or welfare ought to be considered. Initially, these others include family and friends. At the **conventional level of moral development**, the individual learns the importance of conforming to the conventional norms of society. This is the level at which social relationships form and become dominant.

The conventional level is composed of two stages. Stage 3 has been called the "*good boy/nice girl*" *morality stage*. The young person learns that there are some rewards (such as feelings of acceptance, trust, loyalty, or friendship) for living up to what is expected by family and peers, so the individual begins to conform to what is generally expected of a good son, daughter, sister, brother, friend, and so on.

Stage 4 is the *law-and-order morality stage*. Not only does the individual learn to respond to family, friends, the school, and the church, as in Stage 3, but the individual now recognizes that there are certain norms in society (in school, in the theater, in the mall, in stores, in the car, waiting in line) that are expected or needed if society is to function in an orderly fashion. Thus, the individual becomes socialized or acculturated into what being a good citizen means. These rules for living include not only the actual laws (don't run a red light, don't walk until the "Walk" light comes on, don't text or talk on the phone while driving) but also other, less official norms (don't break into line, be sure to tip the server, mute your cell phone in restaurants). At Stage 4, the individual sees that she or he is part of a larger social system and that to function in and be accepted by this social system requires a considerable degree of acceptance of and conformity to the norms and standards of society. Therefore, many organizational members are strongly influenced by society's conventions as manifested in both Stages 3 and 4 as described.

Level 3: Postconventional, Autonomous, or Principled Level At the **postconventional, autonomous, principled level of moral development**, which Kohlberg argues few people reach (and those who do reach it have trouble staying there), the focus moves beyond those "others" who are of immediate importance to the individual to *humankind* as a whole. At the postconventional level of moral development, the individual develops a concept of ethics that is more mature than the conventionally articulated situation. Thus, it is sometimes called the level at which moral principles become self-accepted, not because they are held by society but because the individual now perceives and embraces them as "right."

Kohlberg's third level consists of two stages that differ by whether the individual can just follow rules established by society or others, or engage in his or her own moral reasoning. Stage 5 is the *social-contract orientation*. At this stage, right action is thought of in terms of general individual rights and standards that have been critically examined and agreed upon by society as a whole. Social contracts have influence. There is a clear awareness of the relativism of personal values and a corresponding emphasis on fair processes for reaching consensus.

Stage 6 is the *universal-ethical-principle orientation*. Here the individual uses his or her thinking and conscience in accord with self-chosen ethical principles that are anticipated to be universal, comprehensive, and consistent. These universal principles (for example, the Golden Rule) might be focused on such ideals as justice, human rights, reciprocity, and social welfare. At this stage, the individual is motivated by a commitment to universal principles or guidelines.

Kohlberg suggests that at Level 3 the individual is able to rise above the conventional level where "rightness" and "wrongness" are defined by others and societal institutions and that she or he is able to defend or justify her or his actions on some higher ethical basis. For example, in our society the law tells us we should not discriminate against minorities. A Level 2 manager might not discriminate because to do so is to violate the law and social custom. A Level 3 manager would not discriminate but might offer a different reason—for example, it is wrong to discriminate because it violates universal principles of human rights and justice. Part of the difference between Levels 2 and 3, therefore, is traceable to the motivation for the course of action taken. The authenticity of one's motives is crucial at Level 3.

The discussion to this point may have suggested that we are at Level 1 as infants, at Level 2 as youths, and, finally, at Level 3 as adults. There is some approximate correspondence between chronological age and Levels 1 and 2, but the important point should be made that Kohlberg thinks many of us as adults never get beyond Level 2. The idea of getting to Level 3 as managers or employees is desirable, because it would require us to think about people, products, and markets at a higher ethical level than that generally attained by conventional society. However, even if we never get there, Level 3 urges us to continually ask, "What ought to be?" The first two levels tell us a lot about moral development that should be useful to us as managers. There are not many people who consistently operate according to Level 3 principles. Sometimes a manager or employee may dip into Level 3 on a certain issue or for a certain period of time. Sustaining that level, however, is quite challenging.

If we frame the issue in terms of the question, "Why do managers and employees behave ethically?," we might infer conclusions from Kohlberg that look like those presented in Figure 7-14. These conclusions attempt to generalize about people's reactions to various factors.

Ethics of Care as Alternative to Kohlberg One of the major criticisms of Kohlberg's research was set forth by psychologist Carol Gilligan. Gilligan argued that Kohlberg's conclusions may accurately depict the stages of moral development among men, whom he used as his research subjects, but that his findings are not generalizable to women.[54] According to Gilligan's view, men tend to deal with moral issues in terms that are impersonal, impartial, and abstract. Examples might include the principles of justice and rights that Kohlberg argues are relevant at the postconventional level. Women, on the

FIGURE 7-14 Why Managers and Employees Behave Ethically

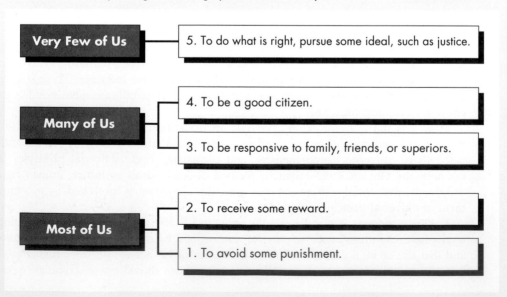

- **Very Few of Us** — 5. To do what is right, pursue some ideal, such as justice.

- **Many of Us**
  - 4. To be a good citizen.
  - 3. To be responsive to family, friends, or superiors.

- **Most of Us**
  - 2. To receive some reward.
  - 1. To avoid some punishment.

other hand, perceive themselves to be part of a network of relationships with family and friends and thus are more focused on *relationship maintenance* and *hurt avoidance* when they confront moral issues. For women, then, morality is often more a matter of caring and showing responsibility toward those involved in their relationships than in adhering to abstract or impersonal principles, such as justice. This alternative view of ethics has been called the ethics of care.

According to Gilligan, women move in and out of three moral levels.[55] At the first level, the *self* is the sole object of concern. At the second level, the chief desire is to *establish connections and participate* in social life. In other words, maintaining relationships or directing one's thoughts toward others becomes dominant. Gilligan says that this is the conventional notion of women. At the third level, women recognize their own needs and the *needs of others*—those with whom they have relationships. Gilligan goes on to say that women never settle completely at one level. As they attain moral maturity, they do more of their thinking and make more of their decisions at the third level. This level requires care for others as well as care for oneself. In this view, morality moves away from the legalistic, self-centered approach that some say characterizes traditional ethics.

Some research does not support the view that moral development varies by gender in the fashion described by Gilligan. However, it does support Gilligan's claim that a different perspective toward moral issues is sometimes used. Apparently, both men and women sometimes employ an impartial or impersonal moral-rules perspective and sometimes they employ a care-and-responsibility perspective. This "care perspective" is still at an early stage of research, but it is useful to know that perspectives other than those found by Kohlberg are being considered.[56] More will be said about the ethics of care in the next chapter. In the final analysis, we need to exercise caution when thinking about the applicability of Kohlberg's and Gilligan's research as well as the thousands of studies that have sought to fine tune their research. The value of this research, however, is the idea that moral development levels and stages do occur and that managers need to be aware of and sensitive to this in their approaches to dealing with people and ethics challenges in their organizations.

Different Sources of a Person's Values

In addition to considering the levels of moral development as an explanation of how and why people behave ethically, it is also useful to look at the different *sources of a manager's or employee's values*. Ethics and values are intimately related. We referred earlier to ethics as the set of moral principles or values that drives behavior. Thus, the rightness or wrongness of behavior really turns out to be a manifestation of the ethical beliefs held by the individual. Values, on the other hand, are the individual's concepts of the relative worth, utility, or importance of certain ideas. Values reflect what the individual considers important in the larger scheme of things. One's values, therefore, shape one's ethics. Because this is so, it is important to understand the many different value-shaping forces that influence employees and managers.

The increasing pluralism of the society in which we live has exposed managers to a large number of values of many different kinds, and this has resulted in ethical diversity. One way to examine the sources of a manager's values is by considering both forces that originate from *outside the organization* to shape or influence the manager and those that emanate from *within the organization*. This, unfortunately, is not as simply done as we would like, because some sources are difficult to pinpoint. This discussion expands on and organizes some of the sources of ethical norms depicted earlier in Figure 7-4.

Sources External to the Organization: The Web of Values The external sources of a person's values refer to those broad sociocultural values that have emerged in society

ETHICS IN PRACTICE CASE

Are People More Ethical When Being "Watched?"

Most people would probably say they would be more honest if they were being watched. This is human nature, isn't it? A team of researchers at Newcastle University in the UK decided to test this proposition by creating an experiment.

The setting for the experiment was the coffee station set up in a department break room where faculty and staff could help themselves to coffee, tea, or milk during the day and then place their payment for the refreshments in a jar or a box. The "honor system" was requested because there was no one at the station to monitor whether people actually paid or not. The department had been using an "honesty box" for people to place their money in for years.

The researchers decided to post the prices for the coffee, tea, and milk on a poster that featured a banner across the top that contained images that were alternated without announcement from week to week. The poster was placed above the coffee station. The alternating images included a set of eyes and a picture of flowers. The image of eyes was varied in their gender and position, but they were always situated so that they appeared to be looking directly at the person.

The research team collected the money each week and recorded how much had been placed in the box. The team calculated that, on average, the amount collected when the "eyes poster" was present was 2.76 times the amount collected when the flowers poster was there. The researchers concluded that the effect of being "watched" had the subconscious effect of improving people's honesty. But, the researchers were surprised at how large an effect resulted from being watched.

Later, the question was raised whether using "watching eyes" could curb dishonest behaviors in other settings. A police department in Birmingham, UK, decided to test whether it worked to deter crime by posting pictures of staring eyes all over the city. Time will tell whether this approach to keeping crime at bay will work.

1. Was it unethical for the research team to conduct this experiment without telling people it was going on?
2. Do the results of the experiment surprise you? What ethical phenomena were at work here?
3. Evaluate the experiment using Kohlberg's levels of moral development. Does the experiment tend to support or refute Kohlberg's findings? Do you think it would make a difference whether the coffee drinkers were men or women?
4. Will the police department experiment work? Why? Why not?

Sources: "'Big Brother' Eyes Encourage Honesty, Study Shows," Newcastle University, http://www.ncl.ac.uk/press.office/press.release/item/?ref=1151491586#.USug4TCkqeY. Accessed April 4, 2013; "Watchful eyes keep you honest," http://www.abc.net.au/science/articles/2011/09/27/3326890.htm. Accessed April 4, 2013; Armenian Medical Network, "When it comes to honesty, the eyes have it," http://www.health.am/ab/more/honesty-the-eyes-have-it/. Accessed April 4, 2013.

over a long period of time. Although current events (scandals, fraud, deception, bribery) seem to affect these historic values by bringing specific ones into clearer focus at a given time, these values are rather enduring and change slowly. It has been stated that "every executive resides at the center of a web of values" and that there are five principal repositories of values influencing businesspeople. These five include religious, philosophical, cultural, legal, and professional values.[57] Each deserves brief consideration.

Religious Values   Religion and faith have long been a basic source of morality in most societies. Religion and morality are so intertwined that William Barclay related them for definitional purposes: "Ethics is the bit of religion that tells us how we ought to behave."[58] The biblical tradition of Judeo-Christian theology forms the core for much of what Western society believes today about the importance of work, the concept of fairness, and the dignity of the individual. Other religious traditions also inform management behavior and action.[59]

Philosophical Values   Philosophy and various philosophical systems are also external sources of the manager's values. Beginning with preachments of the ancient Greeks, philosophers have claimed to demonstrate that *reason* can provide us with principles or morals in the same way it gives us the principles of mathematics. John Locke argued that morals are mathematically demonstrable, although he never explained how.[60] Aristotle with his Golden Rule and his doctrine of the mean, Kant with his categorical imperative, Bentham with his pain and pleasure calculus, and modern-day existentialists have shown us the influence of various kinds of reasoning for ethical choice. Today, the strong influence of moral relativism and postmodernism have influenced some people's values.

Cultural Values   Culture is that broad synthesis of societal norms and values emanating from everyday living. Culture has also had an impact on managers' and employees' thinking. Modern sources of culture include music, movies, television, video games, social networking and the Internet. The melting-pot culture of many countries today is a potpourri of norms, customs, and rules that defy summarization. In recent years, it has become difficult to summarize what messages the culture is sending people about ethics. In an influential book, *Moral Freedom: The Search for Virtue in a World of Choice*, by Alan Wolfe, the author argues that the United States, like other Western nations, is undergoing a radical revolution in morals and is now, morally speaking, a new society.[61] Wolfe thinks the traditional values that our culture has looked upon with authority (churches, families, neighborhoods, civic leaders) have lost the ability to influence people as they once did.

Wolfe goes on to say that as more and more areas of life have become democratized and open to consumer "choice," people have come to assume that they are free to determine for themselves what it means to lead a good and virtuous life. He says that a key element in this new moral universe is nonjudgmentalism, which pushes society to suspend judgment on much immoral behavior or interpret immoral behavior as not the fault of the perpetrator. Thus, although many people may uphold the old virtues, in principle, they turn them into personal "options" in practice.[62] These trends are clearly a departure from the past and are likely impacting the way managers perceive the world of business. Employees, likewise, share these same perspectives and this creates challenges for managers.

Legal Values   The legal system has been and continues to be one of the most powerful forces defining what is ethical and what is not for managers and employees. This is true even though ethical behavior generally is that which occurs over and above legal dictates. As stated earlier, the law represents the codification of what the society considers right and wrong or fair. Although we as members of society do not completely agree with every law in existence, there often is more consensus for law than for ethics. Law, then, "mirrors the ideas of the entire society."[63] Law represents a minimum ethic of behavior but does not encompass all the ethical standards of behavior. Law addresses only the grossest violations of society's sense of right, wrong, and fairness and thus is not adequate to describe completely all that is acceptable or unacceptable. Because it represents our official consensus ethic, however, its influence is pervasive and widely accepted.

In recent years, it has become an understatement to observe that we live in a litigious society. This trend toward suing someone to bring about justice has clearly had an impact on management decision making. Whereas the threat of litigation may make managers more careful in their treatment of stakeholders, the threat of losing tens or hundreds of millions of dollars has distorted decision making and caused many managers and companies to be running scared—never knowing exactly what is the best or fairest course of action to pursue. Therefore, it is easy to see how laws and regulations are among the most influential drivers of business ethics.[64]

Professional Values   These include those emanating from professional organizations and societies that represent various jobs and positions. As such, they presumably articulate the ethical consensus of the leaders of those professions. For example, the Public Relations Society of America has a code of ethics that public relations executives have imposed on themselves as their own guide to behavior. The National Association of Realtors has created its own code of conduct. Professional values thus exert a more specific impact on the manager than the four broader values discussed earlier. Though there is not a generally accepted code of conduct or ethics for general managers, in recent years The Oath Project has sought to establish enhanced professionalization of management by proposing and gaining signatories to a form of a "Hippocratic oath for business" which would help integrate professional conduct and social responsibility into the culture, core values, and day-to-day operations of corporations and academic institutions.[65]

In sum, several sources of values that are external to the organization come to bear on the manager and employees and influence their ethics. In addition to those mentioned, people are influenced by family, friends, acquaintances, and social and current events of the day as depicted earlier in Figure 7-4. People thus come to the workplace with personal philosophies that truly are a composite of numerous interacting values that have shaped their views of the world, of life, and of business.

Sources Internal to the Organization   The external forces constitute the broad background or milieu against which a manager or an employee behaves or acts. There are, in addition, a number of more immediate factors that help to channel the individual's values and behavior. These values grow out of the specific organizational experience itself. These internal (within the organization) sources of a manager's values constitute more immediate and direct influences on one's actions and decisions.

When an individual goes to work for an organization, a *socialization process* takes place in which the individual comes to learn and adopt the predominant values of that organization. The individual learns rather quickly that to survive and succeed, certain norms must be internalized, honored, and perpetuated. Several of these "internal" norms that are prevalent in business organizations include:

- Respect for the authority structure
- Loyalty to bosses and the organization
- Conformity to principles, practices, and traditions
- Performance counts above all else
- Results count above all else

Each of these norms may take on a major influence in a person who subordinates her or his own standard of ethics to those of the organization. In fact, research suggests that these internal sources play a much more significant role in shaping business ethics than do the host of external sources we considered first. *Respect for the authority structure, loyalty, conformity, performance,* and *results* have been historically synonymous with survival and success in business. When these influences are operating together, they form a composite **bottom-line mentality** that is remarkably influential in its impact on individual and group behavior. These values form the central motif of organizational activity and direction.

Underlying the first three norms is the focus on performance and results. This has been called the "calculus of the bottom line."[66] One does not need to study business organizations for long to recognize that the bottom line—profits—is the value that seems to take precedence over all others. Profits "now rather than later" seems to be the orientation that spells success for managers and employees alike. Respect for authority, loyalty, and conformity become means to an end, although one could certainly find organizations and people who see these as legitimate ends in themselves. Only recently are some managers and organizations starting to respond to the "multiple bottom line" or "triple bottom line" perspective introduced in Chapter 2. From the standpoint of sustainability, managers will increasingly need to think and practice beyond that which is dictated by the short-term obsession with quarterly earnings.

Elements of Moral Judgment

A positive way to close out this chapter is to consider what it takes for moral or ethical judgment to develop. For growth in moral judgment to take place, it is necessary to appreciate the key elements involved in making moral judgments. This is a notion central to the transition from the amoral management condition to the moral management condition. Powers and Vogel have suggested that there are six major elements or capacities that are essential to making moral judgments. These **elements of moral judgment** include: (1) moral imagination, (2) moral identification and ordering, (3) moral evaluation, (4) tolerance of moral disagreement and ambiguity, (5) integration of managerial and moral competence, and (6) a sense of moral obligation.[67] Each reveals an essential ingredient in developing moral judgment, which then forms the basis for personal and organizational ethics to be examined in the next chapter.

Moral Imagination

Moral imagination refers to the ability to perceive that a web of competing economic relationships is, at the same time, a web of moral or ethical relationships. Business and ethics are not separate topics but occur side by side in organizations. Those with moral imagination are able to perceive the presence of ethical issues and develop creative ways for dealing with them. Developing moral imagination means not only becoming sensitive to ethical issues in business decision making but also developing the perspective of searching out subtle places where people are likely to be harmfully affected by adverse decision making or behaviors of managers. Moral imagination requires the manager to rise above the everyday stress and confusion and carefully identify the ethical issues and values conflicts that exist in the organization or for which symptoms of problems may be present.

Moral Identification and Ordering

Moral identification and ordering refers to the ability to discern the relevance or nonrelevance of moral factors that are introduced into a decision-making situation. Are the moral issues actual or just rhetorical? The ability to see moral issues as issues that can be dealt with is at stake here. Once moral issues have been identified, they must be ranked, or ordered, just as economic or technological issues are prioritized during the decision-making process. A manager must not only develop this skill through experience but also hone it through repetition and the application of ethics principles. In this prioritizing process, a manager may conclude, for example, that worker safety is more important than worker privacy, though both are important qualities.

Moral Evaluation

Once issues have been identified and ordered, evaluations must be made. *Moral evaluation* is the practical, decision phase of moral judgment and entails essential skills, such as coherence and consistency that have proved to be effective principles in other contexts. Managers need to understand the importance of clear principles, develop processes for weighing ethical factors, and develop the ability to identify what the likely moral as well as economic outcomes of a decision will be. Important here is the foresight of likely consequences of different courses of action.

The real challenge in moral evaluation is to integrate the concern for others into organizational goals, purposes, and legitimacy. In the final analysis, though, the manager may not know the "right" answer or solution, although moral sensitivity has been introduced into the process.

Tolerance of Moral Disagreement and Ambiguity

An objection managers often have to ethics discussions is the amount of disagreement generated and the volume of ambiguity that must be tolerated. This disagreement and ambiguity must be accepted, however, because it is a natural part of ethics discussions. To be sure, managers need closure and precision in their decisions. But in moral discussions the situation is seldom clear, as in many traditional and more familiar decision contexts of managers, such as introducing a new product based on limited test marketing, choosing a new executive for a key position, deciding which computer system to install, or making a strategic decision based on instincts. All of these are risky decisions, but managers have become accustomed to making them in spite of the disagreements and ambiguity that prevail among those involved in the decision or within the individual decision maker. The *tolerance of moral disagreement and ambiguity* is simply an extension of a managerial aptitude that is present in practically all decision-making situations managers face. It includes the ability to hear, discuss, and be respectful toward other people's views.

Integration of Managerial and Moral Competence

The *integration of managerial and moral competence* underlies all that we have been discussing. Moral issues in management do not arise in isolation from traditional business decision making but right in the middle of it. The scandals that major corporations face today did not occur independently of the companies' economic activities but were embedded in and culminated from a series of decisions made at various points in time. Therefore, moral competence is an integral part of managerial competence. Managers are learning—some the hard way—that there is a significant corporate, and in many instances, personal price to pay for their amorality. The amoral manager sees ethical decisions as isolated and independent of managerial decisions and competence, but the moral manager sees every decision as one in which an ethical perspective must be integrated. This kind of future-looking view is essential to sustainable organizations.

A Sense of Moral Obligation

The foundation for all the capacities we have discussed is a *sense of moral obligation*[68] and integrity. This wisdom is the key to the process but it is difficult to acquire. This sense requires the intuitive or learned understanding that moral threads—a concern for fairness, justice, and due process to people, groups, and communities—are woven into the fabric of managerial decision making and are the integral components that hold systems together.

These qualities are perfectly consistent with, and indeed are essential prerequisites to, the free enterprise system as we know it today. One can go back in time to Adam Smith and the foundation tenets of the free enterprise system and not find references to immoral or unethical practices as being elements needed for the system to work. The late Milton Friedman, our modern-day Adam Smith, even alluded to the importance of ethics when he stated that the purpose of business is "to make as much money as possible while conforming to the basic rules of society, both those embodied in the law and *those embodied in ethical custom.*"[69] The moral manager develops a sense of moral obligation and integrity that is the glue that holds together the decision-making process in which human welfare is inevitably at stake. Indeed, the sense of moral obligation is what holds society and the business system together as a sustainable enterprise.

Figure 7-15 summarizes the six elements of moral judgment identified by Powers and Vogel as they might be perceived by amoral and moral managers. The contrast between the two perspectives should be helpful in understanding each element of moral judgment.

FIGURE 7-15   **Elements of Moral Judgment in Amoral and Moral Managers**

Amoral Managers	Moral Managers
Moral Imagination	
See a web of competing economic claims as just that and nothing more.	Perceive that a web of competing economic claims is simultaneously a web of moral relationships.
Are insensitive to and unaware of the hidden dimensions of where people are likely to get hurt.	Are sensitive to and hunt out the hidden dimensions of where people are likely to get hurt.
Moral Identification and Ordering	
See moral claims as squishy and not definite enough to order into hierarchies with other claims.	See which moral claims being made are relevant or irrelevant; order moral factors just as economic factors are ordered.
Moral Evaluation	
Are erratic in their application of ethics if it gets applied at all.	Are coherent and consistent in their normative reasoning.
Tolerance of Moral Disagreement and Ambiguity	
Cite ethical disagreement and ambiguity as reasons for forgetting ethics altogether.	Tolerate ethical disagreement and ambiguity while honestly acknowledging that decisions are not precise like mathematics but must finally be made nevertheless.
Integration of Managerial and Moral Competence	
See ethical decisions as isolated and independent of managerial decisions and managerial competence.	See every evolving decision as one in which a moral perspective must be integrated with a managerial one.
A Sense of Moral Obligation	
Have no sense of moral obligation and integrity that extends beyond managerial responsibility.	Have a sense of moral obligation and integrity that holds together the decision-making process in which human welfare is at stake.

Source: Archie B. Carroll, "In Search of the Moral Manager," *Business Horizons* (March/April 1987), 15. Copyright © 1987 by the Foundation for the School of Business at Indiana University. Used with permission.

Summary

Business ethics has become a serious challenge for the business community over the past several decades. The major ethics scandals of the past two decades affected the public's trust of executives and major business institutions. The Wall Street financial scandals brought the public's trust of business into further question. Polls indicate that the public does not have a high regard for the ethics of business or managers. It is not easy to say whether business's ethics have declined or just seem to have done so because of increased media coverage and rising public expectations. Business ethics concern the rightness, wrongness, and fairness of managerial behavior, and these are not easy judgments to make. Multiple norms compete to serve as standards against which business behavior should be compared.

The conventional approach to business ethics was introduced as an initial way in which managers might think about ethical judgments. One major challenge with this approach is that it is not clear which standards or norms should be used, and thus the conventional approach is susceptible to ethical relativism and misjudgment. Though the conventional approach has value, the varied sources of norms informing decision making can often result in confusion and conflicting expectations.

A Venn diagram model was presented as an aid to making decisions when economics, law, and ethics expectations compete with each other and are in tension. Three models of management ethics are (1) immoral management, (2) moral management, and (3) amoral management. Amoral management is further classified into intentional and unintentional categories. There are two hypotheses about the presence of these three moral types in the management population and in individuals themselves.

Understanding how moral judgment develops is helpful to aspiring managers. A generally accepted view is that moral judgment develops according to the pattern described by Lawrence Kohlberg. His three levels of moral development are (1) preconventional, (2) conventional, and (3) postconventional, autonomous, or principled. Gilligan and others have suggested that men and women use different perspectives as they perceive and deal with moral issues. Care must be exercised in generalizing about the process of moral development.

In addition to moral maturity, managers' ethics are affected by sources of values originating from within the organization as well as from those external to the organization. This latter category includes respect for the authority structure, loyalty, conformity, and a concern for financial performance and results. Together, they represent the "bottom line" mentality.

Finally, six elements in developing moral judgment were presented. These six elements include (1) moral imagination, (2) moral identification and ordering, (3) moral evaluation, (4) tolerance of moral disagreement and ambiguity, (5) integration of managerial and moral competence, and (6) a sense of moral obligation. If the moral management model is to be sustained, these six elements need to be developed and successfully integrated.

Key Terms

bottom-line mentality, p. 208
business ethics, p. 182
compliance strategy, p. 197
conventional approach to business
    ethics, p. 183
conventional level of moral
    development (level 2), p. 203
descriptive ethics, p. 182
elements of moral
    judgment, p. 209
ethical relativism, p. 187

ethical tests approach to business
    ethics, p. 183
immoral management, p. 190
individual hypothesis, p. 200
integrity strategy, p. 194
intentional amoral
    management, p. 196
Kohlberg's levels of moral
    development, p. 207
moral development, p. 202
morality, p. 182
moral management, p. 193

normative ethics, p. 183
population hypothesis, p. 199
preconventional level of moral
    development (level 1), p. 202
principles approach to business
    ethics, p. 183
postconventional, autonomous,
    principled level of moral
    development (level 3), p. 203
unintentional amoral
    management, p. 196

Discussion Questions

1. Give a definition of ethical business behavior, explain the components involved in making ethical decisions, and give an example from your personal experience of the sources of ethical norms that affect you while making these determinations.

2. To demonstrate that you understand the three models of management ethics—moral, immoral, and amoral—give an example from your personal experience of each type. Do you agree that amorality is a serious problem? Explain.

3. Give examples from your personal experience of Kohlberg's Levels 1, 2, and 3. If you do not think

you have ever gotten to Level 3, give an example of what it might be like.

4. Compare your motivations to behave ethically with those listed in Figure 7-14. Do the reasons given in that figure agree with your personal assessment? Discuss the similarities and differences between Figure 7-14 and your personal assessment.

5. From your personal experience, give an example of a situation you have faced that would require one of the six elements of moral judgment.

Endnotes

1. For a history of business ethics, see Richard T. DeGeorge, "The History of Business Ethics," in Marc J. Epstein and Kirk O. Hanson (eds.), *The Accountable Corporation, Business Ethics,* Vol. 2 (Westport, CT: Praeger Publishers, 2006), 47–58.

2. Cathy Booth Thomas, "The Enron Effect," *Time* (June 5, 2006), 34–35.

3. Archie B. Carroll, "Two Scandals and the Decade Isn't Over Yet," *Athens Banner Herald* (November 16, 2008), http://onlineathens.com/stories/111608/bus_356090174.shtml. Accessed April 27, 2013.

4. Gallup Poll, "Ratings of Honesty and Ethics," December 3, 2012, http://www.gallup.com/poll/159035/congress-retains-low-honesty-rating.aspx. Accessed January 28, 2013.

5. Ibid.

6. Ethics Resource Center, "The 2011 National Business Ethics Survey," http://www.ethics.org/nbes/files/FinalNBES-web.pdf. Accessed January 28, 2013.

7. Ibid.

8. Robert Frank and Amir Efrati, "Evil Madoff Gets 150 Years in Epic Fraud," *The Wall Street Journal* (June 30, 2009), A1. Also see, James Bandler and Nicholas Varchaver, "How Bernie Did It,"*Fortune* (May 11, 2009), 51–71.

9. Michael Blumenthal, "Business Morality Has Not Deteriorated—Society Has Changed," *The New York Times* (January 9, 1977).

10. Ibid.

11. Richard T. DeGeorge, *Business Ethics,* 4th ed. (New York: Prentice Hall, 1995), 20–21. See also Rogene A. Buchholz and Sandra B., Rosenthal, *Business Ethics* (Upper Saddle River, NJ Prentice Hall, 1998), 3.

12. DeGeorge, 15.

13. Kenneth E. Goodpaster, "Business Ethics," in Patricia H. Werhane and R. Edward Freeman (eds.), *The Blackwell Dictionary of Business Ethics* (Malden, MA: Blackwell Publishers, 1997), 51–57.

14. Ethics Alarms, "The Donald's Dangerous Ethics: Loyalty Trumps Honesty on Celebrity Apprentice," http://ethicsalarms.com/2012/04/10/the-donalds-dangerous-ethics-loyalty-trumps-honesty-on-celebrity-apprentice/ April 10, 2012. Accessed January 28, 2013.

15. Stephen Miller and Joe Palazzolo, "Scholar argued for moral understanding of the law," *The Wall Street Journal*, February 15, 2013, A6.

16. Mark Gimein, "The Skilling Trap," *BusinessWeek* (June 12, 2006), 31.

17. Ibid., 32.

18. For more on ethics and the law, see William A. Wines, *Ethics, Law, and Business* (Mahwah, NJ: Lawrence Erlbaum Associates, Publishers, 2006).

19. See, for example, Melissa Baucus and Janet Near, "Can Illegal Corporate Behavior Be Predicted? An Event History Analysis," *Academy of Management Journal* (Vol. 34, No. 1, 1991), 9–36; and P. L. Cochran and D. Nigh, "Illegal Corporate Behavior and the Question of Moral Agency," in William C. Frederick (ed.), *Research in Corporate Social Performance and Policy,* Vol. 9 (Greenwich, CT: JAI Press, 1987), 73–91.

20. Mark S. Schwartz and Archie B. Carroll, "Corporate Social Responsibility: A Three-Domain Approach," *Business Ethics Quarterly* (Vol. 13, Issue 4, October 2003), 503–530.

21. Most of the material in this section comes from Archie B. Carroll, "In Search of the Moral Manager," *Business Horizons* (March/April 1987), 7–15. See also Archie B. Carroll, "Models of Management Morality for the New Millennium," *Business Ethics Quarterly* (Vol. 11, Issue 2, April 2001), 365–371.

22. *Dilbert* comic strip, by Scott Adams (September 15, 2007), http://www.dilbert.com. Accessed July 6, 2010.

23. Allan Sloan, "Laying Enron to Rest," *Newsweek* (June 5, 2006), 25–30.

24. "Kenneth Lay," *The Economist* (July 8, 2006), 81.

25. Daily Finance, "Wall Street Applauds as Enron the play dies on Broadway," May 7, 2010, http://www.daily finance.com/2010/05/07/wall-street-applauds-as-enron-the-play-dies-on-broadway/. Accessed March 4, 2013.

26. Andrew Dunn, "Lay, Skilling Assets Targeted by U.S. After Guilty Verdicts" (May 26, 2006), http://Bloom berg.com. Accessed May 26, 2006.

27. Kim Clark and Marianne Lavelle, "Guilty as Charged," *U.S. News & World Report* (June 5, 2006), 44–45.

28. The Enron Blog, "Status of Jeff Skilling," January 10, 2013, http://caraellison.wordpress.com/2013/01/10/status-of-jeff-skilling/. Accessed March 4, 2013.

29. Jean Eaglesham, "The Shadow of Enron Still Lingers," *The Wall Street Journal*, October 17, 2012, C1.

30. Robert Frank and Amir Efrati, "Evil Madoff Gets 150 Years in Epic Fraud," *The Wall Street Journal* (June 30, 2009), A1, A12. Also see "The Madoff Affair: A Sidekick Sings," *The Economist* (August 15, 2009), 64.

31. "Bernie Madoff: The Banks Had to Know What I Was Doing," February 24, 2013, Huffington Post, http://www .huffingtonpost.com/2013/02/24/bernie-madoff-banks_n_ 2754388.html. Accessed March 4, 2013.

32. "Insider trading: Who's next?" *The Economist*, June 23, 2012, 74; Susan Pulliam and Chad Bray, "Trader Draws Record Sentence," *The Wall Street Journal*, October 14, 2011; Daniel Gilbert and Jean Eaglesham, "Stanford Hit with 110 Years," *The Wall Street Journal*, June 15, 2012, C1.

33. "Deloitte & Touche USA 2007 Ethics & Workplace" survey, 2007, Deloitte Development LLC, 16.

34. Ibid., 15.

35. Lynn Sharp Paine, "Managing for Organizational Integrity," *Harvard Business Review* (March–April 1994), 106–117.

36. Ibid., 111–112.

37. Archie B. Carroll, "The Moral Leader: Essential for Successful Corporate Citizenship," in Jorg Andriof and Malcolm McIntosh (eds.), *Perspectives on Corporate Citizenship* (Sheffield, UK: Greenleaf Publishing Co., 2001), 139–151.

38. Stephen Covey, *The Seven Habits of Highly Effective People* (New York: Simon & Schuster, 1989).

39. Carroll (2001); ibid., 145–150.

40. "Deloitte & Touche USA 2007 Ethics & Workplace" survey, 15.

41. Rikki Klaus, "Huntsville Company Saves 50 Jobs by Helping the Community," *WHNT News*, http://www .whnt.com/news/whnt-navistar-jobs-saved-010510,0,451 836.story. Accessed July 6, 2010; Marian Accardi, "Huntsville's Navistar Plant Manager Named to People Magazine's Heroes of the Year List," The Huntsville Times, October 28, 2010, http://blog.al.com/huntsville-times-business/2010/10/huntsvilles_navistar_plant_man .html. Accessed January 30, 2013.

42. Marian Accardi, The Huntsville Times, "Navistar employees return to their plants after nonprofit work," April 19, 2010, http://blog.al.com/breaking/2010/04/post_271.html. Accessed April 4, 2013.

43. Business Enterprise Trust, 1994, "The Business Enterprise Trust Awards (1991 Recipients)," unpublished announcement. To view Merck's video documenting this program, see http://www.merck.com/about/featured-stories/mectizan1.html. Accessed April 4, 2013.

44. Mahzarin R. Banaji, Max H. Bazerman, and Dolly Chugh, "How (Un) Ethical Are You?" *Harvard Business Review* (December 2003), 56–64.

45. Ibid.

46. Max Bazerman, George Loewenstein, and Don A. Moore, "Why Good Accountants Do Bad Audits," *Harvard Business Review* (November 2002).

47. Ibid.

48. Paine, 109–113.

49. Ibid., 107–108.

50. Ibid.

51. Dan Ariely, *The (Honest) Truth about Dishonesty*, Harper: 2012; also see Gary Belsky, "Why (Almost) All of Us Cheat and Steal," *Time Business*, June 18, 2012, 40.

52. Carroll (1987), 7–15.

53. Lawrence Kohlberg, "The Claim to Moral Adequacy of a Highest Stage of Moral Judgment," *The Journal of Philosophy* (Vol. 52, 1973), 630–646.

54. Carol Gilligan, *In a Different Voice: Psychological Theory and Women's Development* (Cambridge, MA: Harvard University Press, 1982).

55. Manuel G. Velasquez, *Business Ethics*, 3d ed. (Englewood Cliffs, NJ: Prentice Hall, 1992), 30. See also Brian K. Burton and Craig P. Dunn, "Feminist Ethics as Moral Grounding for Stakeholder Theory," *Business Ethics Quarterly* (Vol. 6, No. 2, 1996), 136–137.

56. See, for example, Robbin Derry, "Moral Reasoning in Work Related Conflicts," in William C. Frederick (ed.), *Research in Corporate Social Performance and Policy*, Vol. 9 (Greenwich, CT:JAI Press, 1987), 25–49. See also Velasquez, 30–31.

57. George A. Steiner, *Business and Society* (New York: Random House, 1975), 226.

58. William Barclay, *Ethics in a Permissive Society* (New York: Harper & Row, 1971), 13.

59. "Ethic of Reciprocity," http://www.princeton.edu/acha ney/tmve/wiki100k/docs/Ethic_of_reciprocity.html. Accessed April 4, 2013.

60. Marvin Fox, "The Theistic Bases of Ethics," in Robert Bartels (ed.), *Ethics in Business* (Columbus, OH: Bureau of Business Research, Ohio State University, 1963), 86–87.

61. Alan Wolfe, *Moral Freedom: The Search for Virtue in a World of Choice* (New York: W.W. Norton & Co., 2001).

62. John Leo, "My Morals, Myself," *U.S. News & World Report* (August 13, 2001), 10.

63. Carl D. Fulda, "The Legal Basis of Ethics," in Bartels, 43–50.

64. American Management Association, "The Ethical Enterprise: Doing the Right Things in the Right Ways, Today and Tomorrow—A Global Study of Business Ethics 2005–2015," 2006, American Management Association/Human Resource Institute, viii.

65. "The Oath Project," http://www.theoathproject.org/approach. Accessed April 4, 2013.

66. Carl Madden, "Forces Which Influence Ethical Behavior," in Clarence C. Walton (ed.), *The Ethics of Corporate Conduct* (Englewood Cliffs, NJ: Prentice Hall, 1977), 31–78.

67. Charles W. Powers and David Vogel, *Ethics in the Education of Business Managers* (Hastings-on-Hudson, NY:The Hastings Center, 1980), 40–45. Also see Patricia H. Werhane, *Moral Imagination and Management Decision Making* (New York: Oxford University Press, 1999).

68. Ibid.

69. Milton Friedman, "The Social Responsibility of Business Is to Increase Its Profits," *The New York Times* (September 1962), 126 [italics added].

8

Personal and Organizational Ethics

CHAPTER LEARNING OUTCOMES

After studying this chapter, you should be able to:

1. Understand the different levels at which business ethics may be addressed.

2. Differentiate between consequence-based and duty-based principles of ethics.

3. Enumerate and discuss principles of personal ethical decision making and ethical tests for screening ethical decisions.

4. Identify the factors affecting an organization's ethical culture and provide examples of these factors at work.

5. Describe and explain actions, strategies, or "best practices" that management may take to improve an organization's ethical climate.

6. Identify and describe concepts from "behavioral ethics" that affect ethical decision making and behavior in organizations

The ethical issues on which managers must make decisions are numerous and varied. The news media tends to focus on the major ethical scandals involving well-known corporate names. Therefore, Bernie Madoff, Barclay's Bank, Galleon Group, Goldman Sachs, Peregrine Financial Group, and other such high-visibility firms attract considerable attention. As a consequence, many of the day-to-day ethical challenges that managers and employees face in medium-sized and small organizations are often overlooked.

The megascandals of the Enron era and the implicated companies and people during the Wall Street financial scandals and the global financial crisis are not the only issues facing the corporate world, though they may get the most press coverage. Managers encounter day-to-day ethical challenges in such arenas as conflicts of interest, sexual harassment, inappropriate gifts to corporate personnel, unauthorized payments, customer dealings, evaluation of personnel, and pressure to compromise on personal standards. But often these managers have no experience or training in business ethics or ethical decision making to tackle such quandaries.

People today face ethical issues in a variety of settings, but our concern in this chapter is limited to personal and organizational ethics. David Callahan's highly influential book titled *The Cheating Culture: Why More Americans Are Doing Wrong to Get Ahead* talks at length about these ethical issues.[1] Callahan never clearly defines what "cheating" means, but uses its synonyms that are commonly accepted today, including *dishonest, immoral, unethical,* and *corrupt*—all of which characterize the threats we are addressing in this chapter. He argues that the instances of cheating have shot up in today's society due to four essential reasons: rising pressures on people, bigger rewards for winning, temptation, and trickle-down corruption. To these could easily be added the financial pressures people have faced during the recent recession. Each of these factors influences personal and organizational ethics and thus frames the issues that need to be addressed at these levels.

The ethical challenge in business is a daunting one, and progress on this front is vital to sustainable businesses. An ethics officer for a large corporation once said that there are three types of organizations: those that *have had* ethics problems, those that *are having* ethics problems, and those that *will have* ethics problems. Ethical issues appear through all levels of management, in many different types of jobs, and in organizations of all sizes.

A study of managers' desired leadership qualities was conducted by consultant and writer Lee Ellis, who concluded that *integrity* is the quality most sought after in leaders.[2] A retired corporate executive, now business school lecturer, Bill George, former CEO at Medtronic, argued that we need corporate leaders with integrity.[3] But how does one come to have personal integrity, and as a manager, how do you instill it in your organization? Following are some significant challenges: How do you keep your own personal ethics focused in such a way that you avoid immorality and amorality? What principles, concepts, or guidelines are available to help you to be ethical? What specific strategies, approaches, or best practices might be emphasized to bring about an ethical culture in companies and organizations? How is "behavioral ethics" a major factor in decision making?

Ethics Issues Arise at Different Levels

As individuals and as managers, we experience ethical pressures or dilemmas in a variety of settings and at different levels of analysis, including the individual or personal level, the organizational level, the industry level, the societal level, and the global level. These levels expand out from the individual to the global. Some observers believe that "ethics are ethics" regardless of whether they are applied at the personal or the organizational level. To some extent this is true. However, each level of analysis also introduces distinct challenges. To help understand the types of decision situations that are faced at the various levels, it is worth considering them in terms of the types of issues that may arise in different contexts.

Personal Level

First, we all experience *personal-level* ethical challenges. These challenges include situations we face in our personal lives that are generally outside the context of our employment. Questions or dilemmas that we might face at the personal level include the following:

- Should I cheat on my income tax return by overinflating my charitable contributions?
- Should I tell the professor I need this course to graduate this semester when I really don't?
- Should I download music from the Internet although I realize it is someone else's intellectual property?
- Should I connect this TV cable in my new apartment and not tell the cable company?

Wanda Johnson, a 34-year-old single mother of five from Savannah, Georgia, faced a personal-level ethical dilemma when temptation came knocking in the form of a bagful of money that contained $120,000. True story: Johnson, a low-paid custodian at a local hospital, was on her lunch break when she witnessed the bag falling off an armored truck. The bag contained small bills and nobody saw her find it. She could have used the money to pay her outstanding bills. She had recently pawned her television set for cash to keep the bill collectors at bay. What should she do? What would you do?

Johnson later stated that she knew she had to turn it in. After consulting with her pastor, she turned in the money to the police. Johnson reported that her religious upbringing had taught her that was the right thing to do. Later SunTrust Bank rewarded her with $5,000, and EM Armored Car Service, Inc., also promised her an unspecified sum.[4] Would you react to this personal, ethical dilemma in the same fashion as Johnson did? We all face hundreds of such dilemmas throughout our lives.

Organizational Level

People also confront ethical issues at the *organizational level* (or firm level) in their roles as managers or employees. Many of these issues are similar to those we face personally. However, organizational-level issues carry consequences for the company's reputation and success in the community and also for the kind of ethical environment or culture that will prevail on a day-to-day basis at the office. In addition, how the issue is handled may have serious organizational consequences. Examples of issues managers and employees face at the organizational level include the following:

- Should I set high production goals for my work team to benefit the organization, even though I know it may cause them to cut corners to achieve such goals?
- Should I overreport the actual time I worked on this project, hoping to get overtime pay?
- Should I authorize a subordinate to violate company policy so that we can close the deal and be rewarded by month's end?
- Should I misrepresent the warranty time on a product in order to get the sale?

One August, it was revealed that months before people began dying nationwide, managers at the Sara Lee Corporation's Bil Mar plant in Michigan knew they were shipping tainted hot dogs and deli meats. This was an organization-level ethical dilemma. The consumption of tainted food caused a national outbreak of listeriosis in which 15 people were killed, 6 suffered miscarriages, and 101 got sick. Employees of the plant later revealed that several employees, as well as the management, were aware of the shipment of contaminated meat but kept silent. According to a report, a USDA worker had told a Bil Mar employee at the time that the plant was running the risk of getting into trouble if it continued shipping contaminated foods, but the worker replied, "they would never know it was our product since [listeria] has about a two-week incubation period." Before these latest revelations, the company had pleaded guilty to a federal misdemeanor charge, paid a $200,000 fine, and made a $3 million grant to Michigan State University for food safety research.[5]

The presence or absence of unethical practices in an organization goes a long way toward revealing the climate of ethics that exists within it. To illustrate the types of unethical practices that may be evident in organizations, the results of a revealing survey conducted by the Ethics Resource Center documented what managers and employees are up against. In this survey of employees, the following types of misconduct were observed and reported along with the percentage of time these items were mentioned:[6]

- Abusive or intimidating behavior toward employees (23 percent)
- Misreporting actual time or hours worked (20 percent)
- Lying to employees, customers, vendors, or the public (19 percent)
- Withholding needed information from employees, customers, vendors, or the public (18 percent)
- Discriminating on the basis of race, color, gender, age, or similar categories (13 percent)
- Stealing, theft, or related fraud (12 percent)

Each of these categories reveals some of the questionable practices that employees and managers face every day in their work lives.

Industry or Profession Level

A third level at which a manager or an organization might experience business ethics issues is the *industry or profession level.* The industry might be stock brokerage, real estate, insurance, manufactured homes, financial services, telemarketing, electronics, or a host of others. Related to the industry might be the *profession*, of which an individual is a member—accounting, engineering, pharmacy, medicine, journalism, or law. Examples of questions that might pose ethical dilemmas at this level include the following:

•   Is this safety standard we electrical engineers have passed really adequate for protecting the consumer in this age of do-it-yourselfers?

•   Is this standard contract we mobile home sellers have adopted really in keeping with the financial disclosure laws that have recently been strengthened?

•   Is it ethical for telemarketers to make cold calls to prospective clients during the dinner hour when we suspect they will be at home?

An excellent example of an industry-wide ethical problem occurred during the buildup to the Wall Street financial scandals and market collapse in 2008. The mortgage-lending industry got carried away with subprime lending. Granting home loans to individuals who could not meet their payments when their variable interest rates rose turned out to be a questionable and unsustainable practice. The industry became disreputable for its NINJA loans—*No* Income, *No* Job, no *A*ssets. For the sake of keeping up with the competition, firms were granting loans just to keep up with the whirlwind competition and to collect commissions. This practice contributed significantly to the worldwide recession. Many analysts believe the same type of practice is now going on with student loans.

Societal and Global Levels

At the *societal* and *global levels*, it becomes very difficult for the individual manager to have a direct effect on business ethics. However, managers acting in concert through their companies and industries and professional associations can definitely bring about high standards and constructive changes. Because the industry, societal, and global levels are quite removed from the actual practicing manager, in this chapter we will focus our attention primarily on the personal and organizational levels. The manager's greatest impact can be felt through what he or she does personally or as a member of the management team.

In Chapter 10, we will deal with global ethics more specifically—a crucial topic that is increasing in importance as global capitalism has come to define our commercial world.

Personal and Managerial Ethics

In discussing personal and managerial ethics in an educational context it is anticipated that the individual wants to behave ethically or improve his or her ethical behavior in personal and/or managerial situations. Each individual is a stakeholder of someone else—a friend, a family member, an associate, or a businessperson—who is affected by that person's behavior. That "someone else" has a stake in the individual's honesty; therefore, the individual person's ethics are important to that someone else, too. Our discussion aims at those who desire to be ethical and are looking for help in doing so. All the difficulties with making ethical judgments that we discussed in the previous chapter are applicable in this discussion as well.

Personal and *managerial ethics*, for the most part, entail making decisions. Difficult decisions typically confront the individual with a conflict-of-interest situation. A conflict of interest is usually present when the individual has to choose between her or his interests and the interests of someone else or some other group (stakeholders). What it boils down to in the final analysis is answering the question, "What is the right or fair thing to do in this situation?" In other instances, *practices* that managers and organizations employ are embedded with ethical implications. Many ongoing practices were first introduced by someone else at an earlier time, so some managers don't see that each time they continue a questionable practice, they are implicitly deciding that it is appropriate.

In answering the question about the right or fair course of action, it often seems that individuals think about the situation briefly and then go with their instincts. There are, however, guidelines to ethical decision making that one could turn to if she or he really wants to make the best ethical decisions. Some of these guidelines are discussed in this chapter.

In Chapter 7 we indicated that there are three major approaches to ethics or ethical decision making: (1) the conventional approach, (2) the principles approach, and (3) the ethical tests approach. In that chapter, we described the first approach—the conventional approach—which entailed a comparison of a decision or a practice with prevailing norms of acceptability. We also discussed some of the challenges inherent in that approach because of the multitude of value expectations coming to bear on the individual. In this chapter, we will discuss the other two approaches along with other important business ethics concepts.

Principles Approach to Ethics

The principles approach to ethics or ethical decision making is based on the idea that employees and managers desire to anchor their decisions and actions on a more solid foundation than that provided by the conventional approach to ethics. The conventional approach to ethics, you may recall, depended heavily on what people thought and what the prevailing standards were at the time. Several principles of ethics have evolved over time as moral philosophers and ethicists have attempted to organize and codify their thinking and guidelines. These principles are normative in nature as they offer guidance regarding what one ought to do.

What Is an Ethics Principle? From a practical point of view, a principle of business ethics is an ethical concept, guideline, or rule which, if applied when you are faced with an ethical decision or practice, will assist you in taking the ethical course.[7] Ethics principles or guidelines have been around for centuries. The Golden Rule has been around for several millennia. In the 16th century, Miguel de Cervantes, the Spanish novelist and author of *Don Quixote*, uttered an important ethics principle that is still used today: *Honesty is the best policy.*

Types of Ethical Principles or Theories Moral philosophers customarily divide ethics principles or theories into two categories: teleological and deontological. **Teleological theories** focus on the *consequences* or results of the actions they produce. Utilitarianism is the major principle in this category. It recommends taking the action that results in the greatest good for the greatest number. **Deontological theories**, by contrast, focus on *duties*. For example, it could be argued that managers have a duty to tell the truth when they are doing business. The principles of rights and of justice, two major ethics theories we will discuss, seem to be nonteleological in character.[8] **Aretaic theories** are a third, less-known category of ethics, put forth by Aristotle. The term comes from the Greek word *arete*, which means "goodness" (of function), "excellence" (of function), or "virtue." Aristotle saw the individual as essentially a member of a social unit and moral virtue as a behavioral habit, a character trait that is both socially and morally valued.

Virtue theory is the best example of an aretaic theory.[9] Other principles, such as the principle of caring, the Golden Rule, and servant leadership, reflect concerns for duty, consequences, and virtue, or a combination of several principles.

Many different principles of ethics have been put forth, but we limit our discussion here to those regarded as most useful in business applications. Therefore, we will concentrate on the following major principles: *utilitarianism* (consequences based) and *Kant's categorical imperative, rights,* and *justice* (duty based). In addition, we will consider the principles of *care, virtue ethics, servant leadership,* and the *Golden Rule*—approaches that are popular and relevant today.

The basic idea behind the principles approach is that managers may improve their ethical decision making if they factor into their proposed actions, decisions, behaviors, and practices a consideration of certain principles or philosophies of ethics.

Principle of Utilitarianism Many ethicists have held that the rightness or fairness of an action can be determined best by looking at its results or consequences. If the consequences are good, the action or decision is considered good. If the consequences are bad, the action or decision is considered wrong. The **principle of utilitarianism** is therefore a *consequential* principle, or as stated earlier, a *teleological* principle. In its simplest form, **utilitarianism** asserts: "We should always act so as to produce the greatest ratio of good to evil for everyone."[10] Another way of stating utilitarianism is to say that one should take the course of action that represents the "greatest good for the greatest number." Two of the most influential philosophers who advocated this consequential view were Jeremy Bentham (1748–1832) and John Stuart Mill (1806–1873).

The attractiveness of utilitarianism is that it forces the decision maker to think about the general welfare, or the common good. It proposes a standard outside of self-interest by which to judge the value of a course of action. To make a cost-benefit analysis is to engage in utilitarian thinking. Utilitarianism forces us to think in stakeholder terms: What would produce the greatest good in our decision, considering stakeholders such as owners, employees, customers, and others, as well as ourselves? Finally, it provides for latitude in decision making in that it does not recognize specific actions as inherently good or bad but rather allows us to fit our personal decisions to the complexities of the situation.

A weakness of utilitarianism is that it ignores actions that may be inherently wrong. A strict interpretation of utilitarianism might lead a manager to fire minorities and older workers because they "do not fit in" or to take some other drastic action that contravenes public policy and other ethics principles. In utilitarianism, by focusing on the ends (consequences) of a decision or an action, one may ignore the means (the decision or action itself). This leads to a problematic situation where one may argue that the end justifies the means. Therefore, the action or decision is considered objectionable only if it leads to a lesser ratio of good to evil. Another problem with the principle of utilitarianism is that it may conflict with the idea of justice. Critics of utilitarianism say that the mere increase in total good is not good in and of itself because it ignores the *distribution* of good, which is also an important issue. Another stated weakness is that when using this principle, it is very difficult to formulate satisfactory rules for decision making. Therefore, utilitarianism, like most ethical principles, has both advantages and disadvantages.[11]

Kant's Categorical Imperative Immanuel Kant's **categorical imperative** is a duty-based principle of ethics, or as stated earlier, a deontological principle.[12] A duty is an obligation; that is, it is an action that is morally obligatory. The duty approach to ethics refers both to the obligatory nature of particular actions and to a way of reasoning about what is right and what is wrong.[13] Kant's categorical imperative argues that a sense of duty arises from *reason* or *rational nature*, an internal source. By contrast, the *Divine Command* principle maintains that God's law is the source of duties. Thus, we can conceptualize both internal and external sources of duty.

Kant proposed three formulations in his theory or principle. The categorical imperative is best known in the following form: "Act only according to that maxim by which you can at the same time *will* that it should become a universal law." Stated another way, Kant's principle is that one should act only on rules (or maxims) that you would be willing to see everyone follow.[14] Kant's second formulation, referred to as the *principle of ends*, is "so act to treat humanity, whether in your own person or in that of any other, in every case as an *end* and never as merely a means." This has also been referred to as the *respect for person's principle*.[15] This means that each person has dignity and moral worth and should never be exploited or manipulated or merely used as a means to another end.[16]

The third formulation of the categorical imperative invokes the *principle of autonomy*. It basically holds that "every rational being is able to regard oneself as a maker of universal law. That is, we do not need an external authority—be it God, the state, our culture, or anyone else—to determine the nature of the moral law. We can discover this for ourselves."[17] Kant argues that this view is not inconsistent with Judeo-Christian beliefs, his childhood heritage, but one must go through a series of logical leaps of faith to arrive at this point.[18] Like all ethical principles, Kant's principles have strengths and weaknesses and supporters and detractors. In the final analysis, it is his emphasis on *duty*, as opposed to consequences, that merits treatment here. Further, the notion of universalizability and respect for persons are key ideas. The principles of rights and of justice, which we discuss next, seem more consistent with the duty-based perspective than with the consequences-based perspective.

Principle of Rights One major problem with utilitarianism is that it does not handle the issue of **rights** very well. A right may be thought of as a claim or entitlement to something. Utilitarianism implies that certain actions are morally right (i.e., they represent the greatest good for the greatest number) when in fact they may violate another person's rights.[19] **Moral rights** are important, justifiable claims or entitlements. They do not depend on a legal system to be valid. They are rights that people ought to have based on moral reasoning. The right to life or the right not to be killed by others is a justifiable claim in our society. The Declaration of Independence referred to the rights to life, liberty, and the pursuit of happiness. John Locke had earlier spoken of the right to property. Today we speak of human rights, some of which are **legal rights** and some moral rights.

The basic idea undergirding the **principle of rights** is that rights cannot simply be overridden by utility, but only by another, more basic or important right. Let us consider the problem of applying the principle of utilitarianism. For example, if we accept the basic right to human life, we are precluded from considering whether killing someone might produce the greatest good for the greatest number. To use a business example, if a person has the right to equal treatment (not to be discriminated against), we could not argue for discriminating against that person so as to produce more good for others.[20] However, some people would say that this is precisely what we do when we advocate affirmative action.

The principle of rights expresses morality from the point of view of the individual or group of individuals, whereas the principle of utilitarianism expresses morality in terms of the group or society as a whole. The rights view forces us in our decision making to ask what is due each individual and to promote individual welfare. It also limits the validity of appeals to numbers and to society's aggregate benefit.[21] However, a central

FIGURE 8-1

Some Legal Rights and Claimed Moral Rights in Today's Society

Civil rights	Smokers' rights
Minorities' rights	Nonsmokers' rights
Women's rights	AIDS victims' rights
Disabled people's rights	Children's rights
Older people's rights	Fetal rights
Religious affiliation rights	Embryo rights
Employee rights	Animals' rights
Consumer rights	Right to burn the American flag
Shareholder rights	Right of due process
Privacy rights	Gay rights
Right to life	Victims' rights
Criminals' rights	Rights based on appearance

© Cengage Learning

question that is not always easy to answer is: "What constitutes a legitimate right that should be honored, and what rights or whose rights take precedence over others?"

Figure 8-1 provides an overview of many types of rights being claimed in our society today. Some of these are legally protected, whereas others are "claimed" as moral rights but are not legally protected. Managers are expected to be attentive to both legal and moral rights, but no clear guidelines are available to help them sort out which claimed moral rights should be protected, to what extent they should be protected, and which rights should take precedence over others. Sometimes politics becomes involved in this determination. This is one of the limitations of the rights theory.

Rights may be subdivided further into two types: negative rights and positive rights.[22] A **negative right** is the right to be left alone. It is the right to think and act free from the coercion of others; for example, freedom from false imprisonment, freedom from illegal search and seizure, and freedom of speech are all forms of negative rights.[23] A **positive right** is the right *to* something, such as the right to food, to health care, to clean air, to a certain standard of living, or to education. In business, as in all walks of life, both negative and positive rights are played out in both legally and morally claimed forms.

In recent years, some have argued that we are in the midst of a rights revolution in which too many individuals and groups are attempting to urge society to accept their wishes or demands as rights. The proliferation of rights claims has the potential to dilute or diminish the power of more legitimate rights. If everyone's claim for special consideration is perceived as a legitimate right, the rights approach will lose its power to help management concentrate on the morally justified rights. A related problem has been the politicization of rights. As our lawmakers bestow legal or protected status upon rights claims for political reasons rather than moral reasons, managers may become blinded as to which rights or whose rights should be honored in a decision-making situation. As rights claims expand, the common core of morality may diminish, and decision makers may find it more and more difficult to balance individuals' interests with the public interest.[24]

Principle of Justice Just as the principle of utilitarianism does not handle well the idea of rights, it does not deal effectively with the principle of justice either. One way to think about the **principle of justice** is to say that it involves the fair treatment of each person. This is why it is often called the "fairness principle." Most would accept that we have a duty to be fair to employees, consumers, and other stakeholders. But how do you decide what is fair to each person? How do you decide what is "due" each person? Sometimes it is hard to say because people might be given their due according to their *type of work*, their *effort expended*, their *merit*, their *need*, and so on. Each of these criteria might be appropriate in different situations. Today the question of what constitutes fairness has divided people to such an extent that it has been argued that we have a new culture war over fairness.[25]

At one time, the prevalent view was that married male heads of households ought to be paid more than single males or women. Today, however, the social structure is different. Women have entered the workforce in significant numbers, more families are structured differently, and a revised concept of what is due people has changed over time. The fair action is to pay everyone more on the basis of merit than on the basis of needs.[26]

To use the principle of justice, we must ask, "What is meant by justice?" There are several kinds of justice (or fairness). **Distributive justice** refers to the distribution of benefits and burdens in societies and organizations. **Compensatory justice** involves compensating someone for a past injustice. **Procedural justice**, or **ethical due process**, refers to fair decision-making procedures, practices, or agreements.[27]

Ethical Due Process   Procedural justice, or ethical due process, is especially relevant to business and professional organizations. Employees, customers, owners, and all stakeholders want to be treated fairly. They want to believe that they have been treated correctly and equally in decision situations. They want their side of the issue to be heard, and they want to believe that the managers or decision makers took all factors into consideration and weighed them carefully before making a decision. Whether the decision was who should be hired (or fired), who should get a promotion or raise, or who should get a choice assignment, employees want to know that fairness prevailed and not favoritism or some other inappropriate factor. People want to know that their performance has been evaluated according to a fair process. Ethical due process, then, is simply being sure that fairness characterizes the decision-making process. It should be noted, too, that ethical due process is as important, if not more important, than outcome fairness. In other words, people can live with an outcome that was not their preferred result if they believe that the method, system, or procedure used in making the decision was fair.

The term **process fairness** has also been used to describe ethical due process.[28] Three factors have been identified that help to decide whether process fairness has been achieved. First, have people's (employees, customers) input been included in the decision process? The more this occurs, the more fair the process is perceived to be. Second, do people believe the decisions were made and implemented in an appropriate manner? People expect consistency based on accurate information. They see whether mistakes are being corrected and whether the decision-making process was transparent. Third, people watch their managers' behavior. Do the managers provide explanations when asked? Do they treat others respectfully? Do they actively listen to comments being made?[29] Ethical due process, or process fairness, works effectively with all stakeholders, whether they are employees, customers, owners, or others. Almost everyone responds positively to being treated fairly.

Rawls's Principle of Justice   John Rawls, a political philosopher who died in 2002 at the age of 81, became well known for his version of ethical due process.[30] He provided what some have referred to as a comprehensive principle of justice.[31] His theory is based on the idea that what we need first is a fair method by which we may choose the principles through which conflicts will be resolved. The two principles of justice that underlie his theory are as follows:[32]

1. Each person has an equal right to the most extensive basic liberties compatible with similar liberties for all others.
2. Social and economic inequalities are arranged so that they are both (a) reasonably expected to be to everyone's advantage and (b) attached to positions and offices open to all.

According to Rawls's first principle, each person should be treated equally. In other words, it holds that each person should enjoy equally a full array of basic liberties.[33] The second principle is more controversial. It is often misinterpreted to imply that public policy should raise as high as possible the social and economic well-being of society's worst-off individuals. It is criticized by both those who argue that the principle is too strong and those who think it is too weak. The former think that, as long as people enjoy equal opportunity, it is not a case of injustice if some people benefit from their own work, skill, ingenuity, or assumed risks. Therefore, such people are more deserving and should not be expected to produce benefits for the least advantaged. The latter group thinks that the inequalities that may result could be so great as to be clearly unjust. Therefore, the rich get richer and the poor get only a little less poor.[34]

In developing further his second principle, Rawls imagined people gathered behind a "veil of ignorance," unaware of whether they, personally, were rich or poor, talented or incompetent. He then asked what kind of society they would create. He reasoned that the rule everyone would be able to agree on would be to maximize the well-being of the worst-off person, partially out of fear that anyone could wind up at the bottom.[35] This view, of course, had its critics, and it represents an idealistic situation that could not likely be brought about.

Supporters of the principle of justice claim that it preserves the basic values—freedom, equality of opportunity, and a concern for the disadvantaged—that have become embedded in our moral beliefs. Critics object to various parts of the theory and would not subscribe to Rawls's principles at all. Utilitarians, for example, think the greatest good for the greatest number should reign supreme.

Ethics of Care We discuss the concept of **ethics of care** (or the principle of caring) just after our discussion of utilitarianism, rights, and justice because this alternative view is critical of many traditional views. Some traditional views, it has been argued, embrace a masculine approach to perceiving the world and advocate rigid rules with clear lines.[36] The "care" perspective builds on the work of Carol Gilligan, whose criticisms of Kohlberg's theory of moral development were discussed in the previous chapter. Gilligan found that women often spoke in "a different voice" that was more based on responsibility to others and on the continuity of interdependent relationships.[37]

The care perspective maintains that traditional ethics such as the principles of utilitarianism and rights focus too much on the individual self and on cognitive thought processes. In the traditional view, "others" may be seen as threats, so rights become important. Resulting moral theories then tend to be legalistic or contractual.

Caring theory is founded on wholly different assumptions. Proponents who advocate this perspective view the individual person as essentially relational, not individualistic. These persons do not deny the existence of the self but hold that the self has relationships that cannot be separated from the self's existence. This caring view emphasizes the relationships' moral worth and, by extension, the responsibilities inherent in those relationships, rather than in rights, as in traditional ethics.[38]

Several writers have argued that caring theory is consistent with stakeholder theory, or the stakeholder approach, in that the focus is on a more cooperative, caring type of relationship. In this view, firms should seek to make decisions that satisfy stakeholders, leading to situations in which all parties in the relationship gain. Robbin Derry elaborates: "In the corporate environment, there is an increasing demand for business to be attentive to its many stakeholders, particularly customers and employees, in caring ways. As organizations attempt to build such relationships, they must define the responsibilities of initiating and maintaining care. The ethics of care may be able to facilitate an understanding of these responsibilities."[39]

Jeanne Liedtka, by contrast, has questioned whether organizations are able to care in the sense in which caring theory proposes. She contends that to care in this sense, an organization would have to care in a way that is:

- Focused entirely on people, not on quality, profits, or other such ideas that today use "care talk"
- Undertaken with caring as an end, not merely as a means to an end (such as quality or profits)
- Essentially personal, in that the caring reflects caring for other individuals
- Growth enhancing for the cared-for, in that the caring moves the cared-for toward the development and use of their capacities

Liedtka takes the position that caring people could lead to a caring organization that offers new possibilities for simultaneously enhancing the effectiveness and the moral quality of organizations.[40] The principle of caring offers a different perspective to guide ethical decision making—a perspective that clearly is thought provoking and valuable.

Virtue Ethics The major principles just discussed have been action oriented. That is, they were designed to guide our actions and decisions. Another ethical tradition, often referred to as **virtue ethics**, merits consideration even though it is not a principle per se. Virtue ethics, rooted in the thinking of Plato and Aristotle, is a school of thought that focuses on the individual becoming imbued with virtues (e.g., honesty, fairness, truthfulness, trustworthiness, benevolence, respect, and nonmalfeasance).[41] Virtue ethics is sometimes referred to as an aretaic theory of ethics, as defined earlier in the section "Types of Ethical Principles or Theories."[42]

Virtue ethics is a system of thought that is centered in the heart of the person—the manager, the employee, the competitor, and so on. This is in contrast to the principles we have discussed, which see the heart of ethics in actions or duties. Action-oriented principles focus on *doing*. Virtue ethics emphasize *being*. The assumption, of course, is that the actions of a virtuous person will also be virtuous. Traditional ethical principles of utilitarianism, rights, and justice focus on the question, "What should I do?" Virtue ethics focuses on the question, "What sort of person should I *be* or *become*?"[43]

Programs that have developed from the notion of virtue ethics have sometimes been called *character education*, because this particular approach emphasizes character development. Many observers think that one reason why business and society are witnessing moral decline today is that we have failed to teach our young people universal principles of good character. VF Corporation, Josephson Institute of Ethics, and the Ethics Resource Center in Washington all have launched character education programs. It has been argued that character education is needed not only in schools but in corporations as well. Corporate well-being demands character, and business leaders are a vital and necessary force for putting character back into business.[44]

Virtue ethicists have brought back to the public debate the idea that virtues are important whether they be in the education of the young or in management training programs. Virtues such as honesty, integrity, loyalty, promise keeping, fairness, and respect for others are completely compatible with the major principles we have been discussing. The principles, combined with the virtues, form the foundation for effective ethical action and decision making. It has been strongly argued that the ethics of virtue in business is an idea whose time has arrived.[45]

Servant Leadership An increasingly popular approach to organizational leadership and thinking today is **servant leadership**. It is an approach to ethical leadership and decision making based on the moral principle of *serving others first*. Can these two roles—servant and leader—be fused in one person—a manager or leader? What are the basic tenets of servant leadership?

Servant leadership is a model of ethical management—an approach to ethical decision making—based on the idea that serving others such as employees, customers, community, and other stakeholders is the first priority. According to Robert K. Greenleaf, the father of this movement, "It begins with the natural feeling that one wants to serve, to serve first." Next, a conscious choice brings one to "aspire to lead." The model manifests itself in the care taken by the leader to make sure that others' needs are being served.[46]

The modern era of servant leadership is marked primarily by the works of Greenleaf, who spent 38 years of his career working for AT&T. Upon his retirement, he founded the Center for Applied Ethics, which was renamed the Greenleaf Center for Servant Leadership. Greenleaf's "second career" lasted until shortly before his death in 1990. During his time, he became influential in leadership circles as a thinker, writer, consultant, and speaker to many organizations.[47]

Greenleaf takes the strong position that the servant leader is "servant first." Of course, the "servant first" and the "leader first" are the two extremes, and between them there are a number of shadings and blends that define a useful range within the notion of servant leadership.

Ten key characteristics essential for the development of servant leaders have been culled from Greenleaf's writings. Each of these is worth listing because, collectively, they paint a portrait of servant leadership in terms of leader behaviors and characteristics. These characteristics are as follows[48]:

- Listening
- Empathy
- Healing
- Persuasion
- Awareness
- Foresight
- Conceptualization
- Commitment to the growth of people
- Stewardship
- Building community

Each of these characteristics is based on the ethical principle of putting the other person first—whether that other person is an employee, a customer, or some other important stakeholder. Some of these characteristics could be stated as virtues and some as behaviors. Thus, servant leadership embraces several of the ethical perspectives discussed earlier.

Servant leadership builds a bridge between the ideas of business ethics and those of leadership. Joanne Ciulla has observed that people follow servant leaders because they can trust them, and this invokes the ethical dimension.[49] James Autry, a top-selling leadership author, argues that servant leadership is the right way, a better way of being a manager and part of organizational life. He adds, "it will enhance productivity, encourage creativity, and benefit the bottom line."[50] It is also clear that the servant leadership principle is compatible with sustainability within organizations.

The Golden Rule The **Golden Rule** merits consideration because of its history and popularity as a basic and strong principle of ethical living and decision making. A number of studies have found it to be the most powerful and useful to managers.[51] The Golden Rule—"Do unto others as you would have them do unto you"—is a straightforward, easy-to-understand principle. Further, it guides the individual decision maker to behavior, actions, or decisions that she or he should be able to express as acceptable or not based on some direct comparisons with what she or he would consider ethical or fair.

The Golden Rule, also known as the **ethic of reciprocity**, argues that if you want to be treated fairly, treat others fairly; if you want your privacy protected, respect the privacy of others. The key is impartiality. According to this principle, we are not to make an exception of ourselves. In essence, the Golden Rule personalizes business relations and brings the idea of self-perceived fairness into business deliberations.[52]

The popularity of the Golden Rule is linked to the fact that it is rooted in history and religious traditions and is among the oldest of the principles of living. Further, it is universal in that it requires no specific religious belief or faith. Almost since time began, religious leaders and philosophers have advocated the Golden Rule in one form or another. It is easy to see, therefore, why Martin Luther said that the Golden Rule is a part of the "natural law," because it is a moral rule that anyone can recognize and embrace without any particular religious teaching. In three different studies, when managers or respondents were asked to rank ethical principles according to their value to them, the Golden Rule was ranked first.[53]

Leadership expert John C. Maxwell published an insightful book titled *There's No Such Thing as "Business" Ethics: There's Only One Rule for Making Decisions.* The one rule Maxwell advocates is the Golden Rule. According to Maxwell, there are four reasons why managers and all decision makers should adopt the Golden Rule.

1. The Golden Rule is accepted by most people.
2. The Golden Rule is easy to understand.
3. The Golden Rule is a win–win philosophy.
4. The Golden Rule acts as a compass when you need direction.[54]

No single principle is recommended for use always. As one gets into each principle, one encounters a number of challenges with definitions, measurement, and generalizability. The more one understands each principle, the more one realizes how difficult it would be for a person to use each principle consistently as a guide to decision making. On the other hand, to say that an ethical principle is imperfect is not to say that it has not raised important criteria that must be addressed in personal or business decision making. The major principles and approaches we have discussed have raised to our consciousness the importance of the collective good, individual rights, caring, character, serving others first, and fairness.

In summary, the principles approach to ethics focuses on guidelines or concepts that have been created to help people and organizations make wise, ethical decisions. Two ethical categories include the teleological (ends-based) and the deontological (duty-based). Both duty and consequences are important ethical concepts. In our discussion, we have treated the following as important components of the principles-based approach: utilitarianism, rights, justice, caring, virtue, servant leadership, and the Golden Rule. Such principles, or principles-based approaches, cause us to think deeply and to reflect carefully on the ethical decisions we face in our personal and organizational lives. For the most part, these principles are rooted in moral philosophy, logic, and religion. On a more pragmatic level, we turn now to a series of ethical tests that constitute our third major approach to ethics.

Ethical Tests Approach

In addition to the ethical principles approach to guiding personal and managerial decision making, a number of practical **ethical tests** also might be set forth. Whereas the principles have almost exclusively been generated by moral philosophers, the ethical tests discussed here have been culled from the experiences of many people. The ethical tests are more practical in orientation and do not require the depth of moral thinking that the principles do. The answer to the questions should provide ethical guidance. No single test is recommended as a universal answer to the question, "What action or decision should I take in this situation?" However, each person may find one or several tests that will be useful in helping to clarify the appropriate course of action in a decision situation.

To most, the notion of a test invokes the thought of questions posed that need to be answered. Indeed, each of these tests for personal ethical decision making requires the thoughtful deliberation of a central question that gets to the heart of the ethics issue. The answer to the question should help one decide whether or not to pursue the course of action, practice, or decision itself. No single test is foolproof, but each should be helpful. Often, several tests can be used together.

Test of Common Sense With this first test, the individual simply asks, "Does the action I am getting ready to take really make sense?" When you think of behavior that might have ethical implications, it is logical to consider the practical consequences. If, for example, you would surely get caught engaging in a questionable practice, the action does not pass the test of common sense. Many unethical practices have come to light when one is led to ask whether a person really used her or his common sense at all. This test has limitations. For example, if you conclude that you would not get caught engaging in a questionable practice, this test might lead you to think that the questionable practice is an acceptable course of action, when in fact it is not. In addition, there may be other common-sense aspects of the situation that you have overlooked. The test of common sense has been called the **"smell" test** by some. If a proposed course of action stinks, don't do it.

Test of One's Best Self Psychologists tell us that each person has a self-concept. Most people can envision a scenario of themselves *at their best*. This test requires the individual to pose the question, "Is this action or decision I'm getting ready to take compatible with my concept of myself *at my best*?" This test addresses the notion of the esteem with which we hold ourselves and the kind of person we want to be known as. Naturally, this test would not be of much value to those who do not hold themselves in high esteem. To those concerned about their esteem and reputation, however, this could be a powerful test.

Test of Making Something Public (Disclosure Rule) The test of making something public, sometimes called the disclosure rule, is one of the most powerful tests.[55] If you are about to engage in a questionable practice or action, you might pose the following questions: "How would I feel if others knew I was doing this? How would I feel if I knew that my decisions or actions were going to be featured on the national evening news tonight for the entire world to see?" This test addresses the issue of whether your action or decision can withstand public disclosure and scrutiny. How would you feel if all your friends, family, and colleagues knew you were engaging in this action? If you feel comfortable with this thought, you are probably on solid footing. If you feel uncomfortable with this thought, you might need to rethink your position. A variation of this test has been called the "Grandma test." Here the question is, "If my grandmother saw what I was doing, would she approve?"

The concept of public exposure is quite powerful. A poll of managers was taken asking whether the Foreign Corrupt Practices Act would stop bribes abroad. Many of the managers said it would not. When asked what *would* stop bribes, most managers thought that public exposure would be most effective. "If the public knew we were accepting bribes, this knowledge would have the best chance of being effective," they replied. This idea gives further testimony to the strength of the transparency movement that is permeating organizations today.

Test of Ventilation   The test of ventilation is to "expose" your proposed action to others and get their thoughts on it before acting. This test works best if you get opinions from people who you know might not see things your way. The important point here is that you do not isolate yourself with your ethical dilemma but seek others' views. After you have subjected your proposed course of action to other opinions, you may find that you have not been thinking clearly. In other words, ventilate—or share—your ethical quandary, rather than keeping it to yourself. Someone else may say something of value that will help you in making your decision.

Test of Purified Idea   An idea or action might be thought to be "purified"—that is, made acceptable—when a person with authority says or implies it is appropriate. Such a person might be a supervisor, an accountant, or a lawyer. The central question here is, "Am I thinking this action or decision is right just because someone with appropriate authority or knowledge says it is right?" If you look hard enough, you always can find a lawyer or an accountant to endorse almost any idea if it is phrased right.[56] However, these other persons are not the final arbiter of what is right or wrong. Similarly, just because a superior says an action or a decision is ethical does not make it so. The decision or course of action may still be questionable or wrong even though someone else has sanctioned it with her or his approval. This is one of the most common ethical errors people make, and people must constantly be reminded that they themselves ultimately will be held accountable if the action is indefensible.[57]

Test of the Big Four   Another test of your ethical behavior is question whether it has fallen victim to "the Big Four." The Big Four are four characteristics of decision making that may lead you astray or toward the wrong course of action. The four factors are greed, speed, laziness, and haziness.[58] *Greed* is the drive to acquire more and more in your own self-interest. *Speed* refers to the tendency to rush things and cut corners because you are under the pressure of time. *Laziness* may lead you to take the easy course of action that requires the least amount of effort. *Haziness* may lead you to acting or reacting without a clear idea of what is going on. All four of these factors represent temptations that, if succumbed to, might lead to unethical behavior.[59]

Gag Test   This test was provided by a judge on the Louisiana Court of Appeals. He argued that a manager's clearest signal that a dubious decision or action is going too far is when you simply "gag" at the prospect of carrying it out.[60] Admittedly, this test can capture only the grossest of unethical behaviors, but there are some managers who may need such a general kind of test. Actually, this test is intended to be more humorous than serious, but a few might be helped by it. The gag test has also been called the "smell" test by some. Figure 8-2 summarizes the practical ethical guidelines that may be extracted from these ethical tests.

Use Several Tests Together   None of the previously mentioned tests alone offers a perfect way to determine whether a decision, act, or practice is ethical. If several tests are used together, especially the more powerful ones, they do provide a means of examining proposed actions before engaging in them. To repeat, this assumes that the individual really wants to do what is right and is looking for assistance. To the fundamentally unethical person, however, these tests would not be of much value.

FIGURE 8-2 Practical Guidelines Derived from Key Ethical Tests

Ethical Test	Practical Ethical Guideline
Common Sense	If the proposed course of action violates your "common sense," don't do it. If it doesn't pass the "smell" test, don't do it.
One's Best Self	If the proposed course of action is not consistent with your perception of yourself at your "best" don't engage in it.
Making Something Public	If you would not be comfortable with people knowing you did something, don't do it. Don't take a course of action if you think your grandma might disapprove.
Ventilation	Expose your proposed course of action to others' opinions. Don't keep your ethical dilemma to yourself. Get a second opinion.
Purified Idea	Don't think that others, such as an accountant, a lawyer, or a boss, can "purify" your proposed action by saying they think it is okay. It still may be wrong. You will still be held responsible.
Big Four	Don't compromise your action or decision by factors such as greed, speed, laziness, or haziness.
Gag Test	If you "gag" at the prospect of carrying out a proposed course of action, don't do it.

Based on a five-year study of ethical principles and ethical tests, Phillip Lewis asserted that there is high agreement on how a decision maker should behave when faced with a moral choice. He concludes,

In fact, there is almost a step-by-step sequence. Notice: One should (1) look at the problem from the position of the other person(s) affected by a decision; (2) try to determine what virtuous response is expected; (3) ask (a) how it would feel for the decision to be disclosed to a wide audience and (b) whether the decision is consistent with organizational goals; and (4) act in a way that is (a) right and just for any other person in a similar situation and (b) good for the organization.[61]

Implicit in Lewis's conclusion is evidence of stakeholder theory, virtue theory, the Golden Rule, the disclosure rule, and Rawls's principle of justice.

Managing Organizational Ethics

To this point, our discussion has centered on principles, guidelines, and approaches to personal or managerial decision making. Clearly, ethical decision making is at the heart of business ethics, and we cannot stress enough the need to sharpen decision-making skills if amorality is to be prevented and moral management achieved. Now we shift our attention to the *organizational context* in which decision making occurs. Actions and practices that take place within the organization's structure, processes, culture, or climate are just as vital as decision making in bringing about ethical business practices and results. Based on his research, Craig VanSandt has concluded, "Understanding and managing an organization's ethical work climate may go a long way toward defining the difference between how a company does and what kind of organization it is."[62]

To manage ethics in an organization, a manager must appreciate that the organization's ethical climate is just one part of its overall corporate culture. When McNeil Laboratories, a subsidiary of Johnson & Johnson, voluntarily withdrew Tylenol® from the market immediately after the reports of tainted, poisoned products, some people wondered why they made this decision. An often cited response was, "It's the J & J way."[63] This statement conveys a noteworthy message about the firm's ethical work climate or corporate culture. It also raises the question of how organizations and managers should deal with, understand, and shape business ethics through actions taken, policies established, and examples set. The organization's moral climate is a complex entity, and we can discuss only some facets of it in this section.[64]

Figure 8-3 portrays several levels of moral climate and some of the key factors that may come to bear on the manager as he or she makes decisions. What happens within organizations, as Figure 8-3 depicts, is nested in the moral climate of industry, business, and society. Our focus in this section is on the moral climate of the organization. Regardless of the ethics of individuals, organizational factors prove to be powerful in shaping ethical or unethical behavior and practices. Three major questions drive the consideration of managing organizational ethics:

1. What factors contribute to ethical or unethical behavior in the organization?
2. What actions, strategies, or best practices might the management use to improve the organization's ethical climate?
3. What psychological and organizational processes revealed through "behavioral ethics" come into play when ethical decision making and behavior are pursued?

FIGURE 8-3

Factors That Affect the Morality of Managers and Employees

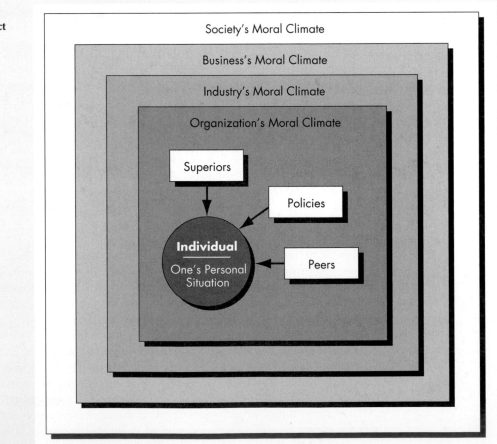

Society's Moral Climate

Business's Moral Climate

Industry's Moral Climate

Organization's Moral Climate

Superiors

Policies

Individual
One's Personal Situation

Peers

Factors Affecting the Organization's Moral Climate

For managers to be able to create an ethical work climate, they must first understand the factors at work in the organization that influence whether or not other managers and employees behave ethically. More than a few studies have been conducted that have sought to identify and to rank the sources of ethical behavior in organizations.

Figure 8-4 summarizes the findings of three landmark, baseline studies.

Although there is some variation in the rankings of the three studies, several findings are worthy of note:

- *Behavior of superiors* was ranked as the number one influence on unethical behavior in all three studies. In other words, the influence of bosses is powerful.
- *Behavior of one's peers* was ranked high in two of the three studies. People do pay attention to what their peers are doing and expecting.
- *Industry or professional ethical practices* ranked in the upper half in all three studies. These context factors are influential.
- *Personal financial need* ranked last in all three studies. But let's not assume it does not matter.

What stands out in these studies from an organizational perspective is the influence of the behavior of one's superiors and peers. Also notable about these findings is that quite often it is assumed that society's moral climate has a lot to do with managers' morality, but this factor was ranked low in the two studies in which it was considered. Apparently, society's moral climate serves as a background factor that does not have a direct and immediate impact on organizational ethics. Furthermore, although it is enlightening to know that personal financial need ranked so low, we should not assume that personal needs and wants are irrelevant. What these findings suggest is that there are factors at work over which managers can exercise some discretion. Thus, we begin to see the managerial dimension of business ethics.

FIGURE 8-4   Factors Influencing Unethical Behavior Question: "Listed Below Are the Factors That Many Believe Influence Unethical Behavior. Rank Them in Order of Their Influence or Contribution to Unethical Behaviors or Actions by Managers."[a]

	Posner and Schmidt Study[b] (N = 1,443)	Brenner and Molander Study[c] (N = 1,227)	Baumhart Study[d] (N = 1,531)
Behavior of superiors	2.17(1)	2.15(1)	1.9(1)
Behavior of one's organizational peers	3.30(2)	3.37(4)	3.1(3)
Ethical practices of one's industry or profession	3.57(3)	3.34(3)	2.6(2)
Society's moral climate[e]	3.79(4)	4.22(5)	
Formal organizational policy (or the lack thereof)	3.84(5)	3.27(2)	3.3(4)
Personal financial need	4.09(6)	4.46(6)	4.1(5)

[a] Ranking is based on a scale of 1 (most influential) to 6 (least influential).
[b] Barry Z. Posner and Warren H. Schmidt, "Values and the American Manager: An Update," *California Management Review* (Spring 1984), 202–216.
[c] Steve Brenner and Earl Molander, "Is the Ethics of Business Changing?" *Harvard Business Review* (January/February 1977).
[d] Raymond C. Baumhart, "How Ethical Are Businessmen?" *Harvard Business Review* (July/August 1961), 6ff.
[e] This item is not included in the Baumhart study.

© Cengage Learning

Pressures Exerted on Employees by Superiors One major consequence of the behavior of superiors and peers is that pressure is placed on subordinates and/or other organizational members to achieve results, and this often requires that they compromise their ethics. In one national study of this topic, managers were asked to what extent they agreed with the following proposition: "Managers today feel under pressure to compromise personal standards to achieve company goals."[65] It is insightful to consider the management levels of the 64.4 percent of the respondents who agreed with the proposition. The results by management level were

- Top management: 50 percent agreed
- Middle management: 65 percent agreed
- Lower management: 85 percent agreed

This study revealed that the perceived pressure to compromise ethics seems to be felt most by those in lower management, followed by those in middle management. In a later study, managers were asked whether they sometimes had to compromise their personal principles to conform to organizational expectations.[66] Twenty percent of the top executives agreed, 27 percent of the middle managers agreed, and 41 percent of the lower managers agreed. In other words, the same pattern prevailed in this second study.

What is especially insightful about these findings is the *pattern of response*. It seems that the lower a manager, or employee, is in the hierarchy, the more he or she perceives pressures to engage in unethical conduct. Although there are several plausible explanations for this phenomenon, one explanation seems particularly attractive—that higher-level managers do not fully understand how strongly their subordinates perceive pressures to go along with their bosses. These varying perceptions at different levels in the managerial hierarchy suggest that higher-level managers may not be tuned in to how pressure is perceived at lower levels. This breakdown in understanding, or lack of sensitivity by higher management to how far subordinates will go to please them, can be conducive to lower-level subordinates behaving unethically out of a real or perceived fear of reprisal, a misguided sense of loyalty, or a distorted concept of their jobs.

Another study of the sources and consequences of workplace pressure[67] produced findings that were consistent with those of the studies reported earlier and provided additional insights into the detrimental consequences of workplace pressure. The following were among the key findings of this study:

- The majority of workers (60 percent) felt a substantial amount of pressure on the job. More than one out of four (27 percent) felt a "great deal" of pressure.
- Nearly half of all workers (48 percent) reported that, due to pressure, they had engaged in one or more unethical and/or illegal actions during the past year. The most frequently cited misbehavior was cutting corners on quality control.
- The sources most commonly cited as contributing to workplace pressure were "balancing work and family" (52 percent), "poor internal communications" (51 percent), "work hours/workload" (51 percent), and "poor leadership" (51 percent).

The National Business Ethics Survey conducted by the Ethics Resource Center found some other insights regarding pressure perceived[68]:

- First-line supervisors and employees were the groups most "at risk" to feel pressure.
- Organizational transitions such as mergers, acquisitions, and restructurings are associated with increased pressure on employees to compromise organizational ethics standards.
- Employees who observe unethical actions more frequently in their organization tend to feel pressure to compromise their ethical standards.

ETHICS IN PRACTICE CASE
More Sales, Lower Ethics?

At my recent job, I held a position as a Customer Service and Sales Representative for a well-recognized bank. My responsibility was to help customers solve issues and concerns they might have on their accounts, but mainly I was to concentrate on selling them bank products. I started out as a teller and worked my way up to Sales Rep. In the training class, we were instructed to concentrate on customer service before anything else, but also told that sales were an important part of the position. We were never told that sales was our primary goal. The goal-setting level in the bank is determined by the amount of sales the bank needs quarterly. However, these goals differ from the requirements of each individual's position. The bank also emphasizes meeting daily sales goals to reach your numbers by the end of the quarter.

As I started working, I realized that it was difficult to meet the daily sales goals. The bank sets goals that are unrealistic for most of us, particularly because the same customers that visit the bank already have the accounts and other bank products they need. Because of the bank's high sales goals, we are pushed to sell to some customers extra checking or savings accounts that sometimes are unnecessary for them. Yet, to achieve our goals we encourage them to open the new accounts by saying it would somehow benefit them. I am not pleased with doing this, because we could easily just convert the existing product to the new one with additional benefits without opening another account. However, not selling them the new products sometimes makes it impossible to meet our sales goal for the quarter.

1. Is it ethical for the bank to keep raising the goals and expect that we keep selling these extra accounts that customers might not really need?
2. What are the ethical issues facing the bank?
3. Is it right for us not to disclose with the customer the idea of keeping the same account and just converting it instead of opening a new one?
4. Should I give in to the pressure of the company to meet the company's goal?

Contributed by Catalina Vargas

- Employees whose organizations have in place key elements of formal ethics programs feel less pressure to compromise standards.

On a troubling note, a later Ethics Resource Center's study found that the percentage of the U.S. workforce perceiving pressure to commit wrongdoing was rising to an all-time high.[69]

Improving the Organization's Ethical Culture

Because the behavior of managers has been identified as the most important influence on the ethical behavior of organization members, it should come as no surprise that most actions and strategies for improving the organization's ethical culture must originate from top management and other management levels. The 2011 National Business Ethics Survey found that the percentage of companies with weak ethical cultures climbed to 42 percent of companies studied—near record levels.[70] The process by which managers strive to improve upon the organization's ethical culture has often been referred to as "institutionalizing ethics" into the organization.[71]

Today, the emphasis is not just on institutionalizing ethics programs. It is more on creating an ethical organizational culture or climate, one in which ethical behavior, values, and policies are displayed, promoted, and rewarded. Ethical culture has more to do with ethical leadership and values than with formal rules or codes. If ethics initiatives are not supported by the surrounding organizational culture, they have less a chance of succeeding. One of the key findings of an earlier National Business Ethics Survey was that formal ethics and compliance programs do have an impact, but the organization's culture is more influential in producing results.[72]

Organizational culture refers to shared values, beliefs, behaviors, and ways of doing things.[73] Part of the culture is driven by formal systems, but much of it is carried on by informal systems. One fact is certain: an ethical culture can be created and can survive only if it has the strong endorsement and leadership of top management, and today, this embraces the board of directors as well.

Compliance vs. Ethics Orientation An organization with a culture of ethics is most likely a mixture of an emphasis on compliance and on such values as integrity or honesty. Early efforts of companies were to avert corporate crime. Compliance emphases took a huge step forward when the **Organizational Sentencing Guidelines** were introduced in 1991 and were revised in 2004 in response to the Sarbanes–Oxley Act. These guidelines began a partnership between companies and the federal government to prevent and deter corporate illegal/unethical practices.[74] These guidelines were created by the U.S. Sentencing Commission, which is an independent agency of the judicial branch of the federal government. The guidelines gave companies incentives for creating strong compliance and ethics programs. It is little wonder, then, that we have seen such programs increase in number and become vital parts of companies' corporate cultures.

Today the discussion is ongoing as to whether a **compliance orientation** or an **ethics orientation** should prevail in companies' ethics programs.[75] Historically, more emphasis has been placed on legal compliance than on ethics. More recently, much concern has been raised about the restrictiveness of a compliance focus. Several concerns articulated about the compliance focus have been identified.[76]

- First, a pure *compliance focus* could undermine the ways of thinking or habits of mind that are needed in ethics thinking. Ethics thinking is more principles based, while compliance thinking is more rule bound and legalistic.
- Second, it has been argued that compliance can squeeze out ethics. An organization can become so focused on following the law that ethics considerations no longer get factored into discussions.
- Third, the issue of "false consciousness" has been raised. This means that managers may become accustomed to addressing issues in a mechanistic, rule-based way, and this may cause them to not consider tougher issues that a more ethics-focused approach might require.[77]

Because of the rule of law and growing litigation, a compliance focus cannot be eliminated. This is so even though some lawyers have claimed that the United States has experienced a "national drift" from the rule of law beginning with the 2008 financial crisis.[78] The approach recommended here is toward developing organizational cultures and programs that aspire to be ethics focused. The importance of both was emphasized in the observation that the ethics perspective is needed to give a compliance program "soul," while compliance features may be necessary to give ethics programs more "body."[79] In short, both are essential.

Best Practices for Improving an Organization's Ethical Culture

In the following sections, we will survey some of the best practices that experts have concluded are vital to improving an organization's ethical culture or climate. Figure 8-5 summarizes a number of best practices for creating such an ethical organization. Top

FIGURE 8-5

Best Practices for
Improving an
Organization's
Ethical Culture

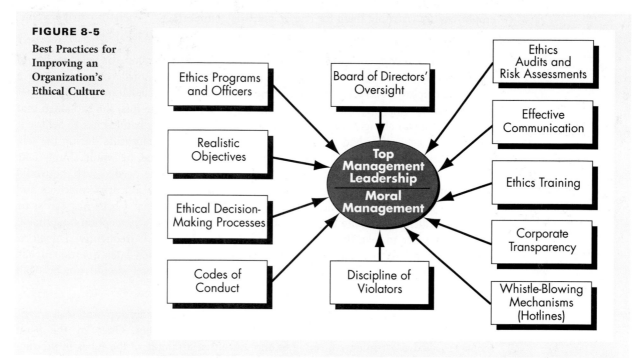

© Cengage Learning

management leadership in the pursuit of moral management is at the hub of these initiatives. Board of directors' oversight has become especially vital in recent years as corporate governance has been discovered to be an integral part of an ethical culture.

There are three key elements that must exist if an ethical organizational culture is to be developed and sustained. These include

1. The continuous presence of **ethical leadership** reflected by the board of directors, senior executives and managers,
2. The existence of a set of **core ethical values** infused throughout the organization by way of policies, processes and practices, and
3. A **formal ethics program** which includes a code of ethics, ethics training and ethics officer and ethics training.[80]

These and other considerations are discussed below.

Top Management Leadership (Moral Management)

Although it has become a cliché, this premise must be established at the outset: *The moral tone of an organization is set by top management.* A poll of communication professionals found that more than half believed that top management is an organization's conscience.[81] This is because managers and employees look to their bosses at the highest levels for their cues as to what practices and policies are acceptable. A former chairman of a major steel company stated it well: "Starting at the top, management has to set an example for all the others to follow."[82] Top management, through its capacity to set a personal example and to shape policy, is in the ideal position to provide a highly visible role model. The authority and ability to shape policy, both formal and implied, forms one of the vital aspects of the job of any leader in any organization. This aspect of becoming a moral manager has been referred to as "role modeling through visible action." Effective moral managers recognize that they live in a fishbowl and that employees are watching them for cues about what's important.[83] There is a striking contrast between weak and strong ethical leadership in business practice today.

Weak Ethical Leadership An example of weak ethical leadership (or role modeling) was found in one of the authors' consulting experiences in a small company where a long-time employee was identified as having embezzled about $20,000 over a 15-year period. When the employee was questioned as to why she had done this, she explained that she thought it was all right because the president of the company had led her to believe it was okay by actions he had taken. She further explained that any time during the fall, when the leaves had fallen in his yard and he needed them raked, he would simply take company personnel off their jobs and have them do it. When he needed cash, he would take it out of the company's petty cash box or get the key to the soft drink machine and raid its coin box. When he needed stamps to mail his personal Christmas cards, he would take them out of the company stamp box. The woman's perception was that it was okay for her to take the money because the president did it frequently. Therefore, she thought it was an acceptable practice for her as well. When later questioned, the president admitted this was all true, and he thought the woman should not be dealt with too harshly.

Strong Ethical Leadership An example of positive ethical leadership was seen in the case of a firm that was manufacturing modern vacuum tubes. One day the plant manager called a last-minute meeting to announce that a sample of the tubes in production had failed a critical safety test. This meant that the safety and performance of the batch of 10,000 tubes was highly questionable. The plant manager wondered out loud, "What are we going to do now?" Ethical leadership was shown by the vice president for technical operations, who looked around the room at each person and then declared in a low voice, "Scrap them!" According to an employee who worked for this vice president, that act set the tone for the corporation for years, because every person present knew of situations in which faulty products had been shipped under pressures of time and budget.[84]

These cases provide a vivid example of how a leader's actions and behavior communicated important messages to others in the organization. In the absence of knowing what to do, most employees look to the behavior of leaders for their cues as to what conduct is acceptable. In the second case, another crucial point is illustrated. When we speak of management providing ethical leadership, it is not just restricted to top management. Vice presidents, plant managers, supervisors, and, indeed, all managerial personnel share the responsibility for ethical leadership.

Two Pillars of Leadership It has been argued that a manager's reputation for ethical leadership is founded on two pillars: perceptions of the manager both as a moral person *and* as a moral manager. Being a *moral person* requires three major attributes: traits, behaviors, and decision making. Important traits are stable personal attributes such as integrity, honesty, and trustworthiness. Critical behaviors—what you do, not what you say—include doing the right thing, showing concern for people, being open, and being personally ethical. Decision making by the moral person needs to reflect a solid set of ethical values and principles. In this activity, the manager would hold to values, be objective and fair, demonstrate concern for society, and follow ethical decision rules.[85]

The idea of the second pillar, being a *moral manager*, was developed and discussed in the previous chapter. According to researchers, moral managers recognize the importance of proactively putting ethics at the forefront of their ethical agenda. This involves three major activities. First, the moral manager must engage in *role modeling* through visible action. Second, the moral manager *communicates about ethics and values*. Third,

---

ETHICS IN PRACTICE CASE

The Anonymous CEO: Strong or Weak Ethical Leader?

John Mackey, CEO of Whole Foods, the country's number one natural and organic grocery store chain, was exposed in July 2007 for having written more than 1,300 anonymous postings on a Web-based Yahoo Finance stock forum between 1999 and 2006. His messages on the discussion forum bashed competitors and praised his own company.

Whole Foods is a giant firm, with 39,000 employees spread over 196 stores in the United States, Canada, and the UK. At the end of fiscal 2006, the company's gross profit margin was 35 percent, compared with 24 percent at Kroger and 29 percent at Safeway. It had sales of $5.6 billion.

Mackey, who took on the pseudonym "Rahodeb" (an anagram of Deborah, his wife), was "outed" by an FTC court filing in July 2007. The Securities and Exchange Commission began an examination of the CEO's postings to determine if he broke any laws. Interestingly, Mackey's alter ego was exposed by the FTC, which filed a lawsuit seeking to block Whole Foods' planned purchase of Wild Oats, its main competitor, on antitrust grounds.

After Mackey apologized to Whole Foods' board, the board announced it would begin an internal investigation of the matter.

In some postings, Mackey (as Rahodeb) bashed Wild Oats, criticizing their former CEO for lack of vision, while noting that it wasn't a profitable company. In a February 2005 posting, Rahodeb apparently wrote with some delight that Wild Oats was going to have to restate its earnings. Rahodeb went on to say that Oats had been misleading its investors for years and that the company was headed for shareholder litigation. He also questioned Wild Oats' leadership regarding its competence and integrity. In spite of these comments, Whole Foods began an effort to acquire Wild Oats, its main rival, in February 2007, but the FTC was seeking to block this purchase on antitrust grounds.

In a public statement posted on Whole Foods' Web site, Mackey claimed that his anonymous postings did not reflect his or his company's policies or beliefs and that some of the views of Rahodeb did not even match his own beliefs.

Mackey explained that he had made the online comments anonymously because he had fun doing it. Some of his defenders have said that his comments were never intended to disclose insider information or to move stock prices.

In 2013, Mackey stimulated another controversy by something he said. To appreciate this it is important to understand that a typical Whole Foods shopper is environmentally conscious. Mackey came out and said that he didn't think global warming was necessarily bad. One writer observed: "Right. That's gonna go over real well with Whole Foods' core customers. 'Climate change is perfectly natural and not necessarily bad.' Uh huh."

1. Were Mackey's anonymous postings representative of a strong, moral leader or a weak, uncertain leader? What insights into his character are revealed by this episode? Is it ethical for a CEO to engage in such deceptions?

2. Do you see Mackey's actions as positive, negative, or indifferent in terms of setting a strong ethical tone for his company?

3. Were Mackey's deceptions just a harmless, fun activity or do they have harmful implications for Whole Foods in the future?

4. Will Mackey's comments about global warming betray the basic beliefs of his environmentally conscious customers?

Sources: David Kesmodel and Jonathan Eig, "A Grocer's Brash Style Takes Unhealthy Turn," *The Wall Street Journal* (July 20, 2007), A1; Greg Farrell and Paul Davidson, "Whole Foods' CEO Was a Busy Guy Online," *USA Today* (July 12, 2007); Shelly Banjo, "For Regulars Poster on Whole Foods Board, A Dramatic Twist," *The Wall Street Journal* (July 18, 2007); Linda Buzzell, "Whole Foods CEO: Shooting Himself in the Foot?" *The Huffington Post* Green Blog, January 29, 2013, http://www.huffingtonpost.com/linda-buzzell/whole-foods-ceo-is-this-g_b_2545344.html. Accessed April 4, 2013.

---

the moral manager needs to *use rewards and discipline effectively.* This is a powerful way to send signals about desirable and undesirable conduct in the workplace.[86]

In a period in which the importance of a sound corporate culture has been strongly advocated, ethical leaders must stress that integrity and morality are vital components of the organization's culture. There are many different ways and situations in which management needs to do this. In general, management needs to create a climate of moral consciousness. In everything it does, it must stress the importance of sound ethical principles and practices.

Ethical Leadership Characteristics Following are 10 features of strong ethical leadership that have been put forth as a framework for understanding what ethical leadership should mean in organizations. Ethical leaders should[87]

- Articulate and embody the purpose and values of the organization
- Focus on organizational success rather than on personal ego
- Find the best people and develop them
- Create a living conversation about ethics, values, and the creation of value for stakeholders
- Create mechanisms of dissent
- Take a charitable understanding of others' values
- Make tough calls while being imaginative
- Know the limits of the values and ethical principles they live
- Frame actions in ethical terms
- Connect the basic value proposition to stakeholder support and societal legitimacy

The leader must infuse the organization's climate with values and ethical consciousness, not just run a one-person show. This point is made vividly clear in the following observation: "Ethics programs which are seen as part of one manager's management system, and not as a part of the general organizational process, will be less likely to have a lasting role in the organization."[88] In short, ethics is more about leadership than about programs.

Effective Communication of Ethical Messages

Management also carries a profound burden in terms of providing ethical leadership in the area of effective communication. We have seen the importance of communicating through acts, principles, and organizational climate. Later we will discuss further the communication aspects of setting realistic objectives, codes of conduct, and the decision-making process. Here, however, we want to stress the importance of communicating principles, techniques, and practices.

Conveying the importance of ethics through communication includes both written and verbal forms of communication as well as nonverbal communication. In each of these settings, management should operate according to certain key ethical principles. Candor, fidelity, and confidentiality are three very important communication principles. *Candor* requires that a manager be forthright, sincere, and honest in communication transactions. It requires the manager to be fair and free from prejudice and malice in the communication. *Fidelity* in communication means that the communicator should be faithful to detail, should be accurate, and should avoid deception or exaggeration. *Confidentiality* is a final principle to be stressed. The ethical manager must exercise care in deciding what information to disclose to others. Trust can be easily shattered if the manager does not have a keen sense of what is confidential in a communication.

Ethics Programs and Ethics Officers

In recent years, many companies have begun creating **ethics programs** within their organizations. These programs frequently embrace both compliance and ethics initiatives and responsibilities. Ethics programs are typically organizational units, people, or departments that have been assigned the responsibility for ethics in the organization. Based upon actual practice, ethics programs typically include the following features[89]:

- Written standards of conduct (e.g., codes of ethics)
- Ethics training
- Mechanisms to seek ethics advice or information
- Methods for reporting misconduct anonymously
- Disciplinary measures for employees who violate ethical standards
- Inclusion of ethical conduct in the evaluation of employee performance.

A key finding in business ethics research has been that ethics programs are increasing in number and that they do make a difference. A major survey disclosed that the impact of ethics programs depends somewhat on the culture in which they are implemented. The study found that the more formal the program's elements, the better the program is. Formal programs make a bigger difference in weak ethical cultures, and, once a strong culture has been established, the formal programs do not have as much impact on results.[90]

Figure 8-6 summarizes the elements that ought to exist in companies' ethics programs in order to comply with the U.S. Sentencing Commission's Organizational Guidelines. Two major benefits accrue to organizations that follow these guidelines. First, following the guidelines mitigates severe financial and oversight penalties. Second, some prosecutors are choosing not to pursue some actions when the companies in question already have sound programs in place that follow these guidelines.[91]

Ethics Officers Ethics programs are often headed by an **ethics officer** who is in charge of implementing the array of ethics initiatives in the organization. In some cases, the creation of ethics programs and designation of ethics officers has been in response to the Federal Sentencing Guidelines, which reduced penalties to those companies with ethics programs that were found guilty of ethics violations.[92] More recently, companies have created ethics programs and hired ethics officers to help them comply with the 2002 Sarbanes–Oxley law or because they were seeking to improve the organization's ethics.

Many companies started ethics programs as an effort to centralize the coordination of ethics initiatives. Many ethics programs and ethics officers initially got started with compliance issues. Only later, in some cases, did ethics or integrity become a focal point of the programs. As suggested earlier, most ethics programs and ethics officers have major corporate responsibility for both legal compliance and ethics practices, and there is some debate as to whether they should be called compliance programs or ethics programs.[93] Major companies that do a lot of their business with the government, such as defense contractors, continue to emphasize compliance. Others strive more for a balance between compliance and ethics.

Just as ethics programs have proliferated in companies, the number of ethics officers occupying important positions in major firms has grown significantly. There are now two major professional organizations that ethics officers may join: Ethics and Compliance Officers Association (ECOA) (http://www.theecoa.org/) and the Society of Corporate Compliance and Ethics (SCCE) (http://www.corporatecompliance.org/).

Raising the Status of Ethics Officers An important concern of some ethics officers has been the tendency of some companies to slide the ethics officer down the organization chart, so direct access to the highest levels of organizational leadership has been decreasing. In other words, the organizational status of the ethics officer has been diminished in some organizations. Another trend has been to move the focus of the ethics officer "downward," that is, spending less time working with or helping to manage the ethics of their superiors, and focusing more on the ethics of lower-level organizational

FIGURE 8-6

Key Elements of Effective Ethics Programs

The U.S. Sentencing Commission has identified these key elements that companies must have in their ethics programs to satisfy the commission's regulatory review. If a company has these key elements in its ethics program, it will be dealt with less harshly should violations arise. Benefits should extend beyond compliance to ethics.

Compliance Standards. Companies are expected to have established compliance standards, which are a key part of detecting and preventing violations of the law. The development of a code of conduct is an initial step in this process. A set of ethical principles that guide decision making will strengthen these standards.

High-Level Ethics Personnel. Companies must assign compliance and ethics programs to senior executives. This person, perhaps called an **ethics officer**, must have the authority, responsibility, and resources to achieve ethics goals.

Avoidance of Delegation of Undue Discretionary Authority. Companies have a responsibility to make sure they do not delegate undue discretionary authority (e.g., access to company funds, investor information, and authority to bind the company to contracts) to individuals who cannot be trusted with such authority. Someone convicted of a previous felony involving company funds would be an example. Background checks are thus becoming much more essential in screening employees.

Effective Communication. Standards and procedures must be effectively communicated. The company has a responsibility to make sure all personnel are aware of ethics codes, standards, policies, and practices. One major way to achieve this communication is through the conduct of ethics training programs.

Systems for Monitoring, Auditing, and Reporting. Companies are expected to have systems and procedures in place for assessing compliance. This may involve a variety of monitoring and auditing systems and reporting systems as well. In other words, companies must take reasonable steps to ensure that compliance is taking place.

Enforcement. Companies are expected to have systems in place to ensure the consistent enforcement of compliance standards. The purpose here is to make sure that everyone is following standards. A high-level executive cannot be treated differently from a low-level executive.

Detecting Offenses, Preventing Future Offenses. Once an offense has been detected, several actions need to happen. If there is an actual violation of the law, the company is expected to self-report the offense and take actions to resolve the issue. The company needs to take further reasonable measures to prevent a similar offense from occurring in the future. The responsible person should be disciplined appropriately. Finally, the company is expected to accept responsibility for the offense as part of good corporate citizenship efforts.

Keeping Up with Industry Standards. Companies are expected, through ethics offices or programs, to keep up with industry practices and standards. This can be done by membership in national or local organizations. At the national level, an example would be the Ethics and Compliance Officer Association (http://www.eoa.org). Many large cities also have their own such organizations. These organizations have as their major purpose the advancement of sound compliance and ethics programs.

Sources: U.S. Sentencing Commission Guidelines, http://www.ussc.gov/index.html. Accessed February 11, 2013; Ethics and Compliance Officer Association, http://www.theecoa.org/. Accessed February 11, 2013.

members rather than senior management.[94] To reverse these trends, it has been recommended that the scope of responsibilities of the ethics office and ethics officers be enlarged to embrace the total organization, including senior management. The phrase "managing ethics upward" has been developed for explaining how the ethics officers should work with their superiors.[95] In light of the large numbers of ethical scandals involving senior-level executives, this idea has genuine value.

The point has been raised by several experts that ethics officers didn't seem to help much during the Wall Street financial scandals that plunged the globe into a serious recession. According to Steve Priest, president of the consulting firm Ethical Leadership, "Many companies did little more than 'check the boxes' on ethics, abiding by the letter of the law by publishing codes of conduct, without really changing the culture of the company or tackling wider ethical issues." He went on to affirm that there is "a wide gulf between how businesspeople define ethics and compliance and how the public sees them."[96]

As valuable as ethics programs and ethics officers are, there is a dangerous downside to their existence. By holding individuals and organizational units responsible for the company's "ethics," managers may tend to "delegate" to these persons/units the responsibility for the firm's ethics. Ethics is everyone's job, and specialized units and people should not be used as a substitute for the assumption of ethical responsibility by everyone in leadership positions.

Setting Realistic Objectives

Closely related to all ethics initiatives and programs being implemented by top management is the need for managers at all levels to set realistic objectives or goals. A manager may quite innocently and inadvertently create a condition leading to unethical behavior on a subordinate's part. Take the case of a marketing manager setting a sales goal of a 20 percent increase for the next year when a 10 percent increase is all that could be realistically and honestly expected, even with outstanding performance. In the absence of clearly established and communicated ethical norms, it is easy to see how a subordinate might believe that she or he should go to any lengths to achieve the 20 percent goal. With the goal having been set too high, the salesperson faced a situation that is conducive to unethical behavior in order to please the superior.

Fred T. Allen, a former executive, strongly reinforced this point:

> *Top management must establish sales and profit goals that are realistic—goals that can be achieved with current business practices. Under the pressure of unrealistic goals, otherwise responsible subordinates will often take the attitude that "anything goes" in order to comply with the chief executive's target.*[97]

Managers must be keenly sensitive to the possibility of unintentionally creating situations in which others may perceive a need or an incentive to cut corners or do the wrong thing. Unrealistic expectations are the primary driver of employees perceiving excessive pressure to achieve goals. This kind of knowledge is what justifies business ethics being a management and leadership topic.

Ethical Decision-Making Processes

Decision making is at the heart of the management process. In fact, decision making is practically synonymous with management. Decision making usually entails a process of stating the problem, analyzing the problem, identifying the possible courses of action that might be taken, evaluating these courses of action, deciding on the best alternative, and then implementing the chosen course of action.

Ethical decision making is not a simple process but rather a multifaceted one that is complicated by multiple alternatives, mixed outcomes, uncertain and extended consequences, and personal implications.[98] It would be nice if a set of ethical principles was readily available for the manager to "plug in" and walk away from, with a decision to be forthcoming. However, that was not the case when we discussed principles that help personal decision making, and it is not the case when we think of organizational decision making. The ethical principles discussed earlier are useful here, but there are no simple formulas revealing easy answers. The key is that managers establish decision-making processes that will yield the most appropriate ethical decisions.

Ethics Screen Although it is difficult to portray graphically the process of ethical decision making, it is possible as long as we recognize that such an effort cannot totally capture reality. Figure 8-7 presents one conception of the ethical decision-making process. In this model, the individual is asked to identify the action, decision, or behavior that is being considered and then work through the model. The decision maker is asked to subject the proposed course of action to an **ethics screen** which consists of several select standards against which the proposed course of action is to be compared. The idea is

FIGURE 8-7

A Process of Ethical Decision Making Using an Ethics Screen

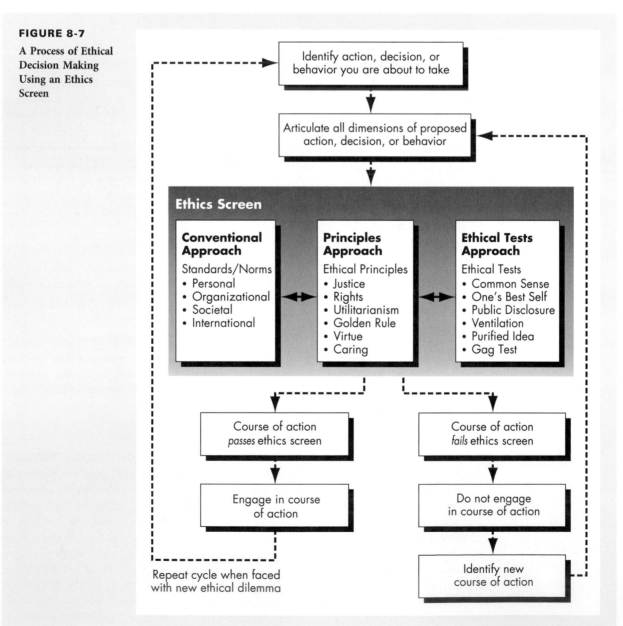

Repeat cycle when faced with new ethical dilemma

© Cengage Learning

that unethical alternatives will be "screened out" and ethical ones will be "screened in." In the ethics screen presented in Figure 8-7, we reference our earlier discussion of the conventional approach (embodying societal standards/norms), the principles approach, and the ethical tests approach to ethical decision making. By using all or a combination of these ethical standards, it is expected that more ethical decisions will be made than would have been made otherwise.

Another useful approach to making ethical decisions is to systematically ask and answer a series of simple questions. This approach is similar to the ethical tests approach presented earlier in the chapter.

Ethics Check   One well-known set of questions merits mention here because of its popularity in the book *The Power of Ethical Management.*[99] The "ethics check" questions are as follows:

1. *Is it legal?* Will I be violating either civil law or company policy?
2. *Is it balanced?* Is it fair to all concerned in the short term as well as the long term? Does it promote win–win relationships?
3. *How will it make me feel about myself?* Will it make me proud? Would I feel good if my decision was published in the newspaper? Would I feel good if my family knew about it?

Ethics Quick Test   Using a brief set of questions to make ethical decisions has become popular in business. For example, Texas Instruments printed its seven-part "Ethics Quick Test" on a wallet card for its employees to carry. The test's seven questions and reminders are as follows[100]:

- Is the action legal?
- Does it comply with our values?
- If you do it, will you feel bad?
- How will it look in the newspaper?
- If you know it's wrong, don't do it.
- If you're not sure, ask.
- Keep asking until you get an answer.

This set of practical questions is intended to produce a process of ethical inquiry that is of immediate practical use and understanding to a group of employees and managers. Many of the items are similar or identical to points raised earlier in the ethical tests approach. These questions help ensure that ethical due process takes place. They cannot tell us for sure whether our decisions are ethical or not, but they can help us be sure that we are raising the appropriate issues and genuinely attempting to be ethical.

Codes of Conduct

The top management has the responsibility for establishing standards of behavior and for effectively communicating those standards to all managers and employees in the organization. The most formal way by which companies and ethics officers have fulfilled this responsibility is through the use of **codes of ethics** or **codes of conduct**. According to Joan Dubinsky, ethics officer at the International Monetary Fund, "a Code of Conduct is the single most important element of your ethics and compliance program. It sets the tone and direction for the entire function. Often, the Code is a standalone document, ideally only a few pages in length. It introduces the concept of ethics and compliance and provides an overview of what you mean when you talk about ethical business conduct."[101]

Virtually all major corporations have codes of conduct today, and the central questions in their usefulness or effectiveness revolve around the managerial policies and attitudes associated with their use.[102] Levi Strauss & Co. and Caterpillar have worldwide codes of ethics. Johnson & Johnson has a worldwide credo. McDonald's has worldwide standards of best practices. Firms that operate in the domestic market have codes that reflect more local concerns.[103]

Some corporate codes are designed around stakeholders. Others are designed around issues.[104] The content of corporate codes typically addresses the following topics: employment practices; employee, client, and vendor information; public information/communications; conflicts of interest; relationships with vendors; environmental issues; ethical management practices; and political involvement.[105] Increasingly, corporate codes of conduct are addressing global issues and relationships with other firms, communities, and governments.[106] Recent research has found that the *quality of code content* plays a crucial role in the effectiveness of codes of conduct and in their ability to transform organizational cultures. Those companies maintaining high quality codes were found to be more often associated with high rankings of corporate social responsibility, ethical behavior, sustainability and public perception.[107]

Both successes and failures have been reported with organizational codes of conduct, but the acid test seems to be whether or not such codes actually become "living documents," not just platitudinous public relations statements that are put into a file drawer upon dissemination. Codes may not be a panacea for management, but when properly developed, administered, and communicated, they serve to raise the level of ethical behavior in the organization by clarifying what is meant by ethical conduct, encouraging moral behavior, and establishing a standard by which accountability may be measured.

Ways of Perceiving Codes A major study of corporate codes by Mark Schwartz revealed that there are a number of different ways in which employees perceive or understand codes of conduct.[108] Schwartz's research yielded eight themes or metaphors that helped to explain how codes influence ethical behavior within organizations.

1. As a *rule book*, the code acts to clarify what behavior is expected of employees.
2. As a *signpost*, the code can lead employees to consult other individuals or corporate policies to determine the appropriateness of behavior.
3. As a *mirror*, the code provides employees with a chance to confirm whether their behavior is acceptable to the company.
4. As a *magnifying glass*, the code suggests a note of caution to be more careful or engage in greater reflection before acting.
5. As a *shield*, the code acts in a manner that allows employees to better challenge and resist unethical requests.
6. As a *smoke detector*, the code leads employees to try to convince others and warn them of their inappropriate behavior.
7. As a *fire alarm*, the code leads employees to contact the appropriate authority and report violations.
8. As a *club*, the potential enforcement of the code causes employees to comply with the code's provisions.[109]

In summary, the code metaphors provide insights into a number of ways in which codes are perceived or viewed by organizational members.

Disciplining Violators of Ethics Standards

To bring about an ethical climate that all organizational members will believe in, management must discipline violators of its accepted ethical norms and standards. A major

ETHICS IN PRACTICE CASE

Sign the New Ethics Code or Quit

Barclay's PLC, the major U.K. bank, was fined £290 million by regulators in the United Kingdom and United States after it was found guilty of manipulating the interbank lending rate LIBOR. In August 2012, a new CEO, Anthony Jenkins, took over after his predecessor Bob Diamond resigned in the wake of the allegations and fines.

As an early order of business, Jenkins decided it was time to change the ethics culture of the bank and to improve the bank's ethics. Jenkins sent a memo to the bank's 140,000 employees informing them that from now on employee performance would be evaluated on a set of ethical standards. The new standards would be part of the bank's code of conduct, and it would be built around five key values: respect, integrity, service, excellence, and stewardship. Jenkins said, "We must never again be in a position of rewarding people for making the bank money in a way which is unethical or inconsistent with our values."

Jenkins has said that the bank's culture has been "too short-term focused, too aggressive, and on occasions too self-serving." Some of the changes introduced included the following: alter the reward structure so that it upholds the company's values; issue a new code of conduct that all employees are expected to sign; create a new "head of compliance" role to help redesign the bank's compensation policies.

Jenkins' message to those who don't desire to make the changes is simple—Barclay's is not the place for you—the rules have changed and you will no longer feel comfortable at Barclay's, and we will not be comfortable with you as our colleagues.

1. What is your evaluation of Jenkin's proposed approach to changing the ethics culture at Barclays?
2. Can an ethics culture change of the magnitude desired be kicked off by a memo? What else is necessary and why?
3. Is a threat of discharge the best way to frame a desire for new, ethical values? How would you recommend the bank take on such a gargantuan ethics program?

Sources: Margot Patrick, "Barclays Vows Culture Shift," *The Wall Street Journal*, February 6, 2013, C3; "Barclays Boss Anthony Jenkins Tells Staff to Sign up to Ethical Code or Quit," *HuffPost Business United Kingdom*, January 17, 2013, http://www.huffingtonpost.co.uk/2013/01/17/barclays-ethical-code-anthony-jenkins-quit-libor-_n_2494463.html?view=screen. Accessed February 10, 2013; ACQ5, "Barclays CEO Tells Staff: Buy into Ethics Code or Leave," http://www.acqmagazine.com/barclays-ceo-tells-staff-buy-into-ethics-code-or-leave/. Accessed April 4, 2013.

reason the general public, and even employees in many organizations, have questioned business's sincerity in desiring a more ethical environment has been business's unwillingness to discipline violators. There are numerous cases where top management officers have behaved unethically and yet were retained in their positions. At lower levels, there have been cases of top management overlooking or failing to penalize unethical behavior of subordinates. This evidence of inaction on management's or the board's part represents implicit approval of the individual's behavior. To be fair, organizations need to communicate their ethics standards clearly and convincingly before taking disciplinary action. But then an organization needs to respond forcefully to the individual who is guilty of deliberately or flagrantly violating its code of ethics.

Based on their research, Treviño, Hartman, and Brown have argued: "The moral manager consistently rewards ethical conduct and disciplines unethical conduct at all levels in the organization, and these actions serve to uphold the standards and rules."[110] The effort on the part of management has to be complete in communicating to all, by way of disciplining offenders, that unethical behavior will not be tolerated in the organization.

A stark example of this point was the discharge by the Boeing Company of its chief financial officer, Michael Sears, and another senior manager for engaging in unethical behavior. Sears, a 34-year veteran of the industry, had been considered a possible successor to then chairman and CEO Phil Condit. The company said that Mr. Sears and the other senior manager had been dismissed when they tried to conceal their alleged misconduct from a team of lawyers hired by the firm to investigate their actions. At the time of the firing, the CEO said, "When we determine there have been violations of our standards, we will act swiftly to address them, just as we have today."[111] In another case, Nortel Networks, North America's largest telecommunications equipment maker, fired its chief executive officer, chief financial officer, and controller for their involvement in accounting problems that had been under scrutiny. The accounting irregularities resulted in the company having to restate its earnings.[112] In the past decade, we have witnessed more and more corporate boards taking disciplinary action with respect to CEO and top management wrongdoing.

Ethics "Hotlines" and Whistle-Blowing Mechanisms

One problem that frequently leads to the covering up of unethical acts by people in an organization is that they do not know how to respond when they witness or suspect a questionable practice. An effective ethical culture is contingent on employees having a mechanism for (and top management support of) reporting violations or "blowing the whistle" on wrongdoers. One corporate executive summarized this point as follows: "Employees must know exactly what is expected of them in the moral arena and how to respond to warped ethics."[113] According to the Ethics Resource Center's 2011 National Business Ethics Survey, whistle-blowing is up among those who have observed wrong behavior.[114]

According to a major ethics and compliance benchmarking survey conducted by the Conference Board, 78 percent of companies had anonymous reporting systems, sometimes referred to as "hotlines." Among companies subject to Sarbanes–Oxley provisions, it was 91 percent.[115] According to a broad-based survey, employees describe various reasons for reporting or not reporting observed violations of ethics. Those who *did* report observations of misconduct gave the following justifications of their actions[116]:

- I thought it was the right thing to do (99 percent).
- I felt I could count on the support of my coworkers (76 percent).
- I believed corrective action would be taken (74 percent).
- I believed that my report would be kept confidential (71 percent).

In this same survey, employees were asked why they *did not* report observations of misconduct. These employees gave the following reasons[117]:

- I didn't believe corrective action would be taken (70 percent).
- I didn't trust that my report would be kept confidential (54 percent).
- I feared retaliation from my supervisor or manager (41 percent).
- I feared retaliation from my coworkers (30 percent).

Hotlines are the most frequent way employees blow the whistle on fraud or related infractions. Such hotlines may be telephone, Web, or e-mail based. In addition, they are typically used without alerting anyone in management about the problem ahead of time. One study tracked incidents at 500 organizations over four years and found that 65 percent of the reports were serious enough to warrant further investigation and 46 percent led to some type of action being taken.[118] One expert on ethics said that such anonymous tips are much more effective than internal audits at shedding light on serious problems. It should also be pointed out that even the best systems won't work if they do not have the support of top management and a corporate culture that is conducive to rooting out wrongdoing.[119]

Ethics hotlines can have a downside risk, however. Ethicist Barbara Ley Toffler has argued that the hotlines may do harm. She suspects that many of the reported wrong-doings are false accusations and that if the company does not handle these issues carefully, it may do a lot of damage to morale.[120]

Business Ethics Training

Today, it is accepted that business ethics training is an essential component of ethics programs. According to a major ethics and compliance benchmarking survey conducted by the Conference Board, more than 77 percent of publically traded companies try to educate their employees on the company's standards and policies through publications and training. A growing number of companies are conducting their training by way of Web-based applications.[121]

ETHICS IN PRACTICE CASE
When Ethics Hotlines Don't Work

Ethics and compliance "hotlines" are designed to give employees an opportunity to internally "blow the whistle" on wrongdoing. Many of them are designed by corporate compliance and ethics offices and some of them are contracted out to independent firms to give employees a greater sense of confidentiality when they report what they see or think is going wrong in the company.

A major corporation that created such a compliance hotline was Olympus Corp., the Japanese camera maker. Olympus Corp. started its compliance hotline soon after Japan passed a whistle-blower protection law in 2004. The hotline office was to handle the receipt of phone calls, letters, e-mails and other forms of reporting from employees. These were to be reports of violations of the law or the company's code of conduct.

Upon investigation, *The Wall Street Journal* learned that the company created an independent panel to look into the use of the hotline and other company irregularities. It was discovered that there were significant problems with how the hotline was being used. It was found, for example, that the two executives who were in charge of the company's hotline were also allegedly behind the concealment of $1.5 billion in company losses.

The panel's report noted that the company's corporate culture was characterized by serious problems. The panel observed a stuffy atmosphere that inhibited employees from speaking openly. The panel concluded that compliance systems were significantly disabled. One employee who used the hotline to report on wrongdoing claimed he was transferred to a less desirable job after issuing a complaint via the hotline. The hotline required employees to report their names in case complaints needed to be investigated further.

When the hotline was initially set up, some recommended that it be administered by external parties so that those reporting complaints would feel more secure about their anonymity. The manager in charge strongly opposed using an outside party to administer the hotline. It was later revealed by a Japanese consumer affairs agency that about two-thirds of the large firms did use outside parties to administer their hotlines.

1. What ethics issues do you see in the company's culture and administration of the hotline?
2. As an employee, would you feel uncomfortable filing an ethics complaint in a system run by the company itself? Could anything be done to ensure your confidentiality?
3. What principles should be followed in designing a company ethics or compliance hotline?

Sources: Juro Osawa, "Olympus Hotline Didn't Blow Whistle," *The Wall Street Journal*, January 4, 2012; "Olympus Hotline Had Flaws," *Asian Wall Street Journal*, January 3, 2012, Allvoices, http://www.allvoices.com/news/11219120-olympus-compliance-hotline-had-flaws. Accessed February 25, 2013; "Ethics Hotlines," In Touch, http://getintouch.com/solutions/compliance-hotlines/. Accessed March 5, 2013.

What are the goals of ethics training? Different companies set different goals, but a typical set of goals for ethics training includes the following:

- To learn the fundamentals of business ethics.
- To learn to solve ethical dilemmas.
- To learn to identify causes of unethical behavior.
- To learn about common managerial ethical issues.
- To learn whistle-blowing criteria and risks.
- To learn to develop a code of ethics and execute an internal ethical audit.[122]

Firms typically use the following materials and formats in their ethics training: codes of ethics (as a training device), lectures, workshops/seminars, case studies, CDs/discussions, and articles/speeches. One major firm, Lockheed Martin, introduced some humor into its initial ethics training by creating the Dilbert-inspired board game, "The Ethics Challenge," for company-wide ethics training. To play the game, players (employees) move around the board by answering "Case File" questions such as "You've been selected for a training course in Florida, and you want to go only for the vacation." Among the answers and their respective points are "Go, but skip the sessions" (0 points), "Ask your supervisor if it would be beneficial" (5 points), and, the Dogbert answer, "Wear mouse ears to work and hum 'It's a Small World After All' all day." Sessions for the company's 185,000 employees were led by supervisors, not ethics officers. The chairman of the company kicked off the training by leading the training of those who reported to him directly.[123]

One former ethics officer of a major corporation has criticized much of the ethics training companies offer. He said that most of this training is being done in the form of a mandatory annual compliance exercise, typically one hour in duration. Often, it is a "check the box" exercise in that management can check off that it is completed for the year. He goes on to say that if such training is not done well, it turns out to be indistinguishable from all the other meetings employees have to attend.[124]

In terms of the effectiveness of ethics training, research has shown that exposure to lengthy programs (for example, 10 weeks) resulted in significant improvements in moral development.[125] Though brief ethics training does not always yield noticeable results, some approaches have demonstrated that improved moral reasoning can be learned in just a few weeks.[126]

Business Roundtable Institute for Corporate Ethics   One of the major limitations of business ethics training has been the exemption of the CEO and other top-level managers from it. This has been changing. The Business Roundtable, an organization of CEOs, developed a business ethics institute targeted toward CEOs.[127] The CEOs who comprise the Business Roundtable are involved in either taking the classes or teaching the classes. The main office for the institute is located at the Darden School at the University of Virginia. The goal of the institute is to help restore public confidence in the marketplace in light of the recent scandals in business. The institute conducts research, creates courses, and offers executive seminars on business ethics. Some skeptics wonder whether this will make a difference or not. Some say that CEOs are pretty set in their ways by the time they reach the pinnacle of their organizations. Optimists are withholding judgment until experience indicates whether the new institute will add significant value or not.[128] Regardless, it is encouraging that CEOs are finally planning to subject themselves to the same kind of training they have always wanted for their subordinates. If ethical leadership truly begins at the top, the institute should provide a useful resource for these organization leaders.

Ethics Audits and Risk Assessments

In increasing numbers, companies today are beginning to appreciate the need to follow up on their ethics initiatives and programs. **Ethics audits** are mechanisms or approaches by which a company may assess or evaluate its ethical climate or programs. Ethics audits are intended to carefully review such ethics initiatives as ethics programs, codes of conduct, hotlines, and ethics training programs to determine their effectiveness and results. Ethics audits are similar to social audits discussed in Chapter 5. In addition, they are intended to examine other management activities that may add to or subtract from the company's ethics initiatives. This might include management's sincerity, communication efforts, incentive and reward systems, and other activities. Ethics audits may employ written instruments, committees, outside consultants, and employee interviews.[129] A popular variation on the ethics audit is the **sustainability audit**. More and more companies today employ this approach for identifying and managing sustainability issues within their organizations. They want to improve the credibility of their sustainability reports and provide greater confidence to all stakeholders.[130] The "Spotlight on Sustainability" reveals more about these audits.

Spurred on by the revised Federal Sentencing Guidelines, companies are increasingly designing and conducting fraud risk assessments of their operations. **Fraud risk assessments** are review processes designed to identify and monitor conditions and events that may have some bearing on the company's exposure to compliance/misconduct risk and to review company's methods for dealing with these concerns. Risk in this context typically refers to the company's exposure to possible compliance, misconduct, and ethics issues. According to recent surveys, the top five subjects of ethics program risk analyses

---

Spotlight on Sustainability

Sustainability Audits Becoming Popular

Sustainability audits are becoming popular today. In some instances they are done in conjunction with ethics audits. Sometimes they are done instead of ethics audits. A sustainability audit is an assessment of the environmental and/or social aspects of the workplace providing a direction for opportunities and potential risks.

Research carried out by Sustainability Training Advice Review has shown that there organizations seeking to become more sustainable are adopting a number of key building blocks, including:

1. Identification of sustainability issues within the organization
2. Sustainability performance measurement and trends
3. Stakeholder engagement, linkages, and systems thinking
4. Values and community issues
5. Change management processes toward sustainability
6. Vision and the future
7. Governance and sustainability audit

If organizations have these sustainability building blocks, this will give a good indication of how the organization is integrating sustainability thinking into its activities. The audit process will assess the extent to which the organization has a process in place to cover each of the areas identified.

Sources: Healthy Homes: Sustainability Audits, http://www.healthyhomereports.com/Healthy%20Homes%20/Sustainability_Audits.html. Accessed February 2, 2010; Sustainability Audit and Review, http://www.sustainabilityconsultants.com/. Accessed April 4, 2013; also see http://www.sustainableni.org/. Accessed April 4, 2013.

include internal policies and processes, employee awareness and understanding of compliance and ethics issues, anonymous reporting systems, disciplinary systems as prevention tools, and employee intent or incentives.[131]

In addition to providing benefits for legal reasons, the conduct of periodic risk assessments provides internal benefits to management. Some of these include the following: detecting compliance and ethics threats and permitting companies to correct problems before they occur or become worse. If problems are not detected and corrected, they may be discovered by regulators, investors, the media, or potential plaintiffs.[132]

Corporate Transparency

One of the most important best practices in the improvement of ethics programs is that of **transparency**. **Corporate transparency** refers to a quality, characteristic, or state in which activities, processes, practices, and decisions that take place in companies become *open or visible to the outside world*. A common definition of transparency is the degree to which an organization

- Provides public access to information
- Accepts responsibility for its actions
- Makes decisions more openly
- Establishes incentives for leaders to uphold these standards[133]

The opposite of transparency is **opacity**, or an opaque condition in which activities and practices remain obscure or hidden from outside scrutiny and review.

Pressures toward transparency have come both from the outside and within companies. From the outside, various stakeholders such as consumers, environmentalists, government, and investors want to know more clearly what is going on within the organizations. The recent business scandals have served as an added outside force. In addition, the Sarbanes–Oxley Act mandated greater transparency. Transparency leads to accountability. From the inside, companies are increasingly seeing how transparency makes sense as an ethics best practice. In their book *The Transparency Edge: How Credibility Can Make or Break You in Business*, Pagano and Pagano state that a transparent management approach—a "what you see is what you get" code of conduct—will increase your company's credibility in the marketplace, build loyalty, and help you gain the trust and confidence of those with whom you work.[134] Another important book on transparency is *The Naked Corporation: How the Age of Transparency Will Revolutionize Business*, by Tapscott and Ticoll. They argue that today corporate transparency is not optional but inevitable. They say companies should "undress for success."[135] As companies become more open enterprises, the public and other stakeholders will come to trust them more because more will be exposed to view.

A major example of the benefits of transparency is that of Chiquita Brands International, which was exposed for a variety of questionable practices such as use of pesticides despite an environmental agreement, secret control over dozens of supposedly independent banana companies, bribery, and lax security that resulted in the use of company boats to smuggle drugs. Chiquita's reaction to this exposure was to turn the company around through a policy of corporate transparency, especially visible in its corporate social responsibility report. The report began to explain the results of external audits and employee surveys, and it helped the company get through bankruptcy proceedings and regain public trust. A point we have made previously is worth repeating here: It all starts at the top. Open leadership is one of the strongest forces behind transparency.[136]

Board of Director Leadership and Oversight

One would think that oversight and leadership of ethics initiatives by the boards of directors of businesses would be a "given." That has not been the case, however, in many instances.[137] The primary impetus for board involvement in and oversight of ethics programs and initiatives has been the megascandals of the past decade that have impacted many major companies. This has been coupled with the passage of the Sarbanes–Oxley Act, which has overhauled federal securities laws to improve corporate governance. Corporate governance was discussed in detail in Chapter 4, but here we want to emphasize the board's role in oversight of corporate ethics, one of the most urgent issues in recent years.

Corporate boards, like top managers, should provide strong ethical leadership. Former SEC Chair William Donaldson said that it is not enough for a company to profess a code of conduct. According to Donaldson, "the most important thing that a board of directors should do is determine the elements that must be embedded in the company's moral DNA."[138] In other words, strong leadership from the board and CEOs is still the most powerful force in improving the company's ethical culture.

According to the ethics and compliance benchmarking survey conducted by the Conference Board, board involvement in ethics programs has risen to 96 percent of companies surveyed.[139] According to another survey of 165 company boards, it is reported that although corporate scandals and Sarbanes–Oxley have been strong forces in bringing about more board involvement in ethics, other factors have motivated it as well. In the United States, general legal developments have increased board scrutiny of ethics programs, but in the United Kingdom, India, and Western Europe, "enhancement of reputation" has often been cited as a reason for closer board scrutiny of corporate ethics. There is also widespread enthusiasm for training board members in ethics, but such enthusiasm does not often result in action.[140]

Although we have not discussed everything that can be done at the organizational level to improve or manage business ethics, the actions suggested represent best practices that can move management a long way toward improving the organization's ethical culture and climate. If management takes specific steps as suggested, many behaviors or decisions that might otherwise have been questionable have a greater chance of being in line with high ethical standards. Thus, ethics can be positively supervised, and managers do not have to treat value concerns as matters out of their influence or control. On the contrary, managers can intercede and improve the organization's ethical climate.[141]

Behavioral Ethics—Striving Toward a Deeper Understanding

In this chapter we have discussed personal and managerial ethics and the challenges involved in managing organizational ethics. At this point, it is helpful to focus on a relatively new field that has been termed **behavioral ethics**. Most of our discussion to this point has been normative in nature. Behavioral ethics, by contrast, helps us to understand at a deeper level many of the behavioral processes that research has shown actually are taking place in people and organizations. Thus, most of these learnings are *descriptive* in nature as they strive to capture insights into processes that have been observed to be taking place in practice. An awareness of these behavioral phenomena greatly adds to our understanding of business ethics and should help us to better design ethics initiatives in organizations.

Bazerman and Gino have defined behavioral ethics as "the study of systematic and predictable ways in which individuals make ethical decisions and judge the ethical decisions of others that are at odds with intuition.…"[142] The approach embraces both intentional and unintentional unethical behaviors. Treviño, Weaver, and Reynolds note that behavioral ethics embrace individual, group, and organizational influences.[143] Behavioral ethics give us insights into how people actually behave in organizations as a result of psychological processes or as a consequence of organizational factors at work. These insights help us overcome problems or better design organizations to offset detrimental consequences.

Following are some of the phenomena that have been observed to fit into the category of behavioral ethics. **Bounded ethicality** tends to occur when managers and employees find that even when they aspire to behave ethically it is difficult due to a variety of organizational pressures and psychological tendencies that intervene.[144] There are limits on people's abilities to be ethical. Tendencies toward bounded ethicality might include claiming credit for a group's work without realizing you are doing it, engaging in implicit discrimination and in-group favoritism, and falling prey to the influence of conflicts of interest.[145] **Conformity bias** has also been observed. This is the tendency people have to take their cues for ethical behavior from their peers rather than exercising their own independent ethical judgment. Another predisposition is **overconfidence bias**. This is the tendency for people to be more confident of their own moral character or behavior than they have objective reason to be. **Self-serving bias** is similar; this is the propensity people have to process information in a way that serves to support their preexisting beliefs and their perceived self-interest.[146]

Other important behavioral ethics patterns include framing, incrementalism, role morality, and moral equilibrium. **Framing** refers to the fact that people's ethical judgments are affected by how a question or issue is posed (framed). It has been found, for example, that when people are prompted to think of an issue as an "ethical" issue they will tend to make more ethical decisions than if they had been prompted to think of the issue as a "business" issue.[147] **Incrementalism** is the predisposition toward the slippery slope. It has been noted that there is a tendency toward making a series of minor ethical misjudgments that can lead to major ethical mistakes.

Role morality is the tendency some people have to use different ethical standards as they move through different roles in life. For example, a person might make more questionable decisions at work when job and profits are at stake than when at home. Finally, **moral equilibrium** has been observed. This is the tendency for people to keep an ethical scoreboard in their heads and use this information when making future decisions. While seeking equilibrium, for example, a person might take moral license on an issue if they think they are running a moral surplus in their overall behavior.[148] While seeking balance, people may rationalize future behavior rather than judging each decision situation on its own merits.

Related to some of these concepts, Bazerman and Tenbrunsel describe ethical breakdowns or barriers that organizational members may experience even as they see themselves as "good people" striving to do what is right.[149] Their five barriers to an ethical organization include the following: **Ill-conceived goals** are poorly set goals that encourage negative behaviors such as sales goals emphasized too much or set too high. **Motivated blindness** is the process of overlooking the questionable actions of others when it is in one's own best interest. This is the self-serving bias described earlier. **Indirect blindness** occurs when one holds others less accountable for unethical behaviors when they are carried out through third parties. The **slippery slope**, mentioned earlier as incrementalism, causes people to not notice others' unethical behavior when it gradually occurs in small increments. Finally, **overcoming values** is the act of letting questionable behaviors pass if the outcome is good. This can occur when managers put more emphasis on results rather than how the results are achieved. It could be played out as the ends justifying the means.

Research into behavioral ethics gives us deeper and richer insights into the challenges of being ethical within our organizational roles and the difficulties of creating an ethical organizational culture while implementing many of the best practices and principles discussed earlier. Behavioral ethics may be seen as an overlay of reality on the normative strategies of improving business ethics. Consequently, they must be taken into consideration when striving to manage business ethics.

Moral Decisions, Moral Managers, and Moral Organizations

In the last two chapters, we have discussed ethical or moral acts, decisions, practices, managers, and organizations. Though the goal of ethics initiatives is to develop moral organizations, sometimes all we get are isolated ethical acts, decisions, or practices, or, if we are fortunate, a few moral managers. Achieving the status of moral standing is a goal, whatever the level on which it may be achieved. Sometimes all we can do is bring about ethical acts, decisions, or practices. A broader goal is to create moral managers in the sense in which they were discussed in Chapter 7 and this chapter. Finally, the highest-level goal for managers may be to create moral organizations, for which many of the best practices discussed in this chapter will need to be successfully implemented. As ethicist Kenneth Goodpaster has reminded us, "The depths of a company's *cultural* commitment to ethical values in the pursuit of economic values are a mark of corporate *moral* development."[150]

The important point here is to emphasize that the goal of managers should be to create *moral decisions, moral managers*, and ultimately, *moral organizations* while recognizing that what we frequently observe in business is the achievement of moral standing at only one of these levels. The ideal is to create a moral organization that is fully populated by moral managers making moral decisions (and practices, policies, and behaviors), but this is seldom achieved. Figure 8-8 depicts the essential characteristics of each of these levels. These challenges become even more specialized when we consider business ethics and technology in Chapter 9 and ethical issues in the global arena in Chapter 10.

FIGURE 8-8

Moral Decisions, Moral Managers, and Moral Organizations

Moral Decision(s)
Single or isolated moral acts, behaviors, policies, practices, or decisions made by a manager or managers of an organization. These are the simplest and most basic form of achieving moral status. The principles of ethical decision making presented should assist in the development of moral decisions.

Moral Manager(s)
A manager or managers who have adopted the characteristics of moral management, and this approach dominates all their decision making. These managers manifest ethical leadership and always occupy the moral high ground. Moral managers will make

moral decisions via the use of ethical principles. In addition, they will learn and use the research of ethics in organizations discussed in this chapter.

Moral Organization(s)
An organization dominated by the presence of moral managers making moral decisions. Moral management has become an integral part of the culture. Moral management permeates all the organization's decisions, policies, and practices. The organization uses the best practices for achieving a moral management culture. Of special importance are moral leadership provided by board of director oversight and top management leadership.

Summary

The subject of business ethics may be addressed at several different levels: personal, organizational, industrial, societal, and international. This chapter focuses on the personal and organizational levels—the levels at which managers can have the most impact. The chapter concludes with insights from the newly emerging field of behavioral ethics.

A number of different ethical principles serve as guides to personal decision making. Ethics principles may be categorized as teleological (ends-based), deontological (duty-based), or aretaic (virtue-based). One of the major deontological principles is the categorical imperative. Major philosophical principles of ethics include utilitarianism, rights, and justice. The Golden Rule was singled out as a particularly powerful ethical principle among various groups studied. Virtue ethics was identified as an increasingly popular concept. Servant leadership was presented as an approach to management that embraced an ethical perspective. Seven practical tests were proposed to assist the individual in making ethical decisions: the test of common sense, the test of one's best self, the test of making something public, the test of ventilation, the test of purified idea, the test of the Big Four, and the gag test.

At the organizational level, factors were discussed that affect the organization's moral culture or climate. It was argued that the behavior of one's superiors and peers along with industry ethical practices were the most important influences on an organization's ethical culture. Society's moral climate and personal needs were considered to be less important. Best practices for improving the firm's ethical climate include providing leadership from management, ethics programs, and ethics officers; setting realistic objectives; infusing the decision-making process with ethical considerations; employing codes of conduct; disciplining violators; creating whistle-blowing mechanisms or hotlines; training managers in business ethics; using ethics audits and risk assessments (which often include sustainability audits); and adopting the concept of transparency and board of director oversight of ethics initiatives.

Behavioral ethics is a newly emerging field which is based upon empirically observed phenomena describing psychological processes that occur when managers and employees strive to do the right thing in their decision making and in their design of an ethical organizational culture. Our knowledge from behavioral ethics serves as a reality check on the implementation of normative processes in business ethics.

The goal of ethics initiatives is to achieve a status that may be characterized not just by isolated moral decisions but also by the presence of moral managers and the ultimate achievement of a moral organization.

Key Terms

aretaic theories, p. 220
behavioral ethics, p. 253
bounded ethicality, p. 254
categorical imperative, p. 221
codes of conduct, p. 245
codes of ethics, p. 245
compensatory justice, p. 224
compliance orientation, p. 236
conformity bias, p. 254
core ethical values, p. 237
corporate transparency, p. 252
deontological theories, p. 220
distributive justice, p. 224
ethical due process, p. 224
ethical leadership, p. 237

ethical tests, p. 228
ethic of reciprocity, p. 228
ethics audits, p. 251
ethics of care, p. 225
ethics officer, p. 241
ethics orientation, p. 236
ethics programs, p. 240
ethics screen, p. 244
formal ethics program, p. 237
framing, p. 254
fraud risk assessments, p. 251
Golden Rule, p. 227
ill-conceived goals, p. 254
incrementalism, p. 254
indirect blindness, p. 254

hotlines, p. 248
legal rights, p. 222
moral equilibrium, p. 254
moral rights, p. 222
motivated blindness, p. 254
negative right, p. 223
opacity, p. 252
Organizational Sentencing Guidelines, p. 236
overcoming values, p. 254
overconfidence bias, p. 254
positive right, p. 223
principle of justice, p. 223
principle of rights, p. 222
principle of utilitarianism, p. 221

procedural justice, p. 224
process fairness, p. 224
rights, p. 222
role morality, p. 254
self-serving bias, p. 254

servant leadership, p. 226
slippery slope, p. 254
"smell" test, p. 229
sustainability audit, p. 251
teleological theories, p. 220

transparency, p. 252
utilitarianism, p. 221
virtue ethics, p. 226

Discussion Questions

1. From your personal experience, give two examples of ethical dilemmas. Give two examples of ethical dilemmas you have experienced as a member of an organization.

2. Using the examples you provided for question 1, identify one or more of the guides to personal decision making or ethical tests that you think would have helped you resolve your dilemmas. Describe how it would have helped.

3. Which is most important in ethics principles—consequences or duty? Discuss.

4. Assume that you are in your first managerial position. Identify five ways in which you might provide ethical leadership. Rank them in terms of importance, and be prepared to explain your ranking.

5. What do you think about the idea of codes of conduct? Give three reasons why an organization ought to have a code of conduct, and three reasons why an organization should not have a code of conduct. On balance, how do you regard codes of conduct?

6. A lively debate is going on in this country concerning whether business ethics can and should be taught in business schools. Do you think ethics can be taught in B school? Justify your point with reasons. Can top managers and board members be taught business ethics?

7. Identify and prioritize the best practices for improving the organization's ethical climate. What are the strengths and weaknesses of each?

8. Which three of the concepts under the field of behavioral ethics do you think are most powerful? Explain why and give examples.

Endnotes

1. David Callahan, *The Cheating Culture: Why More Americans Are Doing Wrong to Get Ahead* (New York: Harcourt, Inc., 2004).

2. Lee Ellis, *Leading Talents, Leading Teams* (Chicago: Northfield Publishing, 2003), 201–204.

3. Bill George, *Authentic Leadership: Rediscovering the Secrets to Creating Lasting Value* (San Francisco: Jossey-Bass, 2003).

4. Dan Chapman, "Woman Rewarded for Act of Honesty," *The Atlanta Journal-Constitution* (September 8, 2001).

5. Jennifer Dixon, "Bosses Knew Shipped Meat Was Tainted, Workers Say," *Chicago Tribune* (August 30, 2001).

6. Ethics Resource Center, *National Business Ethics Survey 2003: How Employees View Ethics in Their Organizations* (Washington, DC: Ethics Resource Center, 2003), 28. Also see http://www.ethics.org.

7. Archie B. Carroll, "Principles of Business Ethics: Their Role in Decision Making and an Initial Consensus," *Management Decision* (Vol. 28, No. 28, 1990), 20–24.

8. John R. Boatright, *Ethics and the Conduct of Business*, 4th ed. (Upper Saddle River, NJ: Prentice Hall, 2003), 31–32.

9. Tom L. Beauchamp, *Philosophical Ethics: An Introduction to Moral Philosophy*, 3d ed. (New York: McGraw-Hill, 2001).

10. Vincent Barry, *Moral Issues in Business* (Belmont, CA: Wadsworth, 1979), 43.

11. Ibid., 45–46.

12. I. Kant, *Groundwork of the Metaphysic of Morals*, trans. H. J. Paton (New York: Harper and Row, 1964).

13. Victoria S. Wike, "Duty," in Patricia H. Werhane and R. Edward Freeman (eds.), *The Blackwell Encyclopedic Dictionary of Business Ethics* (Malden, MA: Blackwell Publishers, Ltd, 1997), 180–181.

14. Boatright, 53.

15. Scott J. Reynolds and Norman E. Bowie, "A Kantian Perspective on the Characteristics of Ethics Programs," *Business Ethics Quarterly* (Vol. 14, No. 2, April 2004), 275–292.

16. Louis P. Pojman, *Ethics: Discovering Right and Wrong* (Belmont, CA: Wadsworth, 1995), 147–148.

17. Ibid., 150.

18. Ibid., 152–153.

19. Manuel C. Velasquez, *Business Ethics: Concepts and Cases*, 3d ed. (Englewood Cliffs, NJ: Prentice Hall, 1992), 72–73.

20. Richard T. DeGeorge, *Business Ethics*, 5th ed. (Upper Saddle River, NJ: Prentice Hall, 1999), 69–72.

21. Velasquez, 73.

22. "Rights: What Are They Anyway?" http://dspace.dial .pipex.com/town/street/pl38/rights.htm. Accessed July 18, 2007.

23. "Negative and Positive Rights," http://www.essays.cc/ free_essays/e4/vak199.shtml. Accessed July 18, 2007.

24. See the following sources for a discussion of these points: David Luban, "Judicial Activism and the Concept of Rights," *Report from the Institute for Philosophy & Public Policy* (College Park, MD: University of Maryland, Winter/Spring 1994), 12–17; George F. Will, "Our Expanding Menu of Rights," *Newsweek* (December 14, 1992), 90; John Leo, "The Spread of Rights Babble," *U.S. News & World Report* (June 28, 1993), 17; and William Raspberry, "Blind Pursuit of Rights Can Endanger Civility," *The Atlanta Journal* (September 14, 1994), A14.

25. Jonathan Haidt, "The New Culture War Over Fairness," *Time*, October 22, 2012, 25.

26. DeGeorge, 69–72.

27. Ibid.

28. Joel Brockner, "Why It's So Hard to Be Fair," *Harvard Business Review* (March 2006), 122–129.

29. Ibid., 123.

30. "John Rawls," *The Economist* (December 7, 2002), 83.

31. John Rawls, *A Theory of Justice* (Cambridge, MA: Harvard University Press, 1971).

32. DeGeorge, 69–72.

33. Michael M. Weinstein, "Bringing Logic to Bear on Liberal Dogma," *The New York Times* (December 1, 2002), 5.

34. Ibid., 72.

35. Ibid., 5.

36. Dahlia Lithwick, "Women: Truly the Fairer Sex," *Newsweek* (April 20, 2009), 13.

37. Robbin Derry, "Ethics of Care," in Werhane and Freeman (1997), 254.

38. Brian K. Burton and Craig P. Dunn, "Feminist Ethics as Moral Grounding for Stakeholder Theory," *Business Ethics Quarterly* (Vol. 6, No. 2, 1996), 133–147. See also A. C. Wicks, D. R. Gilbert, and R. E. Freeman, "A Feminist Reinterpretation of the Stakeholder Concept," *Business Ethics Quarterly* (Vol. 4, 1994), 475–497.

39. Derry (1997), 256.

40. Jeanne M. Liedtka, "Feminist Morality and Competitive Reality: A Role for an Ethic of Care?" *Business Ethics Quarterly* (Vol. 6, 1996), 179–200. See also John Dobson and Judith White, "Toward the Feminine Firm," *Business Ethics Quarterly* (Vol. 5, 1995), 463–478.

41. Alasdair MacIntyre, *After Virtue* (University of Notre Dame Press, 1981). See also Louis P. Pojman, *Ethics:*

Discovering Right and Wrong, 2d ed. (Belmont, CA: Wadsworth, 1995), 160–185.

42. Beauchamp, 2001.

43. Pojman, 161. See also Bill Shaw, "Sources of Virtue: The Market and the Community," *Business Ethics Quarterly* (Vol. 7, 1997), 33–50; and Dennis Moberg, "Virtuous Peers in Work Organizations," *Business Ethics Quarterly* (Vol. 7, 1997), 67–85.

44. Esther F. Schaeffer, "Character Education: A Prerequisite for Corporate Ethics," *Ethics Today* (Summer 1997), 5. Also see Josephson Institute, "Character Counts!" http://charactercounts.org/. Accessed March 5, 2013.

45. Oliver F. Williams and Patrick E. Murphy, "The Ethics of Virtue: A Moral Theory for Business," in Oliver F. Williams and John W. Houck (eds.), *A Virtuous Life in Business* (Lanham, MD: Rowman & Littlefield Publishers, Inc., 1992), 9–27.

46. Robert K. Greenleaf, *Servant Leadership* (New York: Paulist Press, 1977).

47. Greenleaf Center for Servant Leadership, http://www .greenleaf.org/. Accessed February 11, 2013.

48. Larry C. Spears (ed.), *Reflections of Leadership* (New York: John Wiley & Sons, 1995), 4–7.

49. Joanne B. Ciulla (ed.), *Ethics: The Heart of Leadership* (Westport, CT: Praeger Publishers, 1998), 17.

50. James A. Autry, *The Servant Leader* (Roseville, CA: Prima Publishing, 2001), flyleaf.

51. Carroll, 1990, 22. Also see Archie B. Carroll, "One Rule Can Best Guide Practices," in Archie B. Carroll (ed.), *Business Ethics: Brief Readings on Vital Topics* (New York and London: Routledge Publishers, 2009), 170–171.

52. Barry, 50–51.

53. Carroll, 1990, 22.

54. John C. Maxwell, *There's No Such Thing as "Business" Ethics: There's Only One Rule for Making Decisions* (Warner Books, 2003), 24–29.

55. Gordon L. Lippett, *The Leader Looks at Ethics* (Washington, DC: Leadership Resources, 1969), 12–13.

56. "Stiffer Rules for Business Ethics," *BusinessWeek* (March 30, 1974), 88.

57. Lippett, 12–13.

58. Eric Harvey and Scott Airitam, *Ethics 4 Everyone: The Handbook for Integrity-Based Business Practices* (Dallas, TX: The Walk the Talk Company, 2002), 31.

59. Ibid., 31.

60. Frederick Andrews, "Corporate Ethics: Talks with a Trace of Robber Baron," *The New York Times* (April 18, 1977), C49–C52.

61. Phillip V. Lewis, "Ethical Principles for Decision Makers: A Longitudinal Study," *Journal of Business Ethics* (Vol. 8, 1989), 275.

62. Craig V. VanSandt, "The Relationship Between Ethical Work Climate and Moral Awareness," *Business & Society* (Vol. 42, No. 1, March 2003), 144–151.

63. Cited in John B. Cullen, Bart Victor, and Carroll Stephens, "An Ethical Weather Report: Assessing the Organization's Ethical Climate," *Organizational Dynamics* (Autumn 1989), 50.

64. For an excellent discussion, see Deborah Vidaver Cohen, "Creating and Maintaining Ethical Work Climates: Anomie in the Workplace and Implications for Managing Change," *Business Ethics Quarterly* (Vol. 3, No. 4, October 1993), 343–355. See also B. Victor and J. Cullen, "The Organizational Bases of Ethical Work Climates," *Administrative Science Quarterly* (Vol. 33, 1988), 101–125; and H. R. Smith and A. B. Carroll, "Organizational Ethics: A Stacked Deck," *Journal of Business Ethics* (Vol. 3, 1984), 95–100.

65. Archie B. Carroll, "Managerial Ethics: A Post-Watergate View," *Business Horizons* (April 1975), 75–80.

66. Posner and Schmidt, 211.

67. American Society of Chartered Life Underwriters & Chartered Financial Consultants and Ethics Officer Association, "Sources and Consequences of Workplace Pressure: A Landmark Study," unpublished report (1997). See also Del Jones, "48% of Workers Admit to Unethical or Illegal Acts," *USA Today* (April 4–6, 1997), 1A–2A.

68. Ethics Resource Center (2003), 33.

69. Ethics Resource Center, *2011 National Business Ethics Survey: Workplace Ethics in Transition*, Washington: Ethics Resource Center, 2012, 12.

70. Ibid., 12

71. T. V. Purcell and James Weber, *Institutionalizing Corporate Ethics: A Case History, Special Study No. 71* (New York: The President's Association, American Management Association, 1979). See also James Weber, "Institutionalizing Ethics into Business Organizations: A Model and Research Agenda," *Business Ethics Quarterly* (Vol. 3, No. 4, October 1993), 419–436.

72. Ethics Resource Center, 2009 National Business Ethics Survey (Washington, DC: Ethics Resource Center, November 2009), 2.

73. T. E. Deal and A. Kennedy, *Corporate Cultures* (Reading, MA: Addison-Wesley Publishers, 1982).

74. Ronald Berenbeim, "Universal Conduct: An Ethics and Compliance Benchmarking Survey," The Conference Board, 2006, 7.

75. Archie B. Carroll, "Ethics Programs Go Beyond Compliance Strategy," *Business Ethics: Brief Readings on Vital Topics* (New York and London: Routledge Publishers, 2009), 184–185.

76. Ronald E. Berenbeim and Jeffrey M. Kaplan, "Ethics and Compliance … The Convergence of Principle- and Rule-Based Ethics Programs: An Emerging Trend," *The Conference Board, Executive Action Series*, No. 231, March 2007.

77. Ibid., 2.

78. David Skeel, "A Nation Adrift from the Rule of Law," *The Wall Street Journal*, August 22, 2012, A11.

79. Berenbeim and Kaplan, 4.

80. Mark S. Schwartz, "Developing and Sustaining an Ethical Corporate Culture: The Core Elements," *Business Horizons*, January 2013, Vol. 56, No. 1, 39–50.

81. "The Big Picture: Ethics," *BusinessWeek* (June 19, 2006), 13.

82. L. W. Foy, "Business Ethics: A Reappraisal," *Distinguished Lecture Series, Columbia Graduate School of Business* (January 30, 1975), 2.

83. Linda Klebe Treviño, Laura Pincus Hartman, and Michael Brown, "Moral Person and Moral Manager: How Executives Develop a Reputation for Ethical Leadership," *California Management Review* (Vol. 42, No. 4, summer 2000), 134.

84. Harvey Gittler, "Listen to the Whistle-Blowers Before It's Too Late," *The Wall Street Journal* (March 10, 1986), 16.

85. Treviño, Hartman, and Brown, 128–142.

86. Ibid., 133–136..

87. R. Edward Freeman and Lisa Stewart, "Developing Ethical Leadership" (Charlottesville, VA: Business Roundtable Institute for Corporate Ethics, 2006), 3–7.

88. Steven N. Brenner, "Influences on Corporate Ethics Programs" (San Diego, CA: International Association for Business and Society, March 16–18, 1990), 7.

89. National Business Ethics Survey, 2003, 1–2.

90. Ibid.

91. Bruce A. Hamm, "Elements of the US Federal Sentencing Guidelines," http://www.refresher.com. Accessed April 29, 2004; United States Sentencing Commission Guidelines Manual, November 2012, http://www.ussc.gov/Guidelines/2012_Guidelines/Manual_PDF/TitlePage_Citation_ToC.pdf. Accessed March 5, 2013.

92. Susan Gaines, "Handing Out Halos," *Business Ethics* (March/April 1994), 20–24.

93. Roy J. Snell, "Should We Call It an Ethics Program or a Compliance Program?" *Journal of Health Care Compliance* (March/April 2004), 1–2.

94. Michael G. Daigneault, Jerry Guthrie, and Frank J. Navran, "Managing Ethics Upwards," in O. C. Ferrell, Sheb L. True, and Lou E. Pelton (eds.), *Rights, Relationships & Responsibilities* (Kennesaw, GA: Coles College of Business, Kennesaw State University, 2003), 61–69.

95. Ibid., 65–69.

96. Claudia Parsons, "From Madoff to Merrill Lynch, 'Where Was the Ethics Officer,'" *International Herald Tribune* (January 29, 2009).

97. Fred T. Allen, "Corporate Morality: Is the Price Too High?" *The Wall Street Journal* (October 17, 1975), 16.

98. LaRue T. Hosmer, *The Ethics of Management* (Homewood, IL: Richard D. Irwin, 1987), 12–14.

99. Kenneth Blanchard and Norman Vincent Peale, *The Power of Ethical Management* (New York: Fawcett Crest, 1988), 20.

100. Texas Instruments, "The TI Ethics Quick Test" http://www.ti.com/corp/docs/company/citizen/ethics/quicktest.shtml. Accessed February 11, 2013.

101. Joan Dubinsky, "Code Redux Part One: Tips for Writing and Updating Your Corporate Code of Conduct," *Corporate Compliance Insights*, January 31, 2011, http://www.corporatecomplianceinsights.com/corporate-code-of-conduct-guidelines-policy-tips-writing-updating/. Accessed March 5, 2013.

102. Gary Edwards, "And the Survey Said…," in Garone (ed.) (1994), 25.

103. "Codes of Ethics," by Leon V. Ryan, in Patricia Werhane and R. Edward Freeman (eds.), *The Blackwell Encyclopedic Dictionary of Business Ethics* (Malden, MA: Blackwell Publishing, 1997), 114.

104. Institute of Business Ethics, "Developing an Effective Code of Ethics: Content of a Code of Ethics," http://www.ibe.org.uk/index.asp?upid=61&msid=11. Accessed February 11, 2013.

105. "Common Ethics Code Provisions," http://www.ethics.org/resources/common-code-provisions.asp. Accessed July 23, 2007.

106. Cynthia Stohl, Michael Stohl, and Lucy Popova, "A New Generation of Corporate Codes of Ethics," *Journal of Business Ethics* (2009: 90), 607–622.

107. Patrick Erwin, "Corporate Codes of Conduct: The Effects of Code Content and Quality on Ethical Performance," *Journal of Business Ethics*, April 2011, Vol. 99 Issue 4, 535–548.

108. Mark Schwartz, "The Nature of the Relationship Between Corporate Codes of Ethics and Behavior," *Journal of Business Ethics* (Vol. 32, 2001), 247–262.

109. Ibid., 255.

110. Treviño, Hartman, and Brown, *op. cit.*, 136.

111. J. Lynn Lunsford and Anne Marie Squeo, "Boeing Dismisses Two Executives for Violating Ethical Standards," *The Wall Street Journal* (November 25, 2003).

112. Ken Benson, "Nortel Fires 3 Executives Amid Accounting Inquiry," *The New York Times* (April 28, 2004).

113. Allen, 16.

114. 2011 National Business Ethics Survey, 12.

115. Berenbeim, 2006, 6.

116. 2003 National Business Ethics Survey, 44.

117. Ibid., 43.

118. "Ethics: Phoning It In," *CFO* (February 2007), 21.

119. Ibid.

120. Ibid., 22–23.

121. Berenbeim, 2006, 13–14.

122. "Business Ethics Training," *Webucator*, http://www.webucator.com/management-training/course/business-ethics-training.cfm. Accessed February 2, 2010.

123. "At Last: Humor in Ethics Training," *Business Ethics* (May/June 1997), 10.

124. Francis J. Daly, "An Ethics Officer's Perspective," in Marc J. Epstein and Kirk O. Hanson (eds.), *The Accountable Corporation: Business Ethics*, Vol. 2 (Westport, CT: Praeger Publishers, 2006), 186.

125. Thomas M. Jones, "Can Business Ethics Be Taught? Empirical Evidence," *Business & Professional Ethics Journal* (Vol. 8, 1989), 86.

126. David Allen Jones, "A Novel Approach to Business Ethics Training: Improving Moral Reasoning in Just a Few Weeks," *Journal of Business Ethics*, 2009, 88: 367–379.

127. Business Roundtable Institute for Ethics, http://www.corporate-ethics.org/about/. Accessed February 13, 2013.

128. Katherine S. Mangan, "Business Schools and Company CEOs to Create Ethics Center," *Chronicle of Higher Education* (January 30, 2004), A9. Also see Louis Lavelle and Amy Borrus, "Ethics 101 for CEOs," *BusinessWeek* (January 26, 2004), 88.

129. Eric Krell, "How to Conduct an Ethics Audit," *HR Magazine*, April 2010, 55:4, 48–51; Also see Michael Metzger, Dan R. Dalton, and John W. Hill, "The Organization of Ethics and the Ethics of Organizations: The Case for Expanded Organizational Ethics Audits," *Business Ethics Quarterly* (Vol. 3, No. 1, January, 1993), 27–43.

130. *Environmental Leader*, "Big Four Audit Firms Lead Sustainability Assurance Services," June 22, 2011, http://www.environmentalleader.com/2011/06/22/big-four-audit-firms-lead-sustainability-assurance-services/. Accessed March 5, 2013.

131. Ronald E. Berenbeim, "Ethics Programs and Practices: A 20-Year Retrospective," *Executive Action Series*, The Conference Board, No. 207, September 2006, 5; Association of Certified Fraud Examiners, "Fraud Risk Assessment Tool," http://www.acfe.com/frat.aspx?id=6797. Accessed March 5, 2013.

132. Marcia Narine, "Conducting a Risk Assessment—One Approach," Risk Assessments and Compliance Program Benchmarking, The Conference Board, Webcast, V0060-05-CH, November 2, 2005.

133. Ethics Resource Center, 2009 National Business Ethics Survey 20–21; *Investopedia*, "The Importance of Transparency," October 24, 2010, http://www.investopedia.com/articles/fundamental/03/121703.asp#axzz2MhVHuZYp. Accessed March 5, 2013.

134. Barbara Pagano and Elizabeth Pagano, *The Transparency Edge: How Credibility Can Make or Break You in Business* (New York: McGraw Hill Trade, 2003).

135. Don Tapscott and David Ticoll, *The Naked Corporation: How the Age of Transparency Will Revolutionize Business* (New York: Free Press, 2003).

136. Janice Brand, "Book Review: The Naked Corporation," *Darwin Magazine* (May 4, 2004), http://www.darwinmag.com/read/writeon/column.html.

137. Archie B. Carroll, "Slack Corporate Governance Costs Us All," *Business Ethics: Brief Readings on Vital Topics*

(New York and London: Routledge Publishers, 2009), 86–87.

138. Quoted in Curtis C. Verschoor, "Unethical Workplace Is Still with Us," *Strategic Finance* (April 2004), 16.

139. Berenbeim, 5.

140. The Conference Board Press Release, "Boards of Directors Getting More Involved in Companies" Ethics Programs," *PR Newswire* (March 4, 2004).

141. W. Edward Stead, Dan L. Worrell, and Jean Garner Stead, "An Integrative Model for Understanding and Managing Ethical Behavior in Business Organizations," *Journal of Business Ethics* (Vol. 9, 1990), 223–242. See also Robert D. Gatewood and Archie B. Carroll, "Assessment of Ethical Performance of Organization Members: A Conceptual Framework," *Academy of Management Review* (Vol. 16, No. 4, 1991), 667–690.

142. Max H. Bazerman and Francesca Gino, "Behavioral Ethics: Toward a Deeper Understanding of Moral Judgment and Dishonesty," *Harvard Business School Working Papers*, January 26, 2012.

143. Linda Treviño, Gary Weaver, and Scott Reynolds, "Behavioral Ethics in Organizations: A Review," *Journal of Management*, 2006, 32: 951.

144. Robert S. Benchley, "Answering an Ethical SOS," *McCombsToday.org/Magazine,* Fall 2012, 16–21.

145. Ann E. Tenbrunsel, Kristina A. Diekmann, Kimberly A. Wade-Bezoni, Max H. Bazerman, "The ethical mirage: A temporal explanation as to why we are not as ethical as we think we are," *Research in Organizational Behavior* 30, 2010, 153–173.

146. Benchley, 2012, 21.

147. Ibid.

148. Ibid.

149. Max H. Bazerman and Ann E. Tenbrunsel, "Ethical Breakdowns," *Harvard Business Review*, April 2011, 58–65.

150. Kenneth E. Goodpaster, "Examining the Conscience of the Corporation," in Marc J. Epstein and Kirk O. Hanson (eds.), *The Accountable Corporation: Business Ethics*, Vol. 2 (Westport Connecticut: Praeger Publishers, 2006), 102.

9

Business Ethics and Technology

We live in an age dominated by advancing technology. Each new generation experiences technological advances that were not seen by previous generations. The new generation comprising young people, called the iGeneration, is said to have no "off switch" when it comes to technology. For this new group of post-Millennials, technology is said to be a "part of their DNA."[1]

Technology is how we sustain life and make it comfortable. Technology is at the core of most businesses, whether it is used to pursue new products or processes or as a means to achieve other worthwhile ends. But technology, as many have observed, is a two-edged sword. Many positive benefits flow from technological advances. However, advancing technology also poses many new problems and challenges. Futurist John Naisbitt has questioned whether advancing technology has the potential to be a "liberating" or "destructive" force in society. He has said that, at best, technology supports and improves human life, and at its worst it alienates, isolates, distorts, and destroys.[2]

In either case, technology has become such a central part of our lives and doing business in the 21st century that it must be discussed. Moreover, many ethical issues for business and for society have arisen as a result of technological advances. Many believe that technology has developed at a speed that significantly outstrips the capacity of society, government, or business to grasp its consequences or ethics. We will explore some of these issues in this chapter and then discuss additional aspects in ensuing chapters as specific stakeholder groups are considered in more detail.

It is interesting and challenging to brainstorm about what new technologies may have in store for business. And, they are all embedded in a new, complex world of data proliferation and overload. Experts now call this new information universe **Big Data**—an "infinite sea of facts, products, books, maps, conversations, references, opinions, trends, videos, advertisements, surveys"—which is "literally at your fingertips, 24–7, every day from now on."[3] The term Big Data describes the tons of information that are out there and how businesses are striving to put it to work. This information comes from many sources and businesses can obtain it just as it is generated.[4] Big Data is characterized by the 3Vs—high *volume*, high *velocity*, and high *variety*. As one Chief Information Officer (CIO) put it: "We are drowning in Data."[5] For companies, data security and cybercrime have become huge threats and responsibilities.

In this sea of Big Data, one of the hottest topics is social media. Consumers want to use it and companies want to exploit it. A relevant question is what possible social and ethical implications will tools such as Facebook, Twitter, LinkedIn, Pinterest, MySpace, Google Plus+ and Instagram have?[6] As the top-rated tools in social networking, they provide a cyber-meeting space for people wanting to network. Networking tools provide a space where individuals can describe themselves and connect with others. Most young people and college students have a profile on Facebook and the majority of them log on daily.[7] Many log on numerous times a day—some, unfortunately, while driving and walking. The same can be said for many of the other social media. Is the onslaught and overload of the tweets, texts, e-mail and posts making us crazy?[8]

What impact do social networking tools have on business? According to Albert M. Erisman, executive director of www.ethix.org, there are two important ways. First, successful, innovative businesses are established to create social networking tools.. Examples include Facebook, MySpace, Classmates.com, Flickr, and LinkedIn. Second, there are some direct business uses of social networking, and these are increasing over time. For example, LinkedIn.com has more than 200 million members in more than 200 countries and territories around the world. The site provides a way for each individual to connect his or her network of colleagues to other networks of colleagues, enabling exponential growth for their own network. Executives from all Fortune 500 companies are LinkedIn members. One benefit this provides is the sharing of résumés in job searches and recruiting. It also allows connections for business opportunities in buying and selling.[9] One can only speculate what abuses of information are creeping into these systems.

Another relentless issue in the realm of ethics and technology has been the rising extent to which companies are using video cameras mounted in stores to monitor customers' action. We know we are being watched, but do we know how smart these technologies have become? For example, a few Macy's, CVS, and Babies 'R' Us stores have used a system called the Video Investigator. This advanced surveillance software can monitor a customer's movements and compare them between video images and recognize any type of unusual activity. If the shopper removes ten items at once from a shelf, for example, or opens a case that is normally kept closed and locked, the system alerts security guards of the activity. The system can also predict where a shoplifter is likely to hide (e.g., at the end of aisles or behind floor displays).[10] We are, indeed, being watched—more and more. Much of this is for the good. But there can be possible abuses as well.

In this chapter, we explore the subject of technology and business ethics. Technology has become such an integral aspect of our work and consumer lives that special treatment of these topics is warranted. First, we will consider what technology embraces and some of its benefits and challenges. Second, we will briefly discuss the subject of ethics and technology. Finally, we will consider ethical issues connected with two major spheres of technology: computers and information technology and biotechnology.

Technology and the Technological Environment

Technology means many things to many people. In this chapter, **technology** will refer to the "totality of the means employed to provide objects necessary for human sustenance and comfort." It is also seen as a scientific method used in achieving a practical purpose.[11] Technology refers to all the ways people use inventions and discoveries to satisfy their needs and desires. Taken together, these technological advances have made work easier and more productive.[12] But, technology has also introduced new challenges. From a productivity perspective, it is little surprise that businesses have embraced and used technology as much as or more than any other sector of society.

In Chapter 1, we discussed the macroenvironment of business and how this total environment was composed of a number of significant and interrelated segments such as the social, economic, political, and technological environments. The **technological environment** represents *the total set of technology-based advancements or progress taking place in society.* Pertinent aspects of this segment include new products, processes, materials, states of knowledge, and scientific advancements in both theoretical and applied senses. The rate of change and complexity of the technological environment have made it of special interest to business today. Consider the following examples. An electronic greeting card that today plays "Happy Birthday" holds more computing power than existed in the world before 1950. One of today's home video cameras wields more processing power than the old IBM 360, the wonder machine that launched the age of mainframe computers. Computers are being used to aid scientists in comprehending the secrets of matter at the atomic level and to create amazing new materials.[13] In the exploding information technology realm and the burgeoning field of biotechnology, the shape of how we are living, what products we are using, and what processes we are being exposed to is changing at an accelerating pace.

Characteristics of Technology

We have moved from a world characterized by industrial technology to one dominated by information technology and biotechnology. Whatever the technological level of advancement, there are general benefits and undesirable side effects of technology as well as ethical challenges inherent in technological advancements.

Benefits of Technology

Few would dispute that society has benefited greatly from technology and innovation. We live better lives today as employees, consumers, and members of the community due to technology. Technology has helped us gain control over nature and to build civilizations. Through the ages, technology has benefited society in four main ways.[14] First, it has increased society's production of goods and services, a benefit attributable chiefly to the business sector. Second, it has reduced the amount of labor needed to produce goods and services. Third, it has made labor easier and safer. Fourth, higher standards of living have been a direct result of labor-saving technology.[15]

The benefits of technology are vast. In an excellent book, *A Culture of Improvement*, Robert Friedel surveys the entire past millennium of technological advancement. He explains how we have moved from horsepower to jet engines, from Gothic vaults to skyscrapers, from Gutenberg to Google. Friedel helps us see how society has benefited from technological innovation, but he also points out many of the flaws and entanglements that have arisen due to technology.[16]

Side Effects of Technology

Though technologies have benefited people in many ways, there have also been some unanticipated side effects as well—problems, issues, or effects not anticipated before technologies were designed and implemented. One major reason for this is that technologies are often implemented before possible side effects, ethical problems, or downside risks are considered.

Four categories of undesirable side effects of technology are worth noting. First, there is *environmental pollution*. This ranks as one of the most undesirable side effects of technology. Second, there is *depletion of natural resources*. The rapid advance of technology continually threatens the supply of natural resources. Fuel and power shortages have become a way of life. Third is the issue of *technological unemployment*. The most common form of technological unemployment occurs when machines take the place of humans, as we experienced in the automation phase of industrial development and now in the robotic movement. Fourth is the *creation of unsatisfying jobs* due to technology. Many jobs in the technological world fail to give the workers a sense of accomplishment. As jobs are broken down into smaller components, each individual worker is further removed from the finished product that might provide a greater sense of fulfillment and pride. Monotony and boredom can easily set in when jobs are significantly shaped by certain technological processes.[17]

Challenges of Technology

New technologies present many challenges to managers, organizations, and society. Foremost among these is anticipating and avoiding the unwanted side effects. Some side effects cannot be forecast or overcome, of course, but much more could be done to alleviate them. Overcoming the technological determinism that seems to be driving society today would be helpful. For example, one of the most controversial issues today in the realm of biotechnology is that of human cloning. It is difficult to get the scientists and researchers to slow down and talk about the possible consequences (practical and ethical) of human cloning. Many of them seem driven by the technological capacities for achieving it instead of asking the important questions concerning ethics and side effects. One expert said, "If we can clone a human, we will."

Another challenge lies in spreading the benefits of technology, which are primarily restricted to the developed world. The developing nations enjoy few of the benefits of technology enjoyed in the developed nations.[18] Though there is a trend towards U.S. businesses moving production operations back to the states, as multinationals invest in emerging economies the opportunities for technology transfer will remain. The challenge, of course, is to move technologies to other countries in socially responsible ways.

Technology and Ethics

Technology unquestionably has many benefits for humankind. Our perspective at this juncture, however, is to raise the ethical questions that may be related to business development and use of technology and innovation. To do so does not mean that one is against technology. It simply means that one is concerned about the ethical use and implications of technology. Like management decision making and globalization of business, the actions of the business community with respect to technology have ethical implications that should be identified and discussed. Managements need to ask "who will be hurt and in what ways" by technology. Management's goal should be to avoid immoral and amoral practices with respect to technology and to move toward a morally sustainable posture with respect to this potent business resource.

Spotlight on Sustainability

Technology Meets Sustainability

It is increasingly evident that technology is a vital key to sustainability and sustainable development.

Science and Innovation for Sustainability The Forum on Science and Innovation for Sustainable Development is an attempt to sketch out the mushrooming field. Rather than looking broadly at sustainability, the forum focuses on the way in which science, innovation, and technology can be conducted and applied to meet human needs while preserving the life-support systems of the planet. The forum highlights people and programs that are studying nature–society interactions and applying the resulting knowledge to create a sustainability transition around the world.

Advancing *Global Sustainability* **through Technology** An excellent example of technology contributing toward sustainability is the microchip. Intel represents an interesting case study. Intel began working with the Environmental Protection Agency (EPA) to proactively address its industry's impact on global climate change and help support a sustainable future. As demand for computing performance increases, so does the need for more energy-efficient platforms. Intel worked with the EPA to develop the latest ENERGY STAR computer specifications that would deliver higher energy efficiency without compromising performance.

Sources: Forum: Science and Innovation for Sustainability, http://sustsci.aaas.org/. Accessed March 18, 2013; "How Innovation Supports Sustainability," http://www.dowcorning.com/content/publishedlit/solarticles/How_Innovation_Supports_Sustainability.pdf. Accessed March 18, 2013.Intel, "EPA & Intel–Advancing Sustainability," http://www.intel.com/technology/epa/?iid=SEARCH. Accessed February 23, 2013; Energy Star, http://www.energystar.gov/. Accessed March 18, 2013.

Applying business ethics to questions involving technology is simply an extension of our discussions of business ethics up to this point. The goal of managers and businesses striving to be ethical should be to avoid harm and to do what is morally justified and fair. In making ethical judgments, the prevailing norms of acceptability regarding technology must be tested by the principles of fairness and justice, protection of rights, and utilitarianism. The goal should be to reconcile and build bridges over the gap between "what is" and "what ought to be."

Two Key Ethical Issues

There are two key ethical issues in the realm of technology that seem to drive everything. First is the idea of technological determinism. **Technological determinism** is the imperative that "what *can* be developed *will* be developed." When someone once asked, "why do we want to put men on the moon?" the answer was always "because we *can* put men on the moon." In other words, scientists and those who work with advanced technologies are driven to push back the frontiers of technological development without consideration of ethical issues or side effects. The second important concept is that of ethical lag. **Ethical lag** occurs when the speed of technological change far exceeds that of ethical development.[19] Throughout our consideration of technology and ethics, these two phenomena are evident and influential.

Society's Intoxication with Technology

To emphasize the ethical dimension of technology, it is useful to note how society has become obsessed and intoxicated with technology and its power over our lives. Only by fully understanding the magnitude of this relationship society has with technology can we focus on the ethical aspects of it and the actions that should be taken. One way to appreciate what technology is doing to humankind is to consider the thoughts of John Naisbitt, Nana Naisbitt, and Douglas Philips, authors of the influential book *High Tech/High Touch*.[20]

In *High Tech/High Touch*, the authors call upon all members of society to understand and question the place of technology in our lives. They argue that our world has changed from a "technologically comfortable place" into a "technologically intoxicated zone." As the authors analyze the world, they conclude that there are six symptoms of society's intoxication with technology.[21] Some of these touch upon our character as a person, and some touch upon the ethical issues business faces with technology. The six symptoms are as follows:

1. We favor the quick fix. As we perceive a recurring void, we search for something and we want it quickly. Technology promises to detoxify us—to simplify our complex lives, relieve our stress, and calm our nerves. However, this Band-Aid® culture of the quick fix is ultimately an empty one.

2. We fear and worship technology. Our behavior moves us from the extremes of worship at one moment to fear the next. We accept technology, fearing that we will fall behind our competitors or coworkers. We worship technology but then feel frustrated and annoyed when it fails to deliver.

3. We blur the distinction between what is real and what is false. When technology can transform nature, we frequently ask, "Is that real, or is that false?" "Is it authentic or simulated?"

4. We accept violence as normal. Technology has made it possible for us to package violence in the form of merchandise, often spin-offs from television or movies. This violent material is often targeted at children.

5. We love technology as a toy. As affluence finances our play, leisure tends toward diversion—something to fill the time. We live in a culture dominated by consumer technology, where leisure is often passively received. Electronic distractions busy us as we can't find anything worthwhile to do.

6. We live our lives distanced and distracted. The Internet, smart phones, and wireless technologies connect us to the world, but when is it appropriate and when is it a distraction? Technology's bells and whistles are seductive, and they distance us, distract us, and annoy those around us.

The solution to this intoxication with technology is to find the right balance. That is, we need to embrace technology that preserves our humanity and reject technology that intrudes upon it. We need to know when we should push back on technology, in our work and our lives, and when to affirm our humanity. We need to understand that technology zealots are as shortsighted as technology bashers. We need to question the place of technology in our lives.[22]

There are a number of arenas in which specific issues of business ethics and technology might be explored. Research over the past few years reveals two broad categories of issues that now merit consideration: **information technology** and **biotechnology**. Each category is broad and deep, so we can consider them only in an introductory way in this chapter. Each, however, significantly involves business, either directly or indirectly. Within each, there are thousands of technologies that raise ethical questions. Our purpose, therefore, will be to focus on a few that give us a representative sample of ethical issues we face with technology.

Information Technology

Computer-driven information technology, or information technology (IT), as it is most often called, is deeply entrenched in all businesses and stakeholders involved in those businesses. Businesses and people both are affected by technology and are directly involved in pursuits based on technology. We will consider them both. We will discuss two broad areas in this section: *electronic commerce*, or Web-based marketing, and *computer technology in the workplace*, including telecommunications. These areas overlap significantly and are interdependent, so our separation is to lend some order to the discussion.

E-Commerce as a Pervasive Technology

Electronic commerce, often referred to as *e-commerce, e-business*, or *Web-based marketing*, is one of the most significant technological phenomena of our day. It primarily affects consumer stakeholders and competitors of the e-commerce firms. Most experts today are convinced that the Internet has reshaped the way business is conducted around the world. Part of this involves firms selling products and services online. Beyond this, companies are integrating the Internet into every aspect of their businesses.

Business via e-commerce is a multi-trillion dollar business, and 90 percent of it comes from business-to-business (B2B) sales. Consumer transactions are also huge and growing. The pull of e-business is powerful and companies are responding by moving their operations to the Internet. Companies are spending billions of dollars linking customers, sales, and marketing over the Web, increasingly through social networking. In short, electronic commerce is a flourishing business, and the opportunity for questionable practices arises along with this growth.

Online scams Along with the growth of electronic commerce, business ethics problems have arisen as well. The major category of problems is **online scams**. According to Internet Fraud Watch, con artists are taking advantage of the Internet's growth in popularity to bilk the unwary. During one recent year, for example, the top frauds over the Internet included fake check scams, prizes/sweepstakes/free gifts, phishing/spoofing, advance fee loans, friendship scandals, Nigerian money offers, Internet auctions, family/friend imposters, and scholarships/grants.[23] Other scams included credit card fraud, travel and vacation scams, pyramid schemes, and bogus investment opportunities. Virtually all of these scams are delivered via technology: the World Wide Web, telephone and e-mail using technologies such as wire transfers, credit cards, bank account debits, and bank debit cards.[24]

Ongoing Issues in E-Commerce Ethics

Ongoing issues in e-commerce ethics include the following:[25] access, intellectual property, privacy and informed consent, protection of children, security of information, and trust. These ethical issues are not restricted to e-commerce. They also occur in brick-and-mortar businesses. The manifestations and scope of these issues, however, differ from those of traditional businesses. *Access* refers to the difference in computer access between the rich and the poor. *Intellectual property* in e-commerce is illustrated by the ethics of downloading music or books. *Privacy and informed consent* differ in e-commerce. An example is the novel ways companies place cookies on our computers without informed consent. In addition, firms collect online information and merge it with offline information. *Protection of children* is an important ethical issue, and it is illustrated in the issue of pornography. E-commerce makes porn more accessible than through traditional businesses. *Security* is such a major issue that even today some are reluctant to do business on the Web for fear their credit card numbers will be intercepted by someone not associated with the e-commerce business. Finally, *trust* is the basis for practically all business transactions, and it is especially crucial in e-commerce.[26]

Invasion of Consumer Privacy via Electronic Commerce

The average person encounters two forms of Internet electronic commerce: business-to-consumer (B2C) transactions and business-to-business (B2B) transactions. Most of us are quite familiar with B2C transactions when we do personal business on the Internet—buying products and services, arranging credit cards, accessing travel Web sites, and doing financial business such as personal banking. As employees, we also encounter B2B transactions which are anticipated to be the greatest area of e-commerce growth in the coming years. One reason for this is the rapid globalization of commerce. In terms of Web-based marketing to consumers, consumer stakeholders are primarily affected by such issues as database sharing, identity theft, and invasion of privacy. Invasion of privacy is a legitimate concern in all business transactions; however, the special case of electronic commerce or Web-based marketing deserves special attention because of the ease with which data can be stored and transmitted in electronic form. The new world of Big Data has accelerated this trend.

A classic illustration of a potential invasion of privacy was that of DoubleClick Inc., the New York-based Internet advertising company that planned to share customer information with an offline marketing firm. Consumer advocates were up in arms that DoubleClick would betray such confidential information. Another example occurred when Toysmart.com, Inc., went out of business and offered its online customer list for sale, thus violating privacy agreements and understandings previously made with customers. Questions that arose from such situations included "What limits should there be on how online businesses use the information they gather about their customers?" and "What responsibility do companies have to publicly disclose such practices?"[27]

One of the most important ethical issues with respect to doing business over the Internet is the question of invasion of consumer privacy.[28] Business executives and private citizens alike are spending more time today thinking about consumer privacy. Figure 9-1 summarizes some of the concerns that privacy advocates and law enforcement experts have about the Internet's threat to privacy.

Some of the technological means by which companies invade consumers' privacy include the use of cookies and spam. **Cookies** are those little identification tags that Web sites drop on our personal computer hard drives so they can recognize repeat visitors the next time we visit their Web sites.[29] Surveys show that some consumers don't know what cookies are; others are aware of them but don't take the time to block them.[30]

Spam is unsolicited commercial e-mail. It is sent through "open-relays" to millions of persons. It takes a toll on Internet users' time, their resources, and the resources of Internet service providers (ISPs). Another problem is that spammers have begun to send advertisements via text messages to cell phones.[31] Many consumers interpret the receipt of *spam* as a rude invasion of their privacy. Opening our e-mail mailboxes only to find a few dozen unsolicited ads is annoying, at the least, and an invasion of privacy to many. Also, some companies experiment with pop-up pulsing background ads that never go away. Interestingly, dozens of companies make programs that protect our e-mail privacy, block cookies, and filter spam and porn, but very few consumers bother to use them.[32]

Collection and use of personal information is a serious invasion of privacy with respect to electronic commerce. Though non-Internet companies have engaged in this practice for years, everything seems magnified in the e-world in which we now live. None of us really knows how much personal information is collected, saved, swapped, or sold in e-commerce. Thousands of retailers, from department stores to catalog companies, collect and store personal information, from asking customers for their Zip codes to collecting names, addresses, household income, and purchasing patterns through a store credit card. Retailers also share, exchange, and even sell their customer databases to other companies. In short, the average consumer has very little control over what is

FIGURE 9-1 Major Threats to Consumers' Privacy Posed by the Internet

Threats to Privacy	Description
Social networks	Social networks allow individuals to establish connections and store information remotely. Default privacy settings provide too much personal information online. This information creates a field day for identity thieves, hackers, scammers, debt collectors, employers, marketers, data miners, and governments.
Hackers	Organized cybercriminals known as hactivists participate in phishing, online shopping fraud, banking fraud, and other deceptions.
Behavioral advertising	HTTP cookies, flash cookies, sites that respawn HTTP cookies with Flash (KISSmetrics), and HTML5 Local storage (more flexible than standard HTTP cookies). These are a few of the methods used for tracking online users. These techniques create a behavioral profile of you that is then used for exploitation.
Data stealing	Done through rogue applications on social networking sites—computers that harbor botnets. (Coreflood) and smartphone malware (DroidDream) are a couple that may be after you.
Facial recognition technology	Once used for security and surveillance. Now in the public realm with apps such as Social Camera and Scene Tap. Facebook deployed Facial-recognition software allows Facebook to gather data or recognize your face. Then people can be searched for using a picture.
GEO-Tags	Used when photos or videos are taken with a GPS equipped device (e.g., smartphone). Photos are embedded with a geo-tag revealing exact location of where taken. Revelation of geo-locational data on social networking sites creates danger of social surveillance and stalking.

Sources: "Cocoon's 2011 List of Top Internet Privacy Threats," http://blog.getcocoon.com/2011/10/13/cocoons-2011-list-of-thetop-10-internet-privacy-threats/. Accessed February 23, 2013; "The Top Ten Online Privacy Threats," http://www.mywot.com/en/blog/156-the-top-10-online-privacy-threats. Accessed February 23, 2013; Reputation.com, "The Top Five Threats to Your Online Privacy," http://www.reputation.com/reputationwatch/articles/top-five-threats-your-online-privacy. Accessed February 23, 2013.

done with his or her personal data once it is collected.[33] A continuing concern is **identity theft** or someone tampering with one's financial accounts. Less serious is the inundation of marketing attempts, both online and offline, that consumers are subjected to as a result of information being distributed.

Botnet scams, one of the latest techniques by which hackers get access to personal and corporate information, are exploding in numbers. *Bots* are computers that have been compromised by unethical hackers. A network of bots, called a *botnet*, is created by e-mails that get distributed by these compromised computers, and these are controlled by a central computer called the command-and-control server.[34] Experts say that on any given day now, 40 percent of the 800 million computers hooked up to the Internet are infected and made a part of botnets that continue to distribute e-mail spam and malware, steal sensitive data, bombard Web sites, and spread fresh infections.[35] Recently, it was estimated that 73 percent of e-mails contained spam, one in 106 e-mails contained a virus, and one in 99 e-mails contained some form of a phishing attack. These numbers increase every year. Botnets are not only the way our personal information is compromised, but they represent the greatest threat to data security for businesses and governments today.[36]

At a personal level, many individuals are losing their privacy through the use of **social networking sites** such as Facebook, Twitter, LinkedIn, Pinterest, and others. Cybercriminals are now accessing social networking accounts and stealing personal information. Social networks provide a rich repository of information that cybercriminals can use to fine-tune their other computer attacks. Twitter accounts are likewise vulnerable to data theft. Once stolen credentials occur, they often appear on eBay-like hacking forums where they are sold in batches of 1,000. By one account, 1,000 Facebook user names and passwords, guaranteed to be valid, were selling for up to $200. Cyber scammers can acquire e-mail addresses, contact lists, birthdates, home towns, and mothers' maiden names, which all then become useful for targeting specific victims.[37]

Government's Involvement in Consumer Privacy Protection The federal government has become involved in protecting consumers' privacy, but many observers believe it is not doing enough.[38] The Financial Services Modernization Act of 1999 was the breakthrough legislation that permitted banks, insurers, and brokers to join forces. Under the law, it is now possible for consumers to get their credit cards, checking accounts, investments, home loans, and health insurance from one company. This is convenient for consumers. However, the law also empowered these companies to develop exceptionally detailed profiles of their customers just by merging files about their income, assets, debts, health, spending habits, and other personal data. Increasingly, this sensitive data is becoming a public commodity.[39]

Over the past several years, a number of different bills designed to protect consumer privacy on the Internet have been filed but have not yet been passed. Many of the legislators have been uncertain whether a broad privacy bill is even needed or what it should look like. In February 2012, the White House issued a proposed Consumer Privacy Bill of Rights.[40] Figure 9-2 summarizes its provisions. Like so many proposals, the proposed Privacy Bill of Rights had not been adopted into law by Congress.

The Federal Trade Commission (FTC) is the primary government agency concerned with protecting consumers' privacy today. Under the FTC Act, the commission guards against unfairness and deception. The primary legislation now governing consumers' privacy includes the Financial Services Modernization Act (Gramm–Leach–Bliley Act), concerned with financial privacy; the Fair Credit Reporting Act; and the Children's Online Privacy Protection Act.[41] Other legislation regulating consumer and employee privacy may come soon, but Congress seems preoccupied with other priorities.

In 2012, the FTC issued its most recent report on what it considers to be the "best practices" companies should follow in protecting consumer privacy. Each of these recommended best practices are just one part of the FTC's recommended privacy framework:[42]

1. *Privacy by Design*. Companies should "build in" privacy at every stage of product development.
2. *Simplified Choice for Consumers and Businesses*. Consumers should be given the ability to make decisions about their data at a relevant time and context, including through a Do Not Track mechanism, while reducing the burden on businesses of providing unnecessary choices; and
3. *Greater Transparency*. Make information collection and use practices transparent.

With this report, the FTC has called on companies to act now to implement best practices in protecting consumers' privacy. FTC argues that privacy protection should be the default setting for commercial data practices. The FTC has again called on Congress to enact baseline privacy legislation.[43]

FIGURE 9-2 Proposed Consumer Privacy Bill of Rights

The proposed Consumer Privacy Bill of Rights would apply to personal data and contain the following provisions:

1. INDIVIDUAL CONTROL: Consumers have a right to exercise control over what personal data companies collect from them and how they use it.

2. TRANSPARENCY: Consumers have a right to easily understandable and accessible information about privacy and security practices

3. RESPECT FOR CONTEXT: Consumers have a right to expect that companies will collect, use, and disclose personal data in ways that are consistent with the context in which consumers provide the data.

4. SECURITY: Consumers have a right to secure and responsible handling of personal data.

5. ACCESS AND ACCURACY: Consumers have a right to access and correct personal data in usable formats, in a manner that is appropriate to the sensitivity of the data and the risk of adverse consequences to consumers if the data is inaccurate.

6. FOCUSED COLLECTION: Consumers have a right to reasonable limits on the personal data that companies collect and retain.

7. ACCOUNTABILITY: Consumers have a right to have personal data handled by companies with appropriate measures in place to assure they adhere to the Consumer Privacy Bill of Rights.

Sources: Consumer Data Privacy in a Networked World: A Framework For Protecting Privacy and Promoting Innovation in the Global Digital Economy, February 23, 2012, Washington, DC: The White House, http://www.whitehouse.gov/sites/default/files/privacy-final.pdf. Accessed February 25, 2013.

Business Initiatives with Consumer Privacy Protection. There are a number of different ways companies are striving to protect the privacy of their customers in electronic commerce.

Ethical Leadership First, business needs to recognize the potential ethical issues involved in electronic commerce and be committed to treating customers and all affected stakeholders in an ethical fashion. This commitment and ethical leadership undergirds all other initiatives. This ethical leadership must begin with the board of directors, the CEO, and top management. Every principle discussed in Chapter 8 about top management leadership applies to this discussion as well.

Privacy Policies Companies may take the initiative with their own carefully crafted privacy policies designed to protect customers. An example of this might be a company deciding to do more than the law requires. A company that has gone to great lengths to explain its privacy policy to customers and guests is the Walt Disney Company. On its Web site, it provides the following statement regarding its privacy policy:

> *Our updated policy is designed to provide greater transparency into our privacy practices and principles, in a new format that is easier to navigate, read and understand. We continue to treat your personal information with care and respect.*[44]

One of the most significant advances in privacy policies has been made by Microsoft. Microsoft has decided to amend its privacy policies so that consumers will have greater control over what the company does with information it gathers about their online purchasing behavior.[45] The company plans to allow certain users to decline to receive ads tailored to their Web-surfing habits, and it will also sever the connections recorded between information about a computer and the Web searches carried out from that machine after about a year and a half.[46] These initiatives on the part of Microsoft are commendable, but they only scratch the surface of the issue on customer privacy.

Chief Privacy Officers   An innovative approach to protecting consumers' privacy has been the increasing use of a **chief privacy officer (CPO)** in a number of major companies. Companies including American Express, Sony Corporation, Citigroup, IBM, and Facebook have appointed their own privacy chiefs.[47] It has been estimated that there are now more than 2,000 such positions around the country, and their numbers may swell in the next few years.[48] In other companies, these responsibilities are falling under the administration of a chief technology officer.

It is the primary responsibility of the CPO to keep a company out of trouble, whether in a court of law or in the court of public opinion. This includes developing Internet policies, helping their companies avoid consumer litigation, creating methods of handling and resolving consumer complaints, and assessing the risk of privacy invasion of company activities and practices. Because the position is relatively new at most companies, these newly appointed individuals are still trying to figure out what they need to be doing.[49] The job is a challenging one. CPOs must balance their customers' right to privacy with the employer's need for information for financial purposes.[50] CPOs were all the rage in the early 2000s, but the economic downturn has slowed down the movement. As the economy is perking back up, CPOs, once again, will likely become popular.

CPOs also play a role in helping to ensure employee as well as consumer privacy. CPOs are relevant to the section of this chapter on the workplace and they are brought up again in Chapter 18, where employees' rights to privacy are discussed further.

Data Security   One of the clearest ways companies can protect the information of their customers is through data security systems and practices. It turns out that data breaches are on the rise. Data security and cybercrime are among the biggest threats companies face today. FBI Director Robert Mueller told the Senate Select Committee on Intelligence that cyber-espionage and computer crime soon could surpass terrorism as the primary threat facing America and developed nations.[51]

Companies are struggling to keep customer and employee data secure. Cybercriminals are using more sophisticated techniques, including botnets, for breaking into businesses. Businesses are creating, storing, and sharing more data than ever before, and many employees simply do not understand the value and personal nature of the data they work with and the countless ways that data can fall into the wrong hands. These challenges make data security extremely difficult. Companies don't lose their data; they lose the customers' and employees' data and most of these groups seem powerless to stop it. Even though 44 states have laws requiring businesses to disclose data breaches, one major study showed that these laws do not reduce the incidents. Penalties are not large enough to deter security breaches. Either government needs to create stronger incentives, or companies need to become more ethical with respect to protecting private data.[52]

Data breaches that have occurred in recent years point out the strong need for companies, governments, and individuals to make data security a number one priority. Companies have an ethical responsibility to protect data in spite of the lack of severe penalties for failing to do so.

Questionable Businesses and Practices   Several questionable businesses and practices have been made possible by electronic commerce and the use of the Internet. Three business categories that are viewed as questionable by many include Web-based pornography, Internet gambling, and Web-based downloading of music, movies, books, and other copyrighted digital materials. Many ethical questions have been raised concerning Internet porn and Internet gambling. The Internet porn industry has become so controversial that the U.S. Supreme Court is now hearing cases as to whether the industry is violating the Child Pornography Prevention Act of 1996 and the Communication Decency Act.

Illegal Downloading   The illegal downloading of music, movies, television shows, and other copyrighted works continues to be a serious, questionable practice because it represents theft of intellectual property. This practice received significant media coverage in early 2013 when Aaron Swartz, an Internet activist, hanged himself just before facing felony charges and 30 years in prison for illegally downloading five million academic journal articles from an MIT database that required charges for access. Prosecutors were using the 1986 Computer Fraud and Abuse Act, an anti-hacking law, to charge Swartz with criminal offenses.[53]

Recently, the Copyright Alert System created by the film and music industries has been initiated to catch consumers who may be engaging in theft using peer-to-peer software. Under the new system, complaints will trigger Internet service providers—for example, Verizon, AT&T, Comcast—to notify a customer whose Internet address has been detected sharing files illegally. Then, the individual will be given a limited number of chances to stop before the Internet provider will take more extreme steps, such as temporarily slowing their connection. Time Warner Cable has stated that after the first four notifications it will lock down the offenders' browser until they call and show that they understand what they have done and will agree to stop.[54] Proponents of the new technology claim the focus is on educating consumers and they admit that it is unlikely to deter extreme violators. Already, five Internet service providers have agreed to participate in the program.[55]

For the past several years, university students in the United States have been a leading target of a litigation campaign carried out by the Recording Industry Association of America (RIAA). RIAA is the music industry trade group that has found university campuses to be hotbeds of file-sharing activity.[56] In reflecting on this issue, one student observed that downloading was so easy and there is so much free content on the Internet that it's hard to discriminate between illegal downloading, streaming free content, and just copying something from a friend's laptop. The student went on to observe that when a product is digital, it doesn't feel like stealing. Over the past decade, peer-to-peer technology companies have transformed continuously and speedily, making it ever more complicated to police.[57] In spite of this, laws and ethics are being violated and these examples illustrate how Internet technology has threatened legitimate businesses.

Monitoring Technology   Another practice that has raised many questions is the use of technology to monitor consumers as they use a company's products. An extreme example of the monitoring technology was illustrated when an individual rented a vehicle from Acme Rent-a-Car in New Haven, Connecticut, only to find out later that he was the unwitting victim of a global positioning system (GPS) device planted in the minivan he leased. The surveillance device recorded him speeding in three states at rates from 78 to 83 mph, and each violation, digitally recorded, automatically added a $150 charge to his bill.[58] Unbeknownst to most car owners today, black boxes, officially called Event Data Recorders (EDR) are being installed in virtually all recent-model cars and these track your seat belt use, speed, steering, braking, and other data. These EDRs are about the size of a deck of cards. They were initially designed to analyze the cause and effects of crashes to improve safety, but their data has many other potential uses by insurance companies, police, lawyers, and others. Ninety-six percent of all new cars already have them.[59] The use of GPS, EDR, and other technologies is becoming commonplace and consumers need to be aware of how they are being tracked.

Phishing   One of the most serious problems in the realm of computer scams against consumers continues to be the ongoing scam identified as **phishing**. An example of this occurred when a hacker who goes by the cyber name of Robotector sent an e-mail with the subject line "I still love you" to three million people. Within the message had been planted a small computer virus that, when executed, began to record user names and passwords each time their owner visited more than 30 online banks or payment Web sites. Then, this information was secretly e-mailed back to Robotector. This technique is called "phishing" because it lures prey (computer users) with convincing bait into revealing passwords and other private data. The Anti-Phishing Working Group, an industry association, reports that more than 50,000 reports of phishing scams per month were being reported by late 2012.[60] These are just a sampling of the kinds of controversial ethical issues that arise in connection with electronic commerce. As the Smart Revolution takes over all our consumer products, there will be plenty to worry about in the realm of consumer privacy.[61]

The Workplace and Computer Technology

Whereas computer-based information technology creates ethical issues for consumer stakeholders with respect to electronic commerce and Web-based marketing, employee stakeholders also are significantly affected by technology in the workplace. We will discuss these issues in more detail, especially employee privacy, in Chapter 18.

Biometrics   After a decade of talk, the newly emerging field of biometrics is starting to take off, especially in commercial applications. **Biometrics** is the use of body measurements, such as eye scans, fingerprints, or palm prints for determining and confirming identity. The technology of biometrics typically conjures up images of Big Brother surveillance tactics, and it has met resistance in cases where the government has wanted to use it for identification purposes. What seems to be speeding up its use, however, are commercial applications that provide assistance for consumers.[62] Resistance to government applications continues to be strong.

Only in the past several years there has been an explosion of applications in the commercial use of biometrics.[63] In several places now, consumers can scan their fingers or wave their palms over a scanner to gain access to accounts and safe deposit boxes or to make purchases. In Japan, contactless palm scanners are now being used when people want to withdraw cash from a cash point. In the Netherlands, a Dutch bank will be rolling out a system whereby customers may use their voices through voice analysis technology in a telephone banking system. Already, one can purchase laptop computers and mobile phones that come with built-in finger scanners. Other domestic applications include biometric door locks, garage locks, and safe locks. Even online services now respond to the rhythm and other characteristics of a person's typing, using a template of your "keystroke dynamics." There are flash drives that work only when activated by your thumbprint.[64] In short, biometrics is revolutionizing the way business is conducted and is expected to grow in the future.

Like most technologies, biometrics has many advantages and some possible downside risks. At the moment, the focus has not been on the legal and ethical risks associated with biometrics, but this is an issue that companies, consumers, and employees will want to watch carefully in the future. The potential abuses and invasions of privacy are many and must be watched carefully. It is an issue that top managers and privacy officers will want to monitor closely.

ETHICS IN PRACTICE CASE

Personal Technology in the Workplace

Increasingly, especially in small businesses, companies are permitting employees to use their own personal technology on the job. Smartphones, laptops, and tablets are the primary technologies being used. As of 2012, 35 percent of small companies and close to 50 percent of large companies were permitting the use of personal technology on the job, according to Ponemon Institute LLC, a technology-research organization in Michigan.

The benefits to small businesses are several. If companies allow employees to use personal technologies at work, they do not have to spend as much on technology resources themselves. Plus, many employees are more comfortable using their own equipment, and it is portable so they can take it with them. Companies also benefit because the employees in possession of their personal devices are "always working."

But, the use of many gadgets leads to many risks. One major risk is that lost or stolen devices can lead to huge headaches for companies. Once lost or misplaced, others can access company information some of which may be confidential or proprietary. Most companies do not implement basic policies such as requiring lock codes on the personal devices when they are used at work.

Another big issue is misappropriation. Personal devices make it much easier for employees to take information when they leave. Thus, private information may get in the hands of competitors. Viruses and other malware is another troubling issue. Frequently, employees do not keep virus protection on their personal devices up to date and an infected device could create problems throughout a company's network.

As work steadily spills into personal lives and companies continue to allow personal devices to be used on the job, the dividing line between work lives and personal lives begins to blur. This will pose additional problems for organizational members in the future.

1. What are the ethical issues at stake when companies permit employees to use personal technologies on the job? What are the implications for all stakeholders?
2. On balance, should companies continue to allow personal technological devices on the job or should they disallow them? If they allow them, what policies should be put in place?

Sources: Ponemon Institute, "Risk of Insider Fraud," http://www.ponemon.org/blog/risk-of-insider-fraud-second-annual-study. Accessed April 27, 2013; Laura Petrecca, "Always Working," *USA Today*, March 7, 2013, 1A; Emily Maltby, "Many Gadgets, Many Risks," *The Wall Street Journal*, November 12, 2012, R6; Barry Levine, "BYOD Alert: Personal Smartphones Heavily Used at Work," CMS Wire, March 25, 2013, http://www.cmswire.com/cms/information-management/byod-alert-personal-smartphones-heavily-used-for-work-company-compensation-or-security-not-so-much-020185.php. Accessed April 27, 2013.

Other Technology Issues in the Workplace

Surveillance extends beyond companies monitoring e-mail and Internet usage. In addition to these activities, other forms of surveillance include monitoring faxes, using video cameras in the workplace, drug testing, doing online background checks, logging photocopies, and recording phone calls. Each of these poses implications that must be considered from an ethical perspective.

The world of security via computers and technology entered a new era on September 11, 2001, as a result of the terrorist attacks on the World Trade Center in New York and the Pentagon in Washington, DC. People's attitudes changed somewhat as they realized that heightened security checks are needed to guard against terrorist attacks. These added security measures have begun in public institutions (airports, government buildings, and large entertainment venues), and they are spilling over into the employment arena as companies become more cautious about their own security. There is already evidence that some use of face-recognition technology, "active" badges that track where you are, and other such technology-driven security measures have landed squarely in the workplace.

There is further evidence that 9/11 spurred the development of smarter high-tech tools that are currently on the market and will in the future come to market for business use.[65]

Cell Phones and Texting. Although e-mail and the Internet most often create ethical problems in the workplace, the use of company-sponsored cell phones by employees represents one of the fastest-growing technologies with increasing ethical and legal implications. The use of a cell phone is no longer a private matter as job pressures are leading more and more employees to use the phones while driving. Because companies now make cell phones available to their employees, this issue spills over into the business arena and becomes a business ethics topic. Actually, cell phone use while driving is a public matter, because it significantly raises the risk of accidents that cause harm to others on the streets.[66] Increasingly, states are cracking down on drivers using cell phones and texting while driving. States are imposing much higher fines and companies are taking notice. More than 30 states already consider texting a primary offense.[67]

A case that dramatically brought this issue to public attention was reported in *The Wall Street Journal*. A San Francisco-based attorney was working the kind of fast-paced day that is becoming increasingly common. She was totaling her billable hours on her cell phone for her employer while driving to a scheduled 10 P.M. meeting with a client. This was typical for her—continuing to use her cell phone to perform work tasks and to make business calls while driving home. This night was out of the ordinary, however. As she talked, her car swerved and struck a 15-year-old girl who was walking on the shoulder of the road, throwing her fatally injured body down an embankment. The attorney later said she didn't even realize she had hit someone. She said it wasn't until morning when she was watching the news while dressing for work that she realized what she had done. She turned herself in and pleaded guilty to hit and run—a felony. The victim's family sought $30 million in damages from her employer.[68] In settlement, a jury ordered her to pay the victim's family $2 million. She also served one year in jail after pleading guilty to leaving the scene of an accident. Upon conviction, she also forfeited her license to practice law.[69] What appeared to her to be a simple, innocent daily transaction turned into a personal and professional nightmare for her and her employer.

A trend with huge implications for employers is the growing number of employees— managers, salespeople, consultants, lawyers, ad executives, and others—who are using cell phones for talking and texting while driving and chalking up sales or billable hours for the time spent doing so. Hundreds of millions of people in the United States alone subscribe to wireless communication devices. Research has documented that motorists who use cell phones while driving are four times as likely to get into crashes serious enough to injure themselves or others. Text messaging creates a crash risk 23 times worse than driving while not distracted.[70] There are two primary problems with people using such devices while driving. First, drivers have to take their eyes off the road while driving, and second, they can become so absorbed in their conversations that their concentration is severely impaired. This jeopardizes the safety of not only the vehicle's occupants, but also that of pedestrians and other vehicles.[71]

Plaintiffs are more frequently claiming that the employer is partly to blame because it presses employees to work long hours from distant locations, often encouraging them to use cell phones without setting safety guidelines. Research is increasingly documenting the dangers of cell phone talking and texting while driving. A study by an insurance company found that chatty drivers suffered slower reaction times, took longer to stop, and missed more road signs than drivers who were legally drunk. A new term has already been coined for accidents caused by cell phone-using drivers—DWY (driving while yakking).[72]

In a major court case, a New York investment banking firm was sued for damages in federal court by the family of a motorcyclist who was killed when one of its brokers, using a car phone, ran a red light and struck him. Plaintiffs claimed that employer pressure to contact clients after hours contributed to the tragedy, and the company settled the suit for $500,000.[73] Another civil case involving a car crash caused by a driver using a cell phone for business reasons was settled only when the driver's employer agreed to pay the plaintiff $5 million.[74]

Cases such as these—linked to cell phone technology—should raise red flags for employers and individuals concerned about their careers. Not enough companies have the needed policies on cell phone use at this time. It appears that as high-tech tools extend the workplace into every corner of life, too many companies have been leaving the responsibility entirely up to the employees. These cases are tragic examples of what can happen when employees, using technology, become too distracted, pressured, or overfocused on their work.[75] Businesses quickly are moving toward the adoption of policies prohibiting the use of cell phones while driving. One significant decision was made by the California Association of Employers when it recommended that all employers develop a cell phone policy that would require employees to pull off the road before conducting business on their cell phones.[76] A template for company cell phone usage policies has been provided by legalzoom.com.[77]

Robotics. Workers in escalating numbers recently have been losing their jobs due to the growth in the usage of robots in more and more industries. At one time it was thought that the move toward automation would create more jobs than it would displace, but that assumption is being called into question today. Some experts are now saying that the stubbornly high unemployment rates in the United States and Europe are at least partially due to the rise of the machines.[78] Robotics are becoming so advanced today that new questions about their impact on workers are being raised. For example, if robotics can restore one's mobility or sight, do we need to redefine what disability means? This, in turn, might conflict with the assumptions upon which disability rights laws have been established. Research studies are now underway examining how the law might deal with technologies that blur the distinction between humans and machines.[79]

An important editorial in *The Economist* argues that society needs to move quickly in developing ways of dealing with the ethics of robotics. It points out three areas where progress is needed in regulating the development and use of autonomous robots.[80] First, laws are needed to clarify who is at fault if a robotic device causes harm—the designer, programmer, manufacturer, or operator. Second, when ethical systems are embedded into robots, they need to be decision-making schemes that would seem right to most people. Third, collaboration is needed among engineers, ethicists, lawyers and policymakers who left to their own might come up with widely divergent rules.[81] The rise of robotics and its impact on the workplace will need to be monitored closely in the years to come.

Unethical Activities by Employees Related to Technology. In most of the instances described to this point, the employer has had responsibility for the use of technology and its implications. There is another area that should be mentioned: questionable activities that come from the employees. These activities have been aided by computer technologies at work. In a major study of workers, the following are unethical activities employees said they had engaged in during the previous year:[82]

- Created a potentially dangerous situation by using new technology while driving
- Wrongly blamed an error the employee made on a technological glitch
- Copied the company's software for home use
- Used office equipment to shop on the Internet for personal reasons

- Used office equipment to network/search for another job
- Accessed private computer files without permission
- Used new technologies to intrude on coworkers' privacy
- Visited porn Web sites using office equipment

Company Actions. Companies have many options for addressing the kinds of ethical issues described to this point. A major survey of Fortune 500 nonmanagement employees revealed that management should clearly define guidelines for ethical computer use by employees. Options for doing this include company management making these decisions, using the Information Systems Society's code of ethics, and involving employees and users in a collaborative attempt to decide upon computer ethics policies. Only about one-half of those surveyed indicated that company guidelines were written and well known.[83] Beyond this, companies should carefully think about the ethical implications of their use of technology and integrate decisions designed to protect employees into their policies and practices, especially their codes of conduct.

The technologies discussed to this point have been computer facilitated. Therefore, guidelines for employee computer use is helpful in many of the applications described. Several professional societies offer guidelines for computer use. Computer Professionals for Social Responsibility (CPSR) has set forth what it calls its "Ten Commandments of Computer Ethics." These guidelines are informative and useful, and are summarized in Figure 9-3.

Biotechnology

The 20th century's revolution in information technology is merging with the 21st century's revolution in biotechnology. Indeed, Walter Isaacson labeled the 2000s as the "biotech century."[84] At this time, we are undergoing the most significant breakthrough of all time—deciphering the human genome, tens of thousands of genes encoded by three billion chemical pairs in our DNA. Among other achievements, this accomplishment will lead to the next medical revolution, which will not only increase the natural life span of healthy human beings but will also help to conquer cancer, grow new blood vessels, block the growth of blood vessels in tumors, create new organs from stem cells, and much more.[85]

FIGURE 9-3
Ten Commandments of Computer Ethics

The Computer Ethics Institute has set forth the following ten commandments of computer ethics. These should prove useful to employees and employers alike.

- Thou shalt not use a computer to harm other people.
- Thou shalt not interfere with other people's computer work.
- Thou shalt not snoop around in other people's computer files.
- Thou shalt not use a computer to steal.
- Thou shalt not use a computer to bear false witness.
- Thou shalt not copy or use proprietary software for which you have not paid.
- Thou shalt not use other people's computer resources without authorization or proper compensation.
- Thou shalt not appropriate other people's intellectual output.
- Thou shalt think about the social consequences of the program you are designing.
- Thou shalt always use a computer in ways that ensure consideration and respect for your fellow humans.

Sources: Computer Ethics Institute, Computer Professionals for Social Responsibility, "Ten Commandments of Computer Ethics," http://cpsr.org/issues/ethics/cei/. Accessed February 26, 2013; Association for Computing Machinery, "Code of Ethics," http://www.acm.org/about/code-of-ethics. Accessed March 15, 2013.

Spotlight on Sustainability

Is Biotech Agriculture Sustainable?

When we think of sustainable agriculture we typically think of food products that have been organically grown. But, sustainable agriculture is not limited to organic production according to the Biotechnology Industry Organization (BIO). According to BIO, there is currently a new standard being developed under the auspices of the American National Standards Institute that will incorporate any technology that will increase agriculture sustainability. In BIO's perspective, biotech crops are sustainable and also good for the environment. They require fewer pesticides and employ farming techniques which improve soil health and retention of water. Through biotechnology, global pesticide use is down, soil erosion has been reduced, and fuel consumption has been reduced.

According to the Seed Biotechnology Center, genetically engineered (GE) crop varieties offer promising traits which will help increase health and nutrition, sustain farming on marginal lands, and decrease concerns with pests and disease. Currently, there are more than 100 agricultural crops which have been genetically modified in research stations around the world, and five of the most promising traits which are being analyzed in numerous crops include: herbicide tolerance, insect resistance, stress tolerance, nitrogen use efficiency, and nutritional traits.

Sources: "The Sustainability of Biotechnology," Biotechnology Industry Organization, http://www.bio.org/articles/sustainability-biotechnology. Accessed April 2, 2013; "Biotechnology for Sustainability," Seed Biotechnology Center, http://sbc.ucdavis.edu/B4S/B4S.html. Accessed April 2, 2013; "Sustainable Biotechnology," http://sustainablebiotech.wordpress.com/. Accessed April 2, 2013.

The field of biotechnology carries with it significant implications for business and for business ethics, and we can only touch upon these issues here. In fact, we now have a burgeoning growth industry—the biotechnology industry. Biotechnology involves "using biology to discover, develop, manufacture, market, and sell products and services."[86] The biotech industry today consists of small entrepreneurial start-up companies funded largely by venture capitalists, along with dozens of larger, more established companies. Most of the applications of biotechnology are in health care, the pharmaceutical industry, and agriculture.[87] From a sustainability perspective, biotechnology is striving to *heal, fuel,* and *feed* the world.[88]

Bioethics

The field of **bioethics** has emerged that deals with the ethical issues embedded in the commercial use of biotechnology. As new biotech products are developed, thorny ethical issues inevitably arise. In recent years, the question has arisen regarding the federal government's role in bioethics and stem cells. One of the actions former President George W. Bush took was to create a presidential council on bioethics which continues today. A few of the council's ongoing issues of concern include bioethics, biotechnology and public policy, genome sequencing, human subjects research, cloning, genetics, organ transplantation, and stem cells.[89]

On the business front, some biotechnology companies have adopted the idea of bioethics to guide them in their decision making. A question that is being continually raised, however, is whether bioethical decision making is really taking place or whether the companies are using the bioethicists for public relations purposes. Companies such as Geron Corporation have pioneered the idea of a corporate bioethics advisory board. When the Jones Institute for Reproductive Medicine began its research on human embryos, it talked up the idea of panels of bioethicists.

According to William Saletan, who has written extensively about bioethics, the primary tool bioethicists use is *proceduralism*. This involves the establishment of elaborate protocols that ensure that certain classical worries, such as informed consent, are not violated. The focus is on being sure that appropriate procedures are being followed rather than on the actual ethical content of the decisions. This sounds much like the concept of ethical due process discussed in an earlier chapter. The worry continues, however, over whether corporate executives and scientists are deceiving their own consciences by focusing on the *how* rather than the *why*, or the *means* rather than the *end*.[90]

Both critics and supporters say that the use of bioethicists lends companies an air of credibility. The real question is, can they really be objective if they are on a company's payroll? Supporters say "yes," they function like a newspaper ombudsperson who gets paid by the paper to criticize coverage and prevent potential conflicts. Detractors say "no," there's no way around a conflict of interest if money is changing hands. A real danger is that the participation of bioethicists may be interpreted as a stamp of approval.[91]

A public policy expert has observed, "the biotech revolution has surged forward as the defining issue of the new century. On the one hand, it holds out great promise for medical advances enhancing life and health for all humankind. On the other, it raises unprecedented ethical issues." The expert goes on to observe, "the biotech revolution is moving like a steamroller, fueled by huge potential profits, crushing everything—including moral restraint—in its path."[92] It may be too early into the biotechnology revolution to know whether this will turn out to be the case; however, it is important to raise the issue of the balance between costs and benefits early on. Figure 9-4 lists several nonprofit bioethics organizations that may be found on the Web.

Of special interest in this section are two broad realms of biotechnology that help us appreciate some of the challenges in business ethics: **genetic engineering** and genetically modified foods (GMFs). Genetic engineering, primarily of humans, and genetic engineering of agricultural and food products are both part of genetic science. For discussion purposes, however, we will treat them separately. Genetic testing and profiling is another important issue that merits consideration.

Genetic Engineering

Two major areas of genetic engineering, or genetic science, seem to capture the public's imagination today. One is stem cell research, and the second is cloning. Both pose enormous and interesting challenges for business and business ethics.

Stem Cell Research. The basic building blocks that are the progenitors of all other cells were isolated in 1998 by scientists at the University of Wisconsin. These **embryonic stem cells** are the raw materials with which a human body is built. Since their isolation, stem cell research has been proliferating around the world. According to a member of the President's Council on Bioethics, the debate over stem cell research centers on one basic moral question: the moral status of a human embryo—the product of sperm and egg—and what constitutes a human being.[93]

The value of stem cells is that they offer the greatest hope for developing treatments for diseases such as cancer, Alzheimer's, Parkinson's, and juvenile diabetes.[94] Stem cells also can be used to replace other cells in the body that are abnormal or have been destroyed by disease.[95]

President George W. Bush (2001–2009) announced a decision to allow federal government funding for research only on stem cells that had already been harvested. By 2009, however, a majority of Americans supported President Obama's executive order doing away with the rules on federal funding of embryonic stem cell research that were in place under the Bush administration. In a 2012 Gallup poll, 58 percent of citizens surveyed

FIGURE 9-4

Web Sites of
Nonprofit Bioethics
Organizations

Bioethics is an expansive topic and there are many different organizations, especially public action organizations, that provide information regarding specific topics via the World Wide Web. Some of these include the following:

American Society for Bioethics + Humanities (http://www.asbh.org/)
The American Society for Bioethics and Humanities (ASBH) is a professional society of more than 1,500 individuals, organizations, and institutions interested in bioethics and humanities. The purpose of ASBH is to promote the exchange of ideas and foster multidisciplinary, interdisciplinary, and interprofessional scholarship, research, teaching, policy development, professional development, and collegiality among people engaged in all the endeavors related to clinical and academic bioethics and the health-related humanities.

GE Food Alert (http://www.gefoodalert. org/)
This is a Web page that primarily focuses on genetically modified foods (GMFs) and issues related to this topic. The organization defines key terms and posts what it considers are important food alerts and article about foods.

Do No Harm: The Coalition of Americans for Research Ethics (http://www. stemcellresearch.org/)
This organization is a national coalition of researchers, health-care professionals, bioethicists, legal professionals, and others dedicated to the promotion of scientific research and health care that does no harm to human life.

Council for Responsible Genetics (http:// www.councilforresponsiblegenetics.org/)
The council fosters debate on social, ethical, and environmental implications of new genetic technologies. CRG works through the media and concerned citizens to distribute accurate information and represent the public interest on emerging issues in biotechnology. The council publishes "GeneWATCH," a national bulletin on the implications of biotechnology.

Bioethics.net (http://www.bioethics.net/)
This Web page is quite extensive. It hosts the *American Journal of Bioethics.* In service to anyone interested in bioethics, the Web site publishes information on the latest journal publications, events, job opportunities and current news, as well as being a one-stop-shop of popular bioethics blogs.

National Human Genome Research Institute (http://www.genome.gov/A/)
This Web site hosts the Ethical, Legal, and Social Implications (ELSI) Research Program. This program supports basic and applied research that identifies and analyzes the ethical, legal, and social issues surrounding human genetics research.

thought stem cell research was morally acceptable and 33 percent thought it was morally wrong.[96] These data suggest that society is still somewhat divided over the issue. In spite of public opinion, companies and countries continue to push the issue. Companies want to develop cures for diseases and to have bragging rights about their technological superiority. This aggressive competition can lead to unethical practices, even fraud, and this is all the more reason why these issues have to be carefully watched.[97]

Most of the ethical debate over stem cell research has occurred in the public and political arenas, not business. Businesses are moving forward now even though the societal debate is not settled.[98] The pharmaceutical industry is one of the best illustrations of how companies are already moving on research. AstraZeneca and GlaxoSmithKline are two companies are on the cutting edge of stem cell research.[99]

Cloning Stem cell research is well under way. Now, **cloning** continues to be in the news. Some scientists say human cloning is a distant project; however, according to some reports, a few citizens are already lining up to freeze the DNA of their dead loved ones, including pets and racehorses. Several different groups have claimed they are attempting to clone a human being.

Actually, there are at least two debates surrounding cloning and genetic science. First, there is the issue of cloning human beings. Second, there is the issue of cloning animals and plants and using genetics to identify and fight diseases. This second quest is currently the primary focus of science. But it is the fascination with duplicating human beings that arouses the most debate and fear. Surveys in the United States show very little support for human cloning. According to a 2010 Gallup Poll, the last time the polling company pursued this question, 88 percent said cloning human beings was morally wrong while only 9 percent considered it morally acceptable.[100] By contrast, this same poll found that 63 percent thought cloning animals was morally wrong and 31 percent thought it was acceptable.

A variation of human cloning is known as **therapeutic cloning**. Therapeutic cloning uses the same laboratory procedures as reproductive cloning, but its aim is not procreation but rather the creation of a source of stem cells whose properties make them a possible source of replacement tissue for a wide range of degenerative diseases. Opponents of therapeutic cloning are opposed to the creation and destruction of human life for utilitarian ends. In addition, opponents fear the exploitation of women, especially in poor countries, for their eggs. On the other side of the issue, supporters want to give therapeutic cloning a chance because of its possible health advantages.[101]

Possible scenarios of therapeutic cloning have raised nightmare reactions in the minds of some. The chemicals in the human body were once estimated to be worth 89 cents. Now, however, according to the authors of a provocative—and some would say shocking—book, body parts in people and in corpses may be worth millions. In *Body Bazaar: The Market for Human Tissue in the Biotechnology Age*, Lori Andrews and Dorothy Nelkin talk optimistically about the commercialization of the human body in pursuit of new pharmaceuticals, organ transplants, and genetic research on individuals alive or dead. The book has ethicists again asking important questions: Do individuals have "rights" to their blood and tissue? Should body parts be bought and sold? Whose body is it, anyway?[102]

Andrews and Nelkin write, "whole businesses are developing around the body business. Companies have sprung up to make commercial products out of corpses' bones. Some grind up the bones into powder that, when sprinkled on broken live bones, will help them mend." They argue that body parts from the living and the dead are gold mines for pharmaceutical research. Some of the authors' writings raise provocative ethical questions that business must face: Who owns the rights to a corpse? What ethical considerations need to be evaluated when a researcher seeks to do genetic testing on long-deceased individuals? What are the ethical considerations associated with the morbid practice of using human body parts as a means of "expression"? An exhibition that has been on tour in recent years (*Bodies: The Exhibition*) depicts corpses with plasticized body parts, with flaps of skin open to display the anatomical features of the human body. Does this practice debase the sanctity of the human body?[103] Some think so, but tickets to the exhibitions continue to sell.

In an intended humorous insight into where cloning may be heading, a cartoon by Tom Toles depicted a man in an office sticking his head into the office copier; off to the side, there were cloned copies of him coming out of the machine. A sign on the wall stated, "July 2018. The ethical debate, part 2,473,561," and the question posed beneath the cartoon read: "Should employees be allowed to use the office cloning machine for personal business?"

Cloning Animals for Food. The burning issue on the cloning front is that of companies wanting to clone animals for food. Scientists and consumer experts in the United States have been debating whether the country should become the first in the world to allow food from cloned animals onto supermarket shelves. The Food and Drug Administration (FDA) held an open period for public comment on the issue. Thousands of consumers wrote to the FDA protesting allowing cloned foods into the food supply. One consumer said the thought was "unethical, disturbing, and disgusting."[104] Scientists and companies, however, almost completely support cloning for food, indicating they see the technology as an effective, important way to produce higher quality, healthier food. Based on a final risk assessment, FDA scientists issued a report in 2008, in which it concluded that meat and milk from cow, pig, and goat clones and the offspring of any animal clones are as safe as food we eat every day and this remains their latest position on the subject.[105] The FDA does continue to supervise regulations pertaining to this process. A related issue is whether food from cloned animals should be labeled as such. The FDA does not seem to think such labeling is necessary, but opponents say such labels are essential.

Opponents of cloning animals for food come from a large number of different consumer and scientific groups. Consumer advocate organizations such as the Center for Food Safety, Consumers Union, and the Consumer Federation of America, along with environmental and animal welfare groups, have protested the idea. They think there is inadequate data regarding the safety of such a practice and that there needs to be more review of the potential consequences of such a decision. A minority of scientists agree with the consumer groups that cloned animals should not enter the food supply.[106] This is likely to be an emotionally debated ethical issue for some time.

Genetic Testing and Profiling. One of the most questionable applications of biotechnology is in **genetic testing**. Genetic testing has many downside risks, especially from both a legal and an ethical perspective.[107] It is said that someday each of us will have a DNA chip that contains all our genetic information. There are some positives associated with this. It will help each person manage his or her own personal health risks. It will also help a physician predict how well a patient will respond to various therapies. Future drugs will be developed using genetic information so that the therapy will be coupled with the DNA information. The privacy invasion implications are staggering, however, and this continues to be a debated topic. One result of genetic testing can be **genetic profiling**. This provides a perfect means for identifying a person and thus raises questions of privacy and possible discrimination based on genetic factors.[108]

In 2008, then President George W. Bush signed into law the Genetic Information Nondiscrimination Act (GINA) that was intended to protect Americans against discrimination based on their genetic information when it comes to health insurance and employment.[109] Its implementation has been taking effect for several years now. It is too early to tell how vigorously this law will be enforced and whether it will achieve its desired goals.

Genetically Modified Foods

Another major category of biotechnology that carries important and more frequent ethical implications for business is that of **genetically modified foods (GMFs)**. This is especially the case for the multi-billion-dollar agribusiness industry. Many wholesalers and retailers, however, are also involved in the distribution of GMFs. GMFs are also commonly referred to as **genetically engineered foods (GEFs)**. Genetically modified foods are deeply embedded in the global food supply. In the United States, 94 percent of cotton, 93 percent of soybeans, 90 percent of canola, and 88 percent of corn involve crops that are genetically modified.[110] It is readily apparent that most of us are consuming GMFs on a regular basis.

Extreme critics of GMFs call them "Frankenfoods," referring to the parallels with the literary figure Frankenstein. The world today seems to be divided into those who favor

GMFs and those who fear them. Also, a significant number of consumers are simply not informed enough to know but are quick to offer their gut-reaction opinions, usually based on fear rather than facts. Because no one seems to have been "hurt" by GMFs, there is a lot of wild speculation as well as indifference at work in judging the ethics and implications of GMF.

Scant information is available to the public as to the actual safety or lack of safety of these products because field-testing continues and is seldom reported. According to the vice president for food and agriculture at the Biotechnology Industry Organization, "There is still not so much as a single, solitary sniffle or headache positively linked to their consumption."[111] According to the World Health Organization, GMFs currently available on the international market have passed risk assessments and are not likely to present risks for human health. In addition, no effects on human health have been shown as a result of the consumption of such foods by the general population in the countries where they have been approved.[112] Europe set up its own Food Standards Agency and through research has concluded that these technologies are safe.[113] Opponents of GMFs argue that we still do not know for sure that these technologies will be safe over the long term.

Will there be a consumer backlash against biotechnology in food production when the public becomes more familiar with it? Recently, more concern has been expressed about questionable food products, including seafood and vegetables being imported, than GMFs. It is an issue that merits continued close examination for both real and perceived reactions. The debate seems to hinge on whether the perceived pros or cons of GMFs will win out as the arguments are presented and experience is gained.

Labeling of GMFs. Since the safety of GMFs does not seem to be in question by scientific research, the more urgent issue has become the question of whether foods that contain GMFs should be labeled or not when they are sold in grocery stores. Many consumer activists think that, at a minimum, foods that contain genetically engineered ingredients ought to be labeled as such. The Consumer Federation of America Foundation, for example, issued a report recommending mandatory labeling and other ways to improve U.S. biotech food regulations. To date, the FDA has not mandated labeling of GMFs. The FDA has created new rules wherein biotech companies would have to meet with federal regulators before putting a new product on the market, but they would not require special product labels. The FDA has been working on the new guidelines in an attempt to reassure consumers that GMFs are safe.[114]

In spite of inaction on the part of the FDA, the labeling issue will not go away. Proponents of mandatory labeling argue that the consumer has a right to full disclosure about product contents and that the consumers' right to safety argues that such knowledge should be available to them. Of special concern, the organic and natural foods market segment fears that genetically modified crops may be slipping into its products. This market segment strongly supports the Non-GMO Project.[115] The Non-GMO Project has been advocating the *Non-GMO label*, which stands for "nongenetically modified organisms." The Non-GMO Project is a nonprofit collaboration of manufacturers, retailers, processors, distributors, farmers, seed companies, and consumers. The project's shared belief is that "everyone deserves an informed choice about whether or not to consume genetically modified products and our common mission is to ensure the sustained availability of non-GMO choices."[116]

The issue of labeling for GMOs moved center stage when the State of California had Proposition 37 placed on its ballot in fall 2012. Prop 37 would have made California the first state in the United States to require disclosure labels on all foods that contained any genetically engineered ingredients except meat, milk, alcohol or foods sold in restaurants.[117] The organizers of the California initiative were known as the California Right to Know campaign. Some of the companies supporting the initiative were from the natural foods industry and included Nature's Path Foods, Clif Bar, Annie's, and Stonyfield Farm. Once it became apparent that Prop 37 had significant support, opponent companies stepped up to the plate in opposition to the proposal. Opponents included Monsanto, DuPont, Pepsico, Kraft Goods, Coca-Cola, Nestlé, and General Mills, among others.[118] The primary argument by the opponents was that such labels make it seem like the GMO ingredients are unsafe, which they are not. One observer said that such labels would be the equivalent of a skull and crossbones[119] which is a universal identifier of poisonous products. The referendum to compel such labeling in California was narrowly defeated in November 2012 but similar bills are pending in several states to require such labeling.[120] Whole Food Markets, one of the supporters of the labeling proposition announced in early 2013 that on its own it would require all products sold at its stores in the United States and Canada to carry labels indicating whether genetically modified ingredients were contained in products sold by 2018.[121]

ETHICS IN PRACTICE CASE

Whole Foods and GMO Labeling

Whole Foods Market, long known to be a reformist, sustainability-oriented, supermarket chain selling natural products, startled the industry in early 2013 by announcing that it was embarking on a five-year plan to require labeling of genetically modified foods (GMFs) in its stores by 2018. Its decision came months after Proposition 37 in California was narrowly defeated in November 2012. Proposition 37 would have required disclosure labels on all foods that contained genetically engineered ingredients.

The U.S. Food and Drug Administration has found no research to support allegations that genetically engineered ingredients raise safety concerns greater than those found in traditionally grown products. And, the FDA has not issued any regulations requiring GMF labeling. The World Health Organization and the National Academy of Sciences have found no evidence GMFs are unsafe. But, critics persist and say that there still may be some unknown harmful effects that in time will be revealed.

In the California battle, large mainstream companies such as Pepsico, Kraft Foods, Coca-Cola, Nestlé, General Mills and Hershey opposed the labeling measure.

Supporters included smaller, natural foods companies such as Stonyfield Farm, Annie's, Clif Bar, Nature's Path Foods, and Whole Foods. Opponents of GMO labeling fear that such labeling will cause many consumers to think their products containing GMOs are unsafe.

Whole Foods has taken the position that the consumer has a right to know how its foods were produced and whether GMOs are present in any of its foods. The company already has seven stores in the U.K. which already require GMO labeling. The company also supports animal welfare, eco-friendliness, and sourcing origins.

1. Is the Whole Food's decision a sustainable decision? Explain.
2. Do consumers have a right to know whether GMFs are present in products even if research has never found dangers associated with them?
3. Will labeling raise fears among consumers that such foods are unsafe?
4. Do you think Whole Foods honestly thinks GMF labeling ought to occur or is the company doing this as a strategic, marketing decision?

Sources: Whole Foods Market, http://www.wholefoodsmarket.com, Accessed March 11, 2013; BBJ Morning Buzz, "Whole Foods to require genetically modified food labels by 2018," March 11, 2013, http://www.bizjournals.com/boston/blog/mass_roundup/2013/03/whole-foods-label-gmo.html, Accessed March 15, 2013; "Genetically Engineered Foods," Whole Foods Market, http://www.wholefoodsmarket.com/mission-values/environmental-stewardship/genetically-engineered-foods, Accessed March 11, 2013.

The issues of safety and labeling of GMFs will continue. Special-interest groups on both sides of the debate continue to be active in advocating their points of view. The agribusiness industry continues to argue that the foods are safe and that mandatory testing and labeling are not necessary. The FDA does not seem inclined to impose any new requirements on producers. Consumer activists, however, have brought together environmentalists, organic farmers, chefs, and religious leaders, and they continue to lobby for rigorous safety testing and labeling.[122] Whole Foods Market has announced it will require labeling by 2018. Whether other companies follow suit remains to be seen. To be sure, all consumer stakeholders are potentially affected by the outcome of these debates, so it is likely that this issue will be with us for some time. As the economy improves, the organic and natural foods market segment will start to grow again as will the expectation that these products will be differentiated by their non-GMO characteristic.

Summary

Business use of technology today is so dramatic that the topic merits this separate chapter. In this discussion, basic concepts such as technology and the technological environment were introduced and defined. The benefits and side effects or hazards of technology were discussed. The symptoms of society's intoxication with technology were outlined. Questions regarding the ethics of technology were raised in two broad domains: information technology and biotechnology.

In the realm of information technology, characterized by Big Data, the category with the most widespread current impact in business, topics included electronic commerce, invasion of privacy via e-commerce, government's involvement in Internet privacy invasion, and business initiatives. Questions about practices and uses of technology were raised, including particular industries such as the porn industry, Internet gambling,

and Web-based downloading services. Computer technology in the marketplace and workplace have been the most significant areas of application. Questions regarding the ethics of new technologies such as cell phones were also raised. The field of biometrics merits close watch in the future.

The field of biotechnology was discussed with respect to social and ethical implications. A key topic in this sphere included the new field of bioethics. Two arenas of biotechnology were identified and discussed: that of genetic engineering, including a discussion of stem cell research, cloning, and genetic testing and profiling, and the general domain of GMFs. It is anticipated that the debate over food safety and labeling will continue for years as different interest groups raise questions about the appropriateness and safety of GMFs and whether labels on such foods should be required.

Key Terms

Big Data, p. 262

bioethics, p. 280

biometrics, p. 275

biotechnology, p. 267

botnet scams, p. 270

chief privacy officer (CPO), p. 273

cloning, p. 282

cookies, p. 269

electronic commerce, p. 268

embryonic stem cells, p. 281

ethical lag, p. 266

genetic engineering, p. 281

genetic profiling, p. 284

genetic testing, p. 284

genetically engineered foods (GEFs), p. 284

genetically modified foods (GMFs), p. 284

identity theft, p. 270

information technology, p. 267

online scams, p. 268

phishing, p. 275

social networking sites, p. 271

spam, p. 269

technological determinism, p. 266

technological environment, p. 264

technology, p. 264

therapeutic cloning, p. 283

Discussion Questions

1. Can you think of any additional benefits or negative side effects of technology in business that have not been mentioned in this chapter? Discuss.

2. Do you agree that society is intoxicated with technology? Does this pose special problems for business with respect to the ethics of technology? Will such intoxication blind people to ethical considerations in business?

3. Do you think business is abusing its power with respect to invasion of privacy of consumers? Is surveillance of consumers in the marketplace a fair practice? Which particular practice do you think is the most questionable?

4. Is it an exaggeration to question the ethical implications for business of cell phone and text-messaging use? Discuss both sides of this issue.

5. Do you think genetically modified foods (GMFs) raise a legitimate safety hazard? Should government agencies such as the FDA take more action to require safety testing? Do you think labeling unfairly stigmatizes GMFs and make consumers question their safety? Explain your answers.

Endnotes

1. Sharon Jayson, "iGeneration Has No Off Switch," *USA Today* (February 10, 2010), 1D.

2. John Naisbitt, Nana Naisbitt, and Douglas Phillips, *High Tech/High Touch: Technology and Our Search for Meaning* (Nicholas Brealey Publishing Co, 1999).

3. Chuck Raasch, "Instant Information Upends the World," *USA Today*, December 13, 2012, 1A.

4. Steven Rosenbush and Michael Totty, "How Big Data is Changing the Whole Equation for Business," *The Wall Street Journal*, March 11, 2013, R1.

5. John Bussey, "A Transformative Time for Companies—and their CIOs," *The Wall Street Journal*, January 22, 2013, B11.

6. "How college students use Instagram, Facebook and Twitter," http://geniusrecruiter.com/2012/06/22/how-college-students-use-instagram-facebook-and-twitter/, Accessed March 14, 2013.

7. Albert M. Erisman, "Social Networking for Business," http://www.ethix.org/article.php3?id=377. Accessed July 28, 2007.

8. Tony Dokoupil, "Is the Onslaught Making us Crazy?" *Newsweek*, July 16, 2012, 24–30.

9. Tony Dokoupil, "Is the Onslaught Making us Crazy?" *Newsweek*, July 16, 2012, 24–30.

10. Elizabeth Woyke, "Attention Shoplifters: With $30 Billion in Theft, There's a Revolution in Surveillance Systems," *BusinessWeek* (September 11, 2006), 46.

11. *Webster's Ninth New Collegiate Dictionary* (Springfield, MA: Merriam-Webster, Inc., 1983), 1211.

12. "Technology," *The World Book Encyclopedia* (Chicago: World Book, Inc., 1988), 76.

13. Richard L. Daft, *Management*, 5th ed. (New York: The Dryden Press, 2000), 75.

14. "Technology," 77–78.

15. Ibid., 78–79

16. Robert Friedel, *A Culture of Improvement: Technology and the Western Millennium* (Cambridge, MA: MIT Press, 2007). Also see the review of this book, Adam Keiper, "The March of Machines," June 7, 2007, http://www.wsj.online. Accessed July 28, 2007.

17. Ibid., 80.

18. Ibid., 80–81.

19. Beverly Kracher and Cynthia L. Corritore, "Is There a Special E-Commerce Ethics?" *Business Ethics Quarterly* (Vol. 14, Issue 1, January 2004), 77.

20. Naisbitt, Naisbitt, and Phillips.

21. John Naisbitt, "High Tech, High Touch," *Executive Excellence* (Vol. 16, No. 12, December 1999), 5ff.

22. Ibid. Also see Stephen Goode, "Naisbitt Questions the Future of Technology," *Insight* (June 11, 2001), 37–38.

23. NCL's Fraud Center, "Top Scams of 2011," http://fraudresearchcenter.org/wp-content/uploads/2012/02/National-Consumers-League-2011-Top-Scams-of-2011.pdf, Accessed March 18, 2013.

24. Ibid.

25. Kracher and Corritore, 71–94.

26. Ibid., 78–82

27. "Putting the Ethics in E-Business," *Computerworld* (Vol. 34, No. 45, November 6, 2000), 81ff.

28. To appreciate the different issues in which privacy arises, go to the Web site of Privacy Rights Clearinghouse, https://www.privacyrights.org/, Accessed February 25, 2013.

29. The EPIC Cookies Page: http://epic.org/privacy/internet/cookies/, Accessed March 18, 2013.

30. "Privacy Options Are a Blur," *USA Today* (April 10, 2001), 3D.

31. Spam, http://epic.org/, Accessed February 25, 2013.

32. Ibid.

33. Donna De Marco, "What's in a Name?" *Insight* (July 30, 2001), 30–31.

34. "What is a botnet?" Microsoft Safety and Security Center," http://www.microsoft.com/security/resources/botnet-whatis.aspx, Accessed March 18, 2013.

35. Byron Acohido, "An Invitation to Crime," *USA Today* (March 4, 2010), 2A.

36. Bryon Acohido and Jon Swartz, "Botnet Scams Are Exploding," *USA Today* (March 17, 2008), 1B–2B.

37. Acohido, 1A–2A.

38. Roger Grimes, "Privacy protection: The Government Is No Help," *InfoWorld* (June 16, 2006), http://www.infoworld.com/article/06/06/16/79260_25OPsecadvise_1.html. Accessed March 19, 2010.

39. Mike France, "Why Privacy Notices Are a Sham," *BusinessWeek* (June 18, 2001), 82–83. Also see Federal Trade Commission, "Consumer Privacy", http://business.ftc.gov/privacy-and-security/consumer-privacy, Accessed March 18, 2013.

40. "Consumer Data Privacy in a Networked World," The White House, February 23, 2012, http://www.whitehouse.gov/sites/default/files/privacy-final.pdf, Accessed February 25, 2013.

41. Federal Trade Commission, http://business.ftc.gov/documents/bus53-brief-financial-privacy-requirements-gramm-leach-bliley-act, Accessed February 25, 2013.

42. *Protecting Consumer Privacy in an Era of Rapid Change: Recommendations for Businesses and Policy Makers,* FTC Report, March 2012, Report available at http://ftc.gov/os/2012/03/120326privacyreport.pdf, Accessed March 18, 2013.

43. Ibid.

44. Walt Disney Internet Group, Privacy Policy, http://corporate.disney.go.com/corporate/pp.html,. Accessed February 26, 2013.

45. Microsoft Privacy Principles, http://www.microsoft.com/privacy/principles.aspx, Accessed February 26, 2013.

46. Aaron Ricadela, "Microsoft: Privacy Champion?" *BusinessWeek Online,* http://www.BusinessWeek.com Online, July 24, 2007, 1. Accessed February 26, 2013 Microsoft's Privacy Policy, http://www.microsoft.com/about/twc/en/us/privacy.aspx, Accessed February 26, 2013.

47. Michelle Kessler, "Position of Privacy Officer Coming into Public Eye," *USA Today* (November 30, 2000), 1–B. Also see CNN, "Chief Privacy Officer," February 28, 2013, http://articles.cnn.com/keyword/chief-privacy-officer, Accessed March 18, 2013.

48. Jared Sandberg, "The Privacy Officer," *The Wall Street Journal* (July 16, 2001), R10. Also see Steve Ulfelder, "CPOs: Hot or Not?" *Computerworld* (March 15, 2004), 40.

49. Cara Garretson, "Why Your Company Needs a Chief Privacy Officer," *Network World* (May 28, 2007), 20.

50. Ibid.

51. "The Defense Never Rests," *BusinessWeek*, March 19–25, 2012, 70.

52. Ben Worthen, "Data Breaches Are on the Rise with Businesses Rarely Penalized," *The Wall Street Journal* (September 9, 2008), B9.

53. Joe Palazzolo and Spencer Ante, "Activist's Suicide Highlights Tech Law," *The Wall Street Journal*, January 15, 2013, B1.

54. C. S. Stewart and S. Ramachandran, "Warning: Closer Watch on Illegal Downloads," *The Wall Street Journal*, February 26, 2013, B1.

55. Associated Press, "Downloading illegal music or movies? Expect to be put on notice by your Internet Service Provider," *The Washington Post*, February 25, 2013, Accessed February 26, 2013.

56. RIAA, "Scope of the Problem," http://www.riaa.com/physicalpiracy.php?content_selector=piracy-online-scope-of-the-problem, Accessed February 26, 2013.

57. Ibid.

58. Margaret Carlson, "Someone to Watch over Me," *Time* (July 16, 2001).

59. "Safety vs. Privacy: Do you know your new car has a 'black box' to track you?" *USA Today*, January 7, 2013, 6A.

60. APWG: Unifying the Global Response to Cybercrime, http://www.antiphishing.org/, Accessed February 26, 2013.

61. Evgeny Morozov, "Is Smart Making us Dumb?" *The Wall Street Journal*, February 23–24, 2013, C5–6.

62. "Biometrics Gets Down to Business," *The Economist Technology Quarterly* (December 2, 2006), 21–22.

63. "Biometrics: Wobbly ID," *The Economist* (April 2, 2009).

64. Ibid.

65. Aaron Pressman, "Homeland Security 2.0," *BusinessWeek* (January 22, 2007), 73.

66. Insurance Information Institute, "Cellphones and Driving," http://www.iii.org/media/hottopics/insurance/cellphones/. Accessed February 11, 2010.

67. Shawn Ghuman, "States cracking down on drivers using cellphones," *USA Today*, June 26, 2012, 1B.

68. Sue Shellenbargar, "Should Employers Play a Role in Safe Use of Cellphones in Cars?" *The Wall Street Journal* (July 18, 2001), B1.

69. "Jane Wagner," Zoominfo, http://www.zoominfo.com/people/Wagner_jane_16402535.aspx. Accessed February 11, 2010.

70. Risk Management Stay Focused, PCT Market Leadership, http://www.pctonline.com/pct0213-safety-attention-driving.aspx, Accessed February 26, 2013.

71. "Cell Phones and Driving," Insurance Information Institute (August 2007), http://www.iii.org/media/hottopics/insurance/cellphones/. Accessed August 13, 2007. Also see Archie B. Carroll, "Ethical Companies Curb Phone Use While Driving," *Athens Banner Herald* (October 31, 2009).

72. Trish Worron, "Cellphones Don't Ring My Chimes," *The Toronto Star* (January 2004).

73. Shellenbargar, B1.

74. "Cell Phones and Driving," August 2007.

75. Ibid. Also see AnahadO'Conner, "The Distracted American Driver," *The New York Times*, March 15, 2013, http://well.blogs.nytimes.com/2013/03/15/the-distracted- american-driver/, Accessed March 18, 2013.

76. Ibid.

77. Legalzoom.com, "Cell Phone Usage Policy and Guide," http://www.legalzoom.com/legalforms/LegalZoom%20Cell%20Phone%20Usage%20Policy.pdf, Accessed February 26, 2013.

78. Sam Grobart, "What Machines Can't Do," *Bloomberg BusinessWeek*, December 17–23, 2012, 4–5.

79. "You, robot?" *The Economist*, September 1, 2012, 5.

80. "Morals and the machine," *The Economist*, June 2, 2012, 15.

81. Ibid.

82. Mujica, Petry, and Vickery, 286.

83. Thomas Hilton, "Information System Ethics: A Practitioner Survey," *Journal of Business Ethics* (December 2000), 279–284.

84. Walter Isaacson, "The Biotech Century," *Time* (January 11, 1999), 42–43.

85. Ibid.

86. Alison Taunton-Rigby, "Bioethics: The New Frontier" (Waltham, MA: The Sears Lectureship in Business Ethics, Center for Business Ethics, Bentley College, April 19, 2000), 7.

87. Ibid., 7–8.

88. Biotechnology Industry Organization, "What is biotechnology?" http://www.bio.org/articles/what-biotechnology, Accessed March 11, 2013.

89. Presidential Commission for Study of Bioethical Issues, http://bioethics.gov/cms/studies, Accessed March 11, 2013.

90. "Bioethics: Wanna Buy a Bioethicist?" *Christianity Today* (October 1, 2001), 32–33.

91. Nell Boyce, "And Now, Ethics for Sale," *U.S. News & World Report* (July 30, 2001), 18–19.

92. Charles Colson, "The New Tyranny: Biotechnology Threatens to Turn Humanity into Raw Material," *Christianity Today* (October 1, 2001), 128.

93. John Heys, "University Hosts Forum on Ethics of Stem Cell Research," *Knight Ridder Tribune Business News* (March 4, 2004), 1.

94. Tim Friend, "The Stem Cell Hard Sell," *USA Today* (July 17, 2001), 6D.

95. "The Value of Stem Cells," LifeBankUSA, http://www.lifebankusa.com/cord-blood/value.php, Accessed March 11, 2013.

96. Gallup, "Stem Cell Research," http://www.gallup.com/poll/21676/stem-cell-research.aspx, Accessed March 11, 2013.

97. "Value Conflicts in Stem-Cell Research: Governments Struggle with Bioethical Issues," *The Futurist* (January–February 2007), 8–9.

98. Alice Park, "The Quest Resumes," *Time* (February 9, 2009), 36–43.

99. "Potent Medicine: the Use of Stem Cells," *The Economist*, January 12, 2013, http://www.economist.com/news/science-and-technology/21569363-stem-cells-may-transform-development-new-drugs-potent-medicine, Accessed March 11, 2013.

100. "Cloning," *Gallup Poll*, http://www.gallup.com/poll/6028/cloning.aspx, Accessed March 14, 2013.

101. "Pregnant Pause," *The Economist* (January 22, 2004). Also see "What is Therapeutic Cloning," http://www.wisegeek.org/what-is-therapeutic-cloning.htm, Accessed March 14, 2013.

102. Quoted in Elizabeth M. Whelan, "Biomedical Prostitution?" *Insight* (May 28, 2001), 27.

103. *Ibid.* Also see Bodies: The Exhibition, http://www.ticketmaster.com/Bodies-the-Exhibition-tickets/artist/9945 82, Accessed March 14, 2013.

104. Pallavi Gogoi, "Cloning: Scientists vs. Consumers," *BusinessWeek Online* (May 7, 2007), 31.

105. Food and Drug Administration, "Animal Cloning and Food Safety," http://www.fda.gov/ForConsumers/ConsumerUpdates/ucm148768.htm, Accessed March 14, 2013.

106. Gogoi, 31. Also see Center for Food Safety, "Cloned Animals," http://www.centerforfoodsafety.org/campaign/cloned-animals/, Accessed March 14, 2013.

107. Anne Kates Smith, "The Downside of Genetic Testing," *Kiplinger's Personal Finance* (May 2008), 13–14.

108. Taunton-Rigby, 18–19.

109. U.S. Department of Labor, "Genetic Information Nondiscrimination Act of 2008(GINA)" http://www.dol.gov/ebsa/newsroom/fsGINA.html, Accessed March 14, 2013.

110. Julie Jargon and Ian Berry, "Dough Rolls Out to Fight 'Engineered' Label on Food," *The Wall Street Journal*, October 26, 2012, B1.

111. L. Val Giddings, "No: These Crops Pass Multiple Tests Before Approval and Are a Boon to the World's Hungry," *Insight* (August 6, 2001), 43.

112. World Health Organization, "Food Safety: Genetically Modified Foods," http://www.who.int/foodsafety/publications/biotech/20questions/en/, Accessed April 2, 2013.

113. Ian Berry, "Monsanto: Battered, Bruised and Still Growing," *The Wall Street Journal*, January 30, 2013, B5.

114. Jason Chavis, "FDA Regulations on GM Foods," http://www.ehow.com/facts_5554837_fda-regulations-gm-foods.html, Accessed April 2, 2013.

115. William Neuman, "Biotech-Free, Mostly," *The New York Times* (August 29, 2009), B1.

116. Non-GMO Project, http://www.nongmoproject.org/, Accessed March 15, 2013.

117. Elizabeth Weise, "Calif. To vote on labeling genetically modified foods," *USA Today*, October 29, 2012, 3A.

118. Jargon and Berry, 2012, op.cit.

119. Weise, op.cit.

120. "Why Label Genetically Engineered Food?" *The New York Times*, March 14, 2013.

121. "Why Label Genetically Engineered Food?" *The New York Times*, March 14, 2013.

122. For an interesting discussion of the environmentalists' viewpoint, see Jonathan Rauch, "Will Frankenfood Save the Planet?" *The Atlantic Monthly* (October 2003), 103–108.

10
Ethical Issues in the Global Arena

The growth of global business as a critical element in the world economy is one of the most important developments of the past half century. The past two decades, in particular, have been characterized by the rapid growth of foreign direct investment by the United States, by countries in Western Europe, by Japan, and by other developing countries as well, such as China, India, and Russia. Many emerging economies have joined the mix. In the United States, domestic issues have been made immensely more complex by the escalating international growth. At the same time, the **internationalization** of business has created unique challenges of its own. With the rise of global business, international markets have been seen as natural extensions of an ever-expanding global marketplace that must be pursued if firms are to remain competitive.

Peter Drucker referred to the expanded marketplace as the **transnational economy**. He went on to say that if business expects to establish and maintain leadership in one country, it must also strive to hold a leadership position in all developed markets worldwide. This helps to explain the worldwide boom in transnational investments.[1] One useful definition of this transnational or global economy is as follows: trade in goods, a much smaller trade in services, the international movement of labor, and international flows of capital and information.[2]

Everyone has assumed that global business would continue its rapid growth of the past two decades and that, increasingly, companies and countries would become more integrated with the rest of the world. Then, the brakes were slammed with the global economic crisis beginning in 2007–2008. Over the past 20 years, international trade has raced ahead of global economic growth, often at double its pace, but this has changed. Global trade is slowing down. *Fortune* magazine has gone so far as to say that the world is turning inward and that domestic success will start to deliver growth for companies and nations again.[3] A study reported in *The Economist* has shown that both trade and capital flows became less globalized when the economic crisis hit. They demonstrate using the Global Connectedness Index that the economic crisis of 2008 made global connectedness both shallower and narrower.[4]

The past two decades have been characterized by labor arbitrage, developed countries taking advantage of lower wages abroad, especially in the poorer countries. But, as the emerging economies have been booming, rising wages there have made these countries less attractive. For example, pay for factory workers in China climbed by 69 percent between 2005 and 2010. As this trend has spread to many developing nations, the advantages of **offshoring** to these countries has declined.[5] Evidence has already begun to document that many companies are now rethinking their offshoring strategies and some of them are bringing production back home, a process known as "reshoring." Many firms also have realized they went too far in sending work abroad.[6] In addition to foreign wages rising, two other factors have been important also in motivating reshoring—the cost of transporting goods and the riskiness of doing business abroad. Doing business in more corrupt countries such as many of the developing nations has caused managers to rethink the advantages of doing business abroad.[7] In spite of this recent trend slowing down global growth, global business represents such a huge aspect of business today that the issue of doing business abroad will remain substantial in the years ahead.

The complexity introduced by the transnational economy and the globalization of business is seen clearly when ethical issues arise. At best, business ethics is difficult when we are dealing with one culture. Once we bring two or more cultures into consideration, it gets extremely complex. Managers have to deal not only with differing customs, protocols, and ways of operating but also with differing concepts of law and standards of acceptable practices. All of this is then exacerbated by the fact that world political issues become intertwined. What might be intended as an isolated corporate attempt to bribe a foreign government official, in keeping with local custom, could explode into major international political tensions between two or more countries.

Business Challenges in a Multinational Environment

Firms face two major underlying challenges as they operate in a multinational environment. One challenge is that of achieving *corporate legitimacy* as the **multinational corporation (MNC)**, or multinational enterprise (MNE), seeks to be recognized and accepted in an unfamiliar society. A related problem is the fundamentally *differing philosophies* that may exist between the firm's home country and the host country in which it seeks to operate.[8] For firms to be perceived as legitimate in the eyes of a host country they must fulfill their social responsibilities abroad just as they were expected to do so at home. Closely related to the legitimacy issue is the dilemma of MNCs that have quite different cultural or philosophical perspectives from those of their host countries. The philosophy of Western industrialized nations, and thus their MNCs, focuses on economic growth, efficiency, specialization, free trade, and comparative advantage. By contrast, many LDCs have different priorities. Other important objectives for them might include a more equitable income distribution or increased economic self-determination. In this context, the economically advanced nations may appear to be inherently exploitative in that their presence may perpetuate the dependency of the poorer nation.[9] These two challenges set the stage for examining how ethical problems arise in the global environment.

One could well argue that ethical tensions are built into this situation. MNCs attempt to bridge the cultural gaps between two cultures; yet, as they attempt to adapt to local customs and business practices, they at times are assailed at home for not adhering to the standards, practices, laws, or ethics of their home country.

FIGURE 10-1

The Dilemma of the
Multinational
Corporation

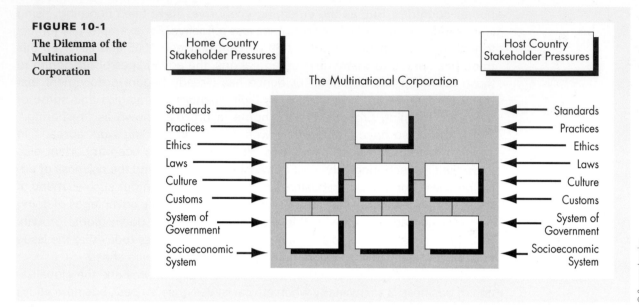

Figure 10-1 graphically depicts the dilemma of MNCs caught between the characteristics and expectations of their home country and those of one or more host countries.
They often find themselves in a totally unmanageable situation, but they cannot be
deterred from finding working solutions.

Spotlight on Sustainability

A Global Ethical Sustainability Movement: Earth Hour

A global event called Earth Hour, which has now become an annual gesture and a combined effort
by almost five million people in more than 100 countries, was observed successfully on March 27,
2010. The event was started in Australia in 2007 by the World Wide Fund for Nature (WWF). The
organization's mission is to stop degrading Earth's natural environment and to create a low-carbon
future for planet Earth.

Earth Hour is a global sustainability movement that was initiated with the hope that each year
will bring about a continued celebration. The first Earth Hour was held in Australia, and after
national acclaim, it gained high international interest, with more and more cities beginning to
sign up for the next Earth Hour campaign.

Earth Hour has now come to be known as the world's largest global climate change initiative.
The event is recognized by millions switching off their lights for one hour. Iconic buildings such
as Sydney Harbour Bridge, the CN Tower in Toronto, Rome's Colosseum, India Gate, the Golden
Gate Bridge in San Francisco, and many more stood in darkness in contemplation of the world's
ethical responsibility to planet Earth. Earth Hour in 2013 was held on March 23, 2013.

Earth Hour now inspires a global community of millions of people in 7,000 cities across 152 countries to switch their lights off to demonstrate a massive support for environmental sustainability. You
can discover the planned Earth Hour in your country by going to: http://www.earthhour.org/.

Sources: Earth Hour, http://www.earthhour.org/. Accessed April 11, 2013; "Earth Hour City Challenge,"
WWF, http://worldwildlife.org/pages/earth-hour-city-challenge. Accessed April 11, 2013.

Ethical Issues in the Global Business Environment

For many companies, most of the ethical problems that arise in the global environment are in the same categories as those that arise in their domestic environments. These ethical issues reside in all of the functional areas of business: production/operations, marketing, finance, accounting, and management. These issues concern the fair treatment of stakeholders—employees, customers, the community, and competitors—and involve product safety, plant safety, advertising practices, human resource management, human rights, environmental problems, business practices, and so on.

These ethical problems seem to be somewhat fewer in developed countries, but they exist there as well. The ethical challenges seem to be more acute in underdeveloped countries, less-developed countries, or developing countries because these countries are at earlier stages of economic development and typically do not have a legal or ethical infrastructure in place to help protect their citizenry. This situation creates an environment in which there is temptation to go with lower standards, or perhaps no standard, because few government regulations or activist groups exist to protect the stakeholders' interests. In the **less-developed countries (LDCs)**, the opportunities for business exploitation and the engagement in questionable practices (by developed countries' standards) are abundant.

We will discuss some prominent categories of ethical issues in the global sphere to provide some appreciation of the development of these kinds of issues for business. First, we will discuss two classic ethical issues that have arisen with regard to questionable marketing and manufacturing safety practices. Then, we will discuss the issue of labor or human rights abuses often found in "sweatshops" (the use of cheap labor in developing countries). This topic has dominated international business discussions for the past couple decades. Lastly, we will consider the special problems of corruption, bribery, and questionable payments. From these examples, we should be able to develop an appreciation of the kinds of ethical challenges that confront all MNCs doing business globally.

Questionable Marketing and Plant Safety Practices

The process of marketing either domestically or abroad creates many ethical challenges for businesses. The most obvious marketing issues are those embedded in the product itself and its promotion. A classic example of a *questionable marketing practice* is the now-infamous infant formula controversy that spanned most of the 1970s, continued into the 1980s and 1990s, and remains an issue today. The *plant safety issue* is best illustrated by examining the Union Carbide Bhopal crisis that began in 1984, continued into the 1990s, and is not completely resolved today. These issues illustrate the endless problems companies can face as a result of mistakes made in global business ethics and how their effects can be felt for decades. It is easy to now predict that BP's oil spill in the Gulf of Mexico may be in this category someday as its repercussions are likely to last for decades.

Questionable Marketing: The Infant Formula Controversy. The **infant formula controversy** is a classic example that illustrates ethical questions that can arise while marketing products abroad. We will briefly review some basic facts about this now-classic case.[10] For decades, physicians working in tropical lands (many of which were LDCs) realized that severe health risks were posed to infants from bottle-feeding as opposed to breast-feeding. Such countries typically had neither refrigeration nor sanitary conditions. Water supplies were not pure, and therefore, powdered infant formula mixed with bacteria-infected water likely led to disease and diarrhea in the bottle-fed infant. Because people in these LDCs are typically poor, mothers tend to over dilute the powdered formula, trying to make it last longer, thus diminishing significantly the amount of nutrition the infant receives. Once a mother begins bottle-feeding, her capacity for breast-feeding quickly diminishes. Poverty also leads the mother to put less expensive substitute products such as powdered whole milk and cornstarch in the bottle. These products are not acceptable substitutes, but they save money. They are nutritionally inadequate and unsatisfactory for the baby's digestive system.

By the late 1960s, it was apparent that in LDCs there was increased bottle-feeding, decreased breast-feeding, and a dramatic increase in the numbers of malnourished and sick babies because of this. The problems began when several of the infant formula companies, aware of the conditions just described, were promoting their products and, therefore, promoting bottle-feeding in an intense way. Such marketing practices as mass advertising, billboards, radio jingles, and free samples became commonplace. These promotional devices typically portrayed the infants who used their products as healthy and robust, in sharp contrast with the reality that was brought about by the conditions mentioned.

One of the worst marketing practices entailed the use of "milk nurses"—women dressed in nurses' uniforms, walking the halls of maternity wards and urging mothers to get their babies started on formula. In reality, these women were sales representatives employed by the companies on a commission basis. Once the infants began bottle-feeding, the mothers' capacity to breast-feed diminished, and they became hooked on the formula.[11]

Although several companies were engaging in these questionable marketing practices, the Swiss conglomerate Nestlé was singled out by a Swiss social activist group in an article entitled "Nestlé Kills Babies." At about the same time, an article appeared in Great Britain entitled "The Baby Killers."[12] From this point on, a protracted controversy developed, with Nestlé and other infant formula manufacturers on one side and a host of organizations on the other side filing shareholder resolutions and lawsuits against the companies. Among the groups that were actively involved in the controversy were church groups such as the National Council of Churches and its Interfaith Center on Corporate Responsibility (ICCR), UNICEF, the World Health Organization (WHO), and the Infant Formula Action Coalition (INFACT). Nestlé was singled out because it had the largest share of the world market and because it aggressively pushed sales of its infant formula in developing countries, even after the WHO developed a sales code to the contrary.[13]

INFACT and ICCR organized and led a national boycott in 1977 against Nestlé that continued for almost seven years. More than 70 American organizations representing doctors, nurses, teachers, churches, and other professionals participated in the boycott. These groups mounted an international campaign aimed at changing these objectionable marketing practices in the LDCs.[14] In 1984, after spending tens of millions of dollars resisting the boycott, Nestlé finally reached an accord with the protesters. The company agreed to make some changes in its business practices. The protesters, in return, agreed to end their boycott but to continue monitoring Nestlé's performance.[15] The infant formula controversy continued through the 1980s and well into the 1990s and 2000s.

The infant formula controversy illustrates the character of questionable business practices by firms pursuing what might be called normal practices were it not for the fact that they were being pursued in foreign countries where local circumstances made them suspect.[16] The infant formula controversy also illustrates the endurance of certain ethical issues, particularly in the global arena.

Later, the AIDS crisis, especially in Africa, put an unusual twist on the infant formula debate. Some have said that UNICEF, the UN agency charged with protecting children, today may be indirectly responsible for thousands of African babies being infected with the deadly AIDS virus. AIDS entered the picture since the early boycotts of Nestlé and others, and it was discovered that HIV-infected mothers could transfer the disease through breast-feeding to their own children. In response to this problem, Nestlé and formula maker Wyeth-Ayerst Labs said they stood ready to donate tons of free formula to the infected women. However, UNICEF refused to give the green light to these gifts. Nestlé claims it had gotten desperate requests from African hospitals for free formula, but the company would not act without UNICEF's approval because it did not want to renew the boycott against the company. The executive director of UNICEF, meanwhile, said that she didn't believe Nestlé and the other infant formula providers had a particular role to play in the AIDS crisis. She thinks they should just comply with the WHO code. [17]

Even today, the International Baby Food Action Network (IBFAN) (http://www.ibfan.org/) continues to advocate safety in feeding babies and lobbies against companies that continue engaging in questionable business and marketing practices.[18] With the AIDS crisis and marketing in the United States to low-income mothers complicating the controversy, it is apparent that no quick solutions are available.

Plant Safety and the Bhopal Tragedy. The Union Carbide **Bhopal tragedy** brings into sharp focus the challenges of multinationals conducting operations in a foreign, particularly less-developed, business environment. The legal issues surrounding this event have not yet been totally resolved and may not be for years to come in spite of earlier agreements reached. On December 3, 1984, the leakage of methyl isocyanate gas caused what many have termed the "worst industrial accident in history." The gas leak killed more than 2,000 people and injured 200,000 others. The tragedy raised numerous legal, ethical, social, and technical questions for MNCs.[19] Observers who have studied this tragedy say the death toll and destruction are many times greater than the "official" numbers indicate. One report is that more than 3,500 were killed in the accident.[20]

Interviews with experts just after the accident revealed a belief that the responsibility for the accident had to be shared by the company and the Indian government. According to Union Carbide's own inspector, the Bhopal plant did not meet U.S. standards and had not been inspected in more than two years. The Indian government allowed thousands of people to live very near the plant, and there were no evacuation procedures.[21]

Many different questions that have implications for manufacturing abroad have been raised by the Bhopal disaster. Among the more important of these issues are the following:[22]

1. To what extent should MNCs maintain identical standards at home and abroad regardless of how lax laws are in the host country?
2. How advisable is it to locate a complex and dangerous plant in an area where the entire workforce is basically unskilled and uneducated, and where the populace is ignorant of the inherent risks posed by such plants?
3. How wise are laws that require plants to be staffed entirely by local employees?
4. What is the responsibility of corporations and governments in allowing the use of otherwise safe products that become dangerous because of local conditions? (This question applies to the infant formula controversy also.)
5. After reviewing all the issues, should certain kinds of plants even be located in developing nations?

At the heart of these issues is the question of differing safety standards in various parts of the world. This dilemma arose in the 1970s, when American firms continued to export drugs and pesticides that had been outlawed in the United States. Pesticides, such as DDT and others that had been associated with cancer, were shipped to and used in LDCs by farmers who may not have understood the dangers of or the precautions needed in using these products. Not surprisingly, poisonings occurred. In 1972, thousands of Iraqis died from mercury-treated grain from the United States. In 1975, many Egyptian farmers were killed and yet others became ill by a U.S.-made pesticide. Asbestos- and pesticide-manufacturing plants that violated American standards were built in several other countries. These companies typically broke no laws in the host countries, but many experts are now saying that the Bhopal tragedy has taught us that companies have a moral responsibility to enforce high standards, especially in developing countries not yet ready or able to regulate these firms.[23]

One major problem that some observers say contributed to the Bhopal gas leak and, indeed, applies to MNCs generally, is the requirement that firms be significantly owned by investors in the host country. Union Carbide owned only 50.9 percent of the subsidiary in Bhopal, India. It has been suggested that this situation may have reduced Union Carbide's motivation and/or capacity to ensure adequate industrial and environmental safety at its Bhopal plant, mainly by diluting the degree of parent control and reducing the flow of technical expertise into that plant. If developing countries continue to insist on a dilution of MNC control over manufacturing plants, this may also diminish the MNC's motivation and incentive to transfer environmental management and safety competence.

Another major problem highlighted by the Bhopal gas leak was the fact that the people of developing countries are often unaware of the dangers of new technology. As one expert observed, countries such as India (at the time) had not "internalized the technological culture."[24] Although the LDCs want technology because they see it as critical to their economic development, often their ability to understand and manage the new technology is in serious doubt.

The complexity and tragedy of the Bhopal gas leak case for its victims, the Indian government, and Union Carbide are attested to by the fact that this issue is unresolved even today. In 1989, Union Carbide extricated itself from relief efforts by agreeing to pay the Indian government $470 million to be divided among victims and their families. By 1993, courts had distributed only $3.1 million of this sum. The overburdened government relief programs in India have been mired in mismanagement and corruption. It has been observed that virtually every level of the relief bureaucracy in India is corrupt. Government officials demanded bribes from illiterate victims trying to obtain documents required for their relief money. Doctors took bribes from victims to testify in their court cases, and unscrupulous agents fished for bribes by claiming they could get victims' cases expedited on the crowded docket. Claims courts that would determine final compensation for victims were not set up until 1992—eight years after the gas leak. Lawyers and officials say it could be another 20 years before this case is settled.[25]

Dow Chemical Co. bought Union Carbide in 2001. Even today the Union Carbide tragedy continues to haunt Dow Chemical more than two decades after the accident. Survivors of the accident and their supporters continue to push Dow to pay more than $1 billion in additional damages for what they claim are unmet medical bills and toxic cleanup.[26] Dow continues to argue that the $470 million settlement it paid in 1989 resolved its outstanding liabilities.[27] The company continues to argue that it never owned nor operated the Bhopal plant, which is now under the control of the state government of Madhya Pradesh, India. It says that the plant site is now owned by the state and that it is up to them to decide what to do with the property.[28]

In 2012, the Madhya high court finally lifted a five-year stay that prevented the summoning of Dow Chemical in the ongoing criminal case in connection with the gas tragedy. The high court has now ruled that it is for the trial court to decide whether Union Carbide had ceased to exist following merger with Dow Chemical or if it still exists as a legal entity.[29] Activists in India insist they will continue to pursue this case until Dow Chemical is held accountable.[30] Current Web pages (http://www.bhopal.org) document that the Bhopal tragedy continues to be of deep concern even today—more than 28 years after the tragedy. Like the infant formula controversy, it is an ethical issue that won't be forgotten.

Factory Fire and Building Collapse in Bangladesh. In a factory fire reminiscent of the Bhopal tragedy, 112 workers were killed in a Tazreen Fashions, Ltd., factory near Dhaka, Bangladesh, in November 2012. This disaster was especially newsworthy because more than 500 Bangladeshi garment workers had died in fires in the past six years according to labor groups. The fire has been called the country's worst industrial accident and it received high-profile news coverage when it was discovered that garments for Walmart were being manufactured there at the time.[31] Walmart says it had found serious fire-safety concerns at the plant in an inspection conducted in 2011 and that it had removed Tazreen from its list of authorized factories "months ago," but that one of its suppliers used the plant without its authorization.[32] A Bangladesh government committee investigation found that the incident was an act of sabotage. In addition, the committee's report disclosed that three mid-level executives from Tazreen Fashions were suspected of stopping workers from leaving during the fire because they wanted to prevent employee theft.[33] Companies such as Walmart are now under the gun even more so to police the safety concerns of factories used.

In April 2013, a garment factory collapsed in Savar, Bangladesh killing more than 1,100 workers. The building housed 5,000 workers who worked in five textile firms. This incident has continued to spotlight Western companies that use factories for low-cost clothes though these companies have not been identified as the guilty parties.[34] The building that collapsed was owned by a local politician who had the building built in 2007 without the required permits. Two of the textile firms located in the multistory building had recently been cleared through an audit by the Business Social Compliance Initiative which was set up a decade ago by the Brussels-based Foreign Trade Association. Unfortunately, most auditing of factories look at working conditions and never get into building structure and safety. The public in Bangladesh has been upset over the lack of safety regulations governing buildings and the ease with which politicians get these structures built.[35]

The lessons from the Bhopal disaster and the two factory disasters in Bangladesh are many and will continue to be debated. In companies around the globe, the Bhopal disaster has stimulated continued controversy in the debate about operating abroad. To be sure, legal and ethical issues are central to the discussions. What is at stake, however, is not just the practices of businesses abroad but also the very question of their presence. Depending on the final outcome of the Union Carbide case, MNCs may decide that the risks of doing certain types of business abroad are just too great.

Sweatshops, Labor Abuses, and Human Rights

No issue has been more consistently evident in the global business ethics debate than the MNCs' use and alleged abuse of women and children in cheap-labor factories in developing countries. In the Tazreen factory fire just described, for example, it was reported that even though Bangladesh has become the world's second-largest exporter of garments behind China, it also pays some of the lowest wages in the world. In Bangladesh, the minimum wage for garment workers is less than $37 per month.[36] The major players in this controversy, large corporations, have highly recognizable names—Nike, Walmart,

Gap, Kmart, Reebok, J. C. Penney, and Disney, to name just a few. The countries and regions of the world involved include Southeast Asia, Pakistan, Indonesia, Honduras, Dominican Republic, Thailand, China, Bangladesh, the Philippines, Mexico, and Vietnam. Sweatshops have not been eliminated in the United States, either, but the most serious problems seem to be in the developing countries.[37]

Though **sweatshops**—characterized by child labor, low pay, poor working conditions, worker exploitation, and health and safety violations—have existed for decades, they have grown in number in the past couple decades as global competition has heated up and corporations have sought to lower their costs and increase their productivity. A landmark event that brought the sweatshop issue into sharp focus was the 1996 revelation by labor rights activists that part of Walmart's Kathie Lee Collection, a line of clothes endorsed by then-prominent U.S. talk-show host Kathie Lee Gifford, was made in Honduras by seamstresses slaving 20 hours a day for 31 cents an hour.

The revelation helped turn Gifford, who was unaware of where the clothes were being made or under what conditions, into an anti-sweatshop activist.[38] The Nike Corporation also became a lightning rod for social activists concerned about overseas manufacturing conditions, standards, and ethics. A major reason for this was the company's high profile and visibility, extensive advertising using athletic superstars, as well as the stark contrast between the tens of millions of dollars Nike icons Michael Jordan and Tiger Woods earned and the several dollars a day wage rate the company's subcontractors once paid their Indonesian workers.[39]

Critics of sweatshop labor practices, including social activist groups, labor unions, student groups, and grassroots organizations, have been speaking out, criticizing business abusers and raising public awareness. These critics claim many businesses exploit children and women by paying them poverty wages, working them to exhaustion, punishing them for minor violations, violating health and safety standards, and tearing apart their families. Many of these companies counter that they offer the children and women workers a superior alternative. They say that although their wage rates are embarrassing by developed-world standards, those rates frequently equal or exceed local legal minimum wages, or average wages.

Defenders of sweatshops further say that because so many workers in LDCs work in agriculture and farming, where they make less than the average wage, the low but legal minimums in many countries put sweatshop workers among the higher-paid ones in their areas.[40] A study conducted by economists found that MNCs generally paid more, often a lot more, than the wages offered by locally owned companies. In one study, it was found that affiliates of U.S. MNCs pay a wage premium that ranges from 40 percent to 100 percent more than the local average pay in low-income countries.[41] When these wages are compared to the developed world, however, they seem embarrassing and abusive.

A number of different initiatives have begun seeking to redress these problems in sweatshops. The Fair Labor Association and SA8000 merit closer consideration.

Fair Labor Association (FLA). The sweatshop issue has been so prominent in the past 20 years that to improve their situations or images, many of the criticized companies have begun working diligently to improve working conditions, further joint initiatives, establish codes of conduct or standards for themselves and their subcontractors, conduct social or ethical audits, or take other steps. In 1996, former President Bill Clinton and Kathie Lee Gifford were instrumental in helping to establish the **Fair Labor Association (FLA)** (http://www.fairlabor.org/), a nonprofit organization of clothing firms, unions, and human rights groups focused on the worldwide elimination of sweatshops. Participating companies make a sustained corporate commitment to the FLA to bring their entire supply chain into the FLA program. Some of the current participating companies include the adidas Group, American Eagle Outfitters, Cutter & Buck, H&M, HanesbrandsInc., New Balance, Puma, and Tumi. Among its various activities, the FLA sets standards through a code of conduct, monitors and reports, and supports compliance.

The FLA is still quite active, but there have been a number of other proposals aimed at eliminating or improving sweatshops. Some call for clothing firms and their contractors to impose a code of conduct that would prohibit child labor, forced labor, and worker abuse; establish health and safety regulations; recognize workers' right to join a union; limit the workweek to 60 hours (except in exceptional business circumstances); and insist that workers be paid at least the legal minimum wage (or the "prevailing industry wage") in every country in which garments are made. Under such proposals, the garment industry would also create an association to police the agreement.

These proposals have some drawbacks, however. For example, the legal minimum wage in many developing countries is below the poverty line. In addition, the "prevailing industry wage" could prove to be a convenient escape clause. Some groups are also concerned that the task force has, in effect, sanctioned 60-hour workweeks and that it will still allow 14-year-olds to work if local laws do. Another big issue will be monitoring the agreements abroad. For example, Liz Claiborne alone has 200 contractors in more than 25 countries. Furthermore, in some countries, like the Philippines, Malaysia, Thailand, and Vietnam, sweatshops go to great lengths to hide their business dealings by "fronting" businesses using false documents to "prove" they pay minimum wages and by intimidating workers to keep quiet.[42]

Social Accountabilty 8000 (SA8000). Another major initiative to improve sweatshop conditions was created by **Social Accountability International (SAI)**. SAI is a nongovernmental, multi-stakeholder organization whose mission is to advance the human rights of workers around the world. SAI had developed one of the world's preeminent social standards—**Social Accountability 8000 (SA8000)**—designed to piggyback on the ISO8000 quality-auditing system of the International Standards Organization (ISO). The standard is now being used in more than 3,000 factories across 65 countries and 66 industrial sectors.[43]

The SA8000 initiative involves a broad spectrum of U.S. and international companies, such as HP, Gap Inc., Walt Disney Company, Chiquita Brands, and Carrefour plus a number of labor and human rights groups. The current standards for SA8000 may be summarized as follows:[44]

1. *Child Labor:* No use or support of child labor.
2. *Forced Labor:* No use of support of forced labor.
3. *Health and Safety:* Provide a safe and healthy work environment; prevent potential occupational accidents.
4. *Freedom of Association and Right to Collective Bargaining:* Respect the right to form and join trade unions and bargain collectively.
5. *Discrimination:* No discrimination based on race, caste, origin, religion, disability, gender, sexual orientation, union or political affiliation, or age; no sexual harassment.
6. *Discipline:* No corporal punishment, mental or physical coercion, or verbal abuse.
7. *Working Hours:* Comply with the applicable law but, in any event, no more than 48 hours per week with at least one day off for every seven-day period; voluntary overtime paid at a premium rate and not to exceed 12 hours per week on a regular basis.

8. *Remuneration:* Respect right of personnel to a living wage; all workers paid at least the minimum wage; wages sufficient to meet basic needs and provide discretionary income.

9. *Management Systems:* Facilities seeking to gain and maintain certification must go beyond simple compliance to integrate the standard into their management systems and practices.[45]

The SA8000 process offers companies the opportunity to be certified. To certify conformance with SA8000, every facility seeking certification must be audited. Thus auditors will visit factories and assess corporate practices on a wide range of issues and evaluate the state of a company's management systems, necessary to ensure ongoing acceptable practices. Once an organization has implemented any necessary improvements, it can earn a certificate attesting to its compliance with SA8000. This certification provides a public report of good practice to consumers, buyers, and other companies and is intended to be a significant milestone in improving workplace conditions.[46]

Campaigns to create "ethical supply chains" have proliferated in recent years as companies have sought to improve working conditions in factories. Richard Locke of MIT decided to study how things really worked and he convinced four major companies to share with him six years of data from their factory audits. After analyzing the data, Locke reached four conclusions. First, codes of conduct, compliance programs, and audits do not deliver sustained improvements in labor conditions over time. They help to highlight the problems but don't remedy them. Second, investments in helping factories improve their managerial and technical capabilities did lead to improved working conditions. Third, for significant and sustained improvements to occur, the company and the suppliers needed to function in a more collaborative way. Fourth, many firms use business models such as just-in-time manufacturing that prevent improved working conditions from occurring.[47]

Individual Company Initiatives In addition to the initiatives by such industry organizations as the FLA and the SAI (SA8000), it is important to highlight some of the efforts by individual companies to address the issues surrounding sweatshops. A number of companies have developed *global outsourcing guidelines* and codes and have made important strides in attempts at self-monitoring their production facilities in developing countries. Companies such as Nike, Levi Strauss & Co., and Gap are notable examples.[48]

In the spirit of transparency, Gap Inc. released a 40-page report in 2004 that offered an unusual look at its factory conditions abroad. It updated this report in its 2007–2008 Social Responsibility Report and again in 2009–2010. Gap's report revealed that the working conditions at many of its 3,000 factories worldwide were far from perfect. The Gap report documented a wide variety of workforce violations at plants making its clothing but revealed even worse conditions at plants vying to win Gap contracts. As a result, the company revoked contracts with 136 factories because of severe or persistent violations. Critics of sweatshops said they were pleased with the move toward greater openness. A representative from the Interfaith Center on Corporate Responsibility in New York described the report as a "major step forward."[49] In 2010, Gap developed a Human Rights Policy and pledged to continue to look for ways to enhance its human rights practices.[50] Gap's strategy has motivated a number of other companies to be more forthright about their factories overseas.

Despite the best of efforts by some companies to improve factory conditions in emerging countries, there is growing evidence that some suppliers have learned how to conceal abuses and continue to get away with unacceptable practices. In a major report, *BusinessWeek* disclosed that many factories, especially in China, have learned how to "game the system" through questionable practices. Some of these practices include

ETHICS IN PRACTICE CASE

Cheating Consultants: Helping Factories to Pass Audits

A new group of consulting firms in China now advertise that they can help Chinese factories pass labor audits being conducted by Western companies. These firms claim they can help generate two sets of books—real ones and fake ones. These consultants are part of a growing cottage industry in China that help factories "appear" to pass the increasingly stringent audits being used to help clean up sweat shops and labor abuses in that country.

Auditors of working conditions in low wage plants have also said they have found documents that might have been used in factories to prep workers with the answers the factory wanted the auditors to hear, this according to the Fair Labor Association (FLA) which conducted an investigation.

The director of the Ethical Trading Initiative, a London-based group, has said that audit fraud is a serious problem. Fake payroll books have become so common that auditors now assume there are at least two sets of books. China Labor Watch, a New York based advocacy group, alleged that one toy factory in China may have bribed its auditor in addition to forging employee time sheets and salary records.

One Chinese consulting firm even advertised on the Internet that it has software available to generate fake factory books. The software also allows the factories to adjust their employee data to present the type of profile the auditors are expecting. The demand for the services of these consulting firms seems to be rising as factories seek to pass the sometimes difficult audit standards.

In their defense, some factory owners in China say it's impossible to meet the MNC's demands for better working conditions while also keeping prices low.

1. Is it ethical to operate a consulting firm that helps factories to lie, cheat, and deceive auditors seeking to monitor working conditions? Could you imagine firms such as this succeeding in your country?

2. What are the implications for the business system in countries that permit this to occur? What happens to the business and society relationship?

3. Should the MNCs striving to create ethical supply chains attempt to interact with and lobby the Chinese government to outlaw consulting firms such as these?

4. Is it possible that we have now reached the point that working conditions cannot be improved while keeping prices low? If so, what comes next?

Sources: Ethical Trading Initiative, http://www.ethicaltrade.org/about-eti, Accessed April 24, 2013; Kathy Chu, "Some Chinese factories lie to pass Western audits," *USA Today*, April 30, 2012, 4B; China Labor Watch, http://www.chinalaborwatch.org/index.html, Accessed April 24, 2013.

keeping double sets of books; scripted responses wherein managers and employees are taught how to answer auditor's questions about hours, pay, and safety practices; and hidden production, whereby plants meet U.S. demands by secretly shifting work to subcontractors that violate pay and safety standards, but these subcontractors are hidden from the auditors.[51]

Sweatshops and labor abuses sharply contrast the "haves" and the "have-nots" of the world's nations. Consumers in developed countries have benefited greatly from the lower prices made possible by cheap labor. It remains to be seen how supportive those consumers will be when prices rise because MNCs improve wage rates and conditions in LDCs. The MNCs face a continuing and volatile ethical issue that is not likely to go away. Their profits, public image, and reputations may hinge on how well they respond. The MNCs must handle a new dimension in their age-old quest to balance shareholder profits with the desires of expanded, global stakeholders who want better corporate social performance. In the age of transparency, we should expect more revelations in the years to come.

Alien Tort Claims Act and Human Rights Violations Looking beyond possible human rights violations in sweatshops, claims that companies may have violated the human rights of foreign nationals could come back to haunt firms that have been accused of more serious human rights abuses. What is at stake is the U.S. courts' interpretation of an obscure piece of legislation known as the **Alien Tort Claims Act (ATCA)**. Though researchers cannot determine why Congress passed this little-known act in 1789, recently it has been the centerpiece of a controversy that may have widespread implications for American firms operating abroad. In the past decade, efforts have been made to use ATCA to sue transnational companies for violations of international law in countries outside the United States. Plaintiffs have argued that ATCA could be used by foreign individuals seeking to sue U.S. firms in U.S. courts for companies' actions abroad. If these suits were to succeed, the ATCA could become a powerful tool to increase corporate accountability around the globe.[52] Some of the companies that have been targeted under this law include Occidental Petroleum of Los Angeles, Del Monte, Chevron, Caterpillar, Ford, IBM, and GM.

Many of the companies have said that they have been unfairly targeted by activists who are using the law to try to remedy the injustices of foreign governments. Many of the lawyers for these companies also say the companies are being blamed for crimes they deplore and know nothing about. The president of the National Foreign Trade Council observed that the ATCA statute was being misused and that it was being exploited by trial lawyers who have seized the law as their new "asbestos" litigation and are hoping to get rich by hitting the jackpot.[53]

In a significant 2013 judgment, the U.S. Supreme Court reined in the scope of the Alien Torts Claims Act. The Court held that the statute cannot be applied to actions that take place overseas thus weakening a device some human rights groups have used against alleged violators in their home countries. The Court held that the ATCA only applies to actions that take place in the United States. The Supreme Court's ruling will shut down many cases that have been ongoing for decades. Several justices expressed the concern that affirming liability in events which took place overseas would make American courts a magnet for distressed foreign plaintiffs for acts unrelated to the United States and could invite foreign courts to encourage judging U.S. corporations for actions outside their own borders.[54]

Corruption, Bribery, and Questionable Payments

It could easily be argued that the most frequent and severe ethical problems with respect to global business are corruption, bribes, and questionable payments. These problems are as old as history itself, but in the past decade governments around the world have escalated their attempts to eliminate them. In the United States alone, the Department of Justice (DoJ) and the Securities and Exchange Commission (SEC), both responsible for the Foreign Corrupt Practices Act prosecutions, filed a record number of cases in 2010 and 2011, the most recent years for which data were available.[55]

Corruption in global business continues to be the overarching problem. It starts with outright bribery of government officials and the giving of questionable political contributions. Beyond these, there are many other corrupt activities: the misuse of company assets for political favors, kickbacks and protection money for police, free junkets for government officials, secret price-fixing agreements, and insider dealing, just to mention a few. All of these activities have one thing in common: They are attempts to influence the outcomes of decisions wherein the nature and extent of the influence are not made public. In essence, these activities are abuses of power.[56] They undermine the system of free trade.

Though one seldom hears an official definition of corruption, such synonyms as dishonesty, sleaze, fraud, deceit, and cheating are typically invoked. Two definitions of corruption that are useful include the following:[57]

- *Behavior on the part of officials in the public sector, whether politicians or civil servants, in which they improperly and unlawfully enrich themselves, or those close to them, by the misuse of the public power entrusted to them. This would include embezzlement of funds, theft of corporate or public property as well as corrupt practices such as bribery, extortion, or influence peddling.* (Transparency International [TI])
- *Corruption involves behavior on the part of officials in the public and private sectors, in which they improperly and unlawfully enrich themselves and/or those close to them, or induce others to do so, by misusing the position in which they are placed.* (World Bank)

Corruption comes in many forms, some petty and some grand. Though hugely lucrative to a few, corruption is incredibly damaging in terms of its effects on stakeholders. It corrodes the rule of law, the legitimacy of government, the sanctity of property rights, and incentives to invest and accumulate. Corruption also is a drag on a country's growth. In fact, corruption has become the biggest problem for developing economies.[58] A major problem, of course, is that those who benefit from corruption most will resist attempts to curb it, and often these are politicians who play decision-making roles.

Bribery has been the subject of ongoing debate, more than any other form of corruption, and the practice merits closer examination. Simply speaking, bribery is the practice of offering something (usually money) in order to gain an illicit advantage. Bribes, of course, are illegal in most places and generally held to be unethical, but it is informative to consider the arguments that have been set forth for and against them. Some business-people continue to argue that bribery is necessary, and some countries of the world continue to assert that they are culturally obligatory or defensible.

Arguments For and Against Bribery Arguments typically given in favor of permitting bribery have included the following: (1) they are necessary for profits in order to do business; (2) everybody does it—it will happen anyway; (3) it is an accepted practice in many countries—it is normal and expected; and (4) bribes are forms of commissions, taxes, or compensation for conducting business between cultures.

Arguments frequently cited against giving bribes include the following: (1) bribes are inherently wrong and cannot be accepted under any circumstances; (2) bribes are illegal in the United States and most developed nations and, therefore, unfair elsewhere; (3) one should not compromise her or his own beliefs; (4) managers should not deal with corrupt governments; (5) such demands, once started, never stop; (6) one should take a stand for honesty, morality, and ethics; (7) those receiving bribes are the only ones who benefit; (8) bribes create dependence on corrupt individuals and countries; and (9) bribes deceive stockholders and pass on costs to customers.[59]

The costs of bribes and other forms of corruption are seldom fully understood or described. Several studies suggest the economic costs of such corrupt activities. When government officials accept "speed" money or "grease payments" to issue licenses, the economic cost is 3 to 10 percent above the licensing fee. When tax collectors permit underreporting of income in exchange for a bribe, income tax revenues may be reduced by up to 50 percent. When government officials take kickbacks, goods and services may be priced 20 to 100 percent higher than they actually could have been. In addition to these direct economic costs, there are many indirect costs—demoralization and cynicism and moral revulsion against politicians and the political system. Due to bribery and corruption, politicians have been swept from office in many countries including Brazil, Italy, Japan, and Korea.[60]

The Foreign Corrupt Practices Act (FCPA) One of the first initiatives by a major government to address the problem of corruption and bribery in international business was the passage of the U.S. **Foreign Corrupt Practices Act** in 1977. Before this, many of the payments and bribes made by U.S.-based MNCs were not illegal. Even so, firms could have been engaging in illegal activities depending on whether and how the payments were reported to the Internal Revenue Service (IRS). With the passage of the FCPA, however, it became a criminal offense for a representative of an American corporation to offer or give payments to the officials of other governments for the purpose of getting or maintaining business. The FCPA specifies a series of fines and prison terms that can result if a company or management is found guilty of a violation.[61] The legislation was passed not only for legal and ethical reasons but also out of a concern for the image and reputation of the United States abroad.

The FCPA differentiates between bribes and facilitating payments, also called **grease payments**. The law does not prohibit so-called grease payments, or minor, facilitating payments to officials, for the primary purpose of getting them to do whatever they are supposed to do anyway. Such payments are commonplace in many countries. The real problem is that some forms of payments are prohibited (for example, bribes), but other payments (for example, grease payments) are not prohibited. The law is sometimes ambiguous on the distinctions between the two.[62]

To violate the FCPA, payments (other than grease payments) must be made corruptly to obtain business. This suggests some kind of *quid pro quo*. The idea of a corrupt *quid pro quo* payment to a foreign official may seem clear in the abstract, but the circumstances of the payment may easily blur the distinction between what is acceptable "grease" (e.g., payments to expedite mail pickup or delivery, to obtain a work permit, border crossings, or to process paperwork) and what is illegal bribery. The safest strategy for managers to take is to be careful and to seek a legal opinion when questions arise.

Figure 10-2 presents a basic distinction, with examples, between bribes (which are prohibited) and grease (or facilitating) payments (which are not prohibited) based on the FCPA.

The FCPA was intended to have and has had a significant impact on the way firms in the United States and many developed countries do business globally. A number of firms

FIGURE 10-2 **Bribes Compared to Grease Payments**

Definitions	Examples
Grease Payments	
Relatively small sums of money given for the purpose of getting minor officials to: • Do what they are supposed to be doing • Do what they are supposed to be doing faster or sooner • Do what they are supposed to be doing better than they would otherwise do	Money given to minor officials (clerks, attendants, or customs inspectors) for the purpose of expediting. This form of payment helps get goods or services through red tape or administrative bureaucracies.
Bribes	
Relatively large amounts of money given for the purpose of influencing officials to make decisions or take actions that they otherwise might not take. If the officials considered the merits of the situation only, they might take some other action.	Money given, often to high-ranking officials. Purpose is often to get these people to purchase goods or services from the bribing firm. May also be used to avoid taxes, forestall unfavorable government intervention, secure favorable treatment, and so on.

that paid bribes to foreign officials have been the subject of criminal and civil enforcement actions, resulting in large fines and, sometimes, suspension and debarment from federal procurement contracting. Sometimes their employees and officers have been imprisoned as well.[63] From 2007 to 2013, the DoJ has been cracking down on bribery abroad at an accelerating pace.[64] The consensus seems to be that the increased prosecutions have been driven by the DoJ's post-Enron enthusiasm and companies' increased reporting of violations under the Sarbanes–Oxley Act.[65]

The DoJ's crackdown on corrupt practices has been broadened in that it is now attempting to catch both U.S. and foreign-based companies. Unbeknownst to many, foreign companies whose securities are publicly traded in the United States now are also subject to the FCPA.[66] The DoJ prosecuted more than four times the number of foreign bribery cases in the past five years than it did in the five years before that. A primary justification for the prosecutions has been the revisions to the FCPA that extended jurisdiction to any foreign company or individual doing business in the United States.[67]

In late 2008, German engineering company Siemens AG and authorities in the United States settled a long-standing bribes-for-business case with a record $1.6 billion fine, almost 20 times higher than the largest previous penalty under the FCPA. Siemens was penalized for routinely offering bribes to win overseas contracts with the following countries—Russia, Argentina, China, and Israel. Many other companies have ongoing investigations of FCPA violations. During 2011–2013, for example, the following major companies were subject to FCPA investigations and settlements: HSBC, Panasonic, Allianz, Ralph Lauren, Eli Lilly, Pfizer, and Walmart.[68]

Figure 10-3 summarizes some of the key features of the antibribery provisions of the FCPA.

FIGURE 10-3

Antibribery Provisions of the Foreign Corrupt Practices Act—Key Features

- In general, the FCPA prohibits American companies from making corrupt payments to foreign officials for the purpose of obtaining or keeping business.
- The U.S. Department of Justice is the chief enforcement agency, with a coordinate role played by the Securities and Exchange Commission (SEC).
- The FCPA's antibribery provisions extend to two types of behavior: making bribes (1) directly and (2) through intermediaries.
- The FCPA applies to any individual firm, officer, director, employee, or agent of the firm and any stockholder acting on behalf of the firm.
- The person making or authorizing the payment must have a corrupt intent, and the payment must be intended to induce the recipient to misuse his or her official position to direct business wrongfully to the payer or to any other person.
- The FCPA prohibits paying, offering, promising to pay, or authorizing to pay or offer money or anything of value.
- The prohibition extends only to corrupt payments to a foreign official, a foreign political party or party official, or any candidate for foreign political office, or anyone acting in an official capacity.
- The FCPA prohibits corrupt payments through intermediaries.
- An explicit exception is made to the bribery provisions for "facilitating payments" for "routine governmental action."
- The following criminal penalties may be imposed: firms are subject to a fine of up to $2 million; officers, directors, stockholders, employees, and agents are subject to a fine of up to $100,000 and imprisonment for up to five years. Fines imposed on individuals may not be paid by the firm.

Source: "Foreign Corrupt Practices Act Antibribery Provisions," U.S. Department of Justice, http://www.osec.doc.gov/ogc/occic/fcparev.html, Accessed April 25, 2013.

The Growing Anticorruption Movement Corruption and bribery in global business is a significant and ongoing topic. With significant increases in global trade and competition, free markets, and democracy over the past decade, this comes as no surprise.[69] Several powerful developments are worthy of mention. Each has contributed to what some have called a growing **anticorruption movement**. By all accounts, the fight against corruption has been a long and continuing march, but progress is being made.[70] The following constitute the major players in the anticorruption movement: Transparency International, OECD Antibribery Initiatives, UN Convention Against Corruption, and individual country initiatives.

Transparency International An innovative special-interest group—**Transparency International (TI)**—was modeled after the human rights group Amnesty International. TI has established itself as the world's foremost anticorruption organization. TI states its vision in the following way:

> *Our Vision: A world in which government, politics, business, civil society, and the daily lives of people are free from corruption."* [71]

TI has defined five priorities in its fight against worldwide corruption. These include fighting corruption in (1) the private sector, (2) politics, (3) public contracting, (4) international anticorruption conventions, and (5) poverty and development. It maintains more than 100 national chapters run by local activists.[72] TI has established two simple principles for businesses striving to root out corruption:

- The enterprise shall prohibit bribery in any form, whether direct or indirect.
- The enterprise shall commit to implementing a program to counter bribery.

According to TI, "These Business Principles are based on a Board commitment to fundamental values of integrity, transparency, and accountability. Enterprises should aim to create and maintain a trust-based and inclusive internal culture in which bribery is not tolerated."[73]

CORRUPTION PERCEPTION INDEX (CPI) One of the primary tools TI uses to combat corruption is its now-famous annual **Corruption Perception Index (CPI)**. The annual CPI has been widely credited with putting TI and the issue of corruption on the international policy agenda. The CPI ranks more than 175 countries by their perceived levels of corruption, as determined by expert assessments and opinion surveys. The result of the ranking is a list of countries in the world ranging from "highly clean" (least corrupt) to "highly corrupt."[74] In TI's 2012 rankings, the most recent available, the "highly clean" countries included Denmark, Finland, and New Zealand. The most "highly corrupt" countries included Somalia, Afghanistan, and North Korea. The United States was ranked 19th from the top. Underperformers in the CPI during 2012 also included some of the Eurozone countries most affected by the world economic crisis—for example, Greece.[75]

BRIBE PAYERS INDEX (BPI) In addition to the CPI, TI also publishes what it calls the **Bribe Payers Index (BPI)**. The BPI ranks leading exporting countries in terms of the degree to which international companies with their headquarters in those countries are likely to pay bribes to senior public officials in key emerging market economies. In that sense, the BPI measures the supply side of bribery in the countries where the bribes are paid. Countries are ranked on a mean score from the answers given by respondents to the following statement: "In the business sectors with which you are most familiar, please indicate how likely companies from the following countries are to pay or offer bribes to win or retain business in this country."[76] Among the major exporting countries of the world, the countries that are perceived to pay more bribes include Russia, China, Mexico, Indonesia, United Arab Emirates, and Argentina.[77] The countries least likely to pay bribes include Netherlands, Switzerland, Belgium, and Germany. The United States ranked tenth from the top in a list of 28 exporting countries studied. [78]

Transparency International hopes and expects that public exposure to its corruption ratings will bring pressure to bear on countries and companies to become less corrupt.

OECD Antibribery Initiatives   Another major development in the growing anticorruption movement is an antibribery treaty and initiative that the 29 industrialized nations of the Organization for Economic Cooperation and Development (OECD) and five other countries agreed to in late 1997. By 2013, 34 countries were subscribed to the OECD Antibribery Convention.[79] The OECD member nations agreed to ban international bribery and to ask each member nation to introduce laws patterned after the U.S. Foreign Corrupt Practices Act. The main thrust of the treaty was to criminalize offering bribes to foreign officials who have sway over everything from government procurement contracts and infrastructure projects to privatization tenders.

In spite of good intentions, the OECD has been criticized for not doing enough quickly enough. It has also been criticized for dramatically failing to live up to its own governance and antisleaze standards. The broader criticism is that the OECD antibribery signatories have failed to follow through on their plans. Implementation and execution have been serious issues for the OECD initiatives.

It may take many years before the OECD Antibribery Convention is fully implemented. However, the OECD represents a significant initiative by a number of major countries in the global battle to eliminate corruption from commercial transactions.

UN Convention Against Corruption (UNCAC)   Another major initiative to combat corruption around the world was passed in 2003. The **UN Convention Against Corruption (UNCAC)** was implemented in December 2005.[80] It created the opportunity to develop a global language about corruption and a coherent implementation strategy. A multitude of international anticorruption agreements already exist; however, their implementation has been uneven and only moderately successful. The UNCAC gives the global community the opportunity to address both of these weaknesses and begin establishing an effective set of benchmarks for effective anticorruption strategies.[81]

From a business perspective, UNCAC claims to hold the potential to become the global framework for combating corruption, which will pave the way for the establishment of a level playing field for all market participants. A central objective of UNCAC is to bring a higher degree of uniformity in the formulation and application of anticorruption rules across the world. For companies doing business in multiple jurisdictions, this agreement aspires to improve legal certainty and facilitate their global compliance efforts, thereby allowing them to fully compete in open markets without being exposed to extortion or unfair practices by their competitors.[82] UNCAC builds on the UN Global Compact, which presented nine principles of conduct in the areas of human rights, labor standards, and environment. A new principle of the Global Compact was adopted, the "10th Principle," which states "Businesses should work against corruption in all its forms, including extortion and bribery."[83] To date, 140 countries have become signatories to UNCAC.[84]

Individual Country Initiatives   In addition to OECD and UNCAC antibribery initiatives, some individual countries have begun antibribery campaigns on their own. Great Britain has its Bribery Act, and France has its Paris-based Financial Action Task Force which monitors member states for their effectiveness in implementing anti-money-laundering laws.[85] Interestingly, many other countries that have begun antibribery campaigns are those that typically do not score very highly on business ethics surveys, for example, Mexico and Russia.

The best way to deal with bribes seems to be to stem the practice before it starts. A major paradox is that the very people who often benefit from illicit payments—the politicians—are the ones who must pass the laws and set the standards against bribes and corruption in the first place. Another factor is that bribes and corruption, whenever possible, need to be exposed. Public exposure, more than anything else, has the potential to bring questionable payments under control. This means that practices and channels of accountability need to be made public.[86]

The CPI and BPI should help in this regard. Beyond these steps, managers need to see that such corruption and bribery are no longer in their best interests. Not only do bribes corrupt the economic system, but they corrupt business relationships as well and cause business decisions to be made on the basis of factors that ultimately destroy all the institutions involved. The OECD treaty and individual country efforts indicate that many countries now understand this important point. Their efforts will not totally eliminate bribery, but they do represent a significant step toward reducing bribery and bringing it under control.

We have by no means covered all the areas in which ethical problems reside in the global business environment. The topics treated have been major ones subjected to extensive public discussion. Examples of other issues that have become important and will probably increase in importance include the issues of international competitiveness, protectionism, industrial policy, political risk analysis, **outsourcing**, and antiterrorism. Also vital will be the dangers of developed countries importing dangerous products from some of the less-developed countries. These issues are of paramount significance in discussions of business's relations with international stakeholders. Other issues that include an ethical dimension are national security versus profit interests, dealing with rogue nations, the use of internal transfer prices to evade high taxes in a country, mining of the ocean floor, stealing intellectual property, and harboring terrorists. Space does not permit us to discuss these issues in detail.

Improving Global Business Ethics

It is clear from the discussion up to this point that business ethics is much more complex at the global level than at the domestic level. The complexity arises from the fact that a wide variety of value systems, stakeholders, cultures, forms of government, socio-economic conditions, and standards of ethical behavior exist throughout the world. Recognition of diverse standards of ethical behavior is important, but if we assume that firms from developed countries should operate in closer accordance with developed countries' standards than with those of developing countries, the strategy of ethical leadership in the world will indeed be a challenging one.

Because the United States and European MNCs have played such a leadership role in world affairs—usually espousing fairness and human rights—these firms have a heavy responsibility, particularly in underdeveloped countries and developing nations. The power–responsibility equation also suggests that these firms have a serious ethical responsibility in global markets. That is, the larger sense of ethical behavior and social responsiveness derives from the enormous amount of power these countries have.

In this section, we will first discuss the challenge of honoring and balancing the ethical traditions of a business's home country with those of its host country. Next, we will discuss the four recommended strategies for conducting business in foreign environments.[87] We will conclude by taking a look at some other steps companies are taking to improve their global ethics.

ETHICS IN PRACTICE CASE

The Beast of Bentonville Bows to Local Customs

In 2012, it was revealed that Walmart, frequently referred to as the "Beast of Bentonville," Arkansas, had bowed to local custom and paid significant bribes in Mexico in efforts to open new stores there. Walmart's Mexican subsidiary, Walmex, was accused of at least 19 instances of paying off local officials to get stores opened in favorable locations. One estimate was that the company paid $24 million in bribes to sidestep local regulations and obtain construction permits for new stores.

Many of the markets that Walmart seeks to penetrate are in developing countries such as Mexico. In many if not most of these markets, corruption is widespread and commonplace. In these countries, bribery is not seen as a serious crime but rather a "way of doing business." One expert observed that in Mexico "the bulk of retailers pay bribes." According to Transparency International, Mexican firms are the third most likely to have to pay bribes, just after Russia and China.

The really bad news for Walmart is the accusation that top executives knew what was going on as early as 2005 and tried to keep it quiet. One report is that e-mails document that CEO, Mike Duke, was aware of the company's actions and that this contradicts earlier claims by senior officials that they were not aware of the bribes being paid. A Walmart spokeswoman has indicated that the company is cooperating with the Securities and Exchange Commission investigation and that the company is committed to having "a strong and effective global anticorruption program everywhere we operate…"

The Walmart bribery accusations are extremely intricate and complex and external and internal investigations are ongoing. One observer has said that what Walmart did in Mexico was mostly grease payments rather than bribes and had the company not tried to cover it up it might have been cleared of FCPA violations.

1. Is it possible for a sprawling corporation such as Walmart to do business in developing countries and not fall victim to local customs such as bribery?
2. What is a company such as Walmart to do when the countries in which it chooses to locate are rife with corruption? Should the company seek to impose U.S. standards whether the locals accept them or not?
3. In a multinational corporation such as Walmart, is it possible that company officials in Bentonville were unaware of what was going on in Mexico?
4. Do your own research on the Walmart bribery accusations and determine which of its activities were "bribes" and which were "grease payments." Be prepared to give examples of each.

Sources: Reuters, "Walmex used bribes to open 19 Mexican stores: NY Times," Monday, December 17, 2012; Anne D'Innocenzio, "E-mails suggest Walmart CEO knew of Mexico bribes in' 05," *The Boston Globe*, January 11, 2013; Hadley Malcolm and Jayne O'Donnell, "Wal-Mart denies it lobbied to change anti-bribery law," *USA Today*, April 26, 2012, 3B; Rana Foroohar, "Walmart's Discounted Ethics," *Time*, May 7, 2012; *The Jakarta Globe*, "Walmart faces big fines amid bribery charges," April 24, 2012; Rob Cox, "Moral Hazard," *Newsweek*, May 7, 2012, 7.

Balancing and Reconciling the Ethics Traditions of Home and Host Countries

One of the greatest challenges that businesses face while operating globally is achieving some kind of reconciliation and balance in honoring both the cultural and moral standards of their home and host countries. Should a business adhere to its home country's ethical standards for business practices or to the host country's ethical standards? There is no simple answer to this question. The diagram presented in Figure 10-4 frames the extreme decision choices businesses face when they consider operating globally. At one extreme, firms may engage in ethical imperialism. At the other extreme, they may engage in cultural relativism. These extreme alternatives deserve further discussion.

Ethical Imperialism   At one extreme in Figure 10-4 is a position often called **ethical imperialism**. This position holds that the MNC should continue to follow its home country's ethical standards even while operating in another country. Because U.S. and Western standards for treating employees, consumers, and the natural environment are quite high relative to the standards in many LDCs, it is easy to see how managers might find this posture appealing.

As reliance on foreign factories has soared in recent years and harsh conditions have been documented by the media, an increasing number of companies, such as Levi Strauss, Nordstrom, Inc., Walmart, and Reebok, have espoused higher standards for foreign factories that cover such issues as wages, safety, and workers' rights to organize. These standards more nearly approximate U.S. views on how such stakeholders ought to be treated rather than some host country's views. Such higher standards could be seen by other countries, however, as the United States attempting to impose its standards on the host country—thus the name "ethical imperialism" for one end of the continuum. Fortunately, the business world seems to be moving in the direction of eliminating corruption and operating according to higher ethical standards.

Cultural Relativism At the other extreme in Figure 10-4 is a position often called **cultural relativism**. This position is characterized by foreign direct investors such as MNCs following the host country's ethical standards. This is the posture reflected in the well-known saying, "When in Rome, do as the Romans do." This position would argue that the investing MNC should set aside its home country's ethical standards and adopt

FIGURE 10-4

Ethical Choices in Home versus Host Country Situations

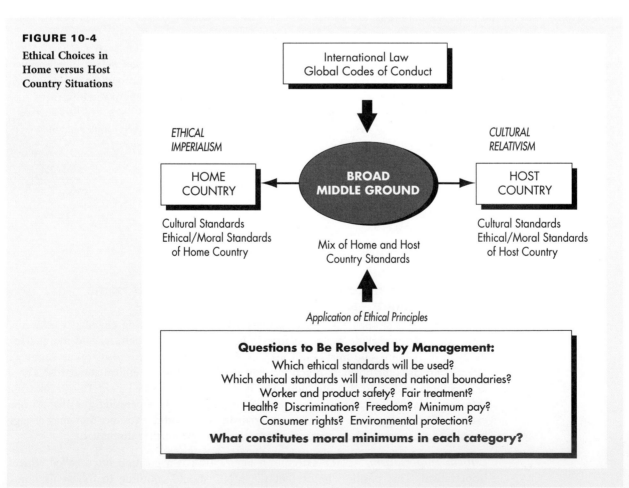

© Cengage Learning

the ethical standards of the host country. For example, if Saudi Arabia holds that it is illegal to hire women for most managerial positions, the investing MNC would accept and adopt this standard, even if it runs counter to its home country's standards. Or if the host country has no environmental protection laws, this position would argue that the MNC need not be sensitive to environmental standards.

It has been argued that cultural relativism holds that no culture's ethics are better than any other's, and that there are, therefore, no international rights or wrongs. If Thailand tolerates the bribery of government officials, then Thai tolerance is no worse than Japanese or German intolerance. If Switzerland does not find insider trading morally repugnant, then Swiss liberality is no worse than American restrictiveness.[88] Most ethicists find cultural relativism to be a case of moral or ethical relativism and, therefore, an unacceptable posture for MNCs to take.

Presented in Figure 10-4 is a series of questions management needs to ask to help determine its stance on home versus host country ethics. Depending on the issue (e.g., health versus minimum pay), companies may be more or less compelled to follow their home country's ethics. Key questions that must be posed and answered include the following: Which ethical standards will be used? Which ethical standards will transcend national boundaries? What constitutes moral minimums with respect to each category of ethical issue?

It may sound like a simplistic solution to say that the MNC needs to operate in some broad middle ground where a mix of home and host country ethical standards may be used. The challenge for managers will be to determine what mix of ethical standards should be used and how this decision should be made. As mentioned earlier, managers will need to ask themselves which moral standards are applicable in the situations they face. Use of ethical principles such as those articulated in the previous chapters—rights, justice, utilitarianism, and the Golden Rule—still apply. Managers will need to decide which ethical standards should transcend national boundaries and thus represent **hypernorms** (transcultural values):[89] safety? health? discrimination? freedom? The safest course of action, of course, is to operate based upon the higher of home versus host ethical standards though this is not always easy to determine especially when a host country invokes a standard as being part of its culture.

Managers will need to decide what will represent their moral minimums with respect to these and other issues. It would be nice to think that international laws and global codes of conduct will make these decisions easier. Though several such codes are available, they may be challenging to apply. In the interim, managers will need to be guided by the ethical concepts at their disposal, possibly with help from some of the strategies to which we now turn.

Strategies for Improving Global Business Ethics

In many instances, major companies work to improve their global business ethics through their global social responsibility programs. Four major strategies or categories of action that could help MNCs conduct global business while maintaining an ethical sensitivity in their practices include:

1. Global codes of conduct
2. Linking ethics with global strategy
3. Suspension of business activities in certain countries
4. Ethical impact statements and audits[90]

1. Global Codes of Conduct Global codes of conduct seek to establish universal principles or guidelines that should be followed while doing business around the world. There are two ways of thinking about global codes of conduct. First, there are specific corporate global codes that individual companies have developed. Second, there are global codes or guidelines that have been developed by various international organizations. Each of these deserves some consideration.

Corporate Global Codes In Chapter 8, we discussed codes of conduct, and that discussion applies in the global sphere as well. While operating on the world stage, MNCs have been severely criticized for employing divergent ethical standards in different countries, thus giving the impression that they are attempting to exploit local circumstances. A growing number of MNCs, however, Chiquita Brands International, Caterpillar Tractor, Allis Chalmers, Johnson's Wax, and Medtronic, have developed and used codes geared toward worldwide operations.

One of the first and most well-known of the corporate global codes is that of Caterpillar Tractor Company. It is now titled "Our Values in Action: Caterpillar's Worldwide Code of Conduct."[91] Caterpillar has been building work machines that have been used the world over for more than 80 years. The company asserts that its code sets a high standard for honesty and ethical behavior for every employee. The code goes into considerable detail and has major sections that cover the following important values that Caterpillar aspires toward: integrity, excellence, teamwork, and commitment.

Other companies do not have comprehensive codes addressing their international operations but rather codes containing sections that address international practices. For example, in its *Standards of Business Conduct*, Northrop Grumman Corporation dedicates a whole section to the subject of "international."[92] In this section it covers Export Controls, Foreign Corrupt Practices Act, and Laws of Other Countries.

Other companies have specific categories of ethical issues in which they address global considerations. For example, Chiquita Banana's Code of Conduct says the following regarding *bribery and corruption:* "Chiquita policy prohibits employees from using improper, unethical, or questionable business practices while conducting business on its behalf. We abide by all international laws, treaties and regulations that forbid bribery of foreign officials, including the U.S. Foreign Corrupt Practices Act."[93]

The GBS Codex Four researchers have published what they have called a Global Business Standards (GBS) Codex.[94] The **GBS Codex** was not intended to be a model code of conduct for global business, but a benchmark for companies wanting to develop their own world-class code. The researchers studied 5 well-known global codes put together by international organizations and 14 codes of the world's largest companies. They analyzed the codes to determine the underlying ethical principles the different codes had in common. The researchers found eight principles, representing worldwide ethical standards, that they thought were basic to the codes studied. The eight principles identified and described standards of conduct in the following categories: *fiduciary, property, reliability, transparency, dignity, fairness, citizenship,* and *responsiveness.*[95] The researchers argued that companies that wanted to assess their current codes of conduct or to create new codes of conduct would find their eight principles useful as a standard by which comparisons could be made. It is still too early to assess the extent to which the GBS Codex has been used in practice.

Corporate codes of conduct are usually just the starting point for companies in dealing with global business ethics. The acid test is whether these codes become living documents that the companies actually use on a daily basis.

Global Codes Created by International Organizations In addition to individual corporate codes, global codes or standards have been developed by a number of international organizations that hope companies will adopt and follow. Some of these codes focus on one specific issue; many provide standards across a number of issue areas. Figure 10-5 summarizes brief information about some of the more prominent of these

FIGURE 10-5 Global Codes and Standards Developed by International Organizations

Codes, Standards, or Guidelines	Brief Description and Web Site
UN Global Compact	The Global Compact's operational phase was launched at UN headquarters in New York on July 26, 2000. Today, thousands of companies from all regions of the world and international labor and civil society organizations are engaged in the Global Compact, working to advance 10 universal principles in the areas of human rights, labor, the environment, and anticorruption. http://www.unglobalcompact.org/, Accessed April 25, 2013.
Caux Round Table Principles for Business	The CRT Principles for Business are a worldwide vision for ethical and responsible corporate behavior and serve as a foundation for action for business leaders worldwide. As a statement of aspirations, the CRT Principles aim to express a world standard against which business behavior can be measured. http://www.cauxroundtable.org/index.cfm?menuid=8, Accessed April 25, 2013.
Global Sullivan Principles of Social Responsibility	The objectives of the Global Sullivan Principles are to support economic, social, and political justice by companies where they do business; to support human rights and to encourage equal opportunity at all levels of employment, including racial and gender diversity on decision-making committees and boards; to train and advance disadvantaged workers for technical, supervisory, and management opportunities. http://thesullivanfoundation.org/about/global-sullivan-principles, Accessed April 25, 2013.
OECD Guidelines for Multinational Enterprises	The guidelines are recommendations addressed by governments to multinational enterprises operating in or from adhering countries. They provide voluntary principles and standards for responsible business conduct in a variety of areas including employment and industrial relations, human rights, environment, information disclosure, combating bribery, consumer interests, science and technology, competition, and taxation. http://www.oecd.org/daf/inv/mne/48004323.pdf, Accessed April 25, 2013.
Global Reporting Initiative Sustainability Guidelines	GRI's guidelines have been updated over the years. They address three major categories of reporting: Human Rights and Reporting, Reporting on Community Impacts, and Gender Reporting. https://www.globalreporting.org/reporting/latest-guidelines/g3-1-guidelines/Pages/default.aspx, Accessed April 25, 2013.

external standards. Among them are the UN Global Compact, Caux Roundtable Principles, Global Sullivan Principles, OECD Guidelines for Multinational Enterprises, and Global Reporting Initiatives.

Two of the most widely used global standards are the **UN Global Compact** and the **Caux Roundtable Principles**. Figure 10-6 summarizes the major specific principles in each.

2. Ethics and Global Strategy The major recommendation regarding ethics and global strategy is that the ethical dimensions of multinational corporate activity should be considered as significant inputs into top-level strategy formulation and implementation.[96] Even more broadly, corporate social policy should be integrated into strategic management.[97] At the top level of decision making in the firm, corporate strategy is established. At this level, commitments are made that will define the underlying character and identity that the organization will have. The overall moral tone of the organization and all decision making and behaviors are set at the strategic level, and management needs to ensure that social and ethical factors do not get lost in the preoccupation with market opportunities and competitive factors.

FIGURE 10-6   UN Global Compact and Caux Roundtable Principles

UN Global Compact	Caux Roundtable Principles
Human Rights Businesses should • Principle 1: Support and respect the protection of internationally proclaimed human rights. • Principle 2: Make sure that they are not complicit in human rights abuses. **Labor Standards** Businesses should uphold • Principle 3: The freedom of association and the effective recognition of the right to collective bargaining. • Principle 4: The elimination of all forms of forced and compulsory labor. • Principle 5: The effective abolition of child labor. • Principle 6: The elimination of discrimination in respect of employment and occupation. **Environment** Businesses should • Principle 7: Support a precautionary approach to environmental challenges. • Principle 8: Undertake initiatives to promote greater environmental responsibility. • Principle 9: Encourage the development and diffusion of environmentally friendly technologies. **Anticorruption** Businesses should • Principle 10: Work against corruption in all its forms, including extortion and bribery.	1. Respect Stakeholders Beyond Shareholders 2. Contribute to Economic, Social, and Environmental Development 3. Respect the Letter and the Spirit of the Law 4. Respect Rules and Conventions 5. Support Responsible Globalization 6. Respect the Environment 7. Avoid Illicit Activities

Sources: UN Global Compact, "The Ten Principles," http://www.unglobalcompact.org/AboutTheGC/TheTenPrinciples/index.html, Accessed April 25, 2013; Caux Round Table, "Principles for Responsible Businesses," http://www.cauxroundtable.org/index.cfm?menuid=8, Accessed April 25, 2013.

If business ethics does not get factored in at the strategic formulation level, it is doubtful that it will be considered at the level of operations where strategy is being implemented. Unfortunately, much current practice has tended to treat ethics and social responsibility as residual factors. A more proactive stance is needed for dealing with ethical issues at the global level. Strategic decisions that may be influenced by ethical considerations in the global sphere include, but are not limited to, product/service decisions, plant location, operations policy, supply chain, marketing policy and practices, and human resource management policies. More and more companies are employing departments and strategies with respect to global corporate social responsibility and global business citizenship.[98]

Levi Strauss & Co   A valuable illustration of ethics being factored into strategic decision making is provided by Levi Strauss & Co. Because the company operates in many countries and diverse cultures, it believes that it must take special care in selecting its contractors and the countries where its goods are produced in order to ensure that its products are being made in a manner consistent with its values and reputation. Years ago, the company developed a set of *global sourcing guidelines* that established standards its contractors must meet.[99] More recently, Levi Strauss took the unprecedented action of publishing on its Web site a list of all active owned-and-operated and contract factories producing the company's branded products. The company's senior vice president for Global Sourcing hopes that such transparency will help to improve working conditions worldwide inside apparel factories and will promote "greater collaboration among brands in shared factories."[100] Levi Strauss & Co.'s Global Sourcing and Operating Guidelines address large, external issues that are outside the control of the company and business partner terms of engagement that apply to individual business partners and their daily operations.[101]

Starbucks   Another example of a company integrating ethical concerns into its corporate strategies is that of Starbucks Coffee Co., the Seattle-based firm. In an innovative pilot program initiated over a decade ago, Starbucks began paying a premium above market price for coffee, with the bonus going to improve the lives of coffee workers. The initial payments were made to farms and mills in Guatemala and Costa Rica, which co-funded health care centers, farm schools, and scholarships for farm workers' children. Starbucks's incentive program was part of a larger "Framework for Action," its plan for implementing its code of conduct.[102] Starbucks began purchasing Fair Trade Certified coffee in 2000. The company has been recognized for helping grow the market for Fair Trade Certified coffee in the United States and bringing it to consumers. By 2012, the company had reached the 93 percent level of ethical sourcing (responsible purchasing practices, farmer loans, and forest conservation). Its 2015 goals include the following: *ethical sourcing* (100 percent of its coffee will be responsibly grown, ethically traded); *environmental stewardship* (100 percent of its cups will be reusable or recyclable); and *community involvement* (it will commit more than 1 million community service hours each year).[103]

3. Suspension of Activities   An MNC may sometimes encounter unbridgeable gaps between the ethical values of its home country and those of its host country. When this occurs, and reconciliation does not appear to be in sight, the responsible MNC should consider suspending activities in the host country. For example, years ago IBM and Coca-Cola established a precedent for this activity by suspending their activities in India because of that country's position on the extent of national ownership and control.[104] In a fight against corruption, Procter & Gamble even closed a Pampers diaper plant in Nigeria rather than pay bribes to customs inspectors.[105]

In 2006, the Ecuadorian government seized control of the operations of Occidental Petroleum prompting the U.S. government to discontinue free trade talks with the country. Officials in the United States claimed that the Ecuadorian government's confiscation of Occidental's operations broke foreign investment laws.[106] Occidental didn't have much choice but to suspend operations because of the treatment it had received. In 2007 and later, a number of companies were having difficulties operating in Venezuela. Former President Hugo Chávez had been leading his country toward "21st century socialism" with rules restricting companies doing business there. According to *BusinessWeek*, former President Chávez forced global oil companies, phone carriers, and power companies to hand over control of key assets. He stated he had plans to nationalize the banks, hospitals, and steel companies. Foreign direct investment plunged in Venezuela over the past several years.[107] Chávez's strong arm tactics caused two major oil companies—ExxonMobil Corp. and ConocoPhillips—to announce their departure from the country.[108] With Chávez's death in 2012, it remains to be seen what other events will take place.

In 2010, Google decided to move its search engine out of China because it no longer thought it to be appropriate to censor searches at the request of the Chinese government.

Google is credited with a clever, strategic decision by moving its search engine to Hong Kong, which is a special administrative region that has broader free-speech protections. This decision allowed Google to adhere to its own privacy principles while also allowing the Chinese government to save face.[109]

Suspension of business in a foreign country is not a decision that can or should be taken too hastily, but it must be regarded as a viable option for those firms that desire to travel on the higher moral road of free trade. Each country is at liberty to have its own standards, but this does not mean that other country's firms must do business in that country. What does ethical leadership mean if it is not backed up by a willingness to take a moral stand when the occasion merits?

4. Ethical Impact Statements and Audits MNCs need to be constantly aware of the impacts they are having on society, particularly foreign societies. One way to do this is to periodically assess the company's impacts. Companies have a variety of impacts on foreign cultures, and ethical impacts represent only a few of these. The impact statement idea derived, in part, from the practice of environmental impact statements pioneered years ago. **Ethical impact statements** are an attempt to assess the underlying moral justifications for corporate actions and the consequent results of those actions. The information derived from these actions would permit the MNCs to modify or change their business practices if the impact statement suggested that such changes would be necessary or desirable.

One form of ethical impact assessment is some firms' attempts to monitor their compliance with their companies' global ethics codes. For example, Mattel Toy Company developed an independent audit and monitoring system for its code. Mattel's monitoring program was headed by an independent panel of commissioners who selected a percentage of the company's manufacturing facilities for annual audits. In one audit, for example, Mattel terminated its relationship with three contractor facilities for refusing to meet company-mandated safety procedures.[110] Mattel continues its auditing of compliance to its code of conduct through its Global Manufacturing Principles.[111]

Corporate Action Against Corruption

An enlightening study conducted by the Conference Board has disclosed some details on companies' recent anticorruption campaigns within their organizations. When asked what was the single most important factor in their company's decision to develop an anticorruption program, the most frequent responses were "senior management leadership and personal convictions," "bribe payments being illegal under their home country laws," "the belief that "bribe payments are wrong," and the impact of "Sarbanes–Oxley Section 404."[112]

The report revealed that there were five vital steps among anticorruption programs that seemed to work best for companies:[113]

1. High-level commitment by top management
2. Detailed statements of policies and operating procedures
3. Training and discussion of policies and procedures
4. Hotlines and help lines for all organizational members
5. Investigative follow-up, reporting, and disclosure

These essential steps, when combined with the strategies for improving global business ethics discussed earlier, go a long way toward establishing a solid foundation for fighting bribery and corruption, the most insidious issues in global business ethics. The good news is that companies are now very much aware of these issues and are moving quickly to address them.

Summary

Ethical dilemmas pose difficulties, in general, for businesses, and those arising in connection with doing business in foreign lands are among the most complex. A cursory examination of major issues that have arisen in global business ethics over the past several decades shows that they rank right up there with the most well-known news stories about business performance. The infant formula controversy, the Bhopal tragedy, corruption and bribery, concern about human rights and sweatshops, and the exploits of MNCs in Third World countries have all provided an opportunity for business critics to assail corporate ethics in the international sphere. These problems arise for a multiplicity of reasons, but differing cultures, value systems, forms of government, socioeconomic systems, and underhanded and ill-motivated business activities have all been contributing factors.

Steps taken by the United States and other major countries to address the issues of corruption and bribery include the Foreign Corrupt Practices Act, the OECD Antibribery Convention, and the UNCAC. Individual country initiatives are also vital, as are the efforts of nonprofit organizations such as Transparency International. A number of different approaches to improving global business ethics were presented. The balancing of home and host country standards were discussed with the extreme options of ethical imperialism or cultural relativism presented and contrasted. Four strategies for improving global business ethics were set forth: (1) global codes of conduct, encompassing corporate codes, the GBS Codex, and global codes created by international organizations; (2) the integration of ethical considerations into corporate strategy; (3) the suspension of activities in the host country; and (4) the use of ethical impact statements and audits. These strategies offer some hope that global business can be better managed. A major study by the Conference Board indicates that companies are taking important actions against corruption within their organizations. Five vital steps being taken against corruption were presented, and these were headed up by high-level commitment by top management.

In spite of the worldwide economic recession, current trends point to a growth in business activity in the transnational economy, and though there is some evidence of a backlash against globalization, these issues will become more rather than less important in the future. Indeed, it could easily be argued that business's greatest ethical challenges in the future will be at the global level.

Key Terms

Alien Tort Claims Act
  (ATCA), p. 304
anticorruption movement, p. 308
Bhopal tragedy, p. 297
Bribe Payers Index (BPI), p. 308
bribery, p. 305
Caux Round Table
  Principles, p. 315
corruption, p. 304
Corruption Perception Index
  (CPI), p. 308
cultural relativism, p. 312
ethical impact statements, p. 318
ethical imperialism, p. 311

Fair Labor Association
  (FLA), p. 300
Foreign Corrupt Practices Act
  (FCPA), p. 306
GBS Codex, p. 314
grease payments, p. 306
hypernorms, p. 313
infant formula controversy,
  p. 295
internationalization, p. 292
less-developed countries
  (LDCs), p. 295
multinational corporations
  (MNCs), p. 293

offshoring, p. 293
outsourcing, p. 310
Social Accountability 8000
  (SA8000), p. 301
Social Accountability
  International (SAI), p. 301
sweatshops, p. 300
transnational economy, p. 292
Transparency International
  (TI), p. 308
UN Convention Against
  Corruption (UNCAC), p. 309
UN Global Compact, p. 315

Discussion Questions

1. Drawing on the notions of moral, amoral, and immoral management introduced in Chapter 7, categorize your impressions of (a) Nestlé, in the infant formula controversy; (b) Union Carbide, in the Bhopal tragedy; and (c) Google, in moving its search engine out of China.

2. As an MNC seeks to balance and honor the ethical standards of both the home and host countries, conflicts inevitably will arise. What criteria do you think managers should consider as they try to decide whether to use home or host country ethical standards? Does it depend on the ethical issue involved? Explain.

3. Differentiate between a bribe and a grease payment. Give an example of each.

4. Conduct research for purposes of updating the latest rankings of Transparency International and the activities of the OECD, UNCAC, and individual country initiatives. How could countries such as China, India, and Russia most effectively improve their TI rankings?

5. What are the major strategies companies might employ in improving global business ethics? What are the key steps research has shown are important to successful company anticorruption efforts?

Endnotes

1. Peter F. Drucker, "The Transnational Economy," *The Wall Street Journal* (August 25, 1987), 38. See also Tammie S. Pinkston and Archie B. Carroll, "Corporate Citizenship Perspectives and Foreign Direct Investment in the U.S.," *Journal of Business Ethics* (Vol. 13, 1994), 157–169.

2. Paul Krugman, cited in Alan Farnham, "Global—Or Just Globaloney?" *Fortune* (June 27, 1994), 97–98.

3. Joshua Cooper Ramo, "Globalism Goes Backward," *Fortune*, December 3, 2012, 135–140; "Globalization: Going Backwards," *The Economist*, December 22, 2012, 136.

4. *The Economist*, December 22, 2012, ibid.

5. *The Economist*, "Moving back to America," May 14th, 2011, 79.

6. *The Economist*, "Here, there and everywhere," January 19, 2013, 3.

7. Rana Foroohar, "Go Glocal," *Time*, August 12, 2012, 26–32.

8. John Garland and Richard N. Farmer, *International Dimensions of Business Policy and Strategy*, 2d ed. (Boston: Kent Publishing Company, 1990), 166–173.

9. Ibid., 172.

10. James E. Post, "Assessing the Nestlé Boycott: Corporate Accountability and Human Rights," *California Management Review* (Winter 1985), 115–116.

11. Ibid., 116–117.

12. Rogene A. Buchholz, William D. Evans, and Robert Q. Wagley, *Management Response to Public Issues* (Englewood Cliffs, NJ: Prentice Hall, 1985), 80.

13. Ibid., 81–82.

14. Oliver Williams, "Who Cast the First Stone?" *Harvard Business Review* (September–October, 1984), 155.

15. "Nestlé's Costly Accord," *Newsweek* (February 6, 1984), 52.

16. For further discussion, see S. Prakash Sethi, *Multinational Corporations and the Impact of Public Advocacy on Corporate Strategy: Nestlé and the Infant Formula Case* (Boston: Kluwer Academic, 1994).

17. Alix M. Freedman and Steve Stecklow, "As UNICEF Battles Baby-Formula Makers, African Infants Sicken, *"The Wall Street Journal* (December 5, 2000).

18. The International Baby Food Action Network, http://www.ibfan.org/index.html, Accessed April 11, 2013.

19. Stuart Diamond, "The Disaster in Bhopal: Lessons for the Future," *The New York Times* (February 5, 1985), 1. See also Russell Mokhiber, "Bhopal," *Corporate Crime and Violence* (San Francisco: Sierra Club Books, 1988), 86–96.

20. Deepti Ramesh and Ian Young, "Tata Boss Proposes Cleanup of Bhopal Site; Survivors Protest," *Chemical Week* (January 17, 2007), 13.

21. Stuart Diamond, "Disaster in India Sharpens Debate on Doing Business in Third World," *The New York Times* (December 16, 1984), 1.

22. Ibid.

23. Ibid.

24. Thomas M. Gladwin and Ingo Walter, "Bhopal and the Multinational," *The Wall Street Journal* (January 16, 1985), 1.

25. Molly Moore, "In Bhopal, a Relentless Cloud of Despair," *The Washington Post National Weekly Edition* (October 4–10, 1993), 17.

26. Jim Carlton and Thaddeus Herrick, "Bhopal Haunts Dow Chemical," *The Wall Street Journal* (May 8, 2003), B3.

27. David Bogoslaw, "Dow Chem Face Holder Proposal on Bhopal Risk at Annual Meeting," *The Wall Street Journal* (May 13, 2004). Matt Kovac, "Dow Chemical: Shareholder Resolutions a Reality of Life," *ICIS Chemical Business Americas* (April 30–May 6, 2007), 10. Accessed August 16, 2007. "Dow Chemical: Liable for Bhopal?" *BusinessWeek* (June 9, 2008), 61–62.

28. Ramesh and Young, op. cit.

29. "Bhopal Gas Tragedy: Dow Chemical may Finally Be held Accountable," October 12, 2012, http://www.downtoearth.org.in/content/bhopal-gas-tragedy-dow-chemical-may-finally-be-held-accountable, Accessed April 11, 2013.

30. "Gas activists plead court to summons Dow Officials," *The Times of India*, March 6, 2013, http://timesofindia.indiatimes.com/city/bhopal/Gas-activists-plead-court-to-summon-Dow-officials/articleshow/18821423.cms, Accessed April 11, 2013.

31. Miguel Bustillo, Tom Wright, and Shelly Banjo, "Tough Questions in Fire's Ashes," *The Wall Street Journal*, November 30, 2012, B1.

32. Syed Al-Mahmood, Tripti Lahiri, and Dana Mattioli, "Fire Warnings Went Unheard," *The Wall Street Journal*, December 11, 2012, B1.

33. Syed Zan Al-Mahmood, "Bangladesh Probe Calls Fatal Fire Act of Sabotage," *The Wall Street Journal*, December 18, 2012, B4.

34. Syed Zain Al-Mahmood and Shelly Banjo, "Deadly Collapse," *The Wall Street Journal*, April 25, 2013, A1.

35. Syed Zain Al-Mahmood and Tom Wright, "Collapsed Factory was built without Permit, *The Wall Street Journal*, April 26, 2013, A9.

36. Syed Zain Al-Mahmood, Kathy Chu and Tripti Lahiri, "After Fire, Pressure on Bangladesh," *The Wall Street Journal*, December 15–16, 2012, B1.

37. Mark Clifford, Michael Shari, and Linda Himelstein, "Pangs of Conscience: Sweatshops Haunt U.S. Consumers," *BusinessWeek* (July 29, 1996), 46–47. See also Keith B. Richburg and Anne Swardson, "Sweatshops or Economic Development?" *The Washington Post National Weekly Edition* (August 5–11, 1996), 19.

38. "Stamping Out Sweatshops," *The Economist* (April 19, 1997), 28–29.

39. Clifford, Shari, and Himelstein, 46.

40. Ibid.

41. Ronald Baily, "Sweatshops Forever," *Reason* (February 2004), 12–13.

42. Ibid.

43. Social Accountability International, http://www.sa-intl.org/index.cfm?fuseaction=Page.ViewPage&pageId=1365, Accessed April 11, 2013.

44. SA8000 Standards. http://www.sa-intl.org/index.cfm?&pageid=937#childlabor, Accessed April 11, 2013.

45. Details maybe found at: http://www.sa-intl.org/index.cfm?&pageid=937#childlabor, Accessed April 11, 2013.

46. SA 8000 Accreditation, http://www.sa-intl.org/index.cfm?fuseaction=Page.ViewPage&pageId=1119, Accessed April 11, 2013.

47. *The Economist*, "Working Conditions in Factories: When the Job Inspector Calls," March 31, 2012.

48. Laura P. Hartman, Denis G. Arnold, Richard E. Wokutch (eds.), *Rising Above Sweatshops: Innovative Approaches to Global Labor Challenges* (Westport, CT: Praeger Publishers, 2003).

49. Amy Merrick, "Gap Offers Unusual Look at Factory Conditions," *The Wall Street Journal* (May 12, 2004), A1.

50. Gap, Inc., Social Responsibility, http://www.gapinc.com/content/csr/html/OurResponsibility.html, Accessed April 24, 2013.

51. Dexter Roberts, Pete Engardio, Aaron Bernstein, Stanley Holmes, and Xiang Ji, "Secrets, Lies, and Sweatshops" (cover story), *BusinessWeek* (November 27, 2006), 50–58. Also see Kathy Chu, "Some Chinese factories lie to pass Western audits," *USA Today*, April 30, 2012, 4B.

52. "Alien Tort Claims Act," *Global Policy Forum*, http://www.globalpolicy.org/international-justice/alien-tort-claims-act-6-30.html, Accessed April 28, 2013; Also see "Alien Tort Claims," *International Law Update* (Vol. 13, April 2007), 66–67.

53. Ibid.

54. Jess Bravin, "High Court Reigns in Scope of Alien Torts Act," *The Wall Street Journal*, April 17, 2013.

55. Kevin McCoy, "Public company foreign bribery cases rarely go to trial," *USA Today*, May 3, 2012, 5B.

56. Bruce Lloyd, "Bribery, Corruption and Accountability," *Insights on Global Ethics* (Vol. 4, No. 8, September 1994), 5.

57. "Corruption Definitions," *Zero Tolerance for Corruption*, http://www.anticorruption.info/other_defs.php. Accessed March 23, 2010.

58. Geoff Colvin, "The Biggest Problem for Developing Economies: Corruption," *Fortune*, May 2, 2011, 48.

59. Ian I. Mitroff and Ralph H. Kilmann, "Teaching Managers to Do Policy Analysis: The Case of Corporate Bribery," *California Management Review* (Fall 1977), 50–52. Also see International Debated Education Association, "Debate: Is Bribery Ever Acceptable?" http://dbp.idebate.org/en/index.php/Debate: Bribery_or_Corruption, Accessed April 25, 2013.

60. "The Destructive Costs of Greasing Palms," *BusinessWeek* (December 6, 1993), 133–138. See also Henry W. Lane and Donald G. Simpson, "Bribery in International Business: Whose Problem Is It?" (Reading 12) in H. W. Lane, J. J. DiStefano, and M. L. Maznevski (eds.), *International Management Behavior*, 4th ed. (Oxford: Blackwell Publishers, 2000), 469–487.

61. "Foreign Corrupt Practices Act," *Department of Justice*, http://www.justice.gov/criminal/fraud/fcpa/, Accessed April 25, 2013.

62. FCPA and Ethics Blog, "When does a grease payment become a bribe under the FCPA?" February 2, 2011, http://tfoxlaw.wordpress.com/2011/02/02/when-does-a-grease-payment-become-a-bribe-under-the-fcpa/, Accessed April 25, 2013.

63. Lay Person's Guide to the FCPA, referred to at http://www.sidley.com/DOJ–SEC-Release-Long-Anticipated-FCPA-Guidance-11-15-2012/, Accessed April 27, 2013.

64. McCoy, 2012.

65. Ibid.

66. Paul Berger, Erin Sheehy, Kenya Davis, and Bruce Yannett, "Is That a bribe?" *International Financial Law Review* (April 2007), 76–78.

67. Emma Schwartz, "Hiking the Cost of Bribery," *U.S. News & World Report* (August 13, 2007), 31.

68. U. S. Securities and Exchange Commission, "SEC Enforcement Actions: FCPA," http://www.sec.gov/spotlight/fcpa/fcpa-cases.shtml, Accessed April 25, 2013.

69. Daniel Henniger, "Capitalism's Corruptions," *The Wall Street Journal*, April 4, 2013, A13.

70. *The Economist*, "The fight against corruption: naming and shaming," October 30, 2010, 65.

71. Transparency International, "Our Vision," http://www.transparency.org/whoweare, Accessed April 25, 2013.

72. Ibid.

73. Ibid.

74. Ibid.

75. TI's Corruption Perception Index, http://www.transparency.org/cpi2012/press, Accessed April 25, 2013.

76. Ibid.

77. TI's Bribe Payer's Index, http://bpi.transparency.org/bpi2011/results/, Accessed April 25, 2013.

78. Ibid.

79. OECD, http://www.oecd.org/about/, Accessed April 25, 2013.

80. United Nations Convention Against Corruption, http://www.unodc.org/unodc/en/about-unodc/index.html?ref=menutop, Accessed April 28, 2013.

81. UNODC, "UN Convention Against Corruption," http://www.unodc.org/unodc/en/treaties/CAC/signatories.html, Accessed April 25, 2013.

82. UN Convention against Corruption, http://www.unodc.org/unodc/en/treaties/CAC/, Accessed April 27, 2013.

83. UN Global Compact, http://www.unglobalcompact.org/AboutTheGC/TheTenPrinciples/index.html, Accessed April 27, 2013.

84. UNODC, "UN Convention Against Corruption," http://www.unodc.org/unodc/en/treaties/CAC/signatories.html, Accessed April 25, 2013.

85. *The Economist*, "The politics of corruption: Squeezing the sleazy," December 15, 2012, 61.

86. Lloyd, 5.

87. Gene R. Laczniak and Jacob Naor, "Global Ethics: Wrestling with the Corporate Conscience," Business (July–September 1985), 3–10.

88. Tom Donaldson, "Global Business Must Mind Its Morals," *The New York Times* (February 13, 1994), F-11. See also Tom Donaldson, "Ethics Away from Home," *Harvard Business Review* (September–October, 1996).

89. Tom Donaldson and Thomas W. Dunfee, "When Ethics Travel: The Promise and Peril of Global Business Ethics," *California Management Review* (Vol. 41, No. 4, Summer 1999), 48–49.

90. Laczniak and Naor, 3–10.

91. Caterpillar, "Our Values in Action: Caterpillar's Worldwide Code of Conduct," http://www.cat.com/cda/files/89286/7/, Accessed April 25, 2013.

92. Northrop Grumman, Standards of Business Conduct, http://www.northropgrumman.com/CorporateResponsibility/Ethics/Documents/pdfs/noc_standards_conduct.pdf, Accessed April 25, 2013.

93. Chiquita Code of Conduct, http://www.chiquita.com/Code-of-Conduct-PDF/ChiquitaCode-FINAL-EN.aspx, Accessed April 25, 2013.

94. Lynn Paine, Rohit Deshpandé, Joshua Margolis, and Kim Eric Bettcher, "Up to Code: Does Your Company's Conduct Meet World-Class Standards?" *Harvard Business Review* (December 2005), 122–133. Also see http://arson04.blogspot.com/2011/07/global-business-standards-codex-gbs-and.html, Accessed April 25, 2013.

95. Ibid.

96. Laczniak and Naor, 7–8.

97. Archie B. Carroll, Frank Hoy, and John Hall, "The Integration of Corporate Social Policy into Strategic Management," in S. Prakash Sethi and Cecilia M. Falbe (eds.), *Business and Society: Dimensions of Conflict and Cooperation* (Lexington, MA: Lexington Books, 1987), 449–470.

98. Donna J. Wood, Jeanne M. Logsdon, Patsy G. Lewellyn, and Kim Davenport, *Global Business Citizenship: A Transformative Framework for Ethics and Sustainable Capitalism* (Armonk, NY: M.E Sharpe), 2006.

99. Robert D. Haas, "Ethics in the Trenches," *Across the Board* (May 1994), 12–13.

100. Quoted in CSRWire.com, http://www.csrwire.com/, Accessed April 27, 2013.

101. Levi Strauss & Co., *Global Sourcing and Operating Guidelines*, http://www.levistrauss.com/sites/levistrauss.com/files/librarydocument/2010/4/CitizenshipCodeOfConduct.pdf, Accessed April 25, 2013.

102. "Starbucks Pays Premium Price to Benefit Workers," *Business Ethics* (March/April 1998), 9.

103. "Ethically sourced coffee goals and progress," http://www.starbucks.com/responsibility/sourcing/coffee, Accessed April 25, 2013.

104. Laczniak and Naor, 8.

105. "The Short Arm of the Law," *The Economist* (March 2, 2002), 63–65.

106. "Ecuador Seizes Oxy," *Multinational Monitor* (May/June 2006), 4.

107. Geri Smith, "Venezuela: A Love-Hate Relationship with Chavez," *BusinessWeek* (June 25, 2007), 42–46.

108. Stanley Reed, "The Problem's Not Peak Oil, It's Politics," *BusinessWeek* (July 9 and 16, 2007), 41–42.

109. L. Gordon Crovitz, "Google's Search Result: Hong Kong," *The Wall Street Journal* (March 29, 2010), A21.

110. Mattel press release (November 20, 1997).

111. Mattel's Global Manufacturing Principles, http://corpo rate.mattel.com/about-us/cr-global.aspx, Accessed April 25, 2013.

112. Ronald E. Berenbeim, *Resisting Corruption: How Company Programs Are Changing, Research Report R-1397-06-RR* (New York: The Conference Board, 2006). http://www.conference-board.org/publications/publicationde-tail.cfm?publicationid=1239, Accessed June 24, 2013.

113. Ibid.

PART **4**

External Stakeholder Issues

Paul Anderson/Images.com/Corbis

11

Business, Government, and Regulation

CHAPTER LEARNING OUTCOMES

After studying this chapter, you should be able to:

1. Articulate a brief history of the government's role in its relationship with business.

2. Appreciate the complex interactions among business, government, and the public.

3. Identify and describe the government's nonregulatory influences, especially the concepts of industrial policy and privatization.

4. Explain government regulation and identify the major reasons for regulation, the types of regulation, and issues arising out of deregulation.

5. Provide a perspective on privatization versus federalization, along with accompanying trends.

"Can governments manage more ethically than capitalism?"[1] As government involvement in business has increased, this question has taken center stage. The government tends to become involved in business after serious problems arise, and there has been no shortage of problems. The first decade of the 21st century was so difficult for people and economies throughout the world that *Time* magazine dubbed it "The Decade from Hell."[2] Of course, the decade's problems were not only financial. Problems ranged from the natural disasters of the Eastern Japan Earthquake and Super Storm Sandy to terrorist attacks and warfare. From a financial perspective, the decade was a debacle, bookended by two major economic meltdowns. The decade began with the tech stock plunge and the Enron, WorldCom, and other scandals: These created a market crash that now seems mild compared with what occurred at the end of the decade.[3] At the end of the decade, as *Time* noted, "a housing bubble fueled by cheap money and excessive borrowing set ablaze by derivatives, so-called financial weapons of mass destruction, put the economy on the brink of collapse."[4] One of the key issues to sort out now that the decade has ended is the role of government in business, and that is the focus of this chapter. The last decade swung the pendulum of government involvement in business from minimal intervenor to major player. The depth, scope, and direction of government's involvement in business have made the relationship of government to business one of the most hotly debated issues today. The government's role, particularly in the regulation of business, has ensured its place among the major stakeholders with which business must establish an effective working relationship if it is to survive and prosper.

This increased level of government involvement in business is likely to remain for some time. The seriousness of the economic crisis revealed systemic weaknesses that have led many to call for structural change with greater protections.[5] At the same time, many worry about the impact of increased government involvement on business's innovation and growth.[6] This chapter and the next examine the relationship between business and government, with the general public assuming an important role in the discussion. Exploring this relationship carefully will provide an appreciation of the complexity of the issues surrounding business or government interactions. From a manager's standpoint, one needs an understanding of the forces and factors involved in these issues before beginning to talk intelligently about strategies for dealing with them. This chapter discusses how government influences business and the next chapter discusses how business influences government.

The Pendulum of Government's Role in Business

To be certain, the government involvement pendulum has swung back and forth for years. Business has never been fond of the government having an activist role in establishing the ground rules under which it operates. In contrast, public sentiment has been cyclical, going through periods when it thought that the federal government had too much power and other periods when it thought that government should be more activistic with regard to business. As an exemplar of a free market economy, the United States serves as a case in point. There have been periods of strong government intervention. For example, in 1791, while serving as Secretary of the U.S. Treasury, Alexander Hamilton pushed for tariffs to protect domestic manufacturers. The purpose was to protect fledgling industries. Then, in the 1860s, President Abraham Lincoln expanded federal powers by opening the American West to settlement.[7] By the 1860s, industrialists like John D. Rockefeller dominated the steel, oil, and banking industries, swinging the pendulum back toward business autonomy.[8]

At the same time, government gave large land grants as incentives for private business to build railroads. Several railroads had grown large and strong through mergers, and people began to use them because their service was faster, cheaper, and more efficient. This resulted in a decline in the use of alternative forms of transportation, such as highways, rivers, and canals. Many railroads began to abuse their favored positions. For example, a railroad that had a monopoly on service to a particular town might have charged unfairly high rates for the service. Competitive railroads sometimes agreed among themselves to charge high but comparable rates. They charged higher rates for shorter hauls, and gave preference to large shippers over smaller shippers. Public criticism of these practices led to the passage of the Interstate Commerce Act of 1887, which was intended to prevent discrimination and abuses by the railroads. This Act marked the beginning of extensive federal government regulation of interstate commerce. It created the Interstate Commerce Commission, which became the first federal regulatory agency and a model for future agencies.[9]

Many large manufacturing and mining firms also began to abuse consumers during the late 1800s. Typical actions included the elimination of competition and the charging of excessively high prices. During this period, several large firms formed organizations known as *trusts*. A trust was an organization that brought all or most competitors under a common control that then permitted them to eliminate most of the remaining competitors by price-cutting, an act that forced the remaining competitors out of business. Then the trusts would restrict production and raise prices. As a response, Congress passed the Sherman Antitrust Act (Sherman Act) in 1890, which became the first in a series of actions intended to control monopolies in various industries. The Sherman Act outlawed any contract, combination, or conspiracy in restraint of trade, and it also prohibited the monopolization of any market. In the early 1900s, the federal government used the Sherman Act to break up the Standard Oil Company, the American Tobacco Company, and several other large firms that had abused their economic power.[10]

The Clayton Antitrust Act was passed in 1914 to augment the Sherman Act. It addressed other abusive practices that had arisen. It outlawed price discrimination that gave favored buyers preference over others and forbade anticompetitive contracts, whereby a company would agree to sell only to suppliers who agreed not to sell the products of a rival competitor. The Act prohibited an assortment of other anticompetitive practices. Also in 1914, Congress formed the Federal Trade Commission, which was intended to maintain free and fair competition and to protect consumers from unfair or misleading practices.[11]

The Great Depression led to President Franklin Roosevelt's New Deal and the creation of more regulatory agencies.[12] Significant legislation included the Securities Act of 1933 and the Securities and Exchange Act of 1934. These laws were aimed at curbing abuses in the stock market, stabilizing markets, and restoring investor confidence in order to prevent a second depression. Significant labor legislation during this period signaled government involvement in a new area. Several examples were the 1926 Railway Labor Act, the 1932 Norris–LaGuardia Act, and the 1935 Wagner Act. During the New Deal period in the 1930s, government took on a new dimension in its relationship with business, actively assuming responsibility for restoring prosperity and promoting economic growth through public works programs. In 1946, this new role of government was formalized with the passage of the Full Employment Act. Prior to the mid-1950s, most congressional legislation affecting business was economic in nature. The 1960s and 1970s continued the trend of government involvement, but the concern was largely with the quality of life.[13] Several illustrations of this include the Civil Rights Act of 1964, the Water Quality Act of 1965, the Occupational Safety and Health Act of 1970, the Consumer Product Safety Act of 1972, and the Warranty Act of 1975.

The pendulum swung back when Ronald Reagan came into office in 1980. Many were growing weary of an active federal role. Throughout the 1980s, the federal government assumed a smaller and smaller role, especially in terms of monitoring and regulating business. It was not without reason, therefore, that in late 1989 *Time* magazine ran a cover story entitled "Is Government Dead?"[14] The "Reagan Revolution" of an inactive federal government had left the public with a desire for government to become active again. It was against this backdrop that George Herbert Walker Bush was elected president in 1988. During the first Bush administration (1988–1992), the country witnessed a growth in the rate of federal government spending.

The Clinton administration (1992–2000) then sought a middle ground, advocating a more activist role for the government in international politics and social concerns, while launching other initiatives to control federal spending. As the economy rebounded in the early 1990s, the peace dividend bore fruit, cost-cutting initiatives took hold, and the rate of government spending slowed dramatically.[15] With the exception of the Americans with Disabilities Act of 1990, the 1990s were characterized by financial deregulation. The repeal of the Glass–Steagall Act, the Commodity Futures Modernization Act, and the revisions to the Community Reinvestment Act all created a more permissive lending environment that, many argue, led to the financial crisis of 2008.[16]

George W. Bush came into office in 2001 on a platform of a reduced role for federal government; however, the attack on the World Trade Center changed everything.[17] Repercussions of the attack, such as the bailout of the troubled airline industry, relief for other distressed industries, the increase in military spending, and the federalization of airport security expanded dramatically both government spending and governmental intervention in business activities.[18] Key examples of this are the USA Patriot Act of 2001 and the Homeland Security Act. In addition, the passage of the Sarbanes–Oxley Act brought stricter regulation to publicly traded businesses.

By the end of the G. W. Bush's second term, the financial crisis prompted bailouts of the financial services and auto industries that were supported by both then-President Bush and President-elect Obama. When Barack Obama became President in 2009, the economic crisis was in full swing and government was involved in business operations at historically high levels. He continued that trend through a variety of initiatives such as efforts to institute new banking regulations and fees to recoup the bailout money. He also made plans to institute a community bank lending fund to encourage loans to small businesses. In its first four years, the Obama administration passed new regulations establishing credit card rules, health-care reform, consumer financial protection, and financial regulatory reform.

Just as the areas in which government has chosen to initiate legislation keep changing, the multiplicity of roles that government has assumed has increased the complexity of its relationship with business. Government is not only a regulator of business that can determine the rules of the game, but it is also a major purchaser with buying power that can affect a business's or industry's likelihood of survival. It can strengthen some businesses and industries while weakening others through the setting of government policy. It can even create new businesses and industries through subsidization and privatization. The range of government roles illuminates the crucial interconnectedness between business and government and the difficulty both business and the public have in fully understanding (much less prescribing) what government's role ought to be in relation to business.

The Roles of Government and Business

We do not intend to philosophize in this chapter on the ideal role of government in relation to business, because this is outside our stakeholder frame of reference. However, we will strive for an understanding of current major issues as they pertain to this vital relationship. For effective management, government's role as a stakeholder must be understood.

The fundamental question underlying our entire discussion of business or government relationships is, "What should be the respective roles of business and government in our socioeconomic system?" This question is far easier to ask than to answer, but as we explore it, some important basic understandings begin to emerge.

The issue could be stated in a different fashion: Given all the tasks that must be accomplished to make our society work, which of these tasks should be handled by government and which by business? This poses the issue clearly, but other questions remain unanswered. If we decide, for example, that it is best to let business handle the production and distribution roles in our society, the next question becomes, "How much autonomy are we willing to allow business?" If our goals were simply the production and distribution of goods and services, we would not have to constrain business severely. In modern times, however, other goals have been added to the production and distribution functions—a safe working environment for those engaging in production, equal employment opportunities, fair pay, clean air, safe products, employee rights, and so on. When we superimpose these goals on basic economic goals, the task of business becomes much more complex and challenging.

Because we do not automatically factor these more socially oriented goals into business decision making and processes, it often falls on the government to ensure that those goals that reflect social concerns be achieved. Thus, whereas the marketplace dictates economic production decisions, government becomes one of the citizenry's designated representatives charged with articulating and protecting the public interest.

A Clash of Ethical Belief Systems

A clash of emphases partially forms the crux of the antagonistic relationship that has evolved between business and government over the years. Although this clash varies

FIGURE 11-1   The Clash of Ethical Systems between Business and Government

Business Beliefs	Government Beliefs
• Individualistic ethic	• Collectivistic ethic
• Maximum concession to self-interest	• Subordination of individual goals and self-interest to group and group interests
• Minimizing the load of obligations society imposes on the individual (personal freedom)	• Maximizing the obligations assumed by the individual and discouraging self-interest
• Emphasizes inequalities of individuals	• Emphasizes equality of individuals

© Cengage Learning

between different countries and cultures, the underlying tension between business and government still holds true. This problem has been termed "a clash of ethical systems." The two ethical systems (systems of belief) are the **individualistic ethic of business** and the **collectivistic ethic of government**. Figure 11-1 summarizes the characteristics of these two philosophies.[19]

The clash of these two ethical systems partially explains why the business or government relationship is adversarial in nature. In elaborating on the adversarial nature of the business or government relationship, Neil Jacoby offered the following comments:

> *Officials of government characteristically look upon themselves as probers, inspectors, taxers, regulators, and punishers of business transgressions. Businesspeople typically view government agencies as obstacles, constraints, delayers, and impediments to economic progress, having much power to stop and little to start.*[20]

Executives continue to express frustration with government. In a recent McKinsey survey of executives from a range of industries and functional specialists, nearly half expressed serious frustration with government involvement in business.[21] The frustrations included concerns that regulators and policy makers do not understand the economics of their industry (41 percent), that government often blames business for society's problems (44 percent), and that it is difficult to determine the best way to work productively with government (44 percent).[22]

The business–government relationship not only continues to be adversarial but it also is more complicated in the 21st century. The goals and values of a pluralistic society continue to be complex, numerous, interrelated, and difficult to reconcile. At the same time, economic conditions compel governments around the world to take a more active role in the economy.[23] As the conflicts among diverse interest groups increase, it becomes more difficult to reconcile trade-off decisions and establish social priorities. An NBC/*Wall Street Journal* poll of adults in the United States underscores the underlying tensions in the relationship. When asked about the role of government in business following the economic crisis, 49 percent said that the government was doing too many things and 45 percent said that the government should do more.[24] The relative pros and cons of government intervention in business continue to serve as fuel for debates.[25]

Interaction of Business, Government, and the Public

This section offers a brief overview of the influence relationships among business, government, and the public. This should be helpful in understanding both the nature of the public policy decision-making process and the current problems that characterize the

FIGURE 11-2

Interaction among Business, Government, and the Public

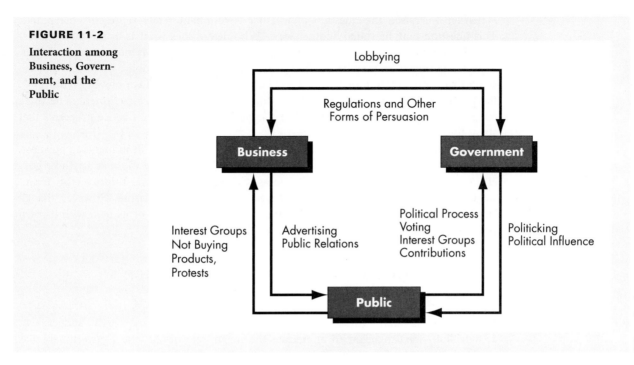

© Cengage Learning

business–government relationship. Figure 11-2 illustrates the pattern of these influence relationships.

One might rightly ask at this point, "Why include the public? Isn't the public represented by government?" In an ideal world, perhaps this would be true. To help us appreciate that government functions somewhat apart from the public, we depict it separately in the diagram. In addition, the public has its own unique methods of influence that we also depict separately.

Government–Business Relationship

Government influences business through regulation, taxation, and other forms of persuasion that we will consider in more detail in the next section. Business, likewise, has its approaches to influencing government, which we will deal with in Chapter 12. Lobbying, in one form or another, is business's primary means of influencing government.

Public–Government Relationship

The public uses the political processes of voting and electing officials (or removing them from office) to influence government. It also exerts its influence by forming special-interest groups (farmers, small business owners, educators, senior citizens, truckers, manufacturers, and so forth) to wield more targeted influence. Government, in turn, uses politicking, public policy formation, and other political influences to have an impact on the public.

Business–Public Relationship

Business influences the public through advertising, public relations, and other forms of communication. The public influences business through the marketplace or by forming special-interest groups (e.g., AARP, Friends of the Earth, American Civil Liberties Union) and protest groups.

Earlier we raised the question of whether government really represents the public. This question may be stated another way: "Who determines what is in the public interest?" In our pluralistic society, determining the public interest is not a simple matter. Whereas government may be the official representative of the public, we should not assume that representation occurs in a straightforward fashion. As we saw in Figure 11-2, the public takes its own initiatives both with business and with government. The three major groups, therefore, are involved in a dynamic interplay of influence processes that strive to define the current public interest.

Our central concern in this chapter is with government's role in influencing business, and we now turn our attention to that topic. We will begin to see more clearly how government is a major stakeholder of business. Government's official priority is in representing the public interest as it sees and interprets the public's wishes. However, like all large bureaucratic organizations, government also takes on a life of its own with its own goals and agenda.

Government's Nonregulatory Influence on Business

By recognizing that the U.S. federal government's proposed 2013 budget was $3.8 trillion, we can begin to appreciate the magnitude of the effect government has on all institutions in society.[26] We limit our treatment to the federal government's influence on business, but we must remain mindful of the presence and influence of state, local, and other governments as well.

Broadly speaking, we may categorize the kinds of influence government has on business as *nonregulatory* and *regulatory*. In the next section, we focus on government regulation, but in this section, let us consider the wide range of *nonregulatory* influences that government has on business.

Two major issues merit consideration before we examine some of the specific policy tools or mechanisms government uses to influence business. These two major issues are (1) industrial policy and (2) privatization. Industrial policy is concerned with the role that government plays in a national economy, and privatization zeroes in on the question of whether current public functions (e.g., public education, public transit, social security, fire service) should be turned over to the private sector (business). Both of these issues have important implications for the business–government relationship. They are both important, because they seem to come into and out of popularity on a regular basis.

Industrial Policy

Industrial policy is "every form of state intervention that affects industry as a distinct part of the economy."[27] This very broad definition by itself does not give us enough focus to understand the concept. Industrial policy has differed over time and across countries in both its philosophy and its actions.[28] In spite of the continuing differences between countries, a global shift in approach to industrial policy has occurred. In his article, "Industrial Policy: A Dying Breed or a Re-emerging Phoenix?," Karl Aiginger notes the gradual demise of the old form of industrial policy:

> *The interest in industrial policy has recently re-emerged, although not for industrial policy as it used to be. Supporting ailing industries, subsidies, and preventing exit will never be completely abandoned, but they are no longer supported by policy makers, evidence, or economic theory. Fortunately, traditional industrial policy has become much more difficult thanks to trade agreements, community law and WTO.[29]*

The newer form of industrial policy is exemplified by Robert Reich in his book *The Next American Frontier*, wherein he argues for a national industrial policy that attempts to identify winning (or sunrise) industries and foster their growth while redirecting resources from losing (or sunset) industries.[30] Reich's book was published when the United States lost significant ground to Japan as the world leader in industrial expansion. Many experts saw the very survival of the U.S. economy at stake in the face of subsidized foreign competition from Japan and other industrialized countries. Indeed, a trade confrontation arose between the United States and Japan over the significant trade imbalances arising out of these issues.

U.S. trade policy is and has been an intensely debated topic.[31] There has always been a strong reaction to any form of industrial policy in the United States because it conflicts with widely held views on the role of government in the economy.[32] During the Reagan (1980–1988) and first Bush (1988–1992) administrations, the notion of industrial policy was not looked upon with great favor. Both these administrations advocated a free market posture rather than government activism via industrial policy. President Bill Clinton, however, supported several actions that typify an active industrial policy. For example, the Clinton administration took an activist stance in promoting the Internet by creating a Framework for Global Electronic Commerce. This framework outlined key principles for supporting the evolution of electronic commerce, identified where international efforts were needed, and designated the U.S. governmental agencies responsible for leading the effort. The administration did this because businesses were wary of becoming involved in the developing Internet because they were unsure of the legal environment and they feared government intervention would stifle Internet commerce.[33]

The George W. Bush administration entered office intending to follow in the footsteps of the early Reagan and Bush administrations by adopting a free-market posture and minimizing government intervention. However, the tragic events of September 11, 2001, prompted extensive new regulations in the areas of homeland security, and the Enron meltdown, as well as the other financial scandals that followed, prompted new regulations in corporate governance. That trend continued with the Obama administration, which entered office during a deep global recession and spent the first four years focused on digging out of an economic hole. These events prompted a stronger industrial policy in areas such as financial services and led to auto industry bailouts, student and mortgage loan intervention, and high-tech investments in non-carbon-based energies.

The trend toward stronger industrial policies is likely to continue for a while as countries work to recover from the after-effects of the global financial crisis. Josh Lerner and William Sahlman recommend a variety of policy decisions that a government can use to revive entrepreneurship at a time when venture capital funding has diminished.[34] These include funding basic research, developing tax policy that rewards risks, and making certain the competitive playing field is level to facilitate new entry.[35] Government can also aid in building the quality of human resources by supporting education and making certain that people who receive a quality education are welcome to remain in the country after graduation.[36] In essence, government must assess the impacts of all policies and decisions on the climate for new enterprises.[37] A strong industrial policy also can help to maintain sustainability amid the challenges of a global downturn. Europe 2020, the European Union's growth strategy for overcoming the financial crisis, focuses on growing in a way that is smart, sustainable, and inclusive.[38] The goal is sustainable growth, leading to "a resource efficient, greener and more competitive economy."[39]

The global financial crisis compelled governments around the world to take an active part in reviving economic growth and restoring financial stability.[40] To do this, governments needed not only to focus on economic reform but also on ways to make government more efficient and effective.[41]

Historically, the U.S. government has opted to minimize government involvement in business, but crises can always change that stance. The recent global financial crisis led to bailouts in the auto, banking, and insurance industries. After the September 11, 2001, terrorist attacks, the crippled airline industry requested bailouts of about $24 billion. Congress passed a bailout program of $15 billion—$5 billion in immediate cash assistance and $10 billion in loan guarantees.[42] Other affected industries soon made requests as well. There is a long history of government stepping in to rescue industries in distress. In 1971 the Lockheed Corporation received $250 million in loan guarantees from Congress. In 1976 the federal government merged seven failing Northeast railroads and then spent about $7 billion to keep the combined entity afloat. In 1979 the Chrysler Corporation received up to $1.5 billion in loan guarantees. In 1989 Congress addressed the Savings and Loan Crisis by closing more than 1,000 S&Ls at a cost of $124 billion.[43]

Some government interventions have been successes while others have faltered. Chrysler paid off its loan seven years early, and the government received a profit of $350 million. However, the Lockheed bailout was rocky from the start. When it was revealed that Lockheed had paid foreign bribes, the government ousted two top executives and proceeded to give Lockheed activities very close scrutiny.[44] In the case of airlines, the U.S. government made $119 million from its equity ownership in the shares of airlines like Frontier.[45] One key to success is for the government to require equity in return for aid: The U.S. government made its profit from the Chrysler bailout due to such an arrangement.[46] It would seem logical then that all government bailouts would include an equity arrangement; however, corporate lobbyists typically block the way.[47]

One of the largest and most controversial bailout was the $182 billion rescue of the American International Group (AIG). The debt was repaid, with $22 billion profit for the government, but it remains in the news. Maurice Greenberg, former AIG CEO, sued the federal government arguing that the bailout was unconstitutional and cheated shareholders.[48] The AIG board voted unanimously not to join the lawsuit, and the government called it frivolous, saying bankruptcy was AIG's only alternative and that would have harmed shareholders more.[49] Lawmakers said that if AIG joined the suit it would "bite the hand that fed them" and "become the poster company for ingratitude and chutzpah."[50]

Because the bailouts arising from the global financial crisis are still playing out, we do not yet know what the final tally will be. It can be difficult to assess their outcome from the news as the bailouts were politically charged events, and so each side slants the figure to their advantage. ProPublica, an independent nonprofit newsroom, is keeping a running tab of the status of the payment to the U.S. bailout recipients (http://projects.propublica.org/bailout/list). Each recipient is listed separately and an overall tally is kept at the top. In total, 936 recipients received $608 billion in total disbursement. At this writing, $367 billion was returned and the government received $183 billion in revenues from dividends, interest, and other fees. Thus, the total net at this writing is −$58 billion.[51]

Few observers today would argue that a strong industrial policy helps firms compete in a fast-moving global economy. Government is not known for being nimble. However, a country without an industrial policy can find itself losing out to countries that are willing to invest in industries they value and in companies they want to have operating within their borders.[52] Most developed countries are not seeking to institute a strong industrial policy, if they can avoid doing so.[53] Nevertheless, government intervention in business continues, sometimes in ways that are appropriate and sometimes not. Various interventions such as "voluntary" restrictions on imports, occasional bailouts for nearly bankrupt companies, and a wide array of subsidies, loan guarantees, and special tax benefits for particular firms and industries constitute an industrial policy by default.[54] Thus, it is important to think carefully about the role of government in business so that a default industrial policy does not emerge.

ETHICS IN PRACTICE CASE

The VOIP Regulatory Dilemma

Voice over Internet Protocol (VOIP) enables users to make telephone calls by using the Internet. As such, it provides regulators with a dilemma—is it a "telecommunications service," due to the fact that a phone call is being made or is it an "information service" because it uses the Internet? The decision has ramifications because, in the United States, telecommunications services are regulated and information services are not. VOIP services have grown in popularity because they are less expensive to operate. With their rise, the use of traditional telephone services has declined. In the United States, that decline in traditional telephone usage has decreased the amount of money in the Universal Services Fund (USF), a fund that provides subsidies for low-income individuals and access for schools, libraries, and rural areas. The growing use of VOIP is also problematic for 911 services because VOIP calls do not provide the caller's location. A controversial concern is whether VOIP should be included in CALEA, the Communications Assistance for Law Enforcement Act, and be required to facilitate government wiretapping and surveillance.

Opponents of VOIP regulation consider it a threat to Internet freedom. They believe that regulating VOIP will stifle innovation and slow the advancement of emerging technologies. Proponents of VOIP regulation argue that a lack of oversight will lead to monopolies and limit affordable access, hurting poor people, small companies, and startups. At present, U.S. regulation of VOIP is a "crazy quilt" of different rules for different types of VOIP in different states.

1. What are the ethical issues in this case? Who are the stakeholders and what are their stakes?
2. When dealing with VOIP, how do you decide between freedom and protection when enhancing one diminishes the other? On what basis are you making your decision?
3. If you were responsible for regulating VOIP, what would you recommend? What trade-offs would you make? What type of industrial policy would your decision be advocating? Be specific.

Sources: Susan Crawford, "Torching California's Broadband Future: Why Your State Is Next," *Wired* (August 27, 2012), http://www.wired.com/business/2012/08/torching-californias-broadband-future-why-your-state-is-next/; Larry Downes, "The Madness of Regulating VOIP," *Forbes* (September 10, 2012), http://www.forbes.com/sites/larrydownes/2012/09/10/the-madness-of-regulating-voip-as-a-public-utility/; Raul Magallanes "Internet Telephony: A Regulatory Oxymoron," *Satellite News* (July 2012), 3.

Interest in the concept of industrial policy ebbs and flows, depending on the political philosophy of the presiding administration and on events in the external environment. Many of the problems that started the current debate are still with us, while new problems have arisen to add further complexity to the issue. Industrial policy (whether coordinated or by default) is a powerful nonregulating approach by government to influence business that is certain to be debated for years to come.

Privatization

Privatization, generally speaking, refers to the process of changing a public organization to private control or ownership.[55] The intent is to capture both the discipline of the free market and a spirit of entrepreneurial risk-taking.[56] To understand privatization, we need to differentiate two functions government might perform: (1) *producing* a service and (2) *providing* a service.[57]

Producing versus Providing a Service   A city government would be *providing* a service if it employed a private security firm to work at the local arena during the state basketball play-offs. This same city government would be *producing* a service if its own police force provided security at the same basketball tournament. The federal government would be providing medical care to the aged with a national Medicare program. The "production" of medical care would be coming from private physicians. The government would be providing and producing medical care if it employed its own staff of doctors, as, for example, the military does. The terminology can be very confusing, but the distinction must be made, because sometimes government provides a service (has a program for and actually pays for a service) and at other times it also produces a service (has its own employees who do it).[58]

The Privatization Debate   Proponents of privatization in both the United States and Europe suggest that the functions of entire bureaucracies need to be contracted out to the private sector. They maintain that government at all levels is involved in thousands of businesses in which it has no real comparative advantage and no basic reason for being involved. They also argue that publicly owned enterprises are less efficient and less flexible than are competitive private firms.[59] Opponents of privatization contend that certain activities cannot be safely or effectively handled by the private sector. They point to the **federalization** of airport security (the return of airport security to the government sector) following the attack on the World Trade Center. Several cities are now considering taking their electric business back from private utilities in order to deal with climate change and power disruptions.[60]

Successful privatization can achieve both financial efficiency and broad social goals. When Argentina privatized its national water system, the results were impressive. Service expanded to reach areas that were previously underserved.[61] Furthermore, far fewer children died from infections and parasitic diseases, and investment in this endeavor soared.[62] When things go badly, however, a public backlash can stunt privatization efforts. Former Chicago mayor Richard Daley received harsh criticism after leasing 36,000 parking meters to a Morgan Stanley-led investor group for 75 years when the new operators moved quickly to quadruple parking rates and eliminate free parking on Sundays.[63] Some cities, such as New York City and Los Angeles, dropped plans to privatize meters after observing the Chicago backlash.[64] The privatization of New Jersey halfway houses has been a recent subject of investigative scrutiny: From 2005 to 2012, 5,100 inmates escaped, some of whom committed murder and other violent crimes shortly thereafter.[65] In contrast, escapes from the state prisons are in single digits each year, if they occur at all.[66]

Privatization efforts are always undertaken with the hope that they will lead to improvements in efficiency and overall performance. In some cases, these hopes are realized, but in others, they are not. Typically, privatization works best when the pursuit of profit does not work against broader social goals or public policy.[67] BP was an unprofitable but safe company when the British government controlled it.[68] It was celebrated as a privatization success until a series of disasters illuminated the corners that had been cut in pursuit of profits. A refinery explosion killed 15 and injured about 170. Then an oil spill in Prudhoe Bay served as a precursor to the biggest oil spill in U.S. history—the Deepwater Horizon explosion that also killed 11 people.[69] However, differences in post-privatization performance can also result from differences in the ways that firms implement privatization programs. The nature of top management, the functioning of the board, and the strategic actions the firms undertake will all contribute to the likelihood of a privatization strategy's success.[70] This was supported by the findings of a study on the efficiency and effectiveness of privatized urban transit services after 25 years of operation. They found no difference between public and private provision of services and concluded that the situation specifics are better predictors of performance than whether the service was public or private.[71]

The two issues, industrial policy and privatization, are largely unresolved and so they continue to be discussed and debated. As we have seen, the success of these efforts is largely dependent on their context—both the environments in which they are adopted and the ways in which they are implemented. It is clear that both industrial policy and privatization will have significant implications for the business–government relationship for years to come.

We now return to our discussion of the ways in which government uses various policies and mechanisms for influencing business.

Other Nonregulatory Governmental Influences on Business

Government has a significant impact on business by virtue of the fact that it has a large payroll and is a *major employer* itself. At all levels, government employs millions of people who, as a consequence of being government employees, see things from the government's perspective. Government is also in the position of being a standard setter; for example, the eight-hour workday began in the federal government.

Government is one of the largest *purchasers* of goods and services produced in the private sector. Some key industries, such as aerospace, electronics, and shipbuilding, are very dependent on government purchasing. Government can exert significant influence over the private sector by its insistence that minorities be hired, depressed areas be favored, small businesses be favored, and so on. Changes in government policy can dramatically change a firm's business environment.[72] For some firms in narrow markets, such as defense, the government dominates and controls whether or not those firms have a good year—indeed, whether or not they survive at all.[73]

Government influences the behavior of business using *subsidies* in a variety of ways. Subsidies are made available to industries such as agriculture, fishing, transportation, nuclear energy, and housing and to groups in special categories, such as minority-owned enterprises and businesses in depressed areas. Quite often, these subsidies have special qualifications attached. Government also influences business, albeit indirectly, by virtue of its *transfer payments*. Government provides money for social security, welfare, and other entitlement programs that totals hundreds of billions of dollars every year. These impacts are indirect, but they do significantly affect the market for business's goods and services.[74]

Government is a major *competitor* of business. Organizations such as the TVA compete with private suppliers of electricity; the Government Printing Office competes with private commercial publishers and printing firms; and the United States Postal Service competes with private delivery services. In areas such as health, education, recreation, and security, the competition between government and private firms exists at all levels—federal, state, and local.

Government loans and *loan guarantees* are sources of influence as well. Government lends money directly to small businesses, housing providers, farmers, and energy companies. Often such loans are made at lower interest rates than those of private competitors. During the global financial crisis, the U.S. Federal Reserve loaned money to undercapitalized banks and the Department of Education essentially acquired the private student loan market.[75]

Taxation is another example of a government influence. Tax deductibility, tax incentives, depreciation policies, and tax credits are tools that are all at the disposal of the government. As a result of the global financial crisis, Italy's Prime Minister Mario Monti implemented a €20 billion program of austerity measures to deal with €1.9 trillion of debt; included in these was an ownership levy on high-performance vehicles.[76] After that, Ferraris and Maseratis began disappearing from Italian streets. The number of second-handhigh-performance cars exported from Italy tripled in the first five months of 2012 and sales of new cars plunged 47 percent.[77]

Monetary policy can have a profound effect on business. In the United States, the Federal Reserve System is independent of the executive branch; however, it often responds to

Spotlight on Sustainability

The Green Guides

As consumers have become increasingly interested in purchasing environmentally friendly products, companies are marketing their products and services as being eco-friendly. Unfortunately, the reality does not always match the claims. In an effort to help marketers avoid making misleading claims, the Federal Trade Commission (FTC) issued revised "Green Guides" that specify what must be true when marketers make specific claims. For example, a firm cannot claim a product is degradable unless, after being disposed in the customary manner, that product will break down completely and return to nature within one year. The FTC also cautions marketers from using terms such as *eco-friendly* or *environmentally friendly*. According to the FTC, those terms connote far-reaching benefits to the environment that few, if any, products actually possess. The Revised Green Guides are available at http://www.ftc.gov/os/2012/10/greenguides.pdf.

Source: "FTC Issues Revised Green Guides," http://www.ftc.gov/opa/2012/10/greenguides.shtm. Accessed February 2, 2013.

presidential leadership or initiatives. Mario Draghi, the president of the European Central Bank (ECB) gave what some observers call "the speech that saved Europe" when he said the ECB would do "whatever it takes" to save the euro.[78] He then did not have to buy Spanish or Italian bonds because his open-ended commitment convinced private investors to buy them.[79]

Finally, *moral suasion* is a government tool. This refers to the government's attempts to "persuade" business to act in the public interest by taking or not taking a particular course of action. These public-interest appeals might include a request to roll back a price hike, show restraint on wage and salary increases, or exercise "voluntary" restraints of one kind or another.

Government's Regulatory Influences on Business

In many ways, government regulation has been the most controversial issue in the business–government relationship. Government regulation has affected virtually every aspect of how business functions. It has affected the terms and conditions under which firms have competed in their respective industries. It has touched almost every business decision ranging from the production of goods and services to packaging, distribution, marketing, and service. Most people agree that some degree of regulation has been necessary to ensure that consumers and employees are treated fairly and are not exposed to unreasonable hazards and that the environment is protected. In fact, businesses have often pushed for greater regulation believing that certain regulations can give them a competitive edge.[80] However, they also think that government regulation has often been too extensive in scope, too costly, and inevitably burdensome in terms of paperwork requirements and red tape. One thing is clear, however: the level of regulation continues to rise.

The annual page count in the *Federal Register* is an imperfect measure of regulatory intensity, but the overall upward trend tells us something about the nature of government and business. The *Federal Register* celebrated its 80th birthday in 2006. In 1936, it contained 2,620 pages; by 2012, the page count had grown more than 30-fold to a staggering 77,249 pages.[81] The page count seems to stay high irrespective of the party in office. The highest count was 83,294 in 2010 at the end of the Clinton presidency. In 2008, the end of the George W. Bush administration, the *Federal Register* 80,700 pages.[82] By 2012, the end of the first term of the Obama administration, it had 77,249 pages.[83]

Regulation: What Does It Mean?

Generally, **regulation** refers to the act of governing, directing according to rule, or bringing under the control of law or constituted authority. Although there is no universally agreed-upon definition of federal regulation, we can look to the definition of a federal regulatory agency proposed years ago by the Senate Governmental Affairs Committee.[84] It described a federal regulatory agency as one that:

1. Has decision-making authority.
2. Establishes standards or guidelines conferring benefits and imposing restrictions on business conduct.
3. Operates principally in the sphere of domestic business activity.
4. Has its head and/or members appointed by the President (generally subject to Senate confirmation).
5. Has its legal procedures generally governed by the Administrative Procedures Act.

The commerce clause of the U.S. Constitution grants to the government the legal authority to regulate. Within the confines of a regulatory agency as outlined here, the composition and functioning of regulatory agencies differ. Some are headed by an administrator and are located within an executive department—for example, the Federal Aviation Administration (FAA). Others are independent commissions composed of a chairperson and several members located outside the executive and legislative branches—such as the Interstate Commerce Commission (ICC), the Federal Communications Commission (FCC), and the Securities and Exchange Commission (SEC).[85]

Reasons for Regulation

Regulations have come about over the years for a variety of reasons. Some managers probably think that government is just sitting on the sidelines looking for reasons to interfere with their business. There are several legitimate reasons why government regulation has evolved, although these same businesspeople may not entirely agree with them. For the most part, government regulation has arisen because some kind of **market failure** (failure of the free enterprise system) has occurred and government, intending to represent the public interest, has chosen to take corrective action. We should make it clear, however, that many regulations resulted from special-interest groups lobbying successfully for them. Four major reasons or justifications for regulations are typically offered: (1) controlling natural monopolies, (2) controlling negative externalities, (3) achieving social goals, and (4) other reasons.

Controlling Natural Monopolies. One of the earliest circumstances in which government felt a need to regulate occurred when a natural monopoly existed. A **natural monopoly** exists in a market where the economies of scale are so great that the largest firm has the lowest costs and thus is able to drive out its competitors. Such a firm can supply the entire market more efficiently and cheaply than can several smaller firms. Local telephone service is a good example, because parallel sets of telephone wires would involve waste and duplication that would be much more costly. The same is true for railroads. Monopolies such as this may seem "natural," but when left to their own devices they could restrict output and raise prices. This potential abuse justifies the regulation of monopolies. As a consequence, we see public utilities, for example, regulated by a public utility commission. This commission determines the rates that the monopolist may charge its customers.[86]

Related to the control of natural monopolies is the government's desire to intervene when it thinks companies have engaged in anticompetitive practices. An example of this was the Justice Department's investigation of the Microsoft Corporation case in which the company was accused of anticompetitive trade practices. Microsoft would bundle new features into its Windows operating system as a way of breaking into new markets. The company then designed the operating system so that it worked more smoothly with Microsoft products than with others—giving it a clear and, according to the courts, unfair marketing advantage.[87] Nearly ten years after the effort to break up Microsoft began, the saga continued. Google filed a complaint alleging that Microsoft's new operating system, Vista, was designed to discourage use of Google's desktop search program.[88] In the end, a settlement was reached and Microsoft made requested changes to Vista.[89] Now, many people are concerned that Google will dominate online computing services in the same way that Microsoft dominated software.[90] The argument presented was that Google arranged search results in a way that highlighted its own services. In 2013, a two-year investigation of Google ended with a unanimous FTC decision that Google had not violated antitrust or anticompetition laws.[91] Google agreed to share more information and not to scrape Web content from rivals.[92] A month later, Google submitted a proposal to the European Commission to settle an antitrust investigation in hopes of reaching a similar decision and settlement from them.[93]

Controlling Negative Externalities.   Another important rationale for government regulation is that of controlling the **negative externalities** (or spillover effects) that result when the manufacture or use of a product gives rise to unplanned or unintended side effects on third parties (the producer and the consumer are first and second parties). Examples of these negative externalities are air pollution, water pollution, and improper disposal of toxic wastes. The consequence of such negative externalities is that neither the producer nor the consumer of the product directly "pays" for all the "costs" that are created by the manufacture of the product. The "costs" that must be borne by the public include an unpleasant or a foul atmosphere, illness, and the resulting health care costs. Some have called these **social costs**, because they are absorbed by society rather than incorporated into the cost of making the product.

Preventing negative externalities is enormously expensive, and few firms are willing to pay for these added costs voluntarily. This is especially true in an industry that produces an essentially undifferentiated product, such as steel, where the millions of dollars needed to protect the environment would only add to the cost of the product and provide no benefit to the purchaser. In such situations, therefore, firms in the industry may even welcome government regulation because it requires all firms competing in a given industry to operate according to the same rules. By forcing all firms to incur the costs, regulation can level the competitive playing field.

Just as companies do not voluntarily take on extra expenditures for environmental protection, individuals often behave in the same fashion. For example, automobile emissions are one of the principal forms of air pollution; but, how many private individuals would voluntarily request an emissions control system if it were offered as optional equipment? In situations such as this, a government standard that requires everyone to adhere to the regulation is much more likely to address the public's concern for air pollution.[94]

Achieving Social Goals.   Government not only employs regulations to address market failures and negative externalities, but it also seeks to use regulations to help achieve certain **social goals** it deems to be in the public interest. Some of these social goals are related to negative externalities in the sense that government is attempting to correct problems that might also be viewed as negative externalities by particular groups. An example of this might be the harmful effects of a dangerous product or the unfair treatment of minorities resulting from employment discrimination. These externalities are not as obvious as air pollution, but they are just as real.

Another important social goal of government is to keep people informed. One could argue that inadequate provision of information is a serious problem and that government should use its regulatory powers to require firms to reveal certain kinds of information to consumers. Thus, the Consumer Product Safety Commission requires firms to warn consumers of potential product hazards through labeling requirements. Other regulatory mandates that address the issue of inadequate information include grading standards, weight and size information, truth-in-advertising requirements, product safety standards, and so on.

Other important social goals that have been addressed include preservation of national security (deregulation of oil prices to lessen dependence on imports), considerations of fairness or equity (employment discrimination laws), protection of those who provide essential services (farmers), allocation of scarce resources (gasoline rationing), and protection of consumers from excessively high price increases (natural gas regulation).[95]

Other Reasons There are several other reasons for government regulation. One is to control **excess profits** by transferring income for the purposes of economic fairness. For example, one observer recently suggested that U.S. defense contractors should pay excess-profits tax for the money they made during the wars in Iraq and Afghanistan.[96] He quoted Franklin D. Roosevelt who said the government should make sure "a few do not gain from the sacrifices of many" and noted that profits of the five largest defense contractors increased 450 percent from 2002 to 2011.[97] This idea is unlikely to take hold, but it provides a good example of a way in which a country can use an excess profits tax if it chooses to do so.

Another commonly advanced rationale for regulation is to deal with **excessive competition**. The basic idea behind this rationale is that excessive competition will lead to prices being set at unprofitably low levels. This action will force firms out of business and ultimately will result in products that are too costly because the remaining firm will raise its prices to excessive levels, leaving the public worse off than before.[98]

Types of Regulation

Broadly speaking, government regulations address two basic types of goals, economic and social; therefore, it has become customary to identify two different types of regulation: economic regulation and social regulation.

Economic Regulation The classical or traditional form of regulation that dates back to the 1800s in the United States is **economic regulation**. This type of regulation is best exemplified by old-line regulatory bodies such as the Interstate Commerce Commission (ICC), which was created in 1887 by Congress to regulate the railroad industry; the Civil Aeronautics Board (CAB), which was created in 1940 to regulate the airline industry; and the Federal Communications Commission (FCC), which was established in 1934 to consolidate federal regulation of interstate communications and, later, the radio, telephone, and telegraph. These regulatory bodies divide along industry lines: They regulate business behavior through controlling and influencing economic or market variables such as prices (maximum and minimum), entry to and exit from markets, and types of services offered.[99]

In the federal regulatory budget today, the major costs of economic regulation are for (1) finance and banking (e.g., Federal Deposit Insurance Corporation and Comptroller of the Currency), (2) industry-specific regulation (e.g., Federal Communications Commission and Federal Energy Regulatory Commission), and (3) general business (e.g., Department of Commerce, Department of Justice, Securities and Exchange Commission, and Federal Trade Commission).[100]

Later we discuss deregulation, a trend that has significantly affected the old-line form of economic regulation that dominated business–government relations in the last century.

Social Regulation The 1960s ushered in a new form of regulation that has come to be known as **social regulation**, because it focuses on the furtherance of societal objectives rather than on markets and economic variables. While economic regulation focuses on markets, social regulation focuses on business's impacts on people. This emphasis addresses the needs of people in their roles as employees, consumers, and citizens.

Two major examples of social regulations having specific impacts on people as employees were (1) the Civil Rights Act of 1964, which created the Equal Employment Opportunity Commission (EEOC), and (2) the creation of the Occupational Safety and Health Administration (OSHA) in 1970. The goal of the EEOC is to provide protection against discrimination in all employment practices. The goal of OSHA is to ensure that the nation's workplaces are safe and healthy.

Examples of major social regulation protecting people as consumers was the 1972 creation of the Consumer Product Safety Commission (CPSC) and the 2011 creation of the Consumer Financial Protection Bureau (CFPB). The CPSC's goal is to protect the public against unreasonable risks of injury associated with consumer products and the CFPB's goal is to protect consumers as they use financial products and services. An example of a major social regulation to protect people as citizens and residents of communities was the 1970 creation of the Environmental Protection Agency (EPA). The goal of EPA is to coordinate a variety of environmental protection efforts and to develop a unified policy at the national level. Figure 11-3 summarizes the nature of economic versus social regulations along with pertinent examples.

Whereas economic regulation aims primarily at companies competing in specific industries, social regulation tends to addresses business practices affecting all industries. However, there are social regulations that are industry specific, such as the National

FIGURE 11-3 Comparison of Economic and Social Regulations

	Economic Regulations	Social Regulations
Focus	Market conditions, economic variables (entry, exit, prices, services)	People in their roles as employees, consumers, and citizens
Industries Affected	Selected (railroads, aeronautics, communications)	Virtually all industries
Examples	Civil Aeronautics Board (CAB)	Equal Employment Opportunity Commission (EEOC)
	Federal Communications Commission (FCC)	Occupational Safety and Health Administration (OSHA) Consumer Product Safety Commission (CPSC) Environmental Protection Agency (EPA)
Current Trend	Reregulation (e.g., Financial Stability Oversight Board)	Reregulation (e.g., Consumer Financial Protection Bureau)

© Cengage Learning

FIGURE 11-4 Major U.S. Regulatory Agencies

Agency	Year Established
Interstate Commerce Commission*	1887
Federal Reserve System (Board of Governors)	1913
Federal Trade Commission	1914
International Trade Commission	1916
Federal Home Loan Bank Board**	1932
Federal Deposit Insurance Corporation	1933
Farm Credit Administration	1933
Federal Communications Commission	1934
Securities and Exchange Commission	1934
National Labor Relations Board	1935
Small Business Administration	1953
Federal Maritime Commission	1961
Council on Environmental Quality	1969
Cost Accounting Standards Board	1970
Environmental Protection Agency	1970
Equal Employment Opportunity Commission	1970
National Credit Union Administration	1970
Occupational Safety and Health Review Commission	1971
Consumer Product Safety Commission	1972
Commodity Futures Trading Commission	1974
Council on Wage and Price Stability	1974
Nuclear Regulatory Commission	1974
Federal Election Commission	1975
National Transportation Safety Board	1975
Federal Energy Regulatory Commission	1977
Office of the Federal Inspector for the Alaska Natural Gas Transportation System***	1979
Transportation Security Administration	2001
Consumer Financial Protection Bureau	2011

*Terminated in 1995. Replaced by the Surface Transportation Board.
**Terminated in 1939. Functions were reassigned to various housing agencies until 1955, when it was redesignated as an independent agency. In 1989, it was abolished and responsibility for oversight of Federal Home Loan Banks was transferred to the Federal Housing Finance Board.
***Abolished by Congress in 1992 and all powers were transferred to the Secretary of Energy.

© Cengage Learning

Highway Traffic Safety Administration (automobiles) and the Food and Drug Administration (food, drugs, medical devices, and cosmetics). Figure 11-4 summarizes the major U.S. independent regulatory agencies along with their dates of establishment. In addition to these, we should remember several regulatory agencies exist within executive departments of the government. Examples of these include the following:

Agency	Department
Food and Health Administration	Health and Human Services
Antitrust Division	Justice
Drug Enforcement Administration	Justice
Occupational Safety and Health Administration	Labor
Federal Highway Administration	Transportation

Government regulation represents a response to a felt need in the environment, so it is not surprising that the most recent regulations are responses to recent major

ETHICS IN PRACTICE CASE
Banning the Big Gulp

New York City Mayor Michael Bloomberg created a firestorm when he proposed a ban on large sugary soft drinks. The proposed ban limited sugary drinks (including sodas, energy drinks, and presweetened iced teas) to cups no bigger than 16 ounces. It does not apply to diet drinks and customers would have been allowed to get refills. The ban only applied to restaurants, movie theaters, stadiums, and arenas. It did not apply to grocery stores, drug stores, or convenience stores because those are regulated by New York State rather than the city.

The purpose of the ban was to stem a rising tide of obesity that has been linked to sugary drinks. The protests did not question the motivation; they attacked the ban on other grounds. Some argued that the ban oversteps the role of government and interferes in a personal decision. Others argued that it would create unfair competition because someone who wants a 20-ounce drink can simply go to a convenience store and buy a bottle there. The NAACP entered a lawsuit against the ban on the grounds that it generates racial discrimination because the smaller establishments to which the ban applies are more likely to be owned by people of color. At the same time, people of color have a higher incidence of obesity and so proponents argue the NAACP should welcome the ban.

1. Who are the stakeholders in this case, and what are their stakes?

2. The ban received approval from the New York City Board of Health, but a state Supreme Court judge subsequently halted it. Mayor Bloomberg vowed to appeal. Irrespective of the legal wrangling, was the ban appropriate? Should the city ever be allowed to institute it?

3. Did the ban represent racial discrimination? Was the NAACP right to join in the lawsuit?

4. Where should government (federal, state, or local) draw the line on what it regulates and what it leaves to the marketplace?

Sources: Chris Dolmetsch, "NYC Judge Told Big-Soda Ban Is Unfair to Small Business," *Bloomberg.com* (January 23, 2013), http://www.bloomberg.com/news/2013-01-23/nyc-judge-told-big-soda-ban-is-unfair-to-small-business.html. Accessed February 4, 2013.; Michael M.Grynbaum," In N.A.A.C.P., Industry Gets Ally Against Soda Ban," *The New York Times* (January 23, 2013), http://www.nytimes.com/2013/01/24/nyregion/fight-over-bloombergs-soda-ban-reaches-courtroom.html?_r=0. Accessed February 4, 2013.

environmental events including the World Trade Center attacks, the financial scandals of Enron and WorldCom, and the global financial crisis. After the attacks, national security was the primary concern. In particular, the collection, protection, and dissemination of information were affected. In response to the financial crises, new economic regulations address issues of corporate accountability. The Enron and WorldCom scandals spawned the Sarbanes–Oxley Act (SOX), which set extensive new reporting procedures and requirements for firms listed on U.S. stock exchanges and instituted severe penalties for firms that fail to comply. Then the global financial crisis gave birth to the Dodd–Frank Act, which reregulated financial markets in an effort to make another economic meltdown less likely and instituted historic new consumer protections.

Issues Related to Regulation

It is important to consider some of the issues that have arisen out of the increased governmental role in regulating business. In general, managers have been concerned with what might be called "regulatory unreasonableness."[101] We could expect that business would just as soon not have to deal with these regulatory bodies; therefore, some of business's reactions are simply related to the nuisance factor of having to deal with a complex array of restrictions. However, other legitimate issues that have arisen over the past few years also need to be addressed.

To be certain, there are benefits of government regulation. Businesses treat employees more fairly and provide them with safer work environments. Consumers are able to purchase safer products and receive more information about them. Citizens from all walks of life have cleaner air to breathe and cleaner water in lakes and rivers. These benefits are real, but their exact magnitudes are difficult to measure. Costs resulting from regulation also are difficult to measure. The **direct costs** of regulation are most visible when we look at the number of new agencies created, aggregate expenditures, and growth patterns of the budgets of federal agencies responsible for regulation. There were 14 major regulatory agencies prior to 1930, more than two dozen in 1950, and 57 by the early 1980s. The most rapid expansion in the number of agencies came in the 1970s, while the most rapid increase in spending came in the 2000s. Figure 11-5 shows the rise in spending for both economic and social regulation in millions of constant 2000 dollars.

In addition to the direct costs of administering the regulatory agencies, there are **indirect costs** such as forms, reports, and questionnaires that business must complete to satisfy the requirements of the regulatory agencies. These costs of government regulation are passed on to the consumer in the form of higher prices. There are also **induced costs**. The induced effects of regulation are diffuse and elusive, but they constitute some of the most powerful consequences of the regulatory process. In a real sense, then, these induced effects are also costs. Three effects are worthy of elaboration.[102]

1. *Innovation may be affected.* When corporate budgets must focus on "defensive research," certain types of innovation are less likely to take place. To the extent that firms must devote more of their scientific resources to meeting government requirements, fewer resources are available to dedicate to new product and process research and development and innovation. However, the relationship is anything but clear. A study showed that deregulation actually had a dramatic negative impact on public interest environmental research by public utilities, whereas regulation can have a

FIGURE 11-5   Regulatory Spending in the United States

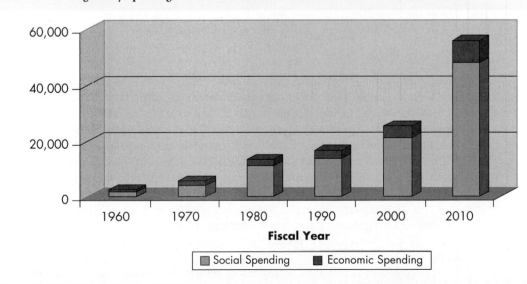

Source: Veronique de Rugy and Melinda Warren, "Regulatory Budget: Annual Report Fiscal Year 2010," *Mercatus Center* (October 2009).

positive impact on pollution abatement research by profit-maximizing firms.[103] The moral of these findings seems to be that organizations will pursue their own interests. Regulation can require firms to lower their pollution and so they can maximize their profits with greater expenditures on research to lower emissions. In contrast, utilities that once received reinforcement for doing research in the public interest may find they no longer have an incentive for that research once they begin to compete on profits.

2. *New investments in plant and equipment may be affected.* To the extent that corporate funds must be used for regulatory compliance purposes, these funds are diverted from uses that are more productive. Environmental and job safety requirements lessen productivity, and uncertainty about future regulations diminishes motivation for introducing new products and processes.[104] Once again, the incentives will play a major part. Investments that aid the firms in complying with regulations are likely to be continued or increased, whereas those that are beyond the scope of the regulation are likely to diminish.

3. *Small business may be adversely affected.* Although not intentional, federal regulations can have a disproportionately adverse effect on small firms because of economies of scale. Large firms have more money, personnel, and resources with which to get the work of government done than small firms do. They can spread the costs over a larger base, whereas small companies can find their resources drained from their efforts to comply.

Robert Reich advised executives who feel the government is breathing down their necks to "Get used to it."[105] That advice is true today, as companies worldwide will be dealing with regulatory concerns for the foreseeable future. In financial services, governments in the United States, Europe, and Japan now hold equity in banks. In housing, the U.S. government has taken over a large portion of outstanding mortgage loans. The controversial bailout of insurance giant AIG made the United States a major participant in insurance markets. In the auto industry, the United States, Canada, Germany, Sweden, and Japan provided tens of billions of dollars in loans and equity. The United States, Europe, and Japan are all subsidizing non-carbon-based energy development. The United States is enacting health care reforms that will affect both the health care and pharmaceutical industries, and it is investing in greater broadband coverage that will affect the telecom industry.

Deregulation

Quite frequently, trends and countertrends overlap with one another. Such is the case with regulation and its counterpart, **deregulation**. From an economic perspective, a continual striving for the balance of freedom and control for business will be best for society. From a political perspective, there is an ongoing interplay of different societal goals and means for achieving those goals. The outcome is a mix of economic and political decisions that seem to be in a constant state of flux. Thus, in the economy at any point in time, trends that appear counter to one another can coexist. These trends are the natural result of competing forces seeking some sort of balance or equilibrium.

This explains how the trend toward deregulation evolved in a highly regulated environment. Deregulation represents a counterforce aimed at keeping the economy in balance. It also represents a political philosophy that prevailed during the period of its origin and growth.

Deregulation is one kind of regulatory reform. It is unique and quite different from the regulatory reform measures discussed earlier, so we treat it separately. Deregulation has taken place primarily with respect to economic regulations, and this, too, helps to explain its separate treatment.

Purpose of Deregulation

The basic idea behind deregulation has been to remove certain industries from the old-line economic regulations of the past. The purpose of this deregulation, or at least reduced level of regulation, has been to increase competition with the expected benefits of greater efficiency, lower prices, and enhanced innovation. These goals are not always met and so debate continues regarding whether deregulation works as a method of maximizing society's best interests. Figure 11-6 outlines the airline industry's experience with more than 35 years of deregulation.

FIGURE 11-6
The U.S. Airline Industry: First to Deregulate

October 24, 1978, was a watershed in aviation history. On that date, President Jimmy Carter signed the Airline Deregulation Act, and the world of aviation changed forever. The Civil Aeronautics Board no longer had the power to determine pricing and set the routes. The industry quickly filled with new carriers and new routes, and the country club atmosphere soon shifted to cutthroat competition. Many airlines went bankrupt or were absorbed by others. Even heavyweights like Eastern and Pan Am tottered until they both went bankrupt in 1991.

In 1974 the cheapest round-trip flight between New York and Los Angeles was $1,442 (in inflation-adjusted dollars). In 2011, the fare for that trip was $268. As a result of lowered prices, the number of U.S. airline passengers grew from 207.5 million in 1974 to 721.1 million in 2010. In sum, more people are flying in the United States, but they are spending far less to do so. Airplanes fly at or near capacity, airports are congested, and security considerations require a much longer waiting time for passengers. All of this contributes to a diminished flying experience for the customer.

The situation is coming to a head as an overtaxed air traffic control system stretches to its limit. The U.S. Air Transport Association expects the number of flights to increase from 45,000 in 2007 to 61,000 in 2016. In the past expansion required simply adding more equipment or hiring more controllers, but the scope of the system has reached maximum capacity and so the entire system requires replacement. The Next Generation Air Transportation System uses a satellite-based navigation and surveillance system. It makes it possible to accommodate more flights and do so more safely and permits pilots to communicate with each other. It also allows planes to save fuel in the process. The technology is available and implementation has begun, but federal funding cuts continually slow implementation. In a deregulated industry, the challenges are great as interest groups line up to oppose major change. Private and executive aircraft do not currently contribute to the system in a way that reflects their actual usage: They do not want their user fees to rise. The closing of older air traffic control centers will mean loss of jobs for some. Regulated airfares corresponded to the distance traveled, but now deregulated fares bear little resemblance to the cost of a flight for the control system. The *Economist* opined, "America was the first to deregulate, but now it's snowed under." The U.S. Congress has some difficult decisions to make to enable the U.S. airline industry to continue to compete in an increasingly challenging environment. Despite the challenges, air travel has never been safer. Worldwide, 2012 was the safest year for air travel since 1945, with fewer than half the crashes and deaths seen in 2000.

U.S. Supreme Court Justice Stephen Breyer helped pass the Airline Deregulation Act of 1978 when he worked as an aide to the late Senator Edward Kennedy. Asking himself whether the effort was worthwhile, Justice Breyer says, "Every major reform brings about new, sometimes unforeseen problems... So we sit in crowded planes, munch potato chips, flare up when the loudspeaker announces yet another flight delay. But how many now will vote to go back to the "good old days" of paying high, regulated prices for better service?"

Sources: Richard Newman, "Deregulation Was Good for Travelers, Hard on Airlines," *The Record*, (Hackensack, NJ, December 7, 2003); "In the Land of Free Flight," *Economist* (June 16, 2007), 5–8; Stephen Breyer, "Airline Deregulation, Revisited," *Bloomberg BusinessWeek* (January 20, 2011), http://www.businessweek.com/stories/2011-01-20/airline-deregulation-revisitedbusinessweek-business-news-stock-market-and-financial-advice. Accessed February 4, 2013.; Jessica Meyers, "Politics, Money Holding Up NextGen," *Politico* (September 26, 2012), http://www.politico.com/news/stories/0912/81660.html. Accessed February 4, 2013; Jad Mouawad and Christopher Drew, "Airline Industry at Its Safest Since the Dawn of the Jet Age," *The New York Times* (February 12, 2013), A1–A3.

The Changing World of Deregulation

A trend toward deregulation began in the 1980s, most notably exemplified in the financial industry, the telecommunications industry, and the transportation (trucking, airline, railroad) industry represented business's first major redirection in 50 years.[106] The result seemed to be a mixed bag of benefits and problems. On the benefits side, prices fell in many industries, and better service appeared in some industries along with increased numbers of competitors and innovative products and services.

Several problems also arose. Although prices fell and many competitors entered some of those industries, more and more of those competitors were unable to compete with the dominant firms. They were failing, going bankrupt, or being absorbed by the larger firms. Entry barriers into some industries were enormous and had been greatly underestimated. Deregulation is generally blamed for the savings and loan industry crisis, which resulted in an unprecedented $124 billion bailout by the U.S. government. Most dramatically, deregulation, specifically the repeal of the Depression-era Glass–Steagall Act that split commercial and investment banking, has been accused of causing the global recession that began in 2008.[107]

Another problem that developed was that a few firms began to dominate key industries. This trend was obvious in transportation, where the major railroad, airline, and trucking companies boosted their market shares considerably during the 1980s. The top six railroads went from about 56 percent of market share to about 90 percent during this time. The top six airlines went from about 75 percent of market share to about 85 percent. The top ten trucking firms went from about 38 percent of market share to about 58 percent. Prior to its breakup, AT&T enjoyed about an 80 percent share of the domestic market and a virtual monopoly in the huge toll-free, big business, and overseas markets.[108]

The dilemma with deregulation is how to enhance the competitive nature of the affected industries without sacrificing the applicable social regulations, that is, to allow for freer competition without lowering health and safety requirements. Unfortunately, the dog-eat-dog competition unleashed by economic deregulation can force many companies to cut corners in ways that endanger the health, safety, and/or welfare of their customers. For example, the trucking industry spent about $37 million on lobbying for rules that industry officials said would save the industry billions.[109] The transportation department then issued rules that increased the maximum allowable hours of driving from 60 to 77 over seven consecutive days and from 70 to 88 hours over eight consecutive days. Maximum daily work hours (which includes loading) were set at 14.[110]

Congress provided very little scrutiny of trucking standards, but the courts were less reticent. Concerned about the relaxed standards, several safety organizations brought a lawsuit to a federal appeals court. A three-judge panel ruled that the Federal Motor Carrier Safety Administration was guilty of "ignoring its own evidence that fatigue causes many truck accidents."[111] They went on to say that "the agency admits that studies show that crash risk increases, in the agency's words, 'geometrically' after the eighth hour on duty" and questioned the legality of the "agency's passive regulatory approach."[112] The American Trucking Association supported the rules, while the Teamsters Union opposed them. The Obama administration reduced drivers' maximum allowable hours of work per week from 82 hours to 70 hours, and made comparable reductions in other fatigue-related issues such as breaks required.[113]

Financial services in the United States were one of the most heavily regulated industries until the passage of the Depository Institutions Deregulation and Monetary Control Act of 1980. It removed caps on deposit interest rates. Gradually, Congress then began to take apart the regulatory barriers that had been in place for decades. The Federal Deposit Insurance Improvement Act of 1991 loosened restrictions on deposit insurance premiums; the Neal–Riegle Interstate Banking Act of 1994 removed geographic restrictions on branches; and the Gramm–Leach–Bliley Act of 1999 created financial holding companies and removed enforced separation of insurance companies and commercial and investment banks.[114] It appeared that the deregulation of financial services would continue until two events, the World Trade Center attacks and the Enron financial scandals, turned the tide.

In response, a variety of agencies within the U.S. government began to issue new financial rules and regulations; The Internal Revenue Service, the FBI, the Justice Department, the Financial Crimes Enforcement Network, and the Federal Reserve each contributed to financial service **reregulation**.[115] Pressure for more regulation followed the economic recession that began in 2008. Most observers believe that the rescinding of the Glass–Steagall Act prompted the meltdown.[116] The Glass–Steagall Act was put in place following the Great Depression. It prevented commercial banks from becoming involved in risky trading activities. The global financial recession motivated the Credit Card Act of 2009 and the Dodd–Frank Wall Street Reform and Consumer Protection Act. The landmark Dodd–Frank financial reform legislation created the Financial Stability Oversight Council (FSOC), which will determine which firms are critical to the financial system and thus should have higher capital requirements. It also creates the Consumer Financial Protection Bureau and allows consumers to sue credit rating agencies that recklessly overlook relevant information.[117]

Summary

Any discussion of business and society must consider the paramount role government plays. Although the two institutions have opposing systems of belief, they interconnect in their functioning in our socioeconomic system. In addition, the public assumes a major role in a complex pattern of interactions among business, government, and the public. Government exerts a host of nonregulatory influences on business. Two influences with a macro orientation include industrial policy and privatization. A more specific influence is the fact that government is a major employer, purchaser, subsidizer, competitor, financier, and persuader. These roles permit government to affect business significantly.

One of government's most controversial interventions in business is direct regulation. Government regulates business for several legitimate reasons, and social regulation has now become more dominant than economic regulation. There are many benefits and various costs of government regulation. A response to the problems with regulation has been deregulation. However, bad deregulation experiences in key industries such as trucking, airlines, telecommunication, financial services, and utilities have led to reregulation and caused many to wonder what the optimal mix of regulation and deregulation should be.

Key Terms

collectivistic ethic of government, p. 330
deregulation, p. 346
direct costs, p. 345
economic regulation, p. 341
excessive competition, p. 341
excess profits, p. 341
federalization, p. 336

indirect costs, p. 345
individualistic ethic of business, p. 330
induced costs, p. 345
industrial policy, p. 332
market failure, p. 339
natural monopoly, p. 339
negative externalities, p. 340

privatization, p. 335
regulation, p. 346
reregulation, p. 349
social costs, p. 340
social goals, p. 340
social regulation, p. 342

Discussion Questions

1. Briefly explain how business and government represent a clash of ethical systems (belief systems). With which do you find yourself identifying most? Explain. With which would most business students identify? Explain.

2. Explain why the public is included as a separate group in the interactions among business, government, and the public. Doesn't government represent the public's interests? How should the public's interests be manifested?

3. What is regulation? Why does government see a need to regulate? Differentiate between economic and social regulation. What social regulations do you think are most important, and why? What social regulations ought to be eliminated? Explain.

4. Outline the major benefits and costs of government regulation. In general, do you think the benefits of government regulation exceed the costs? In what areas, if any, do you think the costs exceed the benefits?

5. What are the trade-offs between privatization and federalization? When would one or the other be more appropriate? What problems might you foresee and what future events would merit a shift in the current mix?

Endnotes

1. Curtis J. Verschoor, "Can Government Manage More Ethically Than Capitalism?" *Strategic Finance* (October 2009), 15–16, 63.

2. Andy Serwer, "The '00s: Goodbye (at Last) to the Decade from Hell," *Time* (November 24, 2009), http://www.time.com/time/nation/article/0,8599,1942834,00.html. Accessed February 9, 2013.

3. Ibid.

4. Ibid.

5. Verschoor, 15.

6. Ibid.

7. Bob Davis, Damian Paletta, and Rebecca Smith, "Sour Economy Spurs Government to Grab a Bigger Oversight Role," *The Wall Street Journal* (July 25, 2008), A12.

8. Ibid.

9. "Antitrust Laws," *The World Book Encyclopedia,* Vol. 1 (Chicago: World Book, 1988), 560. See also "The Interstate Commerce Act" (Vol. 10), 352–353.

10. Ibid.

11. Ibid.

12. Ibid.

13. Alfred L. Seelye, "Societal Change and Business-Government Relationships," *MSU Business Topics* (Autumn 1975), 5–6.

14. "Is Government Dead?" *Time* (October 23, 1989).

15. Michael J. Mandel, "Rethinking the Economy," *BusinessWeek* (October 1, 2001), 28–33.

16. "25 People to Blame for the Financial Crisis," *Time* (November 24, 2009), http://www.time.com/time/specials/packages/article/0,28804,1877351_1877350_1877322,00.html. Accessed February 2, 2013.

17. Paul Magnusson, "Suddenly, Washington's Wallet Is Open," *BusinessWeek* (October 1, 2001), 34.

18. Mandel, 30.

19. L. Earle Birdsell, "Business and Government: The Walls Between," in Neil H. Jacoby (ed.), *The Business–Government Relationship: A Reassessment* (Santa Monica, CA: Goodyear, 1975), 32–34.

20. Neil H. Jacoby, *Corporate Power and Social Responsibility* (New York: Macmillan, 1973), 167.

21. McKinsey & Company, "McKinsey Global Survey," *McKinsey Quarterly* (January 2010), 7.

22. Ibid.

23. Nancy Killefer, "The New Business of Government," *McKinsey Quarterly* (Issue 3, 2009), 7.

24. Naftali Bendavid, "Rage at Government for Doing Too Much and Not Enough," *The Wall Street Journal* (October 13, 2009), A5.

25. http://www.debate.org/opinions/should-the-government-intervene-with-the-free-market-and-save-failing-businesses. Accessed February 2, 2013.

26. Tom Cohen, "President Obama Unveils $3.8 Trillion Budget, "*CNN Politics* (February 13, 2012), http://www.cnn.com/2012/02/13/politics/obama-congress-budget. Accessed February 8, 2013.

27. James Foreman-Peck and Giovanni Frederico, *European Industrial Policy: The Twentieth-Century Experience* (Oxford University Press, 1999).

28. Karl Aiginger, "Industrial Policy: A Dying Breed or a Reemerging Phoenix?" *Journal of Industry, Competition & Trade* (December 2007), 297–323.

29. Ibid.

30. Robert B. Reich, *The Next American Frontier* (New York: Penguin Books, 1983).

31. Clyde Prestowitz, "America's Industrial Policy," *Foreign Policy* (March 6, 2012), http://prestowitz.foreignpolicy. com/posts/2012/03/06/americas_industrial_policy. Accessed February 8, 2013.

32. Ibid.

33. Anonymous, "The Clinton Administration's Framework for Global Electronic Commerce: Executive Summary (July 1, 1997)," *Business America* (Vol. 119, No. 1, January 1998), 5–6.

34. Josh Lerner and William Sahlman, "Reviving Entrepreneurship," *Harvard Business Review* (March 2012), 116–119.

35. Ibid.

36. Ibid.

37. Ibid.

38. http://ec.europa.eu/europe2020/europe-2020-in-a-nutshell/ index_en.htm. Accessed March 17, 2013.

39. http://ec.europa.eu/europe2020/europe-2020-in-a-nutshell/ priorities/sustainable-growth/index_en.htm. March 17, 2013.

40. Killefer, 7.

41. Ibid.

42. Magnusson, 34.

43. Michael Arndt, "What Kind of Rescue?" *BusinessWeek* (October 1, 2001), 36–37.

44. Ibid.

45. Jon Birger, "The Bailout Bounty," *Fortune* (March 5, 2007), 24–26.

46. Ibid.

47. Ibid.

48. Michael J. De La Merced, "Greenberg Forges Ahead With Lawsuit Over A.I.G. Bailout," *The New York Times* (March 12, 2013), http://dealbook.nytimes.com/ 2013/03/12/greenberg-forges-ahead-with-lawsuit-over-a-i-g-bailout/. Accessed March 15, 2013.

49. Michael J. De La Merced and Ben Protess, "A.I.G. Says It Will Not Join Lawsuit Against Government," *The New York Times* (January 9, 2013), http://dealbook. nytimes.com/2013/01/09/a-i-g-says-it-will-not-join-law-suit-against-government/. Accessed March 15, 2013.

50. Michael J. De La Merced, "Lawmakers Warn A.I.G. Not to Join Lawsuit against U.S. *The New York Times* (January 8, 2013), http://dealbook.nytimes.com/2013/ 01/08/lawmakers-warn-a-i-g-not-to-join-lawsuit-against-u-s/. Accessed March 15, 2013.

51. http://projects.propublica.org/bailout/list. Accessed February 3, 2013.

52. Cohen, 2012.

53. Jeffrey Kutler, "Financial Industrial Policy," *Security Industry News* (April 30, 2007), http://www. securitiesindustry.com/issues/20070429/20313-1.html. Accessed February 9, 2013.

54. Ira C. Magaziner and Robert B. Reich, *Minding America's Business: The Decline and Rise of the American Economy* (New York: Vintage Books, 1983), 255.

55. http://www.merriam-webster.com/dictionary/privatize. Accessed February 9, 2013.

56. Shaker A. Zahra, R. Duane Ireland, Isabel Gutierrez, and Michael A. Hitt, "Privatization and Entrepreneurial Transformation: Emerging Issues and a Future Research Agenda," *Academy of Management Review* (July 2000), 509–524.

57. Ted Kolderie, "What Do We Mean by Privatization?" (St. Louis: Center for the Study of American Business, Washington University, May 1986), 2–5.

58. Ibid., 3–5.

59. Steve Coll, "Retooling Europe," *The Washington Post National Weekly Edition* (August 22–28, 1994), 6–7.

60. Diane Cardwell, "Power to the People," *The New York Times*, (March 14, 2013), B1, B4.

61. Eduardo Porter, "When Public Outpeforms Private in Services," *The New York Times* (January 15, 2013), http://www.nytimes.com/2013/01/16/business/when-privatization-works-and-why-it-doesnt-always.html. Accessed February 9, 2013.

62. Ibid.

63. Jason Keller and Jonathan Keehner, "Privatize This!" *BusinessWeek* (March 15, 2010), 54–56.

64. Caroline Porter and Ted Mann, "New York Scraps Privatizing Parking Meters," *The Wall Street Journal* (January 26, 2013), http://online.wsj.com/article/ SB10001424127887323854904578264331152227780.html. Accessed February 3, 2013.

65. Sam Dolnick, "As Escapees Stream Out a Penal Business Thrives," *The New York Times* (June 16, 2012), http://www.nytimes.com/2012/06/17/nyregion/in-new-jersey-halfway-houses-escapees-stream-out-as-a-penal-business-thrives.html?_r=2. Accessed February 9, 2013.

66. Ibid.

67. Porter, http://www.nytimes.com/2013/01/16/business/ when-privatization-works-and-why-it-doesnt-always.html. Accessed February 9, 2013.

68. Tim Sullivan and Ray Fisman, *The Org: The Underlying Logic of the Office* (New York, NY: Hachette Book Group, 2013), 217–247.

69. Ibid.

70. Alvaro Cuervo and Bélen Villalonga, "Explaining the Variance in the Performance Effects of Privatization," *Academy of Management Review* (July 2000), 581–590.

71. Suzanne Leland and Olga Smirnova, "Reassessing Privatization Strategies 25 Years Later: Revisiting Perry and Babitsky's Comparative Performance Study of Urban Bus Transit Services," *Public Administration Review* (September/October 2009), 855–867.

72. Richard Reed, David J. Lemak, and W. Andrew Hesser, "Cleaning Up after the Cold War: Management and

Social Issues," *Academy of Management Review* (Vol. 22, No. 3, July 1997), 614–642.

73. Murray L. Weidenbaum, *Business, Government and the Public,* 3d ed. (Englewood Cliffs, NJ: Prentice Hall, 1986), 5–6.

74. Ibid., 6–8.

75. "Did the Federal Reserve's lending during the recession violate the law?" *Monthly Labor Review* (September 2012), 35–36; Elizabeth Dwoskin and Karen Weise, "The Government Takes Aim at Risky Student Loans," *Bloomberg Businessweek* (July 20, 2012), http://www.businessweek.com/articles/2012-07-20/the-government-takes-aim-at-risky-student-loan. Accessed March 15, 2013.

76. Tommaso Ebhart, "Italy's Austerity Leads to Ferrari Sell-Off," *Bloomberg BusinessWeek* (August 23, 2012), http://www.businessweek.com/articles/2012-08-23/italys-austerity-leads-to-ferrari-sell-off. Accessed March 15, 2013.

77. Ibid.

78. Peter Coy, "The Stitch-Up Artist," *Bloomberg Business-Week* (January 21–27, 2013), 6.

79. Ibid. 6–7.

80. Eric Lipton and Gardiner Harris, "In Turnaround, Industries Push for Regulations after Efforts to Block Them," *The New York Times* (September 16, 2007), A1, 13.

81. http://www.llsdc.org/attachments/wysiwyg/544/fed-reg-pages.pdf. Accessed February 3, 2013.

82. *Federal Register,* "Federal Register Pages Published Annually," http://www.llsdc.org/attachments/wysiwyg/544/fed-reg-pages.pdf.

83. http://www.llsdc.org/attachments/wysiwyg/544/fed-reg-pages.pdf. Accessed February 9, 2013.

84. *Congressional Quarterly's Federal Regulatory Directory,* 5th ed. (1985–1986), 2.

85. Ibid., 2–3.

86. Ibid., 9.

87. "Microsoft: Time to Change," *BusinessWeek* (July 16, 2001), 100.

88. Stephen Labaton, "Microsoft Finds a Legal Defender in Justice Department," *The New York Times* (June 10, 2007), http://www.nytimes.com.

89. Stephan Labaton, "Antitrust Complaints Prompt Changes to Vista," *The New York Times* (June 19, 2007), http://www. nytimes.com/2007/06/19/technology/20softcnd.html.

90. Thomas Catan and Jessica E. Vascellaro, "Google, Microsoft Spar on Antitrust," *The Wall Street Journal* (March 1, 2010), http://online.wsj.com/article/SB20001424052748703510204575086534063777758.html. Accessed February 9, 2013.

91. William Alden, "Google's Antitrust Victory," *The New York Times* (January 4, 2013), http://dealbook.nytimes.com/2013/01/04/googles-antitrust-victory/. Accessed February 3, 2013.

92. Loek Essers, "European Commission Weighs Google Antitrust Settlement," *PCWorld* (February 1, 2013), http://www.pcworld.com/article/2026841/european-commission-weighs-google-antitrust-settlement.html. Accessed February 3, 2013.

93. Ibid.

94. *Congressional Quarterly's Federal Regulatory Directory,* 10–11.

95. Ibid., 12.

96. Walter Pincus, "Excess-profits Tax on Defense Contractors During Wartime Is Long Overdue," *Washington Post* (December 31, 2012), http://articles.washingtonpost.com/2012-12-31/world/36103637_1_defense-contractors-defense-profits-excess-profits-tax. Accessed February 3, 2013.

97. Ibid.

98. Stephen Breyer, *Regulation and Its Reform* (Cambridge, MA: Harvard University Press, 1982), 31–32.

99. Weidenbaum, 178–179.

100. Melinda Warren, "Federal Regulatory Spending Reaches a New Height: An Analysis of the Budget of the U.S. Government for the Year 2001" (St. Louis, Missouri: Center for the Study of American Business, June 2000); derived from the budget of the U.S. government.

101. Graham K. Wilson, *Business and Politics: A Comparative Introduction* (Chatham, NJ: Chatham House, 1985), 39.

102. Ibid., 12–14.

103. Paroma Sanyal, "The Effect of Deregulation on Environmental Research by Electric Utilities," *Journal of Regulatory Economics* (June 2007), 335–353.

104. Ibid., 12.

105. Reich, 98.

106. "Deregulating America," *BusinessWeek* (November 28, 1983), 80–89.

107. Alison Vekshin, "U.S. Senators Propose Reinstating Glass–Steagall Act," *Bloomberg.com* (December 16, 2009), http://www.bloomberg.com/apps/news?pid=newsarchive&sid=aQfRyxBZs5uc. Accessed February 9, 2013.

108. Ibid., 52.

109. Stephen Labaton, "As Trucking Rules Are Eased, a Debate on Safety Intensifies," *The New York Times* (December 3, 2006), 1, 30.

110. Ibid.

111. Ibid., 30.

112. Ibid., 30.

113. http://www.fmcsa.dot.gov/rules-regulations/topics/hos/qanda.aspx. Accessed February 9, 2013.

114. "Financial Deregulation," Chapter 21, *Cato Handbook for Congress: Policy Recommendations for the 108th Congress* (2003), http://www.cato.org/pubs/handbook/hb108/hb108-21.pdf. Accessed February 9, 2013.

115. Richard W. Rahn, "Regulatory Malpractice," *The Cato Institute* (March 27, 2004), http://www.cato.org/publications/commentary/regulatory-malpractice. Accessed February 9, 2013.

116. Vekshin, 2009.

117. David Lawder, "Timeline: Long Road to Implement Financial Reform Bill," *Reuters.com* (July 21, 2010), http://www.reuters.com/article/idUSTRE66K49320100721. Accessed February 9, 2013.

12

Business Influence on Government and Public Policy

As our previous discussion of industrial policy showed, government is a central stakeholder of business. Government's interest, or stake, in business is broad and multifaceted, and its power is derived from its legal and moral right to represent the public in its dealings with business. Today, because of the multiple roles it plays in influencing business activity, government poses significant challenges for business owners and managers. Government not only establishes the rules of the game for business functions but also influences business in its roles as competitor, financier, purchaser, supplier, watchdog, and so on. Opportunities for business and government to cooperate in a mutual pursuit of common goals are present to some extent, but the major opportunity for business is in developing strategies for effectively working with government in such a way that businesses achieve their own objectives. In doing this, business has the responsibility of obeying the laws of the land and of being ethical in its responses to government expectations and mandates. To do otherwise raises the specter of abuse of power.

Attempts by business to influence government are a major and accepted part of the public policy process in the United States. The active participation of interest groups striving to achieve their own objectives drives the U.S. political system. The business sector is behaving, therefore, in a normal and expected fashion when it assumes an advocacy role for its interests. Other groups, be they labor organizations, consumer groups, farmers' groups, doctors' organizations, real estate broker organizations, military groups, women's rights organizations, environmental groups, church groups, and so on, all strive to pursue their special interests with government. Today's pluralism necessitates that all of these groups seek to influence government.

Society would be best served if the system maintained a balance of power; however, a controversial U.S. Supreme Court ruling, *Citizens United*, has upset that balance. Business's power to drive the political agenda in Washington is now virtually unchecked.[1] Power comes with the duty to use it responsibly, and so the need for business to be mindful in its approach to influencing government is greater than ever. Given its inherent wealth and power, business must navigate the political waters thoughtfully, taking care to understand the range of corporate political activity's consequences, for society as well as for business. This qualifies as enlightened self-interest because business, too, needs a healthy and balanced society to thrive.

Corporate Political Participation

Political involvement is broadly defined as participation in the formulation and execution of public policy at various levels of government. As decisions about the current and future shape of society and the role of the private sector shift from the marketplace to the political arena, corporations, like all interest groups, find it imperative to increase their political involvement and activity.[2]

Historically, companies entered into debates in Washington only on an issue-by-issue basis and with no overall sense of a purpose, goal, or strategy. Companies tended to be reactive; that is, they dealt with issues only after they became threats. For example, in its early days Microsoft did not take political participation seriously. While other companies had suites of offices filled with lobbyists looking out for their interests, Microsoft simply had a man traveling around in his Jeep. Then an antitrust case from the U.S. Justice Department convinced the company of the importance of corporate political activity.[3] Today, Microsoft's lobbying expenditures are second only to Google in the computer/Internet industry.[4] Microsoft learned the hard way that political strategies can be as important as competitive strategies in today's marketplace.[5]

In this chapter, we focus on the following major approaches to corporate political activity: (1) lobbying and (2) political spending. As we begin, our perspective will be largely descriptive as we seek to understand these approaches, their strengths and weaknesses, and business's successes and failures with them. We will then explore normative issues in corporate political activity, highlighting areas where there are possible abuses of power and violations of sound ethics.

Business Lobbying

Lobbying is the process of influencing public officials to promote or secure the passage or defeat of legislation. Lobbyists are intensely self-interested. Their goals are to promote legislation that is in their organizations' interests and to defeat legislation that runs counter to that. Business interests, labor interests, ethnic and racial groups, professional organizations, and those simply pursuing ideological goals they believe to be in the public interest are lobbying at the federal, state, and local levels. Our focus is on business lobbying at the federal level, although we must remember that this process also occurs daily at the state and local levels.

Lobbying has been defined as the professionalization of the art of persuasion.[6] Lobbying serves several purposes. It is not just a technique for gaining legislative support or institutional approval for some objective such as a policy shift, a judicial ruling, or the modification or passage of a law. Lobbying may be directed toward the reinforcement of established policy or the defeat of proposed policy shifts. As a tool to get the votes they want, lobbyists can also target the election or defeat of national, state, and local legislators.[7] A lobbyist may be a lawyer, a public relations specialist, a former head of a public agency, a former corporate executive, or a former elected official. In this sense, there is no typical lobbyist.[8] It is clear, however, that more and more businesses, as well as other special-interest groups, are turning to lobbyists to facilitate their involvement in the public policy process.

Lobbying has been called "one of America's most despised professions," and sometimes the label fits.[9] Jack Abramoff was at the center of a corruption and influence peddling investigation that netted 21 people, including legislators, White House officials, lobbyists, and congressional aides.[10] In addition to corruption and tax offenses, the Court found he defrauded Native American tribes of millions of dollars.[11] His crimes were so notorious that he became the subject of a 2010 documentary *Casino Jack and the United*

ETHICS IN PRACTICE CASE
The NRA and the CDC

Trade associations exist to support their member organizations and the industries in which they operate. If another organization begins work that can potentially undermine that industry and lead to a decrease in sales, the trade association will naturally respond and try to put a stop to the work that threatens its industry. This is true across industries but when the trade association is the National Rifle Association (NRA) and the organization posing a threat is the Center for Disease Control (CDC)'s National Center for Injury Prevention and Control (NCIPC), a variety of ethical issues arise.

Prior to the mid-1990s, the NCIPC published a variety of studies that analyzed gun-related injuries and deaths, but then the public health scientists clashed with the NRA and the NRA fought back by lobbying sympathetic lawmakers to take action. The lawmakers first tried to close the NCIPC but, when that failed, they successfully put forth an amendment that removed $2.6 million from their budget—the same amount used the previous year to fund gun-related research—and stipulated that money may not go to research that advocates gun control. Today, the CDC asks funded researchers to let them know if the studies they are conducting involve firearms, and then the CDC forwards that information to the NRA as a courtesy. Arthur Kellermann of the Rand Corp notes, "The (NRA) strategy of shutting down the pipeline of science was effective. It is almost impossible today to get federal funding for firearm injury-prevention research."

1. Do you think the NRA is justified in its actions toward the CDC?
2. Do you think the CDC should pursue gun-related injury research?
3. The NRA contends that the CDC had an anti-gun agenda and that it was playing politics with the research. Does this alter your assessment of the NRA's approach to lobbying?
4. Where do you draw the line regarding lobbying by industry groups? The NRA's actions promote shareholder wealth—is that not the responsibility of a trade group? Are there lines that trade associations should not cross when they lobby and, if so, what are they?

Sources: Michael Luo, "N.R.A. Stymies Firearms Research, Scientists Say," *The New York Times* (January 25, 2011), http://www.nytimes.com/2011/01/26/us/26guns.html?pagewanted=1. Accessed March 15, 2013. "CDC: Politics Affected Gun Violence Research," *The Atlanta Journal Constitution* (December 19, 2012), http://www.ajc.com/news/news/cdc-politics-affected-gun-violence-research/nTZnf/. Accessed March 15, 2013.; James Swift, "Former CDC Director Says NRA "Terrorized" Gun Violence Researchers," *Juvenile Justice Information Exchange* (January 1, 2013), http://jjie.org/former-cdc-director-says-nra-terrorized-gun-violence-researchers/101449. Accessed March 15, 2013.

States of Money as well as a feature film that same year, *Casino Jack*, with Kevin Spacey in the title role. Given the large amounts of money involved, it is not surprising that people will cross the legal and ethical line. In 2012, more than 12,000 lobbyists spent $3.3 billion advocating for a range of interests.[12] A recent study examined lobbying on one specific piece of legislation and found that the return on investment was 22,000 percent.[13]

We should note, however, that lobbying is not inherently evil. Some lobbyists work for nonprofit organizations, supporting causes about which the public would forget without someone representing them in Washington. Other lobbyists work for companies that care about doing the right thing and creating a marketplace in which responsible companies can thrive. Some for-profit lobbyists are doing pro bono work in an effort to remake the profession's tainted image.[14] Lobbyists can serve as educators, providing needed information to elected officials and the public. Lawrence Lessig, who conducts research on public corruption, puts it well, "There's all the difference in the world between a lawyer making an argument to the jury and a lawyer handing out $100 bills to the jurors. That's a distinction the system doesn't understand right now."[15]

Organizational Levels of Lobbying

The business community engages in lobbying at several organizational levels. At the broadest level are **umbrella trade associations**, which represent the collective business interests of the United States. The best examples of umbrella trade associations are the Chamber of Commerce of the United States and the National Association of Manufacturers (NAM). Other umbrella organizations represent subsets of business in general, such as the Business Roundtable, which represents the largest firms in America, and the National Federation of Independent Businesses (NFIB), which represents smaller firms.

At the next level are **sectoral trade associations**, which are composed of many firms in a given industry or line of business. Examples include the National Automobile Dealers Association, the National Association of Home Builders, the National Association of Realtors, PhRMA, the American Bankers Association, the American Chemistry Council, and the American Council of Life Insurers. Also, there are individual **company lobbying** efforts. Here, firms such as IBM, AT&T, Ford, and Delta Airlines lobby on their own behalf. Typically, companies use their own personnel, establish Washington offices for the sole purpose of lobbying, or hire professional lobbying firms or consultants located in Washington or a state capital. To the extent that limited transparency allows, interest groups now rate companies on the nature of their lobbying. For example, in its *Guide to Greener Electronics,* Greenpeace, the independent environment campaigning organization, rated electronics companies on whether they "showed climate leadership" by supporting cuts in global emissions.[16] Finally, companies sometimes form **ad hoc coalitions** to address a particular issue for a period. For example, the Coalition of Gulf Shrimp Industries, an ad hoc coalition of vessel owners and shrimp processors in the United States and Mexico joined together to petition the U.S. Department of Commerce and the International Trade Commission for relief from unfair trade involving subsidized shrimp from other countries.[17]

Figure 12-1 depicts examples of the broad range of lobbying and political interest organizations used by businesses.

FIGURE 12-1

Examples of the Range of Lobbying Organizations Used by Businesses

Broad Representation: Umbrella Trade Associations

- Chamber of Commerce of the United States
- National Association of Manufacturers (NAM)
- Business Roundtable
- National Federation of Independent Businesses (NFIB)
- State Chambers of Commerce
- City Chambers of Commerce

Midrange Representation: Sectoral Trade Associations and Coalitions

- National Automobile Dealers Association
- National Association of Realtors
- American Petroleum Institute American Trucking Association

- National Association of Medical Equipment Suppliers
- Tobacco Institute
- Health Benefits Coalition
- United States Telecom Association

Narrow/Specific Representation: Company-Level Lobbying

- Washington and State Capital Offices
- Law Firms Specializing in Lobbying
- Public Affairs Specialists
- Political Action Committees (PACs)
- Grassroots Lobbying
- Company-Based Coalitions
- Former Government Officials

© Cengage Learning

Spotlight on Sustainability

What Green Rankings Don't Tell You

A corporation's political activities can have a greater impact on the environment than the work it does to make its operations greener. Green rankings can be misleading because they focus on operational impacts, compliance with regulations, and overall practices, while ignoring the firm's political advocacy activities. A recent study compared companies' green rankings to their ranking on political transparency and noted a weak correlation: Some of the companies with higher-than-average green rankings had lower-than-average political transparency rankings. Companies with higher environmental transparency rankings include Duke Energy, Halliburton, Hess, and Newmont Mining. These firms are in the highly environmentally regulated mining, chemical, and energy industries. Firms in those industries typically lobby for more relaxed regulations and so the authors question whether these companies have environmentally friendly political activity to match their environmental transparency. Because disclosure of corporate political activity is not required, there is no way to know the nature of their efforts. The authors suggest that future green rankings should include voluntary disclosure of environment-related lobbying and donations. Otherwise, firms may receive credit for being green when, behind closed doors, they are working against the interests of the environment with their corporate political activity.

Sources: Aaron Chatterji and Michael Toffel, "What Green Rankings Don't Tell You," *Newsweek* (October 22, 2012), http://www.thedailybeast.com/newsweek/2012/10/22/green-rankings-what-sustainability-reports-don-t-tell-you.html. Accessed February 23, 2013; Auden Schendler and Michael Toffel, "The Factor Environmental Ratings Miss." *MIT Sloan Management Review* 53.1 (Fall 2011): 17–18.

We now discuss lobbying in greater detail, beginning with the use of professional lobbyists.

Professional Lobbyists. Lobbyists, sometimes derisively referred to as "influence peddlers," operate under a variety of formal titles and come from a variety of backgrounds. Officially, they are lawyers, government affairs specialists, public relations consultants, or public affairs consultants. Some are on the staffs of large trade associations based in Washington. Others represent specific companies that have Washington offices dedicated to the sole purpose of representing those companies in the capital city. Still others are professional lobbyists who work for large law firms or consulting firms in Washington that specialize in representing clients to the lawmakers.

The Washington lobbyist is frequently a former government official. Some are former congressional staff members or former members of Congress. Others are former presidential staff assistants or other highly placed government officials. The law prohibits many of these individuals from lobbying for one year after leaving office; however, one year is a relatively short apprenticeship for people who are likely to increase their former salaries many times over. For example, after serving as chief architect of the Medicare prescription drug law, former Rep. Billy Tauzin (R-Louisiana), received a lucrative job offer to lobby for the pharmaceutical industry. Pundits suggested that he had already earned his salary when he walked in the door because the Medicare bill provided huge profits for drug makers.[18]

Tauzin began his job as Chairman and CEO of the drug industry trade group, Pharmaceutical Research and Manufacturers of America (PhRMA).[19] He did not register to lobby until after the one-year waiting period mandated by the Ethics Reform Act of 1989. During that waiting year, however, he was able to advise other lobbyists on how to proceed, and he was able to call on his former chief of staff who joined PhRMA with him. Since then, the House Ethics Code added a provision known as "The Tauzin Rule," which prohibited lawmakers from negotiating future employment deals while still working as representatives.[20] Tauzin became the highest-paid health-care lobbyist when he earned $11.6 million for brokering a deal with the Obama administration over health-care reform: He left his position as head of PhRMA after the law was signed.[21]

The revolving door between Congress and lobbying firms may have contributed significantly to the global financial crisis. Deniz Igan and Prachi Mishra followed the track of financial regulation bills in the five-year period before the crisis, classifying them as to whether they promoted deregulation or not.[22] In the years leading up to the financial crisis, they found that bills that were friendlier to the financial industry (i.e., promoted deregulation) were three times more likely to become law; furthermore, the more money lobbyists spent, the more likely legislators were to vote for the bill.[23] What mattered most, however, was the influence of connections—the greatest influence on the likelihood of a legislator voting for a bill was whether or not the lobbyist promoting it has worked for that legislator in the past.[24]

What do business lobbyists actually do? Lobbyists offer a wide range of services that include drafting legislation, creating slick advertisements and direct-mail campaigns, consulting, and, most importantly, gaining access to lawmakers. Access, or connections, seems to be the central product that the new breed of lobbyist is selling—the returned phone call, the tennis game with a key legislator, or lunch with the Speaker of the House. With so many competing interests in Washington today, the opportunity to get your point across in any format is a significant advantage. Lobbyists also play the important role of showing busy legislators the virtues and pitfalls of complex legislation.[25] Figure 12-2 summarizes some of the various activities that business lobbyists accomplish for their clients.

Grassroots Lobbying. In addition to lobbying directly through the use of professional lobbyists, firms and trade associations use what is called **grassroots lobbying**, which refers to the process of mobilizing the "grassroots"—individual citizens who might be most directly affected by legislative activity—to political action. An estimated 40 percent of Fortune 500 companies use grassroots consultants.[26] The better corporate grassroots lobbying programs usually arise in companies whose leaders recognize that people are a firm's most potent political resource. Although firms cannot direct or require people to become politically involved, they persuade and encourage them. Trade associations often use grassroots support by asking members to contact their representatives and maintain contact through social media. They also organize rallies and develop advertisements quickly as the need arises.[27]

FIGURE 12-2

What Business Lobbyists Do for Their Clients

- Get access to key legislators (connections)
- Monitor legislation
- Establish communication channels with regulatory bodies
- Protect firms against surprise legislation
- Draft legislation, slick ad campaigns, and direct-mail campaigns
- Provide issue papers on anticipated effects of legislative activity

- Communicate sentiments of association or company on key issues
- Influence outcome of legislation (promote helpful legislation, defeat harmful legislation)
- Assist companies in coalition building around issues that various groups may have in common
- Help members of Congress get reelected
- Organize grassroots efforts

© Cengage Learning

Grassroots lobbying has become such an effective tool for such a wide range of individual firms and associations that the Public Affairs Council holds an annual National Grassroots Conference.[28] The 2013 agenda includes presentations from companies as diverse as Allstate, Caterpillar, Eli-Lilly, and Volvo, as well as trade groups such as the American Institute of Architects, the National Pork Producers Council, the National Retail Federation, and the Pharmaceutical Research and Manufacturers of America. The growth of technology has ushered in **cyberadvocacy**, a computer-based form of grassroots campaigning. Computers and the Internet have made communication, and thus grassroots lobbying, infinitely easier. Books and consulting services have sprung up to assist organizations in using the Internet to both amass grassroots support and enable grassroots supporters to contact their legislators.

Grassroots lobbying can be highly effective, but the grassroots response should be genuine. Some organizations and trade associations have created fake groups that appear to be grassroots but are largely created and funded by an organization or trade association. These phony "**astroturf lobbying**" efforts give the impression of being the result of a genuine public groundswell, but they are actually orchestrated and funded by professional organizations. The practice once involved the sending of hundreds of phone calls or thousands of identical postcards, letters, or e-mails that arrived on the same day and were rarely effective.[29] Over time, astroturfing has grown more sophisticated and is estimated to be a billion-dollar industry in Washington.[30]

For example, a group called "Americans for Common Cents (ACC)" is actively fighting to keep the penny as a form of currency in the United States. When Canada announced its plan to eliminate the Canadian one-cent coin, ACC issued a press release citing research that showed the majority of people in the United States wanted to keep the penny.[31] The press treated the release as actual news with few news outlets noting that the zinc industry's main lobbyist runs ACC, with support from the vending industry.[32] Zinc is the main material used to make pennies. The news outlets also failed to note that the studies cited were, with one exception, one or two decades old: The only exception was a six-year-old study conducted by Coinstar, a company that makes its money counting coins.[33] Other arguments for keeping the penny include the idea that rounding would cost consumers more money; however a study of 200,000 transactions in 20 locations showed no loss to consumers.[34] In addition to costing 2.4 cents to make, the penny costs businesses time to process. In its busiest locations, Chipotle Mexican Grill rounded customers' final bills to the nearest nickel to keep the line moving quickly: After customers complained, Chipotle changed its policy to always rounding down, which satisfies disgruntled customers while still avoiding having the checkout process slowed down by pennies.[35]

Astroturf lobbying has been around for decades, but over the years it has become increasingly sophisticated.[36] Today's astroturf organizations are more subtle and less likely to show their true origins without investigation from an outside source. Even professional journalists have been duped by astroturf organizations.[37] Until transparency requirements are in place, consumers of information will have to be vigilant in expecting lobbying groups to be transparent and accountable.

Trade Associations. Lobbying at the association level is frequent today. One successful experience worth noting has been the pharmaceutical industry's continued success at blocking Congress's efforts to impose prescription drug price controls and to allow the importation of less expensive drugs. In a true show of the trade association's strength, the pharmaceutical industry was able to have passage written into law that barred the federal government from negotiating the prices of prescription drugs supplied through Medicare Part D. Economist Dean Baker estimates that, even using a conservative scenario, the United States loses about $50 billion each year due to the government's inability to negotiate drug prices in Medicare.[38] President Obama had vilified the costly provision when on the campaign trail; however, his perspective changed during the health-care reform process. PhRMA was able to protect the provision in the health-care reform package in return for other considerations. The pharmaceutical industry agreed to provide $80 billion to close the "doughnut hole" coverage gap for seniors and people with disabilities and subsequently advertised in support of the health care reform legislation.[39] Congress undertook legislation to enable government to negotiate drug prices in 2007, 2010, and 2011 but each time the bill died in committee.[40] At this writing, the Medication Prescription Drug Price Negotiation Act of 2013 has been introduced and is currently in committee. Unfortunately, GovTrack gives it a 6 percent chance of getting past committee and a 1 percent chance of getting enacted.[41]

Trade associations sometimes find themselves in the undesirable role of battling with each other in their attempts to lobby Congress. An example of these types of battles occurred between the credit union and the banking industries regarding the scope of services supplied by credit unions. Credit unions argued that they provide services to individuals and small businesses that traditional banks shun. They contended that they should be able to expand the services they provide to this generally underserved population. Banks countered that credit unions enjoy an unfair competitive advantage by virtue of their exemptions from both taxes and the Community Reinvestment Act (CRA) obligations required of banks. They maintained that large, multiple-employer credit unions should be subject to the same taxes, CRA rules, and safety requirements as banks. Ultimately, the House passed H.R. 1151—the Credit Union Membership Access Act, which relaxed restrictions on credit union membership.[42]

Umbrella Organizations. The umbrella organizations are trade associations, too; however, an umbrella organization has a broad base of membership that represents businesses in several different industries of various sizes. Historically, the two major umbrella organizations in the United States have been the Chamber of Commerce of the United States and the National Association of Manufacturers. Two other prominent organizations include the Business Roundtable and the National Federation of Independent Businesses. Each of these groups has political action as one of its central objectives.

Chamber of Commerce of the United States   The national chamber of commerce was founded in 1912 as a federation of businesses and business organizations. In addition to firms, corporations, and professional members, the chamber has thousands of local, state, and regional chambers of commerce; American chambers of commerce abroad; and several thousand trade and professional associations. Its diversity of membership shows why it is referred to as an umbrella organization.

Historically, the U.S. Chamber of Commerce had been a legislative powerhouse in its ability to influence public policy. Its power gradually waned over the years.[43] When Thomas Donohue became the chamber president, he promised to awaken the "sleeping giant, missing in action from many important battles." One tactic he used to great success was to dispense favors to individual businesses that might not want their company name associated with lobbying efforts. The chamber established the Institute for Legal Reform (ILR) to fight for tort reform. The ILR is funded by large donations from companies typically subject to lawsuits but who do not want to make their support for tort reform public, such as companies in the chemicals and insurance industries.[44] Having spent nearly a billion dollars from 1998 through 2012, the Chamber's lobbying expenditures dwarf those of other individual business groups.[45]

Recently, the chamber has been at odds with many of its former associates. Since 2009, 60 local Chambers of Commerce have either quit or publicly denounced the U.S. Chamber due to its positions.[46] Utilities PG&E, Exelon, and PNM Resources quit the chamber over its opposition to efforts to regulate carbon emissions. The chamber's position on climate change led Apple to resign from the organization and Nike to withdraw from the board, remaining as a member to "debate climate change from within."[47] Nevertheless, if pay is an indication, some members appreciate Donohue's efforts greatly as his pay is now closer to that of a multinational CEO than a head of a trade association.[48]

Business Roundtable Formed in 1972, the Business Roundtable (BRT) is often regarded as an umbrella organization, although it has a restricted membership. It is an association of chief executive officers of leading corporations with a combined workforce of more than 16 million employees in the United States and $7.3 trillion in revenues.[49] The Business Roundtable is different from most groups, such as the U.S. Chamber of Commerce and NAM, in the limitation of participation to chief executive officers (CEOs). Rather than pushing narrow issues that benefit narrow interests, the organization generally selects broader concerns on which to focus. The BRT was once regarded as a sleeping giant, but former president John Castellani turned the organization into a "lobbying juggernaut."[50]

One of the targets for that lobbying activity is the shareholder empowerment movement. Not surprisingly, this association of CEOs prefers that the decision-making power reside in top management. The BRT was active in fighting efforts to empower shareholders through proxy access, a provision included in the Senate's financial regulation bill.[51] Castellani referred to this as the BRT's "highest priority" and noted, "Nearly all of our members have called about this."[52] The push against shareholder democracy has resulted in some criticism of BRT. In *Corpocracy: How CEOs and the Business Roundtable Hijacked the World's Greatest Wealth Machine*, Robert Monks describes a meeting between Castellani and John Connolly of Institutional Shareholder Services (ISS). Castellani went to the ISS office to berate Connolly personally for ISS's recommendation that shareholders withhold proxy votes from compensation committee members who approved a controversial CEO pay package. The title of his book is a clear indication of Monks' assessment of the impact of the BRT. In 2011, Castellani left BRT to head PhRMA and John Engler, former three-term governor of Michigan, became President of BRT.[53]

National Association of Manufacturers (NAM) NAM describes itself as "the preeminent U.S. manufacturers association as well as the nation's largest industrial trade association."[54] Although the membership of NAM has historically been tilted toward firms in the larger smokestack industries, it now includes small and medium-sized firms as well as member associations. The membership of NAM encompasses every industrial sector and all 50 U.S. states.[55] This diversity provides a challenge for NAM because the concerns of small firms often differ from those of the larger, global players.

One example of conflict that can arise is the issue of free trade. The large firms tend to be free trade advocates, a stance with which NAM agrees; however, the small firms are increasingly desirous of protection.[56] The issue came to a head during a meeting of the board. The membership of NAM had voted to fight Chinese currency manipulation because it creates an unfair situation for small U.S. firms that try to compete with Chinese firms or multinational firms operating in China.[57] The NAM board voted to go against the vote of the membership. This led to the creation of a new organization, the American Alliance for Manufacturing, based in Washington. In addition, the Michigan Tooling Association expanded and renamed itself the Tooling, Manufacturing, and Technologies Association.[58]

National Federation of Independent Businesses (NFIB) During the end of the 20th century, the growth of small businesses came to dominate the business news. It should not be surprising, therefore, that the NFIB, as a small business association, also came into a position of power. Although their businesses are small, their influence in Washington is not. When *Fortune* magazine last conducted its ranking of the Power 25 lobbyists, the NFIB ranked third overall and top in business organizations for clout.[59] One of the best ways to appreciate the NFIB's political power is to describe its success at grassroots lobbying.[60] The NFIB made its mark by strong and successful lobbying against former President Clinton's health care plan: They continue in the same vein to oppose aspects of the Obama administration's health care reform that will impact small business.[61] They also serve as the lead organizer of the "Stop the Hit (health insurance tax)" coalition of small business owners that is working to repeal the employer mandate provision.[62]

The NFIB is able to speak with one voice due to the homogeneity of its membership and the many issues that small businesses share because of their size. For this reason, the NFIB avoids the problems faced by the NAM and the U.S. Chamber of Commerce. However, its political activities have cost it any clout it might have had in the Obama administration. The NFIB joined the lawsuit against health care reform, and subsequently lost when the Supreme Court upheld the constitutionality of the law.[63] According to NFIB President and CEO Dan Danner, "It's been a long two-year effort, but I think, certainly from where I am, we'd do it again in a heartbeat."[64]

Coalitions A noteworthy and growing mechanism of political involvement in the public policy process is the creation and use of **coalitions** to influence government processes. A coalition forms when distinct groups or parties realize they have something in common that might warrant their joining forces, at least temporarily, for joint action. More often than not, an issue that various groups feel similarly about creates the opportunity for a coalition. A coalition can work cooperatively with government or it can lobby government when that government does not share the coalition's priorities.

Coalition formation has become a standard practice for firms interested in accomplishing political goals or influencing public policy. If a company or an association wants to pass or defeat particular legislation, it can strengthen its position by enlisting support from an individual or organization that has a similar position on the issue. Coalitions enable members to share their resources and pool their energies when they confront difficult issues. Coalitions also can provide cover for a company that wants to push for its own agenda without necessarily having its name attached to the campaign.

One example of coalition building around a specific issue is the Global Business Coalition against Human Trafficking. Members include Carlson, Delta Air Lines, Exxon Mobil, LexisNexis, ManpowerGroup, Microsoft, NXP, and Travelport.[65] These corporations have joined to share their resources and expertise to work with business and government to fight the growing problem of modern-day slavery.[66] The International Labour Organization estimates that almost 21 million people are victims of forced labor, with 5.5 million younger than 18.[67] The companies' supply chains may contain forced labor and travel and tourism facilities can unknowingly facilitate sex trafficking.[68] The coalition plans to develop training modules for employees and best practices guidelines for corporate leaders.[69] More than 12,000 private employers have signed the Athens accord, a voluntary agreement developed at a meeting of the Business Community against Human Trafficking, held in Athens, Greece.[70] By signing the Accord, companies promise to uphold a zero-tolerance policy toward working with any entity that benefits from human trafficking.[71]

ETHICS IN PRACTICE CASE
Double Irish with a Dutch Sandwich

One way that business affects government is by avoiding taxes by exploiting or creating tax loopholes. Doing this improves corporate profits, meeting one of business's responsibilities. However, businesses also have responsibility to contribute financially to the governments whose resources enable them to grow and prosper. Those contributions are needed to maintain and promote a sustainable world, as evidenced by tax payment being included as a key performance indicator in determining the Global 100 most sustainable corporations. A key question is—where should business draw the line between retaining profits to enhance shareholder wealth and contributing its fair share to government?

As the United States government looks for ways to deal with a growing deficit, greater attention is being paid to the issue of corporate taxation. The Center for Investigative Reporting evaluated the earnings and assets of Silicon Valley tech companies and compared them to taxes paid. It concluded that Silicon Valley giants, such as Apple, eBay, Google and Yahoo, were paying effective global tax rates well below the top U.S. corporate tax rate of 35 percent. Non-tech companies such as General Electric, Coca-Cola, and Procter and Gamble also reduced taxes with offshore holdings. However, because tech companies deal with intellectual property, they are more easily able to shift their intellectual property to tax havens.

In the 1980s, Apple pioneered an accounting method that sent profits to the Caribbean by way of Irish subsidiaries and the Netherlands—hence the title "Double Irish with a Dutch Sandwich." Observers estimate that hundreds of companies employ that tactic today. A U.S. Senate Investigative Panel, headed by Senator Carl Levin (D-MI), is exploring the overall issue of corporate tax avoidance. According to Senator Levin, "The resulting loss of revenue is one significant cause of the budget deficit, and adds to the tax burden that ordinary Americans bear."

1. Who are the stakeholders and how are they affected by these corporate tax-saving strategies?
2. Do companies have a responsibility to pay a fair share of income tax to local, state, and federal governments? Who determines what that fair share should be?
3. Where do you draw the line on tax savings by corporations?
4. The U.K. government has declared that corporate tax avoiders will no longer be able to bid on government contracts. Critics believe that corporations will find a way to work around it. If it were possible to design a foolproof system, would you support the U.K. policy? Would you recommend it to other governments?

Sources: Charles Duhig, "Inquiry into Tech Giants' Tax Strategies Nears End," *The New York Times* (January 3, 2012), http://www.nytimes.com/2013/01/04/business/an-inquiry-into-tech-giants-tax-strategies-nears-an-end.html?_r=0. Accessed February 25, 2013, Matt Orange, "Silicon Valley Firms Shelter Assets Overseas, Avoid Billions in U.S. Taxes," *Center for Investigative Reporting* (February 13, 2013), http://cironline.org/reports/silicon-valley-firms-shelter-assets-overseas-avoid-billions-us-taxes-4203. Accessed February 25, 2013; Prem Sikka, "Big UK Tax Avoiders Will Easily Get Round New Government Policy," *The Guardian* (February 15, 2013), http://www.guardian.co.uk/commentisfree/2013/feb/15/uk-tax-avoiders-wont-stop-new-policy. Accessed February 25, 2013.

Corporate Political Spending

To this point, our discussion of lobbying has focused primarily on interpersonal contact and powers of persuasion. We now turn our attention to corporate political spending and its implications for businesses and their stakeholders. The channels through which corporations can make political contributions are many and varied. In addition to the traditional political action committee (PAC), companies can contribute corporate funds to trade associations and other tax-exempt groups that will subsequently support a particular candidate or cause. Companies can also contribute to Super PACs, political parties, and political committees, both connected and nonconnected to candidates. With this range of options and few meaningful restrictions on corporate involvement, corporate political spending has become "dangerous terrain."[72] Instead of just worrying about contributions to candidates and political parties, firms must now deal with requests from Super PACs, trade associations, and **501(c)(4)** "social welfare" associations, and they must do so carefully.[73] As Bruce Freed and Karl Sandstrom explain:[74]

> *Political spending should not be a casual decision, a choice defaulted to companies' government-relations managers—or to trade associations or c4s. The spending, whether done directly or through third-party groups, needs to reflect the deliberate choices of senior managers and the board. When it comes to political engagement, a company must adhere to its values, keep its broader interests in mind, and understand that giving money to candidates or entities whose behavior is uncertain or at odds with those values and long-term business interests ultimately harms the company and its shareholders. To understand political spending fully is to understand its full consequences.*

Target Corporation, the huge retailer, did not understand the full consequences of its political spending and ended up paying a price. The company contributed to Minnesota Forward, a pro-economic growth political action group, in order to help it support pro-growth political candidates.[75] However, one of those candidates opposed gay marriage, a position that neither Target nor Minnesota Forward endorsed. This led to a boycott of Target stores by gay-marriage activists.[76] Target later apologized for the contribution, noting that the company endorsed the candidate's stance on economic issues and not social issues.[77] The company also said it would do a strategic review of its political donations before moving forward with any more.[78] Supporting a pro-growth candidate was consistent with creating value for Target's shareholders.[79] Minnesota Forward's stance on gay marriage was unrelated to the reason that Target contributed funds to the organization. However, the resultant boycott threatened to harm the company and its shareholders.[80] Target learned the hard way that corporate political spending contains repercussions that extend beyond any single issue.

Arguments for Corporate Political Spending

The most visible and ultimately influential defenders of corporate political spending are the five U.S. Supreme Court justices who shared in the majority opinion in *Citizens United*, the controversial 2010 U.S. Supreme Court ruling that declared government may not restrict independent corporate political expenditures. The logic behind the ruling is that the First Amendment establishes the right to free speech and that not only individuals, but also groups of individuals, have that right. From this perspective, limiting a group's right to political advocacy would violate the free speech of the people who belong to that group. It follows from this logic then that corporations, as well as unions and other groups of people, have the right to express their political opinions and their candidate preferences. Business has an important part to play in society and part of that is speaking up for the needs of business and sharing an economic perspective. In this pluralistic society, business provides a counterbalance to other interest groups who express their own agendas.

Arguments Against Corporate Political Spending

Senator John McCain (R-AZ) became one of the most often quoted critics of corporate campaign spending when he called the *Citizens United* decision "one of the worst decisions I have ever seen… I predict to you that there will be huge scandals associated with this huge flood of money."[81] Senator McCain's comments crystallize one of the key arguments against corporate political spending: Corporations have access to large amounts of money and that creates a serious imbalance of power. Another concern is the possibility of agency problems as managers may promote their own interests rather than the shareholders' interests, or the interests of stakeholders, when promoting candidates or issues. Even when promoting shareholder welfare, the innate self-interest of business gives people pause as business is not likely to focus on the common good. Justice Stevens shared these apprehensions in the dissenting opinion on *Citizens United:* "The financial resources, legal structure, and instrumental orientation of corporations raise legitimate concerns about their role in the electoral process. Our lawmakers have a compelling constitutional basis, if not also a democratic duty, to take measures designed to guard against the potentially deleterious effects of corporate spending in local and national races."[82] The **Golden Rule of Politics** sums up the concerns of those who argue against corporate political spending: "He who has the gold, rules."[83]

Political Action Committees

Political action committees (PACs) are committees organized to raise and spend money for political candidates, ballot initiatives, and proposed legislation. Figure 12-3 shows the top 10 PAC contributors to federal candidates. Most PACs have a political point of view, either conservative or liberal, but many simply focus on a specific issue and try to do so in a nonpartisan manner.[84] In the United States, the Federal Election Campaign Act (FECA) prohibits corporations from making direct contributions to candidates.[85] However, the law has always permitted corporations to form PACs. The U.S. Federal Elections Commission (FEC) differentiates between PACs that are connected and nonconnected. A **connected PAC**, also known as a separate segregated fund, is associated with a specific group or organization and can only raise money from that group. The FEC permits the company or organization sponsoring the PAC to absorb the cost of soliciting contributions, as well as administrative overhead.[86] A **nonconnected PAC** can accept funds from any individual or organization, as well as from a connected PAC, as long as those contributions are legal.[87] Nonconnected PACs are typically formed

FIGURE 12-3 Top 10 PAC Contributors to Candidates (2011–2012)

PAC	Total Amount ($)	Democratic Percentage	Republican Percentage
National Association of Realtors	3,960,282	44	55
National Beer Wholesalers Association	3,388,500	41	59
Honeywell International	3,193,024	41	59
Operating Engineers Union	3,182,887	84	41
National Auto Dealers Association	3,074,000	28	72
International Brotherhood of Electrical Workers	2,853,000	97	2
American Bankers Association	2,736,150	20	80
AT&T, Inc.	2,543,000	35	65
American Association for Justice	2,512,500	96	3
Credit Union National Association	2,487,600	47	52

Source: The Center for Responsive Politics, http://www.opensecrets.org. Based on data released by the FEC on February 18, 2013.

around a specific issue or by specific political leaders. **Leadership PACs** are nonconnected PACs formed by political leaders to support other candidates for office.[88]

Unlike the above PACs that were created through legislation, **Super PACs** resulted from judicial decisions.[89] The first decision occurred in 2010 when the U.S. Supreme Court ruled in *Citizens United v. Federal Election Commission (FEC)* that corporations and labor unions could use the funds from their treasuries to support or oppose political candidates as long as spending is independent, i.e., not coordinated with a candidate.[90] The Court upheld the prohibition against corporations donating directly to candidates.[91] We should note, however, that money spent independently to support or oppose a candidate is as effective as money given to a candidate to spend. In *Speechnow v. Federal Election Commission (FEC)* the Federal Court further clarified the implementation of *Citizens United* by ruling that any government restrictions on the amount corporations can spend would be unconstitutional.[92] Those two rulings spurred the creation of Super PACs, new entities that have transformed the political landscape. Super PACs, officially known as **independent expenditure-only committees**, may raise unlimited amounts of money to support or oppose political candidates.[93] Their financial contributions are unlimited; however, they may not coordinate with or donate directly to a political candidate.[94] Of course, many people question the actual independence of the Super PAC expenditures. Typically, Super PACs are headed by former aides and associates who know the candidate well and so do not need to confer with the candidate to know what he or she would want the Super PAC to do. In addition, the candidate can simply speak to the media and then the Super PAC can simply follow the news for clues as to where to spend the money.

The Impact of Super PACs

Super PACs have facilitated outside spending in politics and the effect of outside spending has been huge. Outside spending in presidential elections has gone from $17 million in 1992 to almost $1.3 billion in 2012. Another item of note is that 72 percent of the money spent in 2010 came from groups that were barred from making political contributions in 2006.[95] In addition, 47 percent of outside spending now comes from donors whose identities are not disclosed.[96] Super PACs are still relatively new and so their full effect is not yet known, but sums of money that large are certain to have a profound impact.

It is important to note that we focus on corporate contributions because the purpose of this chapter is to explore the impact of business on government. However, Super PACs do not stem only from businesses or unions and other interested organizations may also form them.

Agency Issues

As we discussed in Chapter 4, agency problems arise when the actions of managers are not in the shareholders' best interests. Corporate political spending, like all corporate spending, should have the best interests of the firm, its shareholders, and its stakeholders in mind. Political spending should not provide an opportunity for managers to pursue their personal preferences because the money those managers are spending is not their own. Political spending should have a clear association with the firm's best interests rather than the managers' personal points of view.

Agency problems can also arise when managers give the firm's money to a third party, such as a trade association or nonprofit group. These organizations might donate to a candidate whose actions do not serve the interests of the firm's shareholders and stakeholders. Several major drug companies found themselves in this predicament after donating money to PhRMA, the trade association that represents their industry after a Bloomberg report shed light on PhRMA's political donations.[97] The trade association gave $4.8 million to two 501(c)(4) associations that subsequently used that money to support 23 congressional candidates successfully. After being elected, all 23 voted to limit access to and cut federal funding for birth control, as well as to cut medical research funds on which pharmaceutical companies rely.[98] Bayer AG, Johnson & Johnson, Merck, and Pfizer are all leading manufacturers of contraceptives. As members of PhRMA, these companies had contributed part of the money that got those congressional candidates elected.[99] In essence, through the trade association, they had inadvertently supported politicians who voted both to shrink their market and to reduce funding on which they depend. Angry investors berated the firms' managers for belonging to a trade association that used "its members' payments against those same members' best interests."[100]

Political Accountability and Transparency

Political accountability is an assumption of responsibility for political actions and a willingness to be answerable for them. In *Man's Search for Meaning*, Victor Frankl suggests that in addition to the Statue of Liberty on the East Coast of the United States, there should be a Statue of Responsibility on the West Coast because "freedom is only part of the story and half of the truth." He goes on to say, "Freedom is but the negative aspect of the whole phenomenon whose positive aspect is responsibleness. In fact, freedom is in danger of degenerating into mere arbitrariness unless it is lived in terms of responsibleness."[101] In today's political landscape, corporations have unprecedented freedom to pursue their political agendas. Restrictions on the money they can spend are virtually gone and multiple opportunities exist to hide the nature of their activities from public view. This freedom brings forth a duty for corporations to be responsible and, to that end, a movement to promote corporate political accountability has formed.

Some efforts are aimed at putting limits on what companies can spend; these include shareholder resolutions and lawsuits against big spenders. Along these lines, Common Cause filed a complaint against Chevron Corp for making a $2.5 million contribution to a Super PAC. The suit charges that Chevron is in violation of the policy against federal contractors making political contributions.[102] Shareholder resolutions also are growing. 2012 was the second year in a row that shareholder resolutions limiting political spending were the most common proposals.[103] Moreover, political activity resolutions received more shareholder support than any other topic.[104] Shareholders have convinced more than 120 public companies to make their previously hidden political spending transparent, and an additional 31 more companies will hold shareholder votes in 2013.[105] Other efforts involve companies exerting self-restraint: 16 companies have voluntarily agreed to inform investors about their political spending in order to avoid a shareholder vote that would require disclosure.[106] In response to the number and the shareholder support of political activity resolutions, the SEC announced it would propose a disclosure rule.[107]

That announcement set off a politically charged debate. A petition asking for the rule received almost half a million comments, many more any other petition or rule has ever received. The majority of those comments supported the petition.[108] Opposing the petition are some of the largest trade groups. The Chamber of Commerce, National Association of Manufacturers, and the Business Roundtable issued a rare joint letter to Fortune 500 CEOs, asking them to resist shareholder pressure to disclose political spending.[109] Advocates for an SEC rule prefer that disclosure be mandatory because voluntary disclosure is not always as effective. According to the Center for Political Accountability, a review of the extent to which 75 companies complied with their voluntary disclosure

FIGURE 12-4

Key Elements of
Corporate Political
Disclosure and
Accountability

1. Policies
   a. Ways in which we participate in the political process
   b. Who makes spending decisions
   c. Our commitment to publicly disclose all of our expenditures, indirect and direct
2. Disclosure
   a. Itemized Direct Expenditure
      i. State-level candidates and committee contributions
      ii. Ballot measure spending; and
      iii. Independent expenditures
   b. Itemized Indirect Expenditures
      i. Trade association dues and other payments, including special assessments used for political purposes
      ii. Payments to other tax-exempt organizations [527 groups, Super PACs, and 501 (c)(4) "social welfare" organizations] used for political purposes
3. Oversight
   a. Board of directors regularly reviews our spending, direct and indirect, and existing policies.

Source: *The Center for Political Accountability.*

agreements showed that 10 companies were in "significant non-compliance" with the agreed-upon terms.[110] Figure 12-4 provides the Center for Political Accountability's list of the key elements of corporate disclosure and accountability.

Transparency has become a major issue because much corporate political activity today is outside the public view. The Sunlight Foundation coined the term "**dark money**" to refer to the political contributions from undisclosed donors.[111] More than $300 million was spent by dark money donors in the 2012 presidential election, and this does not include money that was not reported to the Federal Election Commission.[112] The *Citizens United* ruling made it easier for donors to stay hidden. Tax exempt "social welfare organizations," known as 501(c)(4)s, are not required to disclose their donors, and so it is impossible to trace the money candidates receive from them back to the source.[113] Another politically active tax-exempt group is the **527**, that is only required to file with the FEC if it is a PAC or political party that expressly advocates for or against a federal candidate.[114] Super PACs are required to disclose their donors but their donors often hide behind other nonprofit groups, creating a vicious cycle of secrecy.[115] Trade associations are another conduit for dark money. In *Hidden Rivers*, the Center for Political Accountability dubbed trade associations "the Swiss bank accounts of American politics." This in-depth examination of the nation's trade associations showed how they have become conduits for unlimited corporate political spending of dark money. Of major concern is the fact that trade associations "are subject to even less disclosure than the much criticized spending of independent political committees (527s)."[116]

The arguments against dark money are undeniable. Advocacy is best understood when one knows the motives of the person making the arguments. Voters have a right to know who is putting forth arguments for and against a candidate or an issue, and dark money denies them that right. In addition, it is a well-known fact that people behave more ethically when their actions are visible to others. As former U.S. Supreme Court Justice Louis D. Brandeis famously explained, "Sunlight is said to be the best of disinfectants; electric light the most efficient policeman."[117] It is not surprising, therefore, that ads funded by dark money tend to be "the most vicious," with nearly 90 percent being negative.[118] According to an Annenberg Public Policy Center study, 26 percent of the ads funded by dark money are deceptive.[119]

Advocates of transparency at the federal level have tried repeatedly to enact legislation to require that donors be identified. Efforts to enact a law in the 111th and 112th

Congresses failed but, at this writing, Rep. Chris Van Hollen (D-MD) is reintroducing the legislation into the 113th.[120] Getting a handle on dark money is not easy because dark money spending often comes in layers. In California, state law requires nonprofit organizations to disclose donors who give money in order to fund political activities. Americans for Responsible Leadership (ARL), a 501(c)(4) based* in Arizona, donated $11 million to assist the Small Business Action Committee (SBAC) to support its effort to defeat two pending propositions. Because the donations were for political activities, the California Fair Political Practices Commission filed suit when ARL refused to disclose its donors saying, "Under California law, the failure to disclose this initially was campaign money laundering."[121] When ARL disclosed its donor, no meaningful light was shed. The donation came from another dark money nonprofit called Americans for Job Security (AJS), whose money came through another nonprofit, The Center to Protect Patient Rights (CPPR).[122] As Brendan Fischer of the Center for Media and Democracy's PR Watch observed, "California managed to peel back one layer of the dark money onion, but discovered little information about who is really bankrolling the operation—they only found more of the dark money onion."[123]

Strategies for Corporate Political Activity

We have discussed the two principal approaches by which business has become politically active—lobbying and political spending. To be sure, there are other approaches, but these are the major ones. In our discussion, we have unavoidably referred to the use of these approaches as part of a strategy. To develop the idea of strategy for political activism, it is important to understand that managers must not only identify useful approaches but also address when and under what conditions these various approaches should be used or would be most effective. We do not want to carry this idea too far, because it is beyond the scope of this book. On the other hand, as managers devise and execute political strategies, it is useful to see political strategy as consistent with their development of stakeholder management capabilities. The purpose of political strategy is "to secure a position of advantage regarding a given regulation or piece of legislation, to gain control of an idea or a movement and deflect it from the firm, or to deal with a local community group on an issue of importance."[124] As with all strategies, it is important to approach political activity in a well-thought-out manner, paying attention not only to the procedures to follow but also to the values inherent in the sought-after outcomes and any repercussions that could follow.

Amy Hillman and Michael Hitt offer three distinct types of strategies that companies use to interact with decision makers in the political arena.[125] They are:

- *Information Strategy*—providing information to policymakers through activities such as lobbying, research projects, position papers, and being an expert witness
- *Financial Incentives Strategy*—making direct financial contributions, providing desired services, reimbursing travel, or paying fees to policymakers
- *Constituency Building Strategy*—mobilizing grassroots or business cohorts to work together through public relations, political education, press conferences, and advertising.

Firms may use any or all of these strategies at any given time. These are all proactive strategies, in which the firm makes a conscious decision to be politically active.[126] Firms can also sit by the sidelines and passively react to changes in political environment, but that strategy is unlikely to serve the business world in today's rapidly changing political environment. What Murray Weidenbaum wrote more than thirty years ago is even truer for business today: Public policy is "no longer a spectator sport for business."[127]

Financial Performance Outcomes

Many studies have been conducted to calculate whether corporate political spending influences political decisions and, ultimately, firm performance. These studies have mixed results. Some find strong support, others find none, and a third group has mixed or marginal findings.[128] A recent meta-analysis found that corporate political activity had a consistent positive relationship with a firm's financial performance.[129] However, generic results are of limited value because the outcomes of corporate political activity occur in a variety of contexts and so researchers have looked for contingencies that might explain differences in returns. For example, another study shows that corporate donations to political campaigns are associated with an increase in firm value of 3.5 percent.[130] The authors speculate that the increase in firm value stems from the economic benefits accruing to the companies from legislation they supported. The return is greatest for firms in the candidate's home state.[131]

In another study, researchers explored the effect of PAC contributions on the regulation of cable television. In support of their hypotheses, they found that PAC contributions were more influential when given to House candidates than to Senate candidates. They explain it in two ways: The more frequent elections of House members make them more susceptible to campaign financing concerns, and the smaller size of the House constituencies (as opposed to the Senate constituencies) means House members have fewer interest groups with which they must contend. Similarly, they found that PAC money was more influential when issues were at the smaller interest-group level, and its importance became diluted when issues moved to the broader arena of the entire House or Senate.[132]

Evidence suggests that corporations are aware of the context in which they operate and adjust their corporate political activity accordingly. Universities do more lobbying when congressional appropriations committee members serve the districts in which they are located.[133] This targeted lobbying is a successful strategy. The universities who engage in lobbying appropriations committee members receive more federal earmarks.[134]

The mixed results of these studies make it difficult to draw a definite connection between corporate political activity and firm performance. Clearly, context matters and so strategies that work in one situation will not necessarily transfer to another. We should even remember that corporate political activity can worsen performance. In a 2013 study of the corporate political activity of 943 firms over a 10-year period, Michael Hadani and Douglas Schuler found very little good news: They likened the hope of reaping corporate profits from corporate political activity to the famously unsuccessful search for El Dorado, the city of gold.[135] They found a negative association between political investments and market performance, with cumulative political investments worsening both market and accounting performance.[136] The only good financial news was for firms in regulated industries. For them, corporate political activity was positively associated with market performance.

Summary

The world is still feeling the after-effects of the global financial meltdown. As a weak economy struggles to get back on its feet, items that were once at the forefront of the legislative agenda have been shelved to deal with issues such as joblessness and business failures. In this challenging environment, corporate political participation has taken on renewed importance.

We discussed the different levels of lobbying, the different types of PACs, and how each can be used responsibly. The 2010 Supreme Court ruling in *Citizens United v. Federal Election Commission* has changed the rules significantly, particularly in terms of corporate political spending. In the midst of these ebbs and flows in restrictions, lobbying and corporate political spending remain a permanent part of the political landscape. Business advocating for its interests is an important part of maintaining the balance of power needed in a pluralistic society. To maintain a true balance of power, however, businesses must advocate in a way that is both ethical and legal. Business has a duty to temper the freedom it now has with responsibility, accountability, and transparency.

We have explored the two major ways companies seek to influence government action—lobbying and corporate spending. While we describe these strategies at a macro level, they each contain a variety of different ways for corporations to take political action. We should remember that politically active firms are inclined to combine various strategies.[137] Companies make political contributions, set up their own lobbyists in Washington offices, contract with outside lobbyists to represent their interests, and join like-minded orga-

nizations to push for change through trade associations and coalitions. Corporate political spending and lobbying are not separate strategies; they are part of an overall approach.[138]

Business's political activity continues to be controversial with the public. As we discussed in Chapter 1, business often receives criticism for using and abusing its power. Nowhere is this more evident than in corporate lobbying and its outcomes. Efforts are underway to rein in some of the power that business now holds in the political action process. As new excesses develop, new regulations and rulings come to address the problems they present. In the meantime, responsible businesses are focused on determining how they can pursue an ethical approach to political participation. This is the ongoing "back and forth" that characterizes the political process.

Key Terms

ad hoc coalition, p. 357
astroturf lobbying, p. 360
Citizens United v. Federal Election Commission (FEC), p. 367
coalition, p. 363
company lobbying, p. 357
connected PAC, p. 366
cyberadvocacy, p. 360
dark money, p. 369
501(c)(4)s, p. 365

527, p. 369
Golden Rule of Politics, p. 366
grassroots lobbying, p. 359
independent expenditure-only committee, 367
Leadership PAC, p. 367
lobbying, p. 355
nonconnected PAC, p. 366
political accountability, p. 368

political action committee (PAC), p. 366
political involvement, p. 355
sectoral trade association, p. 357
Speechnow v. Federal Election Commission (FEC), p. 367
Super PAC, p. 367
transparency, p. 369
umbrella trade associations, p. 357

Discussion Questions

1. Explain lobbying in your own words. Describe the different levels at which lobbying takes place. Why do you think there is a lack of unity among the umbrella organizations?

2. What is a PAC? What are the major arguments in favor of PACs? What are the major types of PACs and how do they differ? In your opinion, are PACs a good way for business to influence the public policy process? What changes would you recommend for PACs?

3. Discuss *Citizens United* and *Speechnow* and their likely effect on future elections. What, if any, reforms would you recommend?

4. What does corporate accountability mean to you? How important is corporate political transparency?

5. What are the limits of corporate political strategy? Are there lines that companies should not cross? If so, what are they?

Endnotes

1. Adam Liptak, "Justices 5-4, Reject Corporate Spending Limit," *The New York Times* (January 22, 2010), http://www.nytimes.com/2010/01/22/us/politics/22scotus.html. Accessed February 23, 2013.

2. S. Prakash Sethi, "Corporate Political Activism," *California Management Review* (Spring 1982), 32.

3. Jeffrey H. Birnbaum, "Microsoft's Capital Offense," *Fortune* (February 2, 1998), 84–86; Dan Carney, "Microsoft's All-Out Counterattack," *BusinessWeek* (May 15, 2000), 103–106.

4. http://www.opensecrets.org/lobby/indusclient.php?id=B12&year=2012. Accessed February 25, 2013.

5. David B. Yoffie and Sigrid Bergenstein, "Creating Political Advantage: The Rise of the Corporate Political Entrepreneur," *California Management Review* (Fall 1985), 124. See also John F. Mahon, "Corporate Political Strategy," *Business in the Contemporary World* (Autumn 1989), 50–62.

6. H. R. Mahood, *Interest Group Politics in America* (Englewood Cliffs, NJ: Prentice Hall, 1990), 52.

7. David D. Kirkpatrick, "Lobbyists Get Potent Weapon in Campaign Ruling," *The New York Times* (January 21, 2010), http://www.nytimes.com/2010/01/22/us/politics/22donate.html?_r=0. Accessed April 13, 2013.

8. Ibid., 53–54.

9. Elizabeth Dwoskin, "Lobbyist on Incremental Mission to Restore Lobbying's Good Name," *Bloomberg BusinessWeek* (June 7, 2012), 78.

10. Keith Matheny, "Abramoff Lists 8 Tips to Overhaul Lobbying Laws," *USA Today* (January 28, 2013), http://www.usatoday.com/story/news/nation/2013/01/28/abramoff-lobby-reform-tips/1870507/. Accessed February 24, 2013.

11. "A Lobbyist in Full," *The New York Times* (June 24, 2010), http://www.nytimes.com/2005/05/01/magazine/01ABRAMOFF.html?pagewanted=all. Accessed February 24, 2013.

12. http://www.opensecrets.org/lobby/incdec.php. Accessed February 24, 2013.

13. Raquel Meyer Alexander, Stephen W. Mazza, and Susan Scholz, "Measuring Rates of Return for Lobbying Expenditures: An Empirical Case Study of Tax Breaks for Multinational Corporations," *Journal of Law and Politics* (Vol. 25, No. 401, 2009), 401.

14. Erich Lichtblau, "Tired of 'Tainted' Image, Lobbyists Try Makeover," *The New York Times* (May 3, 2012), http://www.nytimes.com/2012/05/04/us/politics/tired-of-tainted-image-lobbyists-try-makeover.html?pagewanted=all. Accessed February 24, 2013.

15. Dwoskin, 78.

16. "Greenpeace Rates Electronics Firms on Lobbying," *EnvironmentalLeader.com* (January 7, 2010), http://www.environmentalleader.com/2010/01/07/greenpeace-rates-electronics-firms-on-lobbying/.

17. Ed Lallo, "Coalition of Gulf Shrimp Industries Files for Relief from Subsidized Shrimp Imports," *Louisiana Seafood News,* (January 15, 2013), http://www.louisiana-seafoodnews.com/2013/01/15/gulf-shrimp-coalition-files-for-relief-from-subsidized-shrimp-imports/. Accessed April 13, 2013.

18. "The Glint of the Revolving Door," *The New York Times* (February 5, 2004).

19. M. Asif Ismail, "Spending on Lobbying Thrives: Drug and Health Products Industries Invest $182 Million to Influence Legislation," *Center for Public Integrity Report* (April 1, 2007), http://www.publicintegrity.org/2007/04/01/5780/spending-lobbying-thrives. Accessed March 8, 2013.

20. David Kirkpatrick and Duff Wilson, "Health Reform in Limbo: Top Drug Lobbyist Quits," *The New York Times* (February 11, 2010), http://www.nytimes.com/2010/02/12/health/policy/12pharma.html?_r=0. Accessed March 8, 2013.

21. Alex Wayne and Drew Armstrong, "Tauzin's $11.6 Million Made Him Highest Paid Health-Law Lobbyist," Bloomberg.com (November 20, 2011), http://www.bloomberg.com/news/2011-11-29/tauzin-s-11-6-million-made-him-highest-paid-health-law-lobbyist.html. Accessed February 23, 2013.

22. Deniz Igan and Prachie Mishra, "Making Friends," *Finance and Development* (June 2011), http://www.imf.org/external/pubs/ft/fandd/2011/06/Igan.htm. Accessed February 23, 2013.

23. Ibid.

24. Ibid.

25. Evan Thomas, "Peddling Influence," *Time* (March 3, 1986), 27.

26. Edward T. Walker, "Grass-Roots Mobilization, by Corporate America," *The New York Times* (August 12, 2012), http://www.nytimes.com/2012/08/11/opinion/grass-roots-mobilization-by-corporate-america.html. Accessed February 23, 2013.

27. Jane M. Keffer and Ronald Paul Hill, "An Ethical Approach to Lobbying Activities of Businesses in the United States," *Journal of Business Ethics* (September 1997), 1371–1379.

28. http://pac.org/conferences/grassroots. Accessed February 23, 2013.

29. Jeffrey H. Birnbaum, "Washington's Power 25," *Fortune* (December 8, 1997), 145–158.

30. Daniel Stone, "The Browning of Grassroots," *Newsweek* (August 20, 2009), http://www.newsweek.com/id/212934. Accessed March 8, 2013.

31. Dan Mitchell, "Don't Mess with the Penny Lobby," *CNN Money* (April 11, 2012), http://tech.fortune.cnn.com/2012/04/11/penny/. Accessed February 23, 2013.

32. Ibid.

33. Ibid.

34. Robert M. Whaples, "It's Time to Eliminate the Penny," *CNN.com* (February 12, 2012), http://www.cnn.com/2012/02/17/opinion/whalpes-pennies-economics. Accessed February 23, 2013.

35. Ann Carrns, "Is a Penny Rounded a Penny Lost? Ask Chipotle," *The New York Times* (August 28, 2012), http://bucks.blogs.nytimes.com/2012/08/28/is-a-penny-rounded-a-penny-lost-ask-chipotle/. Accessed February 23, 2013.

36. Daniel Stone, "The Browning of Grassroots," *Newsweek* (August 19, 2009), http://www.thedailybeast.com/newsweek/2009/08/19/the-browning-of-grassroots.html. Accessed February 23, 2013.

37. http://www.sourcewatch.org/index.php/Journalists_who_have_been_taken_in_by_astroturfing. Accessed February 24, 2013.

38. Joseph E. Stiglitz, *The Price of Inequality: How Today's Divided Society Endangers Our Future* (W.W. Norton Company, 2012).

39. Peter Baker, "Obama Was Pushed by Drug Industry, E-Mails Suggest," *The New York Times* (June 8, 2012), http://www.nytimes.com/2012/06/09/us/politics/e-mails-reveal-extent-of-obamas-deal-with-industry-on-health-care.html?pagewanted=all. Accessed February 24, 2013.

40. http://www.govtrack.us/congress/bills/110/hr4; http://www.govtrack.us/congress/bills/111/s3413; http://www.govtrack.us/congress/bills/111/s3413. Accessed February 24, 2013.

41. http://www.govtrack.us/congress/bills/113/s117. Accessed February 24, 2013.

42. Jeffrey Marshall, "Credit Union Battleground Shifts," *US Banker* (April 1998), 10–11. See also Jill Wechsler, "Employers, Healthcare Industry Lash Back at White House, Congress," *Managed Healthcare* (February 1998), 8.

43. Nancy E. Roman, "Chamber of Commerce Hires New Lobbyists to Counter Unions," *Washington Times—National Weekly Edition* (January 11, 1998), 10. See also Douglas Harbrecht, "Chamber of Commerce Battle Cry—Kill All the Lawyers," *BusinessWeek* (March 2, 1998), 53.

44. "The Chamber of Secrets," *The Economist* (April 21, 2012), 77–79.

45. http://www.opensecrets.org/lobby/top.php?indexType=s. Accessed February 24, 2013.

46. http://www.fixtheuschamber.org/issues/local-chambers-vs-us-chamber. Accessed February 24, 2013.

47. Jane Sasseen, "Who Speaks for Business?" *BusinessWeek* (October 19, 2009), 22–24.

48. "The Chamber of Secrets," 79.

49. http://businessroundtable.org/about-us/. Accessed February 24, 2013.

50. Louis Jacobson, "The Roundtable's Turnaround," *National Journal* (June 28, 2003), 2120.

51. Jia Lynn Yang, "CEOs from Far and Wide Band Against Financial Bill Provision," *Washington Post* (May 14, 2010), http://www.fixtheuschamber.org/issues/local-chambers-vs-us-chamber. Accessed February 24, 2013.

52. Ibid.

53. http://businessroundtable.org/about-us/brt-president/. Accessed February 24, 2013.

54. http://www.nam.org/About-Us/About-the-NAM/US-Manufacturers-Association.aspx. Accessed February 24, 2013.

55. Ibid.

56. Timothy Aeppel, "Manufacturer's Group Comes to Capitol Hill to Gain Support," *The Wall Street Journal* (February 12, 2004), A9.

57. "Trade Issues Cause Schism between NAM and American Manufacturers," *Manufacturing Business Technology* (April 2007), 14.

58. Ibid.

59. Jeffrey H. Birnbaum, "Washington's Power 25," *Fortune* (May 28, 2001), 95.

60. Susan Headden, "The Little Lobby That Could," *U.S. News & World Report* (September 12, 1994), 45–48.

61. http://www.nfib.com/advocacy/item/cmsid/1363. Accessed March 8, 2013.

62. Ibid.

63. Kent Hoover, "NFIB Has No Regrets About Lawsuit Challenging Obamacare," *The Business Journals* (June 28, 2012), http://www.bizjournals.com/bizjournals/washingtonbureau/2012/06/28/nfib-has-no-regrets-about-lawsuit.html?page=all. Accessed February 24, 2013.

64. Ibid.

65. Dori Meinert, "Businesses Target Human Trafficking." *HR Magazine* 57, no. 12 (December 2012): 20.

66. Ibid.

67. Ibid.

68. Ibid.

69. Ibid.

70. http://www.ungift.org/doc/knowledgehub/events/Luxor_End_Human_Trafficking_Now.pdf. Accessed March 14, 2013.

71. Dori Meinert, "MODERN-DAY SLAVERY. (Cover Story)." *HR Magazine* 57.5 (2012): 22–27.

72. Bruce F. Freed and Karl J. Sandstrom, "Dangerous Terrain: How to Manage Corporate Political Spending n a Risky New Environment," *The Conference Board Review* (Winter 2012), 20–27.

73. Ibid.

74. Bruce F. Freed and Karl J. Sandstrom, "Navigating Politics," *The Conference Board Review* (Winter 2013), http://tcbreview.com/winter-2013/navigating-politics.html. Accessed February 25, 2013.

75. J. W. Verret, "The SEC Ponders Circumventing Citizens United," *The Wall Street Journal* (January 8, 2013), A5.

76. Ibid.

77. Brian Bakst, "Target Apologizes for Political Donation in Minnesota," *USA Today* (August 8, 2010), http://usatoday30.usatoday.com/money/industries/retail/2010-08-05-target-campaign-donation_N.htm. Accessed March 4, 2013.

78. Ibid.

79. Verret, A5.

80. Ibid.

81. Staff, "McCain Raps High Court's Campaign Finance Ruling," *Associated Press* (January 12, 2012), http://news.yahoo.com/mccain-raps-high-courts-campaign-finance-ruling-123521384.html. Accessed March 4, 2013.

82. Michael Beckel, "Supreme Court Gives Corporations, Unions Power to Spend Unlimited Sums on Political Messaging," *OpenSecretsblog* (January 21, 2010), http://www.opensecrets.org/news/2010/01/supreme-court-gives-corporatio.html. Accessed March 4, 2013.

83. Larry J. Sabato, "PAC-Man Goes to Washington," *Across the Board* (October 1984), 16.

84. http://www.sourcewatch.org/index.php/Political_action_committee. Accessed February 26, 2013.

85. "Court Won't Hear Campaign Contributions Appeal," Boston.com (February 25, 2013), http://www.boston.com/news/politics/2013/02/25/court-won-hear-campaign-contributions-appeal/iy3n3pCviBiMYGSJ0S4FGK/story.html. Accessed February 26, 2013.

86. http://www.fec.gov/pages/brochures/ssfvnonconnected.shtml. Accessed February 26, 2013.

87. Federal Election Commission, *Nonconnected committees* (May 2008), http://www.fec.gov/pdf/nongui.pdf. Accessed February 26, 2013.

88. Ibid.

89. R. Sam Garrett, ""Super PACs" in Federal Elections: Overview and Issues for Congress," *Congressional Research Service* (December 2, 2011), http://www.fas.org/sgp/crs/misc/R42042.pdf. Accessed February 26, 2013.

90. Adam Liptak, "Courts Take On Campaign Finance Decisions," *The New York Times* (March 26, 2010), http://www.nytimes.com/2010/03/27/us/politics/27campaign.html. Accessed February 26, 2013.

91. Adam Liptak, "Courts Take On Campaign Finance Decision," *The New York Times* (March 26, 2010), http://www.nytimes.com/2010/03/27/us/politics/27campaign. html. Accessed March 4, 2013.

92. Ibid.

93. http://www.opensecrets.org/pacs/superpacs.php?cycle=2012. Accessed March 4, 2013.

94. Ibid.

95. Spencer MacColl, "Citizens United Decision Profoundly Affects Political Landscape," *OpenSecretsblog* (May 5, 2011), http://www.opensecrets.org/news/2011/05/citizens-united-decision-profoundly-affects-political-landscape.html. Accessed March 4, 2013.

96. Ibid.

97. Bruce F. Freed and Karl J. Sandstrom, "Navigating Politics," *The Conference Board Review* (Winter 2013), 25–29.

98. Ibid.

99. Ibid.

100. Ibid., 26.

101. Viktor Emil Frankl, *Man's Search for Meaning*, Beacon Press (1956), 132.

102. Taylor Lincoln, "Study Shows Super PACs made mockery of campaign law," *The Hill's Congress Blog* (March 5, 2013), http://thehill.com/blogs/congress-blog/campaign/286219-study-shows-super-pacs-made-mockery-of-campaign-law. Accessed March 8, 2013.

103. http://www.glasslewis.com/blog/glass-lewis-publishes-political-contributions-a-glass-lewis-issue-report/. Accessed March 8, 2013.

104. Lucian A. Bebchuk and Robert J. Jackson, Jr. "Shining Light on Corporate Political Spending," *Georgetown Law Journal* (Vol. 101, April 2013), 923–967.

105. Dave Michaels, "Shareholders Force Firms to Reveal Secret Political Funds," Bloomberg.com (April 25, 2013), http://www.bloomberg.com/news/2013-04-25/shareholders-force-firms-to-reveal-secret-political-funds.html. Accessed April 29, 2013.

106. Ibid.

107. Nicholas Confessore, "S.E.C. Is Asked to Require Disclosure of Donations," *The New York Times* (April 23, 2013), http://www.nytimes.com/2013/04/24/us/politics/sec-is-asked-to-make-companies-disclose-donations.html?hp&_r=0. Accessed April 29, 2013.

108. Ibid.

109. Ibid.

110. Michaels, 2013.

111. Sunlightfoundation.com. Accessed March 4, 2013.

112. Paul Steiberg and Stephen Engelberg, "Dark Money and the 2012 Election," *ProPublica* (November 6, 2012), http://www.propublica.org/article/dark-money-and-the-2012-election-we-need-your-help. Accessed March 5, 2013.

113. Brian C. Mooney, "Ruling Allows Major Political Donors to Hide Identities," *The Boston Globe* (February 15, 2012), http://www.bostonglobe.com/news/nation/2012/02/15/major-political-donors-can-hide-identities/JrQx1lLgLQNJ1Mfuz5LbjN/story.html?camp=pm. Accessed March 5, 2013.

114. http://www.opensecrets.org/527s/types.php. Accessed March 5, 2013.

115. John Dimsdale, "Required Super PAC disclosures don't reveal all," *Marketplace* (February 1, 2012), http://www.marketplace.org/topics/elections/campaign-trail/required-super-pac-disclosures-dont-reveal-all. Accessed March 5, 2013.

116. Center for Political Accountability, "Hidden Rivers (2006): How Trade Associations Conceal Corporate Political Spending, Its Threat to Companies, and What Shareholders Can Do," http://www.political accountability. net/index.php?ht=display/Content-Details/i/1025. Accessed July 2010.

117. http://www.brandeis.edu/legacyfund/bio.html. Accessed March 4, 2013.

118. Michael Scherer, "Dark Money: The Rise of Outside Spending in 2012," *Time* (November 1, 2012), http://swampland.time.com/2012/11/01/dark-money/#ixzz2FX0K5omj. Accessed March 7, 2013.

119. Ibid.

120. Eliza Newlin Carney, "DISCLOSE Advocates Renew Fight," *Roll Call* (January 4, 2013), http://atr.rollcall.com/disclose-advocates-renew-fight/. Accessed March 4, 2013.

121. Ibid.

122. Ibid.

123. Ibid.

124. John F. Mahon, "Corporate Political Strategy," *Business in the Contemporary World* (Autumn 1989), 50–62.

125. Amy J. Hillman and Michael A. Hitt, "Corporate Political Strategy Formulation: A Model of Approach, Participation, and Strategy Decisions," *Academy of Management Review* (Vol. 24, No. 4, 1999), 825–842.

126. Ibid.

127. Murray L. Weidenbaum, "Public Policy: No Longer a Spectator Sport for Business," *Journal of Business Strategy* (Vol. 1, No. 1, 1980), 46.

128. Sean Lux, T. Russell Crook, and Terry Leap. "Corporate Political Activity: The Good, the Bad, and the Ugly," *Business Horizons*, May 2012, 307–312; Frank R. Baumgartner and Beth L. Leech, *Basic Interests: The Importance of Interest Groups in Politics and Political Science* (Chicago: University of Chicago Press, 1995), cited in Jeffrey E. Cohen and John A. Hamman, "Interest Group PAC Contributions and the 1992 Regulation of Cable Television," *The Social Science Journal* (2003), 357–369.

129. Sean Lux, T. Russell Crook and David J. Woehr, "Mixing Business with Politics: A Meta-Analysis of the Antecedents and Outcomes of Corporate Political Activity," *Journal of* Management (Vol. 37, No. 1, 2011), 223–236.

130. Daniel Fisher and William P. Barrett, "All Follow the Money," *Forbes* (April 16, 2007), 48; Michael J. Cooper, Huseyin Gulen, and Alexei V. Ovtchinnikov, "Corporate Political Contributions and Stock Returns" (January 23, 2007). Available at SSRN: http://ssrn.com/abstract=940790. Accessed July 8, 2010.

131. Ibid.

132. Cohen and Hamman, 357–369.

133. De Figueiredo, John M., and Brian S. Silverman. "Academic Earmarks and the Returns to Lobbying." *Journal of Law & Economics* 49.2 (2006): 597–625.

134. Ibid.

135. Michael Hadani and Douglas A. Schuler. "In search of El Dorado: The elusive financial returns on corporate political investments." *Strategic Management Journal* 34, no. 2 (February 2013), 165–181.

136. Ibid.

137. Douglas A. Schuler, Kathleen Rehbein, and Roxy D. Cramer, "Pursuing Strategic Advantage through Political Means: A Multivariate Approach," *Academy of Management Journal* (August 2002), 659–672.

138. Ibid.

13

Consumer Stakeholders: Information Issues and Responses

As businesses are striving to come out of the worldwide recession, they have all been fighting for the hearts and minds of consumers. In nearly all sectors, the pace of consumer spending has slackened over the past several years. Consumers have become more cautious and selective about their spending on the entire gamut of products and services. Even as the economy perks up, some observers say it may be years before consumers return to their pre-recession levels of spending. Other analysts are more optimistic. Some think the new consumer is "down" but "not out." By all measures, however, it is clear that businesses need to pay careful attention to customer stakeholders and especially their fair treatment.

How important are consumers as stakeholders? According to management expert Peter Drucker, there is only one valid definition of business purpose: *to create a customer*.[1] Retaining customers is essential, too. In his book, Frederick Reichheld showed that small increases in customer retention rates can lead to dramatic increases in profits.[2] Clearly, businesses must create and retain customers if they are to succeed in today's competitive marketplace. Therefore, it is not surprising that **customer relationship management (CRM)** has become an important mantra of marketing.[3] Customer relationship management is "the ability of an organization to effectively identify, acquire, foster, and retain loyal profitable customers."[4]

With CRM guiding businesses in their customer relations, one would expect consumers to be pleased, or at least satisfied, with the way they have been treated. Unfortunately, that hasn't been the case. The consumer is still "often ignored"[5] and, in practice, CRM has been said to be "an awful lot of bland talk and not a lot of action."[6] Many believe that, in practice, the customer care revolution has largely been a failure.[7] Most statistics seem to indicate that although product and service quality has improved somewhat, the treatment of customers has been weak.

Getting a fix on whether customers are satisfied or not is no small task. As an important book has told us, "satisfied customers tell three friends, but angry customers tell 3,000."[8] A major reason consumers are not satisfied today is because they are exhausted by all the choices they face and the decisions they must make in their roles as consumers. Whether the consumer is attempting to buy a new pair of jeans or a cup of coffee, the choices are dizzying. With regards to financial affairs, there is too much fine print to read, much less understand. In short, as companies have sought to satisfy customers, they have frustrated them with too much complexity in the products or services offered or the information related to the decision and after-purchase experience. Exhausted customers are seldom satisfied customers.

As the economy is striving to emerge from a serious recession, many companies have begun what has been called "the great trust offensive." This amounts to an effort to rebuild customer confidence in their brands. Companies as diverse as Ford, American Express, and McDonald's have been revamping their marketing policies to win back the most valuable of corporate assets—their customers. This is because customer trust in business collapsed during the recession, after three years of steady growth, according to a major survey of informed citizens.[9] Companies have now realized that it is critical that consumers start spending again in order for the economy to bounce back.

Because we are all consumers, the business-and-consumer stakeholder issue is at the forefront of discussions about business, its relationships with, and its responsibility to the society in which it functions. Products and services are the most visible manifestations of business in society. For this reason, the whole issue deserves careful examination. We devote two chapters to it. In this chapter, we focus on the consumer movement and product information issues—most notably, advertising. In Chapter 14, we consider product and service issues, especially product safety and liability, and business's response to its consumer stakeholders.

The Consumer Movement

The basic expectations of the modern consumer movement were found in the "**consumer's Magna Carta**," or the four basic consumer rights spelled out by President John F. Kennedy in his "Special Message on Protecting the Consumer Interest."[10] Those rights included the right *to safety*, the right *to be informed*, the right *to choose*, and the right *to be heard*.

The **right to safety** concerns many products (insecticides, foods, drugs, automobiles, appliances) that are dangerous. The **right to be informed** refers to the consumer's right to know about a product, its use, and the cautions to be exercised while using it. This right includes the whole array of marketing: advertising, warranties, labeling, and packaging. The **right to choose**, although not of great concern today, refers to the assurance that competition is working effectively and that choices are available. The fourth, the **right to be heard**, was proposed because of many consumers' belief that they could not effectively communicate to business their desires and, especially, their grievances.[11]

Although these four basic rights do not encompass all the responsibilities that business owes to shopper stakeholders, they do capture the fundamentals of business's social responsibilities to consumers. In addition, consumers today want "fair value" for money spent, a product that will meet "reasonable" expectations, a product (or service) with full disclosure of its specifications, a product (or service) that has been truthfully advertised, and a product that is safe and has been subjected to appropriate product safety testing. Consumers also expect that if a product is too dangerous it will be removed from the market, or some other appropriate action will be taken.

For decades, there have been outcries that business has failed in these responsibilities to consumers, often leaving them neglected or mistreated.[12] The roots of consumer activism date back to 1906, when Upton Sinclair published *The Jungle*, his famous exposé of unsanitary conditions in the meatpacking industry.[13] The contemporary wave of consumer activism, however, started to build in the late 1950s, took shape in the 1960s, matured in the 1970s, and continues into the present day in a variety of forms.[14] Today it is called consumerism, consumer activism, or the consumer movement.

The following definition of **consumerism** captures the essential nature of the consumer movement:

Consumerism is a social movement seeking to augment the rights and powers of buyers in relation to sellers.[15]

Although the modern consumer movement is often said to have begun with the publication of Ralph Nader's criticism of General Motors in his book *Unsafe at Any Speed*,[16] the impetus for the movement was actually a complex combination of circumstances. The conditions necessary for bringing about a social movement of any kind were present for the birth of consumerism. These conditions are "structural conduciveness, structural strains, growth of a generalized belief, precipitating factors, mobilization for action, and social control."[17] Additionally, the factors of affluence, education, and awareness mentioned in Chapter 1 also have been at work.

Ralph Nader's Consumerism

Ralph Nader's contribution to the birth, growth, and nurturance of the consumer movement cannot be overstated. Nader arrived on the scene 50 years ago, and he is still the acknowledged father of the consumer movement. The impact of *Unsafe at Any Speed* was momentous. Nader's book not only gave rise to auto safety regulations and devices (safety belts, padded dashboards, stronger door latches, head restraints, air bags, etc.) but it also created a new era—that of the consumer. Nader was thrust into national prominence.

Nader's aforementioned book criticized the auto industry, generally, and General Motors, specifically. Nader objected to the safety of the GM Corvair, in particular. GM could not figure out what motivated Nader, so in 1966 the company hired detectives to trail and discredit him. GM denied having used women as "sex lures" as part of its investigation. However, the company did apologize to Nader at a congressional hearing and paid him $480,000 for invasion of his privacy.

Nader put his money to work and built an enormous and far-reaching consumer protection empire. His legions of zealous activists became known as "Nader's Raiders." Nader popularized public interest law and his activism generated significant growth in the enrollment of law schools. Nader and the consumer movement were the impetus for consumer legislation being passed in the 1970s.

The 1980s, however, did not turn out to be a positive decade for consumers. In the late 1980s, though, Nader began what *BusinessWeek* dubbed his "second coming." Nader successfully campaigned to roll back car insurance rates in California and to squelch a congressional pay raise. These victories vaulted him to a prominence he had not enjoyed in years.[18] In 2000, Nader ran as the Green Party candidate for U.S. president with a campaign that focused on establishing a viable third party, attacking corporate wealth, and protecting the environment. He was unsuccessful in his goal of receiving 5 percent of the total popular vote, which would have made the Green Party eligible to receive federal matching funds in the 2004 presidential election. In the process, however, he raised the ire of Democrats, labor leaders, feminists, and environmentalists who characterized him as a "spoiler" who tipped the election to George W. Bush.[19] When he announced a second run for the presidency in February 2004, the Green Party disavowed him, and a poll found that two-thirds of Americans did not want him to run again.[20]

Ralph Nader continues to be a controversial figure and a strong activist for the consumer voice. His articles appear regularly on Common Dreams, www.commondreams.org, a non-profit newscenter. Nader has been the source of considerable progress for consumers. Consumer complaints did not disappear with the advent of Ralph Nader's activism; instead, they intensified. One of Nader's greatest contributions is that he made consumer complaints respectable.

Consumerism in the 21st Century

Many groups make up the loose confederation known as the consumer movement. The power held by consumers is not the result of organized group lobbying—instead, their efforts today are at the grassroots level. Grassroots activism of consumers has never been stronger. In England, a relatively small group of disgruntled consumers brought the country to a halt by protesting the price of gas. They set up blockades that emptied roads, closed schools, and caused panic buying in supermarkets. The Internet and social media have made it easier for consumer groups to respond to issues more quickly and more forcefully. These tools make it possible to not only inform consumers of concerns that have arisen but also to rally the troops to take action. This is of special concern for global companies with far-flung interests. According to Cordelia Brabbs of *Marketing*, "Global companies find themselves under the watchful eye of their customers. If they fail to behave impeccably at all times, they risk finding their misdemeanors broadcast on a high-speed information network."[21]

Figure 13-1 presents information about some of the leading consumer organizations today.

FIGURE 13-1 **Consumer Organizations Today**

Consumer Organization	Information About Organization
Consumer Voice: An Online Magazine for Consumer Awareness http://www.consumer-voice.org/Index.aspx	Consumer Voice raises awareness in consumers not only about malpractice perpetuated in the marketplace but also about his/her rights. Consumer Voice aims to be the most powerful tool in the hands of the consumer to help fight for value for their money.
Consumerist http://consumerist.com/	Since its founding in 1936, Consumer Reports has fought for a fair, just, and safe marketplace for all consumers and to empower consumers to protect themselves.
Consumer Federation of America http://www.consumerfed.org/	The Consumer Federation of America (CFA) is an association of non-profit consumer organizations that was established in 1968 to advance the consumer interest through research, advocacy, and education.
Consumer Reports http://www.consumerreports.org/cro/index.htm	Consumer Reports is an expert, independent, nonprofit organization whose mission is to work for a fair, just, and safe marketplace for all consumers and to empower consumers to protect themselves.
Consumer Action http://www.consumer-action.org/	Through multilingual financial education materials, community outreach, and issue-focused advocacy, Consumer Action empowers underrepresented consumers nationwide to assert their rights in the marketplace and financially prosper.
Public Citizen http://www.citizen.org/Page.aspx?pid=2306	Public Citizen claims to represent the people's voice in Washington. Since its founding in 1971, PC has delved into many different areas, but its work on each issue shares a major, common goal which is to ensure that all citizens are represented on issues that may affect them.
Center for Science in the Public Interest http://www.cspinet.org/about/mission.html	CSPI is a consumer advocacy organization whose twin missions are to conduct innovative research and advocacy programs in health and nutrition and to provide consumers with current and useful information about their health and well being.

FIGURE 13-2

Examples of
Consumer
Problems with
Business

- The high prices of many products
- The poor quality of many products
- Misleading and deceptive advertising
- Hidden fees
- Poor quality of after-sales service
- Too many products breaking or malfunctioning after purchase
- Misleading packaging or labeling
- The feeling that it is a waste of time to complain about consumer problems

- because nothing substantial will be achieved
- Inadequate guarantees and warranties
- Failure of companies to handle complaints properly
- Too many products that are dangerous
- The absence of reliable information about various products and services
- Not knowing what to do if something is wrong with a purchased product

© Cengage Learning 2015

Figure 13-2 lists some of the most frequently cited examples of consumer's problems with business.

Before we consider more closely the corporate response to the consumer movement and the consumer stakeholder, it is fruitful to analyze some of the issues that have become prominent in the business–consumer relationship and the role that the major federal regulatory bodies have assumed in addressing these issues. We may broadly classify the major kinds of issues into two groups: *product/service information* and the *product/service itself*. As stated earlier, this chapter will focus on product/service information issues such as advertising, warranties, packaging, and labeling. The next chapter focuses on the product or service itself. Throughout our discussion of products, the reader should keep in mind that we are referring to services also.

Product Information Issues

Why have questions been raised about business's social and ethical responsibilities in the area of product information? Most consumers know the answer. Companies understandably want to portray their products in the most flattering light. However, efforts to paint a positive portrait of a product can easily cross the line into misinformation or deception regarding the product's attributes. Consumers Union (CU), an independent, nonprofit testing and information organization, exists to protect consumers' interests. They conduct independent tests of products and report their findings in their print and online editions of *Consumer Reports (CR)*.[22] "Selling It" is a segment in the print edition of *Consumer Reports*; it is designed to "memorialize the excesses in the world of marketing." Quite often the ads are contradictory. The following items are examples of the often humorous absurdities chronicled:

- A headline reads "Eden PURE ranked #1." But it's not by *Consumer Reports*. CR did give the room heater a "good" rating overall. When you read the ad's fine print you find that the Eden PURE's *own* pitchman ranked it #1. His qualifications? He's an actor from the 1990s sitcom "*Home Improvement.*"[23]
- A banner hangs outside a Dunkin' Donuts restaurant, reading "CLOSED to better serve you." How so, by causing you to go to Starbuck's?[24]
- An ad implores the reader to "switch to Verizon high-speed Internet at a super-low price that'll never go up." The ad repeats again, "Guaranteed to Never Go Up." Then, the fine print on the same page reveals: "Rates increase after two years."[25] What part of "never go up" do they fail to understand?
- A box of pudding and pie filling boldly claims to be pistachio flavor and the photo of it is green. When you read the ingredients list, however, it says the nuts are diced *almonds*, the flavor is artificial, and the green color is yellow and blue dyes![26]

- The Zazzle Web site advertises a tee shirt which reads "Grandma to Be." The model wearing the shirt, however, is a male! And, isn't 25 years old too young to be a grandmother?[27]

These cases are actual examples of the questionable and careless use of product information. It is not clear whether the firms that created these communications were intending to deceive, but the information they provided did not match the reality of the product. Business has a legal and an ethical responsibility to provide fair and accurate information about its products or services.

The primary issue with product or service information falls in the realm of advertising. Other information-related areas include warranties or guarantees, packaging, labeling, instructions for use, and the sales techniques used by direct sellers. Information about after-sale service is also a critical issue.

Advertising Issues

The debate over the role of advertising in society has persisted for decades. Most observers have concentrated on the economic function of advertising in our market system, but opinions vary as to whether advertising is beneficial or detrimental as a business function. Critics charge that it is a wasteful and inefficient tool of business, and that our current standard of living would be higher if we could be freed from the negative influences of advertising. These critics argue that advertising raises the prices of products and services because it is an unnecessary business cost, effectively circulating superfluous information that could more readily and cheaply be provided on product information labels or by salespeople in stores. The result is that significant amounts of money are spent with no net consumer benefit.[28]

In response, others have claimed that advertising is a beneficial component of the market system and that increases in the standard of living and consumer satisfaction may be attributed to ads. This camp argues that, in general, advertising is an efficient means of distributing information because consumers need to know about the enormous and ever-changing array of products. From this perspective, advertising is an effective and relatively inexpensive way of informing consumers of new and improved products.[29]

The debate over whether advertising is a productive or wasteful business practice will undoubtedly rage on. As a practical matter, however, advertising has become the lifeblood of the free enterprise system. It stimulates competition and disseminates information that consumers can use in comparison shopping. Additionally, advertising provides competitors with information with which to respond in a competitive manner, and contains a mechanism for immediate feedback in the form of sales response. So, despite its criticisms, advertising does provide social and economic benefits to consumers.

With the availability of thousands of products and their increasing complexity, the consumer today has a real need for information that is clear, accurate, and adequate. **Clear information** is that which is direct and straightforward and on which neither deception nor manipulation relies. **Accurate information** communicates truths, not half-truths. It avoids gross exaggeration and innuendo. **Adequate information** provides potential purchasers with enough information to make the best choice among the options available.[30]

Whereas *providing information* is one legitimate purpose of advertising in our society, another legitimate purpose is *persuasion*. Most consumers today expect that business advertises for the purpose of persuading them to buy their products or services, and they accept this as a part of the commercial system. Indeed, many people enjoy companies' attempts to come up with interesting ways to sell their products. It is commonplace for people to talk with one another about the latest appealing or entertaining advertisement they have seen. Awards are given for outstanding advertisements, as well as for those

ETHICS IN PRACTICE CASE
What Do We Tell the Customer?

While working as a customer service representative at a bank, a huge part of our job is to sell financial products to customers. We have to meet our goal every quarter by opening as many accounts as we can and to sell the bank's products. The branch manager is very tough and we can be written up if we don't reach our goal. Eventually, write-ups can lead to termination. As part of our jobs, we are supposed to make sure the customer is aware of the banking products they are getting or the accounts they are opening. Also, the customer service representative needs to explain the product fully to the customer and leave it up to them to decide if they want to open the account or not.

Some of my coworkers don't explain everything in detail to the customer unless the customer asks. However, I have overheard the whole conversation of one of my coworkers telling a customer to open a lot of accounts combined together because they come as a package. This means the customer will have to open Checking, Savings, Debit Card, Apply for Overdraft Protection, and Credit Card. My coworker didn't give the customer an option to choose from, but rather told her she had to open everything because it's a package—which is not true. The customer had no option; she trusted the employee because he knows better than her. The employee is the one that has more knowledge of what he/she is doing. The customer ended up opening all the accounts.

I was really in shock because I knew what was going on and what I have heard is totally wrong. I also knew that we are supposed to explain the products to the customer and leave the decision up to them as to what accounts they would like to open. I felt so bad that the customer just went by what the employee had said and opened everything, even though she didn't want it, but she believed she had to. In addition, the same coworker always got recognized for selling a lot of products and always reaching his goal. I was in shock and I didn't know how to react.

1. Is it fair to miscommunicate to the customer in this way? Are we being accurate, unambiguous, and clear? What's the harm if the customer opens all the accounts?
2. Should I have gone over to my coworker's desk while he was with the customer and made sure she got the right information? Or, should I have waited until the customer left and then gone to my coworker and told him that what he had done is wrong and unethical?
3. Is this misinformation given to the customer important enough for me to approach my manager and tell her everything I heard, even though the manager pushes us to sell accounts and do whatever it takes?

Contributed by Haidy Elfarra

that are particularly bad. Nevertheless, there is some evidence that the public may be losing its patience with advertising.[31]

Ethical issues in advertising arise as companies step over the line in their attempts to inform and persuade consumer stakeholders. The frequently heard phrase "the seamy side of advertising" alludes to the economic and social costs that derive from advertising abuses, such as those mentioned earlier in the chapter, and of which the reader is probably able to supply ample personal examples.

Advertising Abuses. There are four major types of advertising abuses in which ethical issues surface. These include situations in which advertisers are ambiguous, conceal facts, exaggerate, or employ psychological appeals.[32] These four types cover most of the general criticisms leveled at advertising.

Ambiguous Advertising   One of the simplest ways that companies deceive is through **ambiguous advertising**, in which something about the product or service is not made clear because it is stated in a way that may mean several different things.

An ad can be ambiguous in several ways. One way is to make a statement using **weasel words**, which leaves it to the viewer to infer the message. Weasel words are inherently vague and the company could always claim it was not misleading the consumer. An example of a weasel word is "help." Once an advertiser uses the qualifier "help," almost anything could follow, and the company could claim that it was not intending to deceive. We see ads that claim to "help us keep young," "help prevent cavities," or "help keep our houses germ free." Think how many times you have seen expressions in advertising such as "helps stop," "helps prevent," "helps fight," "helps you feel," "helps you look," or "helps you become."[33] Other weasel words include "like," "virtually," and "up to" (e.g., stops pain "up to" eight hours— which simply means it won't stop pain for more than eight hours). The use of such words makes ads ambiguous. Another way to create an ambiguous ad is through use of legalese, or other excessively complex and vague terminology. To make matters worse, the legalese and complex language is often found in the fine print, which consumers are not inclined to read anyway.

Concealed Facts   A type of advertising abuse called **concealed facts** refers to the practice of not telling the whole truth, or deliberately not communicating information the consumer ought to have access to in order to make an informed choice. Another way of stating this is to say "a fact is concealed when its availability would probably make the desire, purchase, or use of the product less likely than its absence."[34] This is a difficult area because few would argue that an advertiser is obligated to tell "everything," even if that were humanly possible. For example, a pain reliever company might claim the effectiveness of its product in superlative terms without stating that there are dozens of other products on the market that are just as effective. Or an insurance company might promote all the forms of protection that a given policy would provide without enumerating all the situations for which the policy does not provide coverage.

Ethical issues arise when a firm, through its advertisements, presents facts in such a selective way that a false belief is created. As consumers, it is up to us to be informed about factors such as competitors' products, prices, and so on. Of course, judgment is required in determining which ads have and have not created false beliefs. This makes the entire realm of deceptive advertising a challenge. At times it can be considered harmless. For example, a burrito restaurant in a college town ran a humorous newspaper ad with "FREE BEER" in large block letters; underneath in small letters were the words "will not be served." No one accused this company of unlawful deception; however, not all instances of concealed facts are quite so benign. Other concealed facts often occur with respect to hidden fees or surcharges on services. Today, you have to be a sophisticated consumer willing to do timely detective work to root out the rules and policies governing fees companies charge.

An increasingly popular form of concealed advertising is **product placement**, the practice of embedding products in movies and TV shows. Critics call this "stealth advertising." Product placements are everywhere. A recent example finds James Bond sipping a Heineken beer in the movie *Skyfall*.[35] Critics call this "stealth advertising."[36] In another well-known example, the judges in *American Idol* drink from Coke cups, and the "green room" in which contestants wait is now the "Coke Red Room."[37] Ryan Seacrest tells viewers to text message their votes over AT&T Wireless and, in each episode, producers manage to find a new reason for the remaining contestants to sing and dance around a Ford vehicle.[38]

In a variation of product placement, termed **plot placement**, sponsors have paid to make their products integrated into the plotline of a TV show. Revlon played an important part in the plotline of ABC's *All My Children*; Avon was integrated into the plotline of NBC's *Passions*.[39] In one episode of *Biggest Loser*, the dieting contestants hiked from one Subway sandwich shop to another to get a meal as part of the contest rules. The recent product placement of the Apple iPad on *Modern Family* strains credulity.

The Dunphys went on a family mission to get Phil an iPad. At the end of the show, Phil was depicted as stroking his new iPad while uttering "I love you" to the gadget.[40]

These forms of advertising are a response to the "TiVo effect." The popularity of digital video recorders (DVRs) such as TiVo has lessened the time that consumers spend watching commercials. DVRs make it easy and convenient for TV watchers to zap through commercials, so advertisers are looking for new ways to make customers take notice.[41] Even advertising stalwarts like Coca-Cola—with its advertising budget of more than $300 million per year—are relying less on traditional ads, and more on product placement in DVDs and video games.[42]

Free Press is one of a coalition of 50 groups fighting product and plot placements. These groups have appealed to the Federal Communications Commission (FCC) to require networks to disclose such placements, but so far the FCC has passed very few regulations governing them. In their defense, the FCC says they face a delicate balancing act of protecting the public and not undermining the already wobbly economics of television.[43]

Exaggerated Claims   Companies can also mislead consumers by exaggerating the benefits of their products and services. **Exaggerated claims** are claims that simply cannot be substantiated by any kind of evidence. An example of this would be a claim that a pain reliever is "50 percent stronger than aspirin" or "superior to any other on the market." Recently, the Food and Drug Administration has taken several companies to task for exaggerated claims. The FDA rebuked L'Oréal's Lancôme subsidiary for claiming that its antiwrinkle products do more than it can document. Rather than just claiming its products reduce wrinkles, the company claimed that one product "boosts the activity of genes and stimulates the production of youth proteins." The FDA argued that this ad confuses a cosmetics product with a new drug which would require FDA approval. If the company does not comply and change its ads, the FDA may issue injunctions or seize the company's products.[44] In another case, Merck & Co. was ordered to stop using the term "waterproof" in its Coppertone advertising. The company also agreed to stop using the terms "sunblock" and "all day protection" in its advertising because these were considered to be exaggerations of the products' benefits. Merck will pay fines to settle the case.[45]

A general form of exaggeration is known as **puffery**, a euphemism for hyperbole or exaggeration that usually refers to the use of general superlatives. Is Budweiser really the "King of Beers"? Is Wheaties the "Breakfast of Champions"? Does "better ingredients" mean Papa John's has "Better Pizza"? Normally, a claim of general superiority is considered puffery and is allowable. However, companies walk a fine line when engaging in puffery. They need to be certain that no direct comparison is being made.

According to one attorney, "It is no longer enough to take comfort in making the same kinds of claims that have been made in an industry for some time. Those (marketers) making aggressive claims need to consider ways a reasonable consumer will interpret those claims, and marketers need to be able to prove every interpretation that is reasonable."[46]

Most people are not too put off by puffery, because the claims are so general and so frequent that any consumer would know that the firm is exaggerating and simply doing what many do by claiming their product is the best. It has been argued, however, that such exaggerated product claims (1) induce people to buy things that do them no good, (2) result in loss of advertising efficiency as companies are forced to match puffery with puffery, (3) drive out good advertising, and (4) generally result in consumers losing faith in the system because they get so used to companies making claims that exceed their products' capabilities.[47] Another study found that consumers actually have mixed reactions to puffery, and that they don't always react positively to it.[48]

Spotlight on Sustainability

Are Consumers Willing to Pay More for Sustainability?

Two companies recently joined together to publish a report on how consumers viewed the concept of sustainability. Consumers were asked about sustainability with respect to four product categories: purchased food and beverages, household cleaning products, personal care products, and over-the-counter medications. Consumers most often said that sustainability meant "the ability to last over time," and "the ability to support oneself." They linked the concept with "environmental concerns." The consumers also said that terms such as "eco-conscious" and "green" unduly limited the concept of sustainability because they do not account for the variety of economic, social, and environmental issues that real people believe are important in sustaining themselves, their communities, and society as a whole.

The consumers surveyed indicated that they would pay a 20 percent premium for sustainable products. In another study, 40 percent of consumers stated they would not purchase a product if the company did not communicate its sustainability results.

Sources: "Sustainability, Through Consumers' Eyes," http://www.highbeam.com/doc/1G1-214713138 .html. Accessed May 1, 2013; "Consumers Demand Sustainability Results, Survey Says," *Environmental Leader*, October 24, 2012; http://www.environmentalleader.com/2012/10/24/consumers-demand-sustainability-results-survey-says/. Accessed May 1, 2013; Cone Communications Green Gap Trend Tracker, http://www.conecomm.com/research-from-cone. Accessed May 1, 2013.

Psychological Appeals   In advertising, **psychological appeals** are those designed to persuade on the basis of human emotions and emotional needs rather than reason. There is perhaps as much reason to be concerned about ethics in this category as in any other category. One reason is that the products can seldom deliver what the ads promise (i.e., power, prestige, sex, masculinity, femininity, approval, acceptance, and other such psychological satisfactions).[49] Another reason is that psychological appeals can stir emotions in a way that is manipulative and appears designed to take advantage of the consumer's vulnerability. For example, many home security salespeople will watch the newspapers for reports of home break-ins and then call a homeowner with a sales pitch for a new home security system.

Though most advertising strives to appeal to our sight, an increasingly popular form of sensual advertising focuses on consumers' hearing. Neuromarketers have concluded, on the basis of research, that the most effective sounds in terms of their psychological appeals are babies giggling, cell phones vibrating, ATM machines dispensing cash, steaks sizzling on a grill, and a soda being popped and poured.[50] Whether such ploys represent unethical uses of psychological persuasion is debatable.

Specific Controversial Advertising Issues

We have considered four major kinds of deceptive advertising—ambiguous advertising, concealed facts, exaggerated claims, and psychological appeals. There are many other variations on these themes, but these are sufficient to make our point. Later in this chapter, we will discuss the FTC's attempts to keep advertising honest. But even there we will see that the whole issue of what constitutes deceptive advertising is an evolving and amorphous concept, particularly when it comes to the task of proving deception and recommending appropriate remedial action. This is why the role of business responsibility is so crucial if business honestly desires to deal with its consumer stakeholders in a fair and truthful manner.

There are seven specific advertising issues that have become particularly controversial in recent years because of borderline and questionable ethics: comparative advertising, use of sex in advertising, advertising to children, marketing to the poor, advertising of alcoholic beverages, cigarette advertising, health and environmental claims, and ad creep.

Comparative Advertising. One controversial advertising technique that always threatens to affect advertising adversely is **comparative advertising**. This refers to the practice of directly comparing a firm's product with the product of a competitor. Some classic examples of past high-profile comparative campaigns are Coke versus Pepsi, Whopper vs. Big Mac, Subway vs. Quiznos, Avis vs. Hertz, and Papa John's vs. Pizza Hut. A memorable and successful example was the "Get a Mac" campaign. The ads feature two men, Mac and PC, standing in front of a white background. PC is in an ill-fitting jacket and tie, while Mac is in comfortable jeans. The banter between the two characters is a running comparison of the two machines. The cultural icon campaign seems to have struck a nerve with the public: in 2009, *U.S. News & World Report* named the "Get a Mac" campaign one of the best marketing schemes in recent times.[51] It was also named Ad of the Decade by *Adweek*.[52]

Comparative advertising sometimes generates unexpected and undesirable conflicts among companies. Whether out of pride or general business interest, more and more companies are fighting back when they think the competition has overstepped its bounds. Companies may take their adversaries to court, before the FTC, or before voluntary associations, such as the National Advertising Division of the Council of Better Business Bureaus, in attempts to resolve these disputes. Though there can be good reasons to launch comparative ads, they sometimes come at a cost.

Use of Sex Appeal in Advertising. The use of sex appeal in U.S. advertising has been an ongoing ethical issue for decades. It took center stage 40 years ago when several women's groups were offended by a series of television commercials sponsored by a major airline. The controversial use of sex appeal in advertising, however, dates back to at least 1911, when, in a landmark case, Woodbury's used sex to sell soap—and that ad was created by a woman.[53] Today, sexual references and innuendos in advertising have become commonplace, so the issue sparks less controversy. Consumer behavior professor Bruce Stern has observed: "We're moving into an arena that we are becoming numb to things that would have offended us a few years ago."[54]

The most recent trend in sex-appeal advertising campaigns is to target younger and younger girls with the idea that they too can be sexy, and that this will help them be more popular and successful with boys. Victoria's Secret college brand, Pink, has become appealing to high school girls. Other ads are targeting girls as young as 11 and 12 to diet, get hair extensions, eye-lash extensions, and push-up bras. Critics say this is subtly training girls to focus on their external appearance at the expense of developing a fuller identity. It is argued that girls are being overly sexualized in our culture long before they are cognitively and emotionally prepared.[55]

Virtually all studies have shown that the use of sex in advertising works. One study that looked at the use of sex in magazine advertisements over a recent 30-year period revealed the practice was on the ascent, and concluded that it has been effective.[56] Studies seem to indicate that though many oppose the use of sex appeal in ads, their purchasing decisions reflect that sex appeal works.

Ads that portray young women as sex objects can have a serious impact on the physical and mental health of girls. A task force report from the American Psychological Association (APA) studied this issue and found that the media's sexualization of young women can lead to poor self-image as well as depression, eating disorders, and

ETHICS IN PRACTICE CASE

The Comparative Advertising Wars

Comparative advertising traditionally takes place between the features of two brands—Coke vs. Pepsi, McDonald's vs. Wendy's, Starbuck's vs. Dunkin' Donuts. But, now, Walmart has raised the stakes and the battle is between entire stores, not just brands.

Walmart has gotten aggressive with its new advertising campaign. Its new campaign asserts that Walmart has lower prices than specific, named competitors and this has troubled many of them. Several of the targeted retailers, including Toys "R" Us, Best Buy, and some regional supermarket chains, such as Publix, claim Walmart has been citing inaccurate prices and comparing different products such as laptops with different specifications.

Best Buy, the electronics retailer, fingered a Walmart ad for a Dell laptop as being deceptive. Walmart had claimed the laptop cost $251 more at Best Buy. The electronics retailer said that the two laptops in the comparison were different models and that the one it was advertising had a longer battery life. Toys "R" Us told Michigan officials that Walmart was citing inaccurate prices for some of its products. Walmart's rivals also say that Walmart does not carry adequate stock for some of its advertised products and that to compete they have to match prices for products that are in short supply or unavailable at Walmart.

Walmart claims its ads are accurate. One company spokesman was quoted as saying: "We know competitors don't like it when we tell customers to compare prices and see for themselves." He continued: "We are confident on the legal, ethical and methodological standards associated with our price comparison ads."

The FTC has said the following about comparative advertising: "When truthful and non-deceptive [comparison advertising] is a source of important information to consumers and assists them in making rational purchase decisions."

1. When thousands of products and their prices are at stake, does it make sense that comparative advertising at the store level be permitted?
2. Based on what you have read and any further research you choose to do, has Walmart competed fairly with its comparative advertising campaign? Does the fact that so many retailers have complained about Walmart's advertising suggest that there are probably some problems with it?
3. A strong standard for advertising is that it be clear, accurate and adequate. Can comparative advertising as a practice meet these standards? Or, are there too many products with too many subtle variations to make the practice defensible?
4. Should the FTC reconsider its endorsement of comparative advertising? Should restrictions be placed on comparative advertising? If so, what would they be?

Sources: "Competitors Take Issue with Walmart Ads," The City Wire, January 4, 2013, http://www.thecitywire.com/node/25852# .UYpLnbWkobw. Accessed May 8, 2013; Tom Ryan, "Rivals: Walmart Plays Loose with the Truth," Retailwire, January 7, 2013, http://www.retailwire.com/discussion/16499/rivals-walmart-plays-loose-with-the-truth. Accessed May 8, 2013; Ann Zimmerman and Shelly Banjo, "Rivals Object to Wal-Mart Ads," *The Wall Street Journal*, January 4, 2013, B1; FTC, "Statement of Policy Regarding Comparative Advertising," August 13, 1979, http://www.ftc.gov/bcp/policystmt/ad-compare.htm. Accessed May 8, 2013.

low self-esteem.[57] In spite of the fact that sex in advertising is widespread today, the practice still carries serious ethical questions about its appropriateness, and responsible companies must be careful and sensitive to these concerns.

Advertising to Children. A hotly debated ethical issue over the past several decades is advertising to children, especially on television. This practice has sometimes been called "kid-vid" advertising. A typical weekday afternoon or Saturday morning in America finds millions of kids sprawled on the floor, glued to the TV, or staring at the computer. According to one study, the average child in the United States watches 25,000 to 40,000 commercials each year and advertisers spend $15 to $17 billion annually marketing products to children.[58] The statistics in other countries are staggering as well.

Children are the consumers of the future, and companies are eager to influence their spending habits. Merchandisers try to instill brand loyalty at a young age. A vivid example is Mattel's "Cool Shopping Barbie," who came complete with her own personal toy MasterCard, a cash register that had the MasterCard logo, and a terminal through which Barbie could swipe her card to make a purchase. By 2013, Mattel fed Barbie's consumption habits with "Barbie Shopping Games" including "Shopaholic Best Friends," "Barbie Christmas Shopping," and "School Shopping Day."[59] According to William F. Keenan of Creative Solutions, an advertising and marketing agency, "[If you] set the brand by age seven, they will favor the brand into adulthood. One of the smartest places to plant marketing seeds in the consumer consciousness is with kids."[60]

This is particularly troubling given an APA finding that children under the age of eight do not have the cognitive development to understand persuasive intent, making them easy targets.[61] Children have proved to be receptive targets as well. A phenomenon called **age compression**, or "kids getting older younger" (KGOY), has marketers targeting eight and nine year olds with products once meant for teenagers. With the overabundance of ads to which they are exposed, children are tiring of toys much earlier and looking for products that they see teenagers using.[62]

The Children's Advertising Review Unit (CARU) of the Council of Better Business Bureaus was established to respond to public concerns. CARU developed "Self-Regulatory Guidelines for Children's Advertising."[63] The function of the CARU guidelines is to delineate those areas that need particular attention to help avoid deceptive and/or misleading advertising messages to children. The basic activity of CARU is the review and evaluation of child-directed advertising in all media. When advertising to children is found to be misleading, inaccurate, or inconsistent with the guidelines, CARU seeks changes through the voluntary cooperation of advertisers. It does not always get cooperation and sometimes the advertiser appeals to the National Advertising Review Board (NARB).

Recently, the advertising to children of food products that contain sweets and unhealthy ingredients has become a burning issue. As the obesity epidemic among children has become widely known and debated, special interest groups have been criticizing companies for their marketing of these products to children. In addition, the Federal Trade Commission is now watching ads targeted at children more carefully.[64] Today, childhood favorites such as Lucky Charms, Corn Pops, Froot Loops, Cocoa Pebbles, and other cereals are being labeled a public health menace by the Rudd Center for Food Policy and Obesity at Yale University. The center is trying to expose the marketing tactics companies use that make kids clamor for a sugary, calorie-laden start to each day. Obesity researchers now say they have data proving that the least healthy cereals are the ones that are marketed most aggressively to children. The obesity crisis among children in the United States is now established, and researchers believe that TV advertising is a significant contributing factor.[65]

To their credit, some leading cereal makers have responded by reducing calories, fat, and sugar and increasing fiber and vitamins. Kellogg, General Mills, and Quaker's parent company, PepsiCo, are among about 12 of the largest food companies that have promised to market only "better for you" foods to kids under age 12. Skeptics are concerned because the companies themselves are deciding what constitutes "better for you" standards.[66] In addition, a federal working group proposed that food advertising aimed at children be limited to foods that are healthful.[67]

Efforts to curb child-targeted advertising span the globe. The European Union's directive on television regulation bans "programs that might seriously impair the development of minors" but allows unencrypted programming "that might be harmful to minors providing they are preceded by an acoustic warning or made clearly identifiable throughout their duration by means of a visual symbol."[68] The EU prohibits product placement in programming aimed at children and also does not allow words like "only" to be used to describe prices. Additionally, they forbid advertisers from persuading children to ask their parents to buy the product for them.[69] In Australia, children's advertising is forbidden to imply that the people who buy an advertised product are more generous than people who do not buy it. Mexico does not restrict the amount of children's advertising, but tobacco and alcohol advertising are prohibited. In contrast, Denmark permits the advertising of alcoholic beverages to children as long as the beverage's strength is no greater than 2.8 percent, it is not placed in a program directly aimed at children, and no children are shown drinking it.[70]

Regulatory bodies have been trying for decades to get greater supervisory authority with respect to children's advertising. Finally, in 1990, the **Children's Television Act (CTA)** was passed. A grassroots activist group known as Action for Children's Television claimed credit for getting this legislation passed. This act prohibited the airing of commercials about products or characters during a show about those products or characters and limited the number of commercial minutes in children's shows. Critics say the Federal Communications Commission (FCC) created weak rules to enforce the act, thereby sending the message that it was not taking the legislation seriously. Part of the Act required stations and networks to schedule educational programs for children.[71] Much has changed since that act was passed. With the rise of the Internet, social media and smart toys, companies have found new ways to advertise to children. More than two-thirds of all child and teen Internet sites rely on advertising for their revenue. Banner ads were not successful in reaching children, so these Internet sites have employed games, e-mail, and wireless technology in creative ways. The FCC has added new regulations over the last decade that address cable and Internet Web pages.[72]

The issue of obesity and advertising to children seems to be picking up steam. In 2012, New York Mayor Michael Bloomberg's anti-obesity campaign sought to ban large-serving sugary drinks, especially sodas, but this law was struck down in the courts.[73] Both Coca-Cola and Disney have embarked on strategies to reduce calories in products they sell.[74] Time will tell whether these programs will work and be copied by others. And, First Lady Michelle Obama continues to argue the "business case" for healthier food options.[75]

Marketing to the Poor. A variety of businesses have found that significant profits can be obtained from advertising and marketing to poor people. In the subprime credit industry, businesses provide financing to high-risk borrowers at high interest rates. While this gives poorer people greater access to cars, credit cards, computers, and homes, it often ends with the borrower buried under a mountain of debt. The Federal Reserve reported that households earning $30,000 or less paid auto loan interest rates that were 16.8 percent higher than the rates paid by households earning more than $90,000. The past several years have been the worst ever in home mortgage foreclosures and loan defaults. Many of these have come from the subprime mortgage market, where relatively poor people were lured into loans they had little chance of repaying. Several of the deceptive marketing practices mentioned earlier have been involved in these loans: concealed facts, ambiguous advertising, and psychological appeals.

Another technique by which business profits from the poor is in the form of *payday loans*, loans that provide the borrower with an advance on his or her paycheck. As the FTC warns, these loans equal costly cash; for example, a borrower might write a personal check for $115 to borrow $100 for up to two weeks. The payday lender agrees to hold the check until the person's next payday. Then, depending on the plan, the lender deposits the check, which the borrower can redeem by paying the $115 in cash. Alternatively,

ETHICS IN PRACTICE CASE
Should Food Advertising to Children Be Banned?

There is now an ongoing battle between those who think marketing food and beverages to children should be halted and those who believe it's up to parents to make these decisions, not Big Government. Some companies have been attempting to come up with their own standards to decrease unhealthy ingredients and make kids' foods more nutritious.

It is now estimated that one-third of children in the United States are overweight or obese. A number of experts have argued that sugar in soft drinks and fast foods are the major culprits.

We live in a country where cartoon characters tempt kids to eat the wrong foods, where children don't get enough exercise, where parents don't say "no" often enough, and where childhood diabetes is escalating. Commercial advertising assaults children with TV commercials, ads in schools, product placements, and digital marketing. Research shows that this advertising works.

Founded in the year 2000, a nonprofit organization called Campaign for a Commercial Free Childhood (CCFC) is seeking to address the rapidly escalating problem of commercialism encroaching on the lives of children. Starting out as a small group of concerned parents, health professionals, and educators, CCFC has grown into a powerful force seeking to end what it calls the exploitative practice of child-targeted advertising. CCFC has taken on the following issues: marketing to children, advertising in schools, commercializing toys and play, food marketing and childhood obesity, marketing to babies and toddlers, sexualizing childhood, and media violence.

1. Should food and beverage advertising to children be banned? What about for other types of products as well?
2. Is it unethical for food companies to target their ads towards children? In a period when most parents are working, how are children to be protected?
3. Should the federal or state government begin restricting food ads targeted at children? What about for other products?
4. Can companies do enough on their own to adequately address these problems?
5. Of the list of issues CCFC has taken on (listed above), which do you see as the most serious and why?

Sources: Campaign for a Commercial Free Childhood, http://www.commercialfreechildhood.org/. Accessed May 7, 2013; "Food Fight Over Marketing to Kids Misses Key Ingredient," *USA Today*, October 17, 2011, 10A; Josh Golin, "Ban Food Marketing to Kids," *USA Today*, October 17, 2013, 10A; Diane Levin and Christina Asquith, "As Marketing to Children Intensifies, What Can Society Do?" Solutions Magazine, April 12, 2013, http://thesolutionsjournal.anu.edu.au/node/6641. Accessed May 7, 2013.

---

the borrower can roll over the check by paying a fee to extend the loan for another two weeks. In this example, the cost of the initial loan is a $15 finance charge and 391 percent annual percentage rate (APR). If they roll over the loan three times, the finance charge would climb to $60 to borrow $100.[76] Similar tactics are used by many credit card companies, rent-to-own outfits, and used car dealers.

Tax preparation services provide another way of making money from the poor. Many firms provide quick tax refund services for a fee. Advertising "Money Now," they will prepare your tax return and provide you with an advance on your refund. Low-income tax payers have access to a variety of free tax preparation services but many still use this expensive service because they do not understand the price they will pay for receiving an early refund.

BusinessWeek tells the story of a single mother with five children who was making ends meet on $8,500 a year until she was laid off. She borrowed $400 for rent and food from Advance America, a payday loan service; then she renewed the loan every two weeks, eventually paying more than $2,500 in fees before she paid it off. Two months after paying it off, she was anxious for her $4,500 tax refund and so she took out a refund-anticipation loan from Jackson Hewitt. It cost her $453 (10.4 percent) to get that short-term loan.[77] When asked about the price she paid for these loans, the young mother sounded confused, replying, "What do you call it—interest?"[78]

The ethical issue with marketing and advertising to the poor is the vulnerability of this consumer segment. All consumers are vulnerable to a certain extent, because business has more information about its product or service than does the consumer. However, poor people are especially vulnerable because they are likely to be less educated and thus less aware of the true price of the products or services being advertised to them. Nevertheless, businesses continue to push these products. Another vulnerable group of consumers is the elderly, and some of the same tactics are used on them that are used on the poor.

Advertising Alcoholic Beverages. Special issues about advertising to adults also exist. One that has been quite controversial for years is advertising of alcoholic beverages on television. In 1996, Seagram & Sons broke a 48-year voluntary ban on advertising hard liquor on television. The company argued that a standard serving of hard liquor contained the same amount of alcohol as beer or wine, and advertising is allowed for those products.[79] DISCUS (the Distilled Spirits Council of the United States) then rewrote its "Code of Good Practice" to allow member distillers to advertise on radio and television. The Seagram decision created a groundswell for change in all possible directions.

Around 2011, the broadcasters started easing their decades-old voluntary bans that limited their national alcohol advertising to beer and wine on network TV. This reflected more consumer acceptance—or at least less consumer resistance to the ads. Today, many liquor companies are starting to increase their TV marketing budgets by double-digit percentages. The broadcasters have not opened their doors completely; liquor ads mostly run after 11 P.M. But, because they have been running on cable TV for years, critics say that youth exposure to liquor ads on TV already has increased 30-fold between 2001 and 2009. The liquor companies continue to argue that there ought to be a level playing field in their competition with beer and wine. The Federal Trade Commission has said that there is no basis for treating liquor ads differently from ads for beer and wine.[80]

Of course, hard liquor is not the only concern. Ralph Nader's *Public Citizen's Commercial Alert* organization targeted Anheuser-Busch for its use of a variety of cartoon characters in its campaigns. They cited a KidCom market study that showed that the Budweiser frogs were American children's "favorite ads," just as the tobacco-smoking "Joe Camel™" had been their favorite ad some years ago.[81] In 2007, Anheuser-Busch faced criticism over their product, Spykes™. The bright-colored, fruit-flavored malt beverage was sold in attractive two-ounce bottles that resembled beauty products. Critics charged that the beverage was designed to appeal to kids. Amidst criticism, the company decided to withdraw the product from the market.[82]

Although efforts to curb the abuses of alcohol advertising continue, consumer advocates may find they face an uphill battle. There seems to be less public opposition today to alcohol advertising; but the industry will need to remain vigilant, because any attempts at exploitation of youth, for example, are likely to meet considerable criticism and resistance.

Cigarette Advertising. No industry has been under greater attack than the cigarette industry for its products and its marketing and advertising practices. Cigarette makers have been under fire from all sides for decades. Two particularly important issues dominate the debate about cigarette advertising. First, there is the general opposition to promotion of a dangerous product. As the World Health Organization (WHO) puts it, "Cigarettes remain the only legal product that kills half of its regular users when consumed as intended by the manufacturer."[83] The second issue concerns the ethics of the tobacco industry's longstanding advertising to young people and to less-educated consumer markets.

The classic example of the latter concern was when R.J. Reynolds (RJR) was publicly taken to task by several consumer groups for its Joe Camel campaign. One frequently cited study appeared in the *Journal of the American Medical Association*. In this study, it was found that more than half the children age three to six were able to match the Joe Camel logo with a photograph of a cigarette. Six-year-olds were almost as familiar with Joe Camel as they were with a Mickey Mouse logo.[84] In 1997, the FTC ruled three to two that the Joe Camel ads violated the law by targeting children under 18, and asked RJR to remove the cartoon from any venue where a child might see it. RJR canceled the ad campaign.[85] Shortly after that, the government asked Philip Morris to retire the Marlboro Man.[86] Although Joe Camel and the Marlboro Man are gone, the issue of advertising to young people remains.

In 2009, Congress gave the Food & Drug Administration (FDA) oversight of the tobacco industry. The FDA has continued updating its "smoking kills" theme by requiring the tobacco industry to create better warning labels. When R. J. Reynolds started advertising its "Snus," a smoke-free alternative, in pouches, the company was required to run huge ads proclaiming "WARNING: This product can cause mouth cancer." The FDA overreached its limit when it wanted the industry to show "full-color images of diseased lungs, cancerous mouths, corpses, and smoke billowing from a hole in a man's neck." A District Court struck this requirement down, ruling that there is no proof the ads reduce smoking and they are unconstitutional.[87]

In the past couple years, electronic-cigarettes (e-cigs) have increased in popularity, and the tobacco companies have been working hard to promote them. E-cigs vaporize nicotine without burning tobacco, and were estimated to reach $1 billion in sales in 2013. They are a small (2.5 million users), but fast growing rival to traditional cigarettes (45 million users).[88] Some researchers claim e-cigs are less harmful than regular cigarettes. They are gaining traction but are now attracting lots of attention by regulators and state legislatures.[89] Many states are starting to target the e-cigs because they have not been federally regulated. Bills in a number of states would extend smoking bans in public areas to include the e-cigs and not allow minors to buy them.[90] The danger of e-cigs to health has not yet been fully established, but this is a product which will be closely monitored in the future.

Opponents of tobacco and tobacco-related products continue their campaigns against these products and their advertising. The Campaign for Tobacco-Free Kids, an advocacy group, argues that smokeless products are gaining popularity with high school students and that this is dangerous. Some think the flavored versions are specifically targeted towards young people and getting them hooked on the addictive products.[91] Although the industry seems to be striving to make products that are more palatable and appealing, there is still the concern that the smokeless varieties carry significant health risks.

The future will be determined in part by how the FDA decides to deal with flavored smokeless tobacco, e-cigs, and whatever new products come on the market. In 2013, the FDA named a veteran tobacco-industry critic to become the industry's chief regulator. Predictions are that tougher regulatory oversight of the industry will follow.[92] The ethical issues surrounding the promotion of tobacco products show no signs of abating; this will likely be a controversial advertising issue into the foreseeable future.

Health and Environmental Claims. Advertising and labeling practices that make claims about health and environmental safety have taken on growing importance. One reason that these issues have come to the forefront is the renewed enforcement activities of the Food and Drug Administration (FDA), the Federal Trade Commission (FTC), and state attorneys general in cracking down on misleading or unsubstantiated claims. We now live in an environmentally aware and health-conscious society, and consumers' interest in products that are healthful and protect the environment has grown significantly. It is not surprising that these issues have gained so much attention.

Because health and environmental claims attract customers, marketers are tempted to tout claims that they can't back up. Consumers today are undoubtedly frustrated as they scan health claims on so many products. The fronts of boxes are shouting out claims about different nutrients—sugar free, extra fiber, no transfats, gluten-free, added vitamins, fat free, and heart-healthy. In 2010, the FDA embarked on a quest to clean up misleading and deceptive advertising regarding the health claims of food products. The FDA has become concerned that the food claims companies make are not backed by adequate scientific evidence to support the claims. In one high-profile example, the FDA wrote to General Mills, maker of Cheerios, warning about its boasting for some of the cereal's health benefits. The FDA stated, "We have determined [Cheerios] is promoted for conditions that cause it to be a drug." This resulted in late-night comedy spoofs in which it was suggested that consumers may now need a prescription to buy a box of the cereal.[93] For about a decade, the FDA allowed qualified health claims to appear on food labels as long as the company included a disclaimer that described the reliability of the evidence supporting the claim. But the FDA later rescinded this policy on the theory that the disclaimers were confusing.[94] Clearly, the FDA has been taking a more activist stance regarding such health claims on food products.

Regulators in the United States and Europe have become more concerned about a new category of foods that are being called "functional foods." These products make claims to improve your health functioning in specific ways. For example, all supermarkets today carry probiotic yogurts that claim to ease constipation, improve regularity, and fight infections. Or, you might be interested in butter substitutes that declare they reduce your cholesterol, or tomato extracts that argue they can keep your skin young while warding off cancer. Sales growth of these products have been increasing fast, and Nestlé, the world's largest food company, has predicted that functional foods will be a primary source of future sales growth. All this activity has caught the attention of regulators, and they are beginning to investigate whether the health claims are supported or misleading.[95] The temptation for unethical advertising in this sector is significant.

The market for more healthy food products is growing, and a few companies have been taking it upon themselves to progressively plan for the future. One highly visible example is that of PepsiCo, led by CEO Indra Nooyi. Beginning in 2010, Nooyi made it known that she wants PepsiCo to be "seen as one of the defining companies of the first half of the 21st century." She wants her company to be "a model of how to conduct business in the modern world."[96] With respect to her company's products, she wants to help customers wean off of sugar, salt, and fat. In 2010, she unveiled a series of goals to improve the healthiness of PepsiCo products. By 2015, the company seeks to reduce the salt in its leading brands by 25 percent. By 2020, the company wants to reduce the amount of sugar in its drinks by 25 percent, and the amount of saturated fat in certain snacks by 15 percent. The company announced it would be removing all its sugary drinks from schools around the world by 2012. Astutely, Nooyi observed that she wants to prevent the food companies from going the way of the tobacco firms.[97] Over the past several years, PepsiCo has attempted to move in these directions by hiring physicians and PhDs to help develop the new products. PepsiCo's goal is to expand its sales of healthy products at an annual growth rate of 10 percent, which is twice the company's historical average. The company also plans to push new products to undernourished people in India and other developing countries. PepsiCo's goals are ambitious, but if achieved, may set a new standard for food companies striving to be socially responsible while making money.[98]

The FTC has also cracked down on companies making other types of health-related claims for their products. In 2012, for example, Skechers USA Inc. was required to pay $50 million to resolve allegations that it deceived the public by making unsupported claims that its "toning shoes" would help consumers tone their muscles and lose weight. The FTC judged that Skechers' claim that consumers could "get in shape without setting foot in a gym" was deceptive.[99]

Another major controversial advertising practice is **"green advertising"** with which companies claim their products and/or their product packages are environmentally friendly or safe. Within the past decade, many companies have been ramping up their advertising claims about the environmental friendliness of their products—that their products are "green." A 2012 survey by Cone Communications revealed what consumers think a "green/environmentally friendly" message is all about: 54 percent said it is a product that has "a positive or neutral impact on the environment" and 28 percent said it's a product that has "a lighter impact than similar/older products."[100] Another poll asked consumers whether "green eco" labels are misleading. Sixty-three percent said *yes* and 37 percent said *no*.[101] These findings indicate the public perception that some questionable practices are involved in the green advertising industry. In late 2012, the Federal Trade Commission issued new guidelines for "eco-friendly" labeling, mandating that companies better be able to back up their claims.[102]

There have been contradictory studies about whether consumers are willing to pay more for environmentally friendly products. Some studies indicate that customers are willing to pay more up to a point, but that they are not willing to trade off a product's "green" qualities for product performance. Consequently, some companies such as Procter & Gamble are seeking to put consumers on a more sustainable path without compromising product quality or performance. P&G's CEO, Robert A. McDonald, claims his company can actually cut costs while maintaining its environmental goals.[103]

There is no question that the green economy is huge. It was estimated recently to be in excess of $1.04 trillion and growing. This is a gigantic market segment, and the temptation for companies to promote questionable claims is strong. The major consumer challenge is the difficulty in assessing the reliability of claims that products are environmentally friendly or safe. To offset much of the green advertising, an industry of what might be called **"green watchdogs"** has been growing also. Certification groups claiming to verify eco-friendly claims have proliferated. Examples include Green-e, a San Francisco-based nonprofit. The Forest Stewardship Council promises to verify that the wood in your new furniture was actually harvested from a sustainably managed forest. Sustainable Travel International watches to make sure the hotel you stay at is minimizing its garbage.[104]

Other groups claiming to certify the green aspects of products include Energy Star, which is one of the best known eco-labels, evaluating energy savings; EcoLogo, which monitors 150 product categories; EPEAT (Electronic Product Assessment Tool), which covers computers and monitors; and Eco Options, which covers 3,500-plus products sold at Home Depot. While these groups are an emerging force, some use looser standards than others and it is difficult to ascertain how much due diligence each has behind their eco-seals.[105] The fact that these monitoring groups are increasing in number, however, suggests this is an issue that needs to be watched closely by consumers, lest they be duped about the eco-friendliness of products they buy.

Advertisers have come on so fast and strong with their environmental friendly claims that there is a growing **"green fatigue"** developing among some consumers who are growing weary of these claims.[106] The evidence seems to indicate that being green is not enough. Products need to be wallet-friendly as well, especially as the economy struggles to emerge from a recession. Some marketers have noticed a green backlash among consumer attitudes.[107] Companies and advertisers will need to watch carefully the quality of their claims or a real cynicism about environmental claims may develop.

Recently, companies have strived to transition from **green marketing** to marketing for environmental sustainability.[108] Part of this challenge is to create a stronger case, complete with documentation. Four insights along these lines have been presented. First, more reliable metrics are needed to translate environmental commitments into customer value. Second, verifiable product standards and certifications help to communicate this value. Third, these standards need to be developed in concert with multiple stakeholders if they are to be trustworthy. Fourth, environmental sustainability brand value needs to be embedded in sincere, systemic, and organization-wide commitments.[109] It will be challenging for companies to make this transition, and the opportunities for questionable practices will be present all along the way.

Ad Creep. The way that advertising can increasingly be found everywhere one looks is referred to as **ad creep**. Both product placement and plot placement, discussed earlier, are special cases of ad creep. Ads are now going into places that once were not considered acceptable for advertisements. School buses, textbooks, doctors' offices, and historical monuments have all been festooned with advertisements. The traditional term for advertising that is located in nontraditional places is **ambient advertising**, but *ad creep* reflects both the way the ads have grown and the way people often feel about its creators.[110]

A variety of factors contribute to ad creep. A declining network TV audience, increased dispersion from cable and Internet outlets, and soaring network television rates make it difficult to blanket the population with an advertising message. The arrival of digital video recorders (such as TiVo and those of cable TV providers) has made it easier for viewers to speed through ads without watching them. One response to ad-skipping technologies like TiVo has been the insertion of ads into video games. Since most PCs, and an increasing number of video games are connected to the Internet, it will be possible to update advertisements when required.[111]

Furthermore, ad creep generates more ad creep because people become numb to messages in traditional places and so unique new venues are sought—just to get the consumer's attention.[112] Some of the ad creep examples of recent years have been quite bizarre. One extreme example has been the appearance of ads on Japanese girls' thighs. A Japanese PR agency began paying young women to wear advertising stickers on their thighs, between the edge of their miniskirts and their high socks. After choosing a sticker ad, the woman has to wear it for at least eight hours a day for a set period of time in order to receive payment. In another interesting example of ad creep, Papa John's ads were placed outside the peep hole in people's apartments and then the door bell was rung. When the resident peeped out, he or she saw a Papa John delivery boy offering up a box of pizza with a phone number on it.[113]

The seven controversial advertising issues discussed above are simply the tip of the iceberg. Issues have been raised about the marketing of pharmaceutical drugs directly to patients through magazine and television ads. These ads encourage patients to ask their doctor for the prescription drug, to the frustration of doctors everywhere. Concerns have also been raised about the marketing of guns and ammunition, particularly in family stores like Walmart and Kmart. Channel One, a television station that beams educational programming to schools across the country, has been sharply criticized for its commercials, which students end up watching along with the educational programming. Audiences in movies everywhere have bemoaned the inclusion of commercials in the preview clips, as they are captive audiences, unable to change the channel. There is no end to the list of concerns about the advertising practices undertaken today. Business-people must tread carefully to make certain they do not cross the line where their customers become more annoyed with their practices than attracted to their products. Further, serious ethical questions may arise about the types and placements of advertising in the future.

Warranties

From the glamorous realm of advertising, we now proceed to the less glamorous issues of warranties. **Warranties** were initially used by manufacturers to limit the length of time they were expressly responsible for products. Over time, they came to be viewed by consumers as mechanisms to protect the buyer against faulty or defective products. Most consumers have had the experience of buying a hair dryer, a stereo, a computer, a refrigerator, an automobile, a washing machine, a chain saw, or any of thousands of other products, only to find that it did not work properly or did not work at all. That is when warranties and guarantees take center stage.

The law recognizes two types of warranties—implied and express. An **implied warranty** is an unspoken promise that there is nothing significantly wrong with the product and that the product can be used for the purposes intended. An **express warranty** is explicitly offered at the time of the sale. The nature of express warranties can range from advertising claims to formal certificates, and they may be oral or written.

The passage of the Magnuson–Moss Warranty Act of 1975 helped clarify the nature of warranties for consumers. It is still the basic law of the land, although the FTC has amended, clarified, and interpreted it over the years.[114] This act was aimed at clearing up a variety of misunderstandings about manufacturers' warranties—especially whether a **full warranty** was in effect, or whether certain parts of the product or certain types of defects were excluded from coverage, resulting in a **limited warranty**. Also at issue was whether or not the buyer had to pay shipping charges when a product was sent to and from the factory for servicing of a defect.[115] The Warranty Act set standards for what must be contained in a warranty and the ease with which consumers must be able to understand it. If a company, for example, claims that its product has a full warranty, it must contain certain features, including repair "within a reasonable time and without charge."[116] The law holds that anything less than this unconditional assurance must be promoted as a limited warranty.

With the rise of e-commerce, warranties have become an important issue. Companies find that warranties or guarantees are essential when marketing by mail. The internationalization of commerce that has resulted from the Internet has presented new challenges. International e-commerce has been largely unregulated. Scott Nathan, an attorney who specializes in e-commerce law, explains that the "speed 'n' ease" factor heightens the warranty problems. "Because of the lack of international law governing warranties," says Nathan, "be prepared to defend the performance of your polka dot widgets in a foreign court."[117]

An issue of increasing ethical concern is **extended warranties**, service plans that lengthen the warranty period and are offered at an additional cost. Consumer advocates advise against buying most extended warranties because they often cost as much as the original item bought would eventually cost to replace. Eric Antum, editor of *Warranty Week*, explains that retailers might make only $10 on a $400 television, but will then make $50 on a $100 on extended warranty.[118] Not surprisingly, the lure of big profits has led to some hardball sales tactics.

Consumers spend billions of dollars on extended warranties.[119] They have become very popular with car purchases, perhaps because customers are keeping their cars longer. Some customers view the warranties to be insurance, and they are willing to take the risk that the warranty will be worth the price they paid for it. A serious problem today is third-party vendors selling extended warranties on products such as autos. Some of these vendors may go out of business before you try to collect, and some represent scams that never intend to pay off for anyone.[120] Opponents of extended warranties offer the following reasons not to buy them: the manufacturer's warranty is usually sufficient; extended warranties are not always effective; the necessity of repairs is rare; warranties are not cost-effective; and, credit cards can offer better protection.[121]

Of course, if companies simply offer complete satisfaction, with no fine print, the warranty problem is not such an issue. Few companies accomplish this, but one that does is L.L. Bean, whose guarantee says: "Our products are guaranteed to give 100 percent satisfaction in every way. Return anything purchased from us at any time if it proves otherwise. We will replace it, refund your purchase price, or credit your credit card, as you wish. We do not want you to have anything from L.L. Bean that is not completely satisfactory."[122]

Packaging and Labeling

Abuses in the packaging and labeling areas were fairly frequent before the passage of the Federal Packaging and Labeling Act (FPLA) of 1967. The purpose of this act was to prohibit deceptive labeling of certain consumer products, and to require disclosure of certain important information. This act, which is administered by the Federal Trade Commission, requires the FTC to issue regulations regarding net contents disclosures, identity of commodity, and name and place of manufacturer, packer, or distributor. Both the FTC and the Food and Drug Administration (FDA) have direct responsibilities under this act. The Act authorizes additional regulations, when necessary, to prevent consumer deception or to facilitate value comparisons with respect to: the declaration of ingredients, slack filling of packages, "downsizing" of packaging, and use of "cents off" designations. The Act gives the FTC responsibility for consumer commodities. The Food and Drug Administration (FDA) administers the FPLA with respect to foods, drugs, cosmetics, and medical devices.[123]

As we mentioned in an earlier section, the packaging and labeling issue is drawing renewed interest because of health and environmental claims, and advertising law in specific product categories such as pharmaceuticals, food, tobacco, alcohol, and advertising directed at children. One unusual example of how packaging can potentially be dangerous to children is the case of Procter & Gamble's Tide Pods packaging. P&G has agreed to modify its Tide Pods packages, which contain a cleaning product, because the colorful gumball-sized packets have been mistaken for candy and children have ingested them and become very ill. P&G has redesigned the packaging; a double latch will now child-proof it. The company is also considering changing the appearance of the pods so that children will not be attracted to them.[124]

The most high-profile labeling issue to enter the public debate recently has been the horse meat scandal, which captivated most of Europe when it came to light. The issue became public when it was discovered that frozen food products such as lasagna and beef burgers labeled as containing beef actually contained horse meat. As it turns out, horse meat is a delicacy in some European countries such as France and Italy. This isn't the case in Ireland and the U.K. where eating horse meat is considered unsuitable. Though not a safety issue, the horse meat scandal is, at minimum, a labeling issue and raises questions about the food supply chain. The European Union decided to propose a testing campaign in an effort to discover the breadth of the problem.[125]

Other Product Information Issues

It is difficult to catalog all the consumer issues in which product information is a key factor. Certainly, advertising, warranties, packaging, and labeling constitute the bulk of the concerns. In addition to these, however, we must briefly mention several others. Sales techniques in which direct sellers use deceptive information cause problems. Some major laws that address information disclosure issues include the following:

1. *Equal Credit Opportunity Act*, which prohibits discrimination in the extension of consumer credit.
2. *Truth-in-Lending Act*, which requires all suppliers of consumer credit to fully disclose all credit terms, and to permit a three-day right of rescission in any transaction involving a security interest in the consumer's residence (e.g., in the case of home equity loans).
3. *Fair Credit Reporting Act*, which ensures that consumer-reporting agencies provide information in a manner that is fair and equitable to the consumer.
4. *Fair Debt Collection Practices Act*, which regulates the practices of third-party debt collection agencies.

The Federal Trade Commission (FTC)

We have discussed three main areas of product information—advertising, warranties, and packaging or labeling. Both the FTC and the FDA are actively involved in these issues. It is important now to look more closely at the federal government's major instrument, the FTC, for ensuring that business lives up to its responsibilities in these areas. The FTC has broad and sweeping powers, and it delves into several other areas that we refer to throughout the book. The Consumer Product Safety Commission and the FDA are major regulatory agencies, too, but we consider them more carefully in the next chapter, where we discuss products and services more specifically.

The FTC was created in 1914. Its purpose was to prevent unfair methods of competition in commerce as part of the battle to "bust the trusts." Over the years, Congress passed additional laws giving the agency greater authority in the policing of anticompetitive prices. In 1938, Congress passed a broad prohibition against "unfair and deceptive acts or practices." Since then the FTC has also been directed to administer a wide variety of other consumer protection laws including Truth-in-Lending, Fair Packaging and Labeling, Fair Credit Reporting, and Equal Credit Opportunity Acts.[126] Over the course of its history, the FTC has been less active or more active in keeping with the agenda of the administration that was in office and the zeal of the Chairperson. Figure 13-3 provides additional information about the FTC's mission, vision, and how it helps consumers.

The FTC in the 21st Century

In addition to dealing with its ongoing responsibilities, the FTC has had a number of successes in carrying out its mission in the 2000s.[127] An early accomplishment was the creation of the National Do-Not-Call Registry. The registry opened to consumers in 2003 and forbade telemarketers from calling consumers who sign up with the registry. The FTC also instituted a requirement that all companies placing marketing calls have their information available for consumers' caller ID systems. Consumers could then report companies that make calls in violation.[128]

Beginning in 2004, the FTC extracted millions of dollars in settlements from firms that made misleading claims for weight loss products, but opted not to require disclosure of the existence of product placement or the sources of word-of-mouth advertising.[129]

FIGURE 13-3 The Federal Trade Commission

FTC's Mission	To prevent business practices that are anticompetitive, deceptive, or unfair to consumers; to enhance informed consumer choice and public understanding of the competitive process; and to accomplish this without unduly burdening legitimate business activity.
FTC's Vision	A U.S. economy characterized by vigorous competition among producers and consumer access to accurate information, yielding high-quality products at low prices and encouraging efficiency, innovation, and consumer choice.
FTC's Strategic Goals	1. *Protect Consumers*: Prevent fraud, deception, and unfair business practices in the marketplace. 2. *Maintain Competition*: Prevent anticompetitive mergers and other anticompetitive business practices in the marketplace. 3. *Advance Performance*: Advance the FTC's performance through organizational, individual, and management excellence.
FTC's Benefits to Consumer	As a consumer or business person, you may be more familiar with the work of the Federal Trade Commission than you think. The FTC deals with issues that touch the economic life of every American. The FTC is the only federal agency with both consumer protection and competition jurisdiction in broad sectors of the economy. The FTC pursues vigorous and effective law enforcement; advances consumers' interests by sharing its expertise with federal and state legislatures and U.S. and international government agencies; develops policy and research tools through hearings, workshops, and conferences; and creates practical and plain-language educational programs for consumers and businesses in a global marketplace with constantly changing technologies.

Sources: Federal Trade Commission, "About the Federal Trade Commission," http://www.ftc.gov/ftc/about.shtm. Accessed May 4, 2013; FTC Consumer Information, http://www.consumer.ftc.gov/. Accessed May 4, 2013.

The FTC preference was that business self-regulate when possible and that the police action of the FTC be a court of last resort.[130] Beginning in 2009, the FTC argued for a more vigorous enforcement of the FTC Act and moved more aggressively on issues such as health care; advertising and marketing to children; Internet, telecom, and technology; energy; and competition enforcement beyond the Sherman Act. Under the Obama administration, the FTC and other federal consumer protection agencies assumed a more active role than in the recent past. Recently, the FTC has been dealing with such issues as robocalls, telemarketers, phone spam, pyramid schemes, Google's antitrust case, children's online privacy and data brokers.

Recent Consumer Legislation

Though the FTC supervises most consumer regulations with respect to product and service information and advertising, and other laws have been passed that address specific issues, it is useful to briefly consider major consumer legislation that has been passed recently. One of these recent laws is the **Credit Card Act of 2009**. Another is the creation of the Consumer Financial Protection Bureau in 2010.

Credit Card Act of 2009

For many years, consumers have been complaining about the treatment they receive from banks and credit card companies, and it came as no surprise that Congress finally passed new regulations on the industry. The *Credit Card Accountability, Responsibility, and Disclosure Act 2009 (CARD)* was passed by Congress and enacted in February 2010.

The CARD Act met with strong resistance from banks and credit card issuers; their lobbyists claimed that credit would be more expensive and harder to get if the act passed. After three years of enactment the CARD act seems to have had a net positive effect on consumers. After one year of enactment, the Office of the Comptroller of the Currency provided documentation that indicated consumers were being helped more than hurt. One strong benefit was increased transparency on the part of the card issuers. By 2012, one major report by the research organization Demos showed that 9 out of 10 consumers now have sufficient time to react to adverse events such as late fees. One-third of lower to middle income card holders are paying down their balances more rapidly, and the percentage of consumers paying late fees has declined to 28 percent; whereas it was at 50 percent in 2009. The upshot of this study is that after three years, consumers are mostly better off, though some problems continue.[131]

All in all, the new law improves the credit card arrangement for consumers, especially in the realm of information, but does not completely eliminate the need to be very careful about credit card terms before agreeing to them.

Consumer Financial Protection Bureau

The Dodd–Frank Wall Street Reform and Consumer Protection Act of 2010 (Dodd–Frank Act) established the **Consumer Financial Protection Bureau (CFPB)**. Congress enacted this legislation to protect consumers by implementing and enforcing federal consumer financial laws. Among other activities, the CFPB:

- Writes rules, supervises companies, and enforces federal consumer financial protection laws
- Restricts unfair, deceptive, or abusive acts or practices
- Takes consumer complaints
- Promotes financial education
- Researches consumer behavior
- Monitors financial markets for new risks to consumers
- Enforces laws that outlaw discrimination and other unfair treatment in consumer finance

The new agency had considerable support due to the belief by many consumers and political leaders that such an agency was needed in light of the financial misdealing and deceptions of the previous several years. One aim of the bill was that it would police and write rules for financial firms' retail products such as mortgages, bank accounts, and credit cards. The proposed legislation was just one part of the Obama administration's proposed financial reforms.[132] The new protection bureau, patterned in concept after the Consumer Product Safety Commission, which will be discussed in the next chapter, was a key element in financial reform legislation that had been debated in Congress for several years. The basic motivation for the legislation was that greedy banks had exploited naïve consumers, and this led to the credit crisis the country has been experiencing.[133] While much of the debate centered on banks and their role in the financial crisis, lawmakers were also concerned about how to handle other financial consumer businesses, such as payday lenders, debt collectors, check-cashing businesses, title and installment lenders, and pawnbrokers.[134]

Critics of the proposed CFPB included those philosophically opposed to more government regulation and the business community, which saw the new regulator as unnecessary. Lobbying by business associations was vigorous. The U.S. Chamber of Commerce, as well as many of the financial service firms themselves, fought the proposed bureau since the beginning.[135] The majority of consumers and consumer advocacy groups were in favor of the proposed legislation, and business associations that were likely to be impacted were against the new agency.

One of the chief responsibilities of the CFPB is to receive consumer complaints about financial products. During the second half of calendar year 2012, the most recent data available, 91,000 consumer complaints had been registered and they broke down into the follow categories and percentages:[136]

- Mortgages 50%
- Credit cards 20%
- Bank accounts and service 17%
- Student loans 4%
- Consumer loans 4%
- Credit reporting 4%
- Other 1%

In terms of how companies responded to the complaints during this same time period, the following actions were taken by the companies along with indicated percentages:

- Company reported case closed with explanation 65%
- Company reported case closed with monetary relief 15%
- Company reported case closed with no monetary relief 9%
- Company still reviewing 7%
- Company provided administrative response 2%
- Company reported case closed (without relief/explanation) 2%

In terms of consumer feedback concerning company responses, the following opinions were offered:

- Consumer did not dispute company's response 61%
- Consumer disputed company's response 22%
- Pending consumer review of company's response 17%

According to the CFPB, the idea behind publishing these statistics is to heighten everyone's awareness of the issues involved and the progress being made.

Self-Regulation in Advertising

Cases of deceptive or unfair advertising in the United States are handled primarily by the FTC. In addition to this regulatory approach, however, self-regulation of advertising has become an important business response. Under the regulatory approach, advertising behavior is controlled through various governmental rules that are backed by the use of penalties. **Self-regulation**, on the other hand, refers to the control of business conduct and performance by the business itself, or business associations, rather than by government or by market forces.[137] The idea behind self-regulation is that companies will carefully monitor their own advertising for legal and ethical issues, and take the initiative in correcting deficient advertising without the regulatory agencies having to get involved. It is a proactive strategy rather than a reactive one.

Types of Self-Regulation of Advertising

Business self-regulation of advertising may take on various forms. One is **self-discipline**, where the firm itself controls its own advertising. Another is **pure self-regulation**, where the industry (one's peers) controls advertising. A third type is **co-opted self-regulation**, where the industry, on its own volition, involves non-industry stakeholders (e.g., consumer or public representatives) in the development, application, and enforcement of norms. A fourth type is **negotiated self-regulation**, where the industry voluntarily negotiates the development, use, and enforcement of standards with some outside body (e.g., a government department or a consumer association). Finally, a fifth type is **mandated self-regulation** (which may sound like an oxymoron), where the industry is ordered or designated by the government to develop, use, and enforce norms, whether alone or in concert with other bodies.[138]

The National Advertising Division's Program

The most prominent instance of self-regulation by business in the advertising industry is the program sponsored by the National Advertising Division (NAD) of the Council of Better Business Bureaus, Inc. The NAD and the National Advertising Review Board (NARB) were created in 1971 to help sustain high standards of truth and accuracy in national advertising, and still serves today in an effective manner. NAD only reviews national advertisements. It leaves to state and city jurisdictions the responsibility for local advertisements.[139]

The NAD initiates investigations, determines issues, collects and evaluates data, and determines whether an advertiser's claims are substantiated. When the NAD finds that an advertiser's claims are unsubstantiated, the advertiser is asked to undertake modification or permanent discontinuance of the advertising. If an advertiser disagrees with NAD's decision, it can file an appeal with the NARB, which has a reservoir of dozens of men and women representing national advertisers, advertising agencies, and the public sector. The chairman of the NARB selects an impartial panel of five members for each appeal. The parties involved, including NAD, submit briefs expressing their views for discussion at an oral hearing, after which the panel issues a public report.[140] If an advertiser is unwilling to abide by the NARB panel's decision, the advertising at issue may be referred to the FTC.[141] NAD is a low-cost alternative to litigation and it reaches determinations regarding the truth and accuracy of advertising in a fair, impartial, and expeditious manner.[142]

Moral Models and Consumer Stakeholders

It is useful to conclude this chapter by providing insights into how the three types of moral manager models, introduced in Chapter 7, would view consumer stakeholders. Figure 13-4 presents a brief statement as to the likely orientations of immoral,

---

FIGURE 13-4

Three Moral Management Models and Their Orientations Toward Consumer Stakeholders

Model of Management Morality Orientation to Consumer Stakeholders

Immoral Management Customers are viewed as opportunities to be exploited for personal or organizational gain. Ethical standards in dealings do not prevail; indeed, an active intent to cheat, deceive, and/or mislead is present. In all marketing decisions—advertising, pricing, packaging, distribution, warranties—the customer is taken advantage of to the fullest extent.

Amoral Management Management does not think through the ethical consequences of its decisions and actions. It simply makes decisions with profitability within the letter of the law as a guide. Management is not focused on what is fair from the perspective of the customer. The focus is on management's rights. No consideration is given to ethical implications of interactions with customers.

Moral Management Customers are viewed as equal partners in transactions. The customer brings needs and expectations to the exchange transaction and is treated fairly. Managerial focus is on giving the customer fair value, full information, fair guarantee, and satisfaction. Consumer rights are liberally interpreted and honored.

© Cengage Learning

amoral, and moral managers to this vital stakeholder group. As it can be seen in these descriptions, the moral management model best represents the highest ethical standards of consumer treatment and is, therefore, the recommended model for business to follow.

Summary

Consumer stakeholders have always been at the top of the list of business's stakeholders. The issue of consumer stakeholders has come to the forefront during the recent recession and recovery. More and more, businesses are realizing that the economy is built upon consumer spending, and that they need to do all they can do to get consumers spending again. In a consumption-driven society, business must be especially attentive to the issues that arise in its relationships with consumers. It is a paradox that consumerism arose during the very period that the business community discovered the centrality of the marketing concept to business success. The consumer's Magna Carta includes the rights to safety, to be informed, to choose, and to be heard. Consumers, however, expect more than this, and hence the consumer movement, or consumerism, was born. Ralph Nader, considered the father of this movement, made consumer complaining respectable. Since then, the consumer movement has been among the most active of the stakeholder categories and promises to be important in the future.

Product information issues comprise a major area in the business–consumer stakeholder relationship. Foremost among these is advertising. Many issues have arisen because of perceived advertising abuses, such as ambiguity, concealed facts, exaggerations, and psychological appeals. Specific controversial spheres have included, but are not limited to: comparative advertising, use of sex appeal in advertising, advertising to children, marketing to the poor, advertising of alcoholic beverages, advertising of cigarettes, health and environmental claims, and ad creep. Other product information issues include warranties, packaging, and labeling. The major body for regulating product information issues has been the FTC. The FDA and the state attorneys general have become active as well. Recent legislation has included the Credit Card Act and the Consumer Financial Protection Bureau, intended to give consumers greater protection with financial service industry products. On its own behalf, business has initiated a variety of forms of self-regulation with respect to its product and service information, especially advertising.

Key Terms

accurate information, p. 382

ad creep, p. 396

adequate information, p. 382

age compression, p.389

ambient advertising, p.396

ambiguous advertising, p. 383

Children's Television Act (CTA), p. 390

clear information, p. 382

comparative advertising, p. 387

concealed facts, p. 384

Consumer Financial Protection Bureau (CFPB), p. 401

consumerism, p. 379

consumer's Magna Carta, p. 378

co-opted self-regulation, p. 402

Credit Card Act of 2009, p. 400

customer relationship management (CRM), p. 377

exaggerated claims, p. 385

express warranty, p. 397

extended warranties, p. 397

full warranty, p. 397

green advertising, p. 395

green marketing, p. 396

green fatigue, p. 395

green watchdogs, p. 395

implied warranty, p. 397

limited warranty, p. 397

mandated self-regulation, p. 403

negotiated self-regulation, p. 403

plot placement, p. 384

product information, p. 381

product placement, p. 384

psychological appeals, p. 386

puffery, p. 385

pure self-regulation, p. 402

right to be heard, p. 378

right to be informed, p. 378

right to choose, p. 378

right to safety, p. 378

self-discipline, p. 402

self-regulation, p. 402

warranties, p. 397

weasel words, p. 383

Discussion Questions

1. In addition to the basic consumer rights expressed in the consumer's Magna Carta, what other expectations or rights do you think consumer stakeholders have of business? Do consumers have some moral rights that have not yet been articulated in law?

2. What is your opinion of the consumerism movement? Is it "alive and well" or is it fading away? Why has consumerism been such an enduring movement for so long?

3. Give an example of a major abuse of advertising from your own observations and experiences. How do you feel about this as a consumer?

4. Are companies genuinely interested in marketing sustainable products or is this just a marketing strategy that is popular today? Do you think "green fatigue" has set in? If so, what should companies now do?

5. Do the new consumer financial products regulations make sense? In a free market, why shouldn't consumers be left to fend for themselves with respect to consumer financial products?

Endnotes

1. Peter F. Drucker, *Management: Tasks, Responsibilities, Practices* (New York: Harper & Row, 1973), 61.

2. Frederick F. Reichheld, *The Loyalty Effect* (Cambridge, MA: Harvard Business School Press, 1996).

3. Russell S. Winer, "A Framework for Customer Relationship Management," *California Management Review* (Summer 2001), 89–105.

4. "The Customer Is Often Ignored," *Marketing Week* (September 27, 2001), 3.

5. Camilla Ballesteros, "Don't Talk About CRM; Do It," *Marketing Week* (September 27, 2001), 49.

6. Ibid.

7. Scott M. Broetzmann, "Why the Customer Care Revolution Has Failed: How Companies Misuse the Telephone when Responding to Customers" (May 31, 2006), http://www.tmcnet.com/news/2006/04/18/1581418.htm. Accessed August 9, 2010.

8. Pete Blackshaw, Satisfied Customers tell three friends, Angry Customers tell 3,000, Doubleday, 2008.

9. David Kiley and Burt Helm, "100 Best Global Brands: The Great Trust Offensive," *BusinessWeek* (September 28, 2009), 38–42.

10. Robert J. Holloway and Robert S. Hancock, *Marketing in a Changing Environment*, 2d ed. (New York: John Wiley & Sons, 1973), 558–565.

11. Ibid., 556–566.

12. Robert O. Herrmann, "Consumerism: Its Goals, Organizations, and Future," *Journal of Marketing* (October 1970), 55–60.

13. Ruth Simon, "You're Losing Your Consumer Rights," *Money* (Vol. 25, No. 3, 1996), 100–111.

14. For more on the history of the consumer movement, see Archie B. Carroll, Kenneth J. Lipartito, James E. Post, Patricia H. Werhane and Kenneth E. Goodpaster, executive editor, 2012, *Corporate Responsibility: The American Experience*, Cambridge: Cambridge University Press.

15. Philip Kotler, "What Consumerism Means for Marketers," *Harvard Business Review* (May–June 1972), 48–57.

16. Ralph Nader, *Unsafe at Any Speed* (New York: Grossman Publishers, 1965).

17. Kotler, 50. Kotler states that these conditions were proposed by Neil J. Smelser, *Theory of Collective Behavior* (New York: The Free Press, 1963).

18. Rich Thomas, "Safe at This Speed," *BusinessWeek* (August 22, 1994), 40; Douglas Harbrecht and Ronald Grover, "The Second Coming of Ralph Nader," *BusinessWeek* (March 6, 1989), 28.

19. Paul Magnusson, "The Punishing Price of Nader's Passion," *BusinessWeek* (November 20, 2000), 44.

20. Gary Fields, "Leading the News: Nader to Run for President Again; Democrats Fear a Reprise of 2000," *The Wall Street Journal* (February 23, 2003), A3.

21. Cordelia Brabbs, "Web Fuels Consumer Activism," *Marketing* (September 21, 2000), 23.

22. Consumer Reports, http://www.consumerreports.org/cro/index.htm. Accessed April 30, 2013.

23. *Consumer Reports*, January 2013, 63.

24. *Consumer Reports*, December 2012, 75.

25. "Never Say Never," http://www.ConsumerReports.org (September 2009), 63.

26. *Consumer Reports*, September 2012, 63.

27. *Consumer Reports,* October 2012, 63.

28. William Leiss, Stephen Kline, and Sut Jhally, *Social Communication in Advertising* (Toronto: Methuen, 1986), 13.

29. Ibid.

30. William Shaw and Vincent Barry, *Moral Issues in Business*, 12th ed. (Cengage Learning, 2012), 389–414.

31. Stuart Elliott, "A Survey of Consumer Attitudes Reveals the Depth of the Challenge That the Agencies Face," *The New York Times* (April 14, 2004), C8.

32. Shaw and Barry, ibid.

33. Ibid., 404.

34. Shaw and Barry, ibid.

35. Justine Goodman, "5 Hilariously Blatant Examples of Product Placement," November 14, 2012, http://www.maxim.com/movies/5-hilariously-blatant-examples-of-product-placement. Accessed April 30, 2013.

36. Tom Lowry and Burt Helm, "Blasting Away at Product Placement," *BusinessWeek* (October 26, 2009), 60.

37. Dean Foust and Brian Grow, "Coke: Wooing the TV Generation," *BusinessWeek Online* (March 1, 2004).

38. Brian Levin, "American Idol's Launch of Text Voting Shows Mobile Voting Can Survive, Wireless Business and Technology" (January 1, 2000), http://wireless.syscon.com/node/41214. Accessed April 30, 2013.

39. Joe Flint and Emily Nelson, "All My Children Gets Revlon Twist—First Came Product Placement Now TV 'Plot Placement' Yields ABC a Big Ad Buy," *The Wall Street Journal* (March 15, 2002); Leslie Ryan, "Passions Product Pitch; NBC, Avon Weave New Cosmetics Line into Soap Opera's Story," *Television Week* (July 28, 2003).

40. Ingela Ratledge, "Modern Product Placement," *TVGuideMagazine.com* (April 12, 2010).

41. Ronald Grover, Tom Lowry, Gerry Khermouch, Cliff Edwards, and Dean Foust, "Can Mad. Ave. Make Zap-Proof Ads?" *BusinessWeek* (February 2, 2004), 36–37.

42. Ibid.

43. Lowry and Helm, 2009, 60.

44. Jennifer C. Dooren and Emily Glazer, "FDA Rebukes Lancome on Marketing," *The Wall Street Journal*, September 12, 2012, B3.

45. Ben Fox Rubin, "Coppertone to Stop Using 'Waterproof' in Marketing," *The Wall Street Journal*, September 26, 2012, B10.

46. James Heckman, "Puffery Claims No Longer So Easy to Make," *Marketing News* (February 14, 2000), 6.

47. Eli P. Cox, "Deflating the Puffer," *MSU Business Topics* (Summer 1973), 29.

48. "Consumers Have Mixed Reactions to Puffery in Advertising" (January 19, 2010), Phys.Org, http://phys.org/news183128214.html. Accessed May 11, 2013.

49. Shaw and Barry.

50. Jeffrey Kluger, "Now Hear This," *Time* (March 1, 2010).

51. Nicole Martinelli, "Get a Mac Campaign Named One of the Best Marketing Jobs Ever" (January 15, 2009), http://www.cultofmac.com/7091/get-a-mac-campaign-named-one-of-best-marketing-jobs-ever/7091/. Accessed May 9, 2013.

52. Academy of Art University, "Academy Alums 'Get a Mac' Campaign Named Ad of the Decade," http://www.academyart.edu/news/articles/academy-alums-get-mac-named-campaign-decade.html. Accessed May 1, 2013.

53. "Sex in Advertising," April 21, 2012, http://www.cbc.ca/undertheinfluence/season-1/2012/04/21/sex-in-advertising-1/. Accessed May 1, 2013.

54. Hillary Chura, "Spirited Sex; Alcohol Ads Ratchet Up the Sex to Woo Jaded Customers," *Advertising Age* (July 9, 2001), 1.

55. Jill Weber, "Sexy teen lingerie sends all the wrong messages," *USA Today*, March 13, 1003, 8A.

56. Jeanette Mulvey, BusinessNewsDaily, "Why Sex Sells… More than Ever," http://www.businessnewsdaily.com/2649-sex-sells-more.html. Accessed May 1, 2013.

57. American Psychological Association, "Sexualization of Girls," http://www.apa.org/pi/women/programs/girls/report.aspx. Accessed May 1, 2013.

58. "The Ethics of Advertising Aimed at Children," HubPages, http://brandconsultant.hubpages.com/hub/advertisingtochildren. Accessed May 1, 2013.

59. "DressUpGamesite.com, "Barbie Shopping Games," http://www.dressupgamesite.com/games/barbie-shopping-games-2013.htm. Accessed May 1, 2013.

60. "Barbie Gets Her First Credit Card," *Credit Card Management* (January 1998), 6–8.

61. American Psychological Association, http://www.apa.org/topics/children/index.aspx. Accessed May 1, 2013.

62. Jayne O' Donnell, "As Kids Get Savvy, Marketers Move the Age Scale," http://www.usatoday.com/search/jayne%20o'donnell/. Accessed May 11, 2013.

63. Children's Advertising Review Unit, Better Business Bureau, "Self-Regulatory Program for Children's Advertising," 2009, http://www.caru.org/guidelines/guidelines.pdf. Accessed May 1, 2013.

64. Anton Troianovski, "FTC Shines Light on Food Ads, Kids," *The Wall Street Journal*, September 19, 2012, B6.

65. Food Fight over marketing to kids misses key ingredient," *USA Today*, October 17, 2011, 10A.

66. Bonnie Rochman, "Sweet Spot: New Data on How the Least Healthy Cereals Do the Most Marketing," *Time* (November 2, 2009), 55–56.

67. Ilan Brat and Jared Favole, "Food Makers Warned on Claims," *The Wall Street Journal* (March 4, 2010), D2.

68. Bob Jenkins, "Much Ado about Ads," *License!* (November 2006), 72–75.

69. Ibid.

70. Ibid.

71. Ellen Edwards, "Television's Problem Child," *The Washington Post National Weekly Edition* (June 20–26, 1994), 22.

72. U.S. Government Accountability Office, "Children's Television Act," July 14, 2011, http://www.gao.gov/products/GAO-11-659. Accessed May 1, 2013.

73. Michael L. Marlow, "The Skinny of Anti-Obesity Soda Laws," *The Wall Street Journal*, April 1, 2013, A11.

74. Holman W. Jenkins, Jr., "Coke and the Calorie Wars," *The Wall Street Journal*, January 30, 2013, A11; Nanci Hellmich, "Disney Cuts Junk from Its Diet," *USA Today*, June 5, 2012, 1B.

75. Michelle Obama, "The Business Case for Healthier Food Options," *The Wall Street Journal*, February 28, 2013, A15.

76. Federal Trade Commission, "Payday Loans," http://www.consumer.ftc.gov/articles/0097-payday-loans. Accessed May 1, 2013.

77. Grow and Epstein, 62.

78. Ibid.

79. Kirk Davidson, "Look for Abundance of Opposition to TV Ads," *Marketing News* (January 6, 1997), 26–28.

80. Mike Esterl, "Liquor Ads Win Airtime," *The Wall Street Journal*, August 24, 2012, B6.

81. Public Citizen's Commercial Alert, http://www.commercialalert.org. Accessed May 11, 2013.

82. "Spotlight on the Alcohol Industry: Anheuser-Busch pulls Spykes Amid Criticism," June 1, 2007, http://corporationsandhealth.org/2007/06/01/spotlight-on-the-alcohol-industry-anheuser-busch-pulls-spykes-amid-criticism/. Accessed May 3, 2013.

83. WHO, "Regulation Urgently Needed to Control Growing List of Deadly Tobacco Products" (May 30, 2006), http://www.who.int/mediacentre/news/releases/2006/pr28/en/. Accessed May 3, 2013.

84. Eben Shapiro, "FTC Staff Recommends Ban of Joe Camel Campaign," *The Wall Street Journal* (August 11, 1993), B1.

85. Ira Teinowitz, "FTC's Camel Case Hinges on Ad's Power Over Kids," *Advertising Age* (June 2, 1997), 4, 45.

86. Judann Pollack and Ira Teinowitz, "With Joe Camel Out, Government Wants the Marlboro Man Down," *Advertising Age* (July 14, 1997), 3, 34.

87. Mark Joseph Stern, "The FDA's New Cigarette Labels Go Up in Smoke," *The Wall Street Journal*, September 12, 2012, A19.

88. "A Quitter's Market: Electronic-Cigarette Sales Are Up and Big Tobacco Wants In," *Time*, January 21, 2013, 19.

89. Mike Esterl and John Kell, "Big Tobacco Embraces E-Cigs," *The Wall Street Journal*, April 26, 2013, B3.

90. Ibid.

91. Campaign for Tobacco-Free Kids, http://www.tobaccofreekids.org/who_we_are/. Accessed May 3, 2013.

92. Mike Esterl, "FDA Names Critic to Oversee Tobacco," *The Wall Street Journal*, February 23–24, 2013, B4.

93. Scott Gottlieb, "The FDA Takes on Cheerios," *The Wall Street Journal* (March 2, 2010), A23.

94. Ibid.

95. "Regulating Health Food: The Proof Is in the Pudding," *The Economist* (October 31, 2009), 17–18; NCBI, "Health Claim Regulation of Probiotics in the US and EU: Is There a Middle Way?" March 1, 2013, http://www.ncbi.nlm.nih.gov/pubmed/23257017. Accessed May 3, 2013.

96. "Pepsi Gets a Makeover: Taking the Challenge," *The Economist* (March 27, 2010), 67.

97. Ibid.

98. Nanette Byrnes, "Pepsi Brings in the Health Police," *Bloomberg Business*, January 14, 2010, http://www.businessweek.com/magazine/content/10_04/b4164050511214.htm. Accessed May 3, 2013; "Human Sustainability," PepsiCo, http://www.pepsico.com/Purpose/Human-Sus tainability.html. Accessed May 3, 2013.

99. Brent Kendall, "Skechers to Pay $50 Million to Settle Ad Suit," *The Wall Street Journal*, May 17, 2012, B3.

100. USA Today Snapshots, *USA Today*, May 29, 2012, B1.

101. USA Today Snapshots, *USA Today*, March 8, 2012, 1B.

102. Edward Wyatt, "FTC Issues Guidelines for 'Eco-friendly' Labels, New York Times, October 1, 2012, http://www.nytimes.com/2012/10/02/business/energy-environment/ftc-issues-guidelines-for-eco-friendly-labels.html. Accessed May 4, 2013.

103. "Selling Green," *The Wall Street Journal*, March 26, 2012, R8.

104. "The Green Watchdogs," *Smartmoney* (April 2010).

105. Ibid.

106. Hank Campbell, "Climate Hype Gives Way to Green Fatigue," March 4, 2013, http://www.realclearpolitics.com/2013/03/04/climate_hype_gives_way_to_quotgreen_fatiguequot_303214.html. Accessed May 3, 2013.

107. Megan Basham, "Green Fatigue," *World* (March 27, 2010), 59–60.

108. Debra L. Scammon and Jenny Mish, "From Green Marketing to Marketing for Environmental Sustainability," in Pratima Bansal and Andrew J. Hoffman (editors), *The Oxford Handbook of Business and the Natural Environment*, 2012 (Oxford: Oxford University Press), 347–402.

109. Ibid., 353.

110. Carrie McLaren, "Ad Creep," *Print* (November/December 2000), 102–107.

111. "Inserting Advertisements into Video Games Holds Much Promise," *The Economist* (June 9, 2007), 73–74.

112. Ibid.

113. "Ad Creep Creep Is Getting Creepier," March 17, 2013, http://www.buzzfeed.com/copyranter/ad-creep-creep-is-getting-creepier. Accessed May 4, 2013.

114. "A Businessperson's Guide to Federal Warranty Law," Federal Trade Commission, http://business.ftc.gov/documents/bus01-businesspersons-guide-federal-warranty-law. Accessed May 4, 2013.

115. "The Guesswork on Warranties," *BusinessWeek* (July 15, 1975), 51; "Marketing: Anti-Lemon Aid," *Time* (February, 1976), 76.

116. Ibid.

117. Amy Zuckerman, "Order in the Courts?" *World Trade* (September 2001), 26–28.

118. "Stores Make Big Profits on Warranties You Don't Need. Here's a Look at Some of the Hooey You Shouldn't Heed," *Consumer Reports Buying Guide* (2007), 8.

119. Ibid.

120. Neal Templin, "Please Spare Me the Extended Warranty," *The Wall Street Journal* (October 14, 2009), D1.

121. US News Money, "6 Reasons Why You Should Never Purchase an Extended Warranty," April 24, 2012, http://money.usnews.com/money/blogs/my-money/2012/04/24/6-reasons-why-you-should-never-purchase-an-extended-warranty. Accessed May 4, 2013.

122. LLBean, http://www.llbean.com/. Accessed May 4, 2013.

123. "Fair Packaging and Labeling Act," *Federal Trade Commission*, http://www.ftc.gov/os/statutes/fpla/outline. Accessed May 4, 2013.

124. Emily Glazer, "P&G to Alter Tide Pods Packaging," *The Wall Street Journal*, May 26-27, 2012, B3.

125. John Revill and Inti Landauro, "Horse-Meat Scandal Hits Nestle in Europe," *The* Wall Street Journal, February 20, 2113, B4.

126. Federal Trade Commission, "History of the FTC," http://www.ftc.gov/ftc/about.shtm. Accessed May 4, 2013.

127. Ibid.

128. Ibid.

129. Jim Edwards, "FTC Chief Majoras Offers a (Laissez) Faire Deal," *Brandweek* (February 5, 2007), 9.

130. Ibid.

131. Peter Stevens, Investment Geeks, "The Credit CARD Act of 2009 Summary and Effects After 3 Years," November 21, 2012, http://www.investmentgeekz.com/news/credit-card-act-2009.html. Accessed May 5, 2013.

132. "America's Consumer-Protection Bill: Sizzling Away," *The Economist* (October 24, 2009), 85–86.

133. "First, Slap Limits on Bank Leverage," *Bloomberg Businessweek* (March 22, 29, 2010), 26–27.

134. Sewell Chan, "Consumer Groups Urge Regulation of Nonbank Financial Institutions," *The New York Times* (March 6, 2010), B3.

135. Bob Herbert, "Derailing Help for Consumers," *The New York Times* (March 27, 2010), A17.

136. Semi-Annual Report of the Consumer Financial Protection Bureau, July1, 2012–December 31, 2012, March 2013, http://files.consumerfinance.gov/f/201303_CFPB_SemiAnnualReport_March2013.pdf. Accessed May 5, 2013.

137. John F. Pickering and D. C. Cousins, *The Economic Implications of Codes of Practice* (Manchester, England: University of Manchester Institute of Science and Technology, Department of Management Sciences, 1980), 17. Also see J. J. Boddewyn, "Advertising Self-Regulation: Private Government and Agent of Public Policy," *Journal of Public Policy and Marketing* (1985), 129.

138. Boddewyn, ibid., 135.

139. Better Business Bureau, "About NAD," http://www.bbb.org/us/About-NAD/. Accessed May 6, 2013.

140. Advertising Industry Self Regulation, http://www.asrcreviews.org/supporting-advertising-industry-self-regulation/. Accessed May 6, 2013.

141. Edwards, 9.

142. Better Business Bureau, "About National Advertising Division," http://www.bbb.org/us/About-NAD/. Accessed May 6, 2013.

14

Consumer Stakeholders: Product and Service Issues

S am Walton, founder of Walmart, got it right when he said, "There is only one boss. The customer. And he can fire everybody in the company from the chairman on down, simply by spending his money somewhere else."

Product information is a pivotal issue between business and consumer stakeholders, but product and service issues such as quality and safety are more central to consumers' concerns. In other words, the product or service *itself* is a more compelling issue than information about it. The quest to improve product and service quality has been driven by the demands of a competitive marketplace and an increasingly sophisticated consumer base. With product safety, an additional driving force has been the threat of product liability lawsuits and the damage these can inflict, upon both the balance sheet and the reputation. The marketers' challenge has been to meet these market-driven needs, as well as the social and ethical expectations consumers have of them.

The Toyota Motors gas pedal acceleration case provides a dramatic example of the havoc that can result from product quality and safety problems, and how these issues can take years to resolve. Toyota has long had a reputation for *quality*. Now that a *safety* issue has tarnished its reputation, we see the vital interconnection between the two issues. Two issues hurt Toyota when the public learned of the massive recalls of their cars following runaway acceleration problems.

First, there was *the problem itself*. For a company that had enjoyed a golden image and sterling reputation for many decades, it was hard to imagine that 8 million of its cars would eventually have to be recalled because of the possibility of mechanical failure (a quality and safety problem).[1] It came as such an immediate crisis that it has been called "Toyota's 'Tylenol Moment,'" in which the deaths and reports of sticking accelerators were likened to Johnson & Johnson's (J&J) Tylenol® crisis of 1982.[2]

The second issue was Toyota's *slow response*. The company had received complaints about the sticking accelerator pedals from customers in Europe beginning as early as December 2008, and started installing redesigned pedals on new vehicles there in the summer of 2009. Then, in January 2010, the company faced a pedal recall of 2.3 million cars in the United States.[3] The Toyota CEO, Akio Toyoda, eventually apologized for the company's problems, but the slow, plodding, and sometimes inept response left many consumers thinking the company had dragged its feet on an important quality and safety issue that should have been dealt with faster and better.[4] This was in contrast to how the Tylenol case was handled: the parent company J&J quickly recalled the possible cyanide-laced products on a voluntary basis and came out of the crisis looking like a hero for its fast and perceived-to-be socially responsible protection of consumers. A *USA Today*/Gallup Poll revealed that 55 percent of consumers surveyed thought Toyota did not move quickly enough in light of the danger of their products.[5]

In December 2012, Toyota finally agreed to settle a class-action lawsuit against it by agreeing to pay $1.1 billion due to the unintended acceleration of its vehicles. The previous three years of bad experiences had soured it reputation for quality and had seriously undermined its sales globally. The settlement has been said to be the largest ever facing the automotive industry and the company's costs are estimated to exceed $3 billion when all is done.[6]

The Toyota case illustrates vividly how a company's products can cause serious consequences for consumers, as well as financial and reputational harm to the company that may take years to overcome. And, most relevant here, it was all because of quality and safety issues in their products.

Consumers face many issues with companies, but this chapter focuses the discussion on product quality and safety issues. Product quality is both a business and, increasingly, an ethical issue. In connection with safety, we examine the product liability issue and the calls for tort reform. The Consumer Product Safety Commission and the Food and Drug Administration are the government's primary regulatory bodies with respect to these issues, so they are also discussed. Finally, business's response to consumer stakeholders regarding the issues introduced both in Chapter 13 and in this chapter are considered.

Two Central Issues: Quality and Safety

The two central issues—quality and safety—in this chapter represent the overwhelming attention given to product and service issues over the past decade. As the Toyota example so clearly indicates, quality and safety are not separate concepts—safety is one aspect of quality. Its importance, however, merits separate attention.

The Issue of Quality

The concept of *product* quality means different things to different people. Some consumers are interested in the composition and design of a product. Others are more concerned with the product's features, functionality, and durability. All are essential aspects of quality. In general, quality is considered the totality of characteristics and features of a product and may embrace both reality and perceptions of excellence, conformance to specifications, value, and the degree to which the product meets or exceeds the consumer's expectations.

With respect to *service* quality, customers are typically concerned that the service is performed the way expected or advertised, that it is completed on time, that all that was promised has been delivered, that courtesy was extended by the provider, and that the service was easily obtained and consistent from use to use. Some of these issues involve personal judgment and perception, and so one can see how difficult it often is to judge quality.

There are several important reasons for the current and ongoing obsession with product and service quality. A concern for quality has been driven by the average consumer household's family income and consequent demand for good value. With both adults often working outside the home, consumers expect a higher quality of life. In addition, very few have surplus time to hang around repair shops or wait at home for service representatives to show up. This results in a need for products to work as they should, to be durable and long lasting, and to be easy to maintain and fix. The Internet has also made it possible for customers to communicate with other customers about their satisfaction, or dissatisfaction, with a product, and this has heightened consumers' exchange of information and expectations.

Closely related to rising household expectations is the global competitiveness issue. Businesses now contend in a hypercompetitive landscape in which multinational strategies have given way to global strategies, and the solutions that once worked no longer will.[7] As firms jockey for position in these hypercompetitive markets, they vie to attract customers by increasing the value of the product or service. Value can be a subjective calculation, but it typically refers to a comparison of the quality received for the price spent. A Sears Craftsman spark-plug wrench that sells for $29.99 is expected to be of proportionally higher quality than a spark-plug wrench sold at Walmart or Target for $7.95. To increase value, firms try to provide higher quality than their competitors for the same price, offer the same quality at a lower price, or some combination of the two.

Each time a competitor raises the quality and/or lowers the price, other competitors scramble to catch up, and the bar is raised.[8] The greater the competition, the more firms will be jockeying for position, and the more often the bar will be raised. Firms that do not continually improve their quality are certain to be left behind. The above-mentioned story about Toyota shows how quickly, in this highly competitive atmosphere, a well-respected company can derail. Once derailed, it is difficult to catch up because of a lag in reputations. Often, consumer perceptions of quality do not catch up to actual changes in quality for years after the quality improvements have been made.[9]

Service Quality. It should be underscored that our discussion of quality here includes service as well as products. In many developed nations, economies have evolved into the mold of a service economy; and poor quality of service has become one of the great consumer frustrations of all time. Still, there is reason for hope. The American Customer Satisfaction Index has held steady for several years and actually increased slightly in some sectors.[10] This is good news for the companies performing well, because studies have shown a positive relationship between customer satisfaction and long-term stock price values.[11] It is also good news for the economy as it is striving to bounce back from a recession.

On the front line of the new economy, service—bold, fast, imaginative, and customized— is now the ultimate strategic business imperative. Consumers today often swap horror stories about poor service as a kind of ritualistic, cathartic exercise. Consider the following typical examples: repeated trips to the car dealer; poor installation of refrigerator ice makers, resulting in several visits from repair people; returned food to the supermarket, resulting in brusque treatment; fouled-up travel reservations; poorly installed carpeting; no clerk at the shoe department of your favorite department store—and on and on. Shoddy service comes at a price. One study showed that 54 percent of the people interviewed would lose all loyalty to a company that had rude or unhelpful staff. One in 10 said they would walk away if a company did not seem to listen.[12]

ETHICS IN PRACTICE CASE

The Pirated Popcorn

Last year, I worked in a local movie theater to earn money during the summer. Part of my job was to clean the theater between showings, collecting discarded cups, napkins, and popcorn tubs. I thought it was odd when my manager asked that I empty and then bring him discarded popcorn tubs that were in fairly good shape. He would then reuse them—refilling them with popcorn for unsuspecting customers.

I soon learned that the theater paid for its popcorn concession by the number of tubs it used. By reusing the tubs, the theater was able to lower its costs.

However, I was fairly certain that customers would have been upset if they knew what was happening (I knew that I would be).

1. How would you characterize the practice in which the movie theater engaged? Does this practice represent fair customer service? How are customers hurt or adversely affected?

2. Should I have followed my manager's orders and gone along with his request? Was it really such a terrible thing to do?

Dimensions of Quality. At least eight critical dimensions of product or service quality must be understood and acted upon if business is to respond strategically to this factor.[13] These include (1) performance, (2) features, (3) reliability, (4) conformance, (5) durability, (6) serviceability, (7) aesthetics, and (8) perception. *Performance* refers to a product's primary operating characteristics. For an automobile, this would include such items as handling, steering, and comfort. *Features* are the "bells and whistles" of products that supplement their basic functioning. *Reliability* reflects the probability of a product malfunctioning or failing. *Conformance* is the extent to which the product or service meets established standards. *Durability* is a measure of product life. *Serviceability* refers to the speed, courtesy, competence, and ease of repair. *Aesthetics* is a subjective factor that refers to how the product looks, feels, tastes, and so on. Finally, *perceived quality* is a subjective inference that the consumer makes on the basis of a variety of tangible and intangible product characteristics. It should be clarified that these quality dimensions are not distinct. Depending on the industry, situation, type of contract, or specification, several dimensions may be interdependent.[14] To address the issue of product or service quality, a manager must be astute enough to appreciate these different dimensions of quality and the subtle and dynamic interplays among them.

Ethical Underpinnings. An important question is whether quality is a social or an ethical issue, or just a competitive factor that business needs to emphasize to be successful in the marketplace. For many consumers, quality is seen to be something more than just a business issue. Three ethical theories based on the concept of duty that informs our understanding of the ethical dimensions of quality include (1) contractual theory, (2) due care theory, and (3) social costs view. The **contractual theory** focuses on the contractual agreement between the firm and the customer. Firms have a responsibility to comply with the terms of the sale, inform the customer about the nature of the product, avoid misrepresentation of any kind, and not coerce the customer in any way. The **due care theory** focuses on the relative vulnerability of the customer, who has less information and expertise than the firm, and the ethical responsibility that places on the firm. Customers must depend on the firm providing the product or service to live up to the claims about it and to exercise due care to avoid customer injury. The third view, **social costs**, extends beyond contractual theory and due care theory to suggest that, if a product causes harm, the firm should pay the costs of any injury, even if the firm had met the

Spotlight on Sustainability

Sustainable Product Development Is Here to Stay

Companies today are seeking to develop sustainable products. Sustainable products are made to last for an indefinite period and have the least damaging effects on the environment. They are products providing environmental, social, and economic benefits as compared with other commercial products. An excellent example are the Levi's® Eco jeans, by Levi Strauss Europe, which are designed to tap into the consumers' interest in organic and sustainable products. Levi's also brought out a line of RECYCLED blue jeans.

DuPont is another company asserting that sustainable products are here to stay. According to its survey of consumers, 89 percent say that such products meet long-term market needs. DuPont has determined that there is broad market demand for products with an enhanced environmental profile. According to DuPont, sustainable products offer the following major benefits: inherently safer materials, reduced air and water pollution, and decreased energy use. DuPont has concluded that *customer demand* is the primary driver for products with environmental benefits. Other drivers include regulatory compliance, recognition for innovation, and increased market share.

Sources: "Levi's RECYCLED Blue Jeans," Maidsoftampa Blog, http://maidsoftampa.wordpress.com/2010/04/21/levis-recycled-blue-jeans/. Accessed May 8, 2013. DuPont, "Sustainable Products Are Here to Stay," http://www2.dupont.com/inclusive-innovations/en-us/sites/default/files/Customer_survey_fact_sheet.pdf. Accessed May 8, 2013.

terms of the contract, exercised all due care, and taken all reasonable precautions. This perspective serves as the underpinning for strict liability and its extension into absolute liability, which is discussed later.[15]

The Issue of Safety

Business clearly has a duty to consumer stakeholders to sell them safe products and services. The concept of safety, in a definitional sense, means "free from harm or risk" or "secure from threat of danger, harm, or loss." Practically speaking, however, the use of virtually any consumer product or service entails some degree of risk, however remote, that harm will come to the consumer while using the product or service. Today, it is thought to be important that even financial services do not cause damage or financial harm. It is for this reason that the Consumer Financial Protection Bureau discussed in Chapter 13 was passed. An important question that never goes away is "how safe" should a product be made? Many consumers think a company has an ethical responsibility to make a product safer than legally required.

Throughout most of history the legal view that prevailed was *caveat emptor* ("let the buyer beware"). The basic idea behind this concept was that the buyer had as much knowledge of what she or he wanted as the seller and, in any event, the marketplace would punish any violators. The caveat emptor doctrine gradually lost its favor and rationale, because it was frequently impossible for the consumer to have complete knowledge about manufactured goods.[16] Today, businesses are held responsible for all products placed on the market. Thus, we have the doctrine known as *caveat vendor* (**or** *caveat venditor*)—"let the seller beware."[17]

Through a series of legal developments as well as changing societal values, business has become increasingly and significantly responsible for product safety. Court cases and legal doctrine now hold companies financially liable for harm to consumers.

Yet this still does not answer the difficult question, "How safe are manufacturers obligated to make products?" It is not possible to make products totally "risk free"; experience has shown that consumers seem to have an uncanny ability to injure themselves in novel and creative ways, many of which cannot be anticipated. The challenge to management, therefore, is to make products as safe as possible while at the same time making them affordable and useful to consumers. And consumers today expect that if products are found to be unreasonably dangerous, they will be removed from market.

Figure 14-1 presents the top ten ways companies can emphasize safety and avoid product recalls.

Today the public is concerned about a variety of potential or perceived hazards, such as the rise in genetically modified foods and the dangers of living near toxic waste dumps or nuclear plants. Food and drug scares, both real and imagined, have occupied much of the public's attention in the past several years, as questions have been raised about food safety all over the world. In Europe, the horse meat scandal has been at the top of the news. It turns out the horse meat scandal was less about food safety and more about products fraudulently being mislabeled as beef.[18]

In the United States, food safety issues, especially tainted foods, have occupied the news for years. In 2008–2009, salmonella in peanut butter was blamed for nine deaths and Peanut Corporation of America was charged with crimes linked to an alleged cover-up. In 2010 salmonella in eggs traced to Iowa farms sickened close to 2,000 people; criminal probes are still underway. In 2011, Listeriosis linked to cantaloupes from a Colorado farm was blamed for 33 deaths and, once again, a criminal probe is ongoing. In 2012, peanut butter made by Sunland, Inc. was linked to 42 cases of salmonella poisoning. The plant was shut down and the company says it is addressing the problems.[19]

The FDA Food Safety and Modernization Act of 2011, the most sweeping reform of U.S. food laws in 70 years, was signed into law in January 2011. The purpose of the legislation is to ensure that the food supply is safe by shifting from responding to contaminations to preventing them.[20] Unfortunately, the law was held in the White House Office of Management and Budget for two years, where it was rewritten in ways that weakened FDA's oversight, according to *Food Safety News*. Then, a federal judge ordered

FIGURE 14-1
Top Ten List of Product Safety Principles

According to former CPSC chair Ann Brown, the following product safety principles are straight-forward. These principles can be used by corporate decision makers and officials to give direction to their employees who have responsibility for product safety. These principles may also provide impetus to middle managers and all employees to suggest creative safety improvements for their company.

The Top Ten Product Safety Principles are:

1. Build safety into product design.
2. Do product safety testing for all foreseeable hazards.
3. Keep informed about and implement latest developments in product safety.
4. Educate consumers about product safety.
5. Track and address your products' safety performance.
6. Fully investigate product safety incidents.
7. Report product safety defects promptly.
8. If a defect occurs, promptly offer a comprehensive recall plan.
9. Work with the Consumer Product Safety Commission (CPSC) to make sure your recall is effective.
10. Learn from mistakes—yours and others'.

Source: U.S. Consumer Product Safety Commission, "CPSC Chairman Ann Brown Unveils Product Safety Initiative," October 5, 2000, http://www.cpsc.gov/en/Newsroom/News-Releases/2001/CPSC-Chairman-Ann-Brown-Unveils-Product-Safety-Initiative/. Accessed May 8, 2013.

the FDA to work with two food-safety advocacy groups to create a new timetable which would speed up the process. One food safety expert has observed that companies have no reason to slack off on food safety because they will be legally liable and should have a strong economic incentive to inspect their own products and avoid outbreaks.[21]

Product safety is of paramount concern in all manufacturing industries, as the Toyota recalls discussed earlier illustrate. Other recent recalls have involved medical-device flaws such as defibrillator wires, surgical vaginal mesh, and metal hip joints.[22] Manufactured products create hazards not only because of unsafe product design, but also as a result of consumers being given inadequate information regarding the hazards associated with using the products. Consequently, in product liability claims, it is not surprising to find

---

ETHICS IN PRACTICE CASE

Has "Pink Slime" Gotten a Bad Rap?

In the early 1990s, Eldon Roth started a meat processing company named Beef Products, Inc. (BPI). The company would buy tons of fatty meat scrap that was left over after cattle were carved into steaks and roasts. Roth developed a centrifuge that would spin the fat away. The remaining product was then treated with a puff of ammonia hydroxide as a safety measure to kill bacteria. This concoction was frozen into a pink pulp that, when mixed in with ground beef, made it leaner. The product became known as "lean finely textured beef" or LFTB in the industry. Roth's company would then package the product in the form of frozen bricks and sell them to companies as an additive to ground beef, making the resulting beef leaner and cheaper. Among others, McDonald's, Burger King, Taco Bell, Kroger and Walmart were clients.

Roth's company was so successful that it opened plants in Kansas, Texas, Iowa and Nebraska, employing about 1,500 workers. In fall, 2011, Roth was inducted into the Meat Industry Hall of Fame. Roth had been called a genius who ran a company that was on the vanguard of food safety.

In March 2012, someone labeled Roth's product "pink slime" and a food blogger launched an online petition to have it removed from the federal lunch program. ABC News and other media jumped on the story and soon the product was being assailed as unsafe and gross as the story went viral on the blogosphere. As media scrutiny increased, many customers quickly abandoned his product. Roth was forced to suspend production at three plants and lay off half his workers. He is now working hard to keep his company afloat.

After the ABC News reports, BPI initiated an extensive PR campaign seeking to get the truth out. BPI also filed a $1.2 billion lawsuit against ABC News and the reporters. The company claimed more than 200 false or disparaging statements were made about BPI.

For the record, LFTB is not an unsafe product, even in the eyes of food safety advocates. It is an ingredient most of us have eaten many times. The USDA insisted the product was safe but left schools to decide whether to buy meat with or without the textured beef. Iowa Governor Terry Branstad, whose state hosts a BPI plant, said he would call for a congressional investigation of the "smear campaign" against BPI.

1. How can a product that has been characterized as "lean" and less expensive be treated in this way?
2. Do you think LFTB and Roth's company has been treated fairly? Has this product gotten a bad rap by overzealous media reporters and critics?
3. Should those who labeled the product "pink slime" and questioned it unfairly be disciplined in any way? Or, is this just an example of the "market at work" and nothing should be done?
4. What should Roth and his company do now? What further action should the USDA, state governors or other officials take to ensure fair treatment?

Sources: "'Pink Slime' Uproar Overshadows More Serious Food Safety Threats," *USA Today*, April 17, 2012, 8A; "Was a Food Innovator Unfairly Targeted?" *Bloomberg Businessweek*, April 16–22, 2012, 18–20; "Lean Beef or Pink Slime? It's All in a Name," *USA Today*, April 2, 2012, 8A; Josh Sanburn, "One Year Later, the Makers of 'Pink Slime' Are Hanging on and Fighting Back," *Time*, March 6, 2013, http://business.time.com/2013/03/06/one-year-later-the-makers-of-pink-slime-are-hanging-on-and-fighting-back/. Accessed May 13, 2013.

charges based on one or more of several allegations. First may be the charge that the product was improperly manufactured, wherein the producer failed to exercise due care in the product's production, which contributed directly to the accident or injury. Second could be the charge that, though manufactured properly, the product's design could have been defective, in that alternative designs or devices, if used at the time of manufacture, may have prevented the accident. Third, could be that the producer failed to provide satisfactory instructions and/or warnings that could have helped avert accident or injury. Fourth, may be that the producer failed to foresee a reasonable and anticipated misuse of the product and warn against such misuse.[23]

To appreciate the "big picture" of dangerous products, it should be noted that the Consumer Product Safety Commission keeps track of injuries treated in hospital emergency rooms and has identified the following categories of consumer products as being the most frequently associated with hospital-treated injuries:[24]

- Sports and Recreation
- Toys and Children's Products
- Fuel, Lighters and Fireworks
- Furniture and Décor
- Home Maintenance and Construction
- Kitchen and Dining

Whether we deal with consumer products (where there is potential for harm following accidents or misuse) or with food products (where not-so-visible threats to human health may exist), the field of product safety is a significant responsibility and a growing challenge for the business community. No matter how careful business is with regard to these issues, product liability lawsuits have become an industry unto themselves, one intimately linked with product safety discussions. Therefore, we now turn our attention to this vital topic. Product liability has been a monumental consumer issue in the United States for several reasons.

Product Liability

In recent years, the product liability issue (sometimes called products liability), has been one of the most important legal and ethical responsibilities businesses have faced. What is at stake is the responsibility for harm caused by products. **Product liability**, as a legal concept, includes the liability of any or all parties in the chain of manufacture of a product for any damage caused by that product. This includes the manufacture, assembly, wholesaling and retailing of the product. Products containing defects that result in harm to a consumer or someone to whom the product was loaned or given are the subjects of product liability lawsuits.[25]

Reasons for Concern about Product Liability. Product, or products, liability has become a major issue because of the sheer number of cases involving products that have resulted in illness, harm, or death. More than in other countries, U.S. residents tend to file lawsuits and pursue litigation when faced with situations in which they are harmed or dissatisfied.

Another cause for concern has been the size of the financial awards that have been given by the courts. The path-breaking award in the product liability category was the $128.5 million awarded in 1978 in the case of a 19-year-old who at age 13 was severely injured. He was riding with a friend in a Ford Pinto that was hit from behind. The Pinto's gas tank ruptured, and the passenger compartment was filled with flames, killing his friend, and causing burns over 90 percent of his body. The badly scarred teenager underwent more than 50 operations. The jury sought from Ford $666,280 for the dead driver's family and $2.8 million in compensatory damages and $125 million in punitive damages for the survivor.[26] The Pinto case was the beginning, but the awards grew after that. Product liability lawsuits seem to increase in number and size of award as the years pass. The verdicts would indicate that jurors are more inclined to take the side of their fellow citizens, perhaps due to the economic recession, the blame for which many lay at the feet of Wall Street and big business.[27]

It has been estimated that litigation's cost to society is more than $250 billion per year, more than half of which goes to legal fees and costs, and some of which could be spent to hire more teachers, police officers, and fire fighters.[28] The cost of litigation to companies has been said to represent approximately 30 percent of a stepladder's price, 50 percent of a football helmet, and 95 percent of the price of a childhood vaccine. The problem is largely confined to the United States; which is a litigious society. One major study showed that the money firms now pay on lawsuit settlements, damage awards, insurance lawyers and legal defense costs is money they no longer have available to spend on improvements in their processes and products. This decrease in innovation due to tort litigation carries lasting consequences for competitiveness.[29]

Since the Pinto case, multimillion-dollar lawsuits have become commonplace. Over the years, some major companies have been hit so hard by lawsuits that they have filed for protection under Chapter 11 of the federal bankruptcy law. One classic example of this is the Johns Manville Corporation, which faced an avalanche of asbestos-related lawsuits totaling 16,500 suits demanding over $12 billion.[30] Another well-known case is that of A.H. Robins, which filed for protection after facing over 5,000 product liability lawsuits in which women charged that its Dalkon Shield, an intrauterine contraceptive device, had injured them.[31] Dow Chemical, the principal manufacturer of silicone breast implants, entered Chapter 11 bankruptcy due to lawsuits.[32] Other companies encountering large lawsuits have included Union Carbide, with its poison gas leak in Bhopal, India; Dow Chemical, with its Agent Orange defoliant; and Bridgestone/Firestone, with its defective tires. As mentioned earlier in the chapter, one of the largest product liability lawsuits in history occurred when Toyota Motor Corp. recently settled a class action lawsuit against it for $1.1 billion. The Deepwater Horizon Claims Center, which is handling the multi-billion dollar settlement for the BP oil spill, has already paid out more than $2 billion in settlements to individuals and businesses.[33]

Doctrine of Strict Liability. The key legal concept in product liability cases is the **doctrine of strict liability**. In its most general form, the doctrine of strict liability holds that anyone in the value chain of a product is liable for harm caused to the user if the product, as sold, was unreasonably dangerous because of its defective condition. This applies to anyone involved in the design, manufacture, or sale of a defective product. Beyond manufacturing, courts have ruled against defendants representing a broad array of functions, such as selling, advertising, promotion, and distribution.[34] For example, the Department of Transportation (DOT) holds warehouses liable for violations of hazardous materials regulations even when the warehouse relied on information provided by the customer (the depositor) when documenting the shipment.[35] In short, there is no legal defense for placing on the market a product that is dangerous to a consumer because of a known or knowable defect, unless the strict liability is imposed by a statute that allows for an argument of due diligence.[36] To prove due diligence, a company must take every possible precautionary step and follow all industry standards.

The doctrine of strict liability and the expansion of this concept in the courts have been at the heart of the litigation explosion in the United States. As mentioned previously, the social costs view of product quality underlies the concept of strict liability and its extensions. In addition, some hold the strict liability view as utilitarian; that is, society has made a determination that it is better to hold persons responsible for certain actions even without a showing of negligence because the benefits derived (e.g., safety, improved products, accountability) outweigh the burden placed on the defendant in a strict liability lawsuit. In the area of consumer product development, strict liability laws have fostered meaningful safety developments that have prevented innumerable deaths and injuries. Strict liability is not without its cost, however, and the price of consumer goods today reflects this cost-shifting consequence.[37]

Extensions of Strict Liability Rule. Courts in several states and certain countries have established a standard that is much more demanding than strict liability. This concept is known as **absolute liability**. The ruling that established this concept was handed down by the New Jersey Supreme Court in *Beshada v. Johns Manville Corporation* (1982). The plaintiffs in the Beshada case were employees of Johns Manville and other companies who had developed asbestos-related diseases as a result of workplace exposure.[38] The court ruled in this case that a manufacturer could be held *strictly liable* for failure to warn of a product hazard, even if the hazard was scientifically unknowable at the time of manufacture and sale. Therefore, a company cannot use as its defense the claim that it did its best according to the state of the art in the industry at that time. Under this ruling, the manufacturer is liable for damages even if it had no way of knowing that the product might cause a problem later. This has led to what *The Wall Street Journal* termed the "asbestos tort blob," named for the movie *The Blob*, which features a creature that devours everything in its path.[39]

Although the United States has been rightly termed the litigation nation, other countries struggle with the issue as well. For example, the Supreme Court of India upheld the absolute liability of a common carrier, in this case Patel Roadways Ltd., for goods destroyed by fire. The court ruled that, in the case of damage or loss, it is not necessary for the plaintiff to establish negligence.[40] Similarly, leading charities in Great Britain have pressured the prime minister to institute a system of strict financial and legal liability before genetically modified crops can be introduced there.[41]

The absolute liability rule frequently involves cases having to do with chemicals or drugs. For example, a producer might put a drug on the market (with government approval) thinking that it is safe on the basis of current knowledge. Under the doctrine of absolute liability, the firm could be held liable for side effects or health problems that develop years, or even decades, later. The result is that a large amount of uncertainty is injected into the production process.[42] Furthermore, the company's association with the damaging product may be tenuous at best. Decades ago, Crown Cork and Seal, Inc. (CCS), had a brief connection with Mundet Cork Company, a maker of cork-lined bottle caps. Unfortunately for CCS, Mundet also owned a small insulation company. Crown Cork's $7 million investment in Mundet led to thousands of asbestos-related claims filed against it and over $350 million in asbestos-related payments.[43] The asbestos litigation now ranks as the longest running mass tort litigation in the United States. A bill to set up an asbestos trust fund failed in 2006 even as asbestos filings were increasing.[44] More than a half million claims are expected to be filed in the coming years.[45]

Another extension of strict liability is known as **market share liability**. This concept evolved from **delayed manifestation cases**—situations in which delayed reactions to products appear years later after consumption of, or exposure to, the product.[46] Market share liability was derived from the California case in which a group of women with birth defects claimed that the defects had been caused by the drug DES, which their mothers had taken while pregnant years earlier. The women could not name the company that had made the pills their mothers had taken. But in 1980, the California Supreme Court upheld a ruling that the six drug firms that made DES would be held responsible in proportion to their market shares of DES sales unless they could prove that they had not made the actual doses the women had taken.[47] When this verdict was reached, the business press expressed alarm about the potential impact of the decision. Their concern, however, was premature. With very few exceptions, market share liability has been rejected in subsequent non-DES cases and in second-generation DES cases. DES was uniquely suited for delayed manifestation cases because it was a generic product, the entire industry used the same formula, and it was marketed and promoted generically by all industry members. Efforts to apply the concept to cases involving asbestos products, blood products, breast implants, DPT vaccines, polio vaccines, multi-piece tire rims, lead-based paints, and benzene all failed.[48]

Product liability law can be very complex and managers should seek legal advice when faced with uncertain situations. The recommended course of action, of course, is to create safe products and be guided by law and ethics in all phases of the design, production, and distribution process.

Product Tampering and Product Extortion. Two other concerns that have contributed to the product liability discussion are *product tampering* and *product extortion*. The most well known cases involved Tylenol in the 1980s—first in 1982, when seven Chicago people died from taking tainted Tylenol® Extra Strength capsules, and again in 1986, when cyanide-laced bottles of Tylenol were found in New York, and one woman died as a result. James Burke, J&J chairperson at the time, characterized the case as "terrorism, pure and simple."[49] In response to these and other incidents, firms began to employ tamper-evident packaging. Although improvements in packaging have slowed the rate of pharmaceutical product tampering, they have not stopped it. Two Australian pharmaceutical manufacturers received threats from extortionists who were believed to have bought over-the-counter analgesics, poisoned them with strychnine, and returned them to the shelves. Four people were hospitalized, and nationwide product recalls cost the firms millions of dollars.[50]

Adulterated and poisoned products stretch beyond pharmaceuticals. After the 9/11 terrorist attacks, product-tampering concerns centered on anthrax and the possible ways it could be used for extortion and terror. When attorneys at Stoel Rives in Portland, Oregon, mailed 50,000 cards in envelopes with bumpy seeds, some recipients became so scared they dialed 911. Publisher's Clearinghouse mailed packages of powdered detergent to customers, causing alarm in the process.[51] Now that the furor over mail has subsided, attention has shifted to ways in which terrorists might tamper with the food or water supply. Since the 9/11 attacks, food companies have spent hundreds of millions of dollars to upgrade security, institute employee background checks, and install lights and video cameras.[52] In spite of these efforts, some incidents continue to occur.[53]

Product Liability Reform. The problems discussed up to this point have combined to generate calls from many groups for **product liability reform**, also known as **tort reform**. A tort is an act that injures someone in some way, and for which the injured person may sue the wrongdoer for damages. Legally, torts are civil wrongs, not criminal wrongs.[54] The U.S. tort system costs Americans billions of dollars every year. The total estimated cost for a recent year was $252 billion—almost $1,000 for every person in the country. Built into the price of every product is a component to pay for liability insurance and lawsuit defense. Tort risks are the second most important factor when a company decides where to relocate, expand operations, build a new plant, or introduce a new product.[55]

With the recent changes in health care law, many experts believe that changes in tort law are also needed as part of the process of bringing health care costs under control.

However, not everyone agrees that tort reform is needed. On one side are business groups, medical associations, local and state governments, and insurance companies that want to change the system they claim gives costly and unfair advantage to plaintiffs in liability suits. On the other side are consumer groups and trial lawyers who defend the current system as one that protects the constitutional rights of wrongfully injured parties.[56]

The business community's criticisms of the current system illustrate some of the aspects of the controversy. Currently, there is a patchwork of state laws, with the law varying significantly from state to state. Business wants a uniform federal code. It also argues for no punitive damages unless the plaintiff meets tougher standards of proof. Business thinks it should have an absolute shield against punitive damages for drugs, medical devices, and aircraft that meet government regulations. Business also wants a cap placed on how high punitive awards can be. Finally, business wants victorious plaintiffs to be able to recover damages only to the extent that defendants are liable.[57]

On the other side of the issue are consumer and citizen groups and others who support the current system. They say the critics of the product liability laws have exaggerated the problems. These supporters of the current system point out that some of the most infamous injuries inflicted on consumers were remedied mainly through lawsuits, not regulatory action. Examples include the Dalkon Shield, a contraceptive device that made thousands of women infertile; the Pinto's exploding gas tank; the damage to workers exposed to asbestos; tobacco cases; and many lesser-known cases.[58] According to Ralph Nader, trial lawyers are "all that is left to require wrongdoers to be held accountable."[59]

The debate over product liability reform is ongoing. Business claims the current system is inherently inefficient, raises the costs of litigation, and imposes a hidden tax on consumers because it inhibits innovation and dampens competitiveness. Consumer groups argue that the current system has forced companies to make safer products and listen to their customers. Studies show that both sides have valid arguments. The laws have spurred some safety improvements, but they have also hampered innovation.[60] From an ethical perspective, if businesses internalize the notion of product safety and take responsibility for the products and services they sell, the need for legal redress is precluded and the entire business–consumer relationship is far better served.

There are two major government agencies that are dedicated to product safety and both of them have become more activist in recent years—the Consumer Product Safety Commission and the Food and Drug Administration.

Consumer Product Safety Commission

The **Consumer Product Safety Commission (CPSC)** is an independent regulatory agency that was created by the Consumer Product Safety Act of 1972. CPSC works to reduce the risk of injuries and deaths from consumer products by:[61]

1. developing voluntary standards with industry,
2. issuing and enforcing mandatory standards,
3. banning consumer products if no feasible standard would adequately protect the public,
4. obtaining the recall of products or arranging for their repair,
5. conducting research on potential product hazards, and
6. informing and educating consumers through the media, state and local governments, private organizations, and by responding to consumer inquiries.

Figure 14-2 summarizes the Mission, Vision and Goals of the CPSC for the period 2011–2016.

FIGURE 14-2   **Consumer Product Safety Commission (CPSC) Strategic Plan—2011–2016**

MISSION	Protecting the public against unreasonable risks of injury from consumer products through education, safety standards activities, regulation, and enforcement.
VISION	The CPSC is the recognized global leader in consumer product safety.
GOALS	
Goal 1	**Leadership in Safety** Take a leadership role in identifying and addressing the most pressing consumer product safety priorities and mobilizing action by our partners.
Goal 2	**Commitment to Prevention** Engage public and private sector stakeholders to build safety into consumer products.
Goal 3	**Rigorous Hazard Identification** Ensure timely and accurate detection of consumer product safety risks to inform agency priorities.
Goal 4	**Decisive Response** Use the CPSC's full range of authorities to quickly remove hazards from the marketplace.
Goal 5	**Raising Awareness** Promote a public understanding of product risks and CPSC capabilities.

Source: U.S. Consumer Product Safety Commission Strategic Plan—2011–2016, http://www.cpsc .gov//PageFiles/123374/2011strategic.pdf. Accessed May 13, 2013.

The CPSC was created at the zenith of the consumer movement as a result of initiatives taken in the late 1960s. Over the decades, the CPSC has experienced ups and downs and various degrees of activism as various administrations came into office. During some administrations, it was significantly bolstered in its power and budget, and during other administrations, it was downplayed and underemphasized. As with all government agencies, their directors are appointed by the presidents in office at the time and their powers are greatly affected by the budgets given to them by Congress.

In 2009, President Obama appointed a new chair of the CPSC, Inez Moore Tenenbaum. Obama also promised to expand the commission to five members from three and expand its budget significantly. Over the previous years, the CPSC had been criticized for failing to strictly enforce product safety laws, especially those relating to lead content in children's toys. The commission's lax enforcement of these laws was highlighted by scandals involving lead-tainted toys and other defective imports from China. The previous chair and her board have been criticized for being too close to the companies they are supposed to regulate. The CPSC also had been criticized for its slow response to the Chinese drywall problem. For months, homeowners in many different states had complained that the drywall material emits sulfur fumes that fill homes with a "rotten eggs" odor. Finally, a bill was passed that banned any future use of drywall imported from China.[62]

Since Tenenbaum became chair of the CPSC, it has become more activist and has introduced a number of new priorities, including an official blog titled *OnSafety* (http://www.cpsc.gov/onsafety/) that reports the latest product safety information that consumers might need. By 2013, some of the product safety issues being closely watched by the CPSC included infant sleep posturing devices, cadmium in jewelry, swimming pool safety, baby monitors, portable cribs, play pens, ATVs, window screens and blinds, batteries and magnets, fireworks, and spas.[63] Consumers may now connect with these safety warnings on YouTube, Twitter, Flickr, Podcast, and RSS Feed, as well as the blog.[64]

The **Consumer Product Safety Improvement Act (CPSIS) of 2008** is the most recent piece of legislation given to the CPSC for enforcement. This Act provided the CPSC with new regulatory and enforcement tools. CPSIA addresses, among other things, lead, phthalates, toy safety, third-party testing and certification, imports, ATVs, civil and criminal penalties and SaferProducts.gov. It also repeals a funding limitation on the number of CPSC commissioners.[65]

The CPSC continues to play an important role in protecting consumers from unsafe products. The CPSC remains the only clearinghouse available for consumers who have safety concerns with the more than 15,000 products under its care, and it is the only mechanism available for recalling unsafe products. Funding has always been a challenge for the CPSC and this will probably never change. There are always new arrays of products that require monitoring. In its 2014 planned budget, for example, the director proposed new funding for CPSC's import surveillance program, nanotechnology research, outreach and education for small businesses, operating an integrated information technology system, and enhancing the technology capabilities of its testing and evaluation center to benefit the health and safety of consumers.[66]

Food and Drug Administration

The **Food and Drug Administration (FDA)** grew out of experiments with food safety by one man—Harvey W. Wiley—chief chemist for the agricultural department in the late 1800s. Wiley's most famous experiments involved feeding small doses of poisons to human volunteers. The substances fed to the volunteers were similar to those found in food preservatives at the time. The volunteers became known as the "Poison Squad," and their publicity generated a public awareness of the dangers of eating adulterated foods. The **Food and Drugs Act of 1906** was a direct result of the publicity created by Wiley's experiments. The act was administered by Wiley's Bureau of Chemistry until 1931, when the name "Food and Drug Administration" first was used. Today, the FDA resides within the Health and Human Services Department and engages in three broad categories of activity: analysis, surveillance, and correction.

Today, the FDA has broad responsibilities as it regulates:

- Foods
- Human Prescription and Non-prescription Drugs
- Vaccines, Blood products, and other Biologics
- Medical devices
- Electronic products
- Cosmetics
- Veterinary products
- Tobacco products[67]

Figure 14-3 provides information about the FDA and its strategic priorities.

FIGURE 14-3   The Food & Drug Administration (FDA)–Strategic Priorities—2011–2015

FDA Overview	The U.S. FDA is the agency within the U.S. Department of Health and Human Services (HHS) responsible for ensuring the safety and effectiveness of products that account for about 20 cents of every dollar spent by American consumers each year—products that touch the lives of every American every day. These include human and animal drugs, 80 percent of the food supply, biological products, medical devices, cosmetics, radiation-emitting products, and tobacco products.
FDA Mission	FDA is charged with protecting the public health by ensuring the safety, effectiveness, and security of human and veterinary drugs, biological products, and medical devices; ensuring the safety of foods, cosmetics, and radiation-emitting products; and regulating tobacco products.
Mission Specifics	Specifically, FDA is responsible for advancing the public health by: • Helping to speed innovations that make foods safer and make medicines and devices safer and more effective; • Ensuring the public has accurate, science-based information they need to use medicines, devices, and foods to improve their health; • Regulating the manufacture, marketing, and distribution of tobacco products and reducing tobacco use by minors; and, • Addressing the Nation's counterterrorism capability and ensuring the security of the supply of foods and medical products.
FDA Vision	FDA is dedicated to world-class excellence as a science-based regulatory agency with a public health mission. We aim to provide effective and innovative leadership—both domestically and internationally—to protect health, prevent illness, prolong life, and promote wellness
Guiding Principles	These principles govern our deliberations, decision making, and actions and provide the framework for our interactions within FDA, with the public, and with other FDA stakeholders. • Science-Based Decision Making • Innovation/Collaboration • Transparency • Accountability

Source: U.S. Food & Drug Administration, About FDA–Strategic Priorities, http://www.fda.gov/AboutFDA/ReportsManuals-Forms/Reports/ucm227527.htm. Accessed May 13, 2013.

The FDA, like the CPSC, has been controversial over the decades, and its zeal in pursuing its mission has varied widely depending on the administration in office.

In 2009, under President Obama, Margaret A. Hamburg, M.D. was confirmed as commissioner.[68] In 2010, Hamburg expressed concerns over the challenges and opportunities ahead in ensuring safe food and drug imports into the United States. By 2013, Hamburg's and the FDA's major initiatives included globalization, advancing regulatory science, food safety, tobacco, innovation, and transparency.[69]

Two issues have been of considerable interest to consumers today—food safety and tobacco. With food safety, the **Food Safety Modernization Act** (FSMA) gave the FDA a mandate to develop a science-based food safety system that addresses hazards from farm to table—putting greater emphasis on prevention of foodborne illness. The FSMA has been said to be the most sweeping reform in food safety laws in 70 years and was signed into law in January 2011. Its aim is to ensure that the U.S. food supply is safe by shifting the focus from responding to contamination to preventing it.[70] Unfortunately, according to *Food Safety News*, the FSMA sat with the White House Office of Management and Budget for two years, where it was rewritten in ways that weakened the FDA's oversight. However, a federal judge has ordered the FDA to work with two food safety advocacy groups to accelerate the timetable for the law's implementation.[71]

In recent years, outbreaks of food poisoning have included salmonella in peanut butter (2009), salmonella in eggs (2010), Listeriosis in cantaloupes (2011), and salmonella in peanut butter again (2012).[72] In 2013, the FDA proposed extensive food safety rules which would step up hygiene standards to prevent crop contamination, as the agency is seeking to prevent bacterial outbreaks.[73] With respect to tobacco, passage of the **Family Smoking Prevention and Tobacco Control Act** in 2009 gave FDA the authority to regulate the manufacture, distribution, and marketing of tobacco products to protect public health.[74] In 2013, a veteran tobacco industry critic was named the industry's chief regulator and it was expected that the FDA would begin even tougher oversight of the tobacco companies. On the agenda were recommendations for regulating electronic cigarettes and cigars, and more stringent curbs on menthol cigarettes.[75]

Business's Response to Consumer Stakeholders

Business's response to consumerism and consumer stakeholders has varied over the years. It has ranged from poorly conceived public relations ploys at one extreme to well-designed and implemented programs focusing on customer relations, customer satisfaction, customer relationship management and programs focusing on quality such as TQM and Six Sigma at the other. The history of business's response to consumers parallels its perceptions of the seriousness, pervasiveness, effectiveness, and longevity of the consumer movement. When the consumer movement first began, business's response was casual, perhaps symbolic, and hardly effective. Today, the consumer movement has matured, and formal interactions with consumer stakeholders have become more and more institutionalized. Business has realized that consumers today are more persistent than in the past, more assertive, and more likely to use or exhaust all appeal channels before being satisfied. Armed with considerable power, consumer activists have been a major stimulus for more sincere efforts on behalf of business to provide consumers with a forum. These efforts have included the creation of toll-free hot lines, user-friendly Web sites, and consumer service representatives. Today, virtually all successful companies have customer service programs, irrespective of whether they are selling products or services.

Customer Service Programs

It is ironic that the United States is said to now be a service economy, and yet poor customer service seems to be a topic on every consumer's mind today. In recent years, retailers of all types have been pushing the idea of self-service. Many consumers continue to be upset with how businesses keep pushing this concept, whether it be checking out your own groceries, following a computer voice protocol to fix your own cable TV problem, printing your own boarding pass at the air terminal kiosk, or pumping your own gas (except in New Jersey and Oregon where pumping your own gas is forbidden by state law). One writer recently exclaimed "Are we entering a dark, deeply un-American era when we literally have to do everything for ourselves?"[76] But, the other type of consumer dissatisfaction is simply with the way merchants and retailers who claim they are doing things for you, don't do a very good job and sometimes behave unethically.

Even McDonald's Corporation has recently said its own service is broken (rude and unfriendly employees, slow service) and is tackling a major repair job.[77] Companies seem to always be finding new ways to stick the consumer with lousy service.[78]

In spite of customer frustrations with poor to erratic service, consumers today continue to expect high-quality, safe products, and responsive customer service regarding the products and services they buy. Nothing is more frustrating than spending money on a product only to encounter after-sale problems or issues that are not quickly and easily remedied. Experts today argue that companies should strive to develop loyal customers who will always come back, and that the key to customer retention is customer service. Building life-long devotion among customers takes serious commitment and hard work. It also requires that a company create a culture and employ workers who are motivated and committed to delivering outstanding service.

P&G faced a customer relations nightmare when it introduced its new Pampers® diapers. Some consumers said they caused rashes, and even "chemical burns," on their children. Angry consumers even started a crusade against the company on Facebook, and P&G had a delicate line to navigate as it tried to be responsive to consumer concerns and also defend its product, which it claimed was not defective. One strategy P&G followed was to add more customer-service representatives so they could more effectively deal with irate consumers.[79] Since the worldwide economic recession, however, it seems that companies have cut back on customer service employees rather than increasing their numbers.

Companies address customer service in a variety of ways, and it is often dependent on the nature of the products or services and the competitiveness of the market that drive commitment on the part of companies. Companies provide customer service through money-back guarantees, warranties, and offices of consumer affairs, in which are found customer service representatives whose full time job it is to make customers happy. The effective execution of customer service depends on a host of factors, but it is absolutely critical that top management be committed to providing a service as part of its ongoing relationship with the consumer. Management's job is to attract, maintain, and retain customers, and this requires a high degree of dedication and commitment. One merchant which has done a remarkable job at customer service is The Vermont Country Store. It has built its high level customer service around its own "Customer's Bill of Rights." Its first two customer's rights include (1) the right to expect polite and courteous service and (2) the right to always be treated as a priority. Its other customer's rights effectively cover almost any possible concern a customer might have.[80]

There are many principles that drive high-quality customer service, and many guidelines for creating a customer-oriented company. Figure 14-4 presents some key customer service principles and guidelines for developing customer-oriented companies. If companies followed these, customers would justifiably think they have been treated fairly.

Programs such as TQM and Six Sigma have become important strategic responses to product quality and safety issues. These responses merit brief consideration.

Total Quality Management Programs

Total Quality Management (TQM) has many different characteristics, but it essentially means that all of the functions of the business are blended into a holistic, integrated philosophy built around the concepts of quality, teamwork, productivity, customer understanding, and satisfaction.[81] The purpose of TQM is to satisfy customers by focusing on product quality and safety issues. To be successful, a strong TQM program needs to employ principles, practices and techniques that focus on the customer, use continuous improvement, and employ teamwork.[82] It should be noted that the customer, or

FIGURE 14-4

Customer Service Principles and Customer-Oriented Companies

Seven Principles of Customer Service[a]

1. **Keeping your word is where it all begins**. Keeping your word builds trust. Trust is the foundation of all successful relationships.

2. **Always be honest and tell it like it is**. By being honest and telling your customers the truth, you are much more likely to get a positive response to any situation.

3. **Always think proactively, looking around the corner**. Thinking proactively when it comes to customer service boils down to addressing concerns prior to you having to hear from the customer that something needs to be done.

4. **Deal with problems as best you can yourself, never passing the buck**. The more authority employees have to address customer problems, the better it is, because nothing upsets customers more than being passed from department to department.

5. **Do not argue with a customer because it is a lose/lose situation**. The best question to ask yourself is:

What can be done to make the customer feel happy and cared for?

6. **Accept your mistakes, learn from them, and do not repeat them**. Accept that you have made a mistake, evaluate the situation, learn the lesson, and move on. Don't get stuck in an indefinite state of denial.

7. **Consistency is the name of the game for lasting success**. When the customer service principles discussed above are practiced consistently, customers realize over time that the integrity of how you choose to run your business is not to be compromised.

Creating a Customer-Oriented Company[b]

1. Top-down culture and commitment are essential.
2. Identify internal champions and uphold them.
3. Commit resources to the task.
4. Hire the right people.
5. Empower your employees.
6. Make customer service training a priority.

---

[a]Summarized from Imran Rahman, "Seven Service Principles Guaranteed to Create Raving Fans," http://www.dreammanifesto.com/service-principles-guaranteed-create-raving-fans.html. Accessed May 13, 2013.
[b]Summarized from John Allen, "Creating a Service-Oriented Company Takes Commitment," *Houston Business Journal* (April 10, 2009), http://www.gnapartners.com/system/files/private/Creating%20a%20service%20oriented%20company%20takes%20commitment.pdf. Accessed May 13, 2013.

consumer stakeholder, is at the center of the process. Efforts to show a relationship between TQM and financial performance have met with mixed results.[83] The positive impact TQM can have on safety in the workplace, in contrast, has been established.[84]

According to the American Society for Quality (ASQ), a global community of people interested in quality, TQM has a number of established benefits. Some of these include strengthened competitive position, elimination of defects and waste, reduced costs, enhanced market position, and improved customer focus and satisfaction.[85] To be successful, TQM must emphasize eight key elements—Ethics, Integrity, Trust, Training, Teamwork, Leadership, Recognition, and Communication. The first three—Ethics, Integrity, and Trust—constitute the foundation on which all else is built. These three elements foster openness, fairness, and sincerity, and they create the foundation for involvement by everyone.[86]

A vital assumption and premise of TQM is that the customer is the final judge of quality. Therefore, the first part of the TQM process is to define quality in terms of customer expectations and requirements. Quality means different things to different people, and this makes its achievement challenging, but the four attributes of quality that most often seem to be used are *excellence, value, conformance to specifications* and *meeting and/or exceeding expectations*.[87] It is important to remember that customers' perceived quality is not always the same as actual quality and so firms may have to wait for customers to realize that genuine quality improvements have been made.[88]

Opportunities for recognition have helped to propel quality efforts. In the United States and the rest of the industrialized world, the Malcolm Baldrige Award, ISO 9000, and the Deming Quality Award have enhanced the reputations of firms that undertake quality initiatives and complete them successfully. Unfortunately, TQM became a management buzzword, and many of its slogans, such as "Getting it right the first time," were viewed as clichés. It is against this backdrop that other tools developed and became popular, such as Just in Time (JIT) strategy and Business Process Reengineering (BPR). Recently, some analysts have argued that sustainability and TQM are intimately related.

The need for a more rigorous definition of quality was part of the appeal of Six Sigma, which is briefly described.

Six Sigma Strategy and Process

Six Sigma is a development within TQM that has become a way of life for many corporations. *Sigma* is a statistical measure of variation from the mean; higher values of sigma mean fewer defects. The six-sigma level of operation is 3.4 defects per million. Most companies operate around the four-sigma level, that is, 6,000 defects per million.[89]

Six Sigma also is viewed as a general heading under which is grouped a body of strategies, methodologies, and techniques. Scarcely a week goes by without a major corporation adopting Six Sigma as a way of improving quality and reducing costs.[90] Accenture, 3M, Alcoa, Apple Computers, Caterpillar, DuPont, and Ford Motor Company are but a few of the major corporations that have adopted the Six Sigma methodology.[91] Although some deride Six Sigma as "TQM on steroids," it has brought new commitment and energy to the quest for quality in the new millennium. It is even said to have brought "more prominence to the quality world than it has enjoyed since the glory days of the mid-1980s."[92]

Motorola first developed Six Sigma, and Allied Signal later experimented with it, but most observers believe that GE perfected it. One of Six Sigma's strengths has been the clarity of the process and the steps companies must take to adopt it. However, Six Sigma is more than a toolbox with clear instructions. The program also represents a philosophy that stresses the importance of customers as well as careful measurement. Six Sigma practitioners look for facts rather than opinions, and they believe in fixing the process

FIGURE 14-5

A Consumer-Stakeholder Satisfaction Model

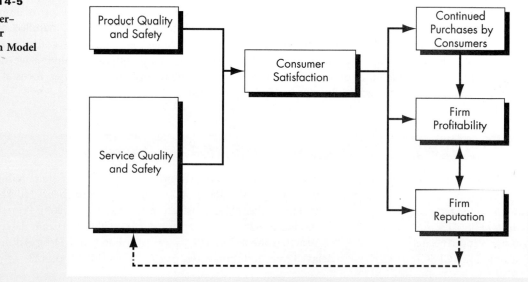

© Cengage Learning

rather than the product.[93] Of course, these underlying principles are the foundation of TQM and most other quality efforts.

Corporations adopting the Six Sigma program must develop "black belts," that is, people specifically trained to fill sponsorship roles, provide assistance, and see the program through. They must also find "champions" at senior levels of management who are committed to shepherding the program when needed.[94]

The basis for all of these quality or safety approaches is the satisfaction of the consumer. Figure 14-5 outlines a **consumer stakeholder satisfaction model** that depicts how product and service quality and safety lead to consumer satisfaction, and the consequences for the firm's profitability, reputation, and continued purchasing by consumers.

Summary

Consumer stakeholders have become concerned with product quality and safety largely because businesses have failed to meet their needs reliably on these two fronts. The situation has been the same with both manufacturing and services. One major challenge has been to identify and understand all the different dimensions of the quality issue. Today, quality may mean performance, features, reliability, conformance, durability, serviceability, aesthetics, perceived quality, or some combination of these dimensions. Product and service quality is both a business and an ethics issue.

An extremely important legal and ethical issue has been the consumer's right to safety. Product safety has become one of the most crucial consumer issues for firms. The product liability crisis has been an outgrowth of business's lack of attention to this issue. Other factors contributing to the product liability crisis have been the number of harmful-product cases, our increasingly litigious society, the size of financial awards given by the courts, and rising insurance rates. A major consequence of these phenomena has been calls for tort reform. Discussions of tort reform are ongoing, but few changes in this process have recently occurred. Product tampering and product extortion have also become safety-related issues. In recent years,

the health and safety issues related to foods, drugs, tobacco, and medical devices have propelled the CPSC and the FDA into prominent roles. The CPSC and FDA play vital roles in product safety, but strong business ethics remains the best practice for dealing with these issues.

Companies today employ a host of different customer service programs, all of which are aimed at creating satisfied customers who will demonstrate loyalty and will return for future purchases. In addition, firms use a variety of approaches that specifically address the issue of quality, primarily in the production process, and these embrace safety as one significant feature. Quality improvement initiatives such as TQM and Six Sigma are being used systematically, but they have not solved all the problems; however, they and other techniques have the potential for addressing the problems in a significant way if they are properly formulated and implemented. In addition to these specific responses, a consumer focus and orientation needs to permeate management decision making if the concerns of consumers are to be handled effectively. In today's business environment, consumers have many choices. Consequently, companies have no alternative but to internalize the consumer focus if they are to succeed.

Key Terms

absolute liability, p. 418

caveat emptor, p. 413

caveat vendor (caveat venditor), p. 413

Consumer Product Safety Commission (CPSC), p. 420

Consumer Product Safety Improvement Act of 2008, p. 422

consumer stakeholder satisfaction model, p. 428

contractual theory, p. 412

delayed manifestation cases, p. 418

doctrine of strict liability, p. 417

due care theory, p. 412

Family Smoking Prevention and Tobacco Control Act (2009), p. 424

Food and Drug Administration (FDA), p. 422

Food and Drugs Act (1906), p. 422
Food Safety Modernization Act (2011), p. 423
market share liability, p. 418

product liability reform, p. 419
product (products) liability, p. 416
Six Sigma, p. 427
social costs view, p. 412

tort reform, p. 419
Total Quality Management (TQM), p. 425

Discussion Questions

1. Identify the major dimensions of quality. Give an example of a product or service in which each of these characteristics is important.
2. What ethical theories can help us to better understand the issue of quality? Discuss.
3. Identify the principal reasons why we have a product liability crisis. Have any reasons been omitted? Discuss.
4. Differentiate the doctrine of strict liability from the doctrines of absolute liability and market share liability. What implications do these views

have for the business community and for future products and services that might be offered?

5. Given the current business and consumer climate, what do you anticipate the future to be for the CPSC and the FDA? What role does politics play in your answer?
6. What is your assessment of business's response to product and service quality and safety? Have they done enough? What is missing from their approaches?

Endnotes

1. Alan Ohnsman, Jeff Green, and Kae Inoue, "The Humbling of Toyota," *Bloomberg BusinessWeek* (March 22, 29, 2010), 33–36.
2. "Toyota's 'Tylenol Moment,'" *Newsweek* (February 15, 2010), 12.
3. James Kanter, Micheline Maynard, and Hiroko Tabuchi, "Toyota's Pattern Is Slow Response on Safety Issues," *The New York Times* (February 7, 2010), 1.
4. David Welch, "Oh, What a (Hideous) Feeling," *Bloomberg BusinessWeek* (February 15, 2010), 21–22.
5. "55% Say Toyota Dragged Its Feet," *USA Today* (March 2, 2010), 1B.
6. Mike Ramsey, "Toyota in $1.1 Billion Gas-Pedal Settlement," *The Wall Street Journal*, December 27, 2012, http://online.wsj.com/article/SB100014241278873246691 04578203440990704994.html. Accessed May 8, 2013.
7. Hermelo, Francisco Diaz, and Roberto Vassolo. "Institutional Development And Hypercompetition In Emerging Economies." *Strategic Management Journal* 31.13 (2010): 1457–1473.
8. Rajaram Veliyath and Elizabeth Fitzgerald, "Firm Capabilities, Business Strategies, Customer Preferences, and Hypercompetitive Arenas," *Competitiveness Review* (Vol. 10, 2000), 56–82.
9. Debanjan Mitra and Peter N. Golder, "Quality Is in the Eye of the Beholder," *Harvard Business Review* (April 2007) 26–28.
10. "ACSI Quarterly Scores," *American Customer Satisfaction Index Commentary*, December 2012, http://www.theacsi.org/acsi-results/acsi-commentary-november-2012. Accessed May 8, 2013.

11. Christopher W. Hart, "Beating the Market with Customer Satisfaction," *Harvard Business Review* (March 2007), 30–32.
12. "Customers Turned Off by Poor Service Levels," *Marketing Week* (March 5, 1998), 11.
13. Chris Akins, "8 Dimensions of Quality," Lean Six Sigma Academy, http://lssacademy.com/2008/05/28/8-dimensions-of-quality/. Accessed May 8, 2013.
14. Ibid.
15. Manuel G. Velasquez, *Business Ethics: Concepts and Cases* (Upper Saddle River, NJ: Prentice Hall, 2002), 335–344.
16. Yair Aharoni, *The No Risk Society* (Chatham, NJ: Chatham House Publishers, 1981), 62–63.
17. "Caveat Venditor," BusinessDictionary.com, http://www.businessdictionary.com/definition/caveat-venditor.html. Accessed May 8, 2013.
18. Cassell Bryan-Low and Ruth Bender, "Label Fears Put Europe on Trail of Horse Meat," *The Wall Street Journal*, February 12, 2013, A9.
19. Brent Kendall and Devlin Barrett, "Four Accused of Salmonella Coverup," *The Wall Street Journal*, February 22, 2013, A2.
20. FDA, "FDA Food Safety and Modernization Act (FSMA)" http://www.fda.gov/Food/GuidanceRegulation/FSMA/default.htm. Accessed May 8, 2013.
21. Liz Szabo, "Issues And answers with FDA's Hamburg," *USA Today*, April 25, 2013, 4-D.
22. Thomas M. Burton, "FDA Plans ID-Tag System to Detect Faulty Devices," *The Wall Street Journal*, April 26, 2012, B3.

23. E. Patrick McGuire, "Product Liability: Evolution and Reform" (New York: The Conference Board, 1989), 6.

24. "U.S. Consumer Product Safety Commission, "Research & Statistics," http://www.cpsc.gov/en/Research–Statistics/. Accessed May 8, 2013.

25. Cornell University Law School, Legal Information Institute, "Products Liability Law: An Overview," http://www.law.cornell.edu/wex/Products_liability. Accessed May 11, 2013.

26. "Ford's $128.5 Million Headache," *Time* (February 10, 1978), 65.

27. "Product Liability Lawsuits Up in 2009," http://www.youhavealawyer.com/blog/2010/01/12/product-liability-lawsuit-verdicts-up/. Accessed May 9, 2013.

28. Matt Kibbe, "America's Ongoing Tort Litigation Nightmare," http://www.forbes.com/sites/mattkibbe/2012/01/19/americas-ongoing-tort-litigation-nightmare/. Accessed May 9, 2013.

29. Kara Sissell, "Study Tallies Tort Litigation's Effect on Innovation," *Chemical Week* (April 4, 2007), 43.

30. Andrew Hacker, "The Asbestos Nightmare," *Fortune* (January 20, 1986), 121.

31. Francine Schwadel, "Robins and Plaintiffs Face Uncertain Future," *The Wall Street Journal* (August 23, 1985), 4.

32. David J. Morrow, "Implant Maker Reaches Accord on Damage Suits," *The New York Times* (July 9, 1998), A1.

33. Richard Thompson, "BP Oil Spill Settlement Payouts Surpass $2 Billion Mark, Administrator Says," *The New Orleans Times Picayune*, May 7, 2013, http://www.nola.com/news/gulf-oil-spill/index.ssf/2013/05/bp_oil_spill_settlement_payout.html. Accessed May 9, 2013.

34. Fred W. Morgan and Karl A. Boedecker, "A Historical View of Strict Liability for Product-Related Injuries," *Journal of Macromarketing* (Spring 1996), 103–117.

35. Ann Christopher, "Avoiding a Hazardous Violation," *Warehousing Management* (August 2001), 20.

36. Kerry Powell, "Liability Language: Know the Difference Between Strict and Absolute," *On-Site* (March 2004), 46.

37. Curt Ward, "What Is Strict Liability?" http://buteralaw.com/newsletters.asp?c=47&id=366. Accessed May 10, 2013.

38. Terry Morehead Dworkin and Mary Jane Sheffet, "Product Liability in the 1980s," *Journal of Public Policy and Marketing* (1985), 71.

39. "The Asbestos Blob, Cont.," *The Wall Street Journal* (April 6, 2004), A16.

40. "Business Line: India Supreme Court Ruling on Damage Liability of Common Carrier," *Businessline* (June 30, 2000), 1.

41. "Charities Appeal to Blair to Stop Use of GM Crops in Britain," *Third Sector* (March 10, 2004), 2.

42. Roger Leroy Miller, "Drawing Limits on Liability," *The Wall Street Journal* (April 4, 1984), 28.

43. Natalie Kosteini, "Top Court Reverses Crown Asbestos Ruling," *Philadelphia Business Journal* (February 23, 2004).

44. Steven T. Taylor, "While the Asbestos Trust Fund May Be Dead (for Now), Litigation in This Area Is Alive and Well," *Of Counsel* (December 2006), 1–15.

45. Ibid.

46. Dworkin and Sheffet, 69.

47. Clemens P. Work, "Product Safety: A New Hot Potato for Congress," *U.S. News & World Report* (June 14, 1982), 62. Also see "What Is Market Share Liability?" *Rottenstein Law Group*, http://www.rotlaw.com/legal-library/what-is-market-share-liability/. Accessed May 11, 2013.

48. Edward J. Schoen, Margaret M. Hogan, and Joseph S. Falcheck, "An Examination of the Legal and Ethical Public Policy Consideration Underlying DES Market Share Liability," *Journal of Business Ethics* (Vol. 24, 2000), 141–163.

49. "Tampering with Buyers' Confidence," *U.S. News & World Report* (March 3, 1986), 46.

50. Damien Thomlinson, "Drug Extortion Highlights Risks," *Business Insurance* (June 26, 2000), 33–37.

51. Dean Foust, Brian Grow, and Sheridan Prasso, "Evolution of the Envelope," *BusinessWeek* (November 5, 2000), 14.

52. Thomas Lee, "Food Service Is on Front Line of Terror War," *St. Louis Post-Dispatch* (September 23, 2002), 8.

53. Daniel Schwartz, "Five Major Product Tampering Cases," *CBC News*, August 2, 2012, http://www.cbc.ca/news/world/story/2012/08/02/f-product-tampering-list.html. Accessed May 11, 2013.

54. "Tort," *The Lectric Law Library's Lexicon*, http://www.lectlaw.com/def2/t032.htm. Accessed May 11, 2013.

55. Matt Kibbe, "America's Ongoing Tort Litigation Nightmare," *Forbes*, January 19, 2012, http://www.forbes.com/sites/mattkibbe/2012/01/19/americas-ongoing-tort-litigation-nightmare/. Accessed May 11, 2013.

56. Peter Waldman and Eileen White, "Battle Rages over Damages, Insurance Rates: States Are Debating Sweeping Changes in Tort Laws," *The Wall Street Journal* (April 15, 1986), 5; See also R. J. Samuelson, "Lawyer Heaven," *The Washington Post National Weekly Edition* (June 27–July 3, 1994), 28.

57. Michele Galen, "The Class Action Against Product Liability Laws," *BusinessWeek* (July 29, 1997), 74. Also see Amy Buttell Crane, "The ABCs of Tort Reform," *Bankrate.com*, http://www.bankrate.com/brm/news/pf/20050727a1.asp. Accessed May 11, 2013.

58. Robert Kuttner, "How Tort Reform Will Hurt Consumers," *San Diego Union Tribune* (June 24, 1994), B7. See also Jerry Phillips, "Attacks on the Legal System: Fallacy of Tort Reform Arguments," *Trial* (February 1992), 106–110; Brian Kabateck and Derek Scott, "Consumer Advocates Block Tort Reform Legislation for the

2012 Session," *Daily Journal*, http://www.kbklawyers.com/consumer-advocates-block-tort-reform-legislation-in-the-2012-session. Accessed May 11, 2013.

59. Stuart Taylor and Evan Thomas, "Civil Wars," *Newsweek* (December 15, 2003), 47.

60. "The Defects in Product-Liability Laws," *BusinessWeek* (July 29, 1991), 88. Also see W. Kip Viscusi, "Does Product Liability Make Us Safer?" *Regulation*, Spring 2012, http://www.cato.org/sites/cato.org/files/serials/files/regulation/2012/4/v35n1-4.pdf. Accessed May 11, 2013.

61. U S. Consumer Product Safety Commission, http://www.cpsc.gov/en/. Accessed May 13, 2013.

62. NewsInferno, "Bill Banning Future Chinese Drywall Use Passes," January 4, 2013, http://www.newsinferno.com/?p=42074. Accessed May 13, 2013.

63. NewsInferno, http://www.newsinferno.com/?s=tenenbaum. Accessed May 13, 2013; Jayne O'Donnell, "CPSC Updates Safety Rules for Children's Products," *USA Today*, May 2, 1013, 5B.

64. http://www.cpsc.gov/. Accessed May 13, 2013.

65. Consumer Product Safety Improvement Act of 2008, http://www.cpsc.gov/en/Regulations-Laws–Standards/Statutes/. Accessed May 13, 2013.

66. U.S. Consumer Product Safety Commission, "Statement of Chairman Inez Tenebaum on the CPSC Fiscal Year 2014 Budget Request," April 18, 2013, http://www.cpsc.gov//Global/About-CPSC/Chairman-Tenenbaum/TenenbaumFY2014BudgetStatement.pdf. Accessed May 13, 2013.

67. FDA, "What Does the FDA Regulate?" http://www.fda.gov/AboutFDA/Transparency/Basics/ucm194879.htm. Accessed May 13, 2013.

68. U.S. FDA, Commissioner's Page, http://www.fda.gov/AboutFDA/CommissionersPage/default.htm. Accessed May 13, 2013.

69. FDA, "Major Initiatives," http://www.fda.gov/AboutFDA/CommissionersPage/default.htm. Accessed May 13, 2013.

70. U.S. FDA, "Food Safety Modernization Act," http://www.fda.gov/Food/GuidanceRegulation/FSMA/default.htm. Accessed May 13, 2013.

71. Liz Szabo, "Issues and Answers with FDA's Hamburg," *USA Today*, April 25, 2013, 4–D.

72. Brent Kendall and Devlin Barrett, "Four Accused on Salmonella Cover-Up," *The Wall Street Journal*, February 22, 2013, A2.

73. Bill Tomson, "FDA Proposes Extensive Food-Safely Rules," *The Wall Street Journal*, January 5–6, 2013, A3.

74. U.S. FDA, "Tobacco Products," http://www.fda.gov/TobaccoProducts/default.htm. Accessed May 13, 2013.

75. Mike Esterl, "FDA Names Critic to Oversee Tobacco," *The Wall Street Journal*, February 22–23, 2013, B4.

76. Joe Queenan, "Die, Die, DIY! Enough of the Self-Service," *The Wall Street Journal*, October 27–28, 2012, C11.

77. Julie Jargon, "McDonald's Says 'Service Is Broken,' Tackles Repair," *The Wall Street Journal*, April 11, 2013, B1.

78. Bill Saporito, "Staying Power: New Ways Companies are Getting Us to Stick with Lousy Service," *Time*, February 4, 2013, 56.

79. Ellen Byron, "Diaper Gripes Grow Louder for P&G," *The Wall Street Journal* (May 14, 2010), B1.

80. The Vermont Country Store, "Customer Bill of Rights," http://www.vermontcountrystore.com/store/company/static/About-Us/Customer-Bill-of-Rights. Accessed May 14, 2013.

81. K. Ishikawa, *What Is Total Quality Control?* (Milwaukee, WI: Quality Press, 1985).

82. James W. Dean, Jr. and David E. Bowen, "Management Theory and Total Quality: Improving Research and Practice Through Theory Development," *Academy of Management Review*, Vol. 19, No. 3, July 1994, 395.

83. Victor B. Wayhan and Erica L. Balderson, "TQM and Financial Performance: What Has Empirical Research Discovered?" *Total Quality Management & Business Excellence* (May 2007), 403–412; Victor B. Wayhan and Erica L. Balderson, "TQM and Financial Performance: A Research Standard," *Total Quality Management & Business Excellence* (May 2007), 393–401.

84. I. Salaheldin Salaheldin and Zain Mohamed, "How Quality Control Circles Enhance Work Safety: A Case Study," *TQM Magazine* (2007), 229–244.

85. ASQ, "Total Quality Management Benefits," http://asq.org/learn-about-quality/total-quality-management/overview/tqm-gets-results.html. Accessed May 13, 2013.

86. "The Eight Elements of TQM," *Six Sigma*, http://www.isixsigma.com/methodology/total-quality-management-tqm/eight-elements-tqm/. Accessed May 13, 2013.

87. Carol A. Reeves and David A. Bednar, "Defining quality: Alternatives and Implications," *Academy of Management Review*, Vol. 19, No. 3, July 1994, 437.

88. Debanjan Mitra and Peter N. Golder, "Quality Is in the Eye of the Beholder," *Harvard Business Review* (April 2007), 26–28.

89. iSixSigma, "What Is Six Sigma?" http://www.isixsigma.com/new-to-six-sigma/getting-started/what-six-sigma/. Accessed May 13, 2013.

90. Michael Hammer and Jeff Godling, "Putting Six Sigma in Perspective," *Quality* (October 2001), 58–62.

91. Asixsigma, "Who Uses Six Sigma?" http://www.asixsigma.com/companies.php. Accessed May 13, 2013.

92. Hammer and Godling, 58.

93. Ibid.

94. Basu, 28–33.

15

Sustainability and the Natural Environment

There are many definitions of **sustainability**. For our purposes, we borrow from the Brundtland Commission (formerly the World Commission on Environment and Development [WCED]) to define sustainable business as "business that meets the needs of the present without compromising the ability of future generations to meet their own needs."[1] The focus of sustainability is the creation of a good quality of life for both current and future generations of humans and nonhumans by achieving a balance between economic prosperity, ecosystem viability, and social justice.[2] The concept is akin to walking lightly on the earth, taking only what is needed, and leaving behind enough for future generations to have access to the same resources. In the words of Maurice Strong, Canadian entrepreneur and a former under-secretary general of the United Nations, "Sustainability means running the global environment—Earth Inc.—like a corporation: with depreciation, amortization and maintenance accounts. In other words, keeping the asset whole, rather than undermining your natural capital."[3]

Sustainability is not just about cutting back and limiting waste, it is a philosophy that embraces a new type of abundance and can inspire greater levels of business creativity.[4] As the sustainability movement grows, creative business people are developing new ways of doing business that benefit all aspects of the **triple bottom line**—people, planet, and profits. The growth of sustainability has been swift. Svenska Cellulosa Aktiebolaget (SCA) conducts an annual Tork Report, in which they ask businesses about their sustainability initiatives. In 2011, 38 percent of businesses had sustainability programs. By 2012, just one year later, that number had increased to 64 percent.[5]

The near doubling of such initiatives in just one year is not surprising when one considers the strong business case for sustainability. In *Green to Gold*, Daniel Esty and Andrew Winston offer three basic reasons for incorporating sustainability into a business's core strategy.[6] First, there are upside benefits. Sustainability requires innovation and entrepreneurship; these qualities can help a firm to move ahead of competitors through new ideas, lower costs, and stronger intangibles, such as trust and credibility. Sustainable companies can even carry less risk, resulting in lower lending rates. Second, companies that ignore the sustainability imperative run the risk of incurring society's wrath once they disregard or endanger the environment or its inhabitants. Union Carbide realized this after the tragedy in Bhopal.

Walmart found that even the largest of firms could not withstand negative public reactions indefinitely. Finally, sustainability is the right thing to do. Oil giant Shell uses an acronym to explain why they do some things that on the surface appear to be costly—TINA (There Is No Alternative). Sustainability is not a luxury, nor is there really a choice.[7] As the sign in Patagonia headquarters says, "There is no business to be done on a dead planet."[8]

This chapter begins by discussing the concept of sustainability and its importance to business. An overview of the growth of the sustainability movement and the drivers of corporate sustainability will follow. We highlight Unilever, a company that has become a leader in sustainability and the principles that guide it. We then narrow the focus to environmental sustainability and the top environmental issues facing business today. The section on environmental ethics begins a discussion of individual and collective responsibility for sustaining the environment. We then explore the role of the government and environmental interest groups in effecting change; look at companies that are leaders in environmentally sustainable business practices; and offer ways in which businesses can develop a strategy aimed at achieving environmental sustainability.

The Sustainability Imperative

Several years ago, a discussion of sustainability would have had to include strong arguments about why businesses would benefit from sustainable practices. Today the need for sustainability is increasingly taken as a 'given' and businesses must simply determine how best to respond. MIT Sloan's Winter 2013 Research Report on *The Innovation Bottom Line* describes sustainability as "both a necessity and an opportunity."[9] *Financial Executive* puts sustainability on CFO to-do lists, points out that shareholder expectations increasingly extend beyond economics to include a firm's social and environmental policies, and notes that 40 percent of shareholder proposals were social or environmental in nature.[10] According to *Triple Pundit*, the business case for sustainability has become increasingly easier to make, that is an "easier sell" for companies of all sizes.[11] **CERES' Roadmap to Sustainability** identifies several key drivers that underscore the movement toward sustainability, presenting both risks and opportunities:[12]

1. Competition for Resources—Demand for resources is growing more quickly than they can be replaced.
2. Climate Change—Businesses must be prepared to not only respond to new policies and regulations regarding emissions, but also take advantage of opportunities to profit from new technologies that reduce emissions or create solutions.
3. Economic Globalization—Wide disparities in social and environmental standards bring risks as well as opportunities.
4. Connectivity and Communications—Stakeholders can monitor and react to sustainability efforts more quickly and effectively. Reputations are more easily and quickly built and destroyed.

One of the foremost advocates of corporate sustainability is Paul Polman, CEO of Unilever. While many business executives are at odds with government, he contends that business, government and nonprofit/non-governmental organizations should be working together to tackle the world's challenges.[13] Since taking the reins of Unilever in 2009, Polman has been charting a dramatic new direction for the company. Concerned that a focus on shareholder wealth maximization would lead to a short-term outlook at odds with the long-term perspective needed for sustainability, he banned quarterly earnings reports, which lowered his percentage of hedge fund investors from 15 percent to 5 percent in three years.[14] Not sorry to see the hedge fund investors go, Polman then actively courted more long-term oriented investment funds. In his words, "Historically, too many CEOs have just responded to shareholders instead of actively seeking out the right shareholders. Most CEOs go to visit their existing shareholders; we go to visit the ones we don't yet have."[15]

Shortly after Polman took over, Unilever embarked on an ambitious ten-year plan. The plan is detailed in Figure 15-1. Begun in 2010, the goals of the plan are to be achieved by 2020. As of 2012, Unilever was making solid progress—the following milestones were reached by the end of 2012:[16]

- Health & Hygiene: 224 million people were reached.
- Improving Nutrition: Majority of products met national standards benchmarks, with 18 percent meeting highest nutritional standards.
- Greenhouse Gases: Greenhouse gas impact was reduced by 6 percent.
- Waste: Waste impact per consumer was reduced by about 7 percent.

FIGURE 15-1

The Unilever Sustainable Living Plan

The Unilever Sustainable Living Plan (USLP) sets out to decouple our growth from our environmental impact, while at the same time increasing our positive social impact. It has three big goals to achieve by 2020—to improve health and well-being, reduce environmental impact, and enhance the livelihoods of people across our value chain. Supporting these goals are seven commitments underpinned by targets spanning our social, environmental, and economic performance across the value chain–from the sourcing of raw materials all the way through to the use of our products in the home.

Improving Health and Well-Being
- Health & Hygiene
  - By 2020 we will help more than a billion people to improve their hygiene habits and we will bring safe drinking water to 500 million people. This will help reduce the incidence of life-threatening diseases like diarrhea.
- Improving Nutrition
  - We will continually work to improve the taste and nutritional quality of all our products. By 2020 we will double the proportion of our portfolio that meets the highest nutritional standards, based on globally recognized dietary guidelines. This will help hundreds of millions of people to achieve a healthier diet.

Reducing Environmental Impact
- Greenhouse Gases
  - Halve the greenhouse gas impact of our products across the lifecycle by 2020.
- Water
  - Halve the water associated with the consumer use of our products by 2020.
- Waste
  - Halve the waste associated with the disposal of our products by 2020.

Enhancing Livelihoods
- Sustainable Sourcing
  - By 2020 we will source 100% of our agricultural raw materials sustainably.
- Better Livelihoods
  - By 2020 we will engage with at least 500,000 smallholder farmers and 75,000 small-scale distributors in our supply network.

Source: Unilever Sustainable Living Plan, http://www.unileverusa.com/sustainable-living/uslp/#PillarGroup3Pillar1. Accessed April 27, 2013.

- Sustainable Sourcing: 36 percent of agricultural raw materials were sustainably sourced.
- Better Livelihoods: 450,000 smallholder farmers trained; 48,000 small–scale Shakti distributors by the end 2012. Project Shakti enables underprivileged rural women to become full-fledged micro entrepreneurs.

It is important to note that Unilever is doing well by traditional measures, as well as by the goals of the Sustainable Living Plan. Unilever's revenues and operating income have risen steadily since Polman took charge. Moreover, share price has outperformed the industry average, enabling Polman to move forward without criticism.[17]

The Natural Environment

For years, businesses conducted their operations with little concern about environmental consequences. Virtually every sector of business in every country was responsible for consuming significant amounts of materials and energy, consequently causing waste accumulation and resource degradation. For instance, forestry firms and companies that process raw materials, such as uranium, coal, and oil, have caused major air, water, and land pollution problems in their extraction, transportation, and processing stages. Manufacturing firms, such as those in steel, petrochemicals, and paper products, have been major sources of air and water pollution. Most major industry sectors have contributed significant levels of pollution with relatively little concern. Businesses have looked the other way, simply labeling the negative consequences of their actions as *externalities*.[18] **Externalities** are side effects or by-products of actions that are not intended and often disregarded.

By labeling the environmental consequences as external to the process, businesses were able to both acknowledge and dismiss the problems they created. The few business environmentalism efforts that existed tended to come from two sources—compliance and efficiency.[19] Environmentalists had one approach available for getting most businesses to treat the environment with greater respect: "mandate, regulate, and litigate." Businesses would stop damaging the environment only when it became illegal and/or unprofitable to do so.[20] In some ways, those days are ending. Companies that were once infamous for the damage they did to the environment are now scrambling to lead the way in environmental initiatives. The reason for the change is simple—environmentalism is now profitable. Companies can make money not only by increasing efficiency but also by inventing entirely new businesses.[21] Nevertheless, businesses still pose hazards to the environment, as evidenced by the devastating impact of the BP oil rig explosion and the Fukushima Daiichi nuclear disaster.

A Brief Introduction to the Natural Environment

Similar to other broad terms, **environment** means many things to many people—trees in the backyard, a family's favorite vacation spot, a mare and her colt in a pasture, a trout stream in the mountains, earth and the other planets and matter in our solar system. This chapter focuses on the natural environment—specifically, what it is, why it is important, how it has become a major concern, and what businesses and other organizations have done both to and for it. It identifies what we mean when we use the term *environment,* and why it has become one of the most significant societal issues of our time. The chapter also describes the variety of responses human organizations, including businesses, have developed to address this issue. Throughout the chapter, the emphasis is on two themes: that humans are a part of their natural environment, and that the environment itself, as well as the issues and human responses related to it, are extremely complex, defying simple analyses.

FIGURE 15-2   Glossary of Important and Helpful Environmental Terms

Bio-Based Product	A product (other than food or feed) that is composed, in whole or in significant part, of biological products or renewable agricultural or forestry materials.
Environment	Broadly, anything that is external or internal to an entity. For humans, the environment can include external living, working, and playing spaces and natural resources, as well as internal physical, mental, and emotional states.
Carbon Footprint	The total amount of greenhouse gases a person, product, or company emits directly or indirectly.
Carbon Neutral	The maintenance of a balance between producing and using carbon dioxide.
Carrying Capacity	The volume of and intensity of use by organisms that can be sustained in a particular place and at a particular time without degrading the environment's future suitability for that use.
Entropy	A resource's carrying capacity has limits that need to be respected for continued use. A measure of disorder of energy, indicating its unavailability for recycling for the same use. Energy tends to break down into lower quality with each use. For instance, a kilowatt of electricity, once it is produced and consumed, can never be used as electricity again and, if stored, will allow far less than 1 kW to be consumed.
Ecosystem	All living and nonliving substances present in a particular place, often interacting with others.
Threshold	The point at which a particular phenomenon, previously suppressed, suddenly begins to be activated. For instance, when a population's carrying capacity threshold is exceeded, the population tends to decrease or even crash as a result of increased morbidity and mortality.
Irreversibility	The inability of humans and nature to restore environmental conditions to a previous state within relevant time frames. Human environment-related actions that appear irreversible are the destruction of a rainforest or wilderness area and the extinction of a species.

© Cengage Learning

To assist you in making environmental business decisions in the future, the chapter presents facts and figures, some of which are technical and scientific, related to environmental issues and responses. These facts and figures are included to help you understand the complexities involved in the business and public environmental issues of today. Because of the influence of business, government, and environmental interest groups and individuals, these and many other technical terms and concepts are discussed in the media and, increasingly, in business and society and business ethics texts. Environmental literacy, whether for business, government, or individual decision making, requires, at minimum, some rudimentary knowledge. Without at least some basic technical information, would-be stakeholder managers abdicate their responsibility to make wise choices, which are potentially critical to the survival of their organizations, as well as to the survival of humans and other species in the natural environment. We call your attention to Figure 15-2, which presents definitions of a few of the most important environmental terms that might be helpful to you now and in the future.

The Impact of Business on the Natural Environment

We will begin with a list of ten fundamental environmental issues. They are:

1. Climate change
2. Energy
3. Water

4. Biodiversity and land use
5. Chemicals, toxics, and heavy metals
6. Air pollution
7. Waste management
8. Ozone layer depletion
9. Oceans and fisheries
10. Deforestation

Each is discussed briefly to give the reader a sense of the issue's complexity and its current status.

Climate Change

No environmental issue has been more contentious than has the subject of **climate change**, which is also known as **global warming**. This is because scientists expect the **greenhouse effect** (i.e., the prevention of solar heat absorbed by our atmosphere from returning to space) to precipitate an unprecedented rate of warming.[22] The debate about climate change's existence has lessened dramatically due to a combination of factors, including Hurricane Katrina, a European heat wave, starving polar bears, and stronger scientific predictions.[23] Climatologists now say with some certainty that human activities are warming the earth at a dangerous level. The Intergovernmental Panel on Climate Change placed the probability that human activities are creating climate change at greater than 90 percent. Just six years earlier, the probability was determined to be 60 percent.[24] The increased confidence in their estimation stems from a longer period of data collected and a greater understanding of the climate system; those two factors have led to more reliable climate models.[25] As discussed in Chapter 12, some CEOs felt so strongly about climate change that they severed ties with the U.S. Chamber of Commerce. Apple, PG&E, Exelon, and PNM Resources all quit the Chamber, and Nike withdrew from its board, because of the Chamber's opposition to efforts to regulate carbon emissions.[26]

The possibility of a swift and radical change in climate is so great that the U.S. Department of Defense highlighted its implications in their most recent *Quadrennial Review*.[27] They reported, "Although they produce distinct types of challenges, climate change, energy security, and economic stability are inextricably linked."[28] They went on to say that "while climate change alone does not cause conflict, it may act as an accelerant of instability or conflict, placing a burden to respond on civilian institutions and militaries around the world."[29] The U.S. military takes climate change so seriously that the Navy SEALS, and other elite forces, are moving actively on a program to have net-zero energy use and net-zero water use in the future.[30]

Figure 15-3 shows growth in global carbon dioxide emissions, measured in million metric tons, from 1900 to 2009.

Energy

A major environmental issue is **energy inefficiency**, or the wasting of precious nonrenewable sources of energy. Nonrenewable energy sources, such as coal, oil, and natural gas, were formed millions of years ago under unique conditions of temperature, pressure, and biological phenomena (hence the term **fossil fuels**). Once these are depleted, they will be gone forever. In addition, because these fuels are not equally distributed around the world, they are the cause of significant power imbalances worldwide, with associated armed conflicts that are typically disastrous for both humans and the natural environment in general.[31] As India, China, and other fast-growth areas in the developing world increase their demand for energy, the depletion of fossil fuels is happening at a quickening pace.

FIGURE 15-3   Global Carbon Dioxide Emissions

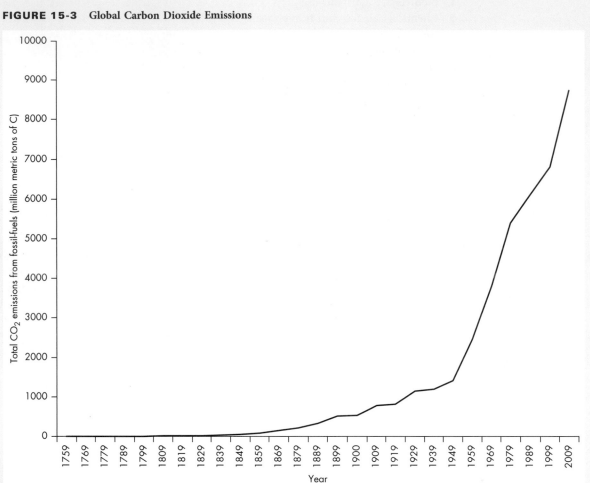

Source: Boden, T.A., G. Marland, and R.J. Andres. 2012. Global, Regional, and National Fossil-Fuel CO_2 Emissions. Carbon Dioxide Information Analysis Center, Oak Ridge National Laboratory, U.S. Department of Energy, Oak Ridge, Tenn., U.S.A. doi 10.3334/CDIAC/00001_V2012

The answer to the nonrenewability problem is to use as little as possible of these energy sources through implementation of sound energy conservation practices, while also shifting to renewable energy sources. Several technologies for tapping these renewable, low-polluting energy sources are becoming economically competitive with nonrenewable sources and so, for business, the energy issue represents not only a challenge but also an opportunity.[32] Many states now mandate that utilities obtain a minimum percentage of their energy supply through renewable energy, and companies ranging from Johnson & Johnson to Fed Ex and Starbucks have committed to buying a portion of their energy from renewable sources.[33] With money now flowing into "clean tech" funds that focus mainly on renewable sources of energy, firms are scrambling to determine how to get a piece of the pie. Not every firm will succeed in this arena, but those that do stand to reap big profits.[34]

Water

Water presents problems in both quality and quantity. The developed world has made significant progress in the quality of water—no longer are waterways so polluted that they risk catching on fire, as the Cuyahoga River did in Cleveland in 1969.[35] Nevertheless, municipal sewage, industrial wastes, urban runoff, agricultural runoff, atmospheric fallout, and overharvesting all continue to contribute to the degradation of the world's oceans and waterways. So, too, do dam sedimentation, deforestation, overgrazing, and overirrigation. The developing world's water quality is far poorer than the water quality of the developed world. In the developing world, a staggering 90 to 95 percent of sewage and 70 percent of industrial waste is untreated as it flows into rivers, lakes, and the ocean.[36] More than a billion people worldwide lack clean water, and the problem shows no signs of abating.[37]

Beyond the issue of pollution, experts now warn that the world is facing a "water bankruptcy."[38] The earth is a closed system with a water supply that is fixed, so as populations grow and crop irrigation increases, supplies become depleted. Pollution renders existing water unusable, further diminishing the supply. A global water crisis brought on by a combination of drought, pollution, mismanagement, and politics has thus developed.[39] No country, no matter how big, is immune from this crisis. In the United States, the giant Ogallala Aquifer, which lies under parts of eight states, is diminishing dramatically due to heavy demand.[40] In China, the Yangtze River is so heavily polluted that a recent World Wildlife Fund report declared the damage to the river's ecosystem to be largely irreversible.[41] The Yellow River has slowed to a trickle for much of the year, leaving nearly 400 million Chinese people, one-third of the country's population, without access to clean water.[42] In India, two-thirds of the 1.1 billion populace lack clean water, and the water table drops six to ten feet each year. If current trends continue, more than half the people in the world could be living in severely water-stressed areas by 2030.[43] This water bankruptcy poses an even bigger threat than the global financial crisis.[44]

Biodiversity and Land Use

An ecosystem's **biodiversity**, that is, the variation of life forms inside the system, serves as a key indicator of its health. According to H.E. Dr. Ali Abdussalam Treki, President of the United Nations General Assembly: "Biodiversity continues to be lost at an unprecedented rate, thus threatening the capacity of the planet to provide the required goods and services." The current rate of extinction is estimated to be 1,000 times higher than the natural rate."[45] Throughout most of time, species died off at a natural rate of one to five in a year; now dozens are becoming extinct each day.[46] Ecosystem and habitat destruction through agricultural and urban development activities and, of course, pollution, have put at risk both wildlife and beneficial plants. Excesses in individual and organizational activities are responsible for significant and tragic ecosystem and species degradation.

Another disturbing environmental issue that human populations face is land degradation. Degradation includes such different multiple facets as desertification, deforestation, overgrazing, salinization, and alkalization. Soil acidification, urban sprawl, and soil sealing, or industrial soil contamination, are part of land degradation as well. According to Dr. Treki, "Seventy per cent of the world's poor live in rural areas. They depend directly on biological resources for as much as 90 per cent of their needs such as food, fuel, medicine, shelter, and transportation. More than three billion people depend on marine and coastal biodiversity, while more than 1.6 billion rely on forests and non-timber forest products for their livelihoods. The degradation of habitat and the loss of biodiversity are threatening the livelihoods of more than one billion people living in dry and subhumid lands, particularly in Africa, the continent most affected by drought and desertificatication."[47] As the population of the world continues to grow, the problems created by the loss of productive soil will only increase.

Chemicals, Toxics, and Heavy Metals

The production of **toxic substances**, whether as constituents of intended products or as unwanted by-products, is an important issue because of its potential for harm. The United States

---

ETHICS IN PRACTICE CASE

Hazardous Waste

I am currently employed at a small company, and from my very first day, I realized that this company is unlike any other electronics manufacturing company in which I have worked since I have been a technician. Very little attention is placed on the operations aspect of their manufacturing process. Most of the equipment, computers, and devices that we use are outdated and very old, including the chairs, benches, carts and tables. Top management sets the culture of the company. The president's main goal is to make a profit by any means necessary, without focusing on aesthetics. His outlook is "we make money and spend very little money," and "if you don't like the way things are done here, don't let the door knob hit you on your ass on the way out."

One of the things that stood out to me right away was how the scrapings, the pieces of solder, and used component parts are disposed. This material is considered hazardous and should not be placed in the regular trash containers, but, of course, this is how it is handled. There should be hazardous containers in place and the solder and other materials should be disposed of properly. Disposing of hazardous materials improperly goes against environmental sustainability. I considered approaching the director of operations and confronting him about the solder disposal but then decided against it because of the nature of the president and the culture of the company.

1. Should I say something to the president, even though I know it will not change his behavior and I could lose my job?
2. Should I blow the whistle outside the company, even though I know the president will know it was me and is likely to fire me?
3. How much should I factor the outcomes of my actions into my decision on whether or not to act?
4. What ethical principle should I use to guide my behavior in this situation? Why?

Source: Contributed Anonymously

Environmental Protection Agency (EPA) defines toxic substances as chemicals or compounds that may present an unreasonable threat to human health and the environment. Human exposure to toxic substances can cause a variety of health effects, including damage to the nervous system, reproductive and developmental problems, cancer, and genetic disorders.[48]

Two problems are central to the toxic substances issue. First, we are not always aware of the effects, especially the long-term and interactive effects, of exposure to the thousands of chemicals produced each year. As we discussed in the previous chapter, strict and absolute liability doctrines hold firms to a high degree of accountability for the effects of toxic substances. Second, toxic substances can be associated with industrial accidents, causing unforeseen widespread biological damage. The Bhopal, India, chemical plant leak; the Chernobyl nuclear power plant meltdown in the former Soviet Union; the *Exxon Valdez* oil spill in Alaska, and the BP oil rig explosion are some well-known environmental disasters involving toxic substances. Less well-known are the 6,500 spills, leaks, fires, and explosions reported to the EPA in just 2010, that is 18 a day.[49]

Air Pollution

The short-term and long-term effects of both outdoor and indoor **air pollution** are wide-ranging and severe.[50] Air pollution leads to acid rain, global warming, smog, and the depletion of the ozone layer. It also causes serious respiratory and other illnesses, so it is not surprising that it rates high in concern according to public opinion polls.[51] In addition to causing human health problems, ambient air pollution is also responsible for a condition called **acid rain**. Acid rain refers broadly to a mixture of wet and dry deposition (deposited material) from the atmosphere containing higher than normal amounts of nitric and sulfuric acids.[52] Both natural sources, such as volcanoes and decaying vegetation, and artificial sources, primarily emissions of sulfur dioxide and nitrogen oxides from fossil fuel combustion, can lead to acid rain.[53] Acid rain causes acidification of lakes and streams, contributes to the damage of trees at high elevations, and accelerates the decay of building materials and paints, including irreplaceable buildings and statues. Before falling to the earth, acid rain degrades visibility and harms public health.[54]

Indoor air pollution is another environmental problem that is becoming an increasing concern, because most people spend the majority of their lives indoors. Indoor air pollution comes from a variety of sources, including oil, gas, kerosene, coal, wood, and tobacco products, and building materials and furnishings such as asbestos-containing insulation, damp carpets, household cleaning products, and lead-based paints.[55] The immediate effects of indoor air pollution are typically short-term and treatable; these include irritation of the eyes, nose, and throat, headaches, dizziness, and fatigue. However, long-term effects that might show up years after exposure can be severely debilitating or fatal. These effects include some respiratory diseases, heart disease, and cancer.[56]

Waste Management

Reduce, Reuse, and Recycle is the waste management mantra. The first goal is to *reduce* the amount of waste discarded, which is source reduction; this is the best form of waste management because in this case the waste is never generated in the first place. The next best option is to *reuse* containers and products—either repairing anything that is broken or giving it to someone who can repair it. Reusing is preferable to recycling because it does not require reprocessing to make the item usable again. *Recycling* is the third best option, but still very valuable. Recycling transforms what once might have been waste into a valuable resource. Business can profit greatly from the boon in recycling. By recycling, businesses are able to cut costs—producing less garbage means lower landfill fees. These efforts also present new business opportunities for the entrepreneur. Figure 15-4

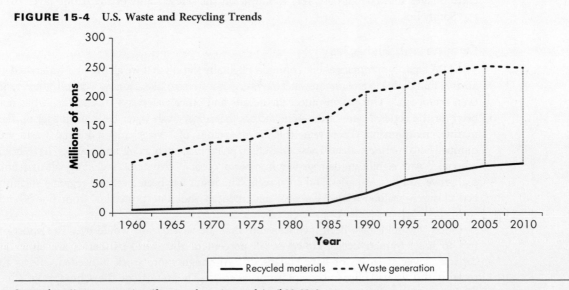

FIGURE 15-4 U.S. Waste and Recycling Trends

Source: http://www.epa.gov/osw/facts-text.htm. Accessed April 28, 2013.

shows the millions of tons of waste generated in the United States compared with the millions of tons of materials that are recycled.

Special consideration must be given to waste that is hazardous. Hazardous waste has properties that make it harmful, or potentially harmful, to human health or the environment. As defined by the EPA, the large and diverse world of hazardous waste includes liquids, solids, contained gases, or sludges.[57] Hazardous wastes can be generated by manufacturing processes, or they can simply result from discarded commercial products, such as cleaning fluids or pesticides.[58] The risk posed by such wastes creates countless causes for concern. Exposure to these wastes in the environment, whether in air, water, food, or soil, can cause cancer, birth defects, and a host of other problems.[59] Another concern is the toxicological effects of a number of new chemicals arriving on the market. Because they are new, we know less about their effects and the measures needed to protect human health and the environment from possible contamination.[60]

Ozone Depletion

Ozone is an oxygen-related gas that is harmful to life near the earth's surface, but is vital in the stratosphere in blocking dangerous ultraviolet radiation from the sun. More than 20 years ago, NASA scientists observed a huge decrease in ozone over Antarctica. They then discovered a "hole" in the ozone layer that had grown as large as the North American continent. Their measurements showed that the flow of ultraviolet light had increased directly under the ozone hole. This phenomenon was attributed to human-produced chemicals—chlorofluorocarbons (CFCs), used in refrigeration, and halons, used in fire extinguisher systems, as well as other ozone-depleting chemicals. A thinner layer of ozone is associated with a higher rate of skin cancer and other illnesses, as well as an increase in problems with agricultural production.

Observers were cautiously optimistic in 2013 when the hole in the ozone layer was at its second smallest point in twenty years.[61] Higher temperatures were mostly responsible, but they hope that a reduction in chemicals will lead to a continuous decrease.[62] For those interested in observing the hole in process, NASA provides "Ozone Watch" (http://ozonewatch.gsfc.nasa.gov/index.html), a Web site with pictures created from satellite images that enable observers to check on the latest status of the ozone layer over the South Pole.

Oceans and Fisheries

The EPA smartly summarizes our common plight, by stating that we all live in a **watershed**— an area that drains to a common waterway, such as a stream, lake, estuary, wetland, aquifer, or even the ocean.[63] Our actions affect the oceans and other waterways, and so far, it has not been for the better. Many of the same factors that affect fresh water have an impact on the marine environments. Each year, trillions of gallons of sewage and industrial waste are dumped into marine waters. These and other pollutants, such as oil and plastics, have been associated with significant damage to a number of coastal ecosystems, including salt marshes, mangrove swamps, estuaries, and coral reefs. The result has been local and regional shellfish bed closures, seafood-related illnesses, and reduced shoreline protection from floods and storms.

Once, it would have been inconceivable that the vast oceans would ever run short of fish to meet human needs. However, 85 percent of the world's fisheries are either at capacity, over capacity, or have collapsed.[64] Although more work is needed, efforts to reclaim the waters have met with some success. The return of the Chesapeake Blue Crab is an example. A variety of efforts, such as shortening the crabbing season, instituting a crabber license buyback program, and banning the raking of hibernating pregnant

Spotlight on Sustainability

There's an App for That

Sustainability software has become a huge growth market. With increased interest in sustainability reporting, and major buyers such as Walmart requiring suppliers to show proof of sustainable practices, companies are looking for ways to improve and monitor their environmental impacts. At the same time, individuals are increasingly interested in achieving a more sustainable lifestyle. Software manufacturers have been designing apps for smart phones to make that task easier. The following apps are free and available for both iPhone and Android users.

Paper Karma

Use your phone to stop unwanted paper mail (coupons, flyers, catalogs, magazines, yellow pages, etc.). Simply take a photo of the mail you do not want and Paper Karma will take care of the rest. Paper Karma contacts the mailer and asks to have your name removed from the distribution list.

GoodGuide

GoodGuide helps consumers find products that are safe, healthy, green, and ethical. The app has the capability to scan bar codes, enabling consumers to decide between products based on their environmental, health, and social impact. Main ratings are provided by qualified scientists, but users may also comment on and review products.

Locavore

Eating local food is not only a way to enjoy the freshest food available, but also a way to reduce one's carbon footprint by minimizing transportation. Locavore identifies the foods that are currently in season, as well as those that are coming into season soon. They also provide information about the food, in-season recipes, and directions to local farmer's markets.

iRecycle

Local recycling options can be hard to locate. iRecycle provides users with the collection points for recycling a range of materials, as well as directions, hours, and the materials collected at each location. Interested users can also connect with other recyclers through Facebook and Twitter.

Seafood Watch

This project of the Monterey Bay Aquarium strives to inform consumers about the fishing practices that are depleting fish populations, destroying habitats, and polluting the oceans. The Seafood Watch app lets consumers search for seafood and sushi so that they can make sustainable seafood choices. It also provides alternatives to seafood on the "Avoid" list. Project Fishmap lets users add names of restaurants and stores where they found sustainable seafood, and find out where others have found it.

Sources: https://www.paperkarma.com/; http://www.goodguide.com/; http://www.getlocavore.com/; http://earth911.com/irecycle/; http://www.montereybayaquarium.org/cr/seafoodwatch.aspx. Accessed March 15, 2013.

females from the bay floor have yielded promising results.[65] The 2010 Winter Dredge Survey estimated the blue crab population at 658 million, which was 235 percent of the 280 million found in a survey two years earlier. EPA Administrator Lisa Jackson said it was "an important indicator of some improvement in the ecosystem." Jackson praised the efforts of Maryland and Virginia, saying they have "shown tremendous leadership in following the science and making the tough decisions that have built a strong foundation for the work ahead."[66]

Deforestation

Although humans depend on forests for building materials, fuel, medicines, chemicals, food, employment, and recreation, the world's forests can be quickly depleted by a variety of human factors. **Deforestation** adds to soil erosion problems and is a major cause of the greenhouse effect. Felled trees are no longer able to absorb carbon dioxide and are sometimes burned for land clearing and charcoal, thereby releasing—rather than absorbing—carbon dioxide. Moisture and nutrient ecosystem cycles can also be severely damaged in deforesting activities, negatively affecting adjacent land and water ecosystems.

Deforestation plays a key role in global warming. Few would be able to guess which country makes the third greatest greenhouse gas emissions after China and the United States. Most would guess Germany because of its industry or Japan because of its cities and high technology. The actual answer is Indonesia; it releases 3.3 billion tons of carbon dioxide a year because of deforestation.[67] Trees absorb carbon dioxide when they are alive and when they die they release it into the air. As a result, deforestation accounts for 20 percent of global carbon emissions—more than the world's trains, boats, and planes combined.[68]

Responsibility for Environmental Issues

Environmental problems such as smog, toxic waste, and acid rain can be described as **"wicked problems"**—that is, problems with characteristics such as interconnectedness, complexity, uncertainty, ambiguity, conflict, and societal constraints. Every wicked problem seems to be a symptom of another problem.[69] Responsibility for such messy situations is difficult to affix, because solutions to wicked problems are seldom complete and final and, therefore, credit for these solutions is seldom given or taken. *Chlorofluorocarbons*, or *CFCs*, for example, were once considered safe alternatives to other, more toxic refrigerants, which is why these ozone destroyers are so ubiquitous in our society's technologies.

When no one takes responsibility, a phenomenon called the **tragedy of the commons** is likely to occur.[70] A "commons" is a plot of land available to all. When the commons is large enough to accommodate the needs of everyone, no problems occur. However, as herders continue to add animals to their herds, the carrying capacity of the commons becomes strained. It is in the self-interest of each herder to allow the animals to graze, even though the cumulative grazing will inevitably destroy the commons. The analogy of a "commons" can be applied to the environment as a whole as well as its many constituent parts. One need only look at the situation with public parks to see how unconstrained use (e.g., vehicles driving anywhere or unrestrained picking of vegetation) can damage a shared resource. As Garrett Hardin points out in his classic article on the tragedy of the commons in the environment, constraints must also be placed on the use of the commons (i.e., our environment), because in the absence of constraints, self-interest is likely to lead individuals and organizations to behave in ways that will not sustain our shared resources.[71]

Environmental Ethics

Nature itself is a polluter and destroyer. The earth's core is continually polluting many bodies of water and airsheds with a full range of toxic heavy metals. The 2010 eruption of Iceland's Eyjafjallajökull volcano melted glaciers, forcing people to flee rising floodwaters, and spewed clouds of dust into the air, snarling air traffic and stranding millions of passengers. Species have been going extinct since life evolved; in a continuous cycle of life and death, nature acts as its own destroyer. Given this fact, what does absolute human environmental sensitivity mean? Humans must consume at least some plants and water to survive. If humans and their organizations need to pollute and destroy at least some of nature for their survival, what is the relative level of degradation that is ethical? Do nonhuman species have any "rights," and, if so, what are they, and how can they be reconciled with human rights? Concerning human rights and the environment, how do we assess the claims of indigenous cultures to the use of their respective environments? Is there any connection between the domination of humans by humans (e.g., the domination of one nation, race, or gender by another) and the domination of nature by humans? This latter question is especially central to several schools of environmental ethical thought, including social ecology, ecofeminism, and environmental justice.

Whose standards will determine what is or is not ethical? Public opinion seems to have been affected by the economic crisis. In a recent GlobeScan poll of 1,000 people each in 22 countries, concern about the environment was found to have hit a 20-year low.[72] However, how much the public will do itself or insist that governments and businesses do to protect the environment is still an unanswered question. How clean do the air and water need to be, and how much is the public willing to pay to meet these standards? As in our earlier discussion of business ethics, values play a major role and can be highly variable in breadth and depth across perspectives, situations, and time.

Following the ethical models discussed in Chapters 7 and 8, we can develop a better idea of what environmental ethics is and how it can be practiced. Kohlberg's model of moral development, for instance, can be used to identify environment-related attitudes and behaviors by developmental level. At the preconventional level in environmental ethics, humans and human organizations can be perceived as being concerned only with self or with their own species and habitats. A conventional level might entail some appreciation of nature, but only when and where such appreciation is commonplace or trendy. A postconventional environmental ethic might include more mature attitudes and behaviors that are more universal (including all species and habitats), of greater duration (including unborn generations), and more consistent (if we humans have a right to survive as a species, why don't all species have that right?).

Similarly, the moral principle of utilitarianism—the greatest good for the greatest number—could be expanded in environmental ethics to the greatest good for the greatest numbers of species and ecosystems. The Golden Rule could read, "Do unto other species as you would have them do unto you." From a virtue ethics perspective, a "Best Self" ethical test could include the question, "Is this action or decision related to the natural environment compatible not only with my concept of myself at my best but also with my concept of myself as a human representing my species at its best?"

In *Who Speaks for the Trees*, authors Sama, Welcomer, and Gerde show that integrating sustainability into a firm's philosophy is a natural extension of stakeholder theory.[73] They expand the concept of the natural environment beyond living things, to the entire ecological system from which the firm obtains resources and to which it bears responsibility for the impacts, both positive and negative, that firm actions have on it. They invoke the ethic of care, discussed in Chapter 8, and explain that organizations that follow

---

ETHICS IN PRACTICE CASE
A Little Green Lie

I work for a telecommunications company as a sales consultant. The environment is very competitive and as "salespeople," we are always required to surpass our quotas and "make money." Lately the company has decided to "go green," which is good for the environment. However, the true motive behind the company's initiative is to save money on paper bills, as the managers have confessed to us. As a way of making us convert customers to paperless billing, they have factored paperless billing conversion into our metrics, which means that if we do not perform we can be reprimanded or fired. One of the area managers suggested we tell customers that the company is no longer sending paper bills and that if they wish to still receive a paper bill they will be charged a fee (which is completely false, paper bills are free to customers). I usually see customers fall for

it and go paperless in order to save money, and the sales consultants who have applied this method are usually our top rankers. The manager said it is not really lying, especially if you are helping selfish customers to help the environment.

1. Global warming and environmental issues have become serious problems. Keeping this in mind, is it right to lie to customers if your main motive is to save the environment and help save trees?
2. Is it okay for the area manager to demand that sales representatives lie?
3. Would it be okay for the sales representative to follow the directions of the manager?
4. What would you do if you were in this position and what would be your motive behind it?

Source: Contributed Anonymously

---

a practice of care would treat the natural environment, which they call the "silent stakeholder," with respect.[74]

The NIMBY Problem

One example of this question of responsibility is the **NIMBY**, or "Not in My Back Yard," phenomenon. This acronym, which can be found on bumper stickers and conference agendas and in newspaper articles, college courses, and many other communication vehicles, reflects human denial of responsibility for the misuse of the environment. The growth of the NIMBY attitude can be seen in the proliferation of other acronyms describing it. *NOTE* or "Not Over There Either," *BANANA* or "Build Absolutely Nothing Near Anything," and *NOPE* or "Not On Planet Earth" were all coined by observers frustrated with the human tendency to avoid assuming responsibility for societal costs.

Examples of NIMBY abound. One is the community that uses ever-increasing amounts of electricity but decides it does not want a power plant that produces electricity located near its homes and schools. Another is a company that generates increasing amounts of waste but is unwilling to pay the full cost of proper disposal. Recently, NIMBY attitudes almost scuttled the United States' first offshore wind farm off the coast of Cape Cod.[75] The project was approved by the Obama administration but, despite more than nine years having elapsed since work on the project began, it still faces court tests ahead.[76] Essentially, NIMBY is an attitude or behavior set based on avoidance or denial of responsibility. When applied to the field of environmental management, NIMBY spells big trouble.

The obvious difficulty with the NIMBY syndrome is that the entities (human individuals, organizations, or both) causing environmental pollution or degradation are not identified as the sources of the problem, and therefore no action is taken to reduce the problem. The NIMBY phenomenon avoids or denies the root cause of the damage and addresses only the symptoms. What results is an attitude of non-responsibility, characterized by an approach of: "I'll create an environmental problem, but I want to have as little as possible to do with solving it." One popular cartoon characterizing the NIMBY problem pictures a stream of polluting, honking cars passing along a highway in front of a huge billboard that reads: "Honk if you love the environment!"

The Role of Governments in Environmental Issues

As we mentioned earlier, governments have played major roles in environmental issues since the inception of such issues. Governments have procured, distributed, and developed habitable lands and other resources; protected, taxed, and zoned natural environment-based areas; and, more recently, exercised regulatory control over how those environments could be used. This section examines how governments in the United States have dealt with environmental challenges, then identifies what has been done in several other countries and at the international level.

Responses of Governments in the United States

Although the U.S. federal government has influenced environmental policy since at least 1899, with its permit requirement for discharge of hazardous materials into navigable waters, the major entrance of the U.S. government into environmental issues occurred in 1970 with the signing of PL 91-190, the National Environmental Policy Act (NEPA). The second section of this act spells out its purposes: "To declare a national policy which will encourage productive and enjoyable harmony between man and his environment; to promote efforts which will prevent or eliminate damage to the environment and biosphere and stimulate the health and welfare of man; and to enrich the understanding of the ecological systems and natural resources important to the Nation."[77]

In addition to establishing these broad policy goals, this legislation requires federal agencies to prepare **environmental impact statements (EISs)** for any "proposals for legislation and other major federal action significantly affecting the quality of the human environment." Environmental impact statements are reports of studies that explain and estimate the environmental impacts of both questionable practices and irreversible uses of resources. These reports propose detailed, reasonable alternatives to these practices and uses.

Business is affected by the NEPA in several ways. First, the federal government pays private consultants to conduct tens of billions of dollars worth of EISs each year. Second, because the federal government is the largest landholder in the United States, private businesses wishing to secure licenses and permits to conduct timber, grazing, mining, highway, dam, and nuclear construction operations likely will be parties to the preparation of EISs. Third, private businesses working under federal government contracts are typically obliged to participate in EIS preparation. Fourth, the NEPA has been used as a model by many state governments, and therefore businesses heavily involved in significant state and local government contracts are likely to be involved in the EIS process.

Also in 1970, the U.S. **Environmental Protection Agency (EPA)** was created as an independent agency to research pollution problems, aid state and local government's environmental efforts, and administer many of the federal environmental laws. These laws can be categorized into three areas—air, water, and land—even though a specific problem of pollution and/or degradation, such as acid rain, often involves two or more of these categories.

Air Quality Legislation. The key piece of federal air quality legislation is the **Clean Air Act**.[78] The overall approach of this act is similar to that used in other areas of federal regulation, such as safety and health legislation, in that standards are set and timetables for implementation are established. In the Clean Air Act, there are two kinds of standards: primary standards, which are designed to protect human health, and secondary standards, which are intended to protect property, vegetation, climate, and aesthetic values. These standards control a variety of air pollutants, including lead, particulates, hydrocarbons, sulfur dioxide, and nitrogen oxide. Businesses that directly produce these substances, such as electric utilities, and those who manufacture products that produce these substances, such as automobile makers, must reduce their emissions to within the set standards.[79]

The Clean Air Act introduced the concept of **emissions trading** (i.e., "**cap and trade**") to the United States. This approach is intended to reduce a particular pollutant over an entire industrial region by treating all emission sources as if they were all beneath one bubble. A business can increase its emissions of sulfur dioxide in one part of a plant or region if it reduces its sulfur dioxide pollution by as much or more in another part of the plant or region. In addition, and as an extension of this bubble analogy, businesses that reduce their emissions can trade these rights to other businesses that want to increase their emissions. Proponents of emissions credit trading hail these policies as free market environmentalism, whereas opponents ridicule them as licenses to pollute. The emissions trading system is part of the Kyoto Protocol, an international agreement that set legally binding targets and deadlines for cutting the greenhouse gas emissions of industrialized countries.[80]

Water Quality Legislation. U.S. government involvement in water quality issues has followed a pattern similar to that of air quality issues. The **Clean Water Act** (also known as the Federal Water Pollution Control Act) was passed in the early 1970s with broad environmental quality goals and an implementation system, involving both the federal and state governments, designed to attain those goals. The ultimate purpose of the Clean Water Act was to achieve water quality consistent with protection of fish, shellfish, and wildlife; as well as ensure safe conditions for human recreation in and on the water. The more tangible goal was to eliminate discharges of pollutants into navigable waters, which include most U.S. rivers, streams, and lakes. These goals were to be accomplished through a pollution permit system, called the National Pollutant Discharge Elimination System, which specifies maximum permissible discharge levels, and often timetables for installation of state-of-the-art pollution control equipment. Another act—the Marine Protection, Research, and Sanctuaries Act of 1972—sets up a similar system for control of discharges into coastal ocean waters within U.S. territory. A third water quality law administered by the EPA, the Safe Drinking Water Act of 1974, establishes maximum contaminant levels for drinking water.[81]

Land-Related Legislation. Land pollution and degradation issues differ from air and water quality issues, because land by definition is far less fluid and therefore somewhat more visible than air and water, so it is more suited to local or regional problem-solving approaches. Consequently, the U.S. federal government, in the Solid Waste Disposal Act of 1965, recognized that regional, state, and local governments should have the main responsibility for nontoxic waste management. The EPA's role in this area is limited to research and provision of technical and financial assistance to these other government levels. However, a 1976 amendment to this act, called the Resource Conservation and Recovery Act, set up a federal regulatory system for tracking and reporting the generation, transportation, and eventual disposal of hazardous wastes by businesses responsible for creating these wastes.[82]

The U.S. government has staked out a much larger role for itself in the area of toxic wastes. The 1976 **Toxic Substances Control Act** requires manufacturing and distribution businesses in the chemical industry to identify any chemicals that pose "substantial risks" of human or other natural environment harm. This act also requires chemical testing before commercialization and the possible halting of manufacture if the associated risks are unreasonable. Because there are more than 70,000 chemicals already in use in the United States and more than 1,000 new chemicals introduced every year, the EPA has prioritized the substances that must be tested to focus on those that might cause cancer, birth defects, or gene mutations.[83]

The other major U.S. government activity in toxic wastes is known as **Superfund**, or, more formally, the Comprehensive Environmental Response, Compensation, and Liability Act of 1980 (CERCLA). Superfund is an effort to clean up more than 2,000 hazardous waste dumps and spills around the country, some dating back to the previous century. Funded by taxes on chemicals and petroleum, this program has established a National Priorities List to focus on the most hazardous sites, and places legal and financial responsibility for the proper remediation of these sites on the appropriate parties. In addition, CERCLA also requires that unauthorized hazardous waste spills be reported, and grants authority to order those responsible to clean up the sites.[84]

One of the most important amendments to the Superfund law, the Emergency Planning and Community Right-to-Know Act of 1986, requires manufacturing companies to report to the federal government annually all of their releases into the environment of any of more than 500 toxic chemicals and chemical compounds. The EPA accumulates these reports and makes them available to the public (at http://www.epa.gov/triexplorer) with the intention that an informed public will pressure manufacturers to reduce these toxic releases.[85]

Endangered Species. The world's species are disappearing at an alarming rate, according to the World Conservation Union, which releases an annual Red List of endangered species.[86] Their 2012 report shows that nearly 11,000 species are now considered threatened with extinction, nearly 2,300 are endangered, and more than 5,000 are vulnerable.[87] "The good news," according to Russ Mittermeier, the head of Conservation International and chairperson of the World Conservation Union's primate group, "is that we still have time to save the majority of [the species], if the conservation community, governments, other organizations, and concerned individuals commit a sufficient amount of resources immediately."[88]

In the United States, responsibility for endangered species is shared by two agencies, the U.S. Interior Department's Fish and Wildlife Service and the Commerce Department's National Marine Fisheries Act. They administer the 1973 **Endangered Species Act (ESA)**. This federal law assigns the responsibility of preventing harm to species considered "endangered" (i.e., facing extinction) or "threatened" (likely to become endangered).[89] Protection of species sometimes means moving them to safe areas when their original habitats have been destroyed by human activities, but it can also mean prevention of these activities, such as mining, construction, and fishing, before such habitat deprivation occurs. This restriction of business activities can be expected to continue as the extinction rate for species climbs, resulting in sometimes intense political conflicts between business interests and environmental groups.[90]

International Government Environmental Responses

The *United Nations Environment Programme (UNEP)* has led the way in identifying global environmental problems and in working toward their resolution. As early as 1977, UNEP was studying the ozone problem and began to lay the groundwork for the

1987 **Montreal Protocol**, in which most of the CFC-producing and consuming nations around the world agreed to a quick phase-out of these ozone-destroying substances. In 2009, the Montreal Protocol achieved universal ratification, the first United Nations treaty to do so.[91] Observers believe that, thanks to the Protocol, the ozone layer should return to pre-1980 levels by 2050 to 2075.[92] The reduction of ozone destroyers brought by the Protocol has helped the world to avoid millions of cases of fatal skin cancer and tens of millions of cases of nonfatal skin cancer and cataracts.[93]

UNEP is also funding research and assisting in information exchange on the protection and more sustainable use of international waters. The Global Waters Assessment will examine the problems surrounding shared transboundary waters, develop scenarios on the future condition of the world's water, and analyze various policy options. UNEP is also the driving force behind efforts to initiate global sound management of hazardous chemicals. These chemicals were an integral part of the Rotterdam Convention, which requires that countries give explicit informed consent before hazardous chemicals cross their borders. UNEP also works to protect the world's biological diversity. Their efforts helped bring the elephant back from the brink of extinction.[94]

Another United Nations initiative is the **Global Compact**, already mentioned in Chapter 10. It brings thousands of companies from across the world society to support universal environmental and social principles. The Global Compact works to advance ten universal principles, three of which involve environmental issues. They are:

7. Business should support a precautionary approach to environmental challenges,
8. Undertake initiatives to promote greater environmental responsibility, and
9. Encourage the development and diffusion of environmentally friendly technologies."[95]

The **Global Reporting Initiative (GRI)** is a collaborating center of the UNEP. GRI spearheaded the development of a sustainability reporting framework that has become the most widely used standard in the world. As we discussed in Chapter 6, the reporting framework outlines the principles and indicators that organizations can use to measure and report their economic, environmental, and social performance.[96]

Other Environmental Stakeholders

Environmental Interest Groups

Perhaps no force in today's society is more responsible for the "greening" of nations around the world than are the many environmental interest groups making up what has come to be known as "the environmental movement." This collection of nonprofit membership and think-tank organizations has been credited with moving the world's governments and businesses, as well as publics, in the direction of environmental responsibility through a host of activities, including demonstrations, boycotts, public education, lobbying, and research.

The history of the environmental movement is instructive. Whereas a few U.S. groups (the National Audubon Society, the Izaak Walton League, and the Sierra Club) were formed in the early 1900s, during the first green wave of the century, many of the largest national and international environmental groups, such as the Environmental Defense Fund (now called Environmental Defense), Greenpeace, and the National Resources Defense Council were created during the second environmental wave, in the late 1960s and early 1970s. Since that time, all of these groups and hundreds of other smaller, more locally focused environmental organizations have grown in size and clout. It was the century's third wave of environmentalism, beginning in the late 1980s, however, that gave many of these groups the power and legitimacy to become credible players in environmental policy-making around the globe.

In this third wave, environmental interest groups have been instrumental in significantly influencing business environmental policy. For example, Environmental Defense is working with Federal Express on building a new generation of vehicles, with DuPont on developing nanotech standards, and with PHH Arval on becoming the first carbon neutral fleet.[97] Other outcomes of relationships between environmental interest groups and business stakeholders have included: corporate selection of environmental group representatives for corporate boards and top management positions, mutual participation in environmental "cleanup" projects, and corporate donations of time and money to environmental groups for their conservation programs. This trend toward cooperation between otherwise adversarial groups is a characteristic of the third green wave, and it sets this wave apart from the two previous environmental eras. That collaboration is discussed in more detail in the section on business environmentalism.

The former chair of the Sierra Club identified three types of major U.S. environmental organizations based on this criterion of cooperation with business. He labeled groups characterized by confrontational behaviors as "radicals," groups that seek pragmatic reform through a combination of confrontation and cooperation as "mainstreamers," and groups that avoid confrontation and are more trusting of corporations as "accommodators."[98] As we mentioned, the differences between the types of groups are beginning to blur as business and environmental activists collaborate increasingly on shared goals. Nevertheless, it is instructive to look at some of the groups that have taken, and sometimes continue to take, a more radical approach.

One group that falls into the radical camp is the Rainforest Action Network (RAN). RAN has been particularly successful in getting large corporations to change their practices. The ways in which RAN has accomplished their goals are described in Figure 15-5. RAN is a small organization, with a budget of only $2.4 million and a staff of just 25. Nevertheless, they have managed to garner the attention of big business in a way that the larger, more

---

FIGURE 15-5   **The Mosquito in the Tent Strategy**

Street Theater	During the holiday season, RAN carolers sang "Oil Wells" to the tune of "Jingle Bells" in front of the Citigroup headquarters on Park Avenue. RAN obtained the access code to the Home Depot intercom and announced to shoppers that they should step carefully, because the wood on Aisle 13 had been ripped from the Amazon Basin and there might be blood on the floors. They had actors, dressed up as Minnie and Mickey Mouse, locked to Walt Disney headquarters with a banner that read, "Disney is destroying Indonesia's rainforest."
Celebrity Endorsements	The night before Citigroup's annual shareholder meeting, RAN began airing commercials showing Ed Asner, Susan Sarandon, Darryl Hannah, and Ali MacGraw cutting up their Citibank credit cards.
Coalitions	RAN doesn't go it alone. They work with other environmental organizations, socially responsible investors, liberal philanthropists, and even sympathetic insiders (which is how they got the Home Depot access code).
Internet Organizing	RAN uses the Internet to both launch their own initiatives and support those of other groups. They urge individuals to contact those whose behavior they want to change and thank those who responded to RAN's requests for action.

Sources: Marc Gunther, "The Mosquito in the Tent," *Fortune* (March 31, 2004), 158–162; Lisa Gerwitz, "It's Not Easy Being Green," *Deal.com* (March 8, 2004), 1. Dan Murphy, "Stunning Reversal? Why 'Big Paper' Just Went Green in Indonesia," *Christian Science Monitor* (February 19, 2013), http://www .csmonitor.com/Environment/2013/0219/Stunning-reversal-Why-big-paper-just-went-green-in-indonesia. Accessed April 27, 2013. See also http://www.ran .org/take-action-online. Accessed April 27, 2013.

established environmental organizations have never managed. They have been described as a mosquito in a tent, "just a nuisance when it starts, but you can wake up later with some serious welts."[99] Environmentalist groups often believe that the threat of confrontation motivates companies to work more cooperatively with them. Greenpeace Research Director Kert Davies says, "What we hear over and over again, especially after a few drinks, is company people telling us, 'We wouldn't be talking to you if we weren't scared of you.'"[100]

A new category that is taking on increased importance are **ecoterrorists**. Ecoterrorists are not included under the radical designation described earlier. Radical groups favor confrontation, but ecoterrorists employ violent acts that involve real or threatened damage to people or property in an attempt to achieve their goals. More than 20 states have passed ecoterrorism laws that increase the penalties for vandalism, arson, and trespassing when ecoterrorism is involved.[101] At the federal level, the "Animal Enterprise Terrorism Act" of 2006 increases penalties for the use of force, violence, and threats involving animal enterprises.[102] "Operation Backfire," the largest eco-terrorism case in U.S. history, resulted in 11 people being charged with domestic terrorism for a five-year period of acts on behalf of the Earth Liberation Front (ELF) and the Animal Liberation Front (ALF).[103] By 2013, two more people were in FBI custody with two remaining at large.[104]

In addition to environmental groups, businesses are paying more attention to the latest green wave because of at least three other stakeholder groups: green consumers, green employees, and green investors.

ETHICS IN PRACTICE CASE
Slow Fashion

Fast fashion is a term that has been applied to clothing that goes from the high fashion catwalk to mainstream clothing stores in record time, enabling the average buyer to wear the latest trends. Zara and H&M are examples of retailers that have made their mark with fast fashion identities, but other retailers have joined the rush to fast fashion in order to provide their customers with the trendiest clothes to wear at moderate prices. The consumer can then afford to get new clothes in the next season when fashion trends inevitably change. Because the expected lifespan is short, fast fashion clothing tends to be made with less care and lower quality materials, cutting corners to make it cheaply and quickly. Of course, when new trends arrive, last year's trends become obsolete and ready for disposal. Making clothing consumes natural resources and yet, because they are made more cheaply, they tend to be thrown out after a year, if not after a few washes. They then find their way to landfills where textiles are posing a serious problem. In North America alone, 12 million tons of textile waste (68 pounds of waste per family) are generated each year.

Slow fashion has entered the scene and is endeavoring to change consumer habits. Slow fashion uses traditional methods of sewing and weaving, quality materials that are natural in origin, and quality handcrafting. The clothing is made to last, and consumers repair, rather than replace, clothing that is slightly damaged. Like the slow food movement, slow fashion promotes a more thoughtful approach to living on the earth in a sustainable way.

1. Is the criticism of fast fashion fair? Should an industry be held accountable for the waste its consumers generate?
2. Do you think slow fashion will become 'fashionable' in the way that fast fashion has? If it does, will its popularity persist or just end up being another fashion trend?
3. What responsibilities do consumers have for sustainability?

Sources: http://www.hearts.com/ecolife/join-slow-fashion-movement/. Accessed April 21, 2013; Maureen Dickson, Carlotta Cataldi, and Crystal Glover, "The Show Fashion Movement: Reversing Environmental Damage," http://www.notjustalabel.com/editorial/the_slow_fashion_movement. Accessed May 9, 2013.

Green Consumers. Individuals referred to as green consumers are actual and potential customers of retail firms, usually in the industrialized countries, who express preferences for products, services, and companies that are perceived to be more environment-friendly than other competitive products, services, and firms. Marketing research firms in these countries have identified a range of green consumerism based on the strengths of these preferences and reported consumer purchases. "Light green" consumers are more likely to make impulsive purchase decisions, while "dark green" consumers are more likely to plan their purchases.[105] Green consumers have been a sought-after segment of the market—young, well-paid, highly educated, Internet savvy, predominately female, and mostly professional or white-collar employees.[106]

Recently, Joel Makower looked back on the 20 years since his book *The Green Consumer* and found that the predictions did not come true. He said that politicians had become more versed in environmental issues and that companies were not only increasingly engaged in environmental responsibility but that some were being truly innovative in their efforts. However, according to Makower, the number of green consumers has not changed drastically since 1990. These are individuals who alter their habits in order to drive markets toward more sustainable offerings. Still, in assessing the past 20 years, he concludes, "I'm not quite ready to proclaim green consumerism dead (though I can't honestly say it's ever been alive and well). There will always be a small corps of true-blue green consumers ready to vote with their dollars—at least for some products." [107]

Why consumers tend not to buy green when they hold such green philosophies is a paradox that has confounded companies. Consumers say that they want environmentally responsible products but sales of those products are often disappointing when they hit the market. Andrew Gershoff and Julie Irwin explored this paradox and found that several issues arise for consumers as they weigh the costs and benefits of green products. One is that consumers question whether green actions will lead to green outcomes: the benefits are hard to observe and marketers are not believed because they are not considered trustworthy.[108] Consumers also question whether it is worth paying a cost today for a benefit that will not occur until the future.[109] Furthermore, consumers tend to believe that there is "a catch" somewhere and may infer tradeoffs that don't even exist.[110] Finally, consumers would prefer to let others bear the costs, knowing that the individual bears the cost but the benefits are shared.[111]

Green Employees. A second stakeholder group with which most businesses are concerned is green employees. Although the popular press has not focused as much attention on green employees as it has on green consumers, there is evidence that employees are playing a major role in promoting environmentalism at work. In addition to union and general employee environmental concerns with plant, warehouse, and office safety and health, employees in many companies have assisted management in going beyond these traditional concerns into areas such as pollution prevention, recycling, energy and environmental audits, and community environmental projects. An important survey of workers in the United Kingdom found that 69 percent welcomed green benefits from environmentally responsible employers, 14 percent would change jobs for a greener benefits package, and 35 percent believed that this would make them more loyal to the firm. In the United States, 33 percent would rather work for an environmentally sound company and more than half thought their company should do more to be eco-friendly.[112]

Green Investors. Another important business stakeholder involved in environmental issues is the green investor. Similar to investors interested in advancing social causes, individuals and organizations sometimes want to put their money where their environmental values are by identifying and utilizing financial instruments that are associated

Spotlight on Sustainability

Living "The Other Low-Carb Life"

Time named the Personal Carbon Footprint one of the "50 best inventions of 2009." Their reasoning was that countries never seem to be able to agree on how to reduce carbon but individuals can move forward on their own. Furthermore, the wealthy people of the world, whether from Indiana or India, produce most of the world's carbon emissions. A strategy focused on rich individuals instead of rich countries might be more effective. Many individuals have begun to make a commitment to the "**carbon neutral**" life by tracking and paying for the CO2 that they spend. Carbon neutrality can be achieved through a combination of minimizing carbon emissions where possible (it is possible to book a carbon neutral flight or have carbon neutral groceries delivered to your home) and then purchasing offsets for the emissions that remain. For example, environmental consultant Guy Dauncey tallies his annual carbon spending when he tallies his taxes. He found that his personal activities caused 13.5 tons of carbon emissions. The going rate for carbon was $10 a ton, and so he arranged to do $135 of work for the Solar Electric Light Fund, a group that helps African villagers use solar power instead of kerosene.

The Nature Conservancy (http://www.nature.org) provides a free carbon footprint calculator that measures how many tons of carbon dioxide and greenhouse gasses are generated by the different choices an individual makes each year. They provide advice on how to evaluate carbon offset options, as well as offering some of these options, such as contributing to the Tensas River Basin Project on the Mississippi River. Their Web site also provides a range of information on global warming along with ways in which individuals can become involved in the issue.

Sources: "The 50 Best Inventions of the Year," *Time* (November 23, 2009), 57–92; Danylo Hawaleshka, "The Other Low-Carb Life," *Maclean's* (June 21, 2004), 54; http://www.nature.org. Accessed April 27, 2013.

---

with environmentally oriented companies. A growing number of mutual funds, stock and bond offerings, money market funds, and other financial instruments have included environmental components in recent years.[113] Shareholder resolutions address concerns that range from toxic emissions to recycling and waste to nuclear power plants and climate change. In 2013, twelve investors with $40 billion in assets sent a letter to the National Federation of Municipal Analysts (NFMA) asking that they increase the disclosure requirements of water utilities.[114] A 2012 survey showed that 83 percent of asset owners and 78 percent of asset managers believe climate change poses a material risk or presents an opportunity in their investment portfolio.[115]

After the *Exxon Valdez* oil spill, several environmental, labor, and social investor groups formed an organization called Ceres. They developed a preamble and a set of ten policy statements called the "Valdez Principles" (later renamed the **Ceres Principles**). These principles were advanced as models for businesses to express and practice environmental sensitivity. In 2010, Ceres reflected on the past and looked toward the future in their "2010 Roadmap to Sustainability."[116] The emphasis is on integrating sustainability through all aspects of the organization. According to Ceres President Mindy S. Lubber, "Business is astute at solving problems, and many of the biggest global challenges we face are social and environmental. As a result, it is business that must lead the way by turning these challenges into opportunities. This means fully integrating sustainability considerations into governance, performance, accountability, R&D and overall business

FIGURE 15-6

Ceres' 21st Century Corporate Vision: 20 Key Expectations

The Ceres' Roadmap presents an integrated approach for embedding environmental and social concerns into the corporate DNA. It focuses on areas where Ceres sees enormous opportunities for impact but it does not cover every aspect of sustainability.

1. **Governance for Sustainability**
   a. Board oversight
   b. Management Accountability
   c. Executive Compensation
   d. Public Policy

2. **Stakeholder Engagement**
   a. Focus Engagement Activity
   b. Substantive Stakeholder Dialogue
   c. Investor Engagement
   d. C-Level Engagement

3. **Disclosure**
   a. Standards for Disclosure
   b. Disclosure in Financial Filings
   c. Scope and Content
   d. Vehicles for Disclosure
   e. Product Transparency
   f. Verification and Assurance

4. **Performance**
   a. Operations
   b. Supply Chain
   c. Transportation and Logistics
   d. Products and Services
   e. Employees

Source: "The 21st Century Corporation: The CERES Roadmap for Sustainability," *Ceres* (Boston, MA: 2010), http://www.ceres.org/resources/reports/ceres-roadmap-to-sustainability-2010/view. Accessed April 28, 2013.

strategy."[117] Figure 15.6 outlines the 20 key expectations in CERES' 21st Century Corporate Vision. It shows how sustainability must be embedded into every aspect of corporate operations to achieve meaningful progress.

Business Environmentalism

Now that caring for the natural environment has become good business, there are countless examples of firms demonstrating that sustainable business practices can not only help the planet but also be a source of competitive advantage. We simply highlight a couple of firms that, to paraphrase an old song, cared about the environment before caring about the environment was "cool."

Patagonia

Patagonia founder and owner Yvon Chouinard has received a variety of accolades, including TriplePundit.com's Most Sustainable CEO award.[118] This is not surprising, because one cannot discuss business sustainability without mentioning Patagonia, the outdoor lifestyle company that is said to be "arguably one of the most environmentally focused companies in the world."[119] Decades before most businesses considered the possibility of recycling, Patagonia had made it an integral part of operations.[120] The company used the mail-order catalog to send messages about the problems of overfishing and genetically modified foods. After discovering they could make their outdoor gear out of discarded plastic soda bottles, founder-owner Yvon Chouinard set about to do an environmental assessment of all their materials. He found that cotton was particularly damaging due to its dependencies on pesticides, insecticides, and defoliants. "To know this and not switch to organic cotton would be unconscionable," says Chouinard.[121] He gave his managers 18 months to make the switch. This was a difficult move in 1994, even for a founder who owned most of the company's stock. Organic cotton was rare at the time, costing 50 to 100 percent more than traditional cotton. The risk was huge because a fifth of Patagonia's products were made from cotton. Suppliers balked and the rank and file grumbled, but Chouinard declared they had to do it or the company would not sell cotton again. As often happens when companies take well-reasoned courageous stands, the risk paid off. Patagonia's cotton sales rose 25 percent and the move set up an organic cotton industry that thrives today.[122]

3M Company

In 2013, 3M was recognized by the U.S. Environmental Protection Agency and U.S. Department of Energy by winning the Sustained Excellence Award for Energy Management for continuous improvement in energy management. 3M is the only industrial company to receive this honor nine years in a row.[123] The 3M Company is one of the best-known multinational companies to have adopted a long-term, comprehensive, beyond-compliance, environmental policy and program. In their own words, "3M's leadership has recognized that the company's long-term success springs from the principles of sustainable development, which include: stewardship to the environment, contributions to society, and the creation of economic value."[124] Begun more than 30 years ago, 3M's Pollution Prevention Pays program was a multiproduct, multiprocess approach to manufacturing. In the program's first year alone, through product reformulation, process modification, equipment redesign, and waste recycling, 3M prevented 73,000 tons of air emissions and 2,800 tons of sludge. They also saved more than $700 million for the company by reducing various pollutants at their sources. The company gives the credit (and financial rewards) for these environmental successes to its employees, who developed more than 4,500 subprojects under this program.[125]

The successes of 3M's environmental efforts are numerous. 3M scientists developed 3M HFEs as a CFC replacement. In just 15 years, 3M cut its volatile organic air emissions by 95 percent, its toxic releases by 94 percent, and its greenhouse gas emissions by 45 percent.[126] It is not surprising, therefore, that 3M has won awards for its environmental excellence. Thirty years ago, 3M's environmental efforts were focused on reducing emissions. Now the company is factoring environmental awareness into all stages of the product's life cycle. Its "Lifecycle Management" program is designed to minimize environmental impact from the product design to customer use and disposal. The *Corporate Responsibility Officer (CRO)* magazine (previously *Business Ethics*) described 3M as having "sustained commitment, innovation, and substantial impact in three decades of environmental stewardship."[127]

Business and Environmental Activist Partnerships

In the past several years, a shift in the relationship between business and environmental activists has occurred. Accommodation is replacing antagonism as the two parties begin to recognize their mutual dependence. Business needs environmental activists to both inform and validate their environmental efforts and activists need business to change the way it operates in order to protect the planet.[128]

Examples of this new partnership abound. Silicon Valley Toxic Coalition activists first communicated their concern to Dell by chaining themselves to computer monitors. They then worked with Dell on their innovative recycling program and other issues of sustainability.[129] According to Coalition founder Ted Smith, "Companies have decided it is better to invite us into the tent than have us outside picketing their keynote speeches. It's a long way from where we started."[130] When the CEOs of ten major corporations met in Washington to issue a call for mandatory carbon emission limits, the presidents of Environmental Defense and the Natural Resources Defense Council (NRDC) were at the table with them.[131]

The strangest of these new bedfellows were Adam Werbach, once the youngest president of the Sierra Club, and Walmart, a company he once called "a new breed of toxin."[132]

Walmart had developed a variety of partnerships. Conservation International helped them to lower energy use and Environmental Defense opened an office in Bentonville, Arkansas, so that they could work more closely with Walmart—though they were careful to take no money from them.[133] However, the partnership between Werbach and Walmart caused a great deal of commotion.

Werbach had been a leader in the environmentalist community since he became the youngest Sierra Club president at the age of 23. His book's title, *Act Now, Apologize Later*, reflected his willingness to act decisively and deal with reactions later. In the case of Walmart, the reaction was intense. Clients of his small consulting firm, Act Now, fired him because they did not want to be associated with anyone who did business with Walmart. Old friends no longer spoke to him; he was even threatened by strangers.[134]

Despite the upset it caused, both parties remained committed to this collaboration. The benefits for Walmart were clear. At a time when some observers were questioning the sincerity of their environmental initiatives, Werbach, now Global CEO of sustainability agency Saatchi & Saatchi S, brought a perception of legitimacy to their efforts. For Werbach, the unprecedented scope of the opportunity was too much to resist. According to Werbach's wife Lyn, "Imagine that struggle of knowing there's an opportunity that has unprecedented reach and not taking it."[135]

Systematic Business Responses to the Environmental Challenge

Various management approaches are available for use in selecting or constructing an environmental strategy. These include management approaches that were discussed in more general terms in earlier chapters, such as crisis management, issues management, and stakeholder management. Because these topics were addressed more fully in Chapters 5 and 6, only their applicability to environmental management is discussed here.

Managers can use crisis management in the environmental area by focusing on two factors: prevention and contingency plans. Issues management can be employed to track public interest in natural environment issues and to develop and implement plans to attempt to ensure that the scope of environmental problems is minimized, and that the firm develops effective responses at each stage in the life cycles of environmental issues. Environmental issues can be developed as part of the environmental impact statement process or as part of the strategic planning macroenvironmental analysis process.

Similarly, stakeholder management applies to environmental management because environmental stakeholders and their stakes can be identified, including the environmental public, environmental regulators, environmental groups, and various entities (human and nonhuman) across the entire natural environment. The follow-up stages of stakeholder management (i.e., planning for and interacting with stakeholders—stakeholder engagement) can then be conducted so that each important environmental stakeholder is given adequate attention after it is identified.

The Future of Business: Greening and/or Growing?

The salient environmental question we all may need to address in the future: "How much is enough?" A common business and, indeed, public policy goal in most human societies has been economic growth. Typically, businesses and societies have needed increasing amounts of either materials or energy, or both, to achieve that economic growth. Limits on growth, similar to limits on human reproduction, at either the macro or micro level, have not been widely popular. One potential problem with unrestrained economic growth worldwide is that, unless technology or people change significantly within a generation, environmental problems change in degree from significant to severe.

The pressures on the environment come from many directions. World population is projected to continue to grow, creating greater demands on food and fuel resources. Large countries such as China and India are industrializing, so they will use increasing amounts of materials and energy. The already industrialized countries continue to maintain the highly consumptive lifestyles that have strained the environment already. As the name implies, the sustainability imperative is of the essence. Business no longer has the luxury of deciding whether or not to respond to it—society in general and the environment in particular can't wait.

Summary

We began by discussing the concept of sustainability and its importance to business. We then outlined the top environmental issues facing business today. Environmental ethics began our discussion of individual and collective responsibility for sustaining the environment. We explored the role of governments and environmental interest groups in effecting change and then looked at companies that are leaders in practicing sustainable business practices. Lastly, we offered ways in which businesses can act toward achieving sustainability.

Although there is a growing consensus about the importance of sustainability, there remain significant differences of opinion on how problems will develop in the future and what should be done to resolve them. The natural environment is crucial for human survival, and a number of complex and interconnected human-induced activities are threatening this environment. Problems such as those profiled in this chapter are potentially endangering nonhuman species and ecosystems, and simultaneously reducing the quality of human life. Individuals and their organizations, including businesses, are directly or indirectly responsible for this situation.

The recent growth in partnerships between business and environmental activists is a promising sign but more changes must come. A minimum baseline of sustainability—meeting the needs of the present without compromising the ability of future generations to meet their needs—should be the bottom line for business as it moves into the future.

Key Terms

acid rain, p. 440
air pollution, p. 440
biodiversity, p. 439
cap and trade, p. 448
carbon neutral, p. 454
Ceres Principles, p. 454
CERES' "Roadmap to Sustainability," p. 433
Clean Air Act, p. 447
Clean Water Act, p. 448
climate change, p. 437
deforestation, p. 444
ecoterrorists, p. 452
emissions trading, p. 448

Endangered Species Act (ESA), p. 449
energy inefficiency, p. 438
environment, p. 435
environmental impact statements (EISs), p. 447
Environmental Protection Agency (EPA), p. 447
externalities, p. 435
fossil fuels, p. 437
Global Compact, p. 450
Global Reporting Initiative (GRI), p. 450
global warming, p. 437

greenhouse effect, p. 437
Montreal Protocol, p. 450
NIMBY, p. 446
ozone, p. 442
Superfund, p. 449
sustainability, p. 432
toxic substances, p. 439
Toxic Substances Control Act, p. 449
tragedy of the commons, p. 444
triple bottom line (TBL), p. 432
watershed, p. 442
wicked problems, p. 444

Discussion Questions

1. What is sustainability? How does sustainability relate to environmentalism?

2. What are several of the most important environmental issues now receiving worldwide attention?

3. Who has responsibility for addressing environmental issues?

4. How can ethics be applied in response to environmental issues?

5. Should businesses and societies continue to focus on unlimited economic growth?

Endnotes

1. "Report of the World Commission on Environment and Development," http://www.un.org/documents/ga/res/42/ares 42–187.htm. Accessed April 30, 2013.

2. W. Edward Stead and Jean Garner Stead with Mark Starik, *Sustainable Strategic Management* (Armonk, NY: M. E. Sharpe, Inc., 2004).

3. Michael de Pencier, "Interview with Maurice Strong," *Corporate Knights: The Canadian Magazine for Responsible Business* (June 4, 2003), http://corporateknights .com/sites/default/files/CK6.pdf. Accessed April 30, 2013.

4. William McDonough and Michael Braungart, *Cradle to Cradle: Remaking the Way We Make Things* (New York: North Point Press, 2002).

5. http://www.torkusa.com/Global/6_North_America/Tork %20Report/Tork%20Report%20Web%202012.pdf. Accessed April 27, 2013.

6. Daniel C. Esty and Andrew S. Winston, *Green to Gold: How Smart Companies Use Environmental Strategy to Innovate, Create Value, and Build Competitive Advantage* (New Haven, CT: Yale University Press, 2006).

7. *Ibid.*

8. Susan Casey, "Éminence Green," *Fortune* (April 2, 2007), 62–70.

9. "The Innovation Bottom Line," *Winter 2013 MIT Sloan Research Report*, http://sloanreview.mit.edu/reports/ sustainability-innovation/. Accessed April 27, 2013.

10. Brendan LeBlanc, "Sustainability Rises on the CFO's To-Do List," *Financial Executive* (March, 2012), 55–57.

11. Leon Kaye, "The Business Case for Sustainability Is Becoming Easier to Make," *Triple Pundit* (March 15, 2013), http://www.triplepundit.com/2013/03/business-case-for-sustainability/. Accessed April 27, 2013.

12. "The 21st Century Corporation: The CERES Roadmap for Sustainability," *Ceres* (Boston, MA: 2010), http:// www.ceres.org/resources/reports/ceres-roadmap-to-sustainability-2010/view. Accessed April 28, 2013.

13. Jo Confino, "Unilever's Paul Polman: Challenging the Corporate Status Quo," *The Guardian* (April 24, 2012), http://www.guardian.co.uk/sustainable-business/ paul-polman-unilever-sustainable-living-plan. Accessed April 27, 2013.

14. *Ibid.*

15. Ibid.

16. Unilever Sustainable Living Plan, http://www.unileverusa .com/sustainable-living/uslp/#PillarGroup3Pillar1. Accessed April 27, 2013.

17. "Captain Planet," *Harvard Business Review* (June 2012), 112–118.

18. Paul R. Ehrlich, Anne H. Ehrlich, and Gretchen C. Daily, *The Stork and the Plow: The Equity Answer to the Human Dilemma* (New Haven, CT: Yale University Press, 1997), 24.

19. Marc Gunther, "Going Green," *Fortune* (April 2, 2007), 44.

20. Ibid., 44.

21. Ibid.

22. William Collins, Robert Colman, James Haywood, Martin R. Manning, and Philip Mote, "The Physical Science Behind Climate Change," *Scientific American* (August 2007), 64–71.

23. "Cleaning Up (Cover Story)," *The Economist* (June 2, 2007), 3–4.

24. Collins et al., 64–71.

25. Ibid.

26. Jane Sasseen, "Who Speaks for Business?" *BusinessWeek* (October 19, 2009), 22–24.

27. The Department of Defense, *The Quadrennial Defense Review Report* (February 2010), http://www.defense .gov/QDR/QDR%20as%20of%2029JAN10%201600.pdf# page=107.

28. Ibid., 84.

29. Ibid., 85.

30. Joshua Zaffos and Daily Climate, "U.S. Military Forges Ahead with Plans to Combat Climate Change," *Scientific American* (April 2, 2012), http://www.scientificamerican .com/article.cfm?id=us-military-forges-ahead-with-plans-to-combat-climate-change. Accessed April 28, 2013.

31. "How a Market Heats Up," *Fortune* (May 29, 2006), 74–75.

32. Wolfram Krewitt, Sonja Simon, Wina Graus, Sven Teske, Arthouros Zervos, and Oliver Schafer, "The 2°C Scenario: A Sustainable World Energy Perspective," *Energy Policy* (October 2007), 4969–4980.

33. Esty and Winston.

34. Esty and Winston.

35. Ibid.

36. Ibid.

37. Mary Carmichael, Sarah Schafer, and Sudip Mazumdar, "Troubled Waters," *Newsweek* (June 4, 2007), 52–56.

38. Geoffrey Lean, "Water Crisis Now Bigger Threat Than Financial Crisis," *The Independent* (March 15, 2009), http://www.independent.co.uk/environment/climate-change/water-scarcity-now-bigger-threat-than-financial-crisis-1645358.html. Accessed April 30, 2013.

39. Carmichael, Schafer, and Mazumdar, 52–56.

40. Esty and Winston.

41. Carmichael, Schafer, and Mazumdar, 52–56.

42. Ibid.

43. Lean, 2009.

44. Ibid.

45. "Message by H.E. Dr. Ali Abdussalam Treki, President of the United Nations General Assembly," http://www.cbd.int/doc/speech/2009/sp-2009-11-09-iyb-welcome-ungatreki-en.pdf. Accessed April 30, 2013.

46. Center for Biological Diversity, http://www.biological diversity.org/programs/biodiversity/elements_of_biodiversity/extinction_crisis/. Accessed June 14, 2013.

47. "Message by H.E. Dr. Ali Abdussalam Treki, President of the United Nations General Assembly," http://www.cbd.int/doc/speech/2009/sp-2009-11-09-iyb-welcome-ungatreki-en.pdf. Accessed April 30, 2013.

48. http://nationalatlas.gov/mld/efct17x.html. Accessed April 30, 2013.

49. Armen Keleyian, "Oil & Gas Industry Spills Happen "All the Time," CBS Evening News (April 12, 2011), http://www.cbsnews.com/8301-18563_162-20053283.html. Accessed April 28, 2013.

50. "Air Pollution Effects," http://www.epa.gov/oar/airpollutants.html. Accessed April 30, 2013.

51. Mark Dolliver, "Environmental Worries Will Never Be Extinct," *Adweek* (March 26, 2007), 35.

52. "What Is Acid Rain," http://www.epa.gov/acidrain/what/index.html. Accessed April 30, 2013.

53. Ibid.

54. Ibid.

55. "Why Should You Be Concerned about Air Pollution?" http://www.epa.gov/air/caa/peg/concern.html. Accessed April 30, 2013.

56. Ibid.

57. http://www.epa.gov/wastes/ Accessed April 30, 2013.

58. Ibid.

59. Ibid.

60. Ibid.

61. Linda Marsa, "Is the Ozone Hole Shrinking?" *Discover Magazine* (April 5, 2013), http://discovermagazine.com/2013/may/02-is-the-ozone-hole-shrinking#.UX2V9KJ-tl8E. Accessed April 28, 2013.

62. Ibid.

63. http://www.epa.gov. Accessed April 30, 2013.

64. http://www.montereybayaquarium.org/cr/cr_seafoodwatch/issues/wildseafood_overfishing.aspx. Accessed April 28, 2013.

65. Alex Dominguez, "Officials: Bay Blue Crab Population up 60 Percent," *Bloomberg BusinessWeek* (April 14, 2010), http://www.businessweek.com/ap/financialnews/D9F32J280.htm. Accessed April 30, 2013.

66. Ibid.

67. Toni Johnson, "Deforestation and Greenhouse-Gas Emissions," *Backgrounder: Council on Foreign Relations* (December 21, 2009), http://www.cfr.org/natural-resources-management/deforestation-greenhouse-gas-emissions/p14919. Accessed April 28, 2013.

68. Bryan Walsh, Zamira Loebis, and Jason Tedjasukmana, "Getting Credit for Saving Trees," *Time* (July 23, 2007), 58–60.

69. David C. Wagman, "Wicked Problems," *Power Engineering* (May 2006), 5.

70. Garrett Hardin, "The Tragedy of the Commons," *Science* (Vol. 162, 1968), 1243–1248.

71. Ibid.

72. Adam Vaughn, "Public Concern for Environment Lowest in 20 Years, "*The Guardian* (February 28, 2013), http://www.guardian.co.uk/environment/2013/feb/28/public-concern-environment

73. Linda M. Sama, Stephanie A. Welcomer, and Virginia W. Gerde, "Who Speaks for the Trees? Invoking an Ethic of Care to Give Voice to the Silent Stakeholder," in S. Sharma and M. Starik (eds.), *Stakeholders, the Environment and Society* (Cheltenham, UK: Edward Elgar, 2004), 140–165.

74. Ibid.

75. Katharine Q. Seelye, "Big Wind Farm Off Cape Cod Gets Approval," *The New York Times* (April 29, 2010), http://www.nytimes.com/2010/04/29/science/earth/29wind.html?scp=2&sq=cape%20cod%20wind%20farm&st=cse. Accessed April 30, 2013.

76. Ibid.

77. Public Law 91–190 (1969), 42 U.S.C. Section 4331 et seq.

78. http://www.epa.gov/air/caa/. Accessed May 9. 2013.

79. http://www.epa.gov/air/caa/peg/understand.html. Accessed May 9, 2013.

80. "Kyoto Protocol," http://unfccc.int/kyoto_protocol/items/2830.php. Accessed May 9, 2013.

81. T. McAdams, *Law, Business & Society*, 3rd. Ed. (Homewood, IL: Irwin, 1992), 784–787, http://www.epa.gov. Accessed April 30, 2013.

82. http://www2.epa.gov/laws-regulations/summary-toxic-substances-control-act Accessed April 30, 2013.

83. Ibid.

84. http://www.epa.gov/superfund/. Accessed April 30, 2013.

85. Ibid.

86. IUCN 2010. *IUCN Red List of Threatened Species. Version 2010.1.* http://www.iucnredlist.org/. Accessed March 10, 2013.

87. Ibid.

88. Ibid.

89. http://www.epa.gov/lawsregs/laws/esa.html. Accessed April 30, 2013.

90. Ibid.

91. http://ozone.unep.org/Publications/MP_Key_Achievements-E.pdf. Accessed April 30, 2013.

92. Ibid.

93. Ibid.

94. http://unep.org. Accessed April 30, 2013.

95. http://www.unglobalcompact.org/AboutTheGC/TheTenPrinciples/humanRights.html. Accessed April 30, 2013.

96. Ibid.

97. http://www.edf.org/approach/partnerships/corporate. Accessed April 30, 2013.

98. M. E. Kriz, "Shades of Green," *National Journal* (July 28, 1990).

99. Mark Gunther, "The Mosquito in the Tent," *Fortune* (March 31, 2004), 158–162; Lisa Gerwitz, "It's Not Easy Being Green," *Deal.com* (March 8, 2004), 1.

100. Sharon Begley, "Good Cop/Bad Cop Goes Green," *Newsweek* (May 4, 2009), 49.

101. Karen Charman, "The U.S. Goes on Green Alert," *OnEarth* (Fall 2003), 8.

102. "Eco-Terrorism," http://www.epw.senate.gov/public/index.cfm?FuseAction=Minority.Blogs&ContentRecord_id=C436B9D1-802A-23AD-4137-FF8D119B7464. Accessed April 30, 2013.

103. Blaine Hardon, "11 Indicted in 'Eco-Terrorism' Case," *Washington Post* (January 21, 2006), http://www.washingtonpost.com/wp-dyn/content/article/2006/01/20/AR2006012001823.html. Accessed April 30, 2013.

104. http://www.fbi.gov/news/stories/2012/december/eco-terrorist-surrenders-two-fugitives-still-at-large/eco-terrorist-surrenders-two-fugitives-still-at-large. Accessed April 28, 2013.

105. "'Light Green' Consumers Differ from 'Dark Green' Consumers," *Environmentalleader.com* (October 21, 2009), http://www.environmentalleader.com/2009/10/21/light-green-consumers-differ-from-dark-greenconsumers/. Accessed April 30, 2013.

106. R. Gardyn, "Saving the Earth, One Click at a Time," *American Demographic* (January 2001), 30–33.

107. Joel Makower, "The Green Consumer, 1990–2010," *Greenbiz.com* (March 29, 2010), http://www.greenbiz.com/blog/2010/03/29/green-consumer-1990-2010. Accessed April 30, 2013.

108. Andrew D. Gershoff and Julie R. Irwin, (2012) "Why Not Choose Green? Consumer Decision Making for Environmentally Friendly Products," in Pratima Ban-sal and Andrew J. Hoffman (eds.) *The Oxford Handbook of Business and the Natural Environment* (Oxford University Press), 366–383.

109. Ibid.

110. Ibid.

111. Ibid.

112. Josephine Rossi, "Show Them the Green," *T+D* (June 2007), 12–13.

113. Barnaby J. Feder, "Funds Want Oil Companies to Report on Climate," *The New York Times* (February 27, 2004), C3.

114. http://www.ceres.org/press/press-releases/investors-seek-stronger-disclosure-by-u.s.-water-providers. Accessed April 30, 2013.

115. http://www.ceres.org/press/press-releases/climate-change-investor-groups-publish-second-report-on-global-investor-practices-relating-to-climate-change. Accessed April 30, 2013.

116. http://www.ceres.org/company-network/ceres-roadmap/ceres-roadmap. Accessed April 30, 2013.

117. Ibid.

118. http://www.triplepundit.com/2010/01/top-tensustainable-ceos/. Accessed April 30, 2013.

119. Esty and Winston, 25.

120. Susan Casey, "Éminence Green," *Fortune* (April 2, 2007), 62–70.

121. Ibid., 67.

122. Ibid.

123. Spark.3m.com/blog/?p=2136. Accessed April 27, 2013.

124. http://solutions.3m.com/wps/portal/3M/en_US/global/sustainability/s/vision-strategy/ceo-statement/. Accessed April 30, 2013.

125. *3M's Pollution Prevention Pays: An Initiative for a Cleaner Tomorrow* (St. Paul, MN: 3M Company, 1991).

126. http://solutions.3m.com/wps/portal/3M/en_US/global/sustainability/s/performance-indicators/environment/ecoefficiency-results/. Accessed April 30, 2013.

127. http://www.thecro.com/awards_winners. Accessed April 30, 2013.

128. John Carey and Michael Arndt, "Hugging the Tree-Huggers," *BusinessWeek* (March 12, 2007), 66–68.

129. Ibid.; http://www.dell.com/Learn/us/en/uscorp1/dell-environment-recycling?c=us&l=en&s=corp&cs=uscorp1&delphi:gr=true. Accessed April 30, 2013.

130. Ibid., 66.

131. Ibid.

132. Danielle Sacks, "Working with the Enemy," *Fast Company* (September 2007), 74–81.

133. Carey and Arndt, 66–68; Sacks, 74–81.

134. Sacks, 74–81.

135. Ibid., 79.

16

Business and Community Stakeholders

CHAPTER LEARNING OUTCOMES

After studying this chapter, you should be able to:

1. Identify and discuss two basic ways of business giving.

2. Discuss reasons for community involvement, various types of community projects, and management of community stakeholders.

3. Explain the pros and cons of corporate philanthropy, provide a brief history of corporate philanthropy, and explain why and to whom companies give.

4. Differentiate between strategic philanthropy, cause-related marketing, and cause branding.

5. Characterize the nature of offshoring and the movement toward reshoring.

6. Address steps that a business or plant might take before a decision to close is made.

7. Identify strategies that a business or plant might employ after a decision to close has been made.

The Oxford English Dictionary has many definitions of the word "community."[1] They all share an underlying theme of commonality. Community members may share a geographic locale, a profession, an ideology, or even a recreational pastime. The actions of business affect a range of communities, and it is important that managers be aware of these impacts and manage in a way that respects the interests of community stakeholders. This chapter primarily focuses on the immediate locale—the town, city, or state—in which a business resides. We should remember, however, that instant communication, speedy travel, and social networking often expand the relevant community to include the region, the nation, or even the world. From the global economic recession, to the devastation of Superstorm Sandy, businesses affect and are affected by events throughout the world.

When we think of business and its community stakeholders, two major kinds of relationships come to mind. One is the positive contribution business can make to the community. Examples of these positive contributions include volunteerism, company contributions, and support of programs in education, culture, urban development, the arts, civic activities, and health and welfare endeavors. On the other hand, business can also cause harm to community stakeholders. It can pollute the environment or put people out of work by offshore outsourcing or closing a plant. Business can abuse its power and exploit consumers and employees. When business causes harm, as with the global financial crisis, it is incumbent upon business to have a positive impact on the community. In a recent Bloomberg *BusinessWeek* report, Michael Porter opined, "As high unemployment, rising poverty, and dismay over corporate greed breed contempt for the capitalist market system.... Serving the intersecting needs of business and the community is the only path to winning back respect for Corporate America."[2]

This chapter concentrates on community involvement and corporate philanthropy as community stakeholder issues. In addition, it discusses the topics of offshore outsourcing and business or plant closings as community stakeholder concerns. This discussion should provide us with an opportunity to explore both the positive and the detrimental effects that characterize business—community relationships. It begins with the positive.

In addition to being profitable, obeying the law, and being ethical, a company may create a positive impact in the community by giving in two ways:

(1) donating the time and talents of its managers and employees and (2) making financial contributions. The first category, **community involvement**, manifests itself in a wide array of voluntary activities in the community. The second category involves corporate philanthropy or business giving. We should note that there is significant overlap between these two categories, because companies quite frequently donate their time and talent and give financial aid to the same general projects. First, we discuss community involvement and the various ways in which companies enhance the quality of life in their communities.

Community Involvement

Business must—not only for a healthier society, but also for its own well-being—be willing to give the same serious consideration to human needs that it gives to its own needs for production and profits. The following argument for increased community involvement from the 2011 UPS Corporate Sustainability Report makes the case for the contributions business can and should make to both the global and the local communities it serves:

> We operate our business to help the global economy operate more efficiently, with a lower carbon impact and better allocation of resources. We're also engaged internationally in the effort to set standards for sustainability and reporting, to help corporations become more transparent about their actions and consequences. At the same time, we are bringing the benefits of our business acumen and infrastructure to individuals and local businesses on a daily basis, millions of times, all around the world... UPS invests in civil society in the same way—from both global and local perspectives. We actively support the world's leading humanitarian relief organizations, including major agencies of the United Nations, and conduct long-term, multinational philanthropic initiatives such as forestry preservation and renewal, community resiliency and road safety. At the same time, we support more than 4,300 non-profits each year, and our people volunteer their time in their communities at an ever-increasing rate.[3]

Business involvement in the community represents enlightened self-interest because businesses are in a position to help themselves in the process of helping others. These dual objectives of business clearly illustrate that making profits and addressing social concerns are not mutually exclusive endeavors. When companies draw upon their strengths, they can make deep and lasting contributions to the communities they serve. Furthermore, when they make community service part of their identities, they can develop greater trust and community. John Lechleiter, Eli Lilly Chairman, President, and Chief Executive Officer drives this point home:

> The business community can—and must—play a vital role in addressing complex societal problems. It's clear that writing a check or donating product alone doesn't have a lasting impact. A growing body of evidence demonstrates that when a company engages with partners in an area in which the company has deep expertise and a vested interest, society benefits and the company enhances its own performance.[4]

Other rationales for business involvement in community affairs provide moral justification beyond that of enlightened self-interest. For example, utilitarian arguments can support corporate giving in that improvement of the social fabric creates the greatest good for the greatest number. This need not contradict the mandates of self-interest, because the corporation is one of the community members that will benefit.[5] Although justifications for corporate involvement in the community are possible from various perspectives, one thing is clear: Business has a moral responsibility to build a relationship with the community and to be sensitive to its impacts on the world around it. The Center for Corporate Citizenship at Boston College has developed a set of seven management practices, processes, and policies that represent a global standard of excellence in community involvement. These are listed in Figure 16-1.

Volunteer Programs

One of the most pervasive examples of business involvement in communities is a volunteer program. Corporate volunteer programs reflect the resourcefulness and responsiveness of business to communities in need of increasing services. They also have become essential for attracting and retaining the best talent in the workforce. Employees not only want to work for 'the good guys,' they want to be the good guys too.[6] According to Kellie McElhaney of the Haas School of Business, "For today's millennials entering the workforce, engagement in sustainability is a must-have, not a nice-to-have. They don't want to be told what the company is doing. They want to do it."[7] Eighty percent of Discover Communications' employees volunteer and, according to Michelle Russo, senior vice president of communications, those employees would revolt if the company ended the program. Russo notes, "We don't lose productivity, we gain it."[8] A recent study by the sustainability accounting firm, Ekos International, found that community engagement is critical for competitive advantage.[9]

There are numerous examples of corporations making a difference in communities through volunteer activities. The Longaberger Company has a longstanding commitment to the American Cancer Society to make and sell "Horizon of Hope" baskets, stuffed with breast cancer literature. The campaign has raised millions of dollars for research and education to combat breast cancer.[10] UPS has a variety of community service initiatives.

FIGURE 16-1

Standards of Excellence in Corporate Community Involvement

Standard 1: Leadership
My company actively and purposefully helps to define needs, set direction, and initiate meaningful change around community or societal issues.

Standard 2: Strategy
My company plans its community involvement and leverages its capacities and strengths to deliver meaningful value to society and to the business.

Standard 3: Integration
My company engages all facets of the business to contribute to and realize the benefit from community involvement.

Standard 4: Infrastructure
My company consistently provides the resources and support needed to ensure the successful execution of its community involvement strategy.

Standard 5: Performance Measurement
My company assesses the effectiveness and impact of its community involvement and uses the results for continuous improvement.

Standard 6: Communication
My company actively and openly communicates in order to inform, influence, and engage internal and external stakeholders.

Standard 7: Community Relationships
My company engages and collaborates with external stakeholders to advance its community involvement strategy.

Source: Center for Corporate Citizenship at Boston College, http://www.bcccc.net/index.cfm?pageId=2096. Accessed April 7, 2013.

Through Neighbor to Neighbor, UPS employees help to improve impoverished communities across the United States and around the world by organizing food drives, working in soup kitchens, and mentoring troubled youth. Community service is part of the Community Internship Program, UPS's senior management level development program, and UPS's Global Volunteer Month provides communities throughout the world with the time and talents of UPS employees. The company urges its employees to volunteer when crises occur and maintains a 20-person logistics emergency team in Asia, Europe, and the Americas. The team is trained in humanitarian relief and continues to draw a paycheck while providing skill-based support in crisis situations.[11]

Many companies support individual volunteering efforts that permit employees to make a volunteer commitment to the community nonprofit of their choice. Known as "Dollars for Doers," these programs magnify the service contributions of the employee by matching employee volunteer hours with a corporate donation.[12] Unlike the traditional matching grant that matched employee donations with corporate funds, "Dollars for Doers" matches hours of service. For example, Campbell Soup donates $500 to nonprofits for every 25 hours an employee volunteers, and IBM provides nonprofits with equipment and services to match employee volunteer hours.[13] In return, companies are likely to harvest healthier and happier employees. Research has shown that volunteers receive physical and emotional benefits from being involved in helping others.[14] Employee volunteers are also more satisfied with, more loyal to, and more proud to work for their companies than non-volunteers.[15]

The overall benefits derived from employee volunteerism are summarized in Figure 16-2.

Managing Community Involvement

For discussion purposes, we are separating our treatment of *managing community involvement* from that of *managing corporate philanthropy*. In reality, however, this separation is impossible to achieve because there are significant overlaps between these two areas. Corporate philanthropy involves primarily the giving of financial resources. Community involvement focuses on other issues in the business–community relationship, especially the contribution of managerial and employee time and talent. This section addresses these broader community issues; a later section of this chapter deals with the more specific issue of managing corporate philanthropy.

Business Stake in the Community When one speaks with corporate executives in the fields of community and civic affairs and examines community affairs manuals and other corporate publications, one sees a broad array of reasons why companies need to keep abreast of the issues, problems, and changes expressed as community needs.

FIGURE 16-2

Benefits of Employee Volunteerism

For the Employee
- Improves morale
- Increases meaningfulness of work
- Develops teamwork and leadership skills
- Improves mental and physical health

For the Corporation
- Builds company image and reputation
- Improves employee attraction and retention

- Develops employee skills
- Builds relationship with and loyalty from consumers

For the Community
- Addresses community needs
- Saves community resources
- Builds pool of future volunteers and contributors
- Builds awareness of community needs

© Cengage Learning 2015

Self-interest and self-preservation provide one rationale. Companies typically have a significant physical presence in the community and so they want to protect that investment. Issues of interest to companies include zoning regulations, the threat of neighborhood deterioration, corporate property taxes, the community tax base, and the availability of an adequately trained workforce.

Companies can support their communities through their daily activities in a variety of ways, including sourcing from local businesses, joining public policy debates, investing in local banks, and locating facilities in places that benefit community development. In addition, companies can develop community action programs that transcend daily operations. For global corporations, the world is the community, so involvement must be at both the global and the local level. Figure 16-3 presents the results of a survey of businesses; identifying businesses' perceptions of the most important issues affecting communities as well as the methods those businesses use to address them.

Developing a Community Action Program The motivation for developing a **community action program** is evident when one considers the stake a firm has in the community. Likewise, the community represents a major stakeholder of business. Therefore, business has an added incentive to be systematic about its relationship with the community. First, the business must get to know the community in which it intends to become involved. The next step is to assess the company's resources to determine what the company is best able to give. Then the company can design a community action program by matching the community needs to the resources the company has available. Finally, as with all corporate endeavors, management should monitor the performance of the community action program carefully and make adjustments where needed.

Step One: Knowing the Community   A key to developing worthwhile community involvement programs is knowing the community in which the business resides. This is a research step that requires management to assess the characteristics of the local area. Every locale has particular characteristics that can help shape social programs of involvement. Who lives in the community? What is its ethnic composition? What is its unemployment level? Are there inner-city problems or pockets of poverty? What are

FIGURE 16-3   Corporate Community Involvement: The Most Important Issues and the Most Common Methods of Addressing Them

Community Investment Issues		Community Investment Methods	
K–12 Education	71%	Volunteerism	86%
Workforce Development	68%	Cause-Related Partnerships	75%
Business Development and Growth	48%	Executive Participation in Community	71%
Higher Education	47%	Nonprofit or Community Board Participation	71%
Transportation or Public Infrastructure	38%	Cash Contributions	65%
Housing	38%	Advocacy	52%
Health and Wellness	38%	Community Advisory Panels	48%
Arts, Parks, Sports	24%	Pro Bono Work	31%
Crimes or Public Safety	22%	Donated Property or Equipment	30%
Other	19%	Community Management	28%

Source: U.S. Chamber of Commerce Survey—Summary of Findings Presented at the 2007 National Partnership Conference: Corporate Community Investment, U.S. Chamber of Commerce.

other organizations doing? What are the most pressing social needs of the area? What is the community's morale?

Knowledge of community leadership is another factor. Is the leadership progressive? Is the leadership cohesive and unified, or is it fragmented? If it is fragmented, the company may have to make difficult choices about the groups with which it wants to affiliate. If the community's current approach to social issues is well organized, "jumping on the bandwagon" may be all that is necessary. If the community's leadership is not well organized, the company may want to provide an impetus and an agenda for restructuring or revitalizing the leadership.

Step Two: Knowing the Company's Resources   Effective addressing of various community needs requires an inventory and assessment of the company's resources and competencies. What are the variety, mix, and range of resources—personnel, money, meeting space, equipment, and supplies? Many companies are willing to give employees time to engage in and support community projects. This involvement may be in the form of managerial assistance, technical assistance, or personnel. Wide spectra of abilities, skills, interests, potentials, and experience exist in most organizations. To put any of these resources to work, however, it is necessary to know what is available, to what extent it is available, on what terms it is available, and over what period of time it is available.

Step Three: Selecting Projects to Support   The selection of community projects for company involvement grows out of the matching of community stakeholders' needs with company resources. Frequently, because there are many possible matches, the company must be selective in choosing from among them. Sometimes companies develop and refine policies or guidelines to help in the selection process. These policies are extremely useful because they further delineate areas in which the company may be involved and provide perspective for channeling the organization's energies most effectively.

Policies and guidelines can go a long way toward rationalizing and systematizing business involvement in the community. Such policy statements can provide a unified focus for company efforts. Guidelines to consider include: fit with the company resources (which project is most consistent with corporate resources and goals?), cost effectiveness (which project makes the best use of resources?), sustainability (will the project continue if the corporate involvement ends?), and employee preferences (with which projects would employees most want to get involved?).

An excellent example of a community project that follows these guidelines is the Ronald McDonald House Charities (RMHC) program sponsored by McDonald's Corporation. The three core programs of RMHC—the Ronald McDonald House, Ronald McDonald Family Room, and Ronald McDonald Care Mobile—are focused on helping families in need. The well-known Ronald McDonald House program provides a "home away from home" for families of seriously ill children receiving treatment at nearby hospitals. Since its inception more than 38 years ago, millions of families around the world have received shelter and solace through the program.[16]

Step Four: Monitoring Projects   Monitoring company projects involves review and control. Follow-up is necessary to ensure that the projects are being executed according to plans and on schedule. Feedback from the various steps in the process provides the information management needs to monitor progress. In later chapters, we elaborate on the managerial approach to dealing with various social issues. The guidelines previously listed, however, provide some insights into the development of business— community stakeholder relationships. As we stated earlier, community involvement is a discretionary or philanthropic activity in our corporate social performance model.

The costs are significant but the potential returns, for both the corporation and the community, are great.

Corporate Philanthropy or Business Giving

The word *philanthropy* comes from the Greek *philien*, which means "to love," and *anthropos*, which means "mankind."[17] Thus the dictionary defines **philanthropy** as "a desire to help mankind as indicated by acts of charity; love of mankind."[18] Corporate philanthropy is "business giving." In this section, we concentrate on the voluntary giving of financial resources by business. One problem with the dictionary definition of philanthropy is that the motive for the giving is characterized as charitable, benevolent, or generous. In actual practice, it is difficult to assess the true motives behind businesses'—or anyone's—giving of themselves or their financial resources.

Not surprisingly, corporate philanthropy took a downturn when the global financial crisis occurred. However, as the economy has rebounded, so has corporate giving. According to a survey conducted by the Committee Encouraging Corporate Philanthropy (CECP) in association with The Conference Board, total giving in 2011was $24.4 million, up significantly from $22.6 million in 2009.[19] Still, the uncertainty in the economy is making firms more cautious. Corporate giving is becoming increasingly focused, with companies giving in a way that is consistent with their core business strategies, skills, and resources.[20]

A Brief History of Corporate Philanthropy

Business philanthropy of one kind or another can be traced back to the 1920s, when the most significant effort to "translate the new social consciousness of management into action" emerged in the form of organized corporate philanthropy.[21] Before World War I, steps had been taken toward establishing systematic, federated fund-raising for community services. The early successes of the YMCA, the War Chests, welfare federations, Community Chests, colleges and universities, and hospitals provided impetus for these groups to organize their solicitations. The business response to the opportunity to help community needs varied. At one extreme, large enterprises such as the Bell Telephone system, with branches, offices, and

---

ETHICS IN PRACTICE CASE
Matters of Good Intentions

A high-level finance computer programmer is sitting at his cubicle working on an upgrade that his manager assigned to him. As he works on his project, he hears one of his peers talking to his wife, who has a major role at a well-known charity organization. The peer tells his wife that he created an account dedicated to funding the charity because the company does not make any contributions at all. He hears his peer say that he did this without getting approval from senior-level management and that the program works by taking very small fractions of cents that have been rounded off and over multiple transactions dumps the fractions of cents into this account made for charity. As he hears his peer explain this to his wife, he wonders to

himself, "what should I do? Should I tell management? He is my friend and technically it is for a good cause... right?"

1. Who are the stakeholders in this situation and what are their stakes?

2. Should the listener report the conversation he overheard to management?

3. Is your answer affected by the fact that the money is going to a good cause?

4. Is your answer affected by the fact that the company gives no money to charity?

Contributed by Steve Coiscou

subsidiaries in thousands of communities, contributed to literally thousands of civic and social organizations. Smaller firms, such as the companies in small mill towns of North Carolina, supported schools, housing projects, religious activities, and community welfare agencies with a degree of enthusiasm that exceeded most 19th-century paternalism.

From 1918 to 1929, the Community Chest movement dominated corporate giving. In the period from 1929 to 1935, there was an attempt to allow business to deduct up to 5 percent of its pretax net income for its community donations. During the years 1935 to 1945, marked by the Great Depression and World War II, business giving did not expand, but it began to grow again from 1945 to 1960. Since about 1960, corporate giving has grown to encompass a variety of initiatives. Now in the 21st century, broader social initiatives continue, but the nature of business giving has taken a turn. The corporate philanthropy watchword is now strategic philanthropy, philanthropy that benefits both society and the corporation that is giving. In a 2012 survey of giving officers, 82 percent said they are more thoughtful and strategic about their corporate philanthropy decisions than in the past: Their funding decisions are increasingly driven by the proximity of the gift to business needs.[22]

A Call for Transparency in Corporate Philanthropy

A major debate has arisen over proposals for legislation that would require companies to disclose which charities they support and how much money they give. Although companies are required to disclose the money they give through foundations because of the tax benefits derived from the foundation's tax-exempt status, companies need not disclose direct donations. This has renewed the age-old debate about the role of business in society. Proponents of disclosure contend that the money belongs to the shareholders and they alone have the right to determine where it will go. Former Representative Paul Gillmor (R-Ohio) said that he introduced legislation to require transparency because he had sat on corporate boards and observed executives distributing corporate assets to their pet charities while ignoring shareholders.

Gillmor's concern was shared by law professors such as Charles M. Elson, who argued that philanthropy often only serves to glorify corporate managers and that, unless the philanthropy clearly benefits the company, it represents a waste of corporate assets. A few nonprofits, such as the American Red Cross, also agreed that disclosure would be good public policy. Surprisingly, the National Society of Fundraising Executives even supported disclosure, arguing that it would help the image of philanthropy, which has been hurt by scandals in recent years.[23] This broad-based support notwithstanding, most corporations and nonprofits had expressed concern that disclosure would have a chilling effect on corporate donations. Their arguments include that charitable giving is a business decision, that disclosure would provide competitors with information about a firm's strategy, that it might incite controversy with special-interest groups, and that the paperwork would become an administrative burden.[24] Gillmor reintroduced his earlier bill in February 2007, but he passed away later that year. No real closure on the issue of corporate philanthropy transparency has been achieved; however, concerns about knowing the source of political donations has given the issue new life.

The fact that corporations are under no obligation to report their charitable giving has led to the rise of "dark money," i.e., political funding received from undisclosed sources, an issue that was discussed in Chapter 12. At this writing, the SEC is revisiting the issue of requiring corporate disclosure of politically-oriented contributions to nonprofits, so the transparency issue continues to receive attention. Shareholder rights advocates, public pension systems, and the AFL-CIO are advocating for greater transparency, while a coalition of the Chamber of Commerce, the Business Roundtable, and the National Association of Manufacturers, as well as other conservative groups, is lobbying against it.[25]

Giving to the "Third Sector": The Nonprofits

According to philanthropist John D. Rockefeller III, business giving is necessary to support what has been called the **third sector**—the nonprofit sector. The first two sectors—business and government—receive support through profits and taxes. The third sector (which includes hundreds of thousands of churches, museums, hospitals, libraries, private colleges and universities, and performing arts groups) depends on philanthropy for support. Philanthropy gives these institutions the crucial margin that assures them of their most precious asset—their independence.[26]

Why Do Companies Give? Perhaps it would be more worthwhile to know why companies give to charitable causes rather than to know how much they give. There are several ways to approach this question. We get initial insights when we consider the three categories of corporate contributions programs identified by the Committee to Encourage Corporate Philanthropy (CECP).[27] The motivations are (1) *Charitable*: community giving for which there is little or no expected benefit for the business, (2) *Community Investment*: Gifts that support long-term strategic business goals while also meeting a critical community need, and (3) *Commercial*: Giving that benefits the business wherein the benefit is its primary motivation. CECP's 2011 report showed an increase in community investment giving and a decrease in charitable giving.[28]

As economic pressures and increased international competitiveness force companies to be more careful with their earnings, we should not be surprised to see the profit motive coexisting with loftier goals in corporate contributions programs. In a subsequent section of this chapter, we illustrate how philanthropy can be "strategic," which means that corporate giving can be aligned with the firm's economic or profitability objectives.

To Whom Do Companies Give? During the course of any budget year, companies receive numerous requests for contributions from a wide variety of applicants. Companies must then weigh both quantitative and qualitative factors to arrive at decisions regarding the recipients of their gifts. By looking at the beneficiaries of corporate contributions, we can estimate the value business places on various societal needs in the community. However, we should note that, because of the lack of transparency in corporate giving which we discussed earlier in the chapter, our figures for giving are simply estimates, and estimates from different sources will vary.

According to the Conference Board, the majority of business giving is distributed mostly among four major categories of recipients in the following order of emphasis: (1) health and human services, (2) education, (3) civic and community activities, and (4) culture and the arts.[29]

A very small percentage of giving went to the environment, with the recipients being environmental interest groups such as the World Wildlife Fund, the Nature Conservatory, and Greenpeace.[30] The small percentage of contributions does not mean business is unconcerned about environmental issues, but rather that its commitment to the environment is less likely to show up in corporate philanthropy and more likely to be found in daily operations, as discussed in Chapter 15. In addition, environmental issues may end up under other categories such as community improvement. A brief discussion of each of these four categories will help explain the nature of business's involvement in philanthropy.

Health and Human Services   Health and human services are critical to the welfare of a community, whether it is the local community in which a business operates or the global community to which we all belong. Major recipients in this category include hospitals, youth agencies, and other local health and welfare agencies. Hospitals represent an obviously important need in most communities. They receive financial support for capital investments (new buildings and equipment), operating funds, and matching employee gifts. Youth agencies include such groups as the YMCA, YWCA, Boy Scouts, Girl Scouts, and Boys and Girls Clubs. These children will grow up, attend college, and move on to employment opportunities, so it is logical for business to include youth as a prominent part of its health and welfare contributions.

Another reason that health and human services are among the largest categories of business giving is the amount donated to federated drives such as the United Way. Dating back to the Community Chest movement, business has traditionally cooperated with federated giving mechanisms. Organizations such as the United Way spend the year evaluating nonprofit programs and determining where dollars would be best spent, with much of the money going to the local community. This saves businesses, particularly smaller local ones, the effort of not only trying to assess the various agencies to which they could make donations but also explaining to stakeholders why they chose one over another. Business hopes, just as the community does, that the consolidated efforts of federated drives will lend some order to the requests of major recipients in the community that business has chosen to support.

Education Corporate contributions in this category go to higher education and K–12 programs.[31] Educational recipients include capital grants (including endowments), unrestricted operating grants, departmental and research grants, scholarships and fellowships, and employee matching gifts. Also included in this category are contributions to educational groups (e.g., the United Negro College Fund and the Council for Financial Aid to Education) and to primary and secondary schools.

As noted earlier, business has a very good reason for supporting higher education—to increase the pool of trained personnel. This has obvious credibility, because higher education institutions do form the resource base from which business fills its managerial and professional positions. K–12 institutions feed into higher education, and so strong preparation at those levels is critical to a strong professional pool down the road. In addition, many workers in the front lines will receive their education primarily from K–12 institutions, and so it is vital that they too be in a position to provide business with a strong and capable workforce.

Civic and Community Activities This category of business giving represents a wide variety of philanthropic activities in the community. The dominant contributions in this category are those given in support of community improvement activities, environment and ecology, nonacademic research organizations (e.g., the Brookings Institution, the Committee for Economic Development, and the Urban League), and neighborhood renewal.

General Mills saw the importance of community involvement when the nickname of Minneapolis changed from the "City of Nice" to "Murderapolis." General Mills executives hired a consultant to analyze crime data and found that Hawthorne, just five miles from the company headquarters, was one of the city's most violent neighborhoods. They devoted thousands of employee hours and $2.5 million to ridding Hawthorne of its problems. As it turned out, the initiatives of General Mills along with a number of other prominent Minneapolis firms led to the development of a program known as Minnesota HEALS (Hope, Education, Law, and Safety) that has grown from a handful of people to dozens of corporate, community, and government groups convening to reduce violence and create hope. Today, Minneapolis is one of the leading cities in America in which business support of the community has become legendary.[32]

Also faced with a city in need of help, Prudential has focused significant philanthropic efforts on supporting the rebuilding of Newark, New Jersey, its headquarters since 1875. In 2012, the Prudential Foundation donated $1.25 million to Newark nonprofit

Spotlight on Sustainability

Greening the Workforce

Community colleges have always been skilled at preparing two-year graduates to enter practical professions because their close ties with industry enable them to be more responsive to industry's needs. These attributes make the two-year college the perfect venue for preparing students to enter green-economy jobs. Recognizing the fit between community colleges and eco-economy job training, businesses are entering into partnerships with community colleges to prepare workers to meet their growing eco-workforce demands. For example, GE donated a small wind turbine to Mesalands Community College in Tucumcari, NM, for their wind energy technician program and promised to hire their first three years of graduates. Johnson Controls constructed a 2,500 solar panel farm at Milwaukee Area Technical College, enabling students there to be trained as the photovoltaic designers and installers that Johnson Controls needs to hire. Experts predict that the expected expansion of environmental policies could increase renewable energy jobs from 9 million in 2007 to 19.5 million in 2030.

Sources: Mina Kimes, "Get a Green Job in Two Years," *Fortune* (November 23, 2009), 32; Jim Morgan, "Mesalands Community College Capitalizes on Wind Resource to Transform a Rural Town," SEED Center (2011), http://www.theseedcenter.org/Colleges-in-Action/Success-Stories/Mesalands-Community-College-Capitalizes-on-Wind-Re. Accessed April 7, 2013.

organizations serving low-income families and at-risk children, as well as $250,000 to the Newark Trust for Education.[33] After Superstorm Sandy devastated Northern New Jersey, the foundation donated $3 million in relief funds to nonprofit agencies assisting the victims, and it pledged to match employee contributions to the cause.[34] According to Lata Reddy, the foundation's president, "The mission of the Prudential Foundation is to promote strong communities and improve the social outcomes in the places where we work and live."[35]

Culture and the Arts   Business support for the arts has been decreasing, and the forecast is not good. Americans for the Arts predicts a "dire drop" in future funding because of the global economic recession.[36] Companies faced with layoffs may feel they cannot afford to support the arts, but that outlook is short sighted. The arts provide brand recognition, ensure community development, and are key to promoting the community as a great place to live and work.[37]

Americans for the Arts conducted a recent economic impact study of the nonprofit arts and culture industry in the United States and found good reason for business to support the arts as part of supporting the community. Using findings from 182 regions representing all 50 states and the District of Columbia, they found that U.S. nonprofit arts and culture organizations generated $61.1 billion of economic activity on top of the $74.1 billion in event-related expenditures by their audiences.[38] As they note, this yield is far greater than the $4 billion they receive in collective arts allocations.[39]

Giving in Times of Crisis   In addition to the four categories previously mentioned, firms are expected to make charitable donations when crises occur in the firm's community, the nation or the world at large. We covered the general issues related to responding to a crisis in Chapter 6, noting that some firms are able to respond so well to a crisis that they can be counted on to lend a hand to others in need. For example, Walmart and Home Depot stood out in their ability to bring relief following the devastation of

Hurricane Katrina, as did Fed Ex, by providing the Federal Emergency Management Agency (FEMA) with a radio antenna to set up communications. We also discussed Prudential's response to the havoc that the 2011 earthquake off the Pacific coast of Tōhoku wreaked on Japan.

This level of giving tends to follow most disasters. According to the U.S. Chamber of Commerce, U.S. businesses donated $566 million to help communities suffering from the effects of the Indian Ocean tsunami.[40] Corporations also stepped up when Superstorm Sandy ravaged the Northeastern United States. According to the Business Civic Leadership Center of the U.S. Chamber of Commerce, businesses pledged more than $141 million in support of recovery efforts, with two-thirds in the form of monetary donations to organizations like the Red Cross and Feeding America.[41]

Some observers worry that in times of crisis, corporate philanthropy becomes a zero-sum game, in that contributions that go to alleviate the crisis then do not go to other causes that need them as well. Typically, giving has increased from year to year irrespective of external events; however, one statistic should give us pause. In the two weeks following the attack on the World Trade Center, corporations gave more than $120 million to relief funds—an unprecedented level of corporate giving.[42] According to a survey by the *Chronicle of Corporate Philanthropy*, however, corporate giving subsequently declined.[43] Other concerns surround the possibility of donor fatigue following crises for which corporations and individuals open their checkbooks. There has been some evidence of this. In the first two weeks after the disaster, Hurricane Katrina garnered $409 million in corporate donations and the Indian Ocean tsunami received $300 million; however, after two weeks, the corporate philanthropy directed toward the Haiti earthquake was only $122 million.[44]

Managing Corporate Philanthropy

As performance pressures on business have continued and intensified, companies have had to turn their attention to *managing* corporate philanthropy. Early on, managers did not subject their contributions to the same kinds of rigorous analysis given to expenditures for plants and equipment, inventory, product development, marketing, and a host of other budgetary items. This began to change in the early 1980s because cutbacks in federal spending on charitable causes created an increasing need for contributions by business. At the same time, however, the economy was struggling through its worst recession in 50 years. It became increasingly clear that business had to reconcile its economic and social goals, both of which were essential.[45]

Now, even as we begin to recover from the global recession, the pressure on businesses to be more businesslike in their philanthropy remains. There are two aspects to this. The first is to base giving on business skills, resources, and capabilities to enhance philanthropic outcomes. The second is to focus on philanthropy that will enhance corporate profitability while also making a positive difference in the community at large. This strategic approach to philanthropy follows an ethic of enlightened self-interest and is clearly on the rise. In the most recent CECP survey, the data show that companies are engaging in more focused giving, targeted to their core strategic interests.[46] That trend will only grow as recovery from the recession makes it more necessary to align philanthropic goals with strategic priorities.[47]

Community Partnerships As a broad response to this growing need to reconcile financial and social goals, the concept of **community partnerships** evolved. A community partnership occurs when a for-profit business enters into a cooperative arrangement with a nonprofit organization for their mutual advantage. Businesses see in community partnerships the opportunity for simultaneous achievement of economic and philanthropic objectives. Business skills and resources are often exactly what a community non-profit organization needs to achieve its mission. A good example of that is National Safe Place.

National Safe Place is a youth outreach program with two purposes, (1) educating young people about the dangers of running away or trying to resolve difficult, threatening situations on their own, and (2) providing safe havens and resources for youth in crisis.[48] They have created a variety of Safe Place locations (e.g., schools, fire stations, libraries, grocery and convenience stores, public transit, YMCAs, and other appropriate public buildings) where young people can get help and be safe. The locations display the yellow and black diamond-shaped Safe Place sign. Corporations that have skills and resources that can help with the Safe Place programs have partnered with the nonprofit. These include Sprint, CSX Movers, Southwest Airlines, QT, and the National Association of Convenience Stores.[49]

Community partnerships take on many different forms. Partnership options include sponsorships, vendor relationships, licensing agreements, and in-kind donations.[50] Other options are strategic philanthropy and cause-related marketing. We now consider strategic philanthropy and cause-related marketing in more detail.

Strategic Philanthropy **Strategic philanthropy** is an approach by which corporate giving and other philanthropic endeavors of a firm are designed in a way that best fits with the firm's overall mission, goals, or objectives. This implies that the firm has some idea of what its overall strategy is, and that it is able to articulate its missions, goals, or objectives. One goal of all firms is profitability. Therefore, one requirement of strategic philanthropy is to make as direct a contribution as possible to the financial goals of the firm. Philanthropy has long been thought to be in the long-range economic interest of the firm. Strategic philanthropy simply presses for a more direct or immediate contribution of philanthropy to the firm's economic success.

An important way to make philanthropy strategic is to bring contribution programs into sharper alignment with business endeavors. This means that each firm should pursue those social programs that have a direct rather than an indirect bearing on its success. Thus, a local bank should logically pursue people-oriented projects in the community in which it resides; a manufacturer might pursue programs having to do with environmental protection or technological advancement.

A third way to make philanthropy strategic is to ensure that it is well planned and managed rather than handled haphazardly and without direction. Planning ensures that efforts have clearly delineated goals, are properly organized and staffed, and are administered in accordance with certain established policies. Figure 16-4 presents recommendations for best practices in the implementation of a philanthropy program.

FIGURE 16-4

Attributes of an Effective Strategic Philanthropy Program

An effective strategic philanthropy program should have the following attributes:

1. The program should fit with the company's strategic goals and mission.
2. The program should be connected with the community involvement programs.
3. The budget and infrastructure should be sufficient to meet goals

4. Company policies and guidelines for should be made clear.
5. Employees should be involved in philanthropy-related activities.
6. Stakeholders should be made fully aware of the program.
7. Long-term business–nonprofit partnerships should be developed.

© Cengage Learning 2015

Strategic philanthropy must find the zone of overlap where the philanthropy provides both social and economic benefits. In an important *Harvard Business Review* article, Michael Porter and Mark Kramer argued that few companies have effectively taken advantage of the competitive advantage corporate philanthropy can provide. They consider strategic philanthropy to be a myth—simply semantics that help companies to rationalize their contributions. To be truly strategic, philanthropy must be congruent with a company's competitive context, which consists of four interrelated elements: factor conditions, demand conditions, the context for strategy and rivalry, and related and supporting industries.[51]

Factor Conditions   These are the available inputs for productions. Porter and Kramer point to DreamWorks as an example of a company that uses strategic philanthropy to improve its factor conditions effectively. They created a program that provides training to low-income and disadvantaged youth in the skills needed to work in the entertainment industry. Of course, the societal benefits of an improved educational system are clear. While providing these social benefits, DreamWorks also enhances the labor pool from which they can draw. This not only strengthens the company but the industry as a whole as well.[52] The Clorox example of improving the community surrounding their headquarters through partnership with the community foundation also addresses factor conditions by improving the general quality of life and the local infrastructure.

Demand Conditions   These are concerned with the nature of the company's customers and the local market. Philanthropy can influence the local market's size and quality. Porter and Kramer point to Apple's long-held policy of donating computers to public schools. By introducing young people and their teachers to computers, Apple expands their market. They also increase the sophistication of their customer base, which benefits a differentiated product such as the ones Apple sells.[53] Similarly, Burger King focuses its philanthropic efforts on highly focused programs to help students, teachers, and schools.[54] This program enhances name recognition in its target population of consumers.

The demand for capitalism with a conscience is growing. In response to a global survey by public relations firm, Edelman, 47 percent of respondents said that every month they buy a product from a company that supports a good causes: That is a 47 percent increase in two years.[55] In the same survey, 72 percent of consumers said they would recommend a company that contributes to good causes: That is a 38 percent increase since 2010.[56] In a 2013 survey, 74 percent said that a firm's social consciousness was a very important or somewhat important determinant of where they shop and buy.[57] The upsurge in social consciousness is partly in response to the influence of Millenials, people born from 1982 to 2004, who were impacted by the recession and have learned to use social media to be more informed consumers.[58] An indication of their influence is that Rolling Stone and Participant Media are creating a new cable network, Pivot, that is aimed at Millenials and "built on a philosophy that entertainment can inspire and accelerate change."[59]

Whole Foods has developed a strategic philanthropy program that affects both factor and demand conditions, enabling the company to reap benefits along the length of the value chain. In the factor market, Whole Foods has designed a system for sourcing products from developing countries while maintaining product standards. It developed a strict set of criteria for its suppliers to adhere to and contracted with TransFair USA and the Rainforest Alliance, two respected third-party certifiers, to ensure the suppliers met these criteria. These certified products receive a Whole Trade logo so that customers know which products come from the developing world and meet the criteria. Its customers value these attributes and so Whole Foods' demand conditions also improve as a result of their efforts.[60]

Context for Strategy and Rivalry   This can be influenced by strategic philanthropy. Porter and Kramer point to the many corporations that support Transparency International as examples of firms using philanthropy to create a better environment for competition. As discussed in Chapter 10, Transparency International's mission is to reveal and deter corporate corruption around the world. The organization measures and publicizes corruption while pushing for stricter codes and enforcement. By supporting Transparency International, corporations are helping to build a better competitive environment—one that rewards fair competition.[61]

Related and Supporting Industries   These can also be strengthened through strategic philanthropy, thereby enhancing the productivity of companies. American Express provides an excellent example of a firm that uses philanthropy to strengthen its related and supporting industries. For almost 20 years, American Express has funded travel and tourism academies in secondary schools. The program trains teachers, supports curricula, and provides both summer internships and industry mentors. A strong travel industry translates into important benefits for American Express.[62]

Now let us turn our attention to a special kind of strategic philanthropy that has become quite prevalent in recent years: cause-related marketing.

Cause-Related Marketing   There is some debate as to whether cause-related marketing is really philanthropy. Porter and Kramer argue that it is marketing and nothing more.[63] However, because cause marketing represents a close linkage between a firm's financial objectives and corporate contributions, it is discussed here. Stated in its simplest form, **cause-related marketing** is the direct linking of a business's product or service to a specified charity. Each time a consumer uses the service or buys the product, a donation is given to the charity by the business.[64] Thus some observers refer to cause-related marketing as "quid pro quo strategic philanthropy."

The term cause-related marketing was coined by the American Express Company to describe a program it began in 1983 in which it agreed to contribute a penny to the restoration of the Statue of Liberty every time a customer used one of its credit cards to make a purchase. The project generated $1.7 million for the statue restoration and a substantial increase in usage of the American Express card.[65] Since that time, companies have employed this same approach to raise millions of dollars for a wide variety of local and national causes.

Recently, cause-related marketing has given way to a new concept, **cause branding**. Cause branding represents a longer-term commitment than cause marketing. It also relates more directly to the firm's line of business and the target audience. Avon Products, Inc. has become a recognized leader in cause branding. Its target audience is women, so it has developed an array of programs to raise awareness of breast cancer, a disease that mostly affects women. The company raises money for programs that provide low-income women with education and free screening. Avon sells products featuring the pink ribbon that represents breast cancer awareness, and then donates the proceeds from these products to nonprofit and university programs.[66]

Cause branding has become a successful marketing tool. A Cone/Roper *Cause-Related Trends Report: Evolution of Cause Branding* showed that 61 percent of consumers felt companies should make cause branding part of their regular business.[67] Moreover, 83 percent of Americans feel more positively disposed toward companies that support a cause about which they care, and 76 percent of consumers are more likely to select the more socially responsible brand when price and quality are equal. The benefits do not apply only to consumers: Employees react to cause branding as well. In companies with cause programs, 87 percent of employees indicate they feel strong loyalty, while only 67

ETHICS IN PRACTICE CASE

Competition in the Workplace

I have been interning for a multibillion-dollar nonprofit organization since January. As a Supply Chain intern, my primary responsibility is to analyze potential suppliers. I use data to determine the cheapest supplier that can properly provide my organization with a product or service. These analyses have saved my organization thousands of dollars each year. This money can be placed back into our grant-making program to help people who are in need of our assistance.

This May, my boss has hired a second intern to assist with the supplier analyses. My boss split my desk in half and told me that I would be sharing my office with the new intern. I welcomed the notion of having someone to work with and discuss ideas.

My boss instructed that we share supplier information with each other, but not our opinions. Instead, he preferred that we come to our own separate conclusions. When the analyses are due, the other intern and I present our findings to my boss. If we come to different conclusion and choose different suppliers, my boss carefully weighs both options and chooses the best supplier.

When my co-intern first started at the foundation, I willingly shared all of my supplier research such as the price, capabilities, references, financial status, etc. Although the other intern had not shared information with me, I merely thought he was still growing accustomed to his new position. However, when presenting our findings to my boss, my co-intern used data and statistics that he had *never* shared with me. My boss often asked why I had not included this data in my analyses.

On several occasions, I would ask my co-intern why he had withheld information from me. He would ignore or avoid the question each time. I know that my co-intern is withholding information from me because he is competitive and wants to impress my boss.

I feel that my co-intern is taking advantage of my research in order to outperform me. I often want to withhold my research as well, but I do not want to hinder potential cost savings for my nonprofit organization. I do not want to sacrifice possible grant-making money for my own benefit, but I also do not want my boss to think my work is below average.

1. Is it productive to have competition in the workplace?
2. Is my boss right in assigning the same project to my co-intern and me? Are there better options to increase our productivity?
3. Should I sacrifice my performance for the benefit of my organization?
4. What actions do you recommend I should take to resolve this issue?

Contributed by Zachary Greytsman

---

percent feel strong loyalty in firms that do not have cause programs.[68] The findings of a recent Cone/Roper Executive Study show that cause branding strengthens internal corporate cultures and has a dramatic influence on employee pride, morale, and loyalty.[69]

Proponents of cause-related marketing argue that everyone involved in it comes out a winner. Business enhances its public image by being associated with a worthy cause, and increases its sales at the same time. Nonprofit organizations get cash for their programs as well as enhanced marketing and public visibility made possible by business's expertise.

Critics of cause-related marketing fear that the needs of capitalism will overshadow the cause. These concerns cropped up in the promotion of the "RED™" project. The rock star Bono devised the RED project, a plan to have firms launch versions of their products that follow the RED guidelines and donate a portion of their proceeds to The Global Fund to Fight AIDS, Tuberculosis, and Malaria. None of the brands were permitted to charge a premium for RED products, but the percentage of profits to be donated was not specified.[70] *Advertising Age* created a stir by reporting that firms involved in the project had spent as much as $100 million to promote the products, while the money raised amounted to only $18 million.[71] RED spokespeople countered that the $100 million estimate was high and many observers concurred; however, they were unapologetic about the possibility that expenditures might exceed contributions, because the project was founded on the idea that self-interest can be a method of fundraising for charity.[72] Non-profit advocates expressed concern, however, that cause-related marketing like the RED project might crowd out philanthropic contributions if people feel that buying a RED item is a substitute for charitable giving.[73] A parody of the RED commercials on http://www.buylesscrap.org expresses the concerns of cause marketing critics and ends with an opportunity to donate directly to the nonprofit organizations designated to receive RED funds.[74]

Clearly, the criticism has not hurt the cause branding movement. Some firms are now going blue for autism awareness month. Brands are encouraged to shine a blue light to show their support. Build a Bear Workshop is making a blue Teddy Bear in honor of the cause and the Empire State Building was lit in all blue. Jet Blue, which already has the color in its name, initiated a "Wings for Autism" program that helps families to familiarize their autistic children with the sights and sounds of air travel so that they can be more comfortable flying.[75]

Global Philanthropy The size of a company's workforce in international markets is the greatest determinant of the size of their charitable contributions to those markets. It should come as no surprise, then, that as corporate operations have become increasingly globalized, so has corporate philanthropy. Firms responding to a 2011 CECP survey indicated that their global philanthropic giving has grown as their involvement in global operations have grown.[76] International development is one of the areas that saw increased funding, even in the recessionary times.[77]

Businesses want to protect the communities in which they operate, keeping them healthy and environmentally sound. Businesses also develop infrastructure to facilitate the flow of goods and services. According to Stephen Jordan of the U.S. Chamber of Commerce Business Civic Leadership Center, companies are increasing their corporate philanthropy to "create a culture of opportunity" in the developing world. He said, "Ninety-six percent of opportunity is outside our borders.... Increasingly, companies ... want to grow their customer base in emerging markets."[78]

The Loss of Jobs

We now shift our focus to the issue of job loss. In the preceding sections, we considered the ways in which business firms might have positive, constructive, and creative impacts on community stakeholders. Firms can also have detrimental impacts on communities. Pervasive examples of such negative effects include mass job layoffs where jobs are moved elsewhere, or business or plant closures without careful consideration by management of the community stakeholders affected. We will address the issue of offshoring first and then take a more in-depth look at business and plant closings.

From Offshoring to Reshoring

The word **outsourcing** refers to the relocation of business processes to a different company. **Offshoring** refers to the relocation of business processes to a different country, while **reshoring** is the returning of business processes to their original location. Offshoring became popular when new technologies such as high-speed data links and the Internet made it easier to do white-collar work overseas, where labor was cheaper. In the late 19th century, the advent of railroads had just as transforming an effect. A writer for Scribner's in 1888 said that life had changed more in the past 75 years than it had since Julius Caesar, "and the change has chiefly been made by railways."[79] Railroads destroyed industries and whole towns, in addition to jobs. There was no longer a need for icehouses or local meatpacking plants, so they closed. While new markets opened for U.S. grain, cotton farmers lost market share to cheaper Egyptian and Indian cotton. Steamboat towns faded, and struggling farmers began to resent their dependence on the wealthy railroads.[80]

Almost 40 years ago, concerns over offshore outsourcing focused on blue-collar occupations, primarily factory workers, and it was mostly a problem in the United States. Then the Internet Boom of the 1990s made it a white-collar issue with information technology workers being particularly hard hit.[81] A programmer who made $11,000 in India or $8,000 in Poland or Hungary could do the work of a programmer who made $80,000 in the United States.[82] This represented huge savings for firms dealing with global competition.

In spite of the savings involved, however, offshoring was not a panacea for companies. The problems that developed from shipping jobs overseas often ended up outweighing the cost savings. Capital One ended a contract for a 250-person call center in New Delhi when they found that workers would boost their sales by offering unauthorized lines of credit.[83] Similarly, Dell brought a tech support center back to the United States after customers complained of thick accents and poor service.[84] Stanley Furniture moved its manufacturing facilities back to the United States after a 2008 recall of cribs made in Slovenia.[85] Even GE, the pioneer of offshoring, has found that the costs of offshoring often outweigh the benefits. GE Chairman and CEO Jeff Immelt refers to outsourcing as "yesterday's model."[86] GE has returned production of refrigerators, washing machines and heaters from China back to Kentucky, shifted much of its IT work back to the United States, and is hiring hundreds of new IT engineers at a new center in Michigan.[87] Google, Caterpillar, Ford Motor Company, and Apple are all planning to bring some production back or add new capacity to the United States.[88]

In a special issue on outsourcing and offshoring, *The Economist* identified some reasons why the offshoring trend has shifted toward reshoring:[89]

1. **Cost advantages diminished**—Labor costs in China and India have risen 10 to 20 percent a year for the past decade, while more automation has reduced labor's share of the cost of operations.[90]
2. **Distance brings disadvantages**—Shipping goods long distances is increasingly expensive and takes time to complete. Distance from R&D can hamper innovation.[91]
3. **Proximity to customers is key**—Companies need to be close to customers to customize production and quickly respond to changes in demand. Lenovo, a Chinese company, has moved some computer production to the United States to be responsive to American consumers.

Michael Porter, Harvard Business School Professor and competitive strategy expert, compares the 1990s rush toward offshoring to the mergers and acquisitions of the 1980s. Many companies pursued mergers and acquisitions that were not sound strategy and they paid a price. Those painful experiences resulted in greater corporate discipline, and the mistakes made in offshoring are likely to have the same impact on future strategy.[92]

Business and Plant Closings

Although the right to close a business or plant has long been regarded as a management prerogative, the business shutdowns of the past two decades—especially their dramatic effects—have called attention to the question of what rights and responsibilities business has in relation to employee and community stakeholders. The literature on business social responsibility and policy has documented corporate concern with the detrimental impact of its actions. Indeed, business's social response patterns have borne this out.

Management expert Peter Drucker suggested the following business position regarding social impacts of management decisions:

> *Because one is responsible for one's impacts, one minimizes them. The fewer impacts an institution has outside of its own specific purpose and mission, the better does it conduct itself, the more responsibly does it act, and the more acceptable a citizen, neighbor, and contributor it is.*[93]

This raises the question of whether business's responsibilities in the realm of plant closings and their impacts on employees and communities are any different from the host of responsibilities that have already been assumed in areas such as employment discrimination, employee privacy and safety, honesty in advertising, product safety, and concern for the environment. From the perspective of the employees affected, their role in plant and business closings might be considered an extension of the numerous employee rights issues.

Business essentially has two opportunities to be responsive to employee and community stakeholders in shutdown situations. It can take certain actions *before the decision* to close is made and other actions *after the decision* to close has been made.

Before the Decision to Close Is Made   Before a company makes a decision to close down, it has a responsibility to itself, its employees, and its community to thoroughly and diligently study whether the closing is the only option available. A decision to leave should be preceded by critical and realistic investigations of economic alternatives.

Diversification   Sometimes it is possible to find other revenue streams to help the company cope with the slim margins of manufacturing. SRC Holdings was making only 2 to 3 percent a year but needed a profit of 4 percent to compete effectively. SRC chief executive John P. Stack explains, "We took our manufacturing discipline into the service sector to develop new sources of revenue.… Without creating these other businesses, we couldn't have survived. Manufacturing has very slim margins but if a company innovates the margins can be incredible."[94] In 2013, having weathered multiple economic storms, SRC took pride in being "the oldest employee-owned remanufacturer to OEM's in North America."[95]

New Ownership   After a careful study has been made, it may be concluded that finding new ownership for the plant or business is the only feasible alternative. Two basic options exist at this point: (1) find a new owner or (2) explore the possibility of employee ownership.[96] A company has an obligation to its employees and the community to try to sell the business as a going concern instead of shutting down. This is often not possible, but it is an avenue that should be explored. Quite often, the most promising new buyers of a firm are residents of the state who have a long-term stake in the community and are willing to make a strong commitment. Ideally, local organizations and the government will be able to offer incentives to companies willing to bring jobs to the area.

For example, when the Grumman Olson facility closed in Lycoming County, Pennsylvania, several parties joined together to bring jobs back to the area. The local chamber of commerce worked with the state to develop an incentive package that included job creation tax credits and customized job training at the local college. Specialized Vehicles Corporation (SVC) bought the facility, promising to prioritize employment of the displaced workers of Grumman Olson.[97]

Employee Ownership   The idea of a company selling a plant to the employees as a way of avoiding a closedown is appealing at first glance. In the United States, more than a thousand companies are **employee owned**. Most of these companies are very small. The National Center for Employee Ownership (NCEO) lists the 100 largest employee-owned companies, defined as having more than 50 percent employee ownership, and, in 2012, the smallest on the list only have about 1,000 employees.[98] Although employee ownership is not a major trend in the current environment, it is instructive to understand its history and record of success and failure to appreciate fully the pros and cons of the practice.

Employee ownership experiences have not always been favorable.[99] In numerous cases, employees have had to take significant wage and benefit reductions to make the business profitable. Some companies, however, have met with better success. Publix Supermarkets is both employee and family owned. Employees own 31 percent of the firm, and the family of founder George W. Jenkins own most of the remaining shares.[100] Most observers credit their employee ownership with earning Publix the number one supermarket ranking on the American Customer Satisfaction Index for each of the 14 years it has been in existence. Publix employees are known for bending over backwards to please customers.[101] In 2012, Publix topped the list as the largest employee-owned company in the United States.

In an instructive case of employee ownership, United Airlines became America's largest employee-owned corporation in 1994. In one of the nastiest and most prolonged corporate battles ever, shareholders of UAL Corp., the parent of United Airlines, awarded employee groups 55 percent of the company's stock in exchange for a $4.9 billion bundle of wage and productivity concessions. U.S. labor leaders hailed this new arrangement in worker control as a model alternative to the way companies usually battle to control costs. However, the success of the new firm was by no means ensured, because the airline has been buffeted for more than a decade by infighting among employee groups, repeated forays by outside potential buyers, and takeover attempts.[102] Furthermore, it still had all the problems inherent in being a legacy carrier. From the beginning, there were problems: workers resented taking pay cuts in exchange for loans to buy the stock, and the flight attendants union opted not to join the ESOP because of concerns about the pay cuts involved and other policies. Problems began in 2000, when the airline pilots conducted a slowdown during contract negotiations. Then the machinists' union threatened to strike, and United took them to court.[103] By 2001, when the attack on the World Trade Center shook the airline industry, the ESOP had ended and United was in no better position than firms without employee-owners were. In 2002, United filed for bankruptcy.[104] It emerged from bankruptcy in 2006 after paying more than $335 million in fees.[105]

Some critics argue that United Airlines failed as an employee-owned enterprise because workers thought employee ownership would mean they no longer needed to be concerned about labor–management issues. Research has shown that employee ownership can provide a firm with competitive advantage; for employee ownership to work, however, it is critical that employees believe they have a part to play in leading the company. A positive ownership culture provides employees with access to information, the power to exert influence, a sense of fairness, and a feeling of ownership and entrepreneurship.[106] It should be noted, however, that the period following the World Trade Center attacks was difficult for all large airlines, and so there are limits to the inferences one can make about the impact that employee ownership had on United.

After the Decision to Close Is Made There are a multitude of actions that a business can take once the decision has been made that a closedown or relocation is unavoidable. The overriding concern should be that the company makes sincere efforts to mitigate the social and economic impacts of its actions on employees and the community. Regardless of the circumstances of the move, some basic planning can help alleviate the disruptions felt by those affected. There are several actions that management can take, including[107]:

1. conducting a community-impact analysis;
2. providing advance notice to the employees or community;
3. providing transfer, relocation, and outplacement benefits;
4. phasing out the business gradually; and
5. helping the community attract replacement industry.

Community-Impact Analysis   Because management is responsible for its impacts on employees and the community, a thorough community-impact analysis of a decision to close down or move is in order. The initial action should be to identify realistically those aspects of the community that would be affected by the company's plans. This entails asking questions,[108] such as:

1. What groups will be affected?
2. How will they be affected?
3. What is the timing of initial and later effects?
4. What is the magnitude of the effect?
5. What is the duration of the impact?
6. To what extent will the impact be diffused in the community?

Once these questions have been answered, management is better equipped to modify its plans so that negative impacts can be minimized and favorable impacts, if any, can be maximized.

Advance Notice   One of the most often discussed responsibilities in business- or plant-closing situations is the provision of advance notice to workers and communities. The national advance-notice law is called the **Worker Adjustment and Retraining Notification Act (WARN)**. Figure 16-5 provides an overview of WARN.

Companies will sometimes try to get around the WARN requirements. Computer Associates, a New York-based software developer was sued by its employees, who charged that the company tried to disguise mass layoffs as individual firings to avoid having to comply with the advance notice required by WARN.[109] There is a fine line between staggering employee layoffs legally and doing it to avoid the notice requirements of WARN. Courts try to determine what employers knew at the time of the layoffs. If they deem that the employers knew they would be laying off more than 50 employees at a time, the firm is considered to be in violation of WARN. Employees who sue successfully under WARN may get back pay and benefits for up to 60 days. The penalty for not giving adequate notice is $500 per day. The only acceptable reasons for not providing a 60-day notice are (1) action being taken by the employer, which, if successful, would have postponed or eliminated the need for layoffs, (2) business circumstances that the employer could not reasonably have foreseen, and (3) natural disasters.[110]

An investigation by *The Blade*, a newspaper from Toledo, Ohio, found that WARN often falls short of its goals. Judges threw out more than half of the 236 lawsuits filed since 1989.[111] Only about one-quarter of the more than 8,000 closings in one year were subject to WARN requirements and only about one-third of those employers subject to the requirements actually provided proper warning.[112] Since the bill's inception, legislators have tried to strengthen the law by closing loopholes and giving it some teeth. One key problem is that the Labor Department has no enforcement power over the WARN Act, so displaced employees must hire their own attorneys to hold their former employers accountable.[113]

FIGURE 16-5

The Worker Adjustment and Retraining Notification Act (WARN)

The Worker Adjustment and Retraining Notification Act (WARN) protects workers, their families, and communities by requiring most employers with 100 or more employees to provide notification 60 calendar days in advance of plant closings and mass layoffs.

Employee entitled to notice under WARN include managers and supervisors, as well as hourly and salaried workers. WARN requires that notice also be given to employees' representatives, the local chief elected official, and the state dislocated worker unit.

Advance notice gives workers and their families some transition time to adjust to the prospective loss of employment, to seek and obtain other jobs, and, if necessary, to enter skill training or retraining that will allow these workers to compete successfully in the job market.

• Generally, WARN covers employers with 100 or more employees, not counting those who have worked less than six months in the last 12 months and those who work an average of less than 20 hours a week.

• Employees entitled to advance notice under WARN include managers and supervisors as well as hourly and salaried workers.

• Regular federal, state, and local government entities that provide public services are *not* covered by WARN.

The Department of Labor's (DOL) Employment and Training Administration (ETA) administers WARN at the federal level, and some states have plant closure laws of their own. DOL has no enforcement role in seeking damages for workers who did not receive adequate notice of a layoff or received no notice at all. However, they can assist workers in finding a new job or learning about training opportunities that are available.

Source: The U.S. Department of Labor, http://www.dol.gov/compliance/laws/comp-warn.htm. Accessed April 8, 2013.

Communication expert Hugh Braithwaite offers advice on communicating with employees being laid off.[114]

1. *Be complete.* Employees will try to fill any holes in your story, and that is how rumors begin.
2. *Be consistent.* Information will become muddled if the story keeps changing.
3. *Inform affected employees first.* Provide a thorough "exit kit" that provides all information the employee might need to smooth their transition.
4. *Inform retained employees.* Recognize that survivors have challenges too and provide ample opportunity for their questions to be asked and answered.

Transfer, Relocation, and Outplacement Benefits   Enlightened companies are increasingly recognizing that the provision of separation or outplacement benefits is in the long-range best interest of all parties concerned. Everyone is better off if disruptions are minimized in the lives of the firm's management, the displaced workers, and the community. Outplacement benefits have been used for years as companies have attempted to remove redundant or marginal personnel with minimum disruption and cost to the company, and maximum benefit to the individuals involved. Now these same benefits are being used in business and plant closings.

Gradual Phase-Outs   Another management action that can significantly ameliorate the effects of a business shutdown is the gradual phasing out of the business. A gradual phase-out buys time for employees and the community to adjust to the new situation and to solve some of their problems.

When the semiconductor industry took a deep downturn, Sony Electronics found it necessary to close its plant in San Antonio. They let their employees go in phases as they gradually wrapped up their customer orders. Affected workers were given 60 days' notice. This did not come as a surprise because, as one worker noted, "It was fairly well-known that the company was sick for a quite a while."[115] When asked about worker reactions, one employee said, "There were a few who were upset but some of them actually requested to be included in Phase 1 (job cuts). They wanted to get their severance packages and get on with their lives."[116] Sony provided workers with severance pay based on years on the job. They also extended benefits packages, outplacement services, and job transfers, where possible, to other Sony plants in the United States. In addition, each departing worker received a DVD player.[117]

Helping to Attract Replacement Industry   The principal responsibility for attracting new industry falls on the community, but the management of the closing firm can provide cooperation and assistance. The closing company can help by providing inside information on building and equipment characteristics and capabilities, transportation options based on its experience, and contacts with other firms in its industry that may be seeking facilities. Helping the community attract replacement industry has the overwhelming advantage of rapidly replacing large numbers of lost jobs. In addition, because attracted businesses tend to be smaller than those that closed, this strategy enables the community to diversify its economic base while regaining jobs.[118]

Survivors: The Forgotten Stakeholders   When job losses occur, attention is understandably placed on the workers who lose their employment and the many repercussions that loss holds for them. Their needs must come first because they bear the brunt of the impact. However, those who retain their jobs—whether they are the remaining employees at a downsized plant or the workers at a plant that survived consolidation—are in need of support as well. Even the managers who conducted the layoffs will not emerge unscathed. A recent study of managers who issued WARN notices found that they had an increase in health and sleep problems: They reported feelings of depersonalization, and a greater intent to quit, with emotional exhaustion playing a role in their difficulties.[119]

All survivors are likely to evidence a variety of negative actions, perceptions, and behaviors. These include depression, guilt, stress, uncertainty, decreased loyalty, and lower enthusiasm.[120] Firms must attend to these concerns of survivors if they are to emerge stronger after job cuts. They can do this by providing[121]:

1. Emotional support—assuring employees that they are important.
2. Directional support—communicating the direction the company is going and the employees' place in that journey.
3. Tactical support—presenting new goals and objectives for the employees.
4. Informational support—answering all questions about the layoff and future plans.

One of the most important actions a firm can take when providing informational support is to answer employees' questions clearly and completely. Michael Fox, senior vice president of Ogilvy Public Relations, has worked with firms that are conducting layoffs. He says, "You've got a good chance at preserving loyalty and lessening anxiety if you've always been pretty open and transparent with information. Tell (remaining employees) how the decision was made.., the layoffs were based on performance reviews, or longevity or the loss of a big customer. If a decision seems arbitrary or unclear, it will only make resentment worse."[122] It is also important that the survivors believe the laid off employees were treated well. When United Technologies paid for a year of college courses for laid-off employees, the remaining employees felt better about staying on the job.[123]

We are only just touching the surface of the stakes and stakeholders involved in the plant-closing issue, the impacts that business closings have on employees and communities, the public's reaction to the problem, and types of corresponding actions that management might take. It is important for businesses to take positive steps to be responsive to their employees and communities. Furthermore, business closings and their adverse consequences are issues that business should continue to address in the future, lest more public problems culminate in new laws, or another knotty regulatory apparatus.

Summary

Community stakeholders are extremely important to companies, and the global economic recession has heightened the importance of business's attending to community stakeholder needs. In many ways, business can provide support in difficult times. Companies may donate the time and talents of managers and employees (volunteerism). Because business has a vital stake in the community, it engages in a variety of community projects. Community action programs are a key part of managing community involvement.

Business also contributes to community stakeholders through philanthropy. The third sector, or nonprofit sector, depends on business's support. Companies give for a variety of reasons—some altruistic, some self-interested. Major recipients of business giving include health and welfare, education, civic activities, and culture and the arts. As companies have attempted to manage their philanthropy, two major types of corporate giving have been emphasized: (1) strategic philanthropy, which seeks to improve the overall fit between corporate needs and charitable programs, and (2) cause-related marketing, which tightens the linkage between a firm's profits and its contributions. Cause-related marketing represents a unique joining of business and charity with the potential for great benefit to each.

Just as firms have beneficial effects on community stakeholders, they can have detrimental effects as well.

Business or plant closings are a prime example of these detrimental effects. Loss of jobs is the primary way in which these effects are manifested. Plant closings have a pervasive influence in the sense that a multitude of community stakeholders—employees, local government, other businesses, and the general citizenry—are affected. There is no single reason why these closings occur, but among the major reasons are economic conditions, consolidation of company operations, outsourcing, outmoded technology or facilities, changes in corporate strategy, and international competition.

Before management makes the decision to close a facility, it has a responsibility to itself, its employees, and the community to study thoroughly whether closing is the only or the best option. Finding a new owner for the business and pursuing the possibility of employee ownership are reasonable and desirable alternatives. After the decision to close has been made, responsible actions include community-impact analysis; giving advance notice; providing transfer, relocation, or outplacement benefits; phasing out operations gradually; and helping the community attract replacement industry. Finally, the needs of survivors must be met as the firm continues operations. Companies have an added incentive to be responsive to the business-closing issue, because state and federal governments are closely watching the manner in which firms are handling this problem.

Key Terms

cause branding, p. 476

cause-related marketing, p. 476

community action program, p. 466

community involvement, p. 463

community partnerships, p. 473

employee owned, p. 481

offshoring, p. 478

outsourcing, p. 478

philanthropy, p. 468

reshoring, p. 478

strategic philanthropy, p. 474

third sector, p. 470

Worker Adjustment and Retraining Notification Act (WARN), p. 482

Discussion Questions

1. Outline the essential steps involved in developing a community action program.

2. Explain the pros and cons of community involvement and corporate philanthropy, provide a brief history of corporate philanthropy, and explain why and to whom companies give.

3. Differentiate among strategic philanthropy, cause-related marketing, and cause branding. Provide an example of each not discussed in the text.

4. Identify and discuss briefly what you think are the major trade-offs that firms face as they think about offshoring and reshoring. When substantial layoffs are involved, what are firms' responsibilities to their employees and their communities?

5. In your opinion, why does a business have a responsibility to employees and community stakeholders in a business or plant closing decision?

Endnotes

1. "Community" *Oxford Dictionaries* (April 2010). Oxford University Press. http://oxforddictionaries.com/us/definition/amercan_english/community. Accessed April 9, 2013.

2. "Michael Porter on Inner City Business," *Bloomberg BusinessWeek* (May 27, 2010), http://www.businessweek.com/smallbiz/content/may2010/sb20100526_383016.htm.

3. *UPS Corporate Sustainability Report 2011*, http://www.responsibility.ups.com/community/Static%20Files/sustainability/2011_UPS_CSR_Report.pdf. Accessed April 7, 2013.

4. http://www.lilly.com/Responsibility/our-approach/Pages/our-approach.aspx. Accessed April 7, 2013.

5. Bill Shaw and Frederick Post, "A Moral Basis for Corporate Philanthropy," *Journal of Business Ethics* (October 1993), 745–751.

6. Susanne Gargiulo, "Why Everyone Wants To Work For The Good Guys," *CNN.com* (November 8, 2012), http://edition.cnn.com/2012/11/07/business/global-office-csr-volunteer/index.html?c=&page=1. Accessed April 7, 2013.

7. Ibid.

8. Ibid.

9. Ibid.

10. http://www.longaberger.com/horizonofhope//. Accessed April 7, 2013.

11. Jayne O'Donnell, "UPS Workers Head to Haiti to Provide Relief," *USA Today* (January 25, 2010), 48.

12. Ryan Scott, "Is Your Company Doubling Down on its Employee Volunteers?" *Forbes* (October 9, 2012), http://www.forbes.com/sites/causeintegration/2012/10/09/is-your-company-doubling-down-on-its-employee-volunteers/. Accessed April 13, 2013.

13. Ibid.

14. Angela Haupt, "Volunteering Does a Body Good," *U.S. News and World Report* (November, 2010), 72.

15. http://www.deloitte.com/view/en_US/us/About/Community-Involvement/volunteerism/impact-day/f98eec97e6650310VgnVCM2000001b56f00aRCRD.htm#. Accessed April 13, 2013.

16. Ronald McDonald House of Charities, "Who We Are," http://www.rmhc.com/who-we-are/(2013). Accessed April 7, 2013.

17. Cecily Railborn, Antoinette Green, Lyudmila Todorova, Toni Trapani, and Wilborne E. Watson, "Corporate Philanthropy: When Is Giving Effective," *The Journal of Corporate Accounting and Finance* (November/December 2003), 47–54.

18. *Webster's New World Dictionary* (Cleveland: World Publishing Company, 1964), 1098.

19. The Conference Board, "Corporate Giving Continues to Grow in Dollars and Sophistication," (June 5, 2012), http://www.conference-board.org/press/pressdetail.cfm?pressid=4507. Accessed April 7, 2013.

20. Ibid.

21. Morrell Heald, *The Social Responsibilities of Business: Company and Community 1900–1960* (Cleveland: Case Western Reserve University Press, 1970), 112.

22. CECP, *Giving in Numbers* (2012 Edition). http://www.corporatephilanthropy.org/pdfs/giving_in_numbers/GIN2012_finalweb.pdf. Accessed April 7, 2013.

23. Adam Bryant, "Companies Oppose Disclosure of Details on Gifts to Charity," *The New York Times* (April 3, 1998), A1.

24. Ibid.

25. Nicholas Confessore, "S.E.C. Gets Plea: For Companies To Air Donations," *The New York Times* (April 24, 2013).

26. John D. Rockfeller III, "In Defense of Philanthropy," *Business and Society Review* (Spring 1978), 26–29.

27. Giving in Numbers 2011, *Committee to Encourage Corporate Philanthropy,* http://www.corporatephilanthropy.org/pdfs/giving_in_numbers/GIN2012_finalweb.pdf. Accessed April 7, 2013.

28. Ibid.

29. Ibid.

30. Ibid.

31. Ibid.

32. Wilfred Bockelman, *Culture of Corporate Citizenship: Minnesota's Business Legacy for the Global Future* (Lakeville, MN: Galde Press, Inc., 2000), 15–16.

33. http://foundationcenter.org/pnd/news/story.jhtml?id=387000012. Accessed April 24, 2013.

34. http://www.dailyfinance.com/2012/11/05/prudential-donates-3-million-for-immediate-support/. Accessed April 24, 2013.

35. http://foundationcenter.org/pnd/news/story.jhtml?id=387000012. Accessed April 24, 2013.

36. Bob Diddlebock, "To Give or Not to Give," *Time* (May 11, 2009), 10.

37. "Prudential Foundation Announces $1.25 Million in Grants," Philanthropy News Digest (July 30, 2012), http://foundationcenter.org/pnd/news/story.jhtml?id=387000012. Accessed April 7, 2013.

38. http://www.artsusa.org/information_services/research/services/economic_impact/iv/national.asp. Accessed April 7, 2013.

39. Ibid.

40. Elizabeth Kelleher, "U.S. Companies Step Up the Business of Giving Overseas," http://www.america.gov/st/developenglish/2006/April/20060411182239berehellek0.1802027. html. Accessed April 7, 2013.

41. http://bclc.uschamber.com/site-page/hurricane-sandy-corporate-aid-tracker. Accessed April 7, 2013.

42. Louis Lavelle, "Giving as Never Before," *BusinessWeek* (October 1, 2001), 10.

43. Ian Wilhelm, "Corporate Giving Takes a Dip," *Chronicle of Philanthropy* (July 24, 2003).

44. "Corporate Kindness," *Newsweek* (February 15, 2010), 14.

45. James J. Chrisman and Archie B. Carroll, "Corporate Responsibility: Reconciling Economic and Social Goals," *Sloan Management Review* (Winter 1984), 59–65.

46. Margaret Coady, "CECP Releases Giving in Numbers: 2012 Edition," (November 27, 2012), http://www.corporatephilanthropy.org/press-room/cecp-insights/item/32-cecp-releases-giving-in-numbers-2012-edition.html. Accessed April 7, 2013.

47. Carolyn Cavicchio, "The 2010 Philanthropy Agenda: Is the Pressure Easing?" *The Conference Board* (March 2010).

48. http://nationalsafeplace.org/what-is-safe-place/. Accessed April 7, 2013.

49. http://nationalsafeplace.org/about-us/our-partners/. Accessed April 9, 2013.

50. Richard Steckel and Robin Simons, *Doing Best by Doing Good* (New York: Dutton Publishers, 1992).

51. Michael Porter and Mark Kramer, "The Competitive Advantage of Corporate Philanthropy," *Harvard Business Review* (December 2002), 56–69.

52. Ibid.

53. Ibid.

54. http://www.bk.com/cms/en/us/cms_out/digital_assets/files/pages/BK_CR_Report.pdf. Accessed April 9, 2013.

55. Bruce Horovitz, "Be Kind and They Will Come," *USA Today International Edition* (March 27, 2013), A1–A2.

56. Ibid.

57. Ibid.

58. Ibid.

59. http://www.participantmedia.com/2013/03/rolling-stone-participant-medias-pivot-join-forces-celebrate-greatest-generation/. Accessed April 13, 2013.

60. Jenny McTaggart, "Whole Foods Steps Up Sourcing Standards," *Progressive Grocer* (April 15, 2007), 12–13.

61. Porter and Kramer, 56–69.

62. Ibid.

63. Ibid.

64. Patricia Caesar, "Cause-Related Marketing: The New Face of Corporate Philanthropy," *Business and Society Review* (Fall 1986), 16.

65. Martin Gottlieb, "Cashing In on a Higher Cause," *The New York Times* (July 6, 1986), 6-F.

66. Michelle Wirth Fellman, "Cause Marketing Takes a Strategic Turn," *Marketing News* (April 26, 1999), 4–8.

67. Peggy Bernstein, "Philanthropy, Reputation Go Hand in Hand," *PR News* (January 17, 2000), 1–8.

68. 1999 Cone/Roper Cause-Related Trends Report.

69. Public Service Advertising Research Center, http://www.psaresearch.com/causebranding.html. Accessed April 9, 2013.

70. David Benady, "Paved with Good Intentions (Cover Story)," *Marketing Week* (March 15, 2007), 24–25.

71. Mya Frazier, "Costly Red Campaign Reaps Meager $18m (Cover Story)," *Advertising Age* (March 5, 2007), 1–43.

72. Benady, 24–25.

73. Ibid.

74. Ibid.

75. Sheila Shayon, "Brands Go Blue for Autism Awareness Month," *brandchannel* (April 5, 2013), http://www.brandchannel.com/home/post/2013/04/05/Brands-Autism-Awareness-040513.aspx. Accessed April 7, 2013.

76. CECP, *Giving in Numbers* (2012 Edition), http://www.corporatephilanthropy.org/pdfs/giving_in_numbers/GIN2012_finalweb.pdf. Accessed April 7, 2013.

77. Carolyn Cavicchio, "The 2010 Philanthropy Agenda: Is the Pressure Easing?" The Conference Board (March 2010).

78. Kelleher, 2006. Accessed April 7, 2013.

79. Bob Davis, "Wealth of Nations: Finding Lessons of Outsourcing in Four Historical Tales," *The Wall Street Journal* (March 29, 2004), A1.

80. Ibid.

81. "Where America's Jobs Went," *The Week* (March 18, 2011), http://theweek.com/article/index/213217/where-americas-jobs-went. Accessed April 8, 2013.

82. Dale Kasler, "Outsourcing Reaps Winners, Losers in U.S. Economy," *The Sacramento Bee* (April 26, 2004).

83. Brad Stone, "Should I Stay or Should I Go," *Newsweek* (April 19, 2004), 52–53.

84. Ibid.

85. Sarah Kabourek, "Back in the USA," *Fortune* (September 28, 2009), 30.

86. "Welcome Home," *The Economist* (January 19, 2013), http://www.economist.com/news/leaders/21569739-outsourcing-jobs-faraway-places-wane-will-not-solve-wests. Accessed April 8, 2013.

87. Ibid.

88. "Here, There, and Everywhere," *The Economist* (January 19, 2013), http://www.economist.com/news/special- report/21569572-after-decades-sending-work-across-world-companies-are-rethinking-their-offshoring. Accessed April 8, 2013.

89. Ibid.

90. Ibid.

91. Ibid.

92. Ibid.

93. Peter F. Drucker, *Management: Tasks, Responsibilities, Practices* (New York: Harper & Row, 1974), 327–328.

94. Susan Diesenhouse, "To Save Factories, Owners Diversify," *The New York Times* (November 30, 2003), 5.

95. http://srcholdings.com/. Accessed April 9, 2013.

96. Archie B. Carroll, "When Business Closes Down: Social Responsibilities and Management Actions," *California Management Review* (Winter 1984), 131.

97. Vincent J. Matteo, "The Chamber View," *Williamsport Sun-Gazette* (July 7, 2003), 2.

98. The Employee Ownership 100: America's Largest Majority Employee-Owned Companies (June 2012), http://www.nceo.org/articles/employee-ownership-100. Accessed April 8, 2013.

99. Terri Minsky, "Gripes of Rath: Workers Who Bought Iowa Slaughterhouse Regret That They Did," *The Wall Street Journal* (December 2, 1981), 1.

100. "The Opposite of Wal-Mart," *The Economist* (May 5, 2007), 79.

101. Ibid.

102. Kenneth Labich, "Will United Fly?" *Fortune* (August 22, 1994), 70–78.

103. Suzanne Cohen, "United Airlines ESOP Woes," *Risk Management* (June 2001), 9.

104. Greg Schneider, "Owner Role Always Tense for United Employees," *The Washington Post* (December 10, 2002), E1.

105. "United's Bankruptcy Tab: $335 Million-Plus in Fees," *USA Today* (October 3, 2006), http://www.usatoday.com/travel/news/2006-03-10-ual-bankruptcy-fees_x.htm. Accessed April 9, 2013.

106. Cohen, 9.

107. Carroll, 132.

108. Grover Starling, *The Changing Environment of Business* (Boston: Kent, 1980), 319–320.

109. Loretta W. Prencipe, "Impending Layoffs Need Warning," *Info World* (April 9, 2001), 15.

110. Ibid.

111. James Drew and Steve Eder, "Without Warning: Flaws, Loopholes Deny Employees Protection Mandated by WARN Act," *The Blade* (July 15, 2007), http://www.toledoblade.com/business/2007/07/15/Without-warning-Flaws-loopholes-deny-employees-protection-mandated-by-WARN-Act.html Accessed April 9, 2013.

112. Ibid.

113. James Drew and Steve Eder, "Different Workers Face the Same Problem with the WARN Act," *The Blade* (July 17, 2007), http://www.toledoblade.com/business/2007/07/17/Different-workers-face-the-same-problem-with-the-WARN-Act.html. Accessed April 9, 2013.

114. Kelly M. Butler, "Going above and beyond Advance WARNing," *Employee Benefit News* (February 2009), 7.

115. Greg Jefferson, "Sony Lays Off 120 Workers, Moves Closer to Closing San Antonio Plant," *San Antonio Express-News* (August 8, 2003), 1.

116. Ibid.

117. Ibid.

118. Cornell University Workshop Report, 28–30.

119. Leon Grunberg, Sarah Moore, and Edward S. Greenberg, "Managers' Reactions to Implementing Layoffs: Relationship to Health Problems and Withdrawal Behaviors," *Human Resource Management* (Summer 2006), 159–178.

120. Suzanne M. Behr and Margaret A. White, "Layoff Survivor Sickness," *Executive Excellence* (November 2003), 18.

121. Ibid.

122. "Survivor Guilt: How the Corporate Ax Affects Remaining Employees," *PR News* (March 12, 2001), 1.

123. Ibid.

Internal Stakeholder Issues

17

Employee Stakeholders and Workplace Issues

CHAPTER LEARNING OUTCOMES

After studying this chapter, you should be able to:

1. Identify the major changes occurring in the workforce today.

2. Outline the characteristics of the new social contract between employers and employees.

3. Explain the employee rights movement and its underlying principles.

4. Describe and discuss the employment-at-will doctrine and its role in employee rights.

5. Discuss the right to due process and fair treatment.

6. Describe the actions companies are taking to make the workplace friendlier.

7. Elaborate on the freedom-of-speech issue and whistle-blowing.

C hanging times and the changes they bring to society's values always have an impact on the workplace. In times of financial difficulty, such changes become even more pronounced, and that is the case with employee stakeholders today. Although external stakeholders such as government, consumers, the environment, and the community continue to be major facets of business's concern for the social environment, considerable attention is now being paid to employee stakeholders—their status, their treatment, their rights, and their satisfaction. This should come as no surprise. Employees are essential to the creation of firm value and the financial success it provides, and so companies have a moral responsibility to create value for employees in their workplace experience and lives. Doing so is also cost effective, because increasing morale and reducing turnover improves a company's bottom line.[1]

The development of employee stakeholder rights has been a direct outgrowth of the kinds of social changes that have brought other societal issues into focus. The history of work has been one of steadily improving conditions for employees. Today's issues are quite unlike the old bread-and-butter concerns of higher pay, shorter hours, more job security, and better working conditions. These expectations still exist, but more complex workplace trends and issues have assumed increased importance. The economic recession has heightened the impact of issues such as pay levels, number of hours worked, employee health care, and retirement benefits, as companies try to reduce costs in order to stay competitive, and employees strive to maintain their standard of living in difficult times.[2]

In the new millennium, two major themes or trends characterize the modern relationship between employees and their employers: the evolution of the social contract and the expansion of employee rights. First, we will discuss the evolving **social contract** between organizations and workers, which is different from contracts of the past. Second, we will consider the continuing trend toward more expansive employee rights. We will describe how the changes in the workplace have precipitated a renewal in the employee rights movement.

Because the subject of employee stakeholders and workplace issues is very extensive, we dedicate two chapters to these topics. In this chapter, we discuss some of the workplace changes that have been taking place, the emerging social contract, and the employee rights movement. Three employee rights issues, in particular, are discussed here: the right not to be fired without good cause, the right to due process and fair treatment, and the right to freedom of speech in the workplace. In Chapter 18, we will extend our discussion to the related issues of the expectations and rights of employees to privacy, safety, and health. These two chapters should be considered a continuous discussion of employee stakeholders, wherein economic, legal, and ethical responsibilities are all taken into consideration.

The New Social Contract

Fifty years ago, the trend was that employees stayed in the same job in the same company for years, and those companies rewarded employees' loyalty by offering job stability, a decent wage, and good benefits.[3] Today, the average person born in the United States between 1957 and 1964 has held 11.3 jobs.[4] Three out of four workers aged 16 to 19, and half of the workers between the ages of 20 and 24, have been at their jobs for less than a year.[5] The workforce of today is more mobile, less loyal, and more diverse. From CEOs to factory workers, employees have become aware that their jobs are vulnerable, and so they increasingly view themselves as free agents, bearing sole responsibility for their own careers.[6] Today's employees don't look for a promise of lifetime employment. Instead, they seek competitive pay and benefits, coupled with opportunities for professional growth. At the same time, they desire meaningful work, a vision they can share with the company, clear performance feedback, and a strong, supportive organizational culture.[7] Some analysts argue that a key driver of an organization's ability to survive and thrive into the future will be the social contract that firm has with its employees.[8] Figure 17-1 presents some of the characteristics of the old and new social contracts.

With this new social contract, loyalty is still important. Indeed, when employers treat employees with respect and consideration, they can earn employee loyalty even in (and perhaps especially in) these difficult times. Paul Savardi of Entrepreneur.com explains,

FIGURE 17-1   **The Changing Social Contract between Employers and Employees**

Old Social Contract	New Social Contract
Job security; long, stable career and employment relationships	Few tenure arrangements; jobs constantly "at risk"; employment as long as you "add value" to the organization
Lifetime careers with one employer	Fewer life careers; changing employer common; careers more dynamic
Stable positions/job assignments	Temporary project assignments
Loyalty to employer; identification	Loyalty to self and profession; diminished identification with employer
Paternalism; family-type relationships	Relationships far less warm and familial; no more parent–child relationships
Employee sense of entitlement	Personal responsibility for one's own career/job future
Stable, rising income	Pay that reflects contributions; pay for "value added"
Job-related skill training	Learning opportunities; employees in charge of their own education and updating
Focus on individual job accomplishments	Focus on team building and projects

© Cengage Learning

"Employee loyalty is an earned response to the trust, respect, and commitment shown to the individuals in your company. ... When you demonstrate loyalty to your employees, they'll reciprocate with commitment and loyalty to your business."[9]

The global financial crisis had some unexpected impacts on employee loyalty. The 2010 Kelly Global Workforce Index, a survey of 134,000 employees in 29 countries, found that 27 percent of respondents worldwide believed the economic recession made them feel more loyal to their employers, 10 percent felt less loyal, and 63 percent said it made no difference.[10] In fact, 43 percent of employees said they felt "totally committed" to their current employer.[11] Oddly, recession may have engendered this level of commitment. Even employees who were not happy with their jobs and felt at the mercy of their employers were likely to feel thankful to their employers for giving them jobs when so many people were unemployed.[12] As the economy has begun to rebound, however, that loyalty seems to have faded. The 2012 Kelly Global Workforce Index paints a different picture. Less than one-third (31 percent) of workers believe a career for life with one employer is relevant today, more than half of workers feel it is important to change employers (53 percent), and almost half of the employees surveyed are always actively looking for a new job, even when they are happy with the one they have.[13]

Even before the global financial crisis, the extreme level of global competition was affecting firms around the globe, as workers began to receive an increasingly smaller portion of the economic pie. The U.S. workers' share of gross domestic product fell by 2.5 percent, German workers' share fell by 2.5 percent, and Japan's workers' share dropped 3 percentage points.[14] The financial crisis exacerbated that problem with historic unemployment levels, in addition to heightened underemployment, deteriorating working conditions, and an increase in part-time work. Now, as the economy appears to be rebounding, global unemployment continues to rise.[15] Corporate profits have been soaring, but employees are not sharing in the wealth. In the United States, corporate profits were at their highest share of national income since 1950, while the share that employees received was at the lowest level since 1966.[16]

Training is vital for employees if they are to navigate new waters successfully. In this highly competitive environment, firms need workers with knowledge and the skill to leverage it. To that end, employers have instituted a wide range of training programs and tuition reimbursement programs to keep their employees at the cutting edge of the changing environment.[17] Of course, this does not help laid-off employees, because the firm has no financial incentive for providing training that will enable the person to seek alternative jobs. **Outplacement**, assistance provided to laid-off employees, is an important ethical responsibility of any firm in the new environment, because the duty to treat employees well does not end when they are laid off. Of course, workers also need retraining when they are ineligible for in-house or outplacement resources because they are no longer associated with any firm. Some argue that this is an example of market failure and that the government should step in to help these workers.[18]

It is difficult to say whether the new social contract is bad or good. More than anything else, it represents an adaptation to the changing world and changing business circumstances. In some respects, workers may prefer the new model. Whatever turns out to be the case, we can expect free agent employees to be more proactive about their work environments than the loyal employees of the past once were. It is likely that employee stakeholders' expectations of fair treatment will continue to rise, and we will witness continuing growth in the employee rights movement.

The Employee Rights Movement

In our discussion of employee rights, we will focus on employees in the private sector because of the underlying public sector–private sector dichotomy. The public sector is subject to constitutional control of its power, and so government employees have more protections. In contrast, the private sector generally has not been subject to constitutional control because of the concept of **private property**, which holds that individuals and private organizations are free to use their property as they desire. As a result, private corporations historically and traditionally have not had to recognize employee rights to the same degree, because society honored the corporation's private property rights. The underlying issues for the private sector and its stakeholders then become why, and to what extent, the private property rights of business should be changed or diluted.

A brief comment on the role of labor unions is appropriate here. In general, although labor unions have been quite successful in improving the material conditions of life at work in the United States—pay, fringe benefits, and working conditions—they have not been as active in pursuing civil liberties. We must give unions credit for the gains they have made in converting what were typically regarded as management's rights or prerogatives into issues in which labor could participate. However, we should note that labor unions seem to be disappearing from the U.S. business scene. In 1953, union representation reached its highest proportion of the private employment workforce, at 36 percent.[19] By 2013, the proportion of union members in the private sector had fallen to 6.6 percent, with workers in education, training, library occupations, and protective service occupations holding the highest unionization rates.[20] Although the public sector union rate has a fivefold higher rate of 35.9 percent, it does not have a significant impact on the private sector employee rights we are discussing here. Compared to other countries, the U.S. unionization rate is very low, but OECD statistics suggest that union membership is declining worldwide as well.[21]

The Meaning of Employee Rights

Before we consider specific employee rights issues, we should discuss briefly what we mean by **employee rights**. A lawyer might look at employee rights as claims that one can enforce in a court of law. Many economists would concur that rights are only creations of the law. For our purposes, we will approach employee rights from the "principle of rights" perspective, and viewed from this perspective, rights are justifiable claims that utility cannot override. While we will focus on employee moral rights, we will also consider employee legal rights. Of course, the current recessionary environment has influenced discussion of employee rights. If a right is truly a moral right, it is not contingent on business's ability to provide it. However, the deep cutbacks that arose from the recession have stimulated renewed discussion of the parameters of employee rights.

Employee rights can be positive or negative. Said differently, they can focus on achieving desired outcomes or on prohibiting unwanted outcomes. Richard Edwards has grouped employee rights into three categories: rights that find their source in law, in union contracts, or in employers' promises. Rights provided by the law are called **statutory rights**. These include, for example, the rights established by the Civil Rights Act of 1964 (at a national level) or by the Massachusetts Right to Know Law (at the state level), which grant production workers the right to be notified of specific toxic substances they may be exposed to in the workplace. Union contracts, by contrast, provide workers with rights established through the process of **collective bargaining**. Examples of these rights are seniority preferences, job security mechanisms, and grievance procedures.[22]

ETHICS IN PRACTICE CASE

Should I Say Something?

I was hired as a temporary employee of a toy manufacturing company, and the department I was assigned to was going through some rough changes. The director had recently quit. The new director came from a similar company that had recently filed bankruptcy. She said she had about 20 years in the imports business and knew it like the back of her hand. Naturally, her new employees were relieved and hoped that business would continue as usual.

Months passed and I learned a lot about the imports aspect of our company. In those months, my coworkers noticed that our boss wasn't doing much work. They were used to a hands-on director, like their previous one, who wasn't afraid to pull back her sleeves and dive into the deepest pile of papers to get it sorted through. Soon, work that we thought our new director was supposed to handle started piling up. We also gained a huge customer, whose orders were a task equal to the amount of work we already had. Our director requested another such account. She also put me, the temporary employee, in charge of the new customer. Because huge amounts of work were getting cranked out of our department, we worked 10 hours shifts and Saturdays to get it all done. Then my coworkers started complaining. "All she does is watch YouTube videos all day," one said. "She's always talking on her cell phone," another coworker said.

Another temp was hired to help us out so that we wouldn't have to work on Saturdays.

I was finally hired as a permanent employee. I was elated for about two months to have a job that I could call "home," and coworkers that I could get close to, and not get sad when my assignment ended. But alas, the company started laying off employees. They began to fire most of the temporary employees; then, they fired 11 regular employees. In all, we lost both of our temps and a regular employee in our department. I can't help but feel that it was our director's fault that we had to lose these employees.

1. The reason I got hired was because of my director's strong push to keep me. Should I look the other way when she acts in ways that are not in the company's best interests? Should my loyalty go to my company in general or to the person who hired me?
2. Even after one of my coworkers spoke to our director about her wasting time on the job she continued her habits. Should my coworker have let the director's boss know what was going on?
3. As an employee, do I have any rights in this situation? Do I have any responsibilities?
4. What would you have done in this situation? Why?

Contributed Anonymously

Employer promises are the third source of employees' rights categorized by Edwards. These employer grants or promises are called **enterprise rights**. Typical examples of such enterprise rights might include the right to petition beyond one's immediate supervisor, the right to be free from physical intimidation, the right to a grievance or complaint system, and the right to due process in discipline. Other enterprise rights include the right to have express standards for personnel evaluation, the right to have one's job clearly defined, the right to a "just cause" standard for dismissal, and the right to be free from nepotism and unfair favoritism.[23]

Management provides and justifies enterprise rights, and so the rationale for those rights can be as varied as the managers implementing them. They might reflect the prevailing customs, and thus be necessary for the firm to be competitive. They might extend above and beyond those offered by competing firms, and thus be used as a type of recruiting tool. They may also be given on the basis of some normative ethical principle or reasoning (for example, "This is the way workers ought to be treated"). In this situation, the ethical principles of justice, rights, and utilitarianism, as well as notions of virtue ethics, may be the rationales.

To summarize, employee rights may be based on economic, legal, and/or ethical sources of justification. In this connection, management may provide the employee

FIGURE 17-2   **Three Models of Management Morality and Their Orientations toward Employee Stakeholders**

Model of Management Morality	Orientation toward Employee Stakeholders
Moral Management	Employees are a human resource that must be treated with dignity and respect. Employees' rights to due process, privacy, freedom of speech, and safety are maximally considered in all decisions. Management seeks fair dealings with employees. The goal is to use a leadership style, such as consultative/participative, that will result in mutual confidence and trust. Commitment is a recurring theme.
Amoral Management	Employees are treated as the law requires. Motivational attempts focus on increasing productivity rather than satisfying employees' growing maturity needs. Employees are still seen as factors of production, but a remunerative approach is used. The organization sees self-interest in treating employees with minimal respect. Organization structure, pay incentives, and rewards are all geared toward short- and medium-term productivity.
Immoral Management	Employees are viewed as factors of production to be used, exploited, and manipulated for gain of individual manager or company. No concern is shown for employees' needs/rights/ expectations. Managers pursue a short-term focus in a coercive, controlling, and alienating environment.

© Cengage Learning

rights as part of an effort to display moral management, as discussed in Chapter 7. To illustrate this point further, Figure 17-2 characterizes how moral managers, as well as amoral and immoral managers, might view employee stakeholders.

Following are the job-related rights that are mentioned often and thus merit further discussion here: (1) the *right not to be fired without good cause*, (2) the *right to due process and fair treatment*, and (3) the *right to freedom, particularly freedom of expression and freedom of speech*. In Chapter 18, we will consider the rights to privacy, safety, and health in the workplace.

The Right Not to Be Fired without Cause

A **good cause norm**, the belief that employees should be discharged only for good reasons (i.e., just cause dismissal), prevails in the United States today. This normative belief persists in spite of the fact that it does not match the descriptive reality. Most U.S. employees can be fired for any reason, or for no reason, as long as the firing is not in violation of any discrimination laws. A range of studies have shown the good cause norm to be widely held in a variety of situations, with respondents including undergraduate and graduate students as well as both blue- and white-collar workers.[24] Belief in the good cause norm stands in direct opposition to the employment-at-will doctrine, which many private employers believe is their right. With employers and employees holding such contradictory views, it is easy to see why so many disputes occur, and terms like "unjust dismissals" and "wrongful discharge" have become part of today's employment language.

Employment-at-Will Doctrine

The central issue in the movement to protect workers' jobs involves changing views of the **employment-at-will doctrine**. In the industrialized world, the United States is unique in adhering to this doctrine, which is based on the private property rights of the employer and the principle that the relationship between employer and employee is a voluntary one that can be terminated at any time by either party. This doctrine holds that just as employees are free to quit a company any time they choose, employers can discharge employees for any reason, or no reason, as long as they do not violate federal discrimination laws, state laws, or union contracts. What this doctrine means is that unless you are protected by a union contract (the vast majority of the workforce is not) or by one of the discrimination laws, your employer is free to let you go anytime, for any reason. This doctrine is not widely understood by the workforce. As previously mentioned, most employees in the United States believe that employment law not only should follow a good cause norm but also does so in practice.[25] However, most private employees in the United States are in an at-will employment relationship.[26]

This lack of awareness about at-will employment may provide the answer to a question Louis Uchitelle poses in *The Disposable American*—why is the United States so tolerant of large-scale layoffs?[27] Uchitelle, who writes on economics for *The New York Times*, details the human costs of a system that allows employers to fire or lay off employees at will. Layoffs are traumatic events that inflict significant mental health damage. Uchitelle poses the following question to the American Psychiatric Association, "Why don't you put a warning label on layoffs?"[28]

Legal Challenges to Employment-at-Will Three broad categories of issues that illustrate the legal challenges that have arisen with regard to employment-at-will discharges are (1) public policy exceptions, (2) contractual actions, and (3) breach of good faith actions.[29] States vary in their adoption of exceptions to employment-at-will, creating a patchwork of employment situations around the country. Only three states: Florida, Georgia, and Rhode Island; have never adopted an exception.[30]

A major exception to the long-standing employment-at-will doctrine is known as the **public policy exception**; 43 states recognize this exception.[31] This exception protects employees from being fired because they refuse to commit crimes or because they try to take advantage of privileges to which they are entitled by law. The courts have held that management may not discharge an employee who refuses to commit an illegal act or performs a public obligation, such as serving on a jury or supplying information to the police. This exception sometimes covers whistle-blowers. We will further discuss the case of whistle-blowers later in the chapter.

Workers who believe they have contracts or implied contracts with their employers are protected in the 42 states that recognize the **implied contract exception**.[32] In some instances, the courts hold employers to promises they do not even realize they have made. For example, statements in employee handbooks or personnel manuals, job-offer letters, and even oral assurances about job security can be interpreted as implied contracts that the management is not at liberty to violate. If an employee can prove in court that the hiring manager said, "We do not fire people without a good reason," that can be enough to create an implied contract. Even the use of the term "permanent employee" to mean an employee who had worked beyond a six-month probationary period may be construed as a promise of continuous employment.

Courts have also recognized that employers should hold themselves to a standard of fairness and good faith dealings with employees. This concept is the broadest restraint on employment-at-will terminations. The **good faith principle** suggests that employers may run the risk of losing lawsuits to former employees if they fail to show that employees had every reasonable opportunity to improve their performance before termination. Only 20 states recognize the good faith principle.[33] As previously noted, however, the good faith principle reflects what many already believe is the responsibility of businesses toward their employees. The principle is not a problem for companies if they simply introduce fair ways of taking disciplinary measures and mechanisms for reviewing grievances that provide employees with due process. We will discuss such due-process mechanisms later in the chapter.

ETHICS IN PRACTICE CASE

The Pocketed Purse

At work, we have a warehouse and an office in the building. Right now, we have a program assembling gift sets for the holiday season and extra help has been required and called in. Two or three months ago, a lady from the warehouse working on this project told me that $30 was missing from her purse, which she leaves in the cafeteria, because seasonal help has no other place to put their belongings. She did not make a big deal about it, because she had no idea who took the money. In addition, she did not speak English, and so did not know how to communicate to management what had happened. I asked her if she wanted me to go to management and explain the situation, but she told me not to do that because she had no proof of who did it.

Only a few people in the office, myself included, knew that we have surveillance cameras in the cafeteria. If I spoke up, it meant that the culprit would lose their job when caught. I had no idea who took the money; it could have been one of my close friends at work, or it might have been a person to whom I barely speak. I had an ethical dilemma, because if I just let it go, the person who took the money would get to keep their job, and to me that was not right. It bothered me that someone could go into someone else's belongings and steal from them. In the end, I went to management and told them about the situation. They reviewed the cameras and were able to see who took the money. The young woman who stole the money was fired on the spot.

1. Was it right for me to report the problem to management? Considering all the facts, would you have done the same?

2. In making your decision, were you affected by the fact that the thief could have been one of your friends? Do you have any moral obligations to friends?

3. Did the fact that the woman who was robbed asked you not to say anything affect your decision? Do you feel she had any rights not to be observed via surveillance without her knowledge?

4. What else could you do to rectify the situation?

Contributed by Natalia Santos

Spotlight on Sustainability

Employees Are Key to Sustainability

A study by the National Environmental Education Foundation (NEEF) found that educating employees in environmental and sustainability (E&S) initiatives can attract and retain good talent while also increasing profitability and reducing environmental impact. The study presents a variety of case studies, including eBay. eBay's green team convinced the company to build San Jose, California's largest commercial solar installation. They reduced CO_2 emissions by more than 1 million pounds a year and saved more than $100,000. In a statement, Diane Wood, president of NEEF, said that past environmental education programs focused on employees involved in safety and health. Now they realize they must involve the entire workforce. Human resource management has a critical role to play through the recruitment and selection of the right people and the establishment of policies and incentives that support a sustainability orientation.

Sources: Greenbiz Staff, "Why Bringing Employees on Board Helps Sustainability Projects Succeed," *Greenbiz.com* (February 22, 2010), http://www.greenbiz.com/news/2010/02/22/bringing-employees-board-makes-sustainability-projects-success#ixzz0pS7n8RUA. Accessed May 9, 1013; Linda C. Forbes and John M. Jermier, "The New Corporate Environmentalism and the Symbolic Management of Corporate Culture," in Pratima Bansal and Andrew J. Hoffman (eds.) *The Oxford Handbook of Business and the Natural Environment* (Oxford University Press: New York, 2012).

Moral and Managerial Challenges to Employment-at-Will As previously mentioned, the United States is unique in its adherence to employment-at-will, and most people in the United States believe a norm of good cause applies to employment decisions, so it is not surprising that employment-at-will has been criticized on moral as well as legal grounds. The argument generally used in favor of employment-at-will is that employers invoke their property rights when they terminate an employee. In an interesting rebuttal, Werhane, Radin, and Bowie suggest that the fruits of an employee's labor are that employee's property and so property rights can also be invoked to argue against the appropriateness of employment-at-will.[34]

Using the concept of employee property rights as a foundation, Werhane et al. derive three objections to employment-at-will. First, they argue that employees deserve respectful treatment, which includes explaining the reasons for termination when it occurs. Second, employees do not have the option of being arbitrary or capricious with employers, and so employers should bear the same responsibility in their treatment of employees. A third issue is based on the concept of reciprocity: employees are expected to be trustworthy, loyal, and respectful in their interactions with employers, and so employers should show employees the same consideration.[35]

Employment-at-will can present managerial problems as well. We should not forget the impact that an employment-at-will environment can have on the culture of an organization. Most bad reasons for firing employees, such as discrimination, are already illegal, and managers can always fire an employee for good, justifiable reasons. From this perspective, employment-at-will is not needed, because it simply protects the right of the employer to fire an employee for no reason at all. This creates an odd dynamic. Trust and loyalty are important to effective workplaces, but they are reciprocal relationships. For managers to be able to trust their employees, they must be willing to be trustworthy in return.[36]

Dismissing an Employee with Care

With respect to employee dismissals, management needs to be aware not only of the content of the decision to dismiss, but also of the process for doing it. Treating employees with care is important not only to the terminated employee, but also to the survivors of the process, who then know they will be treated with care if they face a similar situation. Even in difficult times, a positive corporate culture can be preserved with thoughtful treatment of employees. Steve Harrison offers some do's and don'ts for dismissing employees in a responsible manner. The following are some specific recommendations for actions[37]:

1. *Fire employees in a private space.* Don't terminate an employee in a way that enables coworkers to see what is happening or that forces them to "walk a gauntlet" in front of them.
2. *Be mindful of employees' logistics.* How will they get closure on their projects? How will they get home that day?
3. *Preserve employees' dignity.* If you must lay off a trusted and valuable employee for economic reasons, don't cancel passwords or confiscate IDs and cell phones immediately.
4. *Choreograph the notification in advance.* The purpose of the meeting should not be a surprise.
5. *Use transparent criteria for layoffs.* The rationale for terminations should be clear both to those laid off and to the survivors.

The following are some of the actions managers should *not* take when dismissing employees[38]:

1. *Don't fire on a Friday.* Terminated employees would not have access to support services on weekends and so would have to cope on their own.
2. *Don't say that downsizing is finished.* It is impossible to know for sure that the downsizing has ended, and being wrong about that would make subsequent layoffs more difficult for all concerned.
3. *Don't terminate an employee via e-mail.* Although this advice seems obvious, firms have done so to the detriment of their reputations, as well as their former employees.
4. *Stick to the topic and avoid platitudes.* For example, don't say, "This is as hard for me as it is for you"—it isn't.
5. *Don't rush through the meeting.* Being willing to give a person time is a way of communicating that the person matters. Not to give the employee the time needed for the termination rubs salt in the wound.

For effective stakeholder management, organizations must always consider their obligations to employee stakeholders and their rights and expectations with respect to their jobs. Companies that aspire to emulate the tenets of the moral management model will need to continuously reexamine their attitudes, perceptions, practices, and policies with respect to this issue, and take care to dismiss employees only for solid economic or performance related reasons, not arbitrary reasons.

The Right to Due Process and Fair Treatment

One of the most frequently proclaimed employee rights issues of the past decade has been the right to due process. Basically, **due process** is the right to receive an impartial review of one's complaints and to be dealt with fairly. In the context of the workplace, the right to due process is the right of employees to have impartial third parties review the decisions that adversely affect them. Of course, the right not to be fired without just cause would fall into this category of fair treatment; however, in this section we will expand on this concept and discuss other applications.

One major obstacle to the due-process idea is that to some extent it is a bit contrary to the employment-at-will principle discussed earlier. Due process is consistent with the democratic ideal that undergirds the universal right to fair treatment, and so one can argue that without due process, employees do not receive fair treatment in the workplace. Furthermore, the fact that the courts are gradually eroding the employment-at-will principle might serve as an indication that employment-at-will is thought to be unfair. If this is true, the due-process concept makes more sense.

Due Process

Patricia Werhane, a leading business ethicist, contends that, procedurally, due process extends beyond simple fair treatment and should state, "Every employee has a right to a public hearing, peer evaluation, outside arbitration, or some other open and mutually agreed-upon grievance procedure before being demoted, unwillingly transferred, or fired."[39] Due process can range from the expectation that the company treat employees fairly to the position that employees deserve a fair system of decision making when their status in the organization is at stake.

Sometimes unfair treatment happens in such a subtle way that it is difficult to know that it has taken place. What do you do, for example, if your supervisor refuses to recommend you for promotion or permit you to transfer because she or he considers you to be exceptionally good at your job and doesn't want to lose you? How do you prove that a manager has given you a low performance appraisal because you resisted his sexual advances? The issues over which due-process questions may arise can be quite difficult and subtle, and often challenging to prove.

Due process, when formalized, is a system for ascertaining that organizational decisions have been fair.[40] As such, it aligns closely with the concept of procedural justice, or ethical due process, that we discussed in Chapter 8.[41] The following are the main requirements of a due-process system in an organization:[42]

1. It must be a procedure; it must follow rules. It must not be arbitrary.
2. It must be sufficiently visible and so well known that potential violators of employee rights and victims of abuse are aware of it.
3. It must be predictably effective.
4. It must be institutionalized—a relatively permanent fixture in the organization.
5. It must be perceived as equitable.
6. It must be easy to use.
7. It must apply to all employees.

Procedural due process is a concept derived from the 5th and 14th Amendments of the U.S. Constitution. In law, due process requires a balancing act between the interests of the government and those of the individual. In organizations, a similar balancing act occurs. The challenge is to balance the interests of the individual employee with those of the organization.[43]

Alternative Dispute Resolution

Companies can and do provide due process for their employees in several ways. **Alternative dispute resolution (ADR)** is a term that refers to ways of resolving disputes that avoid litigation. Cornell University conducted a 2011 survey of the use of ADR in Fortune 1000 firms to determine if the level of usage had changed in the past fourteen years. The use of ADR had increased, and the top two reasons were that it enabled firms to save time and money.[44] The approaches described here represent some of the ADR methods that have been employed by companies.

Common Approaches One of the most often-used mechanisms is the **open-door policy**. This approach typically relies on a senior-level executive who asserts that her or his "door is always open" for those who think they have been treated unfairly. Alternatively, the organization might assign to an executive of the human resources department the responsibility for investigating employee grievances and either handling them or reporting them to higher management. From the employee's standpoint, the major problems with these approaches are that (1) the process is closed, (2) one person is reviewing what happened, and (3) there is a tendency in organizations for one manager to support another manager's decisions. The process is opened up somewhat by companies that use a **hearing procedure**, which permits employees to be represented by an attorney or another person, with a neutral company executive deciding the outcome based on the evidence. Similar to this approach is the use of a management *grievance committee*, which may involve multiple executives in the decision process.

The Ombudsman A growing due-process mechanism that has become popular for dealing with employee problems is the use of a corporate **ombudsman**, also known as *ombud* or *ombudsperson*. "Ombudsman" is a Swedish word that refers to one who investigates reported complaints and helps to achieve equitable settlements. The ombudsman approach has been used in Sweden since 1809 to curb abuses by government against individuals. In the United States, the corporate version of the ombudsman entered the scene more than 35 years ago, when the Xerox Corporation named an ombudsman for its largest division. General Electric and the Boeing Vertol division of Boeing were quick to follow.[45] More than 200 major corporations have ombudsmen, with many joining after Sarbanes–Oxley (SOX) was passed.[46] SOX contains a lesser known provision that encourages employees to report wrongdoing and prohibits corporate retaliation against those employees.[47]

The ombudsman's task is quite different from that of the human resources manager. Hiring, firing, setting policy, and keeping records are all the responsibilities of the human resources department; the ombudsman does none of these.[48] In contrast he or she is formally and officially neutral and promises client confidentiality.[49] Ombuds can handle the concerns of employees who believe they have witnessed wrongdoing, and do so in a way that keeps the problem from getting out of hand.[50]

The financial crisis was difficult for ombud offices. Charles L. Howard, author of "The Organizational Ombudsman" explains that senior management views ombud offices as non-revenue centers, and so when times are tight they are often cut.[51] Nevertheless, the use of ombuds, while still small, is growing. The Cornell survey reports that Fortune 1000 ombudsman offices increased by more than fifty percent from 1997 to 2011, from ten percent to sixteen percent.[52]

The Peer Review Panel The **peer review panel** is another due-process mechanism currently in use. Eastman Kodak (now Kodak) made good use of the peer review concept when it dealt with a planned workforce reduction of 4,500 to 6,000 people.[53] As Ann Reesman, former general counsel of the Equal Employment Advisory Council, put it, "The benefit of using peer review rather than some external decision maker is that the peer review panel is well-versed in the company culture and how the company operates."[54] In addition, peers tend to find decisions handed down by peers to be trustworthy.[55]

The key to a successful peer review committee is to make sure that the people involved in the process are respected members of the organization. Election, rather than appointment, of committee members is important for participants to trust the independence of the process. Everyone involved in peer review must receive training in relevant areas such as dispute resolution, discrimination, fairness, legalities, and ethics. Representatives of both employees and management should be involved in the decision-making process.[56] Usage of peer review committees grew from ten percent to thirteen percent from 1997 to 2011.[57]

The Future of ADR. The trend toward using ADR is growing, with no end in sight. This growth is spurred partly by the time and money saved by avoiding costly litigation. KBR (formerly Kellogg Brown & Root), a Houston-based construction and engineering firm, estimates that its legal fees dropped 30 to 50 percent since employing ADR, and 70 to 80 percent of the firm's cases were settled within eight weeks (40 percent within a month). Further, the proportion of adverse settlements and the size of the judgments were no different from when they went through the court system.[58] Viewed from the "ethics of care" standpoint, alternative dispute resolution is preferable to the adversarial strategies that preceded it.[59] The 2011 Cornell survey concluded that more than half of the Fortune 1000 use ADR as their principal approach for handling consumer, commercial, and employment disputes.[60]

ADR is not without problems. In particular, many observers have expressed concern that some employers require new hires to sign contracts, waiving their right to sue the

ETHICS IN PRACTICE CASE
A Whistle-Blower's Windfall

Bradley C. Birkenfeld was a private banker at the Swiss bank, UBS. In 2007, he began giving U.S. authorities detailed descriptions of the ways in which UBS was promoting tax evasion. He also confessed to smuggling a client's diamonds inside a tube of toothpaste. According to Birkenfeld, he decided to become an informant when he learned that the bank's activities were illegal and reporting it to the compliance office had no effect. In 2008, he was convicted of conspiracy, for having withheld information about his top client, a property developer, and was sentenced to forty months in prison.

While still in jail, Birkenfeld was awarded $104 million for the role he played in exposing UBS. To date that is the largest amount awarded by the Internal Revenue Service (IRS). UBS paid a $780 million dollar fine and agreed to give the IRS thousands of names of individuals suspected of evading U.S. taxes. The IRS expects to recoup billions of dollars in unpaid taxes as a result of the information that Birkenfeld provided.

1. Is it appropriate for a convicted felon to reap rewards from reporting someone else's crimes?
2. Should the IRS continue to offer rewards for providing information about tax evaders?
3. Was this record-setting reward too big? Was it too small? Support your answer.

Sources: David Kocieniewski, "Get Out of Jail Free? No, It's Better," *The New York Times* (September 12, 2012), A1; Laura Saunders, "Whistleblower Gets $104 Million, *The Wall Street Journal* (September 12, 2012), C1.

firm and accepting pre-dispute **mandatory arbitration** as the alternative. Arbitration is a process where a neutral party resolves a dispute between two or more parties and the resolution is binding. In mandatory arbitration, the parties must agree to arbitration prior to any dispute. Critics of this practice argue that this robs employees of their right to due process. They say that the structure of mandatory arbitration favors the organization and not the employee. Supporters contend that the arbitration process is just as fair as a jury trial while costing much less in time and money. The war against mandatory arbitration continues to wage. President Obama signed into law bills that limit mandatory arbitration in certain circumstances.[61] At this writing, the Arbitration Fairness Act of 2013 is working its way through the U.S. Congress.[62] The concerns regarding arbitration seem to be having an impact. From 1997 to 2011, Fortune 1000 use of arbitration in employment decisions has dropped 42 percent.[63] The reasons cited included the cost and time involved, concern with the arbitrator's quality, opposing party resistance, and the lack of rights to appeal.[64]

Freedom of Speech in the Workplace

According to a 2012 *Bloomberg Businessweek* article, the workplace is a place where "free speech goes to die."[65] In the United States, people are free to say whatever they like, unless they are at work.[66] Political speech is an example. The United States Constitution protects an individual's political free speech from governmental interference. However, in the absence of a state law prohibiting it, no such protection exists to stop an employer's interference. In all but eight states and the District of Columbia, bosses can insist that employees contribute money or time to their favorite candidate and they can fire employees for expressing views that are inconsistent with their own.[67]

In such a restrictive environment, it is easy to see how much courage is needed for employees to speak up when they see something that is wrong. Speaking truth to power is a Quaker phrase for speaking honestly and openly even when powerful parties would prefer that that you keep quiet. For an employee, speaking truth to power requires a great deal of courage. Some protections exist for those that do but, even when those are in place, the person who is speaking freely faces a challenge.

Whistle-Blowing

As stated earlier, the current generation of employees has a different concept of loyalty to and acceptance of authority than that of past generations. The result is an unprecedented number of employees "blowing the whistle" on their employers. A **whistle-blower** is a former or current organization member who discloses "illegal, immoral, or illegitimate practices under the control of their employers, to persons or organizations that may be able to effect action."[68] Four key elements comprise the whistle-blowing process: the whistle-blower, the act or complaint about which the whistle-blower is concerned, the party to whom the complaint or report is made, and the organization against which the complaint is made.[69]

What is at stake is the employee's right to speak out in cases where she or he thinks the company or management is engaging in an unacceptable practice. Whistle-blowing is contrary to the cultural tradition that an employee does not question a superior's decisions and acts, especially in public. The former view held that the employee owes loyalty, obedience, and confidentiality to the corporate employer; however, the current view of employee responsibility holds that the employee has a duty not only to the employer but also to the public and to her or his own conscience. Whistle-blowing, in this latter situation, becomes an important option for the employee should management not be responsive to expressed concerns. Figure 17-3 depicts these two views of employee responsibility.

FIGURE 17-3 Two Views of Employee Responsibility in a Potential Whistle-Blowing Situation

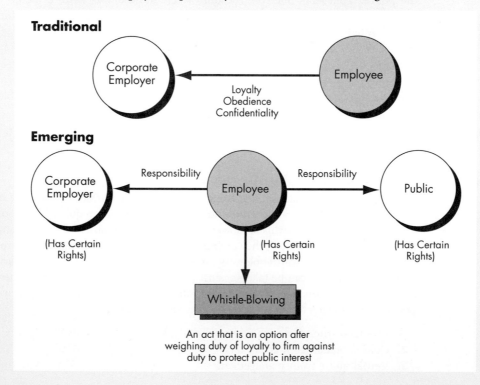

Most whistle-blowers engage in these acts out of a genuine or legitimate belief that certain actions in their organizations are wrong and that they are doing the right thing by reporting them. They may have learned of the wrongful acts by being asked or coerced to participate in them, or through observation or examination of company records. The genuinely concerned employee may initially express concern to a superior or to someone else within the organization. Other potential whistle-blowers may be planning to make their reports for the purpose of striking out or retaliating against the company or a specific manager for some reason. In a survey of studies of whistle-blowers, however, Near and Miceli found the latter to be uncommon. Whistle-blowers were on average more highly paid, with higher job performance than inactive observers were. They were more likely to hold supervisory or professional status, and they had both the role and responsibility to report wrongdoing and the knowledge of channels for doing so.[70]

After Enron and the scandals that followed, whistle-blowers began to receive more recognition. The *Time* Persons of the Year were three women who fit Near and Miceli's description. They named the women "the whistle-blowers": the former Enron vice president Sherron Watkins, who wrote a memo to Enron CEO Kenneth Lay, warning of improprieties in the firm's accounting methods; FBI staff attorney Colleen Riley, who told FBI director Robert Mueller about the bureau having ignored the Minneapolis field office's pleas that they investigate Zacarias Moussaoui, now convicted as a September 11 co-conspirator; and WorldCom's vice president of internal audit, Cynthia Cooper, who told the board that the company had hidden $3.8 billion in losses in falsified books.[71] According to *Time*, these women of "ordinary demeanor but exceptional guts and sense" risked their jobs, health, privacy, and sanity to bring about sea changes in their industries.[72] Some have argued that their designation as whistle-blower is incorrect because they are internal whistle-blowers. Dan Ackerman of *Forbes* writes in *The Wall Street Journal*, "A whistle-blower is someone who spots a criminal inside a bank and alerts the police. That's not Sherron Watkins. What she did was write a memo to the bank robber (Mr. Lay) suggesting he was about to be caught and warning him to watch out."[73] Whatever one's opinion of the nature of their disclosures, it is hard to argue their impact on the business psyche. The media coverage of high-profile cases continues to contribute to a dramatic rise in public awareness of and interest in whistle-blowing. For example, whistle-blower suits filed with the Office of Special Counsel grew from 380 in fiscal year 2001 to nearly 1,000 in 2010: From 2009 to 2010 alone, whistle-blower disclosures increased 37 percent.[74]

Figure 17-4 depicts a checklist to be followed by whistle-blowers before blowing the whistle.

Consequences of Whistle-Blowing

As we mentioned, speaking truth to power is a Quaker phrase for speaking honestly and openly even when powerful parties would prefer that you keep quiet. Doing so is not often easy and, unfortunately, whistle-blowers are not always rewarded for their contributions to the public interest. Although they are now more likely to get some form of protection than they were in the past, whistle-blowers can still pay dearly for their actions. Various types of corporate retaliation can be taken against whistle-blowers. In 2012, the Business Ethics Resource Center "Workplace Ethics in Transition" survey queried 4800 employees, who reported the following top forms of retaliation and their incidence.[75]

1. Excluded from decisions and work activity   64%
2. Cold shoulder from coworkers   62%
3. Verbal abuse from management   62%

FIGURE 17-4

A Checklist to Follow before Blowing the Whistle

The following things should be considered before you blow the whistle:

1. Is there any alternative to blowing the whistle? Make sure you have tried to remedy the problem by reporting up the normal chain of command and have had no success.
2. Does the proposed disclosure advance public interest rather than personal or political gain? Don't act out of frustration or because you feel mistreated.
3. Have you thought about the outcomes of blowing the whistle for yourself and your family? Be prepared for the possibility of disapproval from friends, family, and fellow workers.
4. Have you identified the sources of support both inside and outside the organization on which you can rely during the process? Make sure you know your legal rights and have enlisted the help of others.
5. Do you have enough evidence to support your claim? Even more evidence is needed if you plan to remain anonymous. Be thorough but do not break the law.
6. Have you identified and copied all supporting records before drawing suspicion to your concerns? Remember to keep a factual log both before and after blowing the whistle.

Sources: The Government Accountability Center, http://www.whistleblower.org/storage/documents/Courage_without_Martyrdom_1 .pdf. Accessed May 18, 2013; Kenneth K. Humphreys, "A Checklist for Whistleblowers to Follow," *Cost Engineering* (October 2003), 14; Stephen Martin Kohn, *A Whistleblower's Handbook* (Lyons Press: Guilford, CT, 2011).

4.	Almost lost job	56%
5.	Not given promotion or raise	55%
6.	Verbal abuse from coworkers	51%
7.	Cut in hours or pay	46%
8.	Relocated or reassigned	44%

One person paying the price for speaking up is the whistle-blower whose courage drew worldwide attention when he made public the abuse of Iraqi detainees at Abu Ghraib Prison in Baghdad. Spec. Joseph M. Darby, a former reservist in the 372nd Military Police Company, found out about the abuse by accident when a friend gave him the pictures. He turned them over to the Army's Criminal Investigation Division anonymously. The photographs that documented this abuse shocked the world.[76]

Darby's anonymity was short lived; Defense Secretary Donald Rumsfeld spoke his name when giving congressional testimony—testimony that played on the TV as Darby was having lunch in the mess hall.[77] Fearing retaliation, Darby slept with a gun under his pillow. The army soon opted to send him home ahead of his unit for his safety.[78] Unfortunately, Darby's hometown did not prove a safe haven. The commander of the local Veterans of Foreign Wars post referred to him as a "rat" and a "traitor," and Darby's wife, Bernadette, heard people say her husband was a "dead man" and that he was "walking around with a bull's-eye on his head."[79] Relatives from both sides of the family turned against them.[80]

The army concluded that the Darbys could not return home safely, and so they kept them on an army base with round-the-clock security guards. The Darbys have set up residence in a new town; they don't disclose the location due to ongoing safety concerns. Darby left the army, and he misses it. They both miss their hometown, and they know they will never go home again. When asked if he wishes it were someone other than he who had been given the pictures, Darby says, "No, because if it was someone else it might not have been reported. ... Ignorance is bliss they say but to actually know what they were doing, you can't stand by and let that happen."[81]

Although whistle-blowers frequently suffer severe consequences for speaking out, like the Darbys did, other corporate actions are also possible. One encouraging episode is the case of Mark Jorgensen, who was a manager of real estate funds at Prudential Insurance Company of America.[82] Jorgensen thought he was just being an honest guy when he exposed a fraud running in his company. His world then began to fall apart. His boss, who had once been his friend, abandoned him. His colleagues at work began to shun him. Company lawyers accused him of breaking the law. Jorgensen, who was once a powerful and respected executive in the firm, began to hide out at the local library because he had been forbidden to return to his office. His long and successful career appeared to be dwindling to a pathetic end. Finally, he was fired.

Unlike most whistle-blowers, however, Jorgensen received a phone call from the company chairman at that time, Robert Winters, who wanted to meet with Jorgensen to tell him some startling news: the company now believed him and wanted to reinstate him. Further, the company wanted to force out the boss he had accused of falsely inflating the values of funds that he managed. The turnabout was attributed to Jorgensen's persistence in fighting all odds in his quest to justify his convictions. Coming to the realization that Jorgensen had been right in his allegations all along, Prudential found itself in an unusual situation in business today—siding with the whistle-blower it had fought for months and eventually had fired. The company offered to reinstate Jorgensen in his job, but he elected instead to move on to another company. Prudential paid him a sizable amount to settle his lawsuit.[83] Although we do not read about many stories that end this way, it is encouraging to know that there are some stories that have happy endings. Speaking of endings (that may or may not be happy), Figure 17-5 chronicles Hollywood's treatment of some famous whistle-blowers.

Government's Protection of Whistle-Blowers

Just as employees are beginning to get some protection from the courts through the public policy exception to the employment-at-will doctrine, the same is true for whistle-blowers. The U.S. federal government was one of the first organizations to attempt to protect its own whistle-blowers. A highlight of the **Civil Service Reform Act of 1978** was protection for federal employees who expose illegal, corrupt, or wasteful government activities. Unfortunately, this effort has had only mixed results.[84] It is difficult to protect whistle-blowers against retaliation because so often the reprisals are subtle. An added boost for federal employees came in 1989, when Congress passed the Whistle-Blower Protection Act and the president signed it into law. The effect of this act was to reform the Merit System Protection Board and the Office of General Counsel, the two offices that protect federal employees.[85]

Protection for private employees began to arrive at that point. The U.S. Congress introduced a range of protections for workers in various industries.[86] Typically, the whistle-blower protections were contained in various pieces of legislation that dealt with a range of issues, of which whistle-blowing was just one. As a result, no one piece of legislation provides an umbrella of protection for all whistle-blowers across the country. Even the most recent whistle-blower protections are limited. The Sarbanes–Oxley (SOX) whistle-blower protections apply only to employees in publicly held firms. The Dodd–Frank Wall Street Reform and Consumer Protection whistle-blower protections apply only to employees in the financial industry. Figure 17-6 lists the federal laws that include whistle-blower protections.

Of all of these, SOX whistle-blower protections hold the most promise in that they are not limited to preventing wrongful discharge. In addition to protecting employees who

FIGURE 17-5 Whistle-Blowers Get the Hollywood Treatment

Movie	Stars	Story	Inspiration
The Whistleblower (2010)	Rachel Weisz Vanessa Redgrave	Nebraska police officer serves as peacekeeper in post-war Bosnia and blows whistle on U.N. cover-up of sex trafficking scandal.	Based on the experiences of Kathryn Bolkovac, who worked with the U.N. International Police at a U.K. security company.
The Informant! (2009)	Matt Damon Scott Bakula Joel McHale	Mark Whitacre, an employee at Archer Daniels Midland (ADM), blows the whistle on the lysine price-fixing conspiracy.	This dark comedy is based on *The Informant,* a book by journalist Kurt Eichenwald.
The Insider (1999)	Russell Crowe Al Pacino Christopher Plummer	A successful scientist is fired from a major tobacco company for taking a principled stand. *60 Minutes* is due to report the story, but they cave to corporate pressure.	Based on a *Vanity Fair* article, "The Man Who Knew Too Much." The movie tells the true story of Jeffrey Wigand, who was fired from Brown & Williamson tobacco company.
Silkwood (1983)	Meryl Streep (title role) Kurt Russell Cher Craig T. Nelson	Whistle-blowers try to expose unsafe practices at an Oklahoma nuclear parts factory. A worker becomes contaminated.	Based on the true story of Karen Silkwood, who was a chemical technician at the Kerr-McGee plutonium fuels production plant in Crescent, Oklahoma. As a union member and activist, she was critical of plant safety.
Serpico (1973)	Al Pacino (title role)	Frank Serpico is a nonconformist "hippie cop" in New York City who tries to report graft and corruption to his superiors. When they don't listen, he goes to *The New York Times.*	Based on Peter Maas's book, the movie tells a true story from Serpico's perspective. In the true story, another whistle-blower (David Durk) played a critical role, which is downplayed in the movie.

© Cengage Learning 2015

FIGURE 17-6 Federal Laws with Whistleblower Protections

Clean Air Act	Federal Water Pollution Control Act
Commercial Motor Vehicle Safety Act	Longshore and Harbor Workers' Compensation Act
CERCLA (Superfund Act)	Migrant and Seasonal Agricultural Worker Protection Act
Department of Defense Authorization Act	Occupational Safety and Health Act
Dodd-Frank Wall Street Reform and Consumer Protection Act	Safe Drinking Water Act
Energy Reorganization Act	Sarbanes-Oxley Act (SOX)
Fair Labor Standards Act	Solid Waste Disposal Act
FDA Food Safety Modernization Act	Surface Mining Control and Reclamation Act
Federal Mine Safety and Health Act	Toxic Substances Control Act

Source: Jon O. Shimabukuro and L. Paige Whitaker, "Whistleblower Protections Under Federal Law: An Overview," *Congressional Research Service* (September 13, 2012), 1–21.

were fired, the law has four other important whistle-blower protections for employees in publicly traded corporations[87]:

1. The corporations are required to form independent audit committees and develop confidential procedures for whistle-blowers to follow.
2. The law establishes new ethical standards for attorneys who practice before the SEC that include specification for when the attorney is required to blow the whistle on the client.
3. In a provision that applies to all employees, not only those in publicly held corporations, SOX criminalized retaliation against whistle-blowers who give truthful information to a law enforcement officer by amending the federal obstruction of justice statute.
4. SOX gives the SEC jurisdiction over every aspect of the law, including the whistle-blower provisions, and allows for criminal penalties.

The states vary even more widely in the whistle-blower protection they provide. The **Michigan Whistle-Blowers Protection Act of 1981** was the first state law designed to protect any employee in private industry against unjust reprisals for reporting alleged violations of federal, state, or local laws to public authorities. The burden was placed on the employer to show that questionable treatment was justified on the basis of proper personnel standards or valid business reasons.[88] The Michigan Act spurred similar laws in other states, but the progress has been slow. The National Whistleblower Center finds that only 17 states have whistle-blower protection acts. The rest have only a patchwork of protections for whistle-blowers. As of 2013, the 17 states with whistle-blower protection acts are Arizona, California, Connecticut, Delaware, Florida, Hawaii, Illinois, Indiana, Maine, New Hampshire, New Jersey, North Dakota, Ohio, Rhode Island, South Dakota, Tennessee, and Vermont.[89] Most state courts have recognized a public policy exception to employment at-will, and therefore whistle-blowers have some limited protection from discharge. The normal remedy for wrongful discharge of employees is reinstatement with back pay, with some sympathetic juries adding compensatory damages for physical suffering.[90] As of 2013, the seven states without common law public policy protection for whistle-blowers are Alabama, Georgia, Louisiana, Maine, Montana, New York, and Rhode Island.[91]

The patchwork quilt of whistle-blower protections makes it very difficult for employees to shed light safely on corporate wrongdoing. In some states, whistle-blowers could be fired at will; in other states, they would have to sort through a bewildering assortment of statutes to determine what, if any, protection existed for them. People vary in their need to know they have protection before blowing the whistle. Figure 17-7 describes a study that looks at the differences between people who do the right thing in spite of great personal danger and others who choose not to act.

False Claims Act

A provocative piece of federal legislation that was passed to add an incentive for whistle-blowers in the public interest is the **False Claims Act (FCA)**. The act has *qui tam* (Latin shorthand for "he who sues for the king as well as himself") provisions that allow employees to blow the whistle about contractor fraud and share with the government in any financial recoveries realized by their efforts. It dates back to the Civil War, when the army wanted to find and prosecute profiteers who sold the same horse twice or sold boxes of sawdust while claiming they were guns. Citizens were permitted to sue on the government's behalf and receive 50 percent of the recovery. In 1943, Congress reduced the potential payout dramatically, and so it was seldom used.[92] The act was revised in

FIGURE 17-7

Giving Voice to
Values

Developed at the Aspen Institute Business and Society Program and Yale School of Management, and housed at and supported by Babson College, *Giving Voice to Values* is an innovative curriculum development designed to help business students and practitioners strengthen their abilities to voice their values when situations call them into conflict. The focus is not on determining what the right thing to do is, but rather on determining how to do it. Giving Voice to Values is designed to help students build a tool kit that will enable them to voice their values when ethical challenges arise.

Gentile cites a study of World War II rescuers that shows that moral courage can be strengthened through anticipating ethical challenges that might occur and formulating a response to them. In this study, researchers looked for commonalities among individuals who protected others from the Nazis even when they put their own lives at risk by doing so. They found that people who acted with moral courage when confronted with real danger tended to have earlier life experiences where they anticipated situations in which their values would be challenged and had a respected listener with whom they discussed how they would handle that situation. This act of practicing a response before being put in the difficult situation seemed to strengthen their subsequent ability to handle ethical challenges that occurred.

Sources: Mary C. Gentile, "Giving Voice to Values: Way of Thinking about Values in the Workplace," The Aspen Institute Center for Business Education (September 2008); Perry London, "The Rescuers: Motivational Hypotheses about Christians Who Saved Jews from the Nazis," in J. Macaulay and L. Berkowitz (eds.), *Altruism and Helping Behavior: Social Psychological Studies of Some Antecedents and Consequences* (New York: Academic Press, 1970); Douglas H. Huneke, *The Moses of Rovno* (New York: Dodd, Mead, 1985).

1986 to make recoveries easier to obtain and payouts more generous, thereby encouraging whistle-blowing against government contractor fraud.[93] The 1986 act grew out of outrage in the mid-1980s over reports of fraud and abuse on the part of military contractors, such as $600 toilet seats and country club memberships billed to the government.[94]

What is particularly controversial about the FCA is the magnitude of the financial incentives that individual employees may earn as a result of their whistle-blowing efforts. The law allows individuals to be awarded as much as 15 to 25 percent of the proceeds in cases where the government joins in the action and from 15 to 30 percent of the proceeds in actions that the government does not join.[95] Even with these incentives, however, whistle-blowing is never easy, as the experiences of James Alderson illustrate.

James Alderson had been the chief financial officer of the North Valley Hospital for 17 years when Quorum, a former division of HCA, took over management of the hospital. Quorum created a second set of books and told Alderson to use these secret books to report higher-than-average expenses to the government for reimbursement. Knowing this would be both illegal and unethical, Alderson refused, and five days later he was fired. After learning that other Quorum hospitals were cooking the books, too, Alderson went to Washington and talked to the U.S. Department of Justice. He took documentation with him of the false claims being filed and sued Quorum and HCA under the federal FCA.

HCA eventually paid a total of $840 million, consisting of $745 million in civil damages and $95 million in criminal penalties. They later paid another $881 million to settle all remaining fraud charges and other overpayment claims against the company. Thirteen years after Alderson was fired, the final settlement agreement between HCA and the U.S. Department of Justice was approved. The government received $1.5 billion from those payments, thanks to the efforts of Alderson and other whistle-blowers involved.[96]

There aren't many hospitals in Whitefish, Montana, so Alderson was forced to leave Whitefish to find work in hospital finance. For the next ten years, Alderson tried to earn a living while continuing to gather evidence. Federal officials had told him that he needed evidence that the practices at North Valley were widespread, and the collection of that evidence was his responsibility. Building that evidence consumed Alderson's time and money. In addition to the financial drain, Alderson had made many personal sacrifices, from missing his son's football games to not being at his mother's side when she died.[97] Alderson and his wife Connie kept a low profile. According to Connie, it was just like being in the witness protection program—"the only difference is that we weren't receiving any protection or money to keep us going."[98] Their low profile ended when the television show 60 *Minutes* did a profile of Alderson. After the show aired, Alderson became a pariah in the health care industry. Says Alderson, "Even though I had a major impact in reducing health care fraud by $10 billion annually, I had one hospital CEO tell me to my face that I had ruined the industry and that I had given it a black eye."[99]

Under the FCA, Anderson received $20 million in one settlement and split $100 million with another whistle-blower in another. Alderson commented, "I won't deny that money provided an incentive, but it was only part of the motivation. What Quorum and HCA were doing was wrong, and it took me 13 years and my career to prove it. Fortunately, I received enough money from the settlement to retire."[100] However, Connie Alderson says, "Knowing what I know now and knowing how long it's been, I'm not sure I would have agreed to pursuing the case. I don't think any amount of money is going to take care of what we've been through."[101]

Since 1987, The U.S. federal government has recovered $35 billion due to the FCA, with an additional $7 billion recovered in fines, and $6 billion returned to state Medicaid programs.[102] The FCA has also inspired other similar programs. Twenty-nine states, three large cities and one country have FCAs that are modeled after the federal law. The SEC, the IRS and the CFTC (Commodities Future Trading Commission) all have programs that are modeled on the FCA.[103] The proceeds continue to grow. The year 2012 broke payout records, with $5 billion in FCA penalties and another $1.35 billion in fines.[104]

Management Responsiveness to Potential Whistle-Blowing Situations

Whistle-blowing situations occur after normal, less dramatic, channels of communication have failed. Ideally, employees should always feel free to open up to management about any concerns they have. Even in the best of organizations, however, people hesitate to speak up. Employee self-censorship is common.

In a study of whistle-blower protections, workers in a leading high-technology organization were asked if they felt safe speaking up about problems in the firm. In spite of the fact that this organization had a variety of formal mechanisms, such as an ombudsperson and grievance procedures, half the employees indicated that they did not feel safe speaking up.[105] Their overall concern was with self-preservation. They perceived a risk to speaking up that lead them to conclude, "When in doubt, keep your mouth shut."[106]

In rare instances, employees were afraid to speak out because they had experiences with managers who responded badly to past suggestions. More often, the reticent employees were simply responding to a vague perception of a threat in the work environment. Sometimes they were put off by organizational stories about people who had spoken up and then suddenly were no longer there. Typically, their silence stemmed from untested assumptions.[107]

The findings of this study have clear implications for encouraging free and open speech in the workplace. It isn't enough to remove barriers or put formal mechanisms in place. Significant changes in the organizational culture must occur. The following are suggestions for how to accomplish that goal[108]:

1. Managers must be clear not only to accept suggestions—they must also invite them. Managers can't implement all suggestions, but it is important for managers to acknowledge each one.
2. Managers must refute commonly held assumptions and organizational myths that discourage communication. For example, they can counter the commonly held belief that employees should give managers suggestions in private by explaining that openly discussed ideas are likely to be useful.
3. Managers should tailor rewards so that employees share more directly in any cost savings or sales increase from ideas they offer. Tangible rewards can help employees to overcome intangible concerns.

In an ideal world, employees would automatically speak freely to managers if they saw something wrong happening or had an idea to improve operations. Unfortunately, this world is not ideal. It can be instructive to turn back to Enron, one of the classic cases of corporate malfeasance, and ask what went wrong. Former Enron executive Lynn Brewer suggests that there may be "a little Enron in all of us." The problem at Enron was not "dirty secrets hidden well below the surface, but an open secret."[109] She estimates that about two-thirds of the employees at Enron were aware at some time of unethical behavior in the middle ranks, and believes if Enron employees had been asked if the company was ethical or not, 90 percent would have rated the company "highly unethical."[110] In the name of solving business problems, good people will often do bad things. It is incumbent upon managers to design organizations that enable and empower employees to come forward with information that will either stop wrongdoing or improve company operations long before whistle-blowing is needed.[111]

Summary

Employee stakeholders today are more sensitive about employee rights issues for a variety of reasons. Underlying this new concern are changes in the social contract between employers and employees that have been driven by global competition and a faltering economy. Central among the growing employee rights issues discussed in this chapter are (1) the right not to be fired without good cause, (2) the right to due process and fair treatment, and (3) the right to freedom of speech.

The basis for the argument that we may be moving toward an employee's right not to be fired is the erosion by the courts of the employment-at-will doctrine. More and more, the courts are making exceptions to this long-standing common-law principle. Three major exceptions are the public policy exception, the idea of an implied contract, and breach of good faith. Society's concept of what represents fair treatment to employees is constantly changing.

The right to due process is concerned primarily with fair treatment. Common approaches for management responding to this concern, such as the open-door policy and traditional grievance procedures have been disappointing, and so newer methods such as the ombudsman approach and peer review are becoming more prevalent. Thanks to the passage of SOX, whistle-blowers in the private sector now enjoy some of the protections once accorded only to public sector employees; however, those protections are not a guarantee. Whistle-blowers continue to face a slew of obstacles as they seek to speak out on their concerns. Managers should be genuinely attentive to employees' rights in this realm if they wish to avert major scandals and prolonged litigation. A stakeholder approach that emphasizes ethical relationships with employees can create an organizational environment in which employees feel free to express their concerns openly, lessening the need to blow a whistle.

Key Terms

alternative dispute resolution (ADR), p. 500
Civil Service Reform Act of 1978, p. 506
collective bargaining, p. 493
due process, p. 499
employee rights, p. 493
employment-at-will doctrine, p. 495
enterprise rights, p. 494

False Claims Act (FCA), p. 508
good cause norm, p. 495
good faith principle, p. 496
hearing procedure, p. 500
implied contract exception, p. 496
mandatory arbitration, p. 502
Michigan Whistle-Blowers Protection Act of 1981, p. 508
ombudsman, p. 492

open-door policy, p. 500
outplacement, p. 500
peer review panel, p. 501
private property, p. 493
public policy exception, p. 496
social contract, p. 490
statutory rights, p. 493
whistle-blower, p. 503

Discussion Questions

1. Rank the various changes that are occurring in the workplace in terms of their importance to the growth of the employee rights movement. Briefly explain your ranking.

2. Explain the employment-at-will doctrine, and describe how it is being eroded. Do you think its existence is leading to a healthy or an unhealthy employment environment in the United States? Justify your reasoning.

3. In your own words, explain the right to due process. What are some of the major ways management is attempting to ensure due process in the workplace?

4. If you could choose only one, which form of alternative dispute resolution would be your choice as the most effective approach to employee due process? Explain.

5. How do you feel about whistle-blowing now that you have read about it? Are you now more sympathetic or less sympathetic to whistle-blowers? Explain.

6. What is your assessment of the value of the False Claims Act? What is your assessment of the value of the whistle-blower protections under the Sarbanes–Oxley Act?

Endnotes

1. "Taking Steps to Motivate Your Workers Improves Productivity," *Business Owner's Toolkit* (May 24, 2012), http://www.bizfilings.com/toolkit/sbg/office-hr/managing-the-workplace/motivating-workers-for-productivity.aspx. Accessed May 18, 2013.

2. Phred Dvorak and Scott Thurm, "Slump Prods Firms to Seek New Compact with Workers," *The Wall Street Journal* (October 20, 2009), A18.

3. Diane Lewis, "Out in the Field: Workplace Want Loyal Workers? Then Help Them Grow," *Boston Globe* (July 15, 2001), H2.

4. Number of Jobs Held, Labor Market Activity, and Earnings Growth Among The Youngest Baby Boomers, *Bureau of Labor Statistics News Release* (July 25, 2012), http://www.bls.gov/news.release/pdf/nlsoy.pdf. Accessed May 11, 2013.

5. Carl Bialik, "Seven Careers in a Lifetime? Think Twice, Researchers Say," *The Wall Street Journal* (September 4, 2010), http://online.wsj.com/article/SB10001424052748 7042068045754681628058779990.html. Accessed May 17, 2013.

6. Michelle Conlin, "Job Security, No. Tall Latte, Yes," *BusinessWeek* (April 2, 2001), 62–64.

7. Marla Gottschalk, "Big Idea 2013: A New Social Contract between Employer and Employees," *Linkedin.com* (December 11, 2012), http://www.linkedin.com/today/post/article/20121211110842-128811924-big-idea-2013-a-new-social-contract-between-employer-and-employees. Accessed May 17, 2013.

8. Ibid.

9. Paul B. Brown, "Keeping Good Employees when You Can't Pay Them More," *The New York Times* (August 18, 2009), http://www.nytimes.com/2009/08/18/business/smallbusiness/18toolkit.html?scp=17&sq=company%20loyalty&st=cse. Accessed May 18, 2013.

10. "Employee Loyalty Rises during Global Economic Recession, Kelly International Workforce Survey Finds," *Kelly Services* (March 8, 2010), http://ir.kellyservices.com/releasedetail.cfm?ReleaseID=450036. Accessed May 18, 2013.

11. Ibid.

12. David Lazarus, "As Labor Day Nears, Workers Are Just Thankful to Have a Job," *Los Angeles Times* (September 6, 2009), http://articles.latimes.com/2009/sep/06/business/fi-lazarus6. Accessed May 18, 2013.

13. "The Autonomous and Empowered Workforce," Kelly Services (September 2012, http://www.kellyservices.us/uploadedFiles/Dev_-_Kelly_Services(1)/Accordion/Autonomous%20and%20Empowered%20Workforce.pdf. Accessed May 15, 2013).

14. Denise M. Rousseau and Rosemary Batt, "Global Competition's Perfect Storm: Why Business and Labor Cannot Solve Their Problems Alone," *Academy of Management Perspectives* (May 2007), 16–23.

15. "Global Employment Trends 2013," *International Labour Office* (January 2013), http://www.ilo.org/wcmsp5/groups/public/—dgreports/—dcomm/—publ/documents/publication/wcms_202326.pdf. Accessed May 18, 2013.

16. Nelson D. Schwartz, "Recovery in U.S. Is Lifting Profits, but Not Adding Jobs," *The New York Times* (March 3, 2013), http://www.nytimes.com/2013/03/04/business/economy/corporate-profits-soar-as-worker-income-limps.html?pagewanted=1&_r=0&hp. Accessed May 12, 2013.

17. John Challenger, "Establishing Rules for the New Workplace," *USA Today Magazine* (November 2002), 30–34.

18. Louis Uchitelle, J. T. Battenberg III, and Thomas Kochan, "Employer-Employee Social Contracts: Fashioning a New Compact for Workers," *Academy of Management Perspectives* (May 2007), 5–16.

19. Leo Troy, *The End of Unionism: An Appraisal* (St. Louis: Center for the Study of American Business, Washington University, September 1994), 1–2.

20. "Union Members Summary," *Bureau of Labor Statistics* (January 23, 2013), http://www.bls.gov/news.release/union2.nr0.htm. Accessed May 18, 2013.

21. "Trade Union Density," *OECD* (2012), www.oecd.org/els/emp/OECD-Trade%20Union%20density%202012.xlsx. Accessed May 18, 2013.

22. Richard Edwards, *Rights at Work* (Washington, DC: The Brookings Institution, 1993), 25–26.

23. Ibid., 33–35.

24. Mark V. Roehling, "The 'Good Cause Norm' in Employment Relations: Empirical Evidence and Policy Implications," *Employee Responsibility and Rights Journal* (September 2002), 91–104.

25. Ellen Dannin, "Why At-Will Employment Is Bad for Employers and Just Cause Is Good for Them," *Labor Law Journal* (Spring 2007), 5–16.

26. Tara J. Radin and Patricia H. Werhane, "Employment-At-Will, Employee Rights, and Future Directions for Employment," *Business Ethics Quarterly* (April 2003), 113–130.

27. Louis Uchitelle, *The Disposable American* (New York: Knopf, 2006).

28. Uchitelle, Battenberg, and Kochan, 7.

29. David H. Autor, John J. Donohue III, and Stewart J. Schwab, "The Employment Consequences of Wrongful-Discharge Laws: Large, Small, or None at All?" *American Economic Review* (May 2004), 440–446.

30. "Employment at Will Exceptions by State," *National Conference of State Legislatures* (April 2008), http://www.ncsl.org/default.aspx?tabid=13339. Accessed May 18, 2013.

31. Ibid.

32. Ibid.

33. Ibid.

34. Patricia H. Werhane, Tara J. Radin, and Norman E. Bowie, *Employment and Employee Rights* (Malden, MA: Blackwell Publishing, 2004).

35. Ibid.

36. Dannin, 5–16.

37. Steve Harrison, *The Manager's Book of Decencies: How Small Gestures Build Great Companies* (Columbus, OH: McGraw-Hill, 2007).

38. Ibid.

39. Patricia H. Werhane, *Persons, Rights and Corporations* (Englewood Cliffs, NJ: Prentice Hall, 1985), 110.

40. William M. Haraway, "Employee Grievance Programs: Understanding the Nexus between Workplace Justice, Organizational Legitimacy and Successful Organizations," *Public Personnel Management* (Winter 2005), 329–342.

41. Richard A. Posthuma, "Procedural Due Process and Procedural Justice in the Workplace: A Comparison and Analysis," *Public Personnel Management* (Summer 2003), 181.

42. David W. Ewing, *Freedom Inside the Organization: Bringing Civil Liberties to the Workplace* (New York: McGraw-Hill, 1977), 11.

43. Posthuma, 181–195.

44. http://www.icsuperconference.com/wp-content/uploads/2012/05/Corporate-Perspectives-on-ADR-Day-Two-3-45PM.pdf. Accessed May 18, 2013.

45. "Where Ombudsmen Work Out," *BusinessWeek* (May 3, 1976), 114–116.

46. Allen Church, "Ombudsmen Ease Governance Compliance," *Claims* (December 2004), 63–65.

47. Jonathan A. Segal, "The Joy of Uncooking," *HR Magazine* (November 2002), 52–57.

48. Carolyn Hirschman, "Someone to Listen," *HR Magazine* (January 2003), 46–50.

49. Ibid.

50. Ibid., 46–51.

51. Andrew Singer, "On the Evolving Corporate Ombudsman," *Ethikos* (March/April 2010), 10–12.

52. http://www.icsuperconference.com/wp-content/uploads/2012/05/Corporate-Perspectives-on-ADR-Day-Two-3-45PM.pdf. Accessed May 18, 2013.

53. Margaret M. Clark, "Jury of Their Peers," *HR Magazine* (January 2004), 54.

54. Ibid.

55. Ibid.

56. "Peer-Review Policy Provides Protection," *Credit Union Directors Newsletter* (April, 2004), 7–8.

57. http://www.icsuperconference.com/wp-content/uploads/2012/05/Corporate-Perspectives-on-ADR-Day-Two-3-45PM.pdf. Accessed May 18, 2013.

58. Kay O. Wilburn, "Employment Disputes: Solving Them Out of Court," *Management Review* (March 1998), 17–21. Marc Lampe, "Mediation as an Ethical Adjunct of Stakeholder Theory," *Journal of Business Ethics* (May 2001), 165–173.

59. Marc Lampe, "Mediation as an Ethical Adjunct of Stakeholder Theory," *Journal of Business Ethics* (May 2001), 165–173.

60. http://www.icsuperconference.com/wp-content/uploads/2012/05/Corporate-Perspectives-on-ADR-Day-Two-3-45PM.pdf. Accessed May 18, 2013.

61. Jon Hyman, "Congress Employment Law Agenda: 7 Bills to Watch Closely," *HR Specialist* (March 2010), 7.

62. http://www.govtrack.us/congress/bills/113/hr1844/text. Accessed May 18, 2013.

63. http://www.icsuperconference.com/wp-content/uploads/2012/05/Corporate-Perspectives-on-ADR-Day-Two-3-45PM.pdf. Accessed May 18, 2013.

64. Ibid.

65. Michael Dolgow, "Where Free Speech Goes to Die: The Workplace," *Bloomberg Businessweek* (August 3, 2012), http://www.businessweek.com/articles/2012-08-03/where-free-speech-goes-to-die-the-workplace. Accessed July 3, 2013.

66. Ibid.

67. Ibid.

68. Marcia P. Miceli and Janet P. Near, *Blowing the Whistle: The Organizational and Legal Implications for Companies and Employees* (New York: Lexington Books, 1992), 15.

69. Janet P. Near and Marcia P. Miceli, "The Whistle-Blowing Process and Its Outcomes: A Preliminary Model" (Columbus, OH: The Ohio State University, College of Administrative Science, Working Paper Series 83–55, September, 1983), 2. See also Miceli and Near, 15.

70. Janet P. Near and Marcia P. Miceli, "Whistleblowing— Myth and Reality," *Journal of Management* (1996 Special Issue), 507–526.

71. Richard Layco and Amanda Ripley, "Persons of the Year," *Time* (December 30, 2002), 32.

72. Ibid.

73. Dan Ackerman, "Whistleblower?" *The Wall Street Journal* (December 24, 2002), A10.

74. "FY 2010 Summary of Performance and Financial Information," *Office of the Special Counsel*, http://www.osc.gov/documents/pubs/SPFI%20FY2010.pdf. Accessed May 18, 2013.

75. "National Business Ethics Survey: Workplace Ethics in Transition," *Business Ethics Resource Center* (2012), www.ethics.org/nbes. Accessed May 22, 2013.

76. Elizabeth Williamson, "One Soldier's Unlikely Act," *The Washington Post* (May 6, 2004), A16.

77. http://www.cbsnews.com/stories/2006/12/07/60minutes/main2238188.shtml. Accessed May 18, 2013.

78. Nat Hentoff, "The Abandoned Abu Ghiraib Whistle-blower," *Jewish World Review* (December 26, 2006), http://www.jewishworldreview.com. Accessed May 19, 2013.

79. Ibid.

80. http://www.cbsnews.com/stories/2006/12/07/60minutes/main2238188.shtml. Accessed May 18, 2013.

81. Ibid.

82. Kurt Eichenwald, "He Told. He Suffered. Now He's a Hero," *The New York Times* (May 29, 1994), 1-F.

83. Ibid.

84. Joann S. Lublin, "Watchdog Has Hard Time Hearing Whistles," *The Wall Street Journal* (October 17, 1980), 30.

85. Ana Radelat, "When Blowing the Whistle Ruins Your Life," *Public Citizen* (September/October 1991), 16–20.

86. Jon O. Shimabukuro and L. Paige Whitaker, "Whistle-blower Protections Under Federal Law: An Overview," Congressional Research Service (September 13, 2012), 1–21.

87. Stephen M. Kohn, "Sarbanes–Oxley Act: Legal Protection for Corporate Whistleblowers," National Whistle-blower Center, http://www.whistleblowers.org/index.php?option=com_content&task=view&id=27. Accessed May 19, 2013.

88. Alan F. Westin, "Michigan's Law to Protect the Whistle Blowers," *The Wall Street Journal* (April 13, 1981), 18. Also see Daniel P. Westman, *Whistle Blowing: The Law of Retaliatory Discharge* (Washington, DC: The Bureau of National Affairs, 1991); Robert L. Brady, "Blowing the Whistle," *HR Focus* (February 1996), 20.

89. http://www.whistleblowers.org/index.php?option=com_content&task=view&id=743&Itemid=161. Accessed May 19, 2013.

90. Michael W. Sculnick, "Disciplinary Whistle-Blowers," *Employment Relations Today* (Fall 1986), 194.

91. http://www.whistleblowers.org/index.php?option=com_content&task=view&id=743&Itemid=161. Accessed May 19, 2013.

92. Todd Wilkinson, "After Eight Years, an Insider Gets His Reward," *Christian Science Monitor* (July 24, 2001), 1.

93. Miceli and Near, 247.

94. Andrew W. Singer, "The Whistle-Blower: Patriot or Bounty Hunter?" *Across the Board* (November 1992), 16–22.

95. http://www.taf.org/resource/fca/faq#faq12. Accessed May 19, 2013.

96. Grover L. Porter, "Whistleblowers: A Rare Breed," Strategic Finance (August 2003), 51–53.

97. Kurt Eichenwald, "He Blew the Whistle, and Health Giants Quaked," *The New York Times* (October 18, 1998), 1.

98. Porter, 52.

99. Ibid., 53.

100. Ibid.

101. Ibid.

102. http://www.taf.org/node/455. Accessed May 19, 2013.

103. Ibid.

104. Ashley. Post, "Record Reprimands." *Insidecounsel* 24, no. 254 (February 2013): 12.

105. James R. Detert and Amy C. Edmondson, "Why Employees Are Afraid to Speak," *Harvard Business Review* (May 2007), 23–25.

106. Ibid., 24.

107. Ibid., 23–25.

108. Ibid.

109. Lynn Brewer, "Is There a Little Bit of Enron in All of Us?" *Journal for Quality & Participation* (Spring 2007), 26.

110. Ibid.

111. Ibid.

18

Employee Stakeholders: Privacy, Safety, and Health

CHAPTER LEARNING OUTCOMES

After studying this chapter, you should be able to:

1. Articulate the concerns surrounding the employee's right to privacy in the workplace.

2. Identify the advantages and disadvantages of polygraphs, integrity tests, and drug testing as management instruments for decision-making.

3. Discuss the right to safety and the right to know, and summarize the roles and responsibilities of OSHA.

4. Elaborate on the right to health and safety in the workplace, with particular reference to violence in the workplace, smoke-free workplaces, and family-friendly workplaces.

Besides the issues we discussed in the preceding chapter, there are several others that concern employee stakeholders. The latter are extensions of the concept of employee rights developed in Chapter 17. In this chapter, we will discuss employees' rights to privacy, safety, and a healthy work environment. As we discussed in Chapter 17, the global recession has shifted the balance of power from employees to employers. With jobs being harder to find, employees may be more hesitant to ask that their rights be respected, because they fear losing their jobs and being unable to find new work. Margaret Vickers, editor-in-chief of *Employee Responsibilities and Rights Journal*, notes, "What might have been whined about by workers before their workplace morphed into the workplace-in-recession suddenly becomes acceptable to workers trying to keep their jobs."[1] In this environment, we need to be especially mindful of the rights of employees, as they are increasingly vulnerable in the workplace.[2]

The status of an employee's right to privacy in the workplace today is ill-defined at best. Constitutional protection of privacy, such as the prohibition of unreasonable searches and seizures, applies only to the actions of government, not to those of private sector employers. From a legal standpoint, the meager amount of privacy protection that exists, as with so many employee rights, is a collection of diverse statutes, varying from issue to issue and from state to state. Hence, there is a genuine need for management groups to apply ethical thinking and standards to this increasingly important area.

Employee rights to safety and health are issues of growing intensity, too. In the United States alone, approximately 5,000 employees die from fatal injuries on the job each year, while nearly three million occupational injuries and illnesses are reported.[3] Across the world, there were 2.3 million people killed at work, 6,300 per day.[4] Today's workplace, whether a manufacturing facility or an office complex, can expose workers to a variety of hazards, risks of accidents, and occupational diseases. If normal workplace hazards were not enough, the phenomenon of violence is a serious threat to workplace peace and stability that requires managerial attention. Management should also be aware of the issues affecting employee health in the workplace, as well as the need for family-friendly workplaces and the legal rights employees have under the Family and Medical Leave Act (FMLA).

In this chapter, we continue our consideration of social and ethical issues that have become important to employee stakeholders in recent years. If managers are to be successful in dealing with employees' needs and treating them fairly as stakeholders, they must address these concerns now and in the future.

Right to Privacy in the Workplace

If your workplace were in a private space behind partitions and you knew there was no one in the outer office, would you change into either gym clothes or more formal evening attire at the end of the day? Would you remove some clothing to apply a prescription topical ointment when needed? If you believe you would do so, you must know about Gail Nelson, an administrative assistant who did exactly that, and then found out her employer had secretly videotaped her for months with no apparent justification for doing so.[5]

Nelson's supervisor and coworkers knew she sometimes changed clothes in her office cubicle, an accepted practice. Her concern for privacy was such that she did so only when nobody was in the outer office, and she ensured this by listening carefully for the sound of approaching footsteps. The videotaping never revealed any illegal or unauthorized activity; nevertheless, her employer continued to do it. Furthermore, numerous employees at her workplace had viewed the videotapes. The incident came to light only when a coworker discovered it accidentally and informed her.[6] Even after appeal, the higher court upheld the legality of her employer's surveillance, saying that she did not have a reasonable expectation of privacy because other people were able to walk into the outer office.[7]

Technological developments have made surveillance simpler and less expensive—not only in public places but also in the workplace. What was once only an option for large corporations now is available to every work environment, along with the ethical issues it brings. With this growth in workplace monitoring come new ethical considerations. **Privacy in the workplace** is in flux as the implications of new technological options are considered. At this stage, the private employee has few privacy rights in (and sometimes out of) the workplace.

There are no clear legal definitions of what constitutes privacy or invasion of privacy, but everyone seems to have an opinion when one personally experiences such a situation. Most experts say that privacy means the right to keep personal affairs to oneself and to know how information about one is being used.[8] Business ethicist Patricia Werhane opts for a broader definition. She says that privacy includes (1) the right to be left alone, (2) the related right to autonomy, and (3) the claim of individuals and groups to determine for themselves when, how, and to what extent information about them is communicated to others.[9]

Defining privacy, however, does not settle the issue. In today's world, achieving these ideals is extremely difficult and fraught with judgment calls about our own privacy rights versus other people's rights. This problem is exacerbated by our increasingly computerized, technological world. We gain great efficiencies from computers and new technologies, but we also pay a price. Part of that price is that information about us is stored in dozens of places, including federal agencies (the Internal Revenue Service and the Social Security Administration), state agencies (courts and motor vehicle departments), and many local departments and businesses (school systems, credit bureaus, banks, life insurance companies, and direct-mail companies).

In the realm of employee privacy, the following four important issues stand out as representative of the major workplace privacy issues:

1. Collection and use of employee information in personnel files
2. Integrity testing
3. Drug testing
4. Monitoring of employee work, behavior, conversations, and location by electronic means

Other issues also involve protection or invasion of privacy, but the four listed here account for the majority of today's concerns. Therefore, they merit separate consideration.

Collection and Use of Employee Information by Employers

The collection, use, and possible abuse of employee information are serious public policy issues that warrant scrutiny. Today's government databases, with various agencies mixing and matching data, form a cohesive web of information on individual citizens. In the United States, the **Privacy Act of 1974** set certain controls on the right of the government to collect, use, and share data about individuals. These restrictions were relaxed when the **USA Patriot Act** was signed into law in 2001 in response to the attacks on the World Trade Center and the Pentagon. Many people expressed concern that the Patriot Act gave the government too much latitude, and those concerns were exacerbated when secret documents revealed the broad scope of National Security Agency (NSA) surveillance.[10] However, restrictions still remain on how the government can collect, use, and share personal data. In contrast, very few laws protect the privacy of individuals in the workplace, even as monitoring of employees in the workplace grows. Many privacy advocates say, "You check your privacy rights at the door when you enter the workplace."[11]

The necessity for guidelines regarding the collection of information became abundantly clear when the Equal Employment Opportunity Commission (EEOC) sued Burlington Northern Santa Fe Corporation for conducting secret genetic tests on workers who filed carpal tunnel syndrome claims. The tests came to light when one of the workers, Gary Avery, went to a mandatory medical exam as a follow-up to his successful carpal tunnel surgery. His wife, Janice, a registered nurse, became suspicious when he was asked to give seven vials of blood, more than would be needed for traditional tests. She later learned that the blood was for tests to determine whether her husband had a genetic trait that made him susceptible to the syndrome.[12] Burlington Northern ended up paying $2.2 million to settle the charges.[13]

Background checks of both applicants and current employees have become a source of concern for privacy advocates. States vary in the latitude they allow employers when checking employee backgrounds, but most states, with the notable exception of California, give employers relatively free rein. The overriding principle that should guide corporate decision making with regard to the collection and use of employee information is that companies should collect only absolutely necessary information from employees and use it only in ways that are appropriate. Companies should be careful not to misuse this information by utilizing it for purposes for which it was not intended. Employers have a duty to treat their employee's private information with care, which entails neither releasing it to others nor allowing it to become public through careless management. Employers also have a responsibility to allow employees to correct any inaccurate information.

In 2011, the issue of background checking was tested in the courts. In keeping with a recommendation from the 9/11 Commission, the U.S. Department of Commerce mandated that contract employees with long-term access to federal facilities, such as corporate, college, and think-tank employees who work on government-funded projects undergo a background check. This check included questions about whether they had been involved in illegal drugs and also involved asking their references if there was any reason to question the candidate's "honesty or trustworthiness."[14] Twenty-eight contract employees filed suit against NASA, claiming that the questions violated their right to privacy. The case made it all the way to the U.S. Supreme Court.[15] The Justices ruled unanimously in favor of NASA; however, the decision was very specific to that case and the nature of those employees' work, so the Court did not shed much light on the rights of employees who do less sensitive or lower level work.[16]

The requirements of the **Fair Credit Reporting Act (FCRA)** as it pertains to employers are detailed in Figure 18-1. The Federal Trade Commission (FTC) is responsible for monitoring employer use of consumer reports in the United States. **Consumer reports** is

---

FIGURE 18-1

Consumer Reports Used for Employment

Employers in the United States may use consumer reports both to hire new employees and to evaluate current employees as long as they comply with the Fair Credit Reporting Act (FCRA), Sections 604, 606, and 615. Consumer reports are prepared by consumer reporting agencies (CRAs), and they contain private information about not only credit characteristics but also personal characteristics such as the applicant's or employee's character, reputation, and lifestyle. The reports may include credit payment records, driving records, criminal histories, and even interviews with neighbors, friends, or any associates. The FCRA covers only reports prepared by agencies. For example, if the employer checks references directly, the FCRA does not apply; however, verification by an employment or reference-checking agency is covered. The following are the key provisions as written by the Federal Trade Commission (FTC) to employers.

Key Provisions of the FCRA Amendments

Written Notice and Authorization. Before you can get a consumer report for employment purposes, you must notify the individual in writing—in a document consisting solely of this notice—that a report may be used. You also must obtain the person's written authorization before you ask a CRA for the report. (Special procedures apply to the trucking industry.)

Adverse Action Procedures. If you rely on a consumer report for an "adverse action"—denying a job application, reas-

signing or terminating an employee, or denying a promotion—be aware of the following:

Step 1: *Before* you take the adverse action, you must give the individual a pre-adverse action disclosure that includes a copy of the individual's consumer report and a copy of "A Summary of Your Rights Under the Fair Credit Reporting Act"—a document prescribed by the FTC. The CRA that furnishes the individual's report will give you the summary of consumer rights.

Step 2: After you have taken an adverse action, you must give the individual notice—orally, in writing, or electronically—that the action has been taken in an adverse action notice. It must include

- The name, address, and phone number of the CRA that supplied the report;
- A statement that the CRA that supplied the report did not make the decision to take the adverse action and cannot give specific reasons for it; and
- A notice of the individual's right to dispute the accuracy or completeness of any information the agency furnished, and his or her right to an additional free consumer report from the agency upon request within 60 days.

Certifications to Consumer Reporting Agencies. Before giving you an individual's consumer report, the CRA will require you to certify that you are in compliance with the FCRA and that you will not misuse any information in the report in violation of federal or state equal employment opportunity laws or regulations.

Source: Federal Trade Commission, "Using Consumer Reports: What Employers Need to Know," http://www.ftc.gov/bcp/edu/pubs/business/credit/bus08.shtm. Accessed May 2013.

the official term for employment background checks. They can include credit reports, criminal background reports, and other information from a range of sources. Two significant loopholes exist in the protections that allow employers to bypass the FCRA. First, employers can opt to do the background checks themselves instead of using outside providers. If so, the restrictions do not apply.[17] Second, the restrictions do not apply if an adverse employment decision was made for reasons other than the contents of the background check; employers can simply bypass the requirements by citing different reasons.[18] Another problem is that the FCRA does not apply to the interview process, so an employer can obtain some information by simply asking. For example, a background check may not contain information on an arrest that happened more than seven years earlier. However, nothing prevents an employer from asking an interviewee, verbally or in writing, "Have you *ever* been arrested?"[19] In addition, if a background check is inaccurate, the interviewee affected can dispute its contents; however, an employer is not obligated to act upon a corrected report and reinstate a job offer.[20] Finally, the FCRA does not apply when salaries are $75,000 or more.[21] It is important to note that this discussion refers to federal laws. Some states, such as California, have instituted protections that extend beyond the federal requirements.

The **Equal Employment Opportunity Commission (EEOC)** monitors employer use of background checks too, stepping in when discriminatory practices are thought to have occurred. The EEOC has ruled that employers may not deny a person employment based solely on a criminal record; instead they must factor in business necessity, the seriousness of the offense, and how long ago it occurred.[22] Two background check practices have caused the most problems for the EEOC and, by extension, the employers who are brought into court: (1) blanket no-hire policies based on criminal records or negative credit scores and (2) lack of a correlation between the information from the background check and the actual job for which the person has applied.[23]

Although there are still few guidelines for the collection of employee information in most professions, the health care industry has developed stronger guidelines for the way that collected information is handled in general, and those guidelines cover the use of medical information in employment. Medical information supplied to employers must be relevant to the job and requires the applicant's specific written consent.[24] An employer may require a pre-employment physical, but the Americans with Disabilities Act (ADA) requires that the physical be requested only *after* a job offer. The Act requires employers to protect the confidentiality of applicant and employee medical information, while also making it illegal to base employment decisions on a medical condition that does not affect the employee's ability to perform the essential functions of the job. We discuss the ADA in more detail in Chapter 19.

The Society for Human Resource Management (SHRM) has been surveying employers about background checks and they find that fewer employers are using them. From 2010 to 2012, the percentage of employers using credit checks dropped from 60 percent to 47 percent and the percentage of employers using criminal background checks dropped from 93 percent to 86 percent.[25] Even with this downward trend, employee screening is a big and very profitable business.[26] Screening often goes beyond the checking of public records to include interviews with friends and associates, some of which may be disgruntled; the resulting information can contain errors or even outright lies.[27] According to industry veteran Lester Rosen, "Essentially, it's the Wild Wild West. It's an unregulated industry with easy money and not a huge emphasis on compliance or on hiring quality people to do the screening."[28]

The U.S. federal government is beginning to make moves toward shoring up the system. In 2012, the EEOC issued guidance regarding the use of criminal background checks in hiring. People with criminal backgrounds are not a protected class, i.e., federal anti-discrimination laws do not protect them. However, minorities account for a disproportionate percentage of the jail population and so the EEOC is concerned that criminal background checks will have a disparate impact on minority applicants.[29] The guidance asks employers to make an individualized assessment of each case, taking the following three factors into consideration: (1) the nature and seriousness of the offense, (2) how long ago the offense occurred, and (3) the nature of the job.[30] Businesses have expressed multiple concerns regarding this guidance. They cite studies that show that businesses are actually less likely to hire minority applicants when background checks are banned.[31] The biggest problem for businesses is that they feel they are stuck between a rock and a hard place, because they are still subject to EEOC lawsuits if they require background checks in circumstances where state law requires that the firm not hire someone with a felony conviction.[32] The issue of disparate impact is discussed in more detail in Chapter 19.

Integrity Tests

Early efforts to judge a person's integrity focused on uncovering a lack of integrity, such as might be evidenced when a person lies. The notion of a "lie detector," historians tell us, is nothing new. The Bedouins of Arabia knew that certain physiological changes, triggered by guilt and fear, occurred when a person lied. The outstanding change they observed was that a liar would stop salivating. They developed a simple test in which a heated blade was passed across the tongue of a suspected liar. If innocent, the suspect would be salivating normally and the tongue would not be burned; if the person were lying, the tongue would be scorched. The ancient Chinese used dry rice powder. Someone suspected of lying was forced to keep a handful of rice powder in the mouth. If the powder was soggy when spat out, the person was telling the truth; if it was dry, the person was lying.[33]

In the invasion-of-privacy arena, one of the most controversial issues was the use of the **polygraph**, or lie detector, in business. The polygraph machine measures changes in blood pressure, respiration, and perspiration, sometimes called *galvanic skin response*. The theory behind polygraphy is that the act of lying causes stress, which in turn is manifested by observable physiological changes. The examiner, or machine operator, then interprets the subject's physiological responses to specific questions and makes inferences about whether or not the subject's answers indicate deception.[34] The **Employee Polygraph Protection Act (EPPA)** of 1988 banned most uses in the private sector of the lie detector, but it can still be used by private employers that provide security services, protection of nuclear facilities, shipment or storage of radioactive or toxic waste, public water supply facilities, public transportation, precious commodities, or propriety information. In addition, employers that manufacture, distribute, or dispense controlled substances may use polygraph tests for some of their positions. Government employers are also exempt from the prohibitions on polygraph testing. The federal government may also use polygraph tests for private consultants or experts under contract to various government departments, agencies, or bureaus.[35] It is noteworthy that the spy Aldrich Ames wrote from prison that he passed the U.S. government polygraph test with flying colors; all the while, he was selling U.S. secrets to Russia.[36]

The issue of lie detection is unlikely to diminish as new technologies are created. Research is progressing on the use of magnetic resonance imaging (MRI) brain scans to separate truth from fiction.[37] Other scientists are exploring the use of computers to analyze speech pattern and determine if someone is telling the truth.[38] Still others believe that Google Glass, Google's wearable computer with a head-mounted display, may be able to incorporate an advanced digital lie detector.[39] When these or other new technologies for lie detection develop, new protections for employees will be needed to address them. For now, the ability to detect lies through technology remains an elusive goal.[40]

Many companies now use question and answer **integrity tests** (also known as *honesty tests*), which are a specific type of **personality test**. Integrity tests receive the same kinds of criticisms that led to severe restriction of lie detector testing. However, faced with the elimination of the polygraph and the unavailability of a trustworthy technology option, integrity tests seemed to be a convenient alternative. Critics of integrity tests claim they are intrusive and invade privacy by the nature of their inquiries. Some critics also say that they are unreliable and that employers use them as the sole measure of the fitness of an applicant. Even when these tests are properly administered, opponents charge that employers end up rejecting many honest applicants in their efforts to screen out the dishonest ones.

Management and testing companies claim the tests are very useful in weeding out potentially dishonest applicants. They claim that each question asked has a specific purpose. They also argue that hiring by "gut feeling" is problematic, and integrity tests provide a more objective assessment.[41] There is some evidence that integrity tests provide useful information. A major U.S. retailer used integrity tests in 600 of their 1,900 locations to reduce turnover and shrinkage. After one year, they saw inventory shrinkage—i.e., loss of inventory between manufacturing and sale due to employee theft, shoplifting, or administrative error—fall by more than 35 percent in the stores that used the test, while it rose by 10 percent in the stores that did not. Even though turnover was not a goal of the test administration, they noted a 13 percent decrease in turnover at stores that did use the test and a 14 percent increase in turnover at stores that did not.[42] A large hotel chain found that integrity testing reduced worker's compensation claims significantly, more than compensating for the costs of test administration.[43]

Integrity tests are subject to the same kinds of legal and ethical hurdles that affect polygraph and drug tests. The Civil Rights Act (discussed in Chapter 19) makes it unlawful for any test to have a particularly negative impact on a protected subgroup. From the ADA perspective, medical examinations can be given only after a conditional offer of employment has been made. The EEOC has ruled that integrity tests are not medical examinations, and so they can be given to applicants: psychological examinations are considered medical only if they provide evidence of a mental disorder.[44] Most states apply the federal laws to selection tools. However, Massachusetts and Rhode Island have extended the polygraph statutes to integrity tests. In Massachusetts, integrity tests are against the law, while in Rhode Island they cannot be used as the primary basis for an employment decision.[45]

Companies are increasingly turning to the use of broader personality tests, of which the integrity test is a specific form. **Personality tests** cover areas such as conscientiousness, sociability, introversion, extraversion, emotional stability, maturity, and openness to new ideas.[46] The use of personality tests is raising new concerns about employment discrimination and, as a result, the EEOC has reported that it plans to pay more attention to them in the future.[47]

Even when legal issues surrounding integrity and personality tests are resolved, ethical issues are likely to remain. A test that will identify many of those who would behave unethically at a cost to the firm will also yield "false positives," people labeled as unethical who are good, honest candidates. In statistics, this is called a **type 1 error**, finding an innocent person to be guilty. In contrast, a **type 2 error** finds a guilty person to be innocent. The nature of testing is such that an effort to decrease one type of error will lead to an increase in the other. In other words, the more strictly a test is used to rule out any person who would be guilty of unethical behavior, the greater is the chance that innocent

ETHICS IN PRACTICE CASE

Co-Workers vs. Friendship

I worked in retail for a handful of years, and during that time, I made great lifelong friends. Because I am a hardworking, committed employee, my boss/owner took notice and she promoted me to manager at age 17. My fifth year working at the store, we hired a new employee, Lindsey, and we instantly became great friends. We became so close that we were hanging out outside of work, and Lindsey introduced me to her group of friends. My new group of friends and I became super close; I would see them every day.

Lindsey had a lot of health problems, and she would frequently call out sick Being a manager, I had to take responsibility and cover her shifts, even though I would have other obligations. I requested the Fourth of July weekend off to go to my lake house with my family. At the last minute, however, Lindsey called in sick, and I received a phone call from my boss begging me to cover her shifts, which I did.

On the third of July, my friend Rob invited me to come over to his family BBQ, because he knew I was missing my family BBQ. He told me all of our friends would be there as well, so I planned to head over there after I got out of work. I worked ten hours

that day, I was exhausted, but I wanted to see my friends. I pulled up to his house, and I saw Lindsey's car there, I was extremely confused because Lindsey called in sick for the whole weekend, so why was she there?

Lindsey did not seem the least bit sick; in fact, she was socializing and having the time of her life. I could not believe Lindsey just put me in this horrible position- I missed my family vacation because she did not "feel" like working that weekend. If I ratted her out, I would lose the new friends with whom I had become extremely close. Being her manager, should I tell my boss that Lindsey was faking it, even though we are friends outside of work? Where does the line end between friends and employees?

1. What are the ethical issues in this case?
2. Should I have just gone on my family vacation and not have covered the shift?
3. Should I report Lindsey's behavior? Is there some other action I should take?
4. How should I deal with Lindsey in the future?

Contributed by Madeline Meibauer

people will be judged unethical. It is important, therefore, that integrity tests be used judiciously and that they not be the primary criterion on which employment is based.

Drug Testing

Drug testing is an umbrella term intended to embrace drug and alcohol testing and employer testing for any suspected substance abuse. The issue of drug testing in the workplace has many of the same characteristics as the lie detector and integrity test issues. Companies say they need to do such testing to protect themselves and the public, but opponents claim that drug tests are not accurate and invade the employee's privacy. Concerns about drug testing center around the implications for employee privacy, the inaccuracy of tests, and the impact of drug testing on employee morale.

Quest Diagnostics, a major provider of employment-related drug-testing services, releases an annual index that shows a continued decline in positive drug tests. The most recent results, in 2012, show an all-time low of a 3.5 percent fail rate in urine tests.[48] This represents less than one-third the 13.6 percent level of positivity recorded in 1988, the first year of measurement.[49] Marijuana continues to have the highest positivity rates and that trend is likely to continue. Part of the reason is likely to be that marijuana takes longer to vacate the body than other drugs.[50] In addition, attitudes toward marijuana are changing. Various state marijuana legalization developments have created a confusing situation for companies. The U.S. Drug Enforcement Administration continues to consider marijuana to be a Schedule 1 controlled substance, but the Department of Justice is reviewing the states that have legalized marijuana and is planning to issue a policy on how it will respond.[51] The Respect States' and Citizens' Rights Act of 2013 has been introduced into the House of Representatives, with a provision that the Controlled Substance Act (CSA) cannot preempt state law.[52] As this issue continues to evolve, companies will have to sort out how best to respond to the continuous shifts in the legal landscape.

Arguments for Drug Testing. Proponents of drug testing argue that the costs of drug abuse on the job are staggering. The consequences range from accidents and injuries to theft, bad decisions, and ruined lives. The greatest concern is in industries where mistakes can cost lives—for example, the railroad, airline, aerospace, nuclear power, and hazardous equipment and chemicals industries. Thus, the primary ethical argument for employers conducting drug tests is the responsibility they have to their own employees and the general public to provide safe workplaces and security for the firm's assets.

Arguments against Drug Testing. Opponents of drug testing see it as both a due-process issue and an invasion-of-privacy issue. The due-process issue relates to the sometimes-questionable accuracy of drug tests. Common foods and medications can lead to a false positive, giving the appearance of drug use when the person being tested is actually drug-free. This can create a downward spiral for employees, causing reputational damage, lost income, and considerable expense to try to rebut the allegation of drug use.[53]

Many legitimate questions arise in the drug-testing issue. Do employers have a right to know if their employees use drugs off the job? If employees are performing their jobs satisfactorily, is off-hours drug use a relevant issue? Obviously, a delicate balance is necessary, because employers and employees alike have legitimate interests that must be protected. If companies are going to engage in some form of drug testing, they should think carefully about developing policies that not only will achieve their intended goals but also will be fair to the employees and will minimize invasions of privacy. Such a balance will not be easy to achieve, but must be sought. To do otherwise will guarantee decreased employee morale, more and more lawsuits, and new government regulations.

Guidelines for Drug Testing. If management perceives the need to conduct a drug-testing program to protect other stakeholders, it should carefully design and structure the program so that it will be minimally intrusive of employees' privacy rights. The following guidelines, reflecting the ethical aspects of drug testing, have been developed by the American College of Occupational and Environmental Medicine (ACOEM):[54]

1. Companies should have written policies and procedures, which should be applied impartially.
2. Companies should provide clear documentation of the reason for conducting drug testing (e.g., employee safety, public safety, security).
3. Any employees or applicants that will be affected should be informed in advance of the company's drug use, misuse, and testing policies, as well as their right to refuse to be tested and the consequences of refusal.
4. If testing is conducted on an unannounced and random basis, employees should be made aware of the special safety or security needs that justify this procedure.
5. All tests should be done in a uniform and impartial manner.
6. A licensed physician (MD/DO) should supervise the collection, transportation, and analysis of the specimens, as well as the reporting of results. Stringent legal, technical, and ethical requirements should be observed when reporting results.

7. A licensed and appropriately qualified physician should be designated as the medical review officer (MRO) and should evaluate positive results before a report is made to the employer.

8. An employee or applicant who tests positive should be informed of the positive results by the physician and should have the opportunity to explain and discuss the results before the employer is notified. The procedure for this should be clearly outlined.

9. Any report to the employer should provide only the information needed for work placement purposes or as required by government regulations. The employer should not be told of the specific types or levels of drug found unless required by law. A trained and qualified physician should make that report.

Guidelines shift over time, and so exceptions to these might be considered and/or new guidelines may develop. The major point is that management needs to think through its policies and their consequences very carefully when designing and conducting drug-testing programs.

State and Federal Legislation. Some states and cities have enacted laws (or are considering doing so) to restrict workplace drug testing. Generally, these laws restrict the scope of testing by private and public employers and establish privacy protections and procedural safeguards. Some states do not completely ban drug testing but restrict the circumstances (e.g., for reasonable cause) under which it may be used. They may also restrict drug testing to instances where there is reasonable suspicion of drug use and place limits on the disciplinary actions employers may take. Other states provide discounts on worker's compensation and/or incentives of another kind to organizations that implement drug testing. This patchwork of incongruous state laws complicates drug testing for employers.

At the federal level, the **Americans with Disabilities Act (ADA)** must be considered, because the definition of disability applies to drug and alcohol addiction. The ADA prohibits companies from giving applicants medical exams before they extend those applicants' conditional offers of employment. Pre-hire drug tests, however, are permitted. Philadelphia employment lawyer Jonathan Segal advises employers to extend conditional offers before drug testing. Asking an applicant to explain a positive result on a drug test could easily turn that drug test into a medical exam.[55] He recommends conducting the drug test immediately after making the conditional offer and then delaying employment until the test results are back.[56] Employers would also be well advised to use physicians who are trained to review drug test results to evaluate claims of false positive readings.[57]

Employee Assistance Programs. One of the most significant strategies undertaken by corporate America to deal with the growing alcohol- and drug-abuse problem in the workplace has been **Employee Assistance Programs (EAPs)**. EAPs extend into a variety of employee problem areas such as compulsive gambling, financial stress, emotional stress, marital difficulties, aging, legal problems, AIDS, and other physical, psychological, emotional, and social difficulties. The term **broad brush EAP** describes this comprehensive model.[58] A recent major concern with EAPs has been to integrate them into the company's general health management strategy so that they can become a core strategic component.[59]

EAPs represent a positive and proactive step companies can take to deal with these serious problems. EAPs are designed to be confidential and non-punitive, and they affirm three important propositions: (1) employees are valuable members of the organization, (2) it is better to help troubled employees than to discipline or discharge them, and (3) recovered employees are better employees. It is encouraging that in an era when employees are increasingly exerting their workplace rights, enlightened companies are offering EAPs in an effort to help solve their mutual problems. More information on EAPs can be found at the Employee Assistance Professionals Association Web site, http://www.eap-association.org.[60]

Monitoring Employees on the Job

In the old days, supervisors monitored employees' work activities by peeking over their shoulders and judging how things were going. Technology changed all that, as cameras and listening devices gave way to computers and satellites as options for employee monitoring. Privacy advocates are concerned about the use of technology to gather information about workers on the job, and with good reason. In its most recent survey, the American Management Association (AMA) found that the vast majority of mid- to large-sized firms participate in some type of **employee monitoring**. In some cases, the method is passive, such as installing video cameras in a lobby. However, most companies use more active means of monitoring their workers, such as recording their phone calls or voice mail, reading their computer files, monitoring e-mail or Web access, and video-taping them. Employer monitoring of employees has become the norm in businesses today. The consequence is that millions of workers are laboring under the relentless gaze of electronic supervision.

What Can Be Monitored? According to the most recent AMA survey, 66 percent of employers monitor their employees' Web site visits in order to prevent inappropriate surfing and 65 percent block Web sites they consider to be off-limits. The Web sites of concern to employers include adult sites, games, social networking, entertainment, shopping and auctions, sports, and external blogs. E-mail is monitored by 43 percent of companies, and 73 percent of those use technology, while 40 percent have an individual assigned to monitor and read the e-mail.[61]

As discussed in Chapter 9, the introduction of new technologies creates new opportunities for surveillance by employers. For example, the advent of global positioning system (GPS) technology has made it possible to monitor worker location. Of course, the advent of technology works both ways. Camera phones can possibly serve as a tool that employees can use to monitor their employers. Some companies have moved to ban them from the workplace due to fear of corporate espionage.[62]

The only federal level of privacy protection in the United States is the **Electronic Communication Privacy Act (ECPA) of 1986**. The interception or unauthorized access of a wire, oral, or electronic communication where there is a reasonable expectation of privacy is illegal under this act unless it is covered by one of the statutory exceptions or required by government compulsion. One of the statutory exceptions is the business use exception: the act does not apply if the interception or access occurs as part of the "ordinary course of business." It also does not apply if the person gives consent. An employee working for a company that has disclosed that it will monitor its employees is considered to have given implicit consent. With these broad exceptions, it is not surprising that the ECPA has been ineffective in regulating the monitoring of employees in the workplace.[63] The one clear protection is that employers may not listen to purely personal phone conversations; however, they can monitor a conversation for the time required to determine that the call is personal.[64] States have tried to enact laws to strengthen workplace privacy but with limited success, resulting in a patchwork of state laws.[65]

Efforts to enact a U.S. law specifically geared toward workplace privacy have always been stymied. However, recent court cases may have implications for workplace privacy in the future. One of the key issues is the phrase "reasonable expectation of privacy." In one case, the New Jersey Supreme Court ruled in favor of an employee whose company read e-mails that she sent to her attorney using her personal, password protected, Web-based Yahoo e-mail account on the company's computer.[66] The court unanimously found that the use of a password that she did not save on the employer's hard drive, as well as the attorney client privilege, gave her a reasonable expectation of privacy.[67] The Justices further noted that the company's e-mail policy said, "Occasional personal use is permitted."[68] The Federal Appeals Court ruled against Phillip Hamilton when he tried to get the content of workplace e-mails exchanged between him and his wife rendered inadmissible due to spousal privilege.[69] The court ruled that by not taking steps to protect the e-mails' privacy, he had waived the marital privilege and thus had no reasonable expectation of privacy.[70]

The workplace privacy problem creates dilemmas that are not easily resolved. At this writing, six states have enacted laws that protect employee privacy by prohibiting employers from demanding that employees provide them with Facebook usernames and passwords, and other states are considering similar bills.[71] While this is a positive move in terms of employee privacy, the increased privacy may come at a price. According to the Financial Industry Regulatory Authority (FINRA), these laws may conflict with security rules, thereby decreasing investor protection and increasing the risk of securities fraud.[72] To date, efforts to reconcile the two concerns have not been successful.

Effects of Being Monitored. Invasion of privacy is one major consequence of employee monitoring. Another is unfair treatment. Employees working under such systems complain about stress and tension resulting from their being expected and pressured to be more productive now that their efforts can be more thoroughly observed. The pressure of being constantly monitored is also producing low morale and a sense of job insecurity in many places. Employees have good reason to be concerned. The most recent AMA

ETHICS IN PRACTICE CASE

Sick Day Snoops

In their "Working in America: Absent Workforce" study, Kronos Inc. found that nearly 40 percent of employees have taken sick days when they are not actually sick, and 61 percent of the respondents said their work did not get done when they were absent. In an effort to curb the resultant losses, some businesses are hiring detectives to spy on employees who have called in sick but might be playing hooky. Investigators are looking to determine if the illness or injury actually exists and, if it does, whether it is serious enough to justify the absence.

Rick Raymond is a private detective who has taken on a variety of these cases. He tracked one woman to a theme park where they take roller-coaster riders' pictures as they round a sharp turn. He bought the pictures as proof. He has tracked others to bowling alleys, pro football games, and weddings. He estimates that about 80–85 percent of the people he is hired to follow end up being guilty.

1. The courts have ruled that this practice is legal. Is it ethical?
2. Should limits be placed on the use of private detectives in following employees when they are outside of the office?
3. How would you feel if your boss had you followed?
4. Would you hire a private detective to follow one of your employees?

Sources: "Working in America: Absent Workforce," *Kronos*, http://www.workforceinstitute.org/wp-content/themes/revolution/docs/Working-in-Amer-Survey.pdf. Accessed May 20, 2013; Thomas Chan, "Employers and Insurers Hire Private Eyes to Probe Sick Leave Scams," *South China Morning Post* (May 2, 2013), http://www.scmp.com/news/hong-kong/article/1227821/employers-and-insurers-call-private-investigators-root-out-sick-leave. Accessed May 20, 2013; Eric Spitznagel, "The Sick Day Bounty Hunters," *Bloomberg BusinessWeek* (December 8–December 12, 2010), 93–95.

survey found that not only do the vast majority of major U.S. companies engage in employee monitoring, but also they are now using their findings to make employment decisions: 30 percent have fired employees for misusing the Internet, and 28 percent have terminated employees for misusing e-mail.[73]

Policy Guidelines on the Issue of Privacy

During our discussion of various privacy issues, we have indicated steps that management might consider taking in an attempt to be responsive to employee stakeholders. Frederick S. Lane III, a law and technology expert and author of *The Naked Employee: How Technology Is Compromising Workplace Privacy*, offers an "Employee Privacy Bill of Rights" that sets forth guidelines for developing privacy policies and procedures that uphold the dignity of the employee.[74] To preserve employee rights, firms should:

1. Obtain informed consent from employees and applicants before acquiring information about them
2. Disclose the nature of any surveillance that will occur
3. Set controls so as to avoid casual and unauthorized spread of information
4. Limit the collection and use of medical and health data to that which is relevant to the job
5. Require reasonable suspicion before administering drug tests
6. Respect and preserve the boundary between work and home

Business's concern for protection of the privacy of its employees, customers, and other stakeholders is growing. It is not surprising, therefore, that a new form of corporate executive has appeared on the horizon. As we discussed in Chapter 9, **chief privacy officers (CPOs)** are high-ranking executives responsible for monitoring and protecting the private information held by firms. They differ from security personnel in that they determine what data should be protected, while the security department determines how it will be protected. The CPO is responsible for ensuring that the privacy of individuals is respected.

Workplace Safety

Workers Memorial Day was observed on April 28, 2013. That date is the anniversary of the Occupational Safety and Health Administration and the Federal Coal Mine Health and Safety Act. Sadly, the deaths of 1,127 garment workers in Dhaka, Bangladesh, and 23 coal mine workers in Guizhou province, China, served as a reminder of how much work remains to be done in the area of worker safety.[75] Throughout the world, 6,300 people die each day as a result of injury or illness stemming from the workplace: every 15 seconds, a worker dies from a work-related incident or disease.[76]

The main law that protects the safety and health of workers in the United States is the Occupational Safety and Health Act. This act requires the Secretary of Labor to set safety and health standards that protect employees and their families. Every private employer who engages in interstate commerce is subject to the regulations promulgated under this act.[77] The federal agency responsible for overseeing the safety and health of America's workers is the **Occupational Safety and Health Administration (OSHA)**. Figure 18-2 provides OSHA's list of employer responsibilities for safeguarding employee health and safety.

We will begin by examining the workplace safety problem and the right-to-know laws that have evolved from it. We will look at the issue of workplace violence, which is a serious concern in today's workplace. Then, we will turn to the issue of smoking in the workplace. Finally, we'll end with a discussion of the family-friendly workplace.

FIGURE 18-2

OSHA's List of
Employer
Responsibilities

Employers have the responsibility to provide a safe workplace. Employers *must* provide their employees with a workplace that does not have serious hazards and follow all relevant OSHA safety and health standards. Employers must find and correct safety and health problems. OSHA further requires employers to try to eliminate or reduce hazards first by making changes in working conditions rather than just relying on masks, gloves, earplugs, or other types of personal protective equipment. Switching to safer chemicals, implementing processes to trap harmful fumes, or using ventilation systems to clean the air are examples of effective ways to get rid of or minimize risks. Employers must also:

- Inform employees about chemical hazards through training, labels, alarms,

color-coded systems, chemical information sheets and other methods;
- Keep accurate records of work-related injuries and illnesses;
- Perform tests in the workplace, such as air sampling, required by some OSHA standards;
- Provide hearing exams or other medical tests required by OSHA standards;
- Post OSHA citations, injury and illness data, and the OSHA poster in the workplace where workers will see them;
- Notify OSHA within 8 hours of a workplace incident in which there is a death or when three or more workers go to a hospital; and
- Not discriminate or retaliate against workers for using their rights under the law.

Source: "We Are OSHA We Can Help," OSHA, http://www.osha.gov/Publications/3334we-can-help-sm.pdf. Accessed May 21, 2013.

The Workplace Safety Problem

Two events stand out as milestones in the adjudication of workplace safety problem. The first ranks among the landmark cases on job safety. In Elk Grove Village, Illinois, Film Recovery Systems operated a plant that extracted silver from used hospital x-ray and photographic film. To extract the silver, the employees first had to dump the film into open vats of sodium cyanide and then transfer the leached remnants to another tank. One day, employee Stefan Golab staggered outside and collapsed, unconscious. Efforts to revive him failed, and he was soon pronounced dead from what the local medical examiner labeled "acute cyanide toxicity."[78]

An intensive investigation by attorneys in Cook County, Illinois, revealed a long list of incriminating details: (1) Film Recovery workers seldom wore even the most rudimentary safety equipment, (2) workers were laboring in what amounted to an industrial gas chamber, and (3) company executives downplayed the dangers of cyanide poisoning and removed labeling that identified it as poisonous. The prosecutors took action under an Illinois homicide statute that targets anyone who knowingly commits acts that "create a strong probability of death or serious bodily harm." Three executives at Film Recovery Systems—the president, the plant manager, and the foreman—were convicted of the murder of Stefan Golab and each were sentenced to 25 years in prison. This marked the first ever conviction of managers for homicide in a corporate matter such as an industrial accident.[79] The Film Recovery Systems case marked a new era in managerial responsibility for job safety. Other prosecutions of managers have followed this case. What this clearly signals is not only do employees have a moral right to a safe working environment, but also that managers can face prosecution if they do not ensure that employees are protected.

The second milestone event, which we also discussed in Chapter 10, was the dramatic and catastrophic poisonous gas leak at the Union Carbide plant in Bhopal, India. The death toll topped 2,000, and tens of thousands more were injured. People around the globe were startled and shocked at what the results of one major industrial accident

Spotlight on Sustainability

It's All Connected

Workplace safety is not always mentioned in discussions of business sustainability, but that is beginning to change. Sustainability initiatives encompass environmental, social, and economic considerations—and safety hinges on all three. The lean and green movement combines eliminating waste with respecting people and the environment. As Michael Taubitz writes, "This brings employee safety into the equation because you cannot be lean without being safe" (p. 42). For example, a recent study of ergonomics discovered that the muscle pain and stress experienced by workers in one department of the company stemmed from root causes in another department. Furthermore, factors that were the source of the muscle pain had also affected employees in still other departments. Sustainability's focus on system-wide thinking lends itself to seeing the connections in complex systems and recognizing the resulting interactions and their consequences. However, employee safety and health have received relatively little attention in the sustainability movement, and so the Center for Safety and Health Sustainability launched in June 2011 with the purpose of bringing safety and health into the discussion and practice of sustainability.

Sources: Ash M. Genaidy, Reynold Sequeira, Magda M. Rinder, and Amal D. A-Rehim, "Determinants of Business Sustainability: An Ergonomics Perspective," *Ergonomics* (March 2009), 273–301; Michael A. Taubitz, "Lean, Green, and Safe," *Professional Safety* (May 2010), 39; Center for Safety and Health Sustainability, http://centershs.org/index.php. Accessed May 20, 2013.

could be. Lawsuits sought damages that quickly exceeded the net worth of the company.[80] Seven years after the leak, India's Supreme Court upheld a $470 million settlement that Union Carbide had already paid, and it lifted the immunity from criminal prosecution that it had granted the company two years after the leak occurred. The name "Union Carbide" became inextricably linked with the Bhopal Disaster. In 2001, Union Carbide became a wholly owned subsidiary of Dow Chemical.[81] Twenty-five years after the tragedy, a district court in Bhopal found seven former Union Carbide India Ltd. officials guilty of "causing death by negligence." They were sentenced to two years in prison and fined 100,000 rupees ($2,130). These two events highlighted the necessity of taking steps to protect worker health and safety.

Of course, not all hazards can be anticipated. The 2001 attack on the World Trade Center was a shock and surprise to the world. Shortly after the tragedy occurred, many were wondering what the impact would be on Morgan Stanley, one of the world's biggest brokerages and investment firms. The company was the largest tenant in the World Trade Center, with about 3,700 employees in the two towers. Amazingly, fewer than ten of their employees were among the missing, and only about 50 reported being injured. Company officials credit the evacuation procedures that Morgan Stanley developed after the 1993 bombing of the World Trade Center with saving so many of their employees' lives. The security staff used megaphones to keep people moving despite announcements over the building's public address system that instructed people to return to work. They moved their employees down the smoke-filled stairs (some descended more than 70 flights) and away from the twin towers. The earlier incident in 1993 had alerted them to their vulnerability, and they took the necessary steps to protect the health and safety of as many of their employees as possible.[82] In a world where the unexpected is to be expected, this is the type of preparedness all workplaces should emulate.

Right-to-Know Laws

Prompted by the Union Carbide tragedy in Bhopal and other, less dramatic industrial accidents, workers have demanded to know more about the thousands of chemicals and hazardous substances they are being exposed to in the workplace on a daily basis. Experts argue that employers have a duty to provide employees with information on the hazards of workplace chemicals and to make sure that workers understand what the information means in practical terms. Since the early 1980s, many states have passed **right-to-know laws** and expanded public access to this kind of information by employees and even communities. Although the states took the initiative on the right-to-know front, OSHA followed suit by creating a Hazard Communication Standard that preempted state regulations. This standard requires covered employers to identify hazardous chemicals in their workplaces and to provide employees with specified forms of information on such substances and their hazards. Specifically, manufacturers, whether they are chemical manufacturers or users of chemicals, must take certain steps to achieve compliance with the standard.[83] These steps include the following:

1. Update inventories of hazardous chemicals present in the workplace.
2. Assemble material safety data sheets (MSDSs) for all hazardous chemicals.
3. Ensure that all containers and hazardous chemicals are properly labeled.
4. Provide workers with training on the use of hazardous chemicals.
5. Prepare and maintain a written description of the company's hazard communication program.
6. Consider any problems with trade secrets that may be raised by the standard's disclosure requirements.
7. Review state requirements for hazard disclosure.

In addition to the right-to-know laws, employees have certain workplace rights with respect to health and safety on the job that OSHA provides by law. As in our discussion of the public policy exceptions to the employment-at-will doctrine in the preceding chapter, it should be clear that workers have a right to seek health and safety on the job without fear of punishment or recrimination.

Workplace Violence

Another issue that has become a major problem and is posing challenges to management is escalating violence in the workplace. **Workplace violence** is one of the four leading causes of death in the workplace and the leading cause of death for women.[84] It falls into two categories: (1) violence from an outside source and (2) violence stemming from coworkers. Workplace violence from coworkers cuts across all industries, while certain industries have a greater likelihood of workplace violence from the general public.[85]

In the United States, nearly two million workers report that they are victims of workplace violence each year, and many more victims never report it.[86] The leading cause of death for women in the workplace is homicide.[87] Overall, companies are making few efforts to address it. Despite the seriousness of this issue, nearly 70 percent of workplaces do not have a formal program that addresses workplace violence.[88]

The problem of workplace violence shows no sign of abating. Experts note that a variety of factors promote continued violence including an overall greater tolerance for violence, easily available weapons, economic stress, a difficult job market, and insufficient support systems.[89] In the United States, gun law battles are complicating an already difficult situation. Businesses have historically been able to keep guns out of the workplace with a posted sign, but gun advocates have been testing that in the courts.[90] As is often the case, companies cannot satisfy all stakeholders on this issue. Starbucks has opted not

---

ETHICS IN PRACTICE CASE
When External Stakeholders Attack

Both customers and employees are primary stakeholders and so when one begins to attack the other, stakeholder management becomes even more challenging. The problem of customer violence is real and appears to be growing. Although workplace homicides in the U.S. have declined in general, one form of workplace homicide is on the rise—assaults by customers. The number is relatively low in terms of overall workplace fatalities, but the upward trend is a concern. In their 2013 Survey of Workplace Violence, the Institute of Finance and Management (IOFM) found that 61 percent of the 307 organizations surveyed believe that abuse of employees by customers has become significantly worse in the past

year. Sometimes the abuse is simply verbal but other times it can result in serious injury and even death.

1. Business cannot refer a customer to an EAP as it can with an employee. It also is not possible to screen and select, much less train, customers as one does for employees. What can a business do to protect its employees from violent customers?
2. Why is customer violence on the increase? Is it the fault of the customer, the organization, and/or society?
3. What do you recommend that managers do to stem this growing problem?

Sources: http://www.bls.gov/iif/oshwc/cfoi/work_hom.pdf. Accessed May 21, 2013. "The Customer Isn't Always Right," *Security Director's Report* (June 2013), 1–11. "Master Guide to Workplace Violence," *IOFM* (2013), http://www.iofm.com/research/view/master-guide-to-workplace-violence (cited in *Security Director's Report*, 2013). Accessed May 21, 2013. James Alan Fox, "When Disgruntled Customers Kill," *The Boston Globe* (August 26, 2011), http://boston.com/community/blogs/crime_punishment/2011/08/when_ disgruntled_customers_kil.html. Accessed May 21, 2013.

---

to ban guns, and so employees and some customers have mounted a petition campaign to encourage the company to changes its stance. California Pizza Kitchen opted to ban guns from its establishments, and so it is now facing a boycott by gun advocates.[91]

Who Is Affected? Although no workplace is immune from workplace violence, some workers are at increased risk of workplace violence from the general public. According to OSHA, the workers who are more likely to experience workplace violence include[92]

- Workers who exchange money with the public
- Workers who deliver passengers, goods, or services
- Workers who work alone or in small groups
- Workers who work late at night or very early in the morning
- Workers who work in community settings and homes where they have extensive contact with the public
- Workers who work in high-crime areas

The workers who are direct targets of the violence are not the only people affected. Not only are the family and friends of the victims impacted, but those employees in the workplace who escaped the violence also experience long-term effects. These survivors often spend years dealing with the after-effects.[93] Many fear returning to work; some never do. They will often replay the event in their minds, unable to forget what happened. Victoria Spang is a marketing director who hid in the personnel office when a client of her law firm came in with assault weapons, killing eight people and wounding six. "No one ever forgets. You'd walk by people's cubicles, and they would keep pictures of the victims up. It's a moment in life you'll always remember."[94]

Corporate image can also suffer long-term effects from worker rage. The term "going postal" is a thorn in the side of the U.S. Postal Service. It became part of the lexicon after a series of post office shootings. The phrase continues even after a study commissioned by the post office found that postal workers are no more likely to commit violence than employees in other professions are.[95] In fact, workplace violence can occur in the most unexpected locations. Quiet Huntsville, Alabama, was shocked when a biology professor shot three of her colleagues due to a dispute over her denial of tenure. University spokesperson Ray Garner commented, "This is a very safe campus. … This town is not accustomed to shootings and having multiple dead."[96]

Prevention. The federal Occupational Safety and Health Act (OSHA) has a "general duty clause" that mandates employers to provide safe workplaces; however, it does not set forth specific standards or requirements addressing violence and has stated it will not try to regulate "random antisocial acts."[97] OSHA will apply the general duty clause to determine whether the violent act came from events that should have been foreseen by the company. Specifically, the company will be liable when (1) the employer neglected to keep the workplace free from a hazard, (2) the hazard was one that is generally recognized by the employer or the industry, (3) the hazard was already causing or was likely to cause serious harm, and (4) elimination or removal of the hazard was feasible.[98]

Management has both the legal and moral duty to address the problem of workplace violence. Companies have barely begun to put meaningful safety measures into place, but such measures will become more important in the future. Programs that deal with crises, and long-range efforts to bring about safer workplace environments, will be essential. Figure 18-3 lists OSHA's recommendations for what employers can do to protect their employees from workplace violence.

FIGURE 18-3

OSHA's Recommendations for Preventing Workplace Violence

The best protection employers can offer is to establish a zero-tolerance policy toward workplace violence against or by their employees. The employer should establish a workplace violence prevention program or incorporate the information into an existing accident prevention program, employee handbook, or manual of standard operating procedures. It is critical to ensure that all employees know the policy and understand that all claims of workplace violence will be investigated and remedied promptly. In addition, employers can offer additional protections such as the following:

1. Provide safety education for employees so they know what conduct is not acceptable, what to do if they witness or are subjected to workplace violence, and how to protect themselves.
2. Secure the workplace. Where appropriate to the business, install video surveillance, extra lighting, and alarm systems; minimize access by outsiders through identification badges, electronic keys, and guards.
3. Provide drop safes to limit the amount of cash on hand. Keep a minimal amount of cash in registers during evenings and late-night hours.
4. Equip field staff with cellular phones and hand-held alarms or noise devices, and require them to prepare a daily work plan and keep a contact person informed of their location throughout the day. Keep employer-provided vehicles properly maintained.
5. Instruct employees not to enter any location where they feel unsafe. Introduce a "buddy system" or provide an escort or police assistance in potentially dangerous situations or at night.
6. Develop policies and procedures covering visits by home health-care providers. Address the conduct of home visits, the presence of others in the home during visits, and the worker's right to refuse to provide services in a clearly hazardous situation.

Source: "What Can These Employers Do To Help Protect These Employees," *Workplace Violence OSHA Fact Sheet.* http://www.osha .gov/OshDoc/data_General_Facts/factsheet-workplace-violence.pdf. Accessed May 20, 2013.

The Right to Health in the Workplace

As the public became more health conscious, it was not surprising that companies in the United States became much more sensitive about health issues. In efforts to control runaway health costs, which are rising at an estimated 10 percent per year, these companies took drastic steps, some of which have become controversial. Smoking has been a controversial issue related to health in the workplace and so it merits special attention. Like other issues we have examined, smoking in the workplace has employee rights, privacy, and due-process ramifications.

Smoking in the Workplace

The issue of regulating **smoking in the workplace** began in the 1980s in the United States. The idea that smoking ought to be curtailed or restricted in the workplace is a direct result of the growing anti-smoking sentiment in society in general. Much of the anti-smoking sentiment crystallized when U.S. Surgeon General C. Everett Koop called for a smoke-free society. He proclaimed that smokers were hurting not only themselves but also the nonsmoking people around them, who were being harmed by secondhand, or passive, smoke in the air they breathed. Koop argued that the evidence "clearly documents that nonsmokers are placed at increased risks for developing disease as the result of exposure to environmental tobacco smoke."[99]

Evidence of the need to control smoking in the workplace continues to mount. The U.S. Environmental Protection Agency (EPA) classifies secondhand smoke involuntarily inhaled by nonsmokers from other people's cigarettes as a known human carcinogen: secondhand smoke is responsible for approximately 3,400 lung cancer deaths and an average of 46,000 heart disease deaths in adult nonsmokers annually in the United States.[100] The World Health Organization calls secondhand smoke a health hazard that kills and declares that every individual has the right to breathe smoke-free air.[101] Worldwide, only 5.4 percent of people are protected by comprehensive national smoke-free laws, but the number of people protected is increasing each year.[102]

The Family-Friendly Workplace

Employees are increasingly less willing to spend every waking hour at work and are more committed to having time to spend at home with family. For example, one study found that employees in firms with more family-friendly policies have less workplace-oriented stress, fewer professional-personal life conflicts, and feel more satisfied with their jobs.[103] Companies are searching for more and more ways to help employees achieve **work–life balance**, which is defined as "a state of equilibrium where the demands of a person's personal and professional life are equal."[104]

The 2011 Society for Human Resource Management (SHRM) Employee Benefits Survey showed that companies are endeavoring to maintain **family-friendly** benefits while striving to reduce costs. Family-friendly benefits were largely intact from 2007 to 2011 except for reduced offerings in foster care assistance, elder care referral services and adoption assistance.[105] Some of the most popular family-friendly benefits and the percentage of firms offering them are

1. Dependent care flexible spending accounts   73%
2. Bring a child to work in an emergency   33%
3. On-site mother's room   28%
4. Child care referral service   17%
5. Domestic partner benefits   14%

Although not everyone thinks that companies are becoming as family friendly as they are claiming to be, it is clear that workers are talking more and more about the importance of family-friendly policies, and many leading companies are responding. Even through the economic slump, many companies continued to offer family-friendly environments, and these have become an important part of "best places to work" surveys, which have become popular in recent years.

It is in the context of organizations becoming more "friendly" on their own that we want to discuss a law aimed at health-related issues in the workplace—the FMLA.

Family and Medical Leave Act. The **Family and Medical Leave Act (FMLA)** was made into law in 1993. This act was designed to make life easier for employees with family or health problems. In 2010, the law was expanded to include employees with family members on active military duty.[106] The new amendments extend "qualifying exigency leave" protections to families of active duty service members deployed abroad so that the families can have time to manage the service member's personal affairs while she or he is on active duty. In addition, family members who provide care for injured veterans can receive 26 weeks of leave.[107]

In addition to the expansions noted above, the FMLA grants employees the following rights:[108]

- An employee may take up to 12 weeks of unpaid leave in any 12-month period for the birth or adoption of a child or for the care of a child, spouse, or parent with a serious health condition that limits the employee's performance.
- Employees must be reinstated in their old jobs or be given equivalent jobs upon returning to work; the employer does not have to allow employees to accrue seniority or other benefits during the leave periods.
- Employers must provide employees with health benefits during leave periods.
- Employees are protected from retaliation in the same way as under other employment laws; an employee cannot be discriminated against for complaining to other people (even the newspapers) about an employer's family leave policy.

Employers also have rights under the FMLA.[109] These rights include the following:

- Companies with fewer than 50 workers are exempt.
- Employers may demand that employees obtain medical opinions and certifications regarding their needs for leave and may require second or third opinions.
- Employers do not have to pay employees during leave periods, but they must continue health benefits.
- If an employee and a spouse are employed at the same firm and are entitled to leave, the total leave for both may be limited to 12 weeks.

A study by the Department of Labor showed that the corporate views on the FMLA are mixed—generally positive but with some issues that merit concern. The good news is that the law seems to work well when employees take up to 12 weeks of unpaid leave for a close relative's sickness or the birth or adoption of a child. Problems arise when employees take unscheduled intermittent leave. In addition, defining a *serious medical condition* has been a challenge.[110]

In summary, the FMLA has not been the major problem that many envisioned, and it has accomplished much good. However, clarifying terminology is important if it is to continue to provide workers with the opportunity to fulfill their family responsibilities without sacrificing their careers. Efforts to pass additional family-friendly workplace legislation continue, but in an environment of global recession, it is doubtful that major changes will occur in the near future. Efforts to streamline and clarify the FMLA are more likely to influence the direction corporate policies will take.

Summary

Critical employee stakeholder issues include the rights to privacy, safety, and health. These issues should be seen as extensions of the issues and rights outlined in Chapter 17.

With the development of new technologies, workplace privacy has increasingly become a serious issue. This wealth of available technology presents new challenges for companies as they weigh the importance of knowing their workers' activities against the importance of maintaining trust and morale. Of equal, if not more, importance to employee stakeholders are the issues of workplace health and safety. The workplace safety problem led to the creation of OSHA.

OSHA is the federal government's major instrument for protecting workers on the job. State-promulgated right-to-know laws, as well as federal statutes, have been passed in recent years to provide employees with an added measure of protection, especially against harmful effects of exposure to chemicals and toxic substances. However, existing laws and regulations deal only with known problems. As the world changes, so do the threats to worker health and safety. Since the World Trade Center tragedy, the threat of terrorism has made many companies reassess operations as basic as their mailroom procedures. Other unexpected threats to workers' health and safety are certain to occur and will represent new challenges for managers.

Other major health issues in the current business-employee relationship are smoking and workplace violence. Smoking in the workplace raises issues of employee rights, those of both smokers and nonsmokers. Violence in the workplace is exacting a heavy toll, and businesses must be responsive. The need for employees to take family leave also impacts the work environment. Wise managers will develop policies for dealing with these issues, as well as their privacy and due process implications.

Key Terms

privacy in the workplace,
p. 517
background checks, p. 518
Privacy Act of 1974, p. 518
USA Patriot Act, p. 518
consumer reports, p. 519
Fair Credit Reporting Act
(FCRA), p. 519
Equal Employment Opportunity
Commission (EEOC), p. 520
polygraph, p. 521
Employee Polygraph Protection
Act (EPPA), p. 521

integrity tests, p. 522
personality tests, p. 522
type 1 error, p. 522
type 2 error, p. 522
drug testing, p. 523
Americans with Disabilities Act
(ADA), p. 525
broad brush EAP, p. 525
Employee Assistance Programs
(EAPs), p. 525
Electronic Communication Privacy
Act (ECPA) of 1986, p. 526
employee monitoring, p. 526

Occupational Safety and Health
Administration (OSHA), p. 528
chief privacy officers
(CPOs), p. 528
right-to-know laws, p. 531
workplace violence, p. 531
family-friendly, p. 534
smoking in the workplace,
p. 534
work–life balance, p. 534
Family and Medical Leave Act
(FMLA), p. 535

Discussion Questions

1. In your own words, describe what privacy means and what privacy protection companies should give employees.
2. Enumerate the strengths and weaknesses of the polygraph as a management tool for decision-making. What polygraph uses are legitimate? What uses of the polygraph are illegitimate?
3. What are the two major arguments for and against integrity (honesty) testing by employers? Under what circumstances could management most legitimately argue that integrity testing is necessary?

4. How has technology affected workplace privacy? What are the implications for the social contract between firms and their employees?

5. How has the World Trade Center tragedy affected workplace privacy? What are the long-term implications of that?

6. Which two of the four guidelines on the issue of privacy presented in this chapter do you think are the most important? Why?

7. Identify the privacy, health, and due-process ramifications of violence in the workplace.

Endnotes

1. Margaret H. Vickers, "The 'Workplace-During-Recession' Reminding Us of Employee Rights and Responsibilities," *Employee Responsibilities and Rights Journal* (March 2009), 3–6.

2. Ibid.

3. http://www.bls.gov/home.htm. Accessed May 20, 2013.

4. Center for Safety and Health Sustainability, http://centershs.org/index.php. Accessed May 20, 2013.

5. "NWI Surveillance Bill Enacted—Additional Efforts Underway," *Workrights News* (Fall-Winter 2005/2006).

6. Ibid.

7. http://www.epic.org/privacy/nelson/. Accessed May 20, 2013.

8. "Big Brother, Inc., May Be Closer Than You Think," *BusinessWeek* (February 9, 1987), 84.

9. Patricia H. Werhane, *Persons, Rights, and Corporations* (Englewood Cliffs, NJ: Prentice Hall, 1985), 118.

10. Glenn Greenwood and James Ball, "The Top Secret Rules That Allow NSA to Use U.S. Data Without a Warrant," *The Guardian* (June 20, 2013), http://www.guardian.co.uk/world/2013/jun/20/fisa-court-nsa-without-warrant. Accessed July 4, 2013.

11. http://www.privacyrights.org/ar/Privacy-IssuesList.htm#D (revised January 2013). Accessed May 19, 2013.

12. Steve Bates, "Science Friction," *HR Magazine* (July 2001), 34–44.

13. Joanne Wojcik, "Wired into Workplace Privacy," *Business Insurance* (September 15, 2003), 28.

14. Judy Greenwald, "NASA Background Checks Upheld." Business Insurance 45, no. 4 (January 24, 2011): 3–19.

15. Ibid.

16. Ibid.

17. http://www.privacyrights.org, "Fact Sheet 16: Employment Background Checks" (updated May 2013). Accessed May 20, 2013.

18. Ibid.

19. Ibid.

20. Ibid.

21. Ibid.

22. Ibid.

23. Jim Giuliana, "Recruiting: EEOC Warns About Background Checks," *HR Morning* (January 6, 2010), http:// www.hrmorning.com/recruiting-eeoc-warns-aboutbackground-checks/. Accessed May 20, 2013.

24. http://www.privacyrights.org, "Fact Sheet 16: Employment Background Checks" (updated May 2013). Accessed May 20, 2013.

25. "SHRM Finds Fewer Employers Using Background Checks in Hiring, SHRM Press Release (July 19, 2012), http://www.shrm.org/about/pressroom/PressReleases/Pages/BackgroundChecks.aspx. Accessed May 23, 2013.

26. Chad Terhune, "The Trouble with Background Checks," BusinessWeek (June 9, 2008), 54–57.

27. Ibid.

28. Ibid., 56.

29. Judy Greenwald, "Background Check Policies Under Review by Employers." Business Insurance 46, no. 43 (November 5, 2012), p. 11.

30. https://www.privacyrights.org/fs/fs16-bck.htm. Accessed May 20, 2013.

31. James R. Bovard, "Perform Criminal Background Checks at Your Peril," *The Wall Street Journal* (February 13, 2013), A15.

32. Ibid.

33. Kenneth F. Englade, "The Business of the Polygraph," *Across the Board* (October 1982), 21–22.

34. James H. Coil III and Barbara Jo Call, "Congress Targets Employers' Use of Polygraphs," *Employment Relations Today* (Spring 1986), 23.

35. David E. Terpstra, R. Bryan Kethley, Richard T. Foley, and Wanthanee Limpaphayom, "The Nature of Litigation Surrounding Five Screening Devices," *Public Personnel Management* (Spring 2000), 43–54.

36. Diana Ray, "Can They Fool the Polygraph?" *Insight* (July 2–9, 2001), 18–19.

37. Shalisa Ladd and Jeff L. Berry, "The Potential Role of fMRI in Lie Detection," eRadimaging (January 1, 2013), http://www.eradimaging.com/site/article.cfm?ID=792. Accessed May 20, 2013.

38. Anne Eisenberg, "Software That Listens for Lies," *The New York Times* (December 3, 2011).

39. James Hirsen, "Privacy Concerns Over Google Glass," *Newsmax* (March 18, 2013), http://www.newsmax.com/Hirsen/Privacy-Google-Glass-software/2013/03/18/id/495158. Accessed May 20, 2013.

40. Nick Barron, "Honest to Goodness," *SC Magazine: For IT Security Professionals* (June/July 2009), 17.

41. Gregory M. Lousig-Nont, "Seven Deadly Hiring Mistakes," *Supervision* (April 2003), 18–19.

42. David W. Arnold and John W. Jones, "Who the Devil's Applying Now?" *Security Management* (March 2002), 85–88.

43. Michael Sturman and David Sherwyn, "The Utility of Integrity Testing for Reducing Worker's Compensation Costs," *Cornell Hospital Quarterly* (November 2009), 432–445.

44. Larry R. Seegull and Emily J. Caputo, "When a Test Turns Into a Trial," *ABA Business Law Section* (January/February, 2006), http://apps.americanbar.org/buslaw/blt/2006-01-02/caputo.html. Accessed May 20, 2013.

45. Sturman and Sherwyn, 423–445.

46. Bill Roberts, "Your Cheating Heart," *SHRM HR Magazine* (June 1, 2011), http://www.shrm.org/publications/hrmagazine/editorialcontent/2011/0611/pages/0611roberts.aspx. Accessed May 20, 2013.

47. Joseph Walker, "Do New Job Tests Foster Bias?" *The Wall Street Journal - Eastern Edition*, September 20, 2012., B2,

48. http://www.questdiagnostics.com/home/physicians/health-trends/drug-testing. Accessed May 20, 2013.

49. Ibid.

50. "Drug of Abuse Reference Guide," LabCorp, https://www.labcorpsolutions.com/images/Drugs_of_Abuse_Reference_Guide_Flyer_3166.pdf. Accessed July 5, 2013.

51. Leslie D. Miller, "Changing State Marijuana Laws and Employer Drug Testing Policies," *The Manufacturers Alliance for Productivity and Innovation (MAPI)* (April 23, 2013), http://www.mapi.net/changing-state-marijuana-laws-and-employer-drug-testing-policies. Accessed May 20, 2013.

52. Ibid.

53. Marc D. Greenwood, "FALSE Positives," *Fire Chief* (April 2003), 48–53.

54. ACOEM, "Ethical Aspects of Drug Testing," http://www.acoem.org/guidelines.aspx?id=722 (February 4, 2009). Accessed May 20, 2013.

55. Jane Easter Bahls, "Dealing with Drugs: Keep It Legal," *HR Magazine* (March 1998), 104–116.

56. Ibid.

57. "ADA Claim Fails to Disturb Refusal to Hire Based on Positive Test Results," *Venulex Legal Summary* (2009) 1–3.

58. Eileen Smith, "How to Choose the Right EAP for Your Employee," *Employee Benefit News* (November 1, 2000).

59. Sean Fogarty, "EAPs New Role: A Core Strategic Element," *Employee Benefits Advisor* (April 2010), 40–46.

60. Ibid.

61. http://press.amanet.org/press-releases/177/2007-electronic- monitoring-surveillance-survey/. Accessed May 21, 2013.

62. John P. Mello, Jr., "Camera Phones a Flashpoint of Concern," *Boston Works* (April 11, 2004), G7.

63. Nancy J. King, "Electronic Monitoring to Promote National Security Impacts Workplace Privacy," *Employee Responsibilities and Rights Journal* (September 2003), 127–147.

64. Ibid.

65. http://www.epic.org/privacy/workplace. Accessed May 20, 2013.

66. Susan K. Livio, "N.J. Supreme Court Upholds Privacy of Personal E-Mails Accessed at Work," *NJ.com* (March 30, 2010), http://www.nj.com/news/index.ssf/2010/03/nj_supreme_court_sets_new_ruli.html Accessed May 21, 2013.

67. Ibid.

68. Ibid.

69. http://epic.org/amicus/hamilton/. (December 13, 2012). Accessed May 23, 2013.

70. Ibid.

71. Jessica Goldenberg, "Protecting Privacy or Enabling Fraud? Employee Social Media Password Protection Laws May Clash with FINRA Rules" (May 8, 2013), http://privacylaw.proskauer.com/2013/05/articles/california/protecting-privacy-or-enabling-fraud-employee-social-media-password-protection-laws-may-clash-with-finra-rules/. Accessed May 20, 2013.

72. Ibid.

73. http://press.amanet.org/press-releases/177/2007-electronic-monitoring-surveillance-survey/. Accessed May 21, 2013.

74. Frederick S. Lane, III, *The Naked Employee* (New York: AMACOM, 2003).

75. Calum MacLeod, "Will 1,127 Deaths Move the Needle for U.S. Shoppers?" *USA Today* (May 16, 2013), http://www.usatoday.com/story/news/world/2013/05/16/bangladesh-collapse-labor-garment-factories/2156413/. Accessed May 21, 2013; Christina Larson, "In China, Politically Connected Firms Have Higher Worker Death Rates," *Bloomberg BusinessWeek* (January 28, 2013), http://www.businessweek.com/articles/2013-01-28/in-china-corrupt-officials-and-worker-deaths. Accessed May 21, 2013.

76. http://www.ilo.org/global/topics/safety-and-health-at-work/lang–en/index.htm. Accessed May 21, 2013.

77. http://www.law.cornell.edu/wex/workplace_safety. Accessed May 21, 2013.

78. Joseph P. Kahn, "When Bad Management Becomes Criminal," *Inc.* (March 1987), 47.

79. David R. Spiegel, "Enforcing Safety Laws Locally," *The New York Times* (March 23, 1986), 11F.

80. "Union Carbide Fights for Its Life," *BusinessWeek* (December 24, 1984), 52–56.

81. http://www.unioncarbide.com/about/index.htm (2010).

82. "By the Numbers Operation at Morgan Stanley Finds Its Human Side," *The New York Times* (September 16, 2001), section 3, 8; "War on Terrorism: The Victims—Snapshot of the Briton Who Became an American Hero,

Seconds Before Death," *The Independent* (September 27, 2001), 3.

83. http://www.osha.gov/pls/oshaweb/owadisp.show_document?p_table=FEDERAL_REGISTER&p_id=13349. Accessed May 21, 2013.

84. Cole A. Wist and Hugh C. Thatcher, "Workplace Violence: An American Secret," *Labor Employment and Law* (Winter 2010), 6.

85. Ibid.

86. http://www.osha.gov/SLTC/workplaceviolence/. Accessed May 21, 2013.

87. Ibid.

88. Cammie Chaumont Menendez and Bobbie L. Dillon. "Workplace Violence: Impact, Causes, and Prevention." *Work* 42.1 (2012): 15–20.

89. Wist and Thatcher, 6.

90. "Workplace Violence: New Regulation, Threats and Best Practices," *Security Director's Report* (May 2010), 1–11.

91. Ibid.

92. http://www.osha.gov/OshDoc/data_General_Facts/factsheet-workplace-violence.pdf. Accessed May 21, 2013.

93. Stephanie Armour, "Companies, Survivors Suffer Years after Violence at Work," *USA Today* (July 9, 2003), 3A.

94. Ibid., 3A.

95. Ibid.

96. Sarah Wheaton and Shaila Dewan, "Professor Said to Be Charged after 3 Are Killed in Alabama," *The New York Times* (February 12, 2010), http://www.nytimes.com/2010/02/13/us/13alabama.html. Accessed May 21, 2013.

97. Wist and Thatcher, 6.

98. Ibid.

99. Otto Friedrich, "Where There's Smoke," *Time* (February 23, 1987), 23.

100. http://www.epa.gov/smokefree/healtheffects.html (updated April 30, 2007). Accessed May 21, 2013.

101. Christian Nordqvist, "Second Hand Smoke Kills Says World Health Organization," *Medical News Today* (May 31, 2010), http://www.medicalnewstoday.com/articles/ 190429.php. Accessed May 21, 2013.

102. Ibid.

103. "How Balanced Are You?" *IESE Insight* 12 (2012), 9.

104. Nancy R. Lockwood, "Work/Life Balance: Challenges and Solutions," *HR Magazine* (June 2003), 2–11.

105. http://www.shrm.org/research/surveyfindings/articles/documents/2011_emp_benefits_report.pdf. Accessed May 21, 2013.

106. "Military Expansions in FMLA Are Now Law," *HR Focus* (January 2010), 2.

107. Ibid.

108. http://fmlaonline.com/. Accessed May 21, 2013.

109. Ibid.

110. Mark Schoeff, "Department of Labor Study Reveals FMLA Challenges," *Workforce Management* (July 23, 2007), 8–10.

19

Employment Discrimination and Affirmative Action

**CHAPTER
LEARNING
OUTCOMES**

After studying this
chapter, you should be
able to:

1. Chronicle the U.S.
civil rights movement
and minority progress
in the past 50 years.

2. Outline the essentials
of the federal
discrimination laws.

3. Define disparate
treatment and disparate
impact, and give
examples of each.

4. Elaborate on issues
in employment
discrimination relating
to race, color, national
origin, sex, age, religion,
sexual orientation, and
disability.

5. Identify the different
types of affirmative
action and compare and
contrast them to each
other.

In the two preceding chapters, we discussed employee rights issues that affect virtually everyone in the workplace. In this chapter, we focus on that group of stakeholders whose employment rights are protected by discrimination laws. In the United States, we have **protected groups** who have federal legal protection from discrimination based on aspects such as race, color, religion, national origin, sex (including pregnancy), age, or disability.[1] In addition to these federal protections, 21 states and the District of Columbia have laws that protect individuals from employment discrimination based on sexual orientation.[2] Many of the issues we examine in this chapter have emerged from the general belief that certain employees are likely to face discrimination because of the above-listed attributes and that they have workplace rights that should be protected.

In the United States, federal antidiscrimination laws date back to the U.S. Constitution—in particular, the First, Fifth, and Fourteenth Amendments, which were designed to forbid religious discrimination and deprivation of employment rights without due process. There were also the Civil Rights Acts of 1866, 1870, and 1871, which were based on these amendments. However, none of these acts was ever effective. Most authorities agree that the Civil Rights Act of 1964 was the effective beginning of the employee protection movement, particularly for those special groups that we will discuss in this chapter.

In recessionary times, we must use the term "protected" with utmost care. It is true that the protected groups are protected from discrimination by the law. However, they are not necessarily protected from the impacts of a global economic crisis. In the United States, young minority men bore a disproportionately bigger burden of the layoffs in the recession.[3] This was especially painful, as they had not earned as much as other workers prior to their layoffs.[4] This phenomenon was felt worldwide. In Great Britain, ethnic minorities experienced the greatest rise in unemployment stemming from the recession.[5] The recession also took a great toll on woman and girls, including Nicaraguan women who reduced their food intake; Cambodian girls who were forced to drop out of school and become domestic workers; and young Greek women who faced an unemployment rate of 67 percent, compared with 44 percent for men in 2011.[6] In addition, we must remember that legal protection is often not enough. It is very difficult to identify and prove discrimination.

Civil rights issues among protected groups are subjects of intense debate. Although there is basic acceptance of the idea of groups' workplace rights being protected, the extent of this protection and the degree to which governmental policy should act to accelerate the infusion of protected groups into the workforce and into higher-paying jobs remain controversial topics. To explore these and related issues, we will cover the following major topics in this chapter: the civil rights movement, federal laws that protect against employment discrimination, the meaning of discrimination, a variety of issues related to employment discrimination, and finally, affirmative action in the workplace.

The Civil Rights Movement

It would take volumes to trace thoroughly the historical events that ultimately led to the passage of the first significant piece of civil rights legislation in the modern period—the Civil Rights Act of 1964. The act grew out of conflict that had been apparent for years but that erupted in the 1950s and 1960s in the form of protests and boycotts.[7]

Equal opportunity was supposed to be everyone's birthright, but not everyone shared this American dream. Things began to change because of individuals who had the courage to stand up for their rights as U.S. citizens.

On December 1, 1955, Mrs. Rosa Parks, a black department store worker, was arrested for refusing to yield her bus seat to a white man. Out of that brave act grew another—a bus boycott by African Americans. One of the leaders of the boycott was a young minister, Dr. Martin Luther King, Jr. After the bus boycott came years of demonstrations, marches, and battles with police. Television coverage depicted scenes of civil rights demonstrators being attacked by officials with cattle prods, dogs, and fire hoses. Along with the violence that grew out of confrontations between protestors and authorities came the stark awareness of the economic inequality between the races that existed in the United States at that time.[8] Against this backdrop of African Americans and other minorities being denied their share in the American ideal of equal opportunity in employment, it should have been no surprise that Congress finally acted in dramatic fashion, passing the Civil Rights Act of 1964.[9]

The women's movement began in the 1970s. Women's groups began to see that the workplace situation was little better for women than for African Americans and other minorities. Despite the fact that the labor participation rate for women was growing, women were still occupying low-paying jobs. They were making some small inroads into managerial and professional jobs, but progress was very slow. Women, for the most part, were still in the lower paying "women's jobs," such as bank teller, secretary, waitress, and laundry worker.[10] The 1990s then began with the next major civil rights movement, the disability rights movement. The Americans with Disabilities Act of 1990 (ADA) was designed not only to stop discrimination against people with disabilities, but also to open up access to buildings and transportation, which in turn opened up access to employment.

Now, in the 21st century, new challenges arise while old problems remain. One of the most significant issues arising in the new millennium has been the changing workforce composition. The U.S. Bureau of Labor Statistics projects that, over the 2010 to 2020 period, every race and ethnicity in the labor market will grow, except the percentage of White non-Hispanics in the U.S. workforce, which is expected to decline.[11] The labor force will be older and composed of more women.[12] The challenge for business will be to assimilate this increasingly diverse workforce. Another challenge for business is to determine how to respond to changing social values and the implications of new technologies. Sexual orientation and gender identity are increasingly receiving protected status from states and large organizations, while not being protected at the federal level. This creates challenges for firms with operations throughout the country. Genetic testing has opened the door to other forms of discrimination; federal law now prohibits employers from using genetic information when making hiring, firing, promotion, or job placement decisions. Diversity issues will continue to evolve with time and employers must stay aware of shifts in this changing landscape.

An indispensable way to understand the changing public policy with respect to employment discrimination is to examine the evolution of federal laws prohibiting discrimination. Once we have a better appreciation of the legal status of protected groups, we can more completely understand the complex issues that have arisen with respect to the evolving meaning of discrimination and its relationship to related workforce issues.

Federal Laws Prohibiting Discrimination

This section provides an overview of the major laws that have been passed in the United States to protect workers against discrimination. We will focus our discussion on legislation at the federal level that has been created in the past 60 years. We will discuss issues arising from the various forms of discrimination in more detail later in this chapter. We should keep in mind that there are state and local laws that address many of these same topics, but lack of space prevents their consideration here. Our purpose in this section is to provide an overview of antidiscrimination laws and the major federal agencies that enforce those laws.

Title VII of the Civil Rights Act of 1964

Title VII of the Civil Rights Act of 1964, as amended, prohibits discrimination in hiring, promotion, discharge, pay, fringe benefits, and other aspects of employment on the basis of race, color, religion, sex, or national origin. It was extended to cover federal, state, and local employers and educational institutions by the Equal Employment Opportunity Act of 1972. The amendment to Title VII also gave the Equal Employment Opportunity Commission (EEOC) the authority to file suits in federal district court against employers in the private sector on behalf of individuals whose charges had not been successfully conciliated. In 1978, Title VII was amended to include the Pregnancy Discrimination Act, which requires employers to treat pregnancy and pregnancy-related medical conditions in the same manner as any other medical disability with respect to all terms and conditions of employment, including employee health benefits.[13]

Title VII also prohibits firms from retaliating against employees who file discrimination claims. In 2006, the U.S. Supreme Court strengthened the anti-retaliation provisions of Title VII. The Court ruled that an employee could establish a retaliation claim even when they were not terminated or demoted. Any action that would "cause a worker to think twice" about lodging a discrimination complaint is sufficient (e.g., being transferred to a less desirable position at the same pay).[14] The Court determined that lower courts had established a "jump off the page and slap you in the face" standard that was unacceptable.[15] In 2010, the U.S. Supreme Court ruled unanimously that the lawsuit clock does not begin when a biased hiring test is administered. Instead, it resets each time an employer uses the biased tests to make hiring decisions. The alternative, as Justice Scalia noted when he wrote the court's opinion, would be unending ongoing

FIGURE 19-1

Title VII of the Civil Rights Act of 1964

EMPLOYMENT discrimination based on race, color, religion, sex, or national origin is prohibited by Title VII of the Civil Rights Act of 1964.

Title VII covers private employers, state and local governments, and educational institutions that have 15 or more employees. The federal government, private and public employment agencies, labor organizations, and joint labor–management committees for apprenticeship and training also must abide by the law.

It is illegal under Title VII to discriminate in

- Hiring and firing;
- Compensation, assignment, or classification of employees;
- Transfer, promotion, layoff, or recall;
- Job advertisements;
- Recruitment;
- Testing;
- Use of company facilities;
- Training and apprenticeship programs;
- Fringe benefits;

- Pay, retirement plans, and disability leave; or
- Other terms and conditions of employment.

Under the law, pregnancy, childbirth, and related medical conditions must be treated in the same manner as any other non-pregnancy related illness or disability.

Title VII prohibits retaliation against a person who files a charge of discrimination, participates in an investigation, or opposes an unlawful employment practice.

Employment agencies may not discriminate in receiving, classifying, or referring applications for employment or in their job advertisements.

Labor unions may not discriminate in accepting applications for membership, classifying members, referrals, training and apprenticeship programs, and advertising for jobs. It is illegal for a labor union to cause or try to cause an employer to discriminate. It is also illegal for an employer to cause or try to cause a union to discriminate.

Source: U.S. Equal Employment Opportunity Commission, http://www.eeoc.gov/laws/statutes/titlevii.cfm. Accessed May 29, 2013.

discrimination: "If an employer adopts an unlawful practice and no timely charge is brought, it can continue using the practice indefinitely, with impunity, despite ongoing disparate impact."[16]

Figure 19-1 presents an overview of Title VII's coverage.

Age Discrimination in Employment Act of 1967

The **Age Discrimination in Employment Act (ADEA)** protects workers aged 40 years and older from arbitrary age discrimination in hiring, discharge, pay, promotions, fringe benefits, and other aspects of employment. It is designed to promote employment of people based on ability, rather than age, as well as to help employers and workers find ways to meet problems arising from the impact of aging on employment. The Act does not protect employees under age forty from age discrimination, but it does protect anyone from retaliation for complaining about age discrimination or being closely associated with someone who does.[17]

Like the provisions of Title VII, the ADEA does not apply where age is a **bona fide occupational qualification (BFOQ)**—a qualification that ordinarily might be argued as being a basis for discrimination, but for which a company can legitimately argue that it is job related and necessary. For example, being young can be a BFOQ when the job is playing a child in a TV commercial.[18] The act also does not bar employers from differentiating among employees based on reasonable factors other than age.[19]

Equal Pay Act of 1963

As amended, this act prohibits sex discrimination in payment of wages to women and men who perform substantially equal work in the same establishment. Passage of this landmark law marked a significant milestone in helping women, who are the chief victims of unequal pay, to achieve equality in their paychecks.[20] Figure 19-2 summarizes other details of the **Equal Pay Act of 1963**.

The Equal Pay Act received a great deal of attention in 2007, when the U.S. Supreme Court heard the *Ledbetter v. Goodyear Tire & Rubber Co.* case, in which the plaintiff, Lilly Ledbetter, alleged that she had been paid less than her male counterparts but was unaware of the discrimination until years after the decision on her pay had been made. The question at hand was whether the clock on the statute of limitations began ticking with the original pay decision or whether it was reset each time a paycheck was made.[21] The Supreme Court decided that the statute of limitations began running from the time of the original pay decision, so, in effect, an employee must file a complaint within 180 days of the action that first sets the discriminatory pay, irrespective of its ongoing impact on the employee.[22] The problem with this requirement is that it often takes time for an employee to learn that her pay is lower than her male counterparts. The **Lilly Ledbetter Fair Pay Act of 2009** effectively undid the Court's decision, stipulating that the clock reset each time a discriminatory paycheck was issued.[23]

Rehabilitation Act of 1973, Section 503

This law, as amended, prohibits job discrimination on the basis of a disability. It applies to employers holding federal contracts or subcontracts. In addition, it requires these employers to engage in affirmative action to employ the disabled, a concept we will discuss later in this chapter. Related to this act is the Vietnam Era Veterans Readjustment Assistance Act of 1974, which also prohibits discrimination and requires affirmative action among federal contractors or subcontractors.[24]

FIGURE 19-2

Equal Pay Act of 1963

The Equal Pay Act (EPA) prohibits employers from discriminating between men and women on the basis of sex in the payment of wages where they perform substantially equal work under similar working conditions in the same establishment. The law also prohibits employers from reducing the wages of either sex to comply with the law.

A violation may exist where a different wage is paid to a predecessor or successor employee of the opposite sex. Labor organizations may not cause employers to violate the law.

Retaliation against a person who files a charge of equal pay discrimination, participates in an investigation, or opposes an unlawful employment practice also is illegal.

The law protects virtually all private employees, including executive, administrative, professional, and outside sales employees who are exempt from minimum wage and overtime laws. Most federal, state, and local government workers also are covered.

The law does not apply to pay differences based on factors other than sex, such as seniority, merit, or systems that determine wages based on the quantity or quality of items produced or processed.

Many EPA violations may be violations of Title VII of the Civil Rights Act of 1964, which also prohibits sex-based wage discrimination. Such charges may be filed under both statutes.

Sources: Information for the Private Sector and State and Local Governments: EEOC (Washington: Equal Employment Opportunity Commission), 9. Also see U.S. Department of Labor, Equal Pay Act of 1963, as amended, http://www.dol.gov/oasam/regs/statutes/equal_pay_act.htm. Accessed May 29, 2013.

Americans with Disabilities Act

The **Americans with Disabilities Act (ADA) of 1990**, as amended in 2008, prohibits discrimination based on physical or mental disabilities in private places of employment and public accommodation, in addition to requiring transportation systems and communication systems to facilitate access for the disabled. The ADA was modeled after the Rehabilitation Act of 1973, which applies to federal contractors and grantees.[25] The basic provisions of the ADA are detailed in Figure 19-3.

Essentially, the ADA gives individuals with disabilities civil rights protections similar to those provided to individuals based on race, sex, national origin, and religion. The ADA applies not only to private employers but also to state and local governments, employment agencies, and labor unions. Employers of 15 or more employees are covered.

The ADA prohibits discrimination in all employment practices, including job application procedures, hiring, firing, advancement, compensation, training, and other terms, conditions, and privileges of employment. If a person's disability makes it difficult for him or her to function, firms are expected to make **reasonable accommodations** if doing so does not represent an **undue hardship** for the firm. The act covers qualified individuals with disabilities. Qualified individuals are those who can perform the **essential functions** of the job.[26] The definition of essential function is sometimes difficult to determine. A case in point occurred with golfer Casey Martin when he applied to the Professional Golfer's Association (PGA) for permission to ride a cart in PGA tournaments when other players were required to walk the course. Martin has a rare and debilitating circulatory condition in his right leg that causes him severe pain when he walks. Much controversy ensued over whether walking the golf course was an essential function of playing professional golf. The Supreme Court subsequently ruled that he could use a cart because providing the cart was a reasonable accommodation and his use of the cart would not fundamentally alter the game. In 2013, the U.S. Court of Appeals ruled that a task that is done rarely could still be an essential function if it is in the job description.[27] The court ruled against a trucking supervisor who sued after being terminated because an eye injury meant he could no longer be certified to drive large trucks, an activity he rarely performed in his position.[28] Because driving was included in the job description, the court ruled it was an essential function.[29]

The definition of disability includes people who have physical or mental impairments that substantially limit one or more **major life activities**, such as: "caring for oneself, performing manual tasks, seeing, hearing, eating, sleeping, walking, standing, sitting, reaching, lifting, bending, speaking, breathing, learning, reading, concentrating, thinking, communicating, interacting with others, and working."[30] A disability is defined using a three-pronged approach, with respect to an individual who:[31]

- has a physical or mental impairment that substantially limits one or more major life activities, or
- has a record of a physical or mental impairment that substantially limited a major life activity, or
- is perceived of as having a disability.

The Supreme Court has upheld an individual's right to sue the state under the ADA. Paraplegic and confined to a wheelchair, George Lanc was ordered to appear on the second floor of a court that featured no ramps or elevators. He could not climb the steps and so he crawled up the stairs to comply with the order. When he was ordered to appear in court a second time, Lane refused to crawl or be carried. He was subsequently arrested for failing to appear in court. He filed a $100,000 discrimination suit against the

FIGURE 19-3

The Americans with Disabilities Act

Title I of the Americans with Disabilities Act of 1990 prohibits private employers, state and local governments, employment agencies, and labor unions from discriminating against qualified individuals with disabilities in job application procedures, hiring, firing, advancement, compensation, job training, and other terms, conditions, and privileges of employment. The ADA covers employers with 15 or more employees, including state and local governments. It also applies to employment agencies and to labor organizations. The ADA's nondiscrimination standards also apply to federal sector employees under Section 501 of the Rehabilitation Act, as amended, and its implementing rules.

An individual with a disability is a person who

- Has a physical or mental impairment that substantially limits one or more major life activities;
- Has a record of such an impairment; or
- Is regarded as having such an impairment.

A qualified employee or applicant with a disability is an individual who, with or without reasonable accommodation, can perform the essential functions of the job in question. Reasonable accommodation may include, but is not limited to

- Making existing facilities used by employees readily accessible to and usable by persons with disabilities;
- Restructuring jobs (for parallelism), modifying work schedules, and reassigning to a vacant position;
- Acquiring or modifying equipment or devices; adjusting or modifying examinations, training materials, or policies; and providing qualified readers or interpreters.

An employer is required to make a reasonable accommodation to the known disability of a qualified applicant or employee if it would not impose an "undue hardship" on the operation of the employer's business. Reasonable accommodations are adjustments or modifications provided by an employer to enable people with disabilities to enjoy equal employment opportunities. Accommodations vary depending on the needs of the individual applicant or employee. Not all people with disabilities (or even all people with the same disability) will require the same accommodation. For example,

- A deaf applicant may need a sign language interpreter during the job interview.
- An employee with diabetes may need regularly scheduled breaks during the workday to eat properly and monitor blood sugar and insulin levels.
- A blind employee may need someone to read information posted on a bulletin board.
- An employee with cancer may need to leave for radiation or chemotherapy treatments.

An employer does not have to provide a reasonable accommodation if it imposes an "undue hardship." Undue hardship is defined as an action that requires significant difficulty or expense when considered in light of factors such as an employer's size, financial resources, and the nature and structure of its operation.

An employer is not required to lower quality or production standards to make an accommodation, nor is it obligated to provide personal use items such as glasses or hearing aids.

An employer generally does not have to provide a reasonable accommodation unless an individual with a disability has asked for one. If an employer believes that a medical condition is causing a performance or conduct problem, it may discuss with the employee how to solve the problem and ask if the employee needs a reasonable accommodation. Once a reasonable accommodation is requested, the employer and the individual should discuss the individual's needs and identify the appropriate reasonable accommodation. Where more than one accommodation would work, the employer may choose the one that is less costly or is easier to provide.

It is also unlawful to retaliate against an individual for opposing employment practices that discriminate based on disability or for filing a discrimination charge, testifying, or participating in any way in an investigation, proceeding, or litigation under the ADA.

Sources: EEOC Facts about the Americans with Disabilities Act (Revised September 9, 2008). Also see Department of Justice, Americans with Disabilities Act of 1990, as amended, http://www.ada.gov/. Accessed May 29, 2013.

state of Tennessee. When the Supreme Court upheld his right to sue, it was seen as an indication that the Court was disinclined to let states' rights arguments prevail over civil rights.[32]

As the world of work changes, so do the obligations of companies to protect workers' rights. The ADA requires that firms make their places of business accessible to people with disabilities as long as doing so does not create an undue hardship. As businesses have moved their sales online, advocates for people with disabilities have filed suits to require them to make those websites accessible for people who are blind or deaf. Basically, they are seeking "the digital version of wheelchair ramps and self-opening doors."[33]

Pregnancy discrimination and genetic information nondiscrimination are two issues that fit under the issue of disabilities discrimination. Of course, only women get pregnant, so it would seem logical to categorize pregnancy under gender discrimination, but the law treats pregnancy as a temporary disability. Fetal protection policies are similar in that they represent a concern that unborn children will have future disabilities. Genetic information nondiscrimination is not a protected class per se; however, the protection of that private information protects people from discrimination based on possible future disabilities, so we will discuss it in the context of disabilities as well.

Pregnancy Discrimination. For some time, maternity leave has been an issue for women. In 1987, the Supreme Court upheld a California law that granted pregnant workers four months of unpaid maternity leave and guaranteed that their jobs would be waiting for them when they returned. Justice Thurgood Marshall argued, "By taking pregnancy into account, California's statute allows women, as well as men, to have families without losing their jobs."[34]

The **Pregnancy Discrimination Act of 1978**, an amendment to Title VII, requires employers to treat pregnancy and pregnancy-related medical conditions the same way as any other medical disability with respect to all terms and conditions of employment. Because of the Pregnancy Discrimination Act, the concept of maternity leave is outdated. In fact, companies are advised to make sure they do not have "maternity leave" policies. By using the term "maternity leave," companies imply that maternity is somehow different from other temporary disabilities.[35] A 2012 study shows that the Pregnancy Discrimination Act has had a positive impact upon the labor supply of women with children and, particularly, pregnant women.[36]

Fetal Protection Policies. Another related form of discrimination was identified when the Supreme Court ruled that **fetal protection policies** constituted sex discrimination. The decisive case was *UAW v. Johnson Controls, Inc.* Johnson Controls, like a number of other major firms, developed a policy of barring women of childbearing age from working in sites in which they, and their developing fetuses, might be exposed to such harmful chemicals as lead. Johnson Controls believed it was taking an appropriate action in protecting the women and their unborn children from exposure to chemicals. Eight current and former employees and the United Auto Workers (UAW) union, who argued that the policy was discriminatory and illegal under Title VII of the Civil Rights Act, brought a class-action lawsuit against Johnson Controls. A U.S. district court ruled in the company's favor, and the Chicago-based U.S. Court of Appeals for the Seventh Circuit affirmed that decision. The U.S. Supreme Court later reversed the appellate court, arguing that the policy was on its face discriminatory and that the company had not shown that women were more likely than men to suffer reproductive damage from lead.[37]

Even though the Supreme Court ruled that injured children, once born, would not be able to bring lawsuits against the company, several experts think it likely that such lawsuits will indeed be filed in the future. One expert said, "A mother can waive her own right to sue, but she can't waive the right of a child to bring suit. So, five or ten years down the line you might see children born with cognitive disabilities, and they could independently sue businesses." The UAW does not dispute this possibility and asserts that it should provide a major impetus for companies to make workplaces safer.[38] OSHA has identified reproductive health hazards as an area likely to experience an increase in litigation over time.[39] One thing is clear: companies must take care to assure that their employees are fully informed of all potential risks in the workplace.[40]

Genetic Information Nondiscrimination Act. The **Genetic Information Nondiscrimination Act (GINA)** is unique in that it is the first *preemptive* civil rights law in U.S. history.[41] Anti-discrimination laws typically respond to discrimination that has already happened. Genetic testing is so new that there is no significant history of discrimination; instead, GINA represents an effort to stop genetics-based discrimination before it occurs. The law prohibits employers from requiring, requesting, purchasing, or disclosing employees' genetic information; however, it does not prohibit employees from voluntarily disclosing genetic information to coworkers or to superiors.[42] GINA protects former employees as well as current ones and applies only to employers with fifteen or more employees.[43] Genetic information is defined broadly; it includes not only the information from employee genetic tests and medical history but also information from family members' tests and medical history.[44] Family members need not be blood relatives. The EEOC considered that employers might discriminate against spouses and adopted children because of concern about health care costs.

Civil Rights Act of 1991

The primary objective of the **Civil Rights Act of 1991** was to provide increased financial damages and jury trials in cases of intentional discrimination relating to sex, religion, race, disability, and national origin. Under the original Title VII, monetary awards were limited to such items as back pay, lost benefits, and attorney fees and costs. This 1991 act permitted the awarding of both compensatory and punitive damages. In addition, charges of unintentional discrimination were more difficult for employers to defend, because the Act shifted the burden of proof back to the employer.[45] Note that the act refers only to protected groups under Title VII and does not reference age or the ADEA. When Congress amended Title VII of the Civil Rights Act, it did not make a similar amendment for the ADEA: this has been a source of confusion in the courtroom since then.[46]

In 2010, the U.S. Supreme Court further raised the standard of proof for age discrimination cases in their decision regarding *Gross v. FBL Financial Services.* The court's opinion in *Gross* raised the standard of proof for employees charging age discrimination by disallowing "mixed motives" defenses. In other words, employees must do more than prove age was a motivating factor. Employees must show that "but for" age, the discrimination would not have occurred.[47] Efforts by Congress to enact legislation that would supersede the *Gross* decision have stalled. Speaking in favor of that proposed legislation, EEOC Chair Jacqueline Berrien said, "The *Gross* decision was a startling departure from decades of settled precedent developed in federal district and intermediate appellate courts. It erected a new, much higher (and what will often be an insurmountable) legal hurdle for victims of age-based employment decisions. Indeed, recent case law reveals that *Gross* already is constricting the ability of older workers to vindicate their rights under the ADEA, as well as other anti-discrimination statutes."[48]

Equal Employment Opportunity Commission

As the major federal body created to administer and enforce U.S. job bias laws, the **Equal Employment Opportunity Commission (EEOC)** deserves special consideration. Several other federal agencies also are charged with enforcing certain aspects of the discrimination laws and executive orders, but we will restrict our discussion to the EEOC because it is the most prominent agency in these affairs.

The EEOC has five commissioners and a general counsel appointed by the president and confirmed by the Senate. The five-member commission is responsible for making equal employment opportunity policy and approving all litigation the commission undertakes. The EEOC staff receives and investigates employment discrimination charges and complaints. If the commission finds reasonable cause to believe that unlawful discrimination has occurred, its staff attempts to conciliate the charges or complaints. When conciliation is not achieved, the EEOC may file lawsuits in federal district court against employers.[49] In 2012, the EEOC received 99,412 private sector workplace discrimination charges: retaliation (37,836), race (33,512), and sex discrimination, including sexual harassment and pregnancy (30,356) represented the charges that were filed most frequently.[50]

Expanded Meanings of Employment Discrimination

Over the years, it has been left to the courts to define the word *discrimination*, because it was not defined in Title VII. Over time, it has become apparent that two specific kinds of discrimination exist: **disparate treatment** and **disparate impact.**

Spotlight on Sustainability

Are Sustainability Advocates a New Protected Class?

As head of sustainability for Grainger, one of the United Kingdom's largest property firms, Rupert Dickinson would sometimes find himself in conflicts with other executives at the firm. For example, one top executive left his BlackBerry in London and then ordered a staff person to get on a plane, retrieve it, and bring it back to him. Dickinson believed that wasting jet fuel to return a BlackBerry (and other such environmentally inappropriate actions) were evidence of contempt for his sustainability beliefs. When he was later laid off, Dickinson filed suit. The judge decided that if one genuinely holds a belief in man-made climate change, and its alleged resulting moral imperatives, that can be a "philosophical belief." Grainger contends that Dickinson was let go when organizational restructuring made his position redundant. In the United Kingdom, it is unlawful to discriminate against a person on the grounds of their religious or philosophical beliefs. The case is still unfolding, but businesses are watching it carefully, believing that a finding for the plaintiff is likely to result in more workplace disputes.

Sources: Karen McVeigh, "Judge Rules Activist's Belief on Environment Akin to Religion," *guardian.co.uk* (November 9, 2009), http://www.guardian.co.uk/environment/2009/nov/03/tim-nicholson-climate-change-belief. Accessed May 24, 2013.; Richard Heap, "Beyond Belief," *Property Week* (June 5, 2009), http://www.building.co.uk/professional/beyond-belief/3142268.article. Accessed May 24, 2013; "Climate Change Worker Tim Nicholson Reaches Settlement," *BBC News* (April 15, 2010), http://news.bbc.co.uk/2/hi/uk_news/england/oxfordshire/8621703.stm. Accessed May 31, 2013.

Disparate Treatment

Initially, the word *discrimination* meant the use of race, color, religion, sex, or national origin as a basis for treating people differently or unequally. This form of discrimination is known as unequal treatment, or disparate treatment. Examples of disparate treatment might include refusing to consider African Americans for a job, paying women less than men are paid for the same work, or supporting any decision or rule with a racial or sexual premise or cause.[51] According to this simple view of discrimination, the employer could impose any criteria so long as they were imposed on all groups alike.[52] This view of discrimination equated nondiscrimination with color-blind decision-making. In other words, to avoid this direct kind of discrimination, one would simply treat all groups or individuals equally, without regard for color, sex, or other characteristics.[53]

Disparate Impact

Congress later clarified that its intent in prohibiting discrimination was to eliminate practices that contributed to economic inequality. What it found was that, although companies could adhere to the disparate treatment definition of discrimination, this did not eliminate all of the discrimination that existed. For example, a company could use two neutral, color-blind criteria for selection—a high school diploma and a standardized ability test. Minority group members might be treated the same under the criteria, but the problem arose when it became apparent that the policy of equal treatment resulted in unequal consequences for minorities. Minority members might be less likely to have high school diplomas, and those who took the test might be less likely to pass it. Therefore, a second, more expanded idea of what constituted discrimination was needed.

The Supreme Court had to decide whether an action was discriminatory if it resulted in unequal consequences in the *Griggs v. Duke Power Company* case.[54] Duke Power had required that employees transferring to other departments have a high school diploma or pass a standardized intelligence test. This requirement excluded a disproportionate number of minority workers. The court noted that there were nonminorities who performed satisfactorily and achieved promotions though they did not have diplomas. The court then reached the groundbreaking conclusion that it was the consequences of an employer's actions, not its intentions that determined whether discrimination had taken place. If any employment practice or test had an adverse or differential effect on minorities, it was a discriminatory practice.

An unequal impact, or disparate impact, means that fewer minorities are included in the outcome of the test or the hiring or promotion practice than would be expected by their numerical proportion. The court also held that a policy or procedure with a disparate impact would be permissible if the employer could demonstrate that it was a business- or job-related necessity. In the *Duke Power* case, however, a high school diploma and good scores on a general intelligence test did not have a clearly demonstrable relationship to successful performance on the job under consideration.[55]

The concept of "unequal impact" is quite significant, because it runs counter to so many traditional employment practices. For example, the minimum height and weight requirements of some police departments have unequal impact and have been struck down by courts because they tend to screen out women, people of Asian heritage, and Latinos disproportionately.[56] Several Supreme Court rulings have addressed the issue of the kind of evidence needed to document or prove discrimination. Typically, if a minority group does not have a success rate of at least 80 percent of that of the majority group, the practice may be considered to have an adverse impact unless business necessity can be proven.[57] When this **four-fifths rule** is triggered, the firm will not necessarily be found guilty of having a disparate impact. However, it will be incumbent upon the firm to show that the selection practice is job related and necessary for the business.[58]

The issue of disparate impact is often not easily resolved. For example, the EEOC determined that a strength test given to applicants for positions in a canned meat factory had an unlawful disparate impact; the company appealed the verdict but lost.[59] The job for which the applicants were applying required them to carry 35 pounds of sausage, and lift and load it, while walking approximately four miles a day. The strength test attempted to replicate the work by having applicants carry a 35-pound bar and loading it onto other bars. A nurse observed the test and had ultimate hiring authority based on her observations. Before the company began using the test, about 50 percent of the hires were females. By the time of the verdict, that number had dropped to 8 percent. A drop from 50 percent to 8 percent is dramatic, and that was the first indication that a disparate impact might be operating. On the surface, the relationship of the test to ultimate job responsibilities appeared strong, so it became necessary to determine why the percentage of women who passed the test was so low. The key problem was that the single evaluator (the nurse) added subjectivity to the process, as evidenced by the fact that the number of women hired declined with each testing and that when women and men received similar comments on their testing forms, only men were hired.[60]

The Supreme Court is widely expected to limit disparate impact theory when the opportunity arises. In 2009, the court ruled against the City of New Haven, Connecticut's decision not to certify firefighter exam results. The City of New Haven was concerned about disparate impact because too few minorities passed the test. However, the Supreme Court found that the act of discarding the test adversely affected those who had passed the test. They noted the efforts New Haven had made to create a fair test and ruled that a test should not be considered discriminatory unless there is a strong basis in evidence.[61] In 2013, the Court agreed to hear another case in which the township of Mt. Holly, New Jersey, is fighting a U.S. Fair Housing Act lawsuit from residents of a predominantly minority neighborhood that is scheduled to be demolished: At issue is whether the residents must prove intent to discriminate or disproportionate effect on minorities.[62] At this writing, the two sides are in settlement talks and, if the case is settled, it will be removed from the docket.[63]

Figure 19-4 summarizes the characteristics of disparate treatment and disparate impact.

Issues in Employment Discrimination

The essentials of the major federal laws on discrimination have been presented, and we have traced the evolution of the concept of discrimination. Now it is useful to briefly discuss the different issues that are related to the types of discrimination we have covered. It is also important to indicate some of the particular problems that have arisen with respect to each of the different issues.

FIGURE 19-4

Two Kinds of Employment Discrimination

Disparate Treatment	Disparate Impact
Primary discrimination	Secondary discrimination
Different treatment	Different results
Intentional discrimination	Unintentional discrimination
Biased actions	Neutral actions, biased impact
Different standards for different groups	Different consequences for different groups

Source: http://www.eeoc.gov/policy/docs/factemployment_procedures.html. Accessed May 28, 2013.

Inequality Persists Despite Diversity Efforts

In spite of the efforts previously described, racial and other forms of inequality persist. The reasons are not necessarily rooted in racism. Often, psychological or sociological factors, independent of race, are at play. For example, people have a tendency to be more comfortable with people who share their life experiences and preferences. The uncertainty of business leads us to seek homogeneity in our work groups. Rosabeth Kanter labeled this tendency to replicate ourselves when we hire and promote people as **homosocial reproduction**.[64] Homosocial reproduction explains, for example, why top management teams are typically not diverse.[65]

In her 2013 book, *The American Non-Dilemma: Racial Inequality without Racism,* Nancy DiTomaso explains how favoritism rather than racism can lead to racial inequality in the workplace.[66] She conducted 246 interviews with white men and women in three parts of the country and found that, throughout their lives, they got their jobs with the help and support of someone they knew (or someone their friends or family knew).[67] Almost every opportunity was attached to a connection created by being someone's relative, friend, or acquaintance, but the advantage was forgotten by the people who used that connection. She had to probe them in the interview to find out about it.[68] The friends or family members who provide the connection are almost always the same race as the person receiving the leg up. DiTomaso explains, "The mechanism that reproduces inequality, in other words, may be inclusion more than exclusion."[69]

Race and Ethnicity

Although racial discrimination was one of the first forms of discrimination to attract the focus of the civil rights legislation, it remains a major problem in workplaces in the United States and throughout the world. Although racial discrimination is always hurtful, the nature of its form and impact has been different for people of different races. Race discrimination includes discrimination based on ancestry or physical or cultural characteristics associated with a certain race, such as skin color, hair texture or styles, or certain facial features.[70]

First, it is important to discuss the special situation of Hispanics. The word *Hispanic* fails to capture the diversity in this population and sometimes creates confusion. The term was created by the U.S. government and was first used in the 1980 census. Hispanics are the only major minority group to be classified by the language they speak. They can be black (Cuba's population is 58 percent black), Asian (Peru's former President Fujimori is 100 percent Japanese), or any of a variety of races. Accordingly, many people prefer to be described as Latino (which includes people from Portugal) or as hailing from their country of origin (e.g., of Puerto Rican descent).[71] People who are Hispanic are faced with significant discrimination that can take the form of racial, national origin, and/or color discrimination.[72] To deal with this, and the complicating fact that people can be of mixed race or mixed heritage, the Equal Employment Opportunity Commission now uses seven categories to collect statistics about the U.S. workforce. They are:[73]

- Hispanic or Latino
- White (not Hispanic or Latino)
- Black or African American (not Hispanic or Latino)
- Native Hawaiian or Other Pacific Islander (not Hispanic or Latino)
- Asian (not Hispanic or Latino)
- American Indian or Alaska Native (not Hispanic or Latino)
- Two or More Races (not Hispanic or Latino)

In an increasingly diverse society, people are not easily characterized, but these categories help to give some sense of the aggregate makeup of the work force.

Color

Color bias is another issue that raises challenges in the workplace. As part of the Civil Rights Act of 1964, discrimination based on color has been illegal for a long period of time. As a practical matter, however, color bias has been largely misunderstood. The EEOC has clarified the definition of color discrimination. "Even though race and color clearly overlap, they are not synonymous. Thus, color discrimination can occur between persons of different races or ethnicities, or between persons of the same race or ethnicity. Although Title VII does not define 'color,' the courts and the EEOC read 'color' to have its commonly understood meaning—pigmentation, complexion, or skin shade or tone. Thus, color discrimination occurs when a person is discriminated against based on their lightness, darkness, or other color characteristic. Title VII prohibits race and color discrimination against all persons, including Caucasians."[74]

Most people do not realize that race and color are considered to be separate by law and both are covered by law, so many cases go unreported."[75] Nevertheless, some situations do surface. In June 2009, the EEOC sued a Puerto Rico–based furniture company for allegedly permitting a Puerto Rican store manager to harass a dark-complexioned Puerto Rican sales associate. The manager taunted him about his skin color (e.g., asking why he was "so black") and then fired him for complaining.[76]

Gender

Issues surrounding sex discrimination are different from those involving race, color, and national origin. The major issues for women today include (1) getting into professional and managerial positions and out of traditionally female-dominated positions, (2) achieving pay commensurate with that of men, (3) eliminating sexual harassment, and (4) being able to take maternity leave without losing their jobs. Some progress is being made on each of these fronts but more work remains to be done.

Women in Professional/Managerial Positions. The fact that, in 2013, only 4 percent of Fortune 500 firms are headed by women is an indication that progress in this area has been slow, given the percentage of women in the population.[77] The 2012 Catalyst Census found that one-fifth of Fortune 500 companies had 25 percent or female representation among executive officers; but more than one-fourth of Fortune 500 companies have no female executive officers.[78] In 2012, women held 14.3 percent of executive officer posts and were 8.1 percent of the executive top earners.[79] Some argue that it takes decades to become a CEO, so the pipeline for female CEOs is just starting to fill.[80] Others contend that women bear some responsibility. Sheryl Sandberg raised a media furor with her 2013 book, *Lean In*, which suggests women sabotage themselves by lacking self-confidence and not grabbing opportunities as they arise.[81] Of course, sex discrimination remains a key explanation for the disparity, and that explanation is supported by the scores of studies that show the significant pay discrepancy between men and women in the workplace.[82] One thing is clear: the explanation is not performance-driven. Hedge funds run by women outperform those run by men, male retail investors out-trade but underperform women, and companies with women at the helm outperform those run by men in the S&P 1500.[83] A possible remedy may be found in the rise of "stiletto networks," a phrase coined by author Pamela Ryckman in her 2013 book, *Stiletto Network: Inside the Women's Power Circles That Are Changing the Face of Business.*[84] Ryckman chronicles the groups of successful women throughout the United States who are forming groups to support each other in their careers. That support can range from information and introductions to partnerships and investment.[85]

Equal Pay and Promotion. The year 2013 marked the fiftieth anniversary of the Equal Pay Act. The April anniversary was especially apt because April is the fourth month of the year and women must work almost four extra months in the same jobs to make the same money as men.[86] The difference is from 18 to 23 cents per dollar, depending on the method of calculation.[87] Some observers have tried to explain the discrepancy by arguing that these statistics include women who lost both time and experience through extended maternity leave. However, the Bureau of Labor statistics shows that the gap exists at the start of women's careers, as well as for women who work full time.[88] The gap also exists for women in professional and technical occupations.[89] This issue affects families as well as the worker involved; a 2013 Pew study found that women are the sole or primary earners in 40 percent of households with children. Most are single mothers or domestic partners, but a 2013 Pew study found that wives earn more than their husbands in 22.5 percent of married households with children.[90]

The issues of pay and promotion are not easily untangled; women who are denied promotion will receive lower pay as a result of working in a lower paying position. The Walmart case illustrates this example. Hundreds of thousands of women who worked at Walmart sued the company for lost pay due to "discriminatory wages and career advancement."[91] They first approached the case as a class action but the Supreme Court, in a 5-4 split decision, ruled that they failed to prove the commonality of the claim. Justice Scalia said that they would have needed to point to companywide policies that had an effect on all the women in the class action.[92] The effort continues as plaintiffs file both regional and individual actions. Walmart's issues with gender discrimination are not likely to go away soon.

Sexual Harassment. Sexual harassment in the workplace is a worldwide problem with negative consequences that are pervasive and ongoing. A meta-analysis of sexual harassment studies found that victims of sexual harassment suffered a range of negative outcomes such as decreased job satisfaction, lower organizational commitment, withdrawal from work, poor physical and mental health, and even symptoms of posttraumatic stress disorder.[93]

Data from the EEOC report an escalating number of sexual harassment complaints. In 1986, 2,052 complaints were filed. By 2011, there were 11,363 sexual harassment complaints, 16 percent of which were filed by males.[94] Although the number of complaints in 2011 was still high, it is a decrease from the 15,889 complaints lodged in 1997.[95] With this background, let us now consider what Title VII and the EEOC have to say about sexual harassment as a type of sex discrimination.

The EEOC defines **sexual harassment** in the following way:

Unwelcome sexual advances, requests for sexual favors, and other verbal or physical conduct of a sexual nature constitute sexual harassment when submission to or rejection of this conduct explicitly or implicitly affects an individual's employment, unreasonably interferes with an individual's work performance, or creates an intimidating, hostile, or offensive work environment.

Implicit in this definition are two broad types of sexual harassment. First is what has been called **quid pro quo** harassment. This is a situation where something is given or received for something else. For example, a boss may make it explicit or implicit that a sexual favor is expected if the employee wants a pay raise or a promotion. Second is what has been referred to as **hostile work environment** harassment. In this type, nothing is given or received, but the employee perceives a hostile or offensive work environment by virtue of uninvited sexually oriented behaviors or materials being present in the workplace. Examples of this might include sexual teasing, jokes, or materials, such as pictures or cartoons, being present in the workplace. A 2012 study of EEOC settlements over a ten-year period found that almost all of the cases (98.5 percent) included a hostile environment aspect and most of the cases (89.1 percent) only involved a hostile environment, i.e., did not include a quid pro quo complaint.[96]

To clear up common misconceptions, the EEOC indicates that sexual harassment can occur in a variety of circumstances that include but are not limited to the following:[97]

- The victim as well as the harasser may be a woman or a man. The victim does not have to be of the opposite sex.
- The harasser can be the victim's supervisor, an agent of the employer, a supervisor in another area, a coworker, or a nonemployee.
- The victim does not have to be the person harassed but could be anyone affected by the offensive conduct.
- Unlawful sexual harassment may occur without economic injury to or discharge of the victim.
- The harasser's conduct must be unwelcome.

Figure 19-5 lists the kinds of experiences about which women are typically talking when they say they have been sexually harassed.

The stereotypical view of sexual harassment is of a male supervisor harassing a female subordinate. That scenario played out in the ten-year study of EEOC settlements, but it was not the only story. Harassers in all the settled cases were male, but the victims were not always female.[98] Same sex harassment occurred in 11.2 percent of the cases.[99] As expected, the harasser was a supervisor in 91.2 percent of the cases, but the harasser was a customer in one case and a contractor in another.[100] Most cases involved multiple plaintiffs. The number of plaintiffs ranged from one to one hundred with an average of nine, suggesting a pervasive environment of sexual harassment.[101]

Many people do not realize that Title IX offers protection against sexual harassment in a way that is essentially similar to Title VII. Title IX, the law that bans sex discrimination at schools receiving federal funds, is best known in its sports context for the formula that determines if schools are providing women with fair opportunities to play sports. Schools can be sued for monetary damages under Title IX for knowingly allowing sexual harassment to take place. There are four parts to the burden of proof:

FIGURE 19-5 Examples of Sexual Harassment Complaints	
- Being subjected to sexually suggestive remarks and propositions - Being sent on unnecessary errands through work areas where coworkers have an added opportunity to stare - Being subjected to sexual innuendo and joking - Being touched by a boss while working - Coworkers' "remarks" about a person sexually cooperating with the boss - Suggestive looks and gestures	- Deliberate touching and "cornering" - Suggestive body movements - Sexually oriented materials being circulated around the office - Pornographic cartoons and pictures posted or present in work areas - Pressure for dates and sexual favors - Boss's cruelty after sexual advances are resisted - A boss rubbing employee's back while he or she is typing

Note: It should be noted that these are "complaints." Whether each item turns out to be sexual harassment or not in the eyes of the law is determined in an official hearing or trial.

© Cengage Learning

(1) the school must be aware of the sexual harassment, (2) the school must fail to take steps to stop it, (3) the harassment must deny access to an educational opportunity, and (4) the harassment must take place in an educational setting.[102]

Supreme Court rulings underscore the importance of companies' remaining diligent in their efforts to discourage harassing behavior. For example, the Supreme Court ruled that employers might be held liable even if they did not know about the harassment or their supervisors never carried out any threatened job actions.[103] Clearly, employers must develop comprehensive programs to protect their employees from harassment. When businesses develop comprehensive and clear programs to prevent sexual harassment, they are legally rewarded. The Supreme Court ruled that good faith efforts to prevent and correct harassment are one prong of an "affirmative defense" companies can employ when charged with harassment. The second prong is proving the employee failed to take advantage of opportunities the firm provided for correction or prevention.[104]

In 2009, the Supreme Court expanded the scope of allowable sexual harassment claims when they ruled that an employee who was not the target of the harassment, but was fired for having cooperated with a sexual harassment investigation, should be protected and could sue for retaliation. Justice David Souter, writing for the seven-judge majority, said, "Nothing in the statute requires a freakish rule protecting an employee who reports discrimination on her own initiative but not one who reports the same discrimination in the same words when her boss asks a question."[105]

Other Forms of Employment Discrimination

Much of the attention surrounding employment discrimination has focused on racial and sexual discrimination. However, other important forms of discrimination represent critical issues for business today. It is important for managers to understand the many forms that discrimination can take in an increasingly diverse workforce and where courts currently stand on those issues.

ETHICS IN PRACTICE CASE

Gentleman's Club?

After only a few months of working with a new firm, my supervisor asked me to partake in a trip to Central America to tour our sister facility. The company had recently purchased a plant in Mexico and after several months of production, the main office needed to conduct a full inventory count. It sounded like a great opportunity and I gladly accepted the offer.

While abroad we spent several long days in the warehouse and when the work was finally complete, the Director of Operations took us out to celebrate at the company's expense. Following a nice dinner, a few of us guys were encouraged to continue the evening at a "Gentleman's Club." While there, the senior staff member began to urge us to take part in the extracurricular activities.

The peer pressure was rather intense, as the Director made it clear that either we would all participate or none of us would. Furthermore, he informed us that he would take care of the entire bill.

To the disappointment of some and the relief of others, I explained that I was not feeling well and preferred to return to the hotel. After we returned home the events of that evening were never openly discussed, however a few co-workers always throw me a look of disappointment.

1. Was I wrong to avoid participating in the activities going on? Might I have put my job at risk? Should I have been put in that situation?

2. Does this practice discriminate against any protected groups? Which one(s)?

3. Does this practice discriminate against any non-protected groups?

4. What should I do? Should I report my supervisor to the company? Will not participating in the "activities" affect my career trajectory? Should I care?

Contributed Anonymously

Religious Discrimination. Religious discrimination is a relatively new issue in the workplace, but it is one that is growing quickly: complaints more than doubled in the past fifteen years.[106] According to Jeanne Goldberg, senior attorney adviser for the EEOC, changes in the composition of the workforce have led to changing immigration patterns that increase the number of people from parts of the world with less familiar religious beliefs and practices. "The workforce also is aging," says Goldberg. "The older people get, the more important religion becomes to them."[107]

The Workplace Religious Freedom Act (WRFA) has been introduced each year for more than a decade and is again being reviewed by the U.S. Congress.[108] Its purpose is to disallow workplace restrictions on religious expression when those restrictions are arbitrary and/or unfair. According to the act's sponsor, former Senator John Kerry (D-Massachusetts), "No worker should have to choose between keeping a job and keeping faith with their cherished religious beliefs."[109] Opposition to the act comes mainly from business groups who fear it will be burdensome.[110] This legislation is designed to respond to the increase in incidents of religious bias by requiring employers to do more to accommodate religious beliefs. Under current standards, employers do not have to accommodate an employee's request if it imposes more than a "de minimus," or minimal, cost on the employer. The proposed legislation would raise the definition of undue hardship to "significant difficulty," effectively raising the employer's burden of proof.[111] The proposed standards reduce the requirements for employers to make reasonable accommodation to the three areas in which most requests for accommodation fall: religious clothing, grooming, and scheduling of religious holidays.[112] This narrowing is intended to address previous concerns that the bill was too broad.[113]

Research has shown that religious discrimination is a continuing problem. A 2012 study examined whether employers discriminate against Muslim women who wear the hijab (traditional headscarf). After controlling for location, applicant characteristics, nature of position and clientele, the researchers found that women who applied for a position wearing the hijab were less likely to receive job callbacks and more likely to encounter interviewers who were more negative and less interested.[114] Fortunately, some employers were more welcoming: those who already had a higher level of employee diversity were more likely to provide callbacks.[115]

Sometimes accommodation requires some ingenuity. IBM was faced with a challenge when a newly hired Muslim woman showed up for work the first day wearing the veil and was told she had to have her picture taken for the employee identification badge. For Muslim women, wearing the veil is a sign of modesty, and so the new employee objected on religious grounds to showing her face. IBM officials came up with an accommodation that met the needs of all involved. She had her picture taken in the veil and that was the picture on the employee identification badge she wore each day. In addition, a female photographer took her picture without the veil for a second badge, which she carried in her bag. It was agreed that if she ever needed to show that badge she would only do so to a female security officer.[116]

Retaliation. As noted earlier, no type of case is filed with the EEOC more frequently than those that are in response to retaliation. The same laws that protect individuals from discrimination protect them from being retaliated against for filing a discrimination claim. They also protect someone who is not the target of the discrimination but is retaliated against for supporting a person who files a claim. **Retaliation** can take many forms, including firing, demotion, or harassment. Retaliation also can be intimidation, threats, and untrue negative evaluations, denial of a promotion, negative references, increased surveillance, or any other kind of treatment that would make a person hesitant to file a claim. This prohibition against retaliation only applies to those who file claims on their

ETHICS IN PRACTICE CASE

Bigotry in the Bakery

Since my junior year in high school, I have been working in the same local supermarket. My main job was to get the bread set-up ready before the following day. After working in the bakery for quite some time, I began to notice the differences between how I have been treated compared to other coworkers. At first, I didn't notice the differences, but as time passed, I saw how they were making me do work that others in my department have never done. For example, the manager of the store realized that the ceiling of the bakery department was dirty and had accumulated pesticides. He told me to go up and clean the ceiling; he gave me no mask to protect myself from the pesticides. He just told me to go up and use Windex and clean the ceiling. I was hesitant at first but I completed the task without asking why. At the time, I was still new, so I didn't want to anger my boss. I just did as I was told.

Now, as this continued to happen, I asked my co-workers, who were \white, if they were ever told to complete this task. They all stated that none of them have ever been told to clean the ceiling and don't know of anyone in the store who has. They couldn't believe that I was cleaning the pesticide-laden ceiling.

For the past four years they have been making me do this, and it's not my job to do so. For this job, they should be hiring a cleaning crew to come in at night and clean the store. So I asked another Latino in the store who has been working there for more than 10 years how he is treated. He said that they have asked him do things around the store that aren't in his job description as well. Over the years, I've seen that the manager feels like it is okay for me to clean the ceilings even though that can potentially harm my health. It is not only happening to me, but other Hispanic employees as well. However, I try to be a good employee and listen. The same is true for the other Latinos in the store. They haven't spoken up to the manager, and they continue to perform these tasks.

1. Is this discrimination?
2. If it is, what should I do next? This job is important to me and I don't want to lose it.
3. Will the fact that I agreed to perform these dirty and dangerous tasks affect my case? I was always taught to work hard and earn the money I am paid. Was that the wrong thing to do?

Contributed Anonymously

own behalf and those who oppose discrimination by supporting victims, testifying at proceedings, or calling attention to unlawful practices. It does not apply to whistle-blowers who call attention to illegal acts other than discrimination (although other whistleblower protections may apply in those instances).

Sexual Orientation and Gender Identity Discrimination. Corporations have been faster than governments in instituting protections for lesbian, gay, bisexual, and transgender (LGBT) employees. As of 2013, 88 percent of the *Fortune* 500 companies include **sexual orientation** in their nondiscrimination policies and a majority of them(58 percent) provide domestic partner health insurance benefits to employees.[117] The greatest growth has been in prohibition of gender identity discrimination in the *Fortune* 500. In 2000, only three companies prohibited discrimination based on gender identity, but in 2013, 285 companies (57 percent) had instituted gender identity discrimination protections.[118] The higher a company's *Fortune* ranking, the more likely it is to provide protections for LGBT employees. Of the *Fortune* 10, nine prohibit discrimination based on sexual orientation, eight provide partner health benefits, and six prohibit discrimination based on gender identity.[119]

Business has been generally supportive of proposed federal and state legislation that would extend LGBT protections. The Business Coalition for Workplace Fairness is pushing for federal legislation to extend protections to both sexual orientation and gender identity.[120] The group supports the federal Employment Non-Discrimination Act (ENDA), a bipartisan piece of federal legislation that was reintroduced in the U.S. House of Representatives in 2013. Various versions of ENDA have been introduced in Congress every year since 1994.[121] Companies are also pushing for the Supreme Court to overturn the section of the Defense of Marriage Act (DOMA) that disallows recognition and federal benefits for same sex couples. More than 200 companies, including Citigroup, Apple, Microsoft, and Marriott, have signed a supporting brief that argues that the patchwork of state laws cost the companies time and money because they have to maintain dual policies.[122] The brief also maintains that the law undermines their business because it does not allow companies to treat all their employees equally and fairly.[123]

Gender identity, among other issues, addresses the special challenges for business of the treatment of transgender and transsexual employees. "Transgender" is an umbrella term that refers to people who express a gender that does not match the one on their original birth certificate or physically change their sex through surgery. "Transsexual" refers specifically to a person who is undergoing or has undergone sex change surgery.[124] This is not a new workplace issue. In 1993, the Washington State Supreme Court upheld Boeing Company's 1985 firing of a male software engineer who dressed in women's clothes and insisted on using the women's restroom while the sex-change operation was pending. The court ruled that discomfort with one's biological sex was not a handicap.[125] Since that time, the opinion of the courts and the stance of corporations have begun to change. In June 2004, the Sixth U.S. Circuit Court of Appeals (which covers Michigan, Ohio, Kentucky, and Tennessee) heard the case of a transsexual Ohio firefighter who had been fired. In the first such action by a federal court, the court ruled that Title VII of the Civil Rights Act of 1964 protects transsexuals and that the sex-stereotyping doctrine covers people who change their sex.[126] In 2010, the Eighth Circuit Court decided in favor of a motel clerk whom the company had deemed too masculine for a daytime front desk clerk position.[127] According to InsideCounsel, "The ruling confirms a legal principle that recently has gained support in circuit courts across the country: Although Title VII does not deal with sexual orientation, courts have found that the statute protects individuals from discrimination for breaking gender stereotypes."[128]

The concept of gender identity and its legal protections continues to evolve, but the trend against gender stereotyping carries implications for future protections for various gender identity issues. InsideCounsel offers employers the following advice: "Employers across the nation should be scrutinizing their policies and practices with regard to discrimination against transgender and transsexual people as states pass laws prohibiting discrimination on the basis of gender identity and courts interpret existing civil rights laws to protect those individuals."[129]

Affirmative Action in the Workplace

Affirmative action is the taking of positive steps to hire and promote people from groups that continue to be affected by a legacy of discrimination. The concept of affirmative action was formally introduced to the business world in 1965, when President Lyndon B. Johnson signed Executive Order 11246, the purpose of which was to require all firms doing business with the federal government to engage in affirmative actions to accelerate the movement of minorities into the workforce. Few people realize, however, that the federal government did not make a real commitment to affirmative action until the administration of President Richard M. Nixon, who revived the practice of racially motivated hiring preferences.[130] Companies today have affirmative action programs because they do business with the government, have begun the plans voluntarily, or have entered into them through collective bargaining agreements with labor unions.

The increase in employee diversity in workplaces throughout the world has shifted the debate. Companies are realizing that a diverse workforce is critical to business success;

many companies actively seek a workforce that not only matches the increasingly diverse world, but also draws upon an underutilized talent pool.[131] Affirmative action can become less of an issue when companies actively seek to increase diversity in their companies, as many of them are. Nevertheless, affirmative action remains an issue in access to educational opportunities as well as opportunities for under-represented groups to break new ground.

The meaning of affirmative action has changed since its introduction. It originally referred only to special efforts to ensure equal opportunity for members of groups that were historically subject to discrimination. More recently, the term has come to refer to programs in which members of such groups are given some degree of preference in determining access to positions from which they were formerly excluded.[132] It is important to remember that affirmative action is not just one thing, it can take many forms in a wide range of programs. Daniel Seligman identified four postures in two groupings that define the range that affirmative action may take.[133] He categorized the following affirmative action postures as "soft" or "weak":

1. *Passive nondiscrimination.* This posture involves willingness to treat the races and the sexes alike in matters of hiring, promotion, and pay decisions. This stance fails to recognize that discrimination leaves many prospective employees unaware of or unprepared for present opportunities.
2. *Pure affirmative action.* This posture involves a concerted effort to enlarge the pool of applicants so that no one is excluded because of past or present discrimination. At the point of decision to hire or promote, however, the company selects the most qualified applicant without regard to sex or race. Postures that Seligman termed "hard" or "strong" were as follows:
3. *Affirmative action with preferential hiring.* Here, the company not only enlarges the labor pool but systematically favors minorities and women in the actual decisions as well. This could be thought of as a "soft" quota system.
4. *Hard quotas.* In this posture, the company specifies numbers or proportions of minority group members that must be hired.

Much confusion surrounds the concept of affirmative action, because it was never clear which of the aforementioned views was being advocated by the government. In hindsight, we can now see that the government was advocating positions based on whichever posture seemed most likely to work, or based on the particular candidate and political party in office at the time. Early on, "soft" or "weak" affirmative action (Postures 1 and 2) was advocated. It became apparent, however, that these postures were not effective in getting the results desired. Therefore, "hard" or "strong" affirmative action (Postures 3 and 4) was later advocated. The real controversy over affirmative action began with the use of soft quotas and "preferential hiring" (Posture 3) and "hard quotas" (Posture 4). Today, when people speak of affirmative action, they are typically referring to some degree of preferential hiring, as in Postures 3 and 4. Figure 19-6 summarizes the key Supreme Court decisions to date on affirmative action.

The underlying rationale for affirmative action is the principle of **compensatory justice**, which holds that whenever injustice is done, just compensation or reparation is owed to the injured party or parties.[134] Over the years, deliberate barriers were placed on opportunities for minorities—especially African Americans. These groups were prevented from participating in business, law, universities, and other desirable professions and institutions. Additionally, when official barriers were finally dropped, matters frequently did not improve because inequalities had been built into the system. Thus, the view that we can and should restore the balance through affirmative action became established as a viable option for moving more quickly toward economic equality in the workplace and in our society.[135]

FIGURE 19-6   Key Supreme Court Decisions on Affirmative Action

Year	Case	Issue	General Finding
1978	*Regents of the University of California v. Bakke*	Admission to medical school	Race deemed a legitimate factor but ruled against strict quotas
1979	*United Steelworkers v. Weber*	Admission to private employer training program (Kaiser)	Quotas acceptable if temporary and addressing a clear imbalance
1980	*Fullilove v. Klutznick*	Set asides for minority contractors	Set asides acceptable due to narrow focus and limited intent
1986	*Wygant v. Board of Education*	Layoff policy that protected minorities	Preferential layoffs unacceptable—greater injury than hiring policy
1987	*United States v. Paradise*	Hiring of state troopers in Alabama	Strict quotas accepted only because there was persistent and pervasive racism
1989	*City of Richmond v. Croson*	Construction set asides for black-owned firms	AA unconstitutional unless racial discrimination proven widespread in industry
1995	*Adarand Constructors, Inc. v. Peña*	Federal affirmative action set asides	AA must pass "strict scrutiny" test of compelling interest and narrow tailoring
1996	*Hopwood v. University of Texas Law School*	Admission to law school	Rejected legitimacy of diversity as a goal for AA
2003	*Grutter v. Bollinger*	Admission to law school	Race can be a factor (invalidates *Hopwood*)
2006	*Parents v. Seattle and Meredith v. Jefferson*	School integration	Unconstitutional to consider race when assigning students to schools
2009	*Ricci v. DeStefano*	Firefighter lieutenant and captain exams	Unconstitutional to discard exams due to concerns about disparate impact
2013	*Fisher v. University of Texas*	Admission to the university	Remanded the case to the lower court finding it did not apply the standard of strict scrutiny

© Cengage Learning 2015

The principal objection to affirmative action and the reason it has become and remained controversial is that it leads to **reverse discrimination**. The public, in general, supports affirmative action when it is described as simply providing opportunities for previously disadvantaged groups. When the question is rephrased to include providing preferential treatment to minorities, the approval rate plummets by half.[136] The possibility of reverse discrimination is at the core of the controversy surrounding affirmative action. In the 2009 *Ricci v. DeStefano* case, the Supreme Court ruled that the plaintiffs were victims of reverse discrimination when the city threw out firefighter exams that they had passed out of concern that too few minorities passed the test.

Gilbert Casellas, a former EEOC chair who now represents employers, believes that corporate diversity policies may be "outpacing the law" because companies are now eager to improve their diversity.[137] Companies know that being diverse provides them with advantages, such as recruiting a diverse and talented workforce. Because many companies are actively working to improve their diversity, affirmative action may become less of an issue in the future.

The Future of Affirmative Action

The buying power of minority groups in the United States is increasing dramatically, and that has led to an increase in business's interest in achieving greater diversity. The University of Georgia's Selig Center charts the growth of consumer groups, and their findings are instructive. According to center director Jeff Humphries, "The $1.2 trillion Hispanic market is larger than the entire economies of all but 13 countries in the world."[138] From 2000 to 2012, the growth has been dramatic: African American buying power increased 73 percent compared to a 60 percent increase for Caucasians. This was driven in part by a 61 percent increase in black-owned businesses from 2002 to 2007. During the same period, the buying power of Asian Americans increased 165 percent and is expected to reach $1 trillion by 2017. Companies increasingly seek to be more diverse to get access to all the benefits diversity can bring.

Increasing minority buying power and influence are leading companies to want to undertake voluntary programs to increase the diversity in their workforce and their bottom lines. In one of life's ironies, the EEOC had to warn companies of the dangers of voluntary affirmative action. Former EEOC Chair Naomi Earp said that firms must be careful to not base employment decisions on race or any other protected category, even when the goal is greater diversity. According to Earp, customer preferences have never been an acceptable reason to discriminate in employment and reference to a global market is not sufficient justification either.[139] The legality of some diversity practices remains unsettled, and thus they may be risky. These include offering incentives for managers to achieve a diverse workforce or promoting affinity groups, formed by employees along race or gender lines.[140]

Summary

This chapter addresses several subgroups of employee stakeholders whose job rights are protected by law. The United States became serious about the problem of discrimination by enacting the Civil Rights Act of 1964, which prohibited discrimination based on race, color, religion, sex, or national origin. Laws covering age and disabilities were passed later. Other protections related to disability are prohibitions against pregnancy discrimination and genetic information discrimination. The EEOC was created to assume the major responsibility for enforcing the discrimination laws. Like other federal agencies, the EEOC has had problems. However, on balance it has done a reasonable job of monitoring the two major forms of discrimination: disparate treatment and disparate impact. Discrimination issues discussed in this chapter include issues of racial discrimination, women moving into professional/managerial positions, pay equity, sexual harassment, pregnancy discrimination, fetal protection policies, age discrimi-

nation, and religious discrimination. In addition, new and evolving discrimination issues such as sexual orientation, gender identity, and color bias as separate from race were discussed.

Affirmative action, the taking of positive steps to hire and promote people from groups previously discriminated against, was one of the government's answers to the problem of discrimination. Considerable controversy has surrounded the question of how far affirmative action should go. There is evidence that attitudes toward affirmative action are changing as the global economy brings a more diverse workforce and customer base. However, psychological and sociological aspects of people being people may mean that achieving diversity will be an elusive goal. Firms should follow best practices when designing diversity programs. Moral management and sound stakeholder management require companies to strive to be fair in their employment practices.

Key Terms

affirmative action with preferential hiring, p. 560

affirmative action, p. 559

Age Discrimination in Employment Act (ADEA), p. 543

Americans with Disabilities Act (ADA), p. 545

bona fide occupational qualification (BFOQ), p. 543

Civil Rights Act of 1991, p. 548

color bias, p. 553

compensatory justice, p. 560

disparate impact, p. 549

disparate treatment, p. 549

Equal Employment Opportunity Commission (EEOC), p. 549

Equal Pay Act of 1963, p. 544

Discussion Questions

1. List the major federal discrimination laws and indicate what they prohibit. Which agency is primarily responsible for enforcing these laws?

2. Give two different definitions of discrimination, and provide an example of each.

3. How has the Americans with Disabilities Act (ADA) evolved since its inception?

4. Do you think racial inequality is caused by racism, favoritism, or both? Explain your answer.

5. Do you agree with the Genetic Nondiscrimination Act? Do companies have a right to know and use genetic information about employees? Why or why not?

6. Has the concept of diversity supplanted the concept of affirmative action in leading companies today? Why or why not?

Endnotes

1. "Equal Employment Opportunity (EEO) Terminology," http://www.archives.gov/eeo/terminology.html#r. Accessed May 28, 2013.

2. "Statewide Employment Laws and Policies," http://www.hrc.org/files/assets/resources/Employment_Laws_and_Policies.pdf. Accessed May 28, 2013.

3. Zachary Karabell, "We Are Not in This Together," *Newsweek* (April 20, 2009), 30–32.

4. Ibid.

5. "Ethnic Minorities Badly Hit by Recession," *Equal Opportunities Review* (February 2010), 4.

6. Jessica Prois, "Global Economic Recession Causing More Poverty, Deaths for Females Than Males: Report," *Huff-Post* (January 23, 2013), http://www.huffingtonpost.com/2013/01/23/global-economic-recession-females_n_2534912.html. Accessed July 6, 2013.

7. William F. Glueck and James Ledvinka, "Equal Employment Opportunity Programs," in William F. Glueck, *Personnel: A Diagnostic Approach*, rev. ed. (Dallas, TX: Business Publications, 1978), 593–633.

8. Ibid., 597–599.

9. "Equal Opportunity: A Scorecard," *Dun's Review* (November 1979), 107.

10. Ibid., 108.

11. Mitra Toossi, "Labor Force Projections to 2020: A More Slowly Growing Workforce" (January 2012), http:// www.bls.gov/opub/mlr/2012/01/art3full.pdf. Accessed May 24, 2013.

12. Ibid.

13. EEOC, "Title VII: Enforces Job Rights" (Washington, DC: The U.S. Equal Employment Opportunity Commission, Office of Communications, October 1988), 1.

14. Gerald L. Maatman, Jr., "Supreme Court Rulings Score a Worker Trifecta," *Business Insurance* (October 16, 2006), 26.

15. Ibid.

16. "Supreme Court: Title VII Deadline Clock Resets with Each New Biased Decision," *The HR Specialist* (June 2010), http://www.thehrspecialist.com/article.aspx?articleid=32469. Accessed May 29, 2013.

17. http://www.eeoc.gov/youth/age.html. Accessed May 24, 2013.

18. "Employment Discrimination," http://www.justia.com/employment/employment-discrimination/docs/age-discrimination.html. Accessed May 31, 2013.

19. EEOC, "Age Discrimination Is Against the Law" (Washington, DC: The U.S. Equal Employment Opportunity Commission, Office of Communications, April 1988), 1.

20. EEOC, "Equal Work, Equal Pay" (Washington, DC: The U.S. Equal Employment Opportunity Commission, Office of Communications, October 1988), 1.

21. Harold M. Brody and Alexander Grodan, "The Effect of the Fair Pay Act on Disparate-Impact Cases," *Employment Relations Today* (Winter 2010), 73–78.

22. "A Backpay Bonanza," *The Wall Street Journal* (August 2, 2007), A10.

23. Sheryl Gay Stolberg, "Obama Signs Equal Pay Legislation," *The New York Times* (January 29, 2009), http://www.nytimes.com/2009/01/30/us/politics/30ledbetter-web.html. Accessed May 29, 2013.

24. EEOC, "Equal Employment Opportunity Is the Law" (Washington, DC: The U.S. Equal Employment Opportunity Commission, Office of Communications 1986), 1.

25. Henry H. Perritt, Jr., *Americans with Disabilities Act Handbook* (New York: John Wiley & Sons, 1990), vii.

26. U.S. Department of Justice, Office on the Americans with Disabilities Act, *The Americans with Disabilities Act: Questions and Answers* (Washington, DC: Government Printing Office, 1991), 1. Also see "Disabilities Act to Cover 500,000 More Firms," *The Atlanta Journal* (July 25, 1994), E1.

27. Suzanne E. Peters, "Essential Could Mean Infrequent: A Look at 'Essential Job Function,' Under the ADA," Lexology (April 30, 2013), http://www.lexology.com/library/detail.aspx?g=b859bb3c-8e00-4e04-9fb5-2cfd5a689d96. Accessed May 24, 2013.

28. Ibid.

29. Ibid.

30. http://www.eeoc.gov/laws/regulations/ada_qa_final_rule.cfm. Accessed May 24, 2013.

31. Ibid.

32. Warren Richey, "Court Boosts Civil Rights Law for Disabled," *The Christian Science Monitor* (May 18, 2004), 1.

33. Joe Palazzolo, "Disabled Sue Over Web Shopping," *The Wall Street Journal* (March 21, 2013), B1.

34. Beth Brophy, "Supreme Court Gives Motherhood Its Legal Due," *U.S. News & World Report* (January 26, 1987), 12.

35. Gillian Flynn, "Watch Out for Pregnancy Discrimination," *Workforce* (November 2002), 84.

36. Sankar Mukhopadhyay, "The Effects of the 1978 Pregnancy Discrimination Act on Female Labor Supply." *International Economic Review* 53.4 (2012): 1133–1153.

37. "Under a Civil Rights Cloud, Fetal Protection Looks Dismal," *Insight* (April 15, 1991), 40–41.

38. Ibid.

39. http://www.osha.gov/SLTC/reproductivehazards/. Accessed May 29, 2013.

40. Dan Markiewicz, "Avoid a Costly Court Challenge." *Industrial Safety & Hygiene News* 47.2 (2013), 18.

41. Jessica L. Roberts, "Preempting Discrimination: Lessons from the Genetic Information Nondiscrimination Act." *Vanderbilt Law Review* 63.2 (2010): 437–490.

42. Andrea Davis, "GINA Can't Prevent Employee Disclosure." *Employee Benefit News* 27.1 (2013): 9–10.

43. Thomas H. Christopher, Louis W. Doherty, and David C. Lindsay. "EEOC Issues Final Regulations on Genetic Discrimination in the Workplace." *Employee Relations Law Journal* 36.4 (2011): 45–49.

44. Ibid.

45. John D. Rapoport and Brian L. P. Zevnik, *The Employee Strikes Back* (New York: Collier Books, 1994), 233–234.

46. Ibid.

47. Statement of Jacqueline A. Berrien, Chair U.S. Equal Employment Opportunity Commission, before the Committee on Health, Education, Labor and Pensions, United States Senate (May 6, 2010), http://www.eeoc.gov/eeoc/events/berrien_protecting_older_workers.cfm. Accessed May 29, 2013.

48. http://www.eeoc.gov/eeoc/events/berrien_protecting_older_workers.cfm. Accessed May 29, 2013.

49. http://www.eeoc.gov. Accessed May 29, 2013.

50. "EEOC Reports Nearly 100,000 Job Bias Charges in Fiscal Year 2012," http://www.eeoc.gov/eeoc/newsroom/release/1-28-13.cfm. Accessed May 31, 2013.

51. James Ledvinka, *Federal Regulation of Personnel and Human Resource Management* (Boston: Kent, 1982), 37. Also see W. N. Outten, R. J. Rabin, and L. R. Lipman, *The Rights of Employees and Union Members* (Carbondale, IL: Southern Illinois University Press, 1994), chapter VIII, 154–156.

52. Glueck and Ledvinka, 304.

53. Ledvinka, 37–38.

54. *Griggs v. Duke Power Company*, 401 U.S. 424, 1971.

55. Theodore Purcell, "Minorities, Management of and Equal Employment Opportunity," in L. R. Bittel (ed.), *Encyclopedia of Professional Management* (New York: McGraw-Hill, 1978), 744–745.

56. Yiyang, Wu. "Scaling the Wall and Running the Mile: The Role of Physical-Selection Procedures in the Disparate Impact Narrative." *University of Pennsylvania Law Review* 160.4 (2012): 1195–1238.

57. Mary-Kathryn Zachary, "Discrimination without Intent," *Supervision* (May 2003), 23–26.

58. http://www.uniformguidelines.com/questionandanswers.html. Accessed May 28, 2013.

59. Maria Greco Danaher, "Strength Test Falls," *HR Magazine* (February 2007), 115–116.

60. Ibid.

61. Kathy DeAngelo, "Title VII's Conflicting 'Twin Pillars' in Ricci v. DeStefano, 129 S. Ct. 2658 (2009)," *Harvard Journal of Law and Public Policy* (Winter 2010), 73–78.

62. Carter Dougherty, "Supreme Court Lending Bias Case in Settlement Talks," *Bloomberg News* (July 5, 2013), http://www.bloomberg.com/news/2013-07-05/lending-discrimination-case-at-supreme-court-in-settlement-talks.html. Accessed July 6, 2013.

63. Ibid.

64. Kanter, Rosabeth Moss. *Men and Women of the Corporation* (New York: Basic Books, 1977), 47–68.

65. Sabina Nielsen, "Why Do Top Management Teams Look the Way They Do? A Multilevel Exploration of the Antecedents of TMT Heterogeneity." *Strategic Organization* 7.3 (2009): 277–305.

66. Nancy DiTomaso, *The American Non-Dilemma: Racial Inequality Without Racism* (Russell Sage Foundation: New York, 2013).

67. "Interview with Nancy DiTomaso," *Background Readings*, http://www.pbs.org/race/000_About/002_04-background-03-07.htm. Accessed May 29, 2013.

68. Ibid.

69. Nancy DiTomaso, "How Social Networks Drive Black Unemployment," *The New York Times* (May 5, 2013), http://opinionator.blogs.nytimes.com/2013/05/05/how-social-networks-drive-black-unemployment/. Accessed May 29, 2013.

70. http://www.eeoc.gov/facts/fs-race.html. Accessed May 24, 2013.

71. Marie Arana, "The Elusive Hispanic/Latino Identity," *Nieman Reports* (Summer 2001), 8–9.

72. Alan Fram, "Hispanics Face Most Discrimination in U.S. (POLL)," Huffington Post (May 20, 2010), http://www.huffingtonpost.com/2010/05/21/hispanics-face-most-discr_n_583538.html. Accessed May 24, 2013.

73. https://securercuh01.rcuh.com/000168d/rcuh1.nsf/7b1e3e85b13603260a2564d6001576fd/3ac04973990c5d920a256dd00060286b/$FILE/Definitions_of_Ethnicity_Groups.pdf. Accessed May 24, 2013.

74. http://www.eeoc.gov/facts/fs-race.html. Accessed May 24, 2013.

75. http://www.eeoc.gov/eeoc/initiatives/e-race/caselist.cfm#color. Accessed May 24, 2013.

76. Ibid.

77. http://management.fortune.cnn.com/2013/05/09/women-ceos-fortune-500/. Accessed May 28, 2013.

78. Rachel Soares and Samantha Bonaparte, "2012 Catalyst Census: Fortune 500 Women Executive Officers and Top Earners," http://www.catalyst.org/knowledge/2012-catalyst-census-fortune-500-women-executive-officers-and-top-earners. Accessed May 28, 2013.

79. Ibid.

80. http://www.huffingtonpost.com/regina-e-herzlinger/has-the-glass-ceiling-bee_b_3001344.html. Accessed May 28, 2013.

81. Jodi Kantor, "A Titan's How-To on Breaking the Glass Ceiling," *The New York Times* (February 21, 2013), http://www.nytimes.com/2013/02/22/us/sheryl-sandberg-lean-in-author-hopes-to-spur-movement.html?pagewanted=all. Accessed May 28, 2013.

82. Steven M. Davidoff, "Why So Few Women Reach the Executive Rank," *The New York Times* (April 2, 2013), http://dealbook.nytimes.com/2013/04/02/why-so-few-women-reach-the-executive-rank/. Accessed May 28, 2013.

83. Ibid.

84. Pamela Ryckman, *Stiletto Network: Inside the Power Circles That Are Changing the Face of Business* (AMACOM: New York, 2013).

85. Ibid.

86. Latifa Lyles, "Closing the Equal Pay Gap: 50 Years and Counting" *(Work in Progress)* (April 9, 2013), http://social.dol.gov/blog/closing-the-equal-pay-gap-50-years-and-counting/. Accessed May 28, 2013.

87. "Myth Busting the Pay Gap" *(Work in Progress): The Official Blog of the U.S. Department of Labor* (June 7, 2012), http://social.dol.gov/blog/myth-busting-the-pay-gap/. Accessed May 28, 2013.

88. Ibid.

89. Ibid.

90. Associated Press, "Moms Are Top Earners in 40% of Homes; More Married Women Now Make More Than Husbands, Pew Study Finds," *Cleveland Plain Dealer* (May 29, 2013), http://www.cleveland.com/business/index.ssf/2013/05/moms_are_top_earners_in_40_of.html. Accessed May 29, 2013.

91. http://www.walmartclass.com/staticdata/2.22.10%20Press%20Release.pdf. May 31, 2013.

92. Joan Biskupic, "Supreme Court Limits Walmart Sex Discrimination Case," *USA Today* (June 21, 2011), http://usatoday30.usatoday.com/money/industries/retail/2011-06-20-walmart-sex-bias-case_n.htm. Accessed May 31, 2013.

93. Chelsea R. Willness, Piers Steel, and Kibeom Lee, "A Meta-Analysis of the Antecedents and Consequences of Workplace Sexual Harassment," *Personnel Psychology* (Spring 2007), 127–162.

94. http://www.eeoc.gov/eeoc/statistics/enforcement/sexual_harassment.cfm. Accessed May 29, 2013.

95. Ibid.

96. Jana Szostek, Charles J. Hobson, Andrea Griffin, Anna Rominger, Marilyn Vasquez, and Natalie Murillo. 2012. "EEOC Sexual Harassment Settlements: An Empirical Analysis." *Employee Relations Law Journal* 38, no. 1: 3–13.

97. Ibid.

98. Szostek, et al., 2012.

99. Ibid.

100. Ibid.

101. Ibid.

102. Erik Brady, "Colorado Scandal Could Hit Home to Other Colleges," *USA Today* (May 26, 2004), http://usatoday30.usatoday.com/sports/college/football/big12/2004-05-26-colorado-cover_x.htm?csp=34. Accessed May 29, 2013.

103. Susan B. Garland, "Finally, a Corporate Tip Sheet on Sexual Harassment," *BusinessWeek* (July 13, 1998), 39.

104. Anita Cava, "Sexual Harassment Claims: New Framework for Employers," *Business and Economic Review*

(July–September 2001), 13–16; Ted Meyer and Linda Schoonmaker, "Employers Must Think Outside the Sexual Harassment Box," *Texas Lawyer* (February 12, 2001), 36.

105. Adam Liptak, "Court Expands Ability to Sue in Sexual Harassment Investigations," *The New York Times* (January 26, 2009).

106. http://www.eeoc.gov/eeoc/statistics/enforcement/charges .cfm. Accessed May 29, 2013.

107. Lauren E. Bohn, "Workplace Religious Freedom Bill Finds Renewed Interest," PEW Forum on Religion and Public Life (May 3, 2010), http://pewforum.org/Religion-News/Workplace-religious-freedom-bill-finds-revived-interest.aspx. Accessed May 29, 2013.

108. S.3686–Workplace Religious Freedom Act of 2013, http://beta.congress.gov/bill/112th-congress/senate-bill/3686?q=workplace+religious+freedom+act. Accessed May 29, 2013.

109. John Elvin, "Does Religion Belong in the Workplace?" *Insight on the News* (October 28–November 10, 2003), 16.

110. Ibid.

111. S.3686–Workplace Religious Freedom Act of 2013, http://beta.congress.gov/bill/112th-congress/senate-bill/3686. Accessed May 29, 2013.

112. Ibid.

113. Kelley Holland, "When Religious Needs Test Company Policy," *The New York Times* (February 25, 2007), 17.

114. Sonia Ghumman, and Ann Marie Ryan. "Not Welcome Here: Discrimination Towards Women Who Wear the Muslim Headscarf." *Human Relations* 66.5 (2013): 671–698

115. Ibid.

116. Kelley Holland, "When Religious Needs Test Company Policy," *The New York Times* (February 25, 2007), http://www.nytimes.com/2007/02/25/business/your money/25mgmt.html. Accessed May 29, 2013.

117. Paul Guequierre, "It's Time for ExxonMobil to Join the Rest of Corporate America and Protect Its LGBT Employees," HRC Blog (May 29, 2013), http://www.hrc.org/blog/entry/its-time-for-exxonmobil-to-join-the-rest-of-corporate-america-and-protect-i. Accessed May 29, 2013; http://www.hrc.org/resources/entry/lgbt-equality-at-the-fortune-500. Accessed May 29, 2013.

118. Guequierre (2013).

119. Ibid.

120. http://www.hrc.org/resources/entry/business-coalition-for-workplace-fairness-members. Accessed May 29, 2013.

121. http://www.hrc.org/campaigns/employment-non-discri mination-act. Accessed May 29, 2013.

122. Erik Eckholm, "Corporate Call for Change in Gay Marriage Case," *The New York Times* (February 27, 2013), http://www.nytimes.com/2013/02/28/business/

companies-ask-justices-to-overturn-gay-marriage-ban .html?_r=0. Accessed May 31, 2013.

123. Ibid.

124. http://www.hrc.org/resources/entry/sexual-orientation-and-gender-identity-terminology-and-definitions. Accessed May 29, 2013.

125. "HRC Lauds Federal Court Ruling Asserting Protection for Transsexual Employees Under Existing Law," *Human Rights Campaign Press Release* (June 1, 2004), http://www.hrc.org/press-releases/entry/hrc-lauds-fed eral-court-ruling-asserting-protection-for-transsexual-employe. Accessed May 29, 2013.

126. Christopher Danzig, "Gender Stereotyping Leads to Title VII Claim," *Inside Counsel* (April 2010), 63–64.

127. Ibid.

128. Dave Wieczorek, "Transsexual Employee's Title VII Claim Goes Forward," *InsideCounsel* (May 2006), 77–79.

129. David L. Chappell, "If Affirmative Action Fails … What Then?" *The New York Times* (May 8, 2004), B7; Terry H. Anderson, *The Pursuit of Fairness: A History of Affirmative Action* (New York: Oxford University Press, May 2004).

130. Thomas Nagel, "A Defense of Affirmative Action," *Report from the Center for Philosophy and Public Policy* (College Park, MD: University of Maryland, Fall 1981), 6–9.

131. Glenn Llopis, "America's Most Wanted: What Diversity Can Do for Business," *Forbes* (August 29, 2011), http://www.forbes.com/sites/glennllopis/2011/08/29/americas-most-wanted-what-diversity-can-do-for-business/. Accessed May 31, 2013.

132. Daniel Seligman, "How 'Equal Opportunity' Turned into Employment Quotas," *Fortune* (March 1973), 160–168.

133. Tom L. Beauchamp and Norman E. Bowie (eds.), *Ethical Theory and Business*, 2d ed. (Englewood Cliffs, NJ: Prentice Hall, 1983), 477–478.

134. Ibid., 478.

135. "Public Backs Affirmative Action but Not Minority Hiring Preferences," *PEW Research Center Publications* (June 2, 2009), http://pewresearch.org/pubs/1240/sotomayor-supreme-court-affirmative-action-minoritypreferences.

136. http://pewresearch.org/pubs/1240/sotomayor-supreme court-affirmative-action-minority-preferences. Accessed May 29, 2013.

137. "Voluntary Diversity Plans Can Lead to Risk," *HR Focus* (June 2007), 2.

138. http://www.terry.uga.edu/news/releases/hispanic-consumer-market-in-the-u.s.-is-larger-than-the-entire-economies-of. Accessed May 29, 2013.

139. "Voluntary Diversity Plans Can Lead to Risk," *HR Focus* (June 2007), 2.

140. Ibid., 2.

Case

Case Analysis Guidelines

The guidelines presented below have been designed to help you analyze the cases that follow. The guidelines are presented in three stages, but they are not intended to be a rigid format. Each question is designed to elicit information that will help you in analyzing and resolving the case. Each case is different, and some parts of the guidelines may not apply to every case. The questions for discussion at the end of each case should be addressed in any complete case analysis. Use the Issue/Problem Identification and Analysis/Evaluation steps to focus on generating and defending the most effective set of recommendations possible, because the objective of case analysis is making recommendations. In all stages of the case analysis, use the stakeholder, ethics, sustainability, and corporate social responsibility (CSR) concepts presented in the text.

Issue/Problem Identification

1. Facts and Assumptions. What are the *central facts* of the case and the assumptions you are making on the basis of these facts?

2. Major Overriding Issues/Problems. What are the *major overriding* issues in this case? (What major questions/issues does this case address that merit(s) their/its study in this course and in connection with the chapter/material you are now covering?)

3. Subissues and Related Issues. What *subissues* or *related issues* are present in the case that merit consideration, discussion, and action?

Analysis/Evaluation

4. Stakeholder Analysis. Who are the *stakeholders* in this case, and what are their stakes? (Create a stakeholder map to depict relationships.) What challenges, threats, or opportunities does each stakeholder face? What stakeholder characteristics are at work (legitimacy, power, urgency)?

5. CSR Analysis. What CSRs (*economic, legal, ethica, /philanthropic*) does the company have, and what exactly are the nature and extent of these responsibilities to the various stakeholders?

6. Evaluations. If the case involves a company's or manager's actions, evaluate what the company or manager did or did not do correctly in handling the issue affecting it. How should actions have been handled?

Recommendations

7. Recommendations and Implementation. What *recommendations* would you make in this case? If a company's or a manager's strategies or actions are involved, should they have acted the way they did? What actions should they have taken? What actions should the company or manager take now, and why? Be specific and include a discussion of alternatives (*right now, short-term,* and *long-term*). Identify and discuss any important *implementation considerations.*

CASE 1

Walmart: The Main Street Merchant of Doom*

The small town was in need of a hired gun. The people were tired of dealing with the local price-fixing merchant scum who ran the town like a company store. This low-life bunch of merchants held the people of the town in a death grip and were perceived by the townspeople to overcharge on every purchase. In spite of what appeared to be a case of collusion, the law was powerless to do anything. What competition there was had been effectively eliminated.

Suddenly, coming over the rise and wearing white, their hired man came riding. The women and children buzzed with excitement. The men were happy. Although his methods of getting the job done turned some people's stomachs, the local watering hole buzzed with tales of how this hired gun would change their world for the better, how someday soon they would have the benefits long afforded the big city. But others asked, at what price?

THE MODERN VERSION OF THE "HIRED GUN"

In his final days, the man appeared to be too frail to handle the enormous job. Yet the courage and self-confidence that he instilled in his associates radiated a belief in low prices and good value for all to see. As his associates rode into town, that radiance put to rest the people's fears that things had changed. Sam's spirit, the Walmart Way, had come to town.

Sam Walton, founder, owner, and mastermind of WalMart,[1] now spelled Walmart and often used that way in many advertisements, passed away on April 5, 1992, leaving behind his spirit to ride herd on the colossal Walmart organization. To the consumer in the small community, his store, Walmart, was seen as a friend. On the flip side, many a small-town merchant had been the victim of Sam's blazing merchandising tactics. So what is Walmart to the communities it serves? Is Walmart the consumer's best friend, the purveyor of the free-enterprise system, the "Mother of All Discount Stores," or, conversely, is it really "The Main Street Merchant of Doom"?

---

*This case, originally prepared by William T. Rupp, Austin Peay State University, was revised and updated by Archie B. Carroll, University of Georgia, in 2013.

THE MAN NAMED SAM

Samuel Moore Walton was born on March 29, 1918, near Kingfisher, Kansas. He began attending the University of Missouri in the fall of 1936 and graduated with a degree in business administration. During his time there, he was a member of the Beta Theta Phi fraternity, was president of the senior class, played various sports, and taught what was believed to be the largest Sunday school class in the world, numbering over 1,200 Missouri students.[2]

At age 22, Sam joined JCPenney. One of his first tasks was to memorize and practice the "Penney Idea." Adopted in 1913, this credo exhorted the associate to serve the public; not to demand all the profit the traffic will bear; to pack the customer's dollar full of value, quality, and satisfaction; to continue to be trained; to reward men and women in the organization through participation in what the business produces; and to test every policy, method, and act against the question, "Does it square with what is right and just?"[3]

Sam's First Store

In 1962, at age 44, Sam Walton opened his first Walmart store in Rogers, Arkansas. He took all the money and expertise he could gather and applied the JCPenney idea to Middle America. Sam first targeted small, underserved rural towns with populations of no more than 10,000 people. The people responded, and Walmart soon developed a core of loyal customers who loved the fast, friendly service coupled with consistently low prices. Later, Sam expanded his company into the large cities, often with numerous Walmart's spread throughout every part of the city.

THE STORE THAT SAM BUILT

By 1981, Walmart's rapid growth was evident to all, but it was especially disturbing to Sears, JCPenney, Target, and Kmart, because Walmart had become America's largest retailer. The most telling figures were those of overhead expenses and sales per employee. The overhead expenses of Sears and Kmart ran 29 and 23 percent of sales, respectively, whereas Walmart's overhead expenses ran 16 percent of sales. At this time, the average Sears employee generated $85,000 in sales per year, whereas the average Walmart employee generated $95,000.[4]

By 2001, Walmart Stores, Inc., had become the world's largest retailer with $191 billion in annual sales. The company employed one million associates worldwide through nearly 3,500 facilities in the United States and more than 1,000 stores throughout nine other countries. Walmart claimed that more than 100 million customers per week visited Walmart stores. The company had four major retail divisions—Walmart Supercenters, Discount Stores, Neighborhood Markets, and Sam's Club warehouses. As it entered the 2000s, Walmart had been named "Retailer of the Century" by *Discount Store News*, made *Fortune* magazine's lists of the "Most Admired Companies in America" and the "100 Best Companies to Work For," and was ranked on *Financial Times*' "Most Respected in the World" list.[5] By January 2013, Walmart's sales had grown to $466.1 billion.[6]

Sam the Motivational Genius

Sam promoted the associate—the hourly employee—to a new level of participation within the organization. He offered profit sharing, incentive bonuses, and stock options in an effort to have his Walmart associates share in the wealth. Sam, as the head cheerleader, felt his job was to be the chief proponent of the "Walmart Way." The Walmart Way reflected Sam's idea of the essential Walmart culture that was needed for success. Sam felt that when a customer entered Walmart in any part of the country, he or she should feel at home. Examples of the culture included "exceeding customer expectations" and "helping people make a difference." He was a proponent of the *"Ten-Foot Rule,"* which meant that if a customer came within ten feet of an associate, the associate would look the customer in the eye, greet him or her, and ask if the customer needed help.[7]

As he was growing the business, the courageous Sam borrowed and borrowed, sometimes just to pay other creditors. Arkansas banks that at one time had turned him down later competed with banks that Sam himself owned. Sam, the CEO, hired the best managers he could find. They convinced him to buy an extensive computer network system. This network corporate satellite system enabled Sam to use round-the-clock inventory control and credit card sales control and provided him with information on total sales of which products where and when. This computer control center was about the size of a football field and used a satellite for up-linking and down-linking to each store.

Sam, The Mortal

In 1992, Sam, the mortal, died of incurable bone cancer. At age 73, Sam Walton said that if he had to do it over again, he would not change a thing. He said, "This is still the most important thing I do, going around to the stores, and I'd rather do it than anything I know of. I know I'm helping our folks when I get out to the stores. I learn a lot about who's doing good things in the office, and I also see things that need fixing, and I help fix them. Any good management person in retail has got to do what I do in order to keep his finger on what's going on. You've got to have the right chemistry and the right attitude on the part of the folks who deal with the customers."[8]

SOCIAL AWARENESS: THE "BUY AMERICAN" PLAN

Sam, the innovator, was responsible for two early social responsibility innovations: Walmart's "Buy American" plan and its "Environmental Awareness" campaign.

Walmart's "Buy American" plan was a result of a 1984 telephone conversation with then-Arkansas Governor Bill Clinton. The program was a response to Sam's own enlightenment: He learned that Walmart was adding to the loss of American jobs by buying cheaper foreign goods. Everything Sam stood for came out of his heartfelt obligation to supply the customer with low-cost quality goods, but running counter to this inner driving force was the realization that he was responsible for the loss of American jobs. This contradiction and dilemma drove him to find a solution. His conversation with Governor Clinton inspired Sam to do something about the problem.

In February 1986, about 12 months after the Buy American plan had begun, Sam held a press conference. He showed off all the merchandise Walmart was now buying domestically. He estimated that Walmart's Buy American plan had restored 4,538 jobs to the American economy and its people.[9] The Buy American plan was one of Walmart's early efforts at corporate social responsibility. The Buy American plan morphed over the years into the well-publicized "Made in the USA" campaign in which Walmart called customers' attention to these domestic products with special labels. Ironically, at some point in time, Walmart eventually abandoned this program and became one of the largest purchasers of products made overseas. In fact, the company in time became the country's largest purchaser of Chinese goods in any industry. Some say that by taking its orders abroad, Walmart forced many U.S. manufacturers out of business.[10]

THE "ENVIRONMENTAL AWARENESS" CAMPAIGN

As awareness of the environment was on the rise, Sam looked for a way to involve Walmart in the environmental movement. In August 1989, an ad in *The Wall Street Journal* proclaimed Walmart's "commitment to our land, air and water." Sam envisioned Walmart as a leader among American companies in the struggle to clean up the environment. John Lowne, corporate vice president and division manager for Reynolds Metals Company, stated, "Walmart's move will indeed set a precedent for the entire retail industry. I'm surprised it has taken other retailers this long to follow suit."[11]

Walmart wanted to use its tremendous buying power to aid in the implementation of the campaign. Walmart sent a booklet to manufacturers stating the following:

At Wal-Mart we're committed to help improve our environment. Our customers are concerned about the quality of our land, air and water, and want the opportunity to do something positive. We believe it is our responsibility to step up to their challenge.[12]

In the stores, shelf tags made from 100 percent recycled paper informed customers as to the environmental friendliness of the highlighted product. As a result of these shelf tags and Walmart's advertising, customer awareness had increased, and some environmentally safe product manufacturers were reaping the rewards of increased Walmart orders.

In the *Wal-Mart Associates Handbook*, new associates were indoctrinated with the "Walmart spirit." The section on the *environment* read:

As a responsible member of the community, Wal-Mart's commitments go beyond simply selling merchandise. With environmental concerns mounting world-wide, Wal-Mart has taken action. Home office and store associates are taking decisive steps to help the environment by making community recycling bins available on our facility parking lots. Other action plans include "Adopt-a-Highway" and "Adopt-a-Beach" programs, tree planting and community clean up and beautification. By forming a partnership with our associates, our manufacturers and our customers, we're convinced we can make the world a better place to live.[13,14]

SAM AND THE EARLY MERCHANTS OF MAIN STREET

Not everyone was excited to see Sam and his mechanized Walmart army arrive and succeed. Small merchants across America shuddered when the winds of the "Walmart Way" began to blow in their direction. Kennedy Smith of the National Main Street Center in Washington, DC, said, "The first thing towns usually do is panic." Once Walmart comes to town, Smith says, "Downtowns will never again be the providers of basic consumer goods and services they once were."[15]

Steamboat Springs

Some towns learned to "just say 'no'" to Walmart's overtures. Steamboat Springs, Colorado, was one such city. Colorado newspapers called it the "Shootout at Steamboat Springs." Walmart was denied permission to build on a nine-acre parcel along U.S. Route 40. Owners of upscale shops and condos were very concerned with the image of their resort community, and Walmart, with its low-cost reputation, just did not fit. The shootout lasted for two years, and finally Walmart filed a damage suit against the city. Countersuits followed. A petition was circulated to hold a referendum on the matter. This was the shot that made Walmart blink and back down. Just before the vote, Don Shinkle, corporate affairs vice president, said, "A vote would not be good for Steamboat Springs, and it would not be good for Walmart. I truly believe Walmart is a kinder, gentler company, and, while we have the votes to win, an election would only split the town more."[16]

Iowa City

In Iowa City, Iowa (population more than 50,000), Walmart was planning an 87,000-square-foot store on the outskirts of the town. A group of citizens gathered enough signatures during a petition drive to put a referendum on the ballot to block Walmart and the city council from building the new store (the city council had approved the rezoning of the land Walmart wanted). Jim Clayton, a downtown merchant, said, "Walmart is a freight train going full steam in the opposite direction of this town's philosophy." If businesses wound up closing, Clayton said, "you lose their involvement in the community, involvement I promise you won't get with some assistant manager over at Walmart."[17] Walmart spokesperson Brenda Lockhart commented that downtown merchants can benefit from the increase in customer traffic provided "they offer superior service and aren't gouging their customers."[18] Efforts to stop Walmart and the Iowa City Council were not successful. Walmart opened its Iowa City store on November 5, 1991.

Pawhuska, Oklahoma

In Pawhuska, Oklahoma, as a result of Walmart's entry in 1983 and other local factors, the local "five-and-dime," JCPenney, Western Auto, and a whole block of other stores closed their doors. Four years later, Dave Story, general manager of the local *Pawhuska Daily Journal Capital*, wrote that Walmart was a "billion-dollar parasite" and a "national retail ogre."[19]

Walmart managers have become very active in Pawhuska and surrounding communities since that time. A conversation with the editor of the Pawhuska paper, Jody Smith, and her advertising editor, Suzy Burns, revealed that Walmart sponsored the local rodeo, gave gloves to the local coat drive, and was involved with the local cerebral palsy and multiple sclerosis fund-raisers. On the other hand, Fred Wright, former owner of a TV and record store, said, "Walmart really craters a little town's downtown."[20]

OPPOSITION TO WALMART GETS ORGANIZED

By the 1990s, there were dozens of organized groups actively opposing Walmart's expansion.[21] Some of these groups were and still are run by social activists whose work dates back to the 1960s and 1970s. Instead of protesting the Vietnam War, nuclear proliferation, or the destruction of the environment, they turned their efforts to Walmart specifically and capitalism in general. One of these activists, Paul Glover, who was an antiwar organizer, defined Walmart as the epitome of capitalism, which he despises. For Glover and others, Walmart stands for "everything they dislike about American society—mindless consumerism, paved landscapes, and homogenization of community identity."[22]

Boulder, Colorado Opposition

In Boulder, Colorado, Walmart tried to counter these allegations by proposing a "green" store. Steven Lane, Walmart's real estate manager, said that a "green store" would be built that would be environmentally friendly, with a solar-powered sign out front and other measures to reduce waste and conserve energy. The thoroughness of his plans were called into question by Spencer Havlick, an organizer of the first Earth Day in 1970, suggesting that the entire store be powered by solar energy. Mr. Lane did not respond.[23]

Protest organizers united against the spread of the "Walmart Way" differ from the downtown merchants in that these protesters have no financial stake, though they still regard themselves as stakeholders. These activists are attacking Walmart on a higher, philosophical plane. The accusations ring with a tone of argument that was made by other activists protesting polluting industries (e.g., the coal, nuclear, and chemical industries). These activists accuse Walmart of "strip-mining" towns and communities of their culture and values.

One possible root of this culture clash may be attributed to the unique aspects of the internal corporate culture at Walmart's headquarters. This is a place where competition for the reputation as the "cheapest" is practiced. An example is the competition among employees in procuring the cheapest haircut, shoes, or necktie. Walmart is a place where play-acting as a backwoods "hick" has been an acceptable behavior within the organization. Consequently, as a result of the conflicts between the internal culture of Walmart and the external environment, some analysts believe that a clash of priorities and values was inevitable as Walmart moved into larger, more urban settings.

New England Opposition

Some of the greatest opposition to Walmart's growth came from the New England area. This area holds great promise for Walmart because of the large, dense population and the many underserved towns. These towns are typically underserved in three ways: in variety of product choices, in value, and in convenience. The opposition to Walmart entering these New England markets includes some high-profile names, such as Jerry Greenfield, cofounder of Ben & Jerry's Homemade ice cream, and Arthur Frommer, a well-known travel writer.[24] In addition to New England, other areas, such as resort areas, opposed Walmarts because they have wanted to insulate their unique cultures from what they considered to be the offensive consumerism that is usually generated by Walmart's presence.

Sprawl-Busters

Al Norman, a lobbyist and media consultant, turned opposition to Walmart into a cottage industry. Norman developed a Web site (http://sprawl-busters.com/) that has a vast amount of information for citizens who are fighting to prevent Walmart or other "big box" stores from locating in their cities or neighborhoods. Norman achieved national attention in 1993, when he stopped Walmart from locating in his hometown of Greenfield, Massachusetts. Since then, he has appeared on *60 Minutes*, which called him "the guru of the anti-Walmart movement," and has gained widespread media attention. To this day, Norman remains active in his protests against Walmart and other big box stores. His latest book is *Occupy Walmart*, in which he says that Walmart is the "Mother of all 1% corporations" as the Wall Street movement moves to Main Street.[25]

On the *Sprawl-Busters* Web page, consumers around the country are given the opportunity to detail their fights with Walmart. Examples in 2013 included conflicts in Frederick, MD, Washington, DC, Ridgecrest, CA, Whitehall, MI and Tigard, OR.[26] In actuality, conflicts between Walmart and cities are taking place every day all over the country on a continuous basis.

Sprawl-Busters is not alone in its on-line, focused criticism of Walmart's presence in communities. Another organization, *Hel*Mart*, (http://www.hel-mart.com/about.php) continues it public fight against Walmart and updates criticisms of the company on a regular basis.

CONTINUING CHALLENGES TO WALMART

For its part, Walmart has continued its aggressive diversification and growth pattern. In 2009, *The Wall Street Journal* said that Walmart's image had moved from demon to darling as a result of the strategies the company had employed. But in 2013, questions such as "Is Walmart in Trouble?" continue to be asked.[27]

Figure 1 provides some revealing current statistics about Walmart.

FIGURE 1 Recent Facts and Interesting Information about Walmart

Walmart's Locations

Walmart operates more than **10,800 stores in 27 countries** around the world.
Walmart operates stores under 69 different banners globally.

Walmart's Employees

Walmart employs 2.2 million associates around the world — 1.4 million in the U.S. alone. About **75% of its store management teams** started as hourly associates, and they earn between $50,000 and $170,000 a year — similar to what firefighters, accountants, and some doctors make. Every year, **Walmart promotes about 170,000 people** to jobs with more responsibility and higher pay.

Walmart's Customers

Walmart serves customers more than 200 million times per week. The average family of four spends over $4,000 per year at Walmart. One of every four dollars spent on groceries are spent at Walmart. 90 percent of all Americans live within 15 miles of a Walmart.

Walmart's Financials

For the fiscal year ending January 2013, Walmart **increased net sales by 5% to $466.1 billion** and returned $13 billion to shareholders through dividends and share repurchases.

Walmart's Size

If Walmart were a country, it would be the 26th largest economy in the world. If Walmart was an army, it would have the second largest military in the world, behind China. Walmart is bigger than Home Depot, Kroger, Target, Sears, Costco, and Kmart combined. Walmart's parking lots alone take up roughly the size of Tampa, Florida.

Community Giving

In 2012, Walmart and the Walmart Foundation gave **more than $1 billion** in cash and in-kind contributions around the world. In addition, Walmart, Sam's Club and Logistics associates volunteered more than **2.2 million hours**, generating $18 million to U.S. nonprofits.

Environmental Sustainability

Walmart has three aspirational sustainability goals: to be supplied 100% by renewable energy, to create zero waste, and to sell products that sustain people and the environment.

Hunger and Nutrition

Walmart has committed $2 billion to fight hunger and nutrition in the U.S. The company is striving to make food healthier and more affordable. The company is using its size and scale to help support farmers and their communities to strengthen the global food supply chain.

Sources: Walmart, "Walmart's Facts," http://news.walmart.com/walmart-facts, Accessed May 20, 2013; Walmart, "Corporate & Financial Facts," http://news.walmart.com/walmart-facts/corporate-financial-fact-sheet, Accessed May 20, 2013; Dina Spector, "18 Walmart Facts that will make your head explode," *Business Insider*, February 21, 2013, http://www.businessinsider.com/incredible-facts-about-walmart-2013-2?op=1.

Grocery Sales motivate Clandestine Opposition

In recent years, a new form of opposition to Walmart's growth has emerged. It was disclosed by *The Wall Street Journal* that rival grocery chains had secretly funded opposition to Walmart's entrance into communities because its grocery sales had reached such a large percentage of its total sales. In 2010, 51 percent of Walmart's total revenues came from grocery sales.[28] By year's end in 2012, Walmart's grocery sales had grown to 55 percent of its U.S. sales.[29] What *The Wall Street Journal* learned through investigative research was that in Mundelein, Illinois, a town about 20 miles northwest of Chicago with a population of about 35,000, a grocery chain with about nine stores in the area had hired Saint Consulting Group to secretly operate an anti-Walmart campaign. It was revealed that Saint had developed a specialty in fighting proposed Walmarts in communities and were using techniques it described as "black arts."[30]

Large supermarket chains such as Supervalue, Inc., Safeway, Inc., and Ahold NV retained Saint Consulting to block Walmart's entrance into communities, according to pages of Saint's documents and interviews with employees that the newspaper was able to obtain. It was reported that Saint had jokingly dubbed its staff the "Walmart killers." Supervalue's goal in retaining Saint in the Mundelein, Illinois, case was to block Walmart from competing with its nine Jewel-Osco supermarkets located within the area. City officials claimed that the efforts stalled the development of a major shopping center for three years and cost the community millions in lost sales and sales taxes.[31] It turns out that other grocery chains have employed Saint to block Walmarts in other states. Safeway hired Saint to thwart Walmart superstores in more than 30 towns in California. Earlier, in Pennsylvania, Saint had 53 projects on its books, with most of them targeted toward stopping Walmarts. These were on behalf of Giant Food Stores.[32]

The techniques used by Saint Consulting were usually clandestine. In a typical anti-Walmart project, a Saint executive would drop into the town under an assumed name and take charge of the local opposition to the store. They would flood local politicians with calls, using multiple phone lines to make it look like they were coming from different people. They would hire lawyers and traffic experts to derail the project or stall it. They would flood neighborhoods with flyers outlining the purported evils of a Walmart entering their area and the subsequent traffic and increased police calls that would follow. They would hope that the developer would back off, slow down, or drop the project altogether. They operated in secret. They deployed their strategies under assumed names and never revealed their clients' names because clients didn't want their names publicly known for fear it would draw adverse publicity or lawsuits.[33]

Planet Walmart

The New York Times has argued that Walmart has become a nation unto itself. To document its point, the newspaper stated that if Walmart were an independent nation, it would be China's eighth-largest trading partner. In terms of its low prices and impact, some economists say that the company has single-handedly cut inflation by 1 percent in some years as it has saved customers billions of dollars annually.[34] It is little wonder the newspaper calls the company's growth, size, and dominance "The Walmartization of America."[35] Because of its number one ranking in the *Fortune* 500 listing, based on size, the magazine referred to the company as "Planet Walmart."[36] In the 2012 Fortune 500 listing, Walmart has held on to its #1 position in terms of revenues.[37]

In addition to domestic growth, Walmart continues its growth internationally. Today, Walmart operates 10,800 retail units under 69 banners in 27 countries. International units number 6,194 so it is apparent that global growth is vital to the company.[38] Since U.S. sales have been fairly stable since about 2007, growing around 3 percent per year, the company has increasingly depended on international growth. Emerging markets provide the most significant opportunities for global expansion. In the third quarter of the fiscal year of 2013, Walmart reported 7.6 percent revenue growth from its international business. Brazil, Mexico and China remained the company's key international markets.[39]

Millions of Supporters

In spite of its opponents and the challenges it faces, Walmart draws 100 million customers every week. Each week nearly one third of the U.S. population visits a Walmart. The total amount of money spent every hour of every day is $36 million.[40] By virtually any measure, the popularity of Walmart is staggering.

Many consider the company to be socially responsible in addition to being a provider of thousands of jobs, low prices, and high value and service. Walmart has numerous corporate citizenship initiatives at the local and national levels. Locally, Walmart stores underwrite college scholarships for high school seniors, raise funds for children's hospitals through the

Children's Miracle Network Telethon, provide local fund-raisers money and workforce, and educate the public about recycling and other environmental topics with the help of "Green Coordinators."[41] Over a decade ago, the Walton Family Charitable Support Foundation, the charitable program created by Sam Walton's family, announced what at the time was the largest ever single gift made to an American business school: $50 million to the College of Business Administration of the University of Arkansas. Helen R. Walton, the "first lady" of Walmart, said that she and her husband established the Foundation to support specific charities, including the University.[42]

Global Responsibility and Sustainability Achievements

In its 2013 Global Responsibility Report, Walmart summarized some of its recent achievements[43]:

- Renewable energy now provides 21% of Walmart's electricity globally, and we became the largest onsite green power generator in the United States;
- Walmart and the Walmart Foundation are increasing training, market access, and career opportunities for nearly 1 million women worldwide;
- Walmart and the Walmart Foundation gave more than $1 billion to support organizations that impact local communities around the world;
- The Walmart Foundation became the first partner of Feeding America to donate 1 billion meals (since 2005);
- We saved our customers $2.3 billion on fresh fruits and vegetables since 2011; and
- Walmart committed to hire any honorably discharged U.S. veteran in his or her first year off active duty.

In the realm of community giving, Walmart and the Walmart Foundation gave more than $1 billion in cash and in-kind contributions around the world. This includes $1 billion in cash and in-kind gifts in the United States and $82.2 million in cash and in-kind gifts in international markets. In addition, Walmart, Sam's Club and Logistics associates volunteered more than 2.2 million hours, generating $18 million to U.S. nonprofits.[44]

Walmart's Power and Impact

In spite of its many achievements, article titles from newspapers and magazines consistently raise questions about Walmart's power and impact. Some of these from the 2000s include the following:

"The Wal-Martization of America"[45]
"Is Wal-Mart Too Powerful?"[46]
"Is Wal-Mart Good for America?"[47]
"One Nation under Wal-Mart"[48]
"Wal-Mart Gives Globalization a Bad Name"[49]
"Attack of the Wal-Martyrs"[50]
"Wal-Mart's Midlife Crisis"[51]
"Planet Wal-Mart"[52]

EPILOGUE TO SAM'S STORY

Sam, the hired gun, learned his lessons well. The people who bought at his stores were well satisfied. The downtown merchants who survived learned to coexist with the hired gun's associates. But things would never be the same. The changes had come rapidly. The social fabric of the small town was changed forever. The larger cities continued to fight, but had only limited success.

The hired gun rode on, searching for that next town that needed to be liberated from the downtown price-fixing bad guys. The search has become more complicated as the opposition has risen, but the spirit of Sam rides on.

AN EMBATTLED WALMART: A CONTINUING STREAM OF ISSUES

Walmart's size, power, and impact on local communities is where criticism of the company began. This included the threat of putting other merchants out of business, the creation of urban sprawl, the impact on property values, and the traffic congestion created when the company decides to locate in a particular area. The public and various stakeholders seem to have a love/hate relationship with the company. There is a continuing stream of issues the company faces.

Labor Practices. In addition to anti-sprawl activists and merchants, Walmart continues to face new opposition from competitors, labor unions, other activist organizations, and lawsuits. Its labor practices have been increasingly questioned. The company has been accused of paying wages so low that workers cannot live off them, making employees work "off the clock" without overtime pay, paying few or low benefits, and taking advantage of illegal immigrants. In 2004, the company was hit with a class-action lawsuit alleging gender discrimination against women. This class action lawsuit covered 1.6 million current and former employees, making it the largest private civil rights case in U.S. history. In late 2008, Walmart agreed to pay up to $640 million to settle 63 state class-action lawsuits regarding overtime.[53] In 2011, the U.S. Supreme Court ruled that the huge class-action lawsuit against the company could not move forward as a "class action" and that Walmart was entitled to individual determinations of its employees' eligibility for back pay. This was judged to be a huge victory for Walmart.[54]

Because these labor issues are so expansive and important, they are not addressed in the present case. Another case, focusing primarily on Walmart's labor practices and some of the issues outlined above, has been prepared for separate discussion. Case 32, titled "Walmart and Its Associates," may be discussed immediately following this case or deferred until a more in-depth consideration of employee stakeholders is undertaken in connection with Chapters 17, 18, and 19.

Bribery Scandal in Mexico. In 2012, *The New York Times* broke an investigative story into Walmart's activities as it has tried to expand in Mexico. The allegations stated that Walmart executives had learned of attempts by its Mexican subsidiary, Walmart de Mexico, to bribe Mexican officials to the tune of $24 million in exchange for getting building permits faster and other favors, but chose to cover up these findings. It was alleged that the cover-up scheme went all the way to Walmart headquarters in Bentonville, Arkansas. If Walmart is found guilty of violations of the Foreign Corrupt Practices Act, fines into the millions of dollars and possible prison sentences could be given.[55] In January of 2013, it was reported that e-mails had been found indicating that Walmart senior executives, including then-CEO Mike Duke, learned of the bribery scheme in 2005.[56] Investigation of the charges is ongoing. The company's own internal actions have included a merger of its compliance, ethics, investigations, and legal offices into one organization, which answers to the company's general counsel. This permits the company's review to be closely coordinated and integrated.[57] As Walmart continued its own review, it has said that it was also looking into potential bribery violations in Brazil, China and India.[58] The bribery charges against Walmart may take years to resolve.

Fire in Bangladesh. Though Walmart claimed it was no longer permitting its subcontractors to make clothing at the factories that burned down in 2012 in Bangladesh, the company has been implicated for its lax attention to labor policies and safety standards in sweatshops such as those in Bangladesh. Some of Walmart's brands were found along with a dozen or more Western brands in the charred remains of the fire. Walmart said it had revoked the factory's authorization to make its products months before the fire but that one of its suppliers had given the business to Tazreen Fashions on its own. The case demonstrated how hard it is for companies to monitor and police their suppliers.[59] In early 2013, Walmart announced tougher supplier policies. It has warned suppliers that it is adopting a "zero tolerance policy" for violations of its global sourcing standards and will sever ties with anyone who subcontracts work to factories without the company knowing it.[60]

Buy American More Often. It may be because of consumers' more recent interest in "buying American" or it may be in response to the bad press it received in connection with the fire in Bangladesh, but the nation's largest retailer announced in early 2013 that it was embarking on a program to buy American more often. Walmart officially announced that it would increase sourcing of American-made products by $50 billion over the next decade. The company also said it would help vendors in categories such as furniture and textiles to return production to America that had moved abroad. The challenge for Walmart, according to a spokesman for the American Apparel and Footwear Association, will be in finding vendors who can meet Walmart's price points.[61]

Hyping the "American Success Story." Perhaps in response to all the criticism it has been facing in the past several years, Walmart in early 2013 announced it was embarking on an upbeat advertising campaign, which it claims will try to tell the whole story about Walmart and its success. Walmart has taken a beating in the court of public opinion in recent years in spite of the social responsibility and sustainability initiatives it has supported and awards it has won. "The Real Walmart," as the multimillion dollar campaign has been titled, will be an attempt to talk directly to the public and to tell them their version of the whole story about the company, not just what they read or hear about.[62] The ad campaign will be the company's first purely image-based initiative in recent years, and it will feature national TV ads and a website in which customers, employees and others can share the warm feelings they have about the company. Among the features will be job opportunities at the retailer, efforts to sell more fresh foods, use more renewable energy, and the company's measures to get products to the customer at low prices.[63]

QUESTIONS FOR DISCUSSION

1. What are the major issues in this case? Assess Walmart's corporate social responsibility using the four-part CSR model. Is Walmart socially responsible despite having a devastating impact on small

merchants? What about its impact on communities in terms of sprawl, traffic congestion, and impact on the appearance of the environment? What responsibility, if any, does the company have to these merchants or to the communities it enters?

2. Sam Walton has been called a motivational genius. After reading this case, and with what you have observed at your local Walmart store, explain how this motivational genius empowered the employee. What is the "Walmart Way"? What has happened now that Sam is no longer around to visit the stores?

3. Walmart was an early leader in the area of corporate social responsibility. How do the early "Buy American" program and the "Environmental Awareness" campaign illustrate this? Were these programs actually examples of corporate social responsibility or were they gimmicks to entice customers into the stores? Are the benefits of its more recent corporate citizenship programs offset by the company's detrimental impact on merchants?

4. Walmart continues to find severe resistance to its expansion into New England and California. From Walmart's perspective, draw the stakeholder map. Define the true goals of the opponents of Walmart. Include a consideration of the following: (a) stopping Walmart's expansion, (b) preserving the status quo (e.g., downtown community and social fabric), (c) developing a cause that will pay their bills, (d) fighting for an ideology, or (e) something else. What should Walmart do?

5. What is your assessment of competitors secretly hiring consulting firms to block Walmart's entry into new communities? Is this an ethical practice? Is this a fair practice with respect to competitor stakeholders?

6. Do your own research to update Walmart's situation in the Mexican bribery scandal, the fire in Bangladesh, the plan to "Buy more American," and the campaign to tell its "American Success Story." Has Walmart made progress or have things gotten worse?

7. When you are the largest company in the world, how do you protect yourself against criticism? Does it seem that no matter how hard you try, it's hard to make things better?

ENDNOTES

1. Wal-Mart Stores, Inc. (NYSE: WMT) is the legal name of the corporation. The name "Walmart," expressed as one word and without punctuation, is a trademark of the company and is used analogously to describe the company and its stores.

2. Vance H. Trimble, *Sam Walton: The Inside Story of America's Richest Man* (New York: Penguin Books, 1990), 30. Also see Bob Ortega, *In Sam We Trust* (New York: Times Business, 1998).

3. Ibid., 34.

4. Janice Castro, "Mr. Sam Stuns Goliath," *Time* (February 25, 1991), 62.

5. Walmart's Web page, "News for list of awards," http://corporate.walmart.com/search/?q=list%20of%20awards. Accessed May 20, 2013.

6. Walmart, "Corporate and Financial Facts," http://news.walmart.com/walmart-facts/corporate-financial-fact-sheet. Accessed June 3, 2013.

7. For up-to-date information on Walmart's culture, see "Walmart's Enduring Values," http://news.walmart.com/executive-viewpoints/walmarts-enduring- values. Accessed May 20, 2013.

8. John Huey, "America's Most Successful Merchant," *Fortune* (September 23, 1991), 50.

9. Ibid., 261.

10. "Store Wars: When Walmart Comes to Town," PBS, http://www.pbs.org/itvs/storewars/. Accessed May 20, 2013.

11. Richard Turcsik, "A New Environment Evolves at Wal-Mart," *Supermarket News* (January 15, 1990), 10.

12. Ibid., 10.

13. Walmart Corporation, *Walmart Associates Handbook* (July 1991), 14.

14. Ibid., 14.

15. Dan Koeppel, "Wal-Mart Finds New Rivals on Main Street," Adweek's Marketing Week (November 10, 1990), 5.

16. Trimble, 255.

17. "Just Saying No to Wal-Mart," *Newsweek* (November 13, 1989), 65.

18. Ibid., 65.

19. Karen Blumenthal, "Arrival of Discounter Tears the Civic Fabric of Small-Town Life," *The Wall Street Journal* (April 14, 1987), 1, 23.

20. Ibid., 23.

21. Bob Ortega, "Aging Activists Turn, Turn, Turn Attention to Wal-Mart Protests," *The Wall Street Journal* (October 11, 1994), A1, A8.

22. Ibid., A1.

23. Ibid., A8.

24. Joseph Pereira and Bob Ortega, "Once Easily Turned Away by Local Foes, Wal-Mart Gets Tough in New England," *The Wall Street Journal* (September 7, 1994), B1.

25. "What Is Occupy Walmart?" http://sprawl-busters.com/occupywalmart.html. Accessed May 20, 2013.

26. Sprawl-Busters, Newsflash Blog, http://sprawl-busters.com/search.php?SRCHrecent=1. Accessed May 20, 2013.

27. Ann Zimmerman, "Wal-Mart's Image Moves from Demon to Darling," *The Wall Street Journal* (July 16, 2009), B1; Matthew Yglesias, "Is Walmart in Trouble?" *Slate*, http://www.slate.com/articles/business/moneybox/2013/05/wal_mart_sales_decline_america_s_largest_retailer_is_slipping_as_customers.html. Accessed May 20, 2013.

28. Ann Zimmerman, "Rival Chains Secretly Fund Opposition to Wal-Mart," *The Wall Street Journal* (June 7, 2010), A1.

29. Retail Leader, "Walmart's Grocery Segment Accounts for 55% of U.S. Sales," http://www.retailleader.net/top-story-industry_news-walmart_s_grocery_segment_accounts_for_55__of_u.s._sales-663.html. Accessed May 20, 2013.

30. Zimmerman, ibid.

31. Ibid., A16.

32. Ibid.

33. Ibid.

34. Steven Greenhouse, "Wal-Mart, a Nation unto Itself," *The New York Times* (April 17, 2004), A15.

35. "The Wal-Martization of America," *The New York Times* (November 15, 2003), A26.

36. "First," *Fortune* (May 3, 2010), 27.

37. CNN Money, Fortune 500, "Walmart retook the top spot," http://money.cnn.com/magazines/fortune/fortune500/. Accessed May 20, 2013.

38. Walmart, "Where in the world is Walmart?" http://corporate.walmart.com/our-story/locations. Accessed May 20, 2013.

39. Forbes, "Walmart's slow U. S. growth needs international earnings to drive earnings," February 19, 2013, http://www.forbes.com/sites/greatspeculations/2013/02/19/wal-marts-slow-u-s-growth-needs-international-muscle-to-drive-earnings/. Accessed May 20, 2013.

40. Statistic Brain, "Walmart Company Statistics," http://www.statisticbrain.com/wal-mart-company-statistics/. Accessed May 20, 2013.

41. Walmart Environmental Sustainability, http://corporate.walmart.com/global-responsibility/environment-sustainability. Accessed June 3, 2013.

42. University of Arkansas, http://waltoncollege.uark.edu/about.asp. Accessed June 3, 2013.

43. Walmart, 2013 Global Responsibility Report, http://corporate.walmart.com/global-responsibility/environment-sustainability/global-responsibility-report. Accessed May 20, 2013.

44. Walmart, "Community Giving," http://foundation.walmart.com/. Accessed May 20, 2013.

45. *The New York Times* (November 15, 2003), A26.

46. *BusinessWeek* (October 6, 2003), 100–110.

47. *The New York Times* (December 7, 2003), 1WK.

48. *Fortune* (March 3, 2003), 66–78.

49. Jeffrey E. Garten, "Wal-Mart Gives Globalization a Bad Name," *BusinessWeek* (March 8, 2004), 24.

50. Barney Gimbel, "Attack of the Wal-Martyrs," *Fortune* (December 11, 2006), 125–130.

51. Anthony Bianco, "Wal-Mart's Midlife Crisis," *BusinessWeek* (April 30, 2007), 46–56.

52. "First," *Fortune* (May 3, 2010), 27.

53. Ibid.

54. Jenna Goudreau, Forbes, June 20, 2011, "Walmart Wins Supreme Court Ruling in Historic Sex Discrimination Suit," http://www.forbes.com/sites/jennagoudreau/2011/06/20/wal-mart-wins-supreme-court-ruling-in-historic-sex-discrimination-suit/. Accessed May 20, 2013.

55. David Barstow, "Wal-Mart Hushed Up a Vast Mexican Bribery Case," *New York Times*, April 21, 2012; James B. Stewart, "Bribes without Jail Time," *The New York Times*, April 27, 2012. "Wal-mart Faces Big Fines Amid Bribery Charges," *The Jakarta Globe*, April 24, 2012.

56. Anne D' Innocenzio, "Emails suggest Walmart CEO knew of Mexico bribes in '05" *The Boston Globe*, January 11, 2013.

57. "Walmart: Ethics Unit Remade Amid Bribery Allegations," *The Wall Street Journal*, October 25, 2012, B4.

58. D'Innocenzio, ibid.

59. Miguel Bustillo, Tom Wright and Shelly Banjo, "Tough Questions in Fire's Ashes," *The Wall Street Journal*, November 30, 2012, B1.

60. Shelly Banjo, "Wal-Mart Toughens Supplier Policies," *The Wall Street Journal*, January 22, 2013, B1.

61. Stephanie Clifford, "Walmart Plans to Buy American More Often," *The New York Times*, January 15, 2013.

62. Shelly Banjo, "Wal-Mart Ads Tout 'American Success Story,'" *The Wall Street Journal*, May 4–5, 2013, B3.

63. Ibid.

CASE 2

The Body Shop (A)*

PURSUING SOCIAL AND ENVIRONMENTAL CHANGE

When North American consumers are asked to describe the cosmetics industry, they often respond with words such as "glamour" and "beauty." Beginning in 1976, The Body Shop International PLC (BSI) provided a contrast to this image by selling a range of 400 products designed to "cleanse and polish the skin and hair." The product line included items such as "Honeyed Beeswax, Almond, and Jojoba Oil Cleanser" and "Carrot Facial Oil." Women's cosmetics and men's toiletries were also available. They were all produced without the use of animal testing and were packaged in plain-looking, recyclable packages.[1]

The Body Shop's primary channel of distribution was a network of over 600 franchised retail outlets in Europe, Australia, Asia, and North America.[2] The company had enjoyed annual growth rates of approximately 50 percent until 1990, when net income began to level off. The media raised few questions about this decline in performance, because the firm's social agenda and exotic product line captured most of the public's interest. Indeed, early on, The Body Shop was the poster-child company for the burgeoning corporate social responsibility (CSR) movement.

ANITA RODDICK: FOUNDER

The company's managing director and founder Anita Roddick was responsible for creating and maintaining much of the company's marketing strategy and product development.[3] Roddick believed that The Body Shop was fundamentally different from other firms in the cosmetics industry because, in her own words, "we don't claim that our products will make you look younger, we say they will only help you look your best."[4] She regularly assailed her competitors: "We loathe the cosmetics industry with a passion. It's run by men who create needs that don't exist."[5] During the 1980s, Anita Roddick became one of the richest women in the United Kingdom by challenging the well-established firms and rewriting the rules of the cosmetics industry.

---

* This case was prepared by William A. Sodeman, Hawaii Pacific University, using publicly available information. It was revised by Archie B. Carroll in 2013.

Honors and Awards

Anita Roddick was greatly admired within the business community for the conviction of her beliefs and the success of her company. She received many honors and awards, including the UK Businesswoman of the Year in 1985, the British Retailer of the Year in 1989, and the Order of the British Empire.[6] The firm's customers included well-known celebrities, including Diana, Princess of Wales; Sting; and Bob Weir of the Grateful Dead. Ben Cohen, cofounder and chairman of Ben & Jerry's, described her as an incredibly dynamic, passionate, humorous, and intelligent individual who believes "it's the responsibility of a business to give back to the community ... she understands that a business has the power to influence the world in a positive way."[7]

Roddick opened the first Body Shop store in Brighton, England, as a means of supporting her family while her husband, Gordon Roddick, was taking a year-long sabbatical in America. Gordon, a chartered accountant by trade, was using much of their savings to finance his trip. Anita Roddick had little money to open a store, much less to develop products or purchase packaging materials.[8]

Field Expeditions

Roddick called upon her previous experiences as a resource to get started. Having been a United Nations researcher for several years in the 1960s, she had had many opportunities during field expeditions to see how men and women in Africa, Asia, and Australia used locally grown plants and extracts, such as beeswax, rice grains, almonds, bananas, and jojoba, as grooming products. She knew that these materials were inexpensive and readily obtainable. With some library research, she found several recipes, some of which were centuries old, that used these same ingredients to make cosmetics and skin cleansers. With the addition of inexpensive bottles and handwritten labels, Roddick quickly developed a line of products for sale in her first Body Shop store. She soon opened a second store in a nearby town. When Gordon Roddick returned to the United Kingdom in 1977, The Body Shop was recording sizable profits. At Anita's request, he joined the company as its chief executive officer.[9]

Early Strategy: The Power to Do Good

The Body Shop's early strategy grew out of the company's reliance on cost containment. Roddick was able to afford only 600 bottles when she opened her first store. Since she was looking for the cheapest packaging option, she chose urine sample bottles. Customers were offered a small discount to encourage the return of empty bottles for product refills. This offer was extended to both retail and mail-order customers.[10] The Body Shop could not afford advertising, and Roddick didn't believe in it, so she resolved to succeed without it.[11]

The Body Shop's retail stores were somewhat different from the cosmetic salons and counters familiar to shoppers in highly industrialized nations. The typical retail sales counter relied on high-pressure tactics that included promotions, makeovers, and an unspoken contract with the customer that virtually required a purchase in order for the customer to receive any advice or consultation from a sales counter employee.[12] By contrast, Body Shop employees were taught to wait for the customer to ask questions, be forthright and helpful, and not to press for sales.[13]

According to Roddick, "Businesses have the power to do good. That's why The Body Shop's Mission Statement opens with the overriding commitment, 'To dedicate our business to the pursuit of social and environmental change.' We use our stores and our products to help communicate human rights and environmental issues."[14]

Employees and Hiring Procedures

Store employees were paid a half-day's wage every week to perform community service activities. At the company headquarters in Littlehampton, England, The Body Shop employed an anthropologist, six herbalists, and a variety of others in similar fields. There was nothing that resembled a marketing department. Husbands and wives frequently worked together and could visit their children during the workday at the on-site day-care center.[15] The company's hiring procedures included questions about the applicant's personal heroes and literary tastes, as well as their individual beliefs on certain social issues. On one occasion, Roddick was ready to hire a retail director, but refused to do so when he professed his fondness for hunting, a sport that Roddick despised because of her support for animal rights.[16]

PROSPERITY AND SOCIAL ACTIVISM

As the company prospered, Anita Roddick used her enthusiasm and growing influence on her suppliers and customers. The Body Shop began to produce products in the country of origin when it was feasible and paid the workers wages that were comparable to those in the European Community.[17] Customers were asked to sign petitions and join activist groups that The Body Shop endorsed, mostly in the areas of animal rights and environmental causes. The company said it was contributing significant portions of its earnings to these groups, including Amnesty International and People for the Ethical Treatment of Animals (PETA). Roddick was careful to choose causes that were "easy to understand"[18] and could be communicated quickly to a customer during a visit to a Body Shop store.

Opposition to Animal Testing

An example of The Body Shop's corporate activism was its opposition to a practice that had become common in the cosmetics industry—animal testing. Cosmetics firms were not *required* to perform animal testing of their products to comply with product safety and health regulations. However, many companies voluntarily adopted animal-based testing procedures to guard against product liability lawsuits.[19]

The Body Shop was not worried about such lawsuits, because the product ingredients Roddick chose had been used safely for centuries. In addition, the older recipes had been used for many decades without incident. These circumstances led to the company's rejection of animal-based product testing. Any supplier wishing to do business with The Body Shop had to sign a statement guaranteeing that it had done no animal testing for the previous five years and would never do such testing in the future. The Body Shop used human volunteers from its own staff and the University Hospital of Wales to test new and current products under normal use. The company also volunteered to share the results of its tests on individual ingredients with other cosmetics manufacturers.[20]

Most other cosmetics firms used a variety of procedures to determine the safety of cosmetics products, with two animal-based tests becoming the standard procedures.

The Draize Test　The Draize test involved dripping the substance in question, such as shampoo or a detergent paste, into the eyes of conscious, restrained rabbits and measuring the resultant damage over the course of several days. Rabbits cannot cry, which allowed researchers to complete the tests quickly.

LD50 Test　Another test required researchers to force-feed large quantities of a substance to a sample of laboratory animals. The substance could be a solid (such as lipstick or shaving cream), a paste, or a liquid. The lethal dose of a substance was determined by the amount that had been ingested by an individual surviving animal when 50 percent of the sample had died; hence the name of the test, LD50.[21] Beginning in the 1970s, animal rights groups such as the Humane Society and PETA began protesting the use of these tests by the cosmetics industry. The Body Shop lent its support to these groups' efforts, labeling all animal testing as "cruel and unnecessary." By 1991, alternative procedures that involved far less cruelty to animals had already been developed, but were yet to be approved for industry use.[22]

THE BODY SHOP IN THE UNITED STATES

In the United States, The Body Shop's market share was limited by two factors. First, its prices were significantly higher than those charged for mass-marketed products in drugstores, although they were generally comparable to the prices charged for cosmetics and cleansers at department store sales counters. Second, The Body Shop was constrained by the number of stores it had opened in the United States. By 1991, only 40 stores had been opened in a dozen metropolitan areas across the country. A mail-order catalog and a telephone order line were used to supplement the American retail stores, but they were inadequate substitutes for the product sampling and advice that were readily available at The Body Shop's stores. Roddick maintained that those consumers who sampled Body Shop products became loyal customers: "Once they walk into one of our stores or buy from our catalogue, they're hooked."[23]

Going Public

The Body Shop was taken public in London in 1984, with the Roddicks owning a combined 30 percent of the outstanding stock. The firm's subsequent sales and net income figures grew during 1985–1990 from sales revenue of $15.3 and net income of $1.4 million to $137.7 and $14.7 million, respectively.[24] Without The Body Shop's monetary donations to various social causes, all of these net income figures would be higher than reported in the financial statements. Estimates of the company's annual contributions to outside organizations varied from several hundred thousand dollars to several million dollars.

Industry analysts considered The Body Shop to be a strong performer with the potential to prosper even in an economic downturn. The exotic nature of its products, such as hair conditioner made with 10 percent real bananas and a peppermint foot lotion, would attract consumers who desired affordable luxuries. Analysts regarded the public's desire for personal care products as "insatiable," especially in North America.[25] The addition of the strong emotional appeal of social issues formed the basis for one of the most successful marketing and promotional concepts in the cosmetics industry in decades.

The 20th anniversary of Earth Day, celebrated in 1990, focused media attention on many of the environmental issues that Roddick and The Body Shop regularly addressed. Further, it spurred interest in environmental issues in the commercial sector.

Competition

Several new entrants and existing competitors challenged The Body Shop in the United States and Europe. Among the largest of these firms were Estée Lauder and Revlon. The Limited had opened 50 Bath & Body Works stores, patterned after The Body Shop's outlets and located in shopping malls across the United States. In addition, a British competitor, Crabtree & Evelyn, had held a significant presence in North America and Europe since the mid-1970s.

By 1991, The Body Shop was a successful and profitable firm that had attracted a variety of well-financed competitors. The company faced a genuine threat from these firms because they were all well financed and had a broad range of experience in marketing cosmetics. Each of these firms was well established in the United States, yet no one firm dominated the new product segment that The Body Shop had helped create.

In addition, there were indications that the environmental concerns that attracted customers to The Body Shop might not have permanent drawing power. Roddick had vowed never to sell anything but environmentally friendly cosmetics and grooming products in her stores, but the industry was growing and changing faster than anyone had anticipated. It seemed that The Body Shop needed to take some kind of action to ensure its long-term survival.

THE BODY SHOP'S ADVERTISING CAMPAIGN

The first appearance by Anita Roddick in a U.S. television commercial was in 1993. This came as something of a surprise to long-time Body Shop customers and her competitors in the cosmetics industry. These people believed that Roddick abhorred advertising as a wasteful practice that "created" needs. The company did promote certain nonprofit groups in its stores and catalogs, including Greenpeace, PETA, and

Amnesty International. However, The Body Shop had a policy of not advertising directly to consumers.[26]

American Express Ad

Roddick agreed to endorse an American Express marketing campaign that featured founders of fast-growing retail firms such as BSI and Crate & Barrel. Not coincidentally, all of the firms featured in the campaign accepted the American Express charge card as a payment method. The main message of the campaign was that customers of these stores preferred to use the American Express card and that the store founders also found the card useful in their day-to-day business.

Roddick appeared in three commercials and a series of print advertisements as part of this advertising campaign. The advertisements included Roddick's brief description of the company's purpose and sourcing practices, and used film footage and photographs of her travels in search of exotic new ingredients.

Selling Out?

Although the Roddick commercials received a positive response from advertising industry professionals, some long-time Body Shop customers accused Roddick of "selling out" and breaking her promise never to advertise Body Shop products. Roddick responded that the commercials promoted American Express and did not specifically promote Body Shop products. The advertisements gave The Body Shop valuable publicity in much the same way that Roddick's social activism and personal appearances had done in the past. In 1997, The Body Shop unveiled "Ruby," a voluptuous size 18 doll created to counter media images of thin women.[27]

RODDICK'S ROLE IN THE COMPANY

When asked about her role in the company, founder Anita Roddick stated:

> The purpose of a business isn't just to generate profits to create an ever-larger empire. It's to have the power to effect social change, to make the world a better place. I have always been an activist, I have always been incredibly impassioned about human rights and environmental issues. The Body Shop is simply my stage.[28]

QUESTIONS FOR DISCUSSION

1. In this case, how does The Body Shop address the four components of corporate social responsibility? In The Body Shop, what tensions among these components were at work?

2. Analyze The Body Shop's power using both levels and spheres of power discussed in Chapter 1. How do you assess the company's stated mission?

3. Does The Body Shop employ any questionable practices with respect to hiring? The Body Shop asks potential employees questions about "personal heroes" and individual beliefs. Is it ethical to ask such questions of applicants? Are such questions fair to the applicants?

4. What is your assessment of Anita Roddick's philosophy regarding the "purpose of a business?"

5. What are Anita Roddick's strengths and weaknesses as a leader? Should she stay on in a managing role or step aside and allow a more experienced business person run the marketing operations?

6. Anita Roddick claims that her firm does not advertise, yet it receives free media exposure and publicity through the social causes it champions and her personal appearances. Is this an appropriate approach for a business to follow?

7. What is your opinion of The Body Shop/American Express advertising campaign? Was it a sound business decision on Roddick's part? What does the American Express campaign imply about The Body Shop and its customers? Is this different from the image of the nonprofit organizations that The Body Shop endorses? Did Roddick commit an ethics transgression by advertising through the American Express ad that contravened her earlier statements and policy, or was this different? How should she explain herself?

8. Can a company such as The Body Shop succeed in trying to balance profitability with an obsession for social causes?

ENDNOTES

1. Catalog, The Body Shop (Fall 1990).
2. Laura Zinn, "Whales, Human Rights, Rain Forests—and the Heady Smell of Profits," *BusinessWeek* (July 15, 1991), 114.
3. Ibid., 114.
4. Samuel Greengard, "Face Values," *US Air Magazine* (November 1990), 89.
5. Zinn, 114.
6. Greengard, 93.
7. Ibid., 97.
8. Zinn, 115.
9. Greengard, 94.
10. Ibid.

11. Zinn, 114.
12. Greengard, 90.
13. Maria Koklanaris, "Trio of Retailers Finds Soap and Social Concern an Easy Sell," *The Washington Post* (April 27, 1991).
14. AnitaRoddick.com, http://www.anitaroddick.com/aboutanita.php. Accessed June 3, 2013.
15. Greengard, 90.
16. Zinn, 115.
17. The Body Shop promotional literature, 1991.
18. Zinn, 115.
19. The Body Shop promotional literature, 1991.
20. Ibid.

21. Peter Singer, *Animal Liberation: A New Ethics for Treatment of Animals* (New York: Avon Books, 1975), 48.
22. The Body Shop promotional literature, 1991.
23. Greengard, 89.
24. Compact Disclosure database, 1991.
25. Koklanaris.
26. The materials used in this section are based on Jennifer Conlin, "Survival of the Fittest," *Working Woman* (February 1994).
27. The Body Shop International PLC, "History," *Hoover's Online* (July 7, 2004).
28. Greengard, 97.

CASE 3

The Body Shop (B)*

THE COMPANY'S REPUTATION IS TARNISHED

Between 1991 and 1995, The Body Shop continued to expand its operations. The company had opened 1,200 stores by early 1995.[1] Over 100 company-owned and franchised stores were operating in U.S. shopping malls and downtown shopping districts. During the period from 1991–1994, sales and net income grew from $231 million and $41 million to $330 million and $47 million, respectively.

The Body Shop had moved its U.S. headquarters from Cedar Knolls, New Jersey, to a less expensive and more central location—Raleigh, North Carolina. The original location worked well when The Body Shop opened its first U.S. stores in New York City and Washington, DC, but soon proved to be a logistical problem. In retrospect, Anita Roddick realized that setting up her headquarters in a college town such as Boulder, Colorado, or a city such as San Francisco would have been a better choice than starting from scratch in New Jersey.[2]

PROBLEMS ARISE

The Body Shop had bigger problems to deal with than the location of its national headquarters. The Limited continued to open its chain of Bath & Body Works stores on a nationwide scale. Placement of a Bath & Body Works store in a mall usually precluded The Body Shop from entering the same mall. (There were some exceptions, most notably very large shopping malls such as the Mall of America in Bloomington, Minnesota.) All of The Limited's stores, from Express and Victoria's Secret to Structure and Lerner's, were company owned. This allowed a greater degree of flexibility and speed than was the case with The Body Shop's franchising system. Further, The Limited had started grouping its stores in malls to create its own version of the department store. During the holidays, Express and Structure stores carried special selections of Bath & Body Works products to induce customer trial and develop brand awareness. The Limited's size and power as one of the major retailers in the United States made the company a strong threat to The Body Shop's continued presence in the U.S. retail market.

Confusion

The similarities between The Body Shop and Bath & Body Works stores also created some confusion. Some less-observant customers of The Body Shop were bringing empty Bath & Body Works bottles to The Body Shop to be refilled because Bath & Body Works did not have its own refill policy and the products often seemed similar. The Body Shop protected its slogans, territory, and franchises with an aggressive legal

_____
* This case was prepared by William A. Sodeman, Hawaii Pacific University, using publicly available information. Revised most recently by Archie B. Carroll, 2013.

strategy that included an out-of-court settlement with The Limited in 1993.[3]

More Competition

Other companies had successfully introduced organic or natural beauty products in discount and drugstores, a market segment that The Body Shop had completely ignored in its global operations. Traditional retailers including Woolworths and Kmart had also entered what had come to be known as the minimalist segment of the personal care products industry. Woolworths' entry was an expanded selection of organic bath and body products in its deep-discount Rx Place chain. Kmart's line of naturalistic cosmetics was sold in over 1,800 stores.[4] Other new companies included H_2O Plus, which sold its products in its own retail stores but did not make claims about animal testing as had The Body Shop and Bath & Body Works.

GOOD PRESS

The Body Shop continued to receive new accolades and to hit new heights of prosperity. Anita Roddick published her autobiography, *Body and Soul*, in late 1991. She donated her portion of the royalties to several groups, including the Unrepresented Nations and Peoples Organization, a self-governing group that spoke for Kurds, Tibetans, and Native Americans; the Medical Foundation, which treated victims of torture; and a variety of individual political prisoners. The 256-page book, which was written and designed by Roddick, Body Shop staff, and an outside group, resembled a mixture of catalog and personal memoir. On the final page of the book, where one would expect to see the last page of the index, is the coda of the final chapter. The last line of text, printed in large boldface letters, reads "Make no mistake about it—I'm doing this for me."[5]

Media Attention

Partly as a result of the book's publication, The Body Shop received a great deal of flattering media attention. *Inc.*[6] and *Working Woman*[7] ran cover stories featuring Anita Roddick. *Fortune*[8] and *BusinessWeek*[9] published shorter articles that focused on Anita Roddick and the company's performance. *Time* began its article with a story on Anita's fact-finding mission to Oman, where she obtained a perfume recipe from a local tribe only after participating in an embarrassing local ritual.[10]

BAD PRESS

In 1992, some members of the media began to criticize The Body Shop and the Roddicks. The *Financial Times* gave The Body Shop the dubious honor of headlining its 1992 list of top ten corporate losers after the price of Body Shop stock dipped from $5.20 to $2.70 during September.[11] Stock analysts had reacted to a disappointing earnings report, and the news set some minds to wonder if the company could indeed grow quickly enough to capture a leadership position in the minimalist market, or if there was a minimalist market at all.

In 1993, a British television news magazine telecast a report on The Body Shop. The show alleged that the company knowingly sourced materials from suppliers that had recently performed animal testing. The Body Shop sued the TV station and the production company for libel and won a significant financial award after a six-week court battle. Anita Roddick sat in the courtroom every day and compared the experience to confinement in a "mahogany coffin." The Body Shop won the suit and a huge settlement by proving to the British court that the company had never intentionally misled consumers about the animal-testing policy, which encouraged manufacturers to give up animal testing but not claim that ingredients had never been tested on animals.[12]

JON ENTINE'S EXPOSÉ

In 1994, *Business Ethics* magazine, a well-respected U.S. publication, published a cover story on The Body Shop that built upon many of the allegations that others had presented over the years. The resulting controversy engulfed the journalist, the magazine, and The Body Shop in a new wave of controversy that threatened The Body Shop's already slow expansion into the U.S. market.

In June 1993, journalist Jon Entine had been approached by disgruntled current and former Body Shop staffers about several of the company's practices. After overcoming his initial skepticism and doing some preliminary investigations in Littlehampton, The Body Shop's headquarters, Entine was convinced he had a sound basis on which to develop a story. Entine began his own investigation, which eventually resulted in the *Business Ethics* article.[13] Despite the magazine's admiration for Anita Roddick, it decided the greater good would best be served by publishing the article.

Entine's Allegations

In the lengthy article, Entine made several claims[14]:

- Anita Roddick had stolen the concept of The Body Shop, including the store name, recycling of bottles, store design, catalogs, and products, from a similar store she had visited in Berkeley, California, in

1971, several years before she opened her first Body Shop in Brighton in 1976.

- Roddick had not discovered exotic recipes for some of her products as she had previously claimed: Some were outdated, off-the-shelf formulas that had been used by other manufacturers, whereas others featured unusual ingredients, around which Roddick and company employees had woven fanciful tales of her travels of discovery.
- Many Body Shop products were full of petrochemicals, artificial colors and fragrances, and synthetic preservatives and contained only small amounts of naturally sourced ingredients.
- Quality control was a continuing problem, with instances of mold, formaldehyde, and E. coli contamination reported around the world, thus requiring the use of large amounts of preservatives to give the products stable shelf lives.
- The U.S. Federal Trade Commission had launched a probe into The Body Shop's franchising practices, including deceptive financial data, unfair competition, and misleading company representation. One husband-and-wife franchising team compared the company to the Gambino crime family.
- The Body Shop's "Trade Not Aid" program was a sham, providing only a small portion of The Body Shop's raw materials while failing to fulfill the company's promises to suppliers.
- Between 1986 and 1993, The Body Shop contributed far less than the average annual pretax charitable donations for U.S. companies, according to the Council on Economic Priorities.

Entine published a similar article in a trade magazine, *Drug and Cosmetic Industry*, in February 1995.[15] In this article, he discussed The Body Shop's policies regarding animal testing, citing an internal memo from May 1992. At that time, 46.5 percent of The Body Shop's ingredients had been tested on animals by the ingredients' manufacturers, which was an increase from 34 percent the previous year. This and other practices raised new concerns about the company's slogan "Against Animal Testing" and tainted the company's 1993 victory in its libel suit against the TV program.[16]

Reaction to Entine's Article

The reaction to Entine's *Business Ethics* article was swift and furious. In June, well before the article's publication, Franklin Development and Consulting, a leading U.S.-based provider of social investment services, had sold 50,000 shares of The Body Shop because of "financial concerns."[17] With rumors spreading about the article in early August, the stock fell from $3.75 to $3.33 per share. Ben Cohen, cofounder of Ben & Jerry's and a *Business Ethics* advisory board member, severed his ties with the magazine. The U.S. and British press ran numerous pieces on the article and its allegations. These articles appeared in newspapers and magazines such as *USA Today*,[18] *The Economist*,[19] *The New York Post*,[20] and *The San Francisco Chronicle*.[21] *The London Daily Mail* secured an exclusive interview with one of the founders of the California Body Shop, who described the company's early years and how they eventually came to legal terms with the Roddicks over the rights to The Body Shop trademark.[22]

Entine was interviewed by a small newsletter, the *Corporate Crime Reporter*, in which he defended and explained his research and the article.[23] One point of interest was Entine's claim that Body Shop products were of "drugstore quality," which he based on the company's use of obsolete ingredients and formulas and a *Consumer Reports* ranking that placed Body Shop Dewberry perfume last out of 66 tested.[24] *Corporate Crime Reporter* also noted that another reporter, David Moberg, had brought similar allegations against The Body Shop in a separate article published the same month as Entine's.[25]

Rift in Progressive Community

In January 1995, *Utne Reader* published a forum including commentaries by Anita Roddick, Entine, Moberg, and Franklin Research founder Joan Bavaria. The forum was remarkable in the sense that it presented a structured set of responses to the charges. Editor Eric Utne noted the rift that the article had caused in the progressive business community and described how the Roddicks, Marjorie Kelly, and other parties had begun holding face-to-face meetings to mend their relationships.[26] Entine described the same meetings as "a family gathering a few days after everyone's favorite uncle was found molesting a neighbor's child. The scandal was on everyone's mind, few would openly talk about it, and most hoped that ignoring it would make it fade away. It didn't."[27] Moberg encouraged consumer watchdog groups to do their jobs more carefully, citing the case of the British group New Consumer, which had previously given The Body Shop high ratings.[28] Roddick maintained that the truth had been sacrificed in a rush to judgment but that she had managed to cope with and learn from the experience.[29]

GORDON RODDICK COMES TO THE DEFENSE

Entine's *Business Ethics* article aroused Gordon Roddick to new heights of anger, according to those who knew him. He was now ready to play hard ball.[30]

Early in Entine's investigation, The Body Shop had hired the international public relations firm of Hill & Knowlton (H&K) to launch a counterattack on Entine's credibility and motives.[31] H&K used its contacts at NPR to place an interview with Entine and a follow-up story that included comments from Body Shop supporters on NPR news programs such as "All Things Considered." Attempts by the Body Shop to intimidate *Business Ethics* magazine failed. The editor and publisher, Marjorie Kelly, knew from the beginning that publishing the article was a risk, but she said she had checked and rechecked Entine's sources and was satisfied that his charges were sound. However, if The Body Shop chose to sue the magazine, she also knew that the cost of getting to the summary judgment phase of the trial could put the small magazine out of business.[32]

Gordon's Letter

Gordon Roddick responded to the *Business Ethics* article within a month of its publication by sending a ten-page letter on Body Shop letterhead to all *Business Ethics* magazine subscribers. In this letter, he denied many of the charges made in the article. The letter offered statements by several people that appeared to contradict their own quotations in the article. Roddick seemed to have a reasonable defense for most of Entine's allegations.

Several staff members at *Business Ethics* magazine were not pleased with the letter, which they had received in the mail because they were included as decoys on the subscriber mailing list. This is a common practice in the mailing-list industry to help prevent the misuse of subscriber addresses. The publisher of *Business Ethics* magazine could not recall authorizing the magazine's mailing-list service to rent the list to The Body Shop. It did not take long for the mailing-list company to discover that The Body Shop had obtained the magazine's subscriber list through a third party. Said Ralph Stevens, president of the mailing-list firm, "The Body Shop duped a prominent and legitimate list-brokerage company, a respected magazine, and they duped us…. If this is any indication of the way [The Body Stop does] business, of their regard for honesty and integrity, I give them a failing mark on all counts."[33] In late 1994, The Body Shop hired a business ethics expert to lead a social audit of the company.[34]

THE SITUATION AS OF 1995

By July 1995, Anita Roddick was already considering the possibility of opening Body Shop stores in Cuba, hoping to beat her competitors to that market and at the same time convert the Cubans' social revolution into a profitable yet honorable business revolution.[35] The company was also considering opening retail stores in Eastern European countries. At the same time, the media attention on the company had raised serious concerns among customers, among Body Shop supporters, and within the financial community. Since August 1994, the company's stock price plummeted by almost 50 percent to an all-time low.

Losses

The Roddicks took millions of dollars in paper losses on their holdings, despite having sold a portion of their stock in July 1994.[36] The company faced increased competition from several larger firms, including Procter & Gamble, Avon, Kmart, The Limited, L'Oreal, Crabtree & Evelyn, and Marks & Spencer. Other companies, such as H2O Plus, were making progress in their efforts to open retail stores that featured products similar to those of The Body Shop. The company had hired Chiat/Day to develop advertising campaigns for worldwide use and conduct a marketing study in the United States.[37] There was at least one report that the company was looking for a U.S. advertising agency.[38] The questions that had been raised as a result of media investigations and The Body Shop's responses left some observers wondering what principles the company espoused and if the company could regain its earlier level of success.

Anita's Fame Continued

Anita Roddick continued to be recognized for her leadership on social and ethical causes. Because of her social activism, Roddick won many awards in the mid-1990s. Among them were the following[39]:

1993—National Audubon Society Medal, USA 1994 —Botwinick Prize in Business Ethics, USA
1994—University of Michigan's Annual Business Leadership Award, USA
1995—Women's Business Development Center's First Annual Woman Power Award, USA

QUESTIONS FOR DISCUSSION

1. During the time period of the case, how has The Body Shop continued to address the four components of corporate social responsibility?
2. What is your assessment of the Jon Entine article and his allegations? What is your assessment of The Body Shop's response to Entine's *Business Ethics* article? Has The Body Shop misrepresented itself to stakeholders?

3. Was The Body Shop justified in hiring Hill & Knowlton to conduct a public relations campaign?

4. Has The Body Shop's reputation been damaged by the incidents in this case? How might the company improve its reputation? Do you believe the steps taken by The Body Shop, including the hiring of an advertising agency, will help or hinder these efforts?

5. Describe the roles you believe Gordon and Anita Roddick should play in The Body Shop's future operations. How might a stockholder, a customer, a supplier, and an employee assess the roles that the Roddicks should play?

ENDNOTES

1. Body Language—The Body Shop Web site http://www.the-body-shop.com (May 1995). Current Website is http://www.thebodyshop-usa.com/. Accessed June 3, 2013.

2. Anita Roddick, *Body and Soul: Profits with Principles, The Amazing Success Story of Anita Roddick & The Body Shop* (New York: Crown, 1991), 135–136.

3. Jennifer Conlin, "Survival of the Fittest," *Working Woman* (February 1994).

4. Faye Brookman, "Prototypes Debut," *Stores* (April 1994), 20–22.

5. Roddick, 1991.

6. Bo Burlingame, "This Woman Has Changed Business Forever," *Inc.* (June 1990).

7. Conlin, 29.

8. Andrew Erdman, "Body Shop Gets into Ink," *Fortune* (October 7, 1991), 166.

9. Laura Zinn, "Whales, Human Rights, Rain Forests—and the Heady Smell of Profits," *BusinessWeek* (July 15, 1991), 114–115.

10. Philip Elmer-Dewitt, "Anita the Agitator," *Time* (January 25, 1993), 52–54.

11. Ibid., 54.

12. Conlin, 30–31.

13. Jon Entine, "Shattered Image," *Business Ethics* (October 1994), 23–28.

14. Ibid.

15. Jon Entine, "The Body Shop: Truth & Consequences," *Drug and Cosmetic Industry* (February 1995), 54–64.

16. Ibid., 62.

17. Judith Valente, "Body Shop Shares Plunge on Reports of Sales by Funds and FTC Inquiry," *The Wall Street Journal* (August 24, 1994).

18. Ellen Neuborne, "Body Shop in a Lather over Ethics Criticism," *USA Today* (August 29, 1995), B1.

19. "Storm in a Bubble Bath," *The Economist* (September 3, 1994), 56.

20. Martin Peers, "Journalist's Probe Hits Body Shop," *New York Post* (August 25, 1994), 33.

21. Dirk Beveridge, "Uproar Threatens Body Shop Stock," *The San Francisco Chronicle* (August 25, 1994), D1.

22. Rebecca Hardy, "American Woman Recalls the Heady Days of Her Hippy Perfume Store … And a £2.3m Deal with the Roddicks," *London Daily Mail* (August 28, 1994).

23. "Interview with Jon Entine," *Corporate Crime Reporter* (September 19, 1994), 13–18.

24. Ibid., 17.

25. David Moberg, "The Beauty Myth," *In These Times* (September 19–October 2, 1994).

26. Eric Utne, "Beyond the Body Shop Brouhaha," *Utne Reader* (January–February 1995), 101–102.

27. Jon Entine, "Exploiting Idealism," *Utne Reader* (January–February 1995), 108–109.

28. David Moberg, "Call in the Watchdogs!" *Utne Reader* (January–February 1995), 101–102.

29. Anita Roddick, "Who Judges the Judges?" *Utne Reader* (January–February 1995), 104.

30. Ruth G. Davis, "The Body Shop Plays Hardball," *New York Magazine* (September 19, 1994), 16.

31. Ibid.

32. Maureen Clark, "Socially Responsible Business Brawl," *The Progressive* (March 1995), 14.

33. Ibid.

34. "Ethics Study for Body Shop," *The New York Times* (October 31, 1994), C7.

35. Conlin, 73.

36. "Stake Reduced in Body Shop," *The New York Times* (July 11, 1994), C7.

37. James Fallon, "Body Shop Regroups to Meet Competition in Crowded U.S. Arena," *Women's Wear Daily* (October 21, 1994), 1.

38. Anthony Ramirez, "Body Shop Seeks Its First U.S. Agency," *The New York Times* (June 27, 1995), D7.

39. About Dame Anita Roddick, http://www.anitaroddick.com/aboutanita.php. Accessed June 3, 2013.

The Body Shop (C)*

INTO THE NEW MILLENNIUM

By 1998, The Body Shop International had grown into a multinational enterprise with almost 1,600 stores and 5,000 employees in 47 countries.[1] That year, after several years of lackluster financial performance, Anita Roddick gave the company's CEO post to a professional manager and became executive co-chairman with her husband, Gordon. Anita maintained that job titles were meaningless, anyway.[2] Despite the change, the company's financial performance between 1995 and 1997 continued to be unimpressive:[3] Worldwide sales revenue and operating profits were $303 million and $21 million in 1995 and $377 million and $19 million, respectively, in 1997.

MORE ADVERTISING BECOMES NECESSARY

In 1995–1996, The Body Shop began to experiment with advertising in North American markets. According to one observer, the company originally thought that its brands and human rights agenda would create valuable word-of-mouth promotion among socially conscious consumers and that advertising would not be needed. The Body Shop's anti-advertising strategy largely paid off in the United Kingdom and other European nations, where human rights activism and commerce blended more seamlessly and consumers had fewer brands and retailers than in the United States. The strategy did not work effectively in the United States, where brand differentiation was crucial. In 1997, for example, The Body Shop's same-stores sales in the United States dropped 6 percent, the company's worst performance since entering the U.S. market ten years earlier.[4]

Since it has begun, U.S. advertising for The Body Shop has been piecemeal, often targeted toward the Christmastime holiday sales push. In addition, it has been quirky. For example, Anita Roddick taped a radio spot that slammed the cosmetics industry. In the radio spot, Roddick said, "If more men and more women understood what really makes people beautiful, most cosmetic companies would be out of business."[5]

GETTING ITS ACT TOGETHER

The Body Shop seemed to be trying hard to get its act together in the U.S. market. It hired a new CEO in the fall of 1998 and created the position of vice president for promotions. These were significant moves for the company, but it would take more than advertising to turn things around. The Body Shop typically plays down product efficacy in favor of hyping product ethicality. A case in point is its Mango Body Butter, whose ingredients the company promotes as from a "woman's cooperative in Ghana." Sean Mehegan, a writer for *Brandweek*, summarized the company's dilemma this way: "How much American consumers care about such claims lies at the heart of whether The Body Shop can turn itself around here."[6]

THE BODY SHOP'S SOCIAL AUDITS

In 1994, perhaps in response to the *Business Ethics* magazine article by Jon Entine calling its integrity into question and perhaps on its own initiative, The Body Shop began an elaborate program of annual social audits examining, in particular, its environmental, social, and animal protection initiatives. Through the social audit program, which the company based on mission statements and goals in numerous social performance categories, the company established detailed social and ecological milestones for 1995–1997. In its 218-page *Values Report 1997*, the company reported its progress.[7] This lengthy, landmark document is often held out to be one of the most significant social performance reports ever prepared.

As reported in its *Values Report*, The Body Shop set policies in three areas: human and civil rights, environmental sustainability, and animal protection. In each category, the company set forth a conceptual framework for the auditing process. The auditing process in each category depended heavily on stakeholder interviews. The stakeholders who were interviewed included employees, international franchisees, customers, suppliers, shareholders, and local community/campaigning groups. The company identified the media as a potential stakeholder group for inclusion in future social auditing cycles.[8]

ALLEGATIONS CONTINUE

In 1998, The Body Shop continued to face charges that could threaten its future. The company faced a flood of allegations and lawsuits by franchisees charging fraudulent presentations by the company when they bought their franchises. A number of U.S. franchisees had been angry at what they saw as unfair buyback terms

---

*This case was prepared by Archie B. Carroll, University of Georgia, using publicly available information. Updated 2013.

if they wanted to get out of the business. There was talk of group action that could involve claims in the hundreds of millions of dollars.[9]

An example of the kind of lawsuit being filed was that of Jim White, who was asking for $32 million in damages. He was suing The Body Shop for fraud, fraudulent inducement, and inequitable treatment of franchisees. White claimed that the company offered rock-bottom buyback prices to franchisees caught in a five-year spiral of declining U.S. sales. White claimed he was offered only 20 cents on the dollar and that others were offered as low as 5 cents on the dollar.[10]

INTO THE NEW MILLENNIUM

The early 2000s continued to be tumultuous for The Body Shop. The company continued to grow, but sales and profits were not strong. In the United Kingdom, the company found itself operating in a much more competitive marketplace than in its beginnings 25 years before. Most high street retail chains now are fielding their own "natural" cosmetics and toiletries, and price and promotional battles left the company's products more expensive than those of its rivals.[11]

Conflicts with Franchisees

In September 2001, a major *Fortune* magazine article featured some of the legal difficulties The Body Shop was facing because of conflicts with franchisees. It was reported that eight U.S. Body Shop franchisees, who owned 13 locations, were accusing the parent company of impeding their business. In December 2000, this group filed a lawsuit against the company, asking for damages in the neighborhood of $2 million. One major complaint was that the company-owned stores were getting much better treatment than the franchisee-owned stores. Franchisee owners complained of the company failing to deliver them products while the company-owned stores had no problem getting products. Some franchisee owners saw this chronic out-of-stock problem as a ploy to force them to sell their franchises back for a fraction on the dollar.[12]

Roddicks Step Aside

In 2002, Anita and Gordon Roddick stepped down from their positions as co-chairs of the board of directors. Along with their friend, and early investor, Ian McGlinn, they maintained control of more than 50 percent of the company's voting rights. Anita Roddick was to remain involved in a "defined consultant role." At about this same time, the company had been in discussions with potential buyers of the company,

but these talks were abandoned when offers were below what the company expected.[13] Peter Saunders, former president and CEO of The Body Shop in North America, became the CEO of the company.

Also, during 2002, The Body Shop conducted a global campaign with Greenpeace International on promoting renewable energy. The company furthered its commitment to environmental sustainability through investments in renewable energy, funding of energy-efficient projects in the developing world, and incorporating postconsumer recycled material into its packaging.[14] In 2003, the company started a global campaign to stop violence in the home. In 2003, Anita Roddick was appointed a Dame of the British Empire as part of the Queen's birthday honors.[15]

Sale to L'Oréal

In mid-2006, The Body Shop was sold to France's L'Oréal. Following the sale, Peter Saunders kept his CEO title and founder Dame Anita Roddick remained on the company's board. The plan was that the company would retain its unique identity and values and continue to be based in the United Kingdom. The company would operate independently within the L'Oréal Group and would be led by its own management team, reporting directly to the CEO of L'Oréal.[16] By 2007, the company had 2,100 stores in 55 countries, and two-thirds of them are franchised.[17] It also sells its products via The Body Shop at Home, an in-home sales program in the United Kingdom, the United States, and Australia. In 2007, the company published its *Values Report 2007*, its first since it was acquired by L'Oréal. The company continues to emphasize its five core values: against animal testing, supporting community trade, activating self-esteem, defending human rights, and protecting the planet.[18] The company's most recent values report is *Values Report 2011*.[19]

The company continues to face stiff competition. Its top three competitors are Bath & Body Works, Estée Lauder, and Alliance Boots (the UK's number 1 retail pharmacy). But the company has dozens of other competitors including such familiar names as Alberto-Culver, Avon, Coty, The Gap, Macy's, Mary Kay, Revlon, and Target.[20]

An article in *The Independent*, a newspaper in the United Kingdom, said in 2006 that the Body Shop's popularity plunged after the L'Oréal sale. The article argued that the sale had dented the company's reputation, and it was stated that Dame Anita Roddick had abandoned her principles by accepting the deal with L'Oréal. Roddick claimed that she would eventually give away the £130 million she made from the sale.[21]

Status of Company Criticism

Much of the targeted criticism of The Body Shop for the issues raised earlier, led in part by Jon Entine, has subsided. A review of Jon Entine's Web site, however, shows that he continues to critique The Body Shop and continues to write periodic articles and newspaper columns about the company. Entine's Web site may be accessed at http://www.jonentine.com/the-body-shop.html.

Roddick Turns to Publishing

Roddick published her second book, *Business as Unusual: The Triumph of Anita Roddick and the Body Shop*, in 2001. Also in 2001 she published *Take It Personally: How to Make Conscious Choices to Change the World*. She turned to writing because, she explained, "I'm at the point in my life where I want to be heard." She adds, "I have knowledge and I want to pass it on."[22] In an interview with *Across the Board* magazine, Anita commented on her experiences with professional consultants and executives who are not as concerned as she is about preserving The Body Shop's values. She stated: "The hardest thing for me are the marketing people, because they focus on us as a brand and our customers as consumers. We've never called it a brand; we call it The Body Shop. In 25 years, we've never, ever, ever called a customer a consumer. Customers aren't there to consume. They're there to live, love, die, get married, have friendships—they're not put on this planet to bloody consume."[23]

In 2003 she published *A Revolution in Kindness*. Her last book, published in 2005, was *Business as Unusual: My Entrepreneurial Journey*. She continued to speak and write and raise money for social causes and even developed her own personal Web site, http://www.anitaroddick.com/where you can track everything she did during the final years of her life.

ANITA'S UNTIMELY DEATH

Quite unexpectedly, and as a shock to all, Anita Roddick died on September 10, 2007. She was 64. She died of a brain hemorrhage, according to her family. As *The New York Times* summarized, she was "a woman of fierce passions, boundless energy, unconventional idealism, and sometimes diva-like temperament."[24]

The Future under L'oréal

Upon the sale of The Body Shop to L'Oréal in 2006, *The Independent* (newspaper) in the United Kingdom reported that BSI's popularity had plunged after the sale. An index that tracks public perception of consumer brands found that "satisfaction" with Body Shop had slumped by almost half since the deal by its founder, Dame Anita Roddick, to sell the company to L'Oréal.[25]

Better progress was made in later years. The total number of Body Shop company-owned stores grew from 1,088 in 2010 to 1,111 by year end 2012. Franchised stores increased from 1,517 stores in 2010 to 1,726 by year end 2012. Retail sales were up 3.7% from 2010 to 2012.[26]

In its *Values Report 2011–Striving to Be a Force for Good*, current Executive Chairman Sophie Gasperment said that the theme of the report, "The Values Chain," reflects how the company works as a business with values integrated into everything that is done. She reiterated the company's key values as: defend human rights, support community fair trade, protect our planet, against animal testing, and activate self esteem.[27]

When Anita Roddick sold her business to L'Oréal in 2006, she said that The Body Shop would be a "Trojan Horse." By that she meant that the ethical stance of the smaller group she founded would infiltrate the multinational.[28] Though it is not clear whether this infiltration has occurred, it does appear that the company is operating somewhat independently as one of L'Oréal's divisions and is striving to uphold its socially oriented mission.

In the fall of 2012, rumors were circulating in the cosmetics industry that The Body Shop's performance no longer fit L'Oréal's "profit profile" and that the company was grooming The Body Shop for sale. L'Oréal's chief executive, Jean-Paul Agon was quoted as saying "I very often receive strong offers to buy The Body Shop, which means that it is kind of a treasure."[29]

QUESTIONS FOR DISCUSSION

1. Did Anita Roddick betray her philosophy about advertising by beginning to advertise in U.S. markets? Did this decision have ethical implications? Or is it just a business decision?

2. Did The Body Shop's social auditing program help save the firm's reputation? Did the firm "snap back" from the damage done to its reputation in the mid-1990s?

3. Do the low buyback prices offered to U.S. franchisees reflect poor Body Shop ethics or just the economic reality of risky investments?

4. Is The Body Shop still regarded today as a socially responsible and ethical firm? Research the answer to this question and be prepared to report your findings.

5. At the end of these cases, what is your impression of Anita Roddick? Comment on her strengths and weaknesses and a businessperson and leader. Was the sale of the company to L'Oréal an indication that Roddick's philosophy had finally failed?

6. What will be the likely, longer term impact on The Body Shop's values and priorities under the leadership of L'Oréal and upon Anita Roddick's death? Is it in L'Oréal's best interests to leave the company alone and let it go in the direction Anita had provided it, or should it be brought more into the mainstream of the company?

ENDNOTES

1. "Capitalism and Cocoa Butter," *The Economist* (May 16, 1998), 66–67.

2. Ibid. Also see Ernest Beck, "Body Shop Founder Roddick Steps Aside as CEO," *The Wall Street Journal* (May 13, 1998), B14.

3. *Values Report 1997*, The Body Shop (October 1997), 150.

4. Sean Mehegan, "Not Tested on Humans," *Brandweek* (May 19, 1997), 54.

5. Ibid.

6. Ibid.

7. *Values Report 1997*, 7–12.

8. Ibid., 10–12.

9. Jan Spooner, "Body Shop Faces U.S. Legal Fights," *Financial Mail* (London) (February 22, 1998).

10. Ibid.

11. Harriet Marsh, "Has the Body Shop Lost Its Direction for Good?" *Marketing* (London) (May 10, 2001), 19.

12. Carlye Adler, "The Disenfranchised," *Fortune* (September 2001), 66–72.

13. Sarah Ellison, "Body Shop's Two Founders to Step Aside; Sale Talks End," *The Wall Street Journal* (February 13, 2002), A15.

14. Company Profile: The Body Shop, http://www.thebodyshop-usa.com/. Accessed June 3, 2013.

15. Ibid.

16. Ibid.

17. The Body Shop International PLC, "Overview," *Hoover's Online*. Accessed September 6, 2007.

18. The Body Shop Values Report, http://www.thebodyshop-usa.com/about-us/aboutus_history.aspx. Accessed June 3, 2013.

19. Values Report 2011, http://www.thebodyshop.com/content/pdf/global-values_report.pdf. Accessed June 3, 2013.

20. The Body Shop International PLC, "Overview," *Hoover's Online*. Accessed September 6, 2007.

21. Cahal Milmo, "UK: Body Shop's Popularity Plunges after L'Oréal Sale," *The Independent* (UK), April 10, 2006, http://www.corpwatch.org/article.php?id=13469. Accessed June 3, 2013.

22. Mike Hofman, "Anita Roddick: The Body Shop International, Established in 1976," *Inc.* (April 30, 2001), 61.

23. Matthew Budman, "Questioning Authority," *Across the Board* (January 2001), 15–16.

24. "Anita Roddick, Body Shop Founder, Dies at 64," *The New York Times* (September 12, 2007).

25. "Body Shop's Popularity Plunges after L'Oréal Deal," *The Independent*, http://www.corpwatch.org/article.php?id=13469. Accessed June 3, 2013.

26. The Body Shop Sales and Stores, http://www.loreal-finance.com/eng/brands/the-body-shop. Accessed June 3, 2013.

27. Values Report 2011, http://www.thebodyshop.com/content/pdf/global-values_report.pdf. Accessed June 3, 2013.

28. "Body Shop's Popularity Plunges after L'Oréal Deal," *The Independent*, http://www.corpwatch.org/article.php?id=13469. Accessed June 3, 2013.

29. Neil Craven and Adam Lee-Potter, "L'Oreal is ready to sell high street High Street Chain The Body Shop," October 7, 2012, This is Money.co.uk, http://www.thisismoney.co.uk/money/news/article-2214108/LOreal-ready-sell-High-Street-chain-The-Body-Shop.html. Accessed June 3, 2013.

CASE 5

Engineered Billing

I worked at a private engineering consulting firm that was a one-stop-shop for all engineering disciplines and focused mainly on large corporate or federal projects. Within the engineering community, it was and still is a well-known and respected firm. Upon joining the firm, I was given little instruction regarding how the company was structured and was put to work immediately. My prior position was with a small firm that put a lot of emphasis on producing a quality design and rarely noted the number of hours used for a design. They were only concerned with producing a quality project. My new firm was a stark contrast. I was put in a cubical, given a computer, and I received very little training on how the company operated.

My first weeks of work consisted mostly of me having to figure out how the company structured its files, how to enter billing, and what the company expected in their designs. I had weekly meetings with my boss who went over my time sheets with me and little else. He rarely reviewed my designs, only how many hours I was logging on projects and whether or not they were billable. It seemed that as long as I was making the company money, I was doing a good job. After I spent a month on the job, the lead engineer asked me why I was still billing hours to a project on which I was working. He told me that we had already billed the allotted design hours to this particular project. He then told me that I needed to bill to another project even though I was not working on that project. This came as a shock and I did not really know what to do.

Right or wrong, I stayed late and finished the design on my own time. Luckily, I was offered a job with another firm shortly after this incident, so I was able to remove myself from this situation. I hate to generalize, but to this day, I am more critical of proposals from firms that have a similar structure as this one, which I left years ago.

QUESTIONS FOR DISCUSSION

1. What are the ethical issues in this case?
2. Did I do the right thing even though I lost money in the process?
3. Is it fair of me to judge similar firms more harshly when they submit proposals?

Contributed Anonymously

CASE 6

The Waiter Rule: What Makes for a Good CEO?*

As the topic of corporate governance has been in the news more and more during the past several decade, it is useful to reflect on what boards of directors have to do in terms of their roles and responsibilities. Acting on behalf of shareholders, one of the board's most important jobs is selection of the CEO, who will provide strategic direction for the firm, and in turn, hire the top management team. But how does a board go about hiring a CEO? Certainly, this has got to be one of the toughest in the business world.

In recent years, so many contentious issues have surrounded CEOs that the board's task is no small one. Many CEOs have been implicated in ethics scandals, and many of them have been criticized for what the public considers excessive compensation. Today especially, boards want to be sure they hire CEOs with high integrity and impeccable character. It is a lofty goal and things don't always turn out the way boards wish. With a record number of CEO firings in the past five years, it is little wonder boards of directors are always seeking insights as to how to make these selection decisions.

Employers are always on the alert for guidance, for suggestions, for tips that would make their hiring more successful or run more smoothly. But if an elusive quality such as character is so important, how does

---

* This case was prepared by Archie B. Carroll, University of Georgia. Revised in 2013.

one gauge a prospective CEO's or top executive's character? Or, for that matter, how can we gauge the character of anyone at any level of management?

SWANSON'S UNWRITTEN RULES

In an important *USA Today* article it was revealed that Bill Swanson, CEO of Raytheon (the defense contractor based in Waltham, Massachusetts, that has 80,000 employees and more than $22 billion in annual sales), had published a booklet containing 33 brief leadership observations.[1] The booklet was titled *Swanson's Unwritten Rules of Management*.[2] It turns out that Raytheon has given away close to 300,000 copies of the booklet to members of its own organization and to virtually anyone who inquires about it. The book is filled with common sense maxims, observations, rules, and guidelines; it is considered to be something of a cult hit in corporate America.[3] Among the 33 guidelines or rules compiled in the booklet is one rule that Swanson has said never fails in terms of helping to assess someone's character.

THE WAITER RULE

Known as the "Waiter Rule," the observation says that "A person, who is nice to you but rude to the waiter, or to others, is not a nice person." A number of CEOs and other corporate executives have all agreed with the Waiter Rule. They basically concur that how a privileged corporate executive treats people in subordinate roles, whether they be waiters, clerks, maids, bellmen, golf caddies, or any other service-type worker, reveals insights into the executive's character that should be taken into consideration in hiring decisions.

Former Office Depot CEO Steve Odland recalls that when he was working in a restaurant in Denver many years ago, he spilled a glass of purple sorbet all over the expensive white gown of an apparently important and rich woman. Though it occurred over 30 years ago, he can't get the spill out of his mind. But what struck him most was her reaction to his careless spill. The woman responded in a very kind and understanding way. She kept her composure and in a calm voice said, "It's okay. It wasn't your fault." Years later, Odland recalls what he learned about this incident: "You can tell a lot about a person by the way he or she treats the waiter."[4]

CHARACTER REVEALED

As it turns out, just about every CEO has a waiter story to tell. The opinion they hold in common, moreover, is that the Waiter Rule is a valid way to gain insights into the character of a person, especially someone who may be in a position of authority over thousands of workers. The cofounder of Au Bon Pain (the leading urban bakery and sandwich café), Ron Shaich, became CEO of Panera Bread. He tells the story of interviewing a woman for general counsel, who was "sweet" to him but turned "amazingly rude" to the person cleaning tables. She didn't get the job.[5] She had failed the Waiter Rule.

Author Bill Swanson is quoted as having written, "Watch out for people who have a situational value system, who can turn the charm on and off depending on the status of the person they are interacting with."[6] Related to this observation, Steve Odland, formerly of Office Depot, has been quoted as saying, "People with situational values have situational ethics, and those are people to be avoided."[7]

QUESTIONS FOR DISCUSSION

1. Is character an essential ingredient in ethical leadership? Is it especially important in managers? In leadership, especially among CEOs, is character important? Why?

2. Do you agree with the Waiter Rule? Does it provide useful insights into who might be an ethical or unethical leader? Should corporate boards consider character when hiring someone for the top position?

3. Is using the Waiter Rule too simplistic a guideline for hiring people in important positions such as CEO? Is it too simplistic a guideline for judging one's ethics?

4. Do you have a "Waiter Rule" story or experience to tell?

ENDNOTES

1. Del Jones, "CEOs Vouch for Waiter Rule: Watch How People Treat Staff," *USA Today* (April 14, 2006), B1. Also available at http://usatoday30. usatoday.com/money/companies/management/2006-04-14-ceos-waiter-rule_x.htm. Accessed May 23, 2013.

2. William H. Swanson, *Swanson's Unwritten Rules of Management* (Raytheon, 2005).

3. David Leonhardt, "Rule No. 35: Reread Rule on Integrity," *The New York Times* (May 3, 2006).

4. Jones, Ibid.

5. Ibid.

6. Quoted in Jones (2006).

7. Quoted in Jones (2006).

Using Ex-Cons to Teach Business Ethics*

After the Enron scandal of 2001 and the WorldCom, Tyco, and Adelphia debacles that followed a couple of years later, the business ethics industry really started to take off. Business ethics consulting and training became a booming field of expertise, and those business schools that had not yet started teaching business ethics quickly created new courses to take advantage of the newly energized topic. Business schools that had ethics courses already in their curricula ramped up the number of offerings per year and started looking for innovative and interesting ways to attract students to the courses.

The early wave of ethics scandals brought about two major events that became driving forces in corporate and educational change. First, the Sarbanes–Oxley Act (SOX) was passed by Congress in 2002. SOX elevated the interest in and incentives for stronger financial controls and compliance, and this led to related initiatives in the realm of business ethics. Second, the Federal Sentencing Guidelines were revised in 2004. The U.S. Sentencing Commission revised its guidelines and created a new ruling that rewarded companies for developing ethics programs and offering ethics training. The Commission passed a ruling that among the different factors to be taken into consideration when a company was accused of wrongdoing was whether or not company management had provided ethics training for its employees. If the company had not offered ethics training as part of an ethics program, the company could be more severely disciplined than if it had offered its employees such training.

As a result, the demand for ethics training and education quickly grew in importance on both the business school and corporate fronts. In partial response to this new demand, a new category of ethics education arrived on the scene—the use of ex-cons to teach business ethics via presentations in business schools and companies.

WALT PAVLO: AN EARLY CASE STUDY

Walter A. Pavlo, Jr., had achieved many things by the time he was 40 years old. He had graduated from business school with a master's degree, worked as a manager at MCI, devised a $6 million money laundering scheme,

and served two years in federal prison. Along the way he became divorced and unemployed, and had to move back in with his parents. As *BusinessWeek* reported, it was "a story that should scare any MBA straight."[1]

Walt Pavlo, the convicted white collar criminal, has been called by *ABC News* the "Visiting Fellow of Fraud" for his appearances on many campuses. At an appearance for a business school lecture, Pavlo claimed he was once a God-fearing student who played hard and straight. He told ABC's *Nightline* that he was taught the catechism and Ten Commandments as a child and was taught not to steal, cheat, or curse. He was taught to be honest and truthful in all that he did. Upon completion of his MBA, he got a position at MCI, the communications giant, and started working in the collections department. He became very competitive and began fretting that the next guy might be outperforming him, so he ratcheted up his efforts.[2]

Pavlo eventually became a senior manager at MCI. He was responsible for the billing and collection of almost $1 billion in monthly revenue for MCI's carrier finance division. He had a meritorious employment history. In March 1996, Pavlo, a member of his staff, and an outside business associate began to carry out a fraud involving several of MCI's customers. When completed, the scheme had involved seven customers who were defrauded of $6 million over a six-month period. The money was stashed away in a Grand Cayman bank account.[3]

In explaining his going astray, Pavlo detailed how much pressure he had been under and how he was having a difficult time meeting the targets and goals that had been set for him. He told a colleague about his struggle, and the colleague said that "everybody was cheating" because "that's the way you make it." This became a pivotal moment in Pavlo's life, one that started him down the path to white collar crime.[4] After stealing the $6 million, he began to live according to his newfound means—an expensive new car, hand-tailored Italian suits, and frequent holidays, often to the Cayman Islands.

Six months into the fraud, auditors at MCI realized what he was doing and he was forced to resign. He thought the company would just write off the loss as bad debt to avoid adverse publicity, but his prayers were not answered. MCI brought in the FBI. Knowing he could not withstand a trial, Pavlo made a full confession and was sentenced to three years and five

---

* This case was prepared by Archie B. Carroll, University of Georgia, using public sources. Updated in 2013.

months in prison. He was required to pay recompense from any subsequent earnings for the next 27 years. Pavlo served his time in prison, and after getting out, learned that his wife had filed for divorce. Penniless and homeless, he returned home to live with his parents but found no success in looking for work.[5]

PAVLO'S SECOND CAREER

At the end of one of his unsuccessful job interviews, Pavlo was told he did not get the job but was asked whether he could return to the company and speak to the employees about white collar crime. This was the beginning of his second career. Over the next couple of years, he spoke to the FBI, some of the nation's top accounting firms, professional societies, and numerous business schools. Pavlo was asked by ABC's *Nightline*: "You are a convicted felon and an accomplished liar. Why should anybody listen to you?"

Pavlo responded[6]:

> Before I was a criminal or committed a criminal act, I was someone. I was someone who was on the fast track and did a lot of things right in my life. I've paid a significant price for what I've done, and I tell people that, and I educate people with a cautionary tale about what's going on out there. I'm trying to make a difference, and it's a chance for me to move on with my life and I feel good about my career, for once. For once in my life, I enjoy my work.

THE PROS & THE CONS

The Pros & The Cons, a Web-based company offering up an array of speakers on the subjects of white collar crime, fraud, and business ethics, demonstrates how the use of ex-cons in teaching business ethics has become a profitable enterprise. In addition to Walt Pavlo, the company features several other speakers whose expertise grew out of their having spent time behind bars. Chuck Gallagher embezzled his clients' trust funds, served time in prison, and is now on the lecture circuit. Mark Morze committed an infamous fraud when he bilked banks and investors of $100 million before getting caught and serving time. Nick Wallace served six years in federal prison for bankrupting 69 savings and loan associations. Now, each of these speakers is ready and willing, for a price, to come to your business school or place of employment and share with you the secrets they learned "from behind bars."

These speakers earn thousands of dollars per talk to speak to groups.[7]

Some convicted business people have gone out on their own and written books about their experiences and also lectured to business schools, companies and government. Aaron Beam, one of the co-founders and first Chief Financial Officer of HealthSouth, one of America's most successful health care companies, is a prime example.[8] Beam tells the story of his role in helping to perpetrate one of the biggest frauds in history. After prison time, Beam gives talks on business ethics and how to prevent corporate fraud, but also has to operate a one-man lawn care business to make a living. Beam thinks there are still those who think he is still wealthy, but he denies it. He observes "Trust me—if you can—I would not be mowing lawns in the South Alabama summer heat if it was not necessary."[9]

OPPONENTS TO USING EX-CONS

Not everyone is satisfied with the idea of using ex-cons to speak to business students. Business ethicist, Professor John C. Knapp has said, "I'm disturbed that so many professors seem to be willing to invite Pavlo and other convicted felons into the classroom without verifying that their stories are true. Paying the ex-cons is rewarding them for committing a crime."[10] A reader of *BusinessWeek* chimed in: "Too bad they don't pay $2,500 to honest people who never embezzled a penny to tell students that they shouldn't be crooks."[11]

QUESTIONS FOR DISCUSSION

1. What are the ethical issues in this case?
2. What are the advantages and disadvantages of hiring ex-cons to speak to college students on the subject of business ethics? Is it appropriate for colleges and universities to pay felons to be guest speakers?
3. What do you think you could learn from an ex-con speaking on business ethics?
4. Successful business executives who speak to students on the subject of business ethics typically do not get paid. They do this as a service. Is it wrong to pay ex-cons to speak on their illicit motives and activities?

ENDNOTES

1. Jane Porter, "Using Ex-Cons to Scare MBAs Straight," *Businessweek* (April 24, 2008).

2. Martin Bashir, "Walt Pavlo: The Visiting Fellow of Fraud—Ex-Corporate Criminal Makes a Good Living Talking Up Ethics," *ABC News* (January 30, 2006).

3. "Walter Walt Pavlo," The Pros & The Cons: The Only Speakers Bureau for White-Collar Criminals in the U.S., http://www.theprosandthecons.com/. Accessed June 10, 2013.

4. Bashir.

5. Ibid.

6. Ibid.

7. Christopher S. Stewart, "After Serving Time, Executives Now Serve Up Advice," *The New York Times* (June 1, 2004).

8. Aaron Beam with Chris Warner, *HealthSouth: The Wagon to Disaster*, Fairhope, AL: Wagon Publishing, 2011. Also see "Aaron Beam," http://www.aaronbeam.net/. Accessed June 10, 2013.

9. Ibid., 199.

10. Quoted in Porter (2008).

11. Ibid.

CASE 8

To Hire or Not to Hire*

SELECTING A NEW COMPUTER ANALYST

As a manager in human resources, part of my job is to guide the process by which my company selects new employees. Recently, we selected an applicant to fill a computer analyst position. The supervising manager and a selection panel selected this applicant over a number of others based on her superior qualifications and interview.

BACKGROUND CHECK

However, a routine background check indicated that the applicant had been convicted 18 years earlier for false check writing. The application form has a section where the applicant is asked if he or she has ever been convicted of anything other than a traffic violation. In response to that question, this applicant wrote "no." When informed of this, the supervising manager stated that she would still like to hire the applicant, but asked

_____
* This case was prepared by Tim Timmons.

me for my recommendation. The job does not involve money handling.

QUESTIONS FOR DISCUSSION

1. If the applicant mistakenly thought that her record had been cleared over time and therefore did not lie intentionally, would that make any difference in the hiring decision?

2. Should the fact that the applicant did not tell the truth on one part of the application automatically disqualify her from further consideration?

3. Should the supervising manager be allowed to hire this applicant despite the fact that the applicant lied on her application, provided the manager is willing to take the risk and assume responsibility for the applicant?

4. If the applicant freely admitted the conviction, should she still be considered for the position? Should a minor offense committed 18 years ago, when the applicant was in her early 20s, disqualify her when she is overall the most qualified applicant? What types of convictions, and how recent, should disqualify potential new hires?

CASE 9

You Punch Mine and I'll Punch Yours

When I was in college, I worked part-time one summer at a childcare center that was in a fitness center. Most mornings, I worked from 8 until noon, but some days I was scheduled to work from 7 until 11. My roommate also worked there, and our start times typically varied by that first hour. If I went in at 8 A.M., she had already gone in at 7 A.M. She would leave at 11 A.M., and I would work until noon. One morning when I got in at 8 A.M., she told me that she had punched my timecard for me when she came in at 7 A.M, and if I would punch her out at noon when I left then we would each make a few extra bucks. She thought this would be a great plan. After all, who would know? The folks who actually processed paychecks were in another location; our total hours were just submitted to them every two weeks.

There wasn't anyone who signed off on them, and most of the other folks who worked there paid very little attention to the childcare folks. She said we were only getting minimum wage, so what would it hurt to give ourselves a little raise because we were taking fantastic care of the children.

QUESTIONS FOR DISCUSSION

1. What are the ethical issues in this case?
2. What should I have done in this situation?
3. Should I have confronted my roommate? What should I have said?
4. Should I have gone to management and told them what happened? If I did nothing I would be paid for an hour that I did not work.

Contributed Anonymously

CASE 10

Phantom Expenses*

Jane Adams had just completed a sales training course with her new employer, a major small appliance manufacturer. She was assigned to work as a trainee under Ann Green, one of the firm's most productive sales reps on the East Coast. At the end of the first week, Jane and Ann were sitting in a motel room filling out their expense vouchers for the week.

INFLATING EXPENSES

Jane casually remarked to Ann that the training course had stressed the importance of filling out expense vouchers accurately. Ann immediately launched into a long explanation of how the company's expense reporting resulted in underpayment of actual costs.

She claimed that all the sales reps on the East Coast made up the difference by padding their expenses under $25, which did not require receipts. A rule of thumb used was to inflate total expenses by 25 percent. When Jane questioned whether this was honest, Ann said that even if the reported expenses exceeded actual expenses, the company owed them the extra money, given the long hours and hard work they put in.

FOLLOW THE AGREED-UPON PRACTICE

Jane said that she did not believe that reporting fictitious expenses was the correct thing to do and that she would simply report her actual expenses. Ann responded in an angry tone, saying that to do so would expose all the sales reps. As long as everyone cooperated, the company would not question the expense vouchers. However, if one person reported only actual expenses, the company would be likely to investigate the discrepancy and all the sales reps could

* This case was written by David J. Fritzsche, Penn State Great Valley. Permission to reprint granted by Arthur Andersen & Co., SC.

lose their jobs. She appealed to Jane to follow the agreed-upon practice, stating that they would all be better off, that no one would lose his or her job, and that the company did not really need the money because it was very profitable.

QUESTIONS FOR DISCUSSION

1. What are the ethical issues in this case?

2. Given all the factors, what should Jane have done?

3. What would have been the consequences for Jane and the company if she had accurately reported her expenses? What would the consequences have been if she had inflated her expense account as Ann had urged her to do?

4. What ethical principles would be useful here?

CASE 11

Family Business*

Jane had just been hired as the head of the payroll department at R&S Electronic Service Company, a firm comprising 75 employees. She had been hired by Eddie, the general manager, who had informed her of the need for maintaining strict confidentiality regarding employee salaries and pay scales. He also told her that he had fired the previous payroll department head for breaking that confidentiality by discussing employee salaries. She had also been formally introduced to Brad, the owner, who had told her to see him if she had any questions or problems. Both Brad and Eddie had made her feel welcome.

GREG'S HIGH COMMISSIONS

After three months of employment, Jane began to wonder why Greg, a service technician and Eddie's brother, made so much more in commissions than the other service technicians. She assumed that he must be highly qualified and must work rapidly because she had overheard Brad commending Greg on his performance on several occasions. She had also noticed Brad, Eddie, and Greg having lunch together frequently.

One day, Eddie gave Jane the stack of work tickets for the service technicians for the upcoming week. The technicians were to take whatever ticket was on top when they finished the job they were working on. After putting the tickets where they belonged, Jane remembered that she had a doctor's appointment the next morning and returned to Eddie's office to tell him she would be reporting late for work.

EDDIE SHOWS FAVORITISM

When she entered Eddie's office, she saw Eddie give Greg a separate stack of work tickets. As she stood there, Eddie told her that if she mentioned this to anyone, he would fire her. Jane was upset because she understood that Eddie was giving the easier, high-commission work to his brother. Jane also realized that Eddie had the authority to hire and fire her. Because she had been at the company for only a short time, she was still a probationary employee. This was her first job since college. She wondered what she should do.

QUESTIONS FOR DISCUSSION

1. What are the ethical issues in this case?

2. Is a family business different from other types of businesses with respect to employee treatment?

3. What was Jane's ethical dilemma?

4. What should Jane have done? Why?

---

* This case was written by Marilyn M. Helms, University of Tennessee at Chattanooga. Permission to reprint granted by Arthur Andersen & Co., SC.

CASE 12

Banned If You Do, Banned If You Don't

The old saying that "no good deed goes unpunished" may hold true for corporations sometimes. Chiquita, a U.S. firm best known for its bananas, originated in the late nineteenth century as the United Fruit Company, a firm that was known for bribing officials, damaging the environment, and exploiting workers in the Latin American countries in which it operated.[1]

More recently, Chiquita has invested heavily in social responsibility and sustainability. The company has committed to promoting more women, eliminating sexual harassment from its plantations, and upholding a global union agreement.[2] Sustainability efforts include collaborations such as the one they have with the Rainforest Alliance.[3] Chiquita employs sustainable farming techniques and makes its products available for environmental certification.[4] When Forest Ethics, an environmental group, pressured Chiquita not to use Canadian tar sands fuel, the company agreed to avoid its use in lorries (it already did not use it in its ships).[5]

Environmentalists hailed Chiquita's decision as "courageous" and "an important step." However, the tar sands decision enraged the Canadian oil industry and the people who depend on it. An oil industry lobby group named "EthicalOil.org" called for a boycott of Chiquita's products.[6] According to *The Economist*, this boycott is costing the company "a fortune."[7] They note that neither Dole nor Del Monte has followed Chiquita's lead in avoiding the use of tar sands fuel or signing a global union agreement. Ron Oswald, head of the International Union of Food Workers (IUF), expressed his concern, "It's not sustainable for any company in a competitive sector to make progress and gain no recognition for it."[8]

QUESTIONS FOR DISCUSSION

1. Often an issue has two or more groups whose interests are opposed and still a decision must be made. How should a firm determine which direction to take?
2. Some firms have been able to achieve competitive advantage by doing the right thing. Why has Chiquita not tended to benefit from socially responsible decisions it has made?
3. Why are Dole and Del Monte not following Chiquita's lead?
4. What advice would you give Mr. Oswald?

ENDNOTES

1. Our Complex History, http://web.archive.org/web/20011118092239/ and http://www.chiquita.com/chiquitacr1/6backgrnd/crp92.asp. Accessed June 4, 2013.
2. "Going Bananas," *The Economist* (March 31, 2012), http://www.economist.com/node/21551500. Accessed June 4, 2013.
3. Ibid.
4. Ibid.
5. Ibid.
6. "Going Bananas"
7. Ibid.
8. Ibid.

CASE 13

Location, Location, Location

Our department has two buildings about three miles apart. The extension office operates quite differently from headquarters. Folks seem to come and go as they please, and the atmosphere is casual. April works in the extension office and takes full advantage of this environment to maximize her second income: selling real estate.

Her office—a cubicle in the back of the building—is a disaster area of sales paraphernalia, billing statements from investment properties that she owns, and a smattering of work-related papers. She uses her computer and e-mail account to close deals and is constantly chattering in full voice on her cell phone as she woos potential buyers and schedules appointments. The departmental fax machine and photocopier also come in handy as parts of April's burgeoning real estate endeavors.

Management is aware of April's situation. However, they struggle with the other side of her story. Her job is unique in that it requires her to work in very hot or very cold environments, depending on weather. The storage building from which she must work daily does not have heating or air conditioning, but it must be fully ventilated. The bottles, jerricans, and drums that she handles are heavy, cumbersome, and dangerous. Sometimes the items April handles as a part of her duties are poisonous, extremely flammable, and even carcinogenic. At least once a month she has to don a respirator, a suffocating protective suit, and rubber boots as protection while she consolidates chemicals into larger drums. Temperatures in the suit easily exceed 100 degrees in the summer months. Finally, April is on the low end of the department's salary range, taking home less than $35,000 per year.

April's coworkers understand what her job entails, but her unabashed real estate transactions during work hours are creating a toxic environment for the rest of the staff—many of whom are in the same salary range as April, but with jobs that are not as difficult.

QUESTIONS FOR DISCUSSION

1. What are the ethical issues in this case?
2. What would you advise management to do about this situation?
3. Do April's extremely difficult working conditions factor into your decision?
4. How should management respond to the coworkers?

Contributed Anonymously

CASE 14

Something's Rotten in Hondo*

George Mackee thought of himself as a bright, energetic person with lots of potential. "So why is this happening to me?" he thought. George, with his wife, Mary, and his two children, had moved to Hondo, Texas, from El Paso four years earlier and was now the manager of the Ardnak Plastics plant in Hondo, a small plant that manufactured plastic parts for small equipment. The plant employed several hundred workers, which was a substantial portion of the population of Hondo. Ardnak Plastics Inc. had several other small plants the size of Hondo's. George had a good relationship with his boss, Bill, who was based in Austin, Texas.

THE EMISSIONS PROBLEM

One of the problems George's plant had was that the smokestack emissions were consistently above EPA guidelines. Several months ago, George got a call from Bill, stating that the EPA had contacted him about the problem and fines would be levied. George

*This case was written by Geoffrey P. Lantos, Stonehill College. Permission to reprint granted by Arthur Andersen & Co., SC.

admitted the situation was a continual problem, but because headquarters would not invest in new smokestack scrubbers, he didn't know what to do. Bill replied by saying that margins were at their limits and there was no money for new scrubbers. Besides, Bill commented, other plants were in worse shape than his and they were passing EPA standards.

A QUESTIONABLE SOLUTION

George ended the conversation by assuring Bill that he would look into the matter. He immediately started calling his contemporaries at other Ardnak plants. He found they were scheduling their heavy emissions work at night so that during the day when the EPA took their sporadic readings they were within standards. George contemplated this option even though it would result in increasing air contamination levels.

THE DOUBLE BIND

A month went by, and George still had not found a solution. The phone rang; it was Bill. Bill expressed his displeasure with the new fines for the month and reminded George that there were very few jobs open in the industry. That's when Bill dropped the whole thing into George's lap. Bill had been speaking to the Mexican government and had received assurances that no such clean air restrictions would be imposed on Ardnak if they relocated 15 miles south of Hondo in Mexico. However, Ardnak must hire Mexican workers. Bill explained that the reason for relocating would be to eliminate the EPA problems. Bill told George he had one week to decide whether to eliminate the fines by correcting the current problems or by relocating.

George knew that relocating the plant on the Mexican side would devastate the economy of the city of Hondo and would continue to put contaminants into the air on the U.S. side. When he mentioned the possibility to Mary, she reinforced other concerns. She did not want him to be responsible for the loss of the jobs of their friends and extended families.

QUESTIONS FOR DISCUSSION

1. Who are the stakeholders in this situation, and what are their stakes?
2. What social responsibility, if any, does Ardnak Plastics Inc. have to the city of Hondo?
3. What are the ethical issues in this case?
4. What should George do? Why?

CASE 15

Nike, Inc. and Sweatshops*

Jonah Peretti decided to customize his Nike shoes and visited the NikeiD Web site. The company allowed customers to personalize their Nikes with the colors of their choice and their own personal 16-character message. Peretti chose the word "sweatshop" for his Nikes.

After receiving his order, Nike informed Peretti via e-mail that the term "sweatshop" represents "inappropriate slang" and is not considered viable for printing on a Nike shoe. Thus, his order was summarily rejected. Peretti e-mailed Nike, arguing that the term "sweatshop" is found in *Webster's* dictionary and could not possibly be considered inappropriate slang. Nike responded by quoting the company's rules, which state that the company can refuse to print anything on its shoes that it does not deem appropriate. Peretti replied that he was changing his previous order and would instead like to order a pair of shoes with a "color snapshot of the ten-year-old Vietnamese girl who makes my shoes." He never received a response.[1]

THE PR NIGHTMARE BEGINS

Before Nike could blink an eye, the situation turned into a public relations nightmare. Peretti forwarded the e-mail exchange to a few friends, who forwarded it to a few friends, and so forth. Within six weeks of his initial order, the story appeared in *The Wall Street Journal*, *USA Today*, and *The Village Voice*. Peretti himself appeared on *The Today Show*, and he estimates that 2 million people have seen the e-mail. At the height of the incident, Peretti was receiving 500 e-mails a day from people who had read the e-mail from as far away as Asia, Australia, Europe, and South America.[2,3]

Nike refused to admit any wrongdoing in the incident and stated that they reserved the right to refuse any order for whatever reason. Beth Gourney, a spokesperson for Nike, claimed that Peretti was just trying to create trouble. She said he is not an activist and he doesn't understand the company's labor policy. If he understood the policy he would know that 18 is the minimum age for hiring. She went on to say that Nike does not need to apologize for not using "sweatshop" because company policy clearly says the company can cancel any order within 24 hours of its submission.[4]

Nike, Inc., is no stranger to sweatshop allegations. Since the mid-1990s, the company has been imperiled by negative press, lawsuits, and demonstrations on college campuses alleging that the firm's overseas contractors subject employees to work in inhumane conditions for low wages. As Philip Knight, the CEO and cofounder of Nike, once lamented, "The Nike product has become synonymous with slave wages, forced overtime, and arbitrary abuse."[5]

---

* This case was written initially by Bryan S. Dennis, University of South Carolina Beaufort. Revised and updated in 2010 and 2013 by Archie B. Carroll, University of Georgia.

HISTORY OF NIKE, INC.

Philip Knight started his own athletic shoe distribution company in 1964. Using his Plymouth Reliant as a warehouse, he began importing and distributing track shoes from Onitsuka Company, Ltd., a Japanese manufacturer. First-year sales of $8,000 resulted in a profit of $254. After eight years, annual sales reached $2 million, and the firm employed 45 people. However, Onitsuka saw the huge potential of the American shoe market and dropped Knight's relatively small company in favor of larger, more experienced distributors. Knight was forced to start anew. However, instead of importing and distributing another firm's track shoes, he decided to design his own shoes and create his own company. The name he chose for his new company was "Nike."[6]

Nike's Use of Contract Labor

When the company began operations, Knight contracted the manufacture of Nike's shoes to two firms in Japan. Shortly thereafter, Nike began to contract with firms in Taiwan and Korea. In 1977, Nike purchased two shoe-manufacturing facilities in the United States—one in Maine, the other in New Hampshire. Eventually, the two plants became so unprofitable that the firm was forced to close them. The loss due to the write-off of the plants was approximately $10 million in a year in which the firm's total profit was $15 million. The firm had a successful IPO in 1980, eight years after its founding. Nike went on to become the largest athletic shoe company in the world.[7]

Nike does not own a single shoe or apparel factory. Instead, the firm contracts the production of its products to independently owned manufacturers. Today, practically all Nike subcontracted factories are in countries such as Indonesia, Vietnam, China, and Thailand, where the labor costs are significantly less than those in the United States. Worldwide, over 530,000 people are employed in factories that manufacture Nike products. In an earlier calculation of labor costs for a pair of shoes, the labor costs amounted to less than 4% of the consumer's price for the shoes.[8]

Even in today's hi-tech environment, the production of athletic shoes is still a labor-intensive process. For example, for practically all athletic shoes, the upper portion of the shoe must be sewn together with the lower portion by hand. The soles must be manually glued together. Although most leaders in the industry are confident that practically the entire production process will someday be automated, it may still be

years before the industry will not have to rely on inexpensive human labor.

After some bad press in the early 1990s, Nike sought to improve the working conditions of its plants by establishing a code of conduct for its suppliers.[9] This was not seen as enough by outside critics, however.

Other Firms in the Industry

Nike's use of overseas contractors is not unique in the athletic shoe and apparel industry. All other major athletic shoe manufacturers also contract with overseas manufacturers, albeit to various degrees. Athletic shoe firm New Balance Inc. is somewhat of an anomaly as it continues to operate five factories in the United States and is the only company to continue U.S. production.[10]

Nike spends heavily on endorsements and advertising and pays several top athletes well over a million dollars a year in endorsement contracts. In contrast, New Balance has developed a different strategy. They do not use professional athletes to market their products. According to their "Endorsed by No One" policy, New Balance instead chooses to invest in product research and development and foregoes expensive endorsement contracts.[11]

THE ANTI-SWEATSHOP MOVEMENT

There is one pivotal event largely responsible for introducing the term "sweatshop" to the American public. In 1996, Kathie Lee Gifford, co-host of the formerly syndicated talk show "Live with Regis and Kathie Lee," endorsed her own line of clothing for Walmart. During that same year, labor rights activists disclosed that her "Kathie Lee Collection" was made in Honduras by seamstresses who earned 31 cents an hour and were sometimes required to work 20-hour days. Traditionally known for her pleasant, jovial demeanor and her love for children, Kathie Lee was outraged. She tearfully informed the public that she was unaware that her clothes were being made in so-called sweatshops and vowed to do whatever she could to promote the anti-sweatshop cause.[12]

Nike Is Accused

In a national press conference, Gifford named Michael Jordan as another celebrity who, like herself, endorsed products without knowing under what conditions the products were made. At the time, Michael Jordan was Nike's premier endorser and was reportedly under a $20 million per year contract with the firm.[13] Nike, the number-one athletic shoe brand in the world, soon found itself under attack by the rapidly growing anti-sweatshop movement.

Shortly after the Gifford story broke, Joel Joseph, chairperson of the Made in the USA Foundation,[14] accused Nike of paying underage Indonesian workers 14 cents an hour to make the company's line of Air Jordan shoes. He also claimed that the total payroll of Nike's six Indonesian subcontracted factories was less than the reported $20 million per year that Jordan was receiving from his endorsement contract with Nike. The Made in the USA Foundation is one of the organizations that ignited the Gifford controversy and is largely financed by labor unions and U.S. apparel manufacturers that are against free trade with low-wage countries.[15]

Nike quickly pointed out that Air Jordan shoes were made in Taiwan, not Indonesia. Additionally, the company maintained that employee wages were fair and higher than the government-mandated minimum wage in all of the countries where the firm has contracted factories. Nike avowed that the entry-level income of an Indonesian factory worker was five times that of a farmer. The firm also claimed that an assistant line supervisor in a Chinese subcontracted factory earned more than a surgeon with 20 years of experience.[16] In response to the allegations regarding Michael Jordan's endorsement contract, Nike stated that the total wages in Indonesia were $50 million a year, which is well over what the firm pays Jordan.[17]

Nike soon faced more negative publicity. Michael Moore, the movie director whose documentary *Roger and Me* shed light on the plight of laid-off autoworkers in Flint, Michigan, and damaged the reputation of General Motors chairperson Roger Smith, interviewed Nike CEO Philip Knight for his movie *The Big One*. On camera, Knight referred to some employees at subcontracted factories as "poor little Indonesian workers." Moore's cameras also recorded the following exchange between Moore and Knight:

Moore: Twelve-year-olds working in [Indonesian] factories? That's OK with you?
Knight: They're not 12-year-olds working in factories…the minimum age is 14.
Moore: How about 14, then? Doesn't that bother you?
Knight: No.[18]

Knight, the only CEO interviewed in the movie, received harsh criticism for his comments. Nike alleged that the comments were taken out of context and were deceitful because Moore failed to include Knight's pledge to make a transition from a 14- to a 16-year-old minimum age labor force. Nike prepared its own video that included the entire interview.[19]

Thomas Nguyen, founder of Vietnam Labor Watch, inspected several of Nike's plants in Vietnam in 1998 and reported cases of worker abuse. At one factory that manufactured Nike products, a supervisor punished 56 women for wearing inappropriate work shoes by forcing them to run around the factory in the hot sun. Twelve workers fainted and were taken to the hospital. Nguyen also reported that workers were allowed only one bathroom break and two drinks of water during each eight-hour shift. Nike responded that the supervisor who was involved in the fainting incident had been suspended and that the firm had hired an independent accounting firm to look into the matters further.[20]

Nike Responds

In 1997, Nike hired former Atlanta Mayor Andrew Young, a vocal opponent of sweatshops and child labor, to review the firm's overseas labor practices. Neither party disclosed the fee that Young received for his services. Young toured 12 factories in Vietnam, Indonesia, and China, and was reportedly given unlimited access. However, he was constantly accompanied by Nike representatives during all factory tours. Furthermore, Young relied on Nike translators when communicating with factory workers.[21]

In his 75-page report, Young concluded, "Nike is doing a good job, but it can do better." He provided Nike with six recommendations for improving the working conditions at subcontracted factories. Nike immediately responded to the report and agreed to implement all six recommendations. Young did not address the issue of wages and standards of living because he felt he lacks the "academic credentials" for such a judgment.[22]

Public reaction to Young's report was mixed. Some praised Nike. However, many of Nike's opponents disregarded Young's report as biased and incomplete. One went so far as to state the report could not have been better if Nike had written it themselves and questioned Young's independence.[23,24]

In 1998, Nike hired Maria Eitel to the newly created position of vice president for corporate and social responsibility. Eitel was formerly a public relations executive for Microsoft. Her responsibilities were to oversee Nike's labor practices, environmental affairs, and involvement in the global community. Although this move was applauded by some, others were skeptical and claimed that Nike's move was nothing more than a publicity stunt.[25]

Later that same year, Philip Knight gave a speech at the National Press Club in Washington, DC, and announced six initiatives that were intended to improve the working conditions in its overseas factories. The firm chose to raise the minimum hiring age from 16 to 18 years. Nike also decided to expand its worker education program so that all workers in Nike factories would have the option to take middle and high school equivalency tests.[26] The director of Global Exchange, one of Nike's staunchest opponents, called the initiatives "significant and very positive." He also added, "we feel that the measures—if implemented—could be exciting."[27]

COLLEGE STUDENTS AND ORGANIZED LABOR TAKE ACTION

Colleges and universities have direct ties to the many athletic shoe and apparel companies (such as Nike, Champion, and Reebok) that contract with overseas manufacturers. Most universities receive money from athletic shoe and apparel corporations in return for outfitting the university's sports teams with the firm's products. In 1997, Nike gave $7.1 million to the University of North Carolina (UNC) for the right to outfit all of UNC's sports teams with products bearing the Nike Swoosh logo.[28] Additionally, academic institutions allow firms to manufacture apparel bearing the university's official name, colors, and insignias in return for a fee. In 1998, the University of Michigan received $5.7 million in licensing fees.[29] Most of these contract and licensing fees are allocated toward scholarships and other academic programs. Today, these practices continue and the amounts of money are much larger.

Organized Labor

In 1995, the Union of Needletrades, Industrial and Textile Employees (UNITE) was founded. The union, a member of the AFL-CIO, was formed by the merger of the International Ladies' Garment Workers' Union and the Amalgamated Clothing and Textile Workers Union, and represented 250,000 workers in North America and Puerto Rico. Most of the union members work in the textile and apparel industry. In 1996, UNITE launched a "Stop Sweatshops" campaign after the Kathy Lee Gifford story broke to "link union, consumers, student, civil rights and women's groups in the fight against sweatshops at home and abroad."[30]

In 1997, UNITE, along with the AFL-CIO, recruited dozens of college students for summer internships. Many of the students referred to that summer as "Union Summer…[I]t had a similar impact as Freedom Summer did for students during the civil rights movement."[31] The United Students Against Sweatshops (USAS) organization was formed the following year. It was founded and led by former UNITE summer interns and remains active today.[32]

University Organizations

The USAS established chapters at dozens of universities across the United States. Since its inception, the organization has staged a large number of campus demonstrations that are reminiscent of the 1960s. One notable demonstration occurred on the campus of UNC in 1997. Students of the Nike Awareness Campaign protested against the university's contract with Nike due to the firm's alleged sweatshop abuses. More than 100 students demanded that the university not renew its contract with Nike and rallied outside the office of the university's chancellor. More than 50 other universities, such as the University of Wisconsin and Duke, staged similar protests and sit-ins.[33]

In response to the protests at UNC, Nike invited the editor of the university's student newspaper to tour Nike's overseas contractors to examine the working conditions firsthand. Nike offered to fund the trip by pledging $15,000 toward the student's travel and accommodation costs. Interestingly, Michael Jordan is an alumnus of UNC.[34]

Critics of the USAS contend that the student organization is merely a puppet of UNITE and organized labor. They cite the fact that the AFL-CIO has spent more than $3 million on internships and outreach programs with the alleged intent of interesting students in careers as union activists. The founders of the USAS are former UNITE interns. The USAS admits that UNITE has tipped off the student movement as to the whereabouts of alleged sweatshop factories. Also, in an attempt to spur campus interest in the sweatshop cause, UNITE sent two sweatshop workers on a five-campus tour. They have also coached students via phone during sit-ins and paid for regularly scheduled teleconferences between anti-sweatshop student leaders on different campuses. According to Allan Ryan, a Harvard University lawyer who has negotiated with the USAS, "[T]he students are vocal, but it's hard to get a viewpoint from them that does not reflect that of UNITE."[35]

Many students have denied allegations that they are being manipulated by organized labor and claim that they discovered the sweatshop issues on their own. Others acknowledge the assistance of organized labor but claim it is "no different from [student] civil rights activists using the NAACP in the 1960s."[36] John Sweeney, president of the AFL-CIO, claimed the role of organized labor was not one of manipulation but of motivation. Others assert that the union merely provides moral support.[37]

Regardless of the AFL-CIO's intentions, the students have had a positive impact on the promotion of organized labor's anti-sweatshop agenda over the years. According to the director of one of the several human rights groups that are providing assistance to the students, the sweatshop protests were being carried on the backs of the university students. A major reason for this is that they get more press coverage than do the union people.[38]

In telling the world about itself, in 2013 USAS stated that it "is a national student labor organization fighting for workers' rights with chapters at over 150 campuses."[39] USAS's anti-sweatshop campaign continues under its "Garment Worker Solidarity" initiative.

THE FAIR LABOR ASSOCIATION (FLA)

In 1996, a presidential task force of industry and human rights representatives was given the job of addressing the sweatshop issue. The key purpose of this task force was to develop a workplace code of conduct and a system for monitoring factories to ensure compliance. In 1998, the task force created the Fair Labor Association (FLA) to accomplish these goals. This organization was made up of consumer and human rights groups as well as footwear and apparel manufacturers. Nike was one of the first companies to join the FLA. Many other major manufacturers (Levi Strauss & Co., Liz Claiborne, Patagonia, Polo Ralph Lauren, Reebok, Eddie Bauer, and Phillips-Van Heusen) along with hundreds of colleges and universities also joined the FLA.[40]

FLA Requirements

Members of the FLA must follow the principles set forth in the organization's Workplace Code of Conduct. The Code of Conduct is based on international labor and human rights standards—primarily Conventions of the International Labor Organization (ILO)—and prohibits discrimination, the use of child or forced labor, and harassment or abuse. It also establishes requirements related to health and safety; freedom of association and collective bargaining; wages and benefits; hours of work; and overtime compensation.[41]

The Worker Rights Consortium

The USAS opposed several of the FLA's key components and created the Worker Rights Consortium (WRC) as an alternative to the FLA. The WRC asserts that the prevailing industry or legal minimum wage in some countries is too low and does not provide employees with the basic human needs they require. They proposed that factories should instead pay a higher "living wage" that takes into account the wage required to provide factory employees with enough income to afford housing, energy, nutrition, clothing, health care, education, potable water, child care, transportation, and savings. Additionally, the WRC supports public disclosure of all factory locations and the right to monitor any factory at any time. As of March 2013, 180 colleges and universities had joined the WRC and agreed to adhere to its policies.[42]

Nike, a member and supporter of the FLA, did not support the WRC. The firm states that the concept of a living wage is impractical as "there is no common, agreed-upon definition of the living wage. Definitions range from complex mathematical formulas to vague philosophical notions." Additionally, Nike was once opposed to the WRC's proposal that the location of all factories be publicly disclosed. Nike also has claimed that the monitoring provisions set out by the WRC are unrealistic and biased toward organized labor.[43]

The University of Oregon, Philip Knight's alma mater, joined the WRC in the year 2000. Alumnus Knight had previously contributed over $50 million to the university—$30 million for academics and $20 million for athletics. Upon hearing that his alma mater had joined the WRC, Knight was shocked. He withdrew a proposed $30 million donation and stated that "the bonds of trust, which allowed me to give at a high level, have been shredded" and "there will be no further donations of any kind to the University of Oregon."[44,45]

NIKE COMES AROUND

In May 2001, Harsh Saini, Nike's corporate and social responsibility manager, acknowledged that the firm may not have handled the sweatshop issue as well as it could have and stated that Nike had not been adequately monitoring its subcontractors in overseas operations until the media and other organizations revealed the presence of sweatshops.

We were a bunch of shoe geeks who expanded so much without thinking of being socially responsible that we went from being a very big sexy brand name

*to suddenly becoming the poster boy for everything
bad in manufacturing.*

She added, "We realized that if we still wanted to be
the brand of choice in 20 years, we had certain responsibilities to fulfill."[46]

Oregon Reverses Its Decision

In early 2001, Oregon's state board of higher education
cast doubt on the legality of the University of Oregon's
WRC membership, and the university dissolved its ties
with the labor organization.[47] In September of the
same year, Phil Knight renewed his financial support.
Although the exact amount of Knight's donation was
kept confidential, it was sufficient to ensure that the
$85 million expansion of the university's football sta-
dium would go through as originally planned. In 2000,
the stadium expansion plans suffered a significant set-
back when Knight withdrew his funding. Many of the
proposed additions, such as a 12,000 seat capacity
increase and 32 brand new skyboxes, were possible
largely due to Knight's pledge of financial support.[48,49]

Nike released its first corporate social responsibility report in October 2001. According to Phil Knight,
"[I]n this report, Nike for the first time has assembled
a comprehensive public review of our corporate responsibility practices."[50] The report cited several areas in
which the firm could have done better, such as worker
conditions in Indonesia and Mexico. The report, compiled by both internal auditors and outside monitors,
also noted that Nike was one of only four companies
that had joined a World Wildlife Fund program to
reduce greenhouse admissions. Jason Mark, a spokesperson for Global Exchange, one of Nike's chief critics,
praised the report and stated that Nike is "obviously
responding to consumer concerns."[51]

KASKY V. NIKE, INC.

Nike's problems with fair labor issues continued on a
related front. Labor activist Mark Kasky had sued Nike
in 1998, arguing that Nike had engaged in false advertising when it denied that there was mistreatment of
workers in Southeastern Asian factories. At issue was
the question of whether Nike's defense of its practices
was commercial speech or not; free speech protections
apply only to the latter. The California Supreme Court
ruled that Nike's statements about labor conditions
could be construed as false advertising. Nike appealed
this ruling to the U.S. Supreme Court, which sent it
back to the California court, without making a judgment on the free speech issue. In September 2003,

Kasky and Nike settled the case for a $1.5 million
donation to the FLA.[52] The settlement, however, left
many questions unanswered.[53] Many feared that the
risk of lawsuit would have a chilling effect, causing
firms to no longer release social responsibility reports,
which, unlike the SEC financial reports, are all voluntary.
In 2001, Nike issued a corporate social responsibility
report, but the company announced that, due to the California decision, they would not release a corporate social
responsibility report in 2002–2003. Nike released a
"Community Investment" report detailing its philanthropic efforts instead.[54] The company later released a
corporate responsibility report in 2005–2006 and again
in 2008–2009. The company's most recent Corporate
Responsibility Report was published in 2012.[55]

CRITICS QUIET DOWN BUT DON'T GO AWAY

Nike's critics have not gone away, but they have
quieted down as the company has taken steps to
address many of the criticisms made over the years.
Though the critics are less vocal today compared to
previous periods, there is still some ongoing criticism
of the company. Typical of the continuing opposition
is the organization Educating for Justice (EFJ), which
runs a continuing "Stop Nike Sweatshops" campaign.
In 2006, EFJ planned a film titled *Sweat*. The film, as
described on EFJ's Web site, describes the journey of
two young Americans uncovering the story behind the
statistics about Nike factory workers. Through the lens
of their experiences, they claim viewers will discover
the injustices of Nike's labor practices in the developing world, specifically in Indonesia, and how Nike's
cutthroat, bottom-line economic decisions have a profound effect on human lives.[56] EFJ announced that the
film was going to production in 2009, but in 2013, it
appeared that EFJ was still trying to raise money to
complete the film and to release it for public viewing.[57]

One organization that remains active in taking Nike
to task is "Team Sweat." Team Sweat identifies itself as an
"international coalition of consumers, investors, and
workers committed to ending the injustices in Nike's
sweatshops around the world." It goes on to say "Team
Sweat is striving to ensure that all workers who produce
Nike products are paid a living wage."[58] As of 2013,
Team Sweat was active in the "Nike: Just Pay It" campaign that was being pushed by several anti-sweatshop
organizations.[59] One other organization that conducts
an ongoing campaign against Nike's sweatshops is
Oxfam Australia. Oxfam complains about Nike paying
Tiger Woods $25 million a year while the workers who
make its products receive poverty wages and endure

harsh working conditions.[60] In addition to Nike, Oxfam pursues its initiatives against Puma, Adidas, and Fila.[61]

NIKE LATER GETS POSITIVE RECOGNITIONS

In spite of its controversial record on the issue of sweatshops and monitoring labor practices abroad, Nike has been the recipient of a variety of corporate social responsibility recognitions over the past several years. Many of these awards are for issues other than their labor practices abroad. Among the recent recognitions that Nike has received for its corporate social responsibility and sustainability practices are the following:

> *Corporate Responsibility* magazine (2013): Nike at #22 on its "100 Best Corporate Citizens" list[62]

> Climate Counts (2012): Nike at #1 reducing total emissions across some or all business units[63]

> *Newsweek's* Green Rankings (2010): Nike rated #1 for "green score," and #2 for "reputation score."[64]

In 2013, a new book was published on the subject of improving ethical supply chains, authored by MIT professor Richard Locke. In its research, Locke persuaded four companies held in high regard for their ethical supply chains to open up their books and permit him to study their processes. The four firms he selected were Nike, Coca-Cola, HP, and PVH. Locke said he began studying Nike because he became impressed with their commitment to labor standards but that eventually their efforts fell short.[65] Locke and his associates found the compliance staff and auditors at Nike to be hardworking, serious, and genuinely concerned about the workers. He also thought that with all the time and resources Nike had invested in the problem one would have expected better results. But, while some of Nike's factories were found to be in compliance, others suffered from persistent problems with wages, working hours, and employee health and safety. He summarized: "such disappointing results are common all over the world, in every industry."[66]

QUESTIONS FOR DISCUSSION

1. What are the ethical and social issues in this case?
2. Why should Nike be held responsible for what happens in factories that it does not own? Does Nike have a responsibility to ensure that factory workers receive a "living wage"? Do the wage guidelines of FLA or WRC seem most appropriate to you? Why?
3. Is it fair for Nike to pay endorsers millions while its factory employees receive a few dollars a day?
4. Is Nike's responsibility to monitor its subcontracted factories a legal, economic, social, or philanthropic responsibility? What was it ten years ago? What will it be ten years from now?
5. What could Nike have done, if anything, to prevent the damage to its corporate reputation? What steps should Nike take in the future? Is it "good business" for Nike to acknowledge its past errors and become more socially responsible?
6. What are the motivations of student organizations when they get involved in the anti-sweatshop movement? Why is their activism prevalent on some campuses but not on others?
7. Nike seems to be a much more respected company today than it was back when the anti-sweatshop movement began. What has changed in Nike and the world to explain this? What do its corporate responsibility recognitions say about the company?
8. In light of Richard Locke's research, are truly ethical supply chains ever to be achieved?

ENDNOTES

1. Copy of e-mail exchange found at Department of Personal Freedom Web site, http://www.shey.net/niked.html. Accessed June 5, 2013.
2. Ibid.
3. *ABC News*, "When Nike Just Couldn't Do It," http://abcnews.go.com/Technology/story?id=98680&page=1#.Ua9C50Ckobw. Accessed June 5, 2013.
4. Ibid.
5. Bien Hoa, "Job Opportunity or Exploitation," *Los Angeles Times* (April 18, 1999).
6. Philip Knight, "Global Manufacturing: The Nike Story Is Just Good Business," *Vital Speeches of the Day* 64(20): 637–640.
7. Ibid.
8. These data were presented on an earlier Nike Web site that is no longer available. The site was http://nikeinc.com/.
9. "Working Conditions in Factories: When the Jobs Inspector Calls," *The Economist*, March 31, 2012, 73–74.
10. New Balance, http://www.newbalance.com/Domestic-Manufacturing/about_domestic_manufacturing, default,pg.html. Accessed June 5, 2013.
11. Ibid.
12. David Bauman, "After the Tears, Gifford Testifies on Sweatshops—She Turns Lights, Cameras on Issue," *Seattle Times* (July 16, 1996), A3.
13. Del Jones, "Critics Tie Sweatshop Sneakers to 'Air' Jordan," *USA Today* (June 6, 1996), 1B.

14. Made in USA Foundation, http://www.madeinusa. org/. Accessed June 21, 2010.

15. Ibid.

16. Nike press release (June 6, 1996).

17. Del Jones, 1B.

18. Garry Trudeau, "Sneakers in Tinseltown," *Time* (April 20, 1998), 84.

19. William J. Holstein, "Casting Nike as the Bad Guy," *U.S. News & World Report* (September 22, 1997), 49.

20. VerenaDobnik, "Nike Shoe Contractor Abuses Alleged," *The Atlanta Journal-Constitution* (March 18, 1997), A14.

21. Simon Beck, "Nike in Sweat over Heat Raised by Claims of Biases Assessment," *South China Morning Post* (July 6, 1997), 2.

22. Matthew C. Quinn, "Footwear Maker's Labor Pledge Unlikely to Stamp Out Criticism," *The Atlanta Journal-Constitution* (June 25, 1997), F8.

23. G. Pascal Zachary, "Nike Tries to Quell Exploitation Charges," *The Wall Street Journal* (June 15, 1997).

24. Beck, 2.

25. Bill Richards, "Nike Hires an Executive from Microsoft for New Post Focusing on Labor Policies," *The Wall Street Journal* (January 15, 1998), B14.

26. Knight, 640.

27. Patti Bond, "Nike Promises to Improve Factory Worker Conditions," *The Atlanta Journal-Constitution* (May 13, 1998), 3B.

28. Allan Wolper, "Nike's Newspaper Temptation," *Editor & Publisher* (January 10, 1998), 8–10.

29. Gregg Krupa, "Antisweatshop Activists Score in Campaign Targeting Athletic Retailers," *Boston Globe* (April 18, 1999), F1.

30. UNITE, http://www.unitehere.org/about/apparel. php. Accessed June 5, 2013.

31. Krupa, F1.

32. USAS, http://usas.org/. Accessed June 5, 2013.

33. Wolper, 8–10.

34. Ibid., 8.

35. Jodie Morse, "Campus Awakening," *Time* (April 12, 1999), 77–78.

36. Krupa, F1.

37. Morse, 77–78.

38. Ibid.

39. USAS About Us, http://usas.org/about/mission-vision-organizing/. Accessed June 5, 2013.

40. Fair Labor Association, http://www.fairlabor.org/. Accessed June 5, 2013.

41. Fair Labor Association Workplace Code of Conduct, http://www.fairlabor.org/blog/entry/fair-labor-association-enhances-its-workplace-code-conduct. Accessed June 5, 2013.

42. Worker's Rights Consortium, Affiliated Colleges and Universities, http://www.workersrights.org/ about/as.asp. Accessed June 5, 2013.

43. Nike Web site, http://www.nikebiz.com/labor/index. shtml. Current website is: http://nikeinc.com/search? search_terms=labor. Accessed June 5, 2013.

44. Philip Knight Press Release (April 24, 2000). Found at http://www.nikebiz.com/media/n_uofo. shtml. (Website no longer active.)

45. Louise Lee and Aaron Bernstein, "Who Says Student Protests Don't Matter?" *BusinessWeek* (June 12, 2000), 96.

46. RavinaShamdasani, "Soul Searching by 'Shoe Geeks' Led to Social Responsibility," *South China Morning Post* (May 17, 2001), 2.

47. Greg Bolt, "University of Oregon Ends Relationship with Antisweatshop Group," *The Register Guard* (March 6, 2001).

48. Hank Hager, "Frohnmayer: It's a Very Happy Day for Us," *Oregon Daily Emerald* (September 27, 2001).

49. Ron Bellamy, "Nike CEO to Resume Donations to University of Oregon," *The Register Guard* (September 26, 2001).

50. William McCall, "Nike Releases First Corporate Responsibility Report," *Associated Press State & Local Wire* (October 9, 2001).

51. Ibid.

52. Adam Liptak, "Nike Move Ends Case over Firm's Free Speech," *New York Times* (September 13, 2003).

53. For a more thorough discussion of this controversy, see David Hess and Thomas Dunfee, "The Kasky-Nike Threat to Corporate Social Reporting," *Business Ethics Quarterly* (January 2007), 5–32, and Don Mayer, "Kasky v. Nike and the Quarrelsome Question of Corporate Free Speech," *Business Ethics Quarterly* (January 2007), 65–96.

54. For detailed coverage of this case and its implications, see http://reclaimdemocracy.org/nike/. Accessed June 5, 2013.

55. Sustainable Business Report, http://nikeinc.com/ pages/responsibility. Accessed June 5, 2013.

56. Educating for Justice, SWEAT, http://www. sweatthefilm.org/story.htm. Accessed June 5, 2013.

57. Ibid.

58. Team Sweat, http://www.teamsweat.org/. Accessed June 5, 2013.

59. Team Sweat, https://www.facebook.com/Team Sweat. Accessed June 5, 2013.

60. Oxfam Australia, "Nike," https://www.oxfam.org.au/explore/workers-rights/nike/. Accessed June 5, 2013.

61. Oxfam Australia, https://www.oxfam.org.au/explore/workers-rights/which-brands-are-dodging-the-hard-questions/. Accessed June 5, 2013.

62. CR's 2013 Best Corporate Citizens, http://www.thecro.com/files/100Best2013_web.pdf. Accessed June 5, 2013.

63. Nike Awards and Recognitions, http://nikeinc.com/pages/awards-recognition. Accessed June 5, 2013.

64. Ibid.

65. Boston Review, "Can Global Brands Create Just Supply Chains," May 21, 2013, http://www.bostonreview.net/forum/can-global-brands-create-just-supply-chains-richard-locke?, Accessed June 5, 2013.

66. Ibid.

CASE 16

Coke and Pepsi in India:

ISSUES, ETHICS, AND CRISIS MANAGEMENT*

There is nothing new about multinational corporations (MNCs) facing challenges as they do business around the world, especially in developing nations or emerging markets. Royal Dutch Shell had to greatly reduce its production of oil in Nigeria due to guerrilla attacks on its pipelines. Cargill was forced to shut down its soy-processing plant in Brazil because of the claim that it was contributing to the destruction of the Amazon rainforest. Tribesmen in Botswana accused De Beers of pushing them off their land to make way for diamond mines.[1] Google was kicked out of China, only to be later restored. Global business today is not for the faint of heart.

It should not come as a surprise, therefore, that MNC giants such as Coca-Cola and PepsiCo—highly visible, multibillion dollar corporations with well-known, iconic brands around the world—would encounter challenges in the creation and distribution of their products in some countries. After all, soft drinks are viewed as discretionary and sometimes luxurious products when compared to the staples of life that are often scarce in developing countries.

Whether it is called an issue, an ethics challenge, or a scandal, the situation confronting both Coke and Pepsi in India richly illustrates the many complex and varied social challenges companies may face once they decide to embark on other country's shores. Their experiences in India may predict other issues they may eventually face elsewhere or trials other companies might face as well. With a billion-plus people and an expanding economy, and with markets stagnating in many Western countries, India, along with China and Russia, represent immense opportunities for growth for virtually all businesses. Hence, these companies cannot afford to ignore these burgeoning markets.

INITIAL ALLEGATIONS

Coke and Pepsi's serious problems in India began in 2003. In that year, India's Center for Science and Environment (CSE), an independent public interest group, made allegations that tests they had conducted revealed dangerously high levels of pesticide residue in the soft drinks being sold all over India. The director of CSE, Sunita Narain, stated that such residues could cause cancer and birth defects as well as harm nervous and immune systems if the products were consumed over long periods of time.[2] Further, CSE stated that the pesticide levels in Coke's and Pepsi's drinks were much higher than that permitted by European Union standards. On one occasion, Narain accused Pepsi and Coke of pushing products that they wouldn't dare sell at home.[3]

In addition to the alleged pesticides in the soft drinks, the beverage makers encountered more problems when another special interest group, India Resource Center (IRC), accused the companies of over-consuming scarce water and polluting water sources in the course of their operations in India.[4] IRC intensely criticized the companies, especially

*This case was prepared by Archie B. Carroll, University of Georgia. Updated and revised in 2013.

Coca-Cola, by detailing a number of different "water woes" experienced by different cities and regions of the country. IRC's allegations even more broadly accused the companies of water exploitation and of controlling natural resources, and thus communities. Examples frequently cited were the impact of Coke's operations in the communities of Kerala and Mehdiganj.[5]

In 2004, IRC continued its "Campaign to Hold Coca-Cola Accountable" by arguing that communities across India were under assault by Coke's practices. Among the continuing allegations were communities' experiencing severe water shortages around Coke's bottling plants, significant depletion of the water table, strange water tastes and smells, and pollution of groundwater as well as soil. IRC said that in one community Coke was distributing its solid waste to farmers as fertilizer and that tests conducted found cadmium and lead in the waste, thus making it toxic waste. And the accusation of high levels of pesticides continued. According to IRC, the Parliament of India banned the sale of Coca-Cola in its cafeteria.[6] Another significant event in February 2004 was the government's Joint Parliamentary Committee's "seconding" of CSE's findings.[7] In December 2004, India's Supreme Court ordered Coke and Pepsi to put warning labels on their products. This caused a serious slide in sales for the next several years.[8]

Sunita Narain

One major reason that Indian consumers and politicians respected the allegations of both CSE and IRC was that CSE's director, Sunita Narain, is a well-known activist in New Delhi. Narain was born into a family of freedom fighters whose support of Mahatma Gandhi goes back to the days when Gandhi was pushing for independence in India over 60 years ago. She took up environmental causes in high school. One major cause she adopted was to stop developers from cutting down trees. Her quest was to save India from the ravages of industrialization. She became the director of CSE in 2002.[9]

According to a *BusinessWeek* writer, Narain strongly holds forth on the topic of MNCs exploiting the natural resources of developing countries, especially India. She manifests an alarmist tone that tends toward the end-is-near level of fervency. She is skilled at getting media attention. In 2005, she won the Stockholm Water Prize, one of a number of environmental accolades she has received.[10] In addition, she has been very successful in taking advantage of India's general

suspicion of huge MNCs, dating back to its tragic Bhopal gas leak in 1984.[11] Narain claims she does not intend to hurt companies but only to spur the country to pass stricter regulations.[12]

Sacred Water

Coke and Pepsi's problems in India have been complicated by the fact that water carries considerable significance in India. We are often told about cultural knowledge we should have before doing business in other countries. Businesses wanting to do business in India must understand the cultural significance of water. Although, according to UN sources, the country has some of the worst water in the world (due to poor sewage, pollution, and pesticide use), water carries an almost-spiritual meaning to Indians. Bathing is viewed by many of them to be a sacred act, and tradition for some residents holds that one's death is not properly noted by others until one's ashes are scattered in the Ganges River. In one major poll, Indians revealed that drinking water was one of their major life activities to improve their well-being.[13] Indians' sensitivity to the subject of water has undoubtedly played a role in the public's reactions to the allegations.

COKE'S AND PEPSI'S EARLY RESPONSES

Initially, Coke and Pepsi denied the allegations of CSE and IRC, primarily through the media. Critics contended that the MNCs responses were narrowly tailored to disputing the test results that declared their products unsafe. Coke conducted its own tests, the conclusion of which was that their drinks met demanding European standards.[14] Over the next several years the debate has continued, as the companies questioned the studies and conducted studies of their own. The companies also pointed out that other beverages and foods in the Indian food supply, and indeed water, had trace pesticide levels in it; they sought to deflect the issue in this manner.

The IRC also attacked Coke and Pepsi for not taking the crisis seriously. They argued that the companies were "destroying lives, livelihoods, and communities" while viewing the problems in India as "public relations" problems that they could "spin" away. IRC pointed out that Coca-Cola had hired a new public relations firm to help them build a new image in India, rather than addressing the real issues. According to IRC, the new CEO of Coke, Neville Isdell, immediately made a visit to India, but it was a "stealth" visit designed to avoid the heavy protests that would have met him had the trip been public. IRC also pointed out that Coke had just increased its marketing budget by a sizable amount in India. IRC then laid out the steps it felt Coke should take to effectively address its problems.[15]

PESTICIDE RESIDUE AND PARTIAL BANS

The controversy flared up again in August of 2006 when the CSE issued a new study. The new test results showed that 57 samples from 11 Coke and Pepsi brands contained pesticide residue levels 24 times higher than the maximum allowed by the Indian government. Public response was swift. Seven of India's 28 states imposed partial bans on the two companies, and the state of Kerala banned the drinks completely. Officials there ignored a later court ruling reversing the ban.[16] In 2006, the United Kingdom's Central Science Laboratory questioned the CSE findings. Coca-Cola sought a meeting with CSE that it denied. Also that year, India's Union Health Ministry rejected the CSE study as "inconclusive."[17]

THE COMPANIES RATCHET UP THEIR RESPONSES

As a result of the second major flurry of studies and allegations in 2006, both Coke and Pepsi ratcheted up their responses, sometimes acting together, sometimes taking independent action. They responded almost like different companies than they were before. Perhaps they reckoned this issue was not going to go away and had to be addressed more forcefully.

Coke's Response

Coke started with a more aggressive marketing campaign. It ran three rounds of newspaper ads refuting the new study. The ads appeared in the form of a letter from more than 50 of India's company-owned and franchised Coke bottlers, claiming that their products were safe. Letters with a similar message went out to retailers and stickers were pressed onto drink coolers, declaring that Coke was "safety guaranteed." Coke also hired researchers to talk to consumers and opinion leaders to find out what exactly they believed about the allegations and what the company needed to do to convince them the allegations were false.[18]

Based on its research findings, Coke created a TV ad campaign that featured testimonials by well-respected celebrities. One of the ads featured Aamir Khan, a popular movie star, as he toured one of Coke's plants. He told the people that the product was safe and that if they wanted to see for themselves

they could personally do so. In August and September of 2006, more than 4,000 people took him up on his offer and toured the plants. Opening up the plants sent the message that the company had nothing to hide, and this was very persuasive.[19] The TV ads, which were targeted toward the mass audience, were followed by giant posters with Khan pictured drinking a Coke. These posters appeared in public places such as bus stops. In addition, other ads were targeted toward adult women and housewives, who make the majority of the food-purchasing decisions. One teenager was especially impressed with Khan's ads because she knew he was very selective about which movies he appeared in and that he wouldn't take a position like this if it wasn't appropriate.[20]

In a later interview, Coke's CEO Isdell said he thought the company's response during the second wave of controversy was the key reason the company began turning things around. After the 2003 episode, the company changed management in India to address many of the problems, both real and imagined. The new management team was especially concerned about how it would handle its next public relations crisis. Weeks later, in December 2006, India's Health Ministry said that both Coke's and Pepsi's beverages tested in three different labs contained little or no pesticide residue.

Pepsi's Response

Pepsi's response was similar to Coke's. Pepsi decided to go straight to the Indian media and try to build relationships there. Company representatives met with editorial boards, presented its own data in press conferences, and also ran TV commercials. Pepsi's commercials featured the then president of PepsiCo India, Rajeev Bakshi, shown walking through a polished Pepsi laboratory.[21]

In addition, Pepsi increased its efforts to cut down on water usage in its plants. Employees in the plants were organized into teams, used Japanese-inspired *kaizens*, and suggested improvements to bring waste under control. The company also employed lobbying of the local government.

Indra Nooyi becomes CEO   Pepsi had an advantage in rebuilding its relationships in India, because in October 2006, an Indian-born woman, Indra Nooyi, was selected to be CEO of the multinational corporation. It is not known whether Pepsi's problems in India were in any way related to her being chosen CEO, but the hiring decision definitely helped the PR situation on the subcontinent. After graduating from the prestigious Indian Institute of Management, and later Yale University, Nooyi worked her way up the hierarchy at PepsiCo before being singled out for the top position.[22] She previously held positions at the Boston Consulting Group, Motorola, and ABB Group.

Prior to becoming CEO, Nooyi had a number of successes at Pepsi and became the company's chief strategist. She was said to have a perceptive business sense and an irreverent personal style. One of Nooyi's first decisions was to take a trip to India in December 2006. While there, she spoke broadly about Pepsi's programs to improve water and the environment. The Indian media, beaming with pride, loved her and covered her tour positively as she shared her own heartwarming memories of her life growing up in India. She received considerable praise. Not surprisingly, Pepsi's Indian sales started moving upward.[23]

In the midst of the criticism of Coke and Pepsi, roughly from 2003 to 2006, both companies were pursuing corporate social responsibility (CSR) initiatives in India, many of them related to improving water resources for communities. Still, the conflict took center stage.

A COMMENTARY: WHAT'S GOING ON

Because of all the conflicting studies and the stridency of CSE and IRC, one has to wonder what was going on in India to cause this developing country to so severely criticize giant MNCs such as Coke and Pepsi. Many developing countries would be doing all they could to appease these companies. It was speculated by a number of different observers that what was at work was a form of backlash against huge MNCs that come into countries and consume natural resources.[24] Why were these groups so hostile toward the companies? Was it really pesticides in the water and abuse of natural resources? Or was it environmental interest groups using every opportunity to bash large corporations on issues sensitive to the people? Was it CSE and IRC strategically making an example of these two hugely successful companies and trying to put them in their place?

Late in 2006, an interesting commentary appeared in *BusinessWeek* exploring the topic of what has been going on in India with respect to Coke and Pepsi.[25] This commentary argued that the companies may have been singled out because they are foreign owned. It appears that no Indian soft drink companies were singled out for pesticide testing, though many people believe pesticide levels are even higher in Indian milk and bottled tea. It was pointed out that pesticide residues are present in most of India's groundwater, and

the government has ignored or has been slow to move on the problem. The commentary went on to observe that Coke and Pepsi have together invested $2 billion in India over the years and have generated 12,500 jobs and support more than 200,000 indirectly through their purchases of Indian-made products including sugar, packing materials, and shipping services.[26]

CONTINUING PROTESTS AND RENEWED PRIORITIES AND STRATEGIES

Eventually, the open conflict settled down and sales took an upturn for both companies, but the issue lingers. In June 2007, the IRC continued its attacks on Coca-Cola. It accused the company of "greenwashing" its image in India.[27] The IRC staged a major protest at the recently opened Coke Museum in Atlanta on June 30, 2007, questioning the company's human rights and environmental abuses. They erected a 20-foot banner that read "Coca-Cola Destroys Lives, Livelihoods, Communities" in front of the World of Coca-Cola. Amit Srivastava of the IRC was quoted as saying, "This World of Coke museum is a fairy tale land and the real side of Coke is littered with abuses." A representative of the National Alliance of People's Movements, a large coalition of grassroots movements in India, said, "The museum is a shameful attempt by the Coca-Cola Company to hide its crimes."[28]

Piling On

The protestations by these groups apparently motivated other groups to take action against Coke. It was reported that United Students Against Sweatshops also staged a "die-in" around one of Coke's bottling facilities in India. And more than 20 colleges and universities in the United States, Canada, and the United Kingdom removed Coca-Cola from campuses because of student-led initiatives to put pressure on the company. In addition, the protests in Atlanta were endorsed by a host of groups that participated in the U.S. Social Forum.[29]

Coke's Renewed Priorities

Undaunted, Coca-Cola continues its initiatives to improve the situation in India and around the world. Coke faces water problems around the world because it is the key natural resource that goes into its products. The company now has 70 clean-water projects in 40 countries aimed at boosting local economies. It has been observed that these efforts are part of a broader strategy on the part of CEO Neville Isdell to build Coke's image as a local benefactor and a global diplomat.[30]

The criticism of Coke has been most severe in India. CEO Isdell admits that the company's experience in India has taught some humbling lessons. Isdell, who took over the company after the crisis had begun, told *The Wall Street Journal*, "It was very clear that we had not connected with the communities in the way we needed to." He indicated that the company has now made "water stewardship" a strategic priority, and in a recent 10-K securities filing, had listed a shortage of clean water as a strategic risk.[31] In August 2007, Coca-Cola India unveiled its "5-Pillar" growth strategy to strengthen its bonds with India. Coke's new strategy focuses on the pillars of People, Planet, Portfolio, Partners, and Performance. The company also announced a series of initiatives under each of the five pillars and its "Little Drops of Joy" proposal, which tries to reinforce the company's connection with stakeholders in India.[32]

Though most of the attention recently has been on Coca-Cola, it should also be noted that Pepsi has continued taking steps on a number of projects as well. One novel initiative is that the company now gathers rainwater in excavated lakes and ponds and on the rooftops of its bottling plants in India. The company sponsors other community water projects as well.[33]

Indian Beverage Association Formed

Though Coke and Pepsi are typically fighting one another in their longstanding "cola wars," due to their mutual problems in India they formed the Indian Beverage Association (IBA) in summer of 2010. Because of continuous hostility from regulators and activist groups, the two companies decided that a joint effort to address issues might make sense.[34]

The IBA was formed to address the issues related to the government of Kerala's charge that Coke is polluting the groundwater in the state and other taxation issues that affect both companies. Their issues have been ongoing, but Kerala's government decided to form a tribunal against Coca-Cola, seeking $48 million in compensation claims for allegedly causing pollution and depleting the groundwater level there. Another important issue is the value added tax (VAT) by the Delhi government. The IBA plans to bring in other bottlers and packaging firms that have similar interests and issues in India.[35]

WATER ISSUES CONTINUE

Coke and Pepsi's issues in India, especially surrounding the issue of water, never seem to go away. Beginning in fall 2011, The India Resource Center (IRC) alleged that Pep-

sico's water claims have been "deception with a purpose.[36] According to the IRC, Pepsico's claims of achieving "positive water balance" are misleading and do not stand up to scrutiny. IRC accuses that Pepsico (1) severely underestimates the amount of water it uses in India, (2) has flawed water balance accounting techniques, (3) just doesn't grasp that water issues are local issues in India, (4) has one in four of its plants operating in a water stressed area, and (5) lacks commitment to local water stewardship in India.[37]

In 2012–2013, the IRC's campaigns against Coca-Cola continued as well. According to IRC, fifteen village councils (panchayats) have called upon their government to reject Coca-Cola's application for expansion because it would further worsen the water conditions in the area. They have also called for an end to Coca-Cola's current groundwater extraction in Mehdiganj in the Varanasi district in India. The fifteen panchayats are located within a five kilometer radius of the Coca-Cola bottling plant and are affected by Coca-Cola's bottling operations.[38]

The IRC has taken a strong stance regarding what Coke needs to do to meet the needs of Indians. First, Coke needs to admit the severity of the problems it has created in India and take steps to operationally and strategically correct them. Beyond this, IRC's recommended steps include the following:

- They must permanently shut down the bottling facilities in Mehdiganj, Kala Dera and Plachimada.
- They must compensate the affected community members.
- They must recharge the depleted groundwater.
- They must clean up the contaminated water and soil.
- They must ensure that workers laid off as a result of Coca-Cola's negligence are retrained and relocated in a more sustainable industry.
- They must admit liability for the long term consequences of exposure to toxic waste and pesticide laden drinks in India.

IRC has taken the position that anything short of these steps will make it increasingly difficult for Coca-Cola to do business in India and elsewhere.[39]

QUESTIONS FOR DISCUSSION

1. Identify the ongoing issues in this case with respect to issue management, crisis management, global business ethics, and stakeholder management. Rank these in terms of their priorities for Coca-Cola and for PepsiCo.

2. Evaluate the corporate social responsibility (CSR) of Coke and Pepsi in India.

3. Are these companies ignoring their responsibilities in India, or is something else at work?

4. Why does it seem that Coke has become a larger and more frequent target than Pepsi in India? Did having an Indian-born CEO help Pepsi's case?

5. How do companies protect themselves against the nonstop allegations of special interest groups that have made them a target? Is stakeholder management an answer?

6. Does IRC's list of recommended steps to be taken by Coke appear reasonable? Is IRC an interest group that has gone too far?

7. What lessons does this case present for MNCs doing business in the global marketplace? Enumerate 3–5 lessons and give examples from the case to document them.

ENDNOTES

1. "Beyond India, More Battles," *BusinessWeek* (June 11, 2007), 52.
2. Duane D. Stanford, "Coke's PR Offensive in India Pays Off," *Atlanta Journal Constitution* (December 3, 2006), D1, D9.
3. Diane Brady, "Pepsi: Repairing a Poisoned Reputation in India," *BusinessWeek* (June 11, 2007), 50.
4. AmitSrivastava, "Communities Reject Coca-Cola in India," *India Resource Center* (July 10, 2003), http://www.corpwatch.org/article.php?id=7508. Accessed June 6, 2013.
5. Ibid.
6. Ibid.
7. "Coke and Pepsi in India—Stuck in the Middle with You," October 2006, http://killercoke.org/archives_2006.php. Accessed June 6, 2013.
8. Stanford, D1.
9. Diane Brady, "Pepsi: Repairing a Poisoned Reputation in India," *BusinessWeek* (June 11, 2007), 46–54.
10. Ibid.
11. "Coke and Pepsi in India—Stuck in the Middle with You," ibid.
12. Sunita Narain, Time, http://www.time.com/time/specials/2007/article/0,28804,1652689_1652372_1652366,00.html. Accessed June 6, 2013.
13. Brady, 50.
14. Stanford, D9.
15. "Campaign to Hold Coca-Cola Accountable: Coca-Cola Crisis in India," *India Resource Center* (2004),

http://www.indiaresource.org/campaigns/coke/. Accessed June 6, 2013.
16. Stanford, D9.
17. "Coke and Pepsi in India—Stuck in the Middle with You," ibid.
18. Stanford, D9.
19. Ibid.
20. Ibid.
21. Brady, 54.
22. Ibid., 46.
23. Ibid., 54.
24. Ibid., 48.
25. Brian Bremner and Nandini Lakshman, with Diane Brady, "Commentary India: Behind the Scare over Pesticides in Pepsi and Coke," *BusinessWeek* (September 4, 2006), 43.
26. Ibid.
27. New America Media, "Coke Accused of 'Greenwashing' Its Image in India" (June 8, 2007), http://www.indybay.org/newsitems/2007/06/08/18426206.php. Accessed June 6, 2013.
28. India Resource Center, "Major Protest at Coke Museum in Atlanta" (June 30, 2007), http://www.indiaresource.org/news/2007/1049.html. Accessed June 6, 2013.
29. Ibid.
30. Betsy McKay, "Why Coke Aims to Slake Global Thirst for Safe Water," *The Wall Street Journal* (March 15), 2007.
31. Ibid.
32. Ibid.
33. McKay.
34. AnuradhaShukla, "Taxation issues bring arch rivals Coke and Pepsi on the same platform," India Today, July 6, 2010, http://indiatoday.intoday.in/story/taxation-issues-bring-archrivals-coke-&-pepsi-on-same-platform/1/104338.html. Accessed June 6, 2013.
35. Ibid.
36. India Resource Center, "November 30, 2011, "Deception with Purpose: Pepsico's Water Claims in India," http://www.indiaresource.org/news/2011/pepsipositivewater.html. Accessed June 6, 2013.
37. Ibid.
38. India Resource Center, "Coca Cola," http://www.indiaresource.org/. Accessed June 6, 2013.
39. India Resource Center, "Campaign to Hold Coca-Cola Accountable: Coca-Cola Crisis in India," ibid. Accessed June 6, 2013.

Chiquita: An Excruciating Dilemma between Life and Law*

AN ETHICAL DILEMMA

Assume that you are the top executive for a firm doing business in Colombia, South America. If a known terrorist group threatens to kill your employees unless you pay extortion money, should the company pay it?

If you answer "no," how would you respond to the family of an employee who is later killed by the terrorist group?

If you answer "yes," how would you respond to the family of an innocent citizen who is killed by a bomb your money funded?[1]

BACKGROUND

In many parts of the world, doing business is a dangerous proposition. Such has been the case in the country of Colombia in South America. The danger has been described in the following way: "In Colombia's notoriously lawless countryside, narco-terrorists ran roughshod over the forces of law and order—or collaborated with them in a mutual game of shakedowns, kidnappings, and murders."[2] Foreign companies that choose to do business in many parts of the world are easy targets. These companies have resources, they care about their employees, and many of them have been willing to negotiate with terrorists and just consider it one of the costs of doing business. Security in many of these countries is available only at a price.[3]

Formerly known as United Fruit Company and then United Brands, Chiquita Brands International, based in Cincinnati, Ohio, has faced the kind of situation described above. Today, Chiquita is a global food company that employs more than 20,000 employees across 70 countries in six different continents. The company has strong brand name recognition and premium positioning in the United States and Europe, and operates with solid logistics and an efficient supply chain.[4]

BUYING SECURITY: PROTECTING OUR EMPLOYEES

According to CEO Fernando Aguirre, Chiquita started making payments to paramilitary groups in Colombia beginning in 1997 and extending into 2004. The payments came to a total of about $1.7 million. The company felt it was forced to make these payments because the lives of its employees were at stake.[5] During the period from 2001–2004, the company was making payments to the terrorist group United Self-Defense Forces of Colombia (AUC). AUC was the group's Spanish acronym, by which the group was primarily known. A major complication during this period was that the U.S. government had declared AUC to be a specially designated terrorist organization, making it illegal to provide funds for them, and the Bush Administration had vowed to go after any company that funded terrorist groups.[6]

CHIQUITA TURNS ITSELF IN

Chiquita turned itself in and reported to the government that it had made the payments to AUC during the years indicated.

In 2007, CEO Fernando Aguirre released a public statement outlining what he called "an excruciating dilemma between life and law."[7] Following are some excerpts from his statement:

- In February 2003, senior management of Chiquita Brands International learned that protection payments the company had been making to paramilitary groups in Colombia to keep our workers safe from the violence committed by those groups were illegal under U.S. law.
- The company had operated in Colombia for nearly a century, generating 4,400 direct and an additional 8,000 indirect jobs. We contributed almost $70 million annually to the Colombian economy in the form of capital expenditures, payroll, taxes, social security, pensions, and local purchases of goods and services.
- However, during the 1990s, it became increasingly difficult to protect our workforce. Among the hundreds of documented attacks by left- and right-wing paramilitaries were the 1995 massacre of 28 innocent Chiquita employees who were ambushed on a bus on their way to work, and the 1998 assassination of two more of our workers on a farm while their colleagues were forced to watch.

*This case was written by Archie B. Carroll, University of Georgia. Updated in 2013.

- Despite the harsh realities on the ground, the discovery that our payments were violating U.S. law created a dilemma of more than theoretical proportions for us: the company could stop making the payments, complying with the law but putting the lives of our workers in immediate jeopardy; or we could keep our workers out of harm's way while violating American law.[8]
- Each alternative was unpalatable and unacceptable. So the company decided to do what we believe any responsible citizen should do under the circumstances: We went to the U.S. Department of Justice and voluntarily disclosed the facts and the predicament. The U.S. government had no knowledge of the payments and, had we not come forward ourselves, it is entirely possible that the payments would have remained unknown to American authorities to this day.[9]

In a plea deal, the company was fined $25 million, and in September 2007 it made its first installment payment of $5 million. Chiquita's general counsel said that "this was a difficult situation for the company and that the company had to do it to protect the well-being of our employees and their families." The Department of Justice prosecutor called the payments "morally repugnant" and said that the protection payments "fueled violence everywhere else."[10]

BOARD KNOWLEDGE REVEALED

During the investigation of this incident, it was discovered that the Board of Directors of the company came to know that the questionable payments were going on. A prosecution document, according to the *Miami Herald*, presented the following timeline of events:

2000—Chiquita's audit committee, composed of board members, heard about the payments and took no action.

2002—Soon after AUC had been designated a terrorist organization; a Chiquita employee learned about this and alerted the company.

2003—Chiquita consulted with a Washington attorney who told the company, "Bottom line: Cannot make the payment."

2003—Two months later, Chiquita executives reported to the full board of directors that the company was still making payments. One board member objected and the directors agreed to make the payments known to the Department of Justice.

CHIQUITA'S SOCIAL RESPONSIBILITY INITIATIVES

An interesting description of the company's track record in the area of corporate social responsibility (CSR) makes this case particularly unusual. Jon Entine's account of Chiquita's turnaround as a company is enlightening. Apparently, Chiquita spent at least 15 years living down its longstanding reputation as a "ruthless puppeteer manipulating corrupt Latin American banana republics."[11] Once operating as United Fruit, the company began turning itself around in 1990 and remade itself into a model food distributor, complete with high environmental and ethical standards.

Better Banana Project

In the early 1990s, the company separated itself from its competitors by teaming up with the Rainforest Alliance on sustainability and labor standards. This became known as the Better Banana Project.[12] Rainforest Alliance had the following to say about Chiquita's adoption of the Better Banana Project, "The Rainforest Alliance monitors and verifies that Chiquita's farms abide by strong environmental and social standards, which have positive impacts on rural communities and tropical landscape."[13] The Better Banana Project's ability to be responsive to environmental concerns without threatening the livelihood of companies and employees earned it the 1995 Peter F. Drucker Award for Nonprofit Innovation.

Chiquita also became well known through its publications of its corporate responsibility reports. The company issued public reports on its corporate responsibility efforts each year starting in 2000. In addition, beginning in 2003, the company issued interim updates on its corporate responsibility progress as part of its annual reports to shareholders.

Regarding its CSR initiatives and payments to terrorist groups, CEO Fernando Aguirre pointed to the fact that the company came forward voluntarily to disclose the payments to the paramilitaries as an indication that Chiquita is "completely committed to corporate responsibility and compliance."[14] He noted too that the voluntary action involved considerable cost. In June 2004, Chiquita sold its Colombian farms at a loss of $9 million, in order to bring closure to the issue and remove itself from a difficult situation.[15] The company settled its case with the U.S. Justice Department for $25 million.[16]

LAWSUITS AGAINST CHIQUITA

Chiquita now faces a host of lawsuits related to its time in Colombia. These include one from three U.S. citizens who survived a five-year hostage ordeal by Colombia's notorious FARC paramilitary group.[17] The employees' lawsuit suggests that Chiquita's connection with FARC may have been more proactive than just paying protection money. The suit also claims that Chiquita used its network of local transportation contractors to transport weapons to the group.[18]

These same charges have propelled the largest lawsuit, based on the Alien Torts Claims Act (ATCA), filed by family members of thousands of Colombians who were tortured or killed by paramilitaries in Colombia. Cases from around the country were consolidated and put before a South Florida federal judge.[19] Chiquita asked the judge to dismiss the case arguing that as a victim of extortion, Chiquita was not responsible for the crimes that the paramilitary groups committed.[20] U.S. District Judge Kenneth A. Marra granted Chiquita's motion to dismiss terrorism-related claim; however, he allowed the plaintiffs to move forward with claims against Chiquita for torture, war crimes, and crimes against humanity.[21] If the plaintiffs succeed, the cost to Chiquita could be in the billions.[22]

A TALE OF TWO COMPANIES

The Chiquita payment controversy has been called a "tale of two companies."[23] One face of Chiquita comes across as a defiant, secretive multinational, with lots of resources, determined to break the law to keep its employees safe and its businesses running. The other face of Chiquita builds partnerships with groups such as Rainforest Alliance to support the Better Banana Project and issues frequent corporate social responsibility reports to keep its stakeholders pleased and informed. It tried to extricate itself by turning itself in, paying a huge fine, suffering tremendous embarrassment and loss of reputational capital, and finally selling its farms to help reach closure. Which is the real Chiquita?

QUESTIONS FOR DISCUSSION

1. Go back to the ethical dilemma at the beginning of the case. Which position did you take and why? Did your position change after you read the case?
2. Was Chiquita justified in making the extortion payments to protect its employees? Was the company really between a rock and a hard place? What should it have done?
3. Using your knowledge of business ethics and global practices, what concepts, principles, or ideas from your study have a bearing on this case? Explain how some of them might have guided Chiquita toward better decisions.
4. What is your assessment of CEO Aguirre's statements? Is he sincere or just making excuses?
5. What is your analysis of the Chiquita board of directors' handling of this case? Do you think selling the farms at a loss in Colombia was the right thing to do? Why?
6. If you were the judge in the consolidated case, what would you decide?
7. In the "tale of two companies," which do you think is the real Chiquita and why?

ENDNOTES

1. Denis Collins, Edgewood College, Madison, Wisconsin, posed these questions in an e-mail to an International Association for Business and Society ListServ discussing the Chiquita Banana situation, on June 18, 2007. Used with permission.
2. Rushworth M. Kidder, "Ethical Bananas," *Ethics Newsline* (March 19, 2007), a publication of the Institute for Global Ethics, http://www.globalethics.org/newsline/2007/03/19/. Accessed June 4, 2013.
3. Ibid.
4. "Chiquita Brands International, Inc. SWOT Analysis." *Chiquita Brands International SWOT Analysis* (2012): 1–8.
5. Kidder.
6. Jane Bussey, "Chiquita Disregarded Warnings, Records Show," *The Miami Herald* (April 16, 2007).
7. Fernando Aguirre, "An Excruciating Dilemma between Life and Law: Corporate Responsibility in a Zone of Conflict," *The Corporate Citizen (U.S.* Chamber of Commerce, April 2007), 1–2.
8. Ibid.
9. Ibid.
10. Pablo Bachelet, "Chiquita Pays Fine for Supporting Colombian Terrorist Group," McClatchy Washington Bureau, McClatchy Newspapers, http://www.mcclatchydc.com/2007/09/17/19797/chiquita-pays-fine-for-00+supporting.html#.Ua4Fe9LVB8E. Accessed June 4, 2013.
11. Jon Entine, "Chiquita Counts the Cost of Honesty," *Ethical Corporation* (May 2007), 74.
12. Ibid.

13. http://www.sdearthtimes.com/et1200/et1200s10. html. Accessed June 4, 2013.

14. *The Corporate Citizen* (April 2007).

15. Ibid.

16. Associated Press, "Chiquita Settles Case on Payments to Rebel Groups," *The New York Times* (March 15, 2007), http://www.nytimes.com/2007/03/15/business/worldbusiness/15bananas.html?ref=chiquitabrands internationalinc. Accessed June 4, 2013.

17. Daniel Tencer, "Lawsuit: Chiquita Fruit Company Funded Death Squads in Colombia," *The Raw Story* (April 7, 2010), http://www.rawstory.com/rs/2010/04/07/chiquita-funded-death-squads-colombia/. Accessed June 4, 2013.

18. Ibid.

19. Curt Anderson, "Chiquita Sued Over Colombian Paramilitary Payments," *Seattle Times* (May 30, 2011), http://seattletimes.com/html/nationworld/2015187381_apuschiquitaterrorpayments.html. Accessed June 4, 2013.

20. CNN Wire Staff, "Florida Judge Allows Suits Against Chiquita to Move Forward," *CNNWorld* (June 4, 2011), http://www.cnn.com/2011/WORLD/americas/06/03/florida.colombia.chiquita.lawsuits/index.html. Accessed June 4, 2013.

21. Ibid.

22. Anderson.

23. Jon Entine, 74.

CASE 18

Dole's DBCP Legacy*

Picture yourself as the executive manager of a leading agribusiness company with a dark legacy. What would you do if you found out that 30 years ago your company poisoned thousands of workers around the globe, making them sterile? Now, those workers request justice and compensation. Considering the overall number of affected workers a lost precedent case would skyrocket the potential litigation sum to $45 billion. How do you manage the aftermath of such a crisis? Is it even possible to balance ethical considerations with economic ones when rectifying the company's mistakes could financially threaten the existence of the organization?

THE BANANA SECTOR AND DOLE FOOD COMPANY

With $7.2 billion in revenue in 2011, Dole Food Company is the world's leading producer, marketer, and distributor of fresh fruits and fresh vegetables.[1] Bananas represent the most important product in the company's fresh fruit sales, making Dole one of the largest players in the market. Most banana companies have traditionally had strong ties to Central America, where they often own and operate large-scale plantations or source from independent growers. Dole is no exception; it produces bananas on approximately 32,000 acres of

company-owned land but also relies on around 66,900 acres of independent producers' land.[2]

During the last 50 years, the spread of crop diseases have made the banana sector an industry that increasingly has to rely on chemicals for profitable production. However, many substances have proven to be harmful to workers and the environment and therefore require cautious application. In the past, multinational companies often took advantage of the fact that most bananas are grown in countries that have rather weak public regulations, especially when it comes to occupational health and safety issues. One of the most prominent cases in that context is the use of the pesticide DBCP by Dole in the 1970s and 1980s on banana plantations throughout the world.

CHEMICALS IN THE BANANA SECTOR AND THE RISE OF DBCP

Labeled as an "ancient agricultural menace [that] has plagued farmers worldwide since the dawn of organized agriculture,"[3] nematodes have always been a severe problem for banana production.[4] A banana company that could effectively control for nematodes would have a unique competitive advantage; whoever invented that magic bullet would not file for bankruptcy any time soon.

In the mid-1950s researchers at Shell Chemical Company and Dow Chemical Company discovered that 1,2-Dibromo-3-chloroporpane (DBCP) was a highly effective nematicide.[5]

---

*This case was written by Dennis Klink, Berlin Graduate School for Transnational Studies (BTS), Hertie School of Governance, 2013.

The pesticide was *the* groundbreaking anti-nematode solution modern agriculture had longed for. It effectively killed the worms but left the roots of the plants unharmed. DBCP was especially effective on banana plantations, increasing "banana yields, almost instantly, by 30%."[6] Dow and Shell's enthusiasm did not even wane when test results revealed high toxicity rates and severe potential effects that DBCP could have on the human body:

> *In April 1958, Dr. Hine [from Shell] wrote in a confidential report that "among the rats that died, the gross lesions were especially prominent in lungs, kidneys and testes. Testes were usually extremely atrophied." Dow's preliminary findings came just three months later and echoed Shell's results. Dow's investigation found that [...] "liver, lung and kidney effects might be expected" and that "testicular atrophy may result from prolonged repeated exposure."[7]*

In response, researchers at Dow and Shell drafted an application guideline that outlined a safety level for workplace concentration of DBCP and recommended "impermeable protective clothing if skin contact was likely."[8] Having already initiated the commercial production and marketing of DBCP, such recommendations would, however, tarnish the reputation of the product. It might have occurred to the producers of DBCP that their product would not sell very well if its handling required a full-body protection suit. During the registration process, the safety concerns and the test results were not made public.[9] When DBCP was officially registered in 1964 the product label did not mention the potentially dramatic effects on the human body or the high toxicity of the product.

Banning of DBCP in the United States

By 1975, the United States Environmental Protection Agency (EPA) suspected an increased cancer risk related to DBCP exposure. In the summer of 1977 the issue picked up momentum when a group of employees working on a DBCP manufacturing line in an Occidental Chemical Company factory in California discovered that they were sterile. National media coverage followed and finally, in 1979, DBCP was officially banned in the US. Although, its application on U.S. soil was prohibited, it could still be manufactured in and exported from the United States to other countries. This loophole offered Dole the possibility to continue using DBCP in its overseas operations, in particular on Latin American banana plantations.

Dole and DBCP

After a period of trials, in 1969 Dole began applying DBCP on a large scale. During that time, the production manuals for banana workers and plantation managers did not recommend the use of specific safety equipment such as protective gloves or masks. Moreover, any impacts on sterility or related issues were not mentioned.[10] After the temporary ban in the U.S. in 1977, Dow stopped the production and sale of DBCP. However, instead of following the example, Dole forced Dow to continue with the supply, threatening Dow with a breach of contract suit.[11] The chemical company agreed to further provide the pesticide under the condition of an indemnity agreement. Dole also "promised that new, much more stringent safety precautions would be followed in the field."[12]

As application abroad was legally still permissible, Dole bought up all remaining stocks and used it on its overseas plantations until the very last drop was gone.[13] After DBCP was restricted in Costa Rica in 1979, the company shipped its remaining reserves to Honduras where no DBCP regulations existed. Internal Dole memos, later produced in subsequent lawsuits, show that the company had used DBCP on Nicaraguan supplier farms until 1980 and in the Philippines until 1986.[14]

MANAGEMENT VALUES: ETHICS VERSUS ECONOMICS

In the case of DBCP, Dole's management was confronted with the situation of balancing ethical considerations with economic ones. DBCP helped create outstanding yields and made banana production much more profitable. However, it was very likely that DBCP was harming workers' health. Statements from top executives show how the company approached the issue:

> *In an internal memo dated August 16, 1977, Jack Dement [Castle and Cook; later Dole] worried that a ban on DBCP would drastically reduce banana yields, pointed out that alternative chemicals were only 65% as effective, and emphasized that "there is no evidence that people who apply the chemical, as opposed to those who manufacture it, have been rendered sterile or have been harmed in other ways." [...] The decision to continue using DBCP in Costa Rica for 15 months after the sterility link made news in the United States came from the "highest level of the company" admits retired executive vice president Leonard Marks, Jr. He went on to remark: "You see, DBCP was so important to us. It wasn't a cover up,*

believe me, but hope springs eternal. When the DBCP disclosure began, it was like we were on a freeway, going 65 miles per hour and suddenly there was a sign, 'Detour now'. Well we didn't do that. We thought, what's going on? What shall we do?" Other corporate executives involved in the DBCP saga continued to dispute evidence that it causes sterility. Clyde McBeth, one of those who helped develop DBCP for Shell, says he handled it without safety equipment and suffered no health problems. "Anyways," says McBeth, who has never been to Costa Rica or met any of los afectados, "from what I hear, they could use a little birth control down there."[15]

These values and beliefs of top management had fatal consequences at the plantation level. Dole not only continued using DBCP-based pesticides, but the company also knowingly ignored the additional safety requirements that had been promised to Dow Chemical in order to continue the supply. Dr. Jack de Ment, the executive responsible for Dole's banana pest management worldwide, communicated to national field managers in 1977 that the new requirements such as inhalation masks and gloves are "not operationally feasible [and do] not need to be implemented."[16] As a result, thousands of workers on plantations were exposed to DBCP on a regular basis. A couple of years later, workers in several Central American countries reported sterility, chronic kidney failure and skin disease. Many of the symptoms were similar to the early study results and resembled those of U.S. workers whose complications finally led to the DBCP ban in the United States. Local doctors estimated that in Nicaragua alone around 15,000 workers were exposed in the 70s.[17]

THE BEGINNING OF THE LEGAL BATTLES

Although complaints against Dole and other U.S. companies had already been filed in the 1980s and 1990s, most cases were barred from proceeding under the *Forum Non Conveniens Doctrine*, which dismisses a case based on the argument that the more appropriate locations for litigation are the national courts in the plaintiffs' home country.[18] This procedure offered U.S. companies a strategic opportunity to avoid tort litigation under more stringent home-country regulations. For U.S. multinational companies with their traditionally strong political and economic channels of influence in banana-producing countries, it represented a much more convenient setting.

However, in late 2000 Nicaragua adopted a new law (*Law 364*) basically tailored for dealing with DBCP

litigations and the *Forum Non Conveniens* issue. In contrast to the situation in the past, it created strong incentives for banana companies to avoid tort litigation in Nicaragua.[19] Dole and others now preferred trials at home, a strategic backflip that led to a number of legal battles and out-of-court maneuvers.

TELLEZ VS. DOLE

Tellez vs. Dole, a 2007 DBCP lawsuit, was the first one brought by foreign banana workers against a U.S. corporation in a U.S. court. From a legal point of view, sterility was a strong issue for building a case. It is "both rare in nature and not a common health effect of exposure to other pesticides."[20] Considering study results and the product's history in the United States, lawyers could convincingly demonstrate a causal link between DBCP exposure and sterility. As a result, the jury found Dole guilty in half of the cases and ordered the company to pay U.S. $2.5 million to six Nicaraguan plaintiffs.[21] What followed in subsequent years was a legal battle between the banana workers and Dole, which was trying to have the verdict revised. The stakes were high for Dole because the plethora of potential future plaintiffs could severely affect the company's bottom line. In its 2011 annual report, Dole stated:

> *Claimed damages in DBCP cases worldwide total approximately $45 billion [...], with lawsuits in Nicaragua representing approximately 87% of this amount.*[22]

The development surrounding the legal claims of Nicaraguan workers had become a high priority issue not only involving the company's public image, but also its financial stability and survival. If the company was found guilty, *Tellez vs. Dole* could become a precedence case for further costly claims.

ALTERNATIVE SOLUTIONS

In other countries, Dole was successful in handling the issue through out-of-court settlements. For example in Honduras, Dole has established a workers' program together with the Honduran government in 2007 "that is intended by the parties to resolve in a fair and equitable manner the claims of male banana workers alleging sterility as a result of exposure to DBCP."[23] Dole also offered the implementation of a similar program in Nicaragua. However, in retrospect, we can speculate that two factors significantly constrained that solution. First, the legal environment in Nicaragua and the "special Law 364"[24] made it very likely that tort cases would take place under more stringent U.S.

jurisdiction. Among banana workers and their lawyers, this might have created the expectation that U.S. juries would rather rule in favor of the plaintiffs. Furthermore, a favorable verdict for the banana workers would also translate into high compensation sums. Second, U.S. litigation lawyers had "invested" time and money in Nicaragua. Within the scope of a company-driven compensation program their "revenues" would most likely be lower compared to any U.S. verdict that found Dole guilty. A look at some of the out-of-court tactics used by the plaintiff party makes that point clearer.

Out-of-Court Tactics

Law 364 put companies that had used DBCP under significant pressure. Now, they had to defend their cases under more stringent U.S. jurisdiction. At the same time, the changes in Nicaraguan law opened up a "big market" for U.S. law firms specializing in tort cases. In particular the charismatic personal injury lawyer Juan Dominguez, an exile Cuban and Spanish native speaker, gathered Nicaraguan banana workers systematically for litigation purposes. He organized demonstrations and rallies and even rented a football stadium for one of his events.[25] Dole's reputation was already severely harmed when the company's DBCP practices became public. However, the situation escalated when a Swedish filmmaker produced a documentary about the DBCP story and the *Tellez* case. The film portrayed Dole as a company that stopped at nothing and developed a David versus Goliath plot:

> Juan "Accidentes" Dominguez is on his biggest case ever. On behalf of twelve Nicaraguan banana workers he is tackling Dole Food in a ground-breaking legal battle for their use of a banned pesticide that was known by the company to cause sterility. Can he beat the giant, or will the corporation get away with it? In the suspenseful documentary BANANAS!*, filmmaker Fredrik Gertten sheds new light on the global politics of food.[26]

Dole objected to this particular way of telling the story and tried to stop the screening of *BANANAS!** at the 2009 Los Angeles film festival. It threatened the film festival and the filmmaker with defamation lawsuits. For Dole, the movie was more than a public relations matter. The company was found guilty in six out of twelve cases from the Tellez lawsuit. However, it was challenging the verdict, as half of the cases were dismissed due to a lack of clear evidence. Furthermore, there were a number of similar pending cases that built on the *Tellez vs. Dole* verdict. Consequently, it

was an important precedence case for any future DBCP litigation against the company.

As some authors have argued, in transnational tort litigations companies are attacked on multiple fronts.[27] In those scenarios, bad publicity caused, for example, by public campaigns can shape the perception of decision makers and, in the worst case, influence legal outcomes. For Dole, this was certainly a decisive factor. If the public believed that the DBCP case was a clear-cut issue it would be much more difficult for the company to defend itself in the courtroom. Therefore, the documentary was more than an inconvenient media footnote for Dole.

FROM DBCP TO FREEDOM OF SPEECH

With the defamation threat against the Swedish filmmaker a new issue about Dole and its stakeholders arose. Questionable business practices in Central America were one part of the story. However, now the stakeholders' criticism began to focus on the company's particular interpretation of the First Amendment. Dole was now accused of censorship and *BANANAS!** was promoted as *"The film Dole Food Co. doesn't want you to see."*[28] The filmmakers knew how to play the transnational card and started screening the movie in various European countries. They also showed the film to Swedish members of parliament. Again Dole seemed to have underestimated the dynamics behind the issue. Suddenly, the company found itself in the middle of another unfavorable story. This time, the plot was about a small independent Scandinavian film company that was going to be silenced by a powerful U.S. corporation. Especially in Europe—a premium market for Dole products—the company's image had reached the bottom and economic consequences would follow soon. In 2009, the Swedish fast food chain MAX stopped selling Dole products. MAX CEO Richard Bergfors stated in the Swedish news:

> We don't like Dole's actions. Suing a filmmaker instead of having a dialogue is despicable [...]. I think Dole risks losing more customers on account of their misguided actions. In Sweden we believe in open dialogue and debate. Everyone can make mistakes, but then you have to admit it.[29]

After the event, Swedish retailers announced that they demanded talks with Dole concerning the lawsuit (against the filmmaker!).[30] Finally, in late 2010 a U.S. court ruled that the movie could be screened legally in the United States. The filmmakers had won this battle; Dole had to pay $200,000 to cover the defendant's legal expenses.

Did Dole Go *BANANAS!**?

However, the events that followed Dole's defeat in the law suit against the BANANAS!* filmmaker were much more positive for the company. In 2011, a California court revised the verdict of *Tellez vs. Dole*, arguing that the plaintiff party had fabricated important information and that the whole case was subject to systematic fraud.[31] In addition, similar pending DBCP cases from Nicaragua were dismissed in other U.S. courts.

After the revision of the verdict, some writers speculated that Dole had paid healthy workers to pretend that they were affected, thereby demonstrating that the whole story was based on fraudulent evidence.[32] Others claimed that the plaintiff lawyers were only able to identify a few ex-banana workers who were sterile and who had definitely worked on plantations supplying Dole.[33] They argue that it is "possible, if not likely, that the substantial publicity efforts and other tactics instilled a hope for monetary recovery"[34] among workers in Nicaragua and finally encouraged them "to make dubious claims."[35] Out-of-court tactics might have also influenced the decisions of local judges and others involved in providing evidence.[36] Even today, the truth behind the story has not been discovered and is still subject to popular (and academic) debates. As a result, the question about who is right or wrong is left to public interpretation and re-interpretation.

Soon after the revision of the verdict the company reached an out-of-court settlement with the remaining 38 plaintiffs representing all Nicaraguan DBCP cases filed in the US.[37] Critical scholars have interpreted this development as a "de facto victory for Dole"[38] offering the company the opportunity to pay far less than the total claims of $9 billion. In 2011, the Swedish filmmakers released *Big Boys Go Bananas!**, a follow-up movie showing the legal battle that followed the first movie. So far, the impact of the movie on any subsequent events concerning the DBCP cases has been weak.

QUESTIONS FOR DISCUSSION

1. What are the most important issues throughout Dole's DBCP history? Did Dole appropriately balance economic and ethical considerations in its decision-making?
2. Who are the principal stakeholders of the company? Did Dole treat them differently, and if so, why? What were the key challenges for the company in managing the relationships with those different stakeholder groups?
3. How would you as the top executive of the company handle the situation that pleading guilty in the DBCP cases and rectifying your mistakes from the past could severely harm the company's financial stability?
4. The case tells us that although DBCP was prohibited in the United States, it was legally still possible to manufacture and export the pesticide. Dole took advantage of that situation and used it on many of its plantations in Central America. Some authors have pointed out the fact that when Dole used DBCP in Nicaragua the local worker compensation system "didn't even recognize sterility as a possible injury, and therefore offered no compensation."[39] From that perspective, Dole was in compliance with Nicaraguan and U.S. law. Is legal compliance the only responsibility that should matter in such situations? Can you identify any additional responsibilities that play a role in the Dole case?
5. What does this case reveal about the legal and nonlegal challenges that multinational companies face when doing business abroad? What recommendations would you give to managers in order to avoid situations similar to the Dole case in the future?

ENDNOTES

1. Dole Food Company (2012): Annual Report 2011; http://media.corporate-ir.net/Media_Files/IROL/23/231558/2011DoleAR/docs/Dole-Food-Company-Inc-2011-Form-10-K-As-Filed.pdf. Accessed December 14, 2012.
2. Dole Food Company (2012): Annual Report 2011; http://media.corporate-ir.net/Media_Files/IROL/23/231558/2011DoleAR/docs/Dole-Food-Company-Inc-2011-Form-10-K-As-Filed.pdf. Accessed December 14, 2012.
3. Siegel, Charles S. and Siegel, David S. (1999): The History of DBCP from a Judicial Perspective, in: *International Journal of Occupational and Environmental Health*, Vol. 5(2), 127–135.
4. Nematodes are roundworms that attack the roots of banana plants. Nematode control represents an important production factor impacting the profitability of banana plantations. Studies show that their strong resistance to chemical and biological pest management measures have caused yield losses of up to 30–60% (see e.g., Brooks, Fred (2004): Banana Nematodes—Pests and Diseases

of American Samoa. American Samoa Community College Division; http://www2.ctahr.hawaii.edu/adap/ASCC_LandGrant/Dr_Brooks/BrochureNo9.pdf. Accessed December 16, 2012).

5. Rosenberg, Beth and Levenstein, Charles (1995): Unintended Consequences: Impacts of Pesticide Bans on Industry, Workers, the Public, and the Environment. University of Massachusetts Lowell, The Toxics Use Reduction Institute.

6. Ibid.

7. Siegel, Charles S. and Siegel, David S. (1999): The History of DBCP from a Judicial Perspective, in: *International Journal of Occupational and Environmental Health,* Vol. 5(2), 127–135.

8. Rosenthal, Erika (2004): The DBCP pesticide cases: seeking access to justice to make agribusiness accountable in the global economy, in: K. Jansen & S. Vellema (Eds.): Agribusiness and society: corporate responses to environmentalism, market opportunities and public regulation (177–199). New York, London: Palgrave, Zed Books.

9. Moreover, the managers in charge of product registration disregarded the safety recommendations and declared them "impractical" (Siegel, Charles S. and Siegel, David S. (1999): The History of DBCP from a Judicial Perspective, in: *International Journal of Occupational and Environmental Health,* Vol. 5(2), 127–135).

10. Ibid.

11. Boix, Vicent and Bohme, Susanne R. (2012): Secrecy and justice in the ongoing saga of DBCP litigation, in: *Journal of Occupational and Environmental Health,* Vol. 18(2), 154–161.

12. Siegel, Charles S. and Siegel, David S. (1999): The History of DBCP from a Judicial Perspective, in: *International Journal of Occupational and Environmental Health,* Vol. 5(2), 127–135.

13. Enough pesticide was available because Dole's main competitors stopped using DBCP in 1977 and returned their stocks to the manufacturer (see Moore, Kaitlyn (2011): The true history of Dole, banana plantations, chemical pesticides and human suffering; http://www.naturalnews.com/032794_Dole_bananas.html. Accessed December 16, 2012).

14. Boix, Vicent and Bohme, Susanne R. (2012): Secrecy and justice in the ongoing saga of DBCP litigation, in: *Journal of Occupational and Environmental Health,* Vol. 18(2), 154–161.

15. Rosenberg, Beth and Levenstein, Charles (1995): Unintended Consequences: Impacts of Pesticide Bans on Industry, Workers, The Public, and The Environment. University of Massachusetts Lowell, The Toxics Use Reduction Institute.

16. Siegel, Charles S. and Siegel, David S. (1999): The History of DBCP from a Judicial Perspective, in: *International Journal of Occupational and Environmental Health,* Vol. 5(2).

17. Bérubé, Nicolas and Aquin, Benoit (2005): Chiquita's Children, in: http://www.inthesetimes.com/article/2096. Accessed November 7, 2012.

18. Boix, Vicent and Bohme, Susanne R. (2012): Secrecy and justice in the ongoing saga of DBCP litigation, in: *Journal of Occupational and Environmental Health,* Vol. 18(2), 154–161.

19. For a number of reasons, among others the posting of a $14 million bond by the defendant before the trial, Law 364 made tort trials in Nicaragua much more "unattractive" for foreign corporations. However, it also contained an opting-out clause that would allow the defendant to transfer the case to a U.S. court (Drimmer, Jonathan C. and Lamoree, Sarah R. (2011): Think Globally, Sue Locally: Trends and Out-of-Court Tactics in Transnational Tort Actions, in: *Berkeley Journal of International Law,* Vol. 29(2), 456–527).

20. Rosenthal, Erika (2004): The DBCP pesticide cases: seeking access to justice to make agribusiness accountable in the global economy, in: K. Jansen & S. Vellema (Eds.): Agribusiness and society: corporate responses to environmentalism, market opportunities and public regulation (177–199). New York, London: Palgrave, Zed Books.

21. Boix, Vicent and Bohme, Susanne R. (2012): Secrecy and justice in the ongoing saga of DBCP litigation, in: *Journal of Occupational and Environmental Health,* Vol. 18(2), 154–161.

22. Dole Food Company (2012): Annual Report 2011; http://media.corporate-ir.net/Media_Files/IROL/23/231558/2011DoleAR/docs/Dole-Food-Company-Inc-2011-Form-10-K-As-Filed.pdf. Accessed December 14, 2012.

23. Dole Food Company (2010): Annual Report 2009; http://investors.dole.com/phoenix.zhtml?c=231558&p=irol-reportsannual. Accessed December 14, 2012.

24. Drimmer, Jonathan C/ Lamoree, Sarah R. (2011): Think Globally, Sue Locally: Trends and Out-of-Court Tactics in Transnational Tort Actions, in: Berkeley Journal of International Law, Vol. 29(2), 456–527.

25. Ibid.

26. *About the Film, BANANAS!**, cited from: Drimmer, Jonathan C/Lamoree, Sarah R. (2011): Think Globally, Sue Locally: Trends and Out-of-Court Tactics in Transnational Tort Actions, in: *Berkeley Journal of International Law*, Vol. 29(2), 456–527.

27. Ibid.

28. http://www.bananasthemovie.com. Accessed November 7, 2012.

29. The Local (06.10.2009), http://www.thelocal.se/22484/20091006. Accessed November 7, 2012.

30. The Local (07.10.2009), http://www.thelocal.se/22522/20091007. Accessed November 7, 2012.

31. Dole Food Company (2012): Form 10-K, http://investors.dole.com/phoenix.zhtml?c=231558&p=irol-reportsannual. Accessed November 7, 2012.

32. Boix, Vincent and Bohme, Susanna R. (2012): Secrecy and justice in the ongoing saga of DBCP litigation, *International Journal of Occupational and Environmental Health*, Vol. 18(2), 154–161.

33. Drimmer, Jonathan C/ Lamoree, Sarah R. (2011): Think Globally, Sue Locally: Trends and Out-of-Court Tactics in Transnational Tort Actions,

in: *Berkeley Journal of International Law*, Vol. 29(2), 456–527.

34. Ibid.

35. Ibid.

36. Ibid.

37. Dole Food Company (2012): News Release: Dole Food Company Completes Agreement Terminating 38 DBCPLawsuits, http://investors.dole.com/phoenix.zhtml?c=231558&p=irolnewsArticle&ID=1731957&highlight. Accessed November 7, 2012.

38. Boix, Vincent and Bohme, Susanna R. (2012): Secrecy and justice in the ongoing saga of DBCP litigation, *International Journal of Occupational and Environmental Health*, 18(2):154–161.

39. Rosenthal, Erika (2004): The DBCP pesticide cases: seeking access to justice to make agribusiness accountable in the global economy, in: K. Jansen & S. Vellema (Eds.), Agribusiness and society: corporate responses to environmentalism, market opportunities and public regulation (177–199). New York, London: Palgrave, Zed Books.

CASE 19

Should Directors Shine Light on Dark Money?*

Recent election cycles have brought new challenges for corporations and their boards of directors. In the 2010 U.S. congressional elections, pharmaceutical industry's trade group, PhRMA, donated funds to nonprofit groups that used those funds to help elect 23 representatives who subsequently voted to limit access to contraceptives. Some of those funds came from firms like Pfizer, Bayer, and Merck, all manufacturers of contraceptives. In essence, these firms spent money to promote policies that went against their own financial interests.Similarly, Target Corporation, a company that had positioned itself as an LGBT-friendly corporation, found itself the target of angry employees and customers when they learned about Target's political spending. Target, a sponsor of the annual Twin Cities Gay Pride Festival, donated

money to a business group that supported an anti-gay rights candidate for Minnesota governor. Angry employees and consumers conducted protests outside Target stores and threatened a boycott.

These two examples show how political spending can have dramatic consequences for corporations. Politicians take positions on a range of policies, so the same politician may hold some positions that support and other positions that damage a corporation's best interests. This problem was exacerbated when the U.S. Supreme Court's *Citizen United* decision changed the political spending landscape for corporations. Before that decision, political spending was constrained to political action committees (PACs), and PAC political activity had to be disclosed to the FEC (Federal Election Commission). Now firms can make unlimited contributions directly to candidates or indirectly to 501c4 nonprofits and trade associations, who can then hide both the donors who provided the money and the way the money was spent. Firms are now freer to become politically involved but, as

---

* This case was written by Ann K. Buchholtz, Rutgers University, 2013.

Target and the pharmaceutical companies found out, that freedom comes with risk. Shareholders and other stakeholders are asking firms to be transparent in their political spending. They want to judge those expenditures for themselves to avoid agency problems and other conflicts of interest.

Ira M. Millstein, founder of the Ira M. Millstein Center for Global Markets and Corporate Ownership at Columbia Law School, proposes a new policy for boards of directors to follow in this new landscape. He suggests that (1) Companies should require trade associations of which they are members to report to them on their political spending, (2) Companies should require trade associations of which they are members to disclose the donors who provide the money for their political spending, and (3) Companies should then disclose the information they receive from their trade associations when they disclose their other spending to shareholders and other stakeholders.

QUESTIONS FOR DISCUSSION

1. What is your reaction to the PhRMA problem? What would you do if you were the CEO of a pharmaceutical company? Would you still belong to PhRMA? Would your membership have any conditions attached?
2. What is your reaction to the Target situation? How would you handle it if you were the CEO?

3. Do you agree with Ira Millstein? Should companies require trade associations to disclose this information before they join? Should companies then disclose the information they receive? If a trade association refuses to provide that information, should the company refuse to join?

Sources: Bruce F. Freed and Karl Sandstrom, "Political Spending: Directors Responsible for Protecting Companies," *Directors & Boards* (2013, forthcoming); "Report on the Proceedings of the Roundtable on Corporate Political Accountability: The Importance of Educating Future Business Leaders Post-Citizens United," (February 14–15, 2013), http://politicalaccountability.net/index. php?ht=a/GetDocumentAction/i/7730. Accessed July 13, 2013; Jonathan D. Salant, "Merck, Pfizer Back Lawmakers Who Oppose Company Products," *Bloomberg* (May 31, 2012), http://www. bloomberg.com/news/2012-05-31/merck-pfizer-back-lawmakers-who-oppose-company-products.html. Accessed June 7, 2013. Brian Bakst, "Target Apologizes for Political Donation in Minnesota," *USA Today* (August 5, 2010), http://usatoday30.usatoday. com/money/industries/retail/2010-08-05-target-campaign-donation_N.htm. Accessed June 7, 2013; Bruce F. Freed and Karl J. Sandstrom, "Political Money: The Need for Director Oversight," Conference Board's Executive Action Series(April 2008, No. 263), http://www.politicalaccountability.net/index.php?ht=a/ GetDocumentAction/i/1433. Accessed June 9, 2013.

CASE 20

DTCA: The Pill-Pushing Debate*

What do Tamiflu® and Natazia® have in common? They are both 2013 gold medal winners for their direct-to-consumer advertising (DTCA).[1] Although their brand name recognition does not rival that of Coca-Cola, their names are familiar to consumers across the nation. As flag bearers of the DTCA efforts of the pharmaceutical industry, they are at the fore-

front of the DTCA debate. At this writing, the United States and New Zealand are the only developed countries that permit DTCA of pharmaceuticals. However, the pharmaceutical lobby has been pressuring European regulators to open the European Union to DTCA and so the debate is certain to continue.[2]

Why debate DTCA? In his testimony before the Senate Commerce Subcommittee on Consumer Affairs, Dr. Sidney Wolfe, director of the Public Citizen's Health Research Group, expressed the following concern: "There is little doubt that false and misleading

---

* This case was written by Ann K. Buchholtz, Rutgers University. Updated in 2013.

advertising to patients and physicians can result in prescriptions being written for drugs that are more dangerous and/or less effective than perceived by either the doctor or the patient."[3] The findings of a 2013 CMI/Compas survey of 104 physicians across multiple specialties underscore that concern: 89 percent of the physicians indicated that a patient requested a prescription as a result of seeing a DTCA and 43 percent of the physicians reported changing their prescribing as a result.[4] Only 20 percent agree (5 percent strongly and 15 percent somewhat) that DTCA improves the relationship between a clinician and the patient.[5]

On the positive side, DTCA can help patients. In the CMI/Compas Survey, 48 percent of the same physicians agreed (5 percent strongly and 43 percent somewhat) that DTCA educates patients and 52 percent agreed (9 percent strongly and 43 percent somewhat) that DTCA lessened the stigma of some diseases.[6] Dr. Richard Dolinar, an endocrinologist, says that the ads empower consumers: "Direct-to-consumer advertising is getting patients with diabetes into my office sooner so they can be treated."[7]

With strong arguments for and against DTCA, many people find their opinions evolving. John LaMattina, the former president of Pfizer Global Research and Development, is an expert on the pharmaceutical industry. In a Forbes article entitled, "Maybe It's Time for Drug Companies to Drop TV Ads," he questions whether the negatives of DTCA are starting to outweigh the benefits.[8] He was an early supporter of DTCA based on its education value for the consumer and still believes that benefit remains; however, he now feels that that the ads having too many negative effects due to industry missteps. For example, some of the commercials are not age appropriate for children and so are subject to tighter industry standards.[9] Denis Arnold and James Oakley found that, over a four year period, five major pharmaceutical companies violated industry standards in their marketing of erectile dysfunction drugs, leading to children being exposed to sexually themed advertising over one billion times.[10] Another issue Mattina raises is that the endless listing of negative side-effects creates problems. He quotes Elizabeth Rosenthal's article in *The New York Times*[11]:

When the Food and Drug Administration in the 1990s first mandated that drug makers list medicines' side effects in order to advertise prescription drugs, there was a firestorm of protest from the industry. Now the litany of side effects that follows every promotion is so mind-numbing—drowsiness,

insomnia, loss of appetite, weight gain—as to make the message meaningless.

QUESTIONS FOR DISCUSSION

1. What are the ethical issues in this case?
2. Should DTCA be judged by the same criteria as other advertising? If not, how should it be judged differently?
3. What public policy changes would you advocate regarding DTCA? Should the United States and New Zealand ban them?
4. How will changes in technology and viewing habits change the DTCA issue?

ENDNOTES

1. "Long-Standing DTC National Advertising Awards Honor Diverse Group of DTC Marketing Campaigns," http://www.cvent.com/events/2013-dtc-national-conference/custom-36-16f0d91afe954c9ab932b619722d4642.aspx. Accessed June 2, 2013.
2. Denis G. Arnold and James L. Oakley, "The Politics and Strategy of Industry Self-Regulation: The Pharmaceutical Industry's Principles for Ethical Direct-to-Consumer Advertising as a Deceptive Blocking Strategy," *Journal of Health Politics, Policy and Law* (Advance Publication, February 15, 2013), http://jhppl.dukejournals.org/content/early/2013/02/11/03616878-2079496.full.pdf+html. Accessed June 2, 2013.
3. Sidney M. Wolfe, "Direct-to-Consumer (DTC) Ads: Illegal, Unethical, or Both," *Public Citizen's Health Research Group Health Letter* (September 2001), 3–4.
4. "CMI/Compas Survey Finds Doctors' True Opinions of DTC Advertising" (May 1, 2013), http://www.prweb.com/releases/2013/5/prweb10733538.htm. Accessed June 2, 2013.
5. Ibid.
6. Ibid.
7. Ira Teinowitz, "DTC Regulation by FDA Debated," *Advertising Age* (July 30, 2001), 6.
8. John LaMattina, "Maybe It's Time for Drug Companies to Drop TV Ads," *Forbes* (February 15, 2012), http://www.forbes.com/sites/johnlamattina/2012/02/15/maybe-its-time-for-drug-companies-to-drop-tv-ads/. Accessed June 2, 2013.
9. Ibid.
10. Arnold and Oakley, 2013.
11. Elizabeth Rosenthal, "I Disclose ... Nothing," *The New York Times* (January 21, 2012), SR1. Cited in Mattina, 2012.

CASE 21

Big Pharma's Marketing Tactics*

"Big Pharma" is the name the business press uses for the gigantic pharmaceutical industry. Most of us are familiar with Big Business and Big Government. Now Big Pharma is in the news and has been for several years regarding its marketing, advertising, and sales tactics. As *Time* magazine stated, it's hard to empathize with the drug industry these days because of the high cost of our prescriptions. We either just emptied our wallets in paying for our latest prescription or just returned on a Greyhound bus from Canada, where we bought our prescriptions for less.[1] Public perceptions of the pharmaceutical industry add to its problems. In one major poll, Big Pharma was called greedy as well as shifty, and it was found that most people do not trust the industry to disclose bad news about its products.[2]

Big Pharma has been aware that it faces challenges to its marketing and sales tactics. A major conference was held in Boston, where industry representatives discussed the sale and illegal marketing of drugs for "off label" uses that were not approved by the Food and Drug Administration (FDA). A lawyer from one of the law firms that sponsored the conference said, "Rarely has a conference been more timely."[3] Since that conference, it is uncertain how much progress has been made.

It is hard to imagine Big Pharma cowering before FDA regulators, because the industry has built up an army of lobbyists in Washington, D.C., to protect its interests. Public Citizen, a citizen interest group, reported that the industry had 625 lobbyists—almost one for every member of Congress. Though the public values the drugs the industry makes available for sale, increasingly, the multibillion dollar industry's social responsibilities are being questioned.[4]

THE PHARMACEUTICAL INDUSTRY

The pharmaceutical industry is one of the healthiest and wealthiest in America. However, astronomical drug prices recently have continued to result in push back against the industry. For example, of 12 cancer drugs released in 2012, 11 of them cost more than $100,000. More and more drugs are being offered at this level of pricing, and the more they get away with it the more it becomes a standard that emboldens the

companies to push the envelope on pricing. Anger is percolating about this level of pricing.[5]

The top pharmaceutical companies, according to their 2012 sales data, include the familiar names, with the most profitable at the top of the list[6]:

1. Johnson & Johnson
2. Pfizer
3. Novartis
4. Roche
5. Merck
6. Sanofi
7. GlaxoSmithKline
8. Abbott Laboratories/AbbVie
9. AstraZeneca
10. Bayer Healthcare

Among this group, only Johnson & Johnson ranked #23 among *Fortune*'s "most admired companies in the world in 2012."[7] And, in spite of this relatively high ranking, J&J has increasingly been under the gun in recent years as allegations of questionable marketing of its products have come to light and resulted in huge settlements. For example, in 2012, J&J faced a settlement that may total $2.2 billion to settle charges of illegally marketing Risperdal, which was once the company's top selling drug before generic versions hit the market.[8]

Depending on the study considered and how expenses are calculated, the pharmaceutical industry spends at least as much on advertising as it does on research and development. This includes both professional and direct-to-consumer (DTC) spending by the drug makers.[9] In spite of its size and success, Big Pharma has been called into question for a number of years now for its questionable marketing, advertising, and sales techniques. The charges have included questionable direct to consumers (DTC) advertising (see Case 20) and dubious ethics, and a number of them have resulted in lawsuits. It seems quite amazing, actually, that the pharmaceutical industry has not received more scrutiny.

FROM SCIENCE TO SALESMANSHIP

An overall criticism of Big Pharma is that the industry has abandoned science for salesmanship.[10] That is, the industry has become more concerned with pushing pills to treat minor problems than with developing new and important drugs. An example of this was

---

*This case was written and revised by Archie B. Carroll, University of Georgia. Updated in 2013.

provided in the aggressive marketing by Novartis of its fourth biggest selling drug. Is this drug a lifesaver? No, it's Lamisil, a pill for toenail fungus. Yes, toenail fungus can turn a nail yellow, but apparently no one has died of this illness. On the other hand, a few people may have died taking the drug, as regulators linked the drug to at least 16 cases of liver failure, including 11 deaths. Novartis claimed most of these patients had preexisting illnesses or were on other drugs.[11]

Many patients taking Lamisil were enticed to the drug by a grotesque cartoon creature named Digger the Dermatophyte, who is a squat, yellowish character with a dumb-guy big city accent. In the TV ads, Digger lifts a toenail, creeps beneath it, and declares, "I'm not leavin'!"[12] One group calculated that Novartis spent $236 million on Lamisil ads over three years, but Novartis denies this figure. In the first run of the commercial, Digger is crushed by a giant Lamisil tablet. Regulators thought the ad so overstated the drug's benefits that the company had to pull that particular version of the ad. It has been reported that the drug cured the problem in only 38 percent of patients, but Lamisil's sales increased 19 percent after it.[13] In short, it was alleged that the industry spends a fortune on remedies to cure trivial maladies while its drug research pipelines are running dry. This has been dubbed "salesmanship over science."[14] Others have said it represents marketing and profits being considered more important than consumer safety and wellness.[15]

Another way pharmaceutical firms emphasize sales over science was illustrated when *The New York Times* revealed that drug giant SmithKline Beecham had secretly compared it own diabetes drug, Avandia, to a competing medicine, Actos, which was produced by Takeda. The company discovered that their own drug was riskier, but the company spent the next 11 years trying to cover up the results. According to *The New York Times*, sales of Avandia were crucial to the company and the company failed to disclose the research so it could keep making money.[16] In short, sales trumped science. After an investigation, the FDA review panel recommended that the drug should be kept on the market.[17]

PROMOTIONS TO MED STUDENTS

Big Pharma starts its promotional techniques while the doctors are still students in medical school. There, med students have in the past received free lunches, pens, notepads, and other gifts that are given by the companies. The companies start early in trying to persuade the young doctors to prescribe their products by inundating them with logo-infested products and other

gifts. Some medical students have become fed up with the practice and have resisted the free gifts and have started movements to stop the practice from occurring in the first place.

One med student, Jaya Agrawal, launched a national campaign calling on students to sign a pledge saying they would not accept drug-industry gifts. Medical students on other campuses have organized seminars and lectures on the issue. Agrawal was reminded of how difficult it would be to get everyone to think like her when she moved into an apartment she was planning to share with two other med students and noticed a Big Pharma logo on three different clocks in the apartment.[18]

In recent years, some med schools have banned pharmaceutical reps from giving gifts to their students; some improvements in their graduates being more objective later in terms of prescribing medicines has been evident.[19]

LAWSUITS SPAN MULTIPLE ISSUES

Pricing

The attorneys general in Ohio and Pennsylvania filed lawsuits charging fraud or deceptive sales practices against a number of companies. The State of Ohio claimed five companies provided false wholesale pricing data that led their Medicaid program to pay more than it should have for drugs. The State of Pennsylvania filed suits against Pfizer and 12 other drug makers claiming problems with pricing. They also questioned the free samples and free trips for doctors that the companies allegedly have been providing.[20] The Department of Justice spends a lot of time monitoring companies that may be collecting more from Medicare and Medicaid than they should.[21]

Off-Label Marketing and Prescribing

Companies have been charged with illegally promoting drugs for uses for which they were not approved of by the FDA or ran counter to state consumer protection laws. The result of this is that doctors may be prescribing, and patients may be using, drugs for conditions for which those medicines are not needed, are not appropriate, or might hurt patients.[22]

In a huge 2012 settlement, the biotech giant Amgen agreed to pay $762 million for marketing its anemia drug Aranesp for off-label uses. According to the acting U.S. attorney, Amgen was "pursuing profits at the expense of patient safety."[23] A federal prosecutor in this case said that in some cases Amgen sales people were so indoctrinated to sell the drug for off-label uses that many of them didn't even know that the drug was not approved for the use for which they were selling it.[24]

Another example was the promotion of Paxil. The New York attorney general filed a lawsuit alleging that GlaxoSmithKline (GSK), the world's second largest drug firm, had covered up results from clinical trials of its drug, Paxil, an antidepressant. It was alleged that the drug was at best ineffective in children and at worst could increase suicidal thoughts. GSK denied the charges. The company was charged with "repeated and persistent fraud" in promoting the drug.[25] By December 2009, it was reported that Paxil lawsuit settlements had totaled $1 billion.[26] Paxil lawsuit settlements were continuing into 2013 at unpredictable amounts.[27]

In another case, Glaxo resolved the largest health-fraud settlement in American history when it agreed to a $3 billion settlement for several different criminal and civil charges that included off label marketing as well as the misbranding of two antidepressants. The company was also accused of using spa treatments, trips to Hawaii, and hunting excursions to charm doctors into writing prescriptions for unapproved uses of certain drugs.[28]

The FDA and state attorneys general have been up in arms about drug companies marketing their products for "off-label" uses and continue to pursue companies for these violations.[29] But, the future is uncertain for these types of charges. A U.S. Court of Appeals in December 2012 threw out the conviction of a pharmaceutical salesman for marketing drugs for unapproved uses on the grounds that his actions involved free-speech rights. Big Pharma has argued that it should be legally permitted to make truthful statements about its drugs even if the statements are not related to an FDA-approved use of the drug. The FDA plans to fight this ruling and it will be important to watch over the next several years of litigation.[30]

IMPROPER PAYMENTS AND BRIBES

Sometimes the questionable marketing of drugs entails improper payments or bribes. The Securities and Exchange Commission (SEC) announced that the drug maker Schering-Plough Corporation would pay a $500,000 penalty to settle claims that one of its subsidiaries made improper payments to a Polish charity in a quest to get a Polish government health official to buy the company's products.[31]

The SEC claimed that Schering-Plough Poland donated about $76,000 to a Polish charity over a three-year period. Chudnow Castle Foundation, the charity, was headed up by a health official in the Polish government. Apparently, this information came to light while regulators were investigating several pharmaceutical companies for compliance with the U.S. Foreign Corrupt Practices Act. The SEC charged that the payments were not accurately shown on the company's books and that the company's internal controls failed to prevent or detect them. The SEC said that the charity was legitimate, but that the company made the contributions with the expectation of boosting drug sales. In addition to paying the fine, the company also agreed to hire an independent consultant to review the company's internal control system and to ensure the firm's compliance with the Foreign Corrupt Practices Act.[32]

Johnson & Johnson is another company that has been pursued for improper payments. In its case, the improper payments were in connection with the sale of medical devices in two foreign countries. Johnson & Johnson turned itself in, and the worldwide chairperson of medical devices and diagnostics took responsibility and retired.[33] In a related case, the company was being investigated for possible bribery in its medical device unit in Shanghai, in which it is alleged that the company bribed the deputy chief of the Chinese state FDA.[34]

Even while it was trying to repair the injury to its image in relation to drug-marketing tactics, it was revealed in 2013 that Glaxo is being investigated for allegations that its sales staff in China was involved in general payments to doctors to prescribe their drugs, some for unauthorized uses. China is one of Glaxo's most important markets and the problem is complicated by the fact that the health-care system in China is owned and controlled by the state and that it has a tradition of government patronage and gift-giving.[35]

QUESTIONABLE PAYMENTS TO DOCTORS

Few cases more vividly illustrate the questionable marketing tactics of Big Pharma than that of the allegations made against Schering-Plough. According to an investigation by *The New York Times*, Schering-Plough used the marketing tactic of making payments to doctors in exchange for their commitment to exclusively prescribe the company's medications. One doctor reported receiving an unsolicited check for $10,000 in the mail. He said it had been made out to him personally in exchange for an enclosed "consulting" agreement in which all he had to do was prescribe the company's medicines.[36]

"Shadowy" Financial Lures

Interviews with 20 doctors, industry executives, and observers close to the investigation of Schering-Plough and other drug companies revealed a "shadowy system of financial lures" that the companies had been using to convince the physicians to favor their drugs. In the case of Schering-Plough, the tactics included paying doctors large sums of money to prescribe its drug for hepatitis C and to participate in the company's clinical trials, which turned out to be thinly disguised marketing ploys that required very little on the part of the doctors. The company even barred doctors from participating in the program if they did not exhibit loyalty to the company's drugs.[37]

One doctor, a liver specialist, and eight others who were interviewed, said that the company paid them $1,000 to $1,500 per patient for prescribing Intron A, the company's hepatitis C medicine. The doctors were supposed to gather data, in exchange for the fees, and pass it on to the company. Apparently, many doctors were not diligent in recordkeeping, but the company seemed unconcerned. Another liver disease specialist said that the trials were "merely marketing gimmicks."[38] According to some doctors, the company would even shut off the money if one of the doctors wrote prescriptions for competing drugs, or even spoke favorably about other competing drugs. Other doctors reported being signed up for consulting services and being paid $10,000; the only purpose was to keep them loyal to the company's products.[39]

In response to the allegations against the company, former Schering-Plough CEO Fred Hassan reported that the violations took place before he took office. He went on to outline steps he was taking to get the company on track. This included instituting an "integrity hotline" for employees to report wrongdoing and the creation of a chief compliance officer to report directly to the CEO and the board. Hassan said that compliance has to become "part of the DNA" of a drug company.[40] Another company official said that the company has been "undergoing a company-wide transformation since the arrival of new leadership in mid-2003," which is a "commitment to quality compliance and business integrity."[41]

In 2013, Novartis AG was accused by federal prosecutors of paying kickbacks to doctors to get them to prescribe certain of their brand-name drugs. Novartis disputes the charges and defends its payments to doctors as "accepted and customary practice." Prosecutors claimed that the inducements included lavish dinners, fishing trips off the Florida coast, and outings to expensive restaurants (as well as meals at Hooters) around the country. Though Novartis claimed the speakers' fees were paid to the doctors for educational purposes, some of the dinners in which the "speaking" was taking place appeared dubious. For example, one dinner was attended only by three people, including the doctor/speaker, at a Smith & Wollensky steakhouse in Washington, D.C., and the bill came to $2,016, or $672 per person. The lawsuit alleges that Novartis simply wined and dined doctors at high end restaurants with cosmic prices. In one instance, prosecutors said the company paid a Florida doctor $3,750 for speaking to the same four doctors about a Novartis drug five times in a nine month period.[42]

Paying Questionable Doctors

Some Big Pharma companies have continued to pay doctors with questionable credentials to oversee their drug trials and contribute to marketing. One representative case was a doctor whose medical license was suspended in 1997 by the Minnesota Board of Medical Practice. *The New York Times* reported that from 1997 to 2005, this same doctor was hired by several drug firms to conduct multiple drug trials and he was paid for speaking and consulting fees as well.[43] *The New York Times*' investigation found that 103 doctors in Minnesota who had been disciplined by the Minnesota Board of Medical Practice received a total of $1.7 million in payments for research and marketing services rendered.[44] Though Minnesota was the only state willing to make its records available for inspection, experts say this is a national problem.

GIFTS TO DOCTORS

Over the decades, Big Pharma has managed to give significant sums of gift monies to physicians every year. Though some restrictions have been put in place, it is a continuing issue as the industry has found ways to continue gift-giving. The gift-giving practice has worried a number of attorneys general of the states. Attorney General Anne Milgram of New Jersey summoned together a task force to consider putting limits on the gratuities given to doctors and their staffs. Milgram concluded, "Patients should be getting prescription and device recommendations based on what's best for them, not based on financial incentives doctors receive from companies."[45]

Several years ago, Bristol-Myers Squibb Co. agreed to pay more than $515 million to settle fraud allegations involving gifts to doctors and inflated drug prices, according to the U.S. Department of Justice. The U.S.

Attorney in Boston said that Bristol agreed to settle the charges that doctors were illegally paid to motivate them to prescribe Bristol's drugs. Part of this was the company participating in various programs that included trips to luxurious resorts.[46]

Pharmaceutical companies have given meals, tickets to shows and sporting events, ski and beach vacations disguised as medical education seminars, consulting "jobs" for which the doctors do no work, and other gifts, as part of their marketing strategies for decades. The companies expect something in return. They expect the doctors to prescribe their medicines. It is estimated that there is an army of 88,000 or more pharmaceutical reps, many of them young and beautiful, supplying the doctors and their staffs with gifts and freebies. It is argued that these gifts damage the doctors' integrity.[47]

An article published in *The New England Journal of Medicine* reported on a survey of doctors and found that 94 percent of them had some type of relationship with the drug industry. The most frequent drug-industry ties were food and drinks in the workplace (83 percent), drug samples (78 percent), payments for consulting (18 percent), payments for speaking (16 percent), reimbursement for meeting expenses (15 percent), and tickets to cultural or sporting events (7 percent).[48]

BIG BUCKS, BIG PHARMA

The Media Education Foundation, a nonprofit corporation that produces and distributes educational materials observing the impact and ethics of the media industry, released a hard-hitting film, *Big Bucks, Big Pharma: Marketing Disease and Pushing Drugs*, that continues to be available in 2013.[49]

According to the Media Education Foundation, the 46 minute film, *Big Bucks, Big Pharma* pulled back the curtain on the multibillion dollar pharmaceutical industry to expose the insidious ways that illness is used, manipulated, and in some instances created for capital gain. Focusing on the industry's marketing practices, media scholars and health professionals helped viewers understand the ways in which DTC pharmaceutical advertising glamorizes and normalizes the use of prescription medication, and works in tandem with promotion to doctors. Combined, these industry practices have shaped how both patients and doctors understand and relate to disease and treatment.

Lobbying

Big Pharma is able to ward off most government regulations through the power of its huge lobbying force. The pharmaceutical lobby has defeated most attempts to restrain drug marketing. In September 2007, Congress passed a sweeping drug safety bill, but before it was passed, it was stripped of provisions that were intended to limit the ability of the industry to market directly to consumers. In addition, in 11 states that considered legislation to expose pharmaceutical gift-giving, the bills were either defeated or stalled.[50]

In 2012, it was revealed both by *The New York Times* and *The Wall Street Journal* how successfully Big Pharma had lobbied for its own self-interest and won in the passage of the Affordable Care Act (Obama-Care).[51] According to *The New York Times*, the administration's unlikely collaboration with the drug industry forced unappealing trade-offs. Of particular importance was the industry's writing into the proposed law the provision that the Medicare program could not negotiate prices with the drug industry. The result was there would be no lower prices for drugs in the new legislation.[52] Congress has been fighting this provision for years but has not been successful in its dealings with Big Pharma because of the industry's lobbying power. At this writing, the Medication Prescription Drug Price Negotiation Act of 2013 has been introduced and is currently in committee. Unfortunately, GovTrack gives it a six percent chance of getting past committee and a one percent chance of getting enacted.[53] With respect to the Affordable Care Act, *The Wall Street Journal* complained that "a Pfizer CEO and Big Pharma colluded with the White House at the public's expense."[54] What is clear is that Big Pharma's behind-the-scenes lobbying paid big dividends for the industry.

QUESTIONS FOR DISCUSSION

1. What are the ethical issues in this case?
2. Who are the primary stakeholders in these incidents and what are their stakes?
3. Is there any justification for the marketing tactics described in the case? Which are acceptable and which are questionable?
4. What ethical principles may be violated by the marketing tactics described? Do any of these ethical principles *support* the companies' actions?
5. Big Pharma needs enormous sums of money to conduct R&D and to advance its innovations. Do the ends justify the means because our health is at stake?
6. What response do you think physicians should take when approached regarding some of the schemes presented in this case?
7. What does your personal research indicate is the status of the above cases or that of Big Pharma?

ENDNOTES

1. Daren Fonda and Barbara Kiviat, "Curbing the Drug Marketers," *Time* (July 5, 2004), 40–42.
2. Mark Dolliver, "People Think Big Pharma Is Shifty—In Addition, That Is, to Being Greedy," *Adweek* (May 28, 2007), 28.
3. Ibid., 40.
4. Michael A. Santoro and Thomas M. Gorrie, *Ethics and the Pharmaceutical Industry* (Cambridge: Cambridge University Press, 2005). Also see Public Citizen, "The Other Drug War: Big Pharma's 625 Washington Lobbyists," http://www.citizen.org/congress/article_redirect.cfm?ID=6537. Accessed June 13, 2013.
5. Bernard Munos, "We the people vs the pharmaceutical industry," Forbes, April 29, 2013, http://www.forbes.com/sites/bernardmunos/2013/04/29/the-pharmaceutical-industry-vs-society/. Accessed June 13, 2013.
6. Tracy Staton, "Top Pharma Companies by 2012 Revenues," FiercePharma, March 26, 2013, http://www.fiercepharma.com/special-reports/top-pharma-companies-2012-revenues. Accessed June 13, 2013.
7. *Fortune*'s World's Most Admired Companies 2012, http://money.cnn.com/magazines/fortune/most-admired/2013/list/?iid=wma_sp_full. Accessed June 13, 2013.
8. Jonathan D. Rockoff and Joann S. Lublin, "J&J Penalty May Total $2.2 Billion," *The Wall Street Journal*, July 20, 2012, B3.
9. "Top 10 Pharma Advertising Budgets," FiercePharma, February 26, 2013, http://www.fiercepharma.com/special-reports/top-10-pharma-advertising-budgets-2012. Accessed June 13, 2013.
10. Robert Langreth and Matthew Herper, "Pill Pushers: How the Drug Industry Abandoned Science for Salesmanship," *Forbes* (May 8, 2006), 94–102.
11. Ibid., 94.
12. Ibid.
13. Ibid.
14. Ibid., 96.
15. Dani Veracity, "Pharmaceutical Fraud: How Big Pharma's Marketing and Profits Come before Consumer Safety and Wellness," http://www.naturalnews.com/z020345.html. Accessed June 13, 2013.
16. Gardiner Harris, "Diabetes Drug Maker Hid Test Data on Risks, Files Indicate," *The New York Times* (July 12, 2010), http://www.nytimes.com/2010/07/13/health/policy/13avandia.html?_r=0. Accessed June 13, 2013.
17. "Avandia on Trial," *The Wall Street Journal* (July 16, 2010), A16.
18. Chris Adams, "Student Doctors Protest Largess of Drug Makers," *The Wall Street Journal* (June 24, 2002), B1.
19. Kevin B. O'Reilly, "Pharma Gift Bans for Budding Doctors Have Long Term Impact," amednews.com, February 18, 2013, http://www.amednews.com/article/20130218/profession/130219950/6/. Accessed June 25, 2013.
20. Monica Roman, "Pointing at Big Pharma," *BusinessWeek* (March 22, 2004), 56.
21. Arlene Weintraub, "Big Pharma: Pushing the Pills a Bit Too Hard," *BusinessWeek* (February 26, 2007).
22. Carolyn Susman, "False Marketing of Drugs Raises Red Flags," *Cox News Service* (May 25, 2004).
23. Andrew Pollack and Mosi Secret, "Amgen agrees to pay $762 million for marketing anemia drug for off-label use," *The New York Times*, December 18, 2012, http://www.nytimes.com/2012/12/19/business/amgen-agrees-to-pay-762-million-in-drug-case.html. Accessed June 13, 2013.
24. Ibid.
25. "Business: Trials and Tribulations; Pharmaceuticals," *The Economist* (June 19, 2004), 74.
26. Minara El-Rahman, "Paxil Lawsuits Cost Glaxo $1 Billion in Settlements," December 14, 2009, FindLaw, http://blogs.findlaw.com/injured/2009/12/paxil-lawsuits-cost-glaxo-1-billion-in-settlements.html. Accessed June 13, 2013.
27. Legal Examiner, "Paxil Lawsuit Settlements Continue into 2013, How Much?" LawsuitInformation.org, February 22, 2013, http://lawsuitinformation.org/paxil-lawsuit-settlements-continue-into-2013-how-much-1056. Accessed June 13, 2013.
28. "Mis-selling Drugs: The Settlers," *The Economist*, July 7, 2012, 61.
29. Weintraub, ibid.
30. Thomas M. Burton, "Courts to Weigh Free Speech Rights in Pharmaceutical Marketing Cases," *The Wall Street Journal*, December 6, 2012, B6.
31. Judith Burns, "SEC Settles Bribery Case vs. Schering-Plough Corp.," *The Wall Street Journal* (June 9, 2004).
32. Ibid.
33. Weintraub.

34. Jim Edwards, "J&J's Other Headache: Foreign Bribery Probe Targets Shanghai Unit," *CBS Moneywatch*, June 25, 2010, http://www.cbsnews.com/8301-505123_162-42845025/j038js-other-headache-foreign-bribery-probe-targets-shanghai-unit/. Accessed June 13, 2013.

35. Christopher Matthews and Jessica Hodgson, "Glaxo Probes Claims it Paid Bribes in China," *The Wall Street Journal*, June 13, 2013, B1.

36. Gardiner Harris, "As Doctor Writes Prescription, Drug Company Writes a Check," *The New York Times* (June 27, 2004), 1YT.

37. Ibid.

38. Ibid.

39. Ibid.

40. Fonda and Kiviat, 41.

41. Reuters (June 28, 2004).

42. Chad Bray and Jeanne Whalen, "U.S. Accuses Novartis of Kickbacks," *The Wall Street Journal*, April 27/28, 2013, B1.

43. Gardiner Harris and Janet Roberts, "After Sanctions, Doctors Get Drug Company Pay," *The New York Times* (June 3, 2007), A1.

44. Ibid., 20.

45. Quoted in Arlene Weintraub, "Drug Marketing: Will Pharma Finally Have to Fess Up?" *BusinessWeek* (October 8, 2007).

46. Reuters News Service, "Bristol-Myers Settles U.S. Charges for $515 Million" (September 28, 2007), http://www.reuters.com/article/2007/09/28/justice-pharma-bristol-idUSN2842357320070928. Accessed June 13, 2013.

47. "Gifts from Drugmakers Damage Doctors' Integrity," *USA Today* (February 8, 2006), 10A.

48. Reported in Rita Rubin, "Most Doctors Get Money, Gifts from Industry," *USA Today* (April 26, 2007), 4D. Also see "Doctors Still Chummy with Drug Sales Reps," *AARP Bulletin* (June 2007).

49. "Big Bucks, Big Pharma: Marketing Disease and Pushing Drugs," Media Education Foundation, http://www.mediaed.org/cgi-bin/commerce.cgi?preadd=action&key=224. Accessed June 13, 2013.

50. Weintraub, 36.

51. Peter Baker, "Obama was Pushed by the Drug Industry, E-mails Suggest," *The New York Times*, June 8, 2012. Accessed June 18, 2013; "ObamaCare's Secret History," *The Wall Street Journal*, June 12, 2012, A12.

52. Baker, Ibid.

53. Govtrack, http://www.govtrack.us/congress/bills/113/s117s. Accessed June 25, 2013.

54. *The Wall Street Journal*, June 12, 2012, A12.

CASE 22

Smoke-Free in Tasmania*

The dangers of smoking are well known. According to the World Health Organization (WHO), tobacco kills nearly 6 million people in a year, with more than 5 million deaths stemming from direct tobacco use and more than 600,000 resulting from secondhand smoke.[1] The *2000 Smoke Free Generation Initiative* is an international effort to curb smoking by denying access to tobacco to anyone born after 2000, an idea first proposed in a 2010 *Tobacco Control* paper.[2] The logic in the proposal is that as more people were born after 2000 more people would be banned from access to tobacco. The goal is for a smoke-free generation and, eventually, a smoke-free world. This initiative took a big step forward in Tasmania, an island state in the Commonwealth of Australia, when a motion was put forth that called for ban on cigarette sales to anyone born after 2000. This measure would take effect in 2018, when the first people born in the year 2000

---

*This case was prepared by Ann Buchholtz, Rutgers University.

would reach the age when buying tobacco products had been legal.[3] The Legislative Council, Tasmania's independent Upper House, passed the 2000 Smoke Free Generation initiative proposal unanimously.[4] More hurdles remain, but the mere idea of a generational ban is historic and worthy of discussion.

QUESTIONS FOR DISCUSSION

1. Who are the stakeholders and what are their stakes? How would you deal with the stakeholders whose interests conflict, such as people born after 2000 who want to smoke and people who are affected by secondhand smoke and the other costs that smoking incurs?
2. Is the ban fair? If so, to whom is it fair? To whom is it not fair?
3. Is fairness the issue? If so, whose fairness takes precedence? If not, what ethical principles apply to this case?
4. Is this move within government's responsibility to protect the community or is it an example of government over-reach? Where would you draw the line in terms of what government could and should do to deal with the societal problems that smoking creates?

ENDNOTES

1. http://www.who.int/mediacentre/factsheets/fs339/en/index.html. Accessed June 16, 2013.
2. Deborah Khoo, Yvonne Chiam, Priscilla Ng, AJ Berrick, and HN Koong, "Phasing-Out Tobacco: Proposal to Deny Access to Tobacco for Those Born From 2000", *Tobacco Control* (2010, Vol 19, 355–360).
3. Andrew Darby and Amy Corderoy, "Bid to Ban Cigarettes for Anyone Born After 2000," *Sydney Morning Herald* (August 22, 2012), http://www.smh.com.au/national/bid-to-ban-cigarettes-for-anyone-born-after-2000-20120822-24liy.html. Accessed June 15, 2013.
4. Jonathon Pearlman, "Tasmania Considers Cigarette Ban For Anyone Born After 2000," *The Telegraph* (August 22, 2012), http://www.telegraph.co.uk/news/worldnews/australiaandthepacific/australia/9492504/Tasmania-considers-cigarette-ban-for-anyone-born-after-2000.html. Accessed June 16, 2013.

CASE 23

McDonald's—The Coffee Spill Heard 'Round the World*

The McDonald's coffee spill is the most famous consumer lawsuit in the world. Everyone knows about this case, and the details involved in it continue to be debated in many different venues—classrooms, Web sites, blogs, law schools, and business schools. Regardless, it serves as one of the best platforms in the world for discussing what companies owe their consumer stakeholders and what responsibilities consumers have for their own well-being. Over 20 years later, consumers, lawyers and analysts are still debating the world famous coffee spill case.

Keeping the topic hot is the 2011 documentary film, *Hot Coffee*, which analyzes the famous coffee spill, sets the facts straight, and highlights the ongoing debate about the impact of tort reform on the U.S. judicial system. The film premiered at the 2011 Sundance Film Festival and aired on HBO during June 2011.[1] It won many awards.

STELLA LIEBECK

Stella Liebeck and her grandson, Chris Tiano, drove her son, Jim, to the airport 60 miles away in Albuquerque, New Mexico, on the morning of February 27, 1992. Because she had to leave home early, she and

---

* This case was written by Archie B. Carroll, University of Georgia and updated in 2013.

Chris missed having breakfast. Upon dropping Jim off at the airport, they proceeded to a McDonald's drive-through for breakfast. Stella, an active, 79-year-old, retired department-store clerk, ordered a McBreakfast, and Chris parked the car so she could add cream and sugar to her coffee.[2]

What occurred next was the coffee spill that has been heard 'round the world. A coffee spill, serious burns, a lawsuit, and an eventual settlement made Stella Liebeck (pronounced Lee-beck) the "poster lady" for the bitter tort reform discussions that have dominated the news for more than 20 years. To this day, the issue is subject to a continuing debate.

THIRD-DEGREE BURNS

According to Liebeck's testimony, she tried to get the coffee lid off. She could not find any flat surface in the car, so she put the cup between her knees and tried to get it off that way. As she tugged at the lid, scalding coffee spilled into her lap. Chris jumped from the car and tried to help her. She pulled at her sweatsuit, but the pants absorbed the coffee and held it close to her skin. She was squirming as the 170-degree coffee burned her groin, inner thigh, and buttocks. Third-degree burns were evident as she reached an emergency room. A vascular surgeon determined she had third-degree (full thickness) burns over 6 percent of her body.

Hospitalization

Following the spill, Liebeck spent eight days in the hospital and about three weeks at home recuperating under the care of her daughter, Nancy Tiano. She was then hospitalized again for skin grafts. Liebeck lost 20 pounds during the ordeal and at times was practically immobilized. Another daughter, Judy Allen, recalled that her mother was in tremendous pain both after the accident and during the skin grafts.[3]

According to a *Newsweek* report, Liebeck wrote to McDonald's in August 1994, asking them to turn down the coffee temperature. Though she was not planning to sue, her family thought she was due about $2,000 for out-of-pocket expenses, plus the lost wages of her daughter who stayed at home with her. The family reported that McDonald's offered her $800.[4]

STELLA FILES A LAWSUIT

After this, the family went looking for a lawyer and retained Reed Morgan, a Houston attorney, who had won a $30,000 settlement against McDonald's in 1988 for a woman whose spilled coffee had caused her third-degree burns. Morgan filed a lawsuit on behalf of Lie-beck, charging McDonald's with "gross negligence" for selling coffee that was "unreasonably dangerous" and "defectively manufactured." Morgan asked for no less than $100,000 in compensatory damages, including pain and suffering, and triple that amount in punitive damages.

McDonald's Motion Rejected

McDonald's moved for summary dismissal of the case, defending the coffee's heat and blaming Liebeck for spilling it. According to the company, she was the "proximate cause" of the injury. With McDonald's motion rejected, a trial date was set for August 1994.

As the trial date approached, no out-of-court settlement occurred. Morgan, the attorney, said that at one point he offered to drop the case for $300,000 and was willing to settle for half that amount, but McDonald's would not budge. Days before the trial, the judge ordered the two parties to attend a mediation session. The mediator, a retired judge, recommended McDonald's settle for $225,000, using the argument that a jury would likely award that amount. Again, McDonald's resisted settlement.[5]

THE TRIAL

The trial lasted seven days, with expert witnesses dueling over technical issues, such as the temperature at which coffee causes burns. Initially, the jury was annoyed at having to hear what at first was thought to be a frivolous case about spilled coffee, but the evidence presented by the prosecution grabbed its attention. Photos of Liebeck's charred skin were introduced. (These dramatic photos are shown in the documentary, *Hot Coffee*.) A renowned burn expert testified that coffee at 170 degrees would cause second-degree burns within 3.5 seconds of hitting the skin.

The Defense Helped Liebeck

Defense witnesses inadvertently helped the prosecution. A quality-assurance supervisor at McDonald's testified that the company did not lower its coffee heat despite 700 burn complaints over ten years. A safety consultant argued that 700 complaints—about one in every 24 million cups sold—were basically trivial. This comment was apparently interpreted to imply that McDonald's cared more about statistics than about people. An executive for McDonald's testified that the company knew its coffee sometimes caused serious burns, but it was not planning to go beyond the tiny print warning on the cup that said, "Caution: Contents Hot!" The executive went on to say that McDonald's did not intend to change any of its coffee policies or procedures, saying, "There are more serious dangers in restaurants."

In the closing arguments, one of the defense attorneys acknowledged that the coffee was hot and that that is how customers wanted it. She went on to insist that Liebeck had only herself to blame as she was unwise to put the cup between her knees. She also noted that Liebeck failed to leap out of the bucket seat in the car after the spill, thus preventing the hot coffee from falling off her. The attorney concluded by saying that the real question in the case is how far society should go to restrict what most of us enjoy and accept.[6]

THE JURY DECIDES

The jury deliberated for about four hours and reached a verdict for Liebeck. It decided on compensatory damages of $200,000, which it reduced to $160,000 after judging that 20 percent of the fault belonged to Liebeck for spilling the coffee. The jury concluded that McDonald's had engaged in willful, reckless, malicious, or wanton conduct, which is the basis for punitive damages. The jury decided upon a figure of $2.7 million in punitive damages.

Company Neglected Customers

One juror later said that the facts were overwhelmingly against the company and that the company just was not taking care of its customers. Another juror felt the huge punitive damages were intended to be a stern warning for McDonald's to wake up and realize its customers were getting burned. Another juror said he began to realize that the case was really about the callous disregard for the safety of customers.

Public opinion polls after the jury verdict were squarely on the side of McDonald's. Polls showed that a large majority of Americans—including many who usually support the little guy—were outraged at the verdict.[7] But, of course, the public did not hear all the details presented in the trial.

JUDGE REDUCES AWARD

The judge later slashed the jury award by more than 75 percent to $640,000. Liebeck appealed the reduction, and McDonald's continued fighting the award as excessive. In December 1994, it was announced that McDonald's had reached an out-of-court settlement with Liebeck, but the terms of the settlement were not disclosed due to a confidentiality provision. The settlement was reached to end appeals in the case. We will never know the final ending to this case because the parties entered into a secret settlement that has never been revealed to the public. Because this was a public case, litigated in public and subjected to extensive media reporting, some lawyers think that such secret settlements after public trials should not be condoned.[8]

Debate over Temperature

Coffee suddenly became a hot topic in the industry. The Specialty Coffee Association of America put coffee safety on its agenda for discussion. A spokesperson for the National Coffee Association said that McDonald's coffee conforms to industry temperature standards. A spokesperson for Mr. Coffee, the coffee-machine maker, said that if customer complaints are any indication, industry settings may be too low. Some customers like it hotter. A coffee connoisseur who imported and wholesaled coffee said that 175 degrees is probably the optimum temperature for coffee because that's when aromatics are being released. Coffee served at home is generally 135–140 degrees. McDonald's continued to say that it is serving its coffee the way customers like it. As one writer noted, the temperature of McDonald's coffee helps to explain why it sells a billion cups a year.[9]

LATER INCIDENTS

In August 2000, a Vallejo, California woman sued McDonald's, saying she suffered second-degree burns when a disabled employee at a drive-through window dropped a large cup of coffee in her lap. The suit charged that the disabled employee could not grip the cardboard tray and was instead trying to balance it on top of her hands and forearms when the accident occurred in August 1999. The victim, Karen Muth, said she wanted at least $10,000 for her medical bills, pain and suffering, and "humiliation." But her lawyer, Dan Ryan, told the local newspaper that she was entitled to between $400,000 and $500,000. Attorney Ryan went on to say, "We recognize that there's an Americans with Disabilities Act, but that doesn't give them (McDonald's) the right to sacrifice the safety of their customers." It is not known how this lawsuit was settled.

Suits Go Global

It was also announced in August 2000 that British solicitors have organized 26 spill complainants into a group suit against McDonald's over the piping hot nature of its beverages. One London lawyer said, "Hot coffee, hot tea, and hot water are at the center of this case. We are alleging they are too hot." Since that time other lawsuits have been filed around the world.

Burned by a Hot Pickle

In a related turn of events, a Knoxville, Tennessee woman, Veronica Martin, filed a lawsuit in 2000 claiming that she was permanently scarred when a hot pickle from a McDonald's hamburger fell on her chin. She claimed the burn caused her physical and mental harm. Martin sued for $110,000. Martin's husband, Darrin, also sought $15,000 because he "has been deprived of the services and consortium of his wife." According to Veronica Martin's lawsuit, the hamburger "was in a defective condition or unreasonably dangerous to the general consumer and, in particular, to her." The lawsuit went on to say: "while attempting to eat the hamburger, the pickle dropped from the hamburger onto her chin. The pickle was extremely hot and burned the chin of Veronica Martin." Martin had second-degree burns and was permanently scarred, according to the lawsuit. One report was that the McDonald's owner settled this case out of court.[10]

ISSUE WON'T GO AWAY

The Stella Awards

For more than 20 years now, the coffee spill heard 'round the world continues to be a subject of heated debate. The coffee spill and subsequent trial, publicity, and resolution "prompted a tort reform storm that has barely abated."[11] One school of thought held that it represents the most frivolous lawsuit of all time. In fact, a program called the "Stella Awards" was begun to recognize each year's most outrageous lawsuit. The awards were the creation of humorist Randy Cassingham, and his summaries of award-winning cases may be found on the Stella Awards Website.[12] In actuality, most of the lawsuits he chronicles are far more outrageous than the coffee spill in which Stella Liebeck did get seriously injured. On the other hand, consumer groups are still concerned about victims of what they see as dangerous products, and they continue to assail McDonald's callous unconcern for Stella Liebeck.

In the ensuing decades, lawsuits over spilt beverages have continued to come and go, but most of them have been resolved with less fanfare than Stella's case. As for S. Reed Morgan, the lawyer who successfully represented Stella Liebeck, he has handled only three cases involving beverages since Liebeck's suit. Morgan has turned down many plaintiffs, saying he is interested in such cases only if they involve third-degree burns.

Another Scalded-Granny Case

It was reported in summer of 2004 that Morgan has a new McDonald's coffee case that resembles the Liebeck case. This case involves Maxine Villegas, a grandmother in her 70s, who was a passenger in a car stopped at a drive-through, where coffee splashed on her legs and resulted in third-degree burns. In a deposition, Villegas testified coffee spilled on her legs when her sister was passing her the cup of coffee.[13]

The Villegas case did not turn out to be another Liebeck case. Matt Fleischer-Black, writing in *The American Lawyer*, perhaps summarized it well by saying it was likely to generate jokes on Jay Leno and David Letterman but that in light of the Liebeck case it would keep the coffee industry on alert for another decade to come.[14]

The outcome of the Villegas case has not been made public. Lawsuits of this type are often stretched out over years or get settled with no public announcement.

A Lawsuit in Moscow

Coffee spill cases have even gone global. In fact, a long-running case against McDonald's in Moscow was closed in 2006 by a Moscow court after the claimant withdrew her $34,000 lawsuit. Olga Kuznetsova filed a lawsuit against the company after hot coffee was spilled on her in a Russian McDonald's. Kuznetsova claimed that a swinging door hit her while she was walking out onto the restaurant's terrace with a full tray. She demanded 900,000 rubles (about $34,000) in damages. McDonald's lawyers said she had nobody to blame but herself because the paper cup carried a warning that the coffee was hot. This denial of fault prompted her to go to court.[15]

Suits Continue

There is likely no end in sight for coffee spill-type cases. In a 2013 lawsuit, a woman passenger on Continental Airlines sued the company for $170,550 after a cup of hot coffee was spilled on her during her flight. She claimed the hot coffee resulted in second degree burns and permanent scarring on her inner thighs.[16]

QUESTIONS FOR DISCUSSION

1. What are the major issues in the Liebeck case and in the following incidents? Was the lawsuit "frivolous" as some people thought, or serious business?

2. What are McDonald's social (economic, legal, and ethical) responsibilities toward consumers in the Liebeck case and the other cases? What are consumers' responsibilities when they buy a product such as hot coffee or hot hamburgers? How does a company give consumers what they want and yet protect them at the same time?

3. What are the arguments supporting McDonald's position in the Liebeck case? What are the arguments supporting Liebeck's position?

4. If you had been a juror in the Liebeck case, which position would you most likely have supported? Why? What if you had been a juror in the pickle burn case?

5. What are the similarities and differences between the coffee burn cases and the pickle burn case? Does one represent a more serious threat to consumer harm? What should McDonald's, and other fast food restaurants, do about hot food, such as hamburgers, when consumers are injured?

6. What is your assessment of the "Stella Awards"? Is this making light of a serious problem?

7. What are the implications of these cases for future product-related lawsuits? Do we now live in a society where businesses are responsible for customers' accidents or carelessness in using products? We live in a society that is growing older. Does this fact place a special responsibility on merchants who sell products to senior citizens?

ENDNOTES

1. Hot Coffee, http://www.hotcoffeethemovie.com/. Accessed June 17, 2013.

2. Andrea Gerlin, "A Matter of Degree: How a Jury Decided That a Coffee Spill Is Worth $2.9 Million," *The Wall Street Journal* (September 1, 1994), A1, A4.

3. Theresa Howard, "McDonald's Settles Coffee Suit in Out-of-Court Agreement," *Nation's Restaurant News* (December 12, 1994), 1.

4. Aric Press and Ginny Carroll, "Are Lawyers Burning America?" *Newsweek* (March 20, 1995), 30–35.

5. Howard, 1.

6. "Coffee-Spill Suits Meet ADA," Overlawyered.com, http://www.overlawyered.com/archives/00aug1.html. Accessed June 17, 2013.

7. Gerlin, A4.

8. "The Actual Facts about the McDonald's Coffee Case," The 'Lectric Law Library, http://www.lectlaw.com/files/cur78.htm. Accessed July 16, 2010.

9. Ibid.

10. Associated Press, "Couple Seeks $125,000 for Pickle Burn on Chin," *Athens Banner Herald* (October 8, 2000), 6A. Also see Associated Press, "Couple Sues over Hot Pickle Burn" (October 7, 2000), http://www.washingtonpost.com/wp-srv/aponline/ 20001007/aponline154419_000.htm. Accessed June 17, 2013.

11. Matt Fleisher-Black, "One Lump or Two?" *The American Lawyer* (June 4, 2004).

12. StellaAwards.com, http://www.stellaawards.com/. Accessed June 17, 2013.

13. Fleisher-Black, ibid.

14. Ibid.

15. "Moscow McDonald's Coffee-Spill Case Closed," *RIA Novosti* (January 11, 2006), http://en.rian.ru/russia/20061101/55304783.html. Accessed July 16, 2010.

16. msn.com, "Woman suing airline for $170,550 after her lap was filled with hot joe," June 1, 2013, http://now.msn.com/spilled-coffee-lawsuit-has-continental-airlines-on-the-hot-seat. Accessed June 17, 2013.

CASE 24

The Betaseron® Decision (A)*

The United States Food and Drug Administration's (FDA) approval of interferon beta-1b (brand name Betaseron®), made it the first multiple sclerosis (MS)

* This case was prepared by Ann K. Buchholtz, Rutgers University.
This case was written from public sources, solely for the purpose of stimulating class discussion. All events are real. The author thanks Dr. Stephen Reingold, Vice President Research and Medical Programs at the National Multiple Sclerosis Society, and Avery Rockwell, Chapter Services Associate of the Greater Connecticut Chapter of the Multiple Sclerosis Society, for their helpful comments. All rights reserved jointly to the author and the North American Case Research Association (NACRA). Used with permission.

treatment to get FDA approval in 25 years. Betaseron was developed by Berlex Laboratories, a U.S. unit of Schering AG, the German pharmaceutical company. Berlex handled the clinical development, trials, and marketing of the drug, while Chiron Corporation, a biotechnology firm based in California, manufactured it. The groundbreaking approval of Betaseron represented not only a great opportunity for Berlex but a dilemma. Supplies were insufficient to meet initial demand, and shortages were forecast for three years. With insufficient supplies and staggering development costs, how would Berlex allocate and price the drug?

THE CHALLENGE OF MULTIPLE SCLEROSIS

MS is a disease of the central nervous system that interferes with the brain's ability to control such functions as seeing, walking, and talking. The nerve fibers in the brain and spinal cord are surrounded by myelin, a fatty substance that protects the nerve fibers in the same way that insulation protects electrical wires. When the myelin insulation becomes damaged, the ability of the central nervous system to transmit nerve impulses to and from the brain becomes impaired. With MS, there are sclerosed (i.e., scarred or hardened) areas in multiple parts of the brain and spinal cord when the immune system mistakenly attacks the myelin sheath.

The Impact of MS

The symptoms of MS depend to some extent on the location and size of the sclerosis. Symptoms may include numbness, slurred speech, blurred vision, poor coordination, muscle weakness, bladder dysfunction, extreme fatigue, and paralysis. There is no way to know how the disease will progress for any individual, because the nature of the disease can change. Some people will have a relatively benign course of MS with only one or two mild attacks, nearly complete remission, and no permanent disability. Others will have a chronic progressive course resulting in severe disability. A third group displays the most typical pattern, which is periods of exacerbations, when the disease is active, and periods of remission, when the symptoms recede, yet generally leave some damage. People with MS live with an exceptionally high degree of uncertainty, because their disease can change from one day to the next. Dramatic downturns as well as dramatic recoveries are not uncommon.

THE PROMISE OF BETASERON

Interferon beta is a naturally occurring protein that regulates the body's immune system. Betaseron is composed of interferon beta-1b that has been genetically engineered and laboratory manufactured as a recombinant product. Although other interferons (i.e., alpha and gamma) had been tested, only beta interferon had been shown, through large-scale trials, to affect MS. Because it is an immunoregulatory agent, Betaseron was believed to combat the immune problems that make MS worse. However, the exact way in which it works was yet to be determined.

Research

In clinical studies, Betaseron was shown to reduce the frequency and severity of exacerbations in ambulatory MS patients with a relapsing-remitting form of the disease. It did not reverse damage nor did it completely prevent exacerbations. However, Betaseron could dramatically improve the quality of life for the person with MS. For example, people taking Betaseron were shown to have fewer and shorter hospitalizations. Betaseron represented the first and only drug to have an effect on the frequency of exacerbations.

Administration

Betaseron is administered subcutaneously (under the skin) every other day by self-injection. To derive the most benefits from the therapy, it was important that the MS patient maintain a regular schedule of the injections. Some flu-like side-effects, as well as swelling and irritation around the injection, had been noted. However, these side-effects tended to decrease with time on treatment. In addition, one person who received Betaseron committed suicide, while three others attempted it. Because MS often leads to depression, there was no way to know whether the administration of Betaseron was a factor. Last, Betaseron was not recommended for use during pregnancy.

THE BETASERON DILEMMA

FDA approval for Betaseron allowed physicians to prescribe the drug to MS patients who were ambulatory and had a relapsing-remitting course of MS. An estimated one-third of the 300,000 people with MS in the United States fell into that category, resulting in a potential client base of 100,000. The expedited FDA approval process for Betaseron took only 1 year instead of the customary 3. As a result, Berlex was unprepared to manufacture and distribute the treatment. Chiron Corporation had been making the drug in small quantities for experimental use and did not have the manufacturing facilities to handle the expected explosion in demand. Chiron estimated that it would have enough of the drug for about 12,000 to 20,000 people by the end of the year. By the end of the second year, Chiron expected to be able to provide the drug to 40,000 patients. Depending on demand, it might take about three years to provide the drug to all patients who requested it. Chiron's expanded manufacturing represented the only option for Berlex, because the process required for another company to get FDA approval to manufacture the drug would take even longer.

Pricing

In addition to availability, price was a concern, because successes must fund the failures that precede them.

Betaseron represented years of expensive, risky research by highly trained scientists in modern research facilities. Furthermore, genetically engineered drugs were extremely expensive to manufacture. In the case of Betaseron, a human interferon gene is inserted into bacteria, resulting in a genetically engineered molecule. The stringent quality controls on the procedure take time and are expensive. As a result, the price of Betaseron was expected to be about $10,000 per year for each patient.

Betaseron brought great hope to people with MS and a great quandary to Berlex. How should Berlex handle the supply limitations, the distribution, and the pricing of this drug?

QUESTIONS FOR DISCUSSION

1. What are the ethical issues in this situation? Which issues must Berlex consider first when determining how to distribute Betaseron?
2. Given the shortage of the drug, how should Berlex decide who receives it and who waits? Give a specific plan.
3. How should Berlex handle the logistics of distribution?
4. How should Berlex determine the drug's relative pricing (assume the drug costs about $12,000 per year)?
5. Who, if anyone, should be involved in the decision making?

CASE 25

The Hudson River Cleanup and GE*

One of the major challenges businesses face with respect to government regulations is that often compliance with existing regulations during an earlier period does not protect them against expensive problems that occur or come to light later. The plight of General Electric (GE) with respect to its dumping of PCBs (polychlorinated biphenyls) over 30 years ago is a classic case in point.

For decades, GE had electrical-equipment-making plants along the Hudson River in New York. During the period prior to 1977, GE discharged more than 1.3 million pounds of PCBs into a 40-mile stretch of the Hudson before the chemicals were banned in 1977. In 2001, the PCB-contaminated upper Hudson River had become the largest EPA Superfund site in the nation and has become the most expensive to clean up.[1]

In August 2001, the Environmental Protection Agency (EPA) circulated a draft proposal informing GE that it would have to spend hundreds of millions of dollars to clean up the PCBs that were legally dumped over a 30-year period that ended in 1977.[2] According to *BusinessWeek*, the Bush Administration and the EPA, under fire for its environmental policies, ordered GE to clean up the Hudson in what has been called the biggest environmental dredging project in

U.S. history. The decision reaffirmed a plan developed in the waning days of the Clinton Administration.

A GE representative stated that the company was "disappointed in the EPA's decision," which it said, "will cause more harm than good." Environmentalists, predictably, praised the decision, and the Sierra Club executive director called the decision a "monumental step toward protecting New Yorkers from cancer-causing PCBs."[3]

The cleanup plan became a heated and politically charged debate beginning in fall of 2001, as an investigative report detailed how environmentalists (the Greens) claimed that GE and the EPA used the terrorist attacks on the World Trade Center and Pentagon as a distraction from the priority of the planned cleanup. The Greens charged that GE and the EPA, under the leadership of EPA administrator Christine Todd Whitman, delayed the cleanup and were "negotiating in the shadow of September 11." The executive director of the Clearwater advocacy groups and spokesperson for the coalition said regarding the meetings between GE and EPA, "It smells really bad."[4]

USE OF PERFORMANCE STANDARDS

The Greens charged that a modification of the cleanup plan that would favor GE was in the works. This would be the establishment of "performance standards" to measure the effectiveness of dredging to remove the PCBs. In a change from the original Clinton Administration plan,

* This case was prepared by Archie B. Carroll, University of Georgia. Revised and updated in 2013.

the revised goal of the EPA would be to roll out the dredging project in stages with periodic testing for PCBs. EPA stated: "The performance indicators being considered will include measuring PCB levels in the soil and the water column, as well as measuring the percentage of dredged material that gets re-suspended." The agency added: "Based on these objective scientific indicators, EPA will determine at each stage of the project whether it is scientifically justified to continue the cleanup. PCB levels in fish will be monitored throughout the project as well."[5]

Would GE Be Favored?

Environmentalists believed that the performance standards would be weighted in ways that would favor GE's position and would put an early lid on the project. They communicated to EPA that they did not want any standards built into the project that would offer GE an "out." Environmentalists who met with the EPA claimed they were talking to a brick wall—that their arguments were brushed off. One stated: "That office (EPA), with all due respect, seems to get its information from G.E. It's a political process being handled inside the [Washington] beltway; it's inappropriate and possibly illegal." The Greens stated they planned to start an advertising blitz hammering on its claim that terrorism was used as a cover while the EPA and GE schemed a way to dilute the plan.[6]

THE HUDSON RIVER

Close to 40 miles of the half-mile-wide Hudson River is involved in the planned cleanup. It is a pastoral and wooded stretch of the river that winds in the shadows of the Adirondacks, which provide recreational activities for numerous towns and villages. At one time, these villages were thriving examples of American industrial power. Today, most of the factories, mills, and plants are closed. Like in many other industries, jobs headed south, west, across borders, or across oceans as companies tried to extricate themselves from what they saw as devastating taxes and regulations. Though not obvious to the eye, the hidden problem of hazardous waste pollution has been a significant barrier to redevelopment of the area.[7]

SUPERFUND SITE

In 1983, the upper Hudson was named a Superfund site by the EPA. This meant that GE would be held responsible by law for cleaning up the pollution resulting from years of disposal of pollutants, regardless of whether the disposal was legal at the time. John Elvin, an investigative reporter, claimed that the Hudson River was just one of 77 alleged sites to be in need of cleanup under the EPA's Superfund program. It is believed that there are numerous other sites in addition to the upper Hudson River where PCBs were dumped. In addition to the Hudson River area, the chemicals were used at plants throughout the New England area.[8]

PCBs

PCBs are a large family of fire-retardant chemicals that GE once used in the production of electrical products. There are over 200 variations of the chemical, which were, for the most part, dumped legally in the years before it was determined they posed a possible cancer risk. The PCBs were oily and tarry and were disposed of as fill for roadbeds, housing developments, and other such uses. It was reported that GE often dispensed the material free to residents surrounding its factories. In various forms, the company sold or gave away what is now considered a contaminated waste product to be used as a wood preservative, fertilizer, termite inhibitor, and component in house paints. As for directly dumped wastes, the PCBs are thought to be leaking into groundwater from landfills that GE had put caps on.[9]

PCBs and Their Dangers

According to the EPA, PCBs have been found to cause cancer and can also harm the immune, nervous, and reproductive systems of humans, fish, and wildlife. They think the chemicals are especially risky for children.[10] The director of the Institute for Health and the Environment at the State University of New York at Albany, David O. Carpenter, has been a critic of GE. According to Carpenter, all experts except those allied with GE believe PCBs to be a "probable" cause of cancer in humans. Carpenter has lashed out at GE for "deceitful and unscientific" claims that are "preposterous." Carpenter claims that PCBs are linked to reduced IQ in children, attention deficit disorder, suppressed immune systems, diabetes, and heart disease.[11]

Controversy over Safety

There is controversy over whether PCBs are dangerous or not. Like the EPA, environmental groups believe they are dangerous. A handout from the Friends of a Clean Hudson coalition states strongly: "PCBs are a class of synthetic toxic chemicals universally recognized as among the world's most potent and persistent threats to human health." On the other hand, a former GE employee who worked intimately with PCBs for 25–30 years thinks differently. To put it in layman's terms, he said, "You're talking about a big, fat, slippery, stable molecule that doesn't break down. That's why it was used in lubrication and cooling in the manufacturing process. It's just plain sludge, that's all."[12]

Another hazardous-waste-management expert was reported as saying that he had been in PCBs up to his armpits and so had many others working with GE and other firms. He also affirmed that he had drunk half a glass of PCBs accidentally 25 years earlier. (But, we don't know what happened to him after that period.) The expert went on to say that there are no reported cases of cancer traced to PCBs. He expressed the opinion that this controversy is 25 percent an environmental concern and 75 percent politics in a state and towns abandoned by GE that are left with no industry and a lot of trash. In spite of his views, the expert does think that GE should clean up the "hot spots" where dumping was most severe and the rest of the river should be left to heal on its own.[13]

GE'S POSITION ON CLEANUP PLAN

GE did not accept the EPA's cleanup plan as a done deal. The huge, wealthy company, one of the largest in the world, cranked up a barrage of TV infomercials, radio and TV ads, and initiatives by top-tier Washington lobbyists to sway the public, media, and government. The company fielded an imposing cadre of Washington lobbyists. Among these lobbyists were former Senator George Mitchell, former House Speaker-Designate Bob Livingston, and several other prominent people.[14]

Jack Welch Chimes In

Retired former chief executive officer of GE, the legendary Jack Welch, was negotiating with regulators over this issue as far back as the 1970s. Welch summarized the company's position in a statement he made to GE stockholders while he was the CEO: "We simply do not believe that there are any adverse health effects from PCBs."[15] GE has already spent millions of dollars fighting the proposal to clean up the river. The company contends that the proposed dredging would actually be more destructive, because it will stir up PCBs buried in the mud and recontaminate the river. Supporting GE's position, Rep. John Sweeney said that he would continue to fight the dredging plan because it would have an adverse impact on local residents.[16]

One journalist estimated that GE might end up spending as much fighting the EPA plan as it would if they just went ahead with the cleanup. This raises the obvious question as to why GE would fight the plan. According to John Elvin, investigative reporter, it is because the company thinks it is a precedent-setting case that could leave the company open to a tobacco industry-sized settlement claim. As it turns out, this is only one of the many sites GE used legally to dispose of manufacturing by-products, and PCBs are just one of the many possibly hazardous wastes that the company had to deal with over the years.[17]

CITIZENS' AND ENVIRONMENTAL GROUPS' VIEWS

Many of the residents of the upstate area that would be most affected by a GE cleanup prefer to just leave the situation alone and let the river heal itself. A poll commissioned by GE and administered by Zogby International found that 59 percent of the residents in the region favored letting the river deal with the pollutants naturally. Another poll done by Siena College Research Institute found that 50 percent of all the residents along the entire length of the Hudson wanted the river to be left alone. On the other side of the issue, polls have shown that a large majority of the citizens did want a cleanup.[18] The survey results seem to depend on which citizens are chosen to be polled, how the questions are framed, and who is doing the polling.

Grassroots Opposition

There was even some grassroots opposition to the EPA's dredging plan. An example is found in Citizen Environmentalists Against Sludge Encapsulation (CEASE) and Farmers Against Irresponsible Remediation (FAIR). CEASE proposed acts of civil disobedience to prevent the government from coming onto private property. According to one CEASE activist, "the downstate enviros are only interested in punishing GE at the expense of agriculture, recreation, and other economic interests in our community."[19] FAIR, for its part, asked a federal district court in Albany, New York, for a preliminary injunction blocking the EPA from issuing a final decision until it provided additional information on the impact of the dredging project. But the U.S. District Court for the Northern District of New York ruled that it did not have jurisdiction over the case because the Superfund Amendments and Reauthorization Act of 1986 prohibits judicial review at this point in the case.[20]

Supporters of the Cleanup

For their part, most of the environmental groups continue to think that the cleanup is the right thing to do. Advocates of the cleanup said that the project would be a "gift from heaven" to the rustbelt towns along the

Hudson River. Friends of a Clean Hudson, a coalition of 11 major environmental groups, commissioned a study in which they concluded that thousands of jobs and hundreds of millions of dollars would come into the area once the project was under way. The coalition claimed benefits that could include the creation of close to 9,000 new jobs with annual payrolls of up to $346 million. In a reaction to this report, Rep. Maurice Hinchey, whose district includes a downstate portion of the river, claimed that as a result of the dredging, "tourism will increase, the fishing industry will be revived, thousands of jobs will be created and property values will rise."[21]

According to reporter John Elvin, there are many festering grudges still held against GE in upstate New York. GE was once the centerpiece of the bustling and prosperous area. He contends that GE eventually left the region because of New York's antibusiness environment and that, in recent years, legislators have felt free to tax the company to their heart's content, so the company expressed its own right to pack up and leave. Elvin maintains that many state and local officials, and some citizens, just wanted a last piece of GE's hide—a last chance to make GE pay.[22]

Only time will reveal the whole picture of the ramifications to GE and the contaminated Hudson River. It is obvious from all the interests involved and opinions expressed, however, that it is not totally clear what should take place in the PCB-tainted Hudson River.

WORKING TOWARD A SETTLEMENT

Companies may resist, but government agencies do not go away. Such is the case in the continuing saga of the Hudson River cleanup. In 2001, the Bush Administration ordered a full-scale dredging of a 40-mile stretch of the river. It was to be the largest environmental dredging project in history. GE was expected to pay the estimated $490 million charge for the cleanup and the project was expected to take about a decade, with plans for the dredging to begin in 2005.

In 2003, it was reported that the Hudson River cleanup was moving on schedule, although at the time GE was withholding payments, according to environmental groups. A spokesman for Environmental Advocates, one of 13 concerned groups that formed the Friends of a Clean Hudson coalition said, "contrary to dire predictions of two or three years ago, the project is on track." Critics said that GE had not been cooperative, but the company denied this evaluation of its efforts. At that time, the environmental groups graded the key players in the cleanup. The EPA got a "B" and GE got a "D."[23]

Performance Standards Finalized

In May 2004, the EPA finally released its final quality of life performance standards for the Hudson River cleanup.[24] By March 2004, an environmental progress report was released in which it was stated that more than 290,000 pounds of PCBs had been removed from the Hudson Falls Plant Site. GE installed a comprehensive network of collection and monitoring wells to capture PCBs in the bedrock and prevent them from reaching the river. Also in 2004, the New York State Department of Environmental Conservation (DEC) approved GE's plan to build innovative under-the-river tunnels to capture the final few ounces a day of PCBs that are thought to trickle out of the river bottom near the Hudson Falls Plant.[25]

Dredging Delayed, Backroom Deals

According to environmental groups, GE dragged its feet in moving forward with the cleanup. Initially, dredging was to begin in 2005, but due to GE-requested delays, the start date got pushed back to 2009. Also, the Natural Resources Defense Council (NRDC), an environmental group, claimed that in 2005 the EPA rewarded GE's foot dragging by striking a backroom deal that required GE to commit only to completing Phase 1 of the cleanup—just 10 percent of the total job.[26]

Settlement Reached

On November 2, 2006, the federal district court signed off on the EPA–GE settlement. This agreement allowed for the dredging of the PCB-contaminated river sediments to proceed. GE continued to challenge the EPA over important details, and it continued to press a federal lawsuit challenging the EPA's authority to require GE in the future to complete Phase 2 of the cleanup. If GE got out of the second phase, taxpayers would have to foot the bill to clean up the remaining mess, face protracted legal battles with GE to get it to complete the job, or else be forced to live with a polluted river indefinitely. Much of the upper Hudson River has already been closed to fishing. South of Troy, New York, women of childbearing age and children have been advised not to eat fish at all. And, according to the NRDC, the pollution is spreading, continuing to move downriver from Albany.[27]

PHASE 1 (2009) OF DREDGING PROJECT COMPLETED

After legal squabbling, Phase 1 of the GE dredging project began and was completed in 2009. The work spanned the period of May 15 to November 15, 2009. The task focused on removal of PCB-contaminated sediment from a six-mile stretch of the upper Hudson River. GE removed approximately 10 percent of the contamination scheduled to be dredged during the expected six-year project. During this time, the depth of contamination was found to be greater than expected due to dense logging debris.

In addition to the PCB removal, Phase 1 was intended to allow GE and the EPA to evaluate project progress and to make program adjustments to improve compliance with the EPA's performance standards. The standards were intended to ensure that dredging operations were done safely, with public health being protected at all times.[28]

At the same time that GE had been pursuing Phase 1 of the dredging, it had an outstanding lawsuit filed in 2000 in which it challenged the EPA Superfund law's application to the Hudson River case as unconstitutional. In June 2010, GE lost this lawsuit and its appeal to the U.S. Court of Appeals. A spokesman for the company said, "GE is evaluating the decision and reviewing its options."[29]

PHASE 2 UNDERWAY

The first year of the Phase 2 cleanup occurred during 2011. As of 2013, Phase 2 was in its third year. The remainder of the cleanup is expected to take 3–5 more years to complete.[30]

Progress on the Hudson River cleanup may be monitored on the EPA's Web site: http://www.epa.gov/hudson/.

QUESTIONS FOR DISCUSSION

1. What are the social and ethical issues in this case? Which are major and which are minor?
2. Who are the stakeholders and what are their stakes? Assess their legitimacy, power, and urgency.
3. Do your own research on PCBs. Do your findings clarify their status as being so hazardous they must be removed? Or are they best left where they have settled?
4. Who is responsible for the contaminated Hudson River? GE? EPA? State of New York? Local citizens? What ethical principles help to answer this question?
5. Do research on the EPA Superfund. Does it appear to be fair environmental legislation? Should a company have to pay for something that was legal at the time they did it?
6. Do research on this case and update the case facts. Has anything changed since the facts were presented that affects its resolution?

ENDNOTES

1. James L. Nash, "Compliance Not Good Enough, GE Finds Out," *Occupational Hazards* (September 2001), 47ff.
2. "Hudson River Cleanup," *Business Insurance* (August 6, 2001), 2.
3. Monica Roman, "GE's Hudson River Blues," *BusinessWeek* (August 13, 2001), 40.
4. John Elvin, "Greens Exploit Terror Against GE," *Insight* (November 19, 2001), 22–25.
5. Glenn Hess, "Hudson River Cleanup Could Cost GE About $460 Million," *Chemical Market Reporter* (August 6, 2001), 1, 29.
6. Ibid., 23.
7. Ibid.
8. Ibid., 24.
9. Ibid.
10. Ibid., 1, 29.
11. Elvin, 25.
12. Ibid., 24.
13. Ibid.
14. Ibid., 23.
15. Ibid., 25.
16. Hess, 29.
17. Ibid., 24.
18. Ibid.
19. Ibid.
20. "New York Attacks Push Back Decision on Hudson Dredging," *Chemical Market Reporter* (October 1, 2001), 18.
21. Elvin, 25.
22. Ibid., 22.
23. Yancey Roy, "Environmental Groups Check on Hudson River Cleanup," *Rochester Democrat and Chronicle* (February 7, 2003).
24. Hudson River PCBs Superfund Site, http://www.epa.gov/hudson/. Accessed June 17, 2013.
25. "New York State Approves GE Plan for Hudson River Tunnel Project" (press release) (March 16, 2004), http://www.ge.com/en/company/news/hudson_tunnel.htm.
26. National Resources Defense Council, http://www.nrdc.org/water/pollution/hhudson.asp. Accessed June 17, 2013.
27. Ibid.
28. Environmental Protection Agency, "Hudson River PCBs Superfund Site—Phase 1 Dredging Fact

Sheet" (November 2009), http://www.hudson dredgingdata.com/. Accessed June 17, 2013.

29. William McQuillen, "GE Loses Appeal Challenging EPA Superfund Law Over Hudson River Dredging," *Bloomberg* (June 30, 2010), http://www.bloomberg.com/news/2010-06-29/ge-loses-court-

challenge-to-u-s-s-superfund-law-on-hudson-river-dredging.html. Accessed June 17, 2013.

30. U.S. EPA, Hudson River PBBs Superfund Site, Phase 2 Overview Fact Sheet, Spring 2013, http://www.epa.gov/hudson/pdf/Phase2_Overview-Spring2013.pdf. Accessed June 17, 2013.

CASE 26

Cloud Computing: Earth's Friend or Foe?*

The term "cloud computing" conjures up beautiful visions of nature at its most pristine, but the reality of it is much more mundane. Cloud computing is simply the delivery of computing and storage capacity to customers through shared data networks—rather than being just one thing, it is a group of technologies or practices.[1] Cloud computing is important because it utilizes a range of recently developed technologies and takes advantage of trends (such as the rise of outsourcing) and resources (such as increased bandwidth), making it an important "evolutionary step" in computing.[2] The cloud has arrived and firms are moving inexorably in its direction; however, we are not yet certain of all its effects.

In addition to cloud computing's contributions to business efficiency and global outreach, its positive environmental impact has drawn praise from its proponents. Verdantix, an independent analyst firm, produced a Carbon Disclosure Project study based on detailed information from 11 global firms that have used cloud computing for at least two years.[3] They used the case study information to build a forecast model that predicted by 2020, U.S. companies with revenues of more than $1 billion could cut CO_2 emissions by 85.7 million metric tons annually if they spend 60 percent of infrastructure, platform and software budgets on cloud computing.[4] An addendum to the Carbon Disclosure Project study found that large IT companies in France and the United Kingdom could cut their carbon emissions in half by 2020 if they move their IT systems to the cloud.[5] They

reported that a move to the cloud would save the equivalent of the annual emissions of 630,000 passenger vehicles in France and 4 million in the United Kingdom.[6]

When the reports were issued, some observers praised the environmental benefits that cloud computing would bring. However, others began to question the report's premise. GreenMonk analyst Tom Rafferty notes that most cloud providers do not disclose their energy sources, information that is necessary to determine whether carbon emissions decline.[7] For example, if a company whose energy is generated primarily by nuclear or renewable sources moves its applications to a cloud provider whose energy is generated primarily by coal, then cloud computing will increase, not decrease, its carbon emissions.[8] *The New York Times* conducted a yearlong investigation of the environmental impact of the data centers that provide cloud services. They found that data centers typically run at maximum capacity all of the time and waste about 90 percent of the energy they use. Only six to twelve percent of their electricity provided power for computations. The remaining 88 to 94 percent was used for idling so that they would be able to handle potential surges in activity that could crash their operations if they did not have enough ready power.[9] Data centers' worldwide wattage is the rough equivalent of thirty nuclear power plants.[10] Many of Silicon Valley's data centers are on the list of California's top stationary diesel polluters, and, in Virginia and Illinois alone, at least a dozen major data centers have been cited for air quality violations.

Determining the environmental impact of cloud computing is a difficult task because the industry is cloaked in secrecy. Genuine security concerns keep companies and governments from disclosing the locations of their data centers.[11] Energy use and

_____

*This case was prepared in 2013 by Ann K. Buchholtz, Rutgers University.

technology utilization are also closely guarded secrets. Furthermore, no single government agency is responsible for monitoring the industry.[12] With the rapid growth in cloud computing and the lack of available information on the industry's sustainability, questions about that sustainability are likely to persist.

QUESTIONS FOR DISCUSSION

1. Who are cloud computing's stakeholders and what are their stakes?
2. This case paints two very different pictures of cloud computing's environmental impact. Which one do you think is closer to the truth?
3. If you were in a position to guide the industry, what would you recommend? What advice would you give to a company considering cloud computing?
4. What, if any, recommendations do you have for government action?
5. Things change rapidly in this industry. Collect additional updated information on cloud computing's environmental impact. How have things changed? What do you foresee as the future impact?

ENDNOTES

1. Graeme Philipson, "Why Cloud Computing Is Important," *ITWire* (July 16, 2012), http://www.itwire.com/2012-06-01-13-40-03/browse/c-level/55713-why-cloud-computing-is-important. Accessed June 17, 2013.
2. Ibid.
3. Rosie Reeve and Stuart Neumann, *Cloud Computing–The IT Solution for the 21st Century* (2011), https://www.cdproject.net/Documents/Cloud-Computing-The-IT-Solution-for-the-21st-Century.pdf. Accessed June 26, 2013.
4. Ibid.
5. Rosie Reeve and Stuart Neumann, *An addendum for France & the UK to 'Cloud Computing–the IT Solution for the 21st Century,'* (2011), https://www.cdproject.net/SiteCollectionDocuments/Cloud-Computing-PR-Addendum-UK.pdf. Accessed June 26, 2013.
6. Ibid.
7. Tom Rafferty, "Carbon Disclosure Project's Emissions Reduction Claims For Cloud Computing Are Flawed," GreenMonk: the blog (July 20, 2011), http://greenmonk.net/2011/07/21/carbon-disclosure-projects-emissions-reduction-claims-for-cloud-computing-are-flawed/. Accessed June 26, 2013.
8. Ibid.
9. James Glanz, "Power, Pollution and the Internet," *The New York Times* (September 23, 2012), A1.
10. Ibid.
11. Ibid.
12. Ibid.

CASE 27

New Belgium Brewing: Defining a Business on Sustainability*

When Jeff Lebesch and Kim Jordan expanded from home beer brewing to commercial production in 1991, they envisioned two goals for their new company: they believed they could produce world-class beers, and they believed they could do this while kindling social, environmental and cultural change. In 2012, their company, New Belgium Brewing Company (NBB), has become the third-largest craft brewery in the U.S. and the eighth-largest producer in the overall industry.[1] The brewery also stands as a corporate leader in environmental sustainability, and provides an example of how a company can incorporate environmental concerns into everyday business decisions.[2] However, as NBB continues to expand, the company faces a number of challenges in reaching its environmental goals, many of which it cannot directly control.

HISTORY OF NEW BELGIUM BREWERY

Jeff was inspired to found New Belgium Brewing (NBB) while on a 1989 bike ride through the Belgian countryside.[3] During his trek, he perceived a lack of flavor in American beers compared to those he was drinking in Europe. When he returned home to Colorado he set out on a quest to introduce American beer drinkers to the unique essence found in traditional

*This case was written by Jonathan Bundy, University of Georgia. Updated in 2013.

Belgian brews, from the tart framboise, the light saison and the truly one-of-a-kind trappist ales. Using his home brewing experience, Jeff was able to develop a distinctive recipe for traditional Belgian amber ale. The ale, dubbed Fat Tire in honor of the inspirational bike trip, became the brewery's flagship beer. By 1991, Jeff and Kim formally organized the brewery as New Belgium Brewing Company and began selling the first bottles of Fat Tire around their hometown of Fort Collins, CO.

Kim, serving as the businessperson of the two, engaged in the marketing and distribution operations, selling the beer to friends, neighbors, and local bars and stores. A neighbor provided the watercolors that adorn the beers' labels, a tradition that lives on today. The beers were brewed in the couple's basement, using an 8.5-barrel system (one barrel is 31 gallons) allowing for total production in 1992 of 993 barrels.[4] By 2012, NBB produced over 750,000 barrels and sold in 31 States.[5] In 1991, the company only produced two types of beer, the signature Fat Tire Amber Ale and the darker Abbey Dubbel. Today, NBB regularly produces 21 different styles, 11 being produced year-round. The main brewery is still located in Fort Collins, Colorado and a new second brewery is opening in Ashville, North Carolina.

CORE VALUES

Unique in the founding story of New Belgium Brewing is a commitment to a set of values that were adopted from the beginning. Before initial production and during the planning stages of the business, Kim and Jeff developed a set of core values and beliefs by which they would guide their company. Listed below, it is clear from this set of values that profitability is secondary to a sense of social responsibility. This responsibility is centered on two core concepts: the production of quality beer and beer culture, and a business that can produce this beer while paying attention to environmental and social concerns. All business decisions are made according to the core values and beliefs, and everything is done with the mission "to operate a profitable company which is socially, ethically, and environmentally responsible, and that produces high quality beer true to Belgian styles."[6] The values live on today, unchanged from their original conception, guiding the 300-plus person company into the new era of craft brewing.

Our Core Values and Beliefs[7]

- *Remembering* that we are incredibly lucky to create something fine that enhances people's lives while surpassing our consumers' expectations.

- *Producing* world-class beers.
- *Promoting* beer culture and the responsible enjoyment of beer.
- *Kindling* social, environmental and cultural change as a role model of a sustainable business.
- *Environmental stewardship:* Honoring nature at every turn of the business.
- *Cultivating* potential through learning, high involvement culture and the pursuit of opportunities.
- *Balancing* the myriad needs of the company, our coworkers and families.
- *Trusting* each other and committing to authentic relationships and communications.
- *Continuous*, innovative quality and efficiency improvements.
- *Having fun.*

NEW BELGIUM'S SUSTAINABILITY EFFORTS

In the spirit of the core values, NBB has attempted to implement sustainable efforts in all aspects of the brewing process. Some of NBB's efforts include the following.[8]

Electricity

In 1998, NBB conducted a study to analyze its carbon emissions. It was found that the single largest factor was emissions generated from its electricity consumption—emissions released by coal-fired power plants. In response, NBB owners (which included the founders and approximately 90 employees) unanimously voted to source their electricity from 100% renewable, carbon-free wind sources. At a premium of 57% on its electricity bill, NBB became the first completely wind powered brewery. In addition to the renewable sourcing, NBB has also begun an extensive energy conservation program. In 2008, the company invested $1 million into energy-sparing equipment. NBB also introduced a combination of solar PV, co-generation, metering and control initiatives in an attempt to become a net-zero purchaser of electricity. A further example of its efficiency and conservation efforts includes the development of a 'natural draft cooling' system, which utilizes outside air for refrigeration when the temperature is below 40 degrees. By 2012, these conservation efforts have reduced NBB's electricity consumption by 21%.

Water

The average brewery uses five gallons of water to produce one gallon of beer. NBB's ratio is 4.2:1. The majority of its water use efficiencies come from its conservation efforts.[9] The company has analyzed all of its water consumption activities and has attempted to reduce use at every stage of production. NBB also has invested in an onsite water treatment facility. Wastewater is treated in its "bio-digester" plant before being released into Fort Collins wastewater streams. NBB tries to use this processed water where it can throughout the brewery. In addition, the process creates methane, which is captured and used to co-generate power for the Brewery. NBB hopes that its efforts will help to further reduce its water-to-product ratio to 3.5:1 by 2015.

Waste & Recycling

NBB has made a number of conscious efforts to reduce input materials. NBB is also a believer in recycling; it only sent 5.62% of its waste to landfills in 2011. The majority of its waste consists of spent grain, which is sold as feedstock for cattle. The remainder of its recycled waste includes a combination of glass, cardboard and general office and industrial waste. Because NBB uses amber glass, it is difficult to source recycled glass for new bottles. Amber glass has to be separated from other glass to be successfully recycled, and NBB estimates that its new bottles have a recycled content of only about 10%. However, the company sources its bottle production locally to reduce transportation emissions and is active in advocacy for additional recycling efforts.

Carbon Emissions (Six-Pack of Fat Tire Amber Ale)

New Belgium recently partnered with The Climate Conservancy to assess the greenhouse gases emitted across the lifecycle of its signature Fat Tire Amber Ale.[10] The assessment was born from a goal to reduce the carbon footprint per barrel by 50%. It was found that over half of the total emissions came from 'downstream' activities: distribution and retail storage. The majority of the remaining contribution comes from production and transportation of the raw inputs (barley and hops), bottles, and cardboard. Only 8% is produced directly from brewing activities, with nearly half of this being the actual CO_2 found in the beer itself. Surprisingly, over a quarter of the total carbon equivalent emissions come from refrigeration at retail locations, something that is completely out of the control of NBB. By understanding where the emissions are generated, New Belgium is better able to target specific initiatives to reduce its impact. Some future initiatives include trying to source more organic inputs, more recycled content in their glass and packaging, and better supplier awareness and communication. After a detailed study of the carbon footprint, NBB believes that a reduction of 25% in carbon equivalent emissions is a more realistic goal.

MAKING A BIGGER SPLASH

While NBB is proud of its sustainability efforts, the company also recognizes that much remains to be done. Specifically, NBB wants to make a stronger impact on the upstream (materials sourcing) and downstream (recycling) factors–factors controlled by suppliers and consumers. Beer products, by nature, involve a great deal of packaging, most of which is still ending up in landfills. NBB, as well as the entire craft brewing industry, realizes that it must do what it can to encourage more consumer recycling. One possibility is the enactment of a national "bottle bill," which would require consumers to pay a refundable deposit on glass bottles. When the consumer returns the bottle for recycling they receive their deposit back and thus have a material incentive to recycle. The brewing and packaging industries do not generally support these kinds of bills, and many within the two industries have actively attempted to stop their passage. Opponents see the deposit as a kind of tax or price increase on the product. NBB, however, has shown an inclination for support, saying that "perhaps it is time for the domestic and craft brewers to support Bottle Bills to reduce our industry CO_2 footprint."[11] In the mean time, NBB continues to use as much recycled glass as it can.

An additional effort to impact consumer decisions to recycle is centered on packaging. In an initiative begun in 2008, NBB started selling a small percentage of Fat Tire Amber Ale in lightweight aluminum 12-ounce cans.[12] Because cans weigh less than bottles, they are more efficient to transport around the country. Transporting a bottle emits 20% more greenhouse gases than transporting a can.[13] Consumers are also much more likely to recycle cans than bottles. Studies have shown that over half of all drinking cans are recycled and new cans generally contain more recycled content that new bottles (40% for cans versus 10–30% for bottles).

However, switching from bottles to cans is easier said than done. There are two central issues. The first is perception. As the Brewers Association noted, "Canned beer is commonly associated with mass marketed light American lager beer, budget beer and perceived inferior quality."[14] Additionally, NBB has crafted its image around uniquely styled bottles, complete with the company's embossed logo and watercolor labels. By switching to cans, NBB would have to be willing to sacrifice this unique characteristic of the company. The second issue is the total environmental impact of cans. Even though cans have recycling and transportation benefits, they still have a negative impact on the environment. For example, the mining of bauxite and smelting of aluminum cans are more damaging to the environment than the production of glass bottles.[15] Thus, the environmental benefits of cans over bottles remain unclear.

Despite the negative perceptions and unique environmental issues, canned beer sales are increasing, and today over 50 craft breweries offer canned beer.[16] In addition to making select brews available in cans, in 2012, NBB introduced Shift, a pale lager only available in cans. While a number of sustainability challenges still confront the company, canned beer seems to be an expanding option.

QUESTIONS FOR DISCUSSION

1. What are the ethical issues in this case?
2. What keeps other companies from having the commitment to environmental sustainability that NBB has evidenced?
3. Are you more likely to purchase a product from a company with a strong commitment to sustainability?
4. The benefits of cans over bottles are unclear. Has NBB done the right thing by focusing more on canned beer? Should NBB continue to make a greater commitment to cans? What additional options can NBB explore in the future?
5. Are New Belgium Brewing's Core Values and Beliefs sustainable?

ENDNOTES

1. Press Release, "Brewers Association Releases Top 50 Breweries of 2012," *Brewers Association* (April 10, 2013).
2. "The Green 50: The Integrators," *Inc. Magazine*, (November 1, 2006), 84.
3. Newbelgium.com, http://www.newbelgium.com/brewery/company. Accessed May 19, 2013.
4. Christopher Asher, Elina Bidner and Christopher Greene, "New Belgium Brewing Company: Brewing With a Conscious," *University of Colorado, Graduate School of Public Affairs* (January, 2003), 7.
5. Newbelgium.com
6. Asher, Bidner and Greene, 1.
7. New Belgium Brewing Company, "Company Core Values and Beliefs," http://www.newbelgium.com/brewery/company. Accessed May 19, 2013.
8. The data provided in this section comes from "2007 Sustainability Report," *New Belgium Brewing Company*; and from New Belgium's sustainability website, http://www.newbelgium.com/sustainability.aspx. Accessed May 19, 2013.
9. Asher, Bidner and Green, 11.
10. "The Carbon Footprint of Fat Tire Amber Ale," *The Climate Conservancy*, 2007. See also Jeffery Ball, "Six Products, Six Carbon Footprints," *The Wall Street Journal* (October 6 2008), R1.
11. 2007 Sustainability Report, 10.
12. Steve Raabe, "New Belgium Brewing Turns to Cans," *The Denver Post* (May 15, 2008). Available online at: http://www.denverpost.com/commented/ci_9262005?source=commented-.
13. Brendan Koerner, "Wear Green, Drink Greenly: The Eco-Guide to Responsible Drinking," *Slate* (March 16, 2009). http://www.slate.com/id/2186219, retrieved July 7, 2010.
14. Charlie Papazian, "52 Small Craft Brewers put Beer in a Can," *Brewers Association*. http://www.brewersassociation.org/pages/community/charlies-blog/show?title=52-small-craft-brewers-put-beer-in-a-can, retrieved May 19, 2013.
15. New Belgium's sustainability website, http://www.newbelgium.com/sustainability.aspx. Accessed May 19, 2013.
16. Alissa Walker, "Ditch the Bottle? Microbreweries say Can-Do," *Fast Company* (August 10, 2009). http://www.fastcompany.com/blog/alissa-walker/designerati/real-can-do-attitude-more-microbreweries-saying-no-bottles, retrieved July 7, 2010. See also Papazian.

CASE 28

Safety? What Safety?*

KIRK'S FIRST YEAR

Kirk was a bright individual who was being groomed for the controller's position in a medium-sized manufacturing firm. After his first year as assistant controller, the officers of the firm started to include him in major company functions. One day, for instance, he was asked to attend the monthly financial statement summary at a prestigious consulting firm. During the meeting, Kirk was intrigued at how the financial data he had accumulated had been transformed by the consultant into revealing charts and graphs.

NEW MANUFACTURING PLANT

Kirk was generally optimistic about the session and the company's future until the consultant started talking about the new manufacturing plant the company was adding to the current location and the per-unit costs of the chemically plated products it would produce. At that time, Bob, the president, and John, the chemical engineer, started talking about waste treatment and disposal problems. John mentioned that the current waste treatment facilities could not handle the waste products of the "ultramodern" new plant in a manner that would meet the industry's fairly high standards, although the plant would still comply with federal standards.

COST INCREASES

Kirk's boss, Henry, noted that the estimated per-unit costs would increase if the waste treatment facilities were upgraded according to recent industry standards. Industry standards were presently more stringent than federal regulations, and environmentalists were pressuring strongly for stricter regulations at the federal level. Bob mentioned that since their closest competitor did not have the waste treatment facilities that already existed at their firm, he was not in favor of any more expenditures in that area. Most managers at the meeting resoundingly agreed with Bob, and the business of the meeting proceeded to other topics.

Kirk's Dilemma

Kirk did not hear a word during the rest of the meeting. He kept wondering how the company could possibly have such a casual attitude toward the environment. Yet he did not know if, how, when, or with whom he should share his opinion. Soon he started reflecting on whether this firm was the right one for him.

QUESTIONS FOR DISCUSSION

1. Who are the stakeholders in this case, and what are their stakes?
2. What social responsibility does the firm have for the environment? How would you assess the firm's CSR using the four-part CSR definition presented in Chapter 2?
3. Identify the different competing "standards" at issue in this case. Which standard seems most defensible for this company considering all factors?
4. How should Kirk reconcile his own thinking with the thinking being presented by the firm's management?
5. What should Kirk do? Why?

---

* This case was written by Donald E. Tidrick, Northern Illinois University. Permission to reprint granted by Arthur Andersen & Co., SC.

Felony Franks: Home of the Misdemeanor Wiener*

Hot dog stands in Chicago are a dime a dozen, but entrepreneur Jim Andrews made news when he opened his stand. His hot dog stand was named *Felony Franks*, and it served its' trademarked "misdemeanor wiener" and other jail-themed menu items through a bulletproof revolving glass window. Andrews employed only ex-cons.[1]

THEY NEED HELP: WHY NOT ME?

Though Andrews is a longtime business owner and not an ex-con himself, his mission was to open a restaurant that would help ex-cons get back into the workforce and start new lives for themselves. Andrews had seen how hard it was for felons to find work, so when he opened Felony Franks, he hired ten ex-offenders whose crimes had ranged from drug possession to armed robbery. Andrews had founded the Rescue Foundation in 2003, a nonprofit organization that tries to help formerly incarcerated people by providing them with work and the opportunity to develop business skills. Felony Franks was an extension of the foundation's mission, employing only those people who have served time. One of his goals was to help eliminate the stigma surrounding those who have served time in prison as they attempted to put their lives back together. Andrews said, "they need help," so "why not me?"[2] When Andrews opened his hot dog stand, he said he thought he was doing a community service. Some of his neighbors, however, thought he was the one committing a crime.[3]

THE CLEVER, JAIL-THEMED MENU

In addition to its misdemeanor wiener and Felony Franks, the small store offered a variety of jail-themed foods. Some of the cleverly titled hot dogs included the Chain Gang Chili Dog, Pardon Polish, Cell Mate Dog, and Custody Dog. One of the featured Probation Burgers was called the Warden Special. Side orders were called *Accomplices*, and include the usual round-up of condiments such as cheese sauce, pepper rings, and cheese slices. Other interesting items include Burglar Beef, Freedom Fries, and Guilty Gyros.[4] Near the entrance, customers were presented with their mock list of Miranda rights: "You have the right to remain hungry. Anything you order can and will be used to feed you here at Felony Franks." The servers stood behind bulletproof plastic, which was standard practice in the neighborhood.[5]

According to Andrews, the workers started at $8 an hour and could earn time-and-a-half for overtime. The profits were to be split between the charity to help ex-offenders and a profit-sharing plan for the employees. Before getting his job at Felony Franks, Lydon Walker was unemployed for over a year. The father of five said he didn't know what he would do without the job. He went on to say, "I might be back gangbanging or something or selling drugs."[6]

CRITICISM, PRAISE, FUTURE

Andrews has received both criticism and praise from his neighbors in the community. More than 70 people attended a homeowners' meeting to learn more about the project and to protest it. One concern was expressed by a Roman Catholic priest from Chicago's South Side who claimed that Andrews was exploiting the African-American men working for him.[7] One of Andrews's workers expressed that he does not feel like he is being exploited. He said, "working here allows me to provide for myself and my family." This particular worker used to sell crack and served two years probation for possession of a controlled substance. He went on to say, "I've lived in this neighborhood for 15 years and there's gunfire every other day and you never hear anything about that, but all of a sudden there's all this hoopla about a hot-dog stand."[8]

Alderman Bob Fioretti argued that a "felony means time behind bars" and "we shouldn't be glorifying felonies in this day and age."[9] Fioretti also publicly denounced the business and said he would not approve a curb cut for a drive-through.[10] Alderman Fioretti also refused to allow a sign for the restaurant, a decision that was supported in a split vote by the City Council's Committee on Transportation and the Public Way.[11] Andrews sued the city claiming that the city and Fioretti violated his First Amendment rights by blocking the sign. He settled that case in 2012 for an undisclosed amount after closing the business due to slow sales.[12] He tried to open a Felony Franks in nearby Evanston but he received a similar reception.[13] Now, Felony Franks has gone mobile. Andrews now licenses the Felony Franks name. The first license went to Dennis Justice, one of the owners

---

*This case was written by Archie B. Carroll, University of Georgia. Revised by Ann Buchholtz in 2013.

of American Transportation Systems, and he launched the first food truck in Los Angeles in March 2013.[14] The business still employs ex-offenders and now the sandwich rolls are sourced exclusively from Homeboy Bakery, a bakery with a similar mission.[15]

QUESTIONS FOR DISCUSSION

1. Is Felony Franks just a clever gimmick that will be a passing fad, or a worthy social entrepreneurship venture with lasting potential?
2. Does the community have a legitimate right to complain about a Felony Franks restaurant being located there? Is Felony Franks an asset or a liability to a neighborhood?
3. Will a mobile Felony Franks lessen some of the community concerns that arose in Chicago and Evanston?
4. Will it be possible to maintain the social mission with a licensing format?
5. What do you think will be the future of Felony Franks?

ENDNOTES

1. Eric Horng, "At Felony Franks, Only Ex-Cons Need Apply," *ABC News* (August 2, 2009), http://abcnews.go.com/print?id=8234771. Accessed June 15, 2013.
2. Ibid.
3. Julie Jargon, "Slaw and Order: Hot-Dog Stand in Chicago Triggers a Frank Debate," *The Wall Street Journal* (October 13, 2009), http://online.wsj.com/article/SB125538779820481255.html?KEYWORDS=felony+franks. Accessed June 15, 2013.
4. Ibid.
5. Jargon.
6. Horng.
7. Jargon.
8. Jargon.
9. Ibid.
10. Ashley Kohler and Charlotte Eriksen, "Felony Franks Gives Ex-Cons Second Chance," *Chicago-Storytelling* (June 21, 2010), http://chicagostorytelling.com/2010/06/21/felony-franks-gives-ex-cons-second-chance/. Accessed June 15, 2013.
11. "Felony Franks Sues City to Keep Sign, Escalating Feud with Alderman," *Huff Post Chicago* (May 6, 2011), http://www.huffingtonpost.com/2011/05/06/felony-franks-sues-city-t_n_858700.html. Accessed June 15, 2013.
12. "Felony Franks Settles with City of Chicago," *Chicago Journal* (August 1, 2012), http://www.chicagojournal.com/ news/08-01-2012/Felony_Franks_settles_with_city_of_Chicago. Accessed June 15, 2013.
13. John P. Huston, "Debate over Felony Franks Sizzles in Evanston," *Chicago Tribune News* (July 19, 2012), http://articles.chicagotribune.com/2012-07-19/news/ct-tl-felony-franks-reax-20120719_1_felony-franks-hot-dog-misdemeanor-wiener. Accessed June 15, 2013.
14. Chuck Sudo, "Felony Franks Owner Licensing Name to L.A. Food Truck," *Chicagoist* (February 18, 2013), http://chicagoist.com/2013/02/18/felony_franks_owner_licensing_la_fo.php. Accessed June 15, 2013.
15. http://felonyfranks.com/. Accessed June 15, 2013.

CASE 30

Targeting Consumers (and Using Their Secrets)

Data mining has become a big part of analyzing consumer data that companies collect. Basically, data min-

ing is a computational process of extracting information patterns from data sets and transforming it into more organized uses for the future. Usually this information is used to increase sales, reduce costs, or otherwise improve operations or profits.[1] Obviously, if retailers could predict what consumers might buy in the future based on past purchasing patterns this would be extremely valuable in target marketing.

* This case was prepared in 2013 by Archie B. Carroll, University of Georgia, using publically available information.

The statistical team at Target, the giant national retailer, used data mining techniques to determine whether and when a woman was going to have a baby long before she ever purchased diapers from their stores. The marketing plan was then to target ads towards the woman for purchases she might be thinking about for the future. A conversation with one of Target's statisticians revealed how this worked.

Apparently, Target assigns every customer a Guest ID number and links this with your name, the credit cards you use, addresses, phone numbers, and email addresses they are able to ascertain. They collect all the demographic data they can gather or perhaps buy from others. Their statisticians then decided to analyze the women's purchases who had signed up on Baby Registries in the past and then study their purchasing patterns before their babies were born. They discovered through data analysis that certain purchasing patterns did emerge. For example, the analysts noticed that women started buying huge quantities of lotion during the beginning of their second trimester of pregnancy. They also discovered that women during their first 20 weeks of pregnancy stocked up on calcium, magnesium, and zinc supplements. The analysts also detected that as the woman was approaching her delivery date she bought larger quantities of scent-free soap, cotton balls, hand sanitizer and washcloths.[2]

After their analysis, the Target team concluded that there was a set of 25 products which when analyzed together yielded what they termed a "pregnancy prediction score." They concluded they could closely predict that a woman was pregnant and when the baby was due to be born and could target their ads to the woman based on what they expected her needs at that time would be.[3] By getting the women to shop at Target during an expensive and habit-forming period of her life, she could be made a customer for life.[4]

THE FATHER FROM MINNEAPOLIS

As a result of one set of mailings going out, an angry father showed up at his Target store one day demanding to speak to the manager. In his hands were a fistful of coupons sent to his daughter who lived at home in Minneapolis. His complaint was that his daughter, who was still in high school, was receiving mailed ads for maternity clothes and cribs. He angrily asked the manager "Are you trying to encourage her to get pregnant?"[5]

Not sure what was going on, the manager apologized to the angry father and called him on the phone several days later to apologize again. At this point, the father started changing his tune. He uncomfortably told the manager that he'd had a talk with his daughter and discovered that there were some things going on around his house of which he was unaware. He confessed that he'd discovered that his daughter was due in August and he said that he owed the manager an apology himself.[6]

As a result of *The New York Times* investigating Target's data mining approaches, Target's decision makers finally figured out that some of what they were doing may not be appropriate. They eventually concluded that not everyone wanted them to know this much about their personal lives. They discovered that as long as women didn't know they were being spied on they would use the coupons sent them. But, once they discovered how Target knew to send them these coupons—because of their reproductive status—some of them were quite upset. The company decided to slow down and think about this target marketing scheme a bit more.[7]

Realizing that the company had the ability to create custom advertising booklets, a process that they had used in the past with other products, Target decided to put its ads for baby items in booklets where the baby products were paired with other items such as wine glasses or lawn mowers so that the advertising appeared to be random and not profiled toward an expectant mother. This advertising program was then used.

Target discovered that not too long after this revised advertising approach was begun, its sales in the Mom and Baby category increased impressively.

QUESTIONS FOR DISCUSSION

1. What are the social and ethical issues in this case? Who are the affected stakeholders and what are their stakes?

2. Target's practice of predicting a woman's pregnancy and then exploiting it commercially was legal. Was it ethical? If you were the woman in the case and you learned what Target had done, what terms would you use to describe their practice?

3. Would you feel deceived, tricked, or exploited if a company predicted a purchasing expectation of yours that you felt was private or intimate? What, if anything, would you do about it?

4. How do you evaluate Target's new approach to disguise the ads by mixing them in with other, unrelated ads?

5. Have companies gone too far in their statistical predictions such as that described in this case? Should

companies continue the practice of data mining and seeking to target market to customers based on the patterns they detected?

ENDNOTES

1. "Data Mining: What is Data Mining?" http://www. anderson.ucla.edu/faculty/jason.frand/teacher/ technologies/palace/datamining.htm. Accessed May 29, 2013.

2. Charles Duhigg, "How Companies Learn Your Secrets," *The New York Times*, February 16, 2012, http://www.nytimes.com/2012/02/19/magazine/ shopping-habits.html?src=xps. Accessed May 25, 2013. Also see Kashmir Hill, "How Target Figured out a Teen Girl Was Pregnant Before Her Father Did," *Forbes*, February 16, 2012, http://www.forbes. com/sites/kashmirhill/2012/02/16/how-target-figured -out-a-teen-girl-was-pregnant-before-her-father-did/. Accessed May 25, 2013.

3. Duhigg, ibid.

4. "The Incredible Story of How Target Exposed a Young Girl's Pregnancy," *Business Insider*, February 16, 2012, http://www.businessinsider.com/the- incredible-story-of-how-target-exposed-a-teen-girls- pregnancy-2012-2. Accessed May 25, 2013.

5. Duhigg, 2012, ibid.

6. Ibid.

7. Ibid.

CASE 31

A Moral Dilemma: Head versus Heart*

SITUATION

A 42-year-old male suddenly and unexpectedly died of a brain tumor, leaving behind a wife and a small child. During a review of his employee benefits, it was noted that although he was eligible for an additional company-sponsored life insurance plan used for plant decommissioning purposes, his name was not identified on the insurance rolls.

Evaluation

It was determined that when the employee was promoted to supervisor three years before his death, his paperwork had been submitted to the corporate office for inclusion in the program. Coincidentally, the program was under review at the time, and the employee was not entered into the program due to administrative oversight.

Legal Review

A legal department review determined that the program was offered to certain supervisory employees at the discretion of the company. Therefore, there was no legal obligation to pay.

Dilemma

The death benefit was twice the employee's salary. Because the employee was not enrolled in the life insurance program, if the company were to pay any benefit, it would have to come from the general fund (paid from the business unit's annual operating budget).

To Pay or Not to Pay?

The company could argue that it must start acting like a business and use its head, not its heart. Existing company programs adequately compensate the individual's family; no additional dollars should be paid. On the

*This case was prepared by David A. Levigne.

other hand, it was an administrative oversight that failed to enter the employee into the program.

QUESTIONS FOR DISCUSSION

1. As a manager, you are steward of the company's funds. Are you willing to forgo departmental improvements and potential salary increases to honor this claim? Remember, there is no legal obligation to pay.
2. Would you sense an ethical obligation to pay? Would you be perceived as a weak manager if you do?
3. What are the ethical issues in this case?
4. What action should you take? Why?

CASE 32

Walmart's Labor Practices*

Historically, the primary criticism of Walmart, the world's largest company, has been its impact on communities and small merchants. Anti-sprawl activists and small-town merchants, in particular, have taken issue with the company moving into their communities.[1] In *Case 1—Walmart: The Main Street Merchant of Doom*, these issues were presented in some detail.

In the past decade, however, other issues concerning the company have become important as well and have begun cropping up in the news with increased frequency. In particular, Walmart's labor practices and treatment of its employees have raised many issues in public and business discussions. Paradoxically, Walmart refers to its employees as "associates," a term intended to bestow a more lofty status on its human resources than the term "employees."

Many people do view Walmart as an excellent provider of jobs in communities, and in spite of criticisms that have been raised, people continue to seek out employment with Walmart. Though it has high turnover, it is viewed by countless job seekers as a stable place to work, and some individuals have sought to establish careers at the company. In 2013, Walmart was ranked #27 in the top fifty of the "World's Most Admired Companies" in the annual *Fortune* magazine rankings.[2] In spite of Walmart being ranked highly for years, *Fortune* writer Jerry Useem asked, "Should we admire Walmart?" He continued, "Some say it's evil. Others insist it's a model of all that's right with America. Who are we to believe?"[3] Figure 1 presents some recent corporate facts about Walmart and its associates.

Many different employee-related issues with respect to Walmart have been the focus of a great deal of news coverage in the past few years. The company has been accused of hiring too many part-time workers; offering jobs that are actually dead-ends; paying low wages and substandard benefits; forcing workers to work "off-the-clock," that is, to work overtime without overtime pay; and taking advantage of illegal immigrants. Over the years, the company has also been accused of gender discrimination against women, who occupy most jobs at the company. In addition to fielding allegations of employee mistreatment, Walmart (which currently is not unionized) has fought unions and unionization everywhere it locates.

LOW PAY, HARD WORK, QUESTIONABLE TREATMENT

Walmart is the nation's largest private employer. It employs 2.2 million worldwide—1.3 million in the United States alone.[4] As such, it is not surprising that it has a large number of interactions with employees, and these interactions will be both positive and negative. Walmart claims to offer "good jobs, (and) good careers," but a number of employees have become vocal in recent years about their working conditions at the company. As with many retailers and service industries, Walmart is accused of offering low pay and few benefits. Many of these employees have been angered by the disparity between their low wages and the company's high profits.[5]

One Person's Experience

Journalist Barbara Ehrenreich, author of the best-seller *Nickel and Dimed: On (Not) Getting by in America,"* spent three weeks working at a Walmart to get insights

---

*This case was prepared by Archie B. Carroll, University of Georgia. Updated in 2013.

FIGURE 1   **Recent Facts (2013) about Walmart's Employees/Associates**

Walmart:

- Employs more than 2.2 million "associates" worldwide, more than 1.4 million in the United States alone.
- Depending on the time of year, there are 15,000–50,000 job openings.
- About 75% of store management teams started as hourly associates. They earn between $75,000–$170,000 per year.
- Every year, Walmart promotes about 170,000 people to jobs with higher pay and more responsibility.
- Women make up more than 57% of the U.S. Walmart workforce, 27% of corporate officers, and comprise 20% of the board of directors.
- In the past five years, at Walmart stores in the United States, female co-managers have increased by 134%, female managers have increased by 42%, female market managers have increased by 92% (fiscal year 2013 data).
- Is a *diverse* employer. 37% of associates in the United States are minorities.
- Will offer a job to every returning veteran within the first twelve months of coming off active duty with an honorable discharge.
- Salaries are at or above industry averages.
- Gives eligible employees a 10% discount on general merchandise and select groceries purchased at a Walmart store.
- Offers health care benefits starting at $17.40 per pay period.

Sources: Walmart, "Our People," http://corporate.walmart.com/global-responsibility/diversity-inclusion/our-people, Accessed June 17, 2013; "Diversity and Inclusion," http://corporate.walmart.com/global-responsibility/diversity-inclusion, Accessed June 17, 2013; "Walmart Facts," http://news.walmart.com/walmart-facts, Accessed June 17, 2013; "The Real Walmart," http://www.therealwalmart.com/people-associates.html, Accessed June 17, 2013.

into whether many of the claims she had heard about Walmart's treatment of employees was true. Ehrenreich claimed she'd heard stories about Walmart workers being locked in stores overnight and being asked to work extra hours without overtime pay. During her three weeks there, she said she saw one facet of the mega-retailer that most people who shop there never get to see. She remembered workers having to crouch behind racks of clothing to chat with coworkers because her department head forbade talking among workers during work hours.[6] Ehrenreich complained that it was undignified for women in their 50s to have to resort to such behavior on the job.

Further, she observed that many of the store's cheapest items were often unaffordable to the workers who sold them because of their low pay. She observed: "when you work for a company who you can't afford to buy their product, you're in trouble." She went on, "Here is this store that's oriented toward the lower end of the economic spectrum, but not low enough [for its own workers]." She said on one occasion she had to go to the local food bank and she was mistaken for another Walmart worker who had just been there.[7]

Of course, some people would say that there is nothing wrong with low pay and few benefits if a business can still find workers willing to work there. After all, in a free market, this is the way the economic system works. And,

indeed, one reason Walmart has been so efficient and has contributed to nationwide productivity increases is precisely because of its tight controls on labor costs. The McKinsey consulting group has said that Walmart was responsible for roughly 25 percent of the nation's productivity gains in the 1990s. Their low prices have also contributed significantly to low inflation. Financial guru Warren Buffett expressed the opinion that Walmart has contributed more than any other company to the economic vigor that is found in America.[8]

Working Off-the-Clock and without Breaks

One of the most serious allegations of unfair treatment reported by some Walmart employees is that of being asked to "work *off*-the-clock." This means that employees are pressured to do overtime work for which they do not get paid. One employee reported that he was asked to work off-the-clock by both the store manager and the assistant manager. The allegation is that managers would wait until an employee had clocked out and then say something like, "Do me a favor. I don't have anyone coming in—could you stay here?" Before you knew it, four to five hours passed before you got away.[9] According to Walmart's *2013 Annual Report*, the company had, indeed, been the defendant in several cases pertaining to wage-and-hour class action since 2002.[10]

The Pressure Is On

The company has blamed individual store and department managers for any unpaid overtime. They claim it is against company policy to not pay for overtime. However, there is evidence that managers have been under significant pressure from corporate headquarters to get more work done than can be done with the number of employees allowed. One attorney for an employee said that headquarters collects reams of data on every store and every employee and use sales figures to determine how many hours of labor it wants to allocate to each store. Then, the store managers are required to schedule fewer hours than allotted and their store performance is closely monitored on a daily basis. The store managers, in turn, put pressure on lower managers, and employees start feeling the pressure to work hours without pay. In another case, a former Walmart manager claimed that supervisors had been known to regularly delete hours from time records and even to reprimand employees who claimed overtime hours so the store could keep its labor costs under control.[11]

LABOR UNION RESISTANCE

Because of employee complaints and desires to have higher wages and more generous benefits, Walmart employees have been targeted by union organizers for decades. Walmart's huge size and number of employees allows the firm to increasingly "set the standard for wages and benefits throughout the U.S. economy."[12]

Unionization Attempts

Across the country, workers in many states have tried to get unions organized, but so far they have not had much success. According to one report, employees at more than 100 stores in 25 states have been trying to get union representation. Walmart has tried in various ways to fight the union organizing efforts. The company has engaged in some actions which have been judged to be in violation of federal labor laws. Walmart has been held to be in violation of the law in ten separate cases in which the National Labor Relations Board has ruled that it has engaged in illegal activities such as confiscating union literature, interrogating workers, and discharging union sympathizers.[13] According to one management consultant, Walmart will go to great lengths to keep unions out.

At the time of writing, there are no unions in any part of Walmart. Back in 2000, the meat-cutting department at a Walmart in Jacksonville, Texas, voted to join the United Food and Commercial Workers (UFCW) union, becoming the only Walmart store that had successfully unionized. The company responded quickly. Within two weeks, Walmart totally eliminated its meat-cutting departments throughout the company nationwide.[14] The company claimed it took this action as part of a strategy to have meat cut by outside vendors and supplied differently rather than as a decision to eliminate the union.

The UFCW has been the most aggressive force in trying to unionize Walmart across the country. Several full-time union organizers have traveled the country trying to convince employees to agree to a union vote in their store. The UFCW, which represents 1.4 million workers in the grocery and retail industry, has representatives in many different cities attempting to convince workers to sign a card indicating they want a union vote held at their store. According to the National Labor Relations Board, a workplace needs 30 percent of its workers to sign cards calling for a union election to have one held. Unions often try to get 50 percent of the employees to sign a card, because they want to increase their chances of winning.[15]

Success in Union Resistance

There are several reasons why the unions have not been successful in unionizing Walmart. First, many employees feel intimidated by the company and fear signing on with a union. They fear retaliation of some kind, and many cannot afford to lose their jobs. Second, Walmart has mastered the art and science of fighting unionization. At one point, the company had a "union avoidance program." In this program, the company, with its vast resources, would wear people down and even destroy their spirit.

One consultant said that each Walmart manager is taught to take attempts at union organizing personally and to consider that supporting a union is like slapping the supervisor in the face.[16] Walmart is considered to be a very sophisticated adversary when it comes to fighting unionization. At one point managers had been asked to call a 24-hour hotline if they ever see a hint of unionization taking place, and a labor team can be dispatched to a store under threat at a moment's notice.[17] Third, many Walmarts are located in southern states that do not have a history and tradition of unionization.[18] Regardless, unions in cities in the north continue, most recently in Chicago, ferociously fighting the company's plans to locate in historically union territory, but they have not had great success. These cities are hungry for jobs and cheap products, and these factors seem to win out.[19]

With respect to its position, a Walmart spokesman says that the company is not anti-union, it is "pro-associate."[20] According to writer Karen Olsson, "Walmart has made it clear that keeping its stores union-free is as much a part of the culture as door greeters and blue aprons."[21]

USE OF UNDOCUMENTED IMMIGRANTS

Several years ago, a series of predawn raids by federal agents were conducted in which they rounded up 250 illegal immigrants working as cleaning crews in 61 Walmarts across 21 states. Although technically they were not employees of the company, the company was accused by federal officials of knowing that its contractors were using the illegal immigrants as employees. The Immigration and Customs Enforcement program claimed it has wiretaps revealing that Walmart knew contractors were using undocumented workers in their cleaning crews.[22]

Walmart continues to fight against the charges, because it reports that the company was cooperating with the government for as long as three years in federal investigations in Chicago and Pennsylvania. Walmart reports that it was led to believe that it was not a target of the investigation and that it did not sever its ties with the contractors because federal officials had asked them to leave the relationships in place during their investigations. Walmart claimed that it was told it would be given a heads-up before any arrests were made in its stores, but that did not happen.[23]

Walmart claims that it did what it could to ensure that its contractors were hiring legal workers, both before and after the raid. Antidiscrimination provisions of the immigration code limit an employer's ability to investigate an employee's legal status, the company claimed. The company claimed that as far back as in 1996, the Immigration and Naturalization Service (INS) filed a complaint against Walmart for requiring prospective hires who were not U.S. citizens to show more verification than that required by law. The company paid a $60,000 fine and became very hesitant to ask for more assurances about the status of its contractors' employees, the company claims.[24]

Ending Relationships

Walmart claimed that beginning in 2002 it began to end its relationships with outside cleaning contractors. The company concluded it could typically save money by having its own crews cleaning and polishing the floors.

By October 2003, when the raid occurred, fewer than 700 stores (18 percent) were still using contractors. This was down to half of the stores that were using outside contractors in 2000. The company said it adopted a new written contract in 2002 that included stronger contractual commitment by the outside contractors that they were complying with all federal, state, and local employment laws. The company admitted that it unwittingly may have still been doing business with some of the contractors that were in violation and that their own investigations revealed they were dealing with companies with different corporate identities and names that made it difficult to eliminate suspected violators.[25]

SEX DISCRIMINATION CHARGES

The most serious employee issues Walmart has faced in the past decade have been accusations of gender discrimination against women. In 2001, six women filed a gender bias lawsuit against Walmart, claiming they were discriminated against. The case, *Dukes v. Walmart*, started as an EEOC complaint by Betty Dukes, the lead plaintiff, who claimed she had been trying to get promoted from the cashier ranks for nine years.[26] In a landmark decision in June of 2004, a federal judge in San Francisco ruled that the sex discrimination lawsuit could proceed as a class-action lawsuit, affecting as many as 1.6 million current and former female employees who have worked for the company since December 26, 1998.[27] In February 2007, a federal appeals court upheld the 2004 decision that Walmart must face the class-action bias claim. Walmart appealed the decision but lost. It has been said that the company stands to lose billions of dollars should it be found guilty of sex discrimination.[28] The lawsuit, which has been called the "largest private civil rights case ever,"[29] has the potential to go on for years and doubtless will have significant repercussions for Walmart and other companies in retail and other industries.

The Allegations

Lawyers for the plaintiffs presented various statistical analyses supporting their allegations of sex discrimination. They presented detailed statistical models documenting that Walmart paid their full-time female workers 5–15 percent less than full-time males doing the same jobs. The lawyers also contended that the pay disparities between females and males increased as employees moved up in the management ranks.[30] Plaintiffs also claimed that Walmart's 2001 payroll statistics, the year the lawsuit was filed, also revealed discriminatory patterns such as the following:

- Female workers in hourly jobs earned $1,100 annually less than men.
- Women managers earned $14,500 annually less than their male counterparts.
- 65 percent of Walmart's hourly employees were female, but two-thirds of the company's managers were men.
- On average, it took men just 2.86 years to get promoted to assistant manager, but it took women 4.38 years, despite better performance ratings.[31]

Individual cases also documented allegations of sex discrimination against the company. The case of Gretchen Adams is illustrative. Adams, the mother of four, took an hourly job at the Walmart in Stillwater, Oklahoma, in 1993. Adams was quickly promoted to manager of the deli department, where she supervised 60 workers and flew around the country training hundreds of other workers. She learned that a man she had trained was making $3,500 more than her, and she was told it was "a fluke." She witnessed other men leapfrog past her, and she never landed the job of store manager she says she was promised. Adams claimed she complained and "they told me where to go." She quit the company at the end of 2001.[32]

Other women made sworn statements that Walmart had denied them requests to be placed in a management training position leading to a salaried position, denied them jobs as support managers in favor of men who had less seniority or qualifications, gave promotions to men with less experience, and were fired for not going along with alleged acts of sexual harassment.[33]

A summary of the major sex discrimination allegations against Walmart includes three major areas. First, women claim they have been denied equal promotions. Second, women claim they have been paid less for the same jobs, even when they have more experience. Third, women claim they are subjected to sexist actions and gender stereotyping.[34]

Did Top Management Know?

Lawyers for the plaintiffs are developing the argument that top managers at Walmart knew about the sex bias that was taking place in the company. The lawyers are preparing to argue that women complained to corporate executives, including then CEO Lee Scott, about pay disparities or sexism and received very little response. They also argue that information was shared with board members and that outsiders complained and got little or no response from corporate offices.[35]

The Company's Defense

Walmart has long argued that it treats its female employees fairly. The company has said that women do not apply for promotion as often as men, and this accounts for the underrepresentation of women.[36] The main argument by the company has been its opposition to the lawsuit being categorized as a class-action lawsuit. Walmart argued that decisions about employees are made at the individual store level and that a class-action lawsuit is too unwieldy because the company should be able to present evidence defending itself against each individual plaintiff's claims and that this would not be possible in a class-action trial. Walmart claims that in a class-action lawsuit of this size, it means that store managers will not be given the opportunity to explain how they made individual compensation and promotion decisions.

The company argued in its appeal of the class-action judgment that the class was certified under laws intended to provide injunctive relief, that is, to stop a particular practice, but that the judge ruled that the class can also seek monetary damages that the company does not think applies to the case. Part of the monetary relief could be punitive damages, but for these to apply, it has to be proven that Walmart management "fostered or recklessly ignored discriminatory practices." The judge concluded that whereas the individual decisions were made at specific store locations, there was some evidence of a corporate culture of gender stereotyping that may have affected the decisions made at the store level.[37] Judge Martin Jenkins was not ruling on the merits of the case, but was simply saying there was some evidence of a corporate culture permeating the organization that may be related to the discrimination, and thus he allowed the case to move forward as a class action.

In April 2010, a federal appeals court ruled that the gender discrimination lawsuit could move forward as a class action. It has been estimated that if the company lost this lawsuit, it could cost Walmart upward of $1 billion. In addition, a loss would be a terrible blow to its reputation and much-improved corporate image.[38]

Changes in Labor Practices at Walmart

Partially as a result of criticism and bad publicity Walmart has been receiving in recent years, the company announced some changes that were planned to improve conditions for its workers. In 2004, then CEO Lee Scott outlined the changes at one of its annual shareholders' meeting in Fayetteville, Arkansas, but it may take several years before the true impact of the changes take place and are felt throughout the company.[39]

One change would include the creation of a compliance group to oversee workers' pay, hours, and breaks. The company is also testing a new program that will alert cashiers when it is time for them to take a meal break. Another change is the implementation of a new system that will require employees to sign off on any changes that are made to their time cards. The company also plans to implement software that will force managers to adhere to state employment rules regarding areas such as how late teenagers can work. While announcing these new policies, Scott mentioned several times that he was tired of the adverse publicity that the company was getting.[40]

WALMART'S CHARM OFFENSIVE

Walmart has been battered by adverse publicity in recent years and has been working to improve its image. Some of the articles aimed at the company included the following: "Attack of the Wal-Martyrs,"[41] "Bruised in Bentonville,"[42] and "The Unending Woes of Lee Scott (CEO)."[43] Its economic woes have been chronicled as "Wal-Mart's Midlife Crisis."[44] But, beginning in about 2005, the company ratcheted up its charm offensive by trying to enhance its public image. Then-CEO Lee Scott admitted the company was trying to improve its image by being more open to its critics and trying to take specific steps to improve the way the world perceived the company. He admitted that when growth was easier, they could ignore their critics, but as the share price slowed its growth, the company had to start reaching out and being more responsive to the concerns raised.[45]

Specific Actions

Walmart has sought to improve its image with stakeholders on four fronts. First, in the area of outreach, the company opened offices in eight major cities in an attempt to improve community relations and be responsive to local critics. Second, the company met with several activist groups seeking to improve its environmental impact. Third, the company hired Business for Social Responsibility (BSR), the nonprofit organization, to help it establish better relations with anti-sweatshop advocates and to strengthen its global labor monitoring program. Fourth, the company set up quick-response teams in Washington and at its Arkansas headquarters, with the help of a public relations firm, so that it could be more responsive to public criticism.[46] It appears that Walmart has finally realized the legitimacy of the "stakeholder effect": "As companies grow and develop, some stakeholders become more important than others, and new stakeholders sometimes emerge."[47] In 2009, one writer was exclaiming how Walmart's image had moved from demon to darling, but in the world of public relations, retaining a solid corporate image is a challenging task.[48]

A New CEO

In 2009, CEO Lee Scott relinquished his position, and the board elected Mike Duke to be the new CEO effective February 1, 2009. Scott would remain as chairperson of the board's executive committee until 2011 and would remain active in lobbying for the company and in corporate green initiatives. Duke has a "nice guy" reputation, is very low-key, and is known to be a strategic thinker and risk taker.[49]

In 2010, Walmart continued its emphasis on sustainability and corporate philanthropy. The company unveiled an environmental labeling program for its products in a decision that some say may redefine the design and makeup of consumer goods sold around the globe.[50] And the company also announced that it planned to ramp up its donations to the nation's food banks to a total of about $2 billion over the next five years.[51]

QUESTIONS FOR DISCUSSION

1. Identify and describe the major ethical issues facing Walmart and the likely stakeholders to be affected.
2. Walmart has been said to have excessive power in its relationship with communities. How is its manifestation of power with employees similar to or different than with communities? Which is the most serious issue? Why?
3. Are many of the allegations by employees at Walmart just reflections of the changing social contract between companies and their workers? Are many of the so-called problems just the free-enterprise system at work? Discuss.
4. Regarding the various labor practices discussed in this case, do they reflect immoral or just amoral management actions?
5. Is the practice of being required to "work off-the-clock" an unethical practice or just "to be expected" in the modern world of work? After all, many salaried employees are expected to work "until the job is done" no matter how many hours it takes.
6. Is it wrong for Walmart to fight unionization? Sam Walton always felt the company should function as one big happy family and that unions were to be

resisted. What is your evaluation of the union opposition?

7. Regarding the allegations of sex discrimination, does it sound like the company has been guilty of systemic discrimination?

8. If Walmart can effectively argue that women are contributors to their plight by not applying for promotions or for seeking fewer responsibilities to accommodate family priorities, should the company be held to be in violation of sex discrimination laws because the statistics reveal differences between women and men?

9. Conduct Web-based research on Walmart and update allegations and lawsuits against the company.

ENDNOTES

1. Charles Fishman, "The Wal-Mart Effect and a Decent Society: Who Knew Shopping Was So Important," *Academy of Management Perspectives* (August 2006), 6–25.

2. Fortune's "The World's Most Admired Companies," 2013, http://money.cnn.com/magazines/fortune/most-admired/2013/list/. Accessed June 17, 2013.

3. Jerry Useem, "Should We Admire Wal-Mart?" *Fortune* (March 8, 2004), 118–120.

4. "Walmart Facts," http://news.walmart.com/walmart-facts. Accessed June 17, 2013.

5. Karen Olsson, "Up Against Wal-Mart," *Mother Jones* (March/April 2003), 54–59.

6. Tammy Joyner, "Author Had Eyes Opened at Work," *Atlanta Journal Constitution* (June 27, 2004), Q1.

7. Ibid.

8. George F. Will, "Waging War on Wal-Mart," *Newsweek* (July 5, 2004), 64.

9. Olsson, 58.

10. Wal-Mart's 2013 Annual Report, p. 50, http://az204679.vo.msecnd.net/media/documents/2013-annual- report_;130108806067963477.pdf. Accessed June 17, 2013.

11. Olsson, 58.

12. Ibid., 55.

13. Ibid.

14. Ibid.

15. Cora Daniels, "Up Against the Wal-Mart," *Fortune* (May 17, 2004), 112–120.

16. Olsson, 56.

17. Daniels, 116.

18. Ibid.

19. "Unions vs. Wal-Mart: Belaboured," *The Economist* (May 29, 2010), 30–32.

20. Ibid.

21. Olsson, 58.

22. Ann Zimmerman, "After Huge Raid on Illegals, Wal-Mart Fires Back at U.S.," *The Wall Street Journal* (December 19, 2003).

23. Ibid.

24. Ibid.

25. Ibid.

26. Cora Daniels, "Women vs. Wal-Mart," *Fortune* (July 21, 2003), 79–82.

27. Ann Zimmerman, "Judge Certifies Wal-Mart Suit as Class Action," *The Wall Street Journal* (June 23, 2004), A1.

28. David Kravets, "Wal-Mart Must Face Class-Action Bias Trial: Female Workers Say Men Were Paid More," *USA Today* (February 7, 2007), 3B.

29. Stephanie Armour and Lorrie Grant, "Wal-Mart Suit Could Ripple Through Industry," *USA Today* (June 23, 2004), 4B.

30. Ann Zimmerman, "Wal-Mart Adds to Legal Team," *The Wall Street Journal* (July 1, 2004), B2.

31. Lisa Takeuchi Cullen Wilson, "Wal-Mart's Gender Gap," *Time* (July 5, 2004), 44.

32. Ibid.

33. Stephanie Armour, "Rife with Discrimination: Plaintiffs Describe Their Lives at Wal-Mart," *USA Today* (June 24, 2004), 3B.

34. Ibid.

35. Stephanie Armour, "Women Say Wal-Mart Execs Knew of Sex Bias," *USA Today* (June 25, 2004), 1B.

36. "Wal-Mart: Trial by Checkout," *The Economist* (June 26, 2004), 64.

37. Zimmerman, 2004, B2.

38. Sean Gregory, "Walmart Faces a Gender Discrimination Suit," *Time* (April 29, 2010), http://www.time.com/time/business/article/0,8599,1985549,00.html. Accessed July 31, 2010.

39. Constance L. Hays, "Wal-Mart Plans Changes to Some Labor Practices," *The New York Times* (June 5, 2004), B2.

40. Ibid.

41. Barney Gimbel, "Attack of the Wal-Martyrs," *Fortune* (December 11, 2006), 125–130.

42. Andy Serwer, "Bruised in Bentonville," *Fortune* (April 18, 2005), 84–106.

43. Jon Birger, "The Unending Woes of Lee Scott," *Fortune* (January 22, 2007), 118–122.

44. Anthony Bianco, "Wal-Mart's Midlife Crisis," *BusinessWeek* (April 30, 2007), 46–56.

45. Robert Berner, "Can Wal-Mart Fit into a White Hat?" *BusinessWeek* (October 3, 2005), 94–96.

46. Ibid., 96.
47. R. Edward Freeman, "The Wal-Mart Effect and Business, Ethics and Society," *Academy of Management Perspectives* (August 2006), 38–43.
48. Ann Zimmerman, "Wal-Mart's Image Moves from Demon to Darling," *The Wall Street Journal* (July 16, 2009), B1.
49. Suzanne Kapner, "Changing of the Guard at Wal-Mart," *Fortune* (March 2, 2009), 69–76.
50. Miguel Bustillo, "Wal-Mart to Assign New Green Ratings," *The Wall Street Journal* (July 16, 2009), B1.
51. Associated Press, "Wal-Mart Pledges to Give Food Banks $2B over Five Years," *USA Today* (May 13, 2010), 3B.

CASE 33

The Case of the Fired Waitress*

Ruth Hatton, a waitress for a Red Lobster restaurant in Pleasant Hills, Pennsylvania, was fired from her job because she was accused of stealing a guest-comment card that had been deposited in the customer comment box by a disgruntled couple.[1] The couple, who happened to be black, had been served by Hatton and were unhappy with the treatment they felt they got from her. At the time of her firing, Hatton, age 53, had been a 19-year veteran employee. She said, "It felt like a knife going through me."

THE INCIDENT

The couple had gone to the Red Lobster restaurant for dinner. According to Hatton, the woman had requested a well-done piece of prime rib. After she was served, she complained that the meat was fatty and undercooked. Hatton then said she politely suggested to the woman that prime rib always has fat on it. Hatton later explained, based on her experience with black customers in the working-class area in which the restaurant was located, that the customer might have gotten prime rib confused with spare rib.

Upset Customer Leaves

Upon receiving the complaint, Hatton explained that she returned the meat to the kitchen to be cooked further. When the customer continued to be displeased,

Hatton offered the couple a free dessert. The customer continued to be unhappy, doused the prime rib with steak sauce, and then pushed it away from her plate. The customer then filled out a restaurant comment card, deposited it in the customer comment box, paid her bill, and left with her husband.

Inadvertently Thrown Out

Hatton explained that she was very curious as to what the woman had written on the comment card, so she went to the hostess and asked for the key to the comment box. She said she then read the card and put it in her pocket with the intention of showing it to her supervisor, Diane Canant, later. Hatton said that Canant, the restaurant's general manager, had commented earlier that the prime rib was overcooked, not undercooked. Apparently, the restaurant had had a problem that day with the cooking equipment and was serving meat that had been cooked the previous day and so was being reheated before being served. Later, Hatton said that she had forgotten about the comment card and had inadvertently thrown it out. It also came out that it is against Red Lobster's policy to serve reheated meat, and the chain no longer serves prime rib.[2]

HATTON'S FIRING

Canant said that she fired Hatton after the angry customer complained to her and to her supervisor. Somehow, the customer had learned later that Hatton had removed the comment card from the box. Canant recalled, "The customer felt violated because her card was taken from the box and she felt that her complaint

---

*This case was prepared by Archie B. Carroll, University of Georgia. Updated in 2013.

about the food had been ignored." Referring to the company's policy manual, Canant said Hatton was fired because she violated the restaurant's rule forbidding the removal of company property.

Not a Big Deal

Another person to comment on the incident was the hostess, Dawn Brown, then a 17-year-old student, who had been employed by the restaurant for the summer. Dawn stated, "I didn't think it was a big deal to give her the key (to the comment box). A lot of people would come and get the key from me."[3]

THE PEER REVIEW PROCESS[4]

Hatton felt she had been unjustly fired for this incident. Rather than filing suit against the restaurant, however, she decided to take advantage of the store's peer review process. The parent company of Red Lobster, Darden Restaurants, four years earlier had adopted a peer review program as an alternative dispute resolution mechanism. Many companies across the country have adopted the peer review method as an alternative to lengthy lawsuits and as an avenue of easing workplace tensions.

Success of Peer Review Program

Executives at Red Lobster observed that the peer review program had been "tremendously successful." It helped to keep valuable employees from unfair dismissals, and it had reduced the company's legal bills for employee disputes by $1 million annually. Close to 100 cases had been heard through the peer review process, with only ten resulting in lawsuits. Executives at the company also said that the process had reduced racial tensions. In some cases, the peer review panels have reversed decisions made by managers who had overreacted to complaints from minority customers and employees.[5]

HATTON'S PEER REVIEW PANEL

The peer review panel chosen to handle Ruth Hatton's case was a small group of Red Lobster employees from the surrounding area. The panel included a general manager, an assistant manager, a hostess, a server, and a bartender, all of whom had volunteered to serve on the panel. The peer review panel members had undergone special peer review training and were being paid their regular wages and travel expenses. The peer review panel was convened about three weeks after Hatton's firing. According to Red Lobster policy, the panel was empowered to hear testimony and to even overturn management decisions and award damages.

Testimony Heard

The panel met in a conference room at a hotel near Pittsburgh and proceeded to hear testimony from Ruth Hatton, store manager Diane Canant, and hostess Dawn Brown. The three testified as to what had happened in the incident.

Through careful deliberations, the panelists tried to balance the customer's hurt feelings with what Hatton had done and why, and with the fact that a company policy may have been violated. Initially, the panel was split along job category lines, with the hourly workers supporting Hatton and the managers supporting store management. After an hour and a half of deliberations, however, everyone was finally moving in the same direction and the panel finally came to a unanimous opinion as to what should be done.[6]

QUESTIONS FOR DISCUSSION

1. What are the ethical issues in this case from an employee's point of view? From management's point of view? From a consumer's point of view?
2. Who are the stakeholders, and what are their stakes?
3. As a peer review panel member, how would you judge this case? Do you think Hatton stole company property? Do you think the discharge should be upheld?
4. Do you think the peer review method of resolving work complaints is a desirable substitute for lawsuits? What are its strengths and weaknesses?
5. If you had been Hatton, would you be willing to turn your case over to a peer review panel like this and then be willing to live with the results?

ENDNOTES

1. Margaret A. Jacobs, "Red Lobster Tale: Peers Decide Fired Waitress's Fate," *The Wall Street Journal* (January 20, 1998), B1, B4.
2. Ibid.
3. Ibid.
4. "Peer Review," U.S. Equal Employment Opportunity Commission, http://www.eeoc.gov/federal/adr/peerreview.cfm. Accessed June 17, 2013; Also see ADR Synopsis, http://www.contilaw.com/adrsyn.html. Accessed June 17, 2013.
5. Jacobs, ibid.
6. Ibid.

CASE 34

The Hidden Price of Fast Fashion*

Fast fashion is the term used to describe clothing that goes from the designer to the consumer in record time. The rise of fast fashion revolutionized the fashion industry from one that was based on a "two season shopping calendar" to one with a steady stream of trendy, new, yet inexpensive merchandise designed to entice consumers.[1] Consumer expert Lucy Stone estimates that fast fashion has led British women to buy half their body weight in clothes each year, with the average woman having 22 garments in her closet that she has never worn.[2] According to Elizabeth Cline, author of *The Shockingly High Cost of Fast Fashion*, "Consumers can afford to buy it in quantities that wouldn't have begun to fit in our grandparents' armoires. It's so cheap that it isn't even worth returning if we get home and decide we don't like it."[3] Because of the high volume of sales, the low sales price does not lessen profits; the founder of Zara, a highly successful fast fashion chain, is the third richest person in the world.[4]

As fast fashion has transformed the retail clothing industry, two major concerns have arisen—fast fashion's effect on the environment and on worker safety. The trendiness and the cheapness of the clothing give rise to the environmental issue. The trendiness means that the clothing goes in and out of fashion far more quickly and so consumers are not likely to want to wear the clothing for long. The cheapness means that even if the consumer wanted to keep wearing the clothing, it would be unlikely to last beyond a few washings. Simon Collins, dean of fashion at Parsons The New School for Design, says, "You see some products and it's just garbage. It's just crap and you sort of fold it up and you think, yeah, you're going to wear it Saturday night to your party — and then it's literally going to fall apart."[5]

The speed with which the clothing must be processed and the low prices with which it must be sold drive the worker safety issue. Low prices mean low wages for factory workers and pressure to move quickly can lead to corners being cut in safety measures. The more than 1100 garment workers who were killed in the collapse of the eight story Rana Plaza in Bangladesh had been assembling clothing for H&M, Zara and other fashion retailers, as were the Bangladeshi workers killed in earlier factory fires.[6] Even those retailers that are not at the center of the fast fashion trend feel the pressure to provide clothing more quickly and cheaply. Garments for mainstream companies such as Sears and Walmart were also found in some of the factories that experienced tragedy in Bangladesh.[7]

Fast fashion retailers are beginning to feel pressure to reduce the negative externalities of their operations. In response to increasing public concern, fast fashion firms have begun to initiate programs to mitigate fast fashion's environmental impact. For example, H&M now collects old garments for recycling. The company gives customers a voucher that is good for a discount on future purchases and then sells the clothing to I:CO, a Swiss recycling start-up.[8] The company is also integrating recycled fibers into products in the Conscious Collection brand.[9] Since the multiple tragedies in Bangladesh, fast fashion firms have also begun to address worker safety. International retailers, including H&M and Zara's parent company Inditex, have signed a building and fire safety agreement that is backed by a coalition of labor groups known as IndustriALL.[10] These efforts are commendable, but they are incomplete in that they only address the supply side of fast fashion. Consumers can create a shift in the demand side by engaging in what some have called "mindful shopping," which involves buying fewer clothes in general and only selecting items that are constructed in a way that makes them more likely to last.[11] Elizabeth Cline's website offers suggestions for ways in which consumers can do to become part of the solution to the problems created by fast fashion.[12]

QUESTIONS FOR DISCUSSION

1. Who are the stakeholders in this situation and what are their stakes?
2. Who bears the most responsibility for the problems that have resulted from fast fashion?
3. What solutions do you propose to mitigate fast fashion's negative effects?

ENDNOTES

1. Jim Zarroli, "In Trendy World Of Fast Fashion, Styles Aren't Made To Last," *NPR* (March 11, 2013), http://www.npr.org/2013/03/11/174013774/in-trendy-world-of-fast-fashion-styles-arent-made-to-last. Accessed June 17, 2013.

---

* This case was written by Ann K. Buchholtz, Rutgers University.

2. Paul Sims, "Britain's Bulging Closet: Growth of 'Fast Fashion' Means Women Are Buying HALF Their Body Weight In Clothes Each Year," *The Daily Mail* (May 23, 2011), http://www.dailymail.co.uk/femail/article-1389786/Britains-bulging-closets-Growth-fast-fashion-means-women-buying-HALF-body-weight-clothes-year.html. Accessed June 17, 2013.

3. Zarroli.

4. Ibid.

5. Ibid.

6. Elizabeth Wellington, "Mirror, Mirror: Fighting 'Fast Fashion': Consumers Must Insist on Safe Style," philly.com (May 23, 2013), http://articles.philly.com/2013-05-23/news/39448203_1_april-24-collapse-rana-plaza-bangladesh. Accessed June 17, 2013.

7. Renee Dudley, ArunDevnath, and Matt Townsend, "The Hidden Cost of Fast Fashion: Worker Safety," *Bloomberg Businessweek* (February 7, 2013), http://www.businessweek.com/articles/2013-02-07/the-hidden-cost-of-fast-fashion-worker-safety. Accessed June 17, 2013.

8. Oliver Batch, "H&M: Can Fast Fashion and Sustainability Ever Really Mix?" *The Guardian* (May 3, 2013), http://www.guardian.co.uk/sustainable-business/h-and-m-fashion-sustainability-mix. Accessed June 17, 2013.

9. Ibid.

10. Charlie Campbell, "Retailers Sign Bangladesh Garment Factory Safety Deal," *Time* (May 14, 2013), http://world.time.com/2013/05/14/retailers-sign-bangladesh-garment-factory-safety-deal-as-collapse-rescue-efforts-wind-up/.

11. Wellington.

12. Elizabeth Cline, "Ten Simple Tips for a More Ethical & Sustainable Wardrobe," http://www.overdressedthebook.com/where-to-shop/. Accessed June 17, 2013.

CASE 35

Looksism at A&F*

"Candidly, we go after the cool kids. We go after the attractive all-American kid with a great attitude and a lot of friends. A lot of people don't belong [in our clothes], and they can't belong. Are we exclusionary? Absolutely.[1]

When Abercrombie & Fitch (A&F) CEO Michael Jeffries said these words in a *Salon* interview, relatively few took notice. Years later, *Business Insider* unearthed the quote and included it in an article about A&F's unwillingness to make clothing for larger women.[2] In the words of Robin Lewis, that 2006 spark then became a 2013 conflagration.[3] The quote went viral through social networks, Twitter, You Tube, and blogs. As a result, A&F stores around the country found themselves to be targets of boycotts and protest.[4] This time the issue was A&F's unwillingness to carry larger sizes, but that is not the only "exclusion" for

which A&F has been called to task. A&F has a long history of being charged with discrimination for its attempts to promote a consistent A&F look.

Looksism, i.e., appearance-based discrimination, is always an ethical issue, but when it begins to affect protected groups, it can be a legal issue as well.[5] A decade ago, a coalition of four organizations filed an employment discrimination lawsuit against A&F. The coalition filing the lawsuit included the Mexican American Legal Defense Fund, the Asian Pacific American Legal Center, the NAACP Legal Defense and Educational Fund, and the law firm of Lieff Cabraser Heimann & Bernstein, LLP. The nine plaintiffs to the lawsuit claimed that A&F discriminated against people of color, including Latinos, Asian Americans, and African Americans, in its hiring practices, job assignments once hired, compensation, termination, and conditions of employment—they settled the case for $50 million minus attorney fees and costs.[6] In 2009, an Oklahoma teen successfully sued A&F for not hiring her after telling her that her *hijab*, a headscarf she wore in keeping with her Muslim beliefs, was not consistent with the

---

*This case was written by Archie B. Carroll, University of Georgia. Updated in 2013.

A&F "look."[7] More recently, a corporate jet pilot who claimed A&F fired him and then replaced him with a younger man charged A&F with age discrimination.[8] Then a Denver judge ruled that the entrances to A&F's surfing-themed Hollister stores violated the Americans with Disabilities Act (ADA)'s requirements for accessibility.[9] In 2011, the firm even insulted the *Jersey Shore* cast by offering to pay them if they would stop wearing A&F clothing.[10]

Retail consumer expert Robin Lewis pondered why a 2006 quote, which was largely ignored after its utterance, would create such a firestorm seven years later.[11] Of course, the speed with which messages can go around the world is a factor, but he also wonders if a change in societal values could be a factor as well. Might the backlash be due to an increased sensitivity toward exclusion and a desire to be more inclusive in an increasingly diverse world?[12] Celebrities like Miley Cyrus publicly joined the boycott and comedians like Ellen DeGeneres made the A&F issue part of their routines.[13] Greg Karber, an L.A. filmmaker, created a short video called "Fitch the Homeless", in which he drives to poor areas to give A&F clothing to poor people to "rebrand" the product.[14]

Some observers question whether A&F has now lost its cultural relevance. In a post-economic recession world, is elitism something that A&F's target demographic no longer values? Abe Sauer of *Brandchannel* draws a comparison to the 2012 movie *21 Jump Street*, in which two young police officers go undercover in a high school, thinking that what was cool in 2000 is still cool today.[15] They are confused when the students they meet find the officers' year 2000 conception of 'cool' to be offensive. Those students value compassion, environmentalism, and earnestness instead. Sauer asks if A&F might be about to learn the same lesson as the officers did.[16]

QUESTIONS FOR DISCUSSION

1. What are the legal and ethical issues in this case?
2. What is your evaluation of the concept of the "A&F look?" Have you personally observed this concept in practice?
3. Are the employment practices of A&F discriminatory? Are they unfair? What ethical principles or precepts guide your analysis?
4. What could A&F and other retailers be doing, that they are not doing, to make their hiring practices less controversial? Is their current policy sustainable?
5. Do you agree with Sauer's *21 Jump Street* metaphor?

6. What advice would you give A&F? Would you invest in the company?
7. Are there other companies that promote a particular look? Are they being discriminatory? Where do you draw the line?

ENDNOTES

1. Benoit Denizet-Lewis, "The Man Behind Abercrombie & Fitch," *Salon* (Januray 24, 2006), http://www.salon.com/2006/01/24/jeffries/. Accessed June 16, 2013.
2. Ashley Lutz, "Abercrombie & Fitch Refuses to Make Clothes for Large Women," *Business Insider* (May 3, 2013), http://www.businessinsider.com/abercrombie-wants-thin-customers-2013-5. Accessed June 16, 2013.
3. Robin Lewis, "A&F: Exclusive or Exclusionary?" *Huff Post Business* (May 31, 2013), http://www.huffingtonpost.com/robin-lewis/af-exclusive-or-exclusionary_b_3360354.html. Accessed June 16, 2013.
4. Ibid.
5. M.S. "Looksism and the Law," *The Economist* (May 24, 2010), http://www.economist.com/blogs/democracyinamerica/2010/05/appearance_discrimination. Accessed June 17, 2013.
6. "$50 Million, Less Attorneys' Fees and Costs, Paid to Class Members in December 2005 in Abercrombie & Fitch Discrimination Lawsuit Settlement," AFjustice.com, http://afjustice.com/. Accessed June 16, 2013.
7. "Abercrombie & Fitch Sued over Head Scarf," CBS News (September 18, 2009), http://www.cbsnews.com/2100-201_162-5320868.html. Accessed June 16, 2013.; David Harper, "Tulsa Federal Judge Rules Against Abercrombie & Fitch In Lawsuit Over Hijab," *Tulsa World* (June 29, 2011), http://www.tulsaworld.com/article.aspx/Tulsa_federal_judge_rules_against_Abercrombie_Fitch/20110629_14_0_atulsa 243432. Accessed July 26, 2013.
8. Sapna Maheshwari, "Models on Abercrombie Jet Had Rules on Proper Underwear," *Bloomberg* (October 18, 2012), http://www.bloomberg.com/news/2012-10-18/models-on-abercrombie-jet-had-rules-on-proper-underwear.html?cmpid=yhoo. Accessed June 16, 2013.
9. Terri Pous, "We, the Underdressed: A Brief History of Discrimination and Indifference in Fashion Retail," *Time* (May 22, 2013), http://style.time.

com/2013/05/22/we-the-underdressed-a-history-of-discrimination-and-indifference-in-fashion/. Accessed June 16, 2013.

10. Abe Sauer, "Why A&F's 'Cool Kids' Stance Will Damage the Brand Now More Than Ever," *Brandchannel* (May 13, 2013), http://www.brandchannel.com/home/post/2013/05/13/Abercrombie-Brand-Damage-051313.aspx. Accessed June 16, 2013.

11. Lewis, 2013.

12. Ibid.

13. "Miley Cyrus and US Stars Boycott Abercrombie & Fitch After Discrimination Of Overweight,"

gulfnews.com (June 16, 2013), http://gulfnews.com/arts-entertainment/celebrity/miley-cyrus-and-us-stars-boycott-abercrombie-fitch-after-discrimination-of-overweight-1.1197732. Accessed June 16, 2013.

14. Sami K. Martin, "Abercrombie & Fitch Homeless Campaign by Greg Karber Gives Store 'New Image'," *CP N. America* (May 15, 2013), http://www.christianpost.com/news/abercrombie-fitch-homeless-campaign-by-greg-karber-gives-store-new-image-95905/. Accessed June 16, 2013.

15. Sauer, 2013.

16. Ibid.

CASE 36

Two Vets, Two Dogs, and a Deadlock*

When a roadside explosion in Afghanistan blew up his Humvee, Russ Murray sustained brain and back injuries as well as post-traumatic stress disorder that made it very difficult to leave his home in Watkinsville, Georgia. Getting Ellie, his service dog, made it possible for him to leave the house, and the two are now inseparable.[1] However, when he visited Clyde's Armory Gun Shop in a nearby town, he was told that Ellie could not come in the store because she was disturbing the owner's security dog, Kit. Kit is a Doberman Pinscher who roams freely from the store to the warehouse and is there to provide security. "I want this to be a safe environment," says Clyde, a veteran who served three combat tours in Iraq.[2] "[Kit] doesn't interact well with other dogs and I cannot have a dog fight in my store."[3] Clyde maintained that he had a right not to allow Russ in with his dog because the store is private property and so, as the owner, he has a right to decide who can enter.[4]

Russ received his service dog from the Dog Tag program of Puppies Behind Bars, an organization that trains prison inmates to raise service dogs for disabled Afghanistan and Iraq war veterans.[5] Ellie, a black lab, is able to respond to about 80 commands—she can pick up items, help with laundry, and call 911.[6] According to Gloria Stoga, president of Puppies

Behind Bars, the organization has placed about 54 dogs with wounded veterans. She notes that the dogs they place are "fully trained service dogs."[7] Russ said he intended to file a complaint under the Americans with Disabilities Act of 1990 (ADA) adding, "I don't want this to happen to anyone else."[8]

Clyde asked Russ to leave the store, and when he refused, two employees escorted him out. Russ then called the police and an officer was dispatched to the scene. In the officer's presence, Clyde told Russ he was barred from the store for two years.[9]

QUESTIONS FOR DISCUSSION

1. With whom do you agree in this dispute? Should Russ have honored Clyde's request to leave or should Clyde have allowed Russ and Ellie into his store?
2. Who are the stakeholders and what are the stakes?
3. What ethical principles apply to this situation?
4. Before doing any more research on service dogs and the ADA, think about what happened. Who is in the right? Is this a violation of the ADA or does the store owner have rights that outweigh ADA concerns?
5. Was a reasonable accommodation attempted? Did the potential accommodation involve undue hardship?
6. Now look up the ADA policy on service animals.[10] Considering this, who is in the right in the above scenario? Does your answer change from the one you gave in Question #1 or 4?

*Contributed by Ann K. Buchholtz, Rutgers University

ENDNOTES

1. Denise Dillon, "Disabled Veteran, Service Dog Told to Leave Gun Shop," MyFoxAtlanta.com (April 9, 2013), http://www.myfoxatlanta.com/story/21926108/veteran-says-gun-shop-owner. Accessed June 15, 2013.

2. Wayne Ford, "Two War Vets Disagree Over 'Service Dog' In Athens Gun Store," Online Athens (April 10, 2013), http://onlineathens.com/local-news/2013-04-10/two-war-vets-disagree-over-service-dog-athens-gun-store.

3. Ibid.

4. Ibid.

5. http://www.puppiesbehindbars.com/home. Accessed June 15, 2013.

6. Ford, 2013.

7. Ibid.

8. Ibid.

9. Ibid.

10. 2013; ADA 2010 Revised Requirements, "Service Animals," http://www.ada.gov/service_animals_2010.htm. Accessed June 15, 2013.

CASE 37

Are Criminal Background Checks Discriminatory?

In April 2012, the Equal Employment Opportunity Commission (EEOC) issued revised guidance on the use of arrest and conviction records in employment decisions. In it, the EEOC warned that the use of criminal background as an exclusion must be "job related and consistent with business necessity."[1] The EEOC noted that arrest and incarceration rates are high for African American and Hispanic men and so a blanket exclusion of applicants with criminal backgrounds is likely to have disparate impact and thus be a violation of Title VII of the Civil Rights Act of 1964.[2]

A year later, June 2013, the EEOC filed its first lawsuits under the revised guidance against Dollar General and a BMW manufacturing plant in South Carolina. Both companies are accused of discriminating against African Americans. In the case of BMW, the issue arose when a new logistics service was hired. The previous service had a policy of only screening convictions that occurred in the past seven years. BMW does not have a screening time limit and ordered the new logistics service to do a new screening. Employees with convictions that violated the BMW policy of no time limit were terminated, even if they had worked for the company for years.[3] The Dollar General case involves two applicants. One had her conditional job offer revoked due to a six-year old conviction, even though she disclosed the conviction in the interview and worked for another retailer in a similar position for four years.[4]

Reaction to the filing of the lawsuit was swift. *The Wall Street Journal* opined, "We would have thought that criminal checks discriminate against criminals, regardless of race, creed, gender or anything else."[5] The editorial goes on to say that one can argue that criminals deserve a second chance but "business owners and managers ought to be able to decide if they want to take the risk of hiring felons."[6] An EEOC spokesperson told the Associated Press, "Overcoming barriers to employment is one of our strategic enforcement priorities... We hope that these lawsuits will further educate the public and the employer community on the appropriate use of conviction records."[7]

QUESTIONS FOR DISCUSSION

1. Do you agree with the EEOC or the WSJ?
2. Are blanket exclusions of people with criminal backgrounds discriminatory or should businesses be given the discretion to make the employment decision when a potential or current employee is found to have a criminal background?
3. How would you determine whether a conviction record is "job related and consistent with business necessity"?
4. What factors would affect your decision? Would it vary by the nature of the conviction? If so, how would it vary? Would it vary by the nature of your business and industry? If so, how would it vary?

ENDNOTES

1. "Consideration of Arrest and Conviction Records in Employment Decisions under Title VII of the

Civil Rights Act of 1964," http://www.eeoc.gov/laws/guidance/arrest_conviction.cfm.

2. Ibid.

3. Tess Stynes, "EEOC Files Suits against BMW Manufacturing, Dollar General," *The Wall Street Journal* (June 11, 2013), http://online.wsj.com/article/BT-CO-20130611-706879.html. Accessed June 16, 2013.

4. Ibid.

5. "Banning Background Checks: The EEOC Says That Screening For Felonies Is Discriminatory," *The Wall Street Journal*, (June 15, 2013), A14.

6. Ibid.

7. Bruce Kennedy, "BMW, Dollar General Hit With Discrimination Suits," *MSN Money* (June 12, 2013), http://money.msn.com/now/blog–bmw-dollar-general-hit-with-discrimination-suits. Accessed June 16, 2013.

CASE 38

A Candy Confession

One summer during high school I worked at a concession stand in a movie theatre. One day I saw the concession supervisor throw a box of chocolate candy to the floor in order to damage the box. He then picked it up and wrote down on the spoiler sheet that it was an unsellable damaged box. He continued to pour some chocolates in a cup for me to have and took the rest of them to the back for him to eat. I knew this was wrong, because the box was in perfect condition right before he smashed it to the ground, but I still ate the chocolates. A couple weeks later, we had a meeting with the food and beverage manager. He mentioned that this month there was a higher number than usual of candy spoilage and he knew that the employees were spoiling the candy purposely. He asked for the guilty employees or witnesses to step forward and admit the wrong doings. My dilemma was that I knew it was ethically wrong that I partook in the activity by eating the candy I was offered but I didn't actually ruin the box myself. What should I do?

QUESTIONS FOR DISCUSSION

1. What are the ethical issues in this case?
2. Does eating the candy make me responsible for the problem?
3. Should I step forward and tell the manager what happened?
4. What would you have done?

This case was prepared by Michelle Allen.

Contributed Anonymously

CASE 39

To Take or Not to Take

As a State employee, I am restricted from receiving excessive gifts because of my opportunity to direct business toward certain vendors. Currently, the State forbids acceptance of gifts that exceed $100 in value. Regardless of the limit, I make it a policy not to receive gifts of any value in order to be equitable to all vendors.

Recently, however, a vendor to whom I frequently provide business (because of the great value in their products and services) offered me two tickets to a sold-out concert for a group that my wife greatly enjoys. With our anniversary approaching, I had tried unsuccessfully to purchase the tickets on my own. The face value of the two tickets does not exceed the $100 limit, but I still do not feel comfortable taking them. I am torn because of the joy it would bring my wife to attend the concert.

QUESTIONS FOR DISCUSSION

1. What are the ethical issues in this case?
2. Should I accept the tickets? On what are you basing that decision?
3. Should I change my practice of refusing all gifts?
4. Should the State's policies be modified regarding gifts? If so, how should they be modified?

This case was prepared by Ken Crowe.

Contributed Anonymously

Tragedy in Bangladesh*

On April 24, 2013, an eight story garment factory building collapsed in Rana Plaza, on the outskirts of Dhaka, Bangladesh. The Rana Plaza building is located in Savar, near Dhaka. The collapse occurred just after work had begun that morning at several companies that were all housed in the building. Roughly 5,000 workers, mostly women, worked in the complex. By that evening, 1,000 people had been rescued and it was reported the next day that at least 119 were killed. This building collapse occurred months after more than 100 workers had died in a fire at the Tazreen Fashions factory near Dhaka.[1]

As the weeks passed, the death toll continued to rise. A month after the accident, it was apparent that over 1,100 garment workers perished in the collapse of the substandard factory building. The gruesome calamity already has been called the worst industrial accident since the Bhopal disaster in 1984 and the worst ever in the garment industry.[2]

What makes the tragedy such a monumental story is that it is the worst event to occur in the decades-long debate over the use of sweat shops and related labor rights issues. These controversial links in supply chains are typically used by well-to-do multinational industries to manufacture cheap products for the Western world.

Since the building collapse occurred and the total costs in lives, injuries, and property losses have begun escalating, the logical questions about responsibility for the tragedy have begun to be raised. In a complex situation such as this, there is considerable finger-pointing and the parties being identified as responsible continue to multiply.

Reports are that the owners of the building had been warned that it was unsafe and one response by the owners was to threaten to fire the people who didn't just keep working.[3] Within a month of the building collapse, the government created a panel to study the accident and the panel issued a 400 page report claiming that substandard building materials, failure to comply with building regulations, and the use of heavy equipment on upper floors were key factors in the disaster. The panel also recommended that the owner of Rana Plaza, Sohel Rana, and the owners of the five garment factories located in the building should be charged with "culpable homicide" for allegedly forcing the employees to return to work on April 24 after cracks had been seen on the exterior of the building the previous day.[4]

The Bangladeshi government has been pressured by many diverse groups to take action to overhaul workplace safety in the aftermath of the building collapse. A more serious problem viewed by others has been the lack of acceptable regulations and their enforcement on the part of the government itself. Many blame the government for not setting and enforcing safety standards in much the same way these types of regulations work in more developed countries. The government has taken some steps in the aftermath of the tragedy. It has shut down 20 sites for safety improvements.[5] One reason the government started working quickly after this tragedy is because it feared losing millions of jobs to another poor country if companies exited en masse.[6]

The government has also said it will broker talks for higher garment industry minimum wages; minimum wages now average about $38 per month. The country of Bangladesh is second only to China in terms of garment manufacturing for the developed world; however, its minimum wages are paltry in comparison to the $138 per month received on average by workers in China.[7]

As so often is the case involving sweatshops and their consequences, however, the primary public discussion about the Rana Plaza disaster quickly turned to the United States' and other wealthy nations' corporations who have taken advantage of the low costs in Bangladesh and are thought to be indifferent to the working conditions in the low-cost providing countries. Product remnants of two companies were found in the rubble of the building collapse: Primark, a cut-rate British brand, and Canada's Loblaw, including its Joe Fresh brand.[8]

Other national brands, though they have not been directly linked to the Rana Plaza fire, are also under the gun to take some significant action on the worker safety front. Among these companies are such familiar names as Walmart, Gap, Dress Barn, H&M, Benetton, J. C. Penney, Mango, Target, Sears, Walt Disney Co., and Nike. These companies are not new to sweatshop allegations and challenges, as they have been using them for decades. Many of them have been striving for years to improve workplace conditions, but the

---

*This case was written by Archie B. Carroll, 2013.

challenges posed in countries such as Bangladesh are formidable. To ensure safe and good practices, does a company need to check the supplier of its supplier's supplier? Is seeing a certificate that a factory is safe an adequate assurance? Should the company send people in to check every safety feature of the building and to observe working conditions? If so, how often?[9]

According to *The Economist*, Western firms can decide to respond to the Bangladeshi tragedy in one of three ways: they can overlook attempts at CSR and just take advantage of cheap labor wherever it exists; they can exit countries like Bangladesh and operate only in countries where risks are less; or, they can stay and try to improve upon conditions there. Interestingly, some companies had already been working according to the third alternative. Walmart had started a fire-safety training academy there even before the disaster. Gap had already announced a plan to help factory owners upgrade their plants. The clothing industry had already held meetings with NGOs and governments seeking to develop a strategy to improve safety in Bangladesh's 5,000 factories.[10] Another reason why companies might stay in Bangladesh is because they are running out of low-cost countries to turn to for their production.

Two major approaches have surfaced for companies to respond to the serious workplace safety situation in Bangladesh—(1) form a group, or an accord, and act together or (2) each company go its own way.

EUROPEAN ACCORD ON FIRE AND BUILDING SAFETY IN BANGLADESH

In mid-May 2013, some of Europe's largest retailers took the first approach and decided to create and sign an accord to improve safety conditions in Bangladesh. The accord would be a legally binding five-year agreement not to hire manufacturers whose factories failed to meet safety standards. The group also agreed to pay for necessary factory repairs and renovations. This agreement was negotiated with global worker-safety advocates, overlapping with the Bangladeshi government in its efforts to raise the minimum wage and make it easier for workers to join unions.[11] Leaders of the accord said they need widespread participation to make the agreement work.

Two of the companies leading the proposed accord include Sweden's Hennes & Mauritz AB (H&M) and Spain's Inditex. H&M is the leading buyer of clothing from Bangladesh's $20 billion garment industry. Observers have said that H&M had no choice but to take the lead since the volume it requires from there is so large.[12] Other signers of the accord include Italy's Benetton Group, Spain's Mango MNG Holdings SL, France's Carrefour SA and the U. K.'s Marks & Spencer.[13]

SHOULD COMPANIES ACT INDEPENDENTLY?

When the European-led accord was being developed, two leading companies, Walmart and Gap, indicated they would not join the accord but would put together their own safety plans for improving conditions in Bangladesh. One major objection they had to the accord was that it was legally binding and it was unclear what all that might mean. Other companies have been reluctant to sign the accord for the same reason.

Walmart's initial plan, which it called a commitment, would involve hiring outside auditors to inspect 279 Bangladeshi factories and publish the results on its website. When warranted, Walmart said it would require the factory owners to make needed renovations or risk being removed from its list of authorized factories. Walmart said that it believed its safety plan would meet or exceed the accord's plan and would get results faster. The company also reported that it had already met and revoked authorization for more than 250 factories in the country. Another part of Walmart's plan was to set up an independent call center for workers to call and report unsafe conditions. Walmart also planned to conduct safety training for every worker in plants making its products.[14]

Though Gap did not agree with the European-led accord, the company indicated that if certain revisions were made to the legally binding agreement, it may join the accord. Other companies initially indicating they would craft their own safety plans for Bangladesh included JCPenney, Sears, and Japan's Fast Retailing Co., operator of the Uniqlo casual clothing chain.[15]

Several companies have decided to downplay their use of manufacturing in Bangladesh because of the risks involved. Nike, for example, has said that Bangladesh is a high risk country for them and they plan to keep their footprint very limited there. Nike said that only eight of the 896 factories it worked with were in Bangladesh. To ensure compliance with its safety requirements, Nike has its own system of grading or judging the suppliers.[16] Walt Disney Co. had told its licensees in March, before the building collapse, that they could no longer produce Disney branded products in Bangladesh because some boxes of Disney sweatshirts were found at the site of the major Tazreen factory fire that had occurred in Bangladesh the previous

November. Disney and Walmart claimed that they didn't know their goods were being produced at the plant that burned and that it wasn't an authorized manufacturer.[17] It is difficult for companies to always know or control where their products are sometimes made because sub-contractors hire sub-contractors, and so on, often without the company's knowledge.

UNITED STATES' RETAILERS AGREEMENT FORMED

Just over a month after saying they would act alone, it was announced in late June 2013 that Walmart, Gap, Inc., VF Corp., Macy's, Sears Holdings and other large U.S. retailers would establish their own accord to improve safety conditions in Bangladeshi garment factories. The agreement would be a $50 million, five year fund for improving safety conditions. There were several key differences between the European-led and the U.S.-led proposals. Whereas the European plan does not require participation of the Bangladeshi government, the U.S. plan does require the government's participation. Another major difference is in the realm of legal liability. The European plan requires signatories to accept broad legal liability whereas the U.S. plan calls for limited legal liability.[18]

The $50 million U.S.-led plan would be contingent upon the Bangladeshi government meeting certain criteria ensuring accountability and compliance for safety improvements. This was included because many safety codes were often ignored by governmental officials responsible for enforcing them. As for legal liability, the U.S. proposal stipulated that signatories to their plan have rather limited legal liability. In the U.S. proposal, firms could be held legally liable if they agree to commit resources and then renege or if they continue to use the unsafe factories.[19] Another major difference between the two plans is the amount of resources required to make improvements. Under the European plan, companies would be required to pay for all upgrades to factories at an estimated cost of $600,000 per factory. In the U.S. plan, companies would set up a $50 million fund to help cover the upgrade costs. The final details regarding the U.S. plan were not available as of this writing.

ARE CONSUMERS THE RESPONSIBLE PARTY?

By implication, the world's consumers of "fast fashion" and other cheaply produced products are identified by some as responsible parties in the tragedy in Bangladesh. Though surveys report that consumers will reward responsible business practices or punish viola-tors, this doesn't happen very often. *USA Today* writer Jayne O'Donnell reports on a 23-year-old woman who says she would pay a little more for her clothes if she knew the companies were "socially responsible in the way that they gave their workers safe conditions and adequate pay." But, O'Donnell observes that this woman may be the exception; consumers will be troubled by these news accounts, but they quickly forget. Consumer psychologist Kit Yarrow is quoted as observing that "denial is a pretty powerful thing if something is beautiful and you really want it."[20]

QUESTIONS FOR DISCUSSION

1. Who are the stakeholders in this case and what are their stakes? What are the ethical issues?
2. Based on your study of the building collapse in Bangladesh, which party or parties do you think are responsible and why?
3. What role does the government of Bangladesh assume in this building collapse and other safety violations?
4. Do Western companies have an obligation to safeguard the safety of workers who make the products they sell?
5. What are the pros and cons of companies working together in an accord to address safety violations versus taking independent action to address the issues in the plants they use? Do both approaches represent sound global corporate citizenship?
6. Which plan would you support as preferred for addressing the factory safety problem in Bangladesh—the European-led Plan or the U.S.-led Plan? What are the pros and cons of each?
7. Do research on this case to bring all the facts up to date. Has anything significant changed? If so, integrate these findings into your analysis.
8. What is your appraisal of companies that decide Bangladesh is too risky a country for them to do business in?
9. What is the responsibility of consumers to the employees in other countries where our products are made? Is the writer correct, "we quickly forget?" What can be done to address this mindset?

ENDNOTES

1. Syed Zain Al-Mahmood and Shelly Banjo, "Deadly Collapse," *The Wall Street Journal*, April 25, 2013, A1.
2. "Disaster at Rana Plaza," *The Economist*, May 4, 2013, 12.
3. Ibid.

4. Syed Zain Al-Mahmood, "Shoddy Materials are Blamed for Building Collapse," *The Wall Street Journal*, May 24, 2012, B4.

5. Syed Zain Al-Mahmoud, "Bangladesh Factory Toll Passes 800," *The Wall Street Journal*, May 9, 2013, A10.

6. Adam Davidson, "Clotheslined," *The New York Times Magazine*, May 19, 2013, 16.

7. Syed Zain Al-Mahmood, "Bangladesh to Raise Workers' Pay," *The Wall Street Journal*, May 13, 2013, B4.

8. *The Economist*, May 4, 2013, ibid.

9. Ibid.

10. Ibid.

11. Shelly Banjo and Christina Passariello, "Promises in Bangladesh," *The Wall Street Journal*, May 14, 2013, B1.

12. Jens Hansegard, Tripti Lahiri, and Christina Passariello, "Retailers' Dilemma: Cut Off or Help Fix Unsafe Factories," *The Wall Street Journal*, May 29, 2013, B1.

13. Shelly Banjo, Ann Zimmerman, and Suzanne Kapner, "Wal-Mart Crafts Own Bangladesh Safety Plan," *The Wall Street Journal*, May 15, 2013. B1.

14. Ibid.

15. Mayumi Negishi, "Uniqlo Won't Join Accord on Bangladesh Labor Safety," *The Wall Street Journal*, May 28, 2013, B1.

16. "Nike's Game Plan for Policing its Suppliers: Try to Avoid Bangladesh," *The Wall Street Journal*, November 30, 2012.

17. Hansegard et al., ibid.

18. Suzanne Kapner and Shelly Banjo, "Plan B for Bangladesh," *The Wall Street Journal*, June 27, 2013, B1.

19. Ibid.

20. Jayne O'Donnell, "Treat Workers Well, or Kiss our Cash Goodbye," *USA Today*, May 23, 2013, 5B.

CASE 41

Software Sojourn

A dedicated employee in our department wanted to keep up with work while on maternity leave and avoid having any leave without pay. However, she did not have the required software installed on her home computer to be able to perform the work. Our company's software licenses do not include coverage for installation on personal computers and a company computer was not available for her to take home. Her supervisor wanted to help her with her leave situation because she is a very good employee and it would be better for our company if she stayed caught up with her work. Therefore, the supervisor decided to allow the employee to install the software on her home computer and the supervisor then monitored the work that the employee performed at home.

When she returned to work from maternity leave, the work was caught up and she told the supervisor that the software was uninstalled.

QUESTIONS FOR DISCUSSION

1. What are the ethical issues in this case?
2. Do you think the employee should have been allowed to install the software on her personal computer?
3. If you were the supervisor, would you have handled this situation differently?

This case was prepared by Chad Cleveland.

Contributed Anonymously

Subject Index

Page numbers in italics refer to figures.

Name Index